THE ENCYCLOPEDIA OF

CRIME

THE ENCYCLOPEDIA OF CRIME

CRIME
OLIVER CYRIAX,
COLIN WILSON &
DAMON WILSON

THE OVERLOOK PRESS
WOODSTOCK & NEW YORK

First published in the United States in 2006 by
The Overlook Press, Peter Mayer Publishers, Inc.
Woodstock & New York

WOODSTOCK:
One Overlook Drive
Woodstock, NY 12498
www.overlookpress.com
[for individual orders, bulk and special sales, contact our Woodstock office]

NEW YORK:
141 Wooster Street
New York, NY 10012

Cataloging-in-Publication Data is available from the Library of Congress

Manufactured in Dubai
ISBN 1-58567-763-9
1 3 5 7 9 8 6 4 2

For Holly and Jake
when they are a bit older

Contents

Introduction

On the walls of a shell-holed operating theatre in Mogadishu are scrawled the words 'It is better to light a single candle than rail against the dark', and it is in this spirit that *The Encyclopedia of Crime* was conceived. The historical sweep of criminal activity extends from the first syllable of recorded time, and its ramifications are without limit. We learn from the Book of Genesis that Cain murdered Abel and, with a liberal interpretation, almost anything can be classified as criminal: social injustice, religious bigotry, colonialism and war. Each day brings new reports of juvenile thuggery, car thefts, miscarriages of justice and husband-kills-wife.

But True Crime has an inverted hierarchy of its own, with the villains ranked in order of dishonour. For Britons, these household names include Crippen, Brady, Hindley, Nilsen and Christie; for Americans, Manson, Bundy, Dahmer, Gein, DeSalvo, Ramirez and Ng are numbered in the premier league. Russia's great contemporary contributor is Chikatilo; Germany's past master, Peter Kürten. Ranged behind them are a few hundred others, the select band of murderers or murder cases containing their nugget of forensic or historical significance.

Scores of these benchmark cases are covered, but not in isolation. The black heart of murder, that prima donna of crimes, beats within a tangled morass in part composed of forensic science, legal technicalities, the art of detection and the social mores of the time. Historically, motive was rarely ambiguous: in rough chronological order, men killed for food, shelter, territory, greed and emotional security. But the more recent phenomenon of sex and serial slayings represents a new compulsion, the practice of killing for fun, and from this dismal notion are suspended the related topics of cannibalism, sadism and torture.

In former times, men burned witches, animated at least in part by the fear that their spells sapped sexual potency. Today, sex murders are often triggered by accusations of impotence or actual impotence. Thus witchcraft, on the surface a subject more fit for the nursery bookshelf, harks back to ancient concepts of justice, the modern ones of sex discrimination, looks sideways to sex crimes, embraces the Salem trials, heralds satanic ritual abuse cases, links up with the modern serial killers and sadists, and must be viewed in the light of false confessions and the claims of recalled memory.

The signposts point in every direction, and, in mapping out this book, I awarded entries to as many destinations as space permitted. Many roads led in unexpected directions through surprising landscapes, often twisted into unusual contours by the machinations of the criminal cartels. As Americans progressively discovered during the 1950s, iniquity is not the exclusive preserve of rugged individualists. It can be organised, whether by the Mafia, the Triads, the Colombian drug cartels or Britain's home-grown Kray twins. Here, too, the cornucopia of evil disgorges a rich, if fetid, harvest: the Mafia alone conjures up tales of Capone, Prohibition Chicago, the glory days of Murder Inc., the Apalachin summit, the Cosa Nostra's Sicilian roots, vendettas, J. Edgar Hoover and his G-men. All are featured, as are the great robberies and the more engaging antics of art forgers and conmen. In passing I have attempted to shed light on some of Crime's more pungent enigmas. How did America come to pass the legislation banning alcohol? What is the best way to crack a safe? How do lethal injections work? Does a head survive decapitation? What exactly is the law of rape? The story of opium?

And who invented hijacking? A gentleman named Yu, it turns out. He too has his place, under Y, at someone else's expense. But True Crime is a broad church. There is more than enough to go round, and in this brief, digression-led volume, where every inclusion entailed a corresponding exclusion, a procession of cursory and unilluminating entries on well-thumbed criminal celebrities never seemed the way to proceed. Here, the famous rub shoulders with forgotten hoods from the third division. Sometimes familiar territory is skated over, making room for lesser-known landmarks or for a glimpse of some hackneyed underworld king in an off-guard moment; sometimes, major stories are divided into more manageable satellite entries and treated in detail; sometimes straightforward biographical narratives alternate with `can-they-be-related?' batches marshalled under a single heading. My guiding intent was somehow to weave a representative patchwork, a tapestry of interconnected criminal endeavour, complete at least in parts.

For a subject so intimately bound up with death, True Crime is far from dead. Disclosures and new evidence continue to emerge on files which might reasonably be regarded as closed years ago. Quite apart from the hosts of 1990s cases, such as Mike Tyson, Anita Hill, Aileen Wuornos and Ivan the Terrible, the stories of Marilyn Monroe, Jack the Ripper, Craig and Bentley, Sir Jock 'Delves' Broughton, the Krays, Henry Lee Lucas, Kennedy and Browne, J. Edgar Hoover, and even Crippen, have benefited from the attentions of scholarship, with their original verdicts confirmed, trimmed or reversed by new research. These fables, where citizens are thrown into the limelight to become public property, are as much part of our collective memory as the wedding of Prince Charles or the assassination of President Kennedy, himself an entrant, and are equally subject to reappraisal. Exhumations continue apace, diaries are discovered, memoirs published, letters and documentation released. Other mysteries await their first resolution, but here too I did not feel duty-bound to sit undecided on the fence.

The study of True Crime would yield few dividends were the precedence of villains graven in stone, or the investigative and judicial process disfigured by one besetting source of error. But every component in a case is open to question. Those of liberal disposition may assume that fabricated police evidence is a likely cause of injustice. This is so, but equally often, only devoted detective work beyond the call of duty ferreted out the killer. Confessions are beaten out of suspects, but even when freely given, may constitute no more than the vapourings of an attention-seeker – whereas, in other contexts, a full and open admission can carry overwhelming weight. Expert witnesses can make astonishing blunders or distort the facts, but they also blow cases wide open. In sum, famous villains may not deserve their reputations, and triumphant acquittals are perfectly consistent with guilt blacker than sin. In the intellectual backwater of crime, no particular qualification ensures immunity from error, and in these democratic circumstances, even at the risk of adding my own misapp-rehensions to the general heap of falsity, I have endeavoured wherever possible to point the way to a verdict.

But on one issue I have nothing to add: the Perfect Crime. The reader will search these pages in vain for a dedicated entry under P or C. Yet the *Encyclopedia* consists of nothing but examples of this genre laid end-to-end, and they all happened to someone else, preferably in another country, a long time ago.

Oliver Cyriax

Foreword

When I first read this book – on a plane to New York in 1996 – I realised that it was much more than an encyclopedia of crime: it was an entertainment. Its eccentric author – with whom I am not acquainted – had a quirky sense of humour and an eye for the ridiculous that kept me chuckling throughout the seven-hour flight. The essence of its charm was a kind of casual association of ideas, and a digressiveness that reminded me of Sterne's *Tristram Shandy*.

It was first published in 1992 and the ideal person to update it would obviously have been the author himself. But apparently he cannot be found or otherwise contacted. I am not in the least surprised. He has probably been seized by a sudden impulse to pursue his profession as solicitor in Tibet, or in some remote part of northern Alaska.

By comparison, my own approach to crime is earnest and pedestrian. But I have at least one qualification for carrying on where Mr Cyriax left off: in the late 1950s, while he was probably still at infants' school, I decided it was about time someone compiled an encyclopedia covering all the most notorious murder cases. The subject of crime had always interested me and I was engaged in writing my first novel, *Ritual in the Dark*, about a mass murderer based on Jack the Ripper. I had collected a considerable library of second-hand books on true crime with titles like *Scales of Justice* or *Murderers Sane and Mad*. But if I wanted to look up some fact about a murderer, such as the date he was hanged, I had to recollect which volume in my crime library contained a chapter about him. So I decided to remedy this deficiency by writing an alphabetical encyclopedia of murder (in association with Pat Pitman), which was published in 1961. Since then many writers have followed suit with encyclopedias of female killers, sex killers, serial killers, even one devoted entirely to Jack the Ripper.

Where Mr Cyriax's intentions differ from mine is in his attitude towards the business of compilation. I suspect he keeps a scrapbook of items that appeal to his sense of humour or oddity, which explains why you will find a piece on inflatable dolls followed by one on informality, one about eccentric judges and a mildly tongue-in cheek account of satanic ritual abuse that sounds so preposterous you suspect he has invented it.

In one case, however, his sense of humour has led him into error. It is in his entry on the Gordon Riots, where he refers to Renwick Williams, 'The London Monster', who in the late 1780s used to slash ladies' clothes, and occasionally the flesh beneath, with a very sharp knife; he was caught in 1790. Mr Cyriax describes how, on the evening before he was hanged, Williams threw a 'Monster Ball' at Newgate Prison, at which his guests ate a cold supper of meat with a selection of wines. It is a marvellous story, but as I read it, I had a vague feeling that it was not quite accurate, and that the Monster was only sentenced to a term in prison.

I confirmed this by consulting Jan Bondeson's standard work on the case, *The London Monster*, which records that the Monster Ball was the invention of the 1790 equivalent of the tabloid press. So I have included here the true history of the Monster, which is just as strange, if not quite as funny, as Mr Cyriax's tale of the ball.

This is a matter hardly worth mentioning except that it enables me to explain how my own attitude to crime differs from that of the original compiler. What fascinates me is that Renwick Williams was the first recorded sexual deviant in the annals of modern crime. He would be followed by Carl Bartle of Augsburg, another slasher of ladies' garments, Andreas Bichel of Regensdorf, who killed women for their clothes, and many other sexually maladjusted individuals who can be found in the pages of Krafft-Ebing's *Psychopathia Sexualis* (1899), the first textbook on sexual perversion.

But why should it all have started when it did? What was there about the late eighteenth century that explains the emergence of the first recorded criminal sex deviant?

Seeking an answer, I consulted a dictionary of history, and learned that 1790 also happens to be the first year of the French Revolution, the year the city of Washington DC was founded, the Forth–Clyde canal was completed, the rotary press was invented, the first steam-powered rolling mill came into operation in England and the year Lavoisier produced the first table of the elements. As this short list makes apparent, important changes were taking place, and Renwick Williams's bizarre acts of deviancy were in some way a part of an emergent pattern of history.

Then I saw the solution. The French philosopher Michel Foucault proposed the useful concept of 'epistemes', which means a cultural period which is quite distinct from what has gone before. We can see at a glance that an immense change has come about between the age of Dr Johnson and the age of Byron, Keats and Shelley. But how does this help us explain why an intelligent but feckless young Welshman should decide to attack ladies' clothes with a sharp knife?

Well, to begin with, we can see that the eighteenth century was an age when attitudes towards sex were healthy and down-to-earth, and that the age of Byron and Shelley is dominated by a feverish romanticism that exalted women into goddesses and objects of infinite desire. When did this change begin?

The date can be given precisely. It was in the year 1740, when a novel called *Pamela* appeared in London bookshops. What makes this so interesting is that *Pamela* was the first novel in our modern sense of the word.

It was written by a middle-aged printer named Samuel Richardson, whose only work up to that date was a teach-yourself volume on writing letters. It was therefore natural that *Pamela* should be written in the form of letters. They were supposedly written by a young servant girl who had just found a job in the home of the local squire, Mr B–. And as the reader eavesdrops over Pamela's shoulder, he becomes quickly aware of something that Pamela is too innocent to recognise: Mr B– has every intention of seducing her. Naturally, he reads on to see whether Mr B– succeeds.

When Mr B– flings her on a bed, even Pamela becomes aware of the nature of his interest in her. She is saved when the housekeeper interrupts. Then he tries to rape her while a procuress holds her hands, but gives up when she has a kind of fit. After several such attempts, Mr B– is so touched by Pamela's goodness that he marries her, and all ends happily.

No one had ever read anything like it. *Pamela* quickly became the first best-seller, and the *Pamela* craze swept across Europe.

This new invention, the novel, had the same kind of impact that the cinema had at the beginning of the twentieth century. It provided ordinary readers, particularly bored housewives whose domestic chores were lightened by a cook and housemaid, with an escape into a world of fantasy, of imagination. It was a kind of magic carpet that would take her into other people's lives.

Although we have no day-to-day record of the life of young Renwick Williams, it is a safe bet that he was an avid reader of novels. And that as a country boy who had come to live in London, he gazed with crude sexual lust at beautifully dressed young ladies like those of the Porter family, his chief accusers. As Cyriax points out in his entry on masturbation: 'Excessive indulgence in this harmless recreation is an early pointer to a budding serial killer.' If Williams had been as well off as his older contemporary James Boswell, he would no doubt have hired prostitutes in the Haymarket and possessed them against the nearest wall. Instead, the peculiar alchemy of frustration led him to slash women's clothes as a form of symbolic rape.

And there was another factor. In 1748 the novelist Henry Fielding, who had been launched on his career by a desire to share Richardson's success, became a London magistrate and founded the Bow Street Runners, London's first semi-official police force. Before that citizens relied on night watchmen to keep order. Now they had these visible representatives of the law, with the power of arrest, to protect them. For disaffected young layabouts like Renwick Williams, it was an additional cause to feel rebellious. As Gauguin put it, 'Life being what it is, one dreams of revenge.'

So the age of sex crime began, and has continued, so that we have appalling representatives like Pee Wee Gaskins, Andrei Chikatilo and the Hillside Stranglers.

There had, of course, been plenty of 'sex monsters' in past centuries: the fifteenth-century Vlad the Impaler of Wallachia, the original Dracula, who once ate dinner among hundreds of impaled bodies (many still alive); his contemporary Gilles de Rais, companion in arms of Joan of Arc, who raped and murdered dozens of peasant children and was burned in 1440; Countess Elizabeth Bathory, who in the sixteenth century killed fifty servant girls to bathe in their blood (which she believed kept her young). But they had been members of the ruling class, who had time and leisure to cultivate their sexual peculiarities. What had started to happen in the nineteenth century was that sex crime had ceased to be the preserve of the rich. Which helps to explain why, in the early twenty-first century, we find ourselves squarely in the midst of the age of the serial killer.

Crime, I have always felt, provides some of the most interesting sidelights on history.

Colin Wilson

Acknowledgements

Among the countless friends who provided support during the two years this volume was under compilation, David Nicholls should be singled out, first among equals, for his pithy reminder of the merits of keeping back-up diskettes; David Wilson, for repeatedly pointing out that, when something had been said once, there was little need to say it again; Simon Rae, for his unflagging support and encouragement; Patricia McClintock, for her profusion of apt and delicate artwork; Jenny England, for her flair in the face of adversity; Lizzie Owen, for persevering with the author photograph until one turned out presentable; Giles and Amanda de Margery, for one thing after another; and, for their various contributions, Anthony Berry, Julian and Charity Birch, Georgina Blomefield, George and James Brenan, Nicholas and Sarah Dent, Gian Douglas-Home, John Farmer, Anna, Jane and Pamela Foreman, Edward Littleton Fox, Jonathan Furber, Andrew Gatling, Joss Graham, Tahar Haddadi, Rupert and Helen Hardy, Richard Harvey, Rica Jones, David Keeling, Sophie Macpherson, Michael Merton, Penny Moore, Graham Morgan, Francis Morris, Sarah Nuttall, Shiela Parker and Penelope Rippon.

My grasp on the entrails of crime would never have been as firm without the kindness of Camille Wolff and Loretta Lay of Grey House Books, who took me under their wing, for months giving me the run of their library, their hospitality and their encyclopedic knowledge. Nor would the *Encyclopedia* have been either started or ended without the dual interventions of my editor, Laura Morris, who, having thought of the idea, told me when to start and, when she realised enough was enough, told me when to stop. I stand amazed at her forbearance, trust and culinary ability throughout, and, perhaps more important, at her finely tuned sense of revulsion which time and again helped weed out gratuitously unpalatable material.

And lastly, my very present help in time of trouble, Holly Nuttall, for her clear guidance, like a shining light.

Oliver Cyriax

A

A6 murder

On 4 April 1962 James Hanratty was executed for the murder of Michael Gregsten. On similar facts today, he would not be convicted. Forty-odd years ago, it seemed inconceivable that a Briton might hang for a crime he was tied to by almost no evidence; reviewing the case in 1964, the writer Charles Franklin observed that the English legal system was 'always thought by most people to be little short of perfect'.

Those days have gone for ever, as have the traffic conditions which gave the murder its extended, dream-like quality. For two hours on the night of 22 August 1961 Michael Gregsten and his lover Valerie Storie drove at gunpoint from Taplow, near Maidenhead, puttering almost alone through Slough and across the ghostly suburbs of north-west London before halting at the killing ground of Dead Man's Hill.

James Hanratty was convicted primarily on the identification evidence of Storie, Gregsten's companion and lover, who survived the ordeal. But only just.

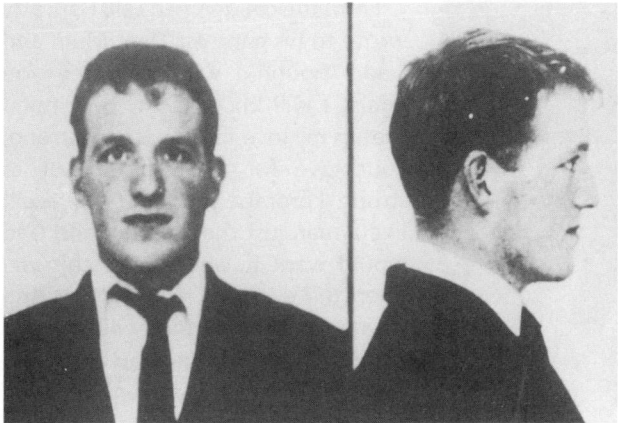

A rare photograph of James Hanratty, the petty criminal hanged for the A6 murder

First Miss Storie was raped in the back seat of the Morris Minor while her lover lay dead in the front; she heard the blood falling out of his head. Then the killer shot her repeatedly at close range, paralysing her from the waist down for the rest of her life.

The incident started at dusk with a sharp tap on the car window. Gregsten wound it down to be confronted by a revolver. 'This is a hold-up,' announced an immaculately dressed stranger. 'I am a desperate man.' Then he climbed into the car. During the next six hours Miss Storie only saw her assailant once with any clarity, for a few seconds, caught in the headlights of a passing vehicle while they were face to face. At the first **identification** parade Miss Storie pulled the wrong man. At the second, she made each suspect say one sentence spoken by the killer: 'Be quiet, will you, I am thinking.' Like the murderer, James Hanratty said, 'Be quiet, will you, I am finking.'

This was not Hanratty's only connection with the killing, but there was little else. As a semi-retarded petty burglar from London, he had no motive for barging into Gregsten's car in a country cornfield at Dorney Reach thirty miles from home. Every contact leaves a trace, but despite spending six hours in the car, there was not a shred of forensic evidence: no fibres from Hanratty's clothes, no mud, no hair, no fingerprints – nothing. Hanratty volunteered to supply samples of everything and, as he expected, received the all clear. Moreover, Hanratty was a competent driver, unlike the murderer. Gregsten and Storie were obliged to show the intruder where the car lights were and how the gears worked.

More recently, it has emerged that Hanratty had a good alibi. This defence was a late entrant at the trial, where it collapsed, but only on a technicality. At first Hanratty could only remember spending the night in question 250 miles away in a bed-and-breakfast in Rhyl overlooking a railway line. This took time to find, and his landlady's credibility was damaged when, in contravention of procedural rules, she spoke to another witness. By then it was too late to dig up further corroboration. But between 1966 and 1971, after Hanratty had gone to the gallows, fourteen witnesses came forward to support, in various ways, the story of his two nights in Rhyl.

Hanratty became enmeshed in the police investigation because on 11 September two .38 cartridge cases from the fatal gun were found in Room 24 of the Vienna Hotel, where he stayed the night before the murder under a false name, as James Ryan. The highly suspicious guest there *after* the murder (when the bullets were discharged, leaving the casings) was probably the actual killer. Peter Louis Alphon, who pronounces 'th' as 'f' when excited, went missing on the night of the murder, gave the police a false alibi and spent the five days after the killing locked in a room at the Alexandra Court Hotel in a highly disturbed state, refusing to come out, talking to himself, pacing the room and rummaging noisily through his wardrobe. Alphon led a nomadic life selling almanacs door to door and was something of a misfit – a mystic and a fascist who has ever since maintained his guilt to whoever will listen, not only claiming that he was paid £5,000 to put the fear of God into Valerie Storie, who was breaking up Gregsten's marriage, but also proving the money's receipt. He was seen in the Old Taplow Inn, where Gregsten and Miss Storie shared their last drink, on the night of the murder.

Alphon is still alive, an unemployed drifter at a cheap King's Cross hotel. He claims he obtained the gun, later found under the back seat of a 36A bus, through a criminal named Charles 'Dixie' France. But Alphon was the man Valerie Storie failed to recognise at the first identity parade on 24 September, conducted in hospital when scarcely off the danger list.

Dapper Peter Alphon, discharged on 4 October 1961

After Alphon's release, the police settled on Hanratty.

Recently published documents show that Miss Storie harboured misgivings before the next parade. 'My memory of this man's face is fading,' she told detectives. 'I am so afraid that when confronted with the man, I may not be able to pick him out.' Second time round, she deliberated twenty minutes before picking Hanratty. 'Oh Mr Acott,' exclaimed Hanratty, without guile, 'I've never killed a man in my life.'

Additional circumstantial evidence against Hanratty came from Charles France. But after helping secure the conviction, France committed suicide as the day of Hanratty's execution approached. France had befriended Hanratty, who took mild liberties with his wife, and it was probably France who told the police that 'Ryan' and Hanratty were the same man.

The cartridge cases from the Vienna Hotel came from the murder weapon, but it is difficult to believe that they were not .planted. First noticed on 11 September, they reposed openly on a chair, which needed moving each time the bed was made, in a room regularly cleaned for nearly three weeks. Today, sixteen boxes of papers remain secret in Scotland Yard. The Crown wants to keep them locked up for a further seventy-five years, and the Yard continues to withhold exhibits which might resolve the issue by **genetic fingerprinting.**

From the condemned cell, Hanratty wrote to his parents: 'Dear Mum and Dad, Though I will never see you again, I will know in my own mind that as my love for you is very strong, your love for me will be just as strong. I promise you that I will face it like a man just the way you and Dad would want it, and I hope this will open the eyes of many people. And what I have said before, will one day be proved to the world. So Mum and Dad until we meet again, you will always be in my thoughts. From your ever loving son, Jim.'

After watching him hang, David

Hanratty's father outside the House of Commons leafleting passers-by, seven years after his son went to the gallows

Lines the Under Sheriff noted how very distressing it was to return to the vacant cell and see Hanratty's pyjamas and half-empty cup of tea, still there.

In fact, to everyone's astonishment, genetic fingerprint tests conducted in 2002 proved Hanratty's guilt beyond doubt. The evidence was presented on a BBC 2 television programme, *The A6 Murder*, on 16 May 2002. The semen stain on Valerie Storie's knickers, and mucus on a handkerchief found wrapped round the murder weapon, a .38 calibre revolver, proved to match the DNA from Hanratty's own exhumed remains (from teeth). Unconvinced, Hanratty's supporters argued that Hanratty's clothing had been taken to court in the same box as the knickers and the handkerchief, and that they could therefore have been contaminated by his skin cells. But even if the sperm stain and the mucus were contaminated, they would also have revealed the genetic profile of the actual killer. And only one profile was revealed.

Hanratty's father died shortly before this evidence came to light.

See also **Concentration**

Accidents

Loosely speaking, murder means killing the victim deliberately. Legal problems can arise when you intend to despatch A, but do away with B by mistake.

In 1907, an English case came to court involving a landlord, Richard Beck, who drank himself to death along with his wife Hilda. The couple took a swig from a bottle of stout spiked with prussic acid, left invitingly open in their rooming house by a crook named Richard Brinkley.

Brinkley, a cabinet-maker, had actually wanted to poison their lodger, Reginald Parker, whom he was meeting for a drink under the pretext of buying his bulldog. But Parker was more concerned to do business. Five pounds were at stake, and they slipped out to examine the animal without starting on the bottle. Meanwhile the Becks returned, feeling thirsty.

In court, the defence pleaded not guilty to murdering the Becks, arguing that Brinkley had no intention of killing them. But he had meant to kill someone, albeit someone else, and the prosecution triumphed through the principle of 'transference of malice aforethought'. Brinkley went to the gallows.

Today, Brinkley would be guilty of Parker's attempted murder; he tried, but failed. Nor was the death of the Becks (where he succeeded but did not try) mere manslaughter. To prove murder simply entails matching the outcome (death) to an intent to take life, and the fact that Brinkley wanted to silence someone else ranked as no more than a personal misfortune. No one else would do, since Parker's testimony (if he lived) threatened Brinkley's exposure as a fraud.

Brinkley had recently persuaded Parker to witness the will of a 77-year-old widow, Johanna Blume from Fulham, with whom he was on friendly terms. Thinking to put her name down for a holiday excursion to the seaside, Blume signed away her property, and when she died two days later on 19 December 1906 Brinkley claimed her entire estate. The relatives contested the will, and disaster loomed unless Parker could be silenced.

On learning of the Becks' deaths, Brinkley's first words to the police were, 'Well, I'll be buggered.' His next sentence was no better considered: 'If anyone says

The exhumation of Johanna Blume

I bought beer they have got to prove it.' But no one, so far, had. Brinkley's past career suggested that Johanna Blume's timely demise – diagnosed as cerebral haemorrhage – was no coincidence. Fourteen years previously Brinkley's wife, Laura Jane, had apparently committed suicide by poisoning herself. Thereafter Brinkley stored a chest of chemicals in his room and, on one occasion, amused himself by poisoning chickens. He made two other attempts on Parker's life, poisoning his whisky and tea. Parker, already a worried man, threw the first on to the fire and refused to touch the second.

Amid mounting excitement the police had Johanna Blume exhumed, but the autopsy's results were unexpectedly negative. Apart from its distinctive odour, prussic acid leaves no marked signs on the organs visible to the naked eye, and theorists have posited a doctor with a defective sense of smell.

See also **Dummy**

Acid Bath Haigh (1909–49)

The confession and trial of John George Haigh in 1949 brightened the austerity of post-war Britain. It was probably the most publicised case of the century, with the *Daily Mirror* going a step too far with headlines like 'Vampire Killer'. The *Mirror*'s editor, Silvester Bolam, wound up in Brixton Prison serving three months for contempt of court.

The murderer, dapper John Haigh, made two serious mistakes. First, he was convinced that under English law the police needed a body in order to obtain a convic-

tion. This is wrong (although it is true that the murderer must be charged with killing a particular individual). This first misconception of Haigh's encouraged his blithe confession: he believed that he had utterly destroyed the body by immersing it in a bath of sulphuric acid. This second notion was equally mistaken. His final victim – 69-year old Olive Durand-Deacon – had indeed turned into a puddle of nasty grey sludge, but enough solid evidence remained to piece together her identity.

Haigh felt so confident that on 20 February he dropped round to Chelsea police station with a friend of Mrs Durand-Deacon's to report his victim's disappearance. An astute woman desk sergeant distrusted his demeanour, and Haigh's record was checked, turning up three prison sentences, one for fraud and two for theft. On 26 February the police forced their way into Haigh's 'factory', a bare brick shed in Crawley with naked lightbulbs, a wooden workbench and a sign outside reading 'Hurstlea Products'. There the officers unearthed three carboys of concentrated sulphuric acid, rubber clothing, a revolver, and a dry cleaning receipt for Mrs Durand-Deacon's Persian lamb coat.

Under questioning Haigh came clean: 'If I told you the truth you wouldn't believe me … Mrs Durand-Deacon no longer exists! She has disappeared completely, and no trace of her can ever be found again … I have

John George Haigh, acid bath killer

destroyed her with acid. You will find the sludge which remains in Leopold Road. Every trace has gone. How can you prove murder if there is no body?'

Given Haigh's detailed confession, the answer was 'without much difficulty' and he was hanged on 6 August 1949 after a one-day trial. His original two-and-a-half-hour statement related how he enticed the crucially plump Mrs Durand-Deacon to his workshop to discuss plans for the manufacture of plastic fingernails. Then he shot her with his .38 Webley, squeezed her body into a forty-gallon drum and went out for tea at Ye Olde Ancient Priors Restaurant. After a poached egg on toast, he pumped sulphuric acid into the tank and, four days later, when he judged the decomposition complete, tipped Mrs Durand-Deacon away as fat into the workshop yard.

'Aha, gallstones!' pronounced an observant Professor Keith Simpson, the Home Office pathologist, standing in Mrs Deacon's residual sludge. The portly victim's gallstones were coated with an indigenous fatty substance that resisted the action of the acid, and the stones now lay amid a liquescent smear some six feet by four permeating the earth to a depth of four inches. Professor Simpson had 475 pounds of the grease and muck dug up and, back at the lab, produced twenty-eight pounds of yellow animal fat, a total of three gallstones, eighteen bones and a set of dentures. The hip bone revealed that the victim was a woman, the fat suggested someone plump, the osteoarthritis indicated late adult age, and the teeth tied the remains unequivocally to Mrs Durand-Deacon.

Despite attempts to sham insanity by imbibing his urine whenever under observation, Haigh was convicted of murder after fifteen minutes' consideration by the jury. Had he held his tongue for a few more weeks, it is unlikely that any evidence would have survived with the exception of the gallstones. But without finding the body from which they were missing, no one could have proved the stones belonged to Mrs Durand-Deacon.

Haigh had previously done away with the entire family McSwann as well as Archie and Rosalie Henderson, appropriating the property of these five victims for the then substantial total of £12,000 in five years. He drove the fifteen-stone Mrs Durand-Deacon to her rendezvous with death in his smart Alvis, but her killing – likewise for profit – netted a mere £100 in jewellery, with a possible £50 due from her coat. The inspiration for his method of body disposal came upon Haigh in a prison workshop, where he rehearsed on mice.

Before execution, Haigh basked in his new-found celebrity, confessing to three more fictitious murders, and professed to have relished drinking his victims' blood. As a child, he was nurtured on Bible stories, mostly those concerned with sacrifice. 'It isn't everybody who can create more sensation than a film star,' he reassured his parents in a letter from prison. 'Only Princess Margaret or Mr Churchill could command such interest.'

Much of the difficulty in putting London's **Kray** twins behind bars in the 1960s turned on the similar dearth of cadavers, which makes it harder to prove that anyone has died. Kray victim Frank 'the Mad **Axeman**' Mitchell just disappeared, and the twins got off. But **Jack the Hat**'s body vanished, and that charge stuck; there were sufficient witnesses. In Haigh's case, the body was found, but in a different shape and form as grease.

Acid doctor

Murders with acid are rare. The so-called 'acid doctor' was a solitary exception, a Californian who tortured his bride of five weeks to death to warn her against the perils of infidelity. As Dr Geza de Kaplany elucidated on his arrest: 'I wanted to take her beauty away. I wanted to put fear into her as a warning against adultery.' He did this on 28 August 1962 in the privacy of a San Jose honeymoon cottage at 1125 Ranchero Way, scorching out her eyes, breasts and genitals with acid, disfiguring 60 per cent of her body with third-degree burns.

His bride was a 25-year-old beauty queen, an ex-show girl and daughter of an Olympic fencing champion; he was a 36-year-old anaesthetist of noble Hungarian blood. Neighbours contacted the police because of the noise, and de Kaplany departed under escort, looking for all the world as though he were going to a dinner party. Inside the apartment was a note: 'If you want to live, 1. Do not shout. 2. Do what I tell you. 3. Or else you will die.'

The wife expired after thirty-three days, though nine specialists worked free of charge to save her; towards the end, her mother stayed at the bedside praying for death.

At the first day of the trial on 14 January 1963, the prosecutor showed de Kaplany a photograph of his dead wife, with the flesh rotting away from her bones.

Her face, brownish-black, had a hard appearance, like overtanned leather. 'No, no, no,' de Kaplany screamed. 'What did you do to her?'

What did *who* do, the court wondered. That same day de Kaplany pleaded guilty; expert witnesses pronounced him a 'paranoid schizophrenic with catatonic features'. Then a Dr Russell Lee disclosed that de Kaplany himself was not the killer; the true culprit was his murderous alter ego, 'Pierre la Roche'. The accused suffered from a split personality, at that time the last word in psychiatry.

In the witness box, de Kaplany confirmed that he had attended the scene of the crime while 'Pierre' poured acid on his wife. Thereafter the trial became hard to follow. No longer clear who was under cross-examination, the defendant – split into two components – offered the court alternative versions of events. 'That evening,' de Kaplany testified, 'Pierre beat her, beat her, beat her. From that point I was vanishing and *I* was dragged and *I* was nowhere, except that I was still aware...'

After thirty-five days the jury found de Kaplany legally sane but medically insane. Sentenced to life, he served thirteen years, and was released in 1975 to follow his new **vocation** as a medical missionary in Taiwan. The parole board (the head of which subsequently resigned) had found him work as a fledgling heart specialist.

In 1991 Briton Cecil Jackson killed his wife in an acid bath. But this was by mistake. Jackson supposed that he had strangled her to death before dumping the body in a tank brimming with hydrochloric acid.

But Dassa Jackson was still alive. Two hours later, pensioners passing the garage thought they heard someone whimpering in pain. They prised open the lockup door to reveal Dassa sitting in a pool of fuming liquid, her clothes in tatters, with a vat-like container steaming in the background. She died in hospital.

See also **MPD**

Acquittals

Easy to obtain in Chicago during the Prohibition era. Most cases never reached court. In 1920 Al Capone first made news immediately after shaking hands with Joe Howard. 'Hi, Al,' said Joe, stretching out his hand in a crowded bar. Then Capone shot him dead; the next day the papers carried the mobster's photograph over the caption 'Tony (Scarface) Capone, also known as Al Brown, who killed Joe Howard by firing six shots into his body in the saloon of Heinie Jacobs at 2300 South Wabash Avenue, in a renewal of the beer war.' But with no further clues, the inquest jury affirmed that Howard was murdered with 'bullets fired from a revolver' by 'unknown white male persons'.

As the Twenties progressed, the gulf between Chicago law and enforcement assumed extraordinary proportions. On 5 May 1926 the authorities made front-page news with a formal statement: 'It has been established to the satisfaction of the State's Attorney's office and the detective bureau that Capone in person led the slayers of McSwiggin ... It has also been found that Capone handled the machine-gun.' No further action was taken. After a few months Capone was officially exonerated and the charge (quite possibly ill-founded) withdrawn.

Securing a conviction proved even more fraught than bringing a case. The future leader of the Irish bootlegging contingent, smiling Dion **O'Bannion**, was apprehended by the police in 1921 on his knees with his tools embedded in the office safe of the Postal Telegraph Building. After distribution of an estimated $30,000 in bribes, the jury dismissed the evidence as inconclusive.

But at least there was a quorum; four years later, when the fearsome duo **Anselmi and Scalise** were arraigned, 234 out of the first 238 potential jurors declined to serve for urgent personal reasons.

Chicago witnesses were habitually intimidated, bribed, or just wilted from the face of the earth. The rare judge not on the take became extremely irritated. On 9 November 1926, a gloomy Judge Harry B. Miller commented on the acquittal of Saltis and Koncil in the teeth of the facts: 'I expected a different verdict on the evidence. I think the evidence warranted a verdict of guilty.'

Chicago's entrammelled reformist mayor, William E. Dever, inaugurated his career with ringing declarations: 'This guerrilla war between hijackers, rum runners and illicit beer pedlars can and will be crushed.' But by the end of Dever's term in 1926 (before things really got under way), gangland killings had topped 130. A total of six suspects came to trial.

Five were discharged. The odd man out was unlucky Sam Vinci, but his fall from grace owed more to loss of self-control than poor planning. At the inquest into his brother's death, Vinci became uneasy that the killer,

John Minnati, might avoid his just deserts. So he shot Minatti with his .45 in open court, earning a 25-year sentence. The evidence against him was simply too strong; but no stronger, one might think, than the amateur video-tape of white policemen subjecting black motorist Rodney **King** to fifty-six truncheon blows in downtown Los Angeles on 3 March 1991. Fear is not the only reason for a verdict of 'not guilty', and when the jury acquitted the lawmen at the first trial, Los Angeles was put to the torch.

Adipocere

A rough guide to the date of death for bodies left outside in the damp. Adipocere is a repellent yellowy-white substance engendered by the stiffening and swelling of a corpse's body fats; mostly, the limbs, chest wall and sometimes the face are affected. Once in place, adipocere maintains the outline body shape in recognisable condition and, three years after burial in 1949, the bodies of Beryl and Geraldine Evans, victims of the **Rillington Place** murders, were clearly identifiable.

In temperate conditions the conversion – also known as saponification – does not happen until some five or six weeks after death. But heat generated from, for instance, maggot infestation, can accelerate the transformation by a week or two.

Maggots adhere to a reasonably precise timetable. Flies cannot lay their eggs until the host body has cooled to about 30°C, a temperature only attained some six hours after death. Sensors in their feet direct them towards moist areas, like orifices, and the first batch of eggs hatches within eight to twenty-four hours, depending on meteorological conditions. The maggots glut on the body, favouring muscular tissues and eschewing fat, and, as they grow, evolve through three distinct stages, known as instars, in the course of ten to twelve days. Then the maggots, gorged on flesh, start to pupate, and the new generation of flies emerges from the pupa after a further twelve days.

These are minimum times, and hence the minimum period elapsed since the corpse's exposure can be computed, as can the maximum time since death: flies are attracted to smells and gases emanating from a fresh body, but after a couple of weeks they lose interest. The particular species infesting the body will show where it has lain.

Advertisements

In fiction, the cracksman John Clay advertised for a fallguy in Conan **Doyle**'s *The Red Headed League*. In real life Charles Henry Schwartz, a bogus Californian inventor, advertised for a murder victim. Schwartz had insured his own life for $185,000, and planned to fake his death. Needing a corpse of comparable physique, he specified that the preferred applicant for the post of chemist's assistant would possess small hands and feet. In the end Schwartz made do with an itinerant missionary, G. W. Barbe, three inches too tall, but death by burning causes appreciable shrinkage.

Schwartz killed Barbe with a blow to the head, extracted an upper right molar for a rough dental match, gouged out the eyes (which were the wrong colour) and burned off his victim's fingerprints with acid (see **Removal**). Then, on 25 July 1925, he blew up his laboratory, the Pacific Cellulose Plant in Walnut Creek, with the dead Barbe inside. A few days later, for good measure, Schwartz broke into his wife's house and stole all their photographs to further complicate identification.

The dead Barbe was horribly charred. But one of his **ears** survived in presentable condition and, perusing a studio negative of Schwartz obtained from nearby Oakland, the investigators realised that the cadaver's ear did not resemble the one in the picture. Thus Barbe's ear, with its distinct Darwinian tubercle, proved his murderer's undoing. The real Schwartz, by then hiding under an assumed name, gave himself away by categorically insisting to his new landlord, out of the blue, that the body in the local laboratory definitely belonged to Schwartz. The police were called, and surrounded the house; Schwartz committed suicide.

His invention consisted of an industrial process for the manufacture of artificial silk. But on investigation, not only were Schwartz's samples indistinguishable from the real thing; they *were* the real thing. Misgivings about his standing as an inventor initially took root because his laboratory was not connected to gas or water.

Other killers have touted for victims, including Belle **Gunness** of Indiana and Carl J. Folk, the American travelling carnival proprietor. But in these cases there was nothing ominous in the wording; Belle Gunness wanted rich suitors, and Folk, a domestic. German insurance fraudster Kurt Tetzner's quest for a corpse led him to advertise for a 'travelling companion', but in the event he killed a hitch-hiker picked up at random.

Aeroplanes

Used on 5 October 1949 by the murderer and racketeer Donald Hume to scatter the remains of his victim, a second-hand car dealer, over the Essex marshes. The corpse was first dismembered and the portions wrapped in three parcels, one of which was unwrapped a fortnight later by a farm labourer out wildfowling in his punt. He came across a sodden bundle on the mud flats.

The segments were reassembled in London by the pathologist Dr Francis Camps. Relying on his wartime experience of pilots whose parachutes had failed to open, Camps suggested that the body had been tipped out of an aircraft, and a police check on the United Services Flying Club at Elstree disclosed that a petty thief, Brian Donald Hume, had recently hired an Auster sports plane, arriving for the day encumbered by two large parcels.

Hume's first explanation was that three desperadoes –

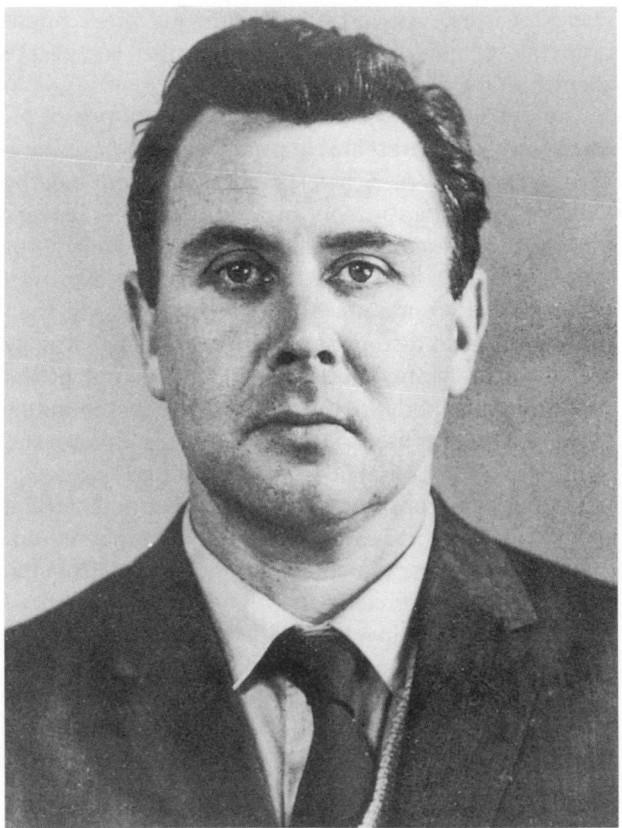

Donald Hume, whose inventive method of body disposal landed him in prison, where he was privy to Timothy Evans's partial confession to the Rillington Place murders

Mac, Greenie and The Boy – took him flying, compelling him to jettison what they swore were the wrapped components of an illicit printing press from a petrol coupon scheme. But the carpet in Hume's flat betrayed extensive bloodstaining.

Halfway through the Old Bailey trial the judge died. At the end of the second court case, the jury could not agree, and during the third, the murder charges were dropped when Hume pleaded guilty to the lesser charge of accessory to murder.

Released in 1958, Hume published his confession in the *Sunday Pictorial* on 1 June, changed his name to Brown, left for Switzerland, shot a man in a Zurich bank robbery on 30 January 1959, received a life sentence, went mad and was repatriated in manacles in April 1988 for hospitalisation. It is not generally known that at the newspaper party celebrating his conviction an effigy of his head was produced, stuffed with baked beans which spilled out on to its mount.

Other miscreants, intent on accomplishing limited objectives regardless of cost, have resorted to aircraft. In 1955 Jack Gilbert Graham, an American insurance fraudster, determined to murder his mother, Mrs Daisie King, for her $150,000 estate. After secreting twenty-six sticks of dynamite in her suitcase together with an activated timer, he managed to take out a last-minute $37,500 policy on her life before the scheduled flight took off from Denver airport on 1 November. All forty-four passengers lost their lives in the explosion.

Graham later admitted to being deeply resentful of his mother's decision to go away over Thanksgiving, and he was gassed at the Colorado State Penitentiary on 11 January 1957. The Canadian Marguerite Pitre was executed for a similar lack of restraint after a Quebec Airways DC3 exploded in mid-air during a flight from Montreal to Seven Islands in September 1949. Twenty-three passengers and air-crew died as a result of a bomb in the forward luggage compartment. Pitre was arrested, widely remembered as the 'fat middle-aged woman' who arrived by taxi and demanded to have a parcel put on board just before take-off. Her aim, in which she succeeded, was to dispose of her lover's wife.

Aiello Brothers

Sicilian gangsters in Chicago who assumed the mantle of the Genna mob, exploiting illiterate immigrant peasants as scab labour and **poisoning** them with rotgut liquor. In 1926 the Aiellos resolved to assassinate Al Capone, and formed a North Side coalition with Moran, Skidmore, Zuta and Bertsche.

The Aiellos broadcast an appeal for volunteers: 'Fifty thousand dollars to anyone who shows us a Capone notch.' Four men tried and four men died, their bodies each found with an unfired gun and a contemptuous nickel placed in their cold right hands. Capone knew someone was gunning for him, but not who, until the Aiellos' next ploy. The chef of the Little Italy Café, a favourite Capone haunt, was offered $10,000 to dose the great man's soup with prussic acid. But he took fright and blabbed.

The next attempt on Capone was inadvertently interrupted by Chief Detective O'Connor's armoured-car squad, which landed Joseph Aiello in jail for questioning about the machine-gun nest installed opposite Hinky Dink Kenna's tobacco shop (where Capone bought his cigars). That night, twenty-five men from the Capone mob besieged the police station angling for a go at Aiello.

'Gunmen defy police: invade law's stronghold' read the headlines the next morning. 'Chicago gun-fighters almost achieved the ultimate in assassination yesterday when they silently encircled the Detective Bureau and waited patiently for the opportunity to kill Joseph Aiello.' Three of Capone's henchmen had themselves arrested and penned in a cell next to Aiello. 'You're dead, friend, you're dead,' Louis Campagna hissed in Sicilian dialect across the bars.

But Joseph survived the night, and was released into hiding. Biding his time, in October 1930 he decided to make a run for it, bought a rail ticket for Texas and telephoned for a taxi to the station. Hurrying from his doorway, Joseph was caught in crossfire by two machine-gunners who between them scored fifty-nine hits. The bullets in his body weighed a pound.

See also **Smokescreen, West Midlands Crime Squad**

Airgun

The intended weapon for the abortive 1917 assassination attempt on the British Prime Minister, Lloyd George. A group of Derby malcontents coalesced around a Mrs Wheeldon, her two daughters and her son-in-law, a chemist. Their watchword was 'Lloyd George must die' and to this end they resolved to shoot the premier with poisoned darts while he played golf at Walton Heath. For poison they chose curare, in regular tribal use in South America for coating arrowheads. It causes death by asphyxia after first paralysing the motor nerve endings of the spinal column.

There was nothing intrinsically wrong with the plan, but its execution was marred by the choice of the marksman, Herbert Booth, an anti-subversion agent from military intelligence. Mrs Wheeldon was sentenced to ten years' hard labour, but Lloyd George regarded the affair as a joke and had her released early.

The case is notable for a unique prosecution collaboration between ballistics and poison experts.

Alcatraz, Birdman of

Robert Franklin Stroud (1887–1963) bears little resemblance to the saintly figure portrayed by Burt Lancaster in the 1961 film. Stroud started out as a pimp in Alaska, and when a bartender refused to pay the $10 due to his girl Kitty O'Brien, Stroud shot him dead.

Sentenced to twelve years in Leavenworth Penitentiary, Stroud was consistently unpopular as a tight-lipped, self-obsessed, predatory homosexual with fellow convicts, one of whom characterised him 'as attractive as a barracuda'. Towards the end of his term, for no known reason Stroud knifed a warder in the mess hall, saying afterwards, 'The guard took sick and died all of a sudden. He died of heart trouble. I guess you would call it a puncture of the heart.' After her laconic boy was sentenced to death, Stroud's mother secured a reprieve from President Woodrow Wilson on condition that he remained in solitary confinement. There he learned about birds, and died the best canary doctor in America.

Britain now has its Fishman of Saughton. The murderer Alex Torbet won an international reputation for his expertise in breeding African tilapia. Stirling University's Institute of Aquaculture established a fishroom inside Saughton Prison, and Torbet demonstrated that the tilapia, with its rapid growth and high protein content, may have a role to play in the alleviation of Third World hunger.

Aliases

Also known as 'monikers'. A few mobster derivations include: Jacob 'Gurrah' Shapiro (for shouting 'Gurrah here'); Sam 'Teets' Battaglia ('I'll bust ya in da teets'); Vincent 'Mad Dog' Coll (shot down children in error during a gunfight); Jack 'Legs' Diamond (outpaced police); and Charles 'Lucky' Luciano (survived being hung by his thumbs and then left for dead with his throat cut). Abe 'Kid Twist' Reles's nickname came from his addiction to munching boxfuls of chocolate candy twists; Vito Gurino was known as 'Chicken Head' because he practised his aim by shooting their living heads off, and Frank Abbanando was always referred to as 'the Dasher' after being chased round the block by an intended victim when his gun misfired. Frank lapped his pursuer, reloaded, and nailed the man in the back of the head.

A false name often has some obvious connection with the criminal. Mme Bosch (executed 1910) gave her married name while making enquiries at the scene of the crime, and the American murderer William A. Dorr (executed 1914) sought to avoid detection under the alias Willis A. Dow.

Allorto and Seller (d. 1889)

French criminals guillotined in front of an audience of sightseers in 1889, the year of the Paris Exhibition. Travel agents Thomas Cook included the double event in their list of scheduled attractions, laying on a special excursion of seven horse-drawn buses, each packed to its full capacity of forty seats.

The tourists were doubtless enjoined to listen attentively. The **guillotine** whipped off a condemned man's head with such despatch that, post-decapitation, his lungs still contained the air from his last breath. Thus the corpse was obliged to exhale and, lacking a windpipe, could be heard whistling through the neck.

This sound was noted by F. Tennyson Jesse, who attended the last public execution at Versailles in 1939, when buskers diverted the drunken crowds and spectators perched in trees. Jesse wrote: 'There came a last exclamation from Weidmann – and that was involuntary – the whistling that always sounds when a head is cut off. For the neck gives out a gasp as the last breath of air leaves the lungs, though the head be already in the basket.' For many years previously it had been general practice to guillotine at dawn, well behind a police cordon.

The guillotine was finally abolished in 1981, when four prisoners awaited its embrace.

The guillotine

Amnesia

It is worth mastering the intricacies of amnesia before running it as a defence. In particular, a blow severe enough for a knock-out causes retrograde amnesia; the disturbance of the brain prevents the event from imprinting on the memory. There is a tiny time-lag between an event and its being stored, and if the system is down at the moment of the command 'save', the mind remains blank. Boxers have no recollection of the blow that stuns them.

In South Africa, successful businessman Ronald Cohen did not know this. Thus his deposition of the struggle on the evening of 5 April 1970, when he tried to ward off the attacker of his beautiful young wife found dead, Cluedo-style, in the library, was marked by total recall of the impact on the back of his head from a hefty wedding present, a ram's head ornament weighing seven pounds. According to Cohen, the killer used it to knock him out.

This untoward 'island of memory' turned Cohen into the murder suspect. There had been no intruder and no fight. In prison serving a twelve-year sentence, the 41-year-old Cohen admitted to killing his wife, half his age, during a quarrel when he accused her of enjoying sexual relations with their children.

Genuine amnesia is a typical response of the perpetrator in domestic murders, often followed by a dissociative telephone call along the lines of 'There's a knife in my hand. I think my wife is dead. You'd better come quick and bring the police.' On interview the killer is likely to say, 'I don't know what happened', and this sincere memory block can persist for some time, occasionally indefinitely. In 1974 the Philadelphia psychologist in the **MacDonald** case cited an English study estimating that 60 per cent of the murderers in their survey were amnesic for the event. Likewise, the best efforts of John Reginald Christie, the British strangler, to furnish a detailed account of his killings leave the reader with the mysterious impression of women dropping dead for no apparent reason. 'She started struggling like anything and some of her clothing got torn. She then fell sort of limp as I had hold of her. She sank to the ground and I think some of her clothing must have got caught round her neck in the struggle. She was just out of the kitchen in the passageway. I tried to lift her up but couldn't. I then pulled her into the kitchen on to a chair. I felt her pulse, but it wasn't beating.'

A form of 'false amnesia' is on the loose in America. This is the phenomenon of 'recovered memory' manifested in satanic **ritual abuse** cases, where those accused of murdering or raping children may shoulder guilt for repeated but forgotten transgressions committed over an extended period. Their accusers believe that their own recollections of the horrible incidents were similarly cloaked for years by a quirk of the unconscious mind, and these are thus unusual crimes, in that neither the victim nor the offender remembers their having happened, until seeing a therapist.

The most celebrated confessor, a puzzled Paul R.

Ingram from Olympia, Washington, began his admissions to his daughters' accusations in 1988 with comments like, 'I can't see myself doing this', or 'There may be a dark side of me I don't know about', and peppered his ensuing statement with vague suggestions that he 'probably' did this, or 'would have' done that. After spending six months peering beyond his memory block into a visualisation of past misdemeanours, Ingram was induced to plead guilty to third-degree rape. Before sentencing, he realised that his amnesia was a false interpolation. He had never molested anyone. But it was too late to recant.

Prosecution witnesses, too, can undergo sudden attacks of forgetfulness. In 1973 Dr Keith Simpson, the Home Office pathologist, overheard an extreme regional variant while in Port of Spain for the trial of Michael X. In the neighbouring court Simpson listened to counsel for the prosecution asking the sole witness to a stabbing for her version of events. After a pause she replied: 'Ah done remember nutt'n. Coconut done fall on my head since, an ah' done know nutt'n.' The case collapsed.

See also **Memory, Rillington Place**

Ampere, one

Tests have shown that an electrical current of one ampere passing through the brain of the average human being will soon make him dead. This is the sort of throughput per second of a 100-watt bulb, but the high resistance of human body-tissue requires voltages in the order of 2,000. This figure must be revised upwards if the victim suffers from tuberculosis, as the lowered level of chlorine in his blood impairs his capacity to conduct. Similar allowances are called for in cold, dry weather, which makes for poor electrical contact.

A sustained electrical jolt raises the blood temperature to about 138 degrees, making restoration of life impossible, the more so as the nervous system is mangled beyond repair. If the scalp is sliced off after death, the dome of the skull underneath is revealed as completely desiccated. Sawing off the top section of the head confirms that the dura encasing the brain has lost its coloration, and when this covering is peeled away the grey matter readily discloses capillary haemorrhaging. In other words, the blood vessels at micro-levels have burst. Lifting out the brain shows that internal bleeding continues far down into its base at

The electric chair

the level of the third and fourth ventricle, and beyond into the spinal cord.

It is said that the victim feels nothing. The theory runs that the electric current coursing into the head arrives at the brain faster than the nerves can relay the information that this sensation hurts. So the brain is paralysed before registering discomfort, and all the twitching and thrashing around in the chair is the muscle spasms of an already unconscious man.

See also **Electric chair**, **Kemmler**, **String**

Ananda VII, King of Siam (1921–45)

The death of the 21-year-old King of Siam in the Year of the Dog 2489 (i.e. 1946) precipitated one of the world's longest and more confusing criminal trials.

On the morning of 9 June the young king was discovered dead in his private suite in the Barompiman Palace by his page Nai Chit. The corpse lay bleeding from a head wound with a pistol close to its outstretched left hand. 'The King's shot himself,' Nai

Chit cried, and thereafter wave upon wave of relatives and court functionaries, nannies, pages and politicians poured into the bedchamber, progressively obliterating the evidence. The weapon, an American .45 Colt automatic, was repeatedly handled and the body (which was divine) withheld from police examination.

The trial became a jamboree for conflicting theories. After the dust from a 1947 *coup d'état* had settled, proceedings started in August 1948. The prosecution called 124 witnesses, including fifteen doctors and scores of experts, none of whom thought to prove either that the bullet embedded in the mattress or the cartridge case on the floor originated from the gun by the King's side. The case unfolded on the basis of interminable woolly conjecture and disputed recollections; during the second year, two defence counsel were arrested for treason and another resigned. The surviving lawyer was called Fat Nasingkhla.

The court sat every other week for three days and not until the summer of 1950 did the defence have their say. In spring the following year the verdict was announced, whereupon the one convicted man – Nai Chit – appealed. This hearing occupied a further fifteen months and the judgment alone (which confirmed Chit's guilt and also condemned two accomplices previously acquitted) took fourteen hours to read.

Appeals to the Supreme Court were despatched in a rapid ten months, leading to the accuseds' execution after nearly six years in custody. Following the death of Dr Niyomsen, the pathologist on the first team of inquiry, his pupils had their lecturer displayed in a beautiful glass case, mounted as a skeleton at the Bangkok Medico-Legal Institute in token of their esteem. The fees of the one English participant, a very frustrated Professor Keith Simpson, were paid in cash, at night, counted out under a lamppost in London's Cromwell Road.

Apart from the king being right-handed, an early indication pointing to murder was that his body was found lying down on a bed. Suicides do not shoot themselves in this relaxed posture; they stand up or sit up.

The longest criminal trial in Britain ended on 6 February 1992 after eighteen months. The £9 million fraud case racked up £3 million in legal fees and involved 375 witnesses; computers helped the jury keep track. The principal defendant, Peter Kellard, was jailed for four years.

Animals

On the European Continent, animals featured regularly as criminals. Between 1120 and 1541 France held eighty trials conducted in the normal way with full legal formalities. The accused appeared in the dock, the Public Prosecutor brought the case, the judge passed sentence, and the executioner killed it.

Sometimes the animals were dressed as people, and in 1386 a sow (condemned for murder) went to the gallows in human clothing. The Saint-Martin de Laon pig, convicted of infanticide in 1494, was sentenced to be 'hanged and strangled on a fork of wood', and the *Petite Chronique de Bâle* records a cross-dressing cockerel which gave birth to an egg. The deviant was burned alive in the market place, along with the egg. Buggered sheep, donkeys and pigs were frequently consigned to the same fate, and as late as 1581 the Nuremberg executioner, Franz Schmidt, recorded in his diary for 6 August, 'George Schörpff, a lecher, guilty of beastliness with four cows, two calves and a sheep, was beheaded for unnatural vice, and afterwards burnt, together with a cow.' Perhaps its three confederates could not be identified, for the concept of individual responsibility was strictly applied.

This principle was established by the brilliant young lawyer, Bartholomé Chassenée, who forged his reputation in 1510 with the case of the Autun rats, arguing that his clients could not be tried unless they were summoned individually. A transcript of a 1520 hearing shows Chassenée in fine fettle trying to save some woodworm threatened with excommunication after they devoured the Bishop of Besançon's throne in the church of Saint-Michel, a mischance which came to light when the seat collapsed under Bishop Hugo's weight on 21 April of that year. Hugo banged his head and went mad.

The woodworm were summoned on 12 August, and on their behalf Chassenée proposed, first, that the court had no jurisdiction (since the defendants were *bestioles* and not people); second, that woodworm could not be tried *in absentia* and, say what the prosecution might about due legal process, no evidence was forthcoming that his clients had either acknowledged the summons or were in a position to travel to court; third, it could not be proved that the woodworm now in the church were the woodworm responsible for demolishing the throne; fourth, that – being woodworm and so framed by God – they were entitled to eat wood, even when inconveniently situated; and fifth,

the remedy sought was inappropriate. *Bestioles* could not be excommunicated because, lacking immortal souls, they had never communicated.

In short, Chassenée behaved in the irritating way that pettifogging lawyers always have, splitting hairs. But the central plank of his submissions – that the defendants were not 'endowed with reason or volition' – shows the issue of personal responsibility already on the legal agenda: and *mutatis mutandis* the same consideration was argued back and forth during Jeffrey **Dahmer**'s trial of 1992.

See also **Budgerigar, Pets**

Anselmi and Scalise (d. 1929)

A Chicago hitman team known as the Homicide Squad. Of a noticeably gorilla-like appearance, John Scalise and Albert Anselmi had barrel-shaped torsos with short legs, dangling arms and scowling, rubbery faces. In 1925 the couple became the unlikely focus of a legal defence fund.

On 13 June 1925, accompanied by Mike Genna, the pair went looking for trouble with the Weiss gang, driving around Chicago's North Side hunting for their rivals. After a brief running gun battle, they committed a traffic offence on Western Avenue. 'Hoodlums,' cried Detective Michael J. Conway, 'let's get after them.'

The patrol car set off in hot pursuit, topping seventy miles an hour. At 59th Street a lorry crossed the gangsters' path; they skidded, mounted the pavement, felled a lamppost and juddered to a halt.

The police car came to rest a few feet distant. 'What's the idea?' demanded Detective Conway, getting out with his gun still in its holster. 'Why all the speed when we were giving you the gong?'

Hundreds of shoppers watched the mobsters respond with a fusillade from repeating shotguns, blowing away Conway's jaw and killing two of his colleagues. The gunmen fled, pursued on foot by the surviving detective, William Sweeney. In a basement shoot-out he fatally wounded Mike Genna, whose dying act was to kick a stretcher bearer in the face. Anselmi and Scalise were arrested soon after on a street-car.

'These men will go straight to the gallows,' announced State Attorney Crowe on the radio. But good Sicilians soon chipped in to the mobsters' $100,000 legal expense fund, and if not, they were shot. Four obstinate local tradesmen were murdered after jibbing when asked for their second or third contributions; one had already donated $10,000, two of the others $2,000 apiece. In retaliation, four 'collectors' were gunned down. Meanwhile the front of Detective Sweeney's house was removed by a bomb and, when the trial began on 5 October, 234 of the first 238 potential jurors declined to serve.

The defence opened with a succinct exposition of the law: 'If a police officer detains you, even for a moment, against your will, and you kill him, you are not guilty of murder ... You may kill him in self-defence and the law cannot harm you.' Nevertheless Anselmi and Scalise were found guilty on a single count of manslaughter (as opposed to two counts of murder) and jailed for fourteen years.

This outrageous judgment was immediately appealed, and on 9 June 1927 the Illinois Supreme Court at last gave due weight to the case's previously neglected element of unwarranted aggression by the *police*. Anselmi and Scalise were released; in those days, virtually the entire apparatus of the state fell under Mob control.

Two years later, on 7 May 1929, the pair were invited as guests of honour to a Sicilian stag-party at Hammond across the state line. During the haze of goodwill and brotherhood over coffee and brandy, Anselmi and Scalise had their skulls beaten to a pulp with a sawn-off baseball bat. Then they were formally shot in the back. 'Scalise threw up his hand to cover his face,' concluded the coroner Dr Eli S. Jones, 'and a bullet cut off his little finger, crashing into his eye.' Their bodies were later dumped by Wolf Lake, Indiana. It had been rumoured that they were plotting against Capone himself.

Scalise and Anselmi were the hitmen who put an end to Dion **O'Bannion**, the troublesome Irish bootlegger. Paid $10,000 apiece in cash, they both received a $3,000 diamond ring, and Scalise sent his back to his Sicilian fiancée. In 1929 their bodies too were shipped home.

See also **Corruption**, **Pax Capone**

Anthropometry

An early method of identification system based on body measurements. Devised by the Frenchman Alphonse Bertillion in the 1880s, the technique was superseded by fingerprinting, not least because the French system was only of retrospective application.

That is, villains hardly ever leave a detailed record of their measurements at the crime scene, so anthropometry's primary role lay in identifying habitual offenders, after arrest, when they re-presented under a new alias hoping to avoid their past records.

Bertillion, a bright but difficult child, was expelled from his Versailles boarding school for setting fire to his desk while trying to cook inside it. His father eventually landed him a clerical job in the Prefecture de Police in Paris, and there Bertillion noticed that the criminals' records portrayed them as little more than large, medium or small.

Bertillion recollected that the statistician Quetelet – author of a tome called *Anthropométrie* – had observed that the chances against any two comparable people being exactly the same height were four to one. Bertillion reasoned that the odds could be lengthened to sixteen to one by taking two body measurements. By extension, the chance against two individuals having fourteen identical measurements, according to the generally quoted figure, worked out at 268,435,454 to one.

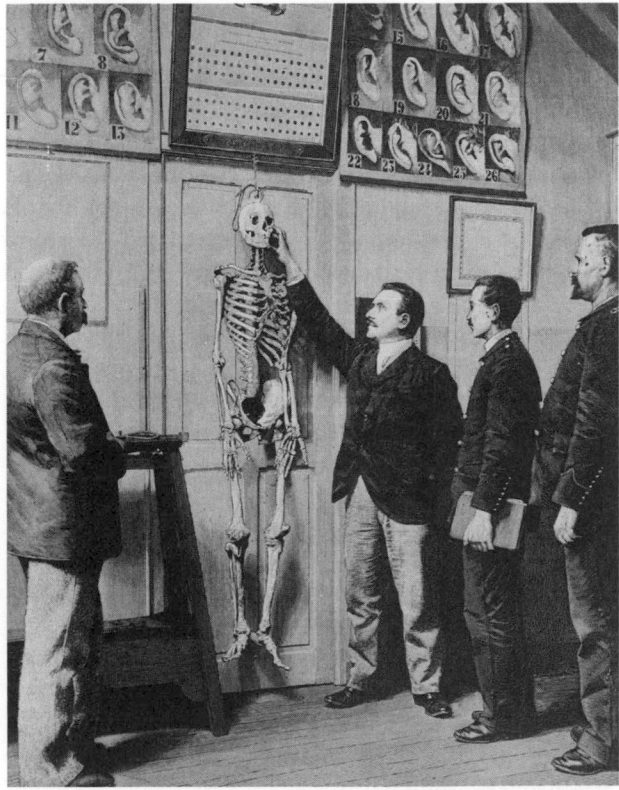

Alphonse Bertillion, founder of anthropometry

Thus was born anthropometry, the science of man-measurement. Bertillion set out to calibrate criminals by size. Using calipers, he perfected the art of measuring his subjects' bones, which, in adults, do not change. The five most important dimensions were the length and width of the skull, the length of the left forearm, the left foot (with the subject standing on one leg) and the left middle finger.

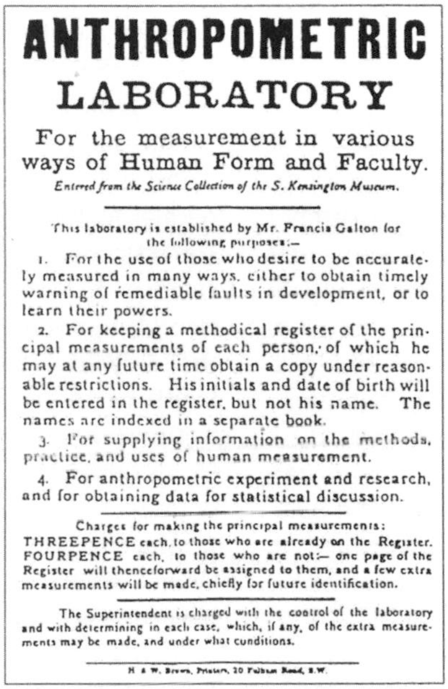

Bertillion's superiors at the Sureté distrusted his scheme; when Bertillion submitted his paper for the second time, the Prefect enquired if it was a joke. But in November 1882 he was granted a three-month experimental run. With time running short, on 20 February 1883 Bertillion at last identified an apparent first offender, M. Dupont, as none other than the M. Martin he had tabulated some weeks previously after an arrest for stealing empty bottles, and by the year's close Bertillion recognised a further fifty recidivists.

Bertillion's system was adopted as standard by all French prison governors. Convicts were routinely measured and their particulars entered into an elaborate cross-referenced filing cabinet with eighty-one drawers. The French press greeted Bertillion's appointment as Director of the Police Identification Service with their customary restraint: 'Bertillionage is the greatest and most brilliant invention the nineteenth century has produced in the field of criminology. Thanks to a French genius, errors of identification will soon cease to exist, not only in France but also the entire world.'

Bertillion went on to categorise the standard face-shapes that would later form the basis of Identikit and, in 1892, triumphantly exposed the anarchist hero Ravachol as none other than the petty thief Koenigstein, wanted for grave-robbery as well as murdering a miser and killing two women shop-keepers by hammering them to death.

In Britain, the Troup Committee of 1893 recommended the establishment of the Anthropometric Registry, and Bertillionage spread throughout the world. But by the turn of the century only 18,000 British criminals had been sized, yielding a meagre 1,300 identifications.

Then in 1901 Albert Ebenezer Fox and his doppelgänger twin Ebenezer Albert Fox (who could not be told apart by Bertillionage) were differentiated by the rival **fingerprinting** system, which produced 1,722 identifications the following year. A year after, in Kansas, two blacks of identical dimensions provided further ammunition for Bertillion's detractors.

His later reputation was severely tarnished by his helping to send the innocent Dreyfus to Devil's Island. Worse, in 1913 he let the thief of the **Mona Lisa** slip through his fingers. By this stage Bertillion kept fingerprints on record but, with no classification system, his immense collection of 100,000 prints served to conceal those of the robber. Bertillion died in 1914. Although buried with national honours, his system survived him by only a few weeks. It was an idea whose time had passed.

Anti-tank mine

The murder weapon in the Eric Brown case, which anticipated the invention of the car bomb. On 23 July 1943 the teenage Eric Brown resolved to rid his family of their bullying father Archibald, an invalid. So he concealed the device – a Hawkins No. 75 Grenade Mine – under the seat of his father's wheelchair, which exploded while Nurse was taking her patient on their daily outing. She had just lit his last cigarette.

After the court heard how Eric wanted to bring some happiness into his mother's life, they found him guilty but mad.

Eric became a criminal because he exploded the mine; more recently, the Burmese army used mines to explode those already convicted. It was a new way of minesweeping: prisoners advanced ahead of the troops to see if they blew up. According to one survivor from the spring campaign of 1992, Maung Mhi Aung, some 6,000 convicts were drafted into hard labour as army porters. More than 800 were seized from Insein Prison

The inset advertisement reads:

ANTHROPOMETRIC LABORATORY

For the measurement in various ways of Human Form and Faculty.

Entered from the Science Collection of the S. Kensington Museum.

This laboratory is established by Mr. Francis Galton for the following purposes:—

1. For the use of those who desire to be accurately measured in many ways, either to obtain timely warning of remediable faults in development, or to learn their powers.

2. For keeping a methodical register of the principal measurements of each person, of which he may at any future time obtain a copy under reasonable restrictions. His initials and date of birth will be entered in the register, but not his name. The names are indexed in a separate book.

3. For supplying information on the methods, practice, and uses of human measurement.

4. For anthropometric experiment and research, and for obtaining data for statistical discussion.

Charges for making the principal measurements: THREEPENCE each, to those who are already on the Register. FOURPENCE each, to those who are not:— one page of the Register will thenceforward be assigned to them, and a few extra measurements will be made, chiefly for future identification.

The Superintendent is charged with the control of the laboratory and with determining in each case, which, if any, of the extra measurements may be made, and under what conditions.

H & W. Brown, Printers, 20 Fulham Road, S.W.

alone, and over 300 human minesweepers died in the battle for Sleeping Dog Hill. Those merely wounded were left to bleed to death or shot out of hand.

See also **Payne**

Apalachin

Location of the Mob convention which led to America's accidental discovery of the **Mafia**. On 13 November 1957, Detective Sergeant Edgar Croswell was summoned to the Parkway Motel in rural Albany to investigate a bad cheque. Meanwhile a local kid, Joseph Barbara Jnr, swaggered into reception to block-book three double rooms for a soft drinks convention.

Croswell's curiosity was fired; he harboured suspicions about Joe's father, Joseph Barbara Snr, who ran the local bottling plant. A big spender living on a palatial estate with a small declared income, Jo Snr had pulled strings up to Governor level over a minor traffic violation the previous year.

Croswell decided to investigate, and walked over to the bottling factory. Everything was quiet, but four big limos were drawn up outside the nearby Barbara homestead. Later that night, the motel rang Croswell. Their delegation of guests had arrived, looking very, very unsavoury: should they refuse admission? Book them in, Croswell advised, and by next morning a dozen burnished limos – Cadillacs, Chrysler Imperials and Lincolns – filled Barbara's drive, with a further twenty-five ranked in the field. Clearly, the well-heeled participants of this convention were no salesmen.

Croswell sneaked into the grounds and jotted down their registration numbers. Rounding the garage corner he ran into a group of delegates. They scattered; he too beat a retreat. On Joe's land he had no authority, but it was a different matter on the highway. Only three roads led from the Barbara property, and two were impassable, the bridges down, flooded.

Croswell ran to his patrol car and set up a road-block before radioing for police support. Meanwhile, the local fish pedlar, Bartolo Guccia, drove up to warn about the police cars straddling the way out. By now the place was like a kicked-over ants' nest. About a dozen senior Mafiosi, in their silk tailored suits, lumbered across the fields to the woods where they were later rounded up, covered in burrs and brambles. The remainder crowded into their limousines and were duly stopped at the road-block.

Croswell hauled off the nation's top hoods to the small Vestal police station and beckoned them one by one to his office for the mild questioning allowed by law – name, occupation and purpose of visit. Most said they were paying their respects to the ailing Joe Barbara Snr; many listed their professions as 'unemployed'; some were prospecting for real estate, others taking the country air. Between them, they carried $300,000 in cash.

But only one was wanted by the law, and this for a parole violation. None was packing a gun. All gave their correct names. With no reason to hold them, they were freed in batches: nineteen mob leaders from upstate New York, twenty-three from New York City, eight from the Midwest, three from over the Rockies, two from the South, two from Cuba and one representative from Italy.

The law had done its utmost; now the press muscled in. If organised crime was a myth, how come sixty underworld figures gathered for an amicable convention? What were they planning? Importing narcotics? What was the FBI doing? What did J. Edgar **Hoover** have to say? An uneasy recollection surfaced about a shadowy organisation called the 'Mafia' – a fearsome secret brotherhood of criminals with its roots in Sicily (see **Inquisition**).

Thirty-four of the Apalachin gangsters within the New York jurisdiction were subpoenaed. The Watchdog Committee's sessions started on 12 December 1957; eleven hoods appeared. Most took the Fifth, with disdain. Jo Riccobono scarcely bothered to get the words right. He said: 'I refuse to answer on the grounds of not to testify against myself. Whether it means the same thing or whether it doesn't, I am not in a position to know.' Tony Maggadino pretended he could not understand English and looked blank. John Montana explained that he gave hundreds of turkeys to the needy every Thanksgiving.

Highlights from the Committee's report were items 1 and 3: '1. The Apalachin meeting is strong evidence that there exists in this country an active association or organisation of criminals ... 3. The incident reveals a serious defect in the state's law enforcement apparatus.' At last the secret was out.

See also **Head, Costello's**

Apologies, ritual

Many of the first wave of English **highwaymen** were former gentlemen ruined by the Civil War who failed to hit on any other socially acceptable way of earning a living.

Apologies for robbing their clients were *de rigueur*. In the words of a contemporary, 'They assure you they are very sorry that poverty has driven them to that shameful recourse, and end by demanding your purse in the most courteous manner', a trait accentuated when the victims were women. On 14 January 1797, the *Morning Chronicle* accorded favourable reviews to a 'very gallant highway robbery lately committed on Wimbledon Common on the person of a young lady'.

Behind the façade of chivalry, highwaymen were as given to brutal violence as any other rogue. But they had learned the part better. In his *Recantation*, Francis Jackson, a seventeenth-century practitioner, advised novices to hone up pretty speeches. He suggested: 'There must be a plausible account given, how you fell into this course of life, fetching a deep sigh, saying "That you were well born, but by reason of your Family falling to decay you were exposed to deep Want, and rather than shamefully beg (for you knew not how to labour), you were constrained to take this course as a Subsistence; that it is your first fault, which you are heartily sorry for, and will never attempt the like again."'

This dual-purpose speech went down almost equally well with victims and – subsequently – the judge. In the absence of fatalities, a highwayman might escape the gallows. Excessive technicalities of procedure served to attenuate the law's severity, and a successful defence, reminiscent of present-day Irish extradition proceedings, could be mounted round the misspelling of the defendant's name. Juries too might take a lenient line, and for richer villains there was always the immunity granted by bribery. In Jackson's words: 'He can't be hanged who hath Five Hundred Pounds at his Command.' But not many had.

Arabin, William St Julian (c. 1775–1841)

British judge at the Old Bailey. According to his contemporaries, Arabin was short-sighted, deaf, eccentric and much given to 'enunciating absurdities with the most perfect innocence'.

Not uncommonly, these attributes lost the accused their liberty or their lives. To a child, on sentencing him to transportation, Arabin said: 'When I first saw you, I knew you well. When you began to cry, I knew you still

better. I'm tired of the sight of you. You must go out of the country.' On another occasion – *R v. Jarvis* 1832 – Arabin muddled the papers of two cases, one for stealing a watch, the other for stealing a handkerchief, provoking the following exchange:

Arabin Well, witness, your name is John Tomkins.
Witness My Lord, my name is Job Taylor.
Arabin Ah! I see you are a sailor, and you live in the New Cut.
Witness No, my Lord, I live at Wapping.
Arabin Never mind your being out shopping. Had you your watch in your pocket on the 10th of November?
Witness I never had but one ticker, my lord, and that has been at the pawn shop for the last six months.
Arabin Who asked you how long you had the watch? Why can't you say yes or no? Well, did you see the prisoner at the Bar?
Witness (a little confused) Yes, of course I did.
Arabin That's right, my man, speak up and answer shortly. Did the prisoner take your watch?
Witness (loudly) I don't know what you're driving at.
Arabin (after a pause, to an elderly barrister at counsel's table who had dined well) Mr Ryland, I wish you would take this witness in hand and see whether you can make anything of him, for I can't.
Ryland (after staring ferociously at the witness) My Lord, it is my profound belief that the man is drunk.
Arabin It's a remarkable coincidence, Mr Ryland. That is precisely the idea that has been in my mind for the last ten minutes.

Perhaps Arabin's most famous pronouncement came during the case of *R v. Chilston and Chandler* in 1832, when he concluded that, 'If ever there was a case of clearer evidence than this of persons acting together, this case is … that case.' After his stint at the Old Bailey, Arabin was elevated to Judge Advocate-General of the Army. His words were transcribed verbatim between 1830 and 1839 by an unofficial rota of ten barristers who believed his *dicta* should be commemorated for posterity.

See also **Trousers**

Arm, James Smith's

A rare example of a celebrity limb. On 25 April 1935 James Smith's arm was safely ensconced in a fourteen-foot tiger shark, itself recently confined to a public aquarium at Coogee Beach, Australia.

At five o'clock that afternoon, the shark regurgitated the contents of its stomach in front of a crowd who thus witnessed the emergence of the tattooed arm, entangled in a length of rope. Dr Coppleson, the local 'sharkologist', advised that the fish had been depressed since its capture and consequently off its food, thereby deferring its normal thirty-six-hour digestive cycle. The arm could have been consumed some days previously while the shark was at sea.

The limb's fingerprints were still intact, and it was soon identified as the property of a forger and petty thief, James Smith, last seen embarking on a fishing trip on 8 April. Basing his decision on an English precedent set in 1276 and ignored ever since, the coroner declined to hold an inquest in the absence of a body. But foul play was obvious since Smith's arm had been detached from the torso with a knife.

The case remains unsolved, although a petty criminal named Patrick Brady was charged. The principal evidence against him was a sworn statement signed by one Reg Holmes. But the court excluded his testimony, ruling it inadmissible because Holmes himself could not be called in cross-examination; he was murdered on 13 June, the day before the inquest. Brady spent over twenty years in prison for various other offences, and died in August 1965 still protesting his innocence. Sydney's then pivotal role in **opium** and heroin smuggling formed the background to the killing. Smith worked as a crewman on the motor launch *Pathfinder*, itself destroyed in an underworld spate of tit-for-tat hijackings, sinkings, tortures and murders. His boat disappeared under water, and so did he, very nearly.

Arsenic

A chemical in widespread use in the dyeing and paper industries and inexplicably popular with the modern poisoner.

Arsenic is hard to administer, almost indissoluble in cold water, which only holds about half of a grain per ounce in suspension A hot beverage can mop up perhaps a hundred times as much, but on cooling nearly 80 per cent precipitates as a visible sediment, curdling any milk in the process; the poisoned cups of tea, coffee and cocoa beloved of fiction are unlikely instruments of doom. Moreover, the effect is unreliable. Although the smallest recorded fatal dose is two grains, Glaister's *Medical Jurisprudence* cites the abortive suicide attempt of a woman who, after ingesting 230 grains, felt no more than quite uncomfortable for three days.

Once suspected, arsenic is particularly easy to identify positively and its traces linger indefinitely in the fingernails, bones and so on. As **Napoleon**'s case exemplifies, a strand of hair – which grows at a uniform rate and likewise absorbs the poison uniformly – can provide a daily calendar of the intake.

On the upside, arsenic is all but tasteless, and readily available to the resourceful; in Victorian times, a fatal dose could be obtained by soaking a single fly-paper in water. The toxin has a cumulative effect, meaning that the victim need not be force-fed in one massive dose, and its incremental results can be mistaken for the symptoms of many ordinary illnesses.

The long heyday of arsenic is attributable to the Arab alchemist Gber who, in the eighth century, distilled a tasteless and odourless white powder called arsenous oxide. For many centuries this afforded poisoners a clear run. The first test for the deadly substance was not developed until 1787 when Johann Metzger of Königsberg produced a deposit on copper plates suspended over the heated poison; and it was only in 1830 that James Marsh, an impoverished English chemist, devised a simple and reliable experiment on which a jury could base a conviction. His device converted arsenous residues in body tissues into arsine gas, which registered as a metallic sheen on a porcelain receptor. With refinement, a 300,000th of an ounce could be detected.

This exactitude led to the confusing finding of minute traces of this common element almost everywhere, including in people. A normal, healthy person is about one ten millionth arsenic by weight; winegrowers and lovers of seafood may house three times that amount. Famous cases include Lafarge (1840), Smethurst (1859), Maybrick (1889), Armstrong (1922) and Frederick Radford (1949), who sent his wife an arsenic fruit pie (via her father Mr Kite) as she lay dying from pulmonary tuberculosis in the Milford Sanatorium at Godalming.

On her deathbed Mrs Radford's misgivings about her husband's gifts of food, which so often preceded her severe stomach cramps, impelled her to hand the partly eaten pie to her friend Mrs Formby, telling her to send it to Scotland Yard for analysis. Instead, Mrs Formby posted it to the Sanatorium's Superintendent, mailing him an explanatory letter under separate cover. The letter went into his secretary's in-tray, arriving on a Saturday, and lay there unread; the handsome fruit pie was placed on the Superintendent's desk. He worked weekends, and bore it home for tea, ate about one sixth and fell seriously ill, vomiting so violently that the blood vessels in his eyes burst. He just survived.

Margery Radford died on 14 April, and on post-mortem her body, wasted to sixty-seven pounds, disclosed a lethal dosage of six and a half grains administered over some 120 days. To the police, her husband said: 'I admit I bought the pies and gave them to Mr Kite to take to my wife. Why should I want to kill my wife? I knew she was going to die anyway.' Radford, an intelligent laboratory assistant, continued: 'I would not be such a fool as to use arsenic with my experience, as I know the police could find it easily enough. If you think I did it, charge me, and let a judge and jury decide.'

A fair challenge – but it was never put to issue. That night, released from questioning, Radford took his life with prussic acid.

See also **Poisoning, Orfila**

Arson

Arson is a recession-led crime, reflecting the endeavours of those with insurance (see **Marine fraud**) to find some way of turning their unsaleable goods or premises into money. The estimated total of British fire claims for businesses in 1991 was £800 million, up 30 per cent on the previous year. The crime is notoriously hard to prove, with probably fewer than one in ten instances leading to conviction.

In the economic boom of 1987 the FBI took a different view, ascribing only 1 per cent of cases to insurance frauds while attributing 49 per cent to 'vandalism', a further 25 per cent to 'excitement' and 14 per cent to 'revenge'.

In a more sombre context, arson is one leg of the 'homicidal triangle' evinced by budding serial killers. David Berkowitz, New York's 'Son of **Sam**', set the prodigious tally of 2,000 fires before raising his sights to shooting courting couples.

Less obvious is the sexual connection. The clearest, almost lyrical evocation of the obscure linkage between watching things burn and making love comes from Peter **Kürten**, the Düsseldorf sadist. 'During the firing of the haystacks,' Kürten wrote, 'the thought that human beings might be burned added to the sensations that I experienced. The shouting of the people and the glare of the fire pleased me. During big fires, I always had an orgasm.'

On the occasions where Kürten did not succeed at first, he tried again: 'If you see in my confession sometimes several arsons in one night, then I had no success with the first or second. I also had an orgasm when I fired the woods. It was a lovely sight when one pine after the other was consumed in the flames fanned by the sharp east wind ... That was wonderful.'

The orthodox explanation goes to the root of the inadequacy and resentment that are the abiding features of the sex and serial killer. Needing someone, or something, to take it out on, they start by maiming animals as a prelude to torturing humans, and similarly find preliminary satisfaction in trashing property. There are many ways of doing this, but apparently it is only fire that induces the sexual criminal to urinate or defecate, a standard reaction with pyromaniacs.

See also **Pets, Sex crimes, Torture**

Assassins

The word derives from 'hasishim', since it was believed that the followers of the Muslim prophet Hasan bin Sabah (c. 1030–1124) doped themselves to the eyeballs before their solitary missions of murder. Word of the Assassins first reached the West through Marco Polo's description of a canny Old Man of the Mountains, whose followers would kill for just one more taste of paradise; these trainee assassins were surreptitiously drugged and then tended for days in a pretty garden by beautiful handmaidens.

In reality, Hasan was a competent leader short of followers. From 1092 onwards he corrected the imbalance in numbers by murdering his opponents one by one, starting with Nizam al-Mulk, and his fanatical disciples were the forebears of the modern terrorist.

The sect fell into its final decline under Rukn al-Din, a pacifist, who surrendered his fortress, the Eagle's Lair, at Alamut in about 1256 and was murdered, kicked to a pulp.

In America today, whatever the democratic theory, not everyone has the opportunity to grow up to be a president. But at least anyone can *kill a* president. In the words of the Stephen Sondheim song, composed for the character of John Wilkes Booth: 'All you have to do is to move your little finger and change the world.' Japanese assassins favour the bomb, and Middle Easterners the knife, but Americans working the dark side of their national dream prefer guns.

According to the stereotype devised by the National Commission on Violence in the 1960s, the typical presidential assassin is a failure at his job or, ideally, does not have one. Likewise his marriage (if any) is unsuccessful, his relationship with his parents strained or non-existent and his demographic profile generally that of a social misfit. Infatuation with a media star, like Jodie Foster, is par for the course.

Mark David Chapman, John Lennon's killer, left an exact account of his impulse to kill. He started his confession by denigrating his hero, the target, but within a few sentences lapsed into self-denigration. 'I came across a book about John Lennon,' he told psychologist Dr Goldstein the day after the shooting on 9 December 1980. 'I didn't hate him but I thought he was a phony. The author made the phony stuff that

Lennon did sound good. I admire him in a way. I wished someone would write a book about me. It sounded like Lennon was an idiot, and he wasn't. It made me think that my life is special and I felt that no one cared about it.'

The underlying self-pity, mimicking the motivation of those who deface works of art, suggests that the destruction of property is a practicable and more considerate alternative to killing people. In a previous attempt to remind the world of his existence, Chapman had a T-shirt printed with the slogan, 'I'm unique. I think for myself.' His obsession focused on Lennon because 'I believed the Beatles. I believed John Lennon. But they were just saying all that stuff. It was all a big hoax. It's ruined my life. It's made me a nobody.'

Recently **Quantico**'s Dr Murray S. Miron opened up the field of 'psycholinguistics' with a computer programme categorising the content of threatening letters, assessing their seriousness and the writer's psychological profile. The technique identified California's 'Masked Marvel' by whittling down the initial suspect list from 7,000 to five.

The cost of Secret Service protection for the US President soared from a 1968 budget of $17.6 million in 1968 to a present-day $475 million, largely because the list of designated 'protectees' has, like the Brazilian civil service, expanded exponentially to take on board an ever-lengthening list of relatives and remote associates.

See also **Dumdums**, **Stalking**

Attaché case, poisoned

The murder weapon for an attempted 1968 killing at London's Old Bailey. As the net closed round East End gangster Ronald **Kray**, he decided to test the loyalty of his inner-circle associate Alan Cooper by insisting, in the style of the Mafia, that he carry out a murder. The target, a small-time villain, had broken the gangland peace by wounding his wife's lover in the groin with a shotgun. The man went to ground, but he was scheduled to take the stand as a witness on another case within a couple of weeks.

The killing posed obvious technical problems. But, accepting the assignment with enthusiasm, Cooper contrived a poisoned pigskin briefcase produced to his design by ex-speedway star 'Split' Waterman. A firm

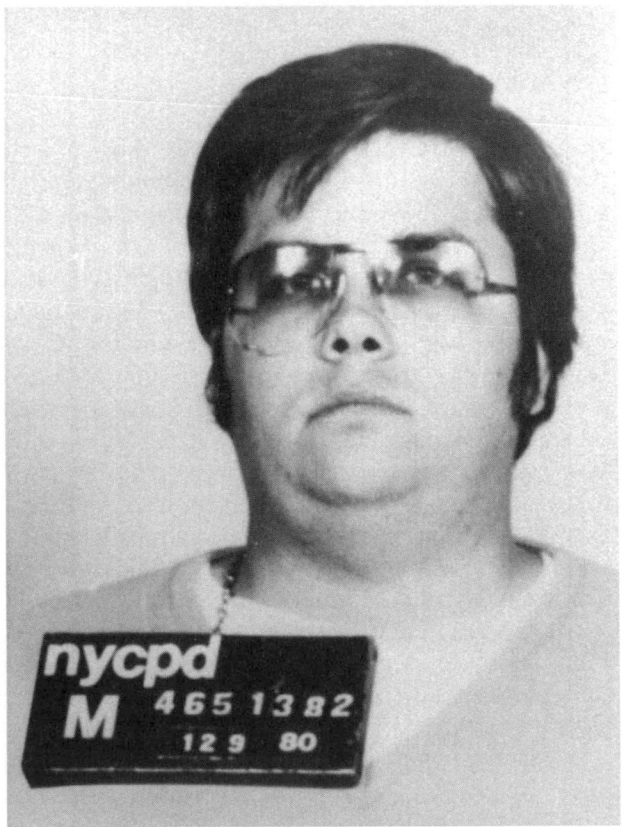

Mark Chapman, Lennon's assassin

tug on a small brass ring by the handle caused a long hypodermic needle to slide forwards, projecting its full length through a hole in the leading corner. Any impact on the needle triggered a spring inside the briefcase, activating the syringe's plunger which squirted out deadly poison.

The plan was to fill the syringe with cyanide; then, in the courtroom jostle, fall in behind the victim, and jab him with the case in the leg. The man would feel little more than a tiny pinprick, and die within seconds of an apparent heart attack. The post-mortem would discern no trace of poison in the stomach.

Ronnie Kray was enthusiastic, but the hitman Paul Elvey bungled the kill, complaining that his mark never showed in the Old Bailey's central lobby. Next the imaginative Cooper suggested a high-powered crossbow with steel-tipped bolts; again, the plan ran into a last-minute snag. In a final scheme – by now hoping to prove the Firm's credentials to the Mafia – Cooper and Ronnie Kray decided to liquidate George Caruana, a West End club-owner of Maltese extraction by wiring up his bright red Mini to a bomb.

This attempt resulted in Elvey's arrest at Glasgow airport carrying thirty-six sticks of dynamite. It emerged that Alan Cooper, an ex-gold smuggler, was an informer working for the US Treasury Department in cahoots with Scotland Yard (or at least part of it). His evidence on these exotic assassinations was highly questionable, but enough to arrest the Kray twins and hold them on remand in the hope of encouraging frightened witnesses to speak. It was a chance, and on 9 May 1968 the Yard took it, pulling in the twins, their brother Charles and fourteen others.

Attorneys

A world away from the glossy television series *LA Law*, South Carolina pays attorneys staving off the death penalty $10 an hour (£5.70) to a maximum of $1,500.

Critics feel this leads to low-grade legal representation. Only serious shortcomings can have inspired the 1987 decision by a District Court in Texas that James Russell (executed in September 1991) 'was not entitled to relief solely because his lawyer may have been intoxicated during the trial'.

At the 1991 pre-execution wake of another capital offender, Andrew Lee Jones, his lawyer reportedly conceded that 'he had failed to give Andrew a proper defence at his trial', belatedly admitting that there was no evidence linking Jones to the offence. Such cases are not uncommon: the unfortunate **Rummel** of Texas, sentenced to life for stealing $120.75, relied on an attorney whose fixed fee was a miserly $250; and on Death Row in Virginia, the murderer Joseph O'Dell launched a similar appeal. 'I represented myself,' O'Dell said, 'and I wasn't competent to represent myself.'

Inadequate defences at initial trials engendered the backlog of appeals now clogging the American system, precipitating the current attack on the 'great writ' of Habeas Corpus. Under a Civil War statute, a defendant could apply for Habeas Corpus Review, often on the grounds of being denied effective legal advice, a tactic avidly adopted by those about to die. In the last sixteen years only 155 of the 3,834 sent to **Death Row** have been executed.

In its more heroic guise, Habeas Corpus freed the American black Jim Montgomery after twenty years inside. Regarded by the Illinois Ku Klux Klan as a trouble-maker, in 1923 Montgomery was jailed on a trumped-up charge of raping a 62-year-old semi-imbecile, Mamie Snow. In 1944 lawyer Louis Kurtner took up the case; he tracked down Mamie's hospital records which disclosed that the examining doctor had detected no signs of **rape**. The hospital nurse confirmed that Mamie was a virgin, and police documents recorded her failure to identify Montgomery in jail. Pardoned on 10 August 1947, he collected the standard 'going-out' fee of $10.

Today, American judges feel that the Habeas Corpus procedure is abused by lawyers trying to save undeserving mass murderers. Rather than reducing their rights of appeal, the courts could streamline the appeal process. About half the time is devoted to typing court transcripts, and a move to videotape may not be premature.

See also **Insane**

Aum Shinrikyo and the Tokyo Subway Attack

On 20 March 1995 a Japanese religious cult prepared to launch an attack that would make it the master of the government. The cult was called Aum Shinrikyo, or Aum Supreme Truth, and its plan was to paralyse Tokyo's nerve centre, the Kasumigazeki, which housed the Tokyo Police Department headquarters building and Japan's major bureaucracies. The original plan had been to attack the police headquarters with a giant laser that would slice it in half, but this had to be abandoned because of technical problems. Plan B was to launch a biological attack on Tokyo by disseminating a steam laden with the botulism virus, which produces a paralysing nerve toxin; this also had to be abandoned because of the problem of producing enough of it in time. For time was short: the cult had been informed by spies planted in the police headquarters that there would be an enormous police raid on 21 March.

So the cult had to fall back on Plan C: a poison-gas attack on the Tokyo underground railway system that would begin at the Kasumigazeki subway below the police headquarters.

Which is why, soon after 7 a.m. on the day before the police raid was due, commuters on the Tokyo subway began to experience a tickling in the throat and a soreness in the eyes and nose, accompanied by a stench like a mixture of mustard and burning rubber. Within minutes, dozens of people were choking or falling to the ground.

The aftermath of the Tokyo subway gas attack

It was happening all over the Tokyo underground system. No one had any idea what was causing it. Fleets of ambulances ferried gasping or unconscious passengers to hospitals – the casualty figure finally reached 5,500. Many seemed to be paralysed and a dozen would finally die. Yet it was not until mid-morning that a military doctor made a cautious and incredible diagnosis: the victims were suffering from poisoning by a nerve gas called sarin, once used by the Nazis in their death camps.

This was not the first such terrorist attack. On 27

June 1994, in the city of Matsumoto in Nagano Prefecture, a similar sarin attack flooded the local hospital. Fortunately the gas had been released into the open air, so fewer people were affected, but seven died nevertheless. The bemused authorities decided it was a matter for the local police only – a decisive factor in allowing the later Tokyo attack to take place.

During the previous six months the police had received dozens of phone calls accusing the Aum Shinrikyo cult of fraud, abduction and brutality. Things had come to a head a month earlier, when a 68-year-old lawyer named Kiyoshi Kariya had been kidnapped in broad daylight by four powerfully built men and bundled into the back of a van. Kariya's sister had been a cult member who had absconded and Kariya had received a threatening phone call demanding to know where she was. After Kariya's disappearance, his son found a note that read: 'If I disappear, I was abducted by Aum Shinrikyo.' A police investigation failed to find either Kariya alive or dead.

By now Aum Shinrikyo was the chief suspect in the gas attack. In spite of his protest – 'We carry out our religious activities on the basis of Buddhist doctrines, such as no killing' – police raided the cult's headquarters on the slopes of Mount Fuji. Most of the cultists had left, taking crates of documents; but the police found a huge stockpile of chemicals such as sodium cyanide and peptone for cultivating bacteria. Yet the cult insisted, through its legal spokesmen, that this was all for legitimate peaceful purposes.

On 23 April, the cult's chief scientist, Hideo Murai, was murdered in front of a crowd of reporters and TV cameramen, stabbed repeatedly in the stomach by a small-time crook named Hiroyuki Jo, who then demanded, 'Isn't anyone going to arrest me?' Police quickly obliged.

But where was the guru? He had vanished without a trace. On 5 May, two months after the sarin attack, a bag left in the toilet of the Shinjuku train station burst into flames. Alert staff doused it with water, but not before it had begun to emit choking fumes. Forensic experts discovered later that, if left undiscovered, it would have given off clouds of hydrogen cyanide gas, called **Zyklon B** by the death-camp Nazis, which would have been sucked through the ventilators on to the platform.

One of the chief suspects was a young cultist called Yoshihiro Inoue, the cult's intelligence chief. He was caught driving a car that contained chemicals for manufacturing high explosives. This left no one in any doubt that the cult's protestations about love and peace were false.

On 16 May, there was another huge police raid on the Mount Fuji headquarters; this time they found a secret room, inside which a large, bearded figure sat cross-legged on the floor in the meditation posture. He admitted: 'I am the guru. Don't touch me, I don't even allow my disciples to touch me.'

Guru Shoko Asahara, whose real name was Chizuo Matsumoto, had been born blind in one eye and partially blind in the other. Raised in a poor home, he had been a brilliant pupil at school. He thought of becoming a radical politician, like Mao Zedong, then began to meditate and claimed that one day he felt the *kundalini* (the sacred energy that electrifies and enlightens the soul) rising up his spine.

This was in the 1980s, which in Japan were rather like the 1960s in Britain and America: a period of popular spirituality that Asahara's biographers have called 'the rush hour of the gods'. Asahara founded a yoga school, which became so profitable that he opened several more. Then he went off to the Himalayas to meditate and had himself photographed with the Dalai Lama, who told him he had the mind of a Buddha. (After Asahara's arrest, the Dalai Lama admitted to being deeply embarrassed by this gaffe.) There in the Himalayas, Asahara claims he experienced enlightenment and achieved psychic powers.

Back in Tokyo he changed the name of his yoga school to Aum Supreme Truth (*Om* or *Aum* is a Sanskrit syllable, pronounced during meditation, which is supposed to encompass the entire universe). Teaching a mixture of Buddhism, Christianity and Hinduism, with the predictions of Nostradamus thrown in for good measure, Asahara, who claimed to be the embodiment of the god Shiva, was soon surrounded by hundreds of followers. Since he assured them that large cash donations would hasten their spiritual enlightenment, he was soon a wealthy man. Brilliant young students from the universities began to join the sect, many of them scientists. However, this mix of science and spirituality produced some odd hybrids; for example, Hideo Murai invented a kind of electric cap which, when placed on the head, supposedly raised the user's level of consciousness.

Yet, despite his apparently unassailable success, desertion roused Asahara to a kind of frenzy. One disciple who announced he was leaving the sect was told

Shoko Asahara of the Aum Shinrikyo cult

he was in need of physical as well as psychological help, and was ordered to drink large quantities of freezing water. After a few pints he went into shock and died. Another disenchanted disciple, Shuji Taguchi, was strangled and his body burned. Another cultist had returned home to his family; in his home he was attacked and his skull smashed with a hammer. The cult assassins also murdered his wife and child.

The sect had a strict celibacy law, but like so many rogue messiahs, the guru could not resist the temptations of the flesh himself. Asahara regularly enjoyed sex with selected female disciples, who were then sworn to secrecy.

During the 1990s, Aum Supreme Truth began to spread all over the world. There had probably not been such a successful pseudo-scientific, hybrid religious cult since Ron L. Hubbard's Scientology. Post-Communist Russia was particularly sympathetic to it; Aum Supreme Truth continues to be a strong movement in Russia, under the new name of Aleph.

World success made Asahara think in terms of world power. In 1993 his chief engineer, Kiyohide Hayakawa, was instructed to try to buy an atomic bomb. In fact, during 1994, Hayakawa made eight trips to Russia trying to buy a nuclear warhead. When he failed, the cult tried to buy a rural area near Tokyo, where there were deposits of uranium. And when this also failed they decided to buy land in Australia. It was half a million acres of scrubland called Banjawarn Station, which the cult bought for $400,000, in cash, after which it paid a further $110,000 for mining rights. There they began testing nerve gas on sheep, whose skeletons were later found by police.

However, rumours that the cult tested the world's first non-governmental atomic bomb in the Australian outback are probably false. A large detonation took place near Banjawarn Station while the cult were camped there. The effect was registered by seismologists hundreds of miles away, but is now thought to have been caused by the atmospheric explosion of a large meteor or a small comet.

As the cult's success increased, so did its paranoia. This mindset seems to have escalated sharply after the interest the police took in the disappearance of Kiyoshi Kariya, and this 'persecution' in turn seems to have triggered the cult's decision to launch the sarin attacks and an attempted *coup d'état*. But why?

Asahara's trial failed to enlighten the public. Placed on the stand in 1996, he refused to enter a plea of either guilty or not guilty. For almost nine years, as the trial ground along with glacial slowness, the ex-guru flatly refused to answer questions with anything but incomprehensible mutterings. In February 2004 he was sentenced to death on multiple counts of murder and attempted murder. Twelve of his followers were also sentenced to death. All thirteen appealed their death sentences, safe in the knowledge that, given the slowness of the Japanese justice system, they might avoid execution for many years, even if their appeals were ultimately unsuccessful.

So, why did they do it? The followers, predictably, said that they were acting on Asahara orders, and were not privy to his divine plan. The guru, through his lawyer, claimed the followers cooked up the whole scheme themselves, without his knowledge. Both the followers and Asahara were lying.

Investigation of the cult's inner teachings revealed that they secretly followed the creed ultimately pursued by so many mad messiahs throughout history: Armageddon is coming, but it needs a few thousand innocent deaths to get it kicked off properly. Shoko Asahara was just a Japanese Charlie **Manson** and Aum

Shinrikyo had become a bloated, over-powerful version of Manson's Family.

Automatism

A defence to murder or, come to that, almost anything. Crimes against the person carry a mental element, known to lawyers as *mens rea*, and clearly the suspension of control by the conscious mind interdicts the formation of any intent to wound or kill.

Instances of automatism are rare, featuring in law students' casebooks more than in the courts. The standard British case (*R v. Clarke* 1972) concerns shoplifting by a woman who argued that extreme depression made her completely absent-minded, the equivalent of saying 'I did it, but I'm not guilty.' This has clear attractions as a defence. Accordingly the burden is on the accused to prove he was, in laymen's parlance, briefly off his head.

A more plausible way of losing mental control is an epileptic seizure. In 1919 a Mrs Perry suffered an attack while filling a kettle and, inverting her intention, laid the kettle down on top of the oven while placing her baby on the fire. Her lawyers were reduced to pleading **insanity**, albeit temporary, with the unfortunate result that Mrs Perry was permanently confined to Broadmoor, the prison for the criminally deranged. This was better than being hanged, but today she would be acquitted on automatism.

Courts take a less sympathetic view of offences committed under the influence of drugs. In 1970 a man called Lipman had a bad trip and hallucinated that he was penned in the centre of the earth. There he assailed a giant snake which, after a fierce tussle, he slew. Coming down, Lipman found he had killed his bedmate. The LSD element reduced his conviction to manslaughter, but he was jailed for six years. Legal commentators regarded this as rather stiff.

Axeman, 'Mad' Frank Mitchell

The **Kray** twins were acquitted of Mad Frank's murder in 1966. Ronnie Kray now says (*Our Story*, 1988) that Mitchell 'is alive and well and living in … I won't reveal where'.

Mad Frank combined an impressive physique with a worryingly small brain. By 1966 he had spent eighteen of his thirty-two years in detention, and his sentence at

Dartmoor was indefinite. The prison governor seemed well-disposed, promising help in extracting an early release date from the Home Office. But the day never came. Meanwhile the Kray twins decided to cut through the red tape, freeing Frank, as one of their protégés, on their own initiative. Their philosophy remains unclear, but they were probably led towards this expansive, benevolent gesture by an associate, 'Mad' Teddy Smith, who was interested in making television 'docudramas'.

Despite Dartmoor's reputation, it proved one of the easiest jailbreaks on record. First Reg Kray reconnoitred the joint. Using a false name, the notorious gangster wrote offering to bring the aged ex-boxer Ted 'King' Lewis down to hold an afternoon talk for the lags. The bait was taken. On arrival Reggie was treated to a tour of inspection before taking luncheon with the governor and padre. He coped with East End gangsters by the dozen waving in acknowledgement as he strolled round the balconies. With creditable aplomb, Reggie explained that the convicts had mistaken one of his companions (also a dyed-in-the-wool villain) for the comedian Norman Wisdom.

Reggie reported with the all-clear, so the twins sent down a car to pick up Mitchell. It was that easy. As a prisoner, Mad Frank was something of a favourite – a 'trusty' on a very loose rein. He could do more or less what he wanted, and what he wanted was to leave the prison on working parties, which were guarded by a single warder. Dressed in his shirt and denim trousers, he would wander off on to the moors for the day, feed the moorland ponies, go for a ride and perhaps meet his girlfriend, a local schoolmistress, for sex in the heather or a deserted barn. Or he might drop into a pub to fetch the liquor order for his mates. Mitchell once took a cab into nearby Okehampton to go shopping, buying a **budgerigar** for another prisoner.

While out on his rambles, Mitchell telephoned the Krays to complain about prison conditions, and under Teddy Smith's prompting they decided to court underworld popularity with a breakout. Once free, Mitchell could bargain with the Home Secretary on level terms, agreeing to surrender if his case was reviewed.

Hence the car to fetch him on 12 December. The only hitch was that the two members of the Firm assigned to Frank did not have a valid driving licence. Reggie borrowed one so that they could hire a car, a green Vauxhall. Frank's contribution consisted of a conspicuous face-mask made out of his girlfriend's nylon nightdress, and in this he toiled through the mist to the pick-up point.

Six hours passed before the prison authorities realised that anything was amiss. On arrival in London, Frank lay low at a 'safe house', a basement flat in Barking where Lennie Dunn and 'Scotch' Jack Dickson minded him night and day.

Over the ensuing days Frank's status regressed. The *Daily Mirror* and *The Times* published his letters, which included the line 'Sir, I ask you, where is the fairness of this?', but the Home Secretary paid them no regard. The Krays wondered What To Do About Frank, and after the first week they devised the stopgap expedient of an expensive call-girl. Frank bedded this attractive woman for two days; he fell for her, and penned a Christmas card that survived as almost the sole physical memorial to his existence. It said: 'To Lisa, the only one I've ever loved.' Afterwards he became increasingly obstreperous, railing against his confinement. The Krays grew fretful, and on 24 December sent round a van, ostensibly to take him to 'a farm in Kent'.

Frank was never seen again, alive or dead. The Krays were tried for his murder, but the uncorroborated evidence of their henchman Albert Donaghue failed to secure a conviction in the absence of a body.

According to Donaghue, two gunmen lay in wait for Frank inside the van, one with a silenced automatic and the other with a revolver. The van lurched forwards as he grabbed for their weapons. They shot him several times in the body and three more times in the heart. Frank lay still. Then he lifted his head and they shot him twice more in the brain. Afterwards, Donaghue telephoned Reggie Kray.

'The geezer's gone,' he said. Reggie broke down and wept.

B

Bamber, Jeremy (1960–)

A famous British police bungle. In the early hours of 7 August 1985 Jeremy Bamber stole into White House Farm and shot his adopted father and mother, his sister by adoption (a model known as 'Bambi') and her two children.

Bamber left his fingerprints on the rifle, an Anschutz .22 automatic, concealed the silencer (still with blood and hair on it) in the gun cupboard, bolted the farmhouse doors and climbed out through the lavatory window. He bicycled to his cottage and, two hours later, telephoned the police, alleging that his father had just managed to put through a call – before the line went dead – saying that Bambi was on the rampage with a rifle.

While Bamber sat down to a fried breakfast, the police surrounded his parents' farmhouse and, after a four-hour wait, broke in and discovered the five bodies. Soon the search started for the culprit. The helpful Bamber was clearly out of the running, as he had no particular motive other than a £436,000 inheritance; anyway, he was on the telephone to the police at the time he said the killings occurred.

But in practice, Bamber would still have been connected to the phone found off the hook at the farmhouse. Lacking this information, the culprit's identity remained wide open until the first major police breakthrough when they missed the open window through which Bamber made his getaway.

This mistake narrowed the suspects to one of the deceased *inside* the building. Then, against all the odds, detectives overlooked the silencer smeared with Bambi's blood. So the rifle found in her hands could have been a suicide weapon, if only the barrel, when pressed against her neck, was not too long for her to reach the trigger.

But the case did not close around Bambi without further corroboration. Her father fought for his life ferociously, sustaining two black eyes and cuts to his face before the rifle stock was broken over his head. So after careful deliberation a clear picture emerged. According to the police, first the frail and diminutive Bambi, on heavy tranquillisers, beat up her six feet four father, a former fighter pilot, without bruising herself, even on the knuckles. Then she shot him and, placing the rifle barrel against her head, unreeled her arms beyond their natural extent and killed herself with a shot to the brain. But the powder marks to her wounds showed that one bullet was fired with the silencer and the other without. So as soon as Bambi was dead, she unscrewed the silencer and shot herself again in the neck – an open-and-shut case.

Local villagers expressed doubts that 'Bambi' could have murdered her own family. And there were others who shared these doubts. One of them was a police sergeant named Stan Jones, who had noted the curious fact that Sheila had apparently shot herself twice. At least two other people were not convinced that Sheila was the killer. One of these was David Boutflour, Jeremy's cousin, for whom White House Farm had been a second home.

After the police had left, David Boutflour and his sister, Ann Eaton, arrived. They had already had a meeting with the superintendent in charge of the case, Taff Jones, in which they had learned that twenty-four rounds had been fired from the rifle lying across Sheila's body. That meant that the gun must have been reloaded at least twice. Yet – as Ann pointed out – Bambi had absolutely no knowledge of guns. Moreover, the weapon was without its usual silencer; so why had nearby neighbours not heard twenty-four shots being fired?

Superintendent Jones had become irritable, and told them that he was conducting the investigation. Sergeant Stan Jones, who was also present, secretly agreed with the brother and sister, but did not dare to show it.

Now David Boutflour looked inside his uncle's gun cupboard, which was under the stairs. Inside, among boxes of ammunition, he found what he was looking for – the silencer that had belonged to the rifle that killed the Bambers. It was seven inches long and one inch in diameter.

And bloodstains on it proved to belong to Sheila Caffell.

For the brother and sister, this was the crucial piece of evidence. If the silencer had been on the rifle when it killed Bambi Caffell, the barrel would have been far too long for her to reach the trigger. And even if Bambi had found some other means of pulling the trigger – perhaps with her toe – how had she returned the silencer to the gun cupboard after killing herself?

When the silencer was later handed to Sergeant Jones, he noticed a small grey hair, about three-quarters of an inch long, attached to it. It looked very like Neville Bamber's hair. Yet when the sergeant delivered the silencer to the forensic department, Detective Inspector Ronald Cook showed little interest in it, merely pointing out that even if it was Neville Bamber's hair, it could have got on to the silencer at any time. He later lost the hair.

The coroner's inquest concluded that the family had been murdered by Sheila Caffell, who had then shot herself.

Two days later, at the funeral service, Bamber sobbed uncontrollably, while his girlfriend, 22-year-old Julie Mugford, tried to comfort him. She was an infant-school teacher, and Bamber had met her two years earlier; they were now living together in Bamber's cottage. Yet all was not well between the lovers. Julie suspected that Jeremy was becoming tired of her.

The following evening, out for a meal with a friend, Susan Battersby, Julie swore her to silence, then told her that Jeremy had paid someone to carry out the murders.

A few days later, Bamber called on Julie in her room. There was a bitter quarrel which ended with him telling her he was finished with her. Soon afterwards she learned that he was sleeping with yet another former mistress. After two more days in emotional turmoil, during which she told two more friends the story of the 'hitman', she allowed herself to be persuaded to speak to the police. It was a friend named Liz Rimington who

rang Sergeant Jones and told him Julie wanted to talk to him. Jones drove over immediately. The first question he asked was: 'Did Jeremy do it?'

Julie avoided his eyes. 'Yes.'

The next day, Sunday 8 September 1985, Jeremy Bamber was taken to Chelmsford police headquarters for questioning. And in the last week of September, the office of the Director of Public Prosecutions reviewed all the evidence collected by the police and decided it had a *prima facie* case against Jeremy Bamber.

Bamber was convicted on 28 August 1986 and sent down for a minimum of twenty-five years. Colin Wilson, the crime writer, makes the point that 'detection only comes into its own when the investigator is aware he has something to detect'.

In this case Bamber 'packaged' a ready-made solution. He insists on his innocence from prison, not by disputing the facts but by proffering alternative 'scenarios'. From his late teens he **fantasised** about eliminating his family, and in the months preceding the killings he talked of 'rubbing them out' to get his hands on their money, either by burning down White House Farm while they slept or by engaging a London **hitman**. Julie Mugford said he devised 'plot after plot', dismissing the fire scheme because it would destroy too many valuables. Consumed by resentment at his sister's – his *adopted* sister's – £20,000 allowance, Bamber was going nowhere under his own steam; he worked casually as a waiter or barman, while Bambi produced children who constituted further obstructions to his inheritance, and his parents continued their pointless existence as pillars of the local community.

Bath, drowning in the

The correct technique is to seize the victim by the knees and raise the legs in the air. This immerses the head. Tests have shown that no other method is comparably effective.

In 1914 the case against George Joseph Smith (1872–1915) was considered vulnerable when Sir Charles Mathews, the Director of Public Prosecutions, pointed out the difficulty of drowning anyone in the bath who put up the slightest resistance; potential victims could easily keep their heads above water by propping themselves up on their elbows.

The circumstantial evidence against Smith was strong. He had married three times, losing his first wife

Bessie Mundy in 1912 (found dead in the bath), his second – Alice Burnham – passing away the following year (found dead in the bath) and the third, Margaret Lofty, expiring shortly afterwards in December 1914 (found dead in the bath). While Margaret lay dead or dying, Smith played 'Nearer My God to Thee' on the sitting-room organ.

Smith's matrimonial career came to light when the father of Number Two read a *News of the World* item on Number Three: 'A Bride's Tragic Fate'. The evidential hurdle was finding a plausible way of satisfactorily drowning bathers.

Sir Bernard **Spilsbury**, expert witness for the prosecution, set out to solve the riddle. Together with Detective Inspector Arthur Neill he practised on young ladies, attired in bathing suits, who obliged by sitting in a narrow bath while he attempted to drown them. But, just as Sir Charles feared, even the slenderest specimen could not be submerged. Nothing worked until an inspired Neill grabbed his prospect by the knees. She went under immediately and lost consciousness.

At Smith's trial, the public gallery was packed with women, to whom he proved most attractive. He 'married' scores of them, once under the name George Oliver Love; in a typical case, after a brief courtship, Smith would lay his hands on any cash and then, the day after the ceremony, nip out for a stroll from which he never returned. His trial ran for an unprecedented eight days, and it took 112 witnesses and 264 court exhibits to unravel his numerous aliases and deceptions. Smith's motive was money, pure and simple; he netted £2,500 from his first killing.

In those days, baths were not so common. Smith had to insist on lodgings with baths, or buy one himself. He purchased Alice Burnham's on 9 July 1913, beating the price down from £2 to £1 17s 6d, and, after the murder four days later, returned it to the shop scarcely used. 'I did not like the way he asked about the bath,' recalled Mrs Heiss, an astute landlady who refused accommodation to Smith and his third victim.

'Brides in the Bath' Smith was hanged on 13 August 1915, still claiming that the deaths were a tragic coincidence. His last days were spent in almost constant tears, but probably his most trying moments came after each killing, as he stood by the bath, encouraging the local doctor in his endeavours to revive the murder victim.

See also **Exhibits**

That special day. George Joseph Smith in a studio photograph with his first murder victim, Beatrice Mundy

Beach Bodies Case, The

Scott Peterson was either one of the coldest or, perhaps, one of the unluckiest men alive.

In late 2002 he and his wife, Laci, were living a comfortable life in the town of Modesto, California. Scott, aged 30, and Laci, 27, had been college sweethearts. They had been married for five years and lived well on Scott's income as a fertiliser salesman and Laci's wage as a substitute teacher. Best of all, their first child was due to be born in early February 2003. Then, on Christmas Eve, Laci disappeared.

Scott told police he had gone out fishing for the day, sailing his boat from the marina at Berkeley. When he returned that evening, his wife was missing, having left behind her car, her mobile phone and her purse. Laci's only known plan for that day had been to go to buy some groceries and walk the dog in the nearby park.

Neighbours had found the Petersons' dog wandering

in the street at 10 a.m., just half an hour after Scott had left for his fishing trip. Laci had not answered the door when they called to return the animal and, unusually for a California home even in December, all the window curtains were closed. So the neighbours had simply left the dog tethered in the Petersons' backyard.

The police immediately suspected that Mrs Peterson had met with foul play. Eight-month pregnant women do not wander far from home without money or transport. Nor did it seem likely that she had run away; Scott, family friends and Laci's own mother all insisted that the couple had a 'honeymoon' relationship.

Laci's disappearance moved everyone in Modesto: flyers were handed out and thousands interrupted their holiday plans to help comb first the city, then the local countryside. Within days a $500,000 reward for finding Laci was posted, much of it donated by concerned citizens.

Through all this Scott refused to give press interviews, insisting he was too distressed, but he was very active in the search for his wife and unborn baby. Yet the police almost immediately decided that he was the prime suspect in Laci's disappearance. Away from the public eye, investigators found Scott too relaxed and even prone to laughter – hardly the image of an anxious husband. He had also taken out a $250,000 life-insurance policy on his wife, so stood to gain substantially if the police were forced to proclaim her 'missing, presumed dead'.

Nobody but Scott admitted to having seen Laci on the day she disappeared. Police bloodhound handlers insisted that Laci had not left her home on foot, but in a vehicle. Since the Petersons' dog had been found wandering just half an hour after Scott had driven from the house, it seemed most likely that Laci – alive or dead – had left with him. A neighbour told police that she had seen Scott leave the house on the morning Mrs Peterson vanished; Laci had not been with him but, ominously, Scott had loaded something heavy into the truck before driving away.

Yet relatives, including Laci's mother, continued to insist that Scott could never have harmed his pregnant wife. The Petersons had an idyllic marriage, they said, and Scott was keen to be a father – lovingly decorating a nursery for the son that they had already decided to call Conner. How could a man like that be a wife murderer?

Then a woman came forward to reveal that Scott Peterson was not the model husband everyone had

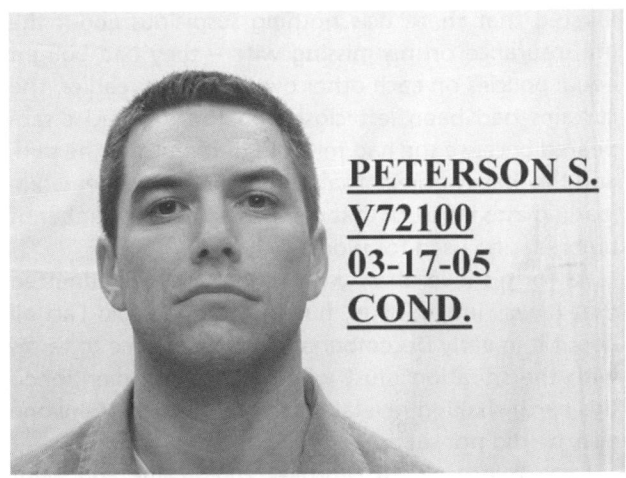

Scott Peterson

believed. Amber Frey, a 28-year-old massage therapist, had met Scott the previous November, when she had been introduced to him by a friend who had earlier met him at a business conference, and believed that he was an eligible bachelor. Amber was a lonely single mother with a two-year-old daughter, so the kind, educated, well-off, supposedly single Scott appeared a perfect catch. They had started a love affair that Scott failed to tell Amber was adulterous.

In fact, the friend who had introduced them, Shawn Sibley, discovered in early December that Scott was married and threatened to tell Amber. Peterson convinced Sibley that he had 'lost his wife' and found the subject too painful to talk about. To placate Sibley, Peterson told Amber the same lie, stressing that all he wanted now was a loving relationship with her. Chillingly, he had added that, come January, he would have a lot more time to spend with her and her daughter. As soon as Amber saw Scott on television, described as Laci Peterson's anxious husband, she put two and two together and rang the police.

Police forensic teams checked the Peterson house and Scott's truck and boat for signs of foul play. Peterson reacted by casually selling his missing wife's SUV to buy a replacement for the truck impounded by the police. He was also reported to be making enquiries with local estate agents about selling the house. It appeared that he didn't think his wife was coming home.

In the face of these negative revelations, Peterson broke his media silence, allowing himself to be interviewed on ABC News by anchor Diane Sawyer. There he insisted that there was nothing suspicious about the life insurance on his missing wife – they had bought equal policies on each other over two years earlier. The curtains had been left closed on the day Laci disappeared because she had felt cold that morning, he said, and the 'heavy object' that his neighbour had seen him loading into his truck that day was actually a number of umbrellas he used for work.

As for his love affair with Amber Frey, he admitted that it was indeed true, but that he had told Laci all about it in early December and she 'had come to terms with the situation'. Just why she had not mentioned this earth-shaking revelation to her mother, or anyone else, he did not say.

Laci's due date, 10 February 2003, came and went with still no sign of her. It was two months before there was a further development in the case, but when it came, on 13 April, it was horrible. The decayed corpse of an eight-month male foetus washed ashore just south of Berkeley Marina, where Scott had gone fishing on the day his wife vanished. The next day the headless, limbless body of a woman was found on the beach, near to where the baby had washed ashore.

DNA tests proved the corpses to be those of Laci and Conner Peterson. The cause of death could not be ascertained, but both had been dead since Christmas. Gas from the decay process had forced the foetus from the mother's body while still at sea. The torso seemed to have originally been weighted down but had evidently escaped its sea anchor.

The police arrested Scott Peterson shortly after the bodies were found. Despite having heard the news of the gruesome discoveries, he was calmly playing golf when officers came for him. He had grown a beard and dyed blond both it and his naturally brown hair. He was also found to be carrying $10,000 – the legal maximum that can be taken from the USA into Mexico without having to notify border officials.

The circumstantial case against Peterson seemed damning, but one important thing stood in his favour – the police had failed to find any physical evidence that he had been involved in the killings. He had wanted to start a new life with Amber Frey, prosecutors insisted, and Laci and the unborn baby had stood in his way so he had killed them; but this was only a theory. They had no proof.

Yet if the prosecution's case was purely circumstantial, what the defence offered the jury was little less than fantastic. Peterson's lawyer told the court that

roving, murderous satanists might have kidnapped Laci as she walked the dog in the park: who else could so brutally murder a heavily pregnant woman?

Unfortunately for Peterson, this defence was about ten years too old. California in the early 1990s had indeed been racked with fears that gangs of satanic ritual abusers were stalking the night, murdering babies and hypnotising witnesses into forgetting what they had seen. But that particular delusion had since fallen out of fashion in the face of a total lack of supporting evidence.

The jury found Peterson guilty of first-degree murder for killing Laci and second-degree murder for killing Conner. The judge took their recommendation and sentenced Peterson to death by lethal injection.

Justice seems to have been served, but it should be remembered that there was absolutely no physical or conclusive witness evidence to indicate that he killed his wife and unborn son. There remains the grim possibility that Scott Peterson – as unattractive a personality as he certainly seemed to be – was innocent.

Benefit of Clergy

An early English legal defence. The gradual extension of this principle, according to Sir James Stephen, the great (if stern) Victorian judge, 'reduced the administration of justice to a sort of farce'.

Originally, Benefit of Clergy exempted those in Holy Orders from the jurisdiction of the ordinary courts, a benign manoeuvre when the death penalty was mandatory for every felony. Its progressive extension to other groups of the population marked an early effort by the legal profession to mitigate the full rigour of the law.

A statute of 1350 extended Benefit of Clergy to minor religious functionaries such as church doorkeepers, exorcists and so on. To avoid limitless immunity for successive murders, from 1487 criminals were branded on the thumb, and second time round the exemption was withheld, unless the supplicant was ordained. In due course, virtually anyone able to read and write was entitled to the concession, except women, and this legal stratagem staggered on down the centuries, saving the life of the playwright Ben Jonson in 1598. As late as 1765, Lord Byron (the poet's great-uncle) avoided his just deserts for the manslaughter of a Mr Chaworth by pointing out that he could read. Particularly heinous crimes – for instance, **petty treason**, piracy and murder in church – stayed beyond forgiveness, and by 1769 some 160 offences were classified as 'non-clergyable', that is, worthy of instant execution. For the remainder, the death sentence was optional.

The procedure involved the defendant falling to his knees and reading out the first verse of the 51st Psalm (the 'neck-verse'), which begins, 'Have mercy upon me, 0 God, according to thy loving kindness'. The more wily illiterates learned the passage by rote. Rather than attempting to discriminate against those who seemed able to read in favour of those who really could, in 1705 the law formally conceded that Benefit of Clergy covered anyone able to memorise the lines. Women only qualified if bona-fide nuns, and not until 1692 did they achieve parity with men.

For many years a replica of a medieval cage discovered in the moat of the Sicilian castle of Hilazzoa was exhibited in Madame Tussaud's Chamber of Horrors. In Sicily, prisoners in holy orders could not be executed; but it was permissible to cage them up until death resulted from hunger, thirst and exposure.

Bernardo and Homolka

In Canada's most sensational murder cases of the 1990s, the defendant was Paul Bernardo, a handsome young businessman in his late twenties, who resembled President Clinton, and his girlfriend and accomplice, Karla Homolka, a pretty blonde, six years his junior, who was accused of being his accomplice in a series of kidnaps, murders and rapes. They were accused of two murders of teenage girls, Leslie Mahaffy and Kristen French, and of the death by drugging of Karla's teenage sister Tammy.

Karla Homolka had been 17 years old in 1987 when she met Paul Bernardo in the dining room of a Howard Johnson's hotel in Scarborough, a suburb of Toronto; she and a girlfriend had booked in for the night. The girls had invited Paul Bernardo and his friend Van Smirnis to their room, and within minutes Bernardo and Karla were in bed, having wild, orgiastic sex. It was obvious that they had some extraordinary chemical affinity. Later it became clear that this affinity was based upon the fact that his sexual tastes veered towards sadism and hers towards masochism. At 16 Karla had allowed a boyfriend to tie her up with his

belt and slap her during sex, and discovered that she enjoyed it. The first time she and Paul were alone in her bedroom, he found handcuffs in her pocket, and asked, 'Are these for me?' Then he handcuffed her to the bed and they pretended he was raping her. As their relationship progressed, she had to pretend to be a schoolgirl – with her hair in pigtails tied with ribbons – and he also liked her to wear a dog collar round her neck when they had sex.

If she showed unwillingness to participate in his fantasies, Bernardo beat her. She soon became expert at explaining away her bruises to her friends and family.

Paul Bernardo

When she met Bernardo, Karla was unaware that he was the man the police referred to as the Scarborough Rapist. Since May 1987 the rapist had been grabbing women who alighted from buses. He liked to rape the victims vaginally and anally, and to humiliate them by calling them names. Often he pounded them with his fists as he raped them. These attacks continued for years after Bernardo met Karla Homolka.

Some time before Christmas 1990, Karla had asked Bernardo – by now engaged to her and living in her home – what he wanted for Christmas, and Bernardo had replied, 'Your sister Tammy.' Tammy was 15, and still at school. Finally, Karla gave way, and obtained drugs from the animal clinic where she worked. On the evening of 23 December 1990, they invited Tammy to join them in watching a film after midnight in the basement 'den', and gave her drugged drinks. When she was unconscious, Bernardo undressed her and raped her on the floor.

It was while Bernardo was having sex with Tammy – filmed by Karla – that he noticed that the girl had stopped breathing, and her face had turned blue. Tammy died in hospital, but no suspicion fell on her sister or Bernardo; the inquest seemed to show that she had drunk too much, and choked on her own vomit.

On Friday 14 June 1991, a 14-year-old schoolgirl named Leslie Mahaffy arrived at her home at 2 a.m. to find herself locked out. Bernardo came across her sitting disconsolately on a bench in her backyard and offered her a cigarette. Then he held a knife to her throat and took her back to the house that he and Karla now shared – they were due to get married in two weeks. There he raped her and videotaped her urinating.

He woke Karla to tell her that he had kidnapped a girl, and told her to go back to sleep. But the next day she had to join in, having lesbian sex with the schoolgirl while Bernardo videotaped them. Leslie was raped repeatedly. When left alone with Karla, Leslie begged her to let her go; Karla replied that if she did, she would be beaten. She gave Leslie two sleeping tablets to 'make her feel better', and while Leslie was asleep, Bernardo looped electrical cord around her throat and strangled her.

Two days later he sawed up the body with an electric saw, encased the pieces in quick-drying cement, then dropped them off a bridge into Lake Gibson, with Karla acting as lookout.

Bernardo now decided to seduce a 15-year-old schoolgirl named Jane, who had been a friend of Tammy's. Jane, invited to the house of the newly-weds, was flattered by the attention of two adults, and developed a schoolgirl crush on Karla. One night she was given drugged liquor, and after she fell asleep Karla anaesthetised her with halothane, obtained from the animal clinic. Bernardo then raped and sodomised her while Karla videoed it; Bernardo was particularly delighted to find that Jane had been a virgin.

Later Bernardo persuaded Jane to perform oral sex on demand.

On 6 April 1992, ten months after the murder of Leslie Mahaffy, Karla accompanied Bernardo as they drove in search of another victim. They passed 15-year-old Kristen French, walking alone on her way home from school, and Karla called to ask her directions. The girl came over to their car as Karla produced a map. Then Bernardo moved behind her and forced her into the car at knifepoint.

After three days of rape and being forced to take part in videotapes in which she had to address Bernardo as 'master', Kristen, like Leslie Mahaffy, was murdered. Her naked body was thrown on a dump site full of old washing machines.

During the New Year of 1993, Bernardo beat Karla more violently than usual, clubbing her with a rubber flashlight and blacking both her eyes. Finally her mother and sister called when Bernardo was out, and insisted on taking her to hospital. After that she agreed to go home with them. To prevent her husband discovering her whereabouts, she moved in with an aunt and uncle.

In late January 1993, after six years, the Toronto police finally solved the Scarborough Rapist case. There had been 224 suspects, among these Paul Bernardo, who resembled an Identikit drawing of the rapist. Bernardo had given a body sample to be compared with the rapist, but had heard nothing further in two years and assumed he was in the clear. In fact, the DNA testing had proceeded slowly and Bernardo was among the last five suspects whose body samples were tested. It was only then that the police knew that Paul Bernardo was the Scarborough Rapist, the man they had been seeking for more than five years.

Instead of arresting Bernardo immediately, they went to interview Karla Homolka. She refused to admit that she knew her husband was the rapist, but when they had gone, she blurted out to her uncle and aunt: 'Christ, they know everything.' Pressed by her aunt, Karla finally told her about the murder of the two schoolgirls.

Bernardo was arrested on 17 February 1993. Karla Homolka turned state's evidence against her husband, in what is known in legal slang as a 'sweetheart deal' – that is, in exchange for a promise of a lighter sentence. She was tried first, and was sentenced to twelve years' imprisonment.

Although aware of their existence, the police had not been able to find the videotapes of the prolonged sexual ordeals of Leslie Mahaffy and Kristen French. But eventually they discovered that Bernardo's lawyer had them, and they were at last handed over. Bernardo's trial opened on 1 May 1995. It was as sensational as everyone had expected, with videotapes showing the rapes and capturing Karla at one point telling Bernardo that she feels proud of him for the death of her sister.

On 1 September 1995, Paul Bernardo was sentenced to life imprisonment, with the proviso that he should serve a minimum of twenty-five years before he could apply for parole.

Berry, James (1852–1913)

British hangman. In his disastrous year of 1885 Berry tangled with the redoubtable John **Lee**, whom he failed to despatch despite three attempts. Then on 30 November, Berry decapitated the murderer Robert Goodale despite reducing the drop to a minimal five feet nine inches; after separation, Goodale's headless trunk descended into the pit underneath the scaffold. The episode reduced the prison governor to tears.

The ensuing Committee of Inquiry recommended a drop to produce a blow of 1,260 pounds to the neck, with a diligent mathematician observing that the weight of the head should be discounted in any calculations since it was situated above the noose.

Berry survived these early disappointments and, by his retirement, had officiated at more than 200 executions, averaging a comfortable £200 a year. Of stout moral fibre, at his interview Berry told the Sheriffs of London he had no qualms about **hanging** an innocent man 'because the crime committed would be that of the law and not mine'. Selected from 1,400 applicants for the post, his business card featured an attractive ivy-leaf motif together with his trade: 'Executioner'. Before killing his clients, he sent them a set of fortifying verses entitled 'For one under sentence of death'.

It was Berry's experience that a good rope improved with service, using one sixteen times and another twelve before presenting both to Madame Tussaud's. Berry also donated a large knife used to behead seven

Berry's business card, printed in black, green and gold

Chinese pirates, an item he obtained in a swap for another rope. On retirement, shorn of glory, Berry was unable to find another profession. Ostracised and threatened by those who recognised him, he depended on anonymity for survival. But his autobiographical *Life Story and Strange Experiences* proved popular enough.

See also **Initiation**, **Recruitment**

Biggs, Ronald (1929–)

A decorator and hopeless small-time thief sentenced to thirty years for his part in the **Great Train Robbery** of 8 August 1963. A last-minute addition to the gang, his role was to supply the substitute train driver (who lost his nerve and flunked the job).

On 8 July 1965 Biggs escaped from London's Wandsworth Prison, scaling the walls with a rope ladder and leaping down on to the roof of a waiting furniture van. The jailbreak came free, but honour among thieves is at a premium, and by the time Biggs was reunited with his wife Charmian and their three children in Australia in January 1966 he was £55,000 out of pocket for extensive plastic surgery in France and the forged passport issued in the name of 'Terence Furminger'. The family lived peaceably for several years in the Melbourne suburbs while Biggs traded incognito as a carpenter, shedding another £30,000 when a surefire investment went wrong. Then, recognised from a newspaper picture, he fled to Brazil just ahead of a police raid.

There he established a new life. But in 1974 an English journalist unearthed his whereabouts and started on a biography; the newspaper executives tipped off the British police, and on 1 February 1974 'Slipper of the Yard' arrived in Rio for the arrest in a blaze of publicity.

But Brazil has no extradition treaty with Britain and, before this obstacle could be **straightened**, Biggs was again beyond the reach of the law. His new girlfriend, Raimunda, announced her pregnancy, and the father of a Brazilian child cannot be deported. A crestfallen Slipper returned to England; a triumphant Biggs blossomed, making a record with the Sex Pistols and taking drinks on a Royal Navy destroyer. Seven years passed before the next attempt on his person.

This time the mastermind was a 36-year-old British ex-serviceman, John Miller, who concocted the idea of remaindering Biggs at auction. Heading a four-man team, Miller knocked Biggs out with Mace gas outside a Copacabana bar, zipped him into a sack and smuggled him out of the country through the northern port of Belem on a chartered yacht. The kidnappers sailed to Barbados, and while the boat stood offshore beyond territorial limits, Miller informed the world's press from his hotel base that Biggs was now 'available' to the highest bidder.

Meanwhile, the yacht's engine broke down. The boat drifted into Barbadian waters to be seized by coastguards; Biggs was thrown into Bridgetown jail to await repatriation and the rest of his thirty-year sentence.

But his best friend from Rio, cockney John Pickston, hired a high-calibre lawyer and, after three weeks' deliberation, Chief Justice Sir William Justice ruled that the longstanding extradition treaty with Britain was invalid. Freed to a welcoming crowd, Biggs paraded through the streets in triumph. He flew back to Rio for an emotional reunion with his little son, to be greeted with a newly issued Brazilian passport and work permit.

In 1992 Biggs starred in a celebrity product-endorsement advertisement on Brazilian TV. The final sequence shows him roaring off into the sunset in a vehicle stacked with mailbags. To the camera, Biggs says: 'When you have a tough job to do and need reliable transport, you can always rely on Land Rover.'

Perhaps this exemplifies Brazil's ambivalent attitude towards law and order. The country is about the size of Europe and, in its further reaches, gun law prevails. It holds the record for the world's highest murder rate, with 104 homicides per 100,000 of the population, as against 1.3 for Britain and nearly 10 for the United States. In 1983 Brazilian killings totalled 370 per day; a productive week in New York during the peak season yields about 60 fatalities.

Biggs suffered a stroke in 2000 and the following year flew back to the UK in a private jet paid for by the *Sun* newspaper. With twenty-eight years of his term left to serve, he was promptly returned to prison. Since then he has had two heart attacks, among other medical crises, and remains in very poor health. Attempts by his lawyers to have his sentence overturned or reduced have failed.

Birch

The size of the 'birch' – a bundle of birch twigs – was precisely regulated by law and varied according to the age of the recipient. Boys over ten were beaten with a cane measuring no more than forty inches long and no heavier than nine ounces, but adults could be chastised by a more expansive instrument, four feet long with a circumference of nine inches and a weight of twelve ounces. Before application, the birch was soaked in water for added pliability. The victim, tied to an easel-like apparatus known as the triangle, was bent over a pad placed on the crossbar and bound by the hands and ankles. In this posture he received anything up to thirty-six blows from a prison officer paid two shillings and sixpence for his pains.

In the 1920s, some 30 per cent of those convicted of robbery with violence received corporal punishment, but by the 1940s this figure dropped to 14 per cent. Birching was finally abolished by the Criminal Justice Act of 1947, whereupon the then Lord Chief Justice, Rayner Goddard, instituted a campaign for its restitution. Sentencing two brothers for robbing two other boys, he observed: 'What they want is a thundering good larruping.'

Thrashings have recently been reintroduced in Singapore, where courts can impose a particularly violent form of caning on prisoners guilty of offences like attempted murder, robbery and rape. 'Prisoners feel like the blood is exploding out of their bodies,' said Tony Poh of the Ministry of Home Affairs. Supposedly, the beatings constitute an effective deterrent. According to Poh: 'Only 5 per cent of prisoners who have been caned are ever charged with another crime. The memory of their suffering lasts all their lives.'

In Japan, teachers face severe disciplinary action for beating pupils to death. Between 1979 and 1981, four students died after their thrashings at a single establishment, the Totsuka Yacht School. One – Makoto Ogawa – was found on post-mortem to have 144 external wounds; his wire teeth-brace was smashed back into his throat. Ten years later the school's headmaster was convicted of manslaughter, but Judge Hiroshi Kojima set him free on a suspended sentence, depicting the pupil's punishment as 'largely legitimate'.

See also **Trousers**

Blackmail

Put on the legal map by Alexander Chaffers in 1872. Historically, blackmail took a long time to emerge because it preys off respectability, and it took some time for civilisation to become respectable. Not until the Victorian era could men be ruined by imputations of fornication and the like.

When the Chaffers case came to court in 1872, the blackmailer was branded as 'an object of contempt to all honest and well-thinking men', but otherwise escaped scot-free. As the law stood, Chaffers had done nothing illegal. His victims' recourse was not to report him to the police but to sue for libel, and since Chaffers's allegations were true, the trial ended not in his but in their contumely. So in 1873 the new offence of 'demanding money with menaces' was created.

Chaffers was a London solicitor who, while taking the air in Kew Gardens, came across the promenading Sir Travers Twiss and his wife. Sir Travers was an eminent barrister and professor; his spouse, the former prostitute Marie Gelas. Sir Travers did not know this. He thought Marie, his wife of some years, was a Van Lynseele, daughter to a Polish major-general. He had married Marie on this basis, presenting her at court to the Prince of Wales and Queen Victoria.

Chaffers recognised Lady Twiss from their shared afternoons in a Belgian brothel, and sent her a bill 'for services rendered', first for £46 and then, when she failed to respond, for £150. Lady Twiss spun Sir Travers a story and he paid Chaffers off with £50, but demands continued to arrive. Finally the blackmailer told his tale to the Lord Chamberlain and deposited a sworn affidavit with the Chief Magistrate at Bow Street. Sir Travers could no longer dismiss Chaffers as a madman with a grudge. He had to sue for libel.

On the trial's eighth day, Lady Twiss withdrew her case and entrained for the Continent. She never saw Sir Travers again. He was disgraced in turn, resigning from all his posts. Sadly, the court hearing had gone well for Lady Twiss, with the respectable witnesses testifying she was Van Lynseele and the less respectable witnesses testifying she wasn't Marie Gelas. But the testimony was probably bribed; presumably Marie found her witnesses under increasing pressure from the threat of perjury.

The word 'blackmail' originally derived from the Highlands of Scotland in Elizabethan times, where it meant unlawful rent ('mail') or 'black-rent'. Chieftains extorted this protection money from local farmers. In the East End of **Jack the Ripper**, blackmail acquired a technical meaning for a blunter form of extortion practised on prostitutes. One exponent was the suspect known as 'Leather Apron'. He carried a sharp knife and demanded money with menaces, threatening: 'I'll rip you up.'

See also **Pedigree Chum**

Blackmail, computer

Probably the most notorious blackmail attempt in the history of computer crime was the brainchild of the American anthropologist Dr Joseph Lewis Popp. Found unfit to face trial in November 1991 after a few days on remand in Brixton jail, Dr Popp took to wearing a cardboard box and threading curlers in his beard 'so that he could detect the radioactivity'. The authorities packed him back to the United States.

In December 1989, Dr Popp mailed out 20,000 floppy disks to World Health Organisation medical researchers and other professional users. The software, entitled *Aids Information – Introductory Diskette*, came with an invoice priced at $189 or $378 (depending on the anticipated usage) from a Panamanian company, and the accompanying leaflet specified that unauthorised use would result in computer malfunction. The disks carried a virus that hid all the pre-existing memory on the user's hard disk.

The operation cost about £10,000 to mount, including postage, with a maximum take in excess of £3 million. But Dr Popp lacked the nerve to see it through; on 21 December he cracked up during a Nairobi–Amsterdam flight after reading the first press reports on the resulting havoc. First Popp thought he had been contaminated in mid-air. Then he accused a colleague in the next seat of being an Interpol agent. Finally, on arrival, he attracted attention by scrawling 'DR POPP HAS BEEN POISONED' on another passenger's briefcase. A Dutch police officer informed the head of Scotland Yard's Computer Crime Unit.

No one knows why Dr Popp did it. After gaining a Harvard doctorate in 1979, he spent a decade with commendable African development agencies like the Flying Doctor Service.

Apart from motivation, the case raises interesting legal considerations. Blackmail entails an 'unwarranted demand'. But Dr Popp hoped to exact his licence fee, neither an unwarranted nor an unreasonable ambition. The alternative charge of criminal damage might cover destroying data. But Dr Popp's virus was designed not to obliterate information but to conceal it. In the event, his mental breakdown meant the issues never came to trial.

In 1991 Chile reported an unusual case of a crime committed not with but by a computer. A few days after the installation of a new system in a Valparaiso bank, a security guard noticed one of the terminals running a horned demon graphic on its own initiative. The machine did for two employees and put a third into a coma. In the words of Police Detective Raul Lopez: 'An evil spirit inhabits that machine and the death of two innocent people proves it. Computer experts tried to examine the terminal, but they had no success. One of them started babbling like a madman when he came within ten feet, and a dozen more were flung to the floor like rag dolls by some unseen force. We can't turn the system off because everyone who tries to blacks out and falls to the floor.'

The ordinarily reliable British magazine, *Computing*, carried this story on 5 December 1991, reporting that the bank faced closure unless the efforts of Father Hector Diaz, an exorcist, bore fruit.

Bloodstains, a short history of

The science of serology was a late-comer. Until the twentieth century, dried human bloodstains could not be 'typed' or even distinguished from animal blood. This afforded a first line of defence obvious to the most dim-witted of killers, with the victim's blood routinely ascribed to the results of skinning a rabbit, spilling woodstain or tearing frogs to pieces.

It was the series of animal blood transfusions by a Dr James Blundell in 1814 that instigated serious scientific inquiry. Some of Blundell's charges prospered, others perished in agony, a pattern repeated when he progressed to humans four years later and, by the turn of the century, the survival rate stood at around one in two. The 1871 tally was 146 fatalities out of 263 transfusions.

The talk was of two antipathetic types of blood, a theory put to the test in 1900 by an Austrian, Dr Karl Landsteiner. Watching for visible signs of coagulation ('clumping'), he mixed the blood of five colleagues into six specimens of a single master sample. Repeating the procedure five more times with different masters, he produced a cross-referenced table suggesting the existence of three types of blood: A, B, and C (subsequently better known as 0). To these was soon added a fourth

group, AB, and the approximate percentages for the overall population were later established as A, 42 per cent; B, 10 per cent; 0, 45 per cent and AB, 3 per cent. The figures vary from one part of a continent to another. Thus 'A' group frequency is high among Europeans, western Asians and Australian aboriginals.

At about that time, following in the footsteps of Pasteur and von Behring, another Viennese doctor discovered the precipitin test, based on the defensive reaction of blood serum (blood minus the cells) to invasion by foreign blood cells. Paul Uhlenhuth established that animal blood (except for apes, which are too closely related) reacts to human blood by throwing a visible white precipitate, and a suspect's bloodstained clothes, soaked in salt water, yielded a sufficient concentration to produce the reaction.

At last the forensic pathologist could tell whether bloodstains originated from the same species as the victim, and today police laboratories carry stocks of anti-sera of the common animals, enabling an immediate check on the truth of a suspect's story.

Over the years, the four blood groups were split into subdivisions, and protein analysis separated out distinguishing factors, or combinations of factors, in ever smaller population categories. In 1925 Landsteiner realised that all body fluids – sweat, saliva, urine, semen and so on – could be similarly 'typed'; about 86 per cent of the population are 'secretors' whose fluids carry tell-tale blood cells. In the post-war era Stuart Kind, a Home Office scientist, devised a simple and reliable way of testing old bloodstains, and today the modern radioimmunoassay technique enables samples, in many cases, to be sexed; female white corpuscles display microscopic drumstick-like shapes.

But although blood-grouping theoretically provided ever narrower differential bands, in practice it failed to deliver results. Not until 1934 was the first major trial settled by forensic serology. Flecks of blood proved too small – or their investigation too complex – for the jury's taste, a depressing contrast with companion disciplines securing convictions from microscopic shreds of cloth, fluff or hair.

	GROUPING SERA		
	Anti – A	Anti – B	Anti –A,B
Group O Cells	●	●	●
Group A Cells			
Group B Cells	●		
Group AB Cells			

Testing for the four main blood groups

And rightly so. Australia's '**dingo**' trial showed that, as late as 1982, experts could mistake paint for blood. Even in the British Backhouse case of 1984, suspicions of foul play revolved around more Holmesian deductions about the *shape* of the blood **drops**, not their composition; common sense suggested that a wounded man fighting for his life (the Backhouse version) would spatter blood around, producing drops with flying tails, rather than the neat, round markings actually found, more characteristic of blood dripping from a stationary casualty.

That same year everything changed when Alec Jeffreys from the University of Leicester unveiled the Holy Grail of Serology: **Genetic fingerprinting**.

Bobettes

American journalese for the swarms of female admirers flocking to the trial of Robert Chambers, the upper-crust 'Preppie Murderer'. With one more turn of the screw, the killer evolves into a love object while behind bars, with **romances** blossoming during prison visits from strangers.

Ordinary women may wonder exactly what it is about multiple murderers and wife-slayers that proves so attractive, for – in the words of Sheila Isenberg, author of *Women Who Love Men Who Kill* – 'There is no serial killer who has not been pursued by dozens of women', and the more presentable one-off cases, like the family murderer Jeff **MacDonald**, are also treated to marriage proposals while awaiting trial. Psychiatrist David Abrahamsen, of the Berkowitz case, puts forward an explanation: 'Most of these women are unhappy, frustrated and dissatisfied. They have low self-image and want to attach themselves to figures they think are powerful.'

There is a curious correspondence between a serial killer – an outcast in pursuit of an identity – and his suitor, an outcast seeking a relationship. Their affairs have much to recommend them. An incarcerated love-object is easy to idealise since there is little prospect of the bond being put to the test or consummated. This combination of celibacy and suffering-through-separation makes an ideal fit for strict Catholics, disproportionately represented among murderers' suitors. The romances occasionally lead to marriage; Ronald **Kray** (with his 'old-world manners and gentlemanly behaviour') wed former kissagram girl Kate Howard in 1989, and when handsome Richard **Ramirez** (the 'Night Stalker') proposed to mother-of-two Christine Lee, she could not say no.

Florida boasts a handful of prisons with matrimonial apartments that start the marriages off on the right foot with regulation forty-two-hour honeymoons. It is when the inmate is freed that trouble begins. The prisoner's gratitude fades, and the relationship is exposed as a fiction; according to prison counsellor Kathryn Parris, 'Most of the women involved with prisoners describe a level of emotional intimacy and passion only found in books.'

Bodies in Barrels Case, The

Australia's worst known case of serial killing took place in Snowtown, a tiny hamlet of less than 1,000 inhabitants about 100 miles north of the city of Adelaide. On 20 May 1999, police investigating a series of local disappearances searched a derelict building in the centre of Snowtown – a former bank – and found six black plastic barrels in the abandoned vault. These contained the remains of eight corpses, some dismembered.

The following day, investigating officers arrested three men in the northern suburbs of Adelaide: John Justin Bunting, aged 32, Robert Joe Wagner, 27, and Mark Ray Haydon, 40. A few days later they also arrested James Spyridon Vlassakis, aged 19. Digging in Bunting's garden uncovered two more corpses.

As the investigation and identification of the victims progressed, a bizarre story emerged. The ringleader of the killers was Bunting, a small but powerful abattoir worker who had decided to murder anyone he suspected of being a paedophile. When just 14, Vlassakis had fallen under the older man's spell when his mother had an affair with Bunting, and several years later was involved in three of the killings, including that of his own half-brother, Troy Youde, whom Vlassakis accused of sexually molesting him.

Robert Wagner was Bunting's contact with the paedophile underground. Meeting him in 1991, one of Bunting's first victims was Wagner's boyfriend, convicted paedophile Barry Lane. Using information gleaned from Wagner and Lane, Bunting set about designing what he called his 'spider wall' – a collection of names connected by pieces of string to indicate who knew whom. It was with this that Bunting plotted his killings.

Tried in September 2003, Bunting was convicted of

eleven murders (although twelve bodies were connected to the case, the jury felt that a woman whose dismembered body was found buried in the garden of Bunting's former home might, as he claimed, have died of natural causes and he merely hid the corpse). Wagner was convicted of being involved in ten of the murders. Both were sentenced to life imprisonment with no chance of parole. Vlassakis, who had pleaded guilty of involvement in three murders at an earlier trial, was given twenty-six years.

Bunting, whatever he told himself and others, was no Robin Hood. Although he targeted paedophiles, often torturing them before strangling and dismembering them, he killed other victims, among them mentally subnormal housewife Elizabeth Haydon, who were plainly not paedophiles. The truth seems to be that he was a sadistic serial killer who focused on those he thought society would not care about. His accomplices were drawn into his spider web of murder by his powerful personality and fear that they might be next on his list.

Body language

Sometimes a dead give-away. Perhaps the most extreme example was the American serial murderer Gerald Stano, who found it hard to lie without backing away, pushing back his chair and crossing his legs, left ankle on right knee. For the truth, he earnestly leaned towards his questioner.

This made police interrogation easy. Had Stano ever met Mary Carol Maher, whose body was found in Florida on 17 February 1980? Yes, he had given her a lift (leaning forwards). By herself? No, she was with another girl (back, legs crossed). Where had they gone? To a nightclub called 'Fannie Farkel's' (back, legs crossed). Did he have sex with her? Yes (leaning forwards).

The questioning turned to whether Mary Carol resisted his advances. When Stano was asked, 'She could hit pretty hard, couldn't she?', he leaned forwards and replied, 'You're damned right she could.' But the next question, 'So you hit her?', propelled him backwards as he crossed his legs and demurred, 'No, I let her out.' And so it continued until, angled forwards, Stano confessed and then, inclined backwards, recanted.

The inquiry took a macabre twist when Stano was asked about a missing black prostitute, Toni Van Haddocks. Did Stano know anything about her? No

(back, legs crossed). How often did he pick up black girls? He didn't (back, legs crossed). So what about Toni? Stano adopted his posture for deceit and said, 'That's the only one I ever picked up.' At this stage the investigating officer, Detective Crowe, experienced a sinking feeling that he was dealing with a serial killer.

Eventually Stano admitted to murdering thirty-four women between 1969 and 1980, generally leaving his 'signature' at the site by the careful, ritualistic display of branches arranged round the corpse. On 2 September 1981 Stano was jailed for seventy-five years for six murders, but a subsequent trial awarded the death sentence. Quoted in the *New York Times* as saying, 'I just can't stand a bitchy chick', according to the Florida police he thought only of three things: 'stereo systems, cars, and killing women'.

Bodysnatchers

A grisly British occupation. In 1540 Henry VIII granted a charter to the Company of Barber Surgeons entitling them to the bodies of four felons a year for dissection. As long as surgeons were content to develop anatomical theories without reference to their patients' actual physique, this allotment – bolstered to twelve by the Murder Act of 1752 – proved sufficient, and until the end of the eighteenth century, bodysnatching remained a tiny trade supplying the demand of a dozen or so anatomical pioneers. The rest of the profession practised, if at all, on model skeletons made of papier-mâché.

For centuries there was no legal sanction against bodysnatching; since a corpse did not constitute 'property', nothing was actually stolen. But the legal framework changed with the 1788 case of *R v. Lynn*. Lord Kenyon, the presiding judge, suddenly and erroneously recollected a 1744 precedent involving St Andrew's churchyard, and ruled that, in truth, to disturb a grave was a misdemeanour. He fined Mr Lynn, a surgeon, £10.

In fact the 1744 case dealt with the theft of lead coffins, but as a result Lynn's conviction avoided classification as a felony since it lacked the element of theft: the victim's clothes and coffin were left in the tomb. This nice legal distinction had practical ramifications, since felonies entailed a mandatory death sentence, making convictions an unlikely outcome on even the clearest evidence. But misdemeanours carried a real threat of enforcement, and after 1788 doctors preferred to pay others to do their dirty work.

This untoward change in the law combined with a vast expansion in the medical profession to foster the novel industry of bodysnatching. The number of medical students quintupled to 500, and their new professors wanted them each to try their hands on at least two bodies before qualifying. This put the quota for London alone at 300 corpses a year, at the very period when the rate of criminal executions was declining. One contemporary commentator on this problematic statistical area stated that 'in all Great Britain, from 1805 to 1820, there were executed eleven hundred and fifty criminals, or about seventy-seven annually'.

Resurrectionists, resurrection men or sack-em-up men came into being to supply the shortfall. Doctors might pay two to three guineas for a full-sized body ('large', three feet or more), with children ('large small') or babies ('foetuses') at a guinea or less. Prices inflated steadily, by 1812 attaining four guineas for a 'large' and doubling again by 1828.

The trade, despite its illegality and the endemic bouts of gang warfare, was efficiently administered and controlled by racketeers, notably the ex-boxer Ben Crouch. Like any other wholesaler, at the start of each academic term Crouch negotiated directly with the medical schools' professors, agreeing prices and quantities for the forthcoming term. Crouch ran a tight ship, beating up rivals, turning them in to the law or, if all else failed, spoiling a rival's graveyard (his source of supply) by digging up the graves and heaving the rotting corpses on to the ground. As a last resort he would break into hospitals and shred cadavers purchased from other purveyors.

After his retirement in 1817, Crouch was summoned by the 1827 Select Committee when an alarming legal development resulted in a fine for a medical student, rather than the uncouth bodysnatcher. The Committee estimated that ten full-time resurrectionists were working in London, together with about 200 freelances. Asked if bodies could be imported from the Continent, Crouch attested that the trade was already international, with bodies crossing the borders between England, Ireland and Scotland. Customs sometimes impounded putrefying corpses too long in transit.

The construction of operating theatres in four major London hospitals at the end of the 1820s bolstered demand, forcing the bereaved to mount watch over their relatives' gravesides until the cadaver had sufficiently decayed to be worthless. Spring-guns and mantraps proliferated in the churchyards; a castellated watchtower from this era can still be seen in Edinburgh's New Calton Burial Ground. Outlandishly deep graves became popular, particularly among boxers, who believed that their exceptional musculature was favoured by the anatomists; pugilist Tom 'the gas man' Hickman was buried eighteen feet down. The rich too remained relatively immune in their deeper graves.

An experienced team, working hard in relays, could spirit away a corpse in a quarter of an hour. To prevent outsiders jumping on the bandwagon, the resurrectionist cartel circulated disinformation, suggesting that the body was best extracted through a shaft excavated to a point adjacent to the head of the coffin. They recommended that the coffin's wooden top next to the deceased's cranium should be banged out, the corpse's arms folded down, and the body eased out like toothpaste from a tube. In fact, the real bodysnatchers dug straight down, attached hooks and cords to the coffin itself, which they raised by the head to ground level, and then broke open the lid.

Earnings were good; one gang of six or seven confederates grossed over £1,000 in a single year from the sale of 312 bodies. **Burke and Hare** took bodysnatching a step further, murdering people rather than

The rear of Burke's lodgings, his window marked A

digging them up. In the aftermath of their 1829 trial, a Member of Parliament, Henry Warburton, framed 'A Bill for Preventing the Unlawful Disinterment of Human Bodies', which became law in 1832. It enabled the legal custodians of a corpse – notably unwanted cadavers in the workhouses – to release it for dissection. Bodysnatching ceased forthwith, although Warburton's name was reviled long after by doctors. With its emphasis on a proper inspectorate and by putting an end to the illegal trade, his Bill decreased supply.

In modern Thailand, the days of bodysnatchers may be numbered. In April 1991 the Thai cabinet was poised to suspend the two charities responsible for collecting the corpses of Bangkok's murder and accident victims. The charities were paid by the number of bodies delivered to the morgue. It seems that the system, which in principle entailed handing in those *found* dead, was subject to abuse.

Bolero, Ravel's

A **fingerprint** case from the twilight zone. Ravel's Bolero was the music played by a 1961 **ghost** in northern England. The nocturnal spirit displayed such mastery of the violin that a Manchester widow realised that the other occupant of her home – her sleeping son – could not be responsible.

David Cohen of the Society of Psychical Research was summoned. The seances that followed in the small terraced house featured the standard levitating table, together with the more unusual manifestation of a luminous tambourine zooming round the darkened room, supported by sporadic appearances from a disembodied pair of spirit hands. The tambourine was real, and the ghostly hands might have belonged to one of the sitters round the table. To eliminate fraud, Cohen resolved to check the tambourine for fingerprints, and called in Sergeant Rowland Mason of the Manchester Fingerprint Bureau.

Mason was said by colleagues to possess second sight, and on his second visit he touched the spirit's hands. They felt real, if dry and scaly, but subsequent examination revealed no fingerprints on the tambourine, and findings were similarly negative when he prepared it with mercury dust.

Mason recognised that subterfuge had failed, so he asked the spirit's permission to take its fingerprints on a chemically sensitised pad. The ghost agreed, giving Mason a firm impression at the next session. By now the local police were in a frenzy of excitement, and Mason's ghostly imprints were developed amid intense anticipation. But they amounted to no more than three parallel scratch marks suggestive of fingernails or perhaps a bird's claw.

Forsaking fingerprinting, Mason brought in a Constable John Cheetham to try infra-red photography. The spirit posed for a snap, producing an excellent likeness of an empty armchair with an indentation in its back cushion made by the otherwise invisible head, a photograph revered by the Manchester police for its strange, suggestive powers. Sadly the investigation went no further. The *Daily Mail* got wind of the story, and the Chief Superintendent called a halt to avoid public ridicule.

This odd tale is told by Detective Chief Inspector Tony Fletcher of the Manchester Fingerprint Bureau in his *Memories of Murder* (Weidenfeld, 1986).

Bones, ground

Dr Joseph Mengele, Auschwitz's 'Angel of Death', is definitely dead. He drowned in a Brazilian swimming accident on 7 February 1979.

In February 1992, a master sample of genetic material derived from his son, Rolf Mengele, a German lawyer, was matched with the graveyard skeleton of his supposed father. A new technique enabled the extraction of the tiny amounts of DNA left in Mengele's bones after years of decomposition and provided a positive match with a probability in excess of 1:500. Similar investigations were recently conducted on the supposed bones of Tsar Nicholas and his family found in a pit at Ekaterinburg; the master blood sample came from a distant relative, the Duke of Edinburgh.

The pioneering work for this type of case identified the remains of Karen Price, a Welsh schoolgirl whose murderers were convicted ten years after the killing. Her body lay buried in the rear garden of Cardiff's 29 Fitzhamon Embankment for eight years before building workers deepening a trench sliced into a roll of carpet in 1989. Inside was a skeleton dressed in socks, bra and panties.

Traditional forensic techniques led to identification of the body and thus to the arrest of the killer. But to prove the case in court required firmer evidence.

Analysis of the corpse's rotting clothing showed that the victim wore a Levi-Strauss sweatshirt first marketed in December 1980. Other garments, like her 'Karman Ghia' slacks, were on sale in the Cardiff area during the early 1980s. The fact that her teeth were still developing put her age at about 15, and 'Dr Zak' (Zakaria Erzinclioglu) of Cambridge University pronounced that the presence of a well-established colony of woodlice to eat the fungus gathering round the skeleton's exposed bones indicated that its soft tissues had first been consumed by Phorid flies (the so-called 'coffin flies'), and that the combined processes must have taken a good five years. This placed the murder between early 1981 (the sweatshirt) and 1984 (the Phorid flies), enabling the police to question the inhabitants of 29 Fitzhamon Embankment.

No. 29 had been knocked together with No. 27, and the two houses partitioned into bedsits and small flats for a floating population of lodgers. Some 700 people lived there during the 1980s. But one of the sergeants assigned to the case had seen a television programme about an archaeological technique, **facial reconstruction**, and in December 1989 a sculptured head of 'Little Miss Nobody' was commissioned from Richard Neave of Manchester University. Photographs of her clay bust were distributed to the press and television, and within two days a social worker put a name to the face: 15-year old Karen Price, who absconded from a children's home some eight years previously.

The BBC's *Crimewatch UK* broadcast an appeal for help. Among the viewers was one of Karen's murderers, Idris Ali. In the company of friends, Ali rashly exclaimed, 'I knew her … I used to go around with her', and was persuaded to go to the police.

The sorry tale soon unravelled. Karen Price, the disturbed child of a broken marriage, had been in care since the age of ten. During 1981, aged 15, she repeatedly absconded from her Pontypridd assessment centre and drifted into a life of prostitution in a run-down area of Cardiff. Sixteen-year-old Idris Ali acted as her pimp, and one client was doorman Alan Charlton. Sometime in July 1981 the two men took Karen back to Charlton's basement flat in Fitzhamon Gardens and ordered her to pose for pornographic photographs. When she refused, Charlton went berserk and strangled her. Idris Ali helped him dig the garden grave.

This was fine for the police, but insufficient for the courts. The first forensic hurdle involved extracting the DNA from the skeleton. Erika Hagelberg, an Oxford

biochemist, began with a clean-up, sandblasting Karen's bones. Then she ground the residue into a fine powder at low temperatures. This revealed plenty of DNA, 99 per cent from contaminating fungus and bacteria. So the human component was amplified by the polymerase chain-reaction test.

But standard genetic identification is based on DNA sections between 1,000 and 10,000 units long, and nothing this large had survived intact. So in concert with Professor Alec Jeffreys, Hagelberg devised a miniaturised process that read sections of a mere 100 units

In addition to the novelty of the minute samples and the polymerase chain-reaction test, the trial was the first to present an analysis from decayed bone as court evidence. On 26 February 1991 Alan Charlton (who played 'the greater part' in the killing) was sentenced to life imprisonment, and Idris Ali detained 'during Her Majesty's pleasure'.

Bonnie and Clyde (1910–34; 1909–34)

A couple of small-time hoods (then known as Clyde and Bonnie). Their largest haul came to no more than $2,500, and one month their takings totalled $76. Clyde was driving shoeless on 23 May 1934 when the 187 bullets smacked into their old jalopy; Bonnie, clutching a half-eaten sandwich, wore no pants under her dress. But as word of their death spread, the roads for miles around were jammed with cars. An estimated 9,000 sightseers flooded into Arcadia, Louisiana, and when the truck towing their car broke down, schoolchildren thrust their hands into the vehicle to smear their fingers in blood, pulled tufts from Bonnie's hair and tore shreds from her dress. Thousands shuffled past their bullet-torn corpses displayed in a local furniture store. Their car was still being exhibited forty years later at $2.50 a time. It was sold in 1973 for $175,000, and is said to be at the Hacienda Nàpoles in the possession of Pablo **Escobar**, Colombia's cocaine billionaire.

Bonnie was tiny, no more than four feet ten. She came from a background of narrow respectability in the small Texas town of Rowena. Although no particular rebel, she threatened to razor her best friend when aged ten, tattooed her boyfriend's name, Roy Thornton, on her thigh at 15 and married him a year later. But she never achieved independence from her mother, and Thornton made himself scarce. In 1929 he was sentenced to five years for robbery, and in January

1930, bored and lonely, Bonnie met young Clyde Barrow in West Dallas.

Clyde, the sixth of eight children, grew up in wretched poverty on a Telico farmstead. As a child he was unsupervised, unpunished and neglected, nearly suffocating once and nearly drowning on another occasion. His family scraped and saved even to buy a ukulele costing $1.98, and his parents frequently billeted him with relatives to save money. He landed in trouble several times for torturing animals, and by 1926 was a member of the juvenile Root Square Gang, who cut their teeth on stealing tyres and matured to robberies in Waco and Sherman.

Clyde had already escaped three times from police gunfire and that, to a romantic young girl, meant glamour. So she took him home to meet her mother, and there, next morning, he was arrested. But Bonnie had hopes for the future, writing as he awaited trial, 'I want you to be a man, honey, and not a **thug**. I know you are good and I know you can make good ... We are young and should be happy like other boys and girls.'

Her love for Clyde dragged her down. On 11 March

1930, at his request, she broke into a fellow-prisoner's house, searching for a hidden Colt .32, and smuggled it into his Waco jail. Clyde escaped, but was recaptured and sentenced to fourteen years. He was unexpectedly paroled on 2 February 1932, and within a month Bonnie languished in jail in Kaufman after a joint attempt at robbery misfired. They were caught in the act, fled by car down small dirt roads and got stuck in the mud. So they ran over the fields and, spotting some mules, leapt on to their backs. But the animals refused to budge. So Bonnie and Clyde crawled away down a ditch while bullets flew overhead. Clyde made off looking for a car to steal and, that evening, Bonnie was picked up trudging alone down a country road.

While she was awaiting trial, Clyde killed for the first time, on 27 April shooting 61-year-old John Bucher for no good reason; he had already opened the **safe** to his general store. On 17 June Bonnie was released by a grand jury. Clyde's next killing came on 5 August, during a pointless gun battle after he attracted a sheriff's attention at a Stringtown country dance. Instead of telling the lawman to drop his weapon, Clyde shot him, and continued to blaze away in the dark, killing a deputy and wounding a dancer before driving off in such disarray that he crashed the first car and wrote off its hijacked replacement. The next morning he had Bonnie collected and driven to his hideout, an abandoned farmhouse near Grand Prairie. That night he described their future with the words, 'Driving, just driving from now till they get us. Kansas, Missouri, Oklahoma, Mexico – Texas, always Texas, where we were born.' Scarcely out of their teens, Bonnie and Clyde spent the rest of their days in stolen cars, on the run, robbing grocery stores and making furtive visits to Bonnie's mother.

It is no easy thing to be an armed robber if your first and invariable reaction is panic. Nor is it an enviable life. The only place Bonnie and Clyde felt safe was in a car. They lived in them, sometimes sleeping inside, sometimes camping rough, robbing gas stations for pocket money. On 11 October 1932 they killed a man, Howard Hall, during a $28 raid which also netted a few vegetables. On 25 December 1932, after Christmas dinner, they shot salesman Doyle Johnson while stealing his car, abandoning it a few minutes later. From then on, at constant risk of ambush and betrayal, they took care to shoot first. In all, the 'Barrow Gang' claimed a dozen lives. Of a killing of 6 January 1933, Clyde said he felt 'like I always felt, sick inside, sick and

Cartoon from the Dallas Journal *of 9 April 1934*

Clyde Barrow and Bonnie Parker

cold and weak – and a sort of dull wishing I had never been born'. A year later, on 31 March 1934, just outside Grapevine, Texas, an elderly farmer, William Schieffer, watched as two lawmen dismounted from their motorcycles, casually approached a couple sitting by the roadside, and were blasted by shotguns. Schieffer saw Bonnie walk over to a wounded man, fire twice into his face, and reportedly heard her say, 'Look-a-there, his head bounced just like a rubber ball.'

Bonnie and Clyde drove endlessly, leading a nomadic life as motorised versions of their direct predecessors, the Western outlaws. Driving was almost the only thing for which Clyde showed aptitude. He knew the back roads, and they were immune from pursuit if they could cross a state boundary. The police, hampered by low morale and low pay, often had to buy their own weapons and transportation. Their cars were no match for Clyde's stolen Ford V-8s. **Hoover**'s Department of Investigation, with fewer than 300 G-**men**, had still to make its mark.

There was the ambush at the Wharton bridge, the stakeout at West Dallas, the attack on their apartment in Joplin; the capture of a motorcycle policeman who tried to book them for speeding; the drive with their partner W. D. Jones wounded in the head; the kidnapping of a young undertaker and his fiancée during a car theft; the Red Crown Tavern ambush spearheaded by an armoured car, at which Buck was shot in the temple, and Clyde alone unwounded of the four in their car; the crash at Salt Fork River when Bonnie was horribly burned and they dared not contact a doctor – she hovered, in agony, between life and death for a week; the Dexfield Park ambush, where Buck was killed; the abortive Dallas Highway ambush; the Eastham Farm breakout, when Clyde 'sprang' five convicts from Huntsville penitentiary; the bickerings between the gang members; the fast-and-loose Mary O'Dare who advised Bonnie to dope her lover and then, 'While he's out, take his roll and beat it'; Sheriff Smoot Schmid's plan to trap and perhaps squash the gang with a large four-wheel-drive gravel mover; the gunfight outside Commerce, when a 63-year-old constable perished; and the final ambush, led by Ted Hinton, half a mile outside Irvin Methvin's farm in Louisiana.

Bonnie penned the 'Story of Bonnie and Clyde', possibly the best literary composition by a major criminal, and Clyde sent a famous 'since then I have used no other' letter to Henry Ford. 'While I have still got breath in my lungs,' Clyde wrote, 'I will tell you what a dandy car you make. I have drove Fords exclusively when I could get away with one. For sustained speed and freedom from trouble the Ford has got every other car skinned.' Otherwise, the pair were hardly more attractive than **Brady** and **Hindley**, the Moors murderers, and many of John **Dillinger**'s exploits were appropriated by the 1967 film to make Bonnie and Clyde more palatable.

'Johnny and Clyde' was Truman Capote's working title for a proposed exposé of Hoover and his aide, Clyde Tolson.

Bonny, Anne (b. 1700)

Female pirate captain who disappeared from history at the age of 20 after a spectacular early career.

Born in Ireland in 1700 from the illegitimate union of a lawyer and a serving girl, Anne was raised by her father, who emigrated to South Carolina. As a tomboy,

Anne was trained in the rapier; and her father's tracker, an Indian named Charlie Fourfeathers, taught her to handle guns, knives and hatchets. At 13, Anne stabbed her mother's maid. At 15, her breasts assumed 'the size and strength of melons'. At 16, she married a destitute wretch, James Bonny.

Distraught at this dreadful news, Anne's mother died of shock; her father barred her from the house. Anne laid siege to, and then stormed, the parental home, breaking every window; Pa called out the militia. In high dudgeon, the new Mrs Bonny sailed away to New Providence in the Bahamas, on arrival shooting off the **ear** of a huge desperado blocking her way on the pier.

She dispensed with her husband in favour of the local receiver, Chidley Baynard, temporarily single after killing his mistress. By now a friend of Teach and Blackbeard, Anne put to sea as a pirate in a special outfit of velvet trousers and a scarlet silk blouse. A lawful privateering voyage turned to piracy when the drunken Jack 'Calico' Rackham mutinied and took over the ship. Anne became his lover and, after landing to raze her former husband's house and shipyard to the ground, she cruised for two years in *The Queen Royal*, falling for a handsome young sailor to whom, by way of preliminaries, she disclosed that she was a woman, only to learn that he was no man but the disguised pirate Mary Read.

Anne was captured in October 1720 off the Jamaican coast near Negril Point; she was carousing with a crew of turtle fishermen when her ship surrendered to Captain Jack Barnet's sloop. Legend has it that Anne and Mary were the last to lay down their arms and, along with their shipmates, the two women went on trial at St Jago de la Vega, where they were sentenced to death.

Asked as a formality if there was any reason why they should not be executed, the women responded, 'My Lord, we plead our bellies', and were reprieved on account of their pregnancies. Rackham was hanged at Gallows Point. As Anne remarked, 'I am sorry to see you there, Jack, but if you had fought like a man you need not have been hanged like a dog.' Freed within the year, she married a man called Michael Radcliffe, forsook piracy and left for America. She was last heard of moving west with a train of settlers.

Academics at the cutting edge of piratical scholarship are increasingly dubious about accounts of female buccaneers. It seems that these women, in their gorgeous attire, were often men, and that the Caribbean provided an early refuge for the gay community.

Borden, Lizzie (1860–1927)

To murder enthusiasts, 'Lizzie' will always mean Lizzie Borden, the middle-aged spinster absolved of one of history's great 'locked house' murders. On 4 August 1892 Lizzie's elderly father and stepmother were viciously axed to death at their home, 92 Second Street, in prosperous Falls River. The front door was locked, the house surrounded by a high barbed-wire-topped fence, and the only serious suspects were the four people staying in the house. Of these, two were out, one of them fifteen miles away, so only Bridget Sullivan, the maid, and Lizzie Borden, the disaffected 32-year-old daughter of the house, remained as possible killers.

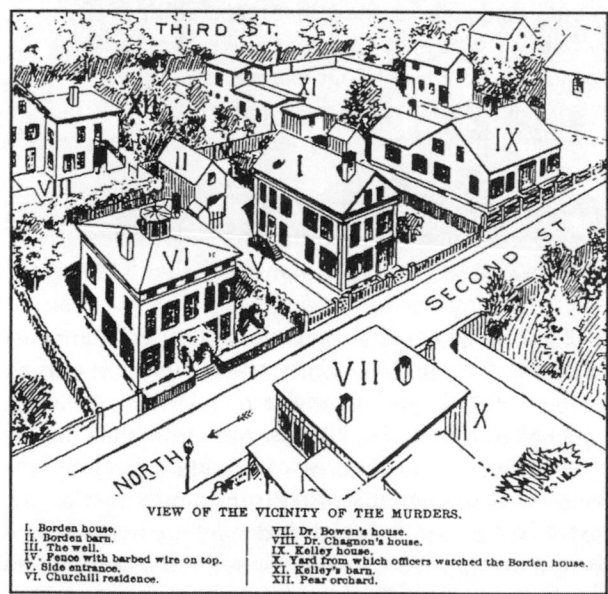

VIEW OF THE VICINITY OF THE MURDERS.

I. Borden house.
II. Borden barn.
III. The well.
IV. Fence with barbed wire on top.
V. Side entrance.
VI. Churchill residence.
VII. Dr. Bowen's house.
VIII. Dr. Chagnon's house.
IX. Kelley house.
X. Yard from which officers watched the Borden house.
XI. Kelley's barn.
XII. Pear orchard.

92 Second Street

The double murder caused an immediate sensation in the highly stratified town; Falls River was one of those prosperous Massachusetts communities where the Durfees and the Braytons spoke only to the Bordens, and the Bordens spoke only to God. By the next day, business had ground to a virtual standstill; jostling crowds gathered on the sidewalk.

On 11 August Lizzie was arrested; it was she who had discovered her father's body, his skull crushed by eleven blows from an axe while he slept on the ground-floor couch, one eye cut in half and his nose severed.

At the time, Lizzie had summoned the maid Bridget with the famous words: 'Come down quick! Father is dead! Somebody came in and killed him!' Checking upstairs, they found Abby Borden – Lizzie's dull, overweight stepmother – killed by twenty-one axe blows to the head. Unlike her husband, who was still dripping gore, Abby's blood had congealed. So she had already been dead for a good hour.

'It must have been done while I was outside in the barn,' said Lizzie. After her arrest she was portrayed in the press as a heroine and martyr, a frail woman hounded by police and prosecutors, and, at her trial in June 1893, the verdict of 'innocent' was greeted with acclaim. Overnight, Lizzie became an idol, inundated with congratulatory messages, courted by clergymen, and headlined in the papers: 'Church and Charity Will Claim Lizzie'.

But two days later, the public mood abruptly changed. With Lizzie off the hook, the conundrum remained. Who had killed her parents? On all the evidence, Lizzie was the only person with the opportunity. Barring an intruder committing a very leisurely double murder, it must have been her.

Amid snide comments about 'self-made heiresses', Lizzie moved upmarket on the proceeds of her father's $250,000 estate, buying a mansion called 'Maplecroft' where she lingered on for another thirty-four years, at first ostracised and then a curiosity, in her later years motoring through the streets in a gleaming limousine with a liveried chauffeur at the wheel.

A century after the killings, the corpses of Lizzie's parents are on the shortlist of proposed exhumations by America's amateur sleuth Professor Starrs. It is now appreciated that a head blow here may produce damage there, so the true number of axe blows may be elucidated. The blade of the fatal axe, on display in the Falls River Museum, is to be microscopically matched against the broken skulls.

The real mystery is how Lizzie escaped the murder charge. She had the motive – money, and an intense dislike of her stepmother, conventionally depicted as a grasping hypochondriac. Before the killings, the atmosphere in the house was terrible. Inner doors were blocked off, and the family ate separately, forcing Bridget to serve each meal twice. Nor was her father a lovable man. A miser and a strict patriarch, he regarded Lizzie as his 'special girl', barring her from contact with outsiders, and commentators have surmised a background of incest. Evidence barred from the trial included two attempts by Lizzie to buy prussic acid to 'mothproof a fur cape' only hours before the murders, and she evidenced her guilt by making inconsistent statements about her whereabouts during the killings.

In court, Lizzie did not testify; her defence hinged on the absence of blood on her clothing. But stepmother Abby died at least an hour before Lizzie's father – ample time to change and freshen up. And the head of her sleeping father lay flush by the door leading from the dining room. Lizzie could have killed Father in one room while standing in another, above and behind.

In any case, Father's blood would not have squirted anywhere in the absence of the *double* circumstance of his heart continuing to beat after an artery had been severed. Even then, Lizzie still had fifteen minutes to make herself presentable before 'finding' the body, and the Sunday after the murders she burned a soiled dress only ten weeks old 'to tidy up her wardrobe'.

Lizzie was not – as she claimed – rummaging in the barn for fishing tackle at the time of the murders. It was suffocatingly hot up in the roof of the outbuilding, almost unendurable after only a few seconds, and the dusty floorboards showed no footprints from her alleged half-hour visit.

Why was Lizzie discharged? The local prejudice ran against executing women. The last one to hang in Massachusetts, Bathsheba Spooner, claimed to be with child, despite expert evidence to the contrary. But on autopsy she was found five months pregnant. Further, on 1 June 1893, a few days before Lizzie's trial, the papers reported another axe murder in Falls River. The *Boston Globe ran* the headline: 'Many Points of Resemblance'.

With Lizzie already locked up, her attorney took full advantage: 'Are they going to claim Lizzie did this too?' In fact, an arrest was made on 4 June, but this was not published until the following day. The news came too late for the jury; the trial had already started.

Brady, Ian (1938–)

The dominant half of the Brady–**Hindley** team, perpetrators of Britain's Moors Murders. Brady swamped Hindley with his personality, and his personality was, in turn, a product of his upbringing. Today's psychological profilers would recognise many constituents of an **'organised'** serial killer's background.

Brady came from the tough Gorbals slums of Glasgow, the illegitimate son of a waitress. His real name was Ian Duncan Stewart. Raised by foster parents, he won a scholarship to an expensive school for children from more prosperous backgrounds. Resentment led to a spate of housebreaking and a disturbing reputation for bullying his juniors; at 13 he was sentenced to two years' probation in the course of which he reoffended ten times, earning a further two years. A teenage drunk, he landed a job in a brewery which culminated in his dismissal for stealing. A spell in a tougher borstal in Hull followed.

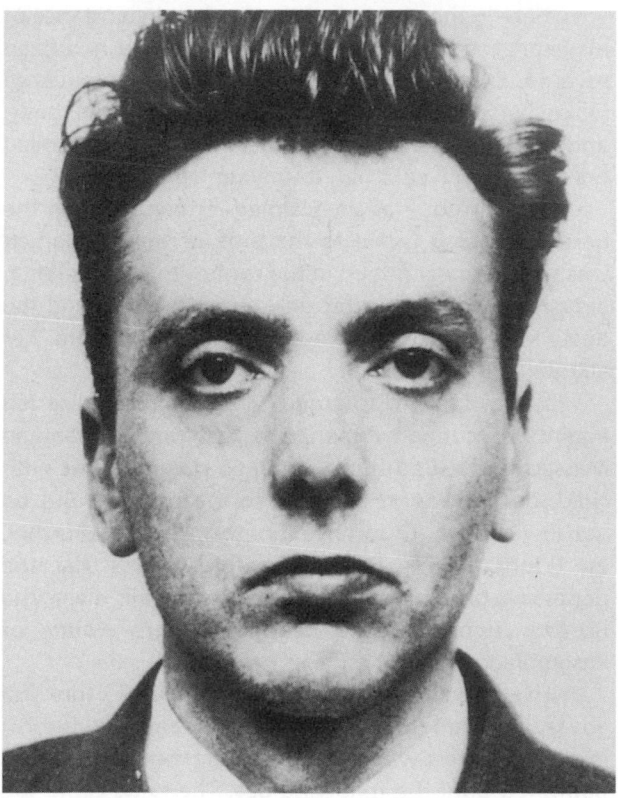

Ian Brady

At 21 Brady found work as a clerk in a Midlands chemical firm. In his youth, he had amused himself with cruelty to animals, lobbing cats out of the tenement windows. Now he devoted himself to a study of the Nazis, True Crime (particularly *Compulsion*, the story of the Leopold and Loeb murder) and the Marquis **de Sade**. He could quote from *Mein Kampf* at length, and amassed a collection of books on leather fetishism, sexual sadism and bondage in an era when these things were hard to come by.

In early 1961 this hardened, vengeful individual dictated a letter at work to an innocent young typist from Gorton: Myra Hindley. The events which followed are described elsewhere, and in 1966 Brady was sentenced to three life terms for murder. Nineteen years later he confessed to two more killings on Saddleworth Moor and, in 1987, provided vague stories about five other murders from his youth, including a woman thrown to her death from a Manchester canal bridge, a man stabbed in Glasgow, and a hitch-hiker shot near Loch Lomond. By then Brady had wasted to eight stone, just skin and bone with shrunken cheeks and his hands devoid of flesh, suffering from delusions, hallucinations and paranoia. Transferred to a mental hospital as a shambling wreck, in a lucid interval he drew parallels with Dostoevsky's *Crime and Punishment*: 'I led the life that other people only think about ... In other words, Raskolnikov's situation was a synopsis of precisely how I was. That's what I believed at the time.'

See also **Fantasising**, **Pets**, **Privilege**, **Tapes**

Brank, brake or scold's head

These days, we hear little of the brank. It was a relatively modern English device, not mentioned until 1623 in Macclesfield.

It consisted of a skeletal metal helmet with a protrusion, sometimes spiked, inserted into the wearer's mouth to immobilise the tongue. The Walton-on-Thames brank bears the inscription 'Chester presents Walton with a bridle/To curb women's tongues that talk too idle.'

An excellent contemporary account survives in Dr Brushfield's recollections from an 1856 lecture. In the village of Congleton, 'There was generally fixed on one side of the large open fireplaces a hook so that when a man's wife indulged her scolding propensities, the husband sent for the town jailor to bring the bridle and had her chained to the hook ... I have often heard husbands say to their wives "If you don't rest up with your tongue I'll send for the bridle and hook you up."' The last record of the Congleton brake's use is in 1824, and for the Shrewsbury brake, 1846.

There is no record of a brank for men, but the

punishment seems mild compared with the fate of disorderly American women who, in the 1860s and '70s, were routinely handed over to gynaecologists for ovariotomy (female castration).

See also **Hopkins, Sexism, Witchcraze**

Brink's

The FBI called it the 'crime of the century'. The *Boston Globe* billed the heist as 'the biggest all-**cash** stick-up in the US'. But the only person to make usable money out of the 1950 robbery at the North Terminal Garage was Joseph F. Dineen, a journalist with the *Boston Globe*. He wrote the book of the crime, filmed as *Six Bridges to Cross*, earning a fee of $150,000.

Brink's was the security firm handling $10 million a day in local payrolls. On 17 January 1950 the thieves made off with $2,775,395, $1,218,211.29 of it in cash. The seven-man team were in and out in seventeen minutes, carting their 1,200 pounds deadweight of loot back home to Adolph 'Jazz' Maffey's. Next morning they went to work as normal, only collecting their share a month later. Then they frittered it away, leaving the police without a lead.

But one of the gang, 'Specs' O'Keefe, entrusted some $90,000 to another member of the team, who later declined to give it back. 'Specs' threatened to blow the gaffe; the gang put out a contract on him with Elmer 'Trigger' Burke, who failed; and Specs did blow the gaffe, on 12 January 1956, only five days before the expiration of the six-year Statute of Limitations. All ten

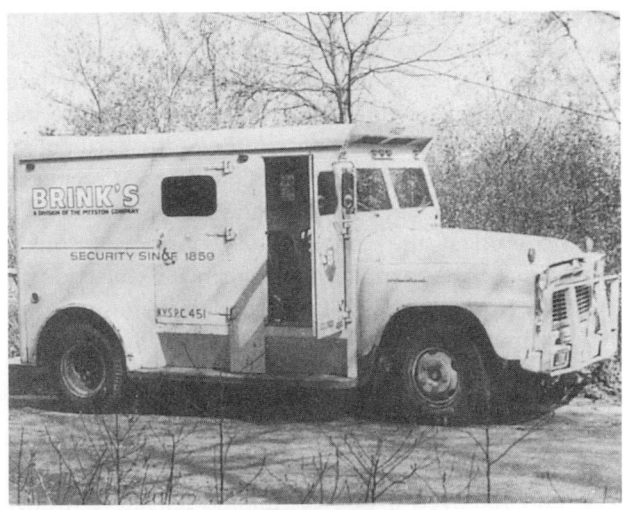

A Brink's van, taken over by bandits with sub-machine guns, yielded $700,000 in Brockton, Massachusetts on 23 May 1967

raiders went to jail. The aftermath of Britain's **Great Train Robbery** is depressingly similar: an unprecedented criminal venture followed by years of filching and misery.

The Brink's break-in was well rehearsed over eighteen months while the gang made a total of twenty-seven night-time sorties, wandering round the premises more or less at will. Five locked doors barred their way to the main counting room; over the months, their locksmith Henry J. Baker removed each lock, cast a duplicate key overnight and then replaced the cylinder. So on the day the raiders walked through to the final wire-mesh grille, donned their rubber masks and chauffeurs' caps, showed their guns and said: 'This is a stick-up.' The FBI investigation into the robbery cost an estimated $29 million.

The co-planner of the robbery was smiling Anthony 'Fats' Pino, an inspirational crook and monumental liar born in 1907. As a child Pino showed unusual promise at pilfering coal for his parents' stove. He sold off the surplus at three cents a pound, earning his first arrest for stealing a street-car ride. When shot in the buttock by the police at the age of 15 after purloining some cake and milk, he already had eight arrests under his belt, as well as three spells on probation and seven months in a reformatory for filching $20. While sitting out World War II in Charlestown prison, he was beaten up by other inmates for stealing the buttons from their uniforms. Released on parole in September 1944, he faced deportation and, to raise the $5,000 bribe to reverse the decision, worked nights as a cart pusher at a Stop and Shop warehouse. In the eight weeks before being sacked, Pino stole $6,000. One morning after his shift, inspired by the sight of the Brink's trucks rumbling up Congress Street towards the Chamber of Commerce building, he thought of doing something worthwhile.

Pino studied the comings and goings at Brink's, wearing a variety of disguises from his collection of stolen costumes, dressing up as a milkman, busboy, chef or doorman. His favourite outfit, stolen from a circus, was the lion tamer's, which he wore only in private. In January 1946 he tailed Truck 48 to a garage and stole a set of keys from the office hook. That February he opened the van door, while the guards were on delivery, and removed a bag containing $3,500; ten days later, he helped himself to $5,000, and thereafter, together with the gang, he embarked on a regular schedule of robberies of the premises to which Brink's made deliveries. In February 1946 the first safe yielded $7,300, and the gang did the rounds of Brink's customers twice, some even three times, netting $600,000 in addition to the $400,000 from the trucks.

In June 1948 Pino married, and while honeymooning in Baltimore he devoted himself to stealing hideous rubber masks from an arcade. Later that year he earned a twelve-month term for stealing a dozen golf balls. Meanwhile the gang agreed to terminate their professional relationship with Brink's by robbing Truck 48 as it loaded on the premises. The raid was set for 7 January 1949, but Brink's moved offices to the North Terminal Garage Building in Prince Street, and a new plan evolved to divest the entire building of cash, dressed as chauffeurs, wearing Pino's masks.

Pino was released from prison in July 1971 and died two years later, still vowing to kill Specs O'Keefe. Brink's remains a favourite target. On 30 March 1976 one of their delivery trucks was stopped on a Montreal street. The gang, who threatened the van with an anti-aircraft gun, made off with $2.8 million.

Budgerigar *et al.*

A long-term prisoner may get permission to keep a budgerigar in his cell. Paid for out of his own pocket, this expensive acquisition indicates a prisoner's acceptance of his sentence. Thereafter he is regarded as quietly settled, *doing his bird*.

A budgerigar may represent the prisoner's most significant relationship and, in the vindictive atmosphere of prison, this constitutes an Achilles heel. Budgies can be assassinated to satisfy a grudge or even be kidnapped: an ounce of tobacco or your bird comes back – dead. In a December 1992 modification, a convict's pet rabbit, 'Lucky', was abducted in a Scottish maximum-security jail and ransomed for two cans of ginger beer.

Rabbits are rarities in mainstream crime. Colleeen Stan, the sex-**slave**, was confined to a hutch-like box, and the eighteenth-century British conwoman Mary Toft conjured rabbits up, but not by pulling them out of a hat.

Delivery was effected with the aid of an accomplice who helped Toft load the struggling creatures into her womb, where they caused such discomfort that their miraculous ejaculation was provoked by painful spasms simulating labour. She hoped for a royal pension, and succeeded in convincing Mr Howard, the local doctor; he confirmed that in one month he had assisted at the birth of twenty live rabbits, provoking widespread awe.

Toft's credibility was much enhanced by her poor education. It was supposed that she lacked the intelligence to mislead sophisticated medical opinion, and rumours of her proclivity reached the household of her sovereign, King George I. He had Toft appraised by no less a luminary than the Royal Surgeon, St Andre, who dissected one of Toft's offspring in the royal presence to prove that they were real rabbits.

Confidence in Toft became a political issue at court, where a cynical Queen's faction took issue with the King and his supporters, and when the Queen despatched her physician, Sir Richard Mannington, to examine the girl, his misgivings were aroused by the pig's bladder she secreted vaginally in error. Toft confessed, and was consigned to Bridewell in 1726; she had briefly made a good living from her exploits.

The murder of Eddie Evans by Ian **Brady** on 6 October 1965 is the only killing known to the author observed by a budgerigar. It was called Joey, and it played no part in the proceedings. Indeed, birds are seldom called in evidence (but see **Carrier pigeons**), except perhaps in Argentina where the eye-witness testimony of a parrot can be decisive. In 1990 Rosella DeGambo brought an action against her husband Carlos, whom she suspected of two-timing, her apprehensions inflamed when the family cockatoo, Bozo, started giggling in an unfamiliar, high-pitched, female voice.

Summoned to the stand, Bozo reacted strongly to photographs of a young beautician who allegedly visited Carlos on the sly. 'Honeybun, I love you!' exclaimed Bozo in apparent recognition of the woman's picture. Bozo added: 'Ruby loves Carlos. Ruby loves her baby.' The husband's secretary was called Ruby.

Despite the protests of Carlos's lawyer, Bozo's evidence was adjudged admissible. But this is a third-hand report of a civil case from another country, noted in the Canadian journal *The Lawyers' Weekly*, summarised in the *Toronto Sun* on 9 March 1990, and digested in the *Fortean Times*.

In America, a 1942 murder case was solved by an eponymous parrot. On 12 July the proprietor of the East Harlem Green Parrot Bar was gunned down in front of twenty customers, none of whom had the good fortune to witness the incident. But the police soon knew the motive. 'Robber, robber,' chanted the parrot. With no further leads, the investigation foundered, but an intrigued detective John J. Morrisey persisted in a study of the bird's linguistic abilities, finding its elocution flawed by a tendency to drop the final consonant, and, further, that its vocabulary was confined to the names of the bar's regular clientele. Checking his files for a likely-sounding Robert, Morrisey came upon a Robert Butler, by then living in Maryland, and on 10 February 1944 Butler was sentenced to seven years after making a full confession.

In Brazil, a 'parrot's perch' denotes a form of **torture** where the victim is suspended in mid-air with his knees bent double over a metal rod and his ankles bound to his wrists.

Bundy, Theodore Robert (1946–89)

This pernicious American serial killer not only depersonalised his victims, he depersonalised himself, preferring to speak of his encounters in the third person. Asked if there was much conversation with his victims, Bundy told the police: 'There'd be some. Since this girl in front of him represented not a person, but again the image, or something desirable, the last thing we would expect him to want to do would be to personalise this person.' So he called them things like 'cargo' or '**throwaways**'. Bundy could not acknowledge his crimes directly, but only 'speculated' about what had happened, hiding behind a fiction of inno-

cence while helping investigators build up a 'picture' of what the killer was like.

It took Bundy years to work up from his first faltering steps as a voyeur, via stalking his quarry home, to overt sexual assaults and thence to rape and finally murder. His first homicide was Lynda Ann Healey on 31 January 1974; his youngest, 12-year-old Kimberley Leach. In July 1974, Bundy killed two in one day, abducting his victims from the crowded beach at Lake Sammamish Park, bringing back the second girl to the house where he had already raped the first, and then raping the second in front of the first before killing both. Returning to his fiancée Cas Richter that evening, Bundy said he felt 'real bad', but later recovered sufficiently to go out to dinner.

Bundy escaped from prison twice, the second time by dieting and then, on New Year's Eve 1977, squeezing through a loose ceiling panel around a light socket and crawling through the overhead space to the jailers' lounge. He might have remained at large indefinitely,

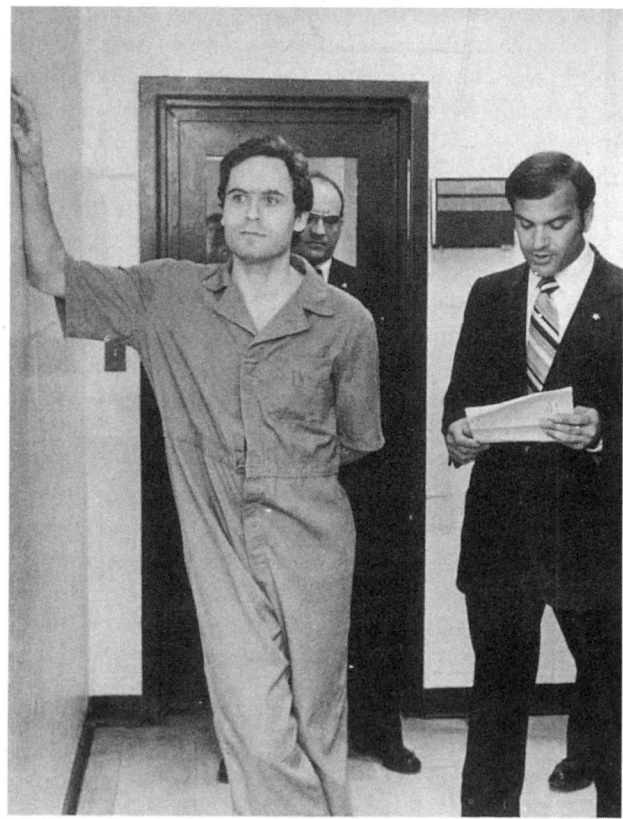

Ted Bundy in a disassociative stance as the County Sheriff indicts him for the Chi Omega slayings

but under his alias Chris Hagen he continued killing. On the night of 15 January 1978 he ravaged four women in a Florida Chi Omega student residential block, moving from room to room in some thirty minutes. Two lived to tell the tale, two were clubbed to death and strangled during vicious sexual assaults. A few minutes later, Bundy broke into a student house a few blocks away. There he attacked ballet student Cheryl Thomas. Her flatmates heard the struggle, and she survived despite massive head injuries.

Next month, during a failed abduction in Jacksonville, the registration number of his stolen white Dodge van was noted. The following day, on 9 February, he kidnapped and murdered schoolgirl Kimberley Leach. The van was found abandoned on 13 February, replete with forensic evidence, and two days later Bundy himself was approached by Patrolman David Lee, his attention caught by an awkwardly parked VW Beetle in a Pensacola side-street at 1.30 a.m. Bundy drove off, was overtaken and arrested at gunpoint. He was sentenced to death the following year and executed nearly ten years later.

Bundy, a good-looking charmer with an easy manner, found work with the Seattle Crime Prevention Advisory Commission before (and while) plunging off the rails. In the words of Barbara Grossman, a TV reporter: 'The first time I saw him I said to myself, "Wow, all he had to do is ask me to go with him and I'd go"' – exactly what many of his victims did, falling for his pick-up **lines**. Grossman was not alone in her assessment; Cathy Swindler, who met Bundy when he was 21, depicted him as 'a figure that people met and loved'. His contemporaries believed him destined for high office, 'a man who might well have been Governor of Washington'.

Too much has been made of Bundy's brilliant future and social talents. His killings formed the counterpoint to his emotional life. The illegitimate son of a respectable secretary, he was left almost alone for the first weeks of life, when the ability to give and receive affection is imprinted. His father's identity remained a secret; his maternal grandfather (with whom he lived until the age of four) was a violent despot. Bundy grew into a keen **masturbator**, formidable liar, a fantasist and a compulsive thief, as an adult once stealing an eight-foot tree from a greenhouse and driving away with his booty sticking out through the car roof. When his lost love, the beautiful, sophisticated and wealthy Stephanie

Brooks, dropped him in 1966, the distress caused a surge in his thieving.

Bundy wanted to impress her by studying Chinese at Stanford University, but his grades were poor and he could not compete with his own standards of success. Reduced to working as a salesman in a department store, he stole for kicks, nurturing an interest in violent pornography. An accidental glimpse of a woman undressing in a lighted room led to a career as a campus Peeping Tom, and by degrees, in between interludes of self-disgust, he sought 'more active kinds of gratification', first following the girls, then tinkering with their cars to disable them, then stalking, weapon in hand, then lying in wait, and finally making his first attack with a piece of wood as his victim fumbled with her keys by her front door. The next stage, in 1973, was forced entry, hiding inside a student's room against her return.

At this stage Bundy's star was temporarily in the ascendant. His acceptance as a law student, coupled with his job at the Crime Commission, imparted a spurious aura of self-confidence and maturity. He won Stephanie Brooks back with a high-power courtship. Dazzled by his new sophistication, she agreed to marry him during Christmas 1973, which they spent in a borrowed condominium at Alpental. But she flew back to California on 2 January, hurt and confused by a change in his manner. She later concluded he had made her fall in love with him for the pleasure of rejecting her.

Maybe this made Bundy feel good: three days later he committed his first rape. It was symbolic; he violated student Sharon Clarke with a metal bed-rod. She was found in a coma the following day, scarcely alive. Then he refused to take Stephanie's bewildered telephone calls. Maybe that made him feel better, and during this phase of satisfying demonstration of power he killed for the first time.

The victims were all attractive Stephanie-clones, sporting the same long hair parted in the middle and the same good, even features. Often penile dominance was not enough; Bundy stuffed his victims' vaginas with twigs and dirt and, on one occasion, sodomised a corpse with an aerosol can. Such activities cannot claim to be primarily sexual. His regular girlfriend during this period, Magan Roberts, reported that she and Bundy progressed through anal sex to bondage and thence to mock **strangulation** with distressing rapidity. Sex became an arena for anger, and Bundy was angry with everyone – his girlfriends, his family and his associates.

After his arrest, Bundy always kept at least one woman under his spell, living for her brief jail visits, running his errands and proclaiming his innocence. When one drifted away, another took her place. But his fragile self-image must have taken a knock after sentence as he walked down the prison corridor towards Death Row. Jeers, threats and howls of execration echoed from the other cells. 'He was scared to death,' said one of the guards. Prisoners regarded him as the lowest of the low, a child molester and sex killer.

Bundy confessed to twenty-three murders. Hours before his electrocution at 7.16 a.m. on 24 January 1989 he gave a radio interview, discoursing on the evils of pornography which, he claimed, caused his crimes – hence the nicknaming of the current Pornography Victims' Compensation Act as the 'Bundy Bill'. His was a popular execution. More than a thousand applicants wrote in asking to witness his death, and outside the Florida State Penitentiary a huge crowd wearing 'Burn, Bundy, Burn' T-shirts let off fireworks in celebration, while the local radio station enjoined listeners to switch off domestic appliances 'to give them more juice down there at the jail'.

See also **Preview**, **References**, **Throwaways**, **de Sade**, **Trolling**

Burke and Hare

A Scottish **bodysnatching** partnership who together despatched sixteen or perhaps seventeen victims, nearly all drunk old wives or drunk old men. The couple made their living by selling the victims' corpses, shocking the Edinburgh citizens so deeply that until the passage of Warburton's 1832 Anatomy Act children were kept off the streets; families huddled indoors long before dark and working men travelled home in groups for safety.

Burke (1792–1829) was of a tolerably amiable disposition, a flautist who never attracted the vilification heaped on his accomplice. Born in County Tyrone, Burke emigrated to Scotland where he worked as a navvy. He took up with Helen McDougal, and ran into Hare (1790–c.1860) at Log's Lodgings in Edinburgh's West Port, a doss-house where the latter was ensconced with the widowed owner, Margaret Laird.

Not long after Burke's arrival, one of the lodgers – a decrepit pensioner called Desmond – died of dropsy. He owed £4 in back rent, a loss the pair more than recouped by marketing his body. The eminent surgeon Robert Knox paid the going rate of £7 10s, representing about six months' wages for a labourer. 'We would be pleased to see you again,' Burke and Hare were told by the hospital.

Thereafter the pair obtained their corpses by murder. The first victim was Joseph the Miller, suffocated with a pillow after being rendered insensible during a companionable drinking session. Their method was for one to lie on top of their 'prospect', keeping him down while the other covered the mouth and nose. This left little trace of violent death, and Knox accepted the murdered bodies in good faith. Joseph the Miller netted a handsome £10. Next came a match-seller; then Abigail Simpson, the salt pedlar; then a young whore Mary Paterson; then more 'drunk auld wives': one-toothed Peggy Haldane and Effy the cinder gatherer. The victims – referred to as 'shots' – were picked up in the Edinburgh streets and, if it seemed their absence would not be missed, befriended and asked back for a drink.

After snapping the spine of a deaf-mute and packing him into a pickled herring barrel along with his grandmother, Burke suffered from sleeplessness, keeping a lighted candle and a bottle of whisky at his bedside. But his partnership with Hare continued, their tally soon including a misguided relative, Mary Haldane, who came to stay for a holiday.

Margaret Laird took a pound from every body-sale as 'rent' for the murder premises which, according to the contemporary Professor Wilson, looked pleasantly 'like a minister's manse'. Similarly, Burke's room 'was one of the neatest and snuggest little places' that Wilson ever saw.

To supplement his income, Burke took in paying lodgers, a tactical error compounded by disposing of popular 'Daft Jamie' Wilson, a mild-mannered but well-known local idiot whose unexplained disappearance had the neighbourhood seething with rumours of a new gang of cannibals like Sawney Beane (see **Cannibalism**).

Burke and Hare sealed their fate with their next murder of 'Madgy or Margaret Campbell or Duffy or M'Gonegal or Doherty'. Whatever her true name, this tiny woman in a conspicuous red gown was unambiguously seen at Burke's lodgings on the evening of her death. Next morning Burke concealed her body in straw under his bed and invited friends in for breakfast, spraying whisky around as a disinfectant. Eventually his guests went about their daily business, leaving Mrs

Burke (left) and Hare (right)

Gray the lodger to wash and sand the floor. There she came across an arm poking out from under the straw.

Her husband dragged out Madgy's body and the couple fled in terror, instantly running into Helen McDougal, who offered them the extravagant hush-money of £1 a week for life. But she could only manage six shillings down. The three discussed it over a drink and the Grays decided to inform the police, but by the time Constable Fisher arrived, the body had vanished. Burke had already flogged it to Knox, and very nearly succeeded in shrugging off Madgy's bloodstains on the straw as a visitor's menstrual bleeding.

A post-mortem on Madgy's recovered body furnished no proof of foul play and Burke realised he had to explain away a corpse, not a murder. After a couple of imaginative false starts (including a tale of a stranger 'in a greatcoat' who arrived with a tea chest out of which, like a conjurer, he produced a body before disappearing) Burke shrewdly admitted everything about Madgy except the manner of her death. He insisted that she had died peacefully overnight. True, he had sold his windfall to Knox, but why not? With no firm evidence of foul play, no fair jury could convict: there was a reasonable doubt.

So the police offered Hare exemption from prosecution if he turned King's evidence. He duly confessed, and the legal proceedings began on Christmas Eve 1828 in the tiny Edinburgh courtroom.

Burke stood accused of three murders, Helen McDougal was indicted as 'art and part' to the killings, and Hare appeared as principal prosecution witness, earning particular disgust for his congenital simper.

The defence opened with a novel gambit, arguing that if the case proceeded then evidence of a nature prejudicial to the defendant's reputation would be aired in public. This was true, but the trial started anyway and continued all night, the judges sipping coffee on the bench as the grim story unfolded; the following morning Burke was sentenced to death. Helen was acquitted. But for police intervention, she would have been torn to pieces, recognised by the crowd at her release on Boxing Day.

Before his execution on 28 January Burke made a full confession, but his regret, though real, was limited to Knox having only made part-payment for the last body. He was hanged on a very short drop in front of a huge gathering, including such luminaries as Sir Walter Scott; to the crowd's gratification, he struggled in protracted agony. The body was exhibited the following day in the medical school, and then dissected. His tanned skin sold at a shilling a square inch for presentation **tobacco** pouches.

Although cleared by a Committee of Inquiry, Knox was suspected by the mob, who strung up his effigy and broke his windows. Attendance at his lectures tapered off and he moved south to the London borough of Hackney as a general practitioner, dispensing free obstetric care to the poor. H. R. F. Keating, the writer of crime fiction, affirms that Knox was last heard of in America as a travelling showman with a band of Redskins.

Hare, smuggled out of Scotland, took a factory job. But he was recognised by his workmates, who hurled him into a **lime** pit. His sight was destroyed, and it seems he made his way to London, where late Victorians recalled seeing him in their youth as a blind beggar around Oxford Street and the British Museum.

See also **Coffins**, **Memorabilia**

Butch Cassidy and the Sundance Kid, the fate of

The recent work of American anthropologist Clyde Snow may have unearthed the bodies of the two men immortalised by Robert Redford and Paul Newman. In the 1969 film the outlaws perished in a doomed act of bravado, charging ranks of massed troops. In reality, a suicide pact is probable.

They died in 1909 in San Vincente, Mexico, where their fate was investigated by the US Bolivian Consul.

Butch Cassidy (front right), the Sundance Kid (front left) in the ill-judged New York photograph of 1900 that put their faces on 'Wanted' posters across the country

He learned from the soldiers in at the kill, that the bandits holed up in a shack and, after an inconclusive gun battle, shot themselves rather than surrender. Today, the closest account comes from a manager of the Chocaya Tin-Silver Mine called Roberts, who told his story to the mining engineer Victor J. Hampton in the 1920s.

During their last day, the gangsters held up a mule train led by a mozo or native guard, making off with both the money from Roberts's mine and one of the pack-animals. Soldiers tracked them down. Hampton recalled: `The soldiers arrived as darkness was closing in. The mozo, who had been the payroll's guard, went inside and found the mule. He came out and told the officer in charge of the detachment that the two Americans cooking inside the hut were surely the robbers. Cassidy and the Kid were in the adobe hut, their rifles outside. They were using a small beehive-type baking oven and could be seen eating in the glow of the candle. The officer led his men into the gate and shouted an order to surrender. That's when the shooting started. Roberts said they found the pair dead the next morning.'

To reduce their risk, the soldiers sent an Indian woman on ahead, carrying a baby. Cassidy lay dead on the floor, and the Kid squatted on his haunches, shot through the eyes. Roberts said that one was wounded going for the rifles, the other committed suicide.

The bodies were buried in the local cemetery, and in January 1992 a local, who had the story from his father, pointed out their supposed grave to Clyde Snow. On excavation, it disgorged the bones of two bodies of Caucasian origin, each with a bullet hole to the skull.

Byrd Junior, James

Homicidal race hate is apparently alive and well in Texas. Thirty years after the assassination of Martin Luther King, many believed that deliberate race violence in the USA was finally becoming a thing of the past. Unfortunately, a murder in Texas showed that some white supremacists still hung on to some old-fashioned 'values'.

In the early hours of 7 June 1998, a middle-aged African-American named James Byrd Junior was walking home from a party in Jasper, Texas, when a pickup truck driven by three white men pulled up and offered him a lift. He climbed into the back of the flatbed and was unsuspicious enough not to try to jump off when he saw that the truck was not heading into town but towards a deserted area, far from any witnesses.

Two of the men beat Byrd, then chained him by his ankles to the back bumper of the truck. The third man then drove the truck three miles to a local cemetery reserved for blacks. The dragging killed Byrd and tore off his head and one arm. What was left of his body was dumped outside the cemetery gates.

The murderers doubtless thought that their 'hands-off' method would mean they would get away with the crime, but police simply had to follow the gruesome trail of blood back to its start to find a dropped lighter, complete with fingerprints and an embossed logo reading 'KKK', for Ku Klux Klan.

The killers turned out to be John William King, 26, Shawn Allen Berry, 24, and Lawrence Russell Brewer, 31. It was King and Berry, both hard-core white supremacists, who had beaten James Byrd and chained his legs to the pickup truck. Brewer drove the truck (and thus could be said to have done the actual killing) but claimed he had done so under duress by the younger men. Brewer had no known involvement with any racist groups.

Why did they kill a man that none of them knew? It

Items Found in King's Apartment

has been conjectured that King, an ex-convict who sported a tattoo of a lynched black man, wanted to start a white supremacist group in Jasper and killed Byrd to advertise his racist ideals.

King and Berry were both sentenced to death by lethal injection, but Brewer escaped with a sentence of life because the jury accepted his claim that he had not been motivated by racism.

Ironically, Ross Byrd, the only son of the murdered man, declared that his father did not believe in the death penalty and campaigned to get the sentence of execution on the killers reduced to life imprisonment.

C

Cadaveric spasm

An important pathological finding. Cadaveric spasm is a form of *rigor mortis* associated with violent death including drowning, when the victim clutches at straws. The fingers grip whatever they held at the time of death with such force that they cannot be prised open.

Since it is impossible to simulate, the condition carries great evidential weight; investigators can be certain that whatever the cadaver's hand holds was there at the moment of expiry. One of G. J. Smith's murdered wives clasped a piece of soap in *prima facie* corroboration of his unlikely tale that she drowned in the **bath.**

This fierce grip must be distinguished from standard *rigor mortis*, a point underlined in 1885 when an apparent suicide's body was discovered in a locked bedroom clutching a revolver. Lacassagne, the great French pathologist, established experimentally that the fingers of a newly-dead corpse *could* be made to encircle objects like a pistol, albeit loosely, and the onset of ordinary *rigor* would temporarily mimic cadaveric spasm as the hand tightened around the butt.

This observation confirmed his suspicions, originally aroused by the corpse's arms, which lay under the bedclothes pulled up to its chin, a point missed by the local Savoy doctors, who diagnosed suicide. But Lacassagne thought it unlikely that the man would blow his brains out *before* tidying up his bedding.

Lacassagne's persistence led to the conviction of the deceased's son, who had shot his father before escaping through a window.

See also **Mortal combat**

Camargo, Daniel (1931–)

The so-called 'Beast of the Andes', currently serving sixteen years – the maximum penalty under Ecuadorian law – for murdering seventy-one or perhaps 150 young girls.

Camargo's story bears suspicious parallels with the life of Henry Lee **Lucas**, the discredited American serial killer. Both were arrested by luck as pathetic hoboes in middle age; both claimed wretched childhoods from broken, violent families; both maintained that they attended school forcibly dressed as a girl; both staked claims to an extraordinary number of murders committed in a very short time, and both were greeted by the police as the answer to a backlog of unsolved killings.

Lucas's **success** in hoodwinking sophisticated American law enforcement agencies suggests that such feats would be easy for well-briefed serial confessors in the Third World. Camargo is intelligent and well-read, fluent in three languages, and one of the things he may have read before his 1986 arrest is the dizzying climb to celebrity that followed Lucas's capture in 1983.

Camargo, born in the Colombian Andes on 22 January 1931, says that his mother died when he was one, his stepmother beat him, his uncle drank, his sister was a bully and his father stole his piggy bank. He left Bogota's Leon XIII College at the age of twelve, married Alcira Castillo when he was 29, and walked out seven years later on the day he discovered her in bed with another man. Then the slide started.

Obsessed with virginity, Camargo forced his next lover to drug young girls with sleeping pills so that he could rape them, and in 1965 he was sentenced to six years after being identified by a victim. On release, by his account he went to Brazil, but according to journalist Alberto Uribe Gomez he stayed in Colombia for a rampage that ended the lives of at least eighty adolescent girls. Not in dispute is his arrest in May 1974 and a twenty-five-year sentence for a single rape and murder.

Ten years into his term on the penal island of Gorgona, Camargo stumbled across an abandoned canoe. After three days at sea, on 26 November 1984 he made shore on the mainland where he evaded capture for fifteen months until his chance arrest, when two inquisitive officers opened his battered suitcase to discover a bundle of bloodstained clothing.

Camargo confessed to seventy-one killings. In his words, 'I took my revenge for several years of humiliation. I took revenge on women's unfaithfulness ... After I spent five years in jail for rape, the only thing I feared was to return there. So I had to kill without leaving traces ... I had an extra shirt with me and when I had blood on my hands I pissed on them.'

His apparent motivation dovetails with the psychological orthodoxy of today: 'Some of my victims fought so violently that they set off my impulse to violence and I couldn't control it. It was a natural prolongation of the sexual impulse which had not always been satisfied through **rape**.' Nor is Camargo a stranger to the concept of the cooling-off period (see **Terminology**). After a murder, he said, 'I swore never to start again. And then it came back. A desire inside me, like a drug. I had to kill another one.'

Asked why he removed one victim's heart, lungs and kidneys, Camargo replied, 'That's an entirely invented story ... At best I might have taken out the heart, the organ of love.'

See also **False confessions, Success**

Cambo, Judge

An eighteenth-century Maltese judge famed for his prowess at distinguishing between **justice** and the law. One day in 1720 Cambo witnessed a murder outside his house and took a good look at the culprit as he ran off, dropping a knife sheath in the process. A passing baker picked up this incriminating clue (matching the dagger left embedded in the victim), and was duly arrested.

As luck would have it, the innocent baker came up for trial before Cambo, who quite properly found the circumstantial evidence insufficient for a conviction. Eschewing personal favouritism, the judge followed standard procedure and subjected the accused – who he knew was not the murderer – to **torture**. When he confessed, the wretch was executed.

This miscarriage of justice came to light when the true culprit admitted the killing on his deathbed. The Grand Master of the Knights of Malta took Cambo to task for condemning a blameless man, but he pointed out it was his duty to uphold the law rather than to act

on knowledge he happened to have acquired in his private capacity. Even so, Cambo lost his job.

Camels, homing

Normal drug couriers are known as '**mules**', except in the border area of Rajasthan where the job is done by camels. These ships of the desert, laden with satchels of heroin strapped to their bellies, are turned loose to plod unescorted through the sands to the border collection point, and their rare interception represents no coup for the police, producing neither arrests nor intelligence. On safe arrival, the **narcotics** are removed and buried to await shipment through India.

In the nineteenth century the daily price for **opium** throughout the subcontinent was formally 'fixed' each morning by the Rajasthan cartel from their desert mansions in Shekhwati. The going rate was broadcast to India after reaching the railway line at Bhowani Junction, where it arrived by bush telegraph, that is, drumming.

Campden Wonder, The

A famous **false confession**. On 16 August 1660 William Harrison, a 70-year-old steward from the village of Chipping Campden, vanished while on his rounds. A bloodstained hat was found, and under interrogation Harrison's servant – John Perry – implicated his brother and mother in the killing. He said they had strangled Harrison with a hair-net and pitched the body into the lake by Wallington's Mill. The three accomplices were tried and executed the following year.

Two years later, in 1663, Harrison turned up alive and well, claiming that a band of highwaymen had beaten him about the head, clapped on handcuffs and escorted him to the coast to be shipped abroad in a convoy and sold as a slave to a Turkish doctor in Smyrna. 'It was my chance to be chosen by a grave physician of eighty-seven years of age,' he said. Harrison's wife – 'a snotty covetous Presbyterian' – hanged herself after his return.

This mysterious train of events, related by Sir Thomas Overbury in his *True and Perfect Account*, highlights the dangers of bringing a murder charge without producing the body. Harrison's story has long excited disbelief; highwaymen were not equipped with handcuffs, and no marauding Turkish traders supplied Smyrna with septuagenarian English slaves. More recently, suspicions grew that the entire story was a fiction: the return of the wanderer is a stock literary theme.

But records surfaced showing that a steward called Harrison stopped signing the local grammar school accounts between April 1660 and October 1663. Other documentation chronicles the delivery on 3 March 1661 of John, Richard and Joan Parry to Gloucester Jail for execution. So Harrison did disappear and the Parrys were hanged.

Today, the phenomenon of Parry's **false confession** is better understood. As for Harrison, he went missing in the year of the King's restoration after the Civil War, when many people found it expedient to make themselves scarce while old scores were settled. If Harrison was not forcibly abducted, then he must have bloodied his own hat, leaving it as a misleading clue.

Cannibalism

Eating people is not against the law provided they are dead. The element of cannibalism adds a macabre dimension to a killing, but the defendant does not face the additional charge that he consumed his victim. Thus men like Chase, Fish and Haarmann were tried for murder, whereas those who – after plane crashes or similar interruptions to their journeys – devour their deceased companions rather than perish from hunger have simply broken a taboo.

It is vital to wait until the prospective meal has expired. On 25 July 1884 Captain John Dudley, starving to death on a drifting lifeboat 1,600 miles off the Cape of Good Hope, resolved to kill the cabin boy Richard Parker for food. The lad was barely alive, but Dudley pipped the Grim Reaper to the post. A replenished Dudley survived his ordeal to make land, only to face a charge of murder. He pleaded 'necessity' by way of defence, but was convicted and sentenced to death. Eventually the Crown relented and let him off with six months.

Cannibalism was practised until recently in parts of Africa. On 11 May 1888 the explorer James Jameson was chatting to the slave trader Tippu-Tib in deepest Congo. Cannibalism was all travellers' tales, said Jameson. By way of reply one of Tippu-Tib's men

fetched a young girl and knifed her. 'Three men then ran forward, and began to cut up the body of the girl,' wrote Jameson in his diary. 'Finally her head was cut off, and not a particle remained, each man taking his piece away down to the river to wash it. The most extraordinary thing was that the girl never uttered a sound, nor struggled, until she fell.' Tippu-Tib resumed the conversation. A CBS correspondent in the Congo during the 1960s recalls tribal feasts where he dined off the flesh of infants (roasted on the spit) who had died of natural causes.

Many other societies continued to eat people into the modern era. Thus the Basuto tribesmen excised the hearts of their enemies and ate them, as did the Sioux Indians. Head hunters sucked out the brains of their prey, and the Zulus consumed the forehead and eyebrows of their foes. The underlying rationale was to imbue the victor with the power of the fallen, and the best documented inheritor of this tradition is Jeffrey **Dahmer**, the Milwaukee serial killer. His love of corpses, in the final phase, extended to eating them. He prepared a total of five meals from their body parts.

Dahmer's words, 'I suppose in an odd way it made me feel as if they were more part of me', grope towards some truth, most notably the tenet at the heart of Christian ritual, the transubstantiation of communion where the faithful partake of Christ's blood and body.

Christianity derives from paganism and the florid rites of pre-history. But the primmer, more pedestrian Protestant doctrines dispense with the elements of primitive mysticism and superstition subsumed in Catholic ritual and iconography, leaving a religion bowdlerised of its pagan roots. On this analysis, throwbacks like Dahmer uncover lineaments of paganism in their unconscious, falling prey to the unacknowledged bogey of cannibalism and erecting primitive shrines in its honour.

Almost the only project ever undertaken by Dahmer was the construction of a home-made shrine in **Oxford Apartments**. There his black table, supposedly corresponding to an altar, was to be flanked by skeletons and adorned by skulls. Numerous Christian places of worship incorporate similar reliquaries. 'What was it a shrine to?' Dahmer was asked. 'Myself,' he replied. It represented a place where he could feel 'at home'. Occasionally members of North American tribes are similarly possessed by the so called 'windigo' spirit, which takes over hunters who spend their harsh lives in

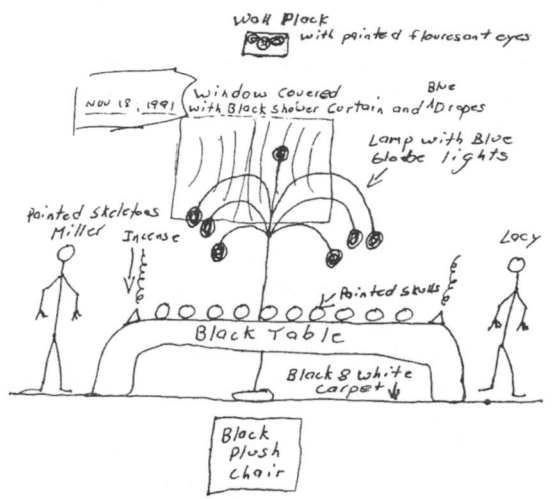

Dahmer's 'shrine', in his own hand

the wilderness, bereft of human companionship and lacking a place to call their own. Indians absorbed by the windigo devoured all who crossed their path. Saskatchewan furnishes a well-attested case from 1879 involving a Cree Indian called Swift Runner. At his trial in Edmonton it was obvious that nothing would shake Swift Runner from his course. 'You might as well hang me,' he said after eating his family, 'because I'm going to kill lots more.'

The Russian serial killer **Chikatilo** laboured under a similar affliction, telling the Rostov Chief of Police: 'I cannot help myself. When the call comes, I must kill.' Both Dahmer and Chikatilo evinced a sexual fascination with their victims' innards. Dahmer made love to the intestines prior to cooking their more digestible parts, but the act of consumption was a leisurely, post-coital confirmation of a relationship during a phase distinct from **dismemberment**. The processing of his victims, elaborated into a ritual extending over hours or days, culminated in a formal meal they shared to the extent that both were present, although one of the participants was merely on the menu. Even then, the bones were destined for incorporation into his shrine.

Dahmer is the thinking man's cannibal; with Chikatilo, eating formed part of the sexual frenzy, an extreme extension of the love-bite which, in the clearest parallel, involved biting off his victims' nipples but progressed to slicing off the tips of tongues, severing the sexual organs or biting off the boys' testicles. In grosser violation of his female victims, Chikatilo excised

the uterus. 'I did not so much chew them as bite them, they were so beautiful and elastic,' he said. This is consumption for sexual rather than liturgical purposes, and the love and the biting are no longer conjoined.

British cases lack conviction. In Scotland the sixteenth-century Sawney Beane supposedly sired an entire incestuous clan of eight sons, six daughters and thirty-two grandchildren, cannibals every one of them. The Beanes inhabited a cave on the Galloway coast, eating 1,500 people in twenty-five years, the bodies 'hung up in rows, like dried beef'. King James I led an expedition of 400 soldiers against them, fought a pitched battle and dragged the clan's surviving members to Leith where they were burned at the stake without trial. There is, however, no historical documentation of these events, and 'Sawney Beane' is almost certainly a legend.

See also **Fish**, **Sagawa**, **Sex crimes**

Canonisation

The latest manifestation of the American crime craze is a new saintly figure: the Victim. Celebrity status awaits 'survivors' who testify on chat shows.

The Central Park Jogger, left for dead after a vicious assault, was honoured by the tribute of flowers from Frank Sinatra. In mid-1992 Rodney **King**, the Los Angeles victim, stood a chance of becoming a movie and merchandising property; he attracted favourable comparison with Martin Luther King's 'I have a dream' speech by saying 'Can't we work together?' in the aftermath of the 1992 riots.

Truman Capote's 1964 *In Cold Blood* made respectable the chronicling of mundane gore. Norman Mailer, with his 1980s dalliance with the convicted murderer Jack Abbott, made it risible. Today, *Vanity Fair* carries regular crime features with glamour photos of leading *mafiosi* like John Gotti by star snapper Annie Leibowitz, and the reversal of the 'Son of **Sam**' law by the Supreme Court left criminals free to profit from their rush into print and celluloid.

On American television a spate of 'reality shows' and televised trials blurred the distinction between real life and entertainment. The FBI retained Robert Stack (of *Untouchables* fame) to host *Unsolved Mysteries*. *The New FBI: The Untold Stories* uses Pernell Roberts (from *Bonanza*). *The American Detective* shows real cops on the job. Celebrities like Mickey Rourke and Anthony

Quinn flocked to John Gotti's **trial**; the televised Kennedy rape trial was selected for video release. *Top Cops* too is just like real life: true stories and voice-overs from the actual policemen involved. The only difference is that the actors are better-looking.

David Simon, a police reporter from the *Baltimore Sun*, has remarked how local jurors, depressed by the quality of real courtroom casting and screenplay, encumber proceedings with interjections of lega-babble culled from *Hawaii Five-0* reruns.

Hinckley's shooting of Ronald Reagan was no less confusing (see **Stalking**). He tried to kill the President because actress Jodie Foster (whom he admired in the film *Taxi Driver*) failed to respond to his letters. The attempt landed him on television, thereby adding to Miss Foster's resonance in her subsequent role in *The Silence of the Lambs*.

Instant television 'docudramas' are big business. On the day of the 1993 World Trade Tower bombing, the FBI logged nineteen calls claiming responsibility while CBS received fifteen from movie producers wanting to cut a deal. An audience of 80 million tuned in to watch the story of Amy Fisher, the 18-year-old 'Long Island Lolita' who shot her lover's wife dead, but the six-month schedule between the murder and its screening as entertainment proved too tight for a quality production. In the words of Professor Robert Kubey from Rutgers University, 'The main issue for Hollywood is, "Can this person sue us?"; not "Are we distorting or offending?"'

The extent to which Britain lags behind the United States in the rush to dramatise personal tragedies can be precisely computed. It is two weeks. Hardly a year after Oxford student Rachel McLean was strangled by her boyfriend and concealed under the floorboards, a reconstruction was filmed for the 1992 television series *Michael Winner's True Crimes*. After Rachel's parents objected that its broadcast might be upsetting, the showing was postponed by a fortnight. A year later, the murder of the Liverpool toddler Jamie Bulger by two ten-year-old children prompted immediate American interest in a two-hour television show. The British researcher charged with obtaining the 'buy-ins' (exclusive rights) to the 'story' from relatives and acquaintances encountered only occasional resistance. He noted, 'The public weren't the problem. Most were only too pleased at the thought of appearing on American television.'

The British True Crime boom owes much to the economic recession. Distressed or anxious readers can comfort themselves with case-histories of warped perpetrators, whose lives are worse than their own, and stories of the victims, brought low more or less at random.

See also **Wuornos**

Cards, collectors'

The latest craze in collectors' cards for American schoolkids is the set of 'Mass Murderers/Serial Killers'. This replaces their former predilection for baseball card series immortalising non-toxic sporting heroes like Babe Ruth. Instead, children can gaze on the visage of Edmund **Kemper** and turn over to find that: 'Edmund as a child showed severe psychological disturbance. At age 13 he cut the family cat into pieces...' Or they can learn about Pogo the Clown, the popular entertainer at Chicago children's parties during the 1970s. The man behind the mask was a local building contractor with a civic streak and an active interest in Democratic politics, John Wayne Gacy, and in the crawl-space under his house he disposed of the bodies of twenty-eight young victims. Their smell finally alerted a policeman on the premises, who had called round to ask about the disappearance of a youth last seen on his way to Gacy's for a job interview.

The card on Jeffrey **Dahmer** is particularly prized.

Carrier pigeons

Trained by an ingenious and unidentified Taiwanese robber in the collection of ransom money, traditionally the most dangerous stage of such operations. Flying off with the victim's money in a pouch hung round its neck, a pigeon can soon shake off police pursuit. 'It is not easy to follow them,' admitted Superintendent Chen Jaioqin, head of the Changwa criminal affairs department in November 1991.

The ruse involved a car thief who telephoned to offer return of the owners' vehicles on receipt of 3,000 Taiwanese dollars. This is only £70 but constitutes the maximum payload for successful take-off.

Victims were directed to a bamboo birdcage in a public park. There they found a homing pigeon sporting a miniature wallet round its neck, together with instructions to fill its pouch with money and turn the bird free.

Disgruntled owners complained to the police that their cars were never returned, probably because they were not stolen by the Birdman of Changwa in the first place. In Taiwan, robbery victims customarily advertise in the classifieds asking for help, making them an easy touch for conmen posing as 'fixers'.

In the 1950s, the New York Mafia employed carrier pigeons to transmit bets for an extensive illegal gambling network, posing the police with serious problems in bringing charges, since the *mafiosi* could simply trip the cages, allowing the only two bits of hard evidence (the pigeons and the rice-paper betting slips) to fly away. Eventually a young plain-clothes detective, Michael Falcione – later a scourge of the Mafia – devised a solution. He bought a falcon. But it was too hungry. It ate the evidence. A better-fed successor eventually brought a pigeon to earth in a state fit for production in court, thereby earning Falcione his nickname: the Falcon.

Cash

For Joe Public, cash is what you buy things with. For a middle-ranking mobster it is what he is forced to spend. There is little else to do with the Niagaras of folding stuff. He cannot buy stocks and shares or real estate (for fear of the IRS); safe-deposit boxes and banks are out (for fear of the IRS and the FBI), and not every hitman fancies the post-impressionists. But pockets are fine for the five or ten thousand dollars of day-to-day pin-money.

So the money is blown. A typical medium-term financial strategy for a *mafioso* involves eating out continually; longer-term investments amount to little more than snappy clothes, like $500 shoes or $2,000 suits, with cars as a good retirement bet. Surplus cash is mopped up by betting, say, $5,000 a card on baccarat, maybe totting up seven-figure losses over the years; the infamous John Gotti ran through $200,000 in the first half of the 1982 football season. But there was plenty more where that came from. Even in the late 1970s, captains with another New York clan, the Bonanno family, pulled in up to $30,000 dollars a week.

The prudent mobster keeps a cache of 'lawyer money' against a rainy day, of necessity entrusted to a partner who – after the eventual arrest – will probably steal it.

Further up the scale, the inflow of drugs money creates problems by its physical size. On Good Friday, 1982, Turkish businessman-turned-informer Paul Waridel was struck by the length of the table in a Lugano bank that supported the two-feet-high stacks of twenty- and fifty-dollar notes. The money was eventually crammed into six voluminous suitcases which, between them, only accounted for $5 million, or 400 kilos of morphine base at wholesale prices.

A few months later, in July, the Merrill Lynch headquarters in Lower Manhattan refused to countenance further deposits of luggage containing low-denomination notes. So the Mafia front-man rang to ask if they would reconsider their position if he lobbed in $50 million cash.

Inevitably, serious drug dealers have recourse to the banking system for transmission of funds, and this leaves a trail. Traffickers increasingly resort to offshore **tax havens**; they buy a company off the shelf, appoint themselves a signatory, fly the money in, and then draw it out, untraceable and freshly laundered.

Cash dispensers

It is easier to extract the cash machine than the cash from the machine.

On 22 April 1992 the London police arrested a London gang red-handed as they levered out a cash dispenser from a Romford building society. They used a fork-lift truck, with a van at the ready to transport the machine away. For the previous raids, netting an estimated total of £200,000, JCBs were employed. All the robberies concentrated on branches of the Abbey National, suggesting either an inside source to notify the outside robbers when the machines were full, or a clear preference for the soft-target setting of the Abbey's hole-in-the-wall machines, installed in glass windows as opposed to brick walls.

This type of bank raid may yet raise complex legal arguments about whether the offence constitutes theft or robbery. The latter is more serious but requires 'breaking-and-entering'. The gang broke, but did not enter.

Cash dispensers are tempting propositions containing up to £60,000 each. Mounted on substantial concrete plinths, they are only secured by a few bolts, which yield easily to the onslaught of heavy machinery. Subsequent manoeuvring of the dispenser is facilitated by its handy rollers. At this stage the problems multiply, one venture coming to grief when – in the course of cutting their dispenser open – the thieves incinerated its contents.

A historical precedent for the take-away robbery dates to 1922 when Matt and George Kimes hit the bank in Pampa, Texas, with a pick-up truck. With their accomplice Ray Terrill, the gang reversed through the front window, tethered the safe to their vehicle and drove away, dragging their 'box' behind them. They netted $35,000.

Cathedral, The

'The Cathedral' was one nickname for Pablo **Escobar**'s lavish hillside prison in Colombia, also known as 'Club Medellin', or 'Club Med' for short. He left on 22 July 1992.

Escobar planned his stockade on the lines of a retirement home, designing a luxury complex of ranches on his own land. Barbed-wire fences and minefields suggested that the prison's function was to keep Escobar in, rather than others out, and the man in charge was no prison governor but Colonel Homero Rodriguez, a specialist in protection, well aware that Escobar's death in captivity could precipitate a civil war. Rodriguez got wind of a plan by the rival Carli cartel for an airstrike on Escobar from an A-37 armed with four 250-pound bombs, and authorised the construction of a concrete bunker. But the attack never came.

Escobar surrendered on 19 June 1991 after negotiating a nine-year sentence for a minor trafficking charge. Effectively, Escobar and fifteen henchmen received military protection to run his cocaine empire from the Club Med's offices with eleven telephone lines, cellular telephones, three radio telephone systems, nine bleepers, fax machines and a flock of microchip-carrying homing pigeons. His primary prison duties thus consisted of murdering rivals and arranging drug distribution, while living at the government's expense, and in July 1992 he summoned two powerful underlings, Galeano and Moncada, for interrogation after growing suspicious that they were welshing on the deal to pay a monthly tithe of $100 million. The pair were killed, along with twenty associates.

Inside Club Med, Escobar lived well. His private suite incorporated a bedroom with a king-size bed; the fitted wardrobes held thirty-seven tailor-made shirts and nine pairs of identical Nike sneakers. His reception area had a padded bar and a balcony with a fixed telescope for the panoramic views. The interiors, dotted with cane sofas covered with scatter cushions, were liberally decorated with potted plants and photographs of Escobar dressed up as a Chicago gangster. Over his bed hung a portrait of the Virgin Mary, and his library included five Bibles. The tiled bathroom, complete with huge jacuzzi and gold-plated taps, bulged with expensive oils and essences from Paris. Other attractions included a fully illuminated football pitch, motorcycles, a gymnasium (with a natural waterfall for showers), a discotheque lined with solar system murals, and a playroom with billiard tables and toys.

In July 1992, as news of Escobar's lifestyle leaked out, embarrassed authorities threatened to send him to a proper prison. It is perhaps an over-dramatisation to say he escaped. Rather, he checked out. His position had become precarious.

President Bush was trailing in the election polls; Escobar might be seized to boost his ratings. Overhead surveillance by DEA planes made Escobar jumpy, as did the price of $1.5 million on his head and the discovery of an AR-15 rifle fitted with a nightscope in the surrounding forest. Then a survivor from the Galeano-Moncada purges went to the police, and on the night of 21 July the Cathedral was surrounded by the military.

Escobar evaded capture, however, by climbing the hillside behind the complex. Sixteen months of freedom was brought to an abrupt end when, on 2 December 1993, he was shot dead in Medellin by Hugo Aguilar, a senior agent in the huge team set up to recapture Escobar.

Cat's eyes, dead

Crucial evidence in the 1893 trial of New York's Dr Robert W. Buchanan. In November 1890 he divorced his first wife for adultery. Her replacement, a fat brothel keeper twice his age called Anna Sutherland, had little to recommend her and indeed became a personal and professional liability. But she was rich, and Dr Buchanan stood to inherit. In 1892, when he booked a passage to Scotland, she threatened to cut him out of her will.

Four days before he was due to sail on 25 April, Anna fell seriously ill and died. The death certificate, issued by a Dr McIntyre, specified 'cerebral haemorrhage', and Buchanan benefited to the tune of $50,000.

A tip-off from a suspicious partner of Anna's alerted the *New York World*. A reporter interviewed Dr McIntyre, who vouchsafed that the prime symptom of morphine poisoning was lacking; the pupils of Anna's eyes, which would have contracted to pin-points with an overdose, were normal. Further enquiries unearthed two highly suggestive facts, first that Dr Buchanan cancelled his ticket ten days before his wife fell ill, not four as claimed, and second that he remarried his former wife three weeks after Anna's death.

Exhumation revealed one tenth of a grain of morphine in her body, the residue of a fatal dose of some five grains. But the pin-point pupils were absent. Then a *New York World* staff writer subjecting Dr Buchanan to a hostile grilling noted that the apparent size of his quarry's eyes was greatly magnified by his thick-lensed spectacles. This reminded the journalist of his childhood when belladonna – administered to a schoolfriend's eyes – achieved the same result.

Dr Robert W. Buchanan

Anna's nurse confirmed that Dr Buchanan had given her patient belladonna drops for no apparent reason, and he came to trial on 20 March 1893. Witnesses testified that he bragged about his method for disguising morphine poisoning, which was put to the test in court. A cat was injected with morphine and then soused in belladonna. It gave its life that another might die, and on 2 July 1895 Dr Buchanan was electrocuted in Sing Sing.

See also **Exhibits**

Champagne

The murder weapon in a 1953 case from New York. When Dr and Mrs Fraden were discovered dead in their apartment after drinking champagne dosed with potassium cyanide, the case was initially viewed as a suicide pact. But it soon emerged that the couple had been poisoned by their son Harlow Fraden, who described his escapade as 'a delightful game'.

Harlow got away with a verdict of serious mental disorder. In his twenties he had struck up a close but platonic relationship with Dennis Wepman; and the two young men egged each other on in fanciful self-indulgence culminating in murder. Wepman too admitted to being 'enthralled'; he felt that by paying close attention to the process of killing he could further his literary ambitions. Perhaps he was right. The long-standing drug addict William Burroughs was highly regarded as a writer, but his wife died after Burroughs (under the influence at the time) accidentally drilled her through the forehead while demonstrating how he thought he could shoot fruit off the top of her head. He has said that this experience helped turn him into an author.

See also **Poisoning, Privilege**

Chaplin, Charles (1889–1977)

Chaplin was buried in a small cemetery at Corsier-sur-Vevey overlooking Lake Geneva; on 2 March 1978 his body disappeared.

A local Bulgarian car mechanic in Switzerland on political asylum, Galtscho Ganev, had been going though a difficult patch. In his own words: 'As a result I decided to hide Charles Chaplin's body and solve my problems.' Ganev failed to grasp the basic point about **kidnapping**: he demanded a ransom of £330,000 from the family if they wanted to see their loved one again, dead. The asking price was soon down by half and the situational dynamics needed bolstering by more traditional threats to kill living members of the family: Geraldine Chaplin's younger brother and sister. But since they had not been kidnapped, this proved beyond Ganev's powers.

Ganev's accomplice was caught after keeping a promise to ring through further demands at exactly 9.30 in the morning; the police captured their man by mounting a watch on 200 local telephone boxes. The main problem with recovering Chaplin's body was that the kidnappers forgot where the coffin was hidden; police officers had to use mine detectors. Ganev was sentenced to four and a half years' hard labour, and the film star's tomb is now protected by a concrete lining; in life, his person formed the target of one of **Hoover**'s many maliciously motivated investigations, the Joan Barry Mann Act case of the 1940s.

Cheerleaders

Wanda Holloway's travails in smalltown Texas began in 1989 when she removed her 14-year-old daughter

Shanna from elementary school and sent her to the Alice Johnson High. This move ensured her eligibility for the 1990 seventh-grade cheerleading tests.

But Wanda learned that her friend and neighbour, Verna Heath, had gone one better. Despite keeping her daughter Amber at the elementary school, Verna persuaded Johnson High to accept her girl for the 1989 Pom-Pom trials.

Wanda protested that this was hardly fair; Amber was not even enrolled at Johnson High. The girls themselves remained friends, even after a playoff for the last two places on the cheerleading squad when the school picked Amber rather than Shanna. But Wanda felt devastated, and Amber's mother noted her altered disposition: 'I felt tension. Wanda was very upset because my daughter got to be cheerleader.'

Wanda would not admit defeat. She campaigned on her daughter's behalf, running off a special set of rulers with printed slogans and handing them out in school. But the Parents' Association said this contravened the rules. Forced to find a way of helping her daughter secretly, in January 1990 she met John Harper – her ex-husband's brother – in the local shopping centre and asked him to have Amber and her mother killed. 'I'm serious about it,' she said. 'I've just got to come up with the money.'

Harper demurred, saying that he did not know anyone who would murder a 13-year-old girl. Wanda replied: 'There's car wrecks. Houses burn down.'

'Yeah, but not on purpose,' objected Harper. But Wanda persisted, and the pair met regularly over the following months. Eventually Harper put forward an offer of $20,000 for the two. Wanda expressed dismay at the expense. 'Lady,' Harper reminded her, 'this ain't no five-and-dime burglary.' So they set about whittling down the cost, and soon he reported that another contact would do the mother for $2,500 and the daughter for an additional $5,000.

But why bother about the girl? With her mother eliminated, Shanna would be too upset to manage the cheerleaders' complicated gymnastic routines. So, on 28 January 1991, the conspirators settled on $2,500 for just the mother. As Wanda said: 'I can't afford to do both. The mother's the one who's screwed me around.' She gave Harper a pair of diamond earrings in part payment and agreed to make up the final $500 within a month of the hit.

Two days later Wanda was arrested. The full story came out at her August 1991 trial. After Wanda's first approach, Harper had gone to the police. 'If anything happened to this woman or little girl,' he said, 'I wanted the cops to hear it from me first.' After initial scepticism a Sergeant Blackwell wired Harper up with a microphone for his last six meetings, and the police had monitored contract negotiations throughout. Harper's packaged bargain, priced at $7,500 for two, was their idea.

At the trial, the defence contended that Harper had proved an enthusiastic salesman. On tape Wanda was heard saying: 'Blow it off. I don't want to go through with this' while Harper cajoled: 'Have I got a deal for you!' The defence argued that Harper was the true instigator from his opening remark to Wanda: 'I can take care of that for you.' In their version, Wanda tried to back off when she realised Harper meant business. She said he turned threatening in an unrecorded telephone conversation, insisting it was too late.

Wanda allegedly realised it was a put-up job when Harper offered to take her earrings in lieu of cash; she handed them over just to be rid of him. In support, the defence produced Harper's estranged wife. She testified against her husband, saying he hoped to worm his way back into his family's favour and back into the family will. Harper's brother was Wanda's ex-husband Tony, the family executor, and – according to Harper's wife – the two had plotted against Wanda in order to regain custody of Tony's children by Wanda. This seems plausible on paper, but the jury did not believe it. Neither did Wanda. After the verdict she sobbed in the dock, saying: 'I lost sight of a wrong from a right.'

Wanda Holloway is currently serving fifteen years. In the late 1960s, her life as a teenager was blighted by the refusal of her God-fearing father to let her join the cheerleaders. He thought their costumes too skimpy.

Chikatilo, Andrei Romanovich (1936–94)

Russian serial killer echoing the personality traits of his Western counterparts. Born in a small Ukrainian village during the era of purges and famines, when millions died, their corpses often littering the streets and fields, Chikatilo heard on his mother's lap that his cousin had been killed and eaten. At primary school he was introverted, unable to admit to short-sightedness; he obtained his first glasses at the age of 30, and wet his bed until he was twelve. His father, captured by the Nazis in the war, was branded an enemy of the people, and Chikatilo lapped up stories of partisan heroes roaming the woods in search of prey.

Humiliated at school, Chikatilo took refuge in Communism, reading *Pravda* to his classmates; his fixation with political dogma verged on a mental disorder. Shy with girls, he vowed to remain pure until marriage. His first attempt at sex failed and, during army service, he was rumoured impotent. Once, while cuddling a girl, she tried to withdraw from his arms, and he climaxed during the few seconds he held on tight. Thereafter he preferred unrequited love, once praising a girl in a newspaper instead of approaching her directly.

Andre Chikatilo, Russian serial killer

Chikatilo was 27 when his sister dragooned him into marriage with a miner's daughter, Fayina. A week later he had his first marital erection. Sex was for making babies – they had two – but otherwise a chore, and fantasies of sexual prowess began to interpose. In 1971 a university degree qualified him as a teacher, but he could not control his class and turned ever more sullen. Girls under twelve exercised increasing allure, and he barged into their dormitories, **masturbating** in his pocket while eyeing pupils in their underwear. In May 1973 he sexually assaulted a girl in the swimming pool. At his next school he molested boys as they slept. To pursue his interests in private, he bought a run-down shack on the edge of town, to which he lured drunks and prostitutes with offers of food and drink. But adults succumbed willingly to his advances, and Chikatilo could not respond.

On 22 December 1978, he befriended Lena Zakotnova, aged nine, in the street. She needed to go to the toilet. Chikatilo took her to his shed and stripped her violently, accidentally drawing blood. This conferred an immediate erection, making the fatal connective spark between blood and sex. So he pulled a knife and stabbed her in the stomach. Each blow brought him closer to orgasm. So he stabbed her again and again.

That night he threw Lena's body into the nearby river; it was found downstream two days later, as was a smudge of blood in the snow by his shack. Chikatilo was questioned, but the police soon arrested another sex offender, Aleksandr Kravchenko, shot in 1984.

Over the next twelve years Chikatilo disposed of fifty-three women and children. In 1981 he became a supply clerk for Rostnovnerud, and his job of travelling the region provided the perfect cover. Rostov, his base, attracted the poor of the surrounding area, and an underclass of teenagers from broken homes slept rough in the railway station, trading their bodies for a drink or a crust of bread. They were outsiders like him but, in his estimation, worse: 'They followed me like dogs.'

On 3 September 1981 Chikatilo met his second victim, Larisa Tkachenko, and offered to take her to a nearby complex of concrete cafes. Probably she had sex in mind, but for Chikatilo one thing now entailed another. On a short cut through a wood, Chikatilo lost his self-control. He strangled her and ejaculated over her body. Then he performed a war dance, whooping round the corpse. 'I felt like a partisan,' he said later.

Chikatilo knew he would kill again. Thereafter he made no attempt at intercourse, but he often inflicted as many as thirty carefully sited stab wounds, slicing up his victims, extracting their organs, and chewing them. Nearly all had their eyes stabbed out, perhaps to avert their shaming gaze.

Chikatilo drew his victims from different ages, sexes and backgrounds. To the police there seemed no link between ageing alcoholic prostitutes and little boys – except that he killed them. But that *was* the link. Chikatilo liked killing people. In November 1984 his twenty-three, highly distinctive murders were united under Operation Forest Path. Moscow's Serbsky Institute produced a profile of an ostensibly normal man, probably married, with a regular job, and sperm found on the shirt of his twentieth victim showed the killer had AB blood.

Killing became a periodic endeavour undertaken for pleasure to satisfy a physiological need and, by the end of 1982, Chikatilo had claimed six more lives. Not until Sasha Chepel's killing (number thirty) in August 1984 were the murders admitted in the local Party daily, *Molot*. The police initially assumed that the culprit was mentally handicapped, and Chikatilo kept his secret from his wife, maintaining that his scratched face and the flecks of blood on his shirt came from handling sheet metal. Given his apathy about sex with her, she never considered him a likely sex killer.

On 14 September 1984 Chikatilo was arrested in Rostov's market after a series of pick-up attempts. In his briefcase was a jar of vaseline, a rope and a long-bladed knife. Chikatilo fitted the killer's rough description, but the files did not show his previous record. He seemed a respectable married man, and was conclusively exculpated when his blood tested group A. Chastened by his escape, in the next two years he only killed twice. By then 26,500 suspects were on file; card number nine was Chikatilo's.

The widely dispersed killings suggested a murderer with access to a car, and in Russia this constituted an eliminating factor. Or maybe the killer had police ID to lure away the tramps who comprised the bulk of his victims. Maybe the skilled incisions indicated a butcher. Investigators checked 5,845 men with previous convictions, particularly sex offences, 10,000 of the mentally ill, 419 homosexuals, 163,000 drivers – 500,000 in all. Among the paperwork languished a 1988 circular, quoting Japanese research that in one case in 10,000, a man's sperm did not match his blood group.

In March 1989 Chikatilo cut off Tanya Ryzhova's head and legs, wrapped her in a bundle and towed her through the snowy streets on a sledge with the help of a passing stranger. Tanya's body was stuffed into pipes by the tracks, and many other victims had been found near the line or last seen at a station. So the police mounted a watch over the platforms, put men picking mushrooms in the nearby woods, and installed officers in holes covered in branches by the side of the track. Decoy policewomen acted as bait, sprawling drunk in the carriages.

On 17 October 1990 Chikatilo killed Vadim Gromov in the forest by Donleskhoz station. Sixty specialists established their headquarters in nearby Shakhti, drafting in the local police and a crack riot squad a hundred strong. Two weeks later Chikatilo struck again, and 600 detectives were deployed along the line through the forests, with three or four officers covering even the most isolated halts.

On 6 November 1990 Sergeant Igor Rybakov at Donleskhoz saw a man in a suit and tie emerge from the nearby woods. When the stranger washed his hands at the water hydrant, Rybakov noticed his bandaged finger and his stained cheek. He asked for his papers and filed a routine report. Five days later a detective at the Gromov site spotted a new piece of ripped pocket dangling from a tree, and a search revealed Sveta Korostik's body, dead for about a week. The killer must have passed through the station, and Rybakov's report named the suspicious stranger as Chikatilo.

Arrested on 20 November, his sperm (but not his blood) tested group AB and he claimed not to have been at Donleskhoz. The following day he conceded a weakness for 'perverted sexual displays in films', admitting he was not 'a complete man'. Of the tramps, he said, 'the question arose of whether these degenerate elements had the right to exist.' On 27 November he said, 'I am ready to give evidence of my crimes, but please do not torment me with details. My psyche could not cope.' Two days later he cracked when a psychologist was sent to discuss his 'problems'. Chikatilo eventually admitted to fifty-three killings and guided investigators to the murder scenes, vaguely hoping that the number of dead would make him a valuable scientific specimen. Indeed, the *Moscow News* reported that the Japanese were interested in acquiring his brain.

Chikatilo appeared at his trial penned in a metal cage with his head shaven. On the first day he delighted photographers by brandishing a porno magazine. Later he became dejected, stripped off and waved his penis in court, shouting 'Look at this useless thing, what do you think I could do with this?' On 15 October 1992 he was sentenced to death. He concluded a rare interview in June 1993 with the words, 'Remember me to my friends, to my colleagues, to everyone I knew. Tell them I am sorry, so sorry…'

Chikatilo was executed with a single shot in the back of the head on 14 February 1994.

China travellers

Early escapees from the first years of the Australian convict settlements. The conditions of brutality and near-starvation encouraged bands of desperate prisoners to vanish into the dunes or make a run for the bush. They headed for China, the fount of milk, honey, opium, silk and yellow girls.

The Irish proved peculiarly susceptible to this fantasy, placing China about a hundred miles north of Sydney on the far side of a wide but navigable river. The first band of twenty men and one woman slipped out of Rose Hill in November 1791. Three believed they came so close to the promised land that on their recapture they ran away again. This time they lost their lives. Others set off, heading for China inland from the beaches of Tasmania, and the phenomenon is reported as late as 1798 with batches of Irishmen sixty-strong setting off for the Orient.

Lacking proper compasses, the China Travellers made their own makeshift version, consisting of a crude circle, drawn on paper or bark, showing the positions of north, south, east and west. And *yes*, they omitted the needle. Mostly the men died, the victims of thirst, hunger or Aboriginal spears. Recaptured survivors faced 500 lashes.

Christmas

A criminal offence in England for sixteen years. The celebration of Christmas was banned on account of its 'carnal and sensual delight' by the Long Parliament of 1644. Cromwell's Puritans abhorred the Christian elements of the Christmas ritual because they were Catholic, the pagan parts because they were pagan, and the festive bits because they were festive. Instead, Christians were directed to fast, and the army sent out yuletide snatch-squads on house-to-house searches for illicit Christmas dinners which they doubtless consumed themselves. In 1647 the ban was extended to Easter and other festivals.

Christmas was reinstated along with Charles II in 1660.

Cicero

In the early 1920s, Cicero was a pleasant Chicago suburb with 50,000 inhabitants, 68 per cent home ownership and its own Rotary and Kiwani clubs.

In 1924 a small-time fixer, Ed Konvalinka, realised there was a danger of the Democrats unseating the Republicans in the coming elections, ending six years of

Republican control over the area's politics and saloons. To ensure election of Klenha's Republican ticket, Konvalinka hit on the scheme of importing an outside electioneering specialist. Local politician Big Ed Vogel approved the plan; together they agreed to approach a young 'mover-and-shaker', Al Capone, offering him free run of the district provided the right candidates were returned.

Capone did a thorough job. According to the Illinois Crime Survey, 'Automobiles filled with gunmen paraded the streets slugging and kidnapping election workers. Polling places were raided by armed thugs and ballots were taken at the point of the gun from the hands of voters waiting to drop them in the box. Voters and workers were kidnapped, taken to Chicago and held prisoner until the polls closed.' Capone's brother Frank was killed in a firefight, and Al shot his way out of trouble with a gun blazing in either hand.

Mayor Klenha and his cronies came sailing through their democratic ordeal with immense majorities. But the day of their election marked their last day in power. Overnight, placid Cicero changed into Mob City, with government by, for and of the bums, sprouting a profusion of dance halls, nightclubs, gambling dens, betting shops, dog tracks and 160 night-and-day bars. There were no whorehouses because of an inter-gang agreement.

Capone ruled the roost. He took $100,000 a week out of Cicero, beat up the editor of one paper, kidnapped the editor of the other and got rough with the Mayor for showing insufficient respect. Once, Capone had to go down to City Hall personally, drag Klenha out of his mayoral office, knock him down the outside steps and then kick him repeatedly. A police-man watched, twirling his nightstick before strolling off. It was said you could tell when you crossed the parish boundary from Chicago to Cicero by sniffing. 'If you smell gunpowder, you're there.'

See also **Hawthorne Castle**, **Pax Capone**

Coffins

A good Chicago mobster deserved a great coffin. When Antonio Lombardo was shot in the head with **dumdums** in 1928 he became the third president of the feudal Unione Sicilione to die by gunfire. He rated a heavy bronze container, crested with a brass eagle, and his funeral train needed twelve pall-bearers.

Another prime example received the body of Frank Capone, Al's brother who lost his life in the line of duty rigging the 1924 **Cicero** elections. Frank went to his grave in a silk-lined silver-plated casket.

Vincent 'the Schemer' Drucci lay in state in a $10,000 silver-and-aluminium affair. **O'Bannion**, the Irish gang leader, went one better. His coffin was rushed to Chicago in a private freight car all the way from Philadelphia. Its design is reminiscent of the showpiece version in Walt Disney's *Sleeping Beauty*, with solid silver-and-bronze airtight walls, and the thick plate-glass on the top made for clear viewing of the smiling killer, who lay in repose on a bed of white satin with tufted cushions. The heavily carved corner posts were of solid silver.

In the nineteenth century the British favoured a baser metal. Iron coffins were constructed to Edward Lillie Bridgman's patented design. His impregnable subterranean containers countered the epidemic of graverobbers, and by 1822 Bridgman was advertising in *Wooler's British Gazette*. 'Many hundreds of bodies will be dragged from their wooden coffins this winter, for the anatomical lectures … The question of the right to inter in iron is now decided … The only safe coffin is Bridgman's Patent wrought-iron one.'

Not unreasonably, the advertisement invited those 'about to inter a mother, husband, child or friend' to consider if they really wanted their loved ones to be dug up by rabble and sliced into bits by medical students. Subsequent advertisements reported a brisk trade. Bridgman charged a hefty £31 10s for his product, which featured interior locking bolts.

The iron slabs and protective railings commonly seen round early Victorian graves served a similar defensive function.

Kidnap victims are often confined under peculiarly grim conditions. Colleen Stan, the sex **slave**, spent years immured in a double-lined wooden crate, and in 1993 Stephanie Slater from Birmingham told the court how, after her abduction in January 1992, she was led into a large darkened garage. 'I hope you are not claustrophobic, because you are going into a box within a box,' her kidnapper said, shovelling Miss Slater into a coffin, itself contained in a large wheelie bin. He cautioned her against any attempt at escape since boulders were balanced overhead and she was ringed by electrodes. In addition, he handcuffed, gagged and blindfolded her.

On her first night, Miss Slater all but froze and, in due course, concluded that she had perished. 'I was so cold, I thought I had died,' she recalled. 'I thought I had gone, completely gone. Then I saw a very, very vivid picture of Christ in front of me in the total blackness.' In court, Miss Slater reduced both the jury and her captor to tears.

See also **Bodysnatchers, Flowers, Neilson**

Colombia, Little

Name given to an area of New York centred on 83rd Street off Roosevelt Avenue. The district is awash with cocaine money, although the local drug of choice is *bazuko*, a cocaine by-product. The incoming consignments of 500 kilos of 'Snow White' are broken up among, say, five Colombians who handle the sub-distribution through a network of Dominicans for the actual street-work. Apparently no one wants to work with Cubans.

Defenestrations in Little Colombia are a regular occurrence. In the words of a detective interviewed in 1992 for *Vanity Fair*, 'You raid Dominicans, you always need a man covering the windows. You've got them all lined up with a gun on them and they start shuffling sideways. You say, "Hey, what the hell are you doing?" And suddenly he's out of the window, three, four, five stories up … You either find a pile of broken bones down there or he staggers away.'

At the Cali cartel in Colombia they assume two fatalities per 500 kilo consignment by the time it reaches the streets. New York police regard Colombian homicides as the hardest to solve; those who break the Wall of **Silence** are 'hit', and if they are not, their families are. The price for murder is $200.

The cocaine comes in to feed the voracious appetite of Wall Street, with Learjet pilots landing it at Westchester for $1,000 per kilo unit. A single successful run earns the intrepid aviator upwards of half a million dollars; New York's total cocaine imports for 1990 were estimated at 400,000 kilos.

Comparatively speaking, New York police relish arresting Colombians; it is high-profile stuff perfect for the evening news bulletins – red Ferraris, stacks of cocaine, guns and cash. Putting a middle-aged, besuited Chinese accountant behind bars for five kilos of heroin does not attract the same kudos. But the Chinese are patient, careful criminals, likely to run in five kilos a week, year in, year out, while the

Colombians go for broke, shipping hundreds of kilos until they are busted, often second time round.

See also **Escobar**

Columbine High School Massacre

Child murderers – adults who kill children – have always troubled the world. But in the late twentieth century an even more disturbing trend arose: children who kill. Easy access to firearms in many areas of the world must be held partially to blame, but many people also believe that global media that portray violence as sexy (while often portraying sex as dirty) are twisting young minds.

The Columbine High School Massacre

At 11.35 a.m. on 20 April 1999, students Dylan Klebold, 17, and Eric Harris, 18, walked into the cafeteria of Columbine High School in Littleton, Colorado, and opened fire with semi-automatic handguns. The boys seemed to target pretty girls particularly, but were indiscriminate and ruthless as they fired. Teacher Dave Sanders realised what was happening and, showing great bravery and presence of mind, stood up and herded many children out of the cafeteria to relative safety. The two boys shot him in the back, killing him.

Following the slaughter in the cafeteria, Dylan and Eric walked through the building spraying bullets arbitrarily at cowering students. In just under an hour,

twelve children, as well as the teacher, were killed, and twenty-five injured. Then Harris and Klebold turned their guns on themselves in an apparent suicide pact.

It is not known why they went on a killing spree, as both boys came from pleasant, relatively well-off homes, had no police records and had showed no signs of serious psychological problems. However, it is speculated that the pair resented the fact that they were loners, excluded from most school cliques and thus denied much of a chance to get girlfriends. Some teachers remembered afterwards that both boys had claimed to admire the Nazis. At the time this was ignored as typical teenaged attention-seeking, but it may be significant that the massacre took place on the 110th anniversary of Adolf Hitler's birth.

The massacre at Columbine High School reignited the US debate on gun-control laws, but little has come of it since. Even the suggestion that children should not be allowed any access to guns has been attacked by vociferous elements of the pro-gun lobby.

Concentration

It is said that the prospect of execution concentrates the mind wonderfully. In the case of William **Palmer**, the poisoner, this operated to the exclusion of the general in favour of the particular. His last words on the morning of 14 June 1855, delivered standing on the trap door of the gallows, were 'Are you sure this is safe?'

One can understand Palmer's point; a sentient being facing imminent extinction has the responses of a living person, even though he is, for all practical purposes, dead. On his way to the scaffold Palmer minced along like a dainty schoolgirl, taking great care to avoid getting wet in the puddles from a heavy overnight downpour. George Orwell was struck by precisely the same conduct in his 1931 essay 'A Hanging'.

Orwell watched as a condemned native walked towards the gallows and execution; the man stepped aside to avoid splashing through rainwater. In Orwell's words: 'All the organs of his body were working – bowels digesting food, skin renewing itself, nails growing, tissues forming – all toiling away in solemn foolery. His nails would still be growing when he stood on the drop, when he was falling through the air with a tenth of a second to live ... He and we were a party of men walking together ... and in two minutes, with a sudden snap, one of us would be gone – one mind less, one world less.' These reflections made Orwell appreciate 'the mystery, the unspeakable wrongness, of cutting a life short when it is in full tide'.

In Russia, the apprehension of imminent extinction is infinitely extended. The condemned never learn their date of execution, and the prisoner fears the worst each time footsteps approach his cell. To be ushered into a room is to anticipate a Ministry of the Interior executioner stationed above the door with a specially adapted Makarov service pistol, waiting to fire a nine-gramme bullet down through the top of the skull.

Condemned sermon

Traditionally delivered to prisoners awaiting execution in **Newgate** Chapel. Lest they forgot, the men were seated in a black-painted pew grouped around a coffin.

Edward Wakefield left a contemporary account of a condemned sermon where one listener was clearly off his head. 'At length the Vicar pauses,' Wakefield wrote, 'and then in a deep tone which, though hardly above a whisper is audible to all, says, "Now to you, my poor fellow mortals, who are about to suffer the last penalty of the law"… The dying men are dreadfully agitated… The poor sheep-stealer is in a frenzy. He throws his hands far from him and shouts aloud: "**Mercy**, good Lord! mercy is all I ask; There! There! I see the Lamb of God! Oh, how happy! Oh! This is happy!"'

The service was a popular spectacle with the general public.

See also **Treadwheel**

Condoms

A useful device for drug runners (known as '**swallowers**') who shepherd rubber-clad contraband through Customs in their stomachs. Contrary to the normal pattern, a burst sac means instant death.

Irina Ratushinskaya reports a more unusual application in her account of the Russian gulag: *Grey is the Colour of Hope*. Prisoners keen to smuggle alcohol into labour camps would slip a condom down their throats and attach it with an airtight seal to a long piece of plastic tubing which, poking up into their mouth, was firmly wedged between any surviving set of adjacent molars.

Outside the workcamp, the *zek* was topped up with a syringe by squirting alcohol into his condom via the tube until it expanded to line the duodenum and stomach, his maximum load of three litres sufficient to make seven litres of vodka. Safely through the guards and back in the camp, the *zek's* jubilant colleagues would drain their hero by suspending him head downwards from the barrack rafters with his tube held over a dish.

According to Detective Dick Woodman of the West London Drug Squad, a similar trick is used today by crack dealers on the capital's streets. But the technique is more akin to fishing than ballooning. First the dealer's crack 'rocks' are wrapped in tin foil. Then the sachet is attached to one end of a length of twine; the other is secured to a tooth, and the **narcotics** are lowered into the throat for retrieval on each sale.

Contempt

A Mafia expression of this extreme emotion is to cut off the penis and testicles with a stiletto, leaving them beside the victim's body after first blowing out his brains.

One intended recipient of this treatment was Eliott Ness of the Chicago **Untouchables**, who received a telephone call promising he would shortly be found in a ditch with his 'wang slashed off'. He wasn't.

The regular Mafia punishment for messing with a *capo's* woman was severing the man's penis and then stuffing it into his mouth. One unnamed hood guilty of this breach of etiquette suffered the ultimate in contempt. According to the 1989 book *Mobster*, Carlo Gambino had the man fed, still alive and limbs first, into a large meatgrinder.

See also **Faithful**

Contempt of Court

An offence entitling a judge to mysterious and far-reaching powers. In 1631 an English thief, Noy, was convicted of a felony at the Salisbury Assizes; in a fit of pique he threw a 'brickbat' at Judge Richardson who, dodging the missile, had the prisoner indicted for contempt. Noy was strung up in the presence of the court, with the exception of his offending hand, hacked off for separate display on a gibbet.

These draconian powers were re-examined in 1975. In that year Lord Balogh's son, Stephen, was devilling as an articled clerk in St Albans. He made £5 a day helping out a firm of solicitors involved in an interminable pornography case. The days passed, the boredom rose. Eventually Balogh decided to enliven the proceedings. The court building was state-of-the-art; it had air-conditioning. Balogh pinched a small gas cylinder containing N_2O from a nearby hospital car park and, that night, sneaked on to the court roof. There he located the ventilation ducts which had their outlets in the court below, near the bench where the barristers who had tormented him for days with their tedious speeches would take up their stations the following morning. All that remained was to judge his moment, slip out of court, position the cylinder and open the valve to flood the chamber with nitrous oxide.

Next morning he arrived with his briefcase at the ready. But court officials spotted him skulking on the roof the previous night; they searched his case and discovered the gas canister. That afternoon Balogh was arraigned before Judge Melford Stevenson in the neighbouring courtroom on a charge of contempt. With commendable presence of mind, he argued: 'I am actually in the wrong court at the moment; the proceedings which I intended to subvert are next door. Therefore, it is not contempt against your court for which I should be tried.' Unimpressed, the judge sent him down for the inordinate period of six months. Balogh greeted his sentence with the words: 'You are a humourless automaton. Why don't you self-destruct?'

After a fortnight cooling his heels, Balogh thought his debt to society must surely be paid and appealed via the Official Solicitor. The court's powers came under scrutiny, and it was held that their exercise should be restricted (since the judge was acting as prosecutor, judge and jury) to emergencies where it was 'urgent and imperative to act at once'.

In Balogh's case there was no emergency. No trial had been upset and no proceedings disturbed. So his offence rated not so much as contempt as attempted contempt. Nor was his plan actually workable, since the laughing gas would have been too diluted by the air-conditioning to reduce the court to its proposed state of giggling hysteria. Hence the crime represented an attempt at attempted contempt, and Balogh was released.

Cornhill Burglary, The

A turning point in the story of safes. Until this 1865 burglary, manufacturers were happy to emblazon their steel 'boxes' with impressive seals, the public were happy to buy them, and thieves happy to prise them open. Afterwards, the industry buttressed its damaged reputation by making genuinely secure safes; thirty-six patents were registered in the following year and a host of new entrepreneurs entered the trade.

The **safe** that started the furore was a Milner's List 3 ('Quadruple Patent, Fraud-resisting, recommended for Cash and Valuables, Doors half-inch, Bodies quarter-inch, lined throughout, unequalled Fire-resisting Chambers') installed in John Walker's jewellers at 63 Cornhill, London, where it held some £6,000 worth of gold watches, diamond rings, chronometers, bracelets and so on.

The strongroom, illuminated by gas all night, had walls lined with iron. The interior was visible from the street through holes in the metal window grilles, and mirrors placed round the safe itself ensured that anyone in its vicinity was highly visible. Yet at start of business on Monday 6 February 1865, the Milner was found with its door burst and the contents vanished. The raiders had entered the building on Saturday and were accidentally locked in by Walker as he left for the weekend. The strongroom's iron walls defeated the gang's first assault, but they attacked from another direction, from the basement, emerged through the floor, and then forced the safe open with wedges.

The press revelled in the story ('The enemy applies the principles of war to the acquisition of gold and jewels') linking it to recent raids in Threadneedle Street, Lombard Street and the Strand, and the gang were soon behind bars after one of their women, animated by spite, shopped her man to the police.

Walker decided to sue Milner's, claiming that their product did not match its 'thief-proof' advertisements. It proved an easy matter to produce the safe in open court and demonstrate its flimsy construction, but Walker's case needed the additional support that only a convincing expert witness could provide. Who better than the cracksman himself? Recently convicted Thomas Caseley was released from Millbank Penitentiary to give evidence, and on 14 February 1866 he testified before the Lord Chief Justice and eight counsel (four for the defendant, four for the plaintiff).

Caseley was charm itself, good-looking, self-assured,

and gifted with 'the most amusing coolness'. He explained how the gang had ducked their heads once every nine minutes to avoid being observed by the regular police patrol.

Their success was assured from the moment the first small metal wedge banged into the crack round the safe's door stayed there. For where a small wedge will go, a bigger will follow.

'You have had some experience in opening safes?' counsel enquired. 'Yes, unhappily I have,' Caseley conceded, and then related how 'two of us purchased two of Milner's safes to experimentalise upon, and we succeeded upon one after seven hours ... the other safe was opened in six hours.' It was all done with wedges and bars of ever-increasing size, until finally the 'alderman' or head-bar could be inserted to rip the door off its hinges. As Caseley left the witness box, the Lord Chief Justice remarked, 'It is a pity you did not turn your talents to better account.'

'It is a pity the police did not let me,' Caseley replied. But for all his *sang-froid* he had a fourteen-year sentence to serve, which perhaps inspired the *Daily Telegraph*'s favourable report of his courtroom performance. It helped launch yet another criminal legend, the insouciant cracksman with 'a keen wit ... a fine dramatic instinct, infinite readiness, surprising fluency; the instinct of an actor for effect'.

Walker lost his case despite Caseley's evidence. Nevertheless, public awareness grew that existing safes were not, in fact, safe. And so the modern security industry was born.

See also **Gutshot**

Corruption

There have been corrupt police as long as there have been police, and few more corrupt than Charles Becker. Given control of New York's Special Squad Number One, charged with cleaning up prostitution, graft and gambling, Becker cleaned up, charging 25 cents on every criminal dollar. He was arrested for the murder of Herman 'Beansie' Rosenthal when his henchman, 'Billiard Ball' Jack Rose, landed in jail for the job and Becker failed to secure his release. Billiard Ball sang, and Becker was electrocuted on 7 July 1915.

Chicago was always something special. In the words of Alderman Robert Merriam: 'Chicago is unique. It is the only completely corrupt city in America.' By the mid-1920s the Capone–Torrio gang were doling out $30,000 dollars a week in bribes, mostly paid over the counter on Fridays to an orderly queue of minor government officials, **Prohibition agents** and policemen. Further up the scale the emoluments were higher. Capone is believed to have contributed $250,000 to the election campaign of *laissez-faire* Mayor Big Bill Thompson; and Morgan Collins, police chief from 1923 to 1927, refused $1,000 a day for looking the other way. Despite such setbacks, during Thompson's three terms as Mayor it was Capone and Torrio who controlled Chicago and Cook County's machinery of government.

Another Chicago gang, the Terrible Gennas, ran a Prohibition warehouse at 1022 Taylor Street conveniently situated just four blocks from the Maxwell Street police station. Their business made $150,000 clear a week. Eventually the government extracted a twenty-five-page affidavit from the warehouse manager describing how the premises had run unmolested for years, operating heavy trucks round the clock except during the occasional raid. Police visits were notified in advance, generally in writing, and 'the entire ... enterprise was done with the full knowledge, consent and approval of the law'. Liquor shipments through hostile gang territory merited a prearranged police escort.

By April 1925 the Gennas' bill for police protection money reached $6,500 a month; as a supplementary inducement, alcohol was available to the force at bargain rates. Some 400 uniformed police attended the warehouse each month together with numerous representatives from the State Attorney's office. To prevent fraudulent claims for protection by unallocated personnel, each week the Maxwell Street station submitted a written list of the accredited officers together with a note of their individual star numbers and the amount due; policemen collecting their wages presented their numbered star as identification.

The Gennas' pay-outs were logged in a ledger (subsequently captured) naming the guilty men, but this evidence disappeared after falling into police hands following one of the Anselmi and Scalise trials. No fewer than 187 police were transferred from the Maxwell Street station, but otherwise no action was taken.

Corruption extended to the judiciary. An undated story has a reporter mid-interview with Capone when the gangster learned that one of his men had been arraigned in court. Capone telephoned the offending judge and shouted: 'I thought I told you to release that fellow.'

More recently, a striking example of corruption comes from Mae Sai in Thailand's **'Golden Triangle'**. The town boasts one main street and a single dirt road. The official salary of the Chief of Police is $100 a month; the job can be bought from the local council for $40,000 down together with monthly 'refreshers' pitched at around $12,000. This is significantly less than the backhanders from the heroin traffickers for turning a blind eye; the dusty border town consists mostly of an unbroken line of banks.

See also **Oaths, West Midlands Serious Crime Squad**

Courtesy

The hallmark of the crack English **highwayman**. He did not rob; he collected.

A typical report, from the *Birmingham Gazette* of 6 May 1751, describes a highwayman who behaved 'very civilly to the passengers, told them that he was a stranger in distress, and hoped that they would contribute to his assistance. Each passenger gave him something, to the amount of about £4, with which he was mighty well satisfied, but he returned some half-pence, saying that he never took copper. He warned them that there were two other collectors on the road, but he would see them out of danger, which he did, and begged that they would not at their next inn mention the robbery nor appear against him if he should be taken up hereafter.'

Similar acts of gentility are so widely reported that they must have had a basis in reality. But courtesy ran only skin-deep and amounted to little more than not shooting those who put up no resistance. Outside this convention, and even within it, all was brutality.

The pick of present-day *mafiosi* observe similarly stringent double standards. Sicily's Salvatore 'the beast' Riina, finally arrested in January 1993 after twenty-three years on the run, seemed the embodiment of soft-spoken Old World courtesy. Prosecutors were impressed by the deferential way he rose to his feet whenever they entered the courtroom, and associates recall him weeping as he mused on his **mother**'s early hardships. A good family man, at funerals he reduced hardened mourners to tears with

An idealised version of Old Mob (Thomas Sympson) robbing the Duchess of Portsmouth

his eulogies of those whose assassinations he had blessed, and, as an informer from the Catania Mafia told the police, 'His philosophy is "If someone's finger is hurt, it's better to be safe and cut off his arm."'

Court of Appeal

Not established in Britain until 1907. Until then a condemned man's only hope was to ask the King for a pardon; some monarchs, George III among them, took the Royal Prerogative of **Mercy** very seriously. The 1901 case of Adolph Beck highlighted the need for change.

Beck suffered the misfortune of a criminal lookalike; but since the other man preyed on women, the fact that Beck's double had been circumcised was well established. Beck was uncircumcised, but this conclusive distinction did not suffice to end his seven-year sentence. Public disquiet after Beck's second arrest in 1901 for the misdeeds of his near-twin culminated in the establishment of a court of last resort.

Sadly the first judgment to be overturned by the Court of Appeal protected not the innocent but the guilty. On 21 August 1911 Charles Ellsome, a real low-lifer, stabbed his girl Rose Pender to death. She worked as a whore; he was her pimp, and she left him for an Italian.

Ellsome gave a detailed account of the killing to a friend, the thief Jack Fletcher, and was later arrested. Tried during an afternoon session at the Old Bailey, Ellsome was quite properly found guilty and sentenced to death. But the condemned man appealed on a point of law. Since Fletcher was a thief, he was a questionable witness; his statements needed corroboration. In the summing-up, the judge pointed out that Fletcher's story had never varied: there were no inconsistencies between his initial statements to the police and his evidence in the dock. This constituted internal corroboration.

But Fletcher's initial statements had never been put in evidence at the Old Bailey. True, Fletcher had not wavered from his story but this had not been *proved in court*. A surprised Ellsome had his conviction quashed. Traumatised by the experience, the Court of Appeal allowed a further twenty years to pass before overturning another murder conviction. On 9 January 1923 even the wretched Edith **Thompson** had to swing, condemned for little more than her immoral role in what the Court's President characterised – irrelevantly – as a 'squalid and rather indecent case of lust and adultery'.

This resilient tradition has been maintained more or less intact, and the recent British flood of overturned convictions – the Birmingham Six, the Guildford Four, the Darvell Brothers, Judith Ward, Stefan Kiszkow, the Cardiff Three, the Broadwater Three, the Maguire Seven and Jacqueline Fletcher – may well prove shortlived.

The Court of Appeal's primary function is to uphold British justice. This could explain the February 1993 decision of the Home Secretary, himself a member of the Bar, to uphold the Bar's reputation by refusing leave to appeal in the Carl Bridgewater case. As with other miscarriages of justice, it had been patently obvious for years to anyone who studied the facts that the accused were innocent of Carl's murder, with the additional twist that this particular crime had been committed by someone else who was identifiable.

Carl Bridgewater was a newspaper boy who died from a shotgun blast to the head at Yew Tree Farm on 19 September 1978. Supposedly he interrupted a burglary. A petty thief, Pat Molloy, admitted to being upstairs in the house at the time of the shooting, and three other men – James Robinson, Michael Hickey and his cousin Vincent Hickey – also earned lengthy sentences almost entirely on the strength of Molloy's brief confession, beaten out of him by a corrupt police officer, now deceased, Detective Constable John Perkins of the West Midlands Serious Crime Squad. Molloy withdrew the confession as soon as he was allowed to see a lawyer, and the absurd document was believed by no one, including the Home Office's own expert, Eric Sheppard. Nevertheless it was far and away the prosecution's strongest evidence, and at the trial Molloy was advised to stick to his confession, in the hope of receiving a sentence for manslaughter, rather than recant and risk the stiffer penalty for murder.

James Robinson became involved because Vincent Hickey traded the 'information' in the hope of obtaining bail. A prison officer named Gibson came forward with convincing evidence (obtained in conversation with a prisoner) that the only eye-witness against Robinson was lying.

According to the then Home Secretary, 'Other prison officers do not support Gibson's version of events.' But as Gibson makes clear, no one else was within earshot. Similarly, Michael Hickey was convicted because his cousin Vincent Hickey was found guilty. Why? Because of Molloy's bogus confession, which meant that Vincent's alibi – that he spent the afternoon with his cousin Michael – must be false, and since, however, Vincent *had* spent the afternoon with Michael, then Michael must have spent the afternoon with Vincent. So he must be guilty too.

A long campaign to clear the names of the 'Bridgewater Four' led to a decision in July 1997 by three judges of the Court of Appeal to quash the convictions of the Hickeys, Robinson and Molloy, who had died in prison in 1981. They ruled that the four men had been denied a fair trial because Staffordshire Police fabricated evidence to force Molloy to confess. The judges added that while there was evidence of Vincent Hickey's involvement in the murder on which a jury 'could convict', he should be freed because his original trial was unfair.

See also **Trousers**, **Virtual reality**

Crack

So called after the snap, popple and crack that cocaine 'rocks' make as they burn. It takes six seconds for the body to respond, as chemicals swoosh into the brain's reward centre where pleasure is registered. Thanks to the influx of dopamine and noradrenaline it registers a great deal.

But each hit lasts only a few minutes, and at four hits a rock the whole trip is over in a quarter of an hour, with the user just £20 short (or $5 in the US, or 25 cents in the West Indies) of paradise by doing it all over again. Addicts become unusually venomous in pursuit of their next hit, and when they have had that one, feel like another. Heroin can dampen the pangs of the aftermath.

In Britain, the users' craving spawns petty crime; the inter-dealer violence leads to murder. In the 1992 words of Detective Inspector Francis Sole of Britain's Crack Intelligence Unit: 'In most Metropolitan Police murder and serious crime investigations in the past year, crack has been involved.'

Ordinary dealers can make £2,000 a week, and this sort of money needs guns for protection. The distribution networks, generally controlled by Jamaican **gangs** – 'Yardies' – teeter on the edge of small wars as the epidemic takes root in the inner cities. London's Notting Hill is the home of an estimated 800 crack addicts.

In America, the writer Thulani Davis, discussing black urban violence after the 1992 Los Angeles riots, underscored the drug's corrosive nature. 'The crucially destructive factor was introduced in the Eighties,' she said, 'when crack appeared in black communities. It's one of the worst things that ever happened, because women take it. Mothers ceased to be nurturers and carers, which led to a generation of children receiving no socialisation. Enormous numbers of homeless children are now growing up in our cities exactly as though they were orphans, completely disenfranchised people.' In Britain too, recent studies show that the great majority for whom crack is the primary drug of dependence are black.

Here is a representative selection of what the habit means at street level, taken from 1992 verbatim reportage by American journalists Tim Wells and William Triplett. From a pusher: 'When I first started dealing heroin back in 1978 there wasn't so much unnecessary violence. But these days the young kids out hustling don't understand that. They don't understand the importance of fear. The only things they care about are gold chains and fancy cars. If some dude smokes up some dealer's money, the dealer don't go back with a baseball bat and put fear in the dude. He thinks he's got to save face, so he goes straight back with his gun and kills the dude straight off the top.'

And an addict: 'After four or five months of heavy crack use, I didn't even look like a human being. I lost a lot of weight and my eyes looked all bloodshot and wired out. I looked like a person off the streets. My boyfriend would let me have all the crack I wanted, but he wasn't nice to me anymore. Him and his friends would beat me and rape me … They'd tear off my clothes and screw me, with a bunch of people in the room.'

One of the problems with cocaine is its plethora of production areas and distribution points. Unlike the heroin trade, largely in the hands of organised crime, crack-dealing is open to all-comers, giving rise to the phenomenon of disorganised crime, a free-for-all with a commensurate incidence of random violence.

In the panic which followed the 1989 visit of San Francisco detective Robert Stutman, who issued dire warnings about the new drug wave at a police conference, the British set up a National Crack Squad. But it had little success. Crack can be made from cocaine in an ordinary kitchen with a bit of baking soda; it was as if the authorities were trying to stamp out tea-drinking, but not tea.

See also **Kids**, **Crack**

Craig and Bentley

To the layman, the case of Craig and Bentley has always represented the apotheosis of unreason. The fatal words 'Let him have it, Chris' have passed into British popular history.

On the night of 2 November 1952, Christopher Craig and Derek Bentley broke into the premises of Barlow and Parker in London's Tamworth Road and climbed on to the warehouse roof. Then the police arrived. Detective-Constable Fairfax shinned up a vent pipe and succeeded in nabbing Bentley on the roof. Meanwhile Craig pulled out a revolver and opened fire. In Fairfax's statement: 'Craig was then on the westerly side of the stack. Bentley broke away from me and as he did so, he shouted "Let him have it, Chris." There was a loud report and something hit my shoulder.'

Christopher Craig at sixteen – too young to swing

His accomplice, Derek Bentley, a few days before arrest

So one policeman was down. Moments later, PC Sydney Miles burst on to the roof. Craig continued firing and Miles collapsed forwards, dead, hit in the forehead. Then the cornered Craig jumped from the roof, waking up three days later in hospital. A policeman at his bedside noted down his first words: 'If I hadn't cut a bit off the barrel of my gun I would probably have killed a lot more policemen. That night I was out to kill.'

Murder then ranked as a capital offence. Craig was only sixteen – too young to hang. But Bentley was old enough. And under the legal principle of 'joint ventures' he was as guilty as Craig. In the words of the indictment: 'Bentley incited Craig to begin the shooting and, although technically under arrest… was party to that murder and equally responsible in law.' So Craig, who had committed the murder, received a prison sentence; and Bentley, who had not, swung on 28 January 1953, while a hostile crowd battled at the prison gates, tearing down the Notice of Death as it was posted.

By then it was apparent that Bentley was a sub-normal with an IQ of 66. Born in 1933, he had fallen off a lorry at the age of four and suffered periodic epileptic fits thereafter. He remained illiterate until the end of his days, thinking his first name was spelt 'Derk', and his deputy head teacher at Norbury Manor uncharitably described him as 'an utterly worthless piece of humanity'.

Craig and Bentley's trial was steamrollered through by Lord Chief Justice Goddard, who in effect acted for the prosecution. Puzzling discrepancies in the evidence were dismissed as irrelevant, and, in 1991, the publication of John Parris's *Scapegoat* put forward a troubling new scenario.

According to Parris, Craig did not shoot PC Sydney Miles. He was shot by the police. Of the three officers said to have witnessed the incident – Fairfax, MacDonald and Harrison – two could hardly have seen what transpired, one because it was dark and he was too far away, if he was there at all, and the other because it is extremely unlikely that he ever reached the top of the roof. A fourth police officer, Claud Pain, actually on the roof, was never officially admitted as present.

Officer Fairfax did climb to the top where – as he testified – he collared Bentley. They sheltered together behind the skylights as Craig loosed off sporadic shots from his revolver. Then the officer persuaded Bentley to help make Craig surrender. Bentley warily left his shelter and came within six feet of Craig. 'For Christ's sake, Chris,' he pleaded, 'what's got into you?' He repeated this a number of times, and started edging forwards. 'Fuck off, otherwise I'll shoot you too,' said Craig. Bentley scampered back to Fairfax and safety.

Meanwhile the local police station summoned two Scotland Yard marksmen with rifles. They took up position opposite on the roof of 26 Tamworth Road while Craig went on firing haphazardly. But it was pitch-dark, with no one in clear view for him to fire at, even if he wanted to. Fairfax was only hit by a ricochet, very possibly aimed wide, the bullet stopped by his braces. After a total of six rounds Craig's gun ran out of ammunition. He pulled the trigger four more times, the hammer falling on an empty chamber. 'See, it's empty,' he shouted.

At that moment the police reinforcements appeared, bursting on to the roof through an internal staircase. First up was PC Miles, immediately drilled clean through the forehead by the marksmen on the far side of the street. More shots rang out, and Craig threw himself over the parapet in a bid to escape.

That night the shocked and angry police cobbled together Bentley's confession, forging his signature a total of six times. Over the ensuing days the officers concocted a complete scenario for the gunfight, agreeing who had been where and seen and heard what. In particular, they invented the shout 'Let him have it, Chris' to put a noose round Bentley's neck in revenge for their colleague's death.

These damning words, designed to be legally watertight, had already been tested in court – in the case of *R v. Appelby* which featured in the force's standard bible *Moriarty's Police Law*. *Appelby* set an exact precedent, where a burglar captured by the police urged his mate, still at liberty, to shoot the arresting officer. He did, and the first burglar swung for his pains. The words that hanged him were 'Let him have it', and there was no reason why they should not hang Bentley too.

At the trial, Bentley elected to run a truly fatuous defence, claiming that he had simply popped out that evening for a bus-ride and had no intention of breaking or entering anything. He was rightly regarded as a stupid liar. Out of loyalty he kept quiet about his attempt to disarm Craig.

More important, Craig never disputed that he killed PC Miles. Why should he? He had been firing away, and there was the dead body. True, Craig felt puzzled by this turn of events, later saying, 'What I've never been able to understand is how I shot him between the eyes when he was facing away from me and was going the other way.'

The truth is that Craig could only have fired six rounds. According to Parris's computations, the fatal shot was the seventh one heard, after which there were three or four more shots. Craig's gun was wildly inaccurate, almost incapable of hitting anyone intentionally. When he sawed off the barrel to a stub, he also removed the sights. His ammunition did not fit: he used .45 calibre bullets for a .455 gun. On test, the deflection worked out at six feet either way over a range of thirteen yards.

PC Miles was hit in the head, the bullet entering one side and exiting the other. If fired by Craig this should have shattered the glass panel in the door behind Miles as he emerged on to the roof. But it remained intact. Further, Miles could only have been shot in the forehead if he was looking left as he was turning right. More likely, he looked right and turned right. In this case he could have been shot in the front of the head from the opposite direction, from Tamworth Road, with the expended rounds lodging in the woodwork round the door frame.

Marks were later found, but any bullets had been removed. Further, the best evidence now available is that Miles's head-wound came from .32 to .38 calibre ammunition. Police sharpshooters were issued with .32s.

At the time, the Lord Chief Justice advised against clemency for Bentley. Forty years later the Home Secretary, Kenneth Clarke, rejected a posthumous pardon on the grounds that the jury's verdict was correct on the evidence *then* available.

In July 1998, after forty-six years, the Court of Appeal finally quashed Bentley's conviction. Craig, who had been released in 1962, expressed his regret for his crime and his relief at the verdict.

Crank, The

The crank was introduced to British prisons along with the **Separate System** during the mid-nineteenth century. This pernicious device ranks as an early feat of miniaturisation, enabling prisoners to be stationed outside a small **treadwheel** instead of inside a large one.

The Victorians implemented the principle that convicts needed the moral uplift of work by making them turn a heavy handle attached to a drum-shaped container installed in their cells. The bottom of this inspiring machine – known as a 'crank' – was filled with sand, and the handle rotated an internal system of scoops. These raised the sand to the top of the drum. When the sand reached the top, it fell down to the bottom.

The crank's pressure was adjustable, with a normal setting of around twelve pounds, and a dial in front of the drum registered the number of rotations. A convict failing to meet his target was liable to further punishment, a system open to sadistic abuse. At a rough guess, the standard quota of 10,000 rotations a day took nine hours based on a notional three seconds a turn. Keener staff insisted on prisoners 'earning' their food by demanding, say, 2,000 turns before breakfast, and a Royal Commission in the 1870s discovered an inmate who had qualified for only nine meals in twenty-one days.

The crank featured an adjustable screw to make the job easier or, more likely, harder. By this means the prisoner could be 'wound up' by the 'screws'.

Unlike the treadwheel, the crank had no endproduct. Its use was banned in 1898.

See also **Prison**

Crime passionel

In France, disposing of one's lover or spouse in a fit of passion can constitute a defence to the charge of murder. The court may reduce the offence to manslaughter or, in especially sentimental circumstances, direct an acquittal.

On 12 August 1952 Yvonne Chevalier, the country wife of a rising political star, shot her unfaithful husband Pierre four times with a 7.65mm Mab automatic. It was his first day as a Minister.

Pierre represented something of a paragon, a real French war hero. A doctor by day, by night he ran the local Resistance, leading the attack on the Germans which expelled them from his native Orléans. And now he had been gunned down by his cloddish peasant wife! Feeling ran so high that she had to be tried in distant Rheims. But the public mood changed on hearing Yvonne's side of the story.

Yvonne Chevalier

Yvonne recounted how her husband had long refused to share the marriage bed; how he flaunted his relationship with his mistress, the glamorous Jeanne Perreau; how he rebuffed her time and again at public receptions, refused to see her when she visited him at work, suggested that she take a lover, reacted indifferently to her attempted suicide and finally announced that he was leaving to marry his mistress. 'And you can remain in your own filth,' he shouted, 'I'm a Minister.' On this last occasion, the distraught Yvonne produced the Mab automatic and waved it in his face, threatening to end her life there and then. 'Go ahead,' Pierre replied. 'It will be the first sensible thing you've done in your life.'

'I'm serious,' cried Yvonne. 'Well,' said Pierre, 'for God's sake kill yourself, but wait until I've gone.' Then she shot him four times. Meanwhile her young son, Mathieu, started crying downstairs. Yvonne went down to soothe the child, handed him over to the maid and then returned upstairs where, in a fit of passion, she shot her husband again.

With a defence like this, the prosecution did not dare ask for a penalty of longer than two years. But the French jury found Yvonne innocent of everything, and she left the court to cheers.

British courts are beginning to invoke the 'slow burn' concept of provocation in an effort to mitigate the sentences of women driven to kill their husbands. For a historical yardstick, the Chevalier case comes from the era when the British could find no alternative to condemning Ruth **Ellis**, who shot her lover, to be hanged by the neck until dead.

See also **Sex discrimination**

Criminals

The British judiciary still draws a fairly clear distinction between crime and criminals. A member of the middle classes can commit a crime, but this does not make him a criminal *per se*. Belonging to the right class can diminish the gravity of an offence, and hence the social system now performs the same function as the old **Benefit of Clergy**, of which it is a vestigial relic.

Thus in January 1992, David Vaughan, a former merchant banker with Kleinwort Benson, was convicted on eighteen charges of embezzling a total of £455,280 from his employers. The most he took at one time was £230,000; normally it went in dribs and drabs, a thousand here and a thousand there, and the theft came to light soon after he left for early retirement.

Passing sentence at Knightsbridge Crown Court, Judge Christopher Compton pointed out that the money had not been squandered on loose living; rather, it was *invested* in a bigger and better home so that his family could maintain a standard of living for which Vaughan had insufficient income. It was true that none of the funds had been recovered, but on the plus side the defendant was a devout Christian. In the circumstances, a suspended sentence seemed appropriate, and a relieved Mrs Vaughan said, 'Things are going to be very difficult for us now', as her husband left the court a free man, thereby irritating hundreds of prisoners serving lengthy sentences for robbing parking meters or stealing bicycles.

This does not imply one law for the rich and another for the poor. Although the distinction between a course of fraud undertaken to support one's family in a style to which they are not accustomed, as against a systematic career in theft aimed at unjust enrichment, might be a tricky one, the fact is that some men prey on society whereas others deserve to be rescued by it.

From the defendant's point of view, the crux is a successful presentation of the offence as an extraordinary aberration. From this perspective, Vaughan's case is a creditable exercise in damage-limitation. Probably the Methodist minister came closest to the mark: 'I have never at any time doubted Vaughan's honesty and this is completely out of character.'

In other words, Vaughan may have committed a crime, but he was very far from being a criminal. Full-blown *mafiosi* feel the same, regarding hoodlums working outside the family as crooks and bums.

Crippen, Hawley Harvey (1862–1910)

Sometimes a murder attains the status of a coat peg on which a generation hangs its sense of dread and love of morbidity. For the British, it was Sutcliffe in 1970s, Brady and Hindley in the 1960s, Christie in the 1950s, Jack the Ripper in the preceding century and Hawley Harvey Crippen in between.

Crippen poisoned his wife with hyoscine on 1

February 1910, buried her in the basement, told their friends that she had left him, took up with his mistress, successfully fobbed off the police, lost his nerve, fled to America, was caught, tried and executed.

The case exemplifies the difference between crime and violence. A 'good' murder – of the old–fashioned kind – towers above the run of juvenile muggings, 'drive-bys', or drunken brawls that end in death. Crippen's full story displays the compact drama of a play, unfolding from early suspicions, via the sensational discovery of the body, to the attempted escape ended by the technological marvel of wireless telegraphy. There were unusual names, an unfamiliar poison, a background of domestic duplicity supported by a large cast of secondary characters, a horrible act of dismemberment, an extended charade of concealment, a disguise, and the clash of experts in court, culminating in Crippen's extinction by the hangman's noose. If the entertainment ever seemed base, Crippen's unfailing love for his mistress redeemed it. He was buried holding her photograph and surrounded by her love letters.

Many killings afford only the ephemeral interest of a grisly death or a novel weapon, but Crippen ran the full five acts, absorbing the nation for half a year. The transatlantic pursuit in July 1910 generated such excitement that newspapers carried diagrams each day showing Inspector Dew's *SS Laurentic* gaining on the fugitives' *SS Montrose* at three and a half knots an hour. The chase elevated readers to the status of gods, granting them crucial information denied to the human participants. Cut off at sea and disguised as 'the Robinsons', the Crippens calmly dined at the Captain's table on board the *Montrose*, unaware of their status as objects of international fascination over whom hung the sword of retribution.

No one would remember Crippen had he been arrested at his home, or had he fled and disappeared, or had he lacked the complication of a lover. By his hanging on 23 November 1910, the impedimenta of Edwardian society were laid out for public dissection: love and marriage, home, hypocrisy, ambition, the mistress, the stage, music halls and medicine, the loyal friends, the murderer's fatal mistake, Scotland Yard, detectives, ocean liners, disguises, telegrams, courtroom drama and Justice.

Crippen's was thus a murder of quality, and the better the story is told the more intriguing it becomes, hinging on the finer social niceties. It can be argued,

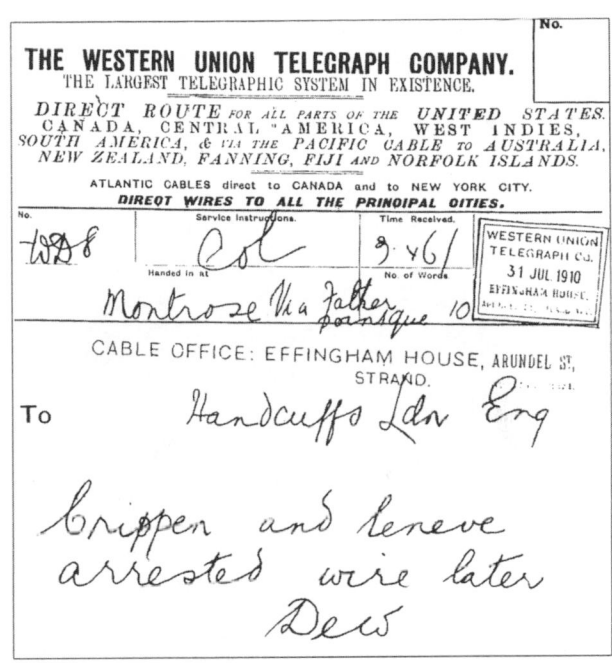

for instance, that his wife Cora was vain on the compelling grounds that she had the house redecorated in shades of pink to better set off her hair, dyed blonde from its natural raven black. But perhaps this was no act of premeditated colour-coordination. Perhaps she just liked pink. But this might suggest poor taste. The reader is willy-nilly caught up in arcane considerations of snobbery. Did Cora ask their lodgers to leave because they disturbed her gentleman-callers? Or because she had aspirations to improve her social standing? And is such a desire compatible with modesty and good sense?

With Crippen, the major actors were fully rounded characters. There are many ways to play their parts. The line adopted by the press was to cast Crippen as the brutal 'cellar murderer', an inhuman monster who disposed of his wife, a flamboyant actress, for the love of his mistress, the beautiful Ethel Le Neve. Closer scrutiny suggests that Crippen was an insignificant little man encumbered by a brassy wife who pretended to have been a music-hall favourite. Behind this version is the kindly, mild-mannered doctor, a model of generosity yoked to a hysterical bully who squandered his money on broken dreams and taunted him with a succession of lovers. This Crippen set the table for their lodgers' breakfasts before going to work while his wife lay in bed, planning her day's flirtations. Here, Ethel is a quiet, modest girl, first Crippen's confidante and then, after seven demure years, his lover.

Then there is Crippen the Quack, salesman for the

Young Ethel Le Neve, briefly the most romanticised woman in the world, wearing a fine hat

Munyon Homoeopathic Home Remedy Co., whose remedies included a nostrum for piles. He was fired when it emerged that he managed a music-hall singer – his wife – and he drifted into work as a bogus ear specialist notable for his filthy equipment and vulgar way of dressing. His firm went into liquidation after a conviction for medical negligence for the death of a locksmith. Crippen acquired the bankrupt stock, and set up in business on his own account with Ethel as his secretary.

The real name of this Ethel was Ethel Neave, who considered Ethel Le Neve more romantic. Her hypochondria earned her the nickname of 'Not very well thank you'. She hated her father, and grew up as

a whining child almost continuously afflicted by delusional bouts of neuralgia, anaemia, headaches and fibrositis. Her biographer brands her as a pathological liar, telling fibs 'from sheer perversity – in fact she seemed incapable of telling the truth'.

Her rival, Cora Crippen, born Kunigunde Mackamotzki, trod the boards under the stage name of Belle Ellmore, by her mid-thirties best described as a monument to corsetry. In her twenties Crippen was content to pay theatres to allow Cora to appear, writers to compose her songs and costumiers to dress her. His support extended to dispensing real £5 notes when Cora's role required her to hold stage money.

As a performer Cora may not have been such a disaster. Producer Clarkson Rose adjudged her perfectly competent: 'She was not a top-rank artist, but, in her way, not bad – a blowsy, florid type of serio', and to the end Crippen funded expensive *toilettes* to fit her for the role of Honorary Treasurer to the Music Hall Ladies' Guild. But Cora drank to excess, adorned the parlour walls with photographs of her lover and was caught in bed with a lodger.

The trial was clear cut, since the quixotic Crippen elected to protect Ethel by denying that his wife had died. He claimed that the body in the basement belonged to someone else, deposited there by a former tenant who somehow included Crippen's pyjama tops in the consignment. This defence introduced a new player into the drama – forensic science – and with it a new public figure, the young pathologist Bernard **Spilsbury**, whose calm, authoritative manner speedily demonstrated that a fragment of skin under the coal cellar floor was derived from a stomach, not a thigh, and that its crease was not a fold but a scar, identical to one that disfigured Cora's stomach. Spilsbury thus put a name to a body that lacked a head, fingers and sexual organs. He became a household name and remained so for decades.

Ethel Le Neve proved no less **durable**. She survived until 1967, but in a different guise. After the trial, briefly the most famous woman in the world, she slipped away to Toronto and changed her name to Harvey before slinking back into Britain, where she took work at Hampton's furniture store near Trafalgar Square. She married a bookkeeper, Stanley Smith, settled down in east Croydon and produced two children, Bob and Nina.

Her offspring had no inkling of their mother's tumultuous past until the seventy-fifth anniversary of the trial in 1985. Six years later they were interviewed for BBC radio; Ethel was described by her daughter as 'straitlaced' and 'perfectly ordinary', and by her son as an 'ordinary housewife sewing on buttons'. He dimly realised that at some stage his mother had 'been' to Canada, but Ethel was too cagey to acknowledge even her assumed name and told her daughter, who once found a book inscribed 'E. Harvey', that it belonged to a friend.

One striking casualty of the case was Cora's body. Spilsbury's notes only record discovering the 'medical organs of the chest and abdomen removed in one mass. Four large pieces of skin and muscle, one from the lower abdomen with old operation scar, four inches long – broader at lower end.' Of the rest – the head, the limbs and bones – from which these components had been excised, there was no trace.

Crown Jewels

The Crown Jewels of England were stolen by the Irishman Colonel Thomas Blood. Born in 1618, the son of a blacksmith, Blood fought with the Parliamentarians in the English Civil War, gaining forfeited estates to the tune of £500 a year. These were reappropriated under the Restoration, confirming his views on the monarchy.

After a series of abortive plots, in 1671 the Colonel disguised himself as a parson and befriended the elderly Mr Edwards, keeper of the Crown Jewels in the Tower of London. Mr Edwards had a lovely daughter, and Blood offered his 'nephew's' hand in marriage. But on 9 May, instead of effecting the promised introduction, Blood gagged the keeper, hit him on the head with a mallet and then ran him through with a sword. Edwards nearly died.

Meanwhile Blood crushed the crown of England flat so that it fitted under his cloak. When the alarm was raised, his accomplices decided to leave the sceptre behind – it took too long to file in half. But the golden orb, symbol of sovereignty, was thrust down a robber's trousers, where it made running difficult. So the orb too was relinquished, the thief melting into the crowd. Next, the squashed crown fell out of Blood's cloak as he rode off

Apprehended in a Hampshire pub, the 'Crown and Cushion', Blood was sent back to the Tower in chains. There he refused to bandy words with anyone except his sovereign. Charles II responded, visiting the prisoner, and subsequently exercised clemency to restore his Irish estates. After release, Colonel Blood remained influential at court, where he continued plotting and scheming until his death in 1680.

Across St George's Channel, the Irish Crown Jewels faded away in July 1907. It soon emerged that the thief had taken an impression of the key to the Dublin Castle safe held by Sir Arthur Vicars, Ulster King of Arms. The most likely culprit was a member of Sir Arthur's staff, Frank Shackleton, Herald of Dublin, a homosexual and a close friend of the Duke of Argyll, King Edward VII's brother-in-law.

The royal connection threatened the throne with scandal and the investigation was cut short, but not before it emerged that Shackleton's lover, Captain Richard Gorges, had been present when a joke was played on Sir Arthur a few weeks before. Sir Arthur drank himself unconscious at a party in the castle, and a friend took his key ring and removed the Crown Jewels as a prank, replacing them on his desk the following morning. Omitting this final stage, Gorges gained access with a key furnished by Shackleton on or about the night of 5 July.

Despite a £1,000 reward, the Insignia of the Order of St Patrick were never recovered. Shackleton was later imprisoned for fraud and died in disgrace, Gorges shot a policeman and outlived his sentence in Dartmoor to die in the 1950s, and Sir Arthur was relieved of his post and killed by the IRA in 1921.

Cuthbert, Cyril (d. 1984)

Police constable from Devon, in charge of the station pay ledger, who became the reluctant founder of Scotland Yard's forensic science laboratory.

For a constable, Cuthbert had an unusual background: an uncompleted medical training and the rudiments of dentistry, rounded off by evening classes in chemistry. On joining the police he developed an interest in criminal medicine, eventually spending half his weekly wages on a thirty-five-shilling microscope, keeping it at home to avoid official reprimands about time-wasting. But his superiors, mindful of his hobby, relegated Cuthbert to the backwater of the Criminal Records Office. Nothing daunted, Cuthbert persisted in helping out his colleagues with their more difficult cases.

Matters came to a head in the 1930s when the Assistant Commissioner, Sir Norman Kendall, received a request for Cuthbert to give evidence in court, referring to him as Cuthbert 'of the Metropolitan Police Laboratory'. Kendall felt outraged by the presumption; there was no police laboratory. He refused permission, but in the end Cuthbert was subpoenaed. By this stage Cuthbert would have left the force had he been able to find another job. But at the trial his well-presented evidence secured a conviction, and his work – reprimanded by Kendall – was commended to the attention of the Police Commissioner, Lord Trenchard.

Trenchard, intrigued to hear of his force's exciting new facility, insisted on a personal tour of inspection. In a panic Cuthbert collected up all his odds and ends, spreading them out in one of the photographic department's cupboards. For added authenticity he borrowed a white coat from a hospital, and Trenchard was so alarmed by this pitiful display that he forced through the establishment of a proper, well-funded facility with lecture halls, dark-rooms and laboratories. A promoted Cuthbert supervised the installation of the apparatus, including microscopes, epidiascope, centrifugal separator, X-ray apparatus, one of the latest reversion spectroscopes and so on.

The new building was opened on 10 April 1935 to highly favourable press comment. But the police themselves were less enthusiastic. 'For the first ten years the lab never really prospered. The "Old Guard" at Scotland Yard were suspicious,' the laboratory's fourth director, Dr Hamish Walls, recollected in 1976. This complaint was repeated in 1987 by the retiring director, Dr Raymond Williams, who considered that the value of forensic science had never been fully acknowledged by the Home Office.

Cutpurse, Moll (c. 1584–1659)

Also known as Mary Frith and Mary Markham, a startling underworld figure so far ahead of her time it is surprising that her life has not been filmed. She was the first bisexual, cross-dressing, pipe-smoking, entrepreneurial highwaywoman, and she may also have been England's first professional actress. Her voice alone resonated so powerfully that it was capable of 'drowning all the city'.

The Roaring Girle.
OR
Moll Cut-Purse.

As it hath lately beene Acted on the Fortune-stage by the Prince his Players.

Written by T. Middleton and T. Dekkar.

My case is alter'd, I must worke for my liuing.

By the age of 26, Moll had sufficiently progressed from her humble beginnings as a pickpocket for the Jacobean dramatists Middleton and Dekker to pen a play in her honour, *The Roaring Girle*. Rather than lose the profits of thieving to the fences, Moll set up as her own receiver, spending her earnings on a large house staffed by three maids and a footman. Moll's critics maintained that she was so big, strong and ugly that there was no real need for her to disguise herself as a man, and she enjoyed a string of lovers both male and female, becoming the first English woman known to have smoked. Still game at the age of 60, Moll overstepped the mark by robbing General Fairfax on Hounslow Heath, shooting him in the arm, and she had to buy her way out of trouble with a massive £2,000 bribe after being captured at Turnham Green, now an underground station on the District Line.

Otherwise Moll kept her nose clean, with a solitary exception in 1612 when she was compelled to do penance at St Paul's Cross, first bracing herself by drinking six pints of sack and then disturbing divine service in the cathedral with her caterwauling.

She died at the age of 75, doling out handsome bequests to her friends along with the unusual injunction that she be buried upside down ('with her breach pointing upwards'). In the words of the contemporary ditty, 'Here's no attraction your fancy greets. But if her features please not, read her feats.'

D

Dahmer, Jeffrey L. (1960–94)

American serial killer and psychological test-bed showing Man stripped bare of everything that makes existence tolerable. Dahmer's negative posture provided no lover, no friends, no contacts, no job, no interests, no conversation, no hobbies, no sports, no occupation, no money, no prospects and nowhere to live. He thus remained utterly unsocialised, and his cavernous emotional interior progressively degraded, the void filling with phantasmagoria.

Dahmer was born on 21 May 1960 to a troubled marriage between a respectable research chemist and an emotional, self-pitying neurotic. A shy child, he seemed forlorn at school. Animals provided an early interest – snakes, toads, rabbits and fish. He kept a heap of bones (which he called 'fiddlesticks') under his house, and was intrigued to feel the same fiddlesticks inside the live animals he handled. His family moved six times before settling into 4480 West Bath Road, Ohio, in 1968, and at the age of ten he first tried bleaching chicken bones. He spent much of his childhood tucked away in a wooden shed up on the hill, collecting insects in pickle jars and preserving them in formaldehyde. He worked his way up through the animal kingdom, via squirrels and raccoons, to large road-kills, carrying their bodies to the woods where they were left to rot. Then he soused the remains in bleach to clean the bones.

His mother, on tranquillisers, set a family precedent by blotting herself out with drugs, and after a spell of hospitalisation she spent her days at home in bed. Dahmer withdrew into unbreakable isolation. At eleven, he talked in a monotone. He turned into a solitary 'class clown', bleating like a sheep during lessons or acting retarded in shops, and he took to drink and **masturbation**. His grades plummeted. By 16 he was regularly drunk in class, his only friend Jeff Six, the local marijuana supplier. The two were continuously stoned. At 17 Dahmer masturbated three times daily; for stim-ulation he used male magazines, focusing on the models' muscular torsos, daydreaming of strangers who lay passively by his side. Like any consumer of pornography, he related not to the models' personalities but to the beautiful shiny pictures. His other preoccupation was with the insides of animals, and later these interests fused when he used the insides of people as pornography.

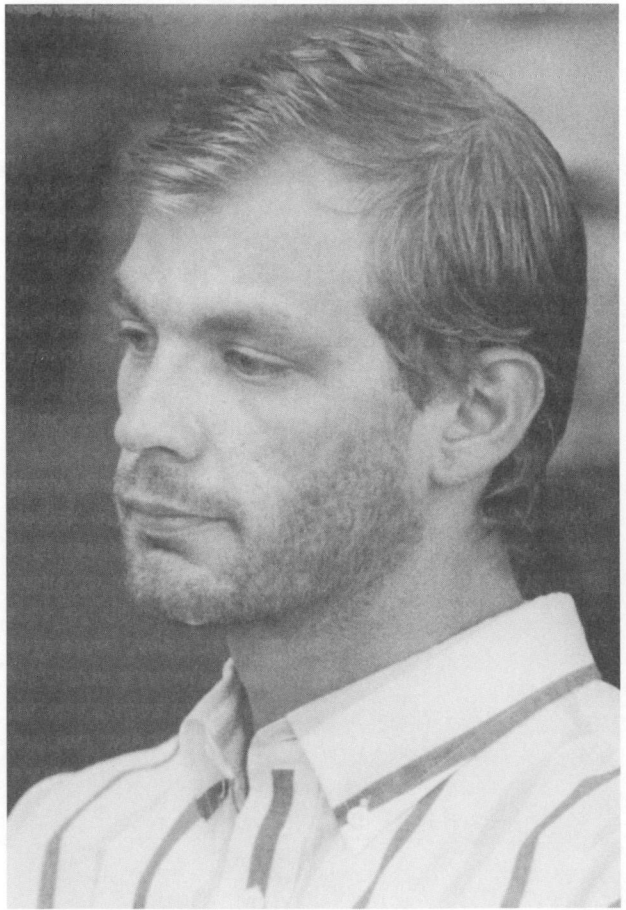

Jeffrey Dahmer, cannibal killer

When Dahmer reached 17, a jogger – an attractive, healthy youth – regularly ran past his house. Dahmer wanted to meet him. Lacking any social skills to detain him, he took a baseball bat and lay in wait, planning to attack as he passed. But the runner never came. The following year his father left home, and on 18 June Dahmer picked up a young hitch-hiker, Stephen Hicks, asked him home and then murdered him rather than allow him to leave. After slitting the body to inspect the innards, Dahmer placed it in some trashbags which he dumped in a nearby ravine.

Thereafter Dahmer renounced life in a brooding descent into self-disgust and withdrawal. His father sent him to Ohio University, where he downed a couple of bottles of whisky a day, never made classes and antagonised his roommates by stacking their furniture in a corner and spreading pizzas over the walls. In December 1978 his despairing father made him enlist as a soldier. But military liquor is half-price and Dahmer drank himself into oblivion, off and on duty. After his discharge in March 1981 he was packed off to his grandmother in West Allis, Wisconsin. Dahmer went to church, read the Bible, and limited his self-abuse to once a week, keeping his cravings at bay, and found work at Milwaukee's Ambrosia Chocolate Factory. But one day in the public library he was handed a note reading 'Meet me in the second level bathroom. I'll give you a blow job.'

Dahmer's veneer of self-control collapsed. His masturbation climbed to four times a day, and he stole a shop mannequin and took it home as a sexual partner. Then he discovered Milwaukee's 'bath-houses' where homosexuals met for anonymous and impersonal sex. But he had difficulty obtaining erections while his partners were awake and, after obtaining sleeping pills on prescription, gave his contacts a heavily doped drink. They passed out for the night; between bouts of masturbation Dahmer put his head to their chest and listened to their heart-beats. But he was banned when an oriental took two days to revive.

So Dahmer searched the obituary columns for a corpse of his own. He attended the funeral of a suitable 18-year-old, and visited the cemetery at night to dig him up. But the ground was frozen. Meanwhile he lived like an automaton, working in order to live in order to work, and an arrest for indecent exposure in September 1986 led to his first psychological assessment. The professionals were unanimous: Dahmer was in a dangerous state, and on 20 November 1987 he killed for the second time. The victim was Steven Tuomi, a black youth he met outside the 219 Club. Dahmer took him to the Ambassador Hotel, offered him a doped drink and woke up the next morning on top of a bloodied body with no recollection of what had happened. He put the corpse in the cupboard, rebooked the room, bought a large suitcase and ferried it by taxi to his grandmother's.

There he stored Tuomi in the basement cellar and dismembered him, keeping the head for two weeks in a blanket on his top shelf. Then he boiled the skull and bleached it. Thereafter Dahmer killed whenever an opportunity presented. His technique hardly varied: first the pick-up – he offered money for sex – then the Irish cream, mixed with coffee and crushed sleeping pills, then the **strangulation**. After the kill he embraced the corpse. In life, contact was harder; as he put it, 'I did my drinking alone, and bar-hopping alone … no one … no one.' Dahmer's next victim was Jamie Doxator. He explained, 'I knew Grandma would be waking up and I still wanted him to stay so I strangled him.' He had anal sex with the corpse, put it in the cellar and went to church. By now he only related to the dead.

Dahmer wanted to keep the heads, and gradually devised the concept of a shrine adorned with bones. Richard Guerrero was killed next, but on 26 September another victim managed to leave before the drugs took effect. The police pressed charges, but their house search missed Guerrero's skull, and Dahmer was found guilty of second-degree sexual assault on 30 January 1989. Before starting his one-year sentence he killed Anthony Sears, storing the body in the upstairs bathroom, mutilating it as a sexual aid and spray-painting the skull.

Dahmer moved into the run-down Oxford Apartments in March 1990. He purchased a long black table and two plastic griffins, laying out the next body on this makeshift altar to take Polaroid snaps. He froze the organs and other preferred items, boiling up the rest in a huge eighty-gallon kettle filled with water and wallpaper stripper, before putting the resulting morass into a large trash container primed with acid. Two weeks later he tipped the slush down the lavatory. This seemed a waste, so the body of Eddie Smith – his next victim – went into the freezer. But it would not dry out properly, and when he tried baking the skull, it exploded. Again, nothing remained.

So Dahmer kept his next victim's head in the fridge, cut up the body, ate some of the flesh, bleached the bones, and tried to reassemble the skeleton. The skull he painted; by now he had three. Of the successors, some he ate in part and one he flayed, hoping to keep the whole skin. But it disintegrated. Normally he slit the bodies from neck to groin, slipped his hands into the chest cavity, and caressed the viscera before having sex with them, either by lowering himself on to the body, or by rubbing himself with the intestines. His Polaroid photospreads became increasingly elaborate; he might lay out the hands, head, and severed genitals in a still life on the kitchen draining board. But the pleasure to be derived from corpses was transitory, and he determined to manufacture '**zombies**' he could keep. He bored through his subsequent captives' skulls and injected fluid into the brain so they would stagger round his apartment in a stupor.

On 19 July Dahmer was sacked from work for absenteeism. By then he showered with two corpses in the tub; there were hearts in the fridge, heads in the freezer, skulls in the filing cabinet, and a body on the bed, crawling with maggots. He was arrested on 23 July after the escape of an intended victim, Tracy **Edwards**.

Dahmer's trial began on 27 January 1992. It seemed clear from the start that he was driven by mental disease and equally clear that he would not be 'let off' as insane. After the verdict Dahmer spoke to the court for the first time. 'Your honour, it is over now,' he said. 'I feel so bad for what I did to those poor families, and I understand their rightful hate ... I take all the blame for what I did ... I have hurt my mother and father and stepmother. I love them all so very much.' Sentenced to a minimum of 900 years, on his first day the prison authorities were inundated by 200 requests for interviews and good wishes from strangers all over the world.

There is a theory that Dahmer's problems originated from a double hernia operation at the age of four, when his abdomen was opened and the doctor rummaged around his insides; the black table on which he laid the bodies of his victims' supposedly mimics the operating table.

Dahmer was murdered in jail in Wisconsin on 28 November 1994, struck on the head with an iron bar by fellow convict Christopher Carver, who explained that he was the Son of God.

Dando, Jill

At 37, Jill Dando was one of the better-known faces on BBC television. As a news, travel and – ironically – crime programme presenter, she offered the public a genial, unaffected, self-evidently good-natured temperament that quickly made her a household name. Then, on the morning of 26 April 1999, she was murdered. Although the crime went unwitnessed, the forensic evidence showed that, as she was entering her west London home, somebody stepped up behind her and fired a single bullet into her head with a silenced pistol.

Naturally there was a public outcry for her killer to be brought to justice, but the London Metropolitan Police investigation ran into an immediate problem: Jill Dando had no enemies and nobody stood to gain from

Jill Dando

Barry George, Jill Dando's killer

gun residue found in Dando's hair. The eleven-person jury found, ten to one, that George was guilty, and the judge sentenced him to life imprisonment.

However, since that conviction, questions have been asked about the case – largely based on circumstantial evidence – brought against George. For example, the only evidence that in any way connected him with the victim was a BBC magazine, found in his flat, that contained a single picture of Jill Dando – hardly, some would say, proof of an obsession. Also, none of the five witnesses could confirm categorically that it was George that they had seen lurking near the victim's flat. In fact, the only conclusive proof was the fragment of chemical that linked George's coat to the murder weapon, which, in 2005, has still not been discovered.

Considering the known pressure the police were working under on the Dando case, some suspect that they simply found a local 'nutter' – Barry George was indisputably obsessed by some celebrities and had a previous police record for sexual violence against women – and planted the key piece of evidence in his coat pocket. This certainly was the line taken in George's appeal against conviction in June 2002, but the judges rejected it.

Database

her death. To their horror, investigators soon realised that the killing was one of those that often prove the most difficult to solve: a motiveless murder.

It was over a year later, on 25 May 2000, that police arrested 40-year-old Barry George and charged him with the murder. In the intervening time investigators had been the butt of a barrage of attacks in the media, many accusing them of incompetence or laziness. Although much of this criticism could be put down to the anger of journalists that 'one of their own' had been killed, the Metropolitan Police evidently felt under considerable pressure. So the arrest of George must have been something of a relief to them.

George's trial started almost a year later, on 5 May 2001. The prosecution presented evidence that George was obsessed with celebrities. They also offered five witnesses, all of whom had made tentative identifications of Barry George as someone they had seen lurking around Jill Dando's flat on the morning of the murder. Finally there was a tiny fleck of chemical, found in the pocket of one of Barry George's coats, that matched

The FBI's Behavioral Science Unit compiled its initial database between 1979 and 1983 from interviews conducted with thirty-six incarcerated sex and serial murderers. No one had thought of talking to these people before. They had been tracked, arrested, tried in court, convicted and sentenced – but never interviewed to find out exactly what they did to their victims.

The unofficial survey was a risky process based on a fifty-seven-page questionnaire which initially involved lengthy one-to-one cell sessions with convicted killers, one of whom (Edmund **Kemper**, a habitual decapitator) told his interrogator, 'I could screw your head off and place it on the table to greet the guard.'

The emphasis in the questioning was more on a murderer's 'how' than his 'why', thus bypassing the notoriously self-serving accounts of motivation which, in any case, do not procure arrests. 'We don't get hung up on why the killer does the things he does,' FBI Special Agent Roy Hazelwood wrote in *Psychology Today*. 'What we're interested in is that he *does* it in a way that leads us to him.' The behaviour at the scene of the crime, manifested by the way the victim (and subsequently the body) was treated, provided clues about the type of assailant.

Of the thirty-six interviewees, twenty-five were serial killers. As to their 'rearing environment', fifteen had been sexually abused in childhood, twelve in adolescence and thirteen as adults. Typically they came from broken homes with a non-caring mother and an absent father. Seventy per cent felt 'sexually incompetent' and relied heavily on pornography, preferring the type featured on the covers of detective magazines, showing a terrified woman, bound and gagged, looking up at her violator. Such images have more to do with sadism and dominance than sex.

To put it another way, these people had terrible childhoods, with a characteristic upbringing of illness, accidents, interference, beatings, abuse, bullying, ridicule, neglect, desertion, resentment, isolation, ostracism, poverty and often head injuries. As yet, there is no serial murderer from a good background.

It transpired that the child, who set fire to buildings or tortured animals, was father to the man, whose emotional focus was random killing. A gradual split emerged between two distinct personality types of killer, the **'organised'** – who plans – and the 'disorganised', who does not: in the initial database sample, the organised/disorganised ratio stood at twenty-four to twelve. The two categories treated their victims in different ways and themselves exemplified different personality traits. Thus *how* the victims were killed indicated *whom* they had been killed by.

The hundreds of indicators from the database survey went on to computer in the form of 'rules' to form the basis of the computer program now known as **'Profiler'**. One of the technique's early success cases was the murder of Francine **Elveson** which ensured that as from 1982 the interviewing of convicted killers became official policy.

See also **Sex crimes**, **Zombie**

Date rape

Date rape has been in the news since 1989, when Dr Koss at the University of Arizona discovered in a nationwide survey of 6,000 students that 15 per cent had been penetrated without their consent. Four out of five of Koss's victims knew their assailant and these findings were mirrored by British studies, the most recent conducted by Cambridge University on 1,600 students nationally, showing that one in five had been raped: a figure exceeding conventional rape figures by a factor of hundreds. Clearly this was helpful in moving the concept of rape out of big city ghettos and into the realms of everyday life. But why the discrepancy?

Indubitably, **rape** – like any other crime – is underreported: the British Home Office figures for 1988 estimate that only 21 per cent of serious sexual offences against adults ever reach the police.

It is likely, if not certain, that date rape has always been with us, but only recently discovered. In the words of Helen Peggs, of Victim Support, women 'are realising that what happened to them was unacceptable and that they were not to blame'. Rape itself still carries the same definition – of unauthorised penile penetration – and thus it is the perception of rape that has broadened.

On the hard feminist line, the concept is extended almost beyond recognition. Germaine Greer has argued that the commonest form is 'rape by fraud – by phoney tenderness or false promises of an enduring relationship'. But Greer acknowledges this as non-criminal and it is, of course, practised by both sexes. A leading QC, Helena Kennedy, dismisses the idea of a halfway house, a 'rapette' as it were, saying that there is no need to differentiate the crime: 'The varying seriousness is reflected in the sentencing.'

On a more practical level, juries tend to take a fairly robust view. According to the barrister John Parris, women jurors frequently argue that the victim 'got what she asked for'.

In four out of five British rape cases the defendant is found not guilty, and with date rape the fact of a previous relationship is often treated as indicative of a consensual element – a tendency only increased by joint ventures such as going out together, having a drink or a meal, returning home, kissing, petting and issuing an invitation to spend the night on the sofa or in the bed – 'but no funny business'.

Juries presumably consider it unduly harsh to brand a man for life when the woman changes her mind only just before, during, or after the act; or where she feels ambivalent but tending more to the negative about actual intercourse. The prosecution's problems are exacerbated by the absence of corroborative evidence such as scratches or torn clothing.

Moira Lasch, the prosecutor in the 1992 Kennedy Smith rape trial (see **Modus operandi**), was reduced to making unsubstantiated allegations to such an extent that the judge threatened her with legal action.

In a sexual relationship of which the cultural essence, for centuries, was that the woman surrendered, there will always be scope for misunderstanding about exactly what constitutes 'consent'. This difficulty is compounded by the predilection of some women to say 'no' when they mean 'yes', a tradition reconfirmed by Charlotte Muehlenhard's recent survey at Texas University where nearly half the female psychology students interviewed admitted to feigning reluctance in the run-up to intercourse to make the man 'more sexually aggressive'.

During the televised hearings of the 1991 Anita Hill–Judge Thomas sexual harassment case that kept Americans glued to their sets, Laura Berman of the *Detroit News* noted a progressive fragmentation of opinion: 'There was this huge gap between what I was reading in the *New York Times* – the standard elitist-feminist line about Anita Hill being this great heroine, and how she reflected the experience of all women – and what I was hearing among women in my own office, out there in middle America, which was a lot of scepticism and speculation about her motives.'

These doubts seem to have been well-founded. Despite Hill's canonisation as a feminist icon, study of her sworn testimony – as dissected in *The Real Anita Hill* by David Brock – shows it either to conflict with the facts or omit them. Nor was Thomas her first harasser. Diane Holt, who worked for her in Washington, commented: 'She always bragged that all the men in the office were coming on to her.' Another lawyer, a former colleague from Oklahoma, says: 'Everything was sexism or sexual harassment. She was obsessed with it … Every time she walked through a crowd someone was grabbing at her breasts. When she really got going, every guy she ever worked with sexually harassed her. The sheer numerosity of it struck me.'

But like so much of the most damning material in *The Real Anita Hill*, this last source remains anonymous. Its author, David Brock, is not an unbiased journalist but a right-wing polemicist and fellow of the Reaganite Heritage Foundation. Many of his verifiable assertions are misleading; for instance, the

lie-detector test passed by Miss Hill was not administered by an inexperienced novice but by the chief of the FBI's polygraph division, and the witnesses cited by Brock as failing to corroborate her evidence were not interviewed by him and, when they were, supported her story.

With his career on hold, Clarence Thomas testified about Anita Hill's allegations to the Senate Judiciary Committee on 11–13 October 1991. The Committee confirmed Thomas as an associate justice of the US Supreme Court by a vote of 52–48.

More than in the assault-by-a-stranger cases, date rape turns on whether the sexual interaction is seen from the man's or the woman's perspective. When a victim clearly and repeatedly expresses her opposition to sex, but her protestations are not believed by the accused, one of two consequences arises. In America, the man goes to prison as a rapist. In Britain, he is acquitted, since from his viewpoint she acquiesced.

US official figures put the annual total of rapes at 85,000. The standard extrapolation from Dr Koss's report, which found that only one date rape case in twenty reached the police, turns that into 1,700,000 rapes per annum or one every 18.55 seconds.

In Britain, the 1991 total of reported rape cases stood at 3,900; if confined to women aged between 16 and 30, this puts the chances of being raped at one in 1,600.

Death, certification of

In Britain all deaths must be certified by a doctor, but it is not necessary to see the body *after* death. Before will do just as well. The law prescribes only that – provided a colleague has seen the actual corpse – the certifying doctor 'should have been in professional attendance during the patient's last illness and within fourteen days of his death'. In 1993, an analysis of 500 British deaths showed that 29 per cent of certificates contained one or more inaccuracies.

In 1978, the American 'Friedgood Bill' banned doctors from signing the death certificates of their own relatives. This was because Dr Friedgood, who murdered his wife with a course of fatal injections, certified her as expiring from a stroke. In an earlier case a Dr Clements got away with signing the certificates of his first three wives, each richer than the last. But when Number Four passed away on 26 May 1947 the cause of death was queried by other doctors, their suspicions aroused by the deceased's pin-point eye pupils, and a second post-mortem confirmed that she had been poisoned with morphine. Clements committed suicide before he could be questioned.

There is of course no law against doctors conducting autopsies on their own murder victims. The crime is the antecedent killing. Thus in 1847 Dr Valorus P. Coolidge proved delighted to sign off his deceased creditor Edward Matthews, whom he had only just finished murdering. In 1855 a similar train of circumstances led to the attempted theft of a very unusual object, the stomach belonging to man called Cook. This had been poisoned by the famous Dr William **Palmer**, called in to assist at the autopsy. Subsequently Dr Palmer tried to bribe the laboratory assistant charged with transporting the stomach to London, begging him to destroy the goods in transit. But to no avail; he went to the gallows on 14 June 1856.

Death, life after

During his late twenties, Britain's Dennis **Nilsen** had plenty of homosexual contacts with strangers. But he found the experience of London's gay scene demoralising; his partners never stayed.

In late 1975 Nilsen had a shot at living with someone, practically kidnapping a young derelict, David Gallichan, who was having trouble in a street brawl. They set up home together, buying a cat, a dog and a budgerigar. Their flat was cosy enough and they cleared the rear garden, where today apple and plum trees still blossom.

But the pair had little in common; both started bedding strangers. When Gallichan – nicknamed 'Twinkle' – left in the summer of 1977, Nilsen had few social outlets. Sometimes he secured casual sex from one of London's gay pubs but normally he went to work, came home, and waited for tomorrow. On Fridays, he waited till Monday. As he put it, 'Loneliness is a long unbearable pain.'

Come the dread hurdle of Christmas 1978, Nilsen spent six days by himself. On the evening of the 30th he could bear it no longer, and walked over to the 'Cricklewood Arms' hoping for company. There he met the man of his dreams – someone who would stay. They returned to Nilsen's flat and drank themselves to sleep. 'I remember thinking,' Nilsen wrote later, 'that I

wanted him to stay with me over the New Year whether he wanted to or not.' Sometime in the early morning Nilsen killed the sleeping youth, strangling him in bed with a necktie.

Nilsen gave the boy – his name never emerged – a bath, and washed his hair. Then he pulled him out of the tub, deposited him on the lavatory seat and towelled him dry. Later, when it was time for bed, Nilsen snuggled the body down, pulling the bedclothes up to the chin.

Next day Nilsen dressed up his dead guest in Y-fronts, a vest and a brand-new pair of socks. He looked so nice that they went to bed together. 'I held him close to me with my arms around him,' Nilsen wrote, 'and I began to remove his pants and explore his body under the blankets (I had an erection all this time).'

But the sex did not work. The boy's body was too cold. Nilsen fell into a deep sleep and that evening he decided to snug the body away under the floorboards. But the corpse would not co-operate; it had *rigor mortis*. This allowed Nilsen to prop him up for the night against the wall. By the following day, the *rigor* had passed off and Nilsen eased him under the floor.

A week later Nilsen pulled his lover out again. In his words: 'I stripped myself naked and carried him into the bathroom and washed the body … I carried the still wet youth into the room and laid him on the carpet.' There was a kind of loving: 'Under the orange side-lights his body aroused me sexually. I knelt over him and **masturbated** on to his bare stomach.'

Then the couple spent one last night together. 'Before I went to bed I suspended him by the ankles from the high wooden platform,' Nilsen recorded. 'He hung there all night, his fingers just touching the carpet. The next day while he was still hanging there upside down I stood beside him and masturbated again.'

At last they parted. The youth's body went under the floorboards for seven months. Nilsen took it out to burn on 11 August 1979 and a few months later he felt ready for his next lover, Kenneth Ockendon, who stayed for two weeks after his demise. They spent hours together sitting in the tiny kitchen, relaxing in the armchairs, or lying side by side on the bed watching television while Nilsen chatted, relating the events of the day, telling the corpse how good it looked. Whenever he wanted, Nilsen could give the body a stroke; but there was nothing sexual, just affectionate caresses.

For the first night Ockendon shared his bed, and next morning Nilsen bought a Polaroid to take some snaps. Soon they settled into a domestic routine. 'Good night, Ken,' Nilsen would say at the end of another companionable evening. Sometimes the body sat docilely on Nilsen's knee and let itself be undressed. Sometimes they shared non-penetrative sex. At night, Nilsen put the corpse to bed in the cupboard, covering it with a curtain for a blanket.

With time, Ockendon decomposed slightly and leaked bodily fluids, but Nilsen wiped the muck away and touched up the face with make-up. It was his standard practice to bathe new visitors in a ritual of purification. Nilsen wrote of another dead victim, Stephen Sinclair: 'He looked really beautiful, like one of those Michelangelo sculptures. It seemed that he was really feeling and looking the best he ever did in his whole life.' Nilsen scrutinised his victims' corpses minutely for hours on end. He wrote: 'Even if I knew the body to be dead, I felt that the personality was still within, aware and listening to me.'

To Nilsen, the murders almost seemed acts of mercy. 'I entertained no thoughts of harming him, only concern and affection for his future and the pain and plight of his life,' he said of Sinclair. 'I remember wishing he could stay in peace like that for ever. I had a feeling of easing his burden.'

The actual killing was not important or particularly gratifying; it constituted a preliminary process enabling Nilsen to transmute base human flesh into something far, far finer. In fact, if he got lucky, as accidentally happened in April 1982 with Carl Stottor, he would not *quite* kill his man. The aftermath of near-strangulation compelled the intended victim to stay all day while Nilsen nursed him back to health.

Nilsen never knew whom he was going to kill; many visitors came to his flat and left unscathed. Many did not; on 27 January 1983 he woke up to note with surprise a dead man seated in his armchair.

When the bodies ceased to be fit for social role-play, Nilsen was in no hurry to be rid of them: he stored them. Even the task of **dismemberment** – revolting enough to make him repeatedly sick – never really destroyed Nilsen's relationship with his victims. A drawing entitled 'The last time I saw Steven [*sic*] Sinclair (final image)' shows Nilsen's farewell glimpse of his friend lying in the kitchen on a plastic sheet. In the picture, Sinclair's upper body is missing, severed at the waist.

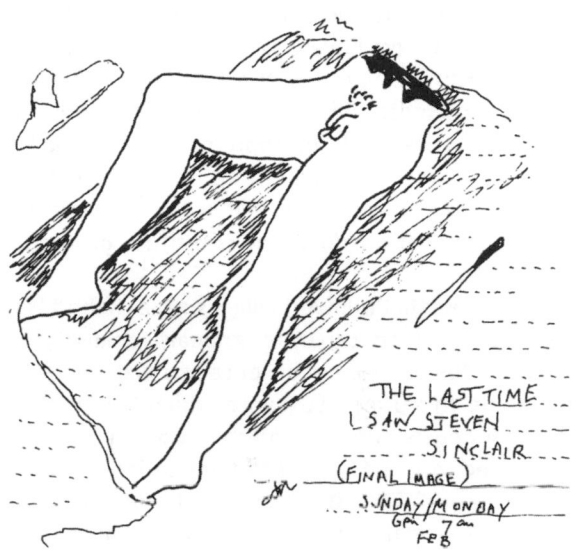

THE LAST TIME I SAW STEVEN SINCLAIR (FINAL IMAGE) SUNDAY/MONDAY FEB 7

In December 1980 Nilsen gave the bodies a great send-off, incinerating his hoard of cadavers on a huge garden bonfire. He noted 'the sparks, heat, hot air, smoke and energy of life arrowing skywards in a great visual display of living natural forces, like some Viking ship glowing westwards to Valhalla'. Nilsen turned his hi-fi speakers face out through the French windows and watched the blaze to the accompaniment of *Tubular Bells*. The neighbourhood children gathered round the flames, and at the day's end Nilsen wrote, 'The sun is setting on the glowing embers and I, weeping, drink the bottle dry.'

By his arrest on 9 February 1983 – 'the day help arrived', as he put it – Nilsen claimed fifteen or sixteen murders; he was desperate for the nightmare to end, no matter how. In prison, he remained a stickler for formality, waiting exactly three months before writing to tender his resignation from the Civil Service.

See also **Mirror**

Death Row

At time of writing, 2,547 men and forty-one women are backed up on America's Death Row. Eight have been there since 1974.

Fifteen states have no capital punishment and, until the death of Robert Harris in April 1992, executions were largely confined to conservative 'renegade' states, like Nevada and Utah. Texas produced a quarter of the total.

Since the reintroduction of the death sentence in 1976, 169 prisoners have been executed. Blacks – who comprise 12.1 per cent of the population at large – account for almost half. Of these, four out of five died for killing white men; in September 1991 'Pee-Wee' Gaskins became the first white for half a century executed for killing a black. But statistical evidence of racial discrimination does not constitute grounds for appeal.

The process that allowed killers such as Robert Harris to lodge fourteen separate appeals, delaying their execution for years or even decades, was rejected by the Senate in a June 1991 vote which barred further legal manoeuvres once a federal judge has ruled that the accused received 'a full and fair hearing' in the original state court. This abolished the traditional ground of appeal that gassing was unconstitutional as a 'cruel and unusual' punishment. In any case, twenty-three states have switched to execution by lethal **injection.**

In 1989 the prisoner's stupidity became another line of defence excluded by a Supreme Court ruling that the mere fact that the condemned man was mentally retarded did not preclude execution, even with a mental age of less than twelve. The 1992 gassing of Robert Harris, the first in the comparatively liberal state of California for twenty-five years, was expected to inaugurate an era of increased throughput.

Some prisoners might welcome a more speedy determination of their fate. The correspondence of Andrew Lee Jones (executed in July 1991) provided a glimpse of his life before death: 'I been here on Death Row since November 15 1984,' he wrote. 'I have had seven execution dates. I don't have any children and I don't have any friends here on Death Row. It don't pay to have one, because it's no telling when he might get executed … Like we are lock down for twenty-three hours a day. We get to go outside three days a week for one hour. Every time I'm out of my cell, I'm handcuff … The cell that I'm in is right in front of the light and it stay on twenty-four hours a day. Like, since I've been here, I have seen men lose their mind … It gets worse in the last few days because they start checking to see if the chair work, and sometimes the lights go dim.'

San Quentin has a holding room for those about to die. Known as the 'death watch cell', it is thirteen paces from the gas chamber. Judging by the level of 'on-off' appeals, this proximity is an important convenience. In 1992 Robert Harris was repeatedly bundled back and forth during the four stays of execution that filled the last day of his life.

The southern states are known as the 'death belt'. Some penitentiaries have truly weird names, like the 'Diagnostic and Classification Center' in Jackson, Georgia, which houses more than a hundred Death Row prisoners.

See also **Attorneys, Lifelines**

Death, time of

The main method of establishing time of death is still body temperature. The interior of a well-fed, clothed, dead adult will not cool down to the ambient temperature for about a day. At first the corpse loses 1°F an hour, but this increases slightly with the passage of time to average out at 1.5°.

In his *Medical Jurisprudence* Glaister presents this formula: (98.4 – rectal/vaginal temperature) divided by 1.5 = approx. hours since death.

The skin and the extremities cool first. Warmth in the armpit continues for about six hours. As a rule, the body loses all its natural heat in eighteen to twenty-four hours, but appropriate allowances must be made; nudes, for instance, cool down twice as quickly as the clothed, and fat people retain body heat better than thin ones.

In sexual cases, readings are often taken from the interior of the abdomen to avoid disturbing evidence in the vagina, and, quite soon, decay radiates out from the corpse's abdomen. According to Glaister: 'A body decomposes in the air twice as quickly as in water, and eight times as rapidly as in earth.' A year outside is generally sufficient to reduce a cadaver to bare bones.

The abdomen turns greenish a couple of days after death as bacteria break down the blood. Then 'marbling' sets in: the veins under the skin gain unusual prominence, imparting a pattern to the body. Next comes gross disfiguration, followed by bloating, with partial disintegration after a month or so. Some poisons, arsenic and alcohol included, act as preservatives.

See also **Adipocere**

Debt, imprisonment for

Often fatal. Initially this draconian sanction was a right reserved to the sole use of the Crown, deployed against those who could but would not pay. By the eighteenth century it was in widespread use and abuse. In 1716 Baston recorded in *Thoughts on Trade and a Public Spirit*: 'tis reckoned there are about 60,000 miserable debtors perishing in prisons in England and Wales', a figure in excess of today's entire British prison population.

Imprisonment for debt made little sense since the prisoner had to pay for his board and lodging. He thus became even poorer or, quite often, dead. In 1792 the Oglethorpe Committee detailed a common Marshalsea sequence whereby an imprisoned wretch soon wore out the kindness of his friends, sold his clothes, ate his last allowance, grew ill, went into the sick ward, lingered for a month or two on charitable rations and then perished. Unquestionably a significant proportion of cases were maliciously inspired for fictitious sums.

Marshalsea and Whitechapel were the principal prisons for defaulters, the former the setting for much of Dickens's *Little Dorrit* and his own father's temporary home. In Elizabethan times, the most desirable jail was the Rules – ordinary London dwellings clustered round the Old Bailey. In effect, the lucky 300 inmates were sent to houses, where they came and went at will. But they remained on the prison register and hence beyond further arrest, since they were already prisoners. Debtors paid to get in. In **Newgate**, the debtors' section went under the name 'Tangiers' since the conditions were reminiscent of the barbarities inflicted by Arab pirates trading on the Barbary Coast. Inmates were called 'tangerines'.

Decline and fall

The **Mafia**'s grip on America is loosening. After the **Pizza Connection** bust of 1984, the FBI estimated the number of 'made' Mafia members had dwindled to 1,700 nationwide together with about a 1,000 associates – about half the strength of the twenty-four Mafia families two decades before. Symbolic of their decline was the wholesale arrest, on 26 February 1985, of the New York Mafia Commission. Its leading lights, mostly respected men with an average age of seventy, were not so much frightened as infuriated, raising their bails, set in Castellano's case at $4 million, in a matter of minutes.

But the defendants were sentenced to 100 years each on 13 January 1987. The dawn raids of 31 March 1988 netted another sixty-four suspected drug traffickers, and on 2 April 1992 the only remaining head of a big American crime family not in jail, John Gotti, was convicted. On the day the Gotti jury retired, 'Little Vic' Orena, the alleged head of the Columbo family, was arrested. In New York two of the five Mafia families are essentially bust and a third is on its knees. The Genovese clan remains largely inviolate, but the mob are on the run or defeated in Kansas City, Philadelphia, Cleveland, Chicago, New Orleans and Boston, with twenty bosses put behind bars in the last ten years.

Legal stratagems have played their part. The conspiracy charges in the Pizza Connection case showed that any one individual could be sentenced for the overall acts of the team; previously, the boss (whose hands, if little else, were clean) remained above the law and only his underlings took the rap. Today the FBI eliminates whole families with a stick-and-carrot approach, on the one hand penetrating the homes of *mafiosi* with electronic surveillance to garner evidence, on the other proffering a workable witness protection scheme to 'turn' mobsters into informers.

Sometimes the hoods can hardly wait. Modern mobsters, even at the highest levels, do not just talk; they wear wires, write books and hire agents to dispense revelations of their lifestyles that today seem increasingly outdated, even quaint.

At the same time, civil RICO (Racketeer Influenced and Corrupt Organizations Act) charges chipped away at the Mob's economic base, in New York breaking its stranglehold on the staples of the Fulton Fish Market, the International Longshoreman's Association and the Teamsters. But this did not happen overnight. RICO's mob-busting potential went largely unappreciated until June 1980 when Professor Robert Blakey held a seminar at Cornell University, explaining to FBI agents how the law could be turned against the Mafia's entire organisational structure. Until then the FBI had concentrated on specific crimes; within a year the Agency was redeployed into nine elite squads, five individually targeted on the Mafia's five New York families.

The onslaught does not bode well for Mafia recruitment. Formerly, the mob's attractions were twofold: there was not much else for poor immigrants to do, and the inner ring possessed legal immunity. In the late 1950s mobster Frank Scalice marketed 'membership' to would-be 'soldiers' for $50,000 a head. Today, these old certainties have faded. In America this represents a golden opportunity for someone else, perhaps the conspicuous Colombian cartels, the violent Jamaican posses or the street-level Dominicans, but more probably the **Triads**.

Elsewhere the Mafia continues to thrive, proliferating from Italy into Germany. During the two years to July 1992, Germany launched sixty-eight investigations into Mafia-related crimes, with twenty-eight Mafia suspects arrested in the most recent three months, mostly on Italian tip-offs. The break-up of the Soviet bloc channelled substantial underworld investments into eastern Germany, where the Mafia crowded in on the ground floor as a substitute form of oppression.

See also **Inquisition**, **Techies**, **Trial**, **Whacks**

de Crespigny, Sir Claude

Latter-day amateur British hangman who in 1886 volunteered to assist **Berry** at the triple execution of three thieves named Rudge, Martin and Baker. The well-heeled Sir Claude paid Berry £10 for the privilege, selecting the alias 'Charles Maddon' for his cameo role.

After the formalities, the prison governor, spotting a man of quality, invited Sir Claude and his boss to tea, and the executioners lingered on for dinner. The incident created quite a *frisson* in Victorian society, and Sir Claude felt constrained to explain his motivation through the columns of *The Times*. Apparently he thought that one day he might attain the post of Sheriff of Essex, and felt it his duty not to ask anyone to do something he would not do himself.

In 1626, another nobleman suffered an adverse experience, this time not as, but at the hands of, a novice. It took twenty-nine blows to slash off the Comte de Chalais' head; the wretched man remained alive after the twentieth stroke. This epic decapitation was conducted by an amateur to save his own neck.

Dementia Americana

Ingenious medical condition said – in court – to afflict rich Americans, making it excusable for them to kill their wives' ex-lovers. The case in question involved one very pretty woman, Evelyn Nesbit, and two very unattractive men, Harry Thaw and Stanford White, America's most distinguished architect.

White designed New York's landmark building, the Madison Square Gardens, on the top of which he was shot on 28 June 1906 while watching a roof-terrace performance of a dreary new musical, *Mam'zelle Champagne*. On the Garden's pinnacle loomed a statue of the naked goddess Diana, rumoured to be a likeness of Evelyn Nesbit sculpted while she was one of White's mistresses. White kept several, throwing dinner parties at which young ladies popped out of immense pies, and by the time of the trial he stood blackened as an unscrupulous roué, a portrayal he was no longer in a position to dispute.

White's first encounter with the 16-year-old Evelyn, then a chorus girl, concluded with her romping Fragonard-style on a velvet-upholstered swing while the architect pushed her higher and higher. Soon White had his quarry half-naked, posing for photographs in a kimono. The final seduction took place while Evelyn, although technically present, lay asleep and quite possibly drugged in a room whose walls and ceilings were lined with mirrors. 'A pounding began in my ears,' she recalled, 'and the room began to spin.'

White's eventual murderer and rival for Evelyn's affections was Harry Thaw, a playboy heir to railroad millions with an $80,000-a-year allowance. Thaw's youthful escapades included stunts like driving a car through a display window, throwing a $50,000 party for the leading whores of Paris and losing $40,000 in a poker game. He ran across Evelyn while she was in tow as White's mistress, and for her it seems a case of money at first sight. The pair absconded to Europe, renting the Schloss Katzenstein where Thaw treated her to a good hiding, ensuring that she was confined to bed for a further three weeks. 'Without any provocation,' she recalled, 'he grasped me by the throat and tore the bathrobe from my body, leaving me entirely nude except for my slippers. His eyes were glaring and he had in his right hand a cowhide whip.' It emerged that Thaw was seriously unbalanced and would beat her savagely at the least provocation. Nevertheless, and despite the additional disincentive of Thaw's cocaine habit, the couple married on 25 April 1905.

According to one account, White arranged the marriage himself at the instigation of Evelyn's parents, persuading Thaw to propose and threatening to expose him on charges of corrupting a minor – Evelyn – if he refused. Whatever Thaw's motivation, they moved into a Pittsburgh mansion where he fostered a penchant for pistols.

A year or so later the Thaws came up to town for the première of *Mam'zelle Champagne* which was, by chance, also attended by Stanford White. The performance was too dull to sit through; the Thaws made for the elevator, Harry pausing on the way to pump three bullets into the architect while the unsuspecting Evelyn waited at the lift.

Thaw rejoined her with the smoking pistol still in his hand. 'Good God, Harry, what have you done?' she asked, and, as guests stampeded for the exits, the stage manager jumped on a table and shouted, 'Go on playing. Bring on the chorus.' The dead man too would have left early, had he not been hoping for an introduction to another chorus girl after the show.

Moments later Thaw was arrested. To the sergeant in charge, who asked 'Why did you do this?', Thaw replied 'I can't say' with no great show of interest. He proved more forthcoming to the District Attorney, commenting, 'I saw him sitting there, big, fat and healthy, and there Evelyn was, poor delicate little thing, all trembling and nervous.'

The aftermath turned into a legal farce. Thaw's novel medical condition of *dementia Americana* was diagnosed by expensive defence doctors and at the first trial the jury could not agree. At the second, in 1908, he was found not guilty by reason of his affliction.

This verdict reflected the successful efforts of the Thaws' press agent to promote a popular morality fable of a wronged waif (Evelyn) seduced by an ageing roué (White) and rescued by a chivalrous knight (Thaw) undergoing a brainstorm. One component of the orchestrated campaign was a Thaw-backed play based on the shooting, culminating with the killer's last-scene declaration from his cell in the Tombs: 'No jury on earth will send me to the chair, no matter what I have done or what I have been, for killing a man who defamed my wife. That is the unwritten law made by men themselves, and upon its virtue I will stake my life.'

Seven years later, with the aid of a waiting limousine, Thaw escaped from his asylum. He was recaptured, but on 16 July 1915 his wealthy family contrived to have him released by reason of his newly certified sanity: he had never been found guilty of murder, now he was no longer mad, so out he came. Thaw lost little time in kidnapping a Kansas City youth, Frederick Gump, and set about him with a horsewhip. This time, the millionaire was not readjudged sane until 1924.

Thaw appointed Delmonico's restaurant as caterers for his spell on remand in New York's Tombs prison; all his meals were shipped in. He died in 1947.

Dempster

A verb, as in 'to be dempstered'. In the 1770s this entailed being hanged, an expression commemorating the name of a contemporary London lackey, fond of giving himself airs, who made his living from other people's misfortunes. He hanged them. A common epithet for his trade was the 'crap merchant'.

Another eponymous hangman, from the sixteenth century, went under the name of Derrick. He was saved from execution by his patron the Earl of Essex, whom he subsequently beheaded. The initial arrangement was that Derrick's life would be spared provided he hanged the twenty or so other felons with whom he had been convicted for rape, and the modern derrick is named after his design for the gallows, suggesting that the condemned were winched to their deaths.

Detection, risk of

Contrary to the tortuous mysteries of fiction, murder remains about the easiest crime to solve. With the exception of the random doodlings of serial killers, only the most extreme personal antagonism will serve as a trigger. Thus the motive, connecting victim to murderer, runs through the fabric of their lives like a scarlet thread, with the culprit's identity flowing naturally from identification of the victim.

Of Britain's 1991 crop of 708 homicides, as at 8 January the following year only sixty-seven (9.46 per cent) had not resulted in charges. Most were cleared up within a few days of the crime. In a July 1992 case, a man loaded the corpse of his common-law wife into the car and drove it as evidence to the local police station at Kingstanding. Experienced homicide detectives will, where possible, first ask of the gaggle of spectators that tends to gather round a body, 'Do you know who did it?' and then, 'Where does he live?'

The crowd may include the murderer. Sex killers, particularly the '**organised**' ones, often haunt the scene of their crime, returning to gloat, and may try to insert themselves peripherally into the investigation. Peter **Sutcliffe**, the Yorkshire Ripper, returned to one of his victims a few days after the attack and tried to remove her head with a hacksaw. Peter **Kürten**, the Dusseldorf sadist, relished the excited throng jostling round his victims' bodies, and in 1931 this trait was turned to advantage by the Rumanian detective Franculescu, baffled by a corpse found behind locked gates in a Bucharest courtyard. The only clue, furnished by the dead man's fingernails, was that his assailant had red hair. After running every other line of enquiry into the ground, Franculescu re-examined the police photograph of the body which showed, in the background, the usual knot of onlookers.

Did any of them have red hair? Yes. And who was it? The murderer, Bardica. As this happened before the invention of colour photography it took some time to work out by patient enquiries, but Bardica eked out the rest of his life in the Kimpolung convict mines.

One of the most obvious reasons for killing someone who is a wife is being her husband. Typical of the domestic cases that parade through the newspapers is that of 47-year-old Hazel Wood, shot fourteen times with her husband's hunting rifle as she lay asleep at home. No great deductive powers were needed to pin the crime on her spouse who, inflamed by jealousy, told friends and relatives that he intended to kill her. Defence lawyers are apt to listen to their clients' protestations of innocence with jaundiced ears. As Bernie Segal, the defence lawyer in the American **MacDonald** case, remarked, 'The police only arrest the obviously guilty. They don't know how to catch the others.'

Over 300 of British cases in 1991 involved domestic disputes and, for 1989, 81 per cent of female and 58 per cent of male victims were killed by someone known to them personally. In America the corresponding figure hovered around 55 per cent overall, well down from the 80 per cent of the Sixties. Thirty-one of the 1991 British killers had committed suicide within a year.

In 1992 the mere fact that a backlog of unsolved murders had accumulated in London led senior Scotland Yard detectives to speculate on the existence of a hitman syndicate, although national newspapers reported that the police were reluctant to state that professional assassins existed for fear of causing public anxiety. Somewhere between five and twenty murders were involved, all sharing an absence of motive, a dearth of clues, and a wall of **silence.**

History provides almost no precedent for the eminent 'consulting detectives' who saunter so brilliantly through the pages of fiction.

The word 'murder' is derived from the Anglo-Saxon 'murdrum', originally a fine imposed on the natives for killing Normans. If the person responsible was not caught, the whole community paid, literally.

Diatoms

Primitive but tough microscopic algae found in unpolluted fresh water and the sea. A corpse dumped in the sea or river fills its air passages with diatoms as the water swamps the lungs. But the diatoms do not penetrate further. In contrast, the continued breathing of a drowning man will, as he struggles, draw the air, water and diatoms into his bloodstream. Once in the system, the acid-resistant silica shells are pumped round to the heart and then distributed throughout the kidneys, stomach, brain and bone marrow.

On post-mortem examination, sample body tissue can be broken down to reveal the diatoms' presence, thereby proving death by drowning. More than 25,000 diatomic varieties of local origin are known to science; hence their identification may indicate the place of death, in one case allowing scientists to show that a corpse washed up on the Belgian coast had fallen off a yacht by the Isle of Wight.

There is 'wet drowning' and 'dry drowning', when death occurs within seconds and little or no liquid is found in the lungs. This happened to Robert Maxwell, the financial fraudster, but traces of diatoms in his bloodstream proved that he was alive when he hit the water, establishing that he had not killed himself *before* falling off the *Lady Ghislaine* near the Canary Islands in November 1991. In dry drowning, a sudden influx of unexpected water through the nose can produce a spasm of the larynx, which in turn squeezes the vagus, the long nerve monitoring blood pressure via a bulb in the neck. In these circumstances the vagus erroneously deduces that blood pressure has reached dangerously high levels, countered by stopping the heart, an instruction issued by the brain forthwith.

Even in wet drowning cases, death may result from heart failure rather than oxygen deprivation. Fresh water sluices into the bloodstream via the lungs, increasing its volume by perhaps 50 per cent in a minute, and the heart cannot take the strain. Sea water, with its higher osmotic pressure, reaches no further than the blood vessels of the lungs. They swell, but this is not fatal of itself, and hence it often proves easier to drown a man in fresh water. There are no reported cases of drowning faked by an *in vivo* infusion of diatoms.

Dickens, Charles (1812–70)

An influential opponent of public hangings. Dickens wrote to *The Times* in 1849 after witnessing the hanging of Frederick and Maria Manning. The spectacle attracted almost unprecedented excitement and 500 constables were drafted in to keep the peace outside Horsemonger Lane jail.

The thrill centred on the novel execution of a husband-and-wife team, with much speculation about who would 'go' first. In the event, they 'went' together. A skeleton summary of Dickens's letter describing the crowd reads: 'levity ... shrillness ... howls ... screeching ... laughing ... prostitutes ... ruffians ... fightings ... faintings ... whistlings ... callousness ... as if the name of Christ had never been heard in the world'.

Dickens's liberal record is hard to fault; when the avant-garde were firmly wedded to the supposedly benevolent prison regime, the **Separate System**, he wrote: 'I hold this slow and daily tampering with the mysteries of the brain to be immeasurably worse than any torture of the body; and because its ghastly signs and tokens are not so palpable to the eye and sense of touch as scars upon the flesh, therefore the more I denounce it.'

Dickens also coined the word 'detective', using it in 1850 for a journalistic series in *Household Words*. The first fictional detective was Inspector Bucket of *Bleak House*, inspired by Inspector Charles F. Field, who accompanied the writer round London's docklands. In the same work, Maria Manning was reshaped as the villainess Hortense.

Maria Manning's execution had a dramatic impact on women's fashion. She dressed in the Sunday staple of black satin for her hanging and, thereafter, black satin was very definitely out. The conviction of Franz Müller fifteen years later for the first British railway murder had the reverse effect. After killing a Mr Thomas Briggs for his gold watch on the 9.50 p.m. from Fenchurch Street Station, Müller swapped his victim's respectable top hat for his own 'beaver'. Müller's headwear was a distinctive truncated version of the topper with a low crown, and after his execution the 'Müller cut-down' enjoyed a brief vogue.

See also **Handkerchiefs**, **Fagin**, **Yuppies**

Dillinger, John Herbert (1902–34?)

A formidable bank robber with good looks and a pleasant manner, who employed his gun sparingly and, when caught by the camera, often appeared relaxed and well turned out. Dillinger's mother died when he was four and he was raised by his father, a strict Quaker disciplinarian who believed in sound thrashings. They moved to Indiana in 1920, and three years later Dillinger joined the navy. He deserted from the *USS Utah* a few months later, and left his new wife, Beryl Hovis, shortly after that, imprisoned for trying to rob the local Mooresville grocer. An ex-con managing his baseball team had cut him in on the deal, and when it misfired Dillinger accepted an offer of a lenient sentence in return for pleading guilty.

Released on parole nearly a decade later, he set about robbing banks, starting in Daleville on 17 July 1933 and eventually extracting a million dollars from at least ten banks dotted through the Midwest. The raids were meticulously planned and rehearsed against the clock; Dillinger's trademark was an athletic spring over the railings protecting the tellers' cages, and his public image benefited from a refusal to take money from customers caught up in the raid, on the grounds that he robbed banks not people. Afterwards he would hightail it over the nearest state boundary and, in the wake of his first five successes, the Chicago police set up a forty-man 'Dillinger Squad'. When caught in September robbing the Bluffton bank and thrown into prison in Lima, Ohio, three of his men turned up posing as prison officials, shot the sheriff, and let him out.

The robberies resumed, clocking up their first fatality during a $20,000 raid on the First National Bank in Chicago when a policeman died. Dillinger was arrested again, this time with three confederates, in Tucson on 27 January 1934 after a tip-off from a detective story fan. Flown to East Chicago, he was locked up in the Crown Point prison, from which he escaped on 3 March, brandishing his famous wooden pistol (blackened with shoe polish) to force the guards to release him before driving off in the sheriff's car; embarrassed officials started the rumour that he wielded a smuggled .38 Colt.

A bent lawyer, Louis Piquett, helped restock the gang with arms and bullet-proof vests; Dillinger submitted to crude facial surgery (to conceal a scar) and tried to burn off his fingerprints with sulphuric acid (see **Removal**). By now almost a national hero, on 13 March 1934, in the company of 'Baby Face' Nelson, he hit the First National Bank of Mason City for $52,000. To cover their escape, Dillinger ordered twenty hostages out at gunpoint and festooned his car with them, standing some on the running boards and putting others on the hood or draping them over fenders and bumpers. A frustrated Police Chief E. J. Patton watched the large tourer lumber out of town.

Acting on a telephoned tip-off, in late April a posse of FBI agents encircled Dillinger in a lodge at the lakeside resort of Little Bohemia, Wisconsin. Closing in after dark under the leadership of Melvin 'Nervous' Purvis, they opened fire on customers leaving the restaurant, killing one diner and wounding two more. 'The fever for action,' Purvis reported, 'dissipated all other emotions.' Dillinger escaped, receiving the accolade of 'Public Enemy Number One' in a poster proclamation of 25 July which pegged a price of $10,000 to his head. The FBI looked increasingly ridiculous. Attorney General Cummings said agents should 'shoot to kill', although Dillinger was not known to have killed anyone himself. But he had irritated **Hoover** with a series of taunting postcards, and his death became a personal priority.

Anna Sage, the 'Lady in Red', was an immigrant brothel madam in trouble with the law. Needing a permit to stay in the United States, she told the police of her date with Dillinger to see *Manhattan Melodrama* at Chicago's Biograph cinema on 22 July. As he emerged from the performance at 10.30 p.m. he found himself ringed by agents. In Purvis's words: 'I was very nervous. It must have been a squeaky voice that called out, "Stick 'em up, Johnny! We have you surrounded." Dillinger drew his .380 automatic pistol, but he never fired it. He dropped to the ground; he had been shot.'

Other reports say Dillinger never went for his gun. As he lay on the pavement, the awestruck crowds dipped their dresses, handkerchiefs and even scraps of paper in his blood.

The ambush represented a great public relations coup for Hoover, helping to establish the FBI as a major investigative force. Hoover kept Dillinger's straw hat, his smashed spectacles and damaged .38 on display in his reception room for decades to come. But the pistol on show – serial number 119702 – never belonged to Dillinger. It did not leave the Colt production line until December 1934, and Dillinger's gang were soon claiming that the FBI shot the wrong man.

When the autopsy records finally materialised after thirty years, they were riddled with discrepancies. The dead man had blue eyes, whereas Dillinger's were grey, and they may have stayed that way for decades afterwards.

Dillinger's associate 'Baby Face' Nelson came to a bloody end in a shootout on a country road near Barrington, Illinois. He killed both the FBI agents who lay in ambush for him, but took seventeen slugs himself. The next day his body was found naked by the roadside, dumped out of the car by his wife.

Hoover's bête noire, John Dillinger, in a 1934 poster

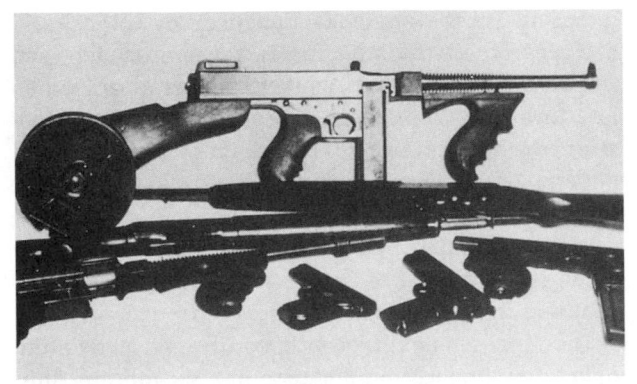

A collection of guns allegedly used by Dillinger

These smalltime hoods were typical FBI targets. Alvin 'Creepy' Karpis, the thief, was another propaganda victim. For years his comments on his own arrest in New Orleans on 1 May 1936 were regarded as sour grapes. Hoover was lionised in the press for personally disarming the gangster, but Karpis grumbled, 'It's an old practice of the FBI to dress up the truth with lies that make them look more clever and powerful than they are. The most obvious flaw in the FBI story of my capture lies in Hoover's own character. He didn't lead the attack on me. He hid until the coast was clear. Then he came out to reap the glory.' It was, however, always conceded that Karpis shambled through the streets bound up with his necktie because the FBI had forgotten the handcuffs.

Years later, Karpis whiled away his term in McNeil Island penitentiary by teaching the steel guitar to a young prisoner named Charles **Manson**, and it was his pupil's musical ability that helped seduce the **Family**'s first members.

Dingo

The disappearance of Lynne (Lindy) Chamberlain's daughter at Ayers Rock on 17 August 1980 launched Australia's sensational 'dingo' case.

During the summer of that year, the encampments and tourist areas round Ayers Rock saw a steady rise in dingo attacks; in early June, several were shot after going for children. On 23 June, little Amanda Cranwell was dragged from her car and just rescued from the animal's jaws by her father. The dingoes became ever bolder, scavenging through tents for food; on 4 August the Chief Ranger posted up warning signs. Then on 15 August a Mr Backhaus-Smith woke to find an unfazed dingo in his tent, and another traveller, Erica Letsch, had the pillow tugged from under her head as she slept. The next day two young tourists were bitten. The day after, the Chamberlain family arrived from Mount Isa. There was Lindy, her husband Michael, and three young children including baby Azaria.

That evening Lindy settled Azaria in her carrying basket and stayed chatting to Bill and Sally Lowe in the tent alongside. Suddenly Bill was alerted by a menacing growl. Then Sally heard the wail of a baby, abruptly cut short.

'I think that is bubby crying,' said Aidan, the Chamberlains' eldest. Lindy covered the few yards to her tent just in time to see a dingo emerging. The animal's lower body was hidden behind a low fence, but Lindy thought it held something in its jaws. It shook its head from side to side before running off. Lindy threw herself into her tent, fearing that Azaria had been savaged. Inside, the central pole was knocked askew, blood was spattered around, and Azaria had vanished. 'A dingo has got my baby,' Lindy screamed.

Within thirty minutes three hundred searchers were combing the bush. With every moment the chances of finding Azaria alive dwindled: she had been snatched by a predator, to be killed and eaten. That night the Chief Ranger and his Aboriginal tracker discovered the animal's tracks. Starting seventeen yards from the tent in a sand dune, the trail consisted of a shallow drag-mark some eight inches wide from Azaria's clothing, with depressions in the sand where she had been rested on the ground. Paw marks circled the tent, bunching outside where Azaria lay as the dingo caught her scent. On 22 August, her mangled and blood-stained jumpsuit was found on the far side of Ayers Rock. Azaria herself was never seen again.

Dingoes may sound fierce in suburban Britain, but in Australia, with its man-eating crocs, they are considered small beer, normally running scared at the word 'shoo'. Baby Cranwell's lucky escape never reached the papers, so the tourist-hardened dingoes of Ayers Rock remained unknown. Azaria became the first reported snatch.

Public reaction played a crucial role; in its initial stages, the case was a trial by media and rumour, and the parents proved fertile targets for gossip. People react in different ways to grief, and Michael was a pastor for the Seventh Day Adventists, his wife a

The Chamberlain family

jumpsuit. These were inexact sciences; by comparison, the eye-witness testimony proved overwhelming, and the coroner ruled that Azaria 'met her death when attacked by a wild dingo'. The alternative of murder seemed a near-impossibility, since Lindy was in view of Bill and Sally Lowe throughout. She could hardly have reached the tent unseen, spirited her child away to the car, slit its throat, concealed the body in something like a camera bag, and returned a few seconds later to continue the conversation.

The coroner's emphatic judgment was televised; the police felt publicly humiliated. But six months later they were vindicated when one of their expert witnesses took Azaria's clothing to London for a second opinion from Professor James Cameron, a renowned forensic pathologist.

His conclusions were dynamite. Azaria's neck had been slit not by a dingo but by a sharp instrument. The bloodstains came from an injury inflicted before her clothing was unbuttoned. And on the back of the babysuit Professor Cameron found the bloodstained imprint of a female hand. On 19 September 1981, during a series of raids on witnesses and suspects, four hundred items were seized from the Chamberlains' house and their car flown by Hercules to Darwin for minute examination.

At the second inquest on 14 December 1981 the Chamberlains heard that bloodstains had been discovered in their vehicle – beneath the scat and, more importantly, in a fine spray under the dashboard, as though caused by a severed artery. Tests showed that this blood could only originate from a child younger than three months. Similarly, minute traces of blood and hairs were detected in the Chamberlains' camera bag, where it now seemed the body had been secreted.

A textile expert confirmed that the ripped jumpsuit was cut rather than torn, and a London odontologist, Bernard Sims, showed that the rips were not what one would expect from a dingo. He also proved that Azaria's head was not clamped in the dingo's jaws (as the defence alleged) because dingoes cannot open their mouths wider than ten centimetres. Further, twenty-five tufts from the jumpsuit were found in the car. But a tuft is a single fibre severed twice and, when a strand has parted at one end, it is no longer taut; accordingly, it cannot be *torn* again. A sharp instrument is needed to cut it twice.

The trial opened on 13 September 1982 and ran for

devout follower. When they tried to reconcile their loss with their faith, regarding Azaria's death as part of God's plan, the average Australian thought it a weird parental stance.

The professionals too turned sceptical; the Mount Isa police reported that Lindy 'appeared not to care for baby ... did not feed it ... dressed it in black ... and did not react like a normal mother'. They disclosed that Azaria meant 'sacrifice in the wilderness'. This was all untrue, but as the rumours grew so the wooden coffin in the family's garage, used by Michael as a prop for anti-smoking classes, evolved into a small white coffin in Azaria's bedroom; soon her clothes on Ayers Rock had been found neatly folded. At school, the Chamberlain children endured taunts of 'Dingoes don't come into our house and steal babies.'

At the inquest on 16 December 1980, expert evidence suggested – on the basis of fairly impromptu tests – that a person, not a dingo, had shredded Azaria's clothing and extracted her body from the nearly two months. It followed a familiar pattern: all the eye-witness evidence (heard first) went the Chamberlains' way. But this was a fading memory after weeks of forensic argument. The prosecution wisely conceded they knew neither why nor exactly how Lindy killed Azaria: they simply knew that she had. The judge summed up broadly in her favour, but juries are entitled to their views, and on 28 October 1982 Lindy was found guilty.

Her initial appeal was turned down in the absence of new evidence, and the second could not hear the new evidence which had then emerged, since its remit was simply to review the legitimacy of the verdict based on the old evidence – largely discredited when, on 24 November 1983, a Seventh Day Adventist, Les Smith, finally found the explanation for the blood-stains under the dashboard.

The stains were not blood but paint. During manu-facture, the wheel arches of the car, a Holden Torana, were coated with a sound-deadening material, Dulux Dufin 1081. In 10 per cent of the models, a burst of spray carried through a drain-hole to the underside of the dashboard. The other microscopic bloodstains under the seat and in the camera bag were only dirt. Serology is an extremely complex science (occupying 108 pages in the final Inquiry) but at base the prose-cution's orthotolidine test was simply a *prima facie* indicator, showing that the traces *might* have been blood. Another thing they might have been was copper dust. The Chamberlains lived in the copper-producing area of Mount Isa, and dirt taken from their street produced an identical reaction.

Similarly, it turned out that dingo teeth *were a* sharp instrument. True, Azaria's clothes had been cut rather than torn, but no one checked whether dingoes cut or tore clothes. Les Smith conducted the first experi-ments, holding out chunks of meat wrapped in cloth, and found that dingo teeth possessed a clean scissor-like action – sharp enough to slice through seat belts in a straight line or sever wire cable. And although dingoes cannot open their mouths wider than a baby's head in theory, they can in practice, as witness a medium-sized dingo videoed grasping a frozen chicken, diameter 13.5cms. Again, experts were baffled by how the dingo managed to undo Azaria's bootees, leaving them in the feet of the jumpsuit, before extracting her body by the head. This was because they had never watched dingoes in action fixing jumpsuits by the feet and shaking out their prey.

The bloodstained female handprint of Professor Cameron's evidence proved invisible. No one else could see it. Likewise the overall pattern of bloodstaining on the jumpsuit was not what Cameron *expected* from a dingo-inflicted wound, but his expectations lacked evidential weight. The 'tuft theory' too had not been submitted to dingoes; given a test-garment to shred, they ripped it into tufts and snippets.

In June 1987, after seven years, two inquests, one trial, two appeals, a £6 million inquiry, and paperwork weighing five tonnes, Lindy Chamberlain won a pardon. Her conviction was quashed on 15 September 1988, and in May 1992 she received A$900,000 compensation.

Dismemberment, reasons for

There are four good reasons for dismembering a corpse. First, to complicate identification. Second, to facilitate transportation of the resulting components. Third, as an act of vengeance where mere killing has constituted insufficient punishment. And finally, for sexual gratification (see **Cannibalism**).

Readers contemplating cutting a body up should set aside a good day for the project. Dennis **Nilsen**, the British serial killer, was an army-trained butcher from the Catering Corps, and he devoted an entire (if leisurely) weekend in February 1983 to carving up Stephen Sinclair into his main chunks.

A great British virtuoso was the British multiple murderer Henry Jeremiah McKenny, a London hard man six feet five inches tall. By the late 1970s McKenny became browned off with life as an armed robber. Whenever an eye-witness described a gangster attend-ing a raid as more than six feet high, the police pulled in 'Big H' for questioning. So one day he observed to his associate John Childs, 'It would be a lot easier to do people in for money.'

They already possessed the know-how. Childs rented a council flat at 13 Dolphin House, Poplar, which had a brick fireplace with a tiny grate, and in October 1974 its living room carpet was covered with polythene to receive the first body: 'Teddy Bear' Eve, killed to facili-tate the takeover of his soft-toy business. The corpse was ferried through the estate at night and then underwent preliminary dissection prior to insertion into a £25 electric meat mincer. But the machine jammed. So they burned Eve bit by bit, and three months later an unlucky witness followed him up the chimney.

In 1978, 'Big H' moved into murder on commission, and when at last the police came by they gazed at the eighteen-inch fireplace of Number 13 in disbelief. It seemed to lack both the capacity and the high-temperature potential for the throughput of the eventual total of six bodies.

Could it be done? Pathologist James Cameron purchased a dead eleven-stone pig. He cut it up and, to his surprise, over the course of thirteen hours, reduced most of it to a heap of ashes, in the process recording a core-heat of 1,000° F. Cameron's only problem came when the intestines released such quantities of fluid that the blaze faltered, but John Childs explained that the secret of Big H's technique was to dry the intestines separately in front of the fire before immolation.

Dismemberment of the living is an exceedingly rare criminal enterprise. John Gotti allegedly divided his neighbour in two with a chainsaw, and on 8 November 1980 Londoner John Bowden devised a plan to divest Donald Ryan, a 47-year-old boxer, of £20. After spending the evening drinking cider together, Bowden battered his friend over the head with a bottle, placed him in a bath and then, while he was still alive, cut off his arms and legs with a saw, a machete and an electric carving knife before disposing of the body in a plastic bag on a waste tip. Neighbours called round by chance to find the door opened by an accomplice, Michael Ward, stripped to the waist and covered in blood. Arrest followed. At the Old Bailey trial, four members of the jury were so affected by the photographic evidence that they fell ill.

See also **Contempt**, **Durability**

Dolphins, sex with

In 1991 Alan Cooper, a British animal rights campaigner, was acquitted of the unusual charge of committing an act of a 'lewd, obscene or disgusting nature' with a wild dolphin. Spectators on a boating trip thought he masturbated it.

The case took five days and amused everyone apart from the defendant. Crucial to Cooper's case was an understanding of what dolphins use their penises for. With humans the penis is of restricted utility. As defence counsel pointed out: 'Men do not employ their penis to push the supermarket trolley. They do not use

it to greet each other.' But things are otherwise in the world of dolphins. A penis is an extra – or only – limb. Mr Cooper explained: 'It's like a flick knife. He flicks it in and out at will.' Expert testimony supported this view. In the words of Dr Dobbs, who had watched the dolphin at play: 'I have seen him catch fish with his mouth, throw it in the air and catch it on his penis.'

The crux was that the dolphin's permanently rigid member had non-sexual applications. The prosecution accepted that when the dolphin hooked divers in the crook of the arm or leg with its penis and towed them round the bay this meant – in the words of Dr Dobbs – no more than 'extending the finger of friendship'. Cooper received two death threats in the run-up to the trial; he was cleared in December 1991.

But experts are not always right. In the correspondence aroused by the case a Mr R. J. Henry from Pearce, Australia, cited anecdotal evidence from his 1974 friendship with a woman dolphin-handler from the Hong Kong Sea World. She told him that male dolphins were, like so many people, 'in a perpetual state of rut and only became tractable if they were regularly masturbated'. Mr Henry asserted that **masturbation** was the standard reward in training, maintaining that the Asian sex industry boasts a number of establishments with specialised dolphinaria catering for Western divers wishing to fraternise with fish.

See also **Animals**

Dominance

Knowledge of 'dominance' is of immense importance in the study of crime.

Zoologists have recognised for a long time that in all animal species, precisely 5 per cent are 'dominant': that is, they possess leadership qualities. This was also known to the explorer H. M. Stanley, who, when asked by Bernard Shaw how many men could lead his party if Stanley fell ill, replied, 'One in twenty.'

The present writer (CW) was told about the 'dominant 5 per cent' by the American author Robert Ardrey. Ardrey explained that during the Korean war there were no escapes of American prisoners. This was because the Chinese observed the prisoners carefully and picked out the dominant ones. These were kept in a separate compound under heavy guard. Once this nucleus of 'troublemakers' had been removed, the other prisoners could be left with virtually no guard at all. The number of dominant prisoners, the Chinese noticed, was always precisely five per cent.

The American psychologist Abraham Maslow, who in 1936 decided to study dominance in women, formed a study group for that purpose. His first finding was significant; they fell into three distinct categories: high-dominance, medium-dominance and low-dominance.

His major findings can be simply stated: sexuality was directly related to dominance. High-dominance women – 5 per cent of the total – were more likely to masturbate, sleep with different men, have lesbian experience and so on. A medium-dominance or low-dominance woman might have a high rating for sex drive, but her sexual experience was usually limited. Low-dominance women (who were difficult to get into the study group) tended to think of sex as being mainly for child-bearing: one low-dominance woman who knew she could not bear children refused sex to her husband, even though she had a strong sex drive. Low-dominance women tended to think of sex as disgusting, or as an unfortunate necessity for producing children, to dislike nudity and to regard the sexual organs as ugly. (High-dominance women usually liked seeing, touching and thinking about the penis, and regarded it as beautiful.)

The choice of men followed similar patterns. High-dominance women liked dominant males and preferred unsentimental, even violent, lovemaking – to be swept off their feet rather than courted. Such women wished to be forced into the subordinate role. One highly dominant woman (whom Maslow admitted to be his most neurotic subject) spent years hunting for a man of superior dominance and married him. Years later she was as much in love with him as at first. 'She actually picks fights in which he becomes violent and which usually end in virtual rape. These incidents provide her with her most exciting sexual experiences.'

Medium-dominance women tended to be scared of highly dominant males; they wanted a husband and father rather than a lover, a 'homey' man, adequate rather than outstanding. The low-dominance women tended to be shy and distrustful about men, while still wanting children; they were found to prefer low-dominance males: 'the gentle, timid, shy man who will adore at a distance for years before daring to speak'. While high-dominance women tended to be realists about sex, middle- and low-dominance women wanted romance, poetry, dim lights and illusions.

When these women are driven to promiscuity by a high sex drive, feelings of guilt are tremendous and may lead to thoughts of suicide.

Maslow discovered that all women prefer a male to be more dominant than themselves, but not too much so. Marriages in which the woman was more dominant than her husband tended to be less successful. He even worked out tests that would enable a couple contemplating marriage to work out if the 'dominance gap' was too great, too small or exactly right.

The connection between criminality and dominance was observed by the zoologist John B. Calhoun in a series of experiments he conducted at Palo Alto, California, in 1954. He enclosed twenty male and twenty female rats in an enclosed area of 1,000 square yards, with ample food and water. It should have been a rat heaven, yet within twenty-seven months it had turned into a hell.

He built four interconnected enclosures, with a narrow bridge between each. As the young rats reached maturity, they began to battle for dominance, and two highly dominant rats finally established themselves in the two end enclosures, together with their harems, allowing only a few very submissive rats to stay. The other rats were forced to content themselves with the middle two cages.

As the population increased, these two cages became overcrowded, with a predominance of males (since the 'sultans' in the end cages had large harems). And as more rats were born, these cages became overcrowded slums.

Now their behaviour became increasingly neurotic: for example, eating habits. Although there was plenty of food and they could eat as often as they liked, they all tried to eat out of the same bowl the moment one of them went towards it, jostling and often biting one another – even though there was another bowl only a few inches away. It was as if they all wanted to be the same, part of a crowd identity.

At this point the females' nest building began to suffer as they became lazier and lazier, and they finally gave it up entirely and let their babies sleep on the bare boards. They also began neglecting their young.

Rat courting behaviour, usually extremely elaborate, also suffered, as gangs of males pursued females, harassing them and even committing rape. The females began losing their babies before they were born, so the population dropped.

Among male rats, some developed into what

Calhoun called 'eccentrics', who lived in 'pathological seclusion', stayed awake all night and slept during the day. A great number, which Calhoun called 'hysterics', ignored all rules of precedence, showing no respect for superior males and returning to the attack until one of them was killed. They often then became cannibals and ate the loser.

In short, overcrowding produced criminal rats. The lesson for our increasingly overpopulated world is worrying.

All this should make it clear that understanding the role of dominance is basic to criminology.

Double jeopardy

It was a pathetic case – of a sort all too common in the crime-ridden state of Illinois – but it proved to highlight what some believe is an iniquity in the legal system: the 'double jeopardy' rule, which makes it illegal to retry a person for any crime if they have already been found not guilty – even if they subsequently make a detailed confession.

In October 1997 Pamela Travis, a 29-year-old mother of toddler twins, was found dead in her Carbondale apartment by maintenance workers investigating a report of smoke. She had been strangled with an electric cable and her corpse set on fire. This evident attempt to destroy the body was largely ineffectual, however. More shocking was that the fire had been set while Pamela's twenty-two-month-old daughters were shut in an adjacent room. If undiscovered, the fire or fumes might have killed them too.

The prime suspect was 35-year-old Gary Stark, an acquaintance of Pamela's and probably her drug dealer. Despite the lack of any conclusive proof against him, the police decided to charge Stark with the crime. The result was a verdict of not guilty owing to lack of evidence.

Six years later Stark was convicted on a number of drug-related charges and sentenced to 235 months (almost twenty years) in prison. Officials then took the opportunity to question him further, during which interview he gave a detailed confession. Pamela Travis had owed him money. They had argued. Stark had killed her with the lighting flex and set the body on fire.

However, because of the double jeopardy rule, upheld by the Fifth Amendment of the US constitution, Stark could not be charged with the murder. Only if substantive new evidence comes to light can a person be retried for the same crime. A confession, which the defendant can retract at any time, is not considered sufficient reason to begin a new trial.

Unjust as this outcome might seem, it should be considered against the alternative: the possibility of tyrannous government authorities being able to continually retry people until they get the guilty result they wish for. A case of a small evil being better than a great one, perhaps?

Dougal, Samuel Herbert (1846–1903)

Samuel Dougal was a pivotal Victorian murderer. His case revolves around a degree of rural isolation and an absence of communications that are today

Samuel Herbert Dougal, conman and killer

inconceivable. But his story has elements that go back further, to a style of imposture and sexual shenanigans of an almost feudal resonance.

In 1899 Dougal killed his common-law wife, 55-year-old Camille Holland, in a moated house in bleakest Essex hours from the nearest railway station, so remote that the local tradesmen never called; Dougal ensured that the postman – the last link with civilisation – did not come too close by meeting him in the lane. There was no one to notice that Camille had disappeared, so after a while Dougal realised that, for financial purposes, he might as well treat her as alive. He learned to forge Camille's signature and for the

Camille Ceile Holland

Camille C. Holland

Miss Holland's undoubted signatures (above) and Dougal's forgeries (below)

Camille C Holland

Camille C. Holland

next four years lived handsomely off her income, toffing it up as a local squire, buying one of the first cars in the district; he referred to it as a 'locomobile'. Meanwhile Dougal recalled his real wife from Ireland, who 'hollandised' herself, assuming Camille's identity and making progressive inroads into her predecessor's wardrobe.

Dougal's victim was that vanished breed – the wealthy spinster, living in semi-retirement. Serving wenches, another historical relic, figure large in the case; Dougal loved them, making them pregnant in droves. In an outlandish twist, Dougal specialised in teaching Essex girls how to cycle in the nude. 'What a picture,' wrote the chronicler of Dougal's 1903 trial, 'in that clayey, lumpy field, the clayey, lumpy girls naked, astride that unromantic object, a bicycle.'

Dougal had a way with women. His first wife bore him four children; she died suddenly in 1885 after eating oysters. His second wife perished of stomach cramps and vomiting the same year. Both may well have been poisoned. In the intervening years Dougal lived with many different women, siring many more children before his third marriage in 1892 to an Irishwoman. But disaster struck with his imprisonment for forging a £35 cheque in the name of 'Lord Frankfort'. The pension from his eleven years' service with the Royal Engineers, previously a steady payer at 2s 9d a day, was forfeit.

Strapped for cash, in early 1899 Dougal attended the Earl's Court Exhibition on the lookout. There he met the well-off, unaccompanied Camille Holland, a resident of a lodging house in fashionable Bayswater. Dougal paid court, and although she knew he had a wife in Dublin, Camille agreed to set up home together.

With Camille's money the couple bought the isolated Moat Farm. They moved in during April 1899 but it at once came forcibly to Camille's attention that her 'husband' had made advances to their 19-year-old servant Florence. The girl took fright when Dougal tried to break down her door and she sheltered overnight in Camille's bed.

Camille apologised for Dougal's conduct, but the girl left the following morning. Camille too could have fled, embarrassed and shamed but alive. She stayed on, and sometime during the next three weeks Dougal shot her in the head, burying the body in a drainage ditch which he then had filled and planted. Learning to forge Camille's handwriting, he released some of her capital and transferred Moat Farm into his own name.

By 1902 Dougal was still at his philandering; he took advantage of dozens of servant girls, including a mother and her three daughters. The real Mrs Dougal

Camille Holland

departed, and his shady background emerged when he attracted public notice by contesting an affiliation order. Camille's nephews came forward; they confirmed that nothing had been heard of their aunt for years. But the bank and solicitors maintained they were in constant correspondence with the vanished woman, and produced her last cheque, dated 28 August

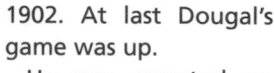

1902. At last Dougal's game was up.

He was arrested on suspicion of murder after his return from a weekend in Bournemouth with yet another woman he had impregnated. The house was searched for Camille's body; the moat dragged and then drained, the grounds probed with long iron rods – all without result. In the absence of the corpse, Dougal regained his bluster and threatened to sue the Chief Constable for £1,000 compensation for disfiguring his land. Then a labourer remembered the old infill of the 1899 ditch. Up came a woman's boot, size 2, with some bones in it, then a skull with a bullet-hole and a round of Union Metallic Ammunition still inside. At the trial the prosecution replicated the hole in the skull by firing bullets into a sheep's head.

It seems that Dougal was remembered by his many *amours* without rancour. He wrote from prison to one old flame suggesting that they hire communal transport for their massed appearance as witnesses at his trial. 'It is a delightful drive through undulating country,' he wrote, 'and at this time of year would be a veritable treat for them all.'

Dougal was hanged on 14 July 1903. As the executioner started to pull the lever the prison chaplain enquired: 'Guilty or not guilty?'

'Guilty,' the hooded Dougal replied. From his photographs he looks a fine, bluff fellow with an Edward VII beard-and-moustache.

Doyle, Sir Arthur Conan (1859–1930)

Conan Doyle, the creator of Sherlock Holmes, meshed with the world of real crime during the case of Oscar Slater, a German Jew wrongfully convicted of the murder of an old lady, Miss Marion Gilchrist, bludgeoned to death for her jewellery. The only evidence linking Slater with the December 1908 killing was eye-witness **identification.**

But of the three crucial witnesses against Slater, one stated, 'It's not the face I went for, it's the walk… I could not tell his face, I never saw his face.' Another succeeded in pointing out Slater as the man wanted by justice when he appeared before her handcuffed between two court officers. The third was near-sighted. None had caught more than the most fleeting glimpse of the culprit as he fled from the murder.

All the twelve witnesses who identified Slater, an obvious foreigner, had previously seen newspaper photographs which showed him to be obviously foreign. In the identity parades, they selected the man most like the accused from an assortment consisting of Slater, an obvious foreigner, standing out like a sore thumb alongside nine plainclothes Scottish policemen and two railway officials. When one witness suggested mixing Slater with men of similar appearance, the officer in charge replied: 'It might be the fairest way, but it is not the practice in Glasgow.'

There was nothing to connect Slater with the deceased, nothing to suggest he was acquainted with her or had heard of her jewellery. His supposed murder weapon – a light tin-tack hammer from Woolworths – was too flimsy for the fearful damage suffered by the victim and, like Slater's clothes, disclosed no bloodstains. He produced a perfectly reasonable alibi and was extradited from America (to which he had travelled openly) only because a bicycle-dealer saw him trying to sell a pawn ticket, allegedly for one of the missing diamond brooches. It was not, but by the time the police ascertained that Slater's brooch had been in pawn since 18 November, well before the killing, they had him fingered as the culprit.

Slater went down on a majority verdict after the judge, Lord Guthrie, explained that 'a man of his kind has not the presumption of innocence in his favour'. The sentence was reduced to life imprisonment two days before the scheduled execution of 27 May 1909.

On release of the trial transcripts, which marched from puzzle to puzzle, Conan Doyle took issue, writing an impassioned booklet entitled *The Case of Oscar Slater*. He showered the newspapers with letters of protest, and approached successive Secretaries of State for Scotland demanding to have the case reopened. The Scottish Office stonewalled and the campaign fizzled out.

Fifteen years later, the publication of *The Truth*

About Oscar Slater resurrected the controversy. Conan Doyle took the opportunity to circularise Members of Parliament, finally forcing a retrial before the Court of Appeal. The conviction was grudgingly set aside on 20 July 1928, leaving Conan Doyle to bear Slater's legal fees of some £1,500, which he guaranteed to get the case off the ground. During the hearing Conan Doyle described Slater's face as 'terrible for the brooding sadness that is in it'.

Conan Doyle's creation of a skilful, if fictional, detective was largely attributable to his lacklustre medical career. His Southsea practice attracted not a single patient and he whiled away his empty hours by composing fiction. In part his inspiration derived from Edgar Allan Poe's detective, Auguste Dupin, who made his debut in *The Murders in the Rue Morgue* in the 1840s. But Conan Doyle had his own plans; as he told a fellow-student in 1880, he wanted a detective based on 'the system of Poe, but greatly simplified and brought down to the level of ordinary people'.

Real police work furnished no precedent; Sherlock Holmes's magnifying glass, his tape measure, his minute study of the crime scene, his monographs on the different types of cigarette ash and the composition of various clays and muds, were all Conan Doyle's invention. When *A Study in Scarlet* came out in 1887 **fingerprinting** and even **anthropometry** still lay in the future, and detection, such as it was, consisted not of assessing the physical evidence, even in blatant cases, but on trapping the culprit red-handed, or accepting hearsay and rumour, or checking suspects one by one in an endless round of elimination (see **Lacenaire**). Juries remained extremely sceptical of any intellectual bias.

Conan Doyle's solitary emphasis on the pre-eminence of logic made him a **court** of last resort for those adjudged guilty who could prove their innocence; he also played a part in the Edalji and Beck cases.

His contribution to **Ripperology** was the theory of Jill the Ripper: since a female midwife could wander bloodstained through the East End streets without attracting attention, the author considered the occupation an ideal disguise for a male killer.

His brother-in-law, the journalist Edward William Hornung, created the gentleman burglar Raffles, who first appeared in the 1899 best-seller *The Amateur Cracksman*.

Drawing and quartering

Until the introduction of the long drop, hanging achieved slow and agonising death through strangulation. It was thus possible to interrupt the process before death supervened and disembowel the victim, compelling him – for instance – to eat his own entrails before chopping the body into quarters. The punishment, reserved for treason, was also known as 'Godly Butchery' since its proponents claimed to find scattered authority for the practice in the Bible. Forgery was considered a direct assault on the apparatus of the state, and many coiners suffered dismemberment.

The victim was sentenced to be 'hanged by the neck until half dead, and then cut down and his entrails to be cut out of his body while living and burned by the executioners. Then his head to be cut off, his body to be divided into quarters and afterwards his head and quarters to be set up in some open places directed.' Clearly the performance had a strong theatrical element, standing as a paradigm for the might of the state and the piecemeal destruction of its enemies.

Efficient workers – butchers were preferred – often removed the innards with such despatch that they could still attract the victim's attention by waving his guts in front of his face. More showy executioners sliced open the chest to excise the heart, which they held out to the populace with the words: 'Behold the heart of a traitor.'

Possibly the first victim was William Marise, pirate, in 1241. The last provincial display happened in Derby in 1813, and seven years later in London the Cato Street Conspirators were decapitated after being hanged; when the executioner dropped the last head, someone from the crowd shouted 'Butterfingers!' As late as 1839, two years into Queen Victoria's reign, the Chartist John Frost was sentenced to the full penalty, later commuted to transportation for life to Australia.

See also **Exactitude**, **Pressing**, **Quartering**

Drops of blood

Drops of blood behave as one would expect, in a Newtonian fashion, and a great deal can be deduced just from their shape. Blood falling vertically makes a circular mark with neat, spiky edges, and the distance fallen can be estimated by the number of pointed 'spines' round the circumference. From a height of about five feet, the blood tends to splodge out towards one side.

Circular **bloodstains** come from a stationary source (since otherwise they would not have fallen vertically). Drops of blood from a moving person (or object) land in the form of exclamation marks, their outline varying according to the speed of impact and direction of travel. Smears on the floor emanating from a bleeding corpse as it is dragged away show which way it went. Lines of blood on the ceiling are flung off when an assailant flourishes an axe overhead. Level trails of blood deposited along the walls suggest a weapon brandished horizontally.

These mundane considerations played a crucial role in the 1984 case of Graham Backhouse. As a hairdresser, Backhouse prospered. But soon after inheriting Widden Hill Farm outside Bristol in middle age and turning his hand to agriculture, he found himself nursing a £70,000 bank overdraft. Meanwhile the traditional hairdresser's perk of extra-marital philandering brought him into bad odour with his neighbours. After a string of abusive telephone calls and poison-pen letters, a worried Backhouse notified the police that on 30 March 1984 his herdsman had found a severed sheep's head impaled on his fence with a note reading 'You next'.

It was no idle threat. On 9 April Backhouse asked his wife to drive into town to collect some antibiotics, and she got into her husband's Volvo and turned on the ignition. This triggered the detonator in a steel pipe packed with the powder from twelve shotgun cartridges, firing 4,000 lead pellets upwards through the driver's seat and removing half her thigh. She was lucky to survive.

This apparent attempt on her husband's life inspired an intensive police investigation, and it transpired that Backhouse was locked in dispute with many of the locals over soured business deals or seductions. One among several suspects was a troubled near-neighbour, Colyn Bedale-Taylor, with whom Backhouse had quarrelled about a right of way. The police provided round-the-clock protection, but after nine days the impatient Backhouse ordered the men off his land.

By the evening of 30 April the police had a corpse on their hands. A bleeding Backhouse related how Bedale-Taylor had called round to Widden Hill Farm on some pretext and, after an amicable cup of coffee in the kitchen, gone berserk. First he accused Backhouse

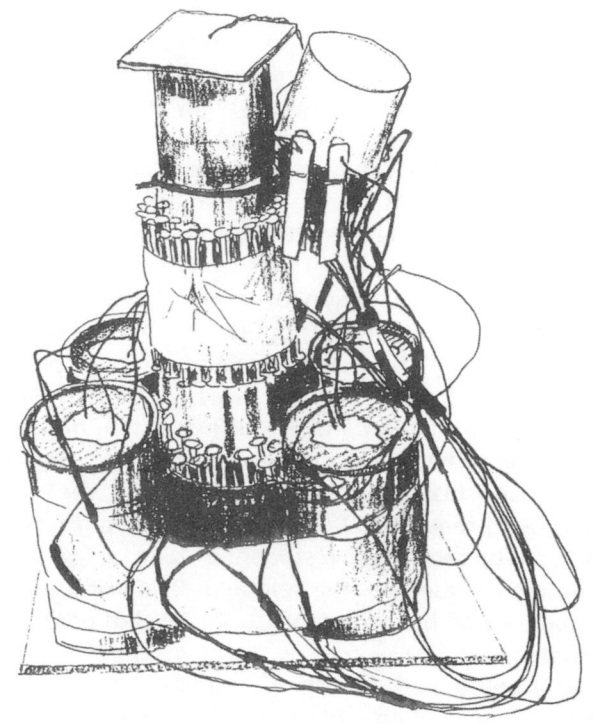

The home-made bomb

of causing his son's death in a car crash two years before. Then he admitted to planting the bomb. Then he pulled a Stanley knife and tried to finish the job, slashing Backhouse across the face and chest as the two men grappled for their lives.

Backhouse struggled free and fled into the hall, where he seized a shotgun. He warned off the advancing Bedale-Taylor, then shot him twice in the chest. A police search of the dead man's land revealed the remainder of the steel pipe used in the car bomb.

But the drops of blood in Backhouse's kitchen were the wrong shape and in the wrong disposition. They should have been spattered around the walls and furniture by the violent fight, producing distinctive 'flying tails'. Instead they lay sedately on the flagstones, forming neat circles with indented edges, as though Backhouse deliberately stood still and allowed his blood to spill evenly to the floor.

On further examination, one of the envelopes containing a threatening letter disclosed a few fibres of wool stuck to the gum under the flap, and the microscope matched them perfectly to fibres from one of Backhouse's own sweaters. In a desk drawer a detective found a notepad, and on one page was a doodle corresponding with indentations carried through to the 'You next' note.

Backhouse had been sending himself threatening letters. The reason? So he could murder his wife and collect her life insurance, recently doubled to £100,000. He could have pulled back from the brink after the failure of the bomb plot, but he may have felt that both the police and his wife needed further proof of innocence. He was sentenced to life imprisonment on 19 February 1985.

Duelling

The German Chancellor Bismarck was quick to take offence in his youth, fighting – some say – twenty-five duels as a student at the University of Gottingen during the 1830s. An unusual affair of honour involved a professor who, given the choice of weapons, selected a matched pair of **sausages**, one of them poisoned. Bismarck declined to participate, but he was game for nearly everything else. Back on his Pomeranian estates after his student excesses, he remained a tearaway, drinking recklessly, womanising and letting loose with a pistol through the bedroom windows of his occasional guests, and all this before he started to cause serious trouble. Bismarck provides a perfect example of the high-dominance, high-ability personality. He became a statesman. His high-dominance, low-ability counterparts grow up as criminals.

Jeffrey Hudson, dwarf by appointment to Queen Henrietta Maria (the first bride of Charles I), killed a man in one duel and defeated a turkey in another. Cyrano de Bergerac, the seventeenth-century French wit, is reputed to have fought and won over 1,000 duels, during one three-month period running through his opponents at the rate of four a week. Between 1601 and 1609 some 2,000 French nobles died in duels.

Affairs of honour were less frequent in England, where the victor stood a reasonable prospect of a murder charge. When Ben Jonson, the Elizabethan playwright, killed an actor with his rapier in a duel in September 1598, he was brought to trial and duly condemned to death. But he pleaded **Benefit of Clergy** on the grounds that he could read as well as write, demonstrating his knack by declaiming from a book handed to him in court. The sentence was commuted to branding, with the letter T (for Tyburn) scorched into his thumb.

In 1654 Oliver Cromwell reaffirmed the illegality of duels, but the practice continued unabated, not least since army regulations obliged officers 'to redeem their honour in a duel' until 1844. The last duel on British soil occurred at Egham in Surrey in 1852, fought by two Frenchmen.

Duffy, John Francis (1954–)

The 'Railway Murderer' was the computer-caught British sex killer who committed his first known **rape** on 10 June 1982. The police had little more to go on than a distinct *modus operandi* coupled with a vague physical description of a small, slightly built man with staring eyes. This fitted hundreds of suspects on their list of 1,999 sex offenders, already whittled down from 4,874 by eliminating improbables and those in prison or dead.

Artist's impression of Duffy

The distinct style of the rapes afforded few clues. Most of the attacks happened on or close to London railway stations, generally in the footpaths and alleys nearby. First the rapist chatted to his victim, then he produced a knife. The woman's hands were bound behind her back, and after the assault he wiped down her privates with a paper tissue and brushed through her pubic hairs with a plastic comb to remove forensic evidence. Apart from the obvious inference of their suspect's familiarity with the railway network, the police had no real pointers.

For the first sixteen attacks the rapist operated in

tandem with a taller partner. Both men wore balaclavas. After a void period in late 1983, the shorter of the two went solo. He had committed a total of twenty-five rapes by 29 December 1985, the day that a London secretary, Alison Day, set off to Hackney Wick station to meet her boyfriend. She never arrived. Two weeks later her body, weighted down with stones, was recovered from a canal a short distance from the station.

Alison had been raped and beaten about the head with a brick. Her hands were tied behind her back, and her assailant tore a strip from her tartan shirt, tied it round her neck, inserted a stick through a turn in her 'collar' and then twisted it round until she died. She was 19.

Other rapes led to murder. On 17 April 1986 a 15-year-old schoolgirl, Maartje Tamboezer, rode her bicycle to the village sweet shop half a mile away. She took a short cut down a narrow lane beside East Horsley station, to be knocked off her bike by a nylon rope across the path. She too had her hands bound; she too was bludgeoned about the head. She too was raped and strangled. This time the killer stuffed her vagina with paper tissues which he set alight to eliminate traces of his spermatozoa. Witnesses saw a small wiry man in a blue parka running for the 6.07 train back to London. Two million railway tickets were collected and examined for the suspect's fingerprints without result.

A month later a third woman died, this time a bride just back from honeymoon. The police correctly considered the Railway Murderer as a latter-day manifestation of the Railway Rapist, and he, in turn, should be among their 2,000 'possibles'. But where?

The year before, in July 1985, a diminutive young man from Kilburn, John Duffy, had broken into the bedroom of his estranged wife and subjected her to a violent rape; later he attacked her new boyfriend. Duffy was released on bail, but the arrest added him to the list as suspect 1594, and a detective took a traumatised 20-year-old rape victim to his court hearing to see if she recognised him. She did not, but it is likely that Duffy saw her and understood the threat posed by survivors.

On 17 May 1986, three weeks after Maartje Tamboezer's murder and the day before the final death, two police officers driving through North Weald in Essex came upon Duffy twenty-five miles from his home, loitering by a tube station. A search revealed a sharp

knife and a wad of paper tissues in his pocket. Duffy explained he was a Zen Budo enthusiast and needed the weapon for martial arts classes. He could not be charged, but by now the investigation had established the rapist's blood group and his phosphoglucomutase reading, enabling the elimination of four suspects out of five. In addition the police had clothes fibres, and knew that the string used to tie up victims was a distinctive type of 'Somyarn' dating from 1982. They could convict the right man, if they could find him.

On 17 July Duffy was called in for routine questioning. He arrived with a solicitor, itself unusual, and, curiouser and curiouser, refused to supply a blood sample. The following day he staggered into West Hampstead police station after being violently attacked in a street mugging, his face bruised and his chest bleeding profusely from a razor slash. A side-effect was partial memory loss, and Duffy committed himself to the psychiatric unit at Friern Barnet Hospital.

The police ploughed on through their other suspects. Meanwhile they contacted David Canter, a

John Duffy and David Mulcahy

psychology professor from Surrey University, to see if an American-style '**profile**' might help. Canter had no previous police experience, but he asked for the witness statements and forensic reports, and two weeks later produced seventeen 'personality indicators' of which thirteen proved well-founded. Many were computer-friendly, allowing instantaneous elimination of whole categories of suspects.

Thus the 'centre of gravity' of the attacks suggested a resident of Kilburn or Cricklewood. Statistical probability put his age between twenty and thirty. The recurring feature of bondage suggested an interest in bondage. Witnesses described their assailant as physically small, and small men given to rape may feel themselves unattractive, particularly if they have acne, and small acned men given to violent rape may be interested in martial arts, and small martial arts hobbyists fascinated by bondage who are given to violent rape are unlikely to have a stable marriage. But they may well keep a collection of hard-core porn and knives and swords. And so on. Detectives keyed the information in, and the computer identified suspect number 1594.

The police now discovered that Duffy was not safely hospitalised, but an outpatient, and while out on 21 October he raped again. Still without hard evidence, Superintendent McFadden ordered his arrest. A search of Duffy's home yielded a collection of knives and 'Kung fu' weapons. In a cupboard at his parents' house the police found a ball of Somyarn. Forensic analysis of thirteen 'foreign' fibres on Alison Day's body proved a perfect match for one of Duffy's sweaters, and a fellow-martial arts devotee, Ross Mockeridge, described how he had been persuaded to subject Duffy to a simulated mugging.

Duffy's wife filled in the picture. She married the former altar boy in June 1980. Amid increasing recriminations they tried hard for a child; he took their failure to procreate as a personal insult and their love life went awry. Before having sex he insisted on tying her hands to replicate rape; the more she struggled the more he liked it. His obsession with bondage and violence bred endless rows, and an attempted reconciliation in the autumn of 1983 corresponded with the temporary cessation of the rapes. Their marriage broke down in June 1985. 'The nice man I had married had become a madman with scary, scary eyes,' said his wife. In 1988 at the Old Bailey, Duffy was sentenced to a minimum of thirty years.

Duffy later confessed to a prison counsellor that he

had had an accomplice in the attacks. But it was not until 1999 that he decided to 'clear his conscience' by naming his fellow-rapist as his schoolfriend David Mulcahy, a married father of four. On 2 February 2001, Mulcahy was given three life sentences for the rape and murder of three women – Alison Day, Maartje Tamboezer and Anne Lock – and for seven other rapes. Duffy had already been given a further sixteen years for rapes not originally disclosed.

Dumdums

Bullets designed to fragment inside the target on impact. Dumdums were first employed in India in 1897, to such terrible effect that their military application was banned by the Hague Convention of 1899. But the Feds in Prohibition Chicago used them, and more recently they constituted the favourite ammunition of both Ronald **Kray** and **van Schoor**, the South African security guard.

The Armalite rifle now achieves the same objective legally. Instead of entering the body cleanly, its high-velocity bullets tumble through. Alternatively, Americans can purchase a type of ammunition known as 'Devastators'. These bullets, developed for sky marshals in hijacking cases, contain a small aluminium canister filled with explosive. John Hinckley Jnr fired them into President Reagan, but they failed to go off.

John Lennon was not so lucky, and it is interesting to see that his assassin, Mark Chapman, thought his plans through to envisioning the dilation of the ammunition – hollow-point Smith & Wesson Plus Ps – within the target body. 'I chose the right type of bullet so that it expanded inside him rather than going in and just laying there,' Chapman told psychiatrists. 'This way, the expansion of the bullet, it instantly damaged more of Lennon's internal organs and death was more quickly there for him.' Chapman's subtext is of caring for his victim, and evidently **assassins** who care use dumdums.

See also **Stalking**

Dummy

One legal constituent of murder is killing with 'malice aforethought'. This requires the formation of intent and there is thus a long line of 'mistake' cases where death was caused without the requisite intention.

Among the more unusual scenarios is the Waterloo Dummy case. It started on the morning of 8 December 1950 when William Donoghue, a 42-year-old bus conductor, stood outside his south London flat staring in horror at a corpse on the landing, muttering: 'Is it a dummy or a body? Take it away.' Later, when the police arrived, Donoghue said: 'If that is a real man, I done it.'

It emerged that Donoghue had been out for a drink the night before. First he downed six or seven bottles of Guinness in the 'Prince Albert'. Still thirsty, he set off for the 'Brunswick Arms', Southwark, where he met an old friend, Thomas Meaney. Together they drank beer laced with gin and then returned unsteadily to Donoghue's flat, rounding off the evening with a bottle of spirits. Donoghue fell asleep in a chair while Meaney dozed off on the bed.

Later that night Donoghue climbed into his bed which – much to his irritation – he found encumbered with some sort of dummy, a person-shaped object presumably put there by his mates as a practical joke. Donoghue threw the 'guy' on the floor and then savaged out its stuffing with his old army bayonet, stabbing it sixteen times. Realistic-looking red gunge oozed out. Then he kicked it on to the landing and went back to his drunken stupor.

Was this murder? Manslaughter? Or an **accident**? Donoghue's urine sample showed 450mg alcohol per cent, sufficient to threaten his own life and enough to bar the formation of any intent to kill. At his trial the prosecution accepted a plea of manslaughter and Donoghue went down for three years.

This case is in sharp contrast to one where a killer drinks for 'Dutch courage' to stiffen his resolve, an aggravating factor indicative of premeditation.

See also **Accidents, Ghost**

Durability

Never underestimate the durability of the human body; no matter what, parts keep on turning up. Killers should clearly visualise the scale of the problem.

A corpse is a large object to conceal and soon broadcasts its presence by the stench. Burial is hard in cities, and in the country the grave is readily distinguishable by traces of disturbed soil. Shallow graves give up their dead. Deep ones take hours to dig, and neighbours think it odd. Transportation to the disposal site is fraught.

Dumping the body in a trunk at Left Luggage is asking for exposure. Hiding a corpse around the house destroys the ambience. **Dismemberment** is a vast task which produces blood and bits everywhere, and even then the chunks have to be concealed. **Acid** does not work. Nor do bombs (see **Payne**). Incineration leaves the **teeth** and often even the **hair**. Identification evidence survives the rivers and the sea. Hence the attractions of faked accidents and **poisoning**. Once the first hurdle of packaging the death as 'natural causes' is surmounted, the problems are over. For a killer with a corpse on his hands, they are just beginning.

John Perry's 1992 experience in Clwyd, Wales, typifies the difficulties caused by an unwanted body. After killing his wife, a Filipina half his age, 52-year-old Perry carried her body to the bathroom to cut her up. The Home Office pathologist Dr Wayte estimated that this task alone would have taken a good twelve hours of intensive effort, but the results were impressive – uniformly diced chunks. The bones Perry sawed and snapped.

Then he started on the cooking. To make it easier to open, the head was baked separately in the double oven. Then Perry drilled and chiselled the skull in two, depositing the contents, together with some twenty gallons of blood and body fluid, in the countryside on repeated night trips. This left a bin full of human organs, two plastic bags stuffed with ancillary material and a container filled with congealed human grease. The house smelled of roasted and decaying flesh, the carpet was covered with blood, and Perry still had fresh gore on his forehead when detectives called to investigate. They had been summoned by neighbours, who noticed an excess of soap suds round the drains.

The police asked Perry where his wife was. He replied, 'I have fed some to the cat.' The family pet thus became the macabre object of photographers' attentions and an excellent portrait appeared in the *Independent*, a paper not normally renowned for its humour. The creature's present whereabouts are not known, but Perry was sent down for life in November 1991.

Durable

Nickname given to the irrepressible Mike Molloy, an Irish inebriate from New York. A syndicate from his

Third Avenue speakeasy in the Bronx reckoned that no one would miss Mike much. He was already aged 60 and, at that, a wreck. So, insuring his life for $1,788 as a healthy 46-year-old, they set about doing him in. It looked like easy money to the five-man team of Kreisberg, Green, Pasqua, Murphy the bartender and Tony Marino, the bar's proprietor; the gang was fresh from their triumph of killing Tony's mistress for her insurance. All they did was get the girl drunk, fix the window open, add water and collect when she died of pneumonia.

For the repeat performance on New Year's Eve 1932, the boys made Mike paralytically drunk on liquor spiked with anti-freeze and left him for dead. But next day Mike staggered back into their lives, desperate for a drink. Over the following days they dosed him with turpentine, and with wood alcohol bumped up with rat poison, and with sardine sandwiches filled with tin tacks. Mike blossomed.

Luckily one of the team – Green – worked as a taxi driver; he ran Mike over, but to no effect. So Green ran him over again. Results were better, a broken shoulder, but still not good enough. So they made Mike very drunk yet again, stripped him, doused him in water, waited until the ice formed and then left his body on the streets to freeze.

When that failed, Mike Molloy must have thought he was having one helluva start to the year. But on 22 February the boys took the Great Survivor out carousing one more time and gassed him with carbon monoxide, stuffing a rubber tube down his throat. Word got out because one of the gang *boasted* of the killing.

On exhumation the conspicuous red blotches on Molloy's skin testified to the cause of death, and all five of his friends went to the **electric chair**.

Dutch, The

Very naive. Dutch liberal policies towards soft drugs in the 1970s attracted the major Chinese heroin traffickers seeking a hospitable European base. Legally speaking, the odds were heavily stacked in the dealers' favour: no *agents provocateurs*, no convictions in the absence of possession, no effective conspiracy laws, no plea-bargaining with informers, no wiretap evidence admissible in court and, until 1977, a maximum sentence of four years for drug trafficking, with remission for good conduct. The prisons were so pleasant they resembled hotels, housing one inmate per cell, with televisions, radios, magazines, books, gymnasia, conjugal visits, full access to telephones, and limited inspection of packages in and out.

In the early 1970s no one in the Dutch police force had seen any heroin, so it was reasonably safe to leave it lying around in buckets. The first haul came in 1971, consisting of a mere two ounces found on a Chinese sailor in a Chinatown gambling den; two years later, when Amsterdam was one of the main conduits for 'China White', total seizures edged towards a pound.

Richard Weijenburg, chief of the intelligence division on Chinese crime, tells a story from the early 1970s when two officers inspected a Chinese restaurant. They ran across millions of dollars' worth of a strange white substance. 'In the kitchen,' recounts Weijenburg, 'they saw a large wicker basket with plastic bags stamped with a tiger on the front.' This was the logo of the Double U-O Globe brand, the world's most famous branded heroin. 'The bags were filled with a white powder and there must have been a hundred large bags in there. The police asked the chef what the bags contained and were told it was a common spice used in the restaurant's cooking. When one of the police asked if he could have some for his wife, an avid cooker, he was politely refused because it was very expensive and hard to get.'

The officers left to go about their business. In 1973 America's exasperated DEA lent a hand in mounting the first big arrest – for fourteen kilos of heroin – which very nearly miscarried when at the critical moment, rather than making the bust, the Dutch police nodded off.

Worried by the growing American intervention, the head of the local 14K **Triad**, nicknamed the Unicorn, was recalled to Hong Kong. He had single-handedly developed the European **narcotics** trade following the American withdrawal from Vietnam; now he needed polishing with an intensive course in socialisation. Back in Amsterdam, a refurbished Unicorn made a big play to the Dutch authorities, stressing his benevolent role as Chairman of the Chinese Overseas Association. Decorated for his contribution to public service, he inveigled his way into the confidence of Amsterdam's Police Commissioner, Gerard Toorenaar, for whom he acted as a personal informer as well as the unofficial peacekeeper of the Chinese community. In return for the Unicorn betraying his rivals,

Toorenaar allegedly issued letters of immunity clearing him of involvement in the heroin trade.

The Unicorn was assassinated on 3 March 1975; by then, the Dutch police were becoming suspicious. But in 1988 they had no more than three full-time officers on the Triad connection – reminiscent of **Hoover**'s taskforce, several strong, devoted to rooting out organised crime in America.

Dutroux, Marc

On 28 May 1996, a twelve-year-old Belgian girl, Sabine Dardenne, disappeared on her way to school. Two men, Michel Lelièvre and Marc Dutroux, had grabbed her and pulled her into a car. She was taken to a house belonging to Dutroux and was chained to a bed for three days. Then she was taken down to a home-made dungeon in the cellar and locked in. Over the next eighty days Sabine was repeatedly raped and underwent

Marc Dutroux, the Belgian paedophile and murderer

psychological torture by Dutroux. (In a grim historical irony, the name 'Sabine' is that of an ancient Italian tribe, the women of whom were kidnapped and forced into sexual slavery by the early Romans.)

Sabine told police that Dutroux, a man who had already served a reduced sentence for paedophilia, had tried to convince her that he was protecting her from a gang of felons who had demanded money from her parents. If she failed to do everything he demanded, he had threatened, he would hand her over to these men, who 'would torture me and kill me after making me suffer'. In a particularly sadistic touch, Dutroux also told Sabine that her parents knew of her whereabouts but had simply abandoned her to her fate. Contradicting this lie, he made her write letters to her family, as if she were on holiday. Of course he never sent them, but read them to find out more details about her home life, to further embroider his manipulative mental games with her. Police found around thirty such letters in his house.

After nearly three months beneath the Dutroux house, Sabine Dardenne was joined by another girl, 14-year-old Laetitia Delhez. A week later, however, both were rescued when police raided the house.

It might have been hoped that the arrest of Dutroux – along with Michel Lelièvre and Dutroux's wife, Michelle – would have ended the horror, but much worse was to come. Police searched another house belonging to Dutroux, but failed to find Julie Lejeune and Mélissa Russo, both aged eight, trapped alive in another home-made dungeon. Officers heard their plaintive cries for help but thought their voices came from children playing in the street outside. The girls both starved to death before another search revealed their location.

Marc Dutroux made no effort to warn the authorities that the trapped girls were there and were in peril. Michelle Dutroux later admitted that she also knew the little girls were trapped and were starving to death. Although free herself at that time, she did nothing to save them because, she said, she was afraid they might attack her if she took them food.

Further searching of one of the basement dungeons in Dutroux's houses unearthed the corpses of Eefje Lambrecks, 17, and An Marchal, 19. Both were abduction victims, like Sabine and Laetitia.

The bungling of the Belgian police staggered the world. Why had they not used sniffer dogs to search Dutroux's second house and thus, almost certainly,

Marc Dutroux's torture chamber cellar

rescue Julie and Mélissa alive? Public fury soon turned to suspicion. It was asked just how Dutroux, an unemployed electrician, could afford to own several houses. Why was he released ten years early from prison after his first conviction for paedophilia? And why did he go unarrested for so long in the face of mounting evidence that he might be connected to the disappearances of children?

Rumours of a paedophile gang, protected by members high up in the Belgian government and police, soon shook the establishment to its roots. There was even talk of Belgium ceasing to exist as a separate country, so horrified were its population by the scandal. It was argued that half the country should become part of the Netherlands, the other should become part of France, and damn the heartless Belgian elite who turned a blind eye to, or even indulged in, monstrous crimes. The fact that police bungling allowed Dutroux to escape in 1998 did not help the scandal; fortunately he was soon recaptured.

In 1996, 275,000 Belgians had joined a march through Brussels protesting apparent police bungling over the Dutroux case and government inactivity over paedophilia. Yet it was partially because of this huge public outcry that Marc Dutroux was not brought to trial until March 2004 – eight years after his arrest. He did not deny his acts of kidnapping and paedophilia, but insisted he was merely a courier for a paedophile gang and it was they, not him, who had strangled the two girls found buried in his cellar. As to just who else was involved in this gang he did not say, only directly accusing his wife, Michel Lelièvre (the man who had helped him kidnap Sabine Dardenne) and Michel Nihoul (a businessman who had helped Dutroux sell drugs).

Nevertheless, Dutroux hinted at a much wider paedophile ring when he told the court that he had once gone hunting abduction victims with 'two policemen'. Rightly or wrongly, the court saw this as an attempt to further delay sentencing and denied Dutroux's defence lawyer's request that the trial be halted while the extent of the ring was fully investigated. Dutroux was sentenced to life imprisonment for kidnapping, rape and murder. His ex-wife Michelle Martin (as she had become) was given thirty years for kidnapping and rape. Michel Lelièvre was given twenty-five years for kidnapping and drug dealing and Michel Nihoul five years for drug dealing and several counts of fraud.

Yet questions remain. Was there a paedophile ring? If so, how far did it extend? Were the Belgian police and government officials linked to it? It seems odd that the jury and three judges felt it necessary to add a caveat to Marc Dutroux's sentence – should the authorities decide to parole him, the government of the day has the right to add ten further years to his sentence to prevent his immediate release. Why did they feel this safety valve was necessary?

E

Ears, severed

Perhaps the best-known ears are J. Paul Getty III's and Lord Erroll's. The former hit the headlines after being sent through the mail to a newspaper in Rome.

Getty had been kidnapped. His captors cut off his ear and consigned it to the mercies of the notorious Italian postal service on 21 October 1973; it was lucky to be received by the press in early November. After further threats that other parts of the kidnapped youth would follow, his grandfather, Paul Getty himself, agreed to a record $2.9 million ransom. Since this was paid as three billion lire, the money was delivered to Calabria by truck.

Lord Erroll's detached ear made a brief appearance in the courtroom scene of the film *White Mischief*. This was no dramatic licence. On the night of 23 January 1941, Josslyn Victor Hay, twenty-second Earl of Erroll, was shot twice in the head from point-blank range with ammunition charged by a black powder propellant, a point demonstrated in court by Erroll's stained ear, handed round in a jar of spirits. 'This really is *too* much. Poor Joss,' said Diana, his ex-lover (see **White Mischief**).

The ear of Donald Merrett's mother became a similar forensic curiosity in 1924 after she was shot in the head while sitting at the desk in a recess of her living room. The police, suspecting suicide, confined her to a secure ward under conditions of near-arrest for her sin, and when she died four days later, her ear (attached to a six-inch slab of flesh) was scrutinised for clues. No scorch marks or traces of 'tattooing' from unburned flecks of powder were found, suggesting that the gun had been at least nine inches from her head at the moment of discharge – unusual for suicides, and it seemed more than a coincidence that her son, who stood to inherit, had been in the room at the time. Donald Merrett purchased the pistol a few days previously, and his mother's last recollection before hearing a bang was of saying: 'Go away, Donald, and don't annoy me.' But the verdict was 'not proven', and Merrett killed twice more before committing suicide in 1954.

In a more mundane incident from October 1991, Scotsman Kenneth Docherty was jailed not for theft but assault. After biting off his opponent's ear in a fight, he ran away with it clenched between his teeth.

The forensic possibilities of earprints are under appraisal by Professor Starrs of George Washington University. Professional criminals wear gloves on a job as a matter of course, but do not appreciate the dangers of listening, with one ear pressed to the door, before effecting entry.

See also **Kidney**

Eastern bloc

With the collapse of the Communist empire, parts of the Soviet Union regressed to the state of brigandage prevalent throughout Europe centuries ago. At the most basic level, customs officials started freelancing, forming themselves into mafia cartels. In late 1991 on the Ukraine/Polish border, vehicles leaving Russia faced a single-line tailback of six miles and a wait of two weeks or more for their turn to be fleeced. Customs officers simply peered into the car and fixed a price – whatever the travellers could pay.

In the words of the Polish writer Ryszard Kapuscinsky: 'The Moscow authorities said they no longer controlled the Ukraine; and the Kiev authorities said that the customs officials were still under the control of Moscow. The truth is they're both right and they're both wrong, because in fact neither has any control. The customs officials operate as free agents, exacting arbitrary tolls without appeal and for themselves alone.'

With these tempting yields, borders became increasingly popular propositions. The Kiev–Minsk–Warsaw train developed a previously non-existent Ukrainian–Byelorussian frontier for the extraction of levies. Heading the other way into Russia, drivers travelled in convoys. Cars on the Byelorussia highway were liable to be shot up, and arrived – if at all – with shattered windscreens.

When the film-maker Piotr Bikont caught the Moscow–Warsaw train, he witnessed the nightly robbery routine. Come the small hours, 'several of the more beefy Russians took to gazing expectantly out of the windows at the endlessly flat, snow-covered terrain, and suddenly, as if on cue, they all heaved themselves up from behind their tables and stalked off to the Russian cars. There they barged into one sleeping compartment after another ... yanked open the windows and proceeded to toss every suitcase, package, purse or unattached bundle out of the train ... And then on to the next compartment, same thing. Their confederates were positioned out there along this particular stretch of railway.'

In Vladivostok, law and order all but disappeared. Conditions were so bad that robbers stole potatoes, digging up whole fields. Students supplemented their monthly grants of £0.50 by turning to prostitution; tourists were openly mugged in city restaurants for their cash, and the import of second-hand cars shipped across the Sea of Japan created Mafia-style gang warfare responsible for about eight bullet-riddled corpses a week.

With the progressive decay of central authority, the infection spread to Moscow by the summer of 1992, with eleven gang-warfare fatalities in one twenty-four-hour period, three gunned down in restaurants. Some were casualties of the Icon Wars; six thousand of these 'wooden roubles' are seized at Moscow's Sheremetyevo Airport each year, on their illegal way out of the country, many for thefts commissioned by Western dealers. Smugglers kill for stock. The month of August saw the recovery of a cement-filled box from the river near Tula. Inside was a dead body, but it had been alive when the concrete poured in.

More fortunate gangsters, who reached the top of the heap, settled in London; the brothers Ruslan and Nasabeck Utsyev paid cash for a luxurious £1 million penthouse with fully fitted cupboards, from one of which their bodies, shot in the head, were retrieved in early 1993. British police suspected that big-time Russian gangsters, with access to limitless supplies of Eastern bloc arms and drugs (some irradiated by Chernobyl), were forging links with both the Mafia and the Colombian cartels.

The Russians act with peculiar savagery. Western gangs generally steer clear of killing journalists, but the Russian investigative reporter Vladimir Glotov turned up dead in his Moscow apartment with his face cut off. Abroad, Russian *mafiosi* appreciate that the worst they face at the hands of the authorities is imprisonment in relatively comfortable conditions.

As an antidote to increasing violence, in 1992 Russia was poised to legitimise the sale of firearms for home use.

See also **Whacks, Zlotys**

Edwards, Tracy (1959–)

A lucky man. On the afternoon of 22 July 1991, 32-year-old Edwards stood chatting to two friends in Milwaukee's Grand Avenue Mall when he was approached by an acquaintance, Jeffrey **Dahmer**.

Dahmer, by that stage virtually destitute, said he felt 'real bored' and offered them $100 each to come back to his house and keep him company. Pressed for details, he added that he wanted to manacle somebody. Edwards accepted, and they took a cab back to Dahmer's home at 213 Oxford Apartments.

Inside the apartment, Edwards commented on the overpowering stench: 'It smells like someone died in here.' They shared a couple of beers but, disturbed by the smell, Edwards became restless. So Dahmer handed him a spiked rum and coke, snapped a pair of handcuffs round his wrist and pulled a knife.

Dahmer easily dragged the groggy Edwards into the bedroom, where they sat on a sheet that appeared to be covered in dried blood and watched *Exorcist II* on video. On the walls Edwards noticed photographs of naked mutilated men, one almost destroyed by acid. Halfway through the tape, Dahmer said, 'I want to show you something', pulled a man's **head** out of a filing cabinet and gave it a good rub. 'This is how I get people to stay with me,' he told Edwards. Then Dahmer pointed to a shelf in the closet, drawing his attention to a pair of severed human hands.

Edwards now observed that Dahmer was trying to force the handcuffs on to his other wrist. It's all right,

Dahmer reassured him, it's just to take a few photographs. Then Dahmer manhandled him to the floor and sat on top with the butcher's knife at his captive's chest. Dahmer said that he intended to cut out Edwards's heart and eat it. Edwards played for time, characterising himself as a friend, and they drifted back into the living room where Dahmer slipped in and out of a reverie.

'It's time, it's time,' Dahmer chanted, brandishing the knife. With his last strength Edwards slugged him in the jaw and then knocked him clear with a karate kick. Edwards reached the door and struggled with the locks while Dahmer scrabbled from behind. He broke free and staggered into the street, running screaming through the night until he flagged down a passing patrol car.

'He's going to kill me, he's going to kill me,' Edwards babbled to the police, but the dangling handcuffs made Officers Rauth and Mueller mistake this strange apparition for a fugitive from justice. Edwards persisted until they checked out his story and found that, indeed, 213 **Oxford Apartments** was a charnel-house.

Within hours Dahmer's grisly secret splashed over the world's press and airwaves. Edwards became a familiar face as he told and retold the story of his escape to the cameras, so much so that police watching the transmissions in Tupelo recognised him as the alleged rapist of a 14-year-old girl. Edwards faces thirty years if convicted.

But at least Edwards survived. Not everyone was so lucky. Only a few days before, on 27 May, 14-year-old Konerak Sinthasomphone ran into Dahmer in the shopping mall. Dahmer offered him a few dollars to pose for some photographs.

Back home Dahmer gave the boy some sleeping pills in a drink. On this occasion, Dahmer's programme included an attempt, with the aid of an electric drill and an injection of muriatic acid, to perform a prefrontal lobotomy. Halfway through, Dahmer realised he had overlooked something important: canned beer. So he left Konerak groaning in semi-consciousness and jogged over to a bar on 27th Street. Meanwhile, Konerak came to and found himself in an apartment reeking of death. Despite the incomplete surgery and his drugged stupor the boy meandered out on to the street, nearly naked, walked into a tree and crumpled to the sidewalk.

Among the crowd that gathered as he lay on the pavement was the returning Dahmer and a concerned neighbour, Nicole Childress. She flagged down a passing patrol car. 'There's this young man,' Childress told the police. 'He's buck naked and he has been beaten up. He can't stand.' The officers summoned an ambulance from the Fire Department. In minutes Engine 32 arrived, but by then the police had decided to send the paramedics back. Konerak did not seem seriously hurt. 'You know this guy?' asked one of the officers, turning to Dahmer.

'I do,' said Dahmer, and explained that Konerak was his 19-year-old lover who had overdone things with a bottle of Jack Daniel's. So the police escorted the couple back to their love-nest, with one of the officers carrying Konerak in his arms because the boy still could not stand. Inside No. 213 the officers put Konerak down in a chair, and left as soon as they could – it smelt like death in there – saying 'Well, you just take care of him.' Dahmer did.

This lamentable chain of events inspired Edwards to file a $5 million lawsuit against the Milwaukee police on 12 September 1991. Edwards claimed for the mental anguish he suffered as a result of the police's failure to apprehend Dahmer sooner.

This was the Sinthasomphone family's second brush with Dahmer; on 30 September 1989 he went down for a second-degree sexual assault on one of Konerak's brothers. Nine years before, the family had risked their lives to reach America from their native Laos, building a boat and making a nighttime run across the Mekong.

Eiffel Tower

Sold not once but twice by the Czechoslovakian-born conman 'Count' Victor Lustig (1890–1947). Part of the scheme's beauty lay in the reluctance of his dupes to complain about their losses. In theory, Lustig could have lived off the trick for life.

In March 1925 Lustig was staying at the luxury Crillon Hotel in Paris when he read a newspaper item on the government's growing concern about the expense of the Tower's upkeep. Forging Ministerial stationery, he approached five scrap merchants, inviting them in strict confidence to the hotel's conference rooms. There he disclosed that they had been selected to pitch for the Tower's demolition and its potential yield of 7,000 tons of scrap. Lustig gave the dealers a personal guided tour of the Tower, arriving incognito so that the staff would not get wind of this sensitive project.

Lustig settled on an ambitious Monsieur Poisson as his dupe and put the deal above suspicion by the authentic Continental touch of demanding a bribe to clinch the contract. Lustig fled the hotel by the back entrance as his victim left by the front. The 'con' went unreported, so next year Lustig did it again.

In the course of his career Lustig – the son of the Mayor of Hostinne – accumulated a total of twenty-five aliases and forty-seven arrests. Before the First World War he spent several years working the trans-atlantic liners as a cardsharp, and in the post-war era netted $25,000 by selling the millionaire Herbert Loller a patent device for duplicating banknotes.

Imprisoned in the Tombs, New York, on 1 September 1935 Lustig escaped by climbing out of a window and down a sheet. After his final conviction in December 1945 for distributing $134 million in forged banknotes, he passed his declining years in the company of Al Capone in the laundry at Alcatraz. They had met before, when Lustig relieved the great man of $50,000 in a 'double-your-money' Wall Street scheme. Thinking things over, Lustig realised that this was rash and went back – money and cap in hand – to Capone, who rewarded him with $5,000 for his honesty.

Scotsman Arthur Ferguson was another talented salesman of larger items. In a six-week period during 1925 he sold Buckingham Palace for £2,000, Big Ben for £1,000 and Nelson's Column for £6,000. The buyers were American tourists, whose homeland must have seemed a source of almost limitless wealth. So he emigrated in late 1925, on arrival attempting to rent out the White House for $100,000 a year to a Texas cattleman.

Before his eventual arrest Ferguson got some way towards disposing of the Statue of Liberty for a six-figure sum to an Australian visitor. But he was identified from a snapshot taken by his client, which clearly showed the conman posing in front of his monumental sculpture of a woman with a tiara holding a torch. Sent down for five years, Ferguson served his time and died in 1938 in prosperity in California.

During his younger days he had worked as a repertory actor, once taking the role of a gullible American conned by a trickster.

Eighteenth Amendment

'A noble experiment', according to J. Edgar **Hoover**, but one to which no great thought was given. Prohibition came about almost absent-mindedly.

It followed a long, slow run-up. The revulsion against the wild drinking of the frontier days melded with America's deep-rooted puritanism to produce an anti-drink crusade which, by 1907, turned Georgia teetotal. Other large rural states succumbed: Tennessee, North Carolina, Mississippi, West Virginia and Oklahoma. A Yale professor, Dr Charles Foster Kent, contributed his mite to the cause of abstinence by producing an alcohol-free Bible; he deleted all references to drink, for instance changing the 'flagon of wine' of II Samuel vi, v. 19 to 'a cake of raisins'.

In 1914, the Eighteenth Amendment gained 197 votes in the House of Representatives, with 190 opposed. But the requirement for a two-thirds majority meant that the issue was not recontested until 1917. By then America was undergoing the sobering experience of war with Germany, which owned many of the breweries, thereby bringing drink into further disrepute, and the eventual victory in the contest of arms would, it was known, usher in a utopian era with little need for artificial stimulants. When the Eighteenth Amendment came up for the second time it passed after a mere thirteen hours. A few months later the House of Representatives nodded the proposal through after a day's debate, and by January 1919 the necessary thirty-six states appended their approval. Apart from President Wilson, no one objected much except the American Federation of Labor, belatedly concerned about the working man's glass of beer.

Despite predictions, there was no last-night binge, even in the notoriously wet cities of New York, Chicago, Detroit, New Orleans and San Francisco. At one minute past midnight, on the morning of 17 January 1920, the Eighteenth Amendment became law with very little thought for the morrow. All breweries would close, all imports cease, all bars stop serving, and everyone would stop drinking for ever.

The story rated only a single column halfway down the page in the Chicago *Tribune*: 'Liquor's knell to toll in US at midnight', above an even shorter item, 'US to be dry as Sahara'. The paper carried no editorial on the subject. As the newly appointed Prohibition Commissioner, John F. Kramer, commented: 'This law will be obeyed in cities, large and small, and in villages, and where it is not obeyed it will be enforced.'

Apart from appointing 1,500 **Prohibition Agents** (an average of about thirty a state), almost the only other practical measures were the partial closures of the Chicago City House of Correction and of the *delirium tremens* ward of Cook County Hospital, now surplus to requirements, since lawlessness and alcoholism would soon cease. In this manner, America was delivered to the Mob.

Electric chair

Early electrocution was not a pretty spectacle. 'The man's lips peel back, the throat strains for a last desperate cry, the body arches against the restraining straps,' wrote reporter Don Reid of a Texas execution.

The Ohio electric chair in a bland setting, 1973. Note the telephone for last-minute instructions and the framed Rogues' Galleries

'The features purple, steam and smoke arise from the bald spots on head and leg while the sick-sweet smell of burned flesh permeates the little room.' The smell of burning comes from the electrodes at a temperature high enough to melt copper – 1,940°F.

In Britain the executioner James **Berry** attended a series of experiments conducted in Manchester in 1888 to see if electrocution represented an improvement on hanging. Together with a 'small committee of gentlemen', Berry assisted at the extermination of a dog and a calf. The process was not impressive.

Nowadays the electric chair is made of stout wood and equipped with leather restraining straps. It stands on a thick rubber mat. As a preliminary the prisoner's skull is shaved; then a Tin Man 'death cap' is strapped on his head over a sponge soaked in salt water to maximise electrical contact. The other electrode is clamped to the inside of the victim's left calf, similarly shaved. The exact dosage varies from one account to the next. But Dr Amos Squire of Sing Sing Prison, who presided at 138 executions, writes of '2,000 volts for ten seconds, reduced to 250 volts for from 40 to 50 seconds, then raised to a higher voltage for five seconds'. Then 'a second contact is almost always given, lasting for three to five seconds'.

The chair at Starke penitentiary is known as 'Old Sparky'. It executed Ted **Bundy**. The leather face mask at Louisiana State Penitentiary – and presumably elsewhere – is a little charred round the edges by its former victims. Martha Beck of the 'Lonely Hearts' murders was so fat that she could hardly squeeze into her seat on 7 March 1951.

To avoid the guilt of lawful killing tainting any one individual, at Cook County Jail four identical death switches were installed, only one of them connected.

See also **Kemmler**

Ellis, Ruth (1926–55)

Few cases have the open-and-shut simplicity of the murder of David Blakely by Ruth Ellis who, shortly after 9 p.m. on Easter Sunday 1955, walked down a Hampstead street towards her lover outside the 'Magdala' pub.

As they stood side-by-side, she produced a Smith and Wesson .38 from her handbag. When Blakely tried to run she pulled the trigger twice, and the first bullet struck him from a range of three inches. He stumbled on, and Ruth walked after him. 'Get out of the way, Clive,' she said to a friend, and shot Blakely again. This time he fell to the pavement and she continued pulling the trigger until the six-chamber magazine was empty.

Drinkers rushed out of the pub to see Ruth standing stock-still with a smoking revolver in her hand. 'Phone the police,' she said, and in the second sentence of her statement to Detective Superintendent Crawford later that night she admitted, 'I am guilty.' By 20 June, Ruth was on trial at the Old Bailey for her life. But she did not want it.

Mr Christmas Humphreys, QC, for the prosecution, only asked one question in cross-examination: 'Mrs Ellis, when you fired that revolver at close range into the body of David Blakely, what did you intend to do?' She replied without hesitation: 'It is obvious that when I shot him I intended to kill him.' This excluded any possibility of manslaughter, and thus necessitated a finding of murder. That took the jury fourteen minutes, and the judge was compelled to pass the death sentence, whereupon Ruth smiled faintly. From her cell she wrote to Blakely's mother: 'I shall die loving your son, and you should feel content that his death has been repaid.'

To a friend Ruth confided that the prospect of execution seemed no more alarming 'than having a tooth out'. At 7 a.m. on 13 July she penned her last note: 'Everyone (staff) is simply wonderful in Holloway. This is just to console my family with the thought that I did not change my way of thinking at the last moment. Or break my promise to David's mother.' At 8 a.m. she prayed in front of a crucifix. At 9 a.m. she downed her tot of brandy, thanked the officers for their kindness, and steadily walked the few feet to the Execution Shed.

By then Ruth Ellis was one of the few who did not object to the procedure. As the mother of two children, the younger aged three, it was hard to see the exact way her death contributed to the greater good of society. 'Should hanging be stopped?' demanded the headlines of the *Daily Mirror*. Her supporters included the crime author Raymond Chandler, who wrote to the *Evening Standard*, 'This was a crime of passion under considerable provocation. No other country in the world would hang this woman … This thing haunts me and, so far as I may say it, disgusts me as something obscene. I am not referring to the trial, of course, but to the medieval savagery of the law.'

Ruth Ellis

Lawyers, MPs, friends and relatives campaigned for a reprieve – one petition collected 50,000 signatures – but there were no grounds on which to apply.

Ruth Ellis was perhaps an unlikely target for sympathy. First a waitress, then a nude model, then a club hostess, then a call girl, then an occasional prostitute and manageress of a seedy Knightsbridge drinking club, with one illegitimate child, a broken marriage and several abortions behind her, Ruth ran two lovers, sported a full peroxide rinse typical of a brassy tart, was strung out on tranquillisers and drunk on Pernod.

She killed her feckless lover, ex-public schoolboy David Blakely, after a couple of on-off years together. At the time of his death they were sharing a one-roomed flat in Chelsea with her son. But the rent was 'lent' to Ruth by her back-up lover, company director Desmond Cussen. Blakely had no job and squandered his £7,000 inheritance on motor racing; his last car, The Emperor, fell to pieces on its first track outing.

Sometimes Blakely beat her. Sometimes they made up. Sometimes he proposed. Nothing went anywhere, they drank to excess and eventually Blakely took fright. On Good Friday 1955 he made the momentous decision to stand Ruth up.

Blakely ran into some friends, Carole and Anthony Findlater, who found him sitting sadly in the 'Magdala' public house. Why not, they suggested, make the break with Ruth and forget their date for 7.30 that night? Why not spend the weekend with them in Tanza Road?

Ruth already suspected Blakely of an affair with Carole, and when he failed to materialise she telephoned the Findlaters' flat repeatedly; they replaced the receiver. She made Cussen drive her to Tanza Road, but they would not answer the door. When she stove in the windows of Blakely's car, they called the police and Cussen drove her home.

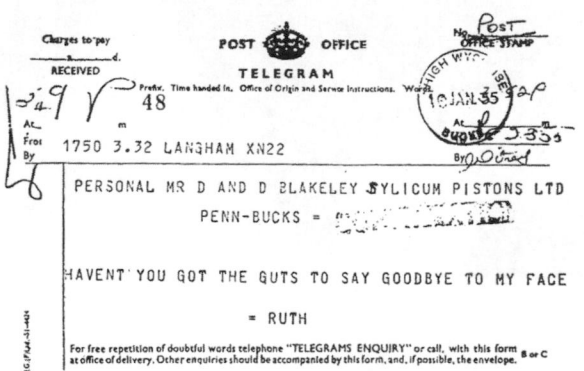

Ruth did not sleep that night, and by ten the following morning, again on station in Tanza Road by the front door, she saw Blakely emerge and get in a car with Anthony Findlater. Leaving her son at London Zoo with enough money for the afternoon, she spent the day driving round town with Cussen, trying to track down her errant boyfriend. That evening she was back at Tanza Road listening from the street as the Findlaters held a small party. Inside she thought she made out David talking to a woman – who laughed. Then some bedroom curtains were drawn. Ruth, overwrought, concluded that the Findlaters were dangling an *au pair* as bait to lure her man away.

That night Ruth again did not sleep. Her thoughts unspooled: 'I had a peculiar feeling I wanted to kill him.' The following evening, blurry-headed but determined, she hit the Pernod. According to a statement made on the last day of her life, 'We had been drinking for some time. I had been telling Cussen about Blakely's treatment of me. I was in a terribly depressed

state. All I can remember is that Cussen gave me a loaded gun … I was in such a dazed state that I cannot remember what was said. I rushed out as soon as he gave me the gun.' Then, by her account, she caught a taxi to the 'Magdala', where she shot her lover dead.

Elveson, Francine (d. 1979)

A New York schoolteacher and murder victim. Her case marked an early success for the FBI's Behavioral Science Unit, who all but identified the murderer from a desk in **Quantico**, 300 miles from the crime scene.

The state of a victim's body can be a good general guide to the killer's age. The teenager tends to kill with the haste and tempestuousness of youth; a murderer of more mature years may take his time. So when Francine Elveson died in a sex attack, it proved possible to estimate her assailant's age.

FBI Agent John Douglas considered that the murderer was unlikely to be far into his thirties since any sex killer (a repetitive occupation) would by then be in prison. On the other hand, the ritualistic posture of Elveson's body on the rooftop of Pelham Parkway House, the severed nipples placed on her chest, and the deliberation with which he forced the umbrella into her vagina suggested a leisurely slaying. This put her attacker between twenty-five and his early thirties, and the knifework had been such a protracted business that the murderer must have known he would be undisturbed. 'He spent hours up there mutilating the body,' recalled Douglas. 'What's strange is that he spent so much time there that he had to defecate on the steps, and he covered it over! Somehow, *that* was repulsive to him … He felt too comfortable there.'

Francine Elveson was accosted while leaving the building for work, and then forced up the stairs. She had not screamed, and all this implied a killer who knew both the building and his victim, the more so since the attack had the personal element of face mutilation. Psychologically, no murderer wants anyone resembling someone he knew left to tell tales, and it is when the killer's identity can be traced through the victim's that the face must be obliterated.

The murderer would be white; sex killings are nearly all intra-racial. The style of the murder did not suggest a good family man. The killer was probably a loner, indubitably a sadist, most likely living by himself and with a predilection for bondage-type hard porn; the body was laid out like a magazine spread. In FBI jargon, the killing was primarily '**disorganised**' and thus the murderer would be an under-achiever.

New York police had already questioned and cleared some 2,000 suspects. One, Carmine Calabro, had given an alibi which withstood the perfunctory scrutiny of the initial screening, but he matched the '**profile**' prepared by Agent Douglas. An unemployed, unmarried 32-year-old actor and high-school drop-out, Calabro shared a pornography collection with his father, a Parkway House resident, and his alibi fulfilled two major requirements. First, it supplied the element of emotional instability: Calabro had been – in theory at least – sequestered in a mental hospital at the time of the murder. And second, the alibi proved easy to break. On closer examination it transpired that the hospital's institutional patients were at liberty to come and go as they pleased. Calabro's **teeth-marks**, corresponding to the bites on the victim's legs, clinched the case and he is currently serving twenty-five years.

In traditional detection the clues lead to a specific individual, with the motive often pointing straight to the killer. Detective work is primarily a physical process – collecting, tagging, logging, examining and so on. But in random murders, nothing connects a particular killer with a particular victim. Instead, the scene-of-the-crime is analysed to find the specific *type* of murderer, creating a theoretical framework against which suspects, in their thousands if necessary, can be compared for exactness of fit. This is both a matter of applied behavioural science and of convenience. Crime scenes do not often contain forensic clues, but murderers inevitably leave behind behavioural clues in the form of the victim's body and exactly how it was treated.

See also **de Sade**

Escape from Alcatraz

Conscientious 1979 Don Siegel movie starring Clint Eastwood and based very closely on the facts. There *were* three escapees, they did scrape away their cell walls with mess-hall cutlery, and the resulting holes were covered with grey-painted bits of cardboard. Just as in the film, the gang left dummy heads in their beds to fool the guards. There was an ascent to a ventilation shaft on the roof, a slide down a drainpipe and – almost certainly – an escape by raft. After that, no more is known. So the film stops.

The three convicts were Frank Lee Morris (who had an IQ of 133) and the two Anglin brothers; their absence was not noticed until the roll call on the following morning. At dawn, on 13 June 1962, a woman saw three men rowing across the San Francisco bay, and a crude paddle was found in the water near Angel Island. The three are regarded as still at large.

Alcatraz Penitentiary – a view from the hills of San Francisco

Their escape led to the prison's closure and the relocation of its inmates to the maximum security penitentiary at Marion, Illinois. Alcatraz witnessed twenty-six attempted breakouts; the previous standard was set on 16 December 1937 by Ralph Roe and 'Sunny Boy' Cole, who certainly made it into the water, but probably not out of it.

Today, the prison is part of the entertainment industry. Parts of *Point Blank* were filmed there, as was *Escape from Alcatraz* itself. In 1992 three-quarters of a million visitors made the trip across the bay for a guided tour. Only two of the thirteen buildings are safe to enter, and the top of the crumbling warden's house is likely to blow off with the next big wind.

Many trippers are struck by the contrast between the harshness of the prison itself and its stunning setting; the tantalising vision of San Francisco shimmers across the bay. On New Year's Eve the inmates could watch the shore fireworks from their five-by-seven cells and even hear snatches of the honking traffic drifting over the waters.

Alcatraz opened in 1934 for the incorrigibles of the American prison system, and for the first five years the regime operated under the 'silent system' discarded elsewhere in the nineteenth century. For the duration of their sentence, prisoners were not allowed to talk.

Escobar, Pablo Emilio (1949–)

Colombia's equivalent of Al Capone, a gangster who made his fortune by meeting the public's needs. Born on a small farm outside **Medellin**, Escobar started in petty crime by stealing gravestones and selling hot cars, and worked briefly as a triggerman for a small Mafia cocaine operation. By the mid-1970s he ran drugs on his own account, and the explosion in demand created the major drug 'cartels' – distribution and insurance services for third-party producers. In Escobar's words, 'You bribe someone here, you bribe someone there, and you pay a friendly banker to bring the money back.'

You also kill people. Alongside the pages of lawyers,

Pablo Escobar, drug baron

accountants, and rural security divisions in Escobar's organisational chart are listed some forty urban extermination squads like *Los Nazis* and *Los Escorpiones*. Escobar opened recruiting offices in the slums so youths could work their way up, if they lived, from minor dirty work to prestigious assassinations at two million pesos each.

Escobar became the undisputed boss of his local trade association. Like the Mafia's governing Syndicate, Escobar's Medellin cocaine cartel regulated the various sub-groups of traders, each retaining their own business networks, their own objectives and their own army, and by the early 1980s Escobar and his friends were making their first millions. As a former girlfriend put it, 'They were peasant boys, adventurers, they were fun. They had lots of airplanes and helicopters and zoos.' The centre of Escobar's empire was the 7,000-acre Hacienda Nàpoles, and guests recall the constant racket of computer games, and the visiting Saudi prince so proficient on jet-skis.

Escobar nurtured political ambitions, in 1982 gaining a Liberal seat in Congress. He believed that his background of poverty tailored him for the Presidency, and he channelled money into public works, building over 200 houses for the homeless and funding the unrivalled social welfare system of Envigado, his home town (see **Zoo**). But he lacked the finesse for non-violent negotiations and, after the patrician power-elite – the 'Men of Always' – forced him out of politics in 1983, he returned to running the cartel with a gun stuck in his belt, playing fast and loose, occasionally telling independent traders that their consignment was 'lost in transit', and deciding who should, and who should not, be killed. By the late 1980s, *Forbes* magazine put his wealth at $3 billion.

Escobar's downfall started in 1989, when a former ally, Luis Carlos Galan, ran for the presidency on a platform including the extradition of cocaine traffickers to the United States. Escobar's name headed the list, and Galan was assassinated. Galan's successor, Virgilio Barca, declared war on the *narcotraficantes*.

Escobar rallied the Medellin city-state behind the banner of non-extradition. Engaged on two fronts, he did battle with his rivals from the Cali cocaine cartel and the government, itself a fairly labyrinthine concept. Car bombings, assassinations, kidnappings, airliners destroyed mid-flight, bounties for dead policemen and helicopter gunship attacks followed in a round of shifting alliances as money changed hands. Army soldiers, on a monthly pittance of $20, were easily bribed, and Escobar's widespread intelligence network infiltrated men and radios into operations supposedly mounted against him. Throughout 1989 the Medellin cartel funded Escobar's campaign, and in 1990 he made the government a tempting offer. He would surrender – provided they shelved plans to deport drug dealers to Miami.

The idea of Escobar behind bars increased Colombia's standing with Washington. But his surrender package involved the construction of a lavish ranch (see **Cathedral**) for a prison. In a back-to-back deal, other cartel members paid him $100 million monthly as compensation for his loss of liberty, and in the autumn of 1990 the Colombian constitution was reworded to make extradition illegal, a deviation accepted by Washington in return for support in the UN for the Gulf War.

Escobar moved into his newly completed retreat overlooking Medellin in June 1990 and left two years later when political realignments threatened real imprisonment. Exiting the rear of La Catedral and ascending a hillside on foot with others, he outwitted a military force sent to seize him. Moving from one safe house to another, he eluded a 3,000-strong team of security agents for sixteen months. But the Medellin Search Block's efforts paid off on 2 December 1993, when he was flushed out of a house in a middle-class district of Medellin. A rooftop shoot-out followed in which Escobar was killed by Hugo Aguilar, a former police colonel heading intelligence operations in the search.

Escobar was a good family man with two children and a longstanding wife, Tata. The best clues to his personality, apart from the gravestones in Medellin's Campos de Paz, and Colombia's 1991 total of 28,284 homicides, come from the Cathedral's interior where Bibles, shrines with candles, tiled portraits of the Virgin Mary and Barbie Barbecue Playsets jostle for space among videos of The **Godfather**, Bullitt, indifferent oil paintings, gold taps, books by Graham Greene and Garcia Marquez and a photograph of Escobar dressed as a Chicago gangster. On the Colombian adage of 'Don't sleep on your own poison', he never indulged in cocaine or **crack**. But he savoured his press, often asking 'What are they saying about Reagan and me?' His real thrill was to fight, taking the war into the enemy's camp, and his primary motivation power. It was certainly not sex, although the two became confused. Asked to whom he would most like to make love, Escobar replied, 'Mrs Thatcher.'

Evidence

Cowed witnesses occasionally testify against all the odds to bring down a criminal empire. This takes courage. By 1935 'Lucky' Luciano was raking in $10 million a year from prostitution. Not surprisingly, the vice squad detectives found none of his 1,200 women prepared to take the stand, and Luciano bragged to newsmen that the investigation would never get anywhere; his girls were just 'gutless whores'.

Mildred Harris, 'Cokey Flo' Brown and the aptly named Nancy Presser took umbrage at this professional slur. They had the guts to testify in court and it took the Second World War to get Luciano out of jail. His sixty-two counts of prostitution earned him a thirty-to-fifty-year sentence, only curtailed by his much-disputed contribution to the cause when he arranged for partisan cover to the Allied landings on Sicily.

In Britain, the **Kray** twins were similarly laid low by a humble barmaid. Their trial's turning point came when she was asked to identify the man who had entered a London pub, 'The Blind Beggar', on the night of 8 March 1966 and put a bullet in George Cornell's head; while the killer remained at large, a whole area of east London stayed under gang law.

In the words of a detective, 'We knew that thirty or so people had seen what had happened, yet there was no one prepared to talk. The bar staff's version was that Cornell had been the only customer. The staff themselves had all been "out the back" when the shooting happened and hadn't seen a thing.'

For months the barmaid (known only as 'Miss X') held her tongue, terrified for her two children and frightened that she herself would be killed if she spoke.

When the trial started on 8 January 1969, she entered the witness box pale and drawn from a legacy of sleeplessness and nightmares; one observer, Professor Keith Simpson, feared she would pass out under the pressure.

Kenneth Jones, QC, took her through the evidence, finally asking: 'Did you see the man who shot Cornell?' There was a pause of several seconds. Then the barmaid raised her arm and pointed: 'It was No. 1 over there. Ronald Kray.'

'Have you any doubt?'

'No – oh no. That was him.'

Witnesses do not always stay the course. In Sicily, an early attempt to break the Wall of **Silence** put thirty *mafiosi* in the dock charged with a total of nine murders when a courageous widow, Rosa Messina, told all she knew to the local magistrates. She had lost her husband and two sons to a **vendetta**, and in 1963 this brave woman was hailed by the international press. On 19 September, amid massive publicity, the court usher at the Assize Court in Palermo called her to the witness box.

But Rosa's nerve failed in the final hours; she was tracked down later that day, quaking with fear in her home village, adamant that even if the police dragged her to court she would utter not a word.

See also **Omerta**

Exactitude

When it came to hanging, **drawing** and quartering, getting the judicial words right mattered. In 1694 an execution was declared void because the sentence failed to specify that the victim's entrails were to be burned while he was still 'living'.

The case (*R v. Walcott*) did not lack interest. On appeal, the Crown contended unsuccessfully that the omitted words were not substantive, being merely *in terrorem* (as a warning), and in any case constituted an impossibility since it was 'inconsistent in nature for a man to be living after his entrails were taken out', an objection overruled on the basis that the court had no discretion to vary the proscribed form of punishment. It was additionally noted that the celebrated Colonel Harrison (one of the regicides who signed the death warrant of King Charles I) had, after his disembowelment, 'strength enough left to strike the executioner'. The sentence was remitted, albeit posthumously, with the action brought by the deceased's son.

Execution Dock

The place at Wapping on the Thames where British pirates were hanged, led to their deaths by an official carrying a silver oar. A special set of gallows, erected for the occasion on the foreshore, stood at the exact point of the low-water mark. This was not just for the convenience of viewers in the boats moored midstream or for the huge crowds watching from the opposite bank. The siting underlined the Admiralty's jurisdiction over all crimes committed on the high seas and waterways up to the low-water mark.

Unlike those executed by the civil authorities on land, the bodies were not immediately cut down but were left to hang until three tides washed over them. One of many sentenced to this fate, Scotsman James Buchanon, was a well-regarded sailmaker who stabbed to death the fourth mate of the *Royal Guardian* on 16 October 1737 while his ship was berthed in the Canton River, China. Returned to England, Buchanon faced his hanging at Execution Dock with courage, leading the singing of the 23rd Psalm before confessing to the crowd that he was a Sabbath-breaker, swearer and drinker who deserved to die for the killing. Then the platform was kicked away from under his feet, whereupon some sixty seamen and friends stormed the scaffold, overthrew the officials, cut Buchanon down and jubilantly carried him away to Deptford. Despite a reward of £200, he was never seen again.

Executive action

What the CIA takes against trouble-makers. It kills them. One failed executive action, an attempt on Castro's life, used Marita Lorenz – a jealous lover – as the assassin. She was issued with poison capsules, which she stored in a jar of cold cream. But they melted.

Castro was long a recipient of American hate mail. One item was the guerrilla leader Che Guevara's severed hands and, with the cessation of the Cold War, a string of more mischievous CIA harassing schemes came to light. In May 1993 Agent Walt Elder described a plot to introduce a drug into Castro's cigar to make his beard fall off, whereupon he would be swept from power on a wave of ridicule.

The CIA's other weird plans included 'Project Artichoke', a post-war experiment in brainwashing which continued into the 1960s, its objective to hypno-programme individuals into performing involuntary acts (like assassinations) of which they subsequently had no recollection. According to the project's Dr William Bryan Jnr, 'You can brainwash a person to do just about anything.' By the late 1960s hypno-programmed killers were ready to go.

But the only operation imputed to the Project was an 'own goal', the 1968 murder of Senator Robert F.

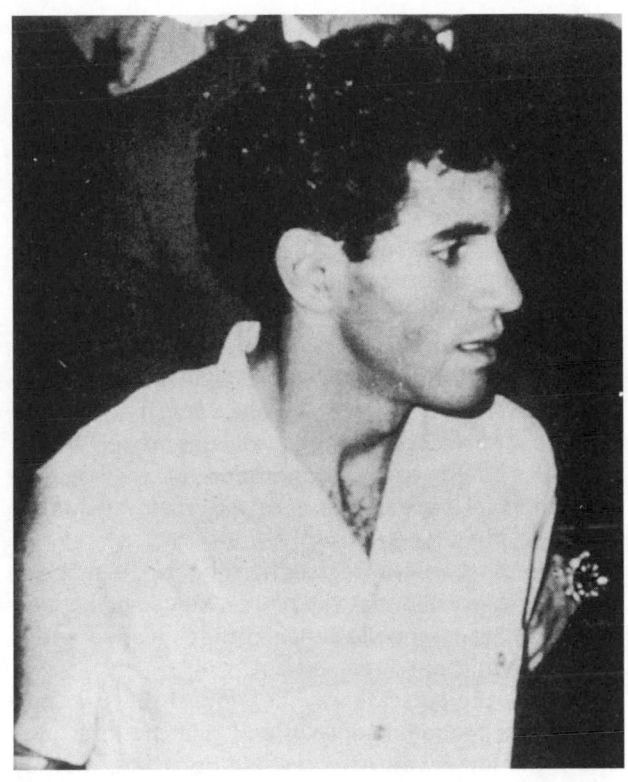

A puzzled Sirhan Sirhan after Robert Kennedy's assassination

Kennedy in a Los Angeles hotel, for which Dr Bryan (now deceased) allegedly claimed responsibility with his successful indoctrination of Sirhan Sirhan. Robert Kennedy's assassination is fertile ground for the conspiracy theorists: Sirhan's trial was blatantly stage managed by the Los Angeles Police Department. The ballistic evidence was inconsistent; inconvenient witnesses were intimidated, testimony suppressed, Officer Sharaga's report falsified, photographic evidence (2,410 pictures) destroyed and the coroner smeared.

Perhaps the LAPD wanted to force the case through before a miasma of conjecture clouded the issues. Alternatively, they may have covered up the fact that Sirhan was not a lone assassin but acted in concert with another couple, one of them probably the so-called 'polka-dot dress girl' seen in the Ambassador Hotel's lobby. The conspiracy scenario has Sirhan shooting at Kennedy and missing, hitting five bystanders instead. The accomplices shot at Kennedy and hit, killing him. This explains numerous discrepancies, like Sirhan's apparent feat of producing ten or perhaps twelve bullets out of an eight-bullet clip. It tallies with the autopsy finding that Kennedy died from shots fired from behind at a range of a few inches; Sirhan opened fire from in front at a range of a couple of feet.

Sirhan was immediately apprehended, but an unknown couple escaped, observed by numerous witnesses, including a bystander, Sandy Serrano, who to this day goes in fear of her life. As for Sirhan, he cannot remember a thing about the attack, and CIA involvement looms large in subsequent police stonewalling.

See also **Hamilton**

Exhibits

Unusual exhibits materialised at the Old Bailey in 1915, when the three baths of George Joseph Smith appeared in evidence. The exact size, shape and angulation of these domestic novelties were described in great detail in the contemporary reports, supplemented by technical illustrations. During the trial Mr Justice Scrutton suggested to the jury that they try the baths out. 'When you examine these baths in your private room,' he said, 'you should put one of yourselves in. Get some one of you who is about the height of five feet nine.'

It was perhaps because of the general scarcity of baths that Smith – who drowned his wives – thought he could get away with murder. He remarked to a Miss Pegler, who unwisely expressed a desire in his hearing to take a dip: 'I should advise you to be careful of those things, as it is known that women often lose their lives through weak hearts and fainting in a **bath**.' Nowadays, no one would believe him.

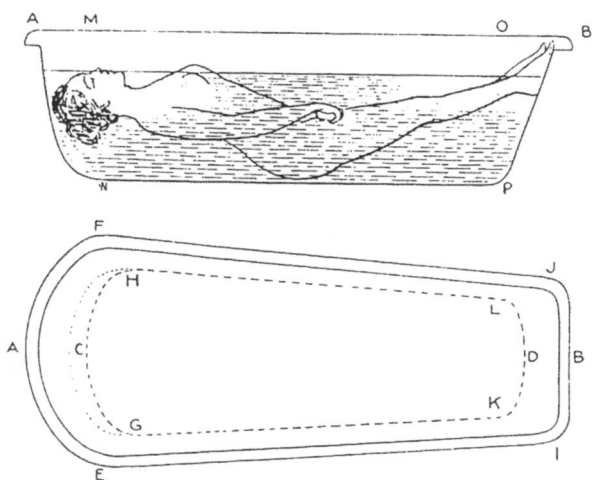

Apparently Smith's persuasive powers were abetted by his eyes, said by his first bigamous wife to have a strange, hypnotic quality. 'He had an extraordinary power over women,' she recalled. 'This power lay in his eyes. When he looked at you for a minute or two you had the feeling you were being magnetised. They were little eyes that seemed to rob you of your will.' At the time of his trial, rumours abounded that Smith had employed hypnotic suggestion to make his wives remove their clothes and drown themselves.

The occasional severed **ear** makes its way into court, and in 1893 a dead cat was put in evidence. During the **Crippen** case of 1910, the defence argued that the identifying scar supposedly found by the pathologist Bernard **Spilsbury** on a piece of the corpse's stomach was no more than a crease in some skin taken from a thigh. For the prosecution, Spilsbury enlivened proceedings by placing the disputed segment of flesh in a soup bowl, and handed it round to the judge and jury, pointing out the vestiges of the rectus muscle attached to the abdominal wall.

Eyes

In criminal folklore, a dead man's eyes retained an imprint of the last thing they saw. The notion (which has some basis in fact, but would never work in practice) survived into the 1920s when – according to the traditional account – Englishman Frederick Browne shot Constable William **Gutteridge**. As the policeman lay groaning on the ground, Browne was disturbed by his continuing gaze. 'What are you looking at me like that for?' Browne asked, blowing out Gutteridge's eyes with two more shots. This grizzly detail made the killing front-page news throughout Europe.

For the forensic scientist the eyes can provide valuable information, including the rough time of death, and asphyxia produces hundreds of tiny haemorrhages in the eyes in response to the increase in blood pressure. In America, the diameter of the pupils is often recorded during the post-mortem; **insulin** causes the pupils to dilate and morphine will make them contract.

Other famous eyes include 'Bugsy' Siegel's, which bounced across the room after being shot out. The man who made legal history by insisting on his own execution, Gary Gilmore, got his eyes on television to the background of a song called 'Gary Gilmore's Eyes', in reference to his expressed wish to donate his eyeballs to the community. The Russian serial killer **Chikatilo** inflicted vicious eye-wounds that almost became his hallmark. Investigators theorised that these mutilations signified a residual sense of shame as the killer tried to avoid his victims' gaze.

In 1937, eyes formed the highlight of a case from provincial France when the badly mutilated bodies of Madame Lancelin and her daughter were discovered lying on the first-floor landing of their home in Le Mans. Blood was splashed round the walls to a height of seven feet; upstairs, two maids lay huddled naked in a single bed. The elder, Christiane Papin, made a meticulous confession: 'When Madame came back to the house, I informed her that the iron was broken again,' she said. 'When I saw Madame Lancelin was going to jump on me, I leaped at her face and scratched out her eyes with my fingers.'

Then Christiane corrected herself: 'No, I made a mistake when I said that I leaped on Madame Lancelin. It was on Mademoiselle Lancelin that I leaped and it was her eyes that I scratched out.'

She continued: 'Meanwhile, my sister Lea had jumped on Madame Lancelin and scratched her eyes out in the same way. After we had done this, they lay and crouched down on the floor. I then rushed down to the kitchen to fetch a hammer and a knife. With these two instruments, my sister and I fell upon our two mistresses; we struck at the head with the knife, hacked at the bodies and legs and also struck with a pewter pot which was standing on a little table on the landing. We exchanged one instrument for another several times. By that I mean that I would pass the hammer over to my sister, so she could hit with it, while she handed me the knife, and we did the same with the pewter pot...'

At the trial, Christiane demonstrated how she had torn out the eyes with her fingers, tossing the first one down the stairs. During cross-examination, the magistrate asked: 'You knocked Madame Lancelin down with a blow from a pewter pot. As she cried out, your sister came running. What did you say to her?'

'Tear her eyes out,' Christiane replied promptly. Doctors, psychologists and lawyers were baffled. The girls – stolid peasant types – were not mad; they harboured no particular grudge against their employers, with whom they stayed for eleven years; there was no prior plan to kill them; conditions of service and pay were normal; their characters excellent. Nor had they espoused communism.

But they were servants, and this point was overlooked by contemporary commentators. Born and bred as menial skivvies, the Papin sisters spent their lives under the watchful eye of a mistress who checked the polished furniture for dust with a white glove and counted the sugar lumps to guard against theft.

The domestic iron that precipitated the killings had already broken down a few days previously, when Madame docked five francs from the girls' wages for its repair. On the afternoon of 2 February the iron shorted again, provoking the fatal outburst. At the trial, asked whether she 'loved' her employers, Lea appeared not to understand. 'We served them, and that's all,' she said. 'We never spoke to them.'

F

Facial reconstruction

Sometimes the only way of establishing a murder victim's identity is to reconstruct the face from the skull and then see if anyone recognises it.

At the turn of the century, Swiss research culminated in the publication of tables listing the average depth of the overlying soft tissues at twenty-six points on the human face. Today the world leader in this lumbering technology (described in the best-seller *Gorky Park*) is Russia, inspired by the work of anthropologist Professor Mikhail Gerasimov.

Following his acclaimed remodelling of the face of a Cro-Magnon woman unearthed before the Second World War in a Late Upper Palaeolithic grave, Gerasimov was approached by the Moscow head of Forensic Medicine. As a test, they collected a dozen heads, numbered and photographed them, stripped away their flesh and then sent them off to Gerasimov, who correctly and recognisably reconstructed the samples as four Russian men, one Russian woman, three Ukrainians, a Pole, a Chinese, a Caucasian and a man of Baltic origin. Gerasimov went on to make some 140 models for criminal investigation.

Great excitement heralded the technique's first use in Britain during the early 1980s. The body of an unknown woman, dead for some sixteen years, came to light in a house in Bolton, and Detective Chief Inspector Fletcher resolved to attempt a reconstruction, coupled with extensive publicity, to put a name to her face. The make-up by Ruth Quinn of Granada Television aimed for historical veracity by simulating the mid-60s style with an unobtrusive blusher and a choice of six different wigs, and the bust was unveiled at a crowded press conference.

Only seven couples came forward; all had lived in the house where the body was found and, with nothing further to add, were eliminated from the enquiry. Two other leads surfaced, one from an elderly woman who could not identify the photographs for certain because she was blind, and the other from a confident old lady unable to share her information, as she had expired by the time detectives arrived.

In 1990 the police enjoyed greater success with another body. A skull unearthed after eight years in a Cardiff garden was rebuilt into a recognisable face by a medical artist from Manchester University, and police posters prompted two social workers to identify the face as that of Karen Price, a Welsh schoolgirl missing since the summer of 1981. From there, the police work proved easy; they soon had their man, Alan Charlton, but to satisfy the court that they had the right body was another matter. At the trial the prosecution relied on DNA fingerprinting, basing their analysis on a novel technique using samples of decayed **bone**.

Fagin

The model for **Dickens**'s Fagin is reputed to be the Jewish pickpocket and fence known as 'Ikey' (Isaac) Solomon, who operated in London during the 1820s.

In 1827 Ikey was finally convicted of theft. But our exits here are often entries elsewhere; Ikey soon materialised on the far side of the globe. Since the Black Maria that conveyed Ikey from the court to Newgate was driven by his father-in-law, he never reached the prison gates. His wife had just been transported to Australia with their four children, so Ikey set off to rejoin them on an elliptical journey via Denmark, the United States and Rio. On arrival in Tasmania as a free man and something of a criminal celebrity, Ikey invested his loot in a house and some land.

For the time being, he remained immune from prosecution. A warrant for his arrest could only be issued by the Colonial Office, which was in London and hence unaware of his presence in Australia. So he stayed at liberty until the papers could cross the sea and back again. Ikey used his months of grace to buy back his wife, putting up a bond of £1,000 to have her assigned to him as a servant.

In November 1829 Ikey's warrant arrived; he was returned to London for trial, but not before petitioning the Governor for work as an informer. Back in England, Ikey was sentenced to fourteen years' transportation, so by Christmas 1831 he found himself in Hobart again. Reunited with his family under the ticket-of-leave system in 1835, he bickered with his wife incessantly. The pair separated in 1840 and he died ten years later, not a pauper, but poor, with an estate worth £70.

Fahmy, Madame (1891–1971)

British lawyers are rather patronising about the Gallic exemption of the '**crime passionel**'. Like the vanished concept of **Benefit of Clergy**, it makes laws pointless. But in 1923 the beautiful Madame Fahmy escaped scot-free after shooting her brute of a husband, 22-year-old Prince Ali, in their suite at London's Savoy Hotel. Her defence consisted of little more than the considerable eloquence of her counsel, Sir Edward Marshall Hall, in denouncing the millionaire Prince as a cad and a toad.

Hall denigrated Ali as 'a psychopath of revolting depravity, a homosexual and a sadist', and harped on about his 'filthy and perverted taste … vile tempers … and demands for unnatural sexual intercourse'. In those days, such epithets were easily earned by foreigners.

Not in dispute was Ali's great wealth. His annual income never fell below £40,000 and at the end of the war exceeded £100,000. Ali loved speed. In 1923 his stable of cars included one Mercedes, two Rolls-Royces, a Buick, a Berlier, a Renault and a Peugeot, as well as a couple of run-abouts, several motorbikes and a fleet of speedboats. He drove through Cairo like Mr Toad. Then there were the jewels, the villas, palaces, footmen, tapestries, rugs, hashish, and of course his retinue of hangers-on.

Prince Ali first set eyes on Marguerite, ten years his senior, in July 1922. She had an extremely expensive lifestyle and a daughter to support; she needed someone with money. They married the following

The former prostitute Madame Fahmy, begowned in all her glory

year, and within a week things started to go awry. Marguerite's conversion to Islam was no more than skin-deep. She continued to entertain and dress décolletée like an emancipated Parisienne; he carried on like an Egyptian prince, insisting she drape a shawl over her shoulders. During the six months of their stormy marriage Marguerite endured scenes in the Hotel Majestic in Paris and, it seems, the most terrible privation on a Nile cruise ship. She wrote to her lawyer, very likely laying the groundwork for a lucrative divorce, with exaggerated reports of confinement: 'I have to bring you notice of very grave incidents. For the last three days, I have been a prisoner on board. I am absolutely unable to get out. Threats were made.'

By June 1923 there was a record of running around brandishing expensive pistols and late-night matrimonial fisticuffs. Then on 9 July, Ali put Marguerite on drip-feed for shopping, cabling Cartier and Vuitton to prevent delivery of two handbags valued at £4,027 the pair in a period when Britain's finest battleship, the *Queen Elizabeth*, cost about 4 million.

Marguerite had done well for herself financially. Starting her working life as a provincial prostitute, she evolved into a modish Parisian courtesan with the help of the kindly Madame Denart, a brothel keeper who

Cartoon depicting Ali Fahmy (right), his secretary and his secretary's secretary: 'the Light, the Shadow of the Light, and the Shadow of the Shadow of the Light'.

shaped her protégée with instruction in dress sense, conversation, elocution and the piano. Marguerite married well at the age of 27, taking the young and wealthy Charles Laurent for a husband in 1919. After her divorce a year later she was well-off in her own right, and her marriage to Ali made her rich.

According to Marguerite, on the night of 10 July 1923 she fired a warning shot in her husband's general direction during a row. Then, thinking the gun empty, she put the .32 pistol to his face and squeezed the trigger twice more. He fell down dead.

She was taken to Holloway Prison in a taxi. But at the trial she was discharged, her defence contending (with tremendous theatrical panache) that she did not realise that the gun was an automatic. In the words of Marshall Hall: 'An inexperienced person might easily reload the weapon thinking that, in fact, he was emptying it.' That is, loosing off a single bullet to clear the chamber simply resulted in the weapon reloading itself. This was the line taken by Marguerite in the witness box. 'The cartridge having been fired,' she said tortuously, 'I thought the pistol was not dangerous.' In fact Marguerite knew enough about the weapon to cock it by pulling back the sliding breech cover. To fire off each round required the heavy finger-pressure of eight and a half pounds – hardly the sort of gun that goes off by accident or feminine indecision.

After the verdict Marguerite left London for the Continent, hoping to assume control of Ali's estate, valued at £2.5 million. Unfortunately there was no

will, although under the Muslim law of intestacy a male descendant's entitlement stood at somewhere between a quarter and a half of the inheritance. So Marguerite would be in the money – if she could produce a posthumous heir.

And she could, at least on paper. She paid a Dr Kamel £2,500 to sign a birth certificate for a phantom child. When the scheme was exposed, she became the laughing stock of Europe, and wisely departed for the watering hole of Carlsbad. There she earned a name as the 'Queen of the Bohemian Watering Places' and broke into films, in a minor way, playing an Egyptian wife. She died in Paris in 1971, at the age of eighty, without remarrying.

Her lawyer, Sir Edward Marshall Hall, possessed innate theatrical sense, in his closing speeches often addressing the hushed courtroom with his arms outstretched to symbolise the scales of justice, finally dropping into one hand the invisible presumption of innocence, like a golden nugget, to tip the scales in favour of the accused. His courtroom tactics included the use of a noisy throat spray during key points of his opponent's speeches, and in Marguerite's case he achieved marked results by entering into learned confabulations with his own expert witness during the prosecution's testimony, apparently in rebuttal but actually in discussion of the prospects for the shooting season.

Faithful, the

When a Mafia boss got 'hit' in the 1930s, his lieutenants had to burn too. In the words of Joe Valachi, *mafioso* turned informer: 'I asked Vito how come there had to be these killings, and he said that whenever a boss dies, all his faithful have to go with him, but he explained that it was all over now and we didn't have a thing to worry about.'

The elimination of influential opponents is a reasonable tactic, but it does not explain why, in the wake of Salvatore Maranzano's gangland murder in 1931, it was necessary to hammer an iron pipe up Sam Monaco's bottom before throwing him into the Passaic River, nor why Louis Russo's head had to be crushed after his throat was cut. The Mafia have always believed in brutality; when they drag a man across the floor, they do it by the testicles. The body of one unfortunate who crossed the *mafioso* Carmine Fatico (founder of New

York's Bergin Hunt and Fish Club) was believed decapitated until, on autopsy, the police discovered his missing head smashed into the chest cavity.

The aftermath of a gangland coup was always tense while the victors decided who the faithful were; after the first few days, survivors on the losing side put out feelers from their hiding places to establish (without getting themselves shot) whether the new management would take them on the payroll.

See also **Contempt**

Fakes

Two of the most impressive written forgeries of modern times are the 'Hitler Diaries' and Clifford Irving's 'auto'-biography of Howard Hughes. Both share something in common with another famous impostor, the **Tichborne Claimant**, namely massive bulk.

In the Hitler case, the forgery was so amateurish it would scarcely deceive a child. Conrad Kujau was a German conman who earned his first prison sentence in 1963 for counterfeiting twenty-seven Marks' worth of luncheon vouchers, and by the 1970s he started dabbling in paintings of battle scenes and war **memorabilia**; he found their value rocketed if fake documentation was attached. For instance, he would certify that an old jacket had once been worn by the **Führer**.

Certificates were easy to run up with Letraset on modern paper aged with spilt tea, inscribed with a few words from 'Bormann' or 'Hess'; the public display of Nazi material was illegal and collectors did not check too carefully. Then one afternoon in 1978 Kujau sat down and copied out bits from *Hitler's Speeches and Proclamations* into a school notebook. When his pen ran out, he switched to pencil. On the cover he stuck some plastic initials, made in Hong Kong, which read AH. And there it was, a genuine fake Hitler diary. Actually, Kujau slipped up; the letters were 'FH'. But no matter, when he showed his work, an aged collector reverentially accepted it as the real thing.

Eventually word of the notebook's existence reached a gullible reporter, Gerd Heidemann, obsessed with the Nazis, and in January 1981 he dragooned *Stern* magazine into investing two million Marks in twenty-seven Hitler diaries. These did not exist, even as fakes, so Kujau churned out the first batch of three more notebooks in ten days, still sprinkling the pages with tea. At 85,000 Marks per volume, this represented

good money, so Kujau kept on discovering more diaries. In the end, *Stern* parted with 9.3 million Marks for their scoop.

The scale of Kujau's work demanded belief. When the historian Hugh Trevor-Roper verified the diaries, he was so distracted by the quantity of bogus material that he neglected to assess its quality. Well versed in the period, Trevor-Roper knew little German and could not read the manuscripts' pages of archaic script. Had he understood the entries, he would have been appalled by their banality, little more than schoolboy material along the lines of 'Got up. Had breakfast.' But Trevor-Roper relied on appearances.

These were overwhelming. After much cloak-and-dagger business, including an oath of secrecy, in April 1983 Trevor-Roper was ushered into the presence of an entire Hitler archive in a private chamber of the Zurich Handelsbank: a stack of fifty-eight diaries, a boxful of paintings and drawings, letters, notes, memorabilia, and Hitler's First World War helmet, authenticated by Hess. All were fakes, but as the historian leafed through the material, which he could not understand, his doubts 'gradually dissolved'. Trevor-Roper reported in the *Sunday Times*: 'It is these other documents ... which convinced me of the authenticity of the diaries', later explaining that he was 'impressed by the sheer bulk of the diaries. Who, I asked myself, would forge sixty volumes when six would have served his purpose?'

The answer was anyone paid on piece-rate. Given the knack, documents can be forged endlessly. After his exposure for the Howard Hughes fiasco, Clifford Irving commented: 'Once you have the mood, you can go on for ever... I could write sixty volumes of Howard Hughes autobiography and they would pass. Once you can do one page, you can do twenty. Once you can do twenty, you can do a book.' Irving's forgery – described as 'beyond human ability' – sailed through layers of verification.

Apart from Trevor-Roper's historical vetting, the Hitler diaries were subjected to two other batteries of tests. One, the scientific examination of the physical constituents of the notebooks, speedily exposed the fraud, since the paper and bindings contained a chemical whitener discovered in 1955, the red threads on the seals were of polyester and viscose, and the ink of a type unavailable during the war. The chloride evaporation test showed that the diaries had been written within the last few years.

But this was established *after* the diaries started serialisation. Until then *Stern* relied only on journalistic hunches and the flawed reports of three handwriting gurus, their task complicated by several factors. First, they were not informed that by approving a couple of letters, some of them photocopied, they would authenticate an entire set of the world's most important diaries. Second, one of the experts could not speak German, and the other was really an authority on the investigation of biological micro-traces.

But the fatal source of confusion arose when two of the three experts compared the new 'Hitler' extracts against old 'Hitler' material which included samples produced by the same forger: Conrad Kujau. So the writing matched.

It would be vexing if large-scale hoaxes became extinct. But this is unlikely. As the serialisation of the Hitler diaries loomed ever nearer, journalist Phillip Knightley begged his employers at the *Sunday Times* to learn from past experience. Setting out in detail the lessons of the famous Mussolini forgery of 1968, which cost the paper £100,000, he warned: 'You cannot rely on expert authentication. Thomson engaged five experts, including the author of the standard work on Mussolini, the world's greatest authority on paper, a famous handwriting expert, an internationally known palaeographer and an academic who authenticated the Casement Diaries. Not one expert said they were fake.'

His words were ignored. Not only can thorough investigation come up with the wrong answers; in a well-conducted fraud it is psychologically and practically impossible to make the checks at all. Throughout the Hitler scam, the buyers were convinced that the scoop would be mined if anyone discovered their amazing secret. This is the heart of a good con – a deal so dazzling and so profitable that if one word ever leaks out the contract would be snapped up by a million outsiders.

Obsessive secrecy and obsessive urgency became the order of the day at *Stern*. When Kujau received a four-year sentence on 8 July 1985, the judge remarked that *Stern* had acted so recklessly that it was a virtual accomplice. The *Sunday Times* weathered a storm of derision, perhaps taking heart from the example of the *Boston Globe* nearly a century before.

Four months after the sensational **Borden** murders of August 1892, the *Globe*'s ace crime reporter Henry Trickey managed to subvert the private detective –

Edwin D. McHenry – who worked with the police on the case when it first broke. On 9 October 1892, for a mere $500, Trickey secured the prosecution's testimony in its entirety, including verbatim copies of their affidavits.

The following day the entire issue of the *Globe* was devoted to the scoop. 'Lizzie had a secret, Mr. Borden discovered it, then a Quarrel. Startling Testimony of 25 New Witnesses' ran the headlines. The edition sold out.

But the *Globe* had been duped. The witnesses were fictitious, their addresses did not exist, and the story devoid of any factual basis. The fraudulent McHenry disappeared, and on 2 December 1892 the journalist Trickey earned an indictment for interfering with the course of justice. A lesser paper might have gone under.

See also **Morals, Provenance, Ripperology**

Fallout, alcoholic

The effects of America's 'Prohibition' were shattering. By 1930, 550,000 citizens had been arrested for drink offences. Two hundred and thirty thousand served a total of 33,000 years in prison. Thirty-five thousand died of liquor poisoning, and countless more were crippled or blinded. Deaths from alcoholism increased sixfold. Two thousand gangsters and beer runners perished in the fighting, together with 500 **Prohibition agents**. In Chicago alone, the 'Feds' killed twenty-three innocent bystanders by mistake, sometimes with **dumdum** bullets.

Worse, the administration of justice degenerated into a farce, its erratic ferocity typified by such cases as the 1928 jailing for life of Fred Palm from Lansing, Michigan, for possession of a pint of gin. Police and local government became an extension of the underworld. By the time Franklin Roosevelt swept to power on one of history's simplest and most appealing slogans, 'A New Deal and a Pot of Beer for Everyone', the ghetto gangs of Italian and Sicilian immigrants had burgeoned into a criminal empire of confederate Mafia families, based on booze, controlled by their governing Syndicate and intricately interwoven into the nation's social and commercial fabric.

It was only in the mid-1930s, after the FBI's headline successes as the nemesis of the Midwestern bank-robber gangs (see **Dillinger**), that **Hoover** turned his attention to organised crime. He established the Hoodlum Watch, declared Dutch Schultz 'Public Enemy Number One' and in 1936 roundly denounced racketeering as 'a problem which, if not solved, will eventually destroy the security of American industrial life and the faith of our people in American institutions'.

By 1937 Hoover was taking his men into the Mob's financial heartlands, personally leading raids in four states against brothels operated by Italian gangsters. In August he linked one of the arrested pimps to crime boss Lucky Luciano, and correctly identified 'the tide of dirty money that flowed from the houses to the racketeers and through them filtered out to local protectors, policemen, small-time politicians and even ultimately into the coffers of state political machines'. This was fighting talk. Luciano was the architect of the first 1929 **Mafia** convention, and Hoover's onslaught suggested the FBI meant business.

But he abruptly changed tack. In 1938 Hoover announced that the American criminal was 'not of a foreign country, but of American stock with a highly patriotic American name'. He retained and elaborated this fiction, with brief lapses, until the day he died. The Mob flourished; the FBI stood idle. Thus in the 1940s FBI agent Pete Pitchess was contacted by Bugsy Siegel (see **Las Vegas**) who offered to rat on his criminal enemies as a 'deep-throat' informant, but Pitchess neither dared tell the Bureau about the contact nor, after it had taken place, dared file the information under 'Mafia', since it did not exist.

In the 1950s, Agent Neil Welch was driven to despair by wasted investigations confined to the theft of single truckloads of chickens when it was obvious that the Teamsters Union were in cahoots with the Mafia, subjecting the entire national distribution network to illicit taxation. Two years after the 1951 Kefauver Commission (which detected 'a nationwide crime syndicate known as the Mafia'), the FBI's Assistant Director wrote, 'the Maffia [sic] is an alleged organisation ... The organisation's existence in the U.S. is doubtful.' Organised crime, which took root during Prohibition and proliferated unchecked for half a century, was Hoover's most abiding legacy to America.

See also **Eighteenth Amendment**

False confessions

Not just concocted by the police. Often innocent outsiders can hardly wait to get in on the act; false confessions are one of the commonest causes of wrongful imprisonment.

Historically, the classic example is the **Campden Wonder**. Judith Ward provides a contemporary British case; and in July 1992 David McKenzie was dubbed a 'serial confessor' by his defence counsel after admitting to a dozen murders he could not have committed, including one that never happened.

A 1992 work, *The Psychology of Interrogation, Confessions and Testimony*, by the forensic scientist Dr Gisli Gudjonsson, identified three distinct psychological types prone to fabricate confessions. There are the depressives, animated by a sense of guilt and a general desire to be punished for something; the publicity seekers, and the fantasists, who cannot distinguish between illusion and reality. An impressive new subdivision of this category is furnished by the American phenomenon of 'recalled **memory**', where perhaps hundreds of thousands of citizens have, with the aid of their therapists, recalled a similar number of murders at satanic **ritual abuse** ceremonies, without producing a single body.

Covert admiration for **sex** criminals is reflected in the unusually high numbers of false confessions they attract. In America, the horrific 'Black Dahlia' killing of 15 January 1947 elicited twenty-eight confessors in the first few months; what with the victim, 22-year-old Elizabeth Short, being mutilated round the breasts, beaten about the head, slit along the torso, cut in half, exsanguinated and washed clean, it was a very macho claim to make. Imaginative reporters added other 'facts' – that she was covered in cigarette burns, her breasts cut off and words carved into her skin, all this while alive. In fact, she died of the blows to her head before injuries were inflicted on the body.

Elizabeth Short, the Black Dahlia. True Crime writers traditionally characterise female victims as beautiful. Miss Short was.

'Well, I'm *capable of* doing it,' John Andry told detectives after bragging for weeks in a Long Beach bar about carving up cadavers. One step further down the line, on 24 January the police received a pre-emptive false confession from a man walking off the street to surrender, saying, 'I'm afraid I *might* kill a woman.' The eventual total *of* Black Dahlia confessors topped forty, embracing those unborn at the date *of* the murder and several women, Emily E. Carter among them, who entered the San Diego precinct yelling, 'Elizabeth Short stole my man, so I killed her and cut her up!'

Another telling indicator of the deep desire to confess is revealed in pathologist Professor Keith Simpson's autobiography. Simpson describes an unpublicised 1956 murder in Hertfordshire to which he was summoned post-haste by telephone. Three false confessions were logged before he had time to reach the police station.

In a separate category are the involuntary false confessors, those whose psychological weaknesses make them vulnerable to pressure. These are the suggestible: often compliant or anxious inadequates with low self-esteem, low intelligence and poor memory.

One of Britain's 'Birmingham Six', Hugh Callaghan, was a classic 'involuntary' case in a highly susceptible phase. At the time of his arrest, Callaghan was in the midst of a heavy drinking bout. Unemployed for three years, he was undergoing hospital treatment for depression and suffered from a duodenal ulcer. A night in the police cells without food or sleep, followed by abusive accusations from the heavies, proved sufficient to crack his resistance. Callaghan recalls: 'I was totally disorientated. I was physically weak. My hands were shaking. There were four or six guys coming at me, shouting at me. The pressure is so bad you'll do just anything to run away from it. I didn't read the statement when I signed it but I knew I had involved myself in the bombings.'

Judith Ward, convicted for the M62 bombing, broke in much the same way. First the police kept her awake for four nights. Then, she said, 'You get all these people screaming at you. So in the end you think: "Oh God! say what they want, get them off your back."' Another confessor, Pat Molloy, wrote to the **Court of Appeal** on 8 October 1980, detailing the similar circumstances surrounding his 1978 admissions: 'Detective Constable Perkins rushed back in again and struck me a severe blow in the stomach ... I was disturbed by the uniformed staff every half hour banging on the hatch to wake me up. The meals I received were liberally doused with salt and I was not given anything to drink ... In the morning I signed the confession out of revenge on the others and out of fear of more beatings and ill treatment.' Molloy is dead, but his statement secured life sentences for three associates in the Carl Bridgewater case.

See also **Ingram**, **West Midlands Serious Crime Squad**

Family, The

The genesis of Charles **Manson**'s 'Family' was described by the biker and gun-freak Danny DeCarlo. The story began in March 1967, with Manson just out of prison. He hung out on the steps of the Santher Gate entrance to the University of California, playing his guitar. Mary Brummer, 23, with a BA in history, was then an assistant librarian at the University. Unattractive, with a high-buttoned blouse and her nose in the air, she would pass Manson while exercising her poodle.

DeCarlo describes what happened next. 'So one thing led to another. He moved in with her. Then he comes across this other girl. "No, there will be no other girls moving in with me!" Mary says. She flatly refused to consider the idea. After the girl *had* moved in, two more came along. And Mary says, "I'll accept one other girl, but never three!" Four, five, all the way up to eighteen. This was in Frisco. Mary was the first.'

Susan Atkins, a Family stalwart, recorded her first impressions of Manson: 'I was sitting in the living-room, and a man walked in and he had a guitar, and all of a sudden he was surrounded by a group of girls.' Manson started to sing. 'I knew at the time that he was something I'd been looking for... and I went down and kissed his feet.' During their first sexual encounter a few days later, Manson suggested that she regard him as her father. 'I did so,' she noted, 'and it was a very pleasant experience.'

In 1968, the Year of Love, Manson decided to quit the increasingly bad vibes that spilled out as the Haight-Ashbury dream turned sour. He acquired a bus and loaded up his followers for a Magical Mystery Tour – just like the Beatles' album – and set off on the journey that ended in Death Valley at Spahn's movie

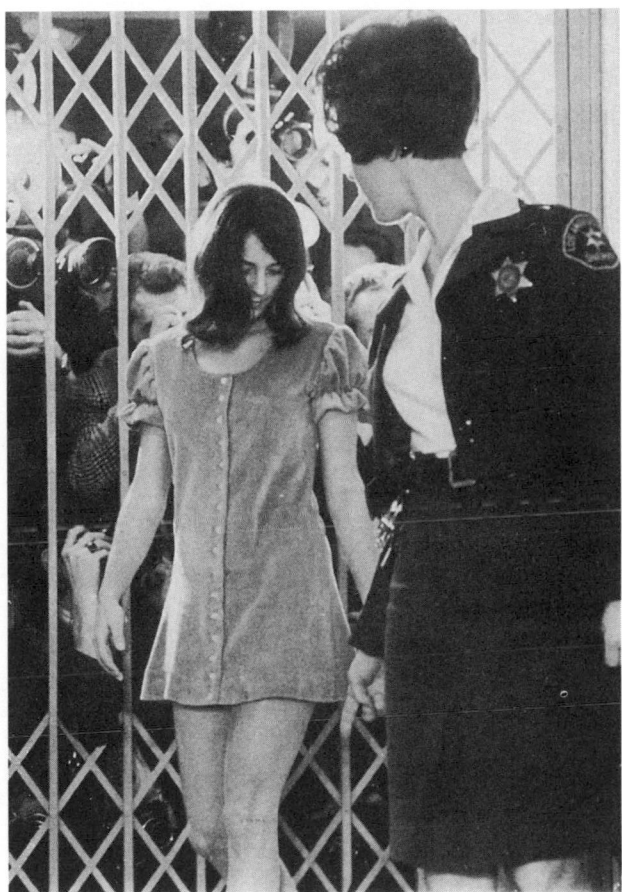

Susan Atkins leaving the courtroom after her arraignment for the Manson slayings. The newspaper men are caged

ranch in the desert. Mary accompanied them, and bore Manson's child, a boy called Michael.

At Spahn's, the Family first took over the Jailhouse Barn, then colonised the outbuildings of the Long Branch Saloon and Rock City Cafe. At its maximum the Family numbered perhaps a hundred members, but the inner core was only twenty-five to thirty strong. Mostly teenage runaways, they were cut off from friends, parents and the framework of their previous life. No books sullied the commune's intellectual freedom and, since time was just a bourgeois convention, clocks were not allowed either. The word 'why' was banned. As Manson pointed out, in conformity with the prevailing orthodoxy of the period, 'Never ask why. Everything is good. Whatever you do is what you're supposed to do. You are following your own karma.'

At first the kids indulged in endless rounds of

lovemaking and drugs and role-play in their desert commune. A rape victim later described her impressions: '20–25 people sitting, standing, lounging around in a living room; men, women, girls, boys and even little children; strobe lights going off and on; things hanging from the walls, everything psychedelic; some on the floor plunking on some types of musical instruments; and they were all drinking out of a dirty jug and smoking something.'

Manson made the Family dress up as pirates and had them slash away at boarders; next day, they would be cowboys fighting Indians, or Mexican knife-fighters, or devils. It was always them-against-us, even to the extent of outstaring snakes in the desert. Later the Family staged the world's first out-door LSD crucifixion ceremony.

But the real gambit was sex. Manson had it seven times a day. Love-vans and mattresses were scattered round the site and, in the hidden gullies and remote woody areas, nudity was the order of dress. Sex 'deconstructed' the girls; they arrived with their middle-class morality intact and finished up in group orgies. Brooks Poston, a Family member, put it this way: 'One of Charlie's basic creeds is that all that girls are for is to fuck.' If a girl was plain, Manson convinced her she looked beautiful; if she wanted a father figure, he turned paternal; and if she needed a leader, he revealed he was Christ. Manson could sniff out an individual's weaknesses.

Manson sent out his sidekick Paul Watkins to collect more girls whenever he ran short, sometimes teeny-boppers from Sunset Strip, sometimes hitch-hikers. Family orgies happened about once a week, starting with drugs. Manson would distribute supplies of 'grass', peyote and LSD. He orchestrated the whole event, beginning the dancing himself; then he stripped and led the naked Family behind him in a long snake while he beat out a rhythm on his drum. Next, they lay naked on the ground, rubbing themselves against each other, until…

Manson, the master of ceremonies, treated the intertwined couplings like plastic art, arranging the combinations into pleasing compositions. In Paul Watkins's words: 'He'd set it all up in a beautiful way like he was creating a masterpiece in sculpture.'

Manson made his disciples 'confront their fears'. Any disinclination or inhibition – whether against homosexuality, lesbianism, buggery or cunnilingus – became the task for the day. Manson initiated one 13-year-old

who did not want to be sodomised while everyone watched by doing just that. The normal ratio stood at five girls to every man; Manson needed the women to lure in the men.

The last orgy happened on 22 July 1969, but by then the sex had tapered off. At the end of 1968 the Family's preoccupation shifted to bloodletting. Manson would intone 'You can't kill kill' and drone on about carnage. 'If you're willing to be killed, you should be willing to kill.' According to a neighbour from nearby Steele Ranch, 'They talked about killing all the time.'

In this deranged atmosphere Manson seized on the release of the Beatles' 'White Album' as a prophecy that he would conquer the world. The Family knew that the end of Western civilisation was nigh – after a fearful bloodbath. By the autumn of 1969 the final Armageddon of the Book of **Revelations** was expected daily. Teams scoured the desert for the 'bottomless pit', their hiding place for the duration. Other squads worked on building look-out posts and fortifications. Stolen beach buggies came pouring in with new recruits, some heavily armed.

By then Sharon Tate and the others were dead (see **White Album**). The final number of Manson's killings remains in doubt; he himself claimed thirty-three.

The gradual evolution of Manson's supposedly loving and peaceful commune into an armed camp follows a traditional and largely American pattern typified by the fate of the Bhagwan's city of love built in Oregon in 1981, where distrust of the local population rapidly turned the encampment into an armed stockade. The Bhagwan went everywhere escorted by guards, and the bitter factional jockeying for position spawned an electronic surveillance system to tap every telephone and every room. The network of spies needed control by an inner clique, one of whom tried to poison 900 of the inhabitants of a nearby town with salmonella in order to induce a fitting degree of respect. The Bhagwan's misadventure ended without loss of life after the FBI were called in amid allegations of financial fraud.

Few quests are more perilous than the pursuit of perfect love, particularly when sought through self-sacrifice and martyrdom. The cult of Jim Jones claimed the lives of 913 disciples in the jungle of Guyana in 1978, and David Koresh, the leader of the Branch Davidians and 'reincarnation' of Christ whose followers were immolated in Waco, Texas, during early 1993, is merely the most recent example.

Fantasies

On 16 July 1973 a crazed teenager, Mary Ellen Jones, burst into a police station in Fort Lauderdale, Florida with a cock-and-bull story about her dead boyfriend. She spun a tale about accepting a lift from a man called 'Eric', who had driven them to his Miami home, forced the pair to strip at gunpoint and then taken photographs while they engaged in 'unnatural' sex acts.

Mary Ellen detailed how Eric had shot her boyfriend Mark Matson dead and then shackled her to a wall in a soundproofed torture-room festooned with whips, padlocks and chains. Eric then embarked on a twenty-four-hour stint of rape. Finally he wearied, saying: 'I've taken a life, but now I'm going to give you your life.' So he had just taken Mary Ellen back to Fort Lauderdale, and here she was.

She was not believed. The police telephoned home, and discovered Mary Ellen's record as a runaway and a compulsive liar. Her mother wired them her fare, and they packed the young attention-seeker back to Kentucky.

The following Saturday, a young Fort Lauderdale boy had better luck when he pointed out to his mother that their neighbour had sat stock-still in his back yard for two days. She telephoned the police: 'I think there's a dead man in the garden next door.' On arrival the officers found the body of Albert Rust; he had poisoned himself with a glass of chocolate cyanide. In his bathroom, a freshly rendered wall behind the shower curtain wept blood.

There, embedded in concrete, the police found the dismembered body of Mark Matson. For the final entry in his diary, the 41-year-old Rust (probably a virgin until his bout with Mary Ellen) wrote in a mood of anti-climax: 'I see no good reason for going on. What would come next? The whole business is not worth it; life is not worth the trouble after all.'

One of John Wayne Gacy's surviving victims encountered a similar credibility gap. The youth related how he had been stopped by a policeman, handcuffed, taken to a house, sodomised, half-drowned in a bath, urinated on and then made to play Russian roulette with his abductor – who predicted, correctly, that the police would never believe his story.

It is often said that 50 per cent of all advertising works, but no one knows which 50 per cent, and it is a pity that truth is no easier to discern. Among current allegations receiving widespread credence are reports of satanic **ritual abuse**. During the late 1980s, America's Erika **Ingram** recalled an extended pattern of rape and extreme sexual violation, convincing the Thurston County Sheriff's Office to press charges against her father. She recounted, 'One time, my mom open my private area and put a piece of died baby inside me. I did remove it after she left, it was an arm [sic].' Erika's father made her 'perform sexual acts with animals including goats and dogs'. On another occasion, 'he urinated all over my body. He didn't defecate on me this time.'

Such recollections landed Erica on television on 2 December 1992, where she recalled satanic ceremonies attended by policemen, judges, doctors and lawyers. 'First, they would start with just, like, chanting,' Erika said. 'Sometimes they would kill a baby.' She mentioned having sex on an altar-like table, and described the ritual abortion performed on her child: 'The baby was still alive when they took it out. And they put it on top of me and then they cut it up. And then, when it was dead, the people in the group ate parts of it.'

Sadly, Erika's impressionable father believed her and in May 1989 pleaded guilty to six counts of rape. He is now serving twenty years.

See also **False confessions**

Fantasising

Serial murderers fantasise on a scale way beyond ordinary daydreaming. The subject matter, too, is different. For the killer, protracted indulgence in sadistic fantasies plays a central emotional role as compensation for his imagined grievances. Mostly his visions are of blood. In the words of crime writer Colin Wilson, 'the basic psychological pattern of the sex criminal is a slow development through fantasy'.

Peter **Kürten** dreamed of weakening railway bridges and watching whole trainloads plunge to their deaths (see **Viaducts**). Or he brooded on individual acts of vileness: 'The long sentence I served when still quite young had a very bad effect on me. I did not masturbate. I got my climax of enjoyment when I imagined something horrible in my cell in the evenings. For instance, slitting up someone's stomach and how the public would be horrified. The thought of wounding was my particular lust.' Two other quotations from the FBI's database interviews echo the same mood: 'I was dreaming about wiping out the whole school' and 'I knew long before I started killing that I was going to be killing. The fantasies were too strong. They were going on far too long and were far too elaborate.'

At these potent levels, the fantasy is poised to erupt into real life. No take-over could be more damaging. The proper place for fantasies is in the head, and their attempted re-creation within the confines of ordinary life, warts and all, brings only contamination in its wake. Nor, for that matter, are fantasies greatly improved by the deadening hand of reality. The two realms are irreconcilably distinct and, during the public debate over the nuclear deterrent, it was argued that it was necessary to descend into a prophylactic hell of the imagination in order to *forestall a* descent in reality.

Ian **Brady**, the sex killer, staged in real life the type of motiveless murder depicted with such fluency in Dostoyevsky's *Crime and Punishment*. But once a fantasy has happened, it is reality, and its original fabulous aura, sullied by enactment, can only be reinstated by variation on repetition. Thus begins an uneasy commerce between the two realms, with the elaborated fantasies bringing only disappointment in their wake.

The serial killer Jeffrey **Dahmer** may have been beyond salvation by the time his sexual daydreams first focused on lying beside the body of another man, calm and still, perhaps even dead, whom he could explore at will. Had these visions remained fantasies, then his life alone would have been poisoned. But Dahmer was, as it were, already heavy with dreams, and no amount of **masturbation** could rub the images away. Bit by bit the ideas developed. Whose body would the stranger be? How could they meet?

Dahmer constructed a scenario in which he picked up a handsome, bare-chested man while cruising the highway – a self-evident fiction, since Dahmer had no car and rural Ohio had no hitch-hikers. But one day in June 1978 the dream happened in real life. As Dahmer drove home in his father's Ford, he saw young Steven Hicks from Illinois thumbing for a lift, standing by the roadside without a shirt. Dahmer picked him up, asked him back for a beer and, when he said he had to leave, killed him. Then, just as in his dreams, Dahmer masturbated over the dead body. So there was a waking dream, death in life.

At his trial, Dahmer's defence counsel laboured manfully to conjure up his dread of receiving disconcerting messages from the Other Side. 'How would you like at age fifteen to wake up and have fantasies about making love to dead bodies?' he asked the jury. 'What kind of person would wish that on another human being? Who do you tell it to? Do you tell it to your mother? To your best friend? None of us can possibly have gotten anywhere near to the fantasy level that this kid was at, at fourteen or fifteen years of age. I would not be Dahmer for one day.'

See also **Ng**, **Sex crimes**, **Zebra**

'Female Offender, The'

Title of an influential 1895 work by the criminologist Cesare Lombroso, who pioneered Social Darwinism by applying the doctrine of 'survival of the fittest' to people. Lombroso suspected that women destined to be murderers developed unusual strength, whereas whores followed their calling because they were particularly attractive.

Such views are difficult to reconcile with direct observation and, after years of studying pictures of female offenders, measuring their crania and quantifying their moles and tattoos, Lombroso seemed no nearer to proving his case. The unequivocal signs of degeneration, like misshapen skulls or thick black primate-like hair, were apparent only in a tiny minority of cases.

Eventually Lombroso realised that women offenders revealed fewer signs of degeneration because they were less highly evolved than men. Hence the female primitives were less conspicuous among their backward sisters. He contended that as women were naturally more law-abiding than men, the rare female criminal was thus genetically male. This meant that women convicts suffered both through application of the law and social ostracism. In his words: 'As a double exception, the criminal woman is consequently a monster.'

The idea passed into the cultural mainstream of received wisdom. The FBI's director, Edgar **Hoover**, claimed: 'When a woman does turn professional criminal she is a hundred times more dangerous than a man … acts with a cold brutality seldom found in a man.' To a New York Round Table audience Hoover went further, assuring them that a female criminal 'always has red hair … She either adopts a red wig or has her hair dyed red.' A case in point was flame-haired Katherine Kelly, wife of George 'Machine-Gun' Kelly, who served twenty-six years in prison for masterminding the 1933 Urschel kidnapping. But this was to put the cart before the horse. It emerged in 1970 that the FBI had suppressed the exonerating report of their own handwriting expert.

See also **G-men**, **Sex discrimination**

Ferrers, Lord Laurence (1720–60)

The star of England's smartest execution. All the Earl's efforts to have his death sentence commuted to the socially acceptable fate of beheading failed; he had to settle for a fashionable **hanging**.

On 5 May 1760, Ferrers was duly taken to Tyburn, but not in the common cart. He was conveyed in his own carriage, drawn by six horses bedecked with black ribbons, and followed by mourning coaches packed with friends. His coachmen wept all the way to the gallows, a set custom-built in the Earl's honour with a central flight of steps leading up to a silken noose beneath which, on a platform covered in black baize, reposed some plump cushions. These allowed the Earl to say his last prayers in comfort. Dressed for the occasion in his wedding suit of white satin, he processed to Tyburn accompanied by a splendid turnout from the Grenadier Guards, with the Life Guards bringing up the rear.

The scaffold incorporated a collapsible platform, precursor of the trap-door. But this innovation only represented a more dignified way of stepping off the gallows; the drop itself was still too short. The Earl's dangling feet touched the ground, and it took him some four minutes to choke to death. The only other hitch came when the Earl handed a tip of £5 to the man he believed to be the hangman. He was not. A fight immediately broke out on the gallows, only broken up by intervention of the Sheriff.

Contemporary engravings show the scaffold ringed by a huge circle of mounted cavalry, with a mobile coffin, drawn by its six horses, waiting in the wings. The day's box-office receipts in the packed grandstand (Madame Proctor's Pews) totalled £500.

Ferrers was overdue for execution. A high-handed, hot-tempered aristocrat, he had a long record of violent assaults on family and domestics. He kicked his wife unconscious, stabbed a servant for impertinence and finally, on 18 January 1760, shot his steward Johnson for suspected embezzlement. It was for this crime that he met his end, condemned by his peers in the House of Lords, where a descendant still sits making speeches about the European Union.

Fielding, Henry (1707–54)

The English novelist and playwright who, after the introduction of official censorship, was reduced in 1748 to taking up work as a magistrate; he landed the job through a friend from Eton.

During his six-year tenure and with the aid of a £600 grant (only half of which he used), Fielding brought the first semblance of law and order to the streets of London. He urged victims of recent robberies to repair forthwith to his offices in Bow Street, whereupon a specially formed group of constables would set off, at a run, in pursuit of the culprit. Hence the 'Bow Street Runners', originally consisting of the only six of the eighty constables in Westminster not on the take.

Fielding himself was scrupulously honest, and strove to introduce the concept of justice into the administration of law (see **Cambo**). The *Covent Garden Journal* contains a report of 'another defendant, who appeared guilty of no crime but poverty, and had money given to her to enable her to follow her trade in the market'.

Fielding's Bow Street snatch-squads proved surprisingly effective, mostly because criminals, unused to the idea of pursuit, were apprehended in scores relaxing in their customary haunts. These arrests came as a shock, since previous attempts at deterrence consisted of the largely academic enactment of a savage penal code, with scant attention paid to its implementation by catching anyone. Fielding reinforced success by advertising, for instance proclaiming on 5 February 1750: 'Near forty highwaymen, street robbers, burglars, rogues, vagabonds and cheats have been committed within a week.'

Fielding's campaign marked the first 'criminalisation' of the criminal. Before, the thief was more of an accepted feature of society, endured if not necessarily admired; thereafter, a felon was expected to use guile and deceit to avoid detection. This new, furtive attitude stood in stark contrast to the traditional values typified by one eighteenth-century highwayman who, at his trial, explained why he had failed to avoid detection: 'Gentlemen do not resort to trickery.'

See also **Horse patrol**

Fifth Amendment

According to the FBI, 'taking the Fifth' was invented by the hoodlum Llewellyn Morris 'Murray' Humphreys (1899–1965), the heir to Capone who eventually rose to become America's Public Enemy Number One.

By 1930 Humphreys controlled some 70 per cent of the Chicago rackets, which produced a gross income of $80 million a year. Nearly thirty years later, Humphreys weighed in as the elder statesman of the Chicago Mob to negotiate the so-called 'Family Pact' with Agent Bill Roemer of the FBI.

The problem started with J. Edgar Hoover's belated 1957 recognition that organised crime existed. This led to the 'Top Hoodlum' programme, and the Mob reacted to the unfamiliar strain of police surveillance by harassing the wives of FBI agents. Roemer only took action when the *mafiosi* stepped up the pressure by shadowing his children on their way to school. He went direct to Humphreys and outlined a deal: you stay away from our families and we will stay away from yours.

The Family Pact remains in force, one aspect of a code which makes the police relatively comfortable when the Mafia are around. Everyone knows where he stands. Disorganised crime, typified by the **crack** trade, is a different ballgame.

Finger

In *Mysteries of Police and Crime* (1898), Major Arthur Griffiths tells the story of a robber who was detected by means of a finger he left behind. The thief was climbing over a factory gate with iron spikes on top when a policeman saw him and shouted. The thief ran away; it was only in the next days that his finger was found on one of the spikes. It had stuck into it as he tried to escape, and his own weight had pulled it off. The fingerprint proved to be in Scotland Yard's collection, and the thief was captured and sentenced to jail.

Fingerprints, discovery of

Fingerprints are patterns formed by papillary ridges which facilitate the discharge of sweat through tiny raised ducts. As early as the 1820s Johann Purkinje, an anatomy professor, observed that every individual's fingerprints were unique. But this unprecedented opportunity for identification held an apparently insoluble problem. If each print was different, how could it be classified? Without categorisation, it would be impossible to find the single matching set in a filing system perhaps millions strong.

As early as 1858 the British magistrate William Herschel used fingerprints successfully in India to prevent illiterate government pensioners from claiming that the money they received last week had in fact been collected by someone else of similar appearance but fraudulent intentions the week before. The idea was not pursued; Herschel's enthusiastic letter to the Inspector-General of Bengal Prisons was politely ascribed to the wanderings of a fevered man weakened by dysentery. But two decades later, in 1880, an acerbic Scottish doctor, Henry Faulds (who afterwards cast himself as the only begetter of fingerprint identification), secured the discharge of a suspect in Tokyo whose prints did not match those found at the crime scene.

The quest was next taken up by Sir Francis Galton. Scheduled to lecture on *Bertillionage* in 1888, he became interested in fingerprints instead. Galton, a highly methodical type who once attempted to tabulate statistically the United Kingdom's distribution of female beauty, contacted Herschel and within three years confirmed that each individual's fingerprints really were unique, or – to be precise – the chances against two identical sets were 64 billion to one.

Ever up-to-the-minute, on 19 February 1939 the *News of the World* tried to boost circulation, venturing a prize of £1,000 for 'the reader who can reproduce a fingerprint identical with any one reproduced at the top of this page'. There were no successful claimants. Forty years previously, Galton too was stymied on the problem of classification. Nevertheless he wrote a book called *Fingerprints* which passed into the hands of Edward Richard Henry, the Inspector-General of the Nepal Police. Henry had grappled with the intricacies of introducing bemused hill-tribes to **anthropometry** with all its paraphernalia of calipers and filing cabinets, and while on leave in England obtained access to Galton's material.

Henry made the conventional observation that each finger displayed the pattern of an arch, a loop or a whorl. Beyond that, and like many before him, he stared at his fingertips in vain. Then, on a railway journey in 1896, he made the breakthrough. Each fingerprint (with the exception of the simple arch) has a 'delta', a roughly triangular space around the central whorl formed by the lines running off to either side. Henry realised that the size of this area has an exact numerical quantity – its width in terms of the number of papillary lines.

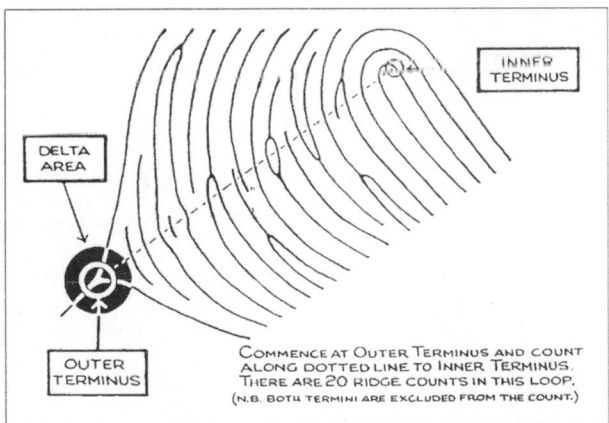

DELTA AREA

INNER TERMINUS

OUTER TERMINUS

COMMENCE AT OUTER TERMINUS AND COUNT ALONG DOTTED LINE TO INNER TERMINUS. THERE ARE 20 RIDGE COUNTS IN THIS LOOP. (N.B. BOTH TERMINI ARE EXCLUDED FROM THE COUNT.)

With the aid of a needle, these were easily counted and the prints then sub-classified according to whether they were whorls or one of the four basic types of arches and loops.

The following year, *Bertillionage* was scrapped throughout India and replaced by the fingerprint system, which soon gave Henry his first arrest. But the culprit, a servant named Charan who had cut the throat of a tea-plantation manager, was cleared of murder because the jury regarded the newfangled evidence as inconclusive. Nevertheless, in May 1901 Henry was appointed Assistant Commissioner at Scotland Yard and founded the Central Fingerprint Branch in July 1902. That year, a total of 1,722 suspects were identified, more than achieved *by Bertillionage* since its inception.

America got off to a slower start. Its first centralised bureau was not established until 1923 when it took over the 800,000 prints from the Leavenworth files, and even this undertaking was crippled by lack of funds for a further year.

Throughout the 1920s American juries remained suspicious of the novel evidence, which was, like so much else, vaguely unconstitutional. The routine fingerprinting of American offenders did not become legal until 1928 and, as the implications sank home, this led to a spate of largely abortive fingerprint **removal**. Today the FBI's library of over 200 million prints handles 30,000 enquiries each day.

Firefights

Careful ballistic work based on pure deductive logic can reconstruct the precise pattern of firefights.

On 4 December 1969 the Cook County Attorney, Edward V. Hanrahan, announced that the Chicago police had been involved in a fierce gun battle with diehard elements of the Black Panthers. Hanrahan described how, following a tip-off, the police arrived at a house in West Monroe Street to search for arms only to be met by a hail of bullets. The gang refused to surrender despite repeated entreaties, and by the time the shooting stopped the building was riddled with some eighty bullet holes. Two Black Panthers lay dead and four were wounded, but providentially the police suffered no casualties. The seven surviving gang members were charged with attempted murder.

At the Panthers' trial, Herbert Leon McDonnell – the defence ballistics expert – reconstructed the precise course of the gun battle. The direction (ingoing/outgoing) of each shot, its flight path and the main firing sequences of the battle were plotted on a scale-drawing of the apartment. McDonnell showed that the first shot had been fired through the apartment door by the police when it was partially open, and the second in response by the Black Panthers when the door was wide open. Thereafter, every single bullet came from the police. The police had decided to kill some Black Panthers, burst into the house unannounced and started firing. Not surprisingly, the Panthers felt their civil rights had been violated and thirteen years later, in 1982, won $1.85 million in damages from Cook County.

The seminal British ballistics case was the 1927 murder of William Walker, a gamekeeper. Towards midnight on 27 October, Walker (together with his underkeeper George Rawlings) caught the local poacher red-handed in a wood near Bath, Whistling

Copse. Shots were exchanged in the moonlight. When the smoke cleared Walker lay dead and Enoch Dix, the poacher, was arrested with a peppering of buckshot down his back.

Dix protested his innocence. With one of the three protagonists dead it was simply his word against the underkeeper's. Or so he thought. He said he had only opened fire by accident as he reeled away under the impact of hits from both barrels of Rawlings's shotgun. But examination of the crime scene showed that most of the pellets fired at Dix were still embedded in the tree trunk by which he had been standing. From the spread of shot in the tree and Dix, it was clear that Rawlings had fired from a range of fifteen yards; to prove the point, firearms expert Robert Churchill banged away with Rawlings's gun at a series of white-washed metal plates, providing the court with a precise computation showing the spread of shot at different ranges.

By contrast, Walker's corpse showed that his fatal wound was inflicted from a range of five yards or less. He had died of a single, closely defined gash to the throat five inches in diameter; the pellets had no time to spread. In other words, the poacher had fired from a range of five yards and been fired at from a range of fifteen. Of course, the gamekeeper could have pulled the trigger first while Dix ran towards him, but since Dix's wounds were to his rear, this entailed charging forward, backwards. The poacher was sentenced to fifteen years.

See also **Hamilton**

Fish, A. H. (1870–1936)

A nauseating American serial murderer still hard at it in his sixties. A father of six, Fish was brought to justice in 1934 by the almost single-handed efforts of Detective Will King of the New York Police.

The murder that brought him down was the June 1928 killing of 10-year-old Grace Budd. Fish got away with the crime itself, but six years later he wrote to Grace's mother describing how he had cut her child's little body into pieces and then eaten it. From a parent's point of view, the missive must mark an all-time nadir. It reads in part, 'Grace sat in my lap and kissed me. I made up my mind to eat her ... How she did kick, bite and scratch! I choked her to death, then cut her in small pieces so I could take my meat

The shambling figure of Albert Howard Fish, multiple murderer and cannibal

to my rooms, cook it and eat it ... How sweet and tender her little ass was, roasted in the oven. It took me nine days to eat her entire body. I did not fuck her tho I could of [*sic*] had I wished. She died a virgin.' Fish cut Grace's flesh into strips which he cooked with 'carrots and onions and strips of bacon'; this excited him sexually.

With the aid of a spectroscope, an otherwise invisible mark on Fish's envelope led Detective Will King – who had kept the case alive all these years – to the New York Chauffeurs' Benevolent Association, where a driver, Lee Siscoski, admitted to stealing office stationery, some of which he had left in a doss-house at 200 East 52nd Street. There the detective found a signature in the register corresponding to the handwriting on Mrs Budd's letter. King rented a room at the top of the stairs and waited for three weeks before he got his man, who surrendered submissively and then tried to razor his captor.

According to the psychiatrist Frederick Wertham, Fish looked every inch 'a meek and innocuous little old man, gentle and benevolent, friendly and polite. If you wanted someone to entrust your child to, he would be the one you would choose.'

This was exactly how he snared Grace. Her father, a doorman in straitened circumstances, advertised for work in the *New York World Telegram*, and on 28 May 1928 a well-dressed elderly gentleman arrived at the family's basement flat in the Chelsea district of Manhattan with an offer of employment at $15 a week. He gave his name as 'Frank Howard' and returned a week later to firm up the details. This time Howard and the Budds had lunch together; he produced a sizeable bankroll, peeled off some bills to send the elder children to the cinema and then volunteered to escort Grace to a children's party given by his sister. Instead, he took her to Wisteria Lodge, an unoccupied house in Greenburgh, choked her, removed her head and then sawed the body in half before carrying the portions home to eat. Wertham related how Fish's account of the culinary process was 'like a housewife describing her favourite methods of cooking. You had to remind yourself that this was a little girl he was talking about.'

A good half of Fish's psyche was resolutely genial. He delighted in his 12-year-old grandson, said, 'I love children and was always soft-hearted', and often read the Bible. But God told him to kill, and his lodgings contained a suitcase packed with press cuttings on another source of inspiration, Fritz Haarmann, the cannibalistic murderer of Hamburg who turned boys into **sausages**. Dr Wertham adjudged Fish mad, but his subject dissented: 'I am not insane, I am just queer.'

Fish confessed to many child murders, sometimes fifteen, sometimes 400, between 1910 and 1934; the true total is anyone's guess since his idea of a good time was highly individual. X-rays revealed a plethora of rusted needles in his testicles. He would thrust them in through his scrotum just for kicks, and he revelled in eating human excrement and setting light to alcohol-soaked cotton wool stuffed into his victims' – or even his own – anus.

Fish also experimented with poking needles into the soft flesh under his fingernails. But it hurt too much. 'If only pain were not so painful,' he complained. To the press he said, 'Going to the electric chair will be the supreme thrill of my life', and this was no mere bravado. Dr Wertham, appealing for clemency, noted, 'This man is not only incurable and unreformable, but unpunishable. In his own distorted mind he is looking forward to the electric chair as the final experience of supreme pain.' He received double value; on 16 January 1936 the first electrical charge failed, supposedly shorting on his intra-testicular stock of twenty-nine needles.

Fish's last words were, 'I don't know why I'm here.' The jury were similarly confused. A majority had concluded that he was legally insane, but they still thought he should die.

See also **Cannibalism**, **Sacher-Masoch**

Flowers

Chicago mobsters said it with flowers. As early as 1924 the passage of Capone's brother Frank to the Great Beyond was soothed by $20,000 worth of flowers. The tradition grew: in 1927 Vincent 'the Schemer' Drucci went to his last resting place preceded by twelve cars piled high with flowers, wreaths, bouquets, flower Bibles and set-piece tributes including a vacant chair of white and purple blossoms bearing the inscription: 'Our pal'.

But it was the Irish gangleader Dion **O'Bannion** who put floral tributes squarely on the map. A keen killer and lover of flowers, in 1922 O'Bannion bought a half-share in William E. Schofield's florists opposite Chicago's cathedral and there the gangleader whiled away shop-opening hours amid the lilies and terracotta vases.

O'Bannion supplied many of the flowers for Mike Merlo, who died on 3 November 1924 from natural causes – almost unprecedented for a President of the Unione Siciliana. A $100,000 cascade of wreaths and orchids descended on Merlo's home, overflowing into the garden to carpet the winter lawn with blooms. Capone sent an $8,000 order; even Merlo's wax effigy, exhibited in the open tourer leading the cortege, was bedecked with flowers.

After he had been shot six times on 10 November while making up one of Merlo's wreaths, it was O'Bannion's turn for a fine send-off. He all but received a state funeral, lying on display in his silver and bronze glass-topped coffin for three days while 40,000 shuffled past to pay their respects in Sbarbaro's Funeral Parlor. According to the *Chicago Tribune*'s funeral correspondent: 'Silver angels stood at the feet with their heads bowed in the light of ten candles that burned in solid golden candlesticks they held in their hands. Beneath the casket, on the marble slab that supports its glory, is the inscription "Suffer the little children to come unto me." And over it all, the perfume of flowers. Vying with the perfume was that of beautifully dressed women of gangland, wrapped in costly furs.'

Twenty-six lorry-loads of flowers followed O'Bannion to his grave at the Mount Carmel Cemetery. Showpieces included a seven-feet-high arrangement in the shape of a heart woven from American Beauty roses, a massive wreath from the Teamsters Union, a duvet of orchids to cover the grave, and a basket of roses labelled 'From Al', suspected of masterminding the hit. Mounted law officers cleared a path through the crowd of 20,000 lining the streets, and the mile-long procession was led by three bands and a police escort. Five municipal judges were among the mourners; the warring gangster chiefs – Torrio, Capone, Moran, Weiss and Drucci – faced each other over the grave. The only flaw came from the Archdiocese's refusal to allow burial on consecrated ground, but even in death O'Bannion coasted round these moral strictures. Within five months he was reinterred next to Archbishops Feehan and Quigley.

The first of the great gangster funerals was accorded to Big Jim Colosimo, underworld boss of Chicago from 1910 to 1920. In his youth, Big Jim laboured as a terrorist, pickpocket and pimp; in maturer years he became Diamond Jim, the Czar of Prostitution with a 'stable' of thirty-five $1 and $2 houses and two rather plusher establishments. When Johnny Torrio had him shot through the head, Colosimo's obsequies were graced by 5,000 mourners. His honorary pallbearers numbered eight Chicago aldermen, three judges, two Congressmen and a State Representative. Hymns were sung by the Apollo Quartet.

In Sicily, the *capo-mafia* Cesare Manzella received an unusual send-off after being blown up in April 1963. All that remained was his hat and one shoe, placed in the coffin alongside a dummy wearing his suit.

Footprints

True footprint evidence is rare in British criminal cases, since most people wear shoes; for the opposite reason, it is fairly common in places like Africa and India.

As with the fingers, the ridges on the soles of the feet are unique to each individual. So when Stephen Tomkinson of Bristol removed all his clothes apart from a pair of goalkeeping gloves prior to a rape, he provided investigators with two clues. They were not just looking for a goalkeeper; they wanted a goalkeeper with corresponding footprints. On 13 April 1992 Tomkinson was sent down for fourteen years on the evidence of a **fingerprint** expert seconded for the occasion.

Until now, the fact that no comparison between the culprit and his footwear was practicable until he and it are caught, vitiated the prospects for foot and shoeprint evidence. But the April 1992 edition of the *Journal of the Forensic Science Society* outlined a device called a pedobarograph which, by encoding images into a computer, showed the pressure patterns on a shoe during a complete step. This allowed assessment of an individual's gait and build from his tread pattern.

In 1946, the body of Dorothy Eggars, recovered from California's San Bernardino Mountains without a head or hands, was identified by the chiropodist who treated her bunions.

Fortuyn, Pim

Even the Dutch admit that their enviably civilised political system is far from exciting. Despite some radical state policies – such as the limited legalisation of both marijuana and voluntary euthanasia – Dutch political life has traditionally tended to emphasise the placid: famously, Queen Beatrix often pedalled around Amsterdam on a bicycle and political revolutions in the Dutch parliament were unheard of – until 2002, that is, when radical politician Pim Fortuyn burst on to the political scene.

Fortuyn was a striking character. Sporting a shaved

Pim Fortuyn

head over invariably immaculate Italian suits, the 54-year-old sociology professor shocked left-wingers by calling for the repeal of anti-discrimination legislation, attacking the Muslim faith as 'backward' and suggesting that immigration into the Netherlands be cut to a quarter its present level (from 40,000 to 10,000 a year). He also shocked traditional right-wingers by being both an open and unrepentant homosexual.

Fortuyn created his own political party in February 2002 and within three months looked close to winning control of the Dutch government. This was partly due to his surprising popularity with younger Netherlanders, many of whom were bored and irritated by the political liberality of their parents' generation. The other reason Fortuyn looked likely to have a shot at winning power was that Prime Minister Wim Kok's government unexpectedly resigned in April 2002. This followed an official report criticising the government's role in the Srebrenica massacre in 1995, when just over 100 lightly armed Dutch peacekeepers failed to stop a large force of Bosnian Serbs from murdering thousands of Muslims.

Then, on 6 May, nine days before the election, Pim Fortuyn was shot dead in a car park.

His killer was almost as odd a political mix as Fortuyn himself. Thirty-three-year-old Volkert van der Graaf was a passionate animal-rights activist who believed it was his moral duty to protect the weak in society. A vegan (one who reveres the sanctity of all life and eats no animal products, or even any type of seed, because that is destruction of potential life), van der Graaf shot Pim Fortuyn five times with a handgun at close range outside a radio studio in the town of Hilversum.

He later confessed that he had struggled with the morality of taking a life but had been pushed over the edge by Fortuyn's pro-discrimination stance and a proposed policy to deregulate fur farming in the Netherlands. 'Something must have gone wrong, something derailed,' he is later reported to have said about his decision to kill Fortuyn.

Thus a vegan humanitarian murdered a gay sociology professor because the second was proposing the most extreme right-wing agenda the Netherlands had seen since the Nazi invasion.

Fortuyn's grieving party went on to win enough parliamentary seats to earn a significant place in a coalition government with the centre-right People's Party for Freedom and Democracy, but within six months their government collapsed because of petty in-fighting within the Pim Fortuyn Party.

Volkert van der Graaf was sentenced to eighteen years in prison.

Franz Ferdinand, Archduke (d. 1914)

Interspersed in the crowd lining the streets of the Bosnian town of Sarajevo on 28 June 1914 were seven conspirators lying in wait for Archduke Franz Ferdinand, heir to Franz Joseph, ruler of the Habsburg monarchy. Resplendent in full-dress uniform topped by plumed headgear, the Archduke motored slowly through the town in an open tourer.

Five of the assassins jibbed at the last moment. One failed to recognise the Archduke, the next felt sorry for his wife, the third was unprepared for the complexities of a moving target, and a fourth fell prey to the delusion that he was standing next to a policeman. Meanwhile their target progressed unharmed through a regular avenue of assassins.

The least reliable of the group, Cabrinovic, proved the most enterprising. He asked a constable: 'Which is His Majesty's car?' and then whipped off the detonator and lobbed the bomb into the designated vehicle. The detonator cap struck the Archduke's wife, bruising her neck. The bomb itself rolled off the folded hood into the street where it exploded under the car behind and made a hole in the paving, injuring a dozen bystanders. Dismayed, the conspirators scattered; a testy Archduke drove on to the Town Hall where he complained: 'I come here on a friendly visit and someone throws a bomb at me.'

The Archduke's humour was quickly restored; he agreed to go to the local hospital to visit the morning's wounded. But since his driver was not informed of the change in plan, the Archduke's car took a wrong turning and then backed slowly past a corner delicatessen where, as it happened, the sixth assassin, Gavrilo Princip, sat despondently, contemplating suicide.

Two years earlier, Princip's attempt to join the Serbian guerrillas had been thwarted by his puny physique. Now, hardly able to believe his good fortune, Princip drew his pistol and shot both the Archduke and his wife. She died instantly. Mortally wounded, the Archduke turned and said: 'Sophie, live for the children.' Then he whispered, 'It is nothing.' Then he died.

Princip and twenty-three other youthful conspirators were rewarded with lengthy jail sentences. Princip himself survived in prison until dying of tuberculosis in 1918. He fared better than millions of others, indirectly killed by the choreography of Ruritanian alliances that led from the Sarajevo assassination to the First World War, the bloodiest conflict the world had ever seen.

After the war, King Zog of Albania proved altogether more fortunate. While Zog was opening Parliament in Tirana, a young assassin rose to his feet from a few benches back and levelled a pistol. The youth had his monarch cold and, in accordance with the blood-feud formalities of the Balkan tradition, embarked on the ritual formula of denunciation before pulling the trigger. But the killer suffered from a very bad stutter and was disarmed.

French Connection, The

Not just a film. The French Connection peaked in 1971 when it delivered about ten tons of heroin to the USA – a strong recovery from the parlous state of the American drugs trade immediately after the Second World War, when the interdiction on shipping, coupled with the prevalence of serious border problems, whittled down the number of heroin addicts to an estimated 20,000.

In the post-war era the Corsicans in France and the Mafia in Sicily retained strong connections with Indochina through the French colonial presence. **Opium** collected from the hill tribes of Southeast Asia was transported to Saigon for processing into morphine before shipment to Marseilles. There, refined into heroin, it was smuggled to the United States in an enterprise undertaken with the connivance of De Gaulle, by way of retaliation for the American failure to rally to the relief of Diem Bien Phu in 1954. Or so the gossip runs. In the words of Agent Thomas C. Tripodi of the Drug Enforcement Agency: 'De Gaulle had to know about it. And he obviously permitted it because he could have stopped it if he wanted to.'

The American crackdown of 1972 ended the French Connection. Among the principals, Sarti was dead, and Ricord, Nocoli, David, Pastou, Catania and Buscetta languished in jail. But nature abhors a vacuum. In one way, the successor to the French Connection was the Sicilian – or '**Pizza**' – Connection; in the other direction, far more important, the Chinese Connection through the **Triads**.

See also **X**, **Operation**

Führer, The (1889–1945)

Adolf Hitler was one of history's greatest war criminals. In addition he may have murdered a young girl in 1931.

At the least, the circumstances invite suspicion. On 19 September 1931 Hitler's half-niece, the attractive 23-year-old Geli Raubal, was found dead in her bedroom in the Munich apartment she shared with Hitler, shot through the chest by a bullet from Hitler's 6.35mm Walther pistol. On her desk lay a letter, broken off midway through a word, with the final 'd' of the *und* omitted. 'When I come to Vienna,' Geli was writing, 'hopefully very soon – we'll drive together to Semmering an...' There the letter ends.

Earlier that day, at lunch, Hitler and Geli had quarrelled violently over whether she could leave for Vienna. Only the previous week, she tried to escape from her claustrophobic life in Hitler's flat, reaching his cottage in Berchtesgaden before receiving orders to return.

Now Geli was dead and, whether it was murder or suicide, a corpse in Hitler's apartment constituted an embarrassment to his meteoric political career. Despite the damage limitation by Hitler's advisers, the periodical *Die Fanfare* ran the headline: 'Hitler's lover commits suicide: bachelors and homosexuals as leaders of the party.'

Long before then, over the weekend, Geli's corpse was spirited down the block's back stairs for a cursory medical examination. Then the sympathetic police hastily announced that Geli had taken her own life. The Bavarian Minister of Justice (already in Hitler's pocket and subsequently well promoted) put an end to any further investigation and the body was shipped to Vienna. There Geli was unaccountably buried on hallowed ground, a right normally denied to suicides.

Meanwhile a distraught Hitler went to earth at an isolated lakeside cottage on the Tegernesse where, in one version, Rudolf Hess snatched a gun out of his hand to prevent suicide. Scandal sheets printed rumours that Hitler had killed Geli; the *Münchner Post* said that 'the nose bone of the deceased was shattered and the corpse evidenced other serious injuries'.

But with the body buried, no police inquiries, and no coroner's report, the story lacked staying power. The only man to pursue it was journalist Fritz Gerlich who, eighteen months later, was ready to reveal the truth in his paper, *Der Gerade Weg*. In March 1933, before he could publish, a squad of fifty stormtroopers burst into his newspaper office, smashed his face, burned his files and bundled him off to Dachau. A month later one of Gerlich's main sources, George Bell, was murdered. Gerlich himself perished during the Night of the Long Knives. But he reportedly smuggled out documentary proof that Hitler had ordered Geli's death; the recipient, Karl von Guttenberg, lodged this dangerous material in a numbered Swiss bank account and then took his secret to the grave as a participant in the July 1944 coup against Hitler.

Who killed Geli? At the heart of her fate is her relationship with 'Uncle Alfie'. It started shortly after his nine-month prison sentence in 1923 when Hitler summoned the 17-year-old Geli and her mother to Munich to act as live-in housekeepers. By

1925 Geli had blossomed: tall, vibrant, a golden girl who turned heads in the street. Hitler squired Geli around town, went riding with her, paid for her music lessons, mooned over her at the opera and, according to Fest (a party leader from Wurttemberg), turned in 'a very plausible imitation of adolescent infatuation'.

Of the seven women with whom Hitler had intimate relations, six committed suicide or seriously attempted it. Before her death in the Bunker in 1945, Eva Braun tried to take her own life in 1932 and 1935. Actress Renate Mueller, later found dead beneath her Berlin hotel window, confided in her director that on her date with Hitler he 'fell on the floor and begged her to kick him ... condemned himself as unworthy ... and just grovelled in an agonising manner ... She finally acceded to his wishes. As she continued to kick him he became more and more excited.'

Heiden, a respected writer on Hitler, calls the future Führer 'a man with masochistic–coprophil inclinations, bordering on what Havelock-Ellis calls undinism'. Geli confided in Otto Strasser, a one-time Nazi insider, on the way back from a Mardi Gras ball in 1931. Strasser recalls: 'Hitler made her undress while he would lie down on the floor. Then she would have to squat down over his face where he could examine her at close range, and this made him very excited. When the excitement reached its peak, he demanded that she urinate on him and that gave him his sexual pleasure.'

It is possible that Geli, trapped in a gilded cage with only Hitler for social and sexual recreation, took her own life. But her last, interrupted letter is the opposite of a suicide note; the girl is looking forward to life. But Geli constituted a serious threat to the future Führer. Two years before, in 1929, Hitler wrote her an explicit and degrading love letter which fell into the hands of his landlady's son. Hitler's fixers managed to buy the missive back. But it was clear that any future revelations by Geli could unleash deeply damaging press smears.

Perhaps Geli was carrying Hitler's child, and killed herself out of grief; for Hitler was just beginning to show an interest in Eva Braun. But if Geli was with child, it is most likely she had spurned Hitler's advances in favour of another admirer, either her suitor in Vienna or an art teacher from Linz, both Jews. Such an alliance would not have gone down well with the leader of the Master Race.

Perhaps Geli Raubal shot herself. Perhaps she was made to shoot herself. Perhaps she was shot on Hitler's orders. Perhaps Hitler shot her. No one knows, and unless her body is exhumed from its zinc coffin in the featureless paupers' burial ground outside Vienna, it is unlikely that anyone ever will.

G

Galvanic research

The scientific hocus-pocus of the *Frankenstein* films once comprised mainstream medical research. On 13 January 1803 the corpse of George Forster, an English murderer, was subjected to an electrical experiment in order to restore him to life. Professor Alkini wired up the cadaver, made a connection and induced the dead Forster to grind his jaw and open one eye. Under further electronic encouragement, the body clenched its right hand and waved its legs around, with the *Criminal Recorder* remarking that this 'showed the eminent and superior powers of Galvanism to be far beyond any stimulant in nature', although Mr Pass, the beadle of the Surgeons' Company who observed the process, died of fright.

More recently, Charles Manson believed in the existence of the Bottomless Pit, and, in the hope of locating the source of evil, today's galvanic researchers evince a fetish for the brains of serial killers. Leonard Lake's (see **Ng**) has been preserved for posthumous study, and the Russian authorities promised that **Chikatilo** would be shot with particular care to avoid damaging his cerebella, for which several psychiatric institutes were in open competition. As Chikatilo said, 'There are two parts to my brain. Part of it says kill and the other part says do not', so it should be relatively straightforward to see which is which.

Gangs

A non-word among the Los Angeles street gangs. 'We'd rather be considered a community inside a community, you know?' said Bone, an Athens Park Blood aged a miraculous 27. 'But the word "gang" puts a stigma on our love. And it's all about love.' This is partly true; the gangs confer a sense of belonging, a family and – perversely – vestigial security.

The main warring factions are the Bloods and the Crips, distinguished by their respective house colours of red and blue. In addition to shooting each other, they shoot themselves; perhaps the biggest of the Crips' internecine feuds was the War of the Stolen Leather Coat, claiming some thirty lives – a toll that stands comparison with major Mafia bloodlettings over multi-million-dollar rackets. In the chilling words of a probation officer, 'By the time they're seventeen, they've done their drive-bys.' Many houses round the South Central district have ramps going up the steps, not because of the high percentage of aged occupants but because so many are paraplegics disabled by the fighting.

An escalation in the bloodletting accompanied the introduction of **crack** in the late 1980s, when disputes abruptly ceased to concern territory and centred on money, corroding traditional restraints on violence. The new wars were fought with assault weapons like the high-velocity Kalashnikov AK-47s, which blasted through not just the target house but the ten houses behind. The gangs themselves never made significant money out of dealing; profits stayed higher up, with the Cubans and Colombians.

After twenty years of fighting, in 1992 the Bloods and the Crips declared a truce. The gangs bonded during the Los Angeles riots against a common enemy, the police.

The expression 'plug uglies' is derived from plug hats, or top hats, and the Plug Uglies were an early New York street gang. Their rivals included the Dead Rabbits and the Shirt Tails, and in Britain of the late eighteenth century it was worth giving a wide berth to 'Macaronis'. A vicious gang of criminal yobs, fond of gambling, drinking, duelling, their direct antecedents were the founders of the Macaroni Club, reserved for young men of fashion who travelled in Italy, on their return daringly introducing pasta to Almack's assembly rooms off St James's. Their criminal namesakes regarded themselves as above the law. Historian Christopher Hibbert cites the case of young Plunket who, exasperated by his wig-maker's refusal to knock more than a guinea off his bill, razored the trades-man's throat from ear to ear.

The word 'hoodlum' is an American creation, coined in San Francisco during the 1870s. Cut-throat gangs formed a scrummage round their intended victim, shouting 'Huddle 'em, huddle 'em', and more recently, the thuggish John Gotti earned a reputation as the 'hoodlums' hoodlum'.

The term 'racketeering' probably derives from American politics. In the late nineteenth century New York City political clubs held boisterous get-togethers called rackets, an idea adopted by local gangs who held rackets of their own, and the racket was that you bought tickets, or else.

Gas chamber

The problem with gassing murderers is that they must collaborate in their own demise. Sympathisers enjoin the condemned man to make things easy by taking a few deep breaths to draw the gas down into his lungs. But even the most obliging type may find this runs contrary to inclination and instinct, and the gas chamber is survivable for as long as the man can hold his breath. At least with hanging, shooting and elec-trocution the state does the job for you.

Death by gas is not pleasant to watch. As Clinton Duffy, Warden of San Quentin, put it: 'In a matter of seconds the prisoner is unconscious. At first there is extreme evidence of horror, pain, strangling. The eyes pop, they turn purple, they drool. It is a horrible sight; witnesses faint.' Observers of Caryl Chessman's execu-tion on 2 May 1960 saw him 'gasping, drooling, rolling his head – surviving the engulfing gas for several seconds'. On 6 April 1992 an Arizona convict took 10 minutes 31 seconds to die.

On 21 April 1992 the final throes of the murderer Robert Harris were viewed by forty-nine spectators. Some were official witnesses, some well-wishers, others quite the reverse. Representing Harris's murder victims were two bereaved mothers, one father and two sisters. All peered into the death chamber through

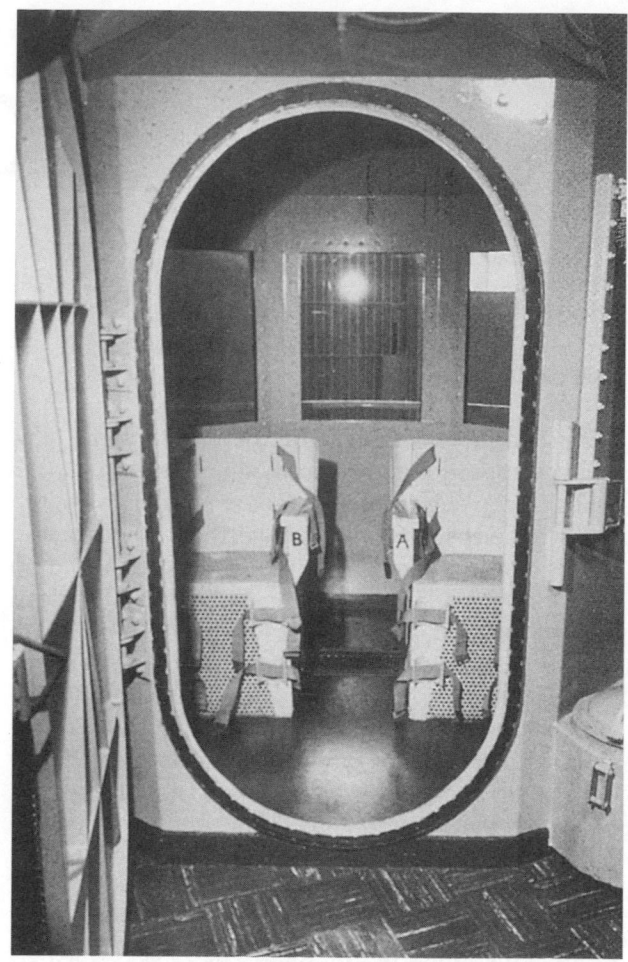

The San Quentin gas chamber, which claimed 194 lives up to 1967. The last moments of Robert Harris in 1992 were recorded on video

the glass panels. Inside, a video-camera whirred to aid post-mortem legal evaluations of whether gassing could be construed as cruel and unusual.

In the words of reporter Dan Morain: 'Harris inhaled four or five times. His head snapped back and then dropped as he strained against the straps. After a minute, his hands appeared relaxed. His mouth was wide open and his face flushed and then almost purple. Whether he was unconscious, in pain or numb, he seemed oblivious two minutes into his execution. But then, as his body seemed to have relaxed, his head rose eerily.'

Gas chamber technology is simple enough. Under the death chair is a tank, linked by a pipe to a reser-voir of sulphuric acid. Above the tank, a pound of cyanide in a gauze bag is suspended on a hook. The condemned man is strapped into the chair, the door locked, and the acid released; presumably the convict hears the trickle. Then the executioner operates a lever, dunking the cyanide in the acid to produce the lethal hydrocyanic gas. Afterwards, a liquid ammonia spray neutralises any gases lingering on the corpse. The procedure was summarised by a placard waved outside San Quentin on the day of Harris's execution: 'Plop, Plop, Fizz, Fizz, Oh, what a relief it is.'

The gas chamber was invented as a humane alternative to the electric chair by a Major D. A. Turner. The first gas execution took place in Nevada in 1924, whereupon the process was adopted by ten states, including California where San Francisco's city authorities tested the apparatus on live pigs; some of the journalists attending the experiment described the procedure as more savage than **hanging, drawing, and quartering.**

In a recent adaptation, a Welsh magistrate constructed a portable gas chamber for personal use out of a plywood hood shaped like a large sewing machine case. He connected it by a pipe to his car exhaust. With the engine running, the device proved capable of despatching the family cat when placed inside and, thinking to replicate the feat with his wife's head, Cranog Jones extended the piping from the garage, over the conservatory and into the marital bedroom.

On the night of 7 December 1991, Margaret Jones awoke to the sound of her Ford Fiesta, eerily loud, as though she had parked upstairs. Crouched at the bedside was her husband, clutching a box about two feet square from which carbon monoxide fumes emanated. 'What are you doing?' she asked, and then tried to ring the police. But the line was dead.

Cranog Jones was sentenced to nine years for attempted murder on 23 April 1993. The couple, married for twenty years, were embroiled in a divorce likely to cost Jones his house. He planned to gas his wife, place her body in the car, and pass off the death as suicide.

Gaskins, Donald 'Pee Wee'

Asked who is the worst serial killer of modern times, many criminologists would answer: 'Pee Wee Gaskins'.

A harmless-looking little man with a high voice, Gaskins enjoyed torturing his victims, mostly hitch-hikers, to death – the total is well over 100.

Born in the backwoods of South Carolina in 1933, Gaskins came to the notice of a writer named Wilton Earle when he was under sentence of death for murdering a fellow-prisoner; he had been sentenced originally for killing a number of 'business associates', people involved with him in a racket involving respraying and selling stolen cars. Earle wrote to ask him if he would like to collaborate on his autobiography. Gaskins invited Earle to visit him in prison, and in unsupervised conversations revealed that he was a sadistic killer who had often cooked and eaten part of his victims – in some cases while they were still alive.

Sent to reform school for burglary as a teenager, Gaskins had been gang-raped by twenty youths. This was the first of many terms in prison, although he later compelled the respect of fellow-inmates when he murdered a particularly dangerous fellow-prisoner, one of the jail's 'power men'. After a prison sentence for raping an under-age girl, he resolved in future to kill women he raped and to hide the bodies. The first time he did this he was so carried away by the sensation of power that he began doing it regularly. His confessions, published by Earle in a book called *Final Truth*, were so appalling that they gave Earle a nervous breakdown. The book was published after Gaskins was electrocuted in September 1991.

When Donald 'Pee Wee' Gaskins was arrested on 14 November 1975 – charged with contributing to the delinquency of a minor – it was for suspected involvement in the disappearance of a 13-year-old girl named Kim Ghelkins, last seen leaving her home in Charleston with an overnight bag.

Kim's parents mentioned a married man named Donald Gaskins, whose stepdaughter was a friend of Kim's.

Twelve years before this, Gaskins had been imprisoned for the statutory rape of a 12-year-old girl named Patsy. A week later he had escaped by jumping from an open window of a second-storey waiting room in the Florence County Courthouse. He was at liberty for six months before being recaptured and sentenced to four years in the South Carolina Central Correctional Institution. In November 1970 he was again questioned by the police, this time about the disappearance of his own 15-year-old niece, Janice Kirby, but denied all knowledge of her.

A month later he had again been under suspicion – this time, of a horrifying sex murder. A 13-year-old girl named Peggy Cuttino, daughter of a prominent local politician, had disappeared in the small town of Sumter; her mutilated and tortured body was found in a ditch. Again Gaskins was questioned and released.

It was when some of Kim Ghelkins's clothes were found in a mobile home rented by Gaskins that a warrant was issued for his arrest.

Yet even when taken into custody, police were unable to find enough evidence to charge him. Just as they were preparing to let him go, his trusted friend Walter Neely suddenly became a born-again Christian, and decided to tell everything he knew. That same afternoon, 4 December 1975, he led the police to the graves of two young men who had been shot in the head and buried in the swamp. The following day he led them to four more corpses, two men and two women. On 10 December he was able to help them locate two more graves.

On 24 May 1976 Gaskins went on trial in the Florence County Courthouse and was sentenced to die in the electric chair.

On Death Row, Gaskins began to think hard about how he could escape execution. One possibility was to confess to more murders, and engage in plea-bargaining. So he confessed to the murder of his niece Janice, and her friend Patty Ann Alsbrook. He claimed he had killed them as a result of an argument when he had caught them taking drugs. (In fact, as he later admitted to Wilton Earle, both had been sex crimes.) In exchange for his confession, Gaskins's death sentence was commuted to life imprisonment. With eleven murders known to his credit, he prepared to face a lifetime behind bars.

In late 1980 there came a welcome diversion. Gaskins was asked if he would murder a fellow-prisoner, Rudolph Tyner, a 24-year-old black drug addict, who had killed an old couple in the course of holding up their grocery store. Tyner was on Death Row, hoping that the sentence would be commuted to life.

The son of Tyner's victims, Tony Cimo, was embittered at the thought of his escaping the electric chair, and decided to take justice into his own hands. Through a friend of a friend, he approached Gaskins. Bored and frustrated, Gaskins rose to the challenge of committing a murder under the nose of the warders.

The first step was to get to know Tyner and gain his trust, which Gaskins did by slipping him reefers. The murder itself was brilliant in its ingenuity. Gaskins suggested he instal a home-made telephone between their cells, running through a heating duct. Tyner's phone contained plastic explosive. When, at a prearranged time, Tyner said, 'Over to you', Gaskins plugged his end of the wire into an electric socket, and the explosion rocked the whole cell block. Tyner was blown to pieces.

At first the authorities believed that it had been an accident. Then rumours of murder began to spread. Soon Tony Cimo was arrested, and confessed everything. He and Gaskins stood trial for the murder of Rudolph Tyner. Cimo received eight years. Gaskins was sentenced to the electric chair.

During his early days in prison, after his arrest for the murder of Kim Ghelkins, Gaskins had often been interviewed by reporters; now he was almost forgotten – a mere car thief and contract killer who had murdered a number of crooked business acquaintances. One or two criminologists had talked about writing about him, but it had all come to nothing. Gaskins disliked his loss of celebrity status; as South Carolina's worst mass murderer, he felt he deserved to be famous.

So when, in 1990, he was approached by Wilton Earle, who felt that his story might be worth telling, Gaskins cautiously agreed. He was running out of appeals, and his appointment with the electric chair could not be long delayed – a year at the most. As he came to trust him, Gaskins agreed to tell Earle what he called 'the final truth'. But there was one stipulation: nothing should be published until after Gaskins had been executed. Among other things, his rape of a small child would disgust his fellow-prisoners.

Earle agreed. What he did not know when they made the agreement was that he was about to hear the most appalling and terrifying story of serial murder in the history of twentieth-century crime. What was revealed over many sessions with the tape recorder was that Gaskins was not simply a killer of crooked business associates; he was a compulsive and sadistic sex killer, whose list of victims amounted to around 120. The story of the 'final truth' was so nauseating and horrific that Earle must have doubted many times whether it could be published,

Gaskins's problem, as it emerged in the tapes, had always been an overdeveloped sex impulse. His need for sex was so powerful and compulsive that, whenever it came on him, he experienced a heavy feeling that rolled from his stomach up to his brain, and down again. He compared it to the pain women suffer before menstruation. When this happened, he would drive up and down the coastal highway looking for female hitch-hikers.

But having served two terms for rape, he had vowed it would never happen again. His solution was simple: to kill his victims. And having raped and killed his first hitch-hiker with a knife, he quickly discovered that torture and murder were becoming an addiction. After a while it made no difference whether the victim was male or female; it was the torture – and the sense of power – that gave the pleasure. In effect, he became a character from one of the novels of the Marquis de **Sade**, working out new ways to satisfy his desire to hurt and degrade.

Gaskins estimated that in the six years between September 1969 and his arrest in November 1975, he committed between eighty and ninety 'Coastal Kills', an average of fourteen a year. He distinguished these murders of hitch-hikers picked up on the coast road from his 'serious murders', those committed for business or personal motives such as revenge.

Hours before his execution on 6 September 1991, Gaskins tried to commit suicide with a razor blade that he had swallowed the previous week and then regurgitated. He was found in time, and given twenty stitches. Soon after midnight he walked into the execution chamber without help, and sat in the chair. After his wrist and ankles had been strapped, a metal headpiece was placed on his skull, with a wet sponge inside it. Before the black hood was placed over his head he gave a thumbs-up salute to his lawyer. Three buttons were then pressed by three men – so that none of them would be sure who had been responsible for the execution.

His body was handed over to his daughter and later cremated.

Gein, Edward (1906–84)

A very strange American. One of the garments that Ed Gein crafted from human skin was a waistcoat. He also made a nipple belt, that is, a belt of nipples.

Gein's ideas on interior decor were equally bizarre. In his room, a wastepaper basket and lampshades

fashioned of human skin jostled for space alongside bowls made from skullcaps. 'You wanted to use them as containers?' asked the incredulous investigator, Joe Wilimovsky, after Gein's 1957 arrest. 'I think you got the right idea,' responded Gein cheerfully, 'I think that's taken from an old Norwegian style.'

Ed Gein, necrophile

Gein came from the rural Midwestern town of Plainsfield. He decorated the interior of his timber house with scatter masks – the skin stripped from faces – and finished off the bedroom with a display of skulls perched on his bedposts. Upholstered chairs, backed with human skin, had strips of fat still visible on the underside.

Another feature not widely copied was the woman's flayed torso slit up either side. Tanned and freestanding, it could be worn in the style of a breast- and back-plate; Gein kept it for those moonlit nights when he pranced round the yard in a state of sexual excitement, draped with the face, hair, breasts and vaginas of his human trophies. In the kitchen he put Mrs Worden's heart fair and square on the stove in the saucepan. On his arrest, her fermenting head was found stashed in a burlap bag, with steam coming out. But basically Gein was a muddled man, storing his stock of nine vulvas in a shoebox. He found that a little sprinkled salt dried them out nicely.

In his capacity as a butcher Gein worked in the

woodshed, hauling up Mrs Worden with a block and tackle by the ankle before eviscerating and decapitating her. It was tidy work; he had dressed the corpse like a carcass in a slaughterhouse when the police found it swinging. In the words of the medical report: 'The body had been opened by a median incision from the manubrium sterni and extending in the mid-line to the area just above the mons veneris … the empty body cavities were glistening and free from blood and appeared as if they had been washed.'

In real life, Gein was a precursor of Jeffrey **Dahmer**, the Milwaukee serial killer and kindred spirit. Both were **cannibals**, both inhabited shadowy inner worlds redolent with primitive superstition, and Gein's home was the 1950s hick equivalent of Dahmer's urban Oxford Apartments. In cinema and fiction, Gein's influence is discernible in more literal characters like Buffalo Bill, the skin-transvestite of *Silence of the Lambs*, and he rates a mention in Bret Easton Ellis's *American Psycho*. Gein also inspired the small-town 'Leatherface' whose handiwork with bodies featured in *The Texas Chainsaw Massacre*. And fifty miles from Plainsfield lived a young writer, Robert Bloch, who worked Gein's story into a novel, *Psycho*, transferring the action to a motel in order to ensure an adequate influx of victims.

Bloch homed in on his anti-hero's Oedipal motivation: there had to be *a reason* for Gein's way of life (see **Lucas**), and his mother's bedroom was the only normal place in the house. It contained a bed, a cedar chest and other furniture, all coated in a thick layer of dust. The room had been nailed shut as a shrine ever since the death of Gein's mother in 1945, twelve years previously. Since then Gein felt that things were unreal. A loner with few social outlets, he never enjoyed sexual relations with anyone and, before she died, Ma Gein drummed into him that sex before marriage was bad and that **masturbation** was worse. During his intensive police debriefing in 1957, Gein devoted hours to discussing his relationship with his mother, dead for more than a decade. She was, he said, 'good in every way'.

Ma kept in touch after she passed on, chatting away for the next year or so while her boy drifted off to sleep; Gein told the police that during this period he developed a fascination with anatomy. He was impressed by contemporary reports of Christine Jorgensen's sex-change operation and toyed with the idea of becoming a woman. Then, in tandem with

another weird local, Gus, Gein opened his first grave to provide material for his medical experiments.

Many of the household knick-knacks and furnishings discovered on Gein's arrest came from grave-robbing. For years he ferreted around in local graveyards, sometimes lugging complete cadavers home, sometimes cutting off the interesting bits as mementoes. But his yearnings were not restricted to predeceased bodies. Although tried for only one murder – Mrs Worden, shot in the head in 1957 – Gein also admitted to killing Mary Hogan. Psychologists were quick to point out that both these women bore a strong resemblance to his mother, but in addition his brother died of a mysterious accident, leaving Gein as sole heir to his mother's estate, and a man called Travis disappeared after Gein offered to take him hunting. Two local girls also vanished without trace. But it was only after the Worden murder that outsiders, in the form of the police, entered Gein's home, finding it bedecked with human remains. At his trial on 6 January 1958, Judge Bunde stated, 'I can't see how my opinion can be anything other than to find this defendant insane', a view judicially confirmed ten years later.

Gein's home was razed to the ground on 30 March 1958 after rumours that it was destined to become a House of Horror tourist attraction. But his 1949 Ford pickup survived, sold at auction for $760 after brisk bidding. The vehicle went straight into harness at local fairs. A placard announced, 'It's here! See the car that hauled the dead from the graves.'

Gein died on 26 July 1984 after decades as an ideal patient at a psychiatric unit. Today, fans can buy latex Gein masks, collect Gein ephemera, or join the Ed Gein Fan Club. Cultists swap Gein jokes: he couldn't operate his farm – all he had left was a skeleton crew. What did he keep in his sewing box? 'Belly buttons.' And how were Gein's folks? 'Delicious.'

Genetic fingerprinting

In 1985 Alec Jeffreys from the University of Leicester discovered DNA fingerprints: the Holy Grail of serology, hailed as the 'forensic breakthrough of the century'.

Jeffreys was studying myoglobin protein when he isolated a block of repeated DNA sequences within the so-called hypervariable region. This is the DNA section responsible not for universal information common to all humans (how to grow arms and legs) but their personal characteristics. These blocks are particular to each individual (with the exception of identical twins) and are derived from bands present in either the mother or the father.

Jeffreys highlighted the hypervariable sections with radioactive probes so they registered on film, producing darkened bands not dissimilar in appearance from supermarket barcodes. At last blood specimens (or any type of genetic material) could be attributed with certainty not to a type of person but to a specific individual. Equally important, they could be unambiguously related to his antecedents and successors.

In its civilian guise, the procedure set to work resolving paternity and immigration disputes. Then in 1987 genetic fingerprinting secured the conviction of the British murderer and rapist Colin Pitchfork, a cake decorator, matching his blood to semen found in his victim. It was a copybook case, with the new wonder-evidence simultaneously exculpating a 17-year-old false confessor. The American author Joseph Wambaugh felt inspired to write: 'The scourge of rape and other violent crimes could largely become a thing of the past.'

In 1988, DNA evidence secured its first conviction in the US when Tommie Lee Andrews went down for two rapes. And in 1989 a British publican, Ian Simms, was convicted of murdering 22-year-old Helen McCourt on the strength of the bloodstains on his discarded clothes. The stumbling block had been to obtain a match with his victim's blood, since her body was never found; the prosecution was only the third British case without a corpse. Ingeniously, a sample taken from her parents tallied at one remove with those found on the murderer.

The most recent figures show that about 15 per cent of the 4,500 DNA tests conducted annually in Britain are for criminal cases. The DNA specimen may be degraded by a body's exposure to poor storage conditions, the process is often complicated by the tiny size of the specimen (see **Bones**), and in closely linked population groups the DNA similarities may exceed the patterns achieved by random mating.

Thus both 'false positives' and 'false negatives' remain a possibility, and the reliability of the DNA test began to be challenged in the courts. In two Australian cases, DNA evidence was ruled non-admissible. In one, it was disputed that the apparent barcode 'match' constituted a true match – they looked the same, but were they identical? In the other, the statistical evidence of probability (once put as high as 1:738,000,000,000,000) was dismissed because it did not include samples from the suspect's ethnic group.

In December 1991, the American journal *Science* suggested that realistic odds could not be calculated without greater knowledge of DNA patterns in ethnic communities. The authors, respected academics, were warned off by a US Department of Justice official and the magazine asked the writers to 'tone down' their findings. These included a Missouri case where the accused was initially found guilty on odds of one in 150 million, a figure the authors revised to one in 256. Six American courts have now excluded DNA evidence, ruling that 'the scientific uncertainty over the role of population sub-structure in calculating the chance of DNA matches is too great to pass the so-called Frye test' by which the admissibility of forensic evidence is judged. Thus the status of genetic fingerprinting is unclear in the United States, but less so in Britain, which has no equivalent of the 'Frye test' to satisfy.

In Britain, where techniques are accepted on an *ad hoc* basis, order prevails. Ethnicity is regarded as a statistical red herring since the odds are so high that the exact number of noughts is irrelevant. Ian Evett, from the Home Office Forensic Science Service, took the most extreme example (a single 'probe' as opposed to the usual four, confined to an Afro-Caribbean sample) and still derived a probability of one in 50,000. The most recent investigations suggest that genetic differences are greater *within* races than *between* them, and in Britain the mere mention of DNA evidence often secures guilty pleas when legal aid committees refuse funds to fight the case.

Nevertheless it is now apparent that 'genetic fingerprinting' is a misnomer. The evidence is subject to technical errors both in carrying out the test and in the inferences drawn from it.

Ghosts

The supernatural provided the key to Allan Pinkerton's most far-fetched case. In 1885 a county clerk and pillar of rectitude, Alexander P. Drysdale, murdered a bank-teller out West and robbed the safe of $130,000.

Pinkerton had his suspicions but not the proof, and called in three operatives to help with the case. It transpired that his youngest sleuth, Green, bore a remarkable resemblance to the murder victim.

Pinkerton turned this to fantastical advantage. He disguised Green as a ghost, caking his hair with blood. Then another assistant, Andrews, inveigled the suspect Drysdale out for a stroll at the witching hour; they made their way at dusk to the local haunted spot of Rocky Creek. There Green put in an appearance as the ghost of the deceased. Drysdale uttered a great shriek but his companion, unperturbed, asserted that there was nothing to be seen.

Soon Pinkerton's third spy, by now a friend of Drysdale's wife, reported that the suspect was prey to nightmares and sleep-walking. Meanwhile, in his capacity as a spirit, Green embarked on a series of nocturnal rambles round Drysdale's house. Finally Pinkerton arrested the murderer and took him to the bank where the disguised Green popped up again, still shamming dead. Drysdale fainted and, with modest encouragement, confessed.

Eighty-one years before the Pinkerton case, Francis Smith was sentenced to death for opening fire on a ghost at point blank range. His target was the notorious sprite of Hammersmith, then a village outside London, and on 3 January 1804 Smith loaded his fowling-piece and went on the prowl with the night-watchman. A few minutes after eleven he cornered a pale spectre in flowing garb lurking near the ghost's usual haunt at the end of Black Cross Lane. Smith brought his gun to his shoulder and challenged the apparition. It did not reply. 'Damn you, who are you?' Smith called. 'Stand, else I'll shoot you.' It advanced towards him. Smith fired.

The phantom had frequented the district for weeks, flitting across the fields as the church bell tolled one in the morning. At the sight, according to a local newspaper, 'Women and children have nearly lost their senses.' A pregnant woman was confined to her bed with shock, and a waggoner driving a team of eight horses fled in terror, deserting his fifteen passengers. One ghost, accosted in Church Lane, was unveiled as an impostor, a girl dressed in white out courting. Another was seen unrobing in Harrow Lane, removing a white sheet. But reliable reports persisted, with many sightings detailing the spirit's eyes flickering like glow-worms, and its nostrils, exhaling fire and smoke. Few would venture out after dark.

Sadly, Francis White's target proved to be Thomas Milward, a young plasterer in his whitened work-clothes which reached to his shoes. Milward's sister told journalists that she had never thought of warning him that he might be mistaken for the ghost, since it had glass eyes and long horns. But even though Smith held his fire to the last moment – as evidenced by the blackened powder on Milward's face – he faced a charge of murder. Three days later he went on trial for his life at the Old Bailey.

Smith was a pleasant, mild-mannered young man, but the Judge, the Lord Chief Baron, made no allowance for the obvious element of mistake (see **Accident**), expounding the law in peculiarly drastic terms. To prove 'malice aforethought' did not entail demonstrating active hatred by the accused; a mere intention to kill sufficed. To their credit, the **jury** paid no attention and returned a verdict of manslaughter. The judge objected that this was wrong, and instructed them to reconsider. This they did, and the Recorder passed the sentence of death. 'Francis Smith,' he reassured the prisoner, 'you have been tried by a most attentive and intelligent jury.' In the normal course of events a grateful Smith would have been hanged the following Monday. But he was reprieved that evening, and on 20 January George III reduced his sentence to one year's imprisonment.

The ghost, caught a week after Milward's shooting, proved to be James Graham, a bootmaker. He had begun his series of nocturnal appearances clad in a sheet with the intention of scaring his apprentices and his lodger, a one-armed postman who had terrorised his children with ghost stories. So Graham waylaid them going home, and enjoyed the impression he created so much that it became a hobby.

The 1970s haunting of 112 Ocean Avenue, Amityville, discloses no firmer basis in the supernatural. In 1974 the house was home to Ronald DeFreo, a well-liked car service manager, his wife and their five children. But their eldest son, Ronnie Jnr, was a spoiled brat with a vicious streak, and on 12 November 1974, aged 23, he slipped barbiturates into the family supper and then shot them dead with a .35 Marlin rifle. His feeble cover story deceived no one, and in December 1975 he was found guilty on six counts of murder. Two weeks later, a Mr and Mrs George Lutz bought 112 Ocean Avenue as a home for their three children and dog.

Twenty-eight days after moving in the Lutzes fled

Ocean Avenue in terror, and their experiences formed the basis for Jay Anson's book, *The Amityville Horror*. Anson, a TV documentary scriptwriter, described how a family friend, Father Frank Mancuso, arrived to bless the house the day they moved in. But the ceremony was suspended when a voice called 'Get out!', and while driving back home Mancuso nearly crashed, and a colleague who shared his car for part of the journey became involved in a serious accident soon afterwards. The Lutz family fell to arguing, and were disturbed by mysterious noises at night; George Lutz stopped washing, and saw a ghostly pig his daughter claimed to keep as a pet. Green slime oozed from the walls, the basements stank of excreta, the lavatory bowls filled with black gunk, and his wife assumed the guise of a toothless hag and levitated.

Lutz became suspicious of the house and researched its history. He learned of the grisly DeFreo murders, and discovered that his home was built on an enclosure for sick and demented Indians. It was their burial ground. Under the front steps he found the entrance to an open cistern, through which, he surmised, evil spirits made their way to infect Ronnie DeFreo Jnr.

Ghost stories are all in the telling, and the slightest distortion turns fact into fiction. No medium is better suited to this transmutation than film, and the smell of excreta, betokening the presence of Satan, may have been indicative only of plumbing problems. We, or our children, have all heard things that go bump in the night, and clever depiction of atmospherics can capture terrors which are none the less baseless.

The Shinnecock Indians never established a compound for their mad or dead anywhere, least of all at 112 Ocean Avenue, and it is surely unlikely that George Lutz, a house broker, was unaware of the DeFreo murders. The killings attracted a blaze of publicity. Lutz, a resident of Suffolk County, purchased 112 Ocean Avenue, presumably at an advantageous price, two weeks after Ronnie Jnr was sentenced at the end of the county's longest trial.

Gibbets

As a rule, gibbeting in irons was reserved for corpses. But occasional reports describe a condemned man as lingering alive in his ironwork after a bungled execution. The gibbeted highwayman John Whitworth was

saved from this fate in 1777 by the guard of a passing stagecoach, who shot him.

The display of the criminal's body was intended as a deterrent, and, after the invention of 'tarring' to act as a preservative, Newgate prison installed a 'kitchen' where the bodies could be processed. Gibbeting remained within the discretion of individual judges until 1752, when hanging in chains became part of the legal sentence, and soon gibbets lined the Thames and the six approach roads to London. The practice was banned in 1834 after reaching new heights the year before, when James Cook, a murderer, was gibbeted from a set of gallows thirty-five feet high in Saffron Lane, Leicester.

At the other end of the scale, in 1762 Peter III ('Peter the Mad') of Russia used a miniature gibbet to execute a rat. The rodent, captured nibbling at one of the emperor's puppets, received the death sentence after a full-scale court-martial; there are some doubts about Peter's mental capacity.

Gibbets were popularly regarded as a cure for toothache; the Spennymore gibbet eventually disappeared completely, removed sliver by sliver for medicinal purposes.

Girl from Botany Bay, The

There was nothing special about Mary Broad's crime or her punishment. A sailor's daughter from Fowey in Cornwall, she stole a cloak, rendering herself eligible for seven years' transportation. She reached Australia alive and there married another convict, William Bryant, in April 1790 giving birth to her second child.

Bryant was a fisherman, and in October 1790 he wangled a chart, a compass, a quadrant and a set of muskets out of a passing Dutch ship. Judging his moment, Bryant stole the governor's six-oar cutter and put out to sea from Port Jackson on the night of 28 March 1791, taking six convicts with him as well as his wife and their two infant children.

In ten weeks they sailed their open boat 3,250 miles north. Hugging the coast, they found themselves blown out to sea, where for three weeks they were lashed by gales and thrown on to the Barrier Reef; they survived on turtles, caulked their boat with soap, fought off hostile natives and headed away from the northernmost tip of Australia into 500 miles of open water, pursued by cannibals in canoes. But on 5 June they made harbour at Koepang, Timor.

There the band of escapees presented themselves to the Dutch governor as shipwrecked mariners and waited for a boat back to England. But Bryant rowed with his wife and, perhaps while drunk, confessed to the governor. They were thrown into prison, and then shipped back to England clapped in irons.

During the harsh voyage both Mary's children died and, on arrival in London, she was bundled off to Newgate to await transportation back to Australia as an escaped felon.

Word of Mary's epic journey leaked out; the press dubbed her 'the Girl from Botany Bay'. Her cause was espoused by James Boswell, Dr **Johnson**'s biographer, who approached both the Home Secretary and the Under Secretary of State on her behalf, and in May 1793 the Girl from Botany Bay received an unconditional pardon. Boswell settled an annuity of £10 on her; she returned to Cornwall and faded from history, but not before giving Boswell a little packet of dried Australian 'sweet tea' that had shared the vicissitudes of her heroic voyage. These few leaves are now in the archives of Yale University.

Glatman, Harvey Murray (d. 1959)

Possibly the ugliest of the sex killers. Glatman possessed an IQ of 130, but the lower half of his face betrayed a slightly inflated, ape-like look which, when coupled with his jug ears, made him unappealing to women. Solo sex was his only recourse, and it took the form of self-strangulation in mock hangings. At the age of 17 his lunges at the opposite sex consisted of snatching their purses in the streets of his hometown in Boulder, Colorado, and then tossing them back. This progressed to making a young girl undress at gunpoint, albeit with a toy gun. Finally a string of robberies – by now with real firearms – on New York women led to a five-year spell in Sing Sing. Released in 1951, he set up a television repair shop in Los Angeles.

The lonely, frustrated Glatman joined a photographic club for the titillation afforded by nude models in studio sessions. Then, on 30 July 1957, he made a service call to the apartment of an attractive young woman, Judy Ann Dull, a model recently arrived from Florida. By chance, he was a photographer for a

New York True Crime magazine. Could he see her portfolio? Would she like a job? How about $50 for a series of bondage pictures in his studio?

Judy Ann agreed, and two days later Glatman drove her to his apartment. He explained that his plans had changed. They would do the shoot there. Would she put her hands behind her back while he bound them? Then he could put on the gag and tie up her legs. She acquiesced, and soon sat helpless in his armchair while he pulled down her sweater, raised her skirt and started to click away. For the first time in his life he had a semi-clad pretty girl in his home.

Whatever his original intentions, Glatman lost his self-control. He tore off her clothes, put a gun to her head, and raped her, twice. Then the pair sat naked on his sofa watching television. She begged him to let her go. She promised not to talk.

But could she be trusted? Glatman's record meant that if she was lying he would be put away for a long time. The logic was inescapable. He loaded her into his car and drove 125 miles into the desert near Idaho. There he took another series of photographs as Judy Ann begged for her life in her underwear. Then he strangled her. Alone with her body, he begged for forgiveness and drove back to Los Angeles in a mood of self-revulsion to await arrest.

But nothing happened. No police came knocking on his door. With time, Glatman's panic and remorse began to mutate. He developed his photographs and sneaked another look. Then he pinned enlargements to his walls.

By the following spring Glatman was ready to kill again. He joined a 'lonely hearts' club under the name of 'George Williams' and on 8 March 1958 he drove 24-year-old Shirley Ann Bridgeford into the desert of Anza State Park, east of San Diego. There he followed the established routine: first the gun, then the rape, then the bondage photo-session, and then the kill. He left Shirley Ann to rot behind a cactus, and four months later, on 23 July 1958, a striptease dancer and nude model, Ruth Rita Mercado, met the same fate. Glatman contacted her through the personal columns of the *Los Angeles Times*. He wanted to let her go, but by now it was even riskier than before. 'Ruth was the only one I liked,' he recalled. 'I didn't want to kill her. I used the rope, the same way.'

By September it was the turn of another model, Joanne Arena. When Glatman offered her a photographic job, she thought his manner 'creepy'. But a friend, Lorraine Vigil, needed the money. Lorraine and Glatman drove off together down the Santa Anna Freeway and, just outside the town of Tustin, he pulled over on to the hard shoulder and produced his gun. Strip, he said.

'I knew he was going to kill me,' Lorraine said later. 'I tried to plead, but I knew pleading wouldn't do any good.' She grabbed for the gun. Glatman shot her in the thigh but she twisted the barrel round until it pointed at him, and the struggling pair tumbled out on to the road.

At that moment a police patrol car came to the rescue. Glatman gave himself up. Sentenced to death after a three-day trial, he refused to lodge an appeal. 'It's better this way,' he said. 'I knew this was the way it would be.'

He was executed on 18 August 1959.

See also **Hansen**

G-men

Abbreviation allegedly coined by Machine Gun Kelly, who was extremely pressed for time. His words were: 'Don't shoot, G-men!' uttered as the FBI agents burst into his bedroom with guns drawn early on the morning of 26 September 1933. The 'G' stood for government.

Kelly died twenty-one years later, still in Leavenworth Penitentiary for the July 1933 **kidnapping** of the Oklahoma oil millionaire Charles F. Urschel, 'snatched' from his porch during an after-dinner hand of bridge.

Urschel had been released on payment of the $200,000 ransom, and he provided the FBI with their crucial clue. Every day during his week of blindfold captivity he listened as two planes droned overhead, one at 9.45 in the morning and the other at 5.45 in the evening. The only intersection where airline timetables showed this to happen in Texas was the town of Paradise.

Urschel proved a meticulous observer. From his room he heard the barnyard sounds of cows and hens, and his drinking water – which had a strong mineral taste – was drawn from a creaking well to the north-west of the house. The FBI flooded Paradise with undercover agents, touring the home-steads kitted out as bankers offering agricultural

loans and found a farm fitting the description, owned by a man called R. G. Shannon. His step-daughter Kathryn was married to a George Kelly, Machine Gun Kelly.

Thirteen men stood trial for Urschel's kidnapping, but Kelly and his wife were still at large when proceedings began. They were caught in a dawn raid in Memphis, Tennessee, after a little girl named Geraldine Arnold confided in a schoolfriend that she had been 'borrowed' by a couple needing a child for the sake of appearances. The playmate told a friend, and the friend told her father, a policeman.

What Kelly actually said when he saw the shotgun pointing at his heart was, 'I've been waiting for you all night.' The phrase 'G-men' was already in popular usage, and **Hoover** concocted the story for publicity.

Despite his ferocious soubriquet, George Kelly was a relatively amiable man who never fired at anyone; it was Kathryn who bought him his gun, Kathryn who landed him a job with a two-bit gang and then – after two feeble bank raids in the towns of Tupelo and Wilmer – Kathryn who talked him into the Big Time with the Urschel kidnapping. But she could not persuade him to kill their captive after the ransom was paid.

Kathryn served twenty-six years. It emerged in 1970 that the FBI had suppressed the handwriting evidence by their own expert, which would have destroyed their case, clearing her of writing the ransom demand notes.

See also **'Female Offender, The'**

Godfather, The

The movie's fictional Don Vito Corleone was derived from the Mafia boss Carlo Gambino, on the outside the very model of an Old World benevolent patrician.

Prior to *The Godfather*'s release, pressure from the newly founded 'Italian-American Civil Rights League' compelled the deletion of all the film's references to the Mafia. The League, which campaigned against the stereotyping of American Italians as gangsters, was the creation of mobster Joseph Colombo, who embezzled the League's funds for distribution to himself and other Mafia bosses. Colombo rose to prominence through Gambino's influence and was murdered in 1971 for his bungling; he died at an open-air League rally in a Mafia hit.

Godmothers

A recent phenomenon in the 'dead-man's-shoes' world of the Italian Mafia. After a family Godfather is rubbed out or jailed, his spouse or sister takes his place as Godmother.

Among these *grandes dames* are old 'Ice Eyes', Rosetta Cutolo, who stepped in when her brother Raffaele was sentenced to life for murder and extortion; Elvira Palumbo, taped nagging her husband during a prison visit: 'Enzo, wouldn't it be better to give that job to someone else? The guy you're talking about can't shoot to save his life'; Pupetta Maresco, who inherited her husband's criminal empire after liquidating his killer; and Anna 'the Black Widow' Mazza, living off the fat of the land in a million-dollar villa surrounded by bodyguards in bulletproof vests.

'Ice Eyes' was captured during Italy's anti-Mafia spasm of 1993. She had been sought ever since escaping from a police raid in September 1981, and was sentenced *in absentia* to nine years in 1990. On 8 February 1993, acting on a tip-off, the police knocked on the door of a fortified villa outside Naples. She came quietly to the entrance saying, 'I am tired of being a fugitive', thus becoming another casualty of the recent confessional spate by former *mafiosi*.

In the summer of 1992 Italy at last established a workable witness protection package (the basic tool of organised crime investigations) offering informers a new name, a new home and a new nose. Special telephone hot-lines enabled those with guilty consciences to confess from the comfort of their own homes; page 166 of domestic Teletext asked repentant viewers to dial Rome 33170804, and in the first nine months some 280 '*penititi*' took the opportunity to shop former associates, a figure standing favourable comparison with the dozen or so who came forward in the previous four decades.

As with the black race riots (see **King**), it is the highly publicised physical outrages that bring retaliation from an incensed populace. The 1963 Italian Mafia crackdown was inspired by the dynamiting of seven policemen with a car bomb, the 1982 campaign by the assassination of General Dalla Chiesa, and the 1990s paroxysm by the devastating 1992 murders of prosecutors Giovanni Falcone and Paolo Borsellino.

They did not die in vain. Despite official reprimands for 'ruining the Sicilian economy', Falcone persevered to become the architect of Palermo's maxi-trial which culminated in 1987 with 350 convictions, reducing the Mafia's wall of **silence** to rubble while maintaining sufficient judicial equilibrium to hand down 114 **acquittals** for lack of evidence. As with the **Pizza Connection** trial, culpability extended into the higher echelons, with nineteen of the most powerful bosses sentenced to life.

Optimistic commentators, many of them astute, consider that the Mob overreached itself with the 1992 Falcone/Borsellino assassinations, and the killings may yet prove the Italian Mafia's worst mistake. In Palermo, between the nineteenth and the twenty-third of every month – the dates of their deaths – the streets are hung with sheets bearing anti-Mafia slogans, and women fast in the Piazza Castelnuovo. The pavement outside Falcone's apartment has become a public shrine.

Golden Triangle, The

Major source, with Afghanistan, part of the Golden Crescent, of the world's opium and heroin. The Middle East is another important producer but nearly all its output is consumed locally.

The Golden Triangle is an area of rugged terrain occupying parts of Thailand, Laos and Burma. The region, about the size of Greece, is dominated by sharp mountain ranges, deep valleys and thick jungle, populated by fierce hill tribes who harvest some 1,500 tons of **opium** annually under **Triad** control. The crop, refined down to 100 tons of heroin, is then distributed worldwide through the Chinese Connection. Each year, a few tons are intercepted, but most law enforcement agencies prefer to concentrate on traditional targets like the Italian Mafia, leaving the Triad distribution network all but untouched.

From the hill farmers' perspective, opium is a perfect crop. With an average yield of two kilos an acre, the harvest is non-perishable and easy to sell. The growers do not go to market: the drug traffickers and opium warlords send their agents to buy at source. Many farmers are addicts – a further incentive to replant – and are bound into economic servitude by accepting loans. Sometimes their payment is in kind, with goods like salt and matches. For cash, the crop fetches about $40 a kilo.

In the Burmese section, the Shan States of the Golden Triangle are a legacy of the British Empire. The area was never colonised and, on gaining independence after the Second World War, Burma inherited a country within a country of thirty-four independent 'Sawbwas' (feudal warlords) indulging in low-scale opium cultivation. American know-how founded the modern industry; the CIA, along with French Intelligence, regarded the creation of independent criminal empires as an excellent buffer against communist expansion.

At harvest time the opium trails with their mule caravans sometimes a mile long are all but invisible, screened by an impenetrable jungle canopy. Nevertheless the opium is brought out at night and, with 40,000 armed insurgents controlling the area, subjugation or control of the Triangle remains a hopeless task. Every jungle laboratory is fiercely defended; in 1987 the US Drugs Enforcement Agency busted a run-of-the-mill lab defended by thirty guards ensconced behind landmines and armed with machine guns, M-16s, Russian AK-47s, M-79 rocket launchers and grenade launchers.

About 80 per cent of the Golden Triangle's narcotics ultimately emerge along the Chiang Mai paved road and its corresponding route to the north, the contraband concealed in ordinary commercial vehicles. In 1987 perhaps seventy tons passed this way. But a big lorry may carry 400 bags of rice, or two tons of fish packed in ice, and a single search takes hours, backing up traffic for miles. American DEA officials depend on the approval of the Thai police, who generally wave the vehicles through after a few minutes. Apparently the local officers meet every one of the FBI's criteria defining organised crime, except that they are not organised.

Some efforts at drug containment are little more than propaganda exercises. For the purposes of cosmetic aerial photography a few hill farmers have taken to planting coffee, but they still harvest opium on the next square of land.

Gordon, Lord George (d. 1793)

A prisoner who brought style to **Newgate**. In 1781, Gordon was tried for high treason following the Gordon Riots. Not only was he innocent of fomenting the disturbances; he got off. But from then on he was a marked man, finally brought to injustice in 1787, sentenced to five years for libel; he had sponsored a petition criticising the British legal system.

Gordon took up private rooms in Newgate, passing his mornings in correspondence and reading before the arrival of his midday guests. Luncheon was served for around half a dozen friends at about 2 p.m., and once a fortnight he threw a formal dinner party, sometimes with music and dancing. Gordon had the benefit of two personal maids, one of them the beautiful Polly Levi, possibly his mistress.

This Newgate story does not end well. After serving his full term Gordon was unable to find the sureties that would have assured his release. In the end he became deranged, adopting the Jewish faith and devoting himself to the bagpipes. He died of jail fever in 1793, intoning the French Revolutionary ditty 'Ça ira'.

It would be a mistake to regard a spell in Newgate as festive, but on 28 August 1790 the prison formed the venue for the so-called 'Monster's Ball', a party thrown by Renwick Williams, of necessity in advance, to celebrate his hanging. Forty guests attended his *thé dansant*, pirouetting until eight in the evening to the accompaniment of violins and flutes. Then the gathering, comprised largely of those who had attempted to provide their host with alibis, sat down to a cold supper with meat and a selection of wines. The following morning Williams – popularly known as the 'Monster of London' – was hanged.

The Gordon Riots form the background to Charles Dickens's *Barnaby Rudge*.

Graphologists

Experts contend that by examining a specimen of handwriting they can discern the characteristics of a thief, rapist or murderer, and spot tell-tale symptoms of impotence, frigidity, deceit, father influence, aggression, homosexuality and the like.

These ideas seem simplistic rather than simple. For instance, handwriting analysis is based on three zones, the upper, the middle and the lower. The 'upper' area is the penstrokes which stick up at the top, the 'lower' those that stick down below and the 'middle' the bits in the middle. These supposedly correspond to the subjects' higher instincts (spiritual and intellectual), lower instincts (sex and the subconscious) and the bits in between (day-to-day attitude). Ideally all three zones should be in proportion, and a lack of balance suggests … a lack of balance.

There are many rules. Small 'a's and 'o's which are not closed at the baseline indicate deceit, as do capital letters which stray leftwards and squiggly 'enrolled' capitals. Inflated capitals suggest an inflated ego. A variable slope denotes an unreliable character; messy writing speaks of a messy mind. Broad 'm's show the extravagant approach of the bluffer, while a cross-bar to a 't' which starts low down at the base reveals that the writer is capable of zipping off in extraordinary directions – in other words, a liar. Narrow loops clambering up the stem a little way without crossing it are a sure sign of sexual anxiety, whereas short spiky underlengths tending towards the right are typical of a stifled sex drive.

To the layman, Jack the Ripper's writing looks a mess, Myra Hindley's is childish, and Himmler's spiky in a robotic way. The same applies to the handwriting of millions of ordinary individuals.

'Revealing' signatures. Crippen's (above) and Himmler's (below), which 'shouts of aggression and a complete lack of warmth or emotion'

But to the professional graphologist even the smallest detail may assume overwhelming significance, especially after the event. Thus the unexceptional signature of the famous British murderer **Crippen** discloses his inferiority complex (by the small capitals), his desire to manipulate others (by the threadlike strokes), his sociability and ardent nature (by the rightwards slant), his craving for prestige (by the heavy pen-pressure) and his domestic discontent (by the small 'g's with their pointed downstrokes).

Except on the Continent, graphology is not thought to have a scientific basis. This is quite distinct from the study of handwriting to detect forgeries, which remains more or less a science.

Great Gatsby *et al.*

The figure of Gatsby was inspired by F. Scott Fitzgerald's New York neighbour in Great Neck, Long Island, a high-profile bootlegger called Larry Fay. The millionaire gambler Arnold Rothstein, responsible for fixing baseball's 1919 World Series (by paying a reputed $70,000 to eight members of the Chicago White Sox), provided the starting point for the character of Wolfsheim, and in real life Rothstein seldom left home with less than $200,000 pocket money in new $1,000 bills.

Dashiell Hammett was another author who stuck to what – and whom – he knew. Hammett was a one-time Pinkerton detective, and Nora Charles, the wisecracking wife in his *Thin Man* series, derives from his lover Lillian Hellman. The husband – a suave, sophisticated metropolitan – is a pen-portrait of Hammett.

The film director D. W. Griffith was a similar stickler for accuracy in his early days. He made the first gangster movie in 1912, *The Musketeers of Pig Alley*, based on the New York murder of gambler Herman 'Beansie' Rosenthal on 21 July of that year. For added verisimilitude, Griffith hired the actual gangsters, 'Kid' Brook and 'Harlem' Tom Evans, to play themselves. But his background research was not always so careful. In *Birth of a Nation* he cast the Ku Klux Klan as social liberators.

Arnold Rothstein's estimated fortune of $50 million just melted away in his bad year of 1928, entering the final tail-spin on 8 September with a three-day poker marathon, when he lost $320,000 to two West Coast gamblers, 'Nigger Nate' Raymond and 'Titanic' Thompson in a game hosted by bookie George 'Hump' McManus. Rothstein welshed on his debts, and it was McManus's duty to collect. On 4 November, Rothstein set off to meet him at New York's Central Park Hotel and was found there with a bullet in his stomach. The police asked Rothstein what had happened. 'I won't talk about it. I'll take care of it myself,' he said, and died. Charges against McManus were dismissed after a chambermaid, on better consideration, withdrew her identification evidence.

In the 1934 film version of the Rothstein story, *Manhattan Melodrama*, the hero was 'blown away' by Clark Gable, and, after watching a screening of this movie on 22 July 1934 in the Chicago Biograph, John **Dillinger** (or someone very like him) died at the hands of the FBI. Crime boss Albert Anastasia was another gangster who met his end in the Central Park Hotel, gunned down in the barber's shop on 25 October 1957 by the infamous Gallo brothers, 'Crazy' Joe, 'Kid Twist' Larry and 'Kid Blast' Albert. The site is now on the tour organised by Sidewalks of New York, an outfit specialising in visits to the Big Apple's crime spots.

'Not a dry eye in the group,' says founder Sam Stafford of his trip to the Dakota apartment building where John Lennon was assassinated. 'There are only two sure things in life – death and taxes, and nobody wants to see where the rich and famous pay their taxes.'

Great Train Robbery

So mesmerised were the British public and authorities by the audacity of the Great Train Robbers that in February 1966 the police announced that they needed the Army's help to guard Durham prison, then holding three of the gang. 'I am satisfied,' declared the Chief Constable of Durham, 'that Goody's friends would be prepared to launch a full-scale military attack, even to the extent of using tanks, bombs, and what the Army calls "limited" atomic weapons.'

Information played the crucial role in the theft: the gang were tipped off that the mail train from Glasgow to London the weekend after the Bank Holiday would be laden with anywhere up to £5 million in used notes. Thus the robbery involved stopping the train and breaking into the second coach behind the engine, the so-called High Value Packages Coach. Compared with busting a bank vault (see **Nice**), the second stage was easy, entailing a few blows from a crowbar, but the first necessitated tampering with two signals, switching one to amber and another, at Sears crossing, to red. Lightbulbs wired up to rogue batteries placed behind the coloured filters did the trick, and the green 'go' signal was masked by a pair of cricket gloves that nearly toppled the government.

For these were worrying times. The Profumo scandal had reached its height with osteopath Stephen Ward committing suicide on 3 August. Scarcely a month before, Kim Philby defected to Russia, turning MI5 into a laughing stock, and England had been humbled at the Fourth Test match at Headingley, with demands for the removal of cricketer E. R. Dexter vying for space with calls for the Prime Minister's resignation. Britain was already on its metaphorical knees by the time the commando-style Great Train Robbery brought the patrician 1950s to a close, at exactly 3.03 a.m. on 8 August 1963.

In obeisance to the signals, the Royal Mail train ground to a halt a few hundred yards short of Bridego Bridge, Buckinghamshire. Fireman David Whitby dismounted to investigate and set off through the dark to the emergency telephone behind the signal gantry. Buster Edwards, a villain, bundled him down the embankment, and moments later the train driver, Jack Mills, was coshed on the head. With the rear coaches uncoupled, the engine and the two front coaches trundled on to Bridego Bridge where the gang smashed through the doors and windows of the High Value Packages Coach, and five Post Office guards were forced to lie on the floor while a human chain passed 120 sacks bulging with banknotes down to a waiting lorry and two Land Rovers.

In twenty-four minutes the Great Train Robbers made off with £2,631,648, about £25 million in today's

Bridego Bridge after the Great Train Robbery, the so-called 'last decent crime'. To the left is the embankment down which the human chain ferried 120 mailbags

terms. Their haul weighed two and a half tons and, split seventeen ways, amounted to a minimum of £150,000 each. When a local policeman, alerted by the blacked-out windows, discovered the gang's abandoned hideout at Leatherslade Farm, among the wealth of fingerprints and forensic clues was a Monopoly game played with real money. Only £50,000 of the loot was recovered, turning up in a telephone box on 11 December, but most of the gang were under lock and key by the end of the year. The following April they received swingeing terms ranging up to twenty-five years – commensurate with the penalty for armed robbery, suggesting that future robbers might as well go equipped with guns to reduce the number of partners, thereby increasing each individual's take. Villains today do not conduct their business in bands of twenty.

Hence the depiction of the Great Train Robbery as 'the last decent crime'. But wealth beyond the dreams of avarice did not bring happiness. On the lam, Buster Edwards was no longer a poor criminal. He was a rich

one, and after three years of frittering his money away on high living in Mexico, he preferred to return to England to face his sentence.

Where are the Train Robbers now? After serving their time, Wisbey, Hussey and Goody went back inside for further offences. Charlie Wilson got himself shot in Spain in 1990. Jimmy White works as a house painter; Buster Edwards runs a flower stall at Waterloo station. That leaves Ronnie **Biggs**, who, after forsaking Rio de Janeiro for the UK in 2001 – for health reasons, many have speculated – was sent back to prison to finish his sentence. In the shadows there may still lurk a handful of unnamed associates. During an August 1993 telephone interview, Biggs confirmed that four gang members escaped, three because they never removed their gloves at Leatherslade Farm and one because his prints were not on file.

Green River Killer (Gary Ridgway)

Gary Ridgway, known for two decades simply as the Green River Killer, is one of America's most prolific serial murderers, having been credited with strangling forty-nine women from America's North-West. In a deal to save himself from the death penalty, he later even offered to give details of fifty-nine murders. Police still believe the actual number is far higher.

On 12 August 1982 a slaughterman discovered a bloated corpse floating in the slow-flowing Green River, near Seattle, Washington State. The police pathologist succeeded in lifting an excellent set of prints from the swollen flesh, which enabled the criminal identification department to name the victim as 23-year-old Debra Lynn Bonner, known as 'Dub'; she was a stripper with a list of convictions as a prostitute. She was the second of literally dozens of women who would be found during the next three years.

The first had been found a month earlier, half a mile downstream, strangled with her own slacks, and had been identified as 16-year-old Wendy Coffield. In spite of her age, she had a record as a prostitute – in fact, as a 'trick roll', someone who sets up her 'johns' (clients) for robbery.

Within three days of the discovery of Debra Bonner, Dave Reichert, the detective in charge of the case, heard that two more bodies had been found in the Green River. Both women were black, both were

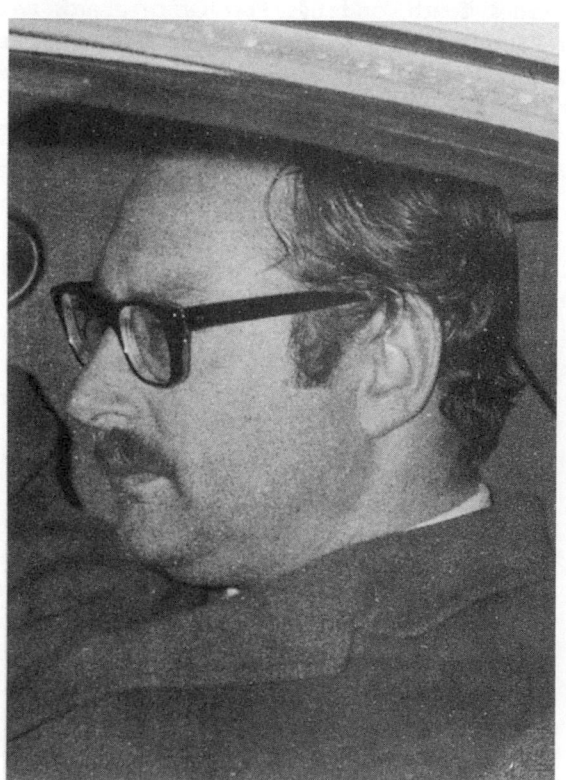

Great Train Robber Bruce Reynolds after his high life in Mexico palled

Gary Ridgway, the Green River Killer

The next – and perhaps the worst – occurred two days later, when a local TV station announced that the riverbank was now under round-the-clock surveillance, thus destroying all chance of catching the killer on a return visit.

The medical evidence on the other two women, Marcia Chapman and Cynthia Hinds, confirmed that the Green River Killer was a 'sick trick'; both women had pointed rocks jammed into their vaginas. Like the others, they were prostitutes working the Strip near Seattle's Sea-Tac airport.

On Saturday 28 August 1982, Kase Lee left her pimp's apartment to 'turn a trick', and vanished. The next day Terri Milligan took an hour off from soliciting to go for a meal; apparently a car pulled up for her as she walked to the fast-food joint and, unwilling to reject business, she climbed in.

The following day 15-year-old Debra Estes – known to the police as Betty Jones – was picked up by a blue and white pickup truck; the man drove her to remote woodland, made her undress at gunpoint, then ordered her to give him a 'blow job'. After that he robbed her of $75 and left her with her hands tied. This man was pulled in by police who recognized the description of his pickup truck, and identified as the attacker. But a lie-detector test established his innocence of the Green River murders. And while he was still in custody, 18-year-old Mary Meehan, who was eight months pregnant, disappeared, and became victim number nine.

Within three weeks of her rape, Debra Estes would become the tenth victim of the Green River Killer. Six more victims in August, October, November and December would bring his total up to at least sixteen – the largest annual total for any American serial killer up to that time.

It would be exceeded in the following year, 1983, when twenty-six women vanished, and the remains of eight of them were found near Sea-Tac airport or close by. In March, special investigator Bob Keppel, known for his brilliant work on the Ted **Bundy** case, was asked to write a report on the investigation. It was devastating, with hundreds of examples of incompetence and failure to follow up leads. For example, when the driving licence of victim Marie Malvar was found at the airport and the police were notified, they did not even bother to collect it – although it might well have contained the killer's fingerprint.

naked, and they had been weighted down to the river bottom with large rocks. They were only a few hundred yards upstream from the spot where Bonner had been found, and had almost certainly been there at the time.

As Reichert walked along the bank towards the place where Bonner had been found, he discovered another body. Like the other two, she was black, and was later identified as 16-year-old Opal Mills. The fact that *rigor mortis* had not yet disappeared meant that she had been left there in the past two days. Which in turn meant that if the police had kept watch on the river, the killer would have been caught.

It was the first of a series of mischances that would make this one of the most frustrating criminal cases in Seattle's history.

In 1984 four victims were found together on Auburn West Hill, six more in wooded areas along State Route 410 and two near Tigard, Oregon, the latter find giving rise to the speculation that the killer had moved. In January a Green River Task Force of thirty-six investigators was formed, with a $2 million budget. (By 1988 the bill had reached $13 million.)

Among the hundreds of suspects interviewed by the police was Gary Leon Ridgway, thirty-five, a mild-looking man with fish-like lips, who worked for the Kenworth Truck Plant and was known to pick up prostitutes – he even admitted to being obsessed by them. He also confessed to choking a prostitute in 1982, but claimed this was because she bit him.

By 1986, with the investigation stalled, Ridgway's file was reopened and his ex-wife interviewed about his preference for sex in the open, often near the Green River. Ridgway was placed under surveillance. And still women disappeared – although no longer with quite the same frequency.

In December 1988 a television special on the case, *Manhunt Live*, led to 4,000 tips from the public and the arrest of 38-year-old William J. Stevens, who had a criminal record. But although both police and media believed the Green River Killer had been arrested, credit card receipts proved Stevens had been else-where at the time of some of the murders, and he was released.

And so throughout the 1990s, the case marked time, while Reichert, the chief investigator, admitted that his obsession with the killer had caused serious problems in his marriage.

Genetic fingerprinting had first been used in 1986, and had led to the solution of many murders. The main problem was likely to occur if there was not enough DNA material for testing, or if it was old. In 2001 a major breakthrough came when the Washington State crime lab acquired the equipment to extract usable DNA from old samples and multiply the quantity by the method known as STR, or short tandem repeats. (This is also known as the PCR, or polymerase chain reaction, which amplifies genetic samples by 'unzipping' the double-stranded DNA molecule and making two exact copies.) Now a major review of samples of semen evidence began. And by September 2001 it had paid off. Semen samples, taken from Opal Mills, Marcia Chapman and Carol Christensen, three of the earliest victims, proved to be from Gary Ridgway. Paint fragments and fibre

evidence taken from the grave of Debra Estes in 1988 were also linked to Ridgway. So when Ridgway was finally arrested on 30 November 2001, he was charged with four counts of murder.

At first pleading innocent, he later agreed to change his plea to guilty to avoid the death penalty.

Ridgway's account of how he became a serial killer occupies the most fascinating chapter of Reichert's book *Chasing the Devil*. As with so many killers, the problems seem to have started with his mother. He was a chronic bed-wetter and she would drag him out of bed and parade him in front of his brothers, then make him stand naked in a tub of cold water. His father seems to have been a timid nonentity. But as an employee of a mortuary he strongly influenced his son's fantasies by describing at length interrupting someone having sex with a corpse. Ridgway began to fantasise about this. When he saw his mother sunbathing he had imagined having sex with her, but now he dreamed of killing her and violating the body.

Like so many serial killers, he was sadistic to animals, and once killed a cat by locking it in a refrig-erator. He also claimed that, as a teenager, he had drowned a little boy by wrapping his legs around him and pulling him under the water. And later he would stab and injure another small boy, although he was never caught.

Sent to the Philippines as a sailor, he began to use prostitutes, and they quickly became a lifelong obsession.

Ridgway had discovered he enjoyed choking when he was quarrelling with his second wife, Marcia, and wrapped his arm round her neck from behind (a method also used by the **Boston Strangler**). In addi-tion he enjoyed tying her up for sex. In 1975 they had a son, Matthew, whom he adored. A religious phase lasted until 1980, when they divorced. During their marriage, he constantly used prostitutes.

He embarked on killing them after his divorce. Because he seemed a mild man they felt no alarm about him and allowed him to get behind them. He often took them back to his house, had sex, then killed them. Later he found he preferred to kill them first and have sex with the bodies. He also confessed to revisiting bodies several times for more sex.

He even admitted to a scheme – never carried out – of overpowering a prostitute, then impaling her with an upright pole in her vagina, a favourite practice of the original Dracula, Vlad the Impaler.

And so this apparently harmless little man was able to carry on killing for many years. Reichert emphasises that Ridgway was full of self-pity, regarding himself as the helpless victim of these sinister urges.

On 5 November 2003 Ridgway pleaded guilty to forty-eight murders and received forty-eight life sentences.

Guillotine

A humanitarian device, which most people know was invented by Dr Guillotin. Less widely appreciated is that the guillotine swiftly became such an object of French veneration that, in Robespierre's 1794 Festival of the Supreme Being, it starred as a quasi-religious totem, appearing draped in blue velvet embroidered with roses. Lord Byron was another great admirer, finding the device 'altogether more impressive than the vulgar and ungentlemanly "new drop"'.

Dr Guillotin (1738–1814) was described by his contemporary Bonneville as 'devoid of either talent or repute', and his mental capacity to give birth to his mechanical marvel is traditionally ascribed to the impulse that expelled him from the womb when his mother suffered a nasty shock, coming unexpectedly upon a criminal undergoing torture on the wheel.

In fact, little inventing was needed; there were precedents aplenty, not least the **Halifax Gibbet**. But the first well-documented claim to mechanical decapitation belongs to the Irish. Holinshed's 1578 *Chronicles* contain a detailed woodcut of a working guillotine, unequivocally affirming its use in the execution of one Murcod Ballagh on 1 April 1307, near Merton.

In France, on 10 October 1789, Dr Guillotin suggested to the Revolutionary Assembly that death without **torture** and by decapitation (hitherto a privilege reserved for nobles) should be the sole means of execution. On 1 December he added a single sentence specifying that this objective 'should be achieved by means of a simple mechanism'. The intention was that loss of life, rather than the pain inflicted while losing it, should constitute sufficient punishment, and even before its invention Dr Guillotin's device became known as the guillotine. But his contribution consisted of proposing that someone should invent it.

The project went forward to various committees, and on 17 March 1792 a droll personage called Dr

Louis submitted a detailed review of beheading round the world, *Avis motive sur la mode de la décolation*. Apart from its imaginative description of the 'standard' English practice of guillotining, the document is packed with interesting *aperçus*. The aged Dr Louis pointed out that botched executions were often conducted with the condemned man kneeling but otherwise unsupported. All too often the first axe-blow simply knocked him sprawling. This observation inspired the corrective invention of the bottom half of the guillotine with its solid restraining platform. Dr Louis continued: 'Everyone knows that cutting instruments have little or no effect when they strike perpendicularly ... You must saw the object to be cut ... You cannot decapitate with a single stroke of an axe or blade of which the cutting edge is horizontal.' This observation entailed the corrective invention of the oblique blade of the top half of the guillotine.

The Legislation Committee were impressed by Dr Louis's report, according him 'the merit of having benefited humanity when the law's blade strikes the head of the guilty'. Over the next few weeks Dr Louis discussed refinements of his gadget at his Sunday-evening salons attended by literati, medical men and politicians, finally submitting a detailed specification to M. Guidon, the state scaffold-builder.

Guidon put in an inflated estimate of 5,600 livres to cover extra payments to his artisans for the unpleasant nature of the work. So on 10 April 1792 the contract went elsewhere, to a German harpsichord-maker, Tobias Schmidt, who threw in a free leather bag for a total price of 960 livres. This little sack was to put the heads in; Schmidt's later inventions included a patent chimney.

According to the unreliable M. Begin (Dr Louis's great-nephew) the new gadget was first tested on 11 April when it removed the heads of two or three sheep. But when the official trials opened three days later using human cadavers, two of the necks were only partially severed, their heads left dangling forwards, the blade embedded in the last few shreds of cartilage. The disappointed party of official observers withdrew to a lunch of capon and excellent wines, specifying an increase in the height of the two uprights and modifying the shape of the blade.

On 21 April a revised model was tried out on 'three corpses of Herculean dimensions' and passed with flying colours. The machine's design never became fixed. According to the executioner Henri **Sanson** in 1811, in one variant 'the body is allowed to fall through a hole in the scaffold into a sort of tomb'. It was alleged (by Guyot de Fère) that Danton asked the retired Dr Guillotin to devise a three-bladed machine. A four-bladed version was actually built and installed in Bordeaux with trap-doors through which the bodies tumbled into waiting carts. In 1793, a M. Guillot (of truncated nomenclature) carried out experiments on a massive nine-bladed installation (which failed). The executioner Heindrecht resisted the proposal to construct an all-metal mobile variant mounted on wheels.

The guillotine's first victim was the highwayman Nicolas Jacques Pelletier, beheaded on 25 April 1792 to ambivalent reviews; *La Chronique de Paris* noted that 'the speed with which it struck' left little by way of improving spectacle. At the height of the Revolution's guillotine fad, its fodder included the corpses of those who had escaped justice by suicide (for instance, Valazé), children (Nantes, 17 December 1793), dummies of notorious émigrés, birds for the dinner table, effigies of reigning monarchs and, allegedly, a dog taught to howl whenever it heard the word 'Republican'.

Guilt

According to FBI agent Howard Teten, the best approach for a policeman interviewing a young suspect in the grip of guilt is to gaze fixedly into his face and enunciate: 'You know why I'm here.' Sadly, Teten's formula was never put to the test. An instinctive 'profiler', Teten devised this approach in response to a frenzied killing of the early 1970s in California. Over the telephone he suggested to the Californian police that the murderer was a lonely teenager living locally – very probably skinny, acned and bursting to confess. Teten advised: 'If you walk round the neighbourhood and knock on doors, you'll probably run into him.'

Teten erred on the side of caution. It was merely necessary to stand close to the killer and say nothing. 'You got me,' conceded a young, acned interviewee on opening his door, before the cop could get a word in edgeways.

Teten joined the FBI National Academy at **Quantico** in 1972 and was a long-time admirer of Dr

Brussel of '**Mad Bomber**' fame. He formed part of the 1973 team that caught sex killer David Meirhofer, an early profiling breakthrough that led to the implementation of VICAP (see Quantico) some ten years later.

Britain's Dennis **Nilsen** proved similarly resilient under interrogation. Returning home on the evening of 8 February 1983, Nilsen found himself confronted by three detectives making enquiries about the human flesh in the drains.

'Good grief, how awful,' said Nilsen. Chief Inspector Peter Jay replied, on a hunch: 'Don't mess around, where's the rest of the body?'

'In two plastic bags in the wardrobe,' Nilsen replied. 'I'll show you.'

Guldensuppe, William (d. 1897)

William Randolph Hearst was a newspaper magnate and gutter press pioneer not always associated with investigative reporting. But in 1897 he played a part in solving the Willie Guldensuppe murder.

Hearst's interest was fired by the discovery on 26 June 1897 of a headless torso wrapped in oilcloth in Brooklyn's East River, and he assigned a team of the *Journal*'s reporters to the case. Journalist George Arnold recognised the calluses on the cadaver's hands as a common characteristic of Turkish bath masseurs and, taken in conjunction with a tattoo, this led to the first breakthrough, the identification of the corpse.

The newspaper tracked down the purchaser of the body's distinctive oilcloth wrapping, and delivered her as a suspect to police headquarters. An unlicensed midwife of majestic proportions called Augusta Knack, she denied any intimate connection with the deceased, saying in the morgue: 'I don't believe those are Willie's **legs**.'

But Hearst knew better. The *Journal* established that Guldensuppe and Knack were lovers and, further, that Augusta had taken up with a barber called Martin Thorn who lost his job after a beating from the masseur. Shortly afterwards, Thorn bought a pistol and swore revenge.

'Murder Mystery Solved By *Journal*,' trumpeted the paper on Thorn's arrest. Then the journalists found the murder cottage. It was quietly situated; the bathroom drained into a pond, and on the day of the murder the local farmer had been perplexed by the way his ducks turned pink.

The lovers had wrapped up Willie's body in a number of parcels, dropping them off from the Greenpoint ferry. Thorn went to the electric chair on 1 August 1898, but Augusta Knack escaped with twenty years. Paroled after ten, she set up a neighbourhood delicatessen, performing much the same function in New York as the Patty Hearst ransom money was later to play on the West Coast.

The full demand for the return of Miss Hearst after her February 1974 kidnapping consisted of a $400 million Food Aid programme for hungry Californians. Eventually this was parleyed down into the mass distribution of $25 lunch boxes, containing emergency rations of chicken, steak, turkey and frozen fish.

Gun control

In America, it is said that 'Guns don't kill people, people kill people.' This view receives typical expression in the 1983 book *Under the Gun*: 'Unless we solve the problem of interpersonal hatred, it may not matter very much what we do about guns ... It definitely does not follow that, in the complete absence of handguns, crimes now committed with handguns would not be committed. The more plausible explanation is that they would be committed with other weaponry.' In fact, from the gun lobby's standpoint it seems that 'few homicides due to shooting could be avoided if a firearm were not immediately present' (*Patterns in Criminal Homicide*, 1958).

So entrenched are these opinions that rational American assessments – for instance *Gun Control* (1987) – of the resulting mayhem proceed with tentative pedantry bordering on the surreal. Thus: 'In addition to providing greater range for the attacker, it is argued, firearms are more deadly than other weapons.' The second of these two contentions is supported by statistical tables.

About 200 million firearms are in circulation in the USA, with about 10 per cent of households owning four or more. Some 60 to 70 per cent of householders with handguns keep them for 'self-protection'. But this is not a good idea. Figures from the Violence Policy Centre show that a handgun is 118 times more likely to be involved in a suicide, a fatal accident or a murder than in eliminating a criminal. Seventy-one per cent of homicides involve friends and acquaintances, and are presumably bitterly regretted; 80 per cent are over domestic disputes like love, money and other transient irritants.

Resistance to armed robbery increases the risk during a commercial attack by a factor of fifty, and during a personal robbery by some fourteen times (*Journal of Legal Studies*, 1986). Accidental killings in the home account for about a thousand lives annually, in addition to the hundreds of thousands of firearms-related injuries and the overall total of a million 'gun incidents' in any given year.

In 1991 these figures included the case of Vicki Childress, an asthma sufferer, who reached under her pillow on the night of 21 October, pulled out what she hoped was her inhaler, and shot herself in the face. She survived, as did Joe Petrowski of Manitobi, shot by his dog. Deputy Sheriff Todd Rollins from Oregon was another survivor; he discovered that he had wounded himself in the right thigh with his 9mm semi-automatic when he awoke drenched in blood the following morning. Rollins got off lightly; in 1989 one in every four of the police officers killed in the line of duty with handguns were victims of their own handguns.

Shortly after the assassination of John Lennon (see **Stalking**), the President's wife Nancy Reagan went on television to oppose gun control, saying that legal restrictions encouraged 'the wrong persons' to obtain guns. She disclosed that she kept a weapon herself, saying it was 'just a tiny little gun. I don't know anything about it', provoking a columnist to enquire whether a tiny little gun fired itsy-bitsy bullets that left the victim just a little bit dead.

Laurette Brunson of Tampa, Florida, encapsulated the arguments in favour of gun control in two sentences. After being wounded by her husband during her wedding reception in April 1992, she said: 'I don't think he meant to shoot me. He just got mad and had a gun in his hand.' Surprisingly, a 1990 Gallup poll found wide support for restrictive measures, with 81 per cent of Americans behind handgun registration and 95 per cent backing a seven-day waiting period before purchase. Virginia's Governor Wilder has sponsored legislation limiting purchasers to one gun per month, but there is little chance of more useful legislation. Congress is terrorised by the National Rifle Association with its annual operating budget of $100 million, and senators who step out of line put their careers at risk.

American schoolroom slang for a gun is a biscuit, burner or cronze. A 'streetsweeper' means a sub-machine-gun.

Gunness, Belle Brynhilde Paulsetter Sorenson (1859–1908?)

Accident-prone professional widow. Belle's father was an itinerant conjurer and in her youth she graced his shows as a tightrope walker. But life on their small Norwegian farm palled and in 1883 she emigrated to America.

The following year she married a Swede, Mads Sorenson. Their union was childless, but she adopted three children: Jenny, Myrtle and Lucy. Then one day in 1900, when two insurance policies overlapped, her husband died of 'an enlarged heart'. Belle collected $8,500 in insurance and left Chicago (where Sorenson's relatives demanded an exhumation) for Austin, Illinois. But her new home, a rooming-house, caught fire, and after collecting the insurance she returned to Chicago to buy a confectionery store.

This too burst into flames. Belle collected the insurance and bought a farm in La Porte, Indiana, with the proceeds. There she met a jovial Norwegian, Peter Gunness. They married, but in 1903 he was involved in a fatal accident which broke his skull when a heavy sausage grinder toppled on to his head. Belle collected the insurance of $4,000. Then, to the general admiration of her neighbours, she settled down to a hard-working routine as a widow, homesteader and mother. Her unhappy personal life attracted some sympathy. Relationships with a succession of farm workers and prospective husbands never prospered; the rejected men disappeared after a few days. Meanwhile she gave birth to Gunness's posthumous son. But as one child arrived, so another left; young Jennie departed in her early teens, sent to Los Angeles to complete her education.

By now Belle had lost her teeth. She weighed about 280 pounds and was reduced to advertising in the matrimonial journals for suitors where, as devotees of Lonely Hearts columns would expect, she depicted herself as rich, good-looking and young. One advertisement ran: 'Comely widow who owns a large farm in one of the finest districts in La Porte County,

Indiana, desires to make acquaintance of gentleman equally well provided, with a view of joining fortunes. No replies by letter considered unless sender is willing to follow answer with a personal visit.' Sometimes she added the tag-line 'Triflers need not apply', and responded in this vein: 'I feel sure you are the one man for me … I am worth at least $20,000, and if you would bring just $5,000 to show you are in earnest we could talk things over.' No one stayed long, but in 1906 a hired hand, Ray Lamphere, added a stable element to her life.

This timid man became Belle's on-off lover. She continued to entertain other suitors; when they arrived, he moved out. In January 1908 the bachelor Andrew Helgelien rode up from Aberdeen in South Dakota. Helgelien stayed for weeks, inflaming Lamphere with jealousy, but shortly after drawing $2,900 in cash from a local bank he too vanished. When Lamphere was overheard remarking to a drinking partner, 'Helgelien won't bother me no more', the locals became suspicious. Meanwhile Helgelien's brother pestered Belle by letter about Andrew's whereabouts. He had not been seen since Belle's note arrived saying, 'My heart beats in wild raptures for you. Come prepared to stay for ever.'

By now Lamphere was quarrelling openly with Belle. She fired him and took on a replacement, Maxon, to run the farm. Lamphere left to live with a woman known as 'Nigger Liz' Smith, but he continued to stalk Belle's land. She had him fined for trespass, and on 27 April she confided in her attorney about her fears for her family's safety. Lamphere had threatened to torch her home.

Early the following morning the farm went up in flames, and in the ashes the searchers found the charred remains of three children aged eleven, nine and five, together with a headless female body with Belle's rings on its fingers. In the smouldering debris were watches and human teeth, and three weeks later a jawbone, with Belle's dentures attached, was discovered in the cellar. Traces of **strychnine** in the woman's body encouraged the coroner towards a finding of 'death by felonious homicide, perpetrator unknown', and Lamphere was charged with the murder of Belle and her family.

Asle Helgelien arrived to look for his brother. Nosing around the fields, his attention was caught by a rubbish pit in the corner of a bog pen, and Sheriff Smitzer set his men digging. They unearthed four bodies with several limbs missing. Andrew Helgelien was one victim, furled in an oilcloth, and young Jennie another. Further excavations brought the total of dismembered corpses to fourteen, including two more children and a human skull dredged from the cesspool. Among the dead were Thomas Lindboe, a labourer from 1905; Henry Gurholdt, a Scandinavian suitor who had brought $1,500 in earnest of his intentions; Olaf Svenherud, a Norwegian admirer; and two others called Budsberg and John Moo. The rest remained nameless.

Meanwhile Belle was seen everywhere and frequently arrested: 'Mrs Gunness Very Numerous' ran the newspaper headline. Lamphere came to trial on 9 November 1908, and after nineteen ballots a divided jury pronounced him guilty of arson. He died in prison of tuberculosis in December 1909, but not before leaving a confession with the prison minister, describing his role as Belle's accomplice in a total of forty-two joint murders. He admitted to chloroforming the Gunness children on the night of the fire and related how Belle had substituted another – presumably spare – female corpse for her own. Then he drove her away, disguised as a man, before doubling back to set fire to the house.

But this story bears a striking resemblance to the theory already advanced in a shocker called *The Mrs Gunness Mystery*. Belle was the possessor of what the crime writer Colin Wilson terms a 'High Dominance' personality (like Brady in the **Brady–Hindley** combination). Lamphere was under her thumb, and one possibility is that they set the scene months before, hoping to be reunited after the fire. Perhaps Belle died in the blaze. Or perhaps she escaped and lived to a ripe old age. The one certainty is that her suitors perished in droves, killed with strychnine and axe or hammer.

Gutshot

Safecrackers' technical term. A gutshot was the basic way of opening a **safe** with explosives. After knocking off the **lock** dial with a hammer, the box was tipped on its back, and the nitroglycerine squeezed into the exposed workings from a pipette; a dropper and a half was more than enough. A detonator laid across the top blew the charge, destroying the lock's innards, and the whole operation took about five minutes.

A variant, the 'ragshot', prevented the explosive from dribbling harmlessly away and, by removing the reliance on gravity, allowed safes to be tackled upright. It entailed inserting a bit of cloth saturated in nitro but, like the gutshot, sometimes fused the lock mechanism solid.

The radical solution of the 'jamshot' blew the safe's door right off. Apart from nitroglycerine, the technique required steady nerves, a bar of well-kneaded soap and a strip of cellophane, pressed in along the top of the door to keep the hairline crack free from the soap. This was worked into a semi-circular 'cup' or dish straddling the gap and, after withdrawal of the cellophane, the nitroglycerine was poured carefully into the cup on the face of the door. The liquid seeped into the crack, trickling round the edge of the doorframe.

In the old days, the safeman lit a fuse dangling into the cup. Timing was all. Needing five seconds to get clear, he had to forecast whether, as he struck his match, the explosive would complete its run round the door by the moment of ignition. Too soon, and some of the nitroglycerine remained in the cup, with not enough in the crack; too late, and it drained away.

This was the golden age of safecracking. Practitioners were underworld kings, revered by their colleagues and the press, like the **highwaymen** of yore. In 1894 the *New York Times* described cracksmen as 'the gentlemen Joes of their trade, who scorn small affairs ... They keep step with science, and they have every new invention at their command.' Down the decades their robberies were celebrated as 'bold', 'daring' and 'expert', and as late as 1965 Britain's *Star* newspaper characterised safecrackers as 'Master Technicians, or even graduates in Crime Technology'.

The advent of electric detonators banished the days of spluttering fuses and turned a craft into a dull, if predictable, science. The final indignity came in the 1960s, when cash payrolls were diluted by increasing reliance on cheques. Safes no longer held enough money to be worth robbing.

Apart from finding the key, the easiest way to open a safe today is with a core drill, a standard building trade item consisting of a water-cooled tube with a diameter anywhere between one and nine inches, tipped with diamond or carbide chips.

Gutteridge, George William (d. 1927)

On the morning of 27 September 1927 the body of Police Constable George William Gutteridge was discovered sprawled in the road outside the Essex village of Howe. He had been shot four times. His right hand clutched a pencil, and his notebook lay nearby. Cartridge cases were scattered on the ground.

The time of death was estimated at four in the morning, when it was still dark. But Gutteridge's torch remained in his pocket, and he needed to see in order to write. His colleagues surmised that he met his death in the glare of car headlights. It soon emerged that a Morris Cowley had been stolen from Dr Edward Lovell's home fourteen miles away, and the vehicle turned up that same evening, abandoned in London, with splashes of blood on the running board.

Seven months later two small-time villains, Frederick Browne and William Kennedy, were convicted at the Old Bailey. The murder weapon had a distinctive damaged breech, and the professional testimony of Robert Churchill represented a major step towards the acceptance of forensic ballistics as a valid discipline.

After the verdict, Browne told the court, 'It will come out later that I had nothing to do with it', and sixty-five years later it has. Frederick Browne was undoubtedly a hardened villain, a violent crook with Essex connections and a car thief to boot, and during the early stages of the investigation, Chief Inspector James Berrett became 'convinced that Browne was mixed up with the murder even if he had not actually committed it'.

Browne was arrested in a dawn raid on 20 January 1928 for an unrelated theft of a Vauxhall car the previous November. At his garage the police found a loaded Webley revolver. Browne casually admitted ownership without being shown the gun in question (later to become Exhibit 31); he had a small arsenal of unlicensed weapons. At this stage there was no hint of a murder charge, but the following day the police uncovered *another* Webley in the garage, which Robert Churchill correctly identified as the fatal weapon (Exhibit 17). Browne had swapped an automatic for this revolver, taking possession on 7 October;

on the day of the shooting Exhibit 17 belonged to an associate, William Kennedy.

Berrett later used Browne's 'sight-unseen' admission to tie him to Exhibit 17, and by the time Browne appreciated his error it was too late for a convincing retraction. But when Browne accepted responsibility for Exhibit 31, the existence of Exhibit 17 was unknown. So Chief Inspector Berrett knew the admission, which hanged Browne, arose from a misunderstanding.

After Kennedy's arrest on 25 January, Berrett extracted the famous confession in which Kennedy, the true murderer, detailed how Browne had shot Gutteridge. Kennedy claimed they had travelled to Essex together to steal a car. On the way back, PC Gutteridge flagged them down and asked for a driving licence.

When Browne prevaricated, Gutteridge demanded, 'Do you know the number of this car?' 'Yes,' said Browne, 'I know the number, but do you?' Kennedy chipped in, 'It's TW6120', and Gutteridge took out his notebook. Then, said Kennedy, 'I heard a report, quickly followed by another one. I saw the policeman stagger and fall over by the bank at the hedge. I said to Browne, "What have you done?", and then saw he had a large Webley revolver in his hand.' *Kennedy's* account went on to describe how *Browne* had shot out Gutteridge's **eyes** as he lay dying.

Where one man's defence is to incriminate another, the two are normally tried separately. On these particular facts, the jury were merely enjoined to disregard Kennedy's statement. But his vivid tale dominated the hearing, and it comprised the only evidence against Browne. He was not seen stealing the Morris Cowley, nor seen travelling in it or to it, nor were his fingerprints detected in it. He was not proved present at the murder and, even if he had been, there was nothing to show he knew his companion was armed. It is almost certain that Browne spent the night of 26 September at home with his wife, as he maintained. But in the course of the trial the two revolvers became inextri-cably muddled, and Kennedy's allegations stuck to Browne like glue. Both were hanged on 31 May 1928.

H

Hair

The year 1857 saw the publication of the first monograph on hair. Magnified some 2,000 times under the microscope, hair became easy to categorise. Emile Villebrun, one of Lacassagne's students, pointed out that animal hair possesses a continuous central core – the medulla, which contains air. With humans the core is only intermittently visible, enabling the two to be differentiated.

Under the microscope, the outer casing – the cuticle – of animal hair displays tiny overlapping scales which vary from species to species, and forensic laboratories now keep quick-recognition charts for animal identification.

Hair thickness can be measured to the nearest hundredth of a millimetre. Its rate of growth is constant, about .44 mm a day and, since hair absorbs poisons such as arsenic, it provides a precise calendar of the dosage inflicted (see **Napoleons**). Its provenance – from pubic area, head or armpit – can be readily established. Head hairs are circular in cross-section, facial hairs triangular, eyebrows taper towards one end, and pubic hairs are triangular or oval (and curly) and tend to drop out during sexual assaults. By the early twentieth century, hair was a forensic discipline in its own right.

Until the advent of **genetic fingerprinting**, hair evidence remained inconclusive, indicating not that the hair did come from a particular person but that it might. 'Consistent with a common source' is the scientist's cautious phrase. Sometimes the common source could be very broad indeed. The pubic hair attributed to Beryl Evans, killed at 10 **Rillington Place**, was identical to that of some 15 to 20 per cent of the population. But the 'co-ed' killer, Edmund **Kemper**, was implicated by old-fashioned hair evidence, as was Ted **Bundy** after being stopped in his Volkswagen in Granger, Colorado, for a traffic violation in August 1975.

Bundy's vehicle was vacuumed from top to bottom, yielding two pounds of dust and debris, and this was shipped to the Quantico laboratories where, spread out on a back-lit glass-topped table, it was minutely scrutinised with an illuminated magnifying glass. Strands were extracted with tweezers, and a comparison microscope produced perfect matches for tresses taken from Melissa Smith (murdered on 18 October 1974) and Caryn Campbell (murdered on 12 January 1975). Bundy was charged with Caryn's murder, but only convicted of the abduction of Carol DaRonch on the strength of her resolute eye-witness testimony.

Things are different today. DNA technology recently secured the conviction of the murderer Patrick Hasset when a hair sample was genetically matched against his semen, which had been removed from his strangled and raped victim fourteen years previously and stored in a freezer (see **Sperm**).

Half-hanged Smith (b. 1662)

John Smith, a Yorkshireman, enlisted in the Second Regiment of Foot Guards and, like many of his fellows, regularly engaged in housebreaking. On 5 December 1705 he was charged at the Old Bailey for the theft of fifty pairs of shoes, 900 yards of cloth, 400 pounds of silk and 148 pairs of gloves. Caught red-handed, he was sentenced to death, and executed at Tyburn on Christmas Eve by a charitable hangman who swung on Smith's feet to expedite his demise.

Somewhere between five and fifteen minutes later – depending on the version – a horseman galloped up to announce that Smith had been reprieved. So he was cut down and taken to a nearby public house where, by a fortunate coincidence, he turned out to be alive. Smith remained under a suspended sentence of death, but on 20 February he received an unconditional pardon after informing on some '350 pickpockets, house breakers, etc, who got to be soldiers in the guards'.

Half-hanged Smith's narrow escape

For many years 'Half-hanged' Smith continued a lucky if not a prudent man. On two occasions he came up on a capital offence; he extricated himself from the first on a legal technicality, and from the second because the prosecutor expired the day before testifying. But in September 1721 he was arrested burgling a warehouse and, despite a plea based on his advanced years, was transported to Virginia where in all probability he died.

Of his near-death experience, Smith said he beheld 'a great blaze or glaring light which seemed to go out at his eyes with a flash, and then lost all sense of pain'. Seeing a radiant haze is a common experience of many survivors of hangings. A Captain Montagnac, from the Religious Wars, spoke of 'a light of which the charm defied description' (although an 1849 contributor to the *Quarterly Review* was probably gilding the lily in his reference to the 'pleasurable feeling' of execution).

Evidence of the incandescent colour is fragmentary, but an Irish youth who recovered from an 1825 hanging for sheep-stealing commented on its scarlet tint. He reported that 'though he felt the jerk of the rope when the ladder was turned, he did not become unconscious. He seemed to have the power of seeing all round, above and below him. Then everything turned a bright red colour, and a sort of half sleepy sensation crept through his frame, till he became insensible.' An unfortunate actor who nearly perished in the course of a stage execution during the 1890s provides partial corroboration: 'Mr H said he felt a burning sensation in the head for a second or two, then everything seemed to become a brilliant red, changing suddenly to a bright green ... Of actual pain, he experienced very little, save for the fact that his head seemed to feel too small.'

This green hue was noted by the British serial killer Ian **Brady**, who knows what Death looks like. In 1985 he told the journalist Fred Harrison: 'I have seen death, a green face, warm, not unattractive ... green, not black – people always associate death with black. The face is not really formed, it's a radiation, a warmth. Warm green.'

Halifax Gibbet

The Halifax Gibbet was an English guillotine, already ancient by the publication of Holinshed's *Chronicles* in 1578.

A local law prescribed that anyone found guilty of a theft valued at more than 1s 1fid should be 'forthwith beheaded on the next market day', and the miscreants perished at the hands of the Halifax Gibbet. The blade of this tremendous engine weighed 7 pounds 12 ounces, and decapitated heads were said to bound a huge distance, anecdotally coming to rest in washerwomen's panniers.

The gibbet incorporated a highly idiosyncratic communal release mechanism, triggered by removal of a pin attached to a rope pulled by 'every man there present' – except in cases involving the theft of animals, when the creatures themselves were roped up and herded away from the gibbet to pull out the pin.

Some twenty-five unfortunates were executed during the reign of Elizabeth I; the last recorded use came in 1640. The gibbet's stone base was rediscovered in 1840 by the Halifax Town Trustees in the course of levelling Gibbet Hall.

A weird echo of the Halifax Gibbet, crossed with the solution to Agatha Christie's *Murder on the Orient Express*, cropped up in the 1740s when a gang of Hampshire smugglers cornered a Customs Officer called Galley and his travelling companion Chater at the inn of Rowland's Castle. After crushing Galley's testicles, the smugglers whipped him to death. It was then proposed that Chater be killed with a pistol, its trigger attached to a length of string. All fourteen gang members would give the fatal tug together. In the event, a simpler expedient was adopted. They threw Chater into a well and dropped rocks on top of him. Seven of the smugglers swung for the killings.

Hamilton, Dr Albert

Early-twentieth-century American charlatan with a bogus doctorate who posed as a ballistics expert when the science was still in its infancy. During the Stielow case of 1915, Hamilton helped obtain a conviction by spotting imaginary but otherwise distinctive scratches on the test bullets, twinning them with the murder ammunition.

The jury accepted the existence of the markings – missing from the pictures produced in court – believing Hamilton's explanation that he had unluckily photographed the wrong side, and Stielow was found guilty of murdering his employer, Charles Phelps.

Phelps was shot dead by a .22 on the morning of 22 March 1915 at his Orleans County farm. Stielow, a farmhand, denied owning a gun, but he was lying. He had a .22, and Hamilton's evidence secured the death sentence.

But the slow-witted Stielow seemed too amiable for a plausible murderer, and after the case was reopened it transpired that his gun was clogged with grease and dirt of some antiquity. The weapon had not been fired for years, and when it was, the test bullets looked quite different from the murder ammunition even to the naked eye. Stielow was

released in 1918, and an assistant on the case, Charles E. Waite, then in middle age, embarked on his life's work, cataloguing the specifications of every type of gun made in America since the first Colt. By 1922 Waite had amassed a collection of some 1,500 weapons, and he established New York's Bureau of Forensic Ballistics, making reliable assessments with the newly invented comparison microscope.

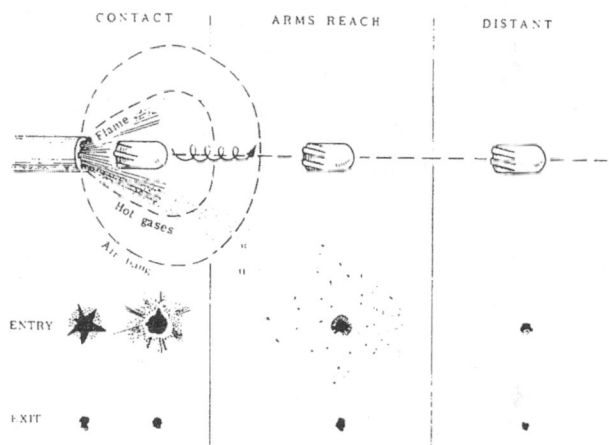

Effects of discharge of firearm with body surface in contact, up to arm's reach, and beyond

One of Waite's notable collaborators, Calvin Goddard, later became the author of the definitive *History of Firearms Identification* (1936), and Goddard too was impelled towards the serious study of ballistics after a spell with Hamilton, who recaptured the limelight during the 1923 **Sacco and Vanzetti** case with an attempt to doctor the evidence. He planned to substitute new guns for old, and set the scene by bringing a pair of Colt revolvers into the courtroom to compare with Sacco's original revolver. Running through some patter, Hamilton dismantled the batch in front of the judge. Then he reassembled them with Sacco's fatal barrel on his own gun, and tried to leave the court with the original exhibit. His ruse failed and the motion for a new trial was rejected.

When falsification is required, scientific findings can still be tailored to fit. Thus the 1968 report on the assassination of Robert Kennedy produced a tidy official account of Sirhan Sirhan's eight bullets which killed the Senator and wounded five others (see **Executive action**). Meticulous diagrams plotted the reconstructed path of each shot. But it is now apparent (as it was then) that ten or possibly twelve bullets had been fired; Sirhan's magazine contained only eight rounds. Witnesses were unanimous in affirming that Sirhan shot at Kennedy from in front at a distance of two to three feet; he certainly never came closer than eighteen inches. But the autopsy showed that the Senator died from gunshot wounds fired from a range of three inches, from the side or behind. Three years later, in 1971, three independent experts affirmed that the fatal bullets (said at the trial to be a perfect match for ammunition fired from Sirhan's gun) could not have come from his weapon.

See also **Firefights**

Hand

Martha Sheward's hand was sniffed out in 1851 by a dog and taken to its master, on an English country walk. But no one knew to whom it belonged, and Sheward's other portions, which turned up all round the Norwich ditches, similarly defied identification when presented to the police. So the entire assortment was pickled, and the jar put into long-term storage in the Norwich Guildhall.

Eighteen years later Martha Sheward's husband, overcome by remorse, felt moved to stand outside the house in Walworth, London, where he first met his wife, and confess her murder to the nearest police-man. The disassembled body in Norwich was produced and, despite subsequent retractions, William Sheward went to the gallows.

The pair had been grindingly poor and quarrelled bitterly over money. Sheward found it galling that shortly after her demise his wife came into a substantial inheritance which she could not claim, being dead. This quirk of fate lay heavy on his mind, and led to his fatal confession.

Half a century later, burglar George Mitchell was arrested after breaking into a crockery warehouse in Clerkenwell. The constable on the beat identified the fixture surmounting one of the spikes on the wooden gate outside the premises as a human finger. It had separated from Mitchell's right hand as he scrambled over the gate and a gold ring snagged on the tip of a spike. The digit, forwarded to the Fingerprint Bureau, acquired a certain measure of renown in the *Police Gazette*, which printed the gate's photograph with a helpful arrow indicating the railing on which it was found. The alert went out for a four-fingered criminal, and Mitchell was arrested a month later on suspicion of pilfering in a crowd at a tramstop. Producing his bandaged hand in proof of innocence, Mitchell not unreasonably objected, 'How could I pick pockets with a hand like this?' The detective replied, 'I don't know about that, but I reckon you've lost a finger. The blokes at the yard are looking after it for you.' Mitchell was sentenced to twelve months' hard labour.

Handkerchiefs

Charles Dickens's **Fagin** constituted a viable financial proposition; it was feasible for a London receiver of stolen goods to prosper by specialising in handker-chiefs. By the early 1800s, a Mrs Diner of Field Lane, Holborn, was reckoned a woman of property, and she dealt exclusively in handkerchiefs for many years, 'buying them from pickpockets of every description. Men, women, boys and girls, but chiefly boys, whose practice it is.' The loft above her shop was crammed to bursting. Mrs Diner remained beyond the short reach of nineteenth-century law by removing the identifying marks and initials from her stock.

In those pre-conglomerate days, London receivers were many and various. Robert Charles was the specialist for stolen ducks. His near neighbour, Edward Memmery from Old Pye Street, preferred pilfered foodstuffs: butter, cheese and bacon. Joshua Roberts of Pump Lane handled hot game. In Tottenham Court Road, Mr Brand concentrated on lead. And a fence called Reed, who had a Rag and Glass shop off Fitzroy Place, ran what amounted to a school for young thieves, starting his pupils off by lending them house-breaking implements.

The young went to prison in droves. Many were transported, some were hanged, 'dying game' in stolen finery, cheered at the gallows by their friends. In 1816, a conservative estimate of 6,000 London boys and girls supported themselves solely by thieving. Known as 'boys on the cross' or 'cross boys', from a middle-class perspective they must have seemed irre-trievably lost, perhaps the 'lost boys' of J. M. Barrie's *Peter Pan*.

Hands up

A succinct formula devised by the remarkable Bill Miner (1847?–1913), who ran away to California 'to become a cowboy' at the age of 13. 'Old Bill's' first stagecoach robbery in 1869 earned him a few hundred dollars and ten years in San Quentin.

After his release, Old Bill travelled, doing a spell in Turkey as the partner of a trader who abducted desert women for resale to harems. Then he worked as a gun runner in Rio before returning to his interrupted career as a stagecoach robber. But in 1881 he was caught again. Sent down for twenty-five years, he gained his freedom in 1901 only to find that the era of the stagecoach had passed.

So at the age of 54, Old Bill took to robbing trains, concentrating on the Canadian Pacific. Jailed for life In 1906, he escaped and held up a bank in Oregon before reverting to railways. Pinkerton's W. H. Minster captured the sexagenarian Miner after a swamp shoot-out and, during his next life sentence, Old Bill escaped three times from the Georgia State Penitentiary.

He spent the final years of his life, like the last Emperor of China, tending a flower garden; in breaks between horticulture, he dictated his life story to a friendly prison detective, and died in his sleep in 1913.

The last person and first woman to rob a stage-coach was Pearl Hart. Obsessed by derring-do dime novels in her twenties, Pearl persuaded the local town drunk to collaborate in a hold-up; and in 1899 the pair stopped a stage somewhere outside Globe, Arizona. They never found out exactly where; inextricably lost, the pair were rounded up by an unarmed posse still with their $450 of loot. She served five years in the Yuma Penitentiary.

Hanging, a short history of

Hanging is thought to be a Persian invention which reached England in the twelfth century. It soon achieved a momentous throughput. In the single year of 1279, Jews alone accounted for 280 executions for clipping coin. According to the historian Stow, some 72,000 criminals were hanged in the reign of Henry VIII when the total population stood at not much more than a couple of million; the 2,000 executions a year represented an annual mortality rate of one in a thou-sand across the population, some ten times the current British road accident rate.

While Edward VI was on the throne (1547–53), hang-ings reached an annual average of 560 at Tyburn alone. Every law day twenty or thirty were executed in a batch. London was referred to as the City of Gallows and it is commonplace to find road directions in Ogilby's *Itinirarium Angliae* with gallows as the nearest reference point. Three sets disfigured the highway between London and East Grinstead, some forty miles distant.

Excessive zeal on 23 March 1738

The habit of doling out the death sentence contin-ued without respite down the centuries. Between 1825 and 1831 a total of 9,136 were condemned to death, but by then only a minority of the sentences were carried out. Of the 410 convicted of horse, sheep and cattle stealing only seventy actually swung, and the proportion of reprieves steadily increased from the mid-eighteenth century, inspiring old lags to reminisce fondly of times past. One, reported by John Townsend – the most famous of the Bow Street officers – remarked: 'Why, Sir, where there is one hung now, there were five when I was young.' But horrors still abounded. In 1833 a boy of nine was killed for poking a stick through a window and stealing tuppence worth of paint.

Thereafter the number of executions fell very rapidly, thanks largely to the work of Sir Robert Peel, who wiped capital offences off the statute books by the score. In 1837, 438 prisoners were capitally convicted, but two years later the figure had dropped to fifty-six. Public executions were banned only in 1868.

For many years it was the custom to dump the bodies of the deceased on the doorsteps of those who had been instrumental in their demise. Thus the Annual Register of 1763 records that the body of Cornelius Sanders was taken to the house of Mrs White in Lamb Street, Spitalfields, from whom he stole the £50 for which he went to the gallows. The mob sacked her house, burning her furniture in the street. In the provinces, civic feasts were often held at public expense to mark executions, a practice which continued in Scotland until the nineteenth century.

The gallows provided work for the lowest of the low, and those who lived by the rope often died by it, with executioners ending up on the scaffold as a matter of routine. Other functionaries were also at risk. On 23 March 1738 a drunken executioner at Hereford was only just restrained from hanging the parson reading from the Book of Prayer.

Family firms – notably the **Pierrepoints** – often dominated the hanging business. Payment was per capita, fixed at ten guineas from the mid-nineteenth century, and last-minute reprieves generated a certain amount of ill-will. Payment came in two instalments, half in advance at the time and the remainder two weeks later for good post-execution conduct. This included not holding court in the local pub afterwards as a freak attraction. During the nineteenth century executioners still received the clothes and personal effects of their victims as a perk, hawking them as souvenirs for a tidy sum. The training course took about a week.

The art of hanging developed very gradually. In the old days at **Tyburn**, the cart holding the accused stopped beneath the gallows; after the noose was fitted, the horse ambled on, leaving the victim to dangle, perishing slowly of asphyxia. Death might not come for many minutes and there are several cases of effective reprieves arriving some time after the victim was hanged. Nor were 'resurrections' unusual. When the murderer William Duell was hanged with four others at Tyburn on 24 November 1740, he revived in time to find himself in one piece (but only just) in the macabre surroundings of a dissection room. He was returned to **Newgate** and transported for life.

Sometimes the executioner pulled on the victim's legs to hasten his demise, and often relatives fought for the corpse to prevent its delivery to the Worshipful Company of Barber-Surgeons for anatomisation.

The most significant technological development, the long drop introduced by William Marwood, produced, in theory at any rate, instantaneous extinction. Almost equally important was the placement of the knot in its optimum location, empirically established, under the angle of the left jaw. This tilted back the chin, thereby assisting in the rupture of the spinal cord. The body was left on the end of the rope for an hour to avoid any chance of premature burial.

Reading the memoirs of the nineteenth-century hangmen it is hard to avoid a dispiriting sense of their professional jealousy about who ranked as the 'best' hangman or 'chief' executioner. Nor do the minor refinements or stylistic variants of each practitioner seem matters for great pride. But in a strange transference of celebrity, the victim's fame rubbed off on to the executioner, who in later periods serialised his memoirs in the newspapers. Public status of the craft was reflected in the hangmen's calling cards. James **Berry** had an attractive card with an ivy-leaf design giving his name and trade of 'Executioner'. William Calcraft's (1800–79) painted shop sign stated 'Boot and Shoe Mender' and, in much larger letters, 'Executioner to Her Majesty'.

Fond of animals, Calcraft hanged people off a three-feet drop, and indulged in one of the more peculiar ruses to segregate his personal from his professional life. On arrival at a prison for a hanging garbed in a black suit, he would change his clothes, donning another black suit of identical design. It is supposed that he purchased these duplicate outfits in multiples, two or three at a time, and perhaps no criminological issue is quite so fraught with insignificance as the speculation over whether he preserved his suits particular to their usage, unless it be the question of erections.

It is widely believed that the victim of a hanging achieves instantaneous erection, which may account for the last words of Dr Thomas Neill Cream, executed on 15 November 1892. 'I am Jack...' he said as the hangman pulled the lever, suggesting that a confession to his true identity as the Ripper was imminent. But Cream was a well-spoken man, and it is equally likely that he was commenting on the phenomenon of involuntary emission ('I am ejaculating').

See also **Initiation**, **Recruitment**

Hansen, Robert (1939–)

Alaskan baker from Anchorage who gave his victims a sporting chance. If they agreed to oral sex he spared them. Only when a woman refused did he strip her at gunpoint. Then Hansen gave his quarry a head start, waiting as she ran off screaming into the frozen woods.

Hansen relished the stalking, sometimes allowing his victim to think she had escaped before flushing her out for the excitement of another chase across the icebound wastes. When his prey became too exhausted to move, he killed her with his .223 Ruger Mini-14 high-velocity hunting rifle.

He tracked naked Paula Golding along a sandy riverbank, following the footprints until he spotted her lying bleeding and exhausted under a stand of brush. Rather than kill outright, he shouted until she staggered to her feet, and then took her on the run with a bullet between the shoulder-blades.

Cats do much the same, growing petulant with mice which won't 'work' any more, hoping to paw them into revived spasms. For Hansen too, nationally recognised for bagging specimen Dall mountain-sheep with a bow and arrow, the thrill was in the hunt. It felt 'like going after a trophy Dall or a grizzly bear'.

In psychological terms, Hansen's move to bigger quarry was motivated by feelings of resentment, in turn provoked by a well-founded perception that he was unattractive. At school, as a pimply, skinny stutterer, Hansen enjoyed little success with girls, and as an adult he preyed on the floating population of busty topless dancers working the red-light district in Anchorage.

Episodes normally began with a bout of torture in the basement of Hansen's pleasant suburban house. Lured to his home by an offer of two or three hundred dollars for oral sex, the unwary soon found themselves handcuffed to a post. Women who demanded money (as though they needed *paying* to have sex) were generally killed, whereas those who admitted servicing Hansen out of carnal desire went free. Maybe thirty or forty victims were released alive after hours, or even days, of sex and torture but, as bar girls on the wrong side of the law, they did not pester the police with complaints.

In 1982 one of the women escaped, declining to get into Hansen's Piper Super Cub at nearby Merrill Field for the flight to the killing ground. She struggled free and ran for her life towards the streetlights where Officer Gregg Baker spotted her on Fifth Avenue. But her detailed report was disbelieved, no more than the word of a frightened teenage hooker against a married local businessman with a teenage daughter. Hansen ran a popular bakery, and two respectable cronies provided an alibi.

A few months later hunters working the Knik River twenty-eight miles from Anchorage noticed a curious mound of earth. Digging a few inches down, they exposed the stiffened body of a naked young woman. Two brass shell casings lay beside her in the shallow grave, and she was easily identified as a 23-year-old topless dancer, Sherry Morrow, missing since November 1981. About this time another body – Paula Golding's – broke through the soil in a half-dug grave on the banks of the River Knik. Paula's clothing showed no bullet holes; she too had been shot while naked in an Alaskan winter. Investigators checking missing-persons reports for other disappearances came across Officer Baker's report, and District Attorney Krumm broke Hansen's alibi by threatening to make his friends repeat their story under oath. A home search located Hansen's .223 Ruger, and tests produced firing-pin marks identical to the shell casings found in the Golding and Morrow graves.

Hansen offered to talk if, by pleading guilty to four murders, he could spare his family the ordeal of a trial. His twelve-hour confession was recorded over two days, and it is possible that he only included 'prostitutes' in his seventeen admitted killings. Krumm commented, 'He liked and respected women who he felt, in his mind, were good', and Hansen may have drawn a veil over the fate of respondents to his advertisements seeking 'a woman to join me in finding what's around the next bend, over the next hill'.

Many of Hansen's victims had simply fallen on hard times. Paula Golding was a secretary until a botulism scare closed the local canneries, and she worked just eight days in a topless bar to make ends meet before Hansen approached her.

On 28 February 1984 he was sentenced to 461 years. Hansen kept a tally of his victims on a little map, marking their graves on the rugged Kenai Peninsula with asterisks.

Harding, John Wesley (1853–95)

A stone-cold killer. Harding was the second son of a Texan Methodist minister, and (in his own words) 'distracted his parents' with his first killing at the age of fifteen. The victim, a black called Mage, seized Harding's bridle. So Harding 'shot him loose'. As he put it, Mage 'kept coming back and every time we would start, I would shoot him again and again until I shot him down'. Harding spent the following ten years on the run, killing three more times before his next birthday, reaching a total of twelve victims before he started to shave, eventually clocking up forty-four notches.

Harding was captured early on and locked up in the log jail at Marshall with an armed prisoner, whose Colt .45 he purchased, enabling him to avoid trial by shooting his guard dead. Then he killed the three soldiers who recaptured him. He sawed his way out of another jail and, in a fight with Mexican cattlemen, claimed five more victims. He lent a hand in the Sutton–Taylor feud, and fell out with Wild Bill Hickok (then the Marshal in Abilene), who took umbrage when Harding killed a fellow-hotel guest through the wall for snoring.

On the night of his twenty-first birthday, on 26 May 1874, Harding killed the Brown County Deputy Sheriff Charles Webb (his thirty-ninth victim), who was prudently trying to shoot him in the back. A posse hanged Harding's cousins Tom and Bud, his brother Joe was strung from a telegraph pole, and two friends were executed by gunfire. Despite the price of $4,000 on his head, Harding himself remained at large for another three years, finally trapped in the smoking car of a Florida train by Texas Rangers when his pistol got caught in his suspenders.

In prison Harding studied algebra, theology and law. On his release in 1894 he set up as an attorney-at-law, portraying himself in the *El Paso Times* as a 'peaceable, dignified man … that never yields except to reason and law'. But he was overheard threatening local lawman Young John Selman for jailing his mistress McRose overnight, and on 19 August 1895 Old John Selman found Harding playing dice in the local bar and blew the back of his head off. Selman successfully pleaded self-defence at his trial.

In the eponymous album, Bob Dylan characterised Harding as a friend to the poor, 'never known to hurt an honest man'. Dylan's music also featured in a 1987 Australian killing, precipitated when Gladys Dickinson asked her son to turn down the volume of the LP *Desire*, which he was playing at four in the morning.

Mistaking his mother for the record's evil character Isis, Richard Dickinson trampled her to death to the accompaniment of the track 'One More Cup of Coffee for the Road'. Then he sprinkled her body with instant coffee grains. Five years later the schizophrenic Richard was let out of prison for the evening to attend a Dylan concert, but not until a medical team evaluated and dismissed the risks of Dylan singing the offending song live.

Hawthorne Restaurant

Site of one of Chicago's most impressive set-piece onslaughts. After the notorious **Cicero** election of 1924, the Hawthorne Inn became known as 'Capone Castle' and, on 20 September 1926, at 1.15 in the afternoon, Capone was finishing lunch in the street-level restaurant, sipping coffee by the window on West Twenty-second Street.

Hymie Weiss planned to take Capone head-on. First he sent in a black tourer, mocked up like a detective bureau car. With its gong clanging, the decoy roared down the road at fifty miles an hour in apparent hot pursuit of escaping mobsters while a heavy on the running board blazed away with blanks from a Thomson sub-machine-gun.

Capone fell for it. The moment the wagon passed, all sixty customers of the packed restaurant – Capone included – dashed to the window to see the fun. They were caught by Weiss's back-up. Ten cars, spaced at three-yard intervals and loaded with

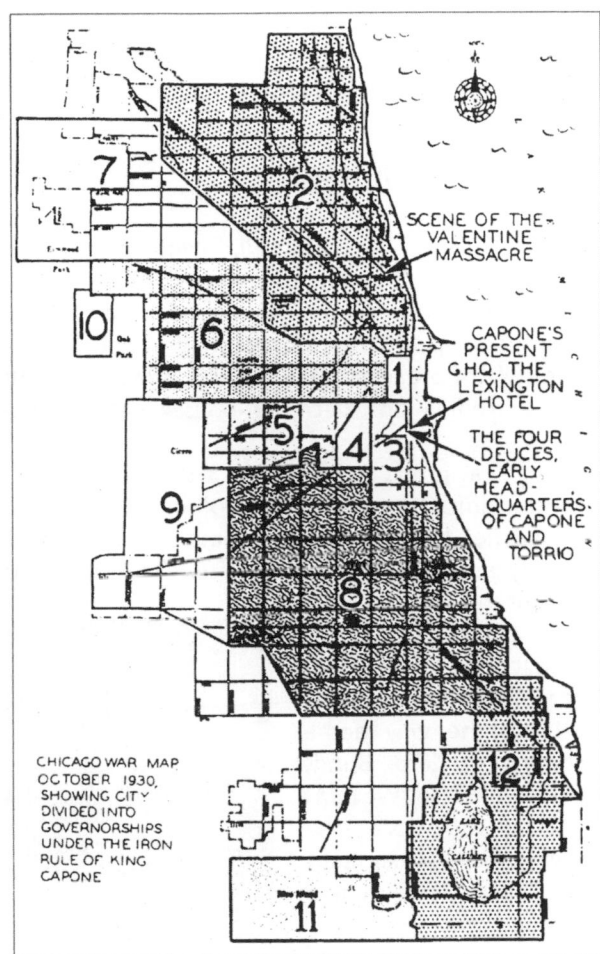

Chicago fiefdoms ruled by Capone in 1930, showing his henchmen's spheres of influence, including: (1) Jake Gusick, (4) Jack McGurn, (8) Spike O'Donnell, (9) Ralph Capone and (10) Joe Montana

machine-gunners, drew up in a slow procession outside the Hawthorne.

Inside, Capone's bodyguard flung his boss to the floor under a table. Weiss's cars opened fire, pouring concentrated streams of bullets through the plate glass, stitching rows of neat horizontal holes in the rear-wall plaster. From the penultimate vehicle stepped a man in brown overalls nursing a Tommy gun. He strolled over to the restaurant, and the final car disgorged his guards, who took up station, with sawn-off shotguns, to either side on the sidewalk. The machine-gunner peered into the entrance, knelt, set the gun to rapid-fire and administered the *coup de grâce*, emptying an entire drum into the premises

from point-blank range, methodically spraying from side to side.

The gunfire ceased, the killers quietly returned to their cars and on a triple blast of the horn the majestic caravan drew away, heading back east towards Chicago. A thousand rounds had been fired. The restaurant was shot to pieces, thirty-five cars were holed and no one died. But a Mrs Freeman, sitting in a nearby parked car, was wounded in the elbow. Her right eye was struck by flying glass; a stray bullet perforated the hat on her husband's head, and their son's overcoat was likewise punctured. In addition, a Capone gunman suffered a shoulder wound.

Two weeks later, on 5 October, Weiss pulled up outside his gang's headquarters above **O'Bannion's** old **flower** shop on North State Street. Accompanied by his bodyguard, his lawyer, their driver and a local politician, Weiss walked across the pavement into a hail of machine-gun crossfire.

Capone's men had rented two overlooking rooms and, to judge by the hundreds of cigarette butts ringing their seats, waited a week for their chance. The gunmen scored twelve hits on Weiss and fifteen on his bodyguard; the two others were badly wounded but survived.

Capone was not questioned. 'It's a waste of time to arrest him,' said Morgan A. Collins, Chief of Police. 'He's been in before on murder charges. He has his alibi.' Capone reimbursed the Hawthorne shopkeepers and shelled out $5,000 dollars to save Mrs Freeman's sight. He could afford it.

See also **Pax Capone**

Head, Billy Moseley's

Said to have been shot in 1974, cut off and driven down to Brighton for exhibition as a trophy to a local publican before its burial at sea.

This was the prosecution's version of events and, at the end of the longest murder trial in English history (November 1976 until June 1977), Bob Maynard and Reg Dudley were sentenced to life imprisonment for murder. The evidence consisted of their own confessions coupled with the testimony of Tony Wild, a violent criminal, who contributed the Gory Head story.

The killing came to light on 5 October 1974 when a birdwatcher observed a torso, minus the hands, wallowing in the Thames near Cold Harbour Point. Detectives suspected that the body belonged to William Henry Moseley, a 37-year-old small-time crook, but it was hard to be sure without the head or fingerprints. The discovery of Moseley's friend and associate Michael Cornwall buried in Chalkdell Wood increased the chance that the two had fallen victim to a gangland feud and, at a second post-mortem on 24 October 1975, Professor James Cameron noted a rare 'metabolic' or pure cholesterol gallstone. Moseley was undergoing treatment for such a condition, and his chest X-ray from a health campaign showed eight points of similarity with a radiograph of the torso.

This painstaking forensic work was not matched by Commander Alan Wickstead's investigation, which earmarked Dudley and Maynard as the culprits. Their life sentences supposedly marked the break-up of one of the big gangs (dubbed '**Murder Inc**.' by the press) inheriting the **Krays**' mantle of terror. Their outfit was credited with four killings and, even in the courtroom, the jury demanded special protection.

In London's East End, Dudley and Maynard went under the sinister epithet of 'Legal and General'. But the nickname was coined in their local pub one day when they arrived wearing mackintoshes and carrying umbrellas, like a couple of gents from an insurance company. Certainly both were criminals, Maynard a petty crook and Dudley a bent jeweller, but there was no weapon, no fingerprints, no forensic evidence, no witnesses to tie them to the killings and, come to that, no gang. Dudley's daughter had married Michael Cornwall, and the two families remain friends, bound together by a joint misfortune rather than sundered by a blood feud. Pundits commented that at the conclusion of the seven-month trial the jury felt that it would be disloyal or even rude to hand down acquittals.

The prosecution witness Wild later admitted that he fabricated his testimony to police specifications in return for a shorter sentence for armed robbery. Maynard's and Dudley's confessions consisted not of detailed admissions but, at best, of a failure to rebut the accusations in detail, and the accuracy of the police interview transcripts has always been disputed.

Perhaps more to the point, Billy Moseley's head turned up on 28 July 1977. But since it was found in a bundle of newspaper in an Islington public lavatory, it could hardly have been washed ashore after a sojourn at sea. On the contrary, judging by its partially defrosted state, it spent the last few years in a deep freeze. Nor had it been shot.

Head, Exxie Wilson's

Discovered beautifully presented, frozen, in an ornate wooden box in a Burbank driveway on 24 June 1980. Its hair had been posthumously washed, the features freshly made up with lipstick, eye shadow and blusher in the style of a Barbie Doll. The sperm in the mouth resulted from a post-decapitation sex session in a shower.

Wilson, a pretty 21-year-old from Little Rock, Arkansas, drifted into life as a Hollywood prostitute with her friend Karen Jones. Douglas Clark, the 'Sunset Strip Slayer', enticed her into the front seat of his car and shot her in the head before cutting it off and driving it away, running over Karen and shooting her to death on the way home. According to Carol Bundy, Clark's accomplice, 'We had a lot of fun with Exxie' once she was safely in their apartment. They kept her head in the refrigerator.

Douglas Clark, serial killer

Carol Bundy was a fat nurse, and she too caught the decapitation habit, severing the head of former lover John Robert Murray and tossing it into a ravine to prevent his sneaking to the police. 'I did it for Doug,' she told investigators. 'I loved him.'

A lonely 37-year-old diabetic on the rebound, Carol allowed Clark to move in the night of their first meeting and thereafter did his shopping, cooking and washing. She lent him her car. She paid an attentive ear to his lurid stories of teenage street-walkers on Sunset Boulevard, and voiced no objection when he brought them to her apartment. She photographed the girls giving him oral sex, and rose to the occasion when Clark produced the bodies of two young runaways he picked up hitch-hiking. She enthused over his making love to their bodies. She applied the make-up to Exxie Wilson's head. She went cruising with Clark and passed him the gun to kill a teenager near Tuna Canyon. She sat with him while he stabbed a girl twenty-seven times in his car in a parking lot and, after telling John Murray too much over a late-night drink, killed him herself.

Carol broke down during a coffee break at her job at a Burbank convalescent hospital. 'I can't take it any more,' she sobbed. 'I'm supposed to save lives, not take them.'

On 28 January 1983 Clark was sentenced to the gas chamber for these and five other murders. Carol received two consecutive life sentences. According to crime writer Colin Wilson, Clark only killed women out of resentment at their failure to bring him to orgasm. The 'right man' phenomenon, a term first coined by science-fiction writer A. E. van Vogt, describes a high-dominance male who cannot bear to admit that he is ever at fault, intellectually, emotionally or physically. Faced with the embarrassment of not being 'right' enough to be sexually competent, such a person is capable of murderous resentment.

See also **Jekyll and Hyde**, **Romances**

Head, Frank Costello's

Shot on 2 May 1957 by Vincent 'the Chin' Gigante in a hotel lobby. Frank Costello was Manhattan's **Mafia** chief, and hence the natural target for a Mafia conspiracy, in this case fomented by the hot-bloods Anastasia and Genovese. They disliked Costello's diplomatic style, which in their view risked turning the Cosa Nostra into a bunch of sissies.

It proved an easy contract. Costello had no retinue of bodyguards, and Gigante's bullet hit him smack in the temple, where it was deflected and veered off round the skull, travelling beneath the skin. After completing the circumnavigation of his cranium, the bullet came upon the original entry hole, through which it exited, leaving Costello with no more than an unusual flesh wound.

Nevertheless, Costello judged it time to retire. In the aftermath, Anastasia indulged in such a rampage of violent killings that he had to be put down, meeting his end riddled with holes in a New York barber's chair on 25 October 1957. The removal of two such senior personnel in rapid order left the Mafia in a turmoil – hence the ill-fated Mob summit at **Apalachin**.

Costello took to the grave the secret of his long-standing, friendly relationship with J. Edgar **Hoover**. The pair first met in the 1930s, when the Director of the FBI was out window-shopping on Fifth Avenue,

and they maintained regular contact through the decades, often meeting in the Waldorf Hotel where both made use of apartments. It was through this conduit that Hoover stage-managed his apparent coup of Louis 'Lepke' Buchalter's arrest on 24 August 1939, in a spirit of continuing peaceful co-existence between the Mafia and the FBI.

Head, John Hayes's

In pre-photographic times, identification was achieved in a relatively direct and robust manner. On 2 March 1726 a severed head, noted on the muddy Thames foreshore near Horse Ferry Wharf in London, was washed, brushed, and impaled on a stake outside St Margaret's, Westminster, with a twofold objective: first, to find out to whom it belonged and second, to arrest anyone 'who might discover signs of guilt on the sight of it'.

But no one recognised it. On becoming excessively decayed for continued public display, the head was immersed in a jar of spirits (most likely gin) and exhibited, on request, to those who thought they might be able to help. In due course someone said it might be John Hayes, a carpenter who had gone missing. His wife Catherine attracted suspicion to herself, lying about her husband's whereabouts, saying variously that he had left for Hertfordshire, gone out for a walk, and fled to Portugal after killing a man in a quarrel. She confirmed the identification, exclaiming in tears, 'Oh, it is my dear husband's head', before embracing the glass container.

Catherine subsequently confessed to murdering her husband after making him very drunk indeed: on six pints of wine. Clearly a high-dominance woman, she compromised two men, Thomas Billings and Thomas Wood, in her plot by depicting her husband as a heartless atheist and the killer of his two children. As a further inducement she offered to share an inheritance of £1,500. The men hatcheted Hayes to death, but it was Catherine's cunning plan to remove the head, complicating identification, and she who held the bucket underneath the neck to catch the sluice of blood. The dismembered trunk turned up in Marylebone pond and, in an early feat of forensic detection, was crudely fitted to the head. The case is well documented, but makes no mention of the sexual bond that today's reader suspects bound the conspirators together.

On 9 May 1726 Catherine Hayes was burned alive and kicking when the executioner was unable to strangle her at the stake before the flames took hold. Her story passed into fiction in Thackeray's 1839 novel *Catherine*.

Head, Lord Lovat's

Reattached for cosmetic reasons. George Selwyn, man of fashion and smart friend of Horace **Walpole**, was addicted to viewing executions; his wide circle of upper-class acquaintances thought the habit in questionable taste.

In Lovat's case, Selwyn stayed the distance. Reproached for sneaking off to watch the removal of the noble lord's head on 8 April 1747, he replied, 'Why, I made amends by going to the undertaker's to see it sewn back again.' The same thing happened to the head of King Charles I.

Lord Lovat, a venerable eighty, was the last man to be executed by the axe in England, and twenty others perished with him when a grandstand by Tower Hill collapsed, crushing both the carpenter who erected it and his wife, selling liquor underneath.

Head, Max Rubin's

An American survivor. Rubin, an ace operative at labour racketeering, had a difference of opinion with Louis 'Lepke' Buchalter, the celebrated boss of **Murder Inc**.

'By the way Max, how old are you?' Lepke enquired in the autumn of 1937. Rubin replied that he was 48.

'That's a ripe age,' said Lepke. A few weeks later, on 1 October 1937, Rubin turned into Gun Hill Road in the Bronx with his head still on his shoulders. A hitman fell in behind, put the muzzle of his revolver on the base of Rubin's neck, adjusted the angulation upwards and pulled the trigger. Rubin heard something go bang. The bullet traversed his neck, emerging via the bridge of his nose between the eyes, and the gunman did not consider a *coup de grâce* worthwhile.

For thirty-eight days Rubin lay in hospital between life and death. Then he staged a full recovery, but his head stayed crooked until the end of its days.

Most survivors of head wounds are shot in the front; many parts of the brain have little to do and, in the absence of infection, it is perfectly feasible to recover from a bullet that enters the head on one side and exits on the other. The business end is at the rear.

Head money

Trouble with Chinese buccaneers prompted the enactment in 1825 of the statute for 'Encouraging the Capture or Destruction of Piratical Ships and Vessels'. Under this Act, the Royal Navy's Treasurer paid £20 for every dead Chinese pirate, a reward known as 'head money' although the heads were not lodged in evidence. The Admiralty accepted any 'sufficient' proof as to quantity. Qualitatively, the issue of whether the foreign seafarers – eliminated on a lawless coast on the far side of the globe – actually were pirates was taken at face value.

Certainly Chinese corsairs were not always able to mount effective resistance; during a couple of days in October 1849, a force under Commander J. C. D. Hay killed 1,700 in the waters near Chokeum without suffering a single fatality.

The cost of the 1825 Act had reached £93,005 by its repeal in 1850, with the more acerbic Members of Parliament asking how claimants *knew* their victims were pirates and wondering aloud about the temptations of the money-for-corpses policy.

See also **Wuornos**

Heads, Jeffrey Dahmer's

No section on heads would be complete without mentioning Jeffrey **Dahmer**.

When the police entered his apartment shortly after midnight on 23 July 1991, they noticed the first one on the bottom shelf of the fridge alongside some pickles and mustard. In the freezer were three more, frozen solid. Another three were packed in a cardboard box marked 'computer equipment', but these, like the two kept in the top drawer of the filing cabinet, were only skulls, with their flesh and skin scraped clean. That was all, apart from the two on the kitchen shelf above the stove where Dahmer was boiling up some hands and a genital organ. He told the police he had eaten Oliver Lacy's heart and biceps after frying them in vegetable oil.

In the words of Dahmer's former schoolmate Dave

Borsvold: 'I kept my distance from him. He was generally one weird dude.'

See also **Torso**

Heads, living

Something funny happened to the head of Charlotte Corday. Charlotte, it will be remembered, assassinated the journalist Marat on 13 July 1793 during the French Revolution.

Immediately after being guillotined, her head was shown to the crowd by an assistant executioner, François le Gros. He slapped her on the cheek in a gesture of **contempt**. It was noted that in her blush of indignation 'both Charlotte's cheeks reddened perceptibly … It cannot be claimed that this flush resulted from the blow itself, for the cheeks of corpses may be struck in this way in vain.' In other words, Charlotte was still 'alive'.

A learned correspondence ensued in the Paris daily Le Moniteur, with the German anatomist S. T. Soemmering professing that the biological technicality of death did not necessarily supervene just because the head was cut off. 'Feeling, the personality, the ego,' Soemmering argued, 'remain alive for some time in the head which has been detached from the victim's body, and there remains the arrière-douleur from which the neck suffers … If the air still circulated through the vocal organs, these heads would speak.'

Most medical men remained sceptical, but the seeds of doubt were planted, and nearly a century later the debate revived after an experiment by three French doctors, the Decaisne brothers and Dr Everard.

After the execution of the murderer Théotime Prunier on the morning of 13 November 1879, the trio started work on his head in the cemetery, trying to get in touch. Putting his mouth very close to the deceased's ear, one doctor tried to rouse Prunier, repeatedly shouting his name. Then they pinched Prunier's cheek; stuffed a brush dipped in ammonia up his nostrils; drew a pencil of silver nitrate over the conjunctiva; and held a lighted candle so close to their subject's eyes that his eyeballs were singed. But nothing worked. Prunier's head was definitely dead.

The following year, Dr Dassy de Lignière experienced better luck with the murderer Menesclou, executed on 7 September 1880. Three hours after his decapitation, Menesclou perked up. With his head receiving the life-support of a blood transfusion from a dog, Menesclou's skin reddened, his features firmed, his eyelids twitched and his lips stammered. De Lignière concluded: 'This head, separated from its body, hears the voices of the crowd. The decapitated victim feels himself dying in the basket. He sees the guillotine and the light of day.'

Twenty-five years later a Dr Beaurieux provided disturbing support for this proposition. At half past five on the morning of 28 June 1905 the freshly guillotined head of the murderer Languille tumbled upright on to its base, semi-sealing the neck and keeping the haemorrhage to a minimum. After Languille's eyelids and lips worked in irregular rhythmic contractions for some five or six seconds, the head seemed to die with the lids half-closing on the eyeballs.

'Languille!' barked Dr Beaurieux. Slowly Languille's head opened its eyes, looked round, saw the doctor, focused on him and returned his gaze. 'I was dealing,' wrote the doctor, 'with undeniably living eyes which were looking at me.'

After a few seconds Languille again shut his eyes. The doctor shouted for the second time; again Languille was roused, and stared 'with perhaps even more penetration than the first time' before a final half-closing of the eyelids. Then his eyes glazed over. Dr Beaurieux's meticulous and convincing report is contained in Archives d'Anthropologie criminelle, vol. XX, 1905.

As late as 1956 the researchers Dr Piedlièvre and Dr Fournier affirmed that death from decapitation 'is not instantaneous … Every vital element survives decapitation … It is a savage vivisection followed by a premature burial.' Since then, countries with advanced medical facilities have ceased research, but in March 1993 a Dr Steven Seddon from Staffordshire volunteered to the Guardian newspaper that a beheaded man's suspension of consciousness results from the interruption of oxygen supply to the cortex.

Thus decapitation simply initiates the process by isolating the head from newly oxygenated blood and, Seddon reported, the cortex only 'shuts down' after some twenty seconds; the process of irreversible brain death takes a further three and a half minutes. The severing of the spinal cord hardly matters; it causes total paraplegia of both the voluntary and involuntary muscles, but in the nether regions to which, by a happy chance, the head is no longer connected. Clearly the accidental 'sealing' of Languille's neck prolonged the presence of arterial blood in his skull, allowing it to drain away rather than gush out, and the sparks of life would persist for longer than normal until the complete 'suffocation' of his brain.

Head, William Gallo's

Gullible but lucky. William Gallo was a small-time hood who, with his associate Ernest 'The Hawk' Rupolo, was assigned to take out Ferdinand 'The Shadow' Boccia in 1934.

The killers' boss, the devious Vito Genovese, awarded Rupolo the task of murdering his partner to tie up the loose ends for $175 all-in. Later, Genovese changed his mind and placed the original Boccia contract with Mafia professionals, and when they killed the 'Shadow', Rupolo believed it was still incumbent on him to murder Gallo.

So one night Rupolo and Gallo went to the movies and, as they strolled home, Rupolo decided to earn his keep. He drew his gun, put it against his partner's head and squeezed the trigger. The weapon misfired, so Rupolo tried again, but it failed again. Meanwhile, Gallo, surprised at the way his friend was holding a pistol to his head and repeatedly pulling the trigger, grew suspicious, and demanded some clarification of his intentions.

Rupolo shrugged off the episode as horseplay with an unloaded weapon, and the pair continued amicably on their visit to a friend. There Rupolo examined his revolver and found that the firing pin had rusted. So he oiled it, and later that night, as they walked another couple of blocks, tried again. This time the gun worked. But since Gallo was only wounded, he experienced no difficulties in identifying his assailant, and Rupolo spent the next ten years in prison.

This was one of the favourite anecdotes of Joe Valachi, the Mafia informer. There is a sequel. In 1937, Vito Genovese staged a tactical withdrawal to Italy, accompanied by $750,000. Seven years later Rupolo was released on parole; shortly afterwards he came up on charges for another shooting. By now it seemed certain that Genovese had left the country for good, so Rupolo had few qualms about incriminating him in the original Boccia murder.

But in 1945 Genovese was repatriated to face trial, where he promptly had the only material witness poisoned. At liberty, Genovese started trading again, creating endless mayhem until his imprisonment in 1958 for a narcotics conspiracy. Meanwhile, Rupolo

made himself scarce, eking out a fearful existence for nearly twenty years as an informer on the run. His tightly bound corpse was found in New York's Jamaica Bay on 17 August 1964, mutilated, with a bullet in the back of his head.

Like many underworld bosses, Vito Genovese was a stickler for appearances. He told one of his enforcers, the toothless Johnny D, 'The next time I see you, I want to see you with some teeth.'

Heaulme, Francis

France's most notorious serial killer of past decades is a textbook example of how to get away with murder by moving from place to place. If it had not been for the instinct of one persistent detective, Jean-François Abgrall, he would almost certainly be killing today.

On Sunday 14 May 1989, the body of a woman was found on Moulin Blanc beach, at Le Relecq-Kerhuon, not far from Brest, in Brittany. The cause of death was a slashed throat and several stab wounds. Considering the time – five in the afternoon on a summer day – it was surprising that there were no witnesses to the murder. The woman was identified from the contents of her handbag as Aline Pérès, a 49-year-old nurse. She was wearing only the bottom part of a bikini, but there had been no sexual attack. Witnesses who saw her sunbathing had noted two poorly dressed men nearby, but added they were not tramps.

The likelihood seemed to be that the killer was one of the drifters, who was staying in a nearby Emmaüs hostel – a kind of Salvation Army hostel – nearby. One of its homeless guests had already left, but was picked up a few days later. He was a tall, thin man of forty named Francis Heaulme. As Abgrall questioned him he kept it casual and informal, and was startled when Heaulme told him he had been in the territorial army and learned to use a knife in combat training. What he then described sounded very like the way that the nurse had been killed. Heaulme also admitted he had mental problems, had been in a psychiatric hospital, that he was a heavy drinker and also that when he was drunk he fantasised about violence. The detective had a sudden intuition that this was the murderer. However, his superior, a major, who was also present, disagreed. He felt that Heaulme's sheer frankness made it unlikely.

His view seemed to be confirmed when Heaulme was able to offer a solid alibi: on the day of the murder he was in a hospital in nearby Quimper after suffering a giddy spell. But when Abgrall went to the hospital and checked, a nurse told him in confidence that someone could have disappeared for a few hours without being noticed, then returned.

Two months later an elderly ex-legionnaire was killed near Avignon, his skull battered with a rock, near the local Emmaüs hostel, and investigation revealed that Heaulme had been staying there at the time. He was picked up, and Abgrall went to interview him. Again Heaulme seemed to delight in dropping hints that he might have been the killer, knowing there was no evidence. But finally, exasperated with questions, he blurted: 'I know you know, but it's all the Gaul's fault', then refused say any more.

It proved to be a vital clue. Abgrall was able to establish that a drifter known as 'the Gaul' – because he looked like the character in the Asterix comic books – had been staying in the local hostel on the day the nurse was murdered. Tracking him down was a long job, and when Abgrall finally succeeded, his superior had decided that Heaulme was not the killer, and refused to let Abgrall go and interview him. However, another opportunity finally arose, and Abgrall got his interview. 'The Gaul' seemed very nervous, but admitted that he was the second man who had been seen on the beach just before the murder, and that when Heaulme had walked towards the woman holding a knife, he had turned and left hastily.

And the next time Abgrall was able to interview Heaulme – three years after the murder – his intuition was proved correct. When he told Heaulme that he had talked to 'the Gaul', Heaulme mistakenly assumed the Gaul had admitted that he had seen him kill the girl, and suddenly confessed to it. Heaulme's love of 'playing games' – offering tantalising clues, then withdrawing them – had brought about his downfall.

In a sense, the case was over. But for Abgrall, the really hard work was just beginning: trying to find out how many murders Heaulme had committed in his years of drifting around France. These, Abgrall finally established, had begun in 1982, on the death of his mother from cancer.

Although Heaulme refrained from further confessions, he enjoyed playing games too much to resist dropping hints – describing violent incidents he claimed to have witnessed ('I saw a man lying face down. There was blood on his back') while disguising places and dates. And it was Abgrall's ability to track

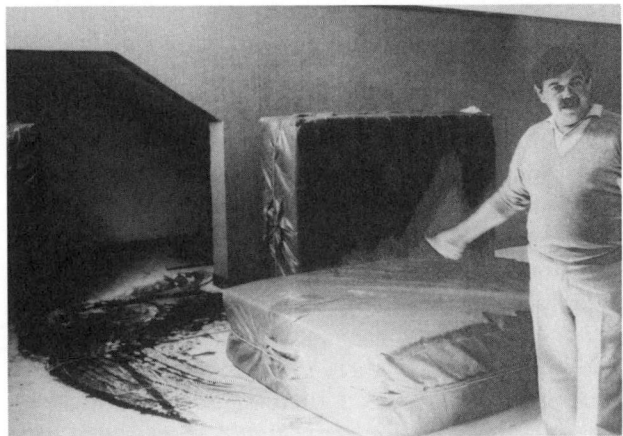

The room where Laurence's body was found

down these incidents with tireless patience, and establish where and when they actually took place, that finally made him aware of the enormous extent of Heaulme's crimes – probably at least forty murders, involving men, women and children. (Heaulme was finally charged with twenty.)

These murders were mostly very sudden and very violent. Heaulme was undoubtedly a psychopath, who often killed on sudden impulse. But some murders were planned. And, even stranger, they were committed with an accomplice. On 7 May 1991, at a fairground, Heaulme met a young man, Michel Guillaume, 19, and his attractive cousin, Laurence, 14, with whom he was already acquainted and about whom he had sexual fantasies. When Laurence left on her moped, her cousin offered to follow in his car and light up the road. Heaulme asked if he could come too. As they drove, Heaulme remarked that she was a 'nice piece of ass' and that he would like to 'give her one'. Her cousin admitted that he felt the same. And Heaulme persuaded him into hitting the rear of the moped and making her crash. They then dragged her into the car and drove to a field, where Heaulme made her undress and told the youth to rape her. When he declined, Heaulme took her away at knifepoint and subjected her to a sexual assault, finally stabbing her thirteen times. Heaulme would eventually receive thirty years for this crime, and the victim's cousin twenty.

From the beginning, Abgrall believed that Heaulme's basic motive was sexual. Medical examination revealed that he was suffering from Klinefelter's Syndrome, in which males have an extra X chromosome, and in which testosterone levels are reduced.

Heaulme also proved to have some physical malformation that would have made rape difficult, as well as a certain ambiguity about his sexual identity, which may explain why many of his victims were male. But one incident left Abgrall in no doubt about Heaulme's sexual drive. In May 1993, after interviewing Heaulme in Metz, he was accompanying him from a photographic session back to prison, and crossing a deserted street. Suddenly Heaulme tensed and stared fixedly, his fists clenched. His eyes were riveted on a girl cycling towards them. Abgrall lost no time in grabbing him and throwing him against the wall. And as the girl vanished, Heaulme relaxed and asked, 'Francis, how can you resist that?' There seems little doubt that if Heaulme had been alone, the girl would have been attacked.

Heaulme appeared in court many times, and had been sentenced to twenty years – the French justice system required him to appear at assizes in places where he had committed crimes – but his main trial began on 21 May 1997, at Draguignan Court of Assizes, where his counsel argued that it was Heaulme's adoration of his mother that triggered the psychosis that turned him into a serial killer. As usual, Heaulme enjoyed playing games and trying to manipulate everybody. He even corrected a policeman who testified that a child had been stabbed eighty-five times: 'No, eighty-three.' He was sentenced to life imprisonment, with a minimum of thirty years.

Abgrall concludes his remarkable book *Inside the Mind of a Killer* by asking whether prison is the right place for Heaulme – a reflection that will have occurred to most of his readers, to whom it seems obvious that Heaulme is rather less than sane.

High finance

Fraud at the highest levels is sometimes depicted as a matter of childish simplicity. In his bitterness at losing the Harrods takeover battle, businessman 'Tiny' Rowland circulated a booklet, *Hero from Zero*, which made nine- or even ten-figure gains seem the work of a moment. At the peripheries of the Harrods–Al Fayed saga, Rowland's confabulations included a story about the son of Carl Hirschmann Snr (an adviser to the world's richest man, the Sultan of Brunei) who he alleged appropriated $100 million. The money, Rowland maintained, was originally intended to put his father in funds to buy the Sultan of Brunei a long-distance 747-SP so that he could fly around with polo ponies and racing cars in an aeroplane. Rowland alleged that Hirschmann's son added the word 'Jnr' after the payee name on the banking forms, and then paid $100 million into his own account.

Another of Rowland's baseless contentions is that the respected financier Al Fayed duped the Sultan of Brunei out of $1.5 billion by the simple expedient of telling him he would, following receipt, place the funds in a joint account.

Money does not grow on trees, but in the nineteenth century the mighty department-store oak of the Sears, Roebuck empire did spring from an acorn of dubious origins. Starting his working life as a railroad telegraph operator, Richard W. Sears dealt in watches on the side, buying them in at $2 and mailing them out at $20 to imaginary customers at non-existent addresses. Sears took care to open the packages 'returned to sender' in his workmates' presence, allowing them to snap up his stock at a bargain $10 each.

It is wrong to underestimate the limitless tenacity and guile exercised by fantasists and conmen in achieving their positions of trust. Nevertheless, at the highest levels the 'sting' itself may bear no clear relationship to complicated financial machinations. When a House of Commons committee reported on Robert Maxwell, who filched £500 million from company pension funds, it described his methodology as 'startlingly simple'. Maxwell was fully entitled to sell the pension fund shares. So he did. But there was nothing to ensure that he gave the sale proceeds back. So he did not.

The latest scam on the international financial markets involves the large-scale sale of 'prime bank notes' at a discount. The scheme has the special allure of free money; buy a dollar for, say, 85 per cent of its face value and see how much more it can be sold for. Translated into inter-bank finance, institutional punters took up millions of dollars' worth of secure debt ('standby letters of credit') at 15 per cent below par. The notes, supposedly issued by major international banks to the privileged few, were traded at a surefire profit in conditions of intense secrecy (somehow connected with furtive 'ethical' investments) under the supervision of the federal authorities in Washington.

If you believe that, you will believe anything.

Buying the notes was effortless, but their sale proved impossible. By late 1992 the South Pacific island of Nauru and the Bank of Croatia had squandered $20 million before calling in the police, and in February 1993 the Salvation Army joined their ranks with an $8.8 million loss.

Highwaymen

A curiously schizophrenic English entity, straddling the realms of fantasy and real life.

Highwaymen comprised the elite – the cavalry, as it were – of eighteenth-century criminals, if only because the ability to acquire a horse was restricted to those of relatively high competence or standing; in their pedestrianised version, robbers were merely footpads. Even Lord Macaulay, the distinguished historian, typecast highwaymen as holding 'an aristocratical position in the community of thieves'.

By the time of the Romantics, highwaymen were elevated to the status of paragons. The writer De Quincey praised their 'strength, health, agility and excellent horsemanship, intrepidity of the first order, presence of mind, courtesy' and concluded: 'The finest men in England, physically speaking, throughout the last century, the very noblest specimens of man, considered as an animal, were the mounted robbers who cultivated their professions on the great roads.'

Highway robberies might go smoothly when the victims handed over their valuables without protest; in general, the prudent highwayman was loath to kill 'for fear of provoking the law to an implacability'. But resistance (or even sometimes compliance) could produce barbarity verging on the psychopathic.

The highwayman Thomas Wilmot thought a passenger slow in handing over a ring and cut off her finger. William Cady was so provoked by a woman who swallowed her wedding ring that he shot her dead and retrieved it via the stomach. Bob Congden murdered his first victim and did away with his landlady together with her baby and maid. Patrick O'Bryan sliced off the nose, lips and ears of a traveller who refused to part with his money, and on another occasion raped, and murdered, and then burned a woman together with her servants.

Notwithstanding, the myth of the cultivated highwayman had some basis in reality. Many were from the upper classes. Smith's contemporary *Complete History of the Lives and Robberies of the Most Notorious Highwaymen* contains two distinct skeins: apocryphal anecdotes lifted from Boccaccio, and fact. Of the fifty-nine practitioners mentioned, thirty-two came from good homes and of these eighteen were the sons of the wealthy, including three Oxbridge men (Brasenose, King's, Trinity) and three law students. The sons of clergymen figure disproportionately.

Highwaymen who were not former students or gentlemen of leisure had almost without exception followed a decent line of work: as goldsmiths, farmers, shoemakers, glovemakers, tailors or servants to the well-off. Footmen – exposed to riches from which they were excluded – often progressed to a career as highwaymen, like many a man of spirit who had exhausted his inheritance on gambling and whores. A wife of mettle might share her spouse's distaste for the world of work. '*Do? Do!*' exclaimed a shocked Mrs Picken in response to her impecunious husband's vacillations about his job prospects, 'Why, what should any man do that wants money and has courage, but go upon the highway!'

Leaping Hornsey toll gate.

"Shout for your lives," cried Patterson, "the turnpike man will hear us—the gate is shut." Dick coolly calculated its height, spoke a few words to Bess, gently patted her neck—stuck spurs into her sides, and cleared the spikes by an inch. No. 2.

The takings might be good, but expenses were high. Mounted robbers were expected to pursue a course of prodigal debauchery, surrounded by conniving innkeepers, whores, dressmakers, tailors, astrologers, hangers-on and wine merchants who made them pay through the nose in return for service and – more important – silence. Few highwaymen ever put by the £500 that was the going rate to bribe their way out trouble.

But prospects were sufficiently attractive to plague the capital with an early form of protectionism when, 'in order to maintain their rights' – according to the Abbé le Blanc writing in the 1720s – highwaymen 'fixed up papers at the doors of the rich people about London, expressly forbidding all persons, of what condition or quality whatsoever, to go out of town without ten guineas and a watch upon them, upon pain of death'.

No police existed to check their activities and not until the reign of William and Mary was the casual system of informers confirmed by Parliament, when a payment of £40 (and the horse) was authorised for information leading to a conviction – a system subject to abuse, culminating in thieftakers like Jonathan **Wild**, who presented gullible young men with the horse, pistol, tuition and even the opportunity with which to commit highway robbery so that he could shop them for the reward. Between 1749 and 1761 some 250 highwaymen were executed at Tyburn, and by 1786 the prize money ran at over £10,000 a year.

Often the corpses were gibbeted, suspended in an iron cage, swinging in the breeze near the scene of their crime. For added longevity the body was coated in tar, making it an attractive proposition for pyromaniacs as well as a local landmark under which, not infrequently, further robberies were committed.

Progressive gentrification of open spaces and heaths eroded the highwaymen's freedom of operation, as did a growing tendency to withhold licences from inns that harboured them. But the highwayman's grip on the English roads was broken by blind John **Fielding** and his introduction of a civilian **Horse Patrol**.

Hindley, Myra (1942–2002)

Myra Hindley was a pleasant working-class Manchester girl, a Catholic convert. She delighted in animals and children, babysat locally and, at 18, was still shocked by bad language.

Myra suffered an early romantic disappointment, breaking off her engagement with Ronnie Sinclair, a low-paid tea blender, dismissing him as too 'immature'. On 16 January 1961, aged 19, she started as a typist at Millwards Merchandising, where her very first letter was dictated by a lanky, good-looking young man in a three-piece suit. He was the Stock Clerk, Scotsman Ian **Brady**, and Myra fell head over heels in love. 'Ian looked at me today' became the first entry in her diary. She wrote later: 'I hope he loves me and will marry me some day.'

Brady seemed quite a catch. Mean and sullen, he looked like Presley, and cut a dashing figure on his motorbike in a long trenchcoat, leather headgear and goggles. Outside work, Brady favoured black shirts; at the office, his suits were a fashionable grey, with just the correct proportion of terylene.

Myra stayed in ignorance of Brady's true character, largely because he proved so unresponsive. Throughout 1961, her diary charts his indifference. On 25 July she noted, 'Haven't spoken to him yet', on 18 October, 'Ian still ignores me', and on 2 December, 'I hate Ian, he has killed all the love I had for him.' But on 22 December Myra wrote triumphantly: 'Out with Ian!', and at the end of the year he walked her home from the office party. Even so, she would not let him through the front door. On New Year's Eve, when Brady presented her father with a bottle of whisky, Myra confided to her diary: 'Dad and Ian spoke as if they'd known each other for years. Ian is so gentle he makes me want to cry.'

Later, as their relationship deepened, Myra noticed that Brady disliked Jews. He preferred things German. On dates, he insisted on German wine. Brady was well versed in the philosophy of the Marquis de **Sade** and the Nazis. He had tape-recordings of Hitler's Nuremberg speeches. Soon Brady was encouraging Myra to read *Mein Kampf*, *Six Million Dead* and *Eichmann*. As the local librarian Barbara Hughes noted: 'He always walked straight to the true crime shelves.'

The couple's sex life started to go awry. After making love a few times Brady wearied of vaginal intercourse. Anal penetration was different. It hurt Myra – but Brady enjoyed it. In the next sexual development she was all but omitted, her participation limited to inserting a candle in his rectum while he masturbated. On at least one occasion – we know, because they took time-lapse photographs – the pair had sex wearing hoods. There are whip marks on her buttocks. On another occasion Ian photographed himself urinating against a curtain.

Brady put Myra wise to a lot of things, like the fact that everyone was corrupt. He explained that God had died; in fact, God was no more than a superstition, a cancer injected into society. Come to that, de Sade believed that rape was no crime, but only a state of mind. According to de Sade, there was little wrong with killing: 'Indeed, such destruction does good, what does it matter to Nature whether a certain mass of flesh which is today a living two-legged animal should, by the action of another two-legged animal, be destroyed?'

For Manchester in the early 1960s, this was exotic stuff; and Hindley too went to Brady's head. Whatever he said, she lapped up. They fed off each other. Soon Myra hated babies, renounced her religion, rejected marriage and scorned social occasions like dances. She bleached her hair and allowed herself to be photographed in jackboots posing as Irma Grese, the 'Beast of Belsen'. Isolated from her own background (see **Family**), she merged her character into Brady's.

Brady basked in the admiration, and by 1963 their *folie à deux* threatened to expand from fantasy into reality. Brady devised a plan for a payroll robbery; Myra would play the driver's part, but she repeatedly

Myra Hindley. This 1965 photo shows her withered at the age of 23

failed her test. Nevertheless she bought a van, and on 16 April Brady wrote to her about his plans to case the joint prior to their raid: 'I shall grasp this opportunity to view the investment establishment situated in Stockport Road, next Friday, to go over details.'

Brady moved in to share Myra's grandmother's house in Bannock Street, and persuaded her to join a pistol club where she bought an unlicensed Webley .45 and a Smith & Wesson .38. But in July 1963 they relegated the robbery to the back burner after Brady outlined an even bolder scheme – to commit the perfect murder.

Killing children was Brady's ambition. They would tour the residential side-streets of Manchester and find someone to abduct. Doing it as a couple in the form of ritualised slaughter would provide a fillip for their relationship. Myra would drive ahead in the van, and when Brady, on his motorbike, spotted a likely-looking prospect he would flash his lights. Myra was to stop and lure the child into the van, offering a reward for help in finding a valuable glove lost on the moors during a picnic.

The victim Brady selected was 16-year-old Pauline Reade. Hindley was on speaking terms with the girl's mother, making the pick-up all the easier. She drove Pauline to the beauty spot of Hollin Brow Hill, introduced her to Brady and left the two together to 'look for the glove' while she found a better parking space. By the time Hindley returned, Pauline lay on the ground with her skirt pulled up, bleeding to death. On 23 November it was the turn of John Kilbride ('lifted' while buying sixpennyworth of broken biscuits) and, seven months later, Keith Bennett and, six months later, Lesley Ann Downey and, ten months later, on 6 October 1965, Edward Evans.

On this occasion they staged a show, inviting Myra's 17-year-old brother-in-law David Smith to witness the killing in the hope of inducting him as a new disciple. Smith owed £14 8s in rent arrears, and Myra and Brady scoured the town for a 'queer to roll'. Instead, they brought back a young homosexual, Eddie Evans, for a drink. Late that night Myra went to fetch Smith, who lived round the corner, and inveigled him back: 'See me home through the houses, it's dark and I'm scared.'

In principle, Smith agreed with Brady and de Sade that 'people are like maggots, small, blind and worthless'. In practice, stunned by the spectacle of Brady axing Evans to pieces amid pools of blood in the living room, he helped lug the body upstairs to Myra's bedroom, and then lingered, mesmerised, while Brady and Hindley chatted over wine and tea. Brady said, 'That was the messiest yet.' Myra remarked, 'Did you notice how when you hit him, his eyes registered astonishment?', propped her blood-covered feet on the mantelpiece and reminisced: 'Ian, do you remember the time we went on the moors with a body in the back…'

Smith left at three in the morning but, far from converted, he sprinted home in a blind panic, threw up and, at 6.10 a.m., rang the police from a phone box, cowering there armed with a screwdriver and carving knife in case Brady was on the prowl.

Brady was arrested after the discovery of Evans's body in a locked room, but no one thought to take Myra into custody for another five days. Neither confessed, and at their trial one of the victims' fathers, Patrick Downey, bought a .32 Webley pistol to kill Brady in court; the pair were tried with shatterproof glass screens behind their backs.

Ann Downey, the picture of sorrow, as the police search the moors for her daughter's body in 1964

Joint killers normally blame each other, but Brady tried to exonerate Hindley. During nine hours of cross-examination, he never acknowledged either his culpability or hers. They both blamed David Smith, no more than an unwilling spectator, and in 1985 Brady confirmed, 'All my evidence was to get her off.' His act of self-sacrifice stored up trouble for the future. After sentence, the pair were separated, and away from Brady's spell Hindley saw herself as others did, not a social pioneer but a monster. She had to hand the raw material of her rehabilitation, Brady's fictionalised testimony.

Thus began a strange double act: the more Hindley proclaimed her innocence as Brady's innocent dupe – always 'out of the room' or 'in the car' at the moment of the killings – the more he recanted, affirming her guilt. In 1979 she submitted a virtual thesis to the Home Secretary, a 30,000-word document requesting parole on the grounds that she was an impressionable young girl serving a sentence for crimes she had little to do with. In January 1985 Brady countered that if he ever 'expanded' on events, Myra 'would never get out in a hundred years'. That year he confessed, for the first time admitting the killings of Pauline Reade and Keith Bennett. The police searched Saddleworth Moors and, under this renewed pressure, in February 1987 Hindley finally confessed. It took seventeen hours, and she remained one of Britain's most hated women until her death in 2002.

In July 1987 Pauline Reade's body was found in a shallow grave 150 yards from the road over the moors. The remains of Keith Bennett were never discovered.

Myra Hindley died in hospital after a chest infection (she was a chain smoker).

See also **Remorse**, **Tapes**

Hirasawa, Sadamichi (1893–1987)

Japanese poisoner who spent a record thirty-nine years on Death Row after his robbery of the Teikoku Bank, Tokyo. It is doubtful whether his technique would work in other countries.

On 26 January 1948 Hirasawa donned an armband of the Welfare Department, walked into the bank and asked the manager to muster the staff for immunisation against amoebic dysentery. Hirasawa presented a doctor's card, and issued each of the sixteen employees with a teacup into which he squirted some cyanide from a syringe.

On the command 'please' they all drank it. Hirasawa waited until everyone was immobilised in agony or dead, and then left with 164,400 yen (about £350). There were twelve fatalities.

Hirasawa died in prison in 1987, aged 95. He avoided the death penalty because his lawyers contended, for decades, that hanging was illegal since the Japanese constitution protected its citizenry from self-destruction (including, by extension, the commission of acts attracting the death penalty). Fundamental doubts persist about his guilt, and in

February 1992 his posthumous lawyers filed their nineteenth request for a retrial, alleging a cover-up. According to documents still to be assessed, the poison used was not sodium cyanide (corresponding to samples found in Hirasawa's house) but acetone cyanohydrin (available only to military personnel).

The 1991 efforts of Seichi Kawaguchi relied on similar fanatical subservience to authority. Kawaguchi, a gifted mass blackmailer, embarked on a programme of standard threats distributed in indiscriminate direct mail shots to some 4,000 candidates. He extracted five million yen (£20,000) from 130 respondents before being reported, and is now awaiting trial. His victims were mostly professional men, their addresses culled at random from trade directories. At his peak, Kawaguchi took on extra staff to help lick the stamps; plagued by heart trouble, he wanted a nice sedentary business.

Hitmen

It is said that hitmen work more for prestige than for cash. The classic statement comes in *Joey*, a 1973 autobiography of an anonymous American killer. The author writes that after his first contract, 'the realization came to me that I was a made individual. I was a force to be reckoned with. A lot of people who had looked down at me as a snot-nosed wise-ass kid would now be speaking of me in different tones. The job paid $5,000.' This is first about kudos, last about cash.

But for a man reduced to 'rubbing out' strangers for money, almost *any* job offer would increase his self-esteem. In 1972 Martin Benitez, a Mexican, told police, 'If I hadn't done it, someone else would. And it was better paid than work as a labourer.' Benitez cut off his victims' heads to show to his clients as proof of completion.

Investigations into the **Murder Inc**. killers found that each was motivated by a personal blend of ambition, fear and sadism. One operative observed of his bosses: 'One of those guys tells me to do something, I do it. If I don't, I'll get myself killed.' Hitman Harry Strauss put himself forward for jobs even when it was not his turn, just to curry favour with the big guys. But Luigi Ronsisvalle, a mob enforcer from Sicily in the 1970s, cast his role in more chivalric terms: 'A man of honour no go around stealing and killing for money. A man of honour, he kill for some reason, to

help people.' He drew the line at drug trafficking: 'You give to me $30,000, and I am sent to kill a person. You kill him, not me. But to move pounds of heroin, you destroy thousands of young American generations.' Of Ronsisvalle's thirteen commissions, the most sordid came in 1977 when he was approached by a policeman with $2,000 collected in a whip-round to finance the hit, and it did indeed concern honour. The officer's sister was married to a compulsive gambler who, unable to cover his last wager in a poker game, had staked his wife. Then he lost the next hand.

The day after the husband brought the two winners back for sex with his mate, she complained to her brother, and in due course Ronsisvalle shot the gambler dead as he left home to go fishing. The following year, Ronsisvalle declined to help the Italian swindler Michele Sindona, who was offering $100,000 contracts on the liquidator and the attorney rummaging through his financial affairs.

The cost of murder varies widely. The Mexican Zosimo Montesino, credited with 150 slayings, charged anywhere between £3 and £150 per job. Prices are higher in the developed world, but first-time buyers should be wary of five-figure asking prices. One of many British cautionary tales befell businessman Malcolm Stanley, who in 1992 negotiated a £30,000 purse for his wife's killing. 'I want a complete termination job, I do not want a hospital job. I want it completely zappo,' said Stanley to the prospective killer, who was, it transpired, an undercover detective.

That same year, Susan Gill, an English businesswoman, went higher, allegedly agreeing a £90,000 fee to have her unfaithful husband eliminated. Again the 'hitman' was a plain-clothes police officer. Similarly, the *agent provocateur* in America's **Cheerleaders** case began bargaining at $20,000.

All these buyers were middle-class, acclimatised to substantial bills from professionals like lawyers and accountants. However one rates their services, there is little of the professional about 'contracts', which in real life are fulfilled by the dregs of society for a pittance. In Britain, it is hardly worthwhile retaining someone; beyond the very limited confines of south London gang warfare, where crooks kill each other with metronomic regularity, mostly over soured drug deals, there is no indigenous hitman tradition. 'Applicants' are posers chancing their arm.

Linda Calvey hired one in November 1990, and it was a waste of time. Known as the 'Black Widow', Calvey agreed on £10,000 with Daniel Reece. After pumping a shot into her lover's elbow, Reece 'froze', and his client snatched the gun back and finished the victim herself.

In 1993, journalist Simon Bell made a determined effort to find a British hitman available to the public. A fortnight passed before he tracked down a contact, 'Ralph', who said, 'If it's an End Job you want … you give me a phone number. You don't get any phone number from me. It may be five or six people down the line.' Ralph mentioned a 'starting price' of between £10,000 and £15,000, largely destined for the intermediaries.

In London's traffic conditions a 'get-away car' is a contradiction in terms. The British hitman of the gang wars goes to work on a motorbike, relying on a pre-planned escape route down a set of stairs or a narrow alley where a back-up bike awaits. The helmet conceals his face.

Killing comes cheap in America. It always has (see **Westies**). Walter Stevens, a Prohibition gunman from Chicago, charged $25 for roughing up a man and twice that for killing him. A quiet, decorous individual, Stevens nursed his invalid wife for twenty years, inveighed against lax morals and the contemporary theatre, adopted three daughters and refused to let them wear lipstick.

In 1993, the going rate in New York's 'Little Colombia' was $200, but there is clear evidence of a two-tier pricing structure: a few dollars for a punk killing and tens of thousands for a prestige Mafia job. Frank Bavosa reportedly netted $40,000 for his February 1987 attempt on Pietro Alfano in Greenwich Village. Nevertheless, Alfano survived his three bullets in the back, albeit paralysed from the waist down.

See also **Dismemberment**, **Head**, **William Gallo's**

Hoover, J. Edgar (1895–1972)

Until recently, Hoover's life provided a shining example of how an individual of almost unbelievable wrong-headedness and limitations could achieve great power. Synonymous with the core values of American society and the safety of the nation, Hoover was eulogised at his death by the Vice-President for his 'dedication to principle and complete incorruptibility'.

Perhaps more than anyone else, Hoover devoted his life to combating the organised crime syndicate whose corrupt tentacles corroded the American Way. In his view, this was the Communist Party, which he pursued tirelessly, from his paper on a 1919 bombing through to the era of Senator McCarthy and beyond.

A decade after McCarthy's demise, Hoover still had most of the FBI on Red Alert, to the extent of putting three harmless septuagenarian Greeks under surveillance for months while they played dominoes. When President **Kennedy** swept to power, Hoover still emphasised that 'The Communist Party USA presents a greater menace to the internal security of this nation than it ever has.' Robert Kennedy, the new Attorney General, riposted, 'It couldn't be more feeble and less of a threat, and besides its membership consists largely of FBI agents.'

FBI anti-Mob staffing levels were risible; in 1992 agent Bill Roemer recalled that just before Kennedy's 1960 election the ten agents assigned to organised crime in Chicago were cut to five. In New York, in 1959, four full-time operatives kept tabs on organised crime; and a hundred times as many toiled on the communist threat.

For Hoover, the 1957 syndicate conference of seventy leading *mafiosi* in **Apalachin** never took place and, when it had, all twenty-five of the FBI reports describing it were shredded. The barrage of press questioning extracted the concession that *something* was going on, leading to his memo of 27 November 1957, quaintly entitled 'The Top Hoodlum Program'. Two more years passed before Hoover finally seemed convinced. In 1959 the FBI bugged the Chicago mob, producing conclusive evidence of the 'Commission', the five leading **Mafia** families who met to arbitrate inter-gang disputes. But Hoover's campaign mysteriously lost impetus, and by 1962 he was again assuring Robert Kennedy that 'No single individual or coalition of racketeers dominated organised crime across the nation.'

Was Hoover really that boneheaded? Not necessarily. It was easier to grab headlines by bagging a few Midwestern bank robbers like John **Dillinger**, Machine-Gun Kelly and Alvin 'Creepy' Karpis, than to tackle the Mob. It was also more expedient. Strong evidence has emerged that the Director's personal life required very careful handling. Apart from the long-rumoured homosexual affair with his aide, Clyde Tolson, with whom he discreetly held hands in public, it now seems that Hoover may have been exposed to continuous Mafia blackmail.

Hoover's homosexuality was common knowledge among the Mob. The clinching detail was the photographs. William Donovan, director of the Office of Strategic Services and himself a target of Hoover's intrigues, allegedly obtained compromising pictures of Hoover and Tolson *in flagrante*, which fell into the Mafia's hands – specifically, Meyer Lansky's hands – and from then on organised crime ceased to exist. It had hardly existed before; Hoover was a long-standing associate of the mobster Frank Costello, whom he met on a regular basis, and it is likely that Costello had known his secret for years (see **Runyon**).

When the 'Top Hoodlum' programme went into reverse, Hoover was seeing a lot of the liquor baron Lewis Rosenstiel, who maintained well-established links with both Costello and Meyer Lansky. Rosenstiel shared Hoover's interest in young boys, and Rosenstiel's wife Susan has claimed that in 1958 she twice met the head of the FBI attending orgies in a private suite at New York's Plaza Hotel. On the first occasion, Hoover was 'wearing a fluffy black dress – very fluffy with flounces, and lace stockings, and high heels, and a black curly wig. He had make-up on, and false eyelashes.' At the next, he sported a red dress with a feather boa draped round his neck, and at about this period Hoover's brief campaign against the Mafia faltered. But prudent commentators have observed that the only person to see Hoover in drag was a gangster's widow, later charged with perjury, and that no photographs have survived.

There is no disputing that Hoover was a vicious blackmailer who corrupted every administration he served, and little doubt that he became increasingly deranged throughout his tenure as Director. After assuming control of the agency in 1924, he welded a corrupt and incompetent force into fearless crime fighters. But by his death, the FBI had returned to its original low morale (see **Prospects**). Neutralised by the Mob, Hoover's principal mission was to cling on to power, and to this end he accumulated enough dirt on President Kennedy's indiscretions to make his dismissal unthinkable.

First came the 1941 'Inga-Binga' tape, recording the future President making love to Inga Arvad (who may have nurtured Nazi sympathies). The year 1959 produced the Pamela Turnure recordings, succeeded by surveillance of Kennedy's relationship with Judith Exner, his use of Mob-controlled whores in Los Angeles, his contacts with Giancana, and Operation Mongoose – the Mafia plot against Castro. Then there was the Angie Dickinson recording from the flight to Palm Springs. Finally Hoover bugged the Lawford house, wiring the living room, bathroom and bedrooms (where **Monroe** and Kennedy met). All this compromising material festered in his files.

Hoover's prurient attentions ran riot over Washington in a series of reports and recordings that reduced national security to a matter of who was sleeping with whom. He degraded the FBI into thought-police, infiltrating more than fifty colleges and universities to oust teachers with left-wing leanings. By his death the Bureau held 883 files on senators and 772 on congressmen, packed with derogatory information that ensured solid support on Capitol Hill, and he broke the lives and careers of those who crossed him. Hoover lived virtually free, milking the FBI as his personal fiefdom, despatching agents to hand-deliver orchids round Washington; having the Exhibits Section do his home building work, painting and maintenance; the Radio Engineering Section to see to his home appliances; and the Recreation Fund to pay for his public relations, personal gifts, accommodation and holiday transport. He lunched gratis daily in Harvey's, one of Washington's best restaurants; at home he went to the lavatory on a special FBI invention, the heated toilet seat; and his particular brand of ice-cream, stockpiled in a basement freezer in the Justice Department, was freighted in by air. Hoover degenerated into what he had set out to destroy, Public Enemy Number One, the most dangerous man in America.

His recruitment policies were particularly unhelpful. He preferred his agents as white, conformist and Protestant – or preferably Mormon – six-footers, and denigrated Dr Martin Luther King, the black civil rights leader, as 'the most notorious liar in the country'. By 1974, after years of racial equality campaigning, one hundred of the FBI's 8,000 agents were black. Fifty were added in the following decade – in agencyspeak, mostly 'house niggers'. Hoover himself directly employed several per cent of the total, one as his chauffeur, another as receptionist and a third, Jim Amos, for old times' sake.

Such racism reflected the FBI's head-in-the-sand

approach to organised crime; it seemed almost a matter of indifference that one bunch of Italian immigrants should exploit another bunch of Italian immigrants, and by the end of Hoover's stewardship the Mafia was deeply entrenched in legitimate business. Today an older and wiser agency cracks down far more quickly on ethnic groups.

Hopkins, Matthew

Mid-seventeenth-century 'witchfinder general' and a rare English manifestation of a predominantly Continental form of hysteria. Hopkins was an Essex lawyer and, after finding an old crone in Manningtree with three teats, he arrested another thirty-one women, successfully descrying nineteen as witches. They were hanged.

Word of Hopkins's special skill spread rapidly. Soon he was paid by the head at £6 a time. He went the whole hog, resorting to 'witchpryking' and the indiscriminate throwing of suspects into ponds to see if they should be executed for floating. Hopkins hanged sixty-eight victims in Bury St Edmunds, raking in £1,000 of blood money in a single year.

In those superstitious times, witches were easy to come by. Conventional wisdom depicted them operating in tandem with a 'familiar' lent by the devil to do their dirty work. The sorcerer's apprentice might be the toad, weasel, rabbit, cat or dog that a seemingly innocuous old woman, living by herself on the edge of poverty, kept as a pet. But Hopkins interpreted the concept of 'familiars' broadly. The mere settling of a fly on a suspect's shoulder was strong evidence of guilt. For Hopkins, a 'third teat' under the arm, or elsewhere, or some other physical irregularity attendant on birth or old age furnished corroboration. He discovered that most communities had their lucrative share of witches.

Unusually, Hopkins was discredited by a courageous man of the cloth, Gaule, who denounced him from the pulpit. Gaule pointed out that torturing witches was a criminal act (or, as one judge said, reviewing the law: 'It is not a legal offence to fly through the air'). Thrown into a pond by an angry crowd, Hopkins died a year later of tuberculosis.

In Europe, men of his ilk were legion, between them responsible for perhaps hundreds of thousands of **Witchcraze** deaths. But in Britain, wrote Reginald Scot

in 1584, 'It is indifferent to say in the English tongue "she is a witch" or "she is a wise woman".'

Hopkins aside, black witches were executed, but not on a lavish scale. In 1563 it was made a capital offence to kill by witchcraft. But murder has always been against the law no matter what the method, and although James I cracked down harder on witches than his predecessor, between 1558 and 1736 (when witchcraft ceased to be a legal offence) no more than 513 cases came before the Courts of the Home Circuit and only 109 persons were hanged.

British witches had to be accused of something specific; it was not enough to just *be* a witch, and thus many English cases lacked the vague Continental razzmatazz of covens and devil worship. Margaret Harker, hanged at Tyburn in 1585, was more mundanely accused of stopping a neighbour's peas from growing by cursing a field. More dramatic cases, like John Palmer (who in 1649 *confessed* to turning himself into a toad) were rarities. In all the trials, a broomstick is mentioned only once, and Britain fell into line with Continental practice only in the late 1980s with a series of baseless satanic **ritual abuse** cases.

Horse, Nails Morton's

Samuel J. 'Nails' Morton was a citizen of style. In the trenches of the First World War he won the Croix de Guerre as a first lieutenant, leading his men over the top despite being wounded twice. In Chicago he found a niche as one of the **O'Bannion** gang, killing two policemen in a cafe, and for recreation he rode daily on the Lincoln Park bridle-paths, mingling with society equestrians.

One morning his stirrup leather parted; he fell and was kicked to death by his cantering steed. Perhaps he was not all bad: on 15 May 1923 the *Daily News* ran the headline, 'Tribute to Nails Morton: Five Thousand Jewish People attended the funeral acclaiming him protector'.

Morton's friends resolved to track down his killer and take their revenge. Two-gun Louis Alterie presented himself at the stable and rented Morton's horse. Then he trotted to the fatal spot, where the O'Bannion mob were assembled, and the horse was ceremonially executed, each gangster firing a shot into its head. Honour satisfied, Alterie telephoned the stables: 'We taught that goddamn horse of yours a lesson.'

Killing horses can be lucrative work. In the words of Tommy Burns, the leading equine hitman arrested on 2 February 1991 after nine years in the trade, 'I got paid a lot more for killing racehorses than many people get for killing people.' Burns received up to $35,000 a time from financially distressed owners anxious to claim windfall profits on their insurance. A typical victim was McBlush, a three-year-old Colt from Connecticut, valued at $100,000 but worth only fifty cents a pound as horsemeat.

Burns attached one end of an electric wire to the animal's ear with an alligator clip, the other to its rectum, and then plugged it in. 'They go immediately,' he reported.

Horse Patrol

The final solution of the English **highwayman** problem, devised by the blind John Fielding who succeeded his brother, the writer Henry **Fielding**, as Justice of the Peace at London's Bow Street in 1753. It is a story of exemplary official blundering.

After soliciting Fielding's proposals for controlling the chronic infestation of highwaymen, and then rejecting them, the government contributed £600 towards an experimental civilian Horse Patrol. Instead of the occasional mounted foray, this was full-time, and by 1763 Fielding had five two-man teams out each night patrolling London's approaches.

No one had tried to *catch* highwaymen before; the only previous recourse involved self-defence or retrospective complaint to the Bow Street Runners, who were, as their name implies, based at Bow Street in central London and in any case on foot. Fielding's men achieved dramatic results, limiting robberies to two in the first fortnight. Both villains were caught, and by the spring of 1764, for the first time in living memory, he had secured the six roads out of London.

Government reaction was swift. They pointed out that as the highways were now crime-free, little would be gained by continuing the patrol, and it was abolished despite Fielding's vociferous protests. Whereupon the relieved highwaymen returned in swarms, and by June 1764 things were as bad as ever with eight incidents in six days.

Grudgingly, the government allowed Fielding another chance. Once again, he miscarried: that is, no one was waylaid while the patrols continued, but when they withdrew his funding for the second time, the highwaymen flooded back. Clearly, the idea was a flop.

Distinguished victims of the ensuing spate of robberies included the Prime Minister, the Prince of Wales, the Duke of York, the Lord Mayor, Admiral Holborn and the Neapolitan Ambassador. Not until 1805 was the patrol reinstated, this time on a permanent footing with the addition of uniformed officers guarding the roads for ten miles round London until midnight. The scheme achieved the usual purgative results.

Hulks

Cheaper than prisons; an unseaworthy vessel could be converted into an intolerable **prison** at a fraction of the cost of a new building. With their patched sides and outcrops of platforms and lean-tos, the vessels resembled bloated slum tenements.

After 1775, the American War of Independence made the transportation of British prisoners to foreign parts problematic. As a temporary expedient, convicts awaiting shipment were packed into the hulks of a couple of motley three-deckers on the Thames.

This stopgap expedient became standard procedure. Over the years more and more criminals were sent to the hulks, until by 1816 a convict establishment of 2,500 festered in five decaying vessels; twelve years later, the total had risen to 4,446. Captain Cook's *Discovery* degraded ungracefully as a prison ship.

Captain Cook's Discovery *at Deptford, where it spent its final ten years as a convict hulk*

After arrival on board, the new prisoners were sodomised as a matter of routine and then had a fourteen-pound iron riveted to the right ankle, extinguishing any hope of escape by swimming. The following day the men were put to work on chain gangs in the Royal Dockyards. Sightseers came to gawp. Of the buggery (see **Tobacco**), Jeremy Bentham wrote: 'An initiation of this sort stands in place of garnish [tips] and is exacted with equal rigour... As the Mayor of Portsmouth, Sir John Carter, very sensibly observes, such things must ever be.'

Conditions on board were terrible. Men and boys, murderers and pickpockets were jumbled together, with the newcomer confined to the lowest of the three decks. There was no air or light, just claustrophobia and guttering candles. At night the hatches were screwed down. Gambling and disease were rife, death rampant, with fellow-prisoners encircling the dying like vultures, eyeing 'anything about the bed, so that they might take it, flannels or money'.

According to George Lee, sentenced to transportation for possession of a forged banknote, 'Nine at a time out of four hundred have lain dead on the shore, the pictures of raggedness, filth and starvation.' Typically, all the officials on board – the captain, the victuallers, the quartermaster and the jailers – were on the take. Even the surgeons were corrupt. Doctors retailed the corpses from the hospital hulk at five or six pounds apiece, and did not always strive officiously to keep their patients alive.

After 1823 the boys were held separately at Chatham on the frigate *Eurylis*, which offered a diet of gruel and potato parings, bullying, scurvy, ophthalmia and the saddest sight of all: child convicts taking silent exercise on deck, trudging round and round, like wizened monkeys.

Hurkos, Peter (b. 1911)

A Dutch psychic detective born with a caul over his head, in Britain superstitiously regarded as evidence that the child is proof against drowning and in Holland a touchstone for the sixth sense. Hurkos showed no exceptional abilities until 1941, when he fell thirty feet off a ladder while painting a house and banged his head.

Coming round, Hurkos found that he had lost his memory but gained X-ray vision. By handling a person's belongings (or making a 'pass' over them with his sensitive hands) he could receive an accurate impression of the owner's personality and background, a process called 'psychometry'.

His local reputation for the recovery of missing objects and people spread, and in 1958 the Miami police called for his assistance in the case of a murdered cab driver. Hurkos flew to Miami and installed himself in the deceased's taxi to soak up a psychic portrait of the killer; he intuited that the culprit was a mariner known as Smitty. Strange to tell, a sailor called Smith was later convicted.

On 29 January 1964, Hurkos came to the aid of the police hunting the Boston Strangler (see **Insatiable**). Presented with 300 case-photographs to study, he placed them face down on a table and scrutinised them carefully by passing his hands over their blank backs. Then he described their contents to the detectives. They knew Hurkos was right because they could look at the photographs face up, and he convinced his remaining detractors when an officer arrived late, claiming that his car had broken down. Not so, said Hurkos, and correctly detailed how the latecomer had stopped to make love to his girlfriend, a divorcee in her late twenties, on her kitchen table.

Six days of gruelling telepathic immersion followed. Hurkos shed fifteen pounds as he seeped into the killer's psyche. Then he 'saw' the murderer. 'I lived through the killings,' he recalled later, 'I lived through the mind of that man.' He presented a detailed description to the police; the suspect weighed 130 to 140 pounds and was slightly built with a pointed nose and a scar on his left arm. 'And he loves shoes.'

So the police picked up a door-to-door shoe salesman, 'Thomas P. O'Brien' (real name withheld). After a face-to-face confrontation with Hurkos, he opted for voluntary psychiatric confinement in the Massachusetts State Mental Centre, and has stayed there ever since. As Hurkos predicted, the killings stopped – until October when Albert DeSalvo was arrested after the final 'Strangler' murder.

Since then Hurkos concentrated on his work as a clairvoyant in the entertainment industry, although he contributed briefly to the 1968 **Manson** case on behalf of the friends of victim Jay Sebring, the hair stylist. A week after the slayings, Hurkos visited the house at 10050 Cielo Drive to cadge some Polaroids of the murder scene from a *Life* photographer. He told the press: 'Three men killed Sharon Tate and the other four and I know who they are. I have identified the killers to the police.' The officers never logged his information, whatever it was, and in due course one man and three women were identified as the murderers. To the papers, Hurkos enlarged that the slayings erupted during a black magic ritual of 'goona goona'.

The author is unaware of any murder case irrefutably solved by psychic intervention.

Hypnosis and crime

Can a person be hypnotised into committing murder? Until the mid-twentieth century, most psychiatrists would have answered no. Then a case came along that proved them wrong.

At 10.15 a.m. on 29 March 1951, a young man in overalls entered the Landsmans Bank in Copenhagen, Denmark, and fired a revolver at the ceiling. Then he tossed a briefcase to Kaj Moller, the chief cashier, and ordered him to fill it with money. When Moller took a step backward, he was shot through the heart. The bandit then gave the same order to the manager, Nils Wisbom. He made the mistake of ducking and was shot through the head. Then, as an alarm sounded, the killer walked calmly from the bank, with an oddly stiff walk, to a padlocked bicycle, on which he rode off into the traffic.

He was followed by a 14-year-old boy, also on a bike. Four miles away, the boy followed the man into a house, whereupon the robber pointed his gun at him, then changed his mind about using it, muttering something about his good angel having deserted him. The boy ran away and flagged down a police car. The building was surrounded and the young man arrested. He gave his name as Palle Hardrup, 28, and had a gun in his pocket. It seemed the police had the bank killer.

Then Chief Inspector Christiansen, in charge of the case, received a tip from a man who asked someone to meet him in a waterfront bar. What the man had to say sounded incredible. It was that, although Hardrup had fired the gun, it was another man who had really pulled the trigger. This other man was called Bjorn Nielsen, and – said the informant – he had a complete psychological hold over Hardrup, who was, in effect, his obedient slave.

They had met in prison, where both had been serving time as Nazi collaborators. That was where the

informant had met them. It was clear that Hardrup was totally dominated by Nielsen and would even give him the meat out of his soup. Nielsen often chalked 'X' marks on the walls, and when Hardrup saw these his eyes would go blank.

The police checked on Nielsen. He proved to be a man of around 40, with a square jaw and deep-set eyes, and had an unshakeable alibi: he had been staying at a hotel in the country with a red-headed dancer at the time of the bank hold-up.

When Nielsen was brought face to face with Hardrup in the presence of Christiansen, it became obvious that Hardrup would say and do whatever he thought Nielsen wanted him to – particularly when Nielsen sat with crossed arms. Nielsen, Hardrup insisted, had nothing to do with the robbery. Nor with an earlier hold-up in the town of Hvidhovre the previous August, when a man later identified as Hardrup had walked out with 61,000 kroner.

An interview with Hardrup's wife, Bente, revealed the extent of Nielsen's domination. Because she told her husband she detested Nielsen and wished he would stop seeing him, Nielsen had torn off her clothes in front of Hardrup and beaten her with his belt, while her normally loving and protective husband simply looked on unmoved. Bente insisted that Nielsen had 'put a spell' on her husband.

She also produced the manuscript of a novel written by Nielsen and her husband, which she had been ordered to type. It was about a sinister politician who totally dominates a weaker man and gets him to commit crimes. But it is the weak man who goes to prison and dies by starving himself to death.

It was this that finally convinced the police psychiatrist, Dr Max Schmidt, that Hardrup had been hypnotised to obey Nielsen like an obedient dog.

But how to de-hypnotise him? Schmidt thought a shock might do it, such as certifying him incurably insane, which would mean a life in a lunatic asylum.

Hardrup was given the medical certificate declaring him insane. His reaction was to shout, 'I'm not crazy. How can anyone say that?' Then he became depressed and brooded for days. Finally, he stopped eating. But after five days of starvation, he asked the guard for a pencil and paper. He began to write the story of his relationship with Nielsen – how, in despair at the defeat of Nazism, in which he believed with religious fervour, he had been given hope when Nielsen told him that all was not yet lost. Together they would create a new political party. He, Nielsen, would be Hardrup's good angel. He then hypnotised Hardrup and told him that whenever he saw the 'X' sign, it was God reminding him of his vow of obedience.

Before he finished his 'confession', his vow of obedience had reasserted itself and he broke off. But what he had said was enough for the prosecutor, who presented his case on 14 July 1954, at the beginning of a three-day trial, during which Hardrup showed himself to be once again under Nielsen's domination. But the jury found Nielsen guilty of Hardrup's crimes, and he was sentenced to life imprisonment. Hardrup, found guilty but not responsible, was transferred to a psychiatric clinic.

Identification evidence

The **Tichborne** Case suggests that, given flair, the similarity required for successful imposture need not be close, a historical deduction confirmed in 1990 by journalist John Louvet on his release by Austrian border command. For months, Louvet travelled round Europe with a picture of his cocker spaniel 'Chummy' as his passport photograph, said by the police to be a 'very good likeness'.

The converse ability to recognise a person from a photograph does not always come naturally. In November 1942 an unknown woman's body, the victim of a vicious strangling, was found near Luton, naked in the shallows of the River Lea, loosely covered in sacking, ankles trussed together and knees strapped to her chest. The left-hand side of her face was crushed by a single blow, but she had probably survived the attack for another half hour; her legs bore traces of bruising from the tight ropes (showing that she was still alive when her lower limbs were bound) but there were no corresponding marks by the time her assailant secured her arms. The woman wore no clothes, no jewellery, no ring and no teeth – even her dentures had been removed. Her blood group was the common 0, she lacked any distinguishing characteristics or deformities, and carried no trace of foreign fibres or hairs.

As an identification aid, the victim's good side was photographed in profile but, despite post-mortem refurbishment, her features were coarsened by the facial bruising, and the pictures must have been as unintelligible as train announcements.

The photographs were shown by the police house-to-house, and the dead woman's sons, aged 14 and 15, failed to recognise their mother, although they had inklings – quashed by their father, the murderer. But the 17-year-old daughter saw the likeness advertised on a cinema screen without evincing so much as a flicker of recognition. Neighbours shook their heads blankly after studying the photographs. Nine times the corpse was wrongly identified, as four different people.

Eventually a name was put to the body by a dry cleaner's tag. The methodical Detective Chief Inspector Chapman had ordered the collection of all the bits of clothing and rags dumped in local garbage tips and dustbins around the date of the killing. Three months into the investigation, the whole collection was minutely re-examined, producing a distinctive section of black coat with a dyer's tag still attached. The trail led to the local branch of Sketchley's, and their books provided the customer's name: Rene Manton. Conclusive evidence was furnished by her dental records.

It took only two days to pin the murder on the husband, Bertie Manton. During an argument on 18 November, she had flung a scalding cup of hot tea in

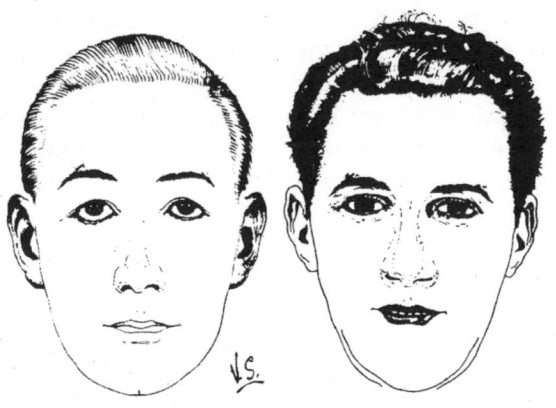

Alternative identikits issued after the A6 mruder. Valerie Storie's version (left) and other witnesses' (right). Although better than nothing, they unleashed hundreds of false sightings

his face, shouting, 'I hope it blinds you.' Manton lost his temper and smashed her head with a heavy wooden stool, but had the presence of mind to tidy up before the children returned from school. He told them Rene had gone to visit their grandmother, and that evening disposed of the body by wheeling it through town, wrapped in sacks on his bicycle's handlebars. The next morning, thinking her departure in midwinter without a coat might look odd, he cut it into pieces and discarded it in a dustbin.

Sentenced to death, Manton was pardoned by the King after presentation of a 26,000-signature petition for clemency. He attempted to preserve the fiction of his wife as still alive by mailing himself letters 'from' her. The messages made mention of Hampstead, misspelled without the 'p' and, in classic style, Chief Inspector Chapman asked Manton to write a sentence in which 'Hamstead' duly appeared.

Even under favourable conditions, eye-witness identifications have long been a source of disquiet. The most troubling recent British case involved a balaclava, the headgear surmounting all four men who burst into the home of 74-year-old Robert Forrest on 17 June 1989. Only the burglars' eyes and mouths were visible through the slits.

Under normal circumstances this might make the robbers hard to recognise. But the tallest intruder wore a black leather jacket, and when Forrest was asked by the police whether anyone in the identification parade 'resembled' his assailants, he saw one who did: the only man in a black leather jacket, unlucky Robert Campbell, now serving five years for armed robbery. The only other evidence against Campbell was an ambiguous confession, later retracted.

In 1992 Professor Graham Davies of Leicester University conducted a scientific study to resolve the thorny issue of whether it is easier to recognise people when their faces are visible. Apparently it is. Professor Davies explains his theory thus: 'The face is the primary source of identification for identification purposes. If you are deprived of that information, you are forced back on other clues, such as voice and body movements, and your chances of making a mistake go up.' The professor convinced doubters by staging a dummy burglary, showing that the ability to recognise hooded raiders rated no higher than chance.

See also **Bloodstains**, **Doyle**, **Fingerprints**, **Genetic fingerprinting**, **Teethmarks** and individual cases.

Inflatable dolls

Beware of imitation women; they are not the same. The Canadian Robert Poulin tried to wriggle off the horns of his dilemma in 1975 by purchasing a blow-up doll. In high hopes he wrote in his diary: 'I no longer think that I will have to rape a girl.'

But he was wrong: the inflatable proved a disappointment. So in October 1975 the 18-year-old Poulin raped and killed schoolgirl Kim Rabat. Then he shot seven classmates before committing suicide, turning the gun on himself.

Canadians have carved out a niche in schoolroom slayings. On 6 December 1989, Marc Lepine entered Room 230 in Montreal University armed with a Sturm Ruger semi-automatic rifle. He separated the women students at gunpoint, ordered the men to leave, and then told the nine female engineering majors that he was there 'to fight against feminists'.

'But we're not feminists,' one student demurred. Then Lepine pulled the trigger, spraying out a thirty-shot clip. Six died. Lepine shot another one in the corridor, three more in the cafeteria, and four in Room 311. Then he removed his anorak, wrapped it round the gun barrel and shot himself upwards through the head. His baseball cap flew off.

Lepine was a 25-year-old at the end of his road. As a child, he was thrashed by his father; as an adult, he was rejected by Montreal University, by the Army and by his girlfriend. His suicide note jumbled up a pathetic desire to appear intelligent with a vendetta against women.

Lepine wrote: 'I continued my studies in a haphazard way for they never really interested me, knowing in advance my fate. Which did not prevent me from obtaining very good marks despite not handing in my theory works and the lack of studying before exams ... The other day, I heard they were honouring the Canadian men and women who fought at the front line during world wars. How can you explain then that women were not authorised to go to the front line? Will we hear Caesar's female legions and female galley slaves who of course took up fifty per cent of the ranks of history, though they never existed.'

His points are no less misconceived than many notions aired in the newspaper correspondence columns, and in fact Lepine sent his suicide note to Francine Pelletier, a columnist for *La Presse*. But Lepine did not kill to get in the papers. Like most mass murderers, he exacted revenge on his supposed oppressors; and he had no desire for them to be any better off than he was shortly to become. As Charles Starkweather said after his 1958 murder rampage across Nebraska and Wyoming: 'Dead people are all on the same level.'

See also **Luby's Cafeteria**, **Terminology**

Informality

American procedure permits judges greater latitude for homilies than their British counterparts. After condemning serial killer Ted **Bundy** to death, the judge continued: 'Take care of yourself, young man. I say that to you sincerely. It's a tragedy to this court to see such a total waste of humanity. You're a bright young man. You'd have made a good lawyer. I'd have loved to have you practise in front of me. I bear you no animosity, believe me. You went the wrong way, partner. Take care of yourself.'

British courts occasionally dispense career advice, notably in 1977 when the Recorder of York Crown Court awarded Mr Philip McCutcheon a conditional discharge, saying: 'I think you should give burglary up. You have a withered hand, an artificial leg and only one eye. You have been caught in Otley, Leeds, Harrogate, Norwich, Beverley, Hull and York. How can you hope to succeed?'

But this is mere badinage compared to the conduct of Judge Fleet of Miami, as reported in the *Daily Post* of 3 July 1992. He opened fire in court, loosing two bullets from his .45 across the accused's head before sentencing him to five years, goaded beyond endurance by the defendant's cry of defiance from the dock after hearing the verdict of 'guilty'.

'Judge Fleet is a bastard, and if I had a gun I would kill him,' Mynette shouted, whereupon the judge produced his weapon, drew a bead on the prisoner and said: 'Get down on your knees – or I will condemn you to death and execute you here and now.' Then he fired his warning shots.

In England, this sort of lapse would never do; nor would the tear jerking that intermittently vitiated the **Dahmer** trial of 1992, when the prosecution handed round photographic portraits of each of the fifteen victims. Since there was no dispute about whether Dahmer had killed them or who they were, the exercise was scarcely germane. Nor could the ritual of allowing relatives of the deceased to hurl abuse at the convicted man prior to sentencing be said to contribute greatly to judicial objectivity.

Ingram, Paul R. (1945–)

America's showcase satanic **ritual abuse** (SRA) offender. For the seventeen years before his 1989 conviction, Ingram led a blameless life in the sheriff's office of Olympia, Washington.

In the late 1970s, the Ingram family found itself drawn to Pentecostalism. Paul was a stern father, and his two daughters, Erika and Julie (born in 1966 and 1970 respectively), were shy with boys. During three years in her late teens, Erika dated only twice, and in August 1988 the sisters attended a two-day retreat sponsored by the Church of Living Water. A charismatic facilitator, Karla Franko, enlightened the teenage audience about sexual abuse, and after the session a number of tremulous girls, Erika among them, declared themselves victims.

Erika left home, telling her mother that she had endured years of forced sex from her father and her two brothers. 'You're the only one who didn't know,' she said. But neither she nor Julie could tell if their ordeal had ceased ten years ago or last month. Apparently traumatised, they only responded to questions after lengthy pauses, and on 28 November 1988 their bemused father was charged. Anxious to co-operate, Ingram said, 'If this did happen, we need to take care of it', and, at his first interrogation, he produced halting snippets like 'I would have removed her clothing'. The police psychologist assured him that, once he confessed, his misdeeds would come flooding back.

Meanwhile Julie wrote to her teacher: 'A lot of men would come over and play poker with my dad, and they would all get drunk and one or two at a time would come into my room to have sex with me.' So a sex ring of paedophiles was at large and, in a gruelling interview, Ingram tried to 'visualise' the rapes. 'I just don't see anything,' he said, enjoined to remember his friends having sex with Julie tied to a bed. 'Let me see if I can get in there. Assuming it happened, she would have had a bed, bedroom, by herself I would think… Uh…' Ten-minute silences came and went while he cudgelled his brains. The interrogators exhorted him to 'choose life over living death', crying, 'God has given you the tools to do this.'

At full stretch, Ingram saw the past, envisioning Julie with her hands tied to her feet. He noticed 'a penis sticking up in the air'. Asked if anyone was taking pictures, he replied, 'Uh, it's possible, let me look. I see, I see a camera … I don't see a person behind that camera … Well, the person that I see is Ray Risch.' So his friend Risch was arrested, and Jim Rabie too, the man behind the waving organ. Ingram said, 'Boy, it's almost like I'm making it up. But I'm not.'

When Rabie was charged, the police pointed out that he remained in the 'denial stage'. 'I must be,' replied Rabie, 'because I honestly do not have any recollection of it happening.' Meanwhile, Ingram reflected, 'If I can't remember this, then I am so dangerous I do not deserve to be let loose.' Soon his **memory** was on the mend, aided by Pastor Bratun who, on 2 December, exorcised his demons. First Ingram remembered that he was the Green River killer. Then he 'saw' Rabie raping his son, Chad. Under questioning, Chad spoke of his childhood dreams: 'People outside my window looking in … short people walking on me.' They reminded him of the Seven Dwarfs.

'You want to believe it's dreams,' urged Detective Schoening. 'You don't want to believe it's real. It was real, Chad.' Well-versed in the ways of SRA, the officers realised that Chad suffered from 'destruction of his sense of reality … total, absolute subservience to the group', and in due course Chad agreed. Conditioned to obliterate the years of abuse, he had not dreamed of having a cloth stuffed in his mouth. It was a real penis. Paul's wife, Sandy, wondered if she too had blanked the past. 'Has my life been a lie? Have I been brainwashed, oppressed – controlled – without knowing it?' she asked her diary in December 1988.

Under further prompting, Erika and Julie hinted at their mother's involvement. 'She'd just watch,' said Erika at first. Afraid of being branded 'in denial', Sandy sought solace from Pastor Bratun. He told her that she was '80 per cent evil', recommending confession, and on 18 December the police located the eldest of the Ingram children, Paul Ross, living in Reno. Paul hated his father, saying 'I'd like to shoot my dad', and depicted a horrific scene glimpsed through a door. His mother was tied to her bed. 'Jim Rabie was screwing her and his dad had his dick in her mouth,' the detectives recorded. Ray Risch and another man were there too, 'jacking each other off'.

But Paul did not think that he, or Erika and Julie, had been molested. Indeed, the Ingrams all remembered different things and, in frustration, Detective Schoening backed Paul against the wall, shouting 'We know you're a victim'. But if Paul was stuck in denial, Erika continued in full flow. Too damaged to answer verbally, she took to writing notes: 'Then he urinated all over my body in bed. He didn't defecate on me this time.'

Meanwhile, Ingram wavered, taking sexual deviation tests in triplicate, basing answers on (i) how he would have replied before his arrest, (ii) before being exorcised by Pastor Bratun, and (iii) afterwards. His results ranged from normal to a monster, but he was keener than ever to be punished after Erika submitted an essay on the full-blown satanic ceremonies he conducted in regalia. Skeletal excerpts read, 'middle of the night … high priestess … dad wore a gown and a hat resembling a viking hat with horns … blood everywhere … sacrifice … chant … baby … dead … They would say, "You will not remember this."'

On 23 January 1989, in disclosures transcribed by a friend, Erika divulged: 'My father made me perform sexual acts with animals including goats and dogs.' But as the case entered its pre-trial phase, the prosecution's testimony was muddled. Julie hid under a table when questioned by attorneys, Erika described the sacrifice of twenty-five babies, and the Thurston County Sheriff's office compiled a wall-chart of Satan's underground, with 225 interconnected headings like 'phibinite cult', 'heavy metal', 'eating faeces', 'urban hysteria', 'buried alive with insects and snakes', 'killing babies', 'eating pets', and 'you will die if you remember'. The Sheriff was overawed by the conspiracy's sheer scale, musing 'It isn't just a matter of people running around and killing babies … When you look at the chart, don't you more or less go, like "Wow"?'

Asked to explain the mind-control devices 'scrambling' the suspects' memories, a Dr Richard Ofshe demonstrated that Ingram was highly suggestible, with an ability to float into trance states and a desire to please authority. He 'remembered' to order. Ofshe suspected a mass folly initiated by the sisters, who unleashed avalanches of new allegations to cover old inconsistencies, outraging one detective so much that, at a court hearing, a private detective had to mount guard in case he tried to shoot the defendants. But Ofshe could not persuade Ingram to recant and, on 13 April 1989, after a convulsive effort, he retrieved the

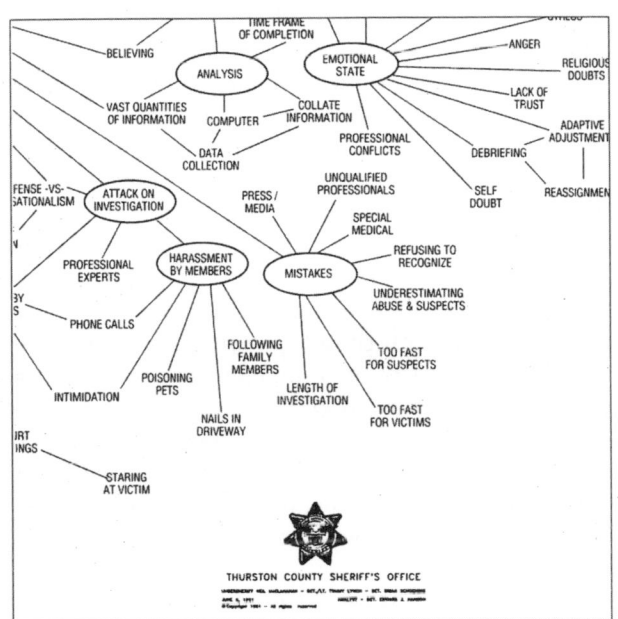

Satan's underground. A corner of the official chart showing how it all fits together

names of ten cultists in the Sheriff's office acting in collusion with the canine unit. Their dogs had raped his wife.

The Sheriff, by now famous on the SRA workshop circuit, lauded the investigation as the first case 'confirmed by an adult offender in the nation's history', and Ingram happily pleaded guilty to six counts of third-degree rape. Then, awaiting sentence, he started a log dividing his recollections into three categories: 'Definitely happened', 'Not so definitely happened', and 'Not sure'. On 19 July, while at prayer, a voice said, 'Let go the rope', and he realised that he had made everything up.

In April 1990, before sentencing, Ingram told the court: 'I stand before you, I stand before God. I have never sexually abused my daughters. I am not guilty of these crimes.' To the judges, he sounded like any other rapist, and they gave him twenty years. 'Satanic abuse is real,' commented the Sheriff, 'this case proves it.'

Initiation rites

The day he gets 'made' is a big one for a *mafioso*. In the typical ritual of the Philadelphia mob (now virtually destroyed), the ceremony was marked by a summons to a luxurious gang house where forty confederates awaited his arrival, seated round a long table sumptuously laden with meatballs, olives and spaghetti.

The *capo* at the head of the table formally demanded of the newcomer: 'Do you know why you're here?', expecting and receiving a 'no'. Next the recruit was advised to disclose any 'bad feelings' about anyone present; again, the prudent response was in the negative. A recitation followed of his working contribution to the family, after which the invitation to join – 'to be one of us' – was extended, together with a token assurance that he could decline and leave as a 'friend'.

Some ceremonial business with the gun and knife lying on the table ensued: would he use these for his colleagues? Yes. Clutching a lighted tissue paper, the new member intoned: 'May I burn like the saints in hell if I ever betray my friends.' For the closing formalities his trigger finger was ritually pricked; then, after kissing his associates, the assembled hoods fell to feasting. Thereafter, the rules were elucidated: no kidnapping, no counterfeiting, no drug dealing on your own behalf. Striking another member meant death. And never so much as look at another member's wife (see **Contempt**).

According to Nick 'The Crow' Caramandi, now under the witness protection scheme: 'It's a strong, deep and very meaningful ceremony. Here are forty guys, we're all killers and we're all one. The ceremony's gorgeous. It's just beautiful. It's a sacred thing. You pray together. We all hold hands.' Salvatore Contorno, inducted in Sicily in 1975, outlined a similar ritual, except that he held a burning picture of a saint; the blood from his finger trickled over the image as it crumbled into ashes.

From that day on, the respect shown by non-members to the new *mafioso* is palpable. His life alters fundamentally. Instead of subjecting the general public to beatings, murder and extortion to gain peer approval, his focus shifts to in-fighting, eliminating rivals in a scramble to expedite promotion: a sort of do-it-yourself dead man's shoes.

Hangmen, too, observe rites of passage, and a British ceremony, now defunct, commemorated the initiation of a public executioner. Probably the last inductee was William Calcraft in 1829, when, after his successful candidacy, he was greeted by the traditional conclave of berobed dignitaries bearing their insignia of office. The Lord Mayor, the Sheriffs and City Marshal, the Governor of Newgate, a Crown Judge and the Town Crier, together with a host of minor functionaries, waited in fearsome solemnity while the bell tolled the funeral knell. Then the Sheriff commanded, 'Bring in a well-sharpened axe', whereupon it was borne in by the Keeper of the Axe. 'Bring in the usual leg-irons, handcuffs and other fetters,' he continued, and these articles were proffered by the Keeper of the Irons. 'Now,' directed the Sheriff, 'bring in the halter and a pair of white caps and the beheading knife.' These too were produced by the relevant Keeper, and at this stage the 'candidate' entered, taking his oath of office kneeling, with his left hand on the axe and his right hand on the Bible, while the Judge kept the great sword of justice poised over him.

After Calcraft had completed the oath, which began with the words, 'I do most solemnly swear to hang or behead, or otherwise destroy, all felons of our Lord the King', a veil bestowing theoretical anonymity was draped over his head and he was hounded out of the assemblage to general groans, with the Judge's final injunction ringing in his ears: 'Get thee hence, wretch!'

Injection, lethal

The lethal injection of today is machine-administered, its operation regulated by a computerised control console fronted with a burnished steel fascia peppered with flashing lights. The contraption is the invention of Fred A. Leuchter, a professional 'execution technologist' who supplies equipment complete with a 'Manual of Operation'.

The business end of the machine embodies a firing sequence of three syringes delivering chemicals into the bloodstream through a single manifold. The first injection of sodium pentothal puts the victim to sleep, the second paralyses his respiratory system, and a final shot of potassium chloride stops the heart. Within nine minutes the prisoner is dead.

Does this hurt? No, but it must be the only part of the sanitised process that is painless. Missouri ordered the first machine in 1988. It came with a full maintenance contract, and fifteen prison officials attended a training course on the theory and practice of execution, compiling a step-by-step guidebook known as the 'Missouri Protocol', now in its thirteenth edition. The manual governs everything that happens to the prisoner from his first isolation in the 'Death Watch' cell to the order for two warders simultaneously to depress the buttons – one of them redundant – to initiate the injection process.

This final act generates huge antecedent requirements in terms of press witnesses, staff witnesses, duty rotas, extra staffing, machine preparation, dress rehearsals, paperwork, medicals, legal appeals and additional security, and the Missouri Protocol covers the countdown in such detail that it is now standard throughout America. A refinement under consideration for the fourteenth edition is the installation of an intercom so that witnesses divided from the death chamber by glass panels can hear the reading of the death warrant. This is followed by the last exchange, 'Do you have anything to say?' and then, 'God bless you.'

Despite the attention to procedural niceties, it is hard for the condemned man to overlook the fact that he is being killed, particularly during his last half-hour as he lies strapped to a trolley with a plug in his anus and a needle in his arm, watching the clock tick the seconds away, waiting for the stay of execution that may still come while his friends and relatives gaze from the far side of the windows.

The first to die from a lethal injection was Missouri's 'Tiny' Mercer in January 1989. When Billy White, a 34-year-old rubbish van driver, was 'turned off' in Huntsville prison on 23 April 1992, medical attendants ferreted around for some forty minutes to find a vein for the needle. White, even then, must have had hopes.

See also **Lunette**

In-laws

A perennial source of detestation. In 1955 Lincoln Sayre of West Virginia decided that he had tolerated his for too long. He resolved to kill his four brothers- and sisters-in-law in one clean sweep.

Sayre was a violent alcoholic who felt that the twenty-four years his relatives spent persuading his wife Hazel to leave him were more than enough. After she walked out for good on 25 August 1955, Sayre moped for five weeks and then, on 30 September, stole a friend's high-powered Japanese hunting rifle fitted with telescopic sights.

For an alibi he faked a hunting trip for wild boar; he would 'return' after his weekend in the woods to be greeted by the news that Phloe Johnson, Alice Martin, Vance Grimes and Elmer Grimes (all of whom he was known to hate) had been slain in four isolated attacks by a mysterious gunman. Sayre supposed that he could talk his way out of any suspicion; after all, he harboured no designs on his mother-in-law and the rifle did not belong to him.

On the morning of 30 September, Sayre was duly seen driving out of town. He doubled back through the woods in his pickup, and at 9.18 that evening he was crouching outside the window of prim Phloe Johnson. While he waited, Phloe entered the living room for her evening tipple of soda and, as she lowered herself into her favourite rocking chair, Sayre shot her through the mouth. A woman came running to the door of the next house. It was Alice Martin. Down went number two, hit in the throat, and Sayre loped away to the home of Vance Grimes, a block away.

Here he encountered his first hitch. Vance had unexpectedly gone out for the evening. So Sayre hurried to nearby Robertsburg to kill Elmer, loosing off a fusillade of shots as his target traversed a window. Then he hightailed it for the woods.

But Sayre had missed Elmer, albeit by inches, so his tally stayed at two. As so often in murder, **detection** took several seconds: the sobbing mother-in-law told the police, 'It was Lincoln Sayre. Nobody else would have done such a thing.' Ballistic evidence tied the bullet to a gun reported missing from his friend's back porch, and on investigation Old Mammy Cole, who worked locally, said she saw Sayre running off with the weapon that morning.

Coming in from the wilds the following evening, Sayre overheard the townsfolk discussing his imminent arrest. He fled, and early the next morning committed suicide.

See also **Oral hygiene treatment**

Inquisition, The

In Sicily, the Inquisition assumed a particularly invidious form. In the absence of any real religious dissent, its heretical net widened to snare bigamists, philosophers, usurers, carnal priests, parvenus and eventually anyone with more money than they needed.

Membership of the Inquisition was restricted to the aristocracy and, on conviction, all the defendant's property was forfeit. So the cult represented oppression of the poor by the rich: arrests on suspicion, an accused presumed guilty, a prosecutor doubling as judge, and a defendant precluded from calling women, children or servants as witnesses in his support – although they could testify against him. Nor was legal representation permissible, since it constituted a seditious challenge to the Inquisition's authority.

For three centuries Sicily groaned under the yoke of religious predators, never fewer than 2,000 of them, whose dominion helped maintain feudalism. The only shield against their random depredations was a subversive brotherhood based on respect for natural justice and true honour, an honoured society or, in other words, the **Mafia** – a term possibly derived from the Arabic word meaning 'place of refuge'.

In later years, the Sicilian Mafia did quite nicely itself. In October 1992, Palermo police confiscated the property of one local family, the Madonias, seizing sixty-two legitimate businesses, 160 apartments, six boats, 202 cars and forty-three plots of land with an aggregate value of $400 million. Since the Madonias are one of two dozen local clans battening on the region, it is not surprising that parts of downtown Palermo, bled dry, look as though they have just been bombed. Indeed, many buildings destroyed by the hostilities of 1943 remain untouched.

Insane

Under English law, a defendant is presumed innocent until proven guilty or insane. This is quite distinct from the technical defence of madness under the McNaghten rules, where the accused avoids *criminal* punishment, a risky defence since it often prefixes an indefinite stay in a secure hospital.

But actual insanity can carry even more drastic repercussions. Here, the accused may be found guilty whether or not he committed the offence. A deranged defendant is adjudged 'unfit to plead': he cannot say whether he wishes to contest the charge, so there can be no trial (see **Pressing**). Detention in psychiatric prison follows. In other words, the mere bringing of the accusation results in a custodial sentence without the customary preliminary of a hearing.

There are only some fifteen English cases a year, which can produce the exciting result of prolonged incarceration for trivial offences the accused may not have committed or, worse, which have not been committed at all. In 1986 Glenn Pearson was sent down indefinitely on a charge of stealing £5 and three lightbulbs, and in 1987 Valerie Hodgson acquired a certain notoriety following release from Wakefield's Newton Lodge secure unit. Two years previously she had confessed to stabbing her father to death and, being mentally handicapped and thus unfit to plead, the court never considered whether she actually had killed anyone. She had not, but this took two years to find out.

In 1992 a sharp-eyed social worker, John Wasson, stumbled on a similar American case. He realised that 94-year-old Junius Wilson, who is black, was not mad but deaf. Wilson was confined to a mental home for sixty-seven years after being branded 'unfit to plead' to a charge of attempted rape in North Carolina. Judging by Jim Montgomery's story (see **Attorneys**), Wilson's 1925 crime may have been a fiction, but despite the absence of a trial he suffered the standard penalty for the period, castration. Prudent British psychiatric cases should likewise take pains never to indulge in mindless acts of petty arson. If the court considers the accused 'of unstable character', it may imprison him for life.

In principle, such a sentence allows the Home Secretary to order the prisoner's early release on recovery – a power he lacks with fixed-term sentences. In practice, petitions are rejected since they entail proving a negative: the appellant must show that he is no longer dangerous. But this proposition is only demonstrable retrospectively, after death.

So he disappears into the bowels of the prison service. Among the missing are a Mr Thornton (Christian name unknown), jailed for life in 1974 after igniting the curtains in a hospital interview room. Also sunk without trace is one Ellis Blogg, last seen in 1980 at his sentencing for burning down a cardboard box.

Insatiable

One of the few **sex** killers motivated largely by sex was the Boston Strangler. The normal sex murder represents the fulfilment of other needs by sexual means, with impotence looming large as a precipitating factor. But Albert Henry DeSalvo (1931–73), the Boston Strangler, suffered from *penile dementia*. He wanted sex all the time. He could make love once and then, right away, do it again. Compulsive recourse to sex, intermingled with casual brutality, permeated his upbringing. His father would bring back prostitutes and take his pleasure in front of the children. He beat his wife senseless, and once broke her fingers one by one. DeSalvo had intercourse with his sisters and, as he matured, wanted sex with any woman he met. His prowess was unusual in matching his desires and, rather than becoming assimilated into a civilising framework, it made a stable relationship unsustainable.

Word of DeSalvo's mesmeric abilities first began to circulate in 1948 when he was a 17-year-old vacationer at Cape Cod. College girls 'would even come up to the motel sometimes looking for me and some nights we would spend the whole night doing it down

Albert DeSalvo inside

on the beach, stopping for a while, then doing it again'. During Army service in Germany, DeSalvo married a Frankfurt girl, but his demands for intercourse six times a day soon exhausted her libido, and his hypersexuality burgeoned into a hideous affliction.

In 1956, a year after he was charged with molesting a nine-year-old girl, DeSalvo settled in Boston. He did the rounds of apartment blocks, persuading women to open their doors to him as a talent scout for a model agency. He took their vital statistics, sometimes with mild molestation and sometimes procuring consensual sex by offering photographic assignments. The police dubbed him the 'Measuring Man'. He was caught on 17 March 1960, sentenced to two years for 'lewd and lascivious behaviour', and released a year later. But his offence was classified as 'breaking and entering'.

Between 14 June 1962 and 4 January 1964, thirteen Boston women were strangled, often after being raped repeatedly – an attribute which might have directed attention towards DeSalvo. The attacker posed as a workman and left his victims ritually displayed with a crude bow tied around the neck with a housecoat, stocking or pillow case. Several victims were sexually assaulted with bottles, and the first five were elderly, aged between 55 and 85. Sometimes investigators found the intruder had ejaculated almost everywhere apart from the vagina, on breasts, thighs and the carpet. But after the killing of Mary Sullivan, the murders ceased.

A rapist continued in operation, an altogether gentler man who occasionally relented and often apologised, and on 27 October he abandoned an assault on a Massachusetts housewife with the words, 'You be quiet for ten minutes … I'm sorry.' His polite demeanour reminded detectives of the 'Measuring Man', and the artist's impression was, for once, clearly recognisable. On arrest, DeSalvo was identified by one of his victims, and routine distribution of his photograph to neighbouring forces precipitated hundreds of complaints about similar incidents by a 'Green Man', named after the colour of his trousers. Police put the number of assaults at 300; DeSalvo estimated his total at 2,000, and both agree that on 6 May 1964 he attacked four women in four different Connecticut towns.

But the Boston Strangler was still believed at large. The city remained in the grip of hysteria, and a Brockton housewife died of fright when a stranger knocked on her door selling encyclopedias. The *Boston Advertiser* offered counselling in an 'Appeal to the Strangler', advising, 'Don't kill again. Come to us for help. You are a sick man.' By then a psychological team had drawn up a complicated **profile** of two or more killers, discernible by their different methodology. Only Dr Brussel, of **Mad Bomber** fame, united their exploits under the umbrella of a single individual with shifting behaviour patterns. 'Over the two-year period

during which he has been committing these murders,' Brussel reported, 'he has gone through a series of upheavals – or, to put it another way, a single progressive upheaval. What has happened to him, in two words, is instant maturity. In this two-year period, he has grown, psychosexually, from infancy to puberty.' Brussel detected a classic victim of the Oedipus Complex. DeSalvo's early concentration on the elderly represented a 'search for potency'. Theoretically, the rapist's unconscious desire for his mother had left him impotent, an inference reinforced by his assaults with broom handles and bottles. The Boston Strangler sought to expunge his mother's image by murdering older women, and the switch to younger women, initiated by his killing of 20-year-old Sophie Clark on 5 December 1962, showed that he had 'found his potency'. So the Boston Strangler was cured: 'This came about, of course, in the most horrible way possible. He had to commit these murders to achieve his growth. It was his only way to solve his problems, find himself sexually, and become a grown man among men.' He stopped killing, Dr Brussel opined, because he was better.

But the Oedipus Complex was by then an intellectual placebo, and although Brussel proved correct in diagnosing the hand of one assailant, it was for the wrong reasons. DeSalvo was not a well man. He continued raping, but stopped killing because, out of some fundamental decency, he could no longer endure the act of murder and preferred to risk capture by letting his victims live. DeSalvo felt particularly disgusted by his defilement of Mary Sullivan. She was only 19, and he left her in a grotesque state with a 'Happy New Year!' card propped against her foot. His penchant for talking to his victims like people – a posture studiously avoided by the likes of Ted **Bundy** – eroded his resolve, the objectives of which fluctuated. DeSalvo would hurry home from a murder to be sure not to miss playing with his children before bedtime.

Sent to the Bridgewater Mental Institute in Massachusetts, DeSalvo was adjudged mentally ill. Meanwhile the vast manhunt for the Boston Strangler dragged on until he bragged to a fellow-inmate, and his detailed confessions to thirteen murders, recorded on fifty hours of tape, convinced investigators of his guilt. But an insane DeSalvo was unfit to stand trial, and if sane, there was no case to answer since he would be advised not to repeat his confession, the only convincing evidence. In a legal compromise, DeSalvo stood trial as the 'Green Man'. Sentenced to life in 1966, he was stabbed to death by an unidentified fellow-inmate in Walpole State Prison on 26 November 1973.

Peter Kürten was similarly oversexed, like Charles Manson, described by Sandy Good as 'perma-rigid'. Of these three, DeSalvo is alone in concentrating his sexual fantasies on sex.

Insulin

A good way of killing people; so good that it seemed perfect until the fine forensic detection of the 1957 Barlow case.

On the evening of 3 May a doctor was summoned to Kenneth Barlow's Bradford home, where his wife's dead body lay in the bath. Barlow said she had been ill and must have passed out and drowned while he dozed in their bedroom. The doctor noticed that her pupils were widely dilated and called the police; when Barlow described his frantic attempts at in-bath artificial resuscitation, the officer noted that his pyjamas were dry.

A preliminary post-mortem investigation excluded drowning. So Elizabeth Barlow had died of something else. But what? Her vital organs were untainted by disease. Poison was suspected, yet exhaustive analysis detected no traces of toxin in the stomach or elsewhere, nor any method of administration. Detectives found syringes in Barlow's house, but this was nothing remarkable; he worked as a male nurse.

As a last resort, the police had the body illuminated by powerful lamps and then minutely inspected, head to toe, with a magnifying glass. And there, in the folded, freckled skin under the right buttock, were two tiny puncture marks.

Barlow had told detectives that on the evening of her death his wife complained of vomiting, sweating and weakness. Specialist advice confirmed that these were common symptoms of hypoglycaemia, a deficiency of blood sugar – the opposite of diabetes, conventionally treated with insulin to drive the blood-sugar level down. Administering insulin to a normal person could induce hypoglycaemia and, in extreme cases, cause death by shock.

There were serious problems with this idea, the first being that it was only a theory and one contra-indicated by the *high* readings of blood sugar in Elizabeth

Barlow's heart. Proof positive entailed discovering insulin in her body. But there was no test; insulin disappears very quickly once in the bloodstream.

Combing through medical literature, the forensic scientists learned that in cases of violent death, the liver releases a massive boost of sugar to help the fight for life. If the victim dies quickly, the residue remains in the stopped heart, exactly the finding with Mrs Barlow. Eventually a Professor Thomson devised a test-by-proxy. Some of her tissue was injected into mice, producing various repercussions (one of which was death) including an identical response of the blood-sugar level to a control group injected with insulin. So although the pathologists could not prove that she had been dosed with insulin, they knew that an insulin injection would produce the same effect. Further research revealed that insulin is preserved by acid. A dead body forms lactic acid in the muscles, and tests on Elizabeth Barlow's buttock yielded eighty-four units of insulin.

The trial hinged on the scientific evidence. Barlow's defence contended that the body manufactures insulin naturally, along with adrenaline, during moments of stress. But the concentration of eighty-four units in his wife's buttock near the point of injection suggested a body-wide count of 15,000 units. According to the prosecution's expert testimony, the maximum natural output is twenty units.

Barlow had strengthened the police's initial suspicions by telling several colleagues that insulin was *the* way to commit a perfect murder. 'If anybody gets a real dose of it, he's on his way to the next world,' he said. Sentenced to life, Barlow was dragged from the dock protesting his innocence; no motive for the killing emerged, but his previous wife expired the year before at the age of 33 with no clear cause of death.

By a strange coincidence, working in the trial judge's chambers at the time of the case was a young Danish lawyer, Claus **von Bülow**.

Iowa

The 1989 explosion in Number Two turret of the battleship *Iowa* exposed the FBI's Behavioral Science Unit to ridicule and contempt. Recommissioned in 1984, the *Iowa* retained its main battery; and shipboard guns – like any other – are subject to periodic explosion whether from enemy action, premature detonation, unstable cordite or machine malfunction.

At 9.53 a.m. on 19 April 1989 the *Iowa* was four rounds into a practice shoot when the hoist officer of Number Two turret shouted, 'Hold up just a minute, we've got a problem here.' At 9.55 the gun turret blew up, killing forty-seven crew.

At first the inquiry drew a blank. Then on 8 May a letter from the sister of a dead crewman, Clayton Hartwig, asked about his parents' entitlement to their son's life insurance policy even though he had assigned it to a shipmate, Kendall Truitt.

So Truitt stood to gain $100,000 from his friend's death, and Hartwig was gun captain on the fatal day. The ordnance inquiry had established that the explosion started between the first and second powder bags in the barrel. Could – or would – Hartwig have put a detonator there?

A 'psychological autopsy' was requested from the FBI's Behavioral Science Unit, widely venerated for its work in profiling serial killers. To crime buffs and the media, pioneering FBI agents like Brooks, Douglas, Hazelwood and Ressler had acquired supersleuth status. But the case was off their patch. It was one thing to analyse fragmentary evidence on a serial killer, but the suspects in this case were professional sailors with reputations and families. For the first time the FBI findings were destined for high-profile critical scrutiny.

On 2 June the FBI took delivery of some 300 dossiers on Truitt, Hartwig, Hartwig's parents, his siblings, schoolmates, and shipmates. They dismissed the idea of murder by Truitt. But Clayton Hartwig had a more suggestive personality. His sister thought him a loner; only in eleventh grade did he develop a close friend, Brian Hoover. Their bond was curiously intense; Hartwig sent Hoover over a thousand letters, gave him $200 a month from his Navy pay, and wrote a will in Hoover's favour in gratitude for his preventing a suicide attempt. The association ended abruptly when Hoover had sex with a mutual friend, and Hartwig's affections switched to Truitt; again, the pair became very close, but they stopped speaking after Truitt married. Then one day Hartwig said, 'Hey Ken, if ever I die you are going to be a rich man.' It was his first mention of the insurance policy.

Hartwig seemed largely asexual, and his letters hinted at rejection, alienation and stress. Like many emotional defectives familiar to the Behavioral Science Unit, he contemplated joining the police (see **Vocations**), and spoke of important – but imaginary – assignments. He discussed suicide with a crew member,

who recalled: 'We came to the conclusion that the quickest way we had ever seen anyone die was by explosion.' Hartwig told shipmates that the powder bags could be detonated with a blow from a hammer. He owned a copy of *Improvised Munitions*, talked of bomb-making, and a sailor saw something like a timing device in his locker. On visits home, Hartwig's conversation dwelt on gun-turret explosions.

The profilers decided that Hartwig was 'a very troubled young man who had low self-esteem'. They concluded: 'In our opinion, it was a suicide. He did so in a place and manner designed to give him recognition and respect that he felt was denied', and on 15 July 1989 Admiral Milligan reported that the explosion was 'a wrongful intentional act'. Hartwig had blown himself up.

The resulting furore could only be assuaged by a full Capitol Hill inquiry. Was not the evidence circumstantial? Were not most young men 'very troubled'? Was not Hartwig in good spirits at the time of his death? How had he ignited the charges? And had the Navy found a clever way of salvaging its billion-dollar battle-

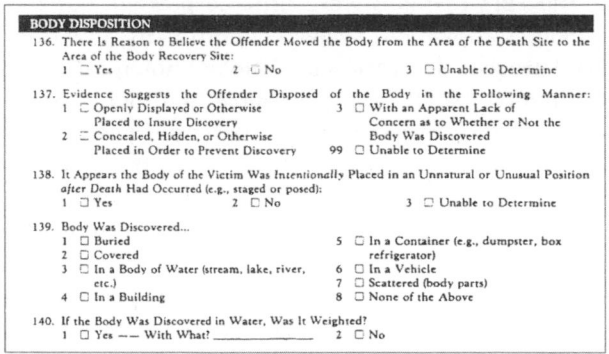

Part of the FBI's profiling questionnaire

ship programme, jeopardised if defective design was responsible for the blast? When the hearings opened on 12 December 1989, the FBI were castigated for being too categorical, for unquestioning acceptance of everything in the Navy's files, for selectivity in reviewing evidence, and for failing to consider whether the explosion was accidental.

Fourteen psychologists testified in summary that suicide by Hartwig was of 'a relatively low probability'. The final report was damning: 'The FBI's psychological analysis procedures are of doubtful professionalism. Their false air of certainty was probably the biggest single factor inducing the Navy to single out Clayton Hartwig.' The *Times* commented: 'Deep within the FBI there exists a unit of people who – without ever talking to you or anyone who knows you – are prepared to go into court and testify that you are a homicidal maniac.'

The outcry prompted renewed investigation into the explosion. The Sandia National Laboratory discovered that a charge could be ignited prematurely by excess ramming speeds, and on 24 May the Navy replicated their results. On 16 October 1991 the Navy conceded it had no proof that the explosion was not an accident and apologised to Clayton Hartwig's family.

So whither the science of profiling? The FBI were not asked to investigate the explosion or query the Navy's findings. Their remit was to give an opinion, based on information received, on whether Hartwig had committed suicide. They thought he had. Their conclusion was not invalidated by an accidental explosion, although it would have been helpful to know it was a possibility. A man with suicidal tendencies can still die in an accident; Hartwig could still have been troubled and depressed.

The FBI's opinions were firmly expressed. But they remained opinions, largely endorsed by the other psychologists. Thus one said: 'The psychological profile drafted by the FBI is very plausible', another, 'Hartwig would appear to be at a high risk for self-destruction', a third, 'Yes, he may have done it. No, the investigation does not present clear, cogent, and compelling evidence that he did do it.' The ridicule directed at the FBI stemmed from a misunderstanding of their role, journalistic over-simplifications, and the Navy's ineptitude. In criminal cases, too, **profilers** rely on evidence from outside experts, and if garbage is put in, it is garbage that comes out.

Ivan the Terrible

The ghoulish war criminal of Treblinka. Ivan the Terrible ran the engine which pumped carbon monoxide into the gas chambers, despatching 850,000 victims in a single year. He derived gratuitous pleasure from his work, smashing the prisoners' skulls with an iron pipe and slashing them with his sword as they passed, slicing off ears, noses, women's breasts. The ears he picked up and gave back, like dropped litter, as the Jews filed to their deaths.

Thirty years after the war, an American journalist returned from the Ukraine bearing a list of some sixty Nazi collaborators resident in the United States. Among them was an 'Ivan Demjanjuk' of the Sobibor death camp, and more than a decade later, after a massively publicised Israeli trial, Cleveland car worker John Demjanjuk was identified as Ivan the Terrible and sentenced to death.

The trial had several bizarre features. Rather like the **Tichborne Claimant** case, which ran for so long that the issues were obscured rather than illuminated, the central issue of identification fell by the wayside. The court deliberated not on whether John Demjanjuk and Ivan the Terrible were one and the same, but on the crimes committed by, and the fitting punishment for, Ivan the Terrible. In the event, John Demjanjuk was convicted for the acts of someone else, Ivan Marchenko.

Two strands of evidence linked Demjanjuk to Treblinka. The first, which occupied fifty days of court time, was equivocal. The prosecution produced an SS identification card showing that Demjanjuk (like thousands of others) had indeed been a concentration camp guard. But at Sobibor, not Treblinka. If the card was genuine, it proved only that Demjanjuk worked in the same country as Ivan the Terrible. The second strand of evidence consisted of direct identification by survivors. Again, this fell into two types, the first of which was fraudulent.

At the June 1981 hearing which stripped him of American citizenship, Judge Frank Battisti held that Demjanjuk was at Treblinka in 1942 and 1943, a finding based on the testimony of Otto Horn, an ex-Nazi. Horn worked with Ivan the Terrible on a daily basis, and the court heard that Horn positively identified Demjanjuk as Ivan.

Had this been true, it would have been powerful evidence. But in the 1980s, the janitor at the US Office of Special Investigations fell into the habit of dumping surplus paperwork in bin-bags outside a McDonald's on Washington's K Street. The documents, removed from the skip by a sympathiser, reached Demjanjuk's son, who unearthed two papers describing in consistent detail what happened at Horn's photo-parade.

Horn identified John Demjanjuk not as Ivan the Terrible but as John Demjanjuk. First Horn was shown a series of photographs and 'studied each of them at length, but was unable to positively identify any of the pictures … The first series of photographs was then placed in a stack, off to the side of the table – with that of Demjanjuk lying face up on top of the pile, facing Horn.'

Next, Horn studied a second set of pictures, including another photograph of Demjanjuk, and he correctly observed that this was the 'same person' as the man at the top of the first stack. In other words, Horn said that Demjanjuk looked like Demjanjuk – no more, no less. By the 1981 hearing this became:

Attorney: Did you in fact identify or recognise someone in those photographs?

Horn: Yes, this Ivan.

So the only valid testimony at the Jerusalem trial came from concentration camp inmates. As the Ivan investigation gathered impetus in the 1970s, several survivors picked out Demjanjuk from photo-spreads, saying (in the words of Eliyahu Rosenberg), 'That man looks very similar to the Ukrainian Ivan' and (Pinchas Epstein), 'This photo reminds me very strongly of Ivan.'

These witnesses were asked not whether they recognised anyone, but whether they recognised anyone as Ivan. In the courtroom's emotional atmosphere, ten years later, Rosenberg confronted Demjanjuk in the dock: 'Ivan. I say so unhesitatingly and without the slightest doubt. This is Ivan from the gas chambers. The man I am now looking at. I saw his eyes. I saw those murderous eyes. I saw that face of his.'

Thus the eleven-month case boiled down to this: Demjanjuk might have followed the right line of work, at the right time, in the right country; and four aged witnesses, separated from Ivan for more than forty years, believed they recognised him. Even with Horn's misleading testimony, the guilty verdict was hardly sustainable.

A contributory factor in Demjanjuk's downfall was his fragmented defence team. *The American Lawyer* stated that Demjanjuk's first attorney had 'little if any experience as a trial lawyer'. His second, the highly respected Dov Eitan, received many death threats and died on 29 November 1989 after unexpectedly plummeting from a fifteenth-storey window. The third, Yoram Sheftel, nearly lost his eyesight in an acid attack two days later. Across the benches, the prosecution case, endlessly padded out by the inclusion of appalling but largely extraneous background material on the Holocaust, fulfilled an important educational function for the coming generation; the hearings were televised, with 250,000 spectators passing through the courts.

After the 'guilty' verdict of April 1988, Demjanjuk's son John took up his father's case. In September 1990 John visited Russia with Sheftel and, through a sympathetic judge, secured the Simferol KGB's file on war criminals, including depositions from Soviet survivors of Treblinka. All sixty-one of these statements identified Ivan the Terrible not as the John Demjanjuk of the SS photo-card but as Ivan Marchenko, last sighted during a June 1943 posting at a prison camp in Trieste.

In 1993 Demjanjuk was allowed to appeal and the Israeli Supreme Court ruled that there was insufficient evidence to show he was Ivan the Terrible. He was returned to the USA, where in 1993 his sentence was overturned following a ruling by the 6th Circuit Court of Appeals that federal prosecutors had committed misconduct by withholding evidence in his case. In 1998 it was ruled that his citizenship could be restored. The following year, however, the US Justice Department filed a new civil complaint against Demjanjuk, without reference to 'Ivan the Terrible', alleging he had been a guard at three Nazi death camps in Germany and Poland. The Justice Department's evidence persuaded the 6th Circuit Court of Appeals to rule that Demjanjuk could be deprived of his US citizenship. He said he would appeal against the decision.

The name 'Ivan the Terrible' was adopted by one of the most feared drug traffickers of Colombia's Cali cartel. He specialised in cutting off his victims' **hands**.

J

Jackson, Michael: The Paedophilia Case

As this book is going to press, America is going through yet another 'celebrity trial of the century'. The once internationally beloved child pop star who went on to create the best-selling music album to date, Michael Jackson is nowadays seen by many people as a bizarre eccentric who lives in a self-created, multi-million-dollar fantasy world: a world that will come crashing down if he is convicted of child molestation.

Born in 1958, Jackson was literally thrust into the entertainment industry at a very young age. His father, Joseph Jackson, was an Indiana mill-crane operator who had long dreamed of becoming a famous blues musician. As this became less and less likely, Joe trained his children to make it where he had failed. He initially put his eldest three sons – Jackie, Tito and Jermaine – on the stage at numerous child talent competitions. Then, in 1962, he added his two youngest boys to the Jacksons' singing act – Marlon and Michael – renaming it the Jackson Five. Michael was just four years old.

In cases of alleged paedophilia, investigators often try to discover if the suspects were themselves sexually abused as children. The idea that abused kids often become abusers themselves is, fortunately, untrue in the vast majority of cases, but it proves correct often enough to remain a useful rule of thumb. There is no known evidence that Michael Jackson was ever sexually abused, but there can be little doubt that his early life was often hellish.

As the Jackson Five became an ever-greater success, so Joe Jackson grimly pushed his sons to work ever harder. The performances, tours and practice sessions were relentless. And Joe Jackson, according to Michael Jackson in a 1993 interview with Oprah Winfrey, often beat his children. 'He was strict; very hard and stern,' Michael Jackson recalled. 'It was difficult to take a beating and then go on stage.'

Michael, as the 'baby' of the group, was the most popular with the public. In 1971 and 1972 he recorded solo singles that did well enough to indicate that he might make it on his own. There was some need; as the Jackson Five's popularity waned in the mid-1970s, it looked as if Michael's long-term career might go down with them.

It was during filming in 1978 of *The Wiz* – an all-black version of *The Wizard of Oz* – that people began to report weird behaviour by the star. Michael, then 19, played the character of the brainless scarecrow, but was said to be 'seeking solace' in the fantasy role – refusing to take off his make-up after shooting and sometimes going home in his full scarecrow costume. His career took another hit when the movie was a tremendous flop.

But the following year he released his solo album *Off the Wall* to great critical and financial success. He was now seen as an adult star in his own right and went on to a gleaming career over the next decade: his 1982 album *Thriller* sold 47 million copies, a world record that has yet to be broken. The media, unsurprisingly, dubbed him 'the King of Pop'.

However, Jackson's eccentricity could hardly be denied; his other press nickname is 'Wacko Jacko'. He took his pet chimp, Bubbles, as his dinner guest to the Oscar ceremonies. His face changed visibly over the years as a result of apparently frequent plastic surgery. This in itself is hardly remarkable for a celebrity, but it soon seemed evident that Jackson's face was looking less African-American and more Caucasian. The fact that his skin also lost most of its pigmentation, turning him almost white, did much to fuel rumours that he was bizarrely trying to escape his birth race. (In fairness, it should be noted that Jackson claims the depigmentation was due to **vitiligo**, a rare epidermal problem that causes random patches of white skin.) His nose became so slim – apparently because of repeated plastic surgery – that some doctors warned publicly that his evidently thin nasal cartilage might collapse completely if damaged in any way.

Then, in 1993, came the first accusation of child molestation. An 11-year-old boy, Jordan Chandler, accused Jackson of sexually abusing him. Details were not made public at the time, but a security guard at Neverland, Jackson's palatial ranch in California, later claimed to have seen Jackson kissing and performing oral sex on the boy.

The following year the case was settled out of court. Jackson paid the Chandler family a reputed $26 million but publicly insisted that he was innocent of all charges.

The suggestion that the darling of millions of female fans was actually a paedophiliac homosexual shook the music industry and damaged Jackson's sales. Cynics were therefore not surprised when, soon after settling the Chandler accusation, Jackson announced he was in love with, and would marry, LisaMarie Presley, daughter of Elvis. The marriage lasted nineteen months. Rumours went about that LisaMarie had been acting as a 'beard' – slang for a wife married to conceal a star's homosexuality.

Jackson's next album, *HIStory*, did reasonably well in the USA and Britain, but controversy continued to dog him. At the 1996 Brit Awards, Jackson, surrounded by choirs of adoring children, was interrupted while performing his 'Earth Song'. Jarvis Cocker, lead singer of the British band Pulp, stormed onstage to denounce Jackson for trying to portray himself as Christ. Jackson later said that he was 'sickened, saddened, shocked, upset, cheated and angry' at Cocker's accusation.

The next year Jackson suddenly announced that he was marrying a nurse, Debbie Rowe, who was already expecting their first child. Cynics wondered aloud if he was just upping the 'beard' gambit, and some questioned the paternity of the child. The lyrics of Jackson's 1983 hit 'Billie Jean' were quoted ironically in the press: 'the kid is not my son…'

The child was a boy, christened Prince Michael Jackson. During the next year, 1998, a daughter was born: Paris Michael Katherine Jackson. Then Jackson divorced Debbie Rowe in 1999. She later said that she had left the two children in the care of their father 'as a gift'.

In 2001 Jackson's next album, the perhaps hubristically titled *Invincible*, was received badly by the critics and sales were sluggish.

Michael Jackson outside court in 2005

A little mystery surrounded the birth in 2002 of Jackson's third child, Prince Michael Jackson II: the identity of the surrogate mother has never been made public, nor was it explained why the supposedly heterosexual Jackson would choose to father a child in this hands-off manner. Jackson was not so shy of publicity for the baby, however, holding him out from a Berlin hotel balcony over a three-storey drop for fans and reporters to see. Although some considered this reckless endangerment of a child, no charges were pressed against Jackson by the city's authorities.

The following year Jackson gave an extended interview to British television. ITV 1's Martin Bashir, famous for his sympathetic interview of Lady Diana Spencer, was allowed into Jackson's Neverland ranch to record his lifestyle there. If Jackson's publicity people had hoped that Bashir would give Michael an easy or sympathetic ride, they were wrong. Jackson's home was shown as a weird pseudo-funfair and Michael himself came across as not only strange-looking but as a wildly extravagant spender (despite the fact that, in 2002, several major banks warned publicly that he was close to bankruptcy). Worse still, Bashir and his director chose to leave in a section where Jackson admitted to sleeping in the same bed with under-aged boys – but affectionately, not sexually, the singer had stressed.

In November 2003 police raided Neverland. Two days later Michael Jackson was arrested and charged with seven counts of sexually molesting a 12-year-old boy and two of giving intoxicants to a minor for the purposes of committing a crime. Released on $3 million bail, Jackson told the press that he would 'slit my wrists' before he would harm a child. He also complained that the arresting police had been 'very rough'.

The pre-trial hearing began on 16 January 2004. Jackson risked annoying Judge Rodney Melville by arriving over twenty minutes late. He pleaded not guilty to the initial charges and to an additional four charges of child molestation and a charge of conspiracy to abduct a child. The trial date was set for January 2005.

Jackson's accuser turned out to be 14-year-old Gavin Arviso, a young cancer victim whom Jackson had often invited to stay, with other members of the Arviso family, at Neverland. He and his family claimed that Jackson not only plied the boy with wine (which Jackson allegedly called 'Jesus juice') and sexually molested him, but they had all been 'coerced' by death threats into praising their persecutor on video.

Dozens of pornographic magazines were found in Jackson's bedroom during a police raid on Neverland in November 2003. Some of these were said to have revealed the fingerprints of Gavin and his little brother, Star. This seemed to confirm their claim that Jackson showed them pornography, although the defence hotly denied this interpretation.

Judge Melville allowed evidence of previous accusations of child molestation to be heard by the jury – for example, the allegations made by Jordan Chandler in 1993. After a four-month-long trial the pop star was cleared on 13 June 2005: not guilty verdicts were reached on all ten charges. The eight women and four men in the jury had deliberated for 32 hours over seven days after listening to 14 weeks of testimony.

The singer, who had suffered health problems and weight loss during the trial, left the courthouse exhausted, too tired to make a statement to the throngs of rejoicing fans.

Jack the Hat

A very English murder. Jack 'the Hat' McVitie was an old-style East End villain in the London of the 1960s.

At the time, the **Kray** twins were campaigning for recognition as 'proper' criminals. Ronnie Kray had already staked his claim, on 8 March 1966, by striding into the bar of the 'Blind Beggar', a large Victorian pub in London's Mile End Road, and shooting George Cornell of the Richardson gang with a 9mm Mauser automatic in front of several dozen witnesses. As Ronnie was fond of recounting, George's head 'burst open'. The way Ronnie saw it, that was how gangsters should deport themselves, killing publicly.

This bravado put his brother Reggie on the spot; Ronnie demanded to know when his twin would 'do his one'. By the autumn of 1966, Ronnie's mania was in full flower. More and more people who 'needed killing' were 'on the **list**'. If the Krays were ever to rank as a serious brotherhood alongside the Mafia, its high-ups should all be killers. The pressure mounted on Reggie to follow his leader.

In the end Jack the Hat drew the short straw. Well past his prime, Jack was prematurely bald (hence the hat), a drunk zonked on pep pills, and definitely not the man to kill Leslie Payne, a former Kray associate and now a suspected informer. But in September 1966 Ronnie issued Jack the Hat with a pistol and a £100 deposit for the hit. Jack bungled the job but hung on to the money, infuriating Ronnie, but Reggie felt so sorry for the old-timer that he advanced another £50.

'You should've paid George Cornell as well,' stormed Ronnie. He wanted his £100 back, and this triggered Jack the Hat's final spiral. Jack went on a blinder and staggered into the Krays' Regency Club – 'North London's Smartest Rendezvous' – brandishing a sawn-off shotgun and threatening to blast the twins. They were not there, but someone blabbed. Ronnie decided Jack the Hat had to go, even if it meant doing it himself.

This was too shaming for Reggie. So on the last Saturday in October, well and truly drunk, he set off for the Regency to shoot McVitie. When his intended victim failed to show, Reggie let the club manager talk him out of his gun and then returned disarmed, mission unaccomplished. Not surprisingly, Ronnie felt let down. He despatched one minion to reclaim the pistol, ordering his henchmen the Lambrianous brothers to scour late-night London, find Jack the Hat, ply him with drink and then bring him for a party to Blond Carol's house in Evering Road, Stoke Newington.

Just before midnight Jack the Hat burst into the house. He was drunk. 'Where's all the birds, all the booze?' he roared. Reggie stepped out from behind the door, wedged the gun against McVitie's head and pulled the trigger. It jammed. Outside, one of the Lambrianous brothers realised what was happening and started to weep. Meanwhile, Reggie pinioned Jack from behind. He broke free and dived through the window into the garden, shattering the glass and frame.

He was pulled back by his legs. 'Be a man, Jack,' shouted Ronnie. 'I'll be a man,' returned Jack, 'but I don't want to die like one.' Now Ronnie held McVitie tight. Clutching a carving knife, Reggie faced the bald, wretched crook. 'Kill him, Reg. Do him,' urged Ronnie. 'Why are you doing this to me, Reg?' said Jack. In reply, Reg shoved the knife into his face below the eye. Then he stabbed him in the guts, then the chest and finished by skewering his throat to the floor.

Within a day or so, Ronnie felt sufficiently composed to talk about how it had all gone, about how Jack looked and the gurgles he made and the amount of blood. Reggie anaesthetised himself with drink, but he had earned his brother's approval.

Jack's body was never found, but after the Krays' arrest on 9 May 1968 one of those present at the killing, Ronnie Hart, turned Queen's evidence, and in March 1969 the twins were sentenced to a minimum of thirty years for the McVitie and Cornell killings.

Both murders were pointless. The Richardson gang had already disintegrated: Cornell was the last survivor. And Jack the Hat was just a drunken nobody. The Krays were enmeshed in make-believe, aiming for the smooth prestige of American gangland killings. They finished up with an East End rough-house while an accomplice, Chrissie Lambrianou, sat blubbing at the horror on the stairs, the venture a prelude to a spiral of self-destructive drinking, remorse, self-pity and prison.

Across the Atlantic, as Ronnie surmised, they did things differently. Of the Dutch Schultz killing in October 1935, the jaunty Joe Valachi recorded: 'Right after this Vito Genovese tells me the Dutchman has got to go ... He says not to go out looking for him, but to shoot him if we happen to bump into him', a distinctive stance within the frame of reference of a small-time London gangster interviewed in 1992:

'There's a lot of instability in drug dealing – the exchange of money, credit. So you need guns. Killing is part of the scene. It's not like the Krays. They didn't need to kill. The only reason they killed is because that's what gangsters did in America. Now blokes have revolvers, semi-automatics ... It's about presenting yourself as someone who will use a gun.'

Jack the Ripper

The benchmark by which all sex killers are judged. Jack the Ripper stands at the gateway to the modern age. Before, men killed for a reason, or so it was assumed. Afterwards, it gradually became apparent that the sexual impulse could entwine round and fuse with violence, engendering the amalgam familiar today as 'sex-and-violence'. In its most extreme form, the mutation becomes the sexual satisfaction that an individual derives from killing, his blood-lust sharpened by social alienation.

Often the point of these assaults is to leave the female body subjugated and humiliated, spread-eagled and disembowelled in a position of ritual supplication. This demonstrates male supremacy more forcibly than intercourse.

The fact that the Ripper was never caught has contributed powerfully to his status as a cultural icon. At large, Jack is imagined as guileful, cunning, and still very much alive, with each new sex killer billed as his successor. As a legend, Jack is enshrined with the immortals, and he materialised – still at it – on another planet, in an episode of *Star Trek*, 'Wolf in the Fold'.

During the 1888 killings, London's Whitechapel resembled an area under siege. Eight newspapers followed the story daily, magazines picked it up, and the penny dreadfuls amplified its reverberations. But despite the contemporary fracas, the Ripper's real populariser was Marie Belloc Lownes's 1913 best-seller *The Lodger*, which ploughed through thirty-one editions, eighteen languages and five films, the first by Hitchcock.

Today, serial killers still take their cue from their Victorian hero. **Kürten** averred that the Ripper exercised a profound influence over him and, like his master, exchanged letters with the newspapers; one of the **Son of Sam**'s few possessions was a book on the Ripper; DeSalvo promised the police he was about to break something really big, 'like Jack the

Ripper', and **Bundy** was designated by the *Reader's Digest* as 'America's Jack the Ripper'. Perhaps this tradition, abetted by the media, inspires emulation rather than aversion.

The facts on Jack are threadbare. There were five accredited killings: Polly Nichols (31 August), Annie Chapman (8 September), Elizabeth Stride and Catharine Eddowes (both 30 September) and Mary Kelly (9 November). All were prostitutes, all had their throats slit, all were mutilated (time permitting), all were killed within a quarter of a square mile in Whitechapel, and all died in the early morning, in the first or the last weekend of the month. None was sexually assaulted.

Any talk of royal suspects, or the Freemasons, barristers or medical men, and any image of plush brothels, should be set beside the district's grinding, unremitting poverty. At maybe tuppence a trick, prostitution was the last bulwark against starvation, with many using their clothes like a house, to keep their possessions in. Catharine Eddowes, the Mitre Square victim, was found on post-mortem with all her belongings in her garments: a blunt table knife, a scrap of red flannel for her pins and needles, and two tin boxes, one for sugar and the other for tea. Annie Chapman, discovered in Hanbury Street, was all but dead on her feet before her fatal

The sketch issued by the press

encounter: undernourished and raddled with chronic diseases of the lungs and brain membranes. Local doss-houses crammed up to eighty into a single dormitory, and many rents were collected daily. The public houses of the area did not close until three in the morning, and opened at six to serve a liquid breakfast. The police ventured into Whitechapel only in groups and, a mile to the east, in the **Ratcliffe Highway**, dared not venture at all.

Jack the Ripper astonished the world by his florid displays. Rather than covering up his transgressions, he broadcast them. The bodies, with their scattered entrails, were left out on exhibition, surrounded by ritually placed objects, often taken from the victim – rings, coins, pills wrapped in paper, and the famous leather apron. He maintained a taunting correspondence with the police, press and citizen groups.

The Ripper's crimes were without historical precedent, leaving commentators bewildered. What was the *point* of the killings? The coroner's suggestion after the inquest on 10 September that 'both Nichols and Chapman had been murdered ... to secure some pathological specimen from the abdomen' was eagerly embraced for its comforting sense of purpose. The London *Times* exhibited typical incomprehension, reporting that the police were 'confronted with a murder of no ordinary character, committed not from jealousy, revenge or robbery, but from motives less adequate than many which still disgraced our society'. The double murder of 30 September demonstrated that the malice was not directed against any particular individual, and represented an exponential leap in horror.

The epicentre of the social tremors was the state of the victims' bodies. The autopsy report on Mary Jane Kelly, by Dr Thomas Bond, reads in part: 'The viscera were found in various parts viz the uterus & Kidneys with one breast under the head, the other breast by the Rt foot, the Liver between the feet, the intestines by the right side & the spleen by the left side of the body. The flaps removed from the abdomen and thighs were on a table ... The whole of the surface of the abdomen and thighs was removed and the abdominal cavity emptied of its viscera. The breasts were cut off, the arms mutilated by several jagged wounds and the face hacked beyond recognition of the features. The tissues of the neck were severed all round down to the bone ... The pericardium was open below and the heart was absent.'

Such savagery was new, in wild excess of any requirement to extinguish life, beyond the previous high-water mark of pointless violence recorded in the Ratcliffe Highway murders seventy years previously. The concept of 'Rippers', together with its alternative, 'stabber', had been popularised by the nineteenth-century press before 1888, but they were faltering antecedents of the modern sex criminal, content merely to stab their victims in the breasts, genitals and buttocks as they walked through the streets. Although commonplace by the 1880s, with exponents in London, Paris, Texas, Moscow and Nicaragua, it was Jack the Ripper who catapulted his exaggerated version into mass cultural consciousness.

For the killings, it is likely that the Ripper stood in front of his victims in the normal position for standing intercourse and then seized them round the neck. This would simultaneously ensure silence and induce unconsciousness. Next he thrust his victim to the ground with the head to his left, and then slit the throat, starting at the far end to direct the blood away.

As to the killer's identity, there is little to go on, but enough to found an industry: **Ripperology**. The police had their suspects, but 1888 was too early for forensic science to play a significant part. *The Times* asserted that a good fingerprint might be 'almost as useful' a clue as a **footprint**, and a proposal to equip constables with rubber-soled shoes to deaden their approach was seriously entertained. The victims' eyes were photographed in case they retained an imprint of the killer (see **Optographs**).

More usefully, rewards were offered and, less usefully, a pair of champion bloodhounds from Scarborough, called Burgho and Barnaby, were assigned to the case. But they got lost on Tooting Common and had to be tracked down by police. Queen Victoria joined the general public condemnation of the force, sending a lengthy missive beginning 'The Queen fears that the detective department is not so efficient as it might be'. But for all the flood of well-intentioned advice, short of catching their man red-handed, there was little the authorities could do.

See also **Ripperology**, **Sex crimes**, **Solution**

Jails, best

With America's prisons filling up with the likes of Ivan Boesky, Leona Helmsley, Michael **Milken** and Mike **Tyson**, a need arose for a guide to the country's best jails. *Playboy* plugged the gap in July 1992 with a listing of the nation's top ten.

Most of the rated prisons are small, some housing only a few dozen inmates, like Olmsted County Jail with its 'tradition of great cooking established by the sheriff's wife'. Over at Evans County Jail in Georgia, the

twenty-five prisoners 'dress in robes and slippers, lounge on down pillows and watch movies. The jail is relatively new; it smells like a new car.' But be warned; Kentucky's Crittendon may have a TV satellite hook-up, but *there is no remote control*.

The place to be seen in Britain is Ford Open Prison in Sussex, as a Category D prisoner. The institution looks like a collective farm for cricketers; huts huddle round the pitch, and inmates trundle their wheelbarrows across the country road intersecting the grounds.

The three city financiers jailed at Ford for the Guinness share-ramping scam founded its reputation as a club for upper-crust lags honing their share portfolios. But the social tone declined after a number of petty offenders and car thieves wormed their way in.

Jake

Prohibition drink. Brewed from Jamaican ginger, jake was some 90 per cent alcohol and allegedly possessed medicinal properties for stomach disorders; hence its availability on prescription in prodigal quantities. A small Texas druggist took delivery of 200 barrels in 1928, and by 1930 jake was in widespread demand throughout Kansas. Indiscriminately sold at thirty cents a shot to previously healthy citizens, it produced the interesting side-effect of selective paralysis.

The condition was manifested by loss of control of the muscles which traditionally ensure that the heel lands before the toes when walking; victims were known as 'jake-trotters'. Frequently the muscles of their thumbs and index fingers wasted away, and initial amusement palled after the Prohibition Bureau estimated the number afflicted nationwide to total 15,000, many of whom in due course recovered partial control of their hands and feet.

See also **Fallout**

Jaws

Despite his nickname of 'Metal Fang', Nikolai Dzhumagaliev from Kazakhstan did not use his white-metal gnashers for the kill.

Nikolai dates back to the pre-*glasnost* era of 1980, so reports are fragmentary. But after his day's work on an Alma-Ata building site, the neatly dressed Nikolai would take a woman for a stroll by the river, rape her, hack her to bits with an axe, light a fire, cook her and then invite friends back for supper with real meat. Such meals were a welcome rarity in the USSR. But Nikolai became careless; it was a mistake to leave a woman's head and intestines exposed on the kitchen table, where they were noticed by two guests.

Charged with seven murders, Nikolai was adjudged insane and sent to a mental institution in Tashkent, from which he escaped in 1989. He was rearrested in Uzbekistan in August 1991.

Jekyll and Hyde

A 60,000-word novella. Robert Louis Stevenson finished the first draft in one three-day stint, as though he were on speed. In fact he was on cocaine, which thus constituted his inspiration, means of production and, in part, the subject. His model for a double life probably came from the career of William Brodie, which Stevenson had already adapted as a stage play, first produced at the Prince's Theatre in London on 2 July 1884.

Brodie was born wealthy and died poor after dissipating his fortune on gambling. From his large house in the Lawnmarket, he played a prominent role in Edinburgh social life as Deacon on the Town Council and a luminary of the exclusive Cape Club. But by 1785, with his money gone, he turned to crime, robbing the houses of his wealthy clients and acquaintances. The following year he formed a gang with three professional thieves and, after a burglary on the Excise Office on 5 March 1788, two confederates were arrested and turned King's evidence. Brodie was hanged on 1 October 1788 before a huge crowd exulting in his fall from grace, and Stevenson's *Jekyll and Hyde* charts his hero's progressive degeneration from high intentions and respectability to a hideous reality from which, one day, there is no return.

In recognition of this tendency, many sadistic killers collaborate in their own capture, using their residual good side (Dr Jekyll) to ensure annihilation of their bad side (Mr Hyde). The youthful serial killer William Heirens expressed this vividly on 10 December 1945, scrawling his message with lipstick on a wall by the dead body of Chicago woman Frances Brown: 'For heavens sake catch me before I kill more I cannot control myself'. He was captured six months later, on 26 June 1946, but not before distributing six-year-old

Suzanne Degnan in five different sewers. Her head was found beneath one manhole cover, with her left leg, right leg, arms and torso occupying four more.

According to graphologists, Heirens's childlike script, with its downward slope and poorly formed letters, shows emotional stress, nervousness and maladjustment

Heirens's sexual drive went haywire during adolescence, when it was his custom to don women's underwear and stare at pictures of Nazi leaders. Arrested for carrying a loaded pistol at the age of 13, he had already accumulated a sizeable home arsenal. His upbringing on matters sexual had been deeply repressive, but sex, like truth, will out. His longings focused on the forbidden, and hence the unlawful, leading to an incremental confusion between sex and crime. Originally this evidenced itself through burglary, when he achieved orgasm as he 'entered' a building through the symbolic vagina of its window.

But one thing leads to another, and on 3 June 1945, while housebreaking, Heirens slashed the throat of Josephine Ross, and from then on murder, in its more strident forms, represented his ultimate pleasure. But he took no pains to avoid capture and was arrested prowling round an empty apartment; routine checks revealed that his **fingerprints** matched those at the murder scenes. His attempt to shift Suzanne's killing on to George Murman (his alter ego) was indicative more of self-disgust and denial than legal manoeuvring (see **MPD**), and he was sentenced to three terms of life imprisonment.

Other sex killers, like Britain's Neville Heath, telephone the police and offer to assist in their enquiries or, like Dennis **Nilsen**, regard their capture as 'the day help arrived', a longed-for curtain-call ending their course of self-destruction. Serial killers often display a kamikaze tendency, with their murders constituting a suicide note, the outcome of acute depression, an inability to relate and an unlived life. 'Low self-esteem' and 'under-achievement' are recurring features of psychological **profiles**.

Apart from sensual gratification, the murders may be motivated by resentment against the world and its failure to take proper cognisance of the killer, whose clever handiwork puts him on the map. But only at the very bottom. It gradually dawns that he is only important for bludgeoning innocent bystanders to death, and even then nobody knows he did it; his lot is worse than when he started (see **Ng**, **Zodiac**).

The killer can only achieve celebrity in his own right after being caught. 'I wanted to be famous … I thought you were never going to catch me,' complained Kenneth Erskine, London's Stockwell Strangler, who throttled seven pensioners in 1986, sodomising five. By this terminal stage, many serial killers welcome or even ask for the death sentence. On 28 January 1983, Douglas Daniel Clark, America's 'Sunset Strip Slayer', presented his own case during the penalty phase of the court proceedings. He appointed himself the thirteenth member of the jury and recommended his execution. 'We have to vote for the death penalty in the case,' he declared. 'The evidence cries out for it.' Numerous other killers have echoed these sentiments.

But Clark felt reasonably safe, since at the time California's last execution was in 1967. Similarly, although the killings may be a suicide note, serial killers rarely take their own lives. To pursue the analogy *à l'outrance*, the **sadism** – a distorted mirror-version of ordinary sexuality – produces the murders which, in a grotesque parody of ordinary existence, represent a displaced plea for help.

Johnson, Dr Samuel (1709–84)

A hard-liner. Johnson characterised the proposed relocation of the gallows to **Newgate** in these terms: '**Tyburn** itself is not safe from the fury of innovation. Executions are intended to draw spectators; if they do not, they do not answer to their purpose. The old method was most satisfactory to all parties; the public was gratified by a procession, the criminal supported by it. Why is all this to be swept away?'

The views of the diarist Samuel Pepys (1633–1703) on **hanging** are perhaps more illuminating. He advocated the use of silken rope, 'it being soft and sleek it do slip close and kills, that is strangles presently, whereas a stiff one do not come so close together and so the party may live longer before being killed'. Pepys was right, but this was not appreciated for nearly two centuries.

Johns, Tommy (1922–88)

Leading but dead Australian sot. Johns celebrated his 2,000th arrest for drunkenness on 9 September 1982 and, shortly before his death, estimated his total at 'nearly 3,000' since 1957, a rate of nearly two arrests a week over a career spanning three decades. Despite these selfless endeavours Johns failed to drink himself into an early grave.

A famous nineteenth-century English drunk was Annie Parker, who served over 400 sentences. She devoted her time inside the Clerkenwell House of Correction to sewing tiny needlework 'samplers' of ivory-coloured lace, delicately emblazoned with religious motifs such as: 'I will instruct thee and teach thee in the way which thou shalt go. I will guide thee with mine eye. Thine home is in heaven.' The words 'Prudence' and 'Temperance' figured in two corners of each cushion. Annie used her hair as thread, giving the embroideries to the prison vicar, who donated them to Scotland Yard's Black Museum.

Jury

Initially comprised exclusively of the accused's personal acquaintances, who were well placed to know if he was guilty. The word derives from the French *juré*, meaning sworn.

In America, the Fully Informed Jury Association's exertions are directed towards publicising the widely unknown power of 'jury veto'. This neglected provision, enshrined in the Constitution as a final check on government powers, entitles jurors to acquit regardless of the evidence, on the basis that they disagree with the law itself.

Jury selection was already big business in America by 1975 when a Duke University psychology professor received $15,000 in the Jeffrey **MacDonald** case to 'profile' potential jurors predisposed to an acquittal.

Nine hundred randomly selected citizens were subjected to telephone interviews including demographic questions about their age, race, marital status, educational background and churchgoing habits, and each factor given statistical weight. The ideal juror, it turned out, was exactly the type which conventional wisdom decreed would be most sympathetic to the prosecution, namely white, conservative and over thirty-five: solid, upstanding citizens like accountants, chemists and ex-policemen.

In the event, MacDonald was convicted after six and a half hours of consideration. A younger, more liberal jury would probably have reached the same conclusion more quickly.

Justice

Easy to achieve in former times, the task simplified by the inviolability of the person of a 'freeman', by definition almost incapable of guilt.

Until the twelfth century, criminal procedure remained a matter of self-assessment. The victim reported an offence to the officers of justice and then made his accusation in court. There the defendant swore on oath that he was innocent, whereupon proceedings terminated in his acquittal. The equivalent commercial process today is known as 'self-regulation'.

The accused's sworn oath was virtually irrefutable as the truth in front of God, thought to intervene continuously in earthly affairs to ensure that wrongs received fitting retribution. Only in the most outrageous cases would the accused's oath require reinforcement from other oath-helpers, called 'compurgators'. But unlike modern witnesses, compurgators did not give testimony as to events; instead, they rendered evidential support by consenting to the swearing of the accused's original oath.

Tricky cases might go one step further, to **mortal combat** where the litigants fought to determine the innocent party. This was the survivor, since it was observed *ex post facto* that God, who moved in mysterious ways, accorded victory to the pure in heart. Nevertheless, prudent litigants often nudged the scales of justice by designating someone bigger and stronger to trade blows on their behalf.

This system was prevalent throughout Christendom until the twelfth century, when the recovery and adaptation of the written body of Roman law introduced a new element: proof. The judgment of man supplanted the judgment of God, inaugurating the familiar process of examining the written record and interrogating witnesses.

The most powerful of all evidence in this uncertain undertaking was a confession, soaring above the vagaries of judges, juries and evasive witnesses, as the *regina probatiorum*, the queen of proofs. It put matters beyond argument; moreover, confessions could be made at any time, in sharp distinction to the fleeting availability of criminals caught red-handed. In cases of inconclusive evidence, the court could rely on the testimony of the one man who *knew first-hand* whether the suspect was guilty, and for some crimes – chiefly capital ones – it was unsafe to convict in the absence of a full admission.

Fortunately, the technology for extracting confessions had long since been mastered, and by the start of the thirteenth century – in the interests of fair play and justice – **torture** was integral to the legal system. It remained in ordinary usage throughout Europe until the 1800s, except in England where it played no official part after 1166. King Henry III instituted the petty jury whose members, confronted by perplexing circumstantial evidence, proved capable of making up their own minds; in other countries, guilt was determined not by the jury but by the judge who, as a state prosecutor, followed the state's rigid hierarchical procedure, of which torture was an established element.

Under English law today, the accused is assumed innocent until proved Irish.

Justification

Murderers often feel obliged to justify their killings to themselves or the police. A common rationalisation is 'obeying voices', often God's but in the case of Son of **Sam**, God spelt backwards. He obeyed a barking dog. Peter **Sutcliffe**, the Yorkshire Ripper, explained that he was animated by the best civic motives (see **Sex crimes**): 'The women I killed were filth ... I was just cleaning the place up a bit.'

The Son of Sam still revelled in his mission during the courtroom proceedings; seeing the parents of his last victim, Stacy Moscowitz, in the spectators' section, he chanted: 'Stacy is a whore, Stacy is a whore. I'll shoot them all.'

In October 1964 John William Stoneley, a 21-year-old cable-maker from Southampton, battered taxi driver George Newbury into unconsciousness with a metal pipe and then, while his victim lay slumped over the wheel, stove in his head with five more blows. The police learned from Stoneley that his victim's demise 'was caused by him not getting help'. At his trial this statement told against him, and he was sentenced to death, later commuted to life imprisonment. Five months into his sentence, Stoneley married a 19-year-old in a brief ceremony with a prison guard for best man.

Sometimes murderers worry that the jury and public do not understand. In 1979 Californian Lawrence Singleton, accused of raping a 15-year-old and chopping off her arms with an axe, explained his ordeal with perfect clarity: 'My night of terror had begun. Everything I did was for survival…' A stubborn jury took the reverse view and found him guilty as charged.

Singleton's last letter to the author Amanda Spake contained a word-for-word rewriting of his indictment, save that his own name was substituted throughout by the true perpetrator of the crime, his victim. In Japan, during 1972, the leader of the Red Army Faction, Hiroko Nagata, worked herself into a similar 'logic grave', killing one of her followers for wearing earrings.

Given the right frame of mind, something can be the motive for anything. On 20 September 1991 Alec Bell was jailed for three and a half years after demolishing a woman's house with a mechanical digger when she refused to heat up his dinner, and in February 1992 Sylvester Simon was convicted of the manslaughter of his 70-year-old friend Cephus John, who denounced him for cheating at dominoes. Similar instances are without number.

Cases where the crime is out of all proportion to its engendering circumstances have always been with us. The leap for mankind was the so-called motiveless murders, where the impulse to kill sprang from the criminal's internal dictates without input from the victim, a trait which came to the attention of criminologists like **Locard** in the 1940s.

K

Kangaroo

A singular disguise. The only land bridge from the penal colony on the Tasman Peninsula was Eaglehawk Neck, a 100-yard isthmus leading to mainland Australia, and in 1831 the Lieutenant-Governor, Sir George Arthur, established a guard station on the narrow strip of land after the first flurry of escapes when desperate convicts walked, crept or waded across to an uncertain future on the mainland.

A former actor as well as a convict, William Hunt decided to dress as a kangaroo for his escape. He had nearly bounded to the safety of Forestier's Peninsula on the far side when he was spotted by two picket guards, who could scarcely believe their luck. At last there would be something decent for dinner. The guards gave chase and levelled their muskets at the animal, which capitulated with the words, 'Don't shoot, I am only Billy Hunt.'

Thereafter Captain Charles O'Hara Booth, the Port Arthur commandant, put a stop to such indignities. To the complement of the nine guard dogs tethered at intervals across the Neck, in 1832 he added a row of oil lamps which illuminated a white background of crushed cockle shells. Behind, Booth constructed a line of sentry boxes together with guard-houses for an increased squad of twenty-five men. When the convicts took to the waters, so did Booth, building seaborne rafts as dog outposts. And according to rumour, when the prisoners tried to bypass the platforms by swimming further out, his guards dumped blood and offal into the sea as a beacon for sharks.

Kelly, Ned (1855–80)

Australian national hero, the inspiration for three movies, a rock opera, several paintings and a jazz suite.

Kelly's father, an Irishman transported for stealing two pigs, was imprisoned in 1865 for rustling, and he died shortly after release, leaving his widow to raise their seven children in squalor. Ned, the eldest, was jailed at 16 after sundry robberies for 'rooting both his spurs' in a constable. Of his chain gang years, Kelly said, 'I'd rather face the gallows than go to jail again.' A fine figure of a man, six feet tall, a good horseman and a skilled boxer endowed with a luxuriant beard, he stayed out of trouble despite stealing some 200 horses. But in September 1877 he was arrested by a Constable Lonigan and dragged across the road by his privates. Kelly bawled, 'If ever I shoot a man, Lonigan, you will be the first.' He was.

The following April Constable Fitzpatrick called at Kelly's slab-and-bark hut to arrest his 17-year-old brother, Dan. According to Fitzpatrick, Ned burst in, took aim from the range of a yard and missed. Meanwhile, the boys' mother banged Fitzpatrick's helmet down over his eyes with a spade; Ned fired again, winging him in the wrist. According to Ned, and this is more likely, he was 400 miles away at the time; Dan duped Fitzpatrick with the oldest trick in the book, crying 'Here comes Ned now', seizing his pistol as he wheeled round. Whichever, Fitzpatrick retired hurt, but his report turned both the Kelly boys into outlaws and landed their mother with a three-year prison sentence.

On 25 October 1878, two noisy search parties set out hunting the Kellys. Informers directed one group to a small clearing by Mount Wombat on Stringybark Creek where Ned ambushed their camp. Constable McIntyre surrendered, but his companion – Lonigan – took to his heels, reaching for his weapon. Kelly blasted him with a shotgun: 'It was him or me. What a pity the bastard had to run.' When the two others, Kennedy and Scanlon, returned they too died in a gunfight, and Kennedy's **ears** were missing when his body was discovered five days later. All Victoria was agog at the news; the confrontation was rehashed as a play, the *Vultures of the Wombat Ranges*, and Kelly's character was cheered to the echo. With £1,000 on his head, an army of police scoured the bush, but rather than lying low, on 9 December 1898 Kelly took over Euroa, a settlement of 300, first investing the station at Faithful's Creek in genial mood, confining twenty-two passengers and staff to the storehouse before riding into town clad in pilfered finery to relieve the bank of £2,060.

Kelly placed the loot in a sugar bag and, after sharing a bottle of whisky with Mr Scott, the manager, insisted on taking him, his wife, seven children and two servants on an outing to Faithful's Creek where he ordered dinner for thirty, delivered a firebrand speech, showed off his riding skills and then, to general acclaim, rode off into the Strathbone Ranges.

Such exploits are the stuff of legend, and the reward was raised to £4,000. On 8 February 1879 Kelly took the town of Jerilderie hostage, locking the local police in their cells, donning their uniforms and forcing the unfortunate Constable Richards to introduce his gang round town as a new contingent hunting the Kellys. Next day, they robbed the Bank of New South Wales of £2,140. Kelly briefly considered burning the mortgages, adding another twist to the legend, but was distracted by the complication that the bank's deedbox also contained pension policies. He hosted another party where, lionised by the townsfolk, he stood drinks all round, alternately threatening to execute Constable Richards on the spot and then magnanimously pardoning him. In sentimental mode, Kelly ordered the return of a gold watch and a favourite horse to their former owners, and he left behind a spirited, unpunctuated note, characterising his detractors as 'a parcel of big ugly

In all his glory

fat-necked wombat-legged narrow-lipped splay-footed sons of Irish bailiffs and English landlords'.

The reward was raised to £8,000. The Kellys had friends everywhere, but eighteen months in the bush took their toll and by June the following year Kelly devised a masterplan to lure a trainload of lawmen into his clutches, derail it and then, invincible in ploughshare armour, gun down the survivors. With all the district's police dead, he would plunder every bank from Benalla to Beechworth. His plan worked like clockwork, but its intended victims did not, and the mistimed scheme backfired.

On 26 June 1880 Kelly baited the trap with the shooting of Aaron Sherritt, an informer, at a hut guarded by four live-in police. Kelly rightly reasoned that this would prompt Melbourne's Captain Standish to despatch reinforcements to Beechworth. But the officers cowered in the hut overnight, and when the news did reach Melbourne, Standish could not be found, and when he was, the engine took hours to work up steam. The train did not leave until 10.15 p.m. on the 27th, twelve hours later than Kelly calculated, and he made his dispositions too soon.

Late on the 26th, Kelly commandeered the Glenrowan Inn by a small railroad halt and ripped up the track a mile down the line on a precipitous embankment. His sixty-two prisoners needed entertaining all morning under mounting tension; games and dancing to a concertina whiled away the hours, but one man of spirit, Thomas Curnow, the local schoolteacher, resolved to avert the impending massacre. He begged Kelly to release him and his family: 'You've got no cause to fear me, I'm with you heart and soul.' Kelly acceded, and at 3 a.m. on the 27th Curnow ran down the track clutching a candle while the Kellys faced their second night without sleep.

Curnow flagged down the pilot engine short of the

Artists were on hand to sketch the battle almost as it unfolded. An accurate depiction of Kelly's capture by Dowsett and Steele

break in the line. The police debouched, as did numerous reporters, artists and several ladies, who were treated to a grandstand view of the shootout. Thirty officers fanned out towards the hotel; the gang donned their armour and lined the verandah, blazing away in the dark for fifteen minutes as the police returned fire from the field's perimeter. 'Come on, I'm Ned Kelly and I'm made of iron,' Kelly taunted his assailants, but he was soon hit in the foot, elbow and hand. Volleys poured through the wooden walls as the hostages lay on the floor.

At 97 pounds, Kelly's armour proved an encumbrance. Hardly able to move, or sight a weapon, or raise a rifle to his shoulder, he shambled out into the fields unobserved, hoping to outflank his tormentors. But at first light he determined to regain the hotel and lumbered from the treeline through the mist like a mythic figure, his coat flapping over the iron plating. Railwayman Jesse Dowsett takes up the story: 'I emptied my revolver at him, but he came on steadily, saying, "Fire away, you bloody dogs, you can't hurt me"... I fired again, hitting him full in the head, but not having the slightest effect ... He seemed to fall backward. I ran up, and jumping over the log, saw Steele and he on the ground. I grasped the revolver from him.' Kelly, bleeding from twenty-five minor and five serious wounds, was asked why he had not deserted his gang to save himself. 'A man would have been a nice sort of **dingo** to walk out on his mates.'

Later that morning the hostages were released, and in the afternoon the hotel was torched. Inside, the other three gang members were already dead. After recuperating in the Melbourne jail infirmary, Kelly was tried on 28 October, charged only with the murder of Lonigan, to which he could have pleaded self-defence. On receiving the death sentence, Kelly steadily addressed Judge Barry from the dock: 'It is quite possible for me to clear myself from this charge if I liked to do so ... I dare say the day will come when we shall go to a bigger court than this. Then we shall see who is right and who is wrong.' A petition 60,000 strong failed to secure a reprieve, and he was hanged on 11 November 1880. 'Such is life,' Kelly said, as they tightened the noose around his neck. Two days later, Judge Barry collapsed and died.

Kemmler, William (d. 1869)

William Kemmler (who hatcheted his girl, Tillie Zeigler, to death on 29 March 1889) was selected as the first victim of the **electric chair**.

A host of curious, besuited physicians attended the experiment at New York's Auburn Prison on 6 August 1890. They awaited Kemmler's arrival expectantly, seated in a circle round his empty chair. He had dressed to the nines in a new suit for his big day, looking 'better than he had ever been before', and the Warden ushered him into the killing room with the announcement, 'Gentlemen, this is William Kemmler.' He walked over to his chair, bowed to the assembled company, and took up his seat.

'Now we'll get ready, William,' said the kindly Warden. As he was strapped in, Kemmler reassured the nervous Deputy Sheriff: 'Don't get excited, Joe. I want you to make a good job of this.' Kemmler wanted everything just so, calling for an adjustment to his skull cap. When all was shipshape, the Warden took his leave: 'Goodbye, William.'

'Goodbye,' replied Kemmler calmly. Then they killed him. But not very well. A thousand volts banged through Kemmler for seventeen seconds; the fascinated doctors gathered round his body. When Kemmler took a deep breath, everyone scattered in panic. Then they gave him the treatment again.

With the exception of the *New York Times*, condemnation of this barbaric implement was universal, and fifteen states adopted electrocution as their official method of execution.

The murderer William G. Taylor survived for longer than Kemmler. On 27 August 1893, after the first electric jolt extended his legs and broke the front part of the chair, a guard fetched a box to prop up the sagging seat. Then the warder threw the switch again, but nothing happened. The generator had burnt out. The groaning Taylor, comatose but still alive, was unstrapped and settled in a cot while the electricians frantically restrung power lines over the prison walls to bleed off the city's current.

But Taylor died before he could be executed; in other words, the sentence had not been carried out. So they executed him dead, installing his corpse in the chair for one last, thirty-second blast.

The first woman to be electrocuted in Pennsylvania was Irene Schroeder who, in tandem with her lover Glenn Dagus, murdered a policeman in 1931. As they tightened her straps, Schroeder was asked if she wanted anything. 'Yes,' she said, 'there is something. Tell them in the kitchen to fry Glenn's eggs on both sides. He likes them that way.'

George Appel, a Chicago gangster, managed a joke while they buckled him in. 'Well folks,' he told the watching press men, 'you'll soon see a baked Appel.'

Kemper, Edmund Emil III (1949–)

The 'co-ed killer', a cornucopia of deviant psychiatric tendencies marked by the usual childhood symptoms including cruelty to animals, especially cats (see **Pets**).

Kemper killed his grandparents in 1964 at the age of 15. Afterwards he said, 'I just wondered how it would feel to shoot grandma', and when grandpa ran into the room he wondered how that would feel too. Released in 1969 by the California Youth Authority against psychiatric advice, Kemper progressed to sadism, murder, necrophilia and cannibalism, finishing with matricide.

For a while the 6ft 9in, 21-stone Kemper confined himself to female university students, picking up hitch-hiking co-eds and cutting off their heads. 'Alive, they were distant, not sharing with me,' he recounted. 'I was trying to establish a relationship. When they were being killed, there wasn't anything in my mind except that they were going to be mine.' To make the girls more truly his, Kemper ate parts of their bodies.

Interiors exerted a strange fascination. Kemper said of his February 1973 victim Rosalind Thorpe: 'She had a rather large forehead, and I was imagining what her brain looked like inside and I just wanted to put a

Ed Kemper, serial killer

bullet in it.' So he did, delivering her to his mother's house at Santa Cruz where he removed her head and gouged the slug out. In life, death was always with him; asked how he would react if he saw a pretty girl on the street, Kemper said: 'One side of me says, "Wow, what an attractive chick, I'd like to talk to her, to date her." The other side of me says, "I wonder how her head would look on a stick."'

Kemper's **mother** was at the root of his problems. She never stopped nagging, so on Easter Saturday 1973 he cut off her head. Then, to make doubly sure, he excised the larynx and stuffed it down the garbage disposal unit. But when Kemper switched the machine on, it clogged and spewed her throat back at him. 'Even when she was dead,' Kemper recalled, 'she was still bitching at me. I couldn't get her to shut up.' Next, Kemper invited his mother's friend, Sarah Hallett, for tea. After crushing her head with a brick, he cut it off and made love to the torso. Then, leaving a note for the police (which concluded 'I got things to do!'), he drove to Colorado to await arrest.

But this proved beyond the capacity of American law enforcement; even though Kemper was stopped for a traffic violation, he had crossed a state boundary and did not feature on the local wanted list. With growing frustration, he made repeated, pleading telephone calls to the Santa Cruz police, eventually persuading them to send the Colorado cops to collect him outside a phone booth.

Convicted of eight murders, Kemper asked for 'death by torture'. But he was running out of steam, like many a serial killer. 'The original purpose was gone,' he later told the police, explaining his decision to surrender. 'It was starting to weigh kind of heavy. The need I had for continuing death was needless and continuous. It wasn't serving any physical or emotional purpose. It was just a pure waste of time. I wore out of it.'

But the homicidal embers still flickered. Sentenced to life, Kemper was interviewed in jail by the FBI for inclusion in their serial killer **database**. He told his questioner, waiting nervously for the long-overdue arrival of a guard to let him out of the cell: 'The rooms are soundproofed here, nobody can hear your screams. By the time you push that button I'll tear you apart ... I could screw your head off and place it on the table to greet the guard.' Heads were Kemper's speciality. As he told the FBI: 'You know, the head is where everything is at, the brain, the eyes, the mouth. That's the person. I remember being told as a kid that if you cut off the head, the body dies. The body is nothing after the head is cut off. The personality is gone.'

With hindsight, it is clear that Kemper was a necrophiliac precursor of Jeffrey **Dahmer**.

Kennedy, John F. (1917–63)

President Kennedy was enmeshed – before, during and after his tenure of office – by intelligence agencies operating to a secret agenda who covertly manipulated governmental policy to their own ends. These included war; and in this warped political context it is not unreasonable to query the official account of his assassination. The original Warren Report, far from being exhaustive, was required by Johnson before the 1964 election, and after only three months the investigators learned that they were supposed to be 'closing doors, not opening them'. The continuing revelations about **Hoover**'s predilection for blackmail and his links with the Mafia, together with the Kennedy–Exner–Giancana–Operation Mongoose–Mafia nexus, hardly inspire confidence.

The leading theories are that Oswald killed the President at his own prompting ('the lone nut' concept), or that Oswald was 'sponsored' by Khrushchev, or Castro, or big business, or the Mafia. Or Oswald was set up as a fall-guy by a disaffected clique within the CIA.

The problem with the 'lone nut' theory is that it involves two lone nuts, the second being Jack Ruby, who had ties with the Mafia and died in custody with (to judge from his words to Chief Justice Warren) his tale still untold. Ruby gained access for a clear shot at Oswald with perfect timing hard to replicate without inside assistance. Nor is Oswald's assassination weapon satisfactory. The 1940s 6.5mm Mannlicher Carcano had a stiff bolt action, a misaligned sight and was notoriously inaccurate. According to the FBI, it took 2.25 seconds to aim and fire. The famous Zapruder film shows Kennedy and Governor Connally taking hits less than two seconds apart, and material from the President's brain splattered backwards on to the car trunk, some impacting on a motorcycle policeman riding behind and to the left.

But firing tests on melons and stuffed skulls show that detritus is not expelled towards the rifle. An alternative point of origin for at least some of the gunfire is the 'grassy knoll'. The evidence is no more than verbal, but it seems persuasive. Thus William Newman, a Korean War veteran, was standing on the pavement between the knoll and the motorcade. He heard the first two shots as no louder than distant firecrackers, and thought they registered a hit. But then he flung himself and his family to the ground as a loud boom rang out from close behind, simultaneous with the disintegration of the President's head.

Doubts remain about Oswald's motivation and the capacity in which he acted, if he acted at all. His palmprints were not found on the rifle until 24 November, and this was after FBI agents – allegedly – visited the funeral parlour to obtain a set of transferable prints. In the seconds following the shooting Oswald was seen unconcernedly strolling around the second-floor lunchroom in the Depository with a bottle of Coca-Cola.

Oswald appears to have trained as an American intelligence agent, and his purported communist sympathies may have been a front. In the days before the assassination, he was seen cloistered with the eccentric David W. Ferrie, an impassioned anti-communist who glued pieces of orange fur to his head to hide his alopecia, and Clay Shaw, a wealthy ex-army officer. Jim Garrison's conspiracy case against Shaw was defeated on 1 March 1969, but not before three of his main informants died, and his investigation formed the mainspring of the recent film *JFK*, which in turn inspired the movie's distributors to issue study guides, further permeating the national consciousness as agreed fact.

In April 1967, Garrison informed the media: 'My staff and I solved the assassination weeks ago. I wouldn't say

Jim Garrison announcing that the trial of Clay Shaw will start on 21 January 1969, nearly two years after indictment

this if we didn't have evidence beyond a shadow of a doubt.' But for Garrison, almost anything constituted evidence. A few hours after complaining to the *Washington Post* on 22 February 1967 that Garrison was persecuting him, Ferrie died. The coroner attributed his death to natural causes – a cerebral haemorrhage resulting from a ruptured blood vessel – but, rather than challenging the autopsy, Garrison arrested Clay Shaw, and within days he announced he had firm evidence linking Shaw to Oswald.

Both their address books contained an identical five-number digit: 19106, Shaw's prefixed by the words 'PO Box' and listed under 'Lee Odom'. When deciphered, Garrison said, the numeral produced Jack Ruby's unlisted telephone number (WH 1-5601) and 'no other number on earth'. This transformation entailed reassembling 19106 by taking digits alternately from each end (making 16901) and then subtracting 1,300. The fact that a man called Odom did have PO Box 19106 (a number only allocated after Oswald's death) failed to shake Garrison's ardour, and, after watching a television programme on 23 February, he devised a scenario where Ferrie, Oswald and Shaw met a man named Perry Raymond Russo in September 1963 to plot the assassination.

Since Ferrie and Oswald (both of whom Shaw denied meeting) were dead, Russo was Garrison's only possible witness. On television Russo affirmed that his partner, Ferrie, had once mentioned that it would be easy to kill a President. But on questioning by a Garrison attorney, Russo maintained that he never heard *Kennedy's* assassination discussed. Nor had he ever met Shaw.

So on 27 February, on Garrison's instructions, Russo was drugged with sodium pentothal and hypnotised, told to imagine a screen in his mind: 'There will be Shaw, Ferrie and Oswald ... They are talking about assassinating somebody.' Under direction, Russo remembered (see **memory**) witnessing the plot, but Garrison knew perfectly well that this contradictory testimony would not withstand cross-examination in court. So he devoted the next twenty-two months to delaying tactics by arresting a broadcaster, Edgar Eugene Bradley, and issuing arrest warrants against three journalists. By the time Shaw's trial began in January 1969, the powers behind Garrison's conspiracy theory had expanded to include homosexuals, anti-Castro Cubans, oil millionaires, the Dallas police, arms manufacturers, White Russians, CIA agents and the invisible Nazi substructure.

Garrison's case against Shaw collapsed, since it was based on a witness, Russo, who had given evidence in support of the defence. Garrison only attended the hearing intermittently, and the sole support for his hypotheses came from a smartly dressed New Yorker, Charles I. Spiesel, who suffered from paranoid delusions. Spiesel went to a party in May 1963, overhearing a plot to kill Kennedy, and was the target of a conspiracy involving fifty hypnotists. He testified that he regularly fingerprinted his daughter to ensure that she was not an impostor. After this fiasco, Garrison continued to home in on 'missing' evidence, asserting what it would reveal when found. There were four frames missing from the Zapruder film, a missing brain, missing bullets, missing gunmen, missing witnesses and unexamined autopsy photographs and X-rays.

Garrison declared that the missing film would show a street sign (now missing) scarred by the marks of a stray bullet, proving the existence of more than one gunman. But on publication they disclosed nothing of the kind. So Garrison said the marks had been airbrushed out. Then he produced newspaper photographs taken ten minutes after the assassination which showed a man. He was wearing a suit. So he was a federal agent. In the first picture the man gazed at the pavement. So he had noticed a bullet, and, in the second, his fist was closed. So he had picked it up. Garrison informed the press that the bullet 'which fell into the grass with pieces of the President's head was in the hands of federal government ten minutes after the President was dead'.

In his 1970 book *A Heritage of Stone* Garrison went further. America was run by 'an invisible government that began and ended with deception', a power elite engaged in thought control operating in another dimension above and beyond mundane reality. This may be true, but not in the way Garrison intended.

A variation on the Mafia connection emerged in 1994 when James E. Files, a prisoner serving a thirty-year sentence for the attempted murder of a policeman, stated that he had fired the shot that killed Kennedy. Files, 21 at the time of Kennedy's death, claimed that a prominent member of the Chicago Mafia, Charlie Nicoletti, hired him to carry out the assassination with him. He said that Nicoletti's bullets struck the President but that it was his own shot to Kennedy's head that killed him.

Files's account has been seriously undermined by, among others, John Stockwell and Edward Jay Epstein, but it has its defenders, prominent among them Wim Dankbaar.

Theories about Kennedy's murder have been the

subject of an undending stream of books, while among the many films that deal with the subject are *Rush to Judgment* (Mark Lane, 1966), *JFK* (Oliver Stone, 1991) and *Thirteen Days* (Roger Donaldson, 2000).

Unravelling the truth behind the assassination would be aided by declassification of material locked away until 2029; by unveiling the Lopez Report (detailing the inquiry into Oswald's supposed Mexico trip shortly before the shooting); and by release of the files on Operation Mongoose and the CIA–Mafia plots. Thirty years after the event, investigation of the killing spirals away into trails where unreliable sources provide glimpses of underworld figures and double agents who may, or may not, have had ulterior motives which governmental agencies perhaps wished to conceal. It is unlikely that the truth will ever be known.

Ketch, John (d. 1686)

Also known as Jack Catch, although his real name was probably Richard Jacquet. He was a seventeenth-century executioner held in execration throughout England for his butchery and incompetence, and his name became generic to his trade, still used to terrorise children in Victorian times. For centuries he survived as a stock character in Punch and Judy performances where he met his just deserts (as in real life) by being hanged. 'While Jeffreys on the bench, Ketch on the gibbet sits' ran the saying.

Specifics of Ketch's early misdeeds have not survived. Dwarfish and pockmarked, he embarked on his career as an executioner in 1663. Like others in the trade, he would have done a bit of whipping, branding and nose-slitting on the side. But he caused widespread revulsion by his habit of clowning on the scaffold, rifling through his victims' pockets and stripping them naked while their bodies still twitched. In 1679 Ketch landed the plum job for the execution of thirty men betrayed by Titus Oates, and traipsed round London hawking a 'Plotters Ballad, being Jack Ketch's incomparable receipt for the cure of traytorous disease'.

Four years later Ketch bungled the decapitation of Lord Russell, condemned for his plan to kidnap Charles II. On the scaffold, Russell offered Ketch (as was customary) a bonus or 'tip' for a clean job. The first blow merely wounded Russell who observed, 'You dog, did I give you ten guineas to use me so inhumanely?', and it took three more swipes to finish the job. In 1785 the Duke of

Monmouth fared worse. Although finally dead after five swings of the axe, his head still needed severing from its trunk with a knife. Monmouth's servant, the stakeholder, walked off without paying Ketch his six guineas.

Ketch was imprisoned twice, once for insulting a sheriff and once for a debt of £22. He celebrated his second release by going on a binge in the course of which he beat a gingerbread woman to death. To general satisfaction, he was hanged in November 1686 by one John Price who, in the manner of the times, later swung from the same gallows.

The Law Journal of 28 August 1926 reports an old case in which a Norwich Court held that to say to a man 'You are Jack Ketch' was *per se* 'undoubtedly actionable as defamation'. And rightly; the innocent lookalike was hurled into a duck pond by an angry mob.

See also **de Crespigny**

Kidd, Captain William (1645–1701)

Hanged twice for a pirate on 23 May 1701 at **Execution Dock**. On the first occasion the halter

The swashbuckling Captain Kidd of legend

snapped, but – despite the crowd's exhortations – Kidd proved unable to make a run for it. He was blind drunk. The second time the rope held, and his body was tarred and gibbeted, swinging from Tilbury Point as a landmark for years to come. The chaplain turned Kidd's temporary respite to good use, remarking that it presented a golden chance to make further supplications to the Almighty.

Despite his fearsome reputation as the 'Arch-pirate and common enemy of mankind', Kidd was more of a scapegoat than a corsair. Born in Scotland, he preyed on the French as a licensed privateer from 1689 to 1691. But after his marriage to a wealthy widow, he moved into a Wall Street mansion and traded as an easygoing merchant skipper, the master of the brigantine *Antiqua*. Then in 1695 this fussy middle-aged man was enticed into accepting a commission as a privateer in an expedition against the pirate Thomas Tew. The backers, a Whig syndicate, comprised most of the British cabinet including the First Lord of the Admiralty and the Lord Chancellor – but not King William IV, who was unable to raise the money. Kidd struck a poor bargain: the backers were to receive 60 per cent of any profits, the King 10 per cent, the crew a standard 25 per cent and Kidd himself (who had to stump up a fifth of the costs) the remaining 15 per cent.

Mathematicians will have noticed that this comes to more than 100, and Kidd was meant to persuade his men to take a reduced share, making it almost impossible to assemble a decent crew and, as Kidd sailed down the Nore in his thirty-gunned frigate, the *Adventure Galley*, he was stopped by *HMS Duchess*, who commandeered his best men in a press gang. On arrival in New York he made up his complement of 155 by signing the scourings of the waterfront, pirates themselves, and set sail on 6 September 1696 amid grim forebodings: 'Twill not be in Kidd's power to govern such a hoarde of men under no pay.'

It was not. Basically, his voyage was a disaster, a three-year 'lost cruise'. The first prize, the Dutch *Rouparelle*, did not come his way for eighteen months. The crew had mutinied long before, in October 1697. Kidd killed one of the mutineers, gunner William Moore, with a blow on the head from a wooden bucket bound with iron hoops. Then he barricaded himself into his cabin and burned the ship's log. Kidd breasted this challenge to his authority, and in January 1698 captured a valuable ten-gunner, the *Quedah*

Captain Kidd

Merchant. She seemed a legitimate quarry, carrying French documentation, and her cargo fetched a handsome £10,000. In November 1698 he set sail for New England.

But unknown to Kidd, the Nine Years War against France had ended, and in any case the *Merchant*'s French passes were papers of convenience. The ship was Armenian, and when Kidd limped into Anguilla he found himself branded as the piratical 'Scourge of the Indies'. But the Governor of New York, the Earl of Bellomont (one of the original syndicate), advised him, 'You may safely come hither... and I make no manner of doubt but to obtain the King's pardon.' Kidd landed at Boston on 4 July 1700 and was told to prepare a report.

Two days later he was arrested and shipped to Britain, where he languished in an underground dungeon at **Newgate** for six months, a pawn in a political power-play. The government was at risk if Kidd revealed the role played by Privy Councillors and three Whig ministers in financing a piratical expedition. They wanted him dead, and in May 1701 a blatantly political hearing indicted him on five counts of piracy and Moore's murder.

The Admiralty impounded his papers, precluding Kidd from producing his two commissions, his original sailing orders from Bellomont and the French passes from the *Quedah Merchant* in his defence. The judge commented, 'For aught I can see, none saw them but himself, if there were any', and he was condemned to death.

Early this century, after two centuries of vilification as a blood-drenched rogue, Kidd's papers were unearthed in a bundle of papers in London's Public Record Office.

Kidnapping, invention of

In the first reported case, dating from 1 July 1874, four-year-old Charlie Ross from Philadelphia was not returned and the ransom of $20,000 not collected; clearly the ploy required fine-tuning to become a paying proposition. To complicate matters, the boy's parents had just gone bankrupt, although they succeeded in raising the money.

Charlie was 'snatched' along with his brother, six-year-old Walter, from the sidewalk outside their home on Washington Lane by two men in a buggy. The kidnappers released Walter the same day, but

Charlie Ross, projected forwards in time. The painting, based on a photograph of the boy at two and a half, was done with suggestions from the Ross family to show him aged four

Charlie was never seen again, and an ex-policeman, William Westervelt, was later convicted on circumstantial evidence. It seems that money formed an ancillary motive; Westervelt preferred to drown Charlie for kicks.

Until the ransom demand for Charlie arrived, no one understood the reason behind the theft; why steal a *baby*? Nearly fifty years passed before the next kidnapping, when the practice aroused so much undesirable publicity that in the 1920s the focus shifted to wealthy businessmen. Although just as valuable to their families, as wage-earners, the public did not miss millionaires as much as their children, and the gangsters suffered less at the hands of the press.

The poverty of the Depression era fuelled the craze, with the *New York Times* reporting in March 1932 that 'abduction for ransom has become a big money crime, taking its place beside the liquor, vice and drug traffic among the prominent rackets of this country'. The practice peaked the year before, with 279 recorded American instances, including the national catastrophe of the Lindbergh kidnapping; the parents were deluged with 38,000 letters in the first week. In New York, a hysterical committee of 600 mothers convened to demand plain-clothes police protection for their children playing in Central Park, and Pinkerton's detective agency quadrupled their operatives in a single week.

Before the Charlie Ross snatch, kidnapping was not a specific legal offence – since no one had committed it, no one had legislated against it. But in its wake, Pennsylvania enacted the first laws which carried the ferocious penalty of twenty-five years in solitary together with a $100,000 fine.

The word 'kidnap' derives from the seventeenth-century English practice of seizing children and transporting them as slaves to the **tobacco** plantations in the American colonies. The American innovation was to make money not by sending children away but by sending them back. Australia did not record its first case until 1960, nine years before Britain.

See also **Ladders**, **Nilsen**, **Public relations**

Kidney, human

On 16 October 1888, George Lusk, the head of the Whitechapel Vigilance Committee, received an unsigned letter. It read [*sic*]:

'From Hell

Mr Lusk sir I send you half the Kidne I took from one woman prasarved it for you tother peice I fried and ate it was very nise I may send you the bloody knif that took it out if you only wate a whil longer.

Signed. Catch me if you can Mishter Lusk.'

The organ, initially dismissed as of canine origin, arrived in a three-inch-square cardboard box preserved in spirits of wine.

The accompanying missive was one of thousands received by Scotland Yard during the Ripper crisis; in one month, 14,000 poured into the Yard and the newspapers. In all, 128 pieces of correspondence purported to be from the killer, suggesting that an appreciable portion of the population considered him a model worth emulating. The consensus is that three missives are from the genuine **Jack** – the one above, and two more, those of 28 and 30 September in which the killer expressed an affinity for **ears**. All three letters evince the same chirpy tone.

In the first, the writer promised: 'The next job I do I shall clip the lady's ears off and send them to the police, just for jolly, wouldn't you.' In the second, he apologised for his failure: 'Double event this time. Number one squealed a bit. Couldn't finish straight off. Had not time to get ears for police. Thanks for keeping last letter back till I got to work again.'

Recent research has cast serious doubt about whether Lusk's kidney came from Catharine Eddowes's body.

See also **False confessions**

Kids, Crack

'Crack' is often the first word assimilated by children in America's inner cities. 'It is when mom gets more and more angry,' according to one five-year-old. The term 'crack kids' denotes children who suffer brain damage while in the womb from their mother's habit.

It was thought that the neurological damage occurred when the drug intake reduced the womb's oxygen supply; as she inhales, the mother feels her unborn child kick madly as though being strangled. But evidence is accruing that the crack chemicals, which invade a woman's bloodstream, wait in the uterus to latch on to the spermatozoa as they turn up. Thus the egg is poisoned *ab initio*.

Some crack kids are violent, others autistic; some are prone to fits, some to rages. A few are born phys-ically impaired with very small heads or deformed hearts and lungs. All experience learning difficulties which first emerge as problems with basic locomotive skills like walking. Collectively, crack kids constitute a 'biological underclass' that is sure to expand with the use of a drug that presents a major problem throughout the developed world.

Killer Bimbos *et al.*

They do not actually kill anyone; Killer Bimbos flock to the ski resort of Aspen, Colorado, in the hope of bedding some celebrity or billionaire. The competition is fierce – and savage internecine Killer Bimbo violence the result. They slash, scratch, bite and attack each other with champagne glasses; over Christmas 1991 at the Aspen Club Lounge, Dewi Sukarno put 'Mini' Osmena in hospital by nearly gouging out her eye. She needed thirty-seven stitches.

'There is no other place with such a concentration of fat wallets and mansions within one square mile,' said Miss Texas USA of Aspen in 1991. Sean Connery took refuge in a wine cellar when charged by a swarm of Killer Bimbos; Michael Caine was mobbed and three bodyguards bitten when they tried to stem an invasion of the Killer Bimbos at an exclusive party. 'There is no doubt,' says David Koch (worth $1.7 billion and suffering from Bimbo Fatigue), 'Aspen is more ferocious and frantic than ever before.' Even the pavements are heated in this socialites' version of **Medellin**, Colombia, and the prison is so comfortable that it reputedly needs walls to keep people out.

First blood went to singer Andy Williams's ex-wife in 1976, when she accidentally shot her lover dead saying: 'Bang! Bang!' Her sentence totalled thirty days inside, served segmentally to dovetail with the school holidays. The following year the Aspen courthouse was the scene of Ted **Bundy**'s celebrated escape. After an interlocutory hearing on 6 June 1977 about the status of the death penalty, Bundy suddenly found himself alone. He sauntered into the law library on the second floor, crossed to a large window, opened it, jumped and ran, thinking 'They don't shoot you in Aspen.' Inside, his absence passed unremarked until a relaxed young woman walked into the Sheriff's office and asked, 'Hey, is it kind of unusual for someone to be leaping out of the courthouse window?'

Despite a sprained ankle, Bundy remained at large for five days, swimming the Roaring Fork River and holing up for one night in a hunter's cabin. But he could not break out of the area with its mountains on all sides. It was on these snowy slopes, years later, that the Ivana Trump/Marla Maples War first blossomed. In 1989 real shots were fired at a paparazzi helicopter hovering over the wedding of Don Johnson (star of TV's *Miami Vice*). Then in 1990 Hunter S. Thompson, the (late) bad man of alternative journalism, landed himself in hot water for allegedly assaulting a girl in a steam tub. And in 1991 Lord White, a sugar grand-daddy and Aspen regular, was charged with assaulting his beautiful companion, Victoria Tucker.

Killer Bimbos are blonde, leggy, and immaculately groomed. Snooty about first-class travel, they are freighted in by private jet, their arrival only marginally preceded by their silicone-enhanced breasts. As short-term sexual assets these accessories are extremely expensive, retailing (according to one exponent at a Christmas 1991 dinner party) at $3,000 a week and a New York condo.

See also **Queen Poison**

King, Rodney (1965–)

Briefly the world's most famous victim, victimised anew by his exploitation as a major financial asset.

King is the ex-convict videotaped during his drubbing from the Los Angeles police on the night of 2 March 1991. From then on he was a made man, the centre of a swirling vortex of agents, lawyers and film-makers who fought tooth-and-nail for a slice of the action. On his first release from jail after the televising of his fifty-six blows, King was so hot a property that he was lucky to hack his way through the crowds of ambulance-chasers. The deal-making mania eventually engulfed Stacey Koon, one of the officers involved in the beating, who signed with a television network, as did Los Angeles police chief Darryl Gates.

As soon as he was safely under contract, King spent his days confined in a secure house in Ventura County, guarded round the clock and dosed with pharmaceuticals under the supervision of his personal psychiatrist. It made King lonely and miserable, but with their client locked away from exploitation and alternative offers, his business advisers could map their commercial strategy. They had King's image to protect; his marketability was seriously dented by an arrest in May 1991 after he engaged the services of a transvestite hooker.

The stakes were high. At one stage the personal injury specialist Stephen Lerman wanted $56 million for the Rodney King 'supersuit', but he later trimmed his demands to a $10 million lump sum plus an annuity. Lerman's fees might have absorbed a third of any receipts; then there were disbursements, like King's advance, his security and living expenses, and the bills due to the medical team of psychiatrist, plastic surgeon and neurologist. Eventually the Los Angeles Council offered $1.5 million in settlement, but Lerman held out for $5 million, and was sacked after negotiations broke down.

Meanwhile the film rights to the Rodney King story were sold to some unknown producers, Triple 7, for a rumoured (and measly) $20,000; they planned a feature film and a domestic mini-series, together with a book of the film and the book of the making of the film. That left the merchandising and endorsement rights; King's Aunt Angela – a Lerman supporter – was warned off producing T-shirts of her nephew's copyrighted face, and his relatives split into warring elements divided between his wife's faction and his own family, with King, a one-man victim corporation, caught in the middle, pulled this way and that by his kith and kin while the media claimed him as a celebrity, spokesperson or cautionary tale. Whether as icon, demon, potential gold-mine, poor businessman or modest retiring citizen, King remains a shy and pleasant man unsuited to the demands of fame; his new lawyer is called Milton Grimes.

The exceptional facet of the King case is that it was captured on tape; otherwise his brutal treatment followed the familiar Los Angeles code for blacks that if you run from the police you are beaten up. But such thrashings play with fire. Although blacks will apparently tolerate economic injustice almost indefinitely, five of America's massive race riots stemmed directly from physical oppression by law enforcement officers: Watts (1965), Newark and Detroit (1967) Liberty City and Brownsville (1980) and South Central itself (1992). That is, race riots are provoked by white policemen, and an examination of the record shows a compelling reason for their addiction to thuggery.

They can get away with it. Police are almost never prosecuted for 'excessive force'. In Los Angeles county, well over a thousand citizens have perished from police gunfire since 1945. But of the fifty-four cases referred to the District Attorney between 1986 and 1990, fifty-three were dismissed and the single exception concerned an officer-on-officer assault.

Thus not one of the 387 shootings by Los Angeles Police Department officers between 1985 and 1991 (which included 153 fatalities) resulted in charges, although numerous survivors received substantial civil damages, with a cumulative total in excess of $20 million.

Similarly, fifty-six of the 202 shootings by the sheriff's department during the corresponding period were seriously questionable (involving, for instance, unarmed victims hit in the back) but again no cases resulted, even for the 1988 execution by a sheriff which the city settled for $1 million out of court. Cynics with long memories can take heart from the 1973 incident when an officer killed a 12-year-old boy while 'playing' Russian roulette, perhaps to secure a confession. He was charged, and two more indictments were laid only last year.

Following the Los Angeles riots, the Christopher Commission reviewing the LAPD monitored dozens of patrol car messages, such as 'I would love to drive down Slauson with a flamethrower. We could have a barbecue' and 'I almost got me a Mexican last night but he dropped the gun too quick.' The hard-core LAPD racist element is thought to constitute no more than 10 per cent of the force, but it is beyond the rule of law.

Kray, Ronald (1933–95) and Reginald (1933–2000)

East End twins, with a strangely cinematic penchant for violence, who controlled the London underworld in the late 1950s and 1960s. They thought Cagney, but filmed Ealing: stock East Enders who drank tea, worshipped their **mother** ('Our Queen'), wore spiv suits from Savile Row, drove flash cars and were on nodding terms with the celebrities of the day.

Not that the twins provided much to laugh at. As children they were boxers and street fighters; as young men they routed Army discipline in head-on conflict (see **Officer material**). By their late teens they were already, in the words of one old villain, 'a thoroughly evil pair of bastards', with a reputation for unrestrained savagery. They loved fighting. As an asso-

ciate said, 'If I was cutting somebody or putting the boot in, I'd usually hold back a bit – never the twins though. If you watched their faces while they did it, you'd see real hate. They always went the limit.'

The young Krays, known locally as the Terrible Twins, with 'Our Queen', their mother Violet

Their first foothold in their early twenties was a rowdy East End snooker hall, the Regal; after a month of brawls the owner installed the Krays as the legal tenants at a weekly rent of £5. The hall became their headquarters; a gang formed round the twins, who led raiding parties for fun, to smash up a dance hall or pub, rather like a club outing. They ruled with fear, holding court martials for breaches of discipline, and Ronnie earned the nickname of 'the Colonel' for his military acumen and network of spies. He accumulated a formidable arsenal, kept at his mother's house – an old Mauser, sawn-off shotguns, revolvers and a Beretta .32. His **swordstick**, Gurkha knives, bayonets, cutlasses and sabres were sharpened on a grindstone in the rear yard. A barber called daily to administer his morning shave while he lounged in a purple dressing gown, and for a while he retained a personal masseur. His yoga fad proved shortlived.

The twins rapidly moved into protection, 'putting the arm on' dozens of local pubs, restaurants, illicit betting shops and unlicensed gambling dens. By 1956 their outfit acquired a name as 'The Firm', and that autumn Ronnie gained tremendous prestige by shooting a docker in the leg after an argument about a car. On 5 November 1956 he received a three-year sentence for causing grievous bodily harm (to another victim), and in prison keeled over into certified madness. On release, in an unstable mental state, he was appalled to find that Reggie had almost gone straight.

Reggie – more diplomatic, more intelligent, less of an out-and-out psychopath – founded a flourishing West End-style club in the East End, 'The Double R', which he fronted in a smoking jacket. He was halfway to quitting the rough-and-tumble of dirty work and Ronnie's bar wars; he '**straightened**' the law and made peace with their old enemies, the Italian gangs of Clerkenwell.

But Ronnie had no time for such trifling; his craving to intimidate and exploit impelled him to demand protection from a club they already owned. He stormed out of inter-gang councils and suddenly all Reggie's administration and self-imposed restraint counted for nothing. It was us-and-them, the twins together against the world, and the Krays' reversion to strong-arm tactics secured a potent victory when they muscled in on Peter Rachman's Notting Hill rent collectors. Rachman tried to buy them off with an ill-considered bouncing cheque and then realised he had to come up with something better fast. It was 'Esmerelda's Barn', a prime Knightsbridge casino, and Rachman agented its takeover from Stephan de Faye in the autumn of 1960. The twins paid £1,000 for an asset producing some £80,000 a year. Their fortunes were made.

But only in theory. Ronnie pined for a plusher version of the Regal billiard hall and ran the Barn into the ground, personally mismanaging credit limits and encouraging admission of riff-raff. He was offered £1,000 a week by the manager (who had been kept on) to stay away. But Ronnie needed a showcase for his violent theatrics, and within a few years the casino went bust. Elsewhere business boomed. The Krays pulled off some fifty 'long-firm frauds' in the early 60s, netting an estimated £100,000 from this source alone in 1962. Their arrest on 10 January 1965 for demanding money with menaces was followed by a bungled prosecution (or perhaps a tampered jury) that made them seem untouchable. By now the Mafia had put out feelers for a reliable outfit to guarantee the well-being of the planeloads of punters they proposed to fly into London on gamblers' junkets. Serious money, in the form of casino and hotel investments, was at stake. Could the twins guarantee protection?

The Krays' only rivals were the Richardson gang (see **Torture**) and, spoiling for a firefight, Ronnie bought two Browning sub-machine-guns. But luck went the

Krays' way. After a couple of skirmishes, an unrelated shootout on 8 March 1966 – the 'Battle of Mr Smith's Club' – put most of the Richardsons into hospital, behind bars or under the ground, leaving the Krays as the undisputed criminal kings of London.

But Ronnie wanted to kill someone. He picked on the one worthwhile survivor from the Richardson debacle, George **Cornell**, who had in any case called him a 'fat poof'. His killing meant that Reggie had to murder **Jack the Hat** to keep up. Then they had Mad Frank the **Axeman** – one of their own – put away, and two more members of the firm – a man called Frost and 'Mad' Teddy Smith – vanished without trace. By now Ronnie was drowning in paranoia verging on madness and the Firm awash with suspicion.

Reg (left) and Ronnie (right), released after thirty-six hours of questioning about George Cornell's murder

A new police commissioner, Sir Joseph Simpson, felt compelled to target the Krays. The full-scale investigation was led by Inspector Leonard 'Nipper' Read (after whom the Krays named their pet boa constrictor, purchased at Harrods) heading a team of fourteen men, and he insisted on legal immunity for informers. When the twins' ex-accountant Leslie Payne panicked, Read interrogated him for three weeks in hope of a charge to lock the twins up until the preliminary hearings. With the Krays out of the way, even temporarily, their terrified victims and associates might give **evidence**.

On 7 May 1968, in the wake of the '**attaché case**' revelations, Read arrested the Krays in an early-morning raid together with a dozen cohorts, charging Ronnie and Reggie with the Cornell and McVitie murders.

One by one members of the Firm talked – first Lennie Dunn, then Billy Exley, then Liza, then the Blind Beggar barmaid, then Albert Donaghue, then Blonde

Carol, then Ronnie Hart. The Krays were jailed for a minimum of thirty years in March 1969. Ronnie served the latter years of his sentence in Broadmoor psychiatric hospital, where he died in 1995.

Reggie, after serving more than the thirty-year prison term he had been given in 1969, was released in August 2000 on compassionate grounds as he had inoperable cancer. He died six weeks later.

Kürten, Peter (1883–1931)

One of the most sinister photographs in all the demonology of crime shows Peter Kürten, the Vampire of Düsseldorf, just standing still, doing nothing, wearing a suit and somehow radiating evil. Proud of his appearance, he used a dab of make-up here and there, staring at himself for ages in the mirror, a compulsion shared with Britain's Peter **Sutcliffe**, the Yorkshire Ripper.

Kürten was adept at obtaining orgasms from unusual stimuli. 'It was not my intention to get satisfaction by sexual intercourse,' he later explained, 'but by killing.' In fact almost anything destructive would do; Kürten set fire to haystacks or woods to bring himself to a climax. What really excited him was blood; if he witnessed a road accident he would ejaculate involuntarily. In adolescence he discovered that the experience of sodomising sheep could be enhanced by stabbing the animal in a frenzy.

In maturer years Kürten regularly experienced emission when seizing a human victim's throat or sticking in the knife (see **Stabs**). If possible, he gulped the blood down as it pumped from the wound; he once gave himself an orgasm in a park by cutting off a swan's head and sticking its spurting neck into his mouth. The gurgling sound was music to Kürten's ears, and just before his execution he told psychiatrist Karl Berg that he looked forward to momentarily hearing his own blood cascading from his trunk into the basket and on to his head.

Kürten spent twenty-four of his forty-eight years in prison. The more he was sentenced, the more he seethed with rage at the inhuman penal conditions. He broke minor prison regulations just to be confined in solitary so that he could better indulge in detailed sadistic daydreams of immense catastrophes when he weakened railway bridges (see **Viaducts**), or introduced bacilli into drinking water, or gave arsenic-laden sweets to schoolchildren. He recalled, 'I would derive the sort of pleasure from these visions that other people got from thinking about a naked woman.'

Kürten's first victim was 13-year-old Khristine Klein, killed on 25 May 1913. The murder is a textbook example of a fascination with blood coupled with the get-even mentality that underpins a serial killer's motivation. 'I heard the blood spurt and drip on the mat beside the bed,' Kürten later recounted. 'It spurted in an arch, right over my hand … Next day I went back to Mulheim. There is a cafe opposite the Kleins' place and I sat there and drank a glass of beer and read all about the murder in the papers. People were talking about it all round me. All this indignation and horror did me good.'

To his Düsseldorf neighbours, Kürten seemed a model citizen – decent, modest, kindly and married. He parted his hair meticulously, buffed his gleaming shoes, and scented himself with eau de Cologne. Children liked him instinctively, and he was finally arrested after befriending a woman stray, Maria Budlick, whom he brought back to his flat for a glass of milk and a sandwich before taking her through the woods, where he assaulted her. But he stopped short of the kill, and within days Maria led the police to his home.

Kürten knew his time was up, but when he notified his wife that he was the 'Beast of Düsseldorf' she thought it a joke. Then, realising he was in earnest, she proposed a suicide pact. But Kürten had a better idea. There was a substantial reward out for his arrest; she might at least earn some money by turning him in. So she did, on 24 May 1931, arranging to meet her husband and the police outside the St Rochus Church.

Kürten was executed on 2 July 1931 for nine murders and seven attempted murders, with the court unable to detect any trace of insanity in his brisk, composed and lucid manner.

His background furnishes all the constituents of a serial killer, and more besides. There is the drunken, brutal father; marital rape; whippings from his mother, the incest and attempted incest, the cruelty to animals, the masturbation of dogs, the buggery of goats and pigs, the **arson**, the rapes, and quite possibly the murder of two children drowned while playing round a raft on the Rhine when he was aged nine.

After his inaugural killing of young Khristine Klein in 1913, Kürten only got into his stride in 1929. He started the year with Rosa Ohliger, a child stabbed thirteen times with a pair of scissors, his favourite weapon. One wound was to the vagina. On 23 August, Kürten killed two children, slitting their throats, and tried to rape and kill a woman, Gertrude Schulte, leaving her for dead.

With such a clear motive for killing – orgasmic gratification – premature ejaculation could be a life-saver; when Kürten climaxed *before* completing a murder, there was no point in continuing the assault. He would shamble off apologetically, mumbling 'That's what love's about.'

It may be that this trait led to Kürten 's arrest, which flowed from Maria Budlick's survival. Just as she was about to lose consciousness, Maria felt her assailant's grip round her throat relax.

'Do you remember where I live?' Kürten asked. 'In case you're ever in need and want my help?'

'No,' gasped Maria, and Kürten quietly showed her out of the woods.

See also **Detection, Fantasising, Organised**

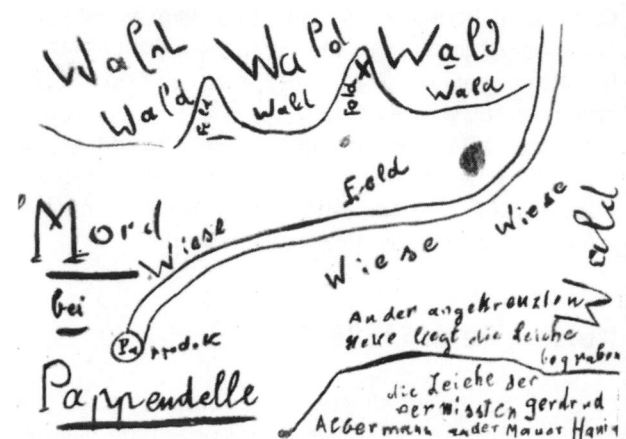

Sketch enclosed by Kürten in the 'murder letter', indicating where the body of Gertrude Alberman would be found

L

Lacenaire, Pierre-François (1800–35)

Poet and murderer who achieved a very brief stay of execution when the guillotine's blade jammed inches above his neck. Lacenaire managed to twist his head round to view the second and final approach of the engine of his destruction.

Lacenaire represented a new kind of criminal, the alienated middle-class intellectual. After a string of convictions for petty theft, he axed an old Parisian woman and her son to death, hoping to steal a hoard of 10,000 francs. All he found was some *bric à brac*. Betrayed by his accomplices, Lacenaire was thrown into prison where, being well-educated and articulate, he attracted fashionable attention, not least for his callow but undeniable sense of style. 'It would have been very disagreeable to be executed by *a provincial* executioner,' he sighed on learning that he would be tried in Paris.

As a free man, Lacenaire composed songs and verses; as a prisoner, he corresponded with the papers, attaining the renown that previously eluded him. In his cell in La Force he conducted Socratic dialogues with an entranced audience of doctors, barristers and journalists. 'There was a day in my life when I had to choose between suicide and crime. I chose crime,' he expounded. In less flamboyant

Pierre-François Lacenaire

mood, Lacenaire described the time in March 1829 when, as a deserter, he exhausted the last of the 500 francs mailed by his mother. 'Within a matter of days, I was reduced to a point at which I almost died of hunger,' he recalled. 'From that moment I became a thief, and in spirit at least a murderer.' This obvious piece of cause-and-effect constituted a novel inversion for an era which assumed that crime caused poverty.

Lacenaire's *Memoirs* – unfinished at his execution – promoted the notion of a neglected man of destiny waging his struggle against a corrupt society, and included a number of modern concepts. **Prisons**, for instance, he dismissed as 'Universities of Crime'. He blamed his misshapen life on the inadequate rearing of his uncaring parents, and lectured visitors on social justice, earning the opposition's favour by his censure of Louis-Philippe's regime. His fame spread to Russia, where the *Memoirs* were released in magazine form by a young editor, Dostoevsky, who was intrigued by his views on crime and punishment.

Lacenaire's capture resulted from one of the great pieces of foot-slogging detection. On 16 December 1834, a neighbour noticed blood seeping under the door of widow Chardon's lodgings at 271 rue St Martin. Inside lay the widow and her son, both dead, and two weeks later a bank messenger was called to the rooms of a man named Mahossier at 66 rue Montorgueil. On entry, the door slammed shut and the boy was pinioned from behind. He broke free and reported the assault to the Sureté, who assigned both cases to Chief Inspector Louis Canler.

The messenger had noticed that one of his assailants, a distinguished man with a silky moustache and a high forehead, had a copy of Rousseau's *Social Contract* protruding from his pocket. Canler visited every cheap hotel in the area, combing their registers for a 'Mahossier', lighting upon the name in a rooming house on the rue du Faubourg. The hotelier remembered little, but on the next line of the ledger the name 'Fizellier' was printed. The two had shared a room, and the proprietor's wife volunteered that Fizellier was a large red-haired man – like someone already under arrest. The imprisoned Fizellier admitted to the bank job, and the hotelier's wife let drop that Mahossier had an alias, Bâton.

The real Bâton, a known homosexual thief, did not resemble Mahossier. Nor was he a great reader. But Canler reasoned that Mahossier must know him – why else appropriate his name? He interrogated all Bâton's associates, finally hearing rumours of an upper-class gentleman with a silky moustache known as 'Gaillard'. But Paris boasted many Gaillards, so Canler toured the hostels to find one whose handwriting matched 'Mahossier's' signature and, after two days, tracked down Gaillard's rooms. The landlady remembered a courteous poet with well-trimmed whiskers.

So Canler returned to Fizellier, who related how an inebriated 'Gaillard' claimed to have axed a widow to death while an accomplice kept watch. Canler now realised that 'Gaillard' figured in both the murder and the bank job. Fizellier was the accomplice for one, and Canler followed his hunch that a stool pigeon, Avril, had played a part in the other. Avril squealed, revealing that Gaillard had a well-to-do aunt in the rue Bar-du-Bec. There Canler located a Madame Gaillard and she, it transpired, had a shady nephew called Pierre-François Lacenaire who, as it happened, was arrested in Beaune on 2 February 1835 for passing a forged bill of exchange.

Brought to Paris, eight months later Lacenaire died with courage and composure.

Ladders

The conclusive evidence in the trial of Richard Bruno Hauptmann, a German carpenter executed for the kidnapping and subsequent murder of nineteen-month-old Charles Lindbergh Jnr.

The kidnapping on 1 March 1931 inaugurated an extended ordeal for the parents which ended only with the grisly discovery of their child's decomposing remains on 12 May 1932. By then the Lindberghs had lived through thirteen ransom demands, one paid in full through their intermediary Dr John F. Condon at St Raymond's cemetery. It was a hoax.

The investigation centred on the wooden scaling ladder, abandoned in the garden after the kidnappers climbed to the second-floor windows of the Lindberghs' New Jersey home. Two years later, 'the greatest feat of scientific detection of all time' (according to *The Trial of Richard Hauptmann*) traced the ladder to Hauptmann. But it now seems the evidence was both inconclusive and fraudulent.

Richard Bruno Hauptmann, electrocuted for the kidnapping and murder of Charles Lindbergh Jnr. To the left, the scrawled ransom note, to the right, the handover instructions

The ladder, crudely made in sections, had three upright runners of North Carolina yellow pine which showed, under the microscope, tiny grooves indicating that the wood was machined in a sawmill with a defective planer. Arthur Koehler, a wood technologist, circularised the 1,598 lumber mills handling yellow pine and pinned the source to the Dorn Lumber Company in South Carolina. They had despatched forty-seven loads of yellow pine to thirty timber merchants, each of which Koehler and Detective Bornmann visited in turn.

One of the wood yards was in the Bronx, and on 19 September 1934 the police arrested a local German carpenter, Richard Bruno Hauptmann, for handling the marked ransom notes, $10 gold certificates. Hauptmann was a regular customer of the Bronx National Lumber and Millwork Company.

This meant that, like other Americans living round the thirty designated timber yards, he could have bought wood from the Lindbergh consignment. The ransom money, laundered on the New York underworld at around forty cents in the dollar, was similarly disseminated into many hands. Hauptmann's $13,000 allegedly came his way through a crooked business partner, Isidor Fisch. This was all very suspicious, but far from conclusive.

The evidence that clinched Hauptmann's fate was Rail Sixteen. The Lindbergh ladder incorporated a section of a different kind of wood – a wide chunk planed down from something like a floorboard. And when Detective Bornmann searched Hauptmann's attic, he came upon a torn-up floorboard with a matching sawn-out section. The interpolated wood from the ladder fitted the plank perfectly, with the four nail holes in Rail Sixteen coinciding with the nail holes in the exposed attic joist. Hauptmann, evidentially tied to the ladder, was buckled into the electric chair on 3 April 1936.

In 1985 Ludovic Kennedy's *The Carpenter and the Airman* established that Hauptmann was framed. At the original hearing the court learned that Hauptmann habitually made the cod Teutonic misspellings exemplified on the ransom note – 'gut' for 'good' and 'singature' for 'signature'. But in the first police test, Hauptmann spelled the text correctly; the detectives insisted that he wrote it again spelled wrongly, producing this second version as evidence. The entire prosecution case was similarly vitiated. One witness altered his story after money changed hands. The telephone number of Lindbergh's intermediary, Dr John Condon, was scrawled on Hauptmann's lavatory door by a journalist, Tom Cassidy, as a joke. Hauptmann's partner Fisch did have strong underworld connections.

As for Rail Sixteen, the cannibalisation of the attic floor only came to light after Hauptmann's wife left the family home, giving the police a free run of the premises. Was it likely that the meticulous, prosperous Hauptmann went up into the roof, prised up the floor and carved out one piece of wrong-sized timber? Or was he framed? Hauptmann's descendants are petitioning for a posthumous pardon.

Another famous ladder, now based in Scotland

Peace's collapsible burgling ladder

Yard's Black Museum, is the collapsible burgling ladder of Charlie Peace, the nineteenth-century murderer.

When folded, it measures fifteen inches by nine by two, fitting comfortably in a briefcase. As a burglar, Peace made his approach from above, roping the top of the ladder to a rooftop chimney and then climbing *down* to effect entry. His crucible for melting the stolen valuables is also housed in the Museum, as is his violin, which he played professionally at private gatherings, thereby casing the joints of the houses he later robbed.

Laing

Long-established British construction company. Laing's motto is 'We Build for People', and in 1987 they accepted an order for two termite-proof gallows for the Abu Dhabi regime. As the Foreign Office pointed out: 'The manufacture of execution equipment in the UK is legal and its export is not subject to any form of control.'

In January 1992 Amnesty International, the human rights organisation, claimed that other British firms were exporting artefacts such as leg-irons and an electronic torture chamber nicknamed (although not by its occupants) 'The House of Fun'. Amnesty opposes the continued trade in lethal **injection** equipment. Indeed, it seems hard to endorse traditional commercial arguments that manufacturers have no idea what, for instance, gallows will be used for. The likely ultimate end-use of small arms may be no more obscure, and Mikhail Kalashnikov's 1993 recommendation that the armaments industry set up a charitable fund for those wounded in conflicts is the thin end of a very large wedge indeed: product liability for weapons manufacturers.

The 1954 edition of a popular book on hanging, *Shadow of the Gallows*, includes a pleasant photograph of elderly craftsmen toiling in a workshop. The caption reads: 'Modern hanging ropes being made at the South London factory which supplies them for Britain and the Empire. The operator is burnishing the metal "eye" which now replaces the slip-knot.'

Landru, Henri Desiré (1869–1922)

French murderer of unusual appearance. On 21 July 1904, in his mid-thirties, Landru collected his first prison sentence. An ostensibly respectable married man, he made a modest living dealing in second-hand furniture and cars, but he could not keep his

Landru, Old Bluebeard

hands off other people's property. Days before the outbreak of the First World War he was sentenced *in absentia* to four years for fraud, his sixth conviction, and only avoided prison by going into hiding under various aliases.

Landru's speciality was inept attempts to swindle elderly widows: fraud by seduction. His three-year sentence in 1910 stemmed from his advertisement for a wife in a Lille newspaper. A Mme Izoret responded, handing over her cashbox (containing 20,000 francs). He reciprocated with his deeds (worthless paper). Landru disappeared, she went to the police, and in prison he must have reflected how much better it would have been if she had disappeared rather than he.

In 1914, posing as the widower Raymond Diard, he charmed an attractive widow, Jeanne Cuchet, in a lingerie store, and they set up home with her 17-year-old son in the Paris suburb of Chantilly, where he appropriated her 5,000 francs savings. Jeanne persisted in the affair, despite the misgivings of her relatives, the discovery that 'Diard' had a track record of fraud, that his real name was Landru, and the revelation that this Landru was, in fact, already married. The Cuchets were last seen on 15 January 1915. Landru almost certainly incinerated their bodies; neighbours saw thick black smoke streaming from his chimney.

Landru hired another villa, where he disposed of a Mme Laborde-Line. Then he rented a pretty stone house, the Villa Ermitage, thirty miles south of Paris in Gambais. He never furnished it properly, but he did instal a large stove in the basement. Landru was no figurative ladykiller – short, bald, middle-aged and handicapped by a bizarre spade-shaped beard – but each day the hostilities on the Western Front created swathes of new widows. In May, Landru advertised in the Parisian *Le Journal* under the name of Freymet: 'Widower with two children, aged 43, with comfortable income, affectionate, serious, and moving into good society, desires to meet widow with a view to matrimony.' During the war years some 300 women succumbed to his blandishments. He escorted his murder victims to Gambais by train, buying himself a return ticket and them a single, thus saving a franc. Every one counted; on average, the murders netted 3,000 francs from the victim's savings or the sale of her trinkets, bonds and furniture. Landru, who killed for money, was permanently broke.

And so it went without mishap until the 1918 disappearance of Mme Anna Colombe (last seen at Gambais with a man called Dupont). The Mayor put her sister, Mlle Lacoste, in touch with the surviving relative of a Mme Celestine Buisson (last seen at Gambais with a man called Freymet). The two women's distinctive descriptions of a small gentleman with a bow tie and large red beard tallied, but the investigation soon reached a dead end. The tenant of the Villa Ermitage had given a false name and address.

But on 12 April 1919, while promenading on the rue de Rivoli, Mlle Lacoste recognised Landru entering a porcelain shop, and the police extracted the customer details from his invoice. Landru had adopted the name of Monsieur Guillet, and taken up lodgings at 76 rue de Rochechouart with a delightful 19-year-old actress, Fernande Segret. She met Landru on a tramcar, thinking him a 'funny old man' until becoming his mistress. As the police dragged him away, Landru bade farewell by bursting into an aria from the Massenet opera *Manon*, 'Adieu, notre petit table'; like '**Acid** Bath' Haigh, who followed in his footsteps, Landru trained as a chorister in his youth.

At the Prefecture, an envelope in Landru's pocket disclosed his true identity. The police examined his little black notebook with growing dismay. On one page, eleven names were listed, four of people known to be missing or presumed dead: the two Cuchets, and Mesdames Buisson and Colombe. The remaining seven had disappeared. Other pages detailed Landru's dealings with 283 women; the mere mention of this figure passed as a joke in France for some time afterwards, and investigators established that Landru had enjoyed 'relationships' with at least 179 respondents. On 29 April the Villa Ermitage was searched and the gardens excavated, but the only remains in the grounds came from two dogs which, Landru said, he had kindly agreed to **strangle** on behalf of their owner, Mlle Merchardier (one of the vanished eleven). 'It is the gentlest and easiest of deaths,' he reassured the court, speaking like one who knew.

Apart from 295 unidentified bones in the cinders near the basement furnace, some clothes, buttons, and forty-seven teeth, no bodies were ever found, and this evidential hiatus allowed Landru to taunt the prosecution. His frequent appearances before the magistrates became a popular diversion. The music-halls nicknamed him Old Bluebeard, the Ladykiller and the Red Man of Gambais, and Fernande Segret's stage career briefly blossomed. Landru played to the gallery, crammed with women, offering his seat in the dock to a latecomer who could not find a space. But it was gallows humour, and it upset the jury.

Landru was convicted on 30 November 1921 of eleven murders. His victims' relatives and the members of the jury signed a petition for mercy, but he went to the guillotine on 25 February 1922, protesting his innocence. Forty-one years later the daughter of one of his trial lawyers removed a picture frame from a presentation drawing by Landru to find a confession, translated in the *Daily Express* as 'I did it. I burned their bodies in my kitchen oven', and in the *News of the World* as 'The trial witnesses are fools. I killed the women inside the house.'

In 1965, Landru's life was filmed. A surprise member of the first-night audience was the aged Fernande Segret, long presumed dead. After the trial she had withdrawn to the Lebanon, working as a governess. Returning forty years later to sue the film's producers for 200,000 francs, she won 10,000, but her renewed notoriety prompted a fatal plunge into the castle moat at Flers-de-l'One. Her suicide note read: 'I still love him, but I am suffering too greatly. I am going to kill myself.'

Of all the attempts to make murder pay, Briton Frederick Henry Seddon made history's most avaricious attempt to squeeze out the last penny. After duping Eliza Barrow out of £1,500 in 1911, he poisoned her with arsenic, augmenting his take with a final twelve shillings levied from the undertaker as commission for introducing the business.

Las Vegas

The invention of Benjamin 'Bugsy' Siegel (1906–47), a mobster from Williamsburg, Brooklyn, who first made his name as a New York bootlegger. He was among the four who on 15 April 1931 executed one of the last old-time bosses, Joe Masseria, in a Coney Island restaurant during a meal with Lucky Luciano.

Siegel moved to Hollywood and apparent respectability in 1936, spattering his underwear with monograms and parking a Cadillac, a Buick and a Dusenberg in the drive of his $250,000 mansion. He lined his bathroom with red marble, the principal bed was mounted on a two-foot dais, and the house concealed three secret refuges behind sliding partitions operated by hidden buttons.

Siegel's children enrolled in the best schools. They took riding lessons; he joined the Hillcrest Country Club and tussled nightly with the *Reader's Digest* feature 'It pays to increase your wordpower'. As mobsters go, Bugsy had a real sense of refinement and courtliness; his charisma won friends like Cary Grant, George Raft, Jimmy Durante and Jack Warner, and Grant took Bugsy as his role model for the 1940s movie *Mr Lucky*.

After bedding numerous starlets in his love nest at the Garden of Allah, Bugsy romanced the Countess di Frasso (née Dorothy Taylor, an American heiress) who, sadly, was married. The Countess whirled Bugsy away on a European tour, passing her mobster off as a baronet from an old English family.

It was a business trip. Bugsy had acquired – or rather, had been duped into buying – the rights to an awesome new explosive, 'Atomite', which he felt sure would interest Mussolini. He was right: the dictator produced a $40,000 advance payment for an exclusive licence. But at the formal demonstration in front of the Italian War Office, the detonator was pressed only to produce a tiny detumescent wisp of smoke. Mussolini demanded his money back and demoted Bugsy and his Countess socially, summarily ejecting them from their guest accommodation in Rome's Villa Madam into the mansion's converted stables. Into their vacated quarters went another pair of visitors, Goebbels and Goering.

This prompted Bugsy's next idea. 'I'm gonna kill him, and that dirty Goebbels too,' he told Dorothy. But she talked him down, pointing out that her Italian husband would be blamed for the murders. The course of world history might have been very different if Bugsy had stuck to unmarried women, and this crime of omission remained one of his great regrets.

Bugsy's first stab at finding treasure in the sand started in September 1938, when he set sail in a three-masted rented schooner, the *Metha Nelson*, on an expedition to Cocos Island 300 miles off Costa Rica, where $90 million of pirate gold was surely buried. They had a treasure map, property of an individual called Bill Bowbeer.

In eighty-five-degree temperatures, through tropical cloudbursts, in the choking jungle, the crew set to work with spades, explosives and heavy drills. 'We drilled through rocks and shale,' recalled one crew member. 'The climate was murderous but we couldn't stop. We dynamited whole cliffs.' But the island extended over eight square miles. After ten days Bugsy called a halt and cruised back to reality and the limelight of the press. The glare of amused newspaper interest led to exposure of his murky past, and the public's worst suspicions were confirmed by rumours about his November 1939 killing of Big Greenie Greenburg for his efforts to chisel $5,000 out of the boys from **Murder Inc**. Siegel had to resign from his clubs. Later, he admitted to a career total of twelve homicides: 'But don't worry, we only kill each other.'

With the advent of war, Siegel's eyes strayed over the state line to the small township of Las Vegas with its population of 6,000, mostly Hoover dam construction workers and descendants of the early Mormons. As well as a street of brothels unromantically entitled 'Block 16', Vegas had a group of sawdust joints where gambling was legal. Siegel looked at the dross but saw glittering lights. He envisaged a future of hydro-electric power driving the air conditioning in glittering hotels accessed by Highway 91 and – maybe – mass air travel.

Together with the new woman in his life, the archetypal moll Virginia Hill, Siegel developed his fantasy. He sold his Trans America wire service to the Vegas joints; then he bought into them. Next he acquired thirty acres of desert for a few dollars, set up the Nevada Projects Corporation, and secured Mob finance. In December 1945, work started on his casino-hotel, 'The Flamingo'.

It is easier to shoot people for not running a tight construction site than to run one yourself. Siegel's penthouse suite needed rebuilding at a cost of $22,500 when he noticed that the planned ceiling height was only five feet eight. The air conditioning throughout proved too noisy; it was ripped out and replaced, and the kitchen reconfigured at a cost of $30,000. The boiler room was too small, building materials just walked off site, it rained in the desert for nine days nonstop and the construction budget mushroomed from $1.5 million to $6 million. Mob pressure intensified and in December 1946 Siegel opened before the hotel was finished.

The first night was catastrophic. Nobody who was anybody came, apart from George Raft whose career had already faded. Nobody stayed; the rooms were not ready. Many guests could not even secure admission; Siegel imposed arbitrary dress restrictions, and he refused to allow the fountains to be turned on for fear of disturbing a cat and her six kittens trapped in a water sump. Over the next two weeks the casino was taken to the cleaners by professional gamblers, losing $300,000 across the tables. Siegel closed 'The Flamingo'; the Mob closed Siegel.

In a December 1946 meeting at the Hotel Nacional in Havana, Siegel's backers heard that their man had syphoned off $600,000 cash from the casino. In the words of Lucky Luciano: 'There was no doubt in Meyer's mind that Bugsy had skimmed this dough from his building budget ... Lansky said, "There's only one thing to do with a thief who steals from his friends. Benny's got to be hit."'

He was. At 10.30 p.m. on 20 June 1947, a .30/30 carbine fired nine rounds through the open window of Virginia Hill's house. Six hit Siegel, the first one bouncing his eye fifteen feet across the room and plastering it to the tiled floor. The eyelashes separated from the eyelids, and were later found glued to the door jamb. Thus did Siegel become only the third person to be killed in exclusive Beverly Hills in thirty-five years.

Within minutes, Siegel's backers were at 'The Flamingo' announcing a change of ownership. It was territory the Mob never relinquished; in 1965 Caesar's Palace was built with $20 million from the Teamster pension funds which were, in the New York and New Jersey branches, under the control of Mafia stooges for the Genovese family.

Only five mourners attended Siegel's funeral. A few days later, on 2 July, Virginia Hill attempted suicide in Paris, and she went on trying until she finally succeeded in March 1966 in a small village outside Salzburg, where she swallowed pills beside a little mountain stream.

The recent film of Siegel's life, *Bugsy*, correctly stresses that only the unwary used his nickname to his face. It does not mention that most of his Hollywood income was creamed from the Film Extras' Union. The 1993 disclosures of J. Edgar **Hoover**'s troubled sexuality affirm that additional support for Siegel came from the Director of the FBI who 'helped get the OK' for 'The Flamingo'. Returning a favour to Meyer Lansky would be a plausible motive; Lansky was one of many *mafiosi* reputedly blackmailing Hoover, and Lansky remained at liberty until he died in 1983. His immunity from

federal prosecution continued until 1970, two years before Hoover's death. Even then, the IRS and not the FBI spearheaded the attack – which failed.

In May 1992 Siegel's car, a 1933 V-12 Packard, went to auction with an estimate of $25,000.

Lawnmower

The intended murder weapon in the Whybrow and Saunders case of 1991. This English couple, who were lovers, planned to rid Susan Whybrow of her wealthy husband in a faked accident. He planted the seed of his undoing by reading his wife an excerpt from the *Daily Telegraph*, describing an unusual fatal mishap in which a gardener fell off a tractor-type lawnmower into a ditch.

Whybrow and Saunders concocted a plan, primarily over the car telephone, to drown their victim in the duckpond and then claim he had plummeted into the depths on his lawnmower with the throttle open. Hoping to lull her husband into unsuspecting satiety, she baited the trap by expressing an interest in making love on the floor. But this prompted Mr Whybrow to undress. Realising that nude lawnmowing would look suspicious, she told him to put his clothes on again and, while thus engaged, Saunders attacked from behind. But their prey broke free and escaped, swimming across the lake to arrive at a neighbour's house bedraggled with weeds.

In March 1991 the conspirators were convicted of attempted murder. Elizabeth Saunders was previously better known for her support of the local church.

Lee, John (1865–1933?)

The man they could not hang. John Lee was one of three servants looking after an elderly widow, Emma Keyse, in her two-storey thatched cottage near Torquay. Early on the morning of 16 November 1885 a fire broke out, and upstairs they discovered their employer's brutally murdered body soaked in paraffin, her throat cut so violently that the knife notched the anterior aspect of her vertebrae.

Lee was arrested on strong but circumstantial evidence. Miss Keyse had accepted Lee back into her employ despite his conviction for stealing silver, but she gave him a boy's rate for a man's job, and shortly before her death denigrated his work, cutting his wages by sixpence to two shillings a week.

His two colleagues were women, and the killing bore the stamp of an 'inside job': no signs of forcible entry, nothing stolen, and weapons – a hatchet and knife – which came from the pantry.

Lee told the police that, like the other retainers, he slept through the blaze. But his bloodstained clothes reeked of paraffin, and a human hair, similar to Miss Keyse's, adhered to one of his bloodied socks. Lee lied in the witness box, invoking his excellent relationship with the deceased and maintaining that he had cut himself on a broken window, and it took the jury only forty minutes to find him guilty. Unruffled by the verdict, he said to the judge, 'The reason, my Lord, why I am so calm and collected is because I trust in my Lord and he knows that I am innocent.'

The night before his execution, Lee dreamed that he would not die. It is unlikely that this is unusual, but Lee envisioned standing on the trap-door while it failed to open three times, and told his warders so before the noose was placed round his neck in Exeter jail on 23 February 1886.

Berry the hangman pulled the lever, but the floor beneath Lee's feet did not open, and the Chaplain, Reverend John Pitkin, read stolidly from the Book of Common Prayer as the lever was jerked to and fro. Then Berry asked Lee to stand to one side while he sent for an axe, saw and plane and, when the mechanism was functioning perfectly, the pinioned and hooded Lee was put back on the spot.

Berry gave the handle such a mighty yank that it bent. Again the trap-doors stayed shut, even when the warders stamped on them, and Lee was directed to wait in the basement until the trap-door was eased again. On the third attempt, still nothing happened. 'The noise of the bolts sliding could be plainly heard, but the doors did not fall,' wrote Berry in his memoirs.

As the Chaplain observed, 'For the third time I had concluded the service; for the third time the prisoner had felt the agonies of death; for the third time the responsible officers had failed to put him to death.' He announced that he would tarry no longer, thus terminating the proceedings. Lee, somewhat disgruntled, was escorted to his cell where he assured the Chaplain that he wanted to die, and the following day wrote to his sister saying he remained in hopes of being hanged.

But it was not to be. Against some opposition, the

Lee's apologia, putting forward an unconvincing account of his innocence

Home Secretary Sir William Harcourt commuted the sentence to life imprisonment. Lee's later history is vague, but he was released in December 1907 and married a nurse, Jessie Augusta Bulleid. Their union failed in 1912, and he died in obscurity in Milwaukee in 1933.

Of his brush with death, Lee concluded, 'It was the Lord's hand which would not let the Law take away my life.' Berry took a different view, believing that the centre of the trap fitted too tightly: 'The woodwork of the doors should have been three or four times as heavy with ironwork to correspond.' Another temporal explanation is foul play. The author Ernest Bowen-Rowlands, in his *In the Light of the Law*, quotes a 'well-known person' who heard from someone, who had it from the old lag in question, 'that in those days it was the practice to have the scaffold erected by some joiner or carpenter among the prisoners. The man inserted a wedge which prevented the drop from working, and when called in as an expert he removed the wedge and demonstrated the smooth working of the drop, only to reinsert it before Lee was placed on the trap.' This sounds plausible, but the information is fourth-hand.

Leg, stabbed

Perhaps the most unusual of the many clues that could have solved the **Manson** case sooner. As a rule, legs do not get stabbed much.

On 31 July 1969, nine days before the Tate murders, two homicide detectives were summoned to investigate the murder of Gary Hinman, a 34-year-old music teacher stabbed in his Los Angeles house. A coded message was scrawled on his wall, in his blood, 'Political piggy', and there was thus a chance that his death might be linked to the Tate murders, when the victims were stabbed in their Los Angeles house, with a coded message scrawled on the wall, in their blood: 'Pigs'.

Hinman was murdered for his unreasonable attitude. He had rebuffed Manson, saying: 'I'm sorry Charlie. I'm not going to sell all my things and come and follow you.' After the killing, Manson's hit squad, including Susan Atkins, felt so hungry that they sat down to cherry cake and coffee in the nearby Topanga Kitchen.

On 6 August, Officers Guenther and Whitely pulled in a youth, Bobby Beausoleil, still with blood on his shirt, still driving Hinman's 1965 Volkswagen bus. He was charged with murder. Two days later the officers read the details of the Tate massacre and were struck by the uncanny similarities. But Guenther and Whitely worked for the Los Angeles County Sheriff's Office, and the Manson killings were handled by the highbrows in the Los Angeles Police Department, who were unimpressed by Whitely's hunches. Sergeant Jess Buckles responded: 'We know

what's behind these murders. They're part of a big dope transaction.'

Before his arrest, Hinman's killer Beausoleil had shacked up in Death Valley on an old movie set at Spahn's ranch, where a hippy commune centred on a man called Charlie who believed he was Jesus Christ. And as it happened, on 9 August the encampment was raided on suspicion of car theft, and thus Manson was in custody at the time he should have been arrested on suspicion of murder. But everyone was released.

The Tate killings remained unsolved nearly two months later when the local Inyo County police paid another visit to Spahn's ranch about some stolen dune buggies. This time they corralled twenty-six **Family** members, one of them a young woman called Susan Atkins. As the police cars bumped over the desert, two frightened girls emerged from the bushes begging for police protection. They were fleeing the wrath of the Family, they said, and feared for their lives. One of the women was Kitty Lutesinger, Bobby's Beausoleil's 17-year-old ex-girlfriend, long wanted for questioning about the Hinman killing.

At the County Sheriff's Office, Kitty Lutesinger admitted being present at Hinman's during the murder, but in another room. She said she accompanied Bobby and a girl, Susan Atkins, who later mentioned knifing a man three or four times in the legs.

But Hinman's legs were unmarked. So the police reasoned that the legs stabbed by Susan Atkins belonged to someone else.

The officers recollected a recent case: Voytek Frykowski, one of the Tate Massacre victims, knifed fifty-one times. It was hardly a surprise that some of the wounds strayed on to his limbs, but when Officer Whitely pestered the LAPD once again, they were no more interested than before.

Lie detector

The first generation of this device was the 'hydrosphygmograph', and the second the 'cardio-pneumo-psychogram'; the third wave was known as the 'polygraph'.

The cardio-pneumo-psychogram became the 'lie detector' for short. In 1921 William Marston of Fordham University published an article reiterating his belief that lies affected the blood pressure; a progressive

Californian Chief of Police, August Vollmer, prevailed upon his sergeant to run up a version based on the traditional blood-pressure armband. The machine was responsive to small fluctuations, and during a mock interrogation instantly penetrated Vollmer's fibs: 'It registered every time I lied – about not liking roast beef and about going to bed before midnight.'

Rumours of the machine's omniscience reached such a pitch that local criminals broke down and confessed at the mere sight of the device. Nationwide publicity followed the Hightower case of 1921.

William A. Hightower was a nut. On 2 August 1921 he kidnapped a priest, Father Patrick E. Heslin, from his home just outside San Francisco; later he crushed his victim's skull with a blow to the head, burying him near Salada beach close to a billboard of a man frying pancakes.

Despairing of the ransom, Hightower resolved to collect the advertised reward by selling information about Heslin's whereabouts. Who could have been better placed? On 10 August Hightower presented himself at Archbishop Hanna's house and recounted how he had stumbled across Heslin's scarf while digging for bootleg liquor in the sand. Heslin's body, Hightower said, had to be nearby; he did not know *exactly* where, but somewhere close.

Hightower led the police to the scarf on the beach, discoursing the while on his invention of the machine-gun and his patent substitute for candied fruit. Then, predicting the very spot where Heslin lay, Hightower seized a spade and set to. 'Be careful,' cautioned Police Chief O'Brien, 'you might damage his face.'

'That's all right,' Hightower reassured the policeman, 'I'm digging at his feet.'

Hightower insisted on his innocence despite this inadvertent confession. So Vollmer's lie detector was brought to the San Mateo jail, where it hardened a very strong suspicion into certainty. Hightower was sentenced to life imprisonment, convicted on overwhelming evidence.

In 1926 a refinement of Vollmer's machine expanded its repertoire to take simultaneous readings of blood pressure, pulse, breathing rate and sweat. But by 1930 it emerged that suspects have a limited inventory of adrenalin. Prolonged exposure to questioning exhausts the stock, allowing placid body-responses during the most monstrous falsehoods. This led to the introduction of three-minute interrogation sessions. But J. Edgar **Hoover** did not

hold with the new device and in 1935 the machine-wonder took a further knock when the Illinois rapist Gerald Thompson passed its scrutiny with flying colours. Asked whether he had killed 'Mildred', Thompson said 'no' and the lie detector stayed steady.

Later Thompson explained that he had outwitted the machine by thinking of a different Mildred, whom he had not killed. Those with advanced powers of self-deception posed additional problems. A madman, when asked if he was **Napoleon**, lied. He said 'No', and the machine spotted the attempted deception. In 1960 multiple killer Chester Weger took a risk which paid off when he washed down aspirin with Coca-Cola before taking the test. More disturbingly, the innocent can register as guilty through worries about the machine's accuracy.

According to Chris Gugas, founder of the National Board of Polygraph Examiners, the modern polygraph is all but infallible in the hands of a properly trained operative. A 1950s study of 4,280 criminals showed a success rate of 95 per cent, exculpating the innocent as well as incriminating the guilty. But the equipment is expensive, at over $10,000 including training, and is inadmissible in a court of law unless both sides agree or the judge so demands.

The complicating factor is that the machine's results need interpretation. What the operator looks for is a sequence where the subject's nervous tension mounts as he approaches the leading question and then tails off. This requires a properly structured sequence of questions, a properly trained user, and a proper interpretation: factors which reintroduce by the back door the subjective element the machine removed by the front. The subject's state of mind can be critical. Psychological pressure, or his own inadequacies, can induce the misapprehension that he is guilty, particularly when allegations are of 'denial' and 'suppressed **memory**'. In the **Ingram** satanic ritual abuse case of 1989, the lie detector indicated that suspect Jim Rabie's assertions of innocence were false; and by then, for all he knew, perhaps they were.

See also **False confessions, Lombroso**

Lime

Powdered calcium oxide, also known as quicklime. It is worth ordering the right chemical for the right job. Quicklime strips away the flesh of a body, rendering identification hard or even impossible. But slaked lime (calcium hydroxide) only disposes of the beetles and maggots which would otherwise eat the corpse. It thus acts as a preservative. The error is occasionally made by murderers, who unintentionally present the police with a body in first-class condition. One who made this mistake was Harry Dobkin.

Dobkin's brief matrimonial career began and ended in September 1920, when his arranged marriage to Rachel Dubinski culminated in a separation after three troubled days. During this interlude he fathered a child, and for the next two decades Dobkin was dogged by their misalliance as his luckless wife waylaid him in the London streets pleading for maintenance. On at least four occasions he reacted with violence, and on the afternoon of 11 April 1941 he strangled her after a meeting in a Dalston café.

Rachel and Harry Dobkin on their wedding day

After carving up her body, he buried it the cellar of a Baptist Church off Vauxhall Road, and for good measure sprinkled the remains with slaked lime. This preserved part of her voice box, and not long afterwards the Luftwaffe set fire to the church during the Blitz. On 17 July 1942 a workman completing the demolition unearthed the corpse, and the following day in the Southwark mortuary it was still possible to discern the distinctive fracture to the upper horn of the thyroid cartilage: the hallmark of strangulation. An adjacent blood clot indicated that the damage had occurred in life, and Rachel Dubinski's body was conclusively identified from dental records.

Across the Channel, the French killer Dr Marcel Petiot needed lime in bulk for his victims, and during the early stages of the police investigation his brother (the supplier) claimed that Marcel wanted the quicklime to exterminate cockroaches. Since he delivered 400 kilos (over a third of a ton), the brother was initially charged with conspiracy to murder.

Petiot created a lime pit to treat the bodies with which he fuelled the stove of his home in Paris's smart XVIth *arrondissement*. An outhouse contained one heap of bodies marinating in quicklime; another lime pit suppurated in the stable, and when Petiot was accused in 1945 of twenty-seven murders, he angrily dismissed the charges, claiming sixty-three victims.

Bizarrely enough, the Gestapo had also arrested Petiot in 1942, on suspicion that he was a member of the French Resistance. He was held until the following year, when he was released without charge. It seems likely that he had confessed his murderous activities under interrogation, but that his equally homicidal captors regarded him as a commendably enthusiastic French supporter of Nazi policies and methods.

Petiot nearly came to grief the year before, on 11 March 1944 when his chimney went up in flames. Summoned to his home by telephone, Petiot arrived to find the police and fire brigade ensconced in his basement, gazing in consternation at corpses in every stage of decay. Asked if he knew anything about them, Petiot said yes, they were his bodies, adding that it was imperative that he leave at once to alert the Resistance network that their headquarters had been overrun. Off he scurried, and, by the time the police realised that the deaths had no connection with the summary execution of pro-Nazi collaborators, Petiot was nowhere to be found. But this is no place for a prominent serial killer. Eschewing anonymity, Petiot initiated a correspondence with the magazine, *Resistance*, claiming under a new name, but with the same handwriting, that the corpses had been dumped in his home by the Gestapo. On 2 November 1945 he was arrested at his return address.

Petiot inveigled wealthy Jews to his house under the pretext of securing their safe passage out of France. They brought their valuables, perhaps a million pounds in total, and he took their lives, administering fatal **injections** under the guise of complying with foreign inoculation requirements. Petiot slept through some of his trial, but scored telling points when awake. The President of the Court opened by reading the accusation and then observed: 'As a child you were noted for your violent temper.' 'Oh come now,' interrupted Dr Petiot, 'if we start like this we shan't get on very well.'

For much of the time the case went his way. Of the

twenty-seven murders, Petiot asserted that nineteen were German collaborators and the other eight were still alive. His defence, part bluster, part abuse, was based round his membership of the Resistance, the details of which he refused to disclose, and his acquittal as a patriotic hero remained a real possibility to the end. He was executed on 26 May 1946.

Lincoln, President Abraham (1809–65)

The Lincoln conspiracy theory suggests that his assassination was too easy, the assassin's escape incredible, his death suspicious, the investigation bodged, the trials rigged and the true culprit unpunished.

On 14 April 1865, three days after the Civil War ended, Lincoln was killed by John Wilkes Booth, who discharged his derringer at the President from a range of four feet during Act III of *Our American Cousins* at Ford's Theatre, Washington.

Lincoln's bodyguard, John F. Parker, considered the play boring. So he deserted his post and went for a drink, giving Booth access. Yet Parker never received an official reprimand. Similarly, Booth's escape route included a surprisingly clear run over the heavily guarded Anancostia Bridge on his way to Maryland. His flight was further facilitated by a mysterious electrical fault which put all the telegraph wires from Washington out of commission for the two critical hours after the killing.

Booth was eventually cornered in a barn near Bowling Green, Virginia, on 26 April. Told that he could safely surrender, he was shot by a Union soldier, Boston Corbett, who later committed suicide himself. Corbett was rumoured to be in the pay of the Secretary of War, Edwin McMasters Stanton, to whom he handed the diary found on Booth's body. When Stanton – the hub of the web – released the diary to the investigators, eighteen pages were missing. Among the extant pages were Booth's puzzling and perhaps overlooked lines: 'I have a greater desire and almost a mind to return to Washington, and in a measure clear my name, which I feel I can do.'

Stanton was a staunch opponent of Lincoln's plans to reconstruct the South after the bitter Civil War. Following the President's death, Stanton pushed through the conspirators' trials, even securing the death sentence for one of their wives, Mrs Surratt. But he was reluctant to have her husband arrested;

Surratt only returned to America against Stanton's orders after his capture in Egypt. At the trial, Surratt was acquitted, with Stanton's legal friends handling the defence.

Stanton destroyed the master-plate of the only photograph of Lincoln in his coffin. Only one print survived, and this by accident. Later, Lincoln's son burned many of his father's documents, explaining: 'These papers contain the documentary evidence of treason of a member of my father's cabinet ... It is best for all that such evidence be destroyed.'

A more humdrum explanation is that Lincoln was shot by a lone nut, operating in concert with other lone nuts, the half-dozen or so co-conspirators. It was Booth's fourth attempt on the President.

Lines, pick-up

The best way to 'slay' at leisure is to lure the victim into a car. From which flows a simple rule-of-thumb for women threatened with sexual assault or abduction: make a stand outside the assailant's vehicle. Do not get in.

The book *Sexual Homicide* (by John Douglas, Robert Ressler and Anne Rule) contains general recommendations for the early stages of a hijack, advocating a first and invariable response of attempted escape, with verbal confrontation as the next defence and offensive physical resistance as the third.

Three approaches are open to the rapist: the 'blitz' (sudden, overwhelming violence), the surprise (an ambush), and the con, a technique espoused in various guises by the Russian serial killer **Chikatilo**. With runaways, he asked if they were hungry or thirsty. To young boys he offered to show his stamp collection, to their elders, his horror videos. To girls he proposed money for sex. Or Chikatilo fell in alongside and asked, 'Where are you off to? ... Oh, I'm going that way myself let's go together', before suggesting a short cut through the woods. In the words of Rostov's Chief of Police, 'He had something for everyone. For the drunkards, there was vodka. For others he was the friendly teacher who could give them a lift.' He lured his first victim, a nine-year-old girl, to her death by pretending to escort her to his toilet. Chikatilo commented, 'They followed me like dogs.'

Ted **Bundy** was another personable fellow who had no need of violence to snare his prey. To 17-year-old

Carol DaRonch, Bundy posed as Officer Roseland. 'Excuse me miss,' he said, 'we think there's been an attempted burglary of your vehicle. I'd appreciate it if you'd go with me to identify a suspect my partner is holding out.' But instead of driving Carol to a police station, he headed out of town, clapped a set of handcuffs round one of her wrists before she flung herself out on to the road, and pursued her on foot, brandishing a tyre iron, until the approach of another car frightened him off.

Bundy accosted another survivor, Raylene Shepherd, in the lobby of the Viewmount High School theatre in Bountiful, Utah, during the intermission. 'I wonder if I could get you to help me for a minute with my car in the parking lot?' he asked. But Raylene, the drama instructor, was busy. As so often after a rebuttal, Bundy tried again. He was noticed later in the auditorium 'breathing kind of heavily', and that night young Debbie Kent fell for a similar approach.

Then there was Bundy's gambit of the Bad Arm and Books, which he deployed against Janet Carstensen on Washington University's Central Campus. One evening, outside the library, she saw a young man in difficulties carrying a stack of textbooks. In her words: 'He dropped the books and was making a noise (pain) as though his arm was hurting. A castlike bandage was on his arm. I went over to offer him some assistance.'

Bundy pulled this trick on a number of women, but it only got them *to* his vehicle, not *into* it. With Janet Carstensen, he arrived at the car complaining, 'Oh my arm hurts.' Then he opened the door and told her to start the engine. She refused. Bundy turned nasty, snarling 'Get in', and Janet ran off.

Bundy perfected his method with the Bad Arm and Boat. On a hot July afternoon in 1974 he drove to Lake Sammamish ten miles outside Seattle, mingling with the 40,000 swimmers and sun-bathers crowding the beach. Wearing a plaster cast, Bundy first approached Jennifer Rutledge on the sands and said with a deprecating smile that he could not manage his boat with just one arm. Would she help unload his dinghy from the car? As they strolled to the parking lot he introduced himself as 'Ted', chatting about his racketball injury.

But when they reached the car park, Jennifer noticed at once that there was no boat. Bundy pointed to the hillside some miles distant and said, 'Oh, it's up at my parents' house.' At this stage

Jennifer backed out, but later that day Bundy somehow glossed over this problem with both Denise Naslund and Janice Ott. The exact technique in these cases is unknown; both girls are dead.

The Dutch film *The Vanishing* shows the anti-hero trying a Bad Arm and Trailer without success; a Bad Arm and Furniture features in *Silence of the Lambs*.

See **Trolling**

Lingle, Alfred Jake (1892–1930)

An accomplished saver. Thrifty Jake Lingle, an obscure crime reporter with the Chicago *Tribune*, entered a crowded pedestrian subway heading for the Illinois Central suburban railway on 9 June 1930. As he neared the east exit, a man with blond hair dropped behind him, drew a Colt .38 (known as a 'belly-gun') and fired a single shot upwards through Lingle's neck. It traversed the brain before exiting through his forehead, and the killer escaped, his pursuit impeded at the critical moment by a mobster dressed as a priest.

Shell-shocked Chicago reacted with outrage. It was one thing for gangsters to bump off each other, and even to kill law-abiding citizens by mistake. But Lingle's murder represented a new twist in the downward spiral.

The *Tribune* launched a massive hunt for his killers. The paper clubbed together with the *Evening Post* and the *Herald and Examiner* to offer a $55,000 reward. Eight columns of the *Tribune*'s edition of 10 June were devoted to this civic crusade, and on 12 June it editorialised under a clarion heading, 'The Challenge': 'The meaning of this murder is plain ... Mr Lingle was a police reporter and an exceptionally well-informed one ... What made him valuable to his newspaper marked him as dangerous to the killers ... It was very foolish ever to think that assassination would be confined to the gangs who have fought each other for the profits of crime in Chicago ... The *Tribune* accepts this challenge. It is war.'

A humble reporter with a byline-free career, Lingle pulled down $65 a week. As the investigation unfurled, it transpired that he maintained a chauffeur-driven Lincoln, a summer house at Long Beach, a suite of rooms at the stylish Hotel Stevens, a jewellery collection and an expensive gambling habit. A friend of millionaire businessmen, judges and county officials,

Lingle shared golfing holidays and stock market speculations with the Police Commissioner, and died with $9,000 in cash in his pockets, girded with the ultimate symbol of gangster chic, a diamond-studded belt presented by Capone himself.

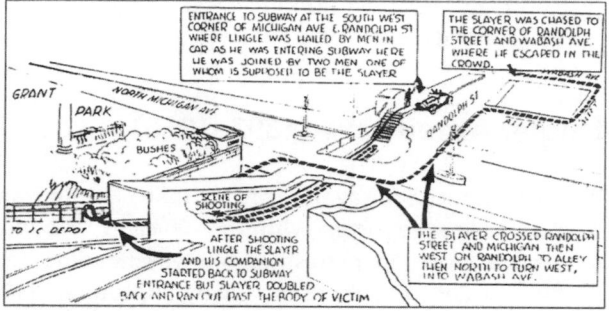

Scene of Lingle's death as he set off towards his favourite racetrack

Lingle's underworld role was as the fixer of police promotions. He mediated between mobland and the political machine as the unofficial Chief of Police. In the words of the Hotel Stevens's house detective, 'He was up there amongst the big boys and had a lot of responsibilities.' A disappointed Chicago returned to its habitual state of lawless torpor.

More than half a century later, on 11 March 1992, New York witnessed a rerun of Lingle's killing when the crusading journalist Manuel de Dios Unanue was gunned down in the restaurant Meson Asturias on 83rd Street to almost identical headlines: 'Slain newsman made criminals quake' and 'He did his job too well – maybe that was deadly'. News organisations sponsored a reward fund that rapidly climbed to $67,000, and a joint task force of the police and federal agencies worked round the clock. The city's Governor, Mayor and ex-Mayor all attended the memorial mass.

At first it was conjectured that Unane was hit on the orders of the Colombian drug lords, whom he constantly harried in the press. But the moral certainties quickly evaporated. 'This case is a nightmare,' said a detective. 'The day after he was shot we hear he was a hero. Two weeks later, he's a dirtbag … Five hundred people hated this guy.' His former employer, the editor of *El Diario*, put in a good word for him, but only one: 'He deserves credit for being consistent. A consistent asshole.'

Lists

On 22 April 1922 a methodical youth, Ernest Walker, wrote out a list:

1 Ring up Sloane Street messenger office for boy.
2 Wait at front door.
3 Invite him in.
4 Bring him downstairs.
5 Ask him to sit down.
6 Hit him on the head.
7 Put him in the safe.
8 Keep him tied up.
9 At 10.30, torture.
10 Prepare for end.
11 Sit down, turn gas on.
12 Put gas light out.
13 Sit down, shut window.

Steps one to twelve proved straightforward. As Walker explained in his intended suicide note: 'I brought him into the pantry and hit him on the head with a coal hammer so *simple*. Then I tied him up and killed him. *I* killed him, *not* the gas. Then I sat down and turned the gas full on. I am as sane as ever I was, only I cannot live without my dear mother. I didn't half give it to that damned boy. I made him squeak. Give my love to Dad and all my friends.'

But step thirteen – when Walker sat there and died – proved a stumbling block. He decided to leave it out, and went to Charing Cross Station instead, catching the 7.35 p.m. to Tonbridge. On arrival, still elated by his brilliant coup, Walker shared the secret of his murder with a constable on the beat. PC Sheepwash noted the dried blood on the youth's hands, and arrested him.

Meanwhile, Raymond Davis was found bleeding from a head wound in the butler's gas-filled bedroom at 30 Lowndes Square, London, with a gag in his mouth. He died the next day. Walker confessed: 'I do not know what made me do it … I hit him with a piece of iron bar. I have felt bad since last Wednesday, and I lost my mother last January, when the flu was about.'

Walker, an 18-year-old-footman, was looking forward to joining his mother on the far side of the grave. But he needed a companion to stiffen his resolve, and devised the scheme of ordering up a boy from the District Messenger Company in Sloane Street (see **Murderee**). Raymond Davis, in his new uniform of a pillbox hat and cape, drew the short straw. At the trial, Walker's list showed clear premeditation, and his letter to the butler started on an upbeat note: 'Dear Mr Pallance, I expect you will be surprised to see what I have done.' Walker was found guilty but insane.

Another famous list was compiled by John George Haigh on the eve of his 1949 encounter with Olive Henrietta Helen Olivia Robarts Durand-Deacon. It went like this:

Large oil drum
Stirrup pump
Rubber gloves
Apron
45 gallons sulphuric **acid**

He dissolved her. The 'Brides-in-the **Bath**' murderer, George Joseph Smith, also committed his thoughts to paper after his murder of Alice Burnham in 1913. In a passage echoing T. S. Eliot's dreary précis of life as no more than 'birth, death and copulation', Smith wrote: 'certificate of birth, certificate of marriage, certificate of death, wife's will, policy, receipt for premium paid, official acceptance, receipt for burial'.

Lividity

Also known as *livor mortis*. A corpse's skin assumes the livid hue of a bruise as the blood gravitates to the body's lower portions. The areas of discoloration, restricted to

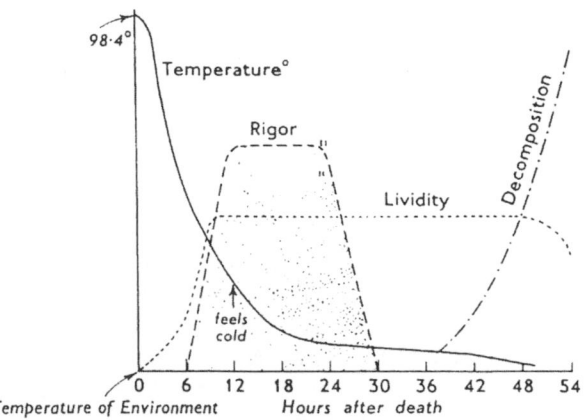

Chart showing the major changes by which the lapse of time after death might be estimated. The first hour often shows little fall in temperature

the body parts not in contact with a hard surface, are established within some twelve hours after death.

A typical supine cadaver exhibits lividity in the small of the back and the posterior aspect of the neck and thighs, the reverse of the symptoms expected from a prone corpse, and when Petrus Hauptfleisch left his mother (whom he had killed) lying face down for some hours before rearranging her the other way up in a staged accident, the local doctor was surprised to find symptoms of lividity on her frontal aspect. Hauptfleisch, a South African, was hanged in 1926.

Locard, Edmond (1877–1966)

Eminent French criminologist whose youthful reading of *The Adventures of Sherlock Holmes* kindled his interest. Against entrenched indifference, in 1910 Locard founded the first police laboratory in Lyon and became a minor celebrity the following year for his conviction of Emile Gourbin.

Gourbin was a bank clerk whose girlfriend, Marie Latelle, lived in a villa on the outskirts of Lyon. Her flirtations gave him pangs of jealousy, making Gourbin the obvious suspect when she was strangled at her parents' home. But he proffered an unbreakable alibi. Medical evidence put Marie's death at around midnight, and Gourbin had passed the whole evening with friends some miles away; they drank deeply, dined well and played cards until one in the morning.

Summoned by the local police, Locard examined Marie's body, detecting abrasion marks on her throat where the murderer's fingers scraped away her skin. He obtained some of Gourbin's fingernail scrapings and, under the microscope, among the traces of epithelial tissue, noticed a strange granular dust. It was powdered rice, a basic cosmetic ingredient, and further analysis disclosed vestiges of other chemicals – iron oxide, zinc oxide, bismuth and magnesium stearate – common in the manufacture of pink face powder.

A police search of Marie's room revealed a box of identical make-up. Gourbin confessed; he had duped his friends by advancing their wall-clock from 11.30 p.m. to 1 a.m. and broken up the evening early. The prosecution argued that this betokened premeditation, and Gourbin was sentenced to death for murder. But he claimed that Marie's death happened accidentally; he altered the clock only because he was bored and wanted to see his girlfriend. He said that at their assignation he asked her to marry him, and when she refused, lost his temper and choked her in a rage. The jury did not believe him.

Locard's guiding tenet was that 'every contact leaves a trace' (the so-called 'Locard Principle'), a philosophy borne out by his 1922 case of the postmen's heads. As he observed, 'Nothing resembles the head of one postman more than the head of another', particularly when viewed from above, and the French postal authorities discovered this empirically during an investigation into the internal theft of registered letters. An enterprising postmaster suspected that the robberies took place in his post office, with the mail opened in the lavatories, and he stationed spies in the attic to watch for suspicious activity. They spotted the thief in action in his cubicle, but his pate was unfamiliar, and the observers banged on the ceiling, dislodging a dusting of fine plaster which drifted on to the culprit's left arm and shoulder.

But the building dust proved invisible on clothing. So the suspect uniform was sent to Locard, who easily detected traces of sulphate of **lime**. Such procedures are routine now, but were cutting-edge technology then, and to this day many laboratory procedures derive from Locard's work. He discovered the distinctive patterning of the microscopic pores in the papillary ridges and is the reputed inventor of the eight-feet-long portable microscope. An account of many of his cases was published in 1922 under the title *Policiers de roman et policiers de laboratoire* and his major work, *Traité de Criminalistique*, came off the presses the following year.

When the seventh volume in the series appeared in 1940, it included a sinister new category, Crime Without a Cause. Locard approached this modern staple with caution, citing a case from 1886 where, against the evidence, a chemist's assistant from Le Havre, Pastré-Beaussier, was absolved of a string of arsenic poisonings after convincing the jury that he lacked any *motive* for murder. The deaths included his employer M. Decamps (who had accused him of petty theft), Mme Decamps, M. Delafontaine (the new owner) and the housekeeper Mme Morisse. Numerous others collapsed with vomiting but recovered, and a simple process of elimination demonstrated that Pastré-Beaussier was the culprit, propelling a reluctant Locard towards the conclusion

that he 'killed for pleasure, and perhaps, after his first murders, from habit'.

See also **Success**, **Young**

Locked-room mystery

The first 'locked-room mystery' was Poe's story 'The Murders in the Rue Morgue'. The first locked-room novel seems to have been John Ratcliffe's *Nena Sahib*. This inspired a real murder.

In 1881 the wife and five children of a Berlin carter named Fritz Conrad were found hanging from hooks in a locked room. It looked as if Frau Conrad, depressed by poverty, had killed her children and committed suicide. Police Commissioner Hollman was suspicious, and when he found out that Conrad was infatuated with a young girl student, he searched the apartment for love letters. He found none, but came upon a copy of *Nena Sahib* and read Ratcliffe's account of a 'perfect murder', in which the killer drilled a tiny hole in the door, passed a thread through it and used this to draw the bolt after the murder; he then sealed up the hole with wax. Hollman examined Conrad's door, and found a similar hole, filled in with sealing wax, to which threads of horsehair still adhered. Confronted with this evidence, Conrad confessed to murdering his wife and children, and was sentenced to death.

Locks, combination

Not since the late nineteenth century could a crook *feel* when the right number was dialled into a combination lock. The countless film plots hinging on safecrackers with sensitive fingers, or sophisticated auditory devices, are baloney. For the last hundred years, the bar releasing the lock has made no contact with the internal dials until the number is correctly set, at which point the safe opens anyway.

A more reliable way of outwitting a combination lock is to find where its owner has written the number, typically in a nearby card index or filing cabinet, under 'S' for 'Safe'. If not, then the words of the American cracksman Harry King afford useful guidance. King 'found it to be the rule among cashiers to use numbers easily divisible. For example, a train of numbers selected would be four, sixteen and thirty-two, or twelve, twenty-four and thirty-six.'

Other safe-owners never revise the original settings dialled in by the manufacturer, likely to be testing sequences such as 10-20-30-40. Or the number corresponds to an anniversary or hobby. Golfers prefer 9-18-36-72, whereas bridge players plump for 4-13-26-52.

This principle allowed the nuclear physicist Richard Feynman to penetrate the Los Alamos safes in the 1940s. Feynman's hobby was lockpicking, and for a lark he postulated that his colleagues would employ a mathematical constant for their combination locks. He tried the base of natural logarithms (2.71828) and the doors to nine cabinets swung wide. 'I accessed the safes which contained all the secrets of the atomic bomb,' he wrote. 'All the schedules for the production of plutonium, the purification procedures, how much material is needed, how the bomb works, how the neutrons are generated, what the design is, the dimensions...'

Unaware of Feynman's success, during the last decade British nuclear weapons scientists still adopted *pi* as the numerical base for their strongboxes. The computer hackers of today, who circumvent electronic security systems by guessing the 'password', operate on a similar mix of cod psychology and intuition.

With combination locks, if all else fails, it is worth filming, photographing, listening or watching as the owner unlocks his door, an approach utilised, on a highly sophisticated level, during the famous 1975 raid on the Bank of America in London's Mayfair.

The gang's inside informant worked on building maintenance and, while checking the ventilation systems prior to an attempt with a thermic lance (which generates heat and smoke), discovered that the lobby overlooking the vault door had a false ceiling.

Above the removable panels was a void some eighteen inches high, enough for an accomplice to crawl into, suspend himself from a cradle and wait all day until the safe was opened. He viewed the operation through a tiny hole with a spyglass, wrote the numbers down and left the building after work hours.

On 24 April 1975 the gang unclicked the vault door and 'caned open' the deposit boxes, described as 'chock-a-block with pound notes and francs and dollars. There was gold this and gold that alongside piles and piles of diamond rings, bracelets and necklaces.' The eight-man team made off with as much as they could carry, valued at £8 million.

On aged domestic safes, the lock should be given a good bang with a heavy hammer. Often the spindle is driven into the case, freeing the handle. A variant, with a long, hard spike, is known as 'punching a can'; it only works with the more elementary safes, but even today is the first thing Americans try.

Lombroso, Cesare (1836–1909)

A former army surgeon and father of modern criminology. His findings, embodied in the science of phrenology, are now discounted.

In 1876 Lombroso rocketed to fame with his publication of *L'Uomo Delinquente*. His revelations were inspired by examination of the brain of the deceased brigand, Vilella.

Just by the spot where Vilella's spine met his cerebellum, Lombroso noted a little concavity, similar to the depression found in the brains of rodents. Lombroso realised that criminals were animals. He wrote: 'At the sight of that skull, I seemed to see, all of a sudden, lighted up a vast plain under a flaming sky, the problem of the nature of the criminal – an atavistic being who reproduces in his person the ferocious instincts of primitive humanity and the inferior animals.'

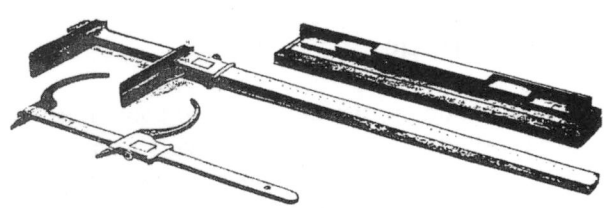

Anthropometric instruments for phrenological purposes

Lombroso distinguished two types of wrong-doers: the environmentally driven 'occasional criminals' and the 'born criminals'. The latter were doomed throwbacks, easily recognisable by their elongated, neanderthal arms. His survey of 7,000 criminal subjects confirmed that criminals had acute eyesight (like birds of prey), heavy jaws, jug ears and asymmetrical faces. They were predisposed to epilepsy and often covered in tattoos.

Lombroso is significant not for what he discovered but for what he investigated, and his mistaken thesis endowed criminology with an aura of respectability. Apart from his views on women (see **'Female Offender'**), his legacy included the 'hydrosphygmo-graph', an aqueous precursor of the **lie detector**. In 1905 he put a mendacious robber, Bersonne Pierre, to the test, sealing his hand in a rubber membrane and inserting it into the glass vessel filled with water. The level visibly altered with each heartbeat, and these fluctuations were transferred to a column of air in another glass tube graduated like an old-fashioned barometer. A revolving drum registered the pulse rate linearly.

Lombroso's contraption correctly predicted that no, Pierre had nothing to do with a railway theft but that, yes, Pierre had relieved a man called Torelli of his passport.

At the 1992 gathering of the British psychological Society, Professor Ian Hunter pointed out that phrenology, the science of cranial bumps, furnishes a good example of researchers' tendency to dismiss evidence which does not support their assumptions ('confirmation bias'). The skull of Descartes was examined by a nineteenth-century phrenologist anxious to get to grips with his magnificent frontal lobes. But Descartes's were of the ordinary variety. So the researcher decided that he was not a great thinker.

London Bridge

Before it fell down, the gatehouse of London Bridge was garnished with up to thirty-five rotting heads impaled on poles. Since the heads were customarily drawn larger than life, this feature is sometimes visible in contemporary engravings of general prospects of London or the Thames.

The **heads** provided snacks for scavenging birds, and for added longevity the trophies were first par-boiled and then dipped in tar. The culinary preparations are described in detail in the seven-teenth-century *History of the Life of Thomas Ellwood*.

Ellwood wrote of his depressing induction to Newgate: 'There lay the quartered bodies of three men who had been executed some days before ... and the reason why their quarters lay so long there was, the relations were petitioning to have leave to bury them, which at length was obtained for the quarters but not for the heads ... I saw the heads when they were

brought up to be boiled. The hangman fetched them in a dirty dust basket, and setting them down among the felons, he and they made sport with them. They took them by the hair, flouting, jeering and laughing at them, and then giving them some ill names, boxed them on the ears and cheeks. Which done, the hangman put them into his kettle, and parboiled them with bay-salt and cumin seeds that keep them from putrefaction and this to keep off the fowls from seizing on them.'

Until 1550, London Bridge provided criminals with an easy avenue of escape. On the south bank of the Thames lay the borough of Southwark, beyond the writ of the city. It consisted mainly of brothels, and a thief had only to walk across the river to dissipate his gains in safety.

London Monster, The

The word 'fetishism' was invented by the nineteenth-century psychologist Alfred Binet, who pointed out that if early sexual excitement is associated with some object, such as a woman's hair or shoes, it may become 'imprinted', so that the same object continues to produce excitement, just as ringing a bell could cause Pavlov's dogs to salivate.

One of the earliest cases of fetishism on record dates from 1790, when London was terrorised by a man who, in the words of the chronicler J. W. von Archenholtz, committed 'nameless crimes, the possibility of whose existence no legislator has ever dreamt of'.

These nameless crimes amounted to creeping up behind fashionably dressed women and slashing at their clothing with a sharp knife, which occasionally caused painful wounds; it was also alleged that he would sometimes hold out a nosegay to young ladies, and as they bent to sniff, would jab them in the face with a 'sharp pointed instrument' hidden among the flowers.

The 'Monster' apparently became obsessed with the pretty daughters of a tavern keeper named Porter, who ran a public bath in St James's Street, off Piccadilly. On the Queen's birthday, 19 January 1790, Anne Porter and her sister Sarah were walking home from a ball in St James's Palace, when a small man with a large nose came up behind them, hit Sarah on the head, then dealt Anne a blow on her right buttock. Indoors, she discovered that she had a nine-inch-long knife wound which was four inches deep in the centre. She and her sister had been accosted by the same man on a number of occasions in the past eighteen months, when he used violent language ('Blast your eyes, you damned bitch, I'll murder you and drown you in your own blood') and made obscene suggestions. Anne was one of many women who had been abused – or slashed – by the 'Monster' since 1788.

Six months later, out walking with her suitor, a 20-year-old fishmonger named Coleman, in St James's Park, Anne recognised the 'Monster' walking nearby. Coleman followed him to a nearby house, accused him of being the attacker and made a kind of 'citizen's arrest'. The man denied being the 'Monster', but Anne Porter fainted when she saw him.

The Monster hardly lived up to his name – he proved to be a slightly built Welshman named Renwick Williams, 23, a maker of artificial flowers, and at Bow Street magistrates court several of his victims identified him. He was remanded to New Prison, in Clerkenwell.

He was tried twice, the reason being that at his first trial, on 8 July 1790, the magistrate decided that his offence should be judged a felony rather than a misdemeanour; a felony was regarded as far more serious and carried a possible death sentence. The magistrate was undoubtedly influenced by the inflamed state of public opinion. Williams was found guilty at this trial, but sentence was deferred. Before that could happen, a panel of judges decided that the offence was, in fact, a misdemeanour. Several newspapers of the time reported that the prisoner had decided to throw a 'Monster Ball' at Newgate Prison to celebrate this reduced charge; The Times, however, dismissed this as an absurd rumour.

At his second trial, in December 1790, Williams insisted that it was a case of mistaken identity; and offered as alibi several fellow-workers who testified that he was in the artificial flower factory until after midnight on the Queen's birthday. The jury chose to disbelieve them, many of his victims having testified to the contrary, and Renwick Williams was sentenced to six years in Newgate Prison for 'damaging clothes'.

During the two years he was attacking women, Williams created a reign of terror: rewards were offered and walls covered in posters describing his activities. The prosecuting counsel talked of 'a scene that is so new in the annals of humanity, a scene so inexplicable, so unnatural, that one might have regarded it, out of respect for human nature, as impossible'.

'The Monster' clearly created a profound sense of psychological shock among his contemporaries, of the kind produced a century later by Jack the Ripper's murders.

Renwick Williams's biographer, Jan Bondeson (The London Monster, 2000), has included a chapter on some later cases of similar attacks. In Paris, where a series of attacks would occur in 1819, the phenomenon was labelled 'piqueurism'. A tailor whose name is not recorded was arrested and sentenced to six months.

In Augsburg, a man who became known as the Mädchenschneider (maiden-cutter) began attacking girls in 1819, jabbing them with sharp instruments. A wine merchant's apprentice named Carl Bartle was arrested, but acquitted for lack of evidence. By 1820 the girl-slicer had become more urbane, and grown a black beard; he would ask a girl if she was married; if she said yes, he bowed and turned away; if she said no, he would jab her with something sharp. The fact that he attacked only 'maidens' suggests a sexual obsession with virgins, and the stabbing as a symbolic method of rape. A bank clerk named Georg Rugener was arrested, having been observed to follow women in the street, but was released when the attacks continued while he was in jail.

Finally, in 1837, the maiden-cutter was arrested before he could get away – and proved to be Carl Bartle. A rather morose man who lived alone, he confessed to the attacks, and described how, the first time he had stabbed a young girl, he had ejaculated. From then on, jabbing his knife into virgins became his main source of sexual pleasure. Like the London Monster, he spent six years in prison.

That 'piquing' women satisfied some basic male aggression becomes clear from the fact that the activities of the piqueur often inspired imitators; an 1820 article on Renwick Williams describes how, during his reign of terror, many 'young blades', often in groups, would whisper obscenities into the ears of well-dressed young women and jab them with a sharp-pointed instrument..

Nowadays, piqueurism is common in places where men and women are packed closely together, such as on the Underground in London or New York. The Los Angeles sexologist Paul de River remarks in Crime and *the Sexual Psychopath* (1958): 'Their sadistic acts of aggression might be called a prelude to homicide.' He remarks that 'they may have feelings of insecurity, inadequacy, frustration and an inferiority complex, and psychologically they are prompted to balance the imbalance – to attempt to overcompensate for their personal deficiencies – through some daring feat or action'. And he says of one of them: 'He inserted the sharp instrument (an ice pick) in the thigh or breast of the female victim with such rapidity that she hardly knew what had happened.' One woman, stabbed in the breasts by a *piqueur*, died instantly as the ice pick penetrated her heart.

Renwick Williams should undoubtedly be classed as the first sex criminal of modern times.

Lottò

An otherwise insignificant hood whose 'death' displays the Sicilian Mafia on peak internationalist form in the early 1920s. Lottò, *a mafioso*, committed a murder in 1922 with such blatant disregard for the niceties of concealment that even in Sicily he courted arrest, posing a serious threat to Mafia prestige. The local chief, Don Calo Vizzini, had Lottò declared insane and confined to a lunatic asylum in Barcelona.

There he 'died', was buried (in a ventilated **coffin**), and on the third day or thereabouts rose again, was issued with false papers and smuggled into the United States. For his provenance, Lottò identified himself to the New York reception committee of *mafiosi* by tendering a yellow silk handkerchief embroidered with the initial 'C', for Calo.

Sicily retains its split personality of grinding, feudal poverty and extensive criminal enterprises, uniting these attributes until recently in the person of Salvatore Riina. A paunchy diabetic dressed in ill-fitting clothes, with a crude haircut and the stubby fingers of a peasant, Riina attempted to pass himself off as a farmhand at his arrest in downtown Palermo, apprehended driving a nondescript Citroën saloon on 15 January 1993. During the two decades he evaded capture, often by living openly in his own home, Riina clocked up convictions *in absentia* for some 150 murders while building a billion-dollar operation in narcotics and money-laundering.

The mere influx of six-figure sums will not loosen a *mafioso*'s stranglehold on the meagre pittance derived from local extortion. The account books of the Madonia family seized by the police a few years ago recorded eighty-five local businesses paying monthly protection of a few hundred dollars – hardly a major income stream for an outfit worth $400 million, but essential to maintain 'domination of the territory'.

See also **Inquisition**, **Vendetta**

Luby's Cafeteria

To date, America's worst mass killer is George Hennard, who drove his blue Ford Ranger truck through the plate-glass window of Luby's Cafeteria in Killeen, Texas, on 16 October 1991.

This dramatic entry into the crowded diner crushed one table and its occupants. Hennard jumped from the vehicle, drew his 9mm Glock semi-automatic and opened fire, calmly and deliberately, reloading as he exhausted each seventeen-round clip, walking through the tables, drilling customers through the head as they scattered to the ground. Hennard killed twenty-two and wounded another twenty-three, and there is no doubt that he would have gone on until his ammunition ran out. He carried a spare pistol with another forty-five rounds.

But it was Hennard's bad luck that two under-cover policemen were on a case almost next door; they reached the cafeteria within a minute of the first shot. In a brief exchange of fire, Hennard took four hits. He staggered to a rear hallway and put a bullet in his brain.

There was little to investigate when the gunfire ceased. The police assigned two dozen detectives to the case, and all they unearthed was Hennard's background. Aged 35, he had not distinguished himself at school, and did not get on with his mother. He had no known friends or girlfriend, and his seaman's licence, his last link with the world of even semi-decent work, had been suspended. At one stage Hennard played the drums, but to a different rhythm from the rest of the group, who chucked him out. Most of his victims were women.

Hennard falls into the classic type of mass murderer – an aggrieved social and sexual failure approaching middle age. His grudge's existence is easy to deduce; almost the only clues to its nature are his babbled words as he gunned down his victims: 'Look at what

Belton's done to me! Tell me people, was it worth it? Wait till those women in Belton see this! I wonder if *they'll* think it's worth it! ... Take that, bitch! ... This is what Belton done to me! Is it worth it? Is it worth it? ... Hiding from me, bitch?'

Hennard lived alone in nearby Belton, and in January 1991 he wrote to two local sisters asking them for a date: 'Please give me the satisfaction of someday laughing in the face of all those mostly white, treacherous female vipers from those two towns who tried to destroy me and my family.' The sisters declined.

See **Terminology**

Lucan, 7th Earl (1934–?)

The rich may have more money, but this does not necessarily make them interesting. As Melissa Wyndham, a girlfriend of one of Lucan's 'Clermont Set', recalls: 'Of course, I thought Lucan was the most depressing person ever. He was fantastically gloomy. He may have had a good point, but I certainly didn't spot it.' Others describe Lucan as charming and intelligent.

Good-looking enough to screen-test for the role of James Bond, Lucan was an addicted gambler who made £20,000 at *chemin de fer* during a two-day winning streak in 1960, on the strength of which he devoted himself full-time to gaming. By the early 1970s he had frittered his fortune away, declining into a bit-part as the Clermont's house player, a lure for other punters.

In 1963 Lord Lucan contracted an ill-fated marriage. He separated from his wife ten years later, and she won custody of their children in a bitter court case while he became enmired in debt and drink. On the night of 7 November 1974, wearing gloves, carrying a ten-inch length of lead pipe and a canvas US mail sack, he stole into his home at 46 Lower Belgrave Street. His wife and children were upstairs watching *The Six Million Dollar Man*. Lucan removed the light-bulb over the stairs and waited in the basement kitchen for his wife to make a cup of tea after putting the children to bed. Shortly after 9 p.m., he heard the descending footsteps and attacked, bludgeoning his victim's head. Blood spurted everywhere. When the body was still, he folded it in two and wedged it into the sack.

Lord Lucan

The rest was easy. Lucan had left time to return to his flat and clean himself up before meeting four friends for an after-theatre supper at the Clermont Club. Then he would drive the corpse to the coast, take it on to a boat and dump it overboard, weighted down, in the middle of the Channel. He had – according to writer Taki Theodoracopoulos – made two practice runs, rehearsing the transfers and timing the journey. Next morning he would learn, from the police or the nanny, that Lady Lucan had disappeared.

Few would be sorry or surprised. Lady Lucan had once fled from a psychiatric hospital, even if only for a few hours, and was widely regarded as difficult and unbalanced. A hotel manager's stepdaughter, she was variously described as tense, joyless and a manic-depressive. The custody battle had cost Lucan £40,000 he did not have. He ran four overdrafts, was borrowing heavily from his friends in the 'Eton Mafia', and received an annual remittance of £12,000 against expenditure of £17,000. With his wife dead, the outgoings on his rented flat and the matrimonial private detectives would cease, and he could reinstate himself in the family home with his children, whom he adored. Posted as a 'Missing Person', Lady Lucan would probably be dismissed, after a judicious interval, as a suicide.

Indeed, eight years later Lady Lucan did try to take her life, and on that night in November 1974, after waiting fifteen minutes for her tea, she called, 'Sandra? Sandra? What's keeping you?' In the dark, Lucan – probably drunk – realised that he had killed the nanny, Sandra Rivett, five feet two like his wife. She had changed her day off because of a boyfriend. Lucan climbed the stairs, stuck his gloved fingers down his wife's throat and battered her round the head. But she fought back, reaching for his balls and squeezing until he stopped. Then she calmed Lucan down and, apparently, they started to chat. While he was in the bathroom damping another towel to tend her wounds, she bolted through the front door and ran to the quiescent 'Plumber's Arms' covered in blood, screaming, 'Murder, murder, he's murdered my nanny.' By the time the police arrived Lucan had disappeared, and he has not been seen since. No one now knows whether he is dead or alive.

After fleeing from Lower Belgrave Street, Lucan drove forty-four miles south to call on Susan Maxwell-Scott. There he downed a few stiff drinks, telephoned his mother, and scribbled a letter to his friend Bill Shand Kydd with a cock-and-bull story about how he had 'interrupted a fight at Lower Belgrave Street and the man left'. The letter continued, 'I will also lie doggo for a bit.' Lucan left Maxwell-Scott at about 1.15 a.m., and his borrowed Ford was discovered two days later, half an hour's drive away at Newhaven, the Channel port.

The car's location suggested that Lucan took the ferry to France. Perhaps this is what he wanted the police to think. Gale-force winds blew that night and, when the ferries resumed, they sailed almost empty. Lucan's photograph was splashed over the headlines and he would have been spotted. He had no access to a speedboat, and no boat was stolen. If he threw himself into the sea, the twenty-foot waves would have regurgitated him somewhere along the coast or, more probably, hurled him straight back. So suicide or conventional flight are both improbable.

But Lucan was part of a coterie of extremely wealthy men. It might have been diverting to give him asylum or spirit him away on a yacht or a private plane. Much is made of Lucan's friends' grand disre-

gard for law and order, but perhaps it is not unusual to wish to keep a friend out of prison.

Detectives searched Warwick Castle, Holkham Hall, the cellar of banker Algy Cluff, John Aspinall's estate, Jimmy Goldsmith's house in Paris and telephoned the wealthy Claus **von Bülow** to ask if he was sheltering Lucan. The fugitive was reliably seen in Cherbourg, Belgium, Brittany, the Netherlands, Ireland, the Orkneys, South Africa and South America.

Today, Lucan's friends are reluctant to talk, and outer members of his circle occasionally let drop remarks like, 'Friends chipped in to pay for the education of his children … Oh, God, I'm not supposed to say that', or, 'There's more, but I can't tell you … We were talking about this down in Mexico at Jimmy's. They said I could only talk about the dinner the night before.'

It has also been proposed, with varying degrees of conviction, that Lucan employed a bungling hitman, that a cover-up concealed Sandra Rivett's death at the hands of a policeman, and that Lucan took his own life in Aspinall's private **zoo** and was fed to the tigers.

Lucan's children have prospered. His wife lives in reduced circumstances, and the affair's aftermath numbered two unexpected casualties. Dominic Elwes, the painter, committed suicide after talking to the press about the Clermont Set, who cut him dead; and Christabel Boyce. She replaced Sandra Rivett as the Lucans' nanny and, in February 1985, in an unrelated incident, her body was found dispersed over the East End. Boyce's husband confessed and was sentenced to six years for manslaughter.

Lucas, Henry Lee (1937–)

A self-proclaimed serial killer from Texas, a penniless drifter remarkable for his ghoulish appearance and grim family background. Lucas was so badly beaten by his mother, a Chippewa Indian prostitute born Nellie Viola Dixon, that he suffered brain damage. She raised him as a girl, and he arrived for his first day at school with permed hair, in a dress. His father froze to death, ejected from home with no legs after a railway accident. Lucas himself sported a down-turned mouth and a glass eye; he tried to kill himself repeatedly, and in 1960 raped and murdered his 74-year-old mother during an argument. He spent four years in a mental hospital on electric shock therapy.

After his release from Michigan's Jackson prison in 1975, Lucas embarked on an eight-year killing spree, for the later stages teaming up with a child sex murderer and pyromaniac, Ottis Elwood Toole. His rampage ended on 9 May 1983 when Ruben Moore, a preacher from the House of Prayer in Stoneberg, tipped off the police that a member of his flock was armed.

Henry Lee Lucas – scourge of the Texas Rangers

Arrested on suspicion, an ill-kempt Lucas confessed to two murders, but hinted at others. As the implications sank in, the Texas Rangers set up a 'Henry Lee Lucas Task Force' to coordinate efforts to unravel his years on the road. Soon Lucas was alluding to sixty killings, and on the day the Rangers opened their telephone lines they fielded seventy long-distance calls from police forces anxious to clear up their unsolved murders. One by one Lucas admitted responsibility for the slayings, providing details only the killer could know.

His turn of phrase was vivid: some victims he 'filleted like fish'. Others he crucified. As he explained: 'Killing someone is just like walking outdoors. If I wanted a victim, I'd just go get one.' And again, 'I've killed by strangulation, knifing, hit and runs, shootings, robbings, stabbings, hangings, every type of crime...' He worked part-time as a contract killer for a shadowy organisation known as 'the Hand of Death', kidnapped children and smuggled them into Mexico and, for sex, would rape people or kill animals and make love to their bodies.

Lucas's grisly body-count multiplied to 150 and, as his prestige as a sweeper-up of unaccounted crimes grew, so the stature of the Task Force soared. In 1984 more than eighty detectives from twenty states booked into a Louisiana Holiday Inn, and for two days the convention studied a special screening of the Henry Lee Lucas videotapes. Speaking to camera, Lucas rambled through a litany of murders and mutilations, and by the time the dust settled some 210 killings were cleared. A detailed computerised ledger provided a chronological record of his wanderings over the interstate highways. In an ordinary month, say October 1979, he killed six times, on the 1st, the 2nd, the 5th, twice on the 23rd and again on the 31st.

As Lucas dredged through his memory the tally climbed to 360 killings. It reached 630, and finally hit 1,000. A media celebrity, he featured in a spate of surprisingly nebulous books. No longer a destitute drifter, he appeared in a three-piece suit with groomed hair and dark glasses. 'It was interview after interview,' he said. 'I was staying on televisiontwenty-four hours a day ... I thought I was the biggest movie star in this country, I think I even beat Elvis Presley.'

Lucas developed a close professional relationship with his 'minders'. 'I was real close to Sheriff Boutwell,' he recalled. 'Like father and son.' He needed careful handling. As Boutwell said, 'If at any time you indicate you disbelieve him ... you'll ruin your credibility with him.' But their restraint brought a rich harvest as day after day they called the press with new reports of cases solved.

Murder is a grim business for relatives of the deceased, and to initiate the grieving process they need to know how their loved one died. The ordeal of Bob and Joyce Lemons ended nine years after the August 1975 killing of their 18-year-old daughter Debra Sue Williamson, when Lucas recounted how he broke into their white suburban bungalow through the patio door and stabbed their daughter to death in her bedroom.

But the Lemons' relief proved short-lived. As they pointed out to the Task Force, although their house was now white it had been green at the time of the killing; the patio door was sealed shut on installation, and their daughter met her death outside in the garden. The Lemons' objections went unheeded. By now Lucas was an unstoppable juggernaut, living high and wide. In his words, 'I was a king, I had everything I wanted, everything possible that a man could want, I had money, I had a colour TV, all kinds of food, stacks of cigarettes.'

Henry Lee Lucas on 4 April 1984, eleven months after his first arrest and well into his confessing spree

Obsessed with the case, the Lemons tracked down Lucas's half-sister, who maintained that he spent the day of Debra Sue's death 2,000 miles from the murder site in Lubbock, Texas. As bereaved parents, the Lemons lacked official standing, and still Lucas piled new iniquities on to his dizzying heap of confessions. 'Every time they would bring a murder case in I would accept it, no matter what it was.'

Meanwhile Vic Feazell, District Attorney from Waco, Texas, landed the job of prosecuting Lucas for three specimen murders. Disturbed that the only evidence was Lucas's own confessions, he too started an investigation.

Feazell obtained copies of Lucas's paycheques, his work records, his applications for food stamps and his traffic tickets, which yielded an indisputable day-by-day record of his whereabouts. It bore no relation to the Task Force log. For 1979 Feazell found that Lucas had cashed forty-three weekly cheques at the Buy-Rite grocery store in Jacksonville. But during that same year the Texas Rangers had him committing forty-six murders in sixteen different states. Killing after killing proved a physical impossibility. A murder of 5 March 1981 in Corpus Christie, Texas, fell on the day that Lucas was selling scrap metal in Jacksonville, Florida. Two claimed murders took place while he was in prison. And so on.

Feazell compiled a meticulous day book with Lucas's actual whereabouts set against the corresponding murder sites and, thus equipped, confronted Lucas in the Huntsville Penitentiary, Texas. Feazell spread out his day book. 'We *know* you didn't do these killings,' he stated. Lucas smiled. 'I was wondering when someone would get wise to this.'

Feazell was in head-on conflict with the Task Force. With its credibility at stake, Feazell found himself targeted by a virulent FBI corruption investigation, and he was dragged off in handcuffs to face accusations of racketeering, burglaries and homicides. Feazell conducted his own defence, vindicating himself and winning a record $58 million in libel damages.

By now Lucas appreciated the drawback of impersonating the world's greatest serial killer. He was on **Death Row** awaiting execution. He started to retract, and his downward revisions of the death toll left the figure of one: his **mother**, a murder for which he had paid the penalty. His terrible childhood remains uncorroborated.

Perhaps Lucas gleaned the names of his supposed victims (when he provided them) from newspaper clippings. But this would involve ambitious forward-planning. A simpler explanation is to hand. As Lucas said, 'I didn't go to the police about these killings, they would bring the murders to me and tell me about them.' By the Task Force's procedure, outside police agencies submitted detailed offence reports; only after receipt was Lucas interrogated, suggesting that he was 'primed' with details.

In Britain, IRA cases revealed a judiciary unable to swallow the bitter pill that the police might be corrupt; in America, the innocence of Lucas would turn the Texas Rangers and a dozen agencies beside into a laughing stock. As Lucas says, 'This is Texas, and I'm trying to fight a legend.'

George W. Bush – the Texas governor who reprieved Henry Lee Lucas's death sentence

On television, Lucas comes across as a likeable, bumbling man who relished his limelight years. 'It's like being a movie star,' he reminisces. 'It's just like playing a part.' But there are tears in his eyes. He may still have to die.

In 1998, Henry Lee Lucas's execution was commuted to life imprisonment by then Governor of Texas – and usually keen proponent of the death penalty – George W. Bush. Lucas died in his sleep of heart failure in 2001. The otherwise admirable film by John McNaughton, *Henry: Portrait of a Serial Killer*, depicts Lucas as a man who just woke up and killed. But he didn't. He just woke up.

See also **False confessions**, **Success**

Luciani, Albino (1912–78)

Also known as Pope John Paul I, who died on 28 September 1978, thirty-three days after his election. Six years later the British investigative author David Yallop published *In God's Name*, a massive research piece whose contents are fairly summarised by the Cataloguing Data on the title verso: '1. Catholic Church – Finance, 2. Organised Crime.'

Yallop assembled a convincing if circumstantial case that the Pope was murdered. It seems that Luciani was bent on rooting out corruption at the Vatican Bank, overturning established Catholic doctrine on birth control and ending the Church's involvement with the illegal but powerful branch of Freemasonry known as P2. Careers and reputations at the highest Vatican levels were at stake; the exposure of massive financial fraud imminent.

Yallop contended that the evening before his death the reformist Luciani discussed a dramatic reshuffle of staff with his Secretary of State, Cardinal John Villot (himself destined for the chop). Next morning, Luciani – previously in good health – was dead, but forty-five minutes *before* the official discovery of the corpse by Villot, the Signoracci brothers, embalmers, were called to the Vatican.

Items beside Luciani's body, including a medicine bottle, vanished. Without troubling to hold an autopsy, a Dr Buzzonetti vaguely passed off the death as 'myocardial infarction' (heart attack); within fourteen hours the body (and any evidence with it) was embalmed. A few days later the hard-liner Karol Wojtyla was elected, the old gang of corrupt cardinals were safe in their sinecures, and Luciani's reforms lay dead in their tracks.

Murder, said Yallop. But his book is a fine example of a conspiracy manufactured out of thin air. None of the main evidential planks bears investigation. Thus the wicked Cardinal Marcinkus was supposedly wandering round the Vatican very early on the morning of the killing: 'What the President of the Vatican Bank, not a renowned early riser, was doing so early remains a mystery,' comments Yallop. In fact, Marcinkus motored early to work every day to avoid the traffic.

Nor were the embalmers summoned to the Vatican with untoward prescience. Old men with failing memories, the Signoraccis' evidence is contradictory and unreliable, with Ernesto later saying· 'It's all confused … it could have been seven in the morning … or … it could have been at ten in the morning … or … at three in the afternoon … I don't know.' It would be easy to put words into their mouths, and there were five doddery brothers in the same line of business to put them into or take them out of.

Again, the Pope's prompt embalming was in anticipation of his imminent public display, spanning several days, quite possibly in sultry weather, and although such conservation might be illegal in Italy, it is lawful – and normal – in the Vatican, a separate country.

There are wider problems, not least that the Vatican is incapable of conspiring to do anything, let alone kill a Pope. In a hive of factional gossip, a concerted cover-up is impossible. Nor was there any point in conniving against Luciani. No clean broom, he was a befuddled old man of 65 out of his depth. His previous administrative experience was restricted to the decaying see of Venice with its small flock of 90,000. Suddenly – and mistakenly – elected Pope, he was plunged into the deep end as the Chief Executive of one of the world's biggest, most demanding businesses.

Luciani did not want the job; he did not understand it; as Pope, he was a provincial embarrassment at his wits' end, and seriously ill to boot. His legs were so swollen that he could not wear shoes – strongly indicative of thrombosis of the inferior vena cava. In his prayers, Luciani begged the Lord to let him die, and on the day of his death complained three times of feeling ill, and of a severe pain in the chest.

Luciani probably took anti-coagulants to improve the circulation in his legs. If he neglected to take his pills, his blood would become more coagulable, making the chest pain of his last afternoon consistent with a minor blood clot in the lungs, and his death that evening consistent with a massive pulmonary embolism. Throughout his brief tenure, Luciani went without the ordinary medical attention that could have saved him. It seems unlikely that he was murdered, but the Vatican staff's failure to provide even basic medical support to such an evidently ailing man could be seen as tantamount to manslaughter by neglect.

Luck, hard

Countless thousands of criminals come to grief each year through no more than hard luck. These stories of unhappy coincidences cumulatively suggest that a life of crime is a high-risk occupation liable to detection one way or the other.

Thus in February 1991 an 18-year-old thief, Freedom A. Hunter from Arizona, achieved simultaneous felonious possession of a chequebook (property of a Nebraska couple) and a driving licence (belonging to one Tim Holt). Using the latter as identification, he went to a drive-in bank with a forged cheque for $275 made out to himself under his new alias. As the bank clerk to whom he handed the cheque was Tim Holt, Freedom Hunter ended up in jail.

Such incidents progressively shade into stories where bad luck is attributable to **stupidity**. On 27 March 1990 the Atlanta *Constitution* reported a striking *faux pas* by William J. Collins. He walked into Atlanta police headquarters and threw a bag of crack down on the desk of Officer V. J. Williams. Shortly before being booked for possession, Collins complained that he was fed up with bad stuff and wanted his supplier arrested.

Many of the more mundane 'hard luck' stories centre on cars – getaway vehicles running out of petrol or being clamped, or fleeing villains flagging down a police car to ask for directions. But despite appearances,

it is not so much that criminals are stupid as that they habitually commit crime. Anyone could get arrested doing it.

Lunette

French term for the wooden halter clamping the condemned man's neck on the **guillotine**; in the plural, *lunettes* means spectacles. At the decapitation of Maitre Georges Sarret on 10 April 1934, the severed head remained affixed to the *lunette* for some ten minutes after the blade got stuck.

Prior to execution, a French convict signed his record-sheet to acknowledge that everything was in order; the prison director added, 'Handed over to M. the Executioner for carrying out of the sentence', whereupon the prisoner, received in operational condition, became the responsibility of his executioner.

America has equally stringent requirements. A man about to have his life removed by the State must be conscious, alert and 'physically able to withstand the shock of execution'. So the day before he dies he receives a medical examination. In the words of Doyle Williams, who survived to tell the tale after the postponement of his 20 March 1991 'event': 'They take your temperature and they weigh you, and the doctor hits your knee to see if you have reflexes. And if I remember right, he took his stethoscope and listened to my heart. I thought it was kind of silly. I said, "What are you going to do if I'm sick?"'

In France the assistant executioner's job was to ensure that his client did not imitate the action of a tortoise, drawing his head back into his shoulders as the blade approached. This he accomplished either by pulling the prostrate victim forwards by the hair or (if bald) the ears, thereby assuring a properly extended neck, and his obsession with settling the condemned man in position accounts for his slang title as 'the photographer'.

M

McCummings, Bernard (1961–)

First mugger to retire a millionaire. In the summer of 1984, 23-year-old Bernard McCummings grabbed an elderly subway passenger at a West Side Manhattan station. By chance, a Transit Police detective standing nearby intervened and shot McCummings twice. One bullet severed his spine, paralysing him from the chest down, but after the trial McCummings was able to serve his thirty-seven-month sentence in a wheelchair.

A police board of inquiry cleared Detective Rodriguez of 'excessive force', accepting that the mugger had lunged for the gun. This was because the departmental proceedings never established that McCummings was hit in the back, a fact which the police captain in charge said he only learned during his cross-examination at the subsequent trial in April 1992. Awarded $4.3 million in damages, McCummings, confined to a wheelchair, lived in a Harlem housing project with his mother while the judgment was appealed.

When the New York Court of Appeals, the state's highest court, upheld the verdict in the spring of 2005 and McCummings got his money, there was a predictable burst of public outrage. 'We had no other choice,' jury foreman Peter Robbins told the media. Another juror said her colleagues realised the plaintiff was a low-life, but they 'had to put that aside' – once they agreed the shooting was unjustified, 'we had to give him an award under the law'.

MacDonald, Dr Jeffrey (1944–)

The front cover of *Esquire*'s March 1970 edition read, 'Lee Marvin is afraid – Evil lurks in California.' Inside were features on the **Manson** slayings and a candlelit LSD orgy presided over by a long-haired 'witch' with a retinue of four. One subscriber to the magazine was 26-year-old Dr Jeffrey MacDonald at the Green Berets' Fort Bragg, and two nights after he drew a neighbour's attention to the articles, the police responded to a late-night emergency call to his home. They found a dazed MacDonald lying by his pregnant wife in the master-bedroom, her skull fractured and both her arms broken. She had thirty-seven stab wounds. 'Pigs' was daubed in blood by the headboard, and down the corridor lay their two children, both stabbed to death. MacDonald gasped, 'Four of them … She kept saying, "Acid is groovy … Kill the pigs."'

MacDonald realised how he had dozed off on the living-room couch at 2 a.m., waking to find himself under attack from intruders wielding knives, an ice-pick and club. One of the men had a moustache, and the girl wore a floppy hat over her long hair. She held a candle. Somehow MacDonald's pyjamas were ripped over his head and became entangled with his hands. As he fainted, he heard Colette, his wife, screaming and his children crying. Coming to, he pulled a knife out of Colette's chest, covered her with his pyjamas and, at 3.42 a.m., called for help.

MacDonald was the boxing team doctor, an Ivy League School graduate and a weightlifter. Perhaps two notes jarred: he aired his suit on the clothesline if he went to a party where guests smoked tobacco. And no one groovy enough to take acid still said 'groovy'. Nor did the forensic evidence tally. Almost a hundred threads from his tattered pyjama tops were found in the three bedrooms – which he went to *after* covering his wife. Some fibres lay *under* Colette's body. But none was shed during the living-room fight, which left MacDonald almost unscathed. His single stab-wound was a slit one centimetre wide, as though self-inflicted with a scalpel, and his home was virtually undisturbed. The greeting cards still stood, and the coffee table found on its side proved top heavy: when investigators knocked it over, it turned upside down.

The MacDonald family all had different blood types. Colette's was present in Kristen's bedroom, Kimberly's in the hall and in the master bedroom, MacDonald's by the hall cabinet housing the scalpels. So the forensic evidence directly contradicted his version of events. 'Step one, you lose your family, step two, you get blamed for it,' he objected on 6 April, and later that day, as he stood in the canteen queue, the radio announced his arrest. MacDonald's in-laws, the Kassabs, rallied to his defence.

The Army hearing discovered that the crime scene had been irreparably compromised. Twelve military police had trampled through MacDonald's apartment; his pyjama bottoms were lost, the lavatory flushed, a bloody footprint destroyed, and scrapings of skin under Colette's fingernails and a blue fibre from Kristen's fingers mislaid. A flower-pot (supposedly found upright) was set back on its base by a medic. A doctor shifted Colette's body and moved the pyjamas, her 'hair' came from her coat collar, and one of MacDonald's from his pony. The police saw a girl in a floppy hat loitering nearby on the night, but nothing was done; Fort Bragg had a population of 50,000 and thirty-one access points, so no roadblocks were set up.

An embarrassed Army cleared the court. Then a man named William Posey recalled that his neighbour – a teenager called Helena, a witchcraft druggy who affected floppy hats – had returned in her Mustang at 4 a.m. with two or three raucous men on the murder night. On the day of the MacDonald funerals, Helena wore black, and draped wreaths from her porch. Later she said of her boyfriend, 'Well, we can't get married until we go out and kill some more people.' Posey testified; Helena was located, but under questioning she betrayed no recollection of the murder night.

MacDonald's lawyer mocked the investigation for its listless pursuit of the Helena lead. Charges against MacDonald were dropped for insufficient evidence, and, in a Newsday interview, he enumerated his nineteen stab wounds. He put out feelers for a book deal with Esquire and the North Carolina Observer, and appeared on television, castigating the Army for framing him. By now he spoke of twenty-three wounds.

Despite MacDonald's veto on taking a lie test, the Kassabs remained stalwart allies. Clearing his name was a prerequisite to renewing the hunt for their daughter's real killers, and Kassab lobbied 500 congressmen on MacDonald's behalf. But he needed the thirteen volumes of Army hearing transcripts to argue his case in detail, and MacDonald seemed reluctant to allow access. Instead, on 18 November, he telephoned: 'All I can say is, one down, three to go.' Next day MacDonald vaguely described how he had tracked down one of the killers and beaten him to death.

This made the Kassabs curious. Who was it? What did the culprit say? Why had MacDonald killed a man who could prove his innocence? Pushed for details, MacDonald said that the girl in the floppy hat was called 'Willie the Witch'; she had left with the moustache man. Two months later Kassab's efforts produced a new investigation, but when Helena was traced, she proved a rambling heroin addict. 'I don't know whether I did it or not,' she said. 'I really and truly don't know anything.' Much of Posey's testimony was untrue.

Background inquiries on MacDonald revealed a domestic martinet addicted to indiscriminate affairs. Re-evaluation of the forensic evidence showed that the smooth knife-holes in MacDonald's torn pyjamas, allegedly deployed in defence while tangled round his hands, were inflicted on a stationary garment. Slits in Colette's clothing showed that the knife MacDonald claimed to have extracted from her chest was never used against her. Its blade matched cuts to his pyjamas, suggesting that he stabbed himself. And some of Colette's blood sprayed on to his pyjamas in circular blobs; the cloth had later been torn in two.

In March 1971 Kassab took delivery of the Army transcripts. He pored over MacDonald's 153-page testimony with mounting disbelief. How had Colette cried, 'Help, help, Jeff why are they doing this to me?', when her throat was cut? If MacDonald was knocked out, where were his contusions? Why wasn't he killed while unconscious? Everyone else had been. Why was only one of his wounds more than 5mm deep? Why were his daughters found on their sides if he gave them mouth-to-mouth respiration? Why deny an ice-pick was in the house?

Kassab secured access to the MacDonald apartment. The ceiling was too low to wield the club overhead. Soundproofing was poor, yet the family above slumbered through the screams. With the lights extinguished it was too dark to see an assailant's moustache. And stamping in the corridor toppled the greeting cards in the dining room.

The new investigation was complete by June 1972, but MacDonald remained at liberty until 1979. By then he had a $350,000 West Coast condominium, drove a Citroën-Maserati, owned a ten-metre yacht, and his many supporters considered him a heroic figure. Although MacDonald's guilt was clear, the Department of Justice evaluated the evidence as circumstantial and the chances of a conviction slim. Nor did MacDonald pose a threat to others. But Kassab's tireless efforts for a prosecution finally bore fruit.

The killings probably began with a bedroom row. Weapons came to hand and Colette's blood spurted on to MacDonald. Kimberly intervened and was killed in her bedroom. Colette revived and tried to protect Kristen. Both were killed. To explain Colette's blood on his pyjamas, MacDonald used them to cover her bleeding body. Then he stabbed her repeatedly, and, when the pyjamas were refolded in replication of the crime-scene photographs, their forty-eight knife-holes could be duplicated by twenty-one ice-pick thrusts, delivered in the pattern of Colette's twenty-one chest wounds.

MacDonald always insisted on his innocence, but an early defence report depicted a selective **amnesiac** with suspect credibility, and his factual statements revealed tiny distortions which, in aggregate, consti-tuted a big lie. In 1970 he was on amphetamines, then considered harmless and pre-scribed for weight loss, and in the month preceding the murders – already lean and fit – he lost a further stone. The side-effects of his probable dosage are insomnia, irritability and hallucinations. On top of his job, MacDonald worked every night of January at one hospital, did weekends at another, applied for a third moonlighting post, and worked out with the boxing team. Before the murder, he stood a twenty-four-hour shift, put in a day at the office, played basketball and stayed up late. Then, something happened.

See also **Jury**

McKinney, Joyce (1948–)

An all-American girl and a regular at Bible camp. Born in 1948, she was voted Miss North Carolina High School by her classmates. But one day in 1975, while driving with a friend in her new Stingray convertible, a handsome young man popped his head through her car window.

In Joyce's words: 'I found myself gazing into the deepest pair of baby-blue eyes. He put Paul Newman to shame. My heart did flip-flops. I turned to my girl-friend and said: "Hey, get out – I'm in love."'

Joyce McKinney maintains a high profile at a movie première with the editor of the Daily Express *in April 1978, a few days before absconding*

Joyce's beau was a 6ft 2in Mormon missionary, Kirk Anderson, and for a time their affair flourished. A besotted Joyce was anxious to please; according to a friend, she visited porn films and live sex acts to amass tips on sensual arousal. When Anderson tired of their Salt Lake City affair, she harassed him, with escalating violence. Anderson's windows were broken, his tyres ripped and his car smashed. He requested a transfer to California, but Joyce followed him. So Anderson took an overseas posting in Britain.

Joyce blamed the tyrannical Mormon Church for stealing her lover; she wanted him back, depro-grammed and freed of sexual inhibitions. So she advertised in an underground magazine for the comprehensive abduction services of 'a muscle man, a pilot and a preacher to help in a romantic adven-ture'. Joyce never assembled the team, but she did have a car crash, and the $15,000 insurance money funded a visit to, or perhaps a raid on, Britain. Arriving with a false passport, she hounded Anderson out of East Grinstead to Reading and thence to Epsom.

It was there she struck on 14 September 1977.

Outside his church, Joyce and a male accomplice hustled Anderson into a car at imitation-gunpoint, put him to sleep with a bottle of chloroform and then motored to Devon for the Cure. At the cottage, Joyce explained her terms. Anderson could go free as soon as he agreed to marriage. Thereafter, what happened depends on whom you believe, but only for one detail. Everyone agrees that Anderson spent three days tied to a bed with chains and a leather strap; that he had oral sex with his ex-lover; that she spreadeagled him on his stomach and gave a back-rub clad in a negligee; that she turned him over, and tied him business side up with ropes, chains and padlocks; that they had intercourse. The dispute centred on that familiar bone of contention, consent.

Joyce said Anderson loved it; he let himself be trussed up and lay there 'grinning like a monkey'. Anderson maintained the sex was forced. 'But he would, wouldn't he?' said Joyce. Anderson would hardly *invite* excommunication.

The element of consent was not crucial. In law, a woman cannot **rape** a man. So when Anderson ran to the police after three days on the rack, Joyce and her accomplice were charged only with abduction and possession of an imitation revolver. From the prison van taking her to court, a tearful Joyce distributed messages to newspapermen, 'Please ask Christians to pray for me', scrawled on the torn-out pages of a Bible. At the preliminary hearing, she was granted bail, but on a curfew, a restriction lifted on 13 March 1978 to enable her to visit the cinema. But she went to America instead, emerging from hiding garbed as a nun to court the popular press. For six years little more was heard. Then in June 1984 the papers announced: 'Sex-in-chains Joyce is at it again.'

By now, Anderson had given up his calling as a missionary; married to a girl called Linda, he worked as an airline company executive. When Joyce stationed herself outside his office, Anderson braced himself for another snatch and called the police; they charged her with disturbing the peace. Joyce carried a notebook detailing Anderson's every move, and through her lawyer, explained that she was 'writing a screenplay about her experiences and wanted to see how the story ended'. For the time being, the story stops there.

See also **Crime passionel**

Maconochie, Alexander (1787–1860)

This son of a Scottish lawyer ranks as one of Australia's unsung heroes. As a young man, Maconochie spent two years from 1811 imprisoned by the French during the Napoleonic Wars; the experience may have been formative.

A quarter of a century later, invited by Sir John Franklin to Australia, Maconochie's colleagues at the Royal Geographic Society commissioned a report on the convict system of Van Diemen's Land. Maconochie correctly depicted its inhabitants as callous slave-owners exploiting convict labour. The system, he wrote, was 'cruel, uncertain, prodigal, ineffectual either for reform or example; can only be maintained in some degree of vigour by extreme severity'.

In Britain, the report's 1838 publication was a bombshell; six months later, when the mails arrived in Australia, it became a scandal. Maconochie was ostracised, libelled and slandered. But he assured London: 'The cause has got me complete ... I will neither acquiesce in the moral destruction of so many of my fellow beings nor in the misrepresentation of myself.'

Maconochie's insight was that all the systematic policies of convict degradation served no purpose. The prisoners had done nothing to deserve their floggings, and were not benefited by them. Other than for the perpetuation of tradition, there was no reason to whip the men within an inch of their lives.

Maconochie devised a disciplinary theory based on a system of marks, as in schools. Points for good conduct would earn convicts better conditions, enabling ascent from solitary confinement to 'social treatment both night and day'. The fiercest punishment was taking marks away, condemning the convict to solitary again. Thus each prisoner's fate lay in his own hands. Maconochie fondly imagined that his scheme would turn the convicts from objects into people, in whom jailers could take a personal interest, and he rounded off his system with proposals for a prison ombudsman.

Maconochie's ideas were as alien as the Coca Cola cans that occasionally drop out of aircraft to land at the feet of stone-age tribesmen. The Australian way was to work convicts to near or actual death, flog them without mercy for misdemeanours like 'looking up from work' and then flog them again for being unable to work after being flogged. But the

Ticket-of-leave, issued to convicts of good behaviour, allowing them to seek employment outside government service

deliberations of the 1838 British Molesworth Committee resulted in Maconochie's surprise appointment as commandant of **Norfolk Island**, the heart of darkness of the Australian penal colony a thousand miles from Sydney.

Maconochie landed in May 1840 to be greeted by the mustered ranks of 1,200 brutalised degenerates who for years had endured a daily round little better than **torture**. In his inaugural speech, Maconochie announced that the old system had ended. Then he outlined his pet plan of schoolboy marks.

After stunned incredulity the compound resounded with cheers. In the words of Thomas Cook, an old hand, 'From that instant, all crime disappeared', and in fact most of these reprobates had been transported for petty theft involving clothes or food.

To celebrate Queen Victoria's birthday on 24 May, Maconochie declared a holiday. He ran little pennants up the prison flagpole, fired off the cannon, threw open the prison gates, allowed the dazed convicts to wander over the island, gave them permission to swim, served special rations for barbecues, issued pannikins of rum and lemon, and staged a play (the comic opera *The Castle of Andalusia*) before winding up the evening with a firework display. Maconochie noted: 'Not a single irregularity,

or anything even approaching an irregularity, took place.'

When trouble started, it was the backlash from the mainland. What about the regime of terror? Where was the hardship? Counter-orders poured in from Sydney. Why had he ignored the regulations about punishment-labour for the new prisoners? On the irksome question of his contravening the law, Maconochie replied: 'It can scarcely be doubted that this Act will be repealed. I never thought of these rules as a guide.'

Instead, he pressed ahead with liberalisation, requisitioning shiploads of encyclopedias, magazines, stories of exploration, history books, poetry and enough Waverley novels to found a library; sheet music, a trumpet, fife, horns, drums, reed accordions and other orchestral instruments; he distributed good conduct marks, dismantled the gallows, threw away the cat-o'-nine tails, built a church, instituted a makeshift synagogue, allocated vegetable plots, held gardening classes, let the men grow **tobacco** and allowed them decent burials with headstones.

The prisoners were transformed. In Cook's *Exile's Lamentations*, Maconochie earns a hundred pages of praise. Another set of memoirs refers to him as an 'angel', stating, 'Justice stares us in the face, the Almighty has now sent us a deliverance.' At a stroke, the Norfolk Island convicts returned to their former identities as ordinary, reasonably docile citizens. Many were former denizens of the Home Counties.

Meanwhile the colonists on the mainland were in a ferment of outrage; in London, Lord Stanley decided to drop his protégé. At the age of fifty-six Maconochie was dismissed from his post, but not before discharging 920 of his prisoners: a mere 2 per cent reoffended in the first two years. After his departure, Norfolk Island was plunged back into the dark ages.

Back in Britain, Maconochie was marginalised, briefly serving as a governor of Birmingham Prison where all his efforts were countermanded. Almost the only person to take him seriously was Charles **Dickens** and he died largely ignored in 1860. His 1846 *Crime and Punishment* remains a classic of modern penology.

See also **Negative blocking**

Mad Bomber

For more than sixteen years George Metesky terrorised New York. His campaign started on 16 November 1940, marked by a dud bomb on a windowsill at a Consolidated Edison plant on West 64th Street. An accompanying note, handprinted in neat capitals, read 'Con Edison Crooks – this is for you.'

Ten years later, on 24 April 1950, the unknown bomber raised his game to devices that exploded, and by 1957 his bomb tally had reached the high fifties. Some were duds. Injuries were few, and for the war years his harassment ceased altogether when, still out of step, he wrote a note vowing: 'I will make no more bomb units for the duration of the war – my patriotic feelings have made me decide this.'

But the underlying trend was for bombs of ever-increasing size, and on 2 December 1956 six cinema-goers were hurt in an explosion at the Paramount Theater in Brooklyn. In January 1957 the Mad Bomber responded to an open letter from the

George Metesky, Mad Bomber

publishers of the *Journal-American* with an explanatory note: 'I was injured on a job at Consolidated Edison plant – as a result I am adjudged totally and permanently disabled – I did not receive any aid of any kind from company – that I did not pay myself – while fighting for my life – section 28 came up.' Section 28 is New York's two-year Statute of Limitations.

Here was the first solid clue – the Mad Bomber had been on Consolidated Edison's payroll. But when a trawl through the company's records drew a blank, Inspector Howard E. Finney called in a Dr James Brussel from New York State's mental health department. Brussel perused the case-files, the photographs of the unexploded devices and the many notes and letters. And this is what he thought.

It was common ground that the bomber was waging a public **vendetta** against Con Ed, blaming the utility for his troubles. So the suspect was paranoid. Most paranoids do not get into their stride until their early thirties. So, by now a middle-aged paranoiac who, to judge by his handwriting, was meticulously, obsessively neat. A clean-shaven type who favoured a double-breasted suit. Buttoned up. And, going by the notes' stilted phraseology, an immigrant. Or, more likely, in view of his age, the first-generation son of an immigrant. A son because most bombers are, statistically, male. And possibly Slavonic, since Slavs, historically, have a taste for bombs. In any case, not German, Italian or Spanish, to judge again by the phrasing. So very probably Slavonic. And hence a Catholic, like most immigrant Slavs. And, like most middle-aged paranoiacs, the Mad Bomber would live either by himself or with an elderly relative. And since he had been seriously ill (according to his letters) for a long time, but remained alive, he either suffered from TB, or chronic heart disease, or cancer.

On arrest, the Mad Bomber proved to be George Metesky, a middle-aged, neatly dressed, paranoid, church-going Catholic Pole, who lived alone with two doting elder sisters and wore his double-breasted suits buttoned. He suffered from TB.

Misleading trimmings of Freudian junk permeated Dr Brussel's analysis. Thus the shape of the bomber's handwritten 'w's, which were tantalisingly plump and round, suggested an obsession with female breasts characteristic of an Oedipus Complex. So Con Ed symbolised *male* authority, and the Bomber's campaign, which included explosive devices left in

James Brussel, first criminal profiler

holes in cinema seats, was motivated by *sexual inadequacy*. Otherwise, Brussel was spot-on.

Brussel's profile did not lead directly to the arrest since, in the meantime, Metesky sent one note too many to the *Journal American*, disclosing the date of his 5 September 1931 accident. His capture followed immediately, and he whiled away the rest of his life in an asylum.

Brussel was dubbed the 'Sherlock Holmes of the Couch' by the press, and the subsequent development of **'profiling'** flowed from attempts to implement his insights on a systematic basis. Brussel stayed ahead of the pack in the Boston Strangler fiasco (see **Insatiable**), when he was the first to realise that the attacks were not the handiwork of two distinct killers but of one. His final 'psychofit' of a strongly built 30-year-old, of average height and clean-shaven, dark-haired, of Spanish or Italian origin, fitted DeSalvo precisely.

Mafia, discovery of

The best-kept secret in the annals of law enforcement. The Mob's existence remained unsuspected by educated Americans until 1950, when Senate Estes Kefauver's investigating committee stubbed its toes on something familiar to every cop and every street-corner punk: 'a sinister criminal organisation known as the Mafia'. Even then this was regarded as a questionable fantasy, with Robert Kennedy in a 1957 cross-examination enquiring of a gangster whether he was 'born into' or had 'married into' the Mob, as though it were the Royal Family.

The core information went on record after the discovery of **Murder Inc**. in 1940, when the killing of a minor hoodlum, 'Red' Alpert, prompted hitman 'Kid Twist' Reles to furnish mountainous evidence that a gang of professional gunmen worked full-time on the orders of Mafia high-ups.

If this was a bombshell, no one heard it. In the words of the case's District Attorney, penned a decade later: 'Kid Twist's confession reached its climax with the incredible disclosure that there existed in America an organised underworld, and that controlled lawlessness across the United States. For the first time in any investigation anywhere, the lid was lifted to lay bare a government within a government, in which the killings and the racket worked hand in hand in a national combine of crime. Law enforcement had hardly any concept even of what a national combination meant. A lot of officialdom, it would appear, still remains in the dark about this danger from within.'

This was because **Hoover**, refusing to acknowledge what he knew to be true, squandered the FBI's resources on communists. New York had four agents working on the Mob, and 400 assigned to the Reds, beavering away on vital issues like whether the head of the Communist Party travelled to work by subway or cab. Meanwhile the Mafia pursued its business undisturbed.

The shooting of the *mafioso* Joe Masseria over supper on 15 April 1930 was a turning point for the Mob, paving the way for the coming generation of hoods. Masseria was one of the last old-timers, believing that every gang should fend for itself, and after the killing, young Lucky Luciano (who shared dinner with Joe but tactfully withdrew to the men's room at the vital moment) assumed the Presidency of the Italian Society. On 11 September 1931 he launched 'Purge Day', a Spaghetti Night of the Long Knives. Thirty-plus of the Mob's older leaders were liquidated. On the East Coast, the Big Six emerged: Costello, Luciano, Adonis, Lepke and Gurrah, Siegel and Lansky, Zwillman and Schultz (who did not last long).

In 1934 Johnny Torrio of Chicago mustered the top shots at a meeting and opened with the proposal, 'Why don't all you guys work up one big outfit?' He continued: 'One guy gets hit, and his troop hits the outfit that did it.' These troublesome inter-gang feuds aroused the attentions of the law. Torrio recommended a Syndicate to end indiscriminate rivalries, with disputes referred to a Commission, which thereafter regulated the myriad rackets in industry, the ports, the rag trade, trucking, labour, strikes, strikebreaking, gambling, the ice business, loan sharking, car-theft, slot-machines, hot dog stands, prostitution, pornography, protection, extortion, construction, narcotics, garbage and the mozzarella trade. In a word, the Mafia was in business, and the Commission's decrees were enforced by Murder Inc. operatives, who killed trouble-makers.

Hoover remained sceptical until the **Apalachin** summit of 14 November 1957, when a New York State detective blundered into a formal conclave of sixty or so mobsters at Joe Barbara's house. Even then, official recognition came slowly; the public first grasped the true extent of organised crime from Joe Valachi's testimony during the McClellan Senate hearings of 1963. Only the year before, on 8 September, FBI agent James Flynn terrorised Valachi by mouthing the dread phrase 'Cosa Nostra'. In the words of the official account: 'Valachi went pale. For almost a minute he said nothing. Then he rasped back hoarsely, "Cosa Nostra! So you know about it."' As late as the early 1970s, Attorney General John Mitchell ordered the word 'Mafia' struck from the Justice Department's vocabulary.

Mafioso *Joe Valachi testifying at the 1963 Senate Investigation Subcommittee*

Times change. In 1984, an alibi witness for the drug trafficker Salvatore Catalano feigned ignorance of the term, saying: 'I don't know what that is. Is it something that one eats?' The court burst out laughing.

See also **Decline and fall**, **Whacks**

Magic Eraser

A 1975 hi-tech gambit in the cocaine business. A Colombian stamp on a passport intensified the chances of arrest, and an Englishman known as 'Dr Richard', with a prototype pigtail and wire-rim spectacles, made his money in Colombia under the trade name Downstream Plastics, selling two aerosols at $5,000 a throw.

The first can sprayed an invisible micron-thin protective layer on to paper documentation; the sheen dried off in a few seconds. A burst from the second aerosol fragmented the coating like a smashed windscreen; the frosted shards could be shaken free, leaving no trace and the paper undamaged. A passport veneered with Magic Eraser allowed removal of the tell-tale Colombian entry and exit stamps after departure but before arrival, and the courier 'Rosalita' used the stratagem for six of her forty-three undefeated trips. The technique had one patent drawback: the whole passport needed treating each time, since it was impossible to foresee on which page an Immigration official would put the stamp. The latent pitfall was that the laminate proved susceptible to heat, as Rosalita discovered when she accidentally left her passport on the windowsill of the Hotel Tequendama in Bogota. The coating baked in the sun, crinkling up on the pages like a fried egg. She binned her passport and abandoned the aerosols.

Rosalita was last heard of in the mid-1980s living in a half-finished apartment in Quinta Paredes, Bogota, with a single-bar electric fire and an expensive habit. If alive, she is now aged 43. She made a number of runs disguised as a nun, Sister Dominica, carrying her cocaine stuffed into crucifixes.

See also **Narcotics**

Male rape

Surprisingly popular among heterosexuals, underlining the point that rape concerns subjugation rather than sex. Nor is it confined to **prison**. A 1990 survey in the *British Journal of General Practice* found that 72 per cent of the victims were acquainted with their assailants socially, regarding them as heterosexual.

Male **rape** differs from the female version in two non-biological respects. First, the maximum penalty is ten years as opposed to life. Second, its exponents are all but immune from prosecution. In the words of the late Richie McMullen, author of *Male Rape: Breaking the Silence on the Last Taboo*: 'If you and I decided that we were going to go out tonight and rape a boy or a man, we could almost guarantee – 99.99 per cent certain – that we would get away with it. We know the victim is not going to report the crime.'

But the humiliation endured by the victims is no different. 'Survivors' recall the usual symptoms of defilement, outrage and depression, frequently coupled with a loss of the will to live. Some burn all their clothes, take to obsessive washing, and are scared to leave home, while their lives collapse around them. Unlike the abscess of female rape, which can be partially lanced by confiding in sympathisers, male victims, lacking a reservoir of social comprehension, have no one to tell because no one understands. One distressed victim telephoned the Rape Crisis Centre, to be told tartly: 'We are for women.'

Malory, Sir Thomas (ca 1400–71)

English Member of Parliament as well as a brigand, robber, horse thief and rapist. After campaigning in France under the Earl of Warwick, Malory ravaged his native county as a gang leader. He extorted money 'by threats and oppression', attempted the murder of the Duke of Buckingham, rustled cattle, ransacked Coombe Abbey and raped Joan Smyth not once but (a few months later) twice. Generally, the law caught up with him and, while serving his third or fourth **Newgate** sentence, Malory amused himself by jottings of fantasies harking back to more chivalric times. Some fourteen years after his unmourned death, the manuscript came into the hands of William Caxton. He thought it had potential.

Malory's *Morte d'Arthur* became an instant best-seller, and stayed so for centuries, profoundly influencing Western culture. The book's elevated tone ensured the posthumous rehabilitation of its author, until the mid-1920s when an American scholar uncovered the truth while researching in the Public Record Office.

Manson, Charles Milles (1934–)

Manson was extremely small, a pint-sized 5ft 2in; so tiny that during the 12 October 1969 raid on the **Family** ranch he nearly avoided detection by hiding in a cupboard – partitioned by a horizontal shelf – under a small hand-basin. But his hair stuck out.

To the Family, even Manson's name was imbued with potency. As Susan Atkins said: 'I want you to dig on his name. Now listen, his name is Manson – *Man's Son!*' That was the name they hooked him under: 'Manson, Charles M., aka Jesus Christ, God'. Manson himself went further, upgrading his middle name from Milles to Willis, producing the aphorism 'Charles' will is Man's Son'. On the ride back to Independence in the police pickup, the arresting officer, Patrolman James Pursell, overheard Manson making utterances 'that caused the others to say "amen" two or three times in unison'. Interrogating the Family women, Deputy District Attorney Vincent Bugliosi was struck by the way the girls smiled almost continuously, repeatedly intoning 'Charlie is love.' Their supine, undifferentiated complaisance reminded him of Barbie Dolls, and initial investigations into the Family's enterprises made little headway. Pressed for details like dates, the girls replied: 'There is no such thing as time.'

Manson was born on or about 12 November 1934, the illegitimate son of a 16-year-old mother. As a child, he experienced 'uncle' after 'uncle' – his mother's new lovers – living in run-down hotel rooms. His first armed robbery came at the age of 13. Confined to juvenile reform school, Manson raped a number of inmates, sodomising one boy with a razor to his throat. By the time he was 32, Manson had clocked up seventeen years behind bars for offences like burglary, car theft and forgery. His overall sentence would probably have totalled less than five years had he been tried for comparable crimes in state rather than federal courts, and it is as though he sought out offences that carried the most severe punishments.

By his Family days, Manson did not think twice about killing. His domination of the group was absolute. Often he dined alone on top of a large rock in the desert while the rest of the Family sat in a reverential circle on the ground, listening to his evocations of the imminent confrontation between blacks and whites.

To trigger this holocaust, he sent out his followers in squads to kill. On 8 August 1969, Manson despatched Susan Atkins, Patricia Krenwinkel, Leslie Van Houten

Charles Manson at the preliminary hearing in Independence, California, March 1969

and Charles 'Tex' Watson to the house of record producer Tony Melcher. He had moved, but they killed the new occupants with the appalling brutality that Atkins afterwards characterised as loving care.

Two days later, Leno LaBianca and his wife Rosemary were done to death under equally gruesome circumstances.

Manson was tried and convicted not for killing, but for masterminding the killings. His comprehension had become inverted. At the trial, he threw his crimes back at his accusers: 'You make your children what they are ... You taught them. I didn't teach them. I just tried to help them to stand up ... These children – everything they have done, they have done for the love of their brothers.' In short, his hands were clean, and any dirt attached to his female disciples. Manson remarked to biker Al Springer, 'Whatever happens the girls will take the rap', and, left to their own devices, they would have shouldered responsibility for planning the slayings.

Defence lawyers decided not to question Atkins, Krenwinkel and Van Houten lest they incriminated themselves on the stand.

'To Charlie, death was no more important than eating an ice-cream,' one Family member recalled, and Manson's true number of murders may be somewhere in the mid-thirties. Recollecting the high points of his 1969 career from the relative tranquillity of 1986, Manson showed some insight into his manipulative skills. At the time of the Tate murders, he was edging towards 40, a father-figure to his teenage acolytes. They may not have known what they were doing, but he certainly did.

Here is Manson in 1986, summarising his 1969 reactions – calculating, self-interested, distant – to the Family's rapturous description of the Tate killings:

'A normal person would find the details of the night's events shocking and horrifying, but I had long ago stopped measuring myself by society's standards ... My only concern was whether it resembled the Hinman killing. Would the police now have reason to believe that Bobby was not the slayer of Hinman? And were the kids, loaded with drugs, clever enough to avoid leaving prints or evidence of their identities? Knowing Sadie and Tex and their flair for dramatic exaggeration, I doubted the slayings went down as they had described. More importantly, did they leave a trail that would lead to the ranch?'

The murders set a new low for the number of **false confessions**; even the most chronic publicity seekers had no desire to be tarred with Manson's brush. He is now eligible for parole.

See also **Leg, stabbed, Revelations, White Album**

Marine fraud

Marine fraud is a cyclical business linked to the ups and downs of world trade; its life-blood is insurance claims.

In boom years shipowners draw perfectly respectable operating profits from their vessel, even if bought on an 80 per cent mortgage. But as with houses, so with ships: come the slump and a $5 million ship tumbles to a fraction of its purchase price. Meanwhile it lies idle and, if unsold, racks up finance and maintenance charges.

In this predicament it makes sense to sink the vessel, the more so since its submersion unlocks windfall profits as well as stopping the loss. Ships are covered on 'valued' policies, with the amount payable agreed in advance, and, to boost premiums, underwriters traditionally endorse over-valuation. A vessel bought for five million, mortgaged for four, and now worth two, may be insured for eight.

The commercial downturn of the early 1980s induced a surprising amount of old Greek tonnage to burst into flames for no apparent reason, typically at lax ports like Piraeus, preferably at the anchorage's far end beyond easy reach of any fire-fighting facilities. The standard explanation was a 'carelessly dropped cigarette falling on an oily rag in the bilges', just within the outer reaches of credibility.

But fires are a risky business. Crews are – rightly – scared of starting them at sea, and in harbour, even in Greece, the blaze is sometimes extinguished, leaving a charred ship which the insurers insist on repairing and an owner no better off. Worse, the **arson** may be detected, particularly if the flare-up began in several 'seats' simultaneously.

So owners turned to sinking their ships outright, developing a scenario that, among investigators, aroused scepticism bordering on derision. The wearying pattern was of a vessel making a ballast run towards Suez, passing relatively close to shore on the pretext of helping the crew conserve their drachmas by taking advantage of cheap VHF rates on calls home.

Despite light seas and clear weather, a Master would receive the astonishing intelligence that his engine room was awash with water. Luckily the discovery normally happened early in the morning, allowing all day for a leisurely sinking and rescue in pleasant conditions. Many losses occurred miraculously close to shore, and one particular tug acquired a reputation in London legal circles for the canny regularity with which it arrived in time to save the crew but just too late to save the ship. In graver cases, owners seeking a more plausible scenario ensured that at least some of the crew drowned.

Legitimate cargo claims flow directly from the Bill of Lading, a pre-printed standard form embellished with a couple of stamps, stating what was – theoretically – loaded on to the ship and hence what sank with it. But the sea-bed is no longer a Black Hole beyond verification. When the MV Lucona foundered with half a dozen crew in 2,000 fathoms in 1977, ROVs (Remote Operated Vehicles) photographed the wreck, establishing not only the cause of loss (a deliberate explosion in number-one hold) but also the fate of its cargo. The containers marked as Uranium Ore Processing Plant and insured for 30 million Swiss francs had spilled over the ocean floor, disgorging scrap farm machinery. The shipowner, Udo Proksch, is now serving a twenty-year sentence for fraud and six murders.

The Honduras have overtaken Panama as the Mecca of slack shipping regulations. Some 90 per cent of the vessels that disappear (with their cargo) by virtue of name-changes are now Honduran-registered. One ship, the *Jupiter 8*, managed two aliases in a single voyage (first the *Joyce* and then the *Wing-Tai*) under the acquiescent eyes of a Chief Officer who, as an unemployed Burmese labourer, had never been to sea before in his life.

Marlowe, Christopher (1564–93)

Marlowe, the Elizabethan playwright, died in a tavern brawl on 30 May 1593 when his companion Ingram Frizer stuck a twelvepenny dagger, via the eye-socket, into his brain. They were arguing over the bill.

But perhaps none of this happened. The conspiracy theory is that Marlowe did not die. The fight was a ruse, a prelude to interring somebody else in his stead. At the time of the taproom squabble, Marlowe was on bail pending his trial for the capital offence of blasphemy. Like Marx and de **Sade**, he held that 'The first beginning of Religioun was only to keep men in awe', and only three days before his death a damning report forwarded to the Privy Council recommended that 'All men in Christianity ought to endeavour that the mouth of so dangerous a member should be stopped'. Marlowe was in fear of his life.

The most extreme theory casts Marlowe's lover, Walsingham, as stage-manager for his boyfriend's vanishing, supplying a substitute corpse and spiriting the playwright away to France. There Marlowe settled down to work; *Venus and Adonis* appeared a few months later. Officially dead, he could not publish under his own name, and coaxed an undistinguished burgher of Stratford, William Shakespeare by name, into 'fronting' his work for a small fee. Later this became common practice in McCarthyite Hollywood.

Or so Calvin Hoffmann proposes in *Murder of a Man Called Shakespeare*. The exotic Shakespeare component goes too far, but Marlowe's death remains suspect. A tamer rendition has the playwright not saved but killed by Walsingham, the Queen's spymaster, to forestall embarrassing sexual disclosures at the writer's trial. Another theory has Marlowe set up and killed by Walsingham's wife.

The truth is probably simpler. All the men in the fatal room were acquaintances of Marlowe's; two – Nicholas Skeres and Robert Poley – came from the shady world of espionage and the third, Frizer, was a fixer, a young man on the make, later pardoned for the killing. Marlowe himself was not only a poet, but also a homosexual spy enmeshed in intrigues: with Walsingham's secret service, with the Earl of Northumberland, with the philosophic paganism of Giordano Bruno, counterfeiting in Holland, anti-Catholic espionage, and the Essex–Raleigh rivalry. Complicated cross-alliances made backing the wrong horse an occupational risk for spies, and it seems that Marlowe was summoned to Deptford for an ultimatum – either implicate Raleigh or take the consequences.

The England of Elizabeth I was a virtual police state where multifarious networks and shifting allegiances meant that players traded scraps of information for preferment. The truth behind Marlowe's death may never be known, but it is unlikely that he died squabbling over a bill. He certainly did not die in a tavern; the house, a private residence, belonged to Widow Bull, a well-connected woman who called Lord Burleigh 'cousin'.

Marsh Test for arsenic

James Marsh, the British chemist who invented an incredibly sensitive test for arsenic – so sensitive that it could detect a thousandth of a milligram – was a scientific prodigy who was never appreciated. He worked all his life for thirty shillings a week at the Royal Military Academy. Frustration turned him into an alcoholic and when he died at 52 he left his wife and children destitute.

The German chemist Johann Metzger had discovered in the 1790s that if a substance containing arsenic is heated, and a cold plate held above it, a white layer – arsenious oxide – would form on the plate. And if the arsenic was heated to red heat, metallic arsenic would be deposited, forming a black layer – the so-called arsenic mirror.

Marsh saw instantly that the trouble with this test is that most of the gas escapes past the dish, and if only a tiny quantity of arsenic is involved, then it has escaped for ever. So he simply devised a sealed apparatus, in which the gas can escape only through a tiny pointed nozzle. First the suspected arsenic compound is dropped into a flask containing zinc and sulphuric acid (which produces hydrogen). The resulting arsine gas, if any, is then heated as it passes along a glass tube; this decomposes it, and the arsenic forms a black 'mirror' as soon as it reaches a cold part of the tube. Or, if the gas is burned as it issues from the nozzle, it forms the mirror on a cold plate. It was simple and obvious, and also extremely sensitive. When he published his result in 1836, the Society of Arts awarded him their gold medal. Poor Marsh would undoubtedly have preferred an appreciation in cash, like the £30 he received from the Board of Ordnance for a percussion cap for naval guns.

When he died in 1846, his achievement was promptly forgotten, so that it is nowadays practically impossible to find his name in a work of reference. Yet he has brought to justice hundreds of murderers.

See also **Orfila**

Masturbation

Excessive indulgence in this harmless recreation is an early pointer to a budding serial killer.

Serial killers cannot (or will not) have relationships with people. So they derive their thrills from pictures; and masturbation over pornographic images forms a prologue to a career as a Peeping Tom and, eventually, sexual assault. The murderer Albert Hamilton **Fish** proved an avid practitioner even in his sixties on Death Row; the prison Chaplain requested him not to 'holler and howl' so loudly while on the job during divine service. One of the prime Ripper suspects – a Polish Jew, Aaron Kosminski – was billed in the Macnaghten Memorandum as a great exponent. First the habit drove him insane. Then it killed him; the Swanson marginalia cites 'self-abuse' as Kosminski's cause of death.

The modern serial killer Jeffrey **Dahmer** did it in public, earning an arrest for 'lewd and lascivious behaviour' on 8 August 1986 for his performance on the banks of the Kinnickinnic River. 'You having a good time?' asked one of the spectators. 'Yeah, I'm having a great time,' Dahmer called back. In all, Dahmer exposed himself in public six times; such exhibitionism is, perhaps, sadistic, compelling bystanders to see something they would rather not.

Masturbation and the serial murderer fit each other like fingers in a glove. Often he kills because he lacks the solace of ordinary human relationships. His sex-drive is normal, his associative powers and social skills low, producing a dearth of sexual partners. Masturbation furnishes the natural outlet, since no one else will consort with him – at least not while alive, and by the time the object of his affections can no longer decline his attentions – in other words, when his victim is dead – the killer is thrown back on the same problem which leads, again, to the same solution. Despite all the excitement and its attendant arousal, he is still by himself and still unsatisfied. Hence the frequent phenomenon of sex killers masturbating on to corpses. The element of disjointed time, where the killer works out of sequence, is exemplified by **Chikatilo**: impotent while his victims were alive, he achieved satisfaction by killing, and then attempted retrospective inter-course, packing his sperm manually into his prey's orifices. Full-blown necrophilia is only a step away.

Murder can become a means to an end where the desire to experience sex, coupled with the inability to have it (which may take the form of impotence when confronted by normal stimuli) engenders extreme frustration. This is vented by the restorative of sadistic murder, which reinstates sexual prowess. Analogously, the absence of sexual power calls for the demonstration of power by other means, for instance, brutality.

New York's serial killer Arthur Shawcross, who claimed eleven victims, was finally caught in 1990 masturbating on a bridge in the forest near the site of his last victim's body; the police kept watch by helicopter against his return. Likewise, Jeffrey Dahmer used his trophies as sexual props. He took the severed head of his first victim, Steven Hicks, up to his bedroom, set it upright on the floor as a stimulant and then sought relief. His behaviour came under scrutiny at his 1992 trial, where the psychiatrist Dr Dietz suggested that 'it facilitated the fantasy of the entire person, the fantasy of the living person to whom the head had belonged, and cut out awareness that the rest of the body was missing'.

But like most psychiatric evidence, this is speculation. Perhaps Dahmer was titillated by the absence of the body. He may have found severed **heads** sexy *per se*. Like the British serial killer, 'Reggie-no-dick' Christie, Dahmer could not achieve erections in the face of the living, and throughout the nine years when he refrained from killing, his frequency of masturbation provided a mental health index. Once a week, under control; four times a day, and an unrequited Dahmer was teetering at the edge.

Masturbation is a starting point for most people's sexual careers; from it, they progress to shared sex. Dahmer's sexual boundaries were more closely confined, extending not to pleasuring a partner, but only to pleasuring himself, using his partner, like a pornographic picture, as a masturbatory aid. Exclusive recourse to this practice produces a dead inner world, where people are objects, and, before raising his sights to corpses, in 1984 Dahmer stole a mannequin from the shop window of the Boston Store in Southridge, keeping it for weeks as a sexual companion.

See also **Torture**, **Zombies**

'Mattress, to go on the'

Mafia expression dating from New York's Castellammares War of 1930 and 1931, when rival gangs shifted from one apartment to another, often at a few minutes' notice as they staked out the opposition for a 'hit' or fled an ambush. The only item the soldiers carried as luggage was their bedding, so 'going on the mattress' meant being at war.

The Castellammares War claimed some sixty lives, ending in complete victory for Salvatore Maranzano after the killing of Joe Masseria. He rashly proclaimed himself *Capo di tuti Capi* at a mass Mob rally held in the Bronx at a hall off Washington Avenue. It was standing space only. A good 500 hoods attended, and Maranzano suspended a crucifix over the platform at the far end of the assembly room and pasted religious paintings to the walls, so that outsiders blundering in would mistake the gathering for a religious convention.

Maranzano held office for only a few months; he was liquidated in the nationwide Mafia purge of September 1931.

Medellin, Colombia

Figures hardly convey the slaughter in this cocaine city-state with a population of around 2 million. More than 300 police officers died in 1990, part of the tally of 5,300 homicides. Of these the majority – some 3,000 fatalities – were concentrated in the age group 14 to 25, and by 1991 the toll for the city and its environs reached 7,900 fatalities, ten times the total for the whole of Britain.

Medellin's youth is wiping itself out. **Hitmen**, drug

gangs, street gangs, death squads, militias, paramilitary squads and extortion brigades fight it out on a neighbourhood basis. Youngsters kill yesterday's friends in endless internecine feuds. The sixth of the seven Mosquera brothers met his end on 28 October 1992; the family's surviving son is temporarily safe, doing time in New York. But he is wanted for murder back home. In February 1993 a vigilante gang, Los Pepes, lined up seven men and machine-gunned them at a petrol station. A boy called Tono, dying of gunshot wounds, was said by Alonso Salazar (a professional chronicler of the epidemic of violence and hence a *violentogos*) 'to almost salivate when he told the stories about all the people he'd killed'.

Wary members of Colombia's elite anti-drug squad mount guard in Medellin after the 2 June 1993 assassination of Escobar's brother-in-law

When Jorge Mario Mejias – another youth who is probably dead by now – was asked what he wanted to do with his life, he replied, '*I'm* a bum. What's the point of making plans if I'm not going to get anywhere anyway? All the **kids** round here are getting killed. We're all going to die.' His brother had already been shot dead. In the words of Victor Gaviria, a local film-maker: 'I think that in the end the kids kill just to see what it's like, they want to know how their own passage from one world into another will be.'

The violence is the outcome of the vicious contrast between local, traditional poverty and the rich pickings from cocaine. The government's war against the drug barons (see **Escobar**) has made things worse. According to one observer: 'There's tremendous unemployment amongst the drug gangs now, and they're all fighting for the available crumbs. All sorts of old scores are getting settled ... Everybody's freelancing.'

The Medellin cartel, with their partiality for death squads, have a reputation for playing rough. By contrast, their rivals in Cali are better known for their fine art collections and sound business sense. When Cali's Rodrìguez Orejuela was jailed in Spain in 1985 he had a 'cultural adviser' flown over to continue his education in the history of art. But the tuition had no perceptible impact on his taste; a visitor to Orejuela's home reported that the lavatory seat had gold coins plastered around its edge.

Cocaine retails locally at around $2,000 per kilo, with two more noughts added by the time it reaches Europe. The cartels have diversified into **opium** and its derivative, heroin. Growing poppies is bad for the environment; the cultivation process on the jungle hillsides drags thousands of acres into an ecological grinder of slash-and-burn agriculture aggravated by indiscriminate bombardment with fertilisers and pesticides.

Medellin's urban warfare has spawned an evocative *argot*, with new terms thrown up as rapidly as the bodies: *narcocondominico* (drug trade apartment), *punketos* (gangs devoted to punk music), *pistolocos* (crazy gunmen), *desechables* (throwaway kids) and *quietos* (corpses).

A good place to see the fun is the casualty ward at the San Vincente de Paul Public Hospital. On weekend nights the taxis ferry in about ninety gunshot victims, a quarter of whom die.

Other regional specialities include a revival of the tradition of **Burke and Hare**. In March 1992 a badly mauled garbage collector barely escaped from the Free University campus in Barranquilla, lured there by security guards who attempted to kill him. A police search of the medical school disclosed a stockpile of ten illicit bodies, together with twenty skulls, the same number of brains, fifteen lungs and twelve limbs. None of the corpses had undergone autopsy by the state pathologist; all had been shot or bludgeoned to death within the preceding two months.

Five security guards were arrested. Police said the killings were for profit, with the bodies sold to the medical students for their 'practicals' at 130,000 pesos each.

Memorabilia

Why not make money out of crime by investing in souvenirs? The revolver used by Jack Ruby to kill Lee Harvey Oswald in November 1963 originally cost $62.50, but on 28 December 1991 it was knocked down at auction to a gun collector for $220,000. The following year, Oswald's hospital body-tag fetched $6,600. The lot included a lock of bloodstained hair and his shoes.

In the late 1970s, an autograph of John Wilkes Booth, Abraham Lincoln's assassin, was worth about £500, twenty times more than that of his law-abiding brother Edwin, the most renowned actor of his day. A square inch of the skin of the graverobber Burke originally retailed at a shilling; in January 1992 a specimen went to auction with an estimated price-tag of £500. Applied pro-rata over the average individual's extent of eighteen square feet, it values Burke's hide at £1,269,000.

In Britain, auctions of hanging impedimenta were common until the turn of the century. The last recorded sale was in 1906 when a length of cord, guaranteed used by **Berry**, realised a disappointing seven shillings. Half a century before, the rope which hanged William **Palmer**, cut into two-inch sections, fetched half-a-crown a piece, and the rope which ended the life of William Corder, the Red Barn murderer, achieved a guinea an inch. According to *The Times* of 1866, Parisian ladies of fashion believed that a segment of a hangman's noose in their pockets conferred good luck at cards.

Hitler's personal guillotine, a decorative focal point, was recovered by Gerd Heidemann of the **fake** Hitler's Diaries three years after its 1989 disappearance from a Hamburg auction house. The thirteen-foot-high machine dates from the French Revolution and, together with Hitler's piano (a 50th birthday present) had an auction estimate of £175,000.

In April 1992 a job lot of Capone memorabilia made £30,000, including an initialled jug at £1,000. A stuffed fish caught by the great man in 1929 went for three times that amount. As a comparative yardstick, **Napoleon**'s penis was reportedly sold for 7,000 francs at a 1977 auction, but Christie's, the fine art dealers, have cast aspersions on its authenticity.

In 1976 an English conman, Barry Edward Gray, purchased a pair of shoes for $3.50 in a junk shop and then offloaded them to the *New York Times* for $50,000 as the former property of the missing US Teamster boss Jimmy Hoffa (whose last resting place, according to hitman Donald 'Tony the Greek' Francos, is six feet under, opposite section 107 of the New York Giants' stadium in the Meadowlands). The newspaper, although out of pocket, can comfort itself with the reflection that their investment must possess a value in excess of Gray's original cost as a memento of his coup.

Memory, recalled

A feature of satanic **ritual abuse** (SRA) cases, based on the supposition that sexual offenders bury the memories of their transgressions as too horrible to contemplate. In 1988 the first influential survey, by psychiatrists Young and Braun, surmised that the 'recovered memories' of their thirty-seven interviewees recorded the real experiences of people suffering from dissociative conditions (like the multiple personality disorder [**MPD**]), often affiliated to an unintegrated sense of identity.

A 1991 paper by a Dr George Ganaway drew different conclusions from the same data. Ganaway argued that highly hypnotisable subjects would, while in a trance, suspend critical judgment and seek to acquiesce to suggestions posed by their therapists. He depicted 'recalled memories' as a colourful 'screen memory' – a Hollywood version of real life, masking mundane forms of genuine abuse and neglect like beating, rape or straightforward deprivation. On this basis, SRA victims correctly identify themselves as damaged, but by something else.

From a sufferer's point of view, the misattribution may not matter. In August 1992, Professor Michael Nash cited a client who, under hypnosis, discovered that he had been shanghaied by aliens. The trauma exposed, the patient recovered. Nash commented, 'Here we have a stark example of a tenaciously believed-in fantasy with all the signs of a previously repressed memory. I work routinely with sexually abused adult women, and I could discern no difference between this patient's clinical presentation ... Worse yet, the patient seemed to recover as he elaborated the report of his trauma (abduction by spaceship) and integrated it into his view of the world.' Nash concluded, 'In terms of clinical utility, it may not really matter whether the event happened or not.' That is, just because a victim believes something, it does not mean it is true, nor does a favourable response to treatment indicate a condition based on actual events.

Paul **Ingram**, the supposed satanic rapist, gave an account of the workings of recalled memory. First he imagined entering a warm, white fog. After a few minutes, images welled up which his interrogators assured him were real because, they said, God would bring the truth. Likewise, Ingram's wife appreciated her questioner's help. 'He kind of prods,' she said. 'When we start, initially he describes a scene to me.' Then she remembered it.

Recalled memory hinges on the theory of repression, originating from Freud. But what did he know? The notion that painful or dangerous memories are blocked from consciousness, thereby inducing irrational conduct, was posited but not proved. Therapists strive to ferry repressed material to the surface, but what is remembered may not be what has happened. Research by Professor Loftus on subjects told of invented incidents by a source regarded as reliable (for instance, an elder brother) shows that they may accept the tales as true and then add details of their own, rapidly achieving a seamless tapestry of fabrication. Thus an acorn of untruth can sprout into an oak of falsehood, a procedure formally entitled the false memory syndrome.

It is a quantum leap from masking a single brief incident (the 'traumatic amnesia' of combat or rape) to blanking protracted episodes of SRA endured time and again over years or decades. To regard their suppression as an equal likelihood produces the curious state where the mere absence of untoward memories is immaterial. On such a *tabula rasa*, false accusations and **false confessions** are writ large.

Mercy

Towards the end of the eighteenth century the disparity between trivial offence and frightful punishment increasingly tormented the British liberal conscience.

Perhaps the most infamous hanging statute was the Waltham Black Act of 1723, a response to minor rural disturbances at Waltham Chase, Hampshire, when protesting labourers poached fish, burned hayricks and the like. The Act made nearly everything punishable by death, creating more than 200 new capital offences: cutting down an ornamental shrub, standing on the highway with a blackened face, setting fire to a hut or poaching a rabbit.

In part, the waning authority of the Church suffered encroachment from a new ritualised orthodoxy, the rule of law. Before the might of the legal system, even its berobed functionaries, the judges themselves, broke down and wept. At the Salisbury Assizes in 1831, during the sentencing of two agricultural protesters, Peter Withers and James Lush, a reporter from the *Dorset County Chronicle* noted, 'The judges were frequently obliged to rest their faces on their extended hands, and even then the large drops were seen falling in quick succession.'

Sometimes the victim petitioned for the offender's pardon. When agricultural worker Thomas Tate was given seven years' transportation for stealing sacks of flour, the farmer William Tidman begged Viscount Sidmouth to let him off the hook in consideration of his wife and four children, 'as I freely forgive him myself'.

Transportees rarely escaped their fate, but hanging was a different matter. Juries bent over backwards to value goods at thirty-nine shillings (forty was a hanging matter), and the proportion of death sentences carried out dwindled from the mid-eighteenth century. In the decade from 1749 to 1758, 365 (69.3 per cent) of London and Middlesex's 527 capital convictions were hanged. For the ten years from 1799, convictions were up to 804 and executions down to 126 (15.7 per cent).

Pardons were granted in batches. Prisoners favoured with leave to appeal 'at the next general pardon' grovelled for their lives. As the Old Bailey's *Post Boy* for 31 August 1700 noted, 'The last day of the sessions 85 criminals pleaded on their knees for the King's most gracious pardon, acknowledging his Majesty's great clemency and mercy; they presented the court with gloves according to custom.' Most were successful.

Villains did not always extend the same courtesy to their monarch. According to William IV, his great-grandfather George II was accosted by a highwayman who scaled the walls of the royal gardens in Kensington. After a hollow show of deference, he deprived the King of his purse, watch and buckles.

See **Court of Appeal**

Milat, Ivan

Ivan Milat has the dubious distinction of being among Australia's worst murderers to date.

On 19 September 1992 two members of a running club from Sydney were running in the Belanglo State Forest when they smelt decaying flesh. A closer look at a pile of branches and rotten leaves revealed a foot poking out. The police who came to the scene quickly discovered this was a double murder, both victims being female.

Ivan Milat, Australian serial killer

It was the beginning of one of the biggest murder investigations in Australia's history.

The bodies proved to be those of a British backpacker, Caroline Clarke, aged 22, who had vanished with her friend Joanne Walters in April 1992. Caroline had been shot ten times in the head. Her companion Joanne had been stabbed fourteen times in the chest and neck; the fact that she had not been shot suggested that there had been two murderers. Both girls had probably been tied up, since there were no defensive wounds on their hands. And it was clear that the killers had taken their time, since there were six cigarette butts lying nearby. The bodies were too decayed for forensic examination to determine if they had been raped.

A wide search of the Belanglo State Forest failed to reveal more bodies, although that was hardly surprising given that it covers 40,000 acres.

But more than a year later, on 5 October 1993, two lots of skeletal remains were found in the forest; they proved to be those of James Gibson and Deborah Everist, both 19, who had vanished four years earlier, on 30 December 1989, when they had set out from Melbourne.

Soon after the discovery, sniffer dogs found the decomposed body of Simone Schmidl, a 20-year-old German girl who had vanished on 20 January 1991. Three days later the dogs found the bodies of two more German backpackers, Gabor Neugebauer, 21, and his travelling companion Anja Habscheid, 20, who had vanished on 26 December 1991. Anja had been decapitated, and the angle of the cut made it clear that she had been forced to kneel while the killer took off her head.

A special team was set up to hunt 'the Backpacker Killer', as he now became known, but they made virtually no progress during the next six months. Then came the break: a workmate of Croat-born Richard Milat reported that he had been heard saying that 'killing a woman was like cutting a loaf of bread'. Milat's brother had a long police record that included sex offences. On 22 May 1994 police arrested 50-year-old Ivan Milat in the Sydney suburb of Eaglevale.

In Ivan Milat's garage police found bloodstained rope of a type that had been used to bind some of the victims, a sleeping bag that proved to belong to Deborah Everist and a camera like the one owned by Caroline Clarke.

Once again the case marked time. Then, on 13 April 1994, investigators received the break they had been hoping for. A young Englishman named Paul Onions, a student from Birmingham, contacted the police and said that in January 1990 he had been attacked by a man who corresponded to Milat's description, near the Belanglo State Forest.

Onions had been hitch-hiking from Sydney on 25 January 1990, when he had encountered a short, stocky man with a drooping moustache, who had given him a lift. But Onions felt instinctively that the man – who called himself Bill – was dangerous. And when 'Bill' stopped the car and got out, Onions got out too – to be confronted by a revolver. He decided to make a run for it, and a bullet whizzed past his head.

Then Onions managed to halt a van by flinging himself in front of it. It was driven by Mrs Joanne Berry, who had her sister and five children in the back. Onions shouted, 'Give me a lift, he's got a gun.' Mrs

Berry let him clamber into the back of the van through the sliding door. When he told her what had happened, she decided to take him to the Bowral Police Station. There Onions reported the attack. Yet, incredibly, the Bowral police succeeded in losing the report on the attempted robbery.

So when, four years later, Onions rang up his local police station in Birmingham and reported the attack, the police lost no time in flying him to Sydney. There he identified Milat as the man who had fired his revolver at him. Onions had left his backpack in the car when he fled, and he later identified a blue shirt found in Milat's garage as his own.

Milat had a long police record. Born in December 1944 to an Australian mother and Croat father, he had been a member of a large family which had been repeatedly in trouble with the law. In his twenties he had been to prison several times for car theft and burglary.

In 1971 he had picked up two female hitch-hikers who were both being treated for depression, and had suddenly turned off the highway, produced a knife and announced that he intended to have sex with them, or he would kill them both. One of the girls, who was 18, allowed him to have sex with her on the front seat. Milat had then driven on to a petrol station and the girl had taken the opportunity to run inside and tell the attendant that she had been raped and the driver was holding her friend. When several employees ran towards the car, Milat pushed the other girl out and drove off at speed, but was later arrested.

He fled to New Zealand to escape the rape charge and also two charges of armed robbery. He was brought back and tried three years later, in 1974, but was cleared of all charges and freed.

In 1979 he again gave a lift to two women near the Belanglo State Forest, and suddenly pulled off the road. When he told them he intended to have sex with both of them, the women managed to jump out of the car, and hid in a ditch. Although Milat searched for them, cursing and swearing, for nearly two hours, he did not succeed in finding them.

Milat's trial began in the New South Wales Supreme Court in Sydney on 25 March 1996. By that time, the press had dubbed him 'Ivan the Terrible'.

What emerged clearly during the trial was that Milat was a 'control freak', whose chief pleasure came from seeing his victims terrified and helpless. It also became apparent that, as he killed more and more victims, he became more sadistic, and enjoyed taking his time over it. He paralysed some of these female victims by stabbing them in the spine, so he could sexually attack them at his leisure. The injuries found on the victims were so appalling that the judge refused to give details during the trial, in order to spare the relatives.

A friend of Milat's ex-wife Karen gave evidence that suggested that Milat was a man who was obsessed by the need to be in the right, a man who demanded total obedience and submission. Milat was obsessive about keeping the house neat and tidy, and when Karen went shopping with a list she had to stick to every item on it or risk his flying into a violent rage. She had to ask him for every penny she spent, account for every minute of her time and bring back receipts for everything. Milat's younger brother, George, reports that Milat would fly into a rage with his wife on the smallest provocation.

When Karen finally walked out on him and he could not find her, he burned down the garage of her parents.

It was shortly after his wife left him in 1989 that Milat began his series of murders.

Milat's barrister suggested in court that the murders must have been committed by Milat's brothers Walter and Richard, and in a television interview on the day after the trial, the two brothers were accused on camera of being accomplices in the murders. Understandably, both denied it.

Milat was found guilty on 27 July 1996 and sentenced to life imprisonment on seven counts of murder. In the maximum-security wing of Goulburn jail, he was placed in solitary confinement after a tiny hacksaw blade was detected in a packet of cigarettes. He declared that he would continue to make every effort to escape.

His brother Boris, tracked down to a secret location by reporters, told them, 'All my brothers are capable of extreme violence. The things I could tell you are much worse than Ivan is supposed to have done. Everywhere he's worked, people have disappeared.'

Asked if he thought Ivan was guilty, he replied, 'I reckon he's done a hell of a lot more.' Pressed to put a figure on it, Boris Milat answered, 'Twenty-eight.'

Milken, Michael

Bond trader with New York's Drexel Burnham and Co. In 1975 his employers set his remuneration at 35 per cent of the profits from his backwater activities dealing in low-grade, unquoted securities – the so-called 'junk bonds'.

Since junk bonds were low-grade, no one else much sold them; as they were unquoted, no one else knew their prices. Milken could buy cheap and sell dear. He could buy back cheaply from companies to whom he had sold dear, and sell dearer. He could buy dear and sell dearer still. By early 1977 Milken had cornered one-quarter of the entire USA market in junk bonds, building a massive buy-and-sell 'spread' into their price. He awarded one-eighth of a point to his salesmen, retaining $29\frac{7}{8}$ points for himself. This made individual sales exceptionally profitable.

But Milken did not just do the occasional deal. He preached and sold the gospel of junk bonds nation-wide. Junk bonds, he argued, carried no higher risk than other securities, but they paid higher interest. Soon everyone wanted them, and they all bought from Milken, fuelling the corporate mania for

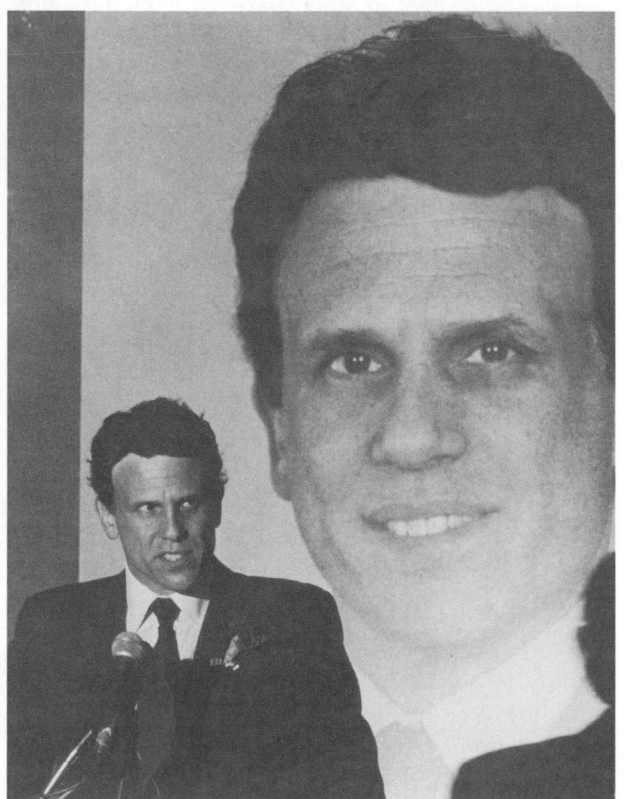

The only good boy in class? Milken urges the 1989 California Forum to push for forgiveness of Latin American debt

takeovers. By 1986 Milken was paying his top men like Jim Dahl $10 million while keeping back $550 million for himself. To boost his income from an increasingly rigged market, in 1984 Milken instigated a tranche of insider-deals with Ivan Boesky.

Or did he? The extent of Milken's guilt remains obscure. In 1983 and 1984, 72 per cent of companies involved in takeovers and mergers saw their stock price rise in the month before going public. Insider-trading was rife. But Milken played no part in it. He was jailed primarily on the evidence of Ivan Boesky, and Boesky – widely regarded as a highly objectionable character – needed a sacrificial scapegoat to lay on the altar of the Securities and Exchange Commission.

In August 1986 Boesky was subpoenaed by the Commission. He rapidly decided to deal, negotiating a settlement in exchange for the downfall of Milken and three other Wall Street figures. Boesky had to act fast; on 14 November 1986, his SEC investigation would become public knowledge. So he telephoned Milken on 1 October, angling for a meeting at the Beverly Hills Hotel, and recorded the call, making a number of heavy references like 'Do you understand what I'm talking about?' He mentioned 'having a kind of like a *private* meeting' so that they could 'spend a little time recalling what we had talked about'.

At the 9 October conference Boesky arrived wired for sound. But the discussion focused mostly on Milken's breakdown of an invoice for $5.3 million for investment banking work. At worst, it was vaguely illustrative of a diffused pattern of manipulation; but two and a half years later, in March 1989, the full indictment against Milken ran to ninety-eight felony counts for a possible total of 520 years in jail.

Milken, ground down piecemeal by a year of legal proceedings, capitulated on 24 April 1990 with guilty pleas to six charges. But the court report noted that the 'Milken Foundations are now among the largest charitable institutions in the country', that Milken himself always made time for family and friends and that his wealth was 'the result of legitimate business activities'. Asked to furnish the judge with three clear-cut examples of Milken's 'pervasive criminality', the prosecutors were unable to link him unequivocally to two crimes, and for the third, an insider-trading case, could not show that a crime had been committed.

Nevertheless on 21 November 1991 Milken was sentenced to ten years at the work camp of

Pleasanton where, *sans toupee*, he shared a four-man 'dorm'. On release, he faced 5,400 hours of community service.

Why such a stiff sentence? Probably because, in the broad view, the harvest of Milken's labours proved catastrophic. Junk bonds lived up to their name, degenerating into junk. But insurance companies, pension funds, savings-and-loans all held them, and the corporate raids and the takeover battles left a billion-dollar legacy of debt, enshrining Milken as 'the Hannibal Lecter of American business' alongside Boesky who, during the peak years between 1984 and 1986, telephoned as a client thousands of times, yelling and screaming abuse. Milken would agree to anything to get Boesky off the phone; hence the imputation of a general criminal alliance, and the narrow picture – that the charges may be based on inaccuracies and factual errors – counted for little.

Milken paid off his $600 million fine in 1990, turned his hand to teaching, and in June 1992 started testifying against former colleague Alan Rosenthal in a bid to shorten his own sentence and secure early release to full-time community service. He was freed after twenty-four months.

What Milken wanted his $1.1 billion fortune for remains unclear. He favoured ready-made clothes, never touched alcohol and despised designer fizz, preferring tap water or fruit juice. The deepest fantasy envisaged by his wife, Lori, was to buy any hardback book she wanted. When she read in November 1986 that her husband was worth $15 million – a gross under-estimate – she told him to 'get rid of it': having so much money 'didn't look good'.

Mirror image

Dennis **Nilsen**, Britain's most prolific serial killer, arrived in London in 1972, aged 25 and almost without friends.

Some five years had elapsed since his first homosexual experience during his Army days, but his most abiding sexual relationship as a Non-Commissioned Officer was with his own likeness. 'By placing a large, long mirror on its side strategically beside the bed,' he noted, 'I would view my own reflection', and from the first he kept his head out of the frame, making believe that he was someone else. Nilsen moved while he watched, but that proved unsatisfactory. 'The pleasure could dwell much longer on a mirror-image which was asleep.' So he stayed inert, gazing at an anonymous, headless version of himself.

Nilsen continued in this vein on settling in London. 'My most fulfilling sexual feasts were savoured with the image of myself in the mirror,' he wrote. 'To detach this image from identifying it directly with me, it evolved from an unconscious body into a dead body.' That is, Nilsen pretended his mirror-image was a stranger's corpse. Then he could **fantasise** that he was someone different, the violator of the inanimate trunk he eyed in the reflection, sometimes suspended by its wrists. This set-up was 'emotional and physical perfection', a great improvement on the unsettling reality of the one-night stands of London's gay scene.

By the summer of 1977, after the failure of his live-in affair with David Gallichan, Nilsen's approach had turned distinctly bizarre. Instead of pretending to be dead, Nilsen dressed up dead: 'I put talc on my face to erase the living colour,' he wrote. 'I smeared charcoal under my eyes to accentuate a hollow dark look. I put pale blue on my lips. I rubbed my eyes to make them bloodshot.' Then he riddled his tee-shirt with imitation bullet holes and dripped simulated gore on to his wounds. He lay there, watching himself playing a corpse with saliva dribbling from his mouth, and dreamed.

Nilsen imagined that he had been shot by the Nazi SS and left for dead in the woods. This much he could see in the reflection. But he still needed to visualise the other actor in the drama: an aged hermit. In Nilsen's words: 'The old man pulls my now naked body off the bed on to the floor. He washes me. He ties my penis and puts some wadding in my anus. He sits me on a chair then he puts me over his shoulder and carries me back into the woods and buries me. Later he returns and digs me up and takes me back to the shack. He masturbates me and my penis comes to life and I ejaculate.'

To imbue his fantasy with life, only one ingredient was lacking: the corpse. Then Nilsen could play the hermit, or whoever, with everything for real. He would have a familial unit of his own, over there, in the reflection.

Nilsen started killing in December 1978 to make his contacts stay so that he could talk to them. Four years later his description of Stephen Sinclair's murder on 27 January 1983 shows his mirror-life in full flower. By then there really were two bodies, one of them really dead.

'I lay beside him, and placed the large mirror at the end of the bed,' Nilsen wrote after the trial. 'I stripped my own tie, shirt and grey cords off and lay there staring at both our naked bodies in the mirror. He looked paler than I did ... I put talcum powder on myself and lay down again. We looked similar now ... He looked sexy but I had no erection. He just looked fabulous. I just stared at both of us in the mirror.'

Later, Nilsen's dog Bleep jumped up on the bed. 'Come on old girl, get your head down,' said Nilsen. 'Stephen is all right now. He's OK.' They started to doze off. Nilsen wrote: 'I turned Stephen's head towards me and kissed him on the forehead. "Goodnight," I said, switched off the bedside light and went to sleep.'

At last Dennis Nilsen was at peace, on the other side of the looking glass.

See also **Chikatilo**

Modus operandi

It is generally agreed that the date-rape case against William Kennedy Smith failed on the first day of the trial, 2 December 1991, when the prosecution was barred from calling evidence of similar assaults by Smith.

The rules against 'similar evidence' are strict. Nothing is more likely to lead a jury to a finding of guilty – on the seventeenth occasion – than to hear the suspect committed (or has been acquitted of committing) the same offence sixteen times before. But the previous instances are not in issue, and evidence of prior acts is only admissible if the crimes show a clear and unique 'signature' or *modus operandi*. If only the accused has a track record of behaving in a particular and idiosyncratic way, it is reasonable to infer that if anyone did the same thing again, he did.

At the Kennedy trial, Patty Bowman's attorney, Ellen Roberts, wanted to put in evidence the stories of three other girls who tangled with William Smith. Roberts adduced the defendant's distinctive behaviour pattern thus: 'The attacks, Judge, on all these women were violent and without provocation. They were pinned down, and they were rough attacks ... He ordered each of them not to resist.' She explained how Smith made a habit of seeking out 'attractive young brunettes' at 'a party, a picnic or a night spot'.

Although not mentioned in court, behind these three attacks glowered a stack of other cases. In the words of *Newsweek*'s Spencer Reiss: 'Lots of us know about lots more. So does Moira Lasch [Miss Bowman's other attorney]. She knows of at least sixteen others. That's the reason she's so venomous. She is convinced she has a real, live rapist on her hands, and she can't fucking pin him.'

Nor could she. As Smith's counsel observed, where else would his client meet girls other than at parties, picnics and night spots? By their nature, all rapes are violent, and many men prefer attractive young women to ugly old ones. Ms Roberts's motion foundered and her client lost the case.

For American detectives, a killer's *modus operandi* has attained investigative rather than legal significance. In the 1960s, Dr James Brussel constructed a psychological portrait of the Boston Strangler (see **Insatiable**) based on the behaviour (or symptomatology) exhibited at the scene of the crime, that is, by the way DeSalvo treated his victims. Britain's L. S. Atcherley of the West Riding Constabulary developed a similar 'MO system' for Scotland Yard from his experience that a criminal's signature was often betrayed by 'small, irrelevant acts which had no relationship at all to the actual commission of the crime and could be accounted for only by the individual'.

See also **Mad Bomber**

Mona Lisa

Probably the most valuable object ever stolen, spirited away by Vicenzo Perruggia, a house painter on friendly terms with one of the Louvre's workmen. On 21 August 1911 he found himself alone in a gallery with the painting, which he simply lifted off the wall. Removing the frame, he slipped the wooden canvas under his smock and walked out through a service exit.

Within a day the theft had been spotted and a squad of a hundred police combed the museum in vain. A clairvoyant attributed the robbery to a 'young man with a thick neck' and suspicion fell on a painter called Picasso – a friend of the poet Apollinaire – whose former secretary was much given to purloining the Louvre's smaller statues (the ears of one of which stood service as a model in *Les*

Demoiselles d'Avignon). Apollinaire spent a week in prison, and Picasso followed in St Peter's footsteps, disentangling himself by denying that he had ever set eyes on his old friend.

For Perruggia, all went smoothly for the next two years while he kept the painting under his bed. Then he attempted to sell it for a reported $95,000 to Alfredo Geri, an Italian art dealer, who inspected the merchandise in Perruggia's *pension*. The picture, stored under a beaten-up pair of shoes, a mangled hat and some plastering tools, looked familiar. Geri went to the police.

The French police triumphant

Perruggia was an Italian immigrant with a grudge against the French, who called him a 'macaroni eater' and dosed his wine with pepper. He received a light prison sentence and the Italian *pension* changed its name to the 'Gioconda'.

See also **Anthropometry**, **Valfierno**

Monroe, Marilyn (1926–1962)

According to Chuck Giancana, Marilyn Monroe died from a doctored suppository. This was considered both safe – since it left no telltale needle marks – and

certain, as there would be nothing in her stomach for any rescuers to pump out.

This new twist is reported in the 1992 book *Double Cross*, by the brother of Mafia Godfather Sam Giancana. The story goes that Marilyn was dangled as bait by the CIA to set up world leaders for blackmail. Meanwhile producer Joseph Schenck, who had Mafia connections, assiduously promoted her career, and by 1960 Marilyn was romantically involved with President John **Kennedy**. Then, in 1962, she fell for his brother Robert. Marilyn became distraught at the way the brothers passed her back and forth like 'a piece of meat', and by July she was threatening to 'blow the lid off the whole damn thing'.

Marilyn now posed a threat to both the Mob and the CIA – who contacted Giancana to have her eliminated. He scheduled the hit to coincide with Robert Kennedy's visit to California planned for the weekend of 4 August. On the night, 'Needles' Gianola and 'Mugsy' Tortorella were stationed outside Marilyn's Brentwood home on electronic surveillance. They saw Kennedy call round, accompanied by another man; they heard Marilyn become hysterical.

Kennedy instructed his friend, a doctor, to give Marilyn a shot to calm her down. When they left, the killers entered the house, taped Marilyn's mouth and inserted the suppository into her anus. Her unconscious body was replaced on the bed; then the tape was removed and her mouth wiped clean. Marilyn died, with Giancana hoping that Kennedy, a crusading Attorney General, would be implicated as the last man to see her alive.

But over their wiretaps 'Needles' and 'Mugsy' heard the cover-up get underway. Kennedy was alerted to Marilyn's death and mobilised a team of FBI agents, ordering Detective Fred Otash to sweep the place clean. And thus Marilyn's murder was passed off to the world as suicide.

Or so the story runs. Variants have the Mob killing Marilyn as a favour to the Kennedys, as part of their mutual support over Cuba. Incidental backing for the rival theory of suicide comes from FBI Agent William Roemer. He bugged Giancana's headquarters and learned that Marilyn was depressed about the events of the previous weekend at the Cal-Neva casino, where she had allegedly been bedded and humiliated by both Giancana and Frank Sinatra in an orgy. Coming on top of the Kennedy 'meat syndrome', she must have found the experience upsetting.

The Giancana murder scenario is compatible with many of the known facts, not least the 'purplish discoloration' of Marilyn's colon noted on autopsy. The Los Angeles Chief of Police, William Parker, a friend of Robert Kennedy, had the death labelled as self-inflicted from the start, allocating the case to the suicide investigation squad. After five days, with her studio's active co-operation, Parker closed the file, and all but thirty pages of the 723-page report into Marilyn's death were destroyed.

A cover-up is beyond doubt, but what was being covered is not clear. The problem with Marilyn's death is her inconclusive autopsy. She died of a Nembutal overdose, with 4.5 per cent barbiturates in her blood. But preliminary examination showed her kidneys were clean, strongly suggesting that her stomach was likewise free of drugs – which would exclude her having taken by mouth the drugs she was supposed to have swallowed. At the time, on post-mortem, Dr Thomas Noguchi ordered microscopic analysis of tissue from her small intestine, and requested tests on her liver, kidneys and stomach. But the tests were never performed; Noguchi learned that Marilyn's organs had been accidentally destroyed.

The exact time of Marilyn's death is suspect. Rather than being found dead at 3.30 in the morning, she may have been discovered comatose at 11.30 p.m. Walter Schaefer, owner of the local ambulance service, maintains that the star was still alive when his ambulance men arrived *before* midnight; according to him, she was driven to the hospital and then returned home after death, allowing time for a 'clean-up' before her official discovery. In confirmation, *rigor mortis* had set in when Sergeant Jack Clemmons arrived at half past three. Marilyn's enigmatic housekeeper, Eunice Murray, now says: 'I don't know why I didn't call the police until 3.30.'

The original suicide theory is hard to sustain. To achieve her blood-level of barbiturates Marilyn needed to gulp down between seventy-five and ninety capsules, a nightmare for someone who simply hated taking pills, particularly without water. There was no glass by her bedside, and the water in the adjoining bathroom was turned off pending plumbing work. In any case Marilyn did not have enough pills. On the best estimate, she was down to twenty-two Nembutals on the morning of 4 August and had no hidden reserves. A week before, her housekeeper drew a blank searching the house for a secret cache,

Marilyn Monroe

and in the days preceding her death Marilyn tried to borrow from friends.

Psychologically, many observers thought Marilyn in fine fettle during her last days. Her psychoanalyst, Dr Ralph Greenson, says: 'Suicide is not an option in this case.' Fox's production chief, one of the last to talk to the star, confirms this view: 'We had hired her back at a salary of half a million dollars. And she was ecstatic.' Nor was the body found in a setting which contra-indicated foul play. Marilyn adhered to a strict bedtime routine, always sleeping in a fresh brassiere, with earplugs and eye mask, in a darkened room with the curtains closed. She was discovered naked and unencumbered, with the curtains open and the lights on.

So it looks like murder, whether by injection, suppository or enema. True, Noguchi detected no needle marks on the body, but medical records show that Marilyn had received two jabs since the preceding Thursday. So Noguchi's examination was not infallible and, in any case, punctures made by fine surgical needles can disappear within a few hours. Recently, Noguchi alluded to other findings. 'I did find evidence which indicated violence. There were bruises on her lower back area – a very fresh bruise – and bruises on her arms.'

A key factor concealed from the American public was Marilyn's association with Robert Kennedy. His presence on the day of her death is still officially denied, but the helicopter company which flew Kennedy out of the area has the flight records of the transfer. The day of her death the FBI pulled General Telephone's records of her frequent calls to Kennedy at the Justice Department in Washington; the papers were recovered only five years ago from a homicide detective's garage.

One of Marilyn's many misfortunes was to pose a serious threat to the political stability of the United States. Just like her scatty screen persona, the girl was always in a muddle. 'How can we carry on a conversation about current events if you can't remember the details?' Kennedy once snapped. So she kept track with a diary full of 'Bobby says this' and 'Bobby says that'. One of the things that Bobby said was that the CIA had hired the Mafia to kill Castro – the administration's deepest secret, of itself enough to have Marilyn killed before she started blabbing.

Then there were the tapes. It seems that the Mob were using Marilyn to provide compromising evidence on the Kennedys. The Hollywood detective Fred Otash was allegedly paid indirectly by the Mafia to install eavesdropping equipment at the star's home. Apparently he recorded exotic love scenes with the President, interspersed with discussions of state secrets, together with similar indiscretions by the Attorney General. In addition, the Lawford house was thoroughly bugged by the FBI for nearly a year during the period that the President bedded Marilyn there. The tapes formed J. Edgar **Hoover's** favourite listening.

England's King Henry II had to demand outright 'Who will rid me of this turbulent priest?' to have Thomas a Becket assassinated. Things are simpler now. 'All the President or Attorney General has to do is *insinuate* displeasure with somebody, and then somebody else picks it up and does it,' said a later Republican Attorney General of Marilyn's death. 'That's the kind of power that really, truly exists.'

So one solution goes like this. Marilyn threatened to expose the President and his brother. On the evening of 4 August 1962, Robert Kennedy made a placatory visit. They quarrelled; she was given a sedative. Kennedy returned to his brother-in-law's house to find Marilyn ranting on the telephone, threatening to call a press conference. Kennedy knew what he'd done, knew what he'd said, and knew of the tapes and the notebooks. So later that evening someone else paid a visit to Marilyn – Hollywood's most famous beauty – and, on behalf of the Attorney General and the President of the United States, killed her.

Her death heralded a remarkable *volte-face* in Kennedy's perspective on Hoover, whose FBI agents helped in the cover-up and in whose hands the incriminating evidence now resided. For years Bobby had derided his weird stance on communism, and on 7 August W. H. Ferry, vice president of the Fund for the Republic, lambasted Hoover's views on the Reds as 'sententious poppycock'. Now Kennedy leapt to Hoover's defence: 'I hope he will continue to serve the country for many years to come.'

See also **Executive action**

Mooney, Tom (b. 1884)

A striking American miscarriage of justice. Mooney, a San Francisco labour leader, was arrested for the July 1916 bombing of the Preparedness Day parade in which nine bystanders died.

At the trial, the evidence showed that Mooney had been both seen and heard by prosecution witness Frank C. Oxman: seen, wedging a satchel against the wall of a Steuart Street saloon, and heard, remarking to his accomplice: 'We must run away, the cops will he after us.' Moments later, the bomb exploded.

Only part of Mooney's defence was a chance photograph of the parade. Produced in court, the picture showed an unmistakable Mooney in the throng exactly 6,008 feet away from the point of detonation. By his side stood his wife, Rena. In the background was a civic clock, showing the precise time of the explosion. Nevertheless Mooney received a life sentence. When it emerged that prosecution witness Oxman was somewhere else at the time of the bombing, ninety miles away, President Wilson commented: 'The utilities sought to get Mooney... With Oxman discredited, the verdict was discredited.'

But California had archaic perjury laws preventing the review of cases based on false evidence. Although discredited, the 'guilty' verdict was immutable (see **Virtual reality**), and Mooney spent twenty-two years in prison before his pardon on 7 January 1939.

See also **Wobblies**

Morals, art forgers'

Morally speaking, art forgery is not always clear-cut. According to the British painter Eric Hebborn, a forger is merely 'an artist working in the style of other people'. He claims to have infused the great art collections with more than a thousand fake Old Masters over the past three decades.

Hebborn, an artist, places the blame squarely on dealers. On the one hand, they commission work in the style of Van Blank, and then pass it off as an original for hefty profits; on the other, they are easily fooled, unwittingly making false attributions. Thus the canvas leaves the artist as a lawful item in its own right; it only becomes a forgery when the dealer ascribes it to the wrong artist. But perhaps Hebborn is disingenuous. He would present a carefully balanced portfolio, with an accomplished fake lurking among the originals, and encourage dealers towards misattribution with vague but suggestive pointers of a **provenance**.

Experts tend to follow experts. When a work is passed by one, it joins the club, accepted by all. Perhaps more difficult than passing off a fake as genuine is exposing a fake as a fake. Owners are reluctant to concede that costly Gainsboroughs are modern facsimiles, and even when this is pointed out by the original artist the response is typically, 'Have you got a degree in Art History?'

In this vein, Hebborn's offer to tour the National Gallery 'outing' his work and other forgeries was rejected. Galleries prefer the idea of false confessions, a concept which opens the door on a world of mirrors more commonly associated with the double and triple agents of espionage. The position is complicated by pranksters like Magritte, who not only repudiated certain of his early paintings but also sanctioned 'copies' of his work. Perhaps not surprisingly, Hebborn was an intimate of Anthony Blunt, Keeper of the Queen's Pictures and Soviet spy.

In his 1991 book *Drawn to Trouble*, Hebborn claimed that only some thirty of his thousand fakes had been identified; he did not disclose what the remaining 970 were, nor where they now hang, although they included eighty Augustus Johns, thirty-seven Castigionis, and works by Walter Sickert, Degas, Picasso and Breughel.

Forgers generally specialise in less expensive items, like preparatory sketches, where expert involvement is of diminished probability. Picasso and Chagall are among the usual 'suspects', with a new frontier opening in the Russian avant-garde.

In his youth, Hebborn was expelled for setting fire to his school in retaliation for being accused of playing with matches. Resentment against the Establishment also fuelled the careers of **Van Meegeren** and of Tom Keating, the British forger who claimed a career total of 2,500 fakes. Keating first took umbrage on discovering that works he was paid £5 to copy finished up in West End galleries for £500 and, as a restorer, witnessed a steady procession of paintings returned to their owners substituted by imitations, with the originals retained for resale. Keating's friends suspect deeper grievances. In his cups, he would discourse at tedious length on his naval service as a stoker in the Second World War, when he was treated with disrespect by the officer class.

Keating's unintended move into forgery seemed a dream come true. Anxious for recognition in his own right, he was disconsolately burning paintings on a bonfire when his girlfriend suggested putting them into a local auction. Experts praised Keating's draughtsmanship to the skies, discerning the hand of Samuel Palmer, and his works changed hands for thousands of pounds each. At his 1979 Old Bailey trial Keating took particular delight in denigrating his output. Of his famous ink-wash of *Sepham Barn* – sold for £9,400 as a genuine Samuel Palmer – he said, 'I am ashamed of this piece of work', dismissing the figure of the shepherd as 'un-Palmerish' and the sheep as 'un-sheeplike'. Similarly, his drawing of *Shoreham Barn* (sold for £2,500) was a doodle. 'That must have taken me about half an hour,' he said.

But when he was good, Keating formed a neutral conduit for the talent of his master. Van Meegeren, too, felt in mystical contact with Vermeer and, at this level of empathy, surely a little artistic licence is allowed. As Keating said, 'I'd sit in my little room waiting for it to happen. I had never drawn a sheep from life but then Palmer's sheep would begin to appear on the paper. With Sam's permission I sometimes signed them with his own name, but they were his, not mine. It was his hand that guided the pen.' Quite.

Mortal combat

An infallible method of apportioning guilt. The last instance occurred in England as late as 1817 during the retrial of Abraham Thornton for the murder of Mary Ashford, a local beauty.

Mary's body was dredged up from a pond the morning after a village dance at Tyburn near the small town of Birmingham. Her bonnet, shoes and neatly folded frock reposed on the bank by her bloodstained stockings. Thornton admitted to deflowering Mary *al fresco* that very night – hence the traces of blood, also found in a nearby patch of grass that bore the impress of a human body lying full length. But Thornton was seen three miles from the pond near the time that Mary must have died, and it seemed that some third party had come upon Mary after her lover departed. Thornton may well have been guilty, perhaps throwing Mary into the water unconscious after a rape, but he was acquitted after only six minutes' deliberation by the jury.

Local feeling ran high. It was still possible to be tried twice for the same offence, and Mary's brother William mounted an appeal. Arraigned in court, Thornton was asked how he pleaded. 'Not guilty,' he cried, 'and I am ready to defend the same with my body.' Then he flung down a glove in front of a surprised Lord Chief Justice, Lord Ellenborough. Thornton correctly stated that this constituted a valid challenge to single combat, and was freed when his accuser, who was smaller, declined to pick up the gauntlet.

Murder aficionados have developed ingenious theories to explain Mary Ashford's demise, sifting the clues provided by the intricacies of footsteps zigzagging across the fields.

The case exudes the attraction of an open-air 'closed room' mystery, one of the most remarkable of which concerned the death of Isidor Fink in New York in March 1929.

Fink ran a laundry from a New York tenement, and inhabited a single room measuring twenty by forty foot at 52 East 133rd Street. His neighbour Locklan Smith heard a disturbance on the evening of 9 March,

and when Patrolman Albert Kattenborg broke into Fink's apartment, he found him dead from two gunshot wounds to the chest, lying in solitude on the floor ten yards from the entrance. Fink's windows were barred and unbroken, the front door of solid construction bolted from inside, as were the windows, and entry was only effected by a small child smashing through the fanlight and wriggling through to release the door.

Cleverly, the dead Isidor Fink was not holding a gun. Nor was a weapon secreted in the apartment. This ruled out Fink either shooting himself or being shot by anyone else inside his home, and although the police made heavy weather of the conundrum, to state the puzzle in these terms is to solve it. Fink must have been shot by someone *outside* his apartment. To allow the bullets access, the door must then have been open and, as it was found locked from the inside, this necessitated locking by Fink, having been shot. And as his body lay some distance away, and there was no one else in the room, he must have gone there under his own steam, and died.

Mothers

One of the many vexations confronting a murderer is the unendurable stench emitted by the victim as decomposition proceeds. In 1954 the teenage New York killers Theresa Gresh and Billy Meyers adopted a radical solution. They encased their cadaver in a plaster-of-Paris sarcophagus and deposited it in the bath as a short-term holding measure.

In a macabre twist, the mummified body was that of Theresa's mother, whom they had bludgeoned and stabbed to death in the hope of removing her as the obstacle to their matrimonial plans. Billy was a 17-year-old schizophrenic homicidal Marine, considered by Mrs Gresh to be an unsuitable spouse for her immature daughter. He went to the chair; Theresa received a twenty-year sentence.

On the feminist analysis, mothers are such well-established scapegoats that a confession to serious sexual crime lacks weight without a token domineering matriarch.

As one astute psychiatrist pointed out to Kenneth Bianchi, the Hillside Strangler, 'If you add the letter s to "mother", you get "smother".' The hypothesis runs that a witch of a mother creates a monster of a son.

Witch-hunts are a regular feature of serial killings, and the Boston Strangler profile (see **Insatiable**) snagged on precisely this misconception.

Feminists maintain that the figure of the wicked matriarch is largely confined to the patriarchal fantasies of film and pulp fiction. Apparently the facts can be safely ignored. When the 'Son of **Sam**' pursued his vendetta in obedience to the dictates of his father – '"Go out and kill" commands father Sam' – the psychiatrist most closely associated with the case deduced that the killings were actuated by Berkowitz's relationship with his mother. Some say that it is only a minor transition from blaming Mother to condemning the victim, particularly female victims of sex crimes who 'ask for it'.

This predisposition has not escaped shrewder killers seeking to prove that their transgressions were not their fault or staking a claim as properly accredited **criminals**. Both Bianchi (see **Romances**) and Henry Lee **Lucas**, the 'wannabe' serial killer, claimed to have suffered sexual abuse from their mothers almost as a talisman of authenticity. Similarly, the 'Co-ed killer' Edmund **Kemper** precluded further investigation into his motivation by blaming his mother: 'Six young women dead because of the way she raised her son, and the way her son is raised and the way he grows up', although no one knows her side of the story because he killed her too.

Who can forget Norman Bates in the dead hand of matriarchy in *Psycho*, or James Cagney on 'top of the world, Ma'? But these are mere films. In fact, mobsters doted on their mamas. Chicago gangster Johnny Torrio endowed his mater in Italy with a coastal estate, retaining fifteen servants to tend to her wishes. She rode around in a chauffeur-driven limo. Hymie 'the Polack', whose crucifix dangled from his neck next to an armpit holster, was another attentive son. Capone too idolised Momma. **O'Bannion** installed his in a fine house, paying weekly visits with stacks of new gramophone records. Dutch Schultz, from New York, said it all with his dying breath: 'Mother is the best bet and don't let Satan draw you too fast.'

The tradition continues, as witness the **Krays**, and, in the 1980s, the New York Bonanno still downed tools on Mother's Day.

See also **Godmothers**

Mozart, Wolfgang Amadeus (1756–91)

Soon after Mozart's death, rumours began to circulate that he had been poisoned by his musical rival, Antonio Salieri. Mozart's widow Constanze laid the theory's cornerstone with an account of her husband's last drive in the Prater in Vienna during the autumn of 1791. 'Mozart began to speak of death and declared he was writing the Requiem for himself,' Constanze reported. "I feel definitely," he continued, "that I will not last much longer. I am sure I have been poisoned. I cannot rid myself of this idea."' Mozart imputed his forthcoming death to ingestion of *aqua toffana*, an arsenous preparation.

Mozart's illness was diagnosed as 'military fever' by his doctors. His body was painfully swollen and he could move only with difficulty. He ran a fever, had 'the taste of death on his tongue', and in the final stages suffered spasms of nausea – symptoms consistent both with kidney disease (progressing to kidney failure, oedema and uraemic poisoning) and a fatal intake of mercury, which attacks the kidneys.

Salieri, the prime candidate for murderer, makes an unlikely poisoner; as a leading composer of the period, he was an important teacher (Beethoven was a pupil), an admirer of Mozart's work and one of the few to attend his funeral. He tutored Mozart's son and engineered his first appointment. Salieri exerted a powerful influence over the distribution of court patronage through his position with the emperor, Joseph II, but merely to possess power to harm in one way is no proof of its exercise in another.

Despite the gossip, Salieri made no deathbed confession, other than inspiring a sickroom visitor to remark, 'Morally speaking Salieri had no doubt by his intrigues poisoned many an hour of Mozart's existence', and the famous discovery of 1953, billed as firm historical evidence by the Soviet musicologist Igor Boelza, consisted of the research of a dead colleague, which Boelza declined to reveal. As with **Jack the Ripper**, this evidential vacuum attracted the spectre of the Freemasons. They killed Mozart. He failed to follow the Masonic line with sufficient rigour in *The Magic Flute* or, in the alternative, divulged too many of their secrets, and was sentenced to death, a conjecture corroborated by the unsurprising deaths of his librettists Schikaneder and Giesecke decades later.

The truth is that Mozart did succumb to poison. At his death he was undergoing treatment for a combination of depression and acute military fever, for which the contemporary remedy was mercury and antimony. Mercury precipitates kidney failure, and in the Vienna of the eighteenth century, antimony was frequently contaminated with arsenic, which kills. Meanwhile the antimony would cause military fever as well as pneumonia and death. Mozart suffered from all three.

With almost every avenue of survival covered, it was asking too much of Mozart to survive his leeches' attentions for more than the fifteen days of his terminal illness. Or so said Dr Ian James in October 1991, addressing the British Association for Performing Arts Medicine.

MPD

Acronym for 'Multiple Personality Disorder'. In 1962 California's **'acid doctor'** was well into his murder trial when he first intimated that, really, his *alter ego* should be held accountable for the killing. 'Let me out of here,' said an astonished policeman as he grasped the nature of the doctor's defence, 'I think I'm going to be sick.'

At the time, psychiatry was a fad tossed into movies to explain the hero's motivation. *Sybil*, based on a woman with no fewer than fourteen personalities, became the forerunner of several MPD films, and in 1979 similar psychological fragmentation formed the defence strategy of the Hillside Strangler, Kenneth Bianchi (see **Romances**).

Although weak-willed, Bianchi was resourceful. He set himself up as a psychiatrist on the basis of a diploma from California State University, culled by submitting a thesis stolen from someone else. Luckily, Bianchi had no patients, so he slid into life as a pimp, and from then on it was downhill all the way.

After his January 1979 arrest, Bianchi stonewalled with impressive sincerity, adamantly denying knowledge of the killings. Then he watched *Three Faces of Eve* on prison television. Soon Bianchi's defence lawyer and psychiatric social worker glimpsed hidden depths in their client, wondering if the most likely explanation for his disavowals was a multiple personality disorder; perhaps the murders were the work of unacknowledged *alter egos*. The authorities called a specialist, and when an excited Professor John G. Watkins from the University of Montana put Bianchi into hypnosis, who should turn up but 'Steve'.

Steve was the Mr Nasty who had spent years inside Kenneth's Mr Nice. Steve spoke through Bianchi with a weird, low voice ingrained with hatred. He held his cigarettes in a different way, first tearing off the filters and gripping the stub between thumb and forefinger. Steve was vengeful and aggressive, and had done those 'jobs' with pleasure. If Kenneth wasn't careful, he would fix him too.

Obviously Bianchi was insane. Another psychological authority was summoned: Ralph B. Allinson, author of *Minds in Many Pieces*, who confirmed the MPD diagnosis. Allinson discovered that 'Steve' even had his own surname: Walker.

Bianchi's insanity meant that he could not be brought to book as the Hillside Strangler, and it was only when Dr Martin T. Orme (like Bianchi, familiar with *Sybil*) subjected him to a simple test that the sham was exposed. Orme introduced a hypnotised Bianchi to an imaginary lawyer. Bianchi leaned

Kenneth Bianchi, the Hillside Strangler, carefully groomed for his courtroom appearance

forwards and shook hands with the invisible attorney. But a subject under hypnosis knows better than to touch his hallucinations. Then Bianchi said to Orme: 'Surely you can see him?' If Bianchi *had* been able to see the lawyer, he would not have known that no one else could.

Next, Orme insinuated that most MPDs had more than two sides to their personalities. And, sure enough, Bianchi's internal family gave birth to another cohabitant, a winning child called Billy. Later, a police sergeant pointed out that 'Steve Walker' and Bianchi were hardly bedfellows of long-standing; it was the name of the psychiatry post-graduate from whom Bianchi stole the thesis. The Hillside Strangler was hastily reappraised and sentenced to five life terms.

The more churlish British school of psychology has long regarded MPDs with warranted scepticism, treating them as hysterics or malingerers. In America, the dysfunction is linked to the rise of satanic **ritual abuse**, where many 'survivors' claim previous MPD diagnoses.

Münchausen by proxy syndrome

An enhanced version of the Münchausen syndrome, when patients persistently seek unnecessary medical attention for themselves. Such individuals need to feel ill. The Münchausen by proxy syndrome happens when they need someone else to feel ill, if necessary by force.

The condition is named after the fictional Baron Münchausen, addicted to fantastical storytelling. The syndrome itself was first noted in 1951, and Professor Roy Meadow of Leeds encountered the first 'proxy' case in 1977. Habitually, the disorder involves grand-mothers suffocating their grandchildren, mothers **poisoning** their offspring, or spouses devoted to nursing their partners with noxious 'medicine'.

In principle, the affliction stops short of murder, but the exact moment is hard to judge. A recent American survey of 117 young victims found ten fatalities, another ten seriously affected in the long term, and ten more unexplained deaths among siblings.

The perpetrator is typically a woman, superficially eager to please but with low self-esteem, often with a history of sexual abuse and marital difficulties. The condition languished in the footnotes of medical liter-

ature until the case of Nurse Beverley Allitt, convicted on 17 May 1993 of four child murders as Britain's worst female serial killer of the century.

Allitt's symptoms dated from childhood when, as an attention seeker, she would arrive at school covered in plasters and bandages. 'We could not tell if she was hurt or not,' recalled a fellow-pupil. As a nurse, Allitt pestered staff with an endless string of minor ailments, aches and sprains of obscure origin, some self-inflicted, attending the casualty department of Grantham and Kesteven Hospital twenty-four times. But the damage was all in her head. During 1990 Allitt took ninety-four days off work, and she progressed to increasingly anti-social behaviour, unattributed at the time, starting fires under her hostel grill and leaving excrement on

Beverley Allitt

display. Then, in the spring of 1991, Allitt seemed to stabilise. Her visits to Casualty ceased.

In fact, she had deteriorated. During this fifty-nine day 'proxy' phase, Allitt switched from molesting herself to attacking babies on Ward Four, accounting for twenty-one unexpected collapses and four fatalities. Afterwards, staying with a friend, Allitt receded into a hinterland where she stole money, embedded a knife in her pillow, poured bleach over the carpets and fed noxious pills to the family pet.

Since the undoubtedly guilty Beverley Allitt was sent first to jail, then to the Rampton high-security mental unit, Professor Meadow has received many plaudits, including a knighthood, for his discovery of Münchausen syndrome by proxy. He has also served as a respected expert witness in many trials involving the suspicious death of infants. However, in recent years his reputation has come under attack.

Some leading paediatricians question the so-called 'Meadow's Law' concerning cot death: this states that 'unless proven otherwise, one cot death is a tragedy, two is suspicious and three is murder'. They feel that it is too glib to be safely used as the basis of clinical or legal judgments. The general public were also angered at revelations made during the acquittal, on appeal, of Sally Clark in 2003. At her original trial, Sir Roy Meadow described the possibility that Clark's two baby sons had died of natural causes as 'one in 73 million', a figure that undoubtedly convinced the jury that she was guilty of infanticide, but later proved to have been vastly overestimated by Meadow.

A number of British mothers, wrongly convicted of killing their children, have since been released on appeal and others plan to apply to the Appeals Court to question the validity of evidence given by expert witnesses like Professor Meadows. And many people now believe that Münchausen by proxy syndrome has been disastrously over-diagnosed – with tragic consequences for bereaved mothers whose only crime was to innocently fall foul of 'Meadow's Law'.

Murder bag

The invention of the great pathologist Sir Bernard **Spilsbury**. Arriving at the bungalow site of the Mahon murder in 1924, Sir Bernard was appalled to see Superintendent Percy Savage rummaging through the victim's remains.

As Savage later recalled, 'Spilsbury … expressed astonishment that I had handled putrid flesh with my bare hands, and he pointed out that I ran a grave risk of septic poisoning. He said that no medical man outside a lunatic asylum would dream of such a thing, and that I ought to at least wear rubber gloves. I told him we were not provided with rubber gloves … We lacked many other things essential to the efficient performance of our duties. If we wanted to preserve human hair on clothing, or soil or dust on boots, we picked it up with our fingers and put it in a piece of paper. We had no tapes to measure distances, no compass to determine direction, no apparatus to take fingerprints, no first-aid outfit, no instrument to find the depth of water, no magnifying glass. In fact we had no appliances available for immediate use on the scene of the crime.'

In conjunction with Sir Bernard, Savage drew up a list of Holmesian impedimenta for inclusion in a 'Murder bag', which thereafter accompanied chief inspectors on their call-outs.

The Mahon trial was distinguished by particularly loathsome medical evidence. In court, Spilsbury ran through a seemingly endless litany of the body parts he had pieced back into a recognisable corpse. In addition to the two-gallon saucepan half-full of a reddish fluid, with a layer of thick grease at the top and a piece of boiled flesh at the bottom, and a hat-box crammed with thirty-seven chunks of flesh, Spilsbury described a suitcase containing four large portions which, carefully assembled, formed practically the whole trunk of a woman. Questioned about the large biscuit tin, Spilsbury responded: 'I found the organs of the chest and of the abdomen in nine separate pieces. Shall I detail all the pieces separately? One long piece was a portion of the large intestine eight inches long.'

'And the second?' enquired counsel. Spilsbury reported that when he squeezed the nipple of the right breast, milky fluid escaped. The victim, Emily Beilby Kaye, had been pregnant.

Patrick Mahon was a dishonest Irishman from Liverpool with good looks and charm. He embezzled from his employers and cheated on his wife, and in 1916 earned a five-year sentence when identified by the charlady of Sunningdale's National Provincial Bank after a break-in. First Mahon knocked her out with a hammer. Then, when she revived, he took her in his arms and romanced her, and in 1924 Mahon won the heart of Miss Kaye. But she discovered his past while cleaning out a drawer lined with the newspaper reporting his trial. When Mahon made her pregnant, she demanded a 'love experiment', spending time together at a bungalow on a bleak stretch of coast near Eastbourne. In anticipation of bliss, Miss Kaye purchased an engagement ring, told her friends she was leaving the country and suggested to Mahon that they sail for South Africa.

Mahon bought a tenon saw and chef's knife before catching a train to Eastbourne on 12 April. It rained, and he shared his **umbrella** with an attractive young woman, Ethel Duncan, making a date for the following Wednesday. On the Tuesday, Mahon killed Miss Kaye, most probably with a violent blow to the head, and set about her dismemberment. Her head he placed on a blazing fire in the kitchen and, as he did so, a thunderstorm burst and the dead eyes flickered open. Mahon ran screaming on to the beach, but by the next day he had regained sufficient composure to escort Miss Duncan to dinner. The following weekend they shared the bed formerly occupied by the late Miss Kaye, next to the room where her corpse lay in a travelling trunk. When Miss Duncan expressed interest in the locked room, Mahon sent himself a telegram and decamped for London, taking his Gladstone bag so he could toss bones out of the train windows. He visited his wife in Richmond, attended the Plumpton races, and returned to Waterloo's Left Luggage to collect his portmanteau. There he was arrested.

His wife, suspicious of Mahon's erratic movements, had handed his luggage ticket to an ex-railway police-man, who found a knife wrapped in a large quantity of bloodstained cloth. The police were waiting for Mahon at Waterloo, and he was hanged on 9 September 1924 for premeditated murder. The prose-cution produced receipts from a hardware store in refutation of his tale that the tenon saw and chef's knife were bought after the killing, and the jury rejected his story of an accidental fall during a scuffle, their deliberations assisted by the absence, among all the body, of the head (suggesting concealment of a vicious injury) and the womb, suggesting attempted concealment of Miss Kaye's pregnancy.

Murderee

Word invented by the writer F. Tennyson Jesse to designate those whose occupation or character makes them particularly subject to lethal force – for instance, prostitutes.

An obliging murderee tumbles into the killer's lap. Thus call-girl Kimberly Diane Martin was simply ordered up, like a pizza, from her escort agency by the Hillside Stranglers. They specified hair and underwear colour, blonde and black respectively.

A broader version of the murderee is the catch-all concept of the innate 'victim', to be contrasted with an 'unvictim'. Janice Hooker, wife of Cameron the **Slavemaker**, said of their house-girl: 'I chose not to be a victim. I hope Colleen makes that choice. Not just to walk out, but to make a total change, to become an unvictim, to take charge.'

It is not only feminists who find the idea of 'choos-ing' not to undergo random sexual assault hard to stomach. But the concept contains a grain of truth. Serial killers, sex killers and sex offenders often select their victims, stalking them perhaps for days. Sometimes a killer nurtures a preference for a certain type whose apparent vulnerability triggers his fantasies (see **Trolling**).

In Britain the term 'murderee' was first popularised by Martin Amis in his novel *London Fields* (see **Rillington Place**). The occupational catchment area has been extended to include **Planning Officers**.

Murder Inc.

Not just a film. Established in New York by Louis 'Lepke' Buchalter in the early 1930s, Murder Inc. provided a nationwide killing service for anyone willing to meet their standard fees of around $500. The customer-base consisted of gangland figures taking out rivals, informers or obstinate businessmen behind with their protection. Thus it was strictly for 'business reasons'.

The **hitmen** often remained in ignorance of the target's identity until afterwards, when they read it in the papers. Body disposal, available for an additional fee, was not included in the basic charge.

Murder Inc.'s exposure came hard on the heels of the 1940 killing of 'Red' Alpert in New York, when informer Harry Rudolph ratted on the hitman, 'Kid Twist' Reles, one of the permanent pay-roll. In the wake of the Kid's confessions it emerged that Murder Inc. had evolved as the enforcement arm of the Mafia Commission, the regulatory body of the leading Mob families. The Commission acted as a loose confederation minimising inter-gang disputes and 'unnecessary' killings. Their decisions had to be respected – hence the need for experts to conduct sanctioned eliminations.

Under Lepke's management the Brooklyn killers acquired a reputation for proficiency, becoming the Mob's semi-official execution squad on $12,000 annual retainers. Work came flowing in, often as fairly casual commissions. According to Reles in 1940: 'Lep gave us eleven contracts for witnesses when he was on the lam. We knocked off seven before Dewey put him on trial last year.' 'Muddy' Kasoff's offhand instructions were: 'This bum is cutting in on my play with the stuff. You guys take him.'

Reles was unperturbed by his arrest for Red Alpert's murder; it was routine, his forty-fourth spell behind bars. The prosecution case looked weak, lacking corroboration, and no one suspected his string of previous killings, which included two black men shot in broad daylight on the streets; one died for failing to wipe a smudge from Reles's front fender after a car-wash, and the other was dilatory in fetching Reles's vehicle from a parking lot. So, when his wife walked into Brooklyn police headquarters on 22 March 1940 announcing, 'My husband wants an interview with the Law', it came as a surprise. But the new Assistant District Attorney, Burton Turkus, had a backlog of 200 unsolved murders on his desk and was eager for help. 'I can make you the biggest man in the country,' Reles told Turkus. 'But I got to make a deal.'

By four in the morning he had his bargain, and Reles started his narrative with the words, 'I can tell you all about fifty guys that got hit; I was on the inside.' He kept talking for twelve days, filling twenty-five shorthand notebooks. The stenographers worked in relays. For the first time the astonished authorities learned of the existence and the workings of Organised Crime – a government within a government.

According to Reles, Murder Inc.'s total body-count ran into the hundreds; about a thousand is a fair estimate. One operative, Pittsburgh Phil, accounted for more than thirty men in more than a dozen cities. Reles preferred to work with an ice-pick; he admitted eighteen Murder Inc. killings. An eventual victim was his former client Muddy Kasoff, one of many seized in a spate of inter-mobster kidnappings, mostly for ransom, sometimes, like Kasoff, for information.

When Kasoff dried up, Reles blew off his head with a shotgun. As Reles explained to the court, recalling his partner's reaction: 'It handed Phil a laugh. We left the bum under a billboard that says "Drive Safely". Lucky was satisfied plenty.' Most photographs of Reles show him laughing.

'Bum' was the hitmen's standard terminology and amounted to a moral disclaimer; there was little wrong with shooting one of them. When Turkus probed deeper into Reles's attitude, he gathered that after the first few, 'you get used to it'.

Reles was given round-the-clock police protection on the seventh floor of a Coney Island hotel. But the Brooklyn District Attorney sold his whereabouts to Mafia boss Anastasia, and on 11 November 1941 Reles was levered out of a window by his police guard, primed with a $100,000 bribe, giving birth to the mobster adage that 'canaries can sing, but they cannot fly'. Lepke, his boss, survived another couple of years before perishing, albeit indirectly, at the hands of associates, when Lucky Luciano gave orders, via Costello and Meyer Lansky, for him to surrender personally to **Hoover** as a sop to public opinion. The plan was to relieve police 'heat' on Mob operations. In return, Lepke was promised lenient treatment. But he

was condemned to die in the electric chair on 15 September 1943.

Murder Inc.'s finest hour came with the destruction of the Dutch Schultz gang on 23 October 1935. Dutch needed killing. A natural hothead, he determined to 'take out' the unusually aggressive New York Special Prosecutor, Thomas E. Dewey. 'Dewey's gotta go,' Schultz used to say. 'He has gotta be hit in the head.' Gangland was aghast at the prospect of the resultant police crackdown, and Charles 'the Bug' Workman accepted the commission. He walked into the Palace Chophouse, Newark, with two automatics blazing, shooting dead three of Schultz's henchman after first mortally wounding Dutch himself, mistaking him for a bodyguard washing his hands in the men's room.

Workman waived his fee for this prestigious assignment and, widely recognised, served twenty-three years. Another walk-on player for Murder Inc. was Oscar 'the Evaporator', renowned for his legendary prowess at atomising hot vehicles so that no trace of evidence survived. For years the Mob paid him $50 per car, leaving Oscar to work the vehicles over with blow-torch and acid until not a scrap of fender or bolt remained. Oscar's prowess was truly legendary; what he actually did was sell the cars on, intact, at $5 each.

A shifty Dutch Schultz Flegenheimer, on charges of income tax evasion in January 1935. He died in a Murder Inc. hit nine months later

Oscar liked poetry; the place to find him was reading in the park, lucky to be alive.

Musicals

By most reckonings, **Jack the Ripper** constitutes an unlikely subject for a musical. The show made its debut on 17 September 1974 at London's Ambassadors Theatre in a production by comedian Brian Rix. It was not a long run, but the stage directions make good reading. Excerpts include: 'He draws a knife across her throat … At this point the cabinet door is flung open and from the cabinet slumps the dead and bloody body of Polly … The Figure cuts Annie's throat … The Ripper creeps up and cuts Lizzie's throat. She is carried off to the "Death March".' The entertainment featured a chorus of massed whores.

The life of Robert Maxwell, the international financial fraudster, is perhaps a more catchy subject. Evan Steadman, who sold his company to Maxwell for £16 million, is hacking a stage version of his patron's life. As Steadman says, 'Not to spend two hours in the company of Robert Maxwell is to deny the fruits of one of life's unrepeatable experiences. Admittedly the fruit goes bad, squashy and then makes you sick. Maxwell was impossible, ruthless, remorseless, but always with a smile, though it wasn't funny for the buggers he didn't buy out for £16 million.'

The broad canvas of opera may be a better vehicle for *The Manson Family*. In the 1992 words of the opera's composer, John Moran from Nebraska: 'The violence of the case doesn't interest me at all. What does interest me is the nature of Manson's personality … In the way of a revivalist preacher, it's not what he says but the way he says it that's so fascinating.' Manson's rhythmical, sing-song delivery is echoed in the music, now available on CD, and his earlier musical career included an abortive joint venture with the Beach Boys, a pop group. One evening in the spring of 1968 their drummer, Dennis Wilson, returned home to find a kneeling Manson inviting him into his own Sunset Boulevard property. Inside, the **Family** were in residence as irremovable, uninvited guests, and their visit cost Wilson about $100,000 in stolen clothes, unreturned loans and a wrecked Ferrari.

Wilson later said: 'Except for the expense, I got on very well with Charlie and the girls.' At any one time, his living room might contain twenty-five nubile 'chicks', all of them deeply into caressing. For food, the Family took Wilson's Rolls-Royce on garbage runs to the San Fernando supermarkets, loading the rear seat with top-grade discarded produce. For music, Manson collaborated with Wilson, writing the song 'Cease to Exist'. But the Beach Boys missed the point. First they changed the words to 'Cease to Resist' and then retitled his offering as 'Never Learn not to Love'.

The New Orleans bandleader and part-time pimp, Jelly Roll Morton, was another artistic beneficiary of crime. Jelly Roll found the Chicago whore-business too tightly controlled for his freelancing, and while in town he was – for the first time in years – compelled to devote himself to music.

See also **Sweeney Todd**

N

Names

No less than anywhere else, Chicago hoodlums had splendid names. Among the more outlandish were: Sam Samoots Amatuna, Bugs Moran, Vincent the Schemer Drucci, Nails Morton, Three-gun Louis Alterie, Mike de Pike Heitler, Tony Mops Volpe, Roger the Terrible Tuohy, Dominic Cinderella, Orchell DeGrazio, Buttons Capone, Mitters Folley, Toots Mondi, Potatoes Kaufman, Slippery Frank Rio, Diamond Joe Esposito, Bummy Goldstein, Jack Greasy Thumb Guzik, Machine-gun Jack McGurn, Eddie the Eagle Baldelli, Orrazzio the Scourge Tropea, and Hop Toad Guinta, so named for his addiction to dancing. John Dingbat O'Berta was a fox-faced Italian with an assumed Irish apostrophe.

Nearly all met violent ends. Cinderella went not to the ball but as one, trussed into a sphere with rope, dropped into a sack and slung in a ditch. He died with his slippers on. Vincent the Schemer Drucci came to grief in an equally mortifying way for a gangster: outraged at being arrested, he got himself shot by a policeman.

The saddest fate was reserved for Roger the Terrible Tuohy. He was not terrible at all. An honest and intelligent young man, he invested his profits from oil leases in a trucking business, and during the early 1920s, like everyone else, moved into bootlegging. His liquor was of high quality, his kegs did not leak, and he kept the local police and politicians in Des Plaines, Illinois, happy with a Special Brew of bottled beer.

Capone decided to take Tuohy over. But the great man's emissaries returned from their visits with awesome tales about the Tuohy gang, an impression Tuohy carefully fostered by stacking his office with borrowed pistols and machine-guns, some loaned by the police, while friends trooped through his rooms talking like plug-uglies. The local garage attendant was primed to ring so that Tuohy could sound fierce when he took the call.

In 1933 **Hoover** denounced Tuohy as one of 'the most vicious and dangerous criminals in the history of American crime', and his capture was hailed as 'a credit to the entire Bureau'. But the FBI were not involved: Tuohy was spotted by an unarmed policeman out on a fishing trip. Nor was Tuohy. He had been framed – perhaps by Capone – for the kidnapping of Chicago businessman John Factor, and he served twenty-six years of his ninety-nine-year sentence before being cleared in 1959. Less than four weeks later he was dead, gunned down in the Chicago streets.

Machine Gun Jack McGurn (real name Jack De Mora) was another near-survivor. After his father's death in 1923 at the hands of the Genna gang, he worked as a hired gun for Capone, concentrating his fire on the Gennas, and he was one of the St Valentine's Day Massacre gunmen. Police charges against McGurn were dropped, but he was indicted for perjury. When he realised that the only witness against him was a girl called Louise Rolfe, he knew what to do. He married her. Then McGurn faded from sight. But seven years to the day after the Valentine's day shooting, he was shot in Chicago's Avenue Recreation Club, still wearing his spats.

Three-gun Louis Alterie survived. A former cowboy, he found Chicago too hot and went back West.

Napoleons

Even before his death on 4 May 1821, Napoleon knew he had been murdered. After months of inexplicable physical degeneration, the Emperor wrote: 'I am dying before my time, murdered by the English oligarchy and its hired assassin.' But historians considered cancer, or any one of a dozen other infections, a more likely explanation.

Then in the 1950s the publication of the St Helena diaries of Napoleon's chief valet, Louis Marchand, gave a detailed description of the day-to-day course of the Emperor's last illness. In 1955, Swedish dentist Sten Forshufvud, who was also a toxicologist, realised that Napoleon's decline exhibited every known characteristic of **arsenic** poisoning: the loss of hair, the swollen feet, the failing legs, the icy chills, the obesity, the alternating bouts of somnolence and insomnia, the enlarged liver found on autopsy and the well-preserved state of the body exhumed in 1840.

Forshufvud's hypothesis could only be verified by analysis of Napoleon's hair. But five grams were needed – about 5,000 strands. Then in November 1959 the journal *Analytical Chemistry* reported a new technique whereby nuclear bombardment of a single hair produced accurate results. The following year, Forshufvud tracked down a lock of the Emperor's hair shaved from his head the day he died; tests conducted in Scotland revealed an arsenic content of 10.38 micrograms per gram – thirteen times the norm. Sectional studies of a 13-centimetre strand (representing about a year's growth) showed that the poison was regularly administered over an extended period, with peaks and troughs ranging from a low of 2.8 micrograms to a high of 51.2. This finding excluded constant exposure to a background source and effectively proved that Napoleon was poisoned.

French historians did their best to disparage and obstruct Forshufvud's work. The principle of a meddlesome Swedish dentist solving major French mysteries was bad enough. The practice was worse. Forshufvud's discovery meant that history's most famous Frenchman had been assassinated by … a Frenchman. Napoleon's British captors could have contaminated his entire St Helena household, but only a member of his immediate entourage was in a position to poison the Emperor alone.

The motive seems clear. After Napoleon's defeat at Waterloo, the Bourbons were reinstated as rulers of France. Napoleon had swept the dynasty away without a single shot in 1815 and, as long as he survived on St Helena, he might do so again.

Among the exiled Emperor's attendants was the improbable figure of Charles Montholon, a playboy aristocrat recently let off the hook by the Bourbons on a serious charge of embezzlement. Oddly, Montholon rallied to the Emperor's banner *after* Waterloo, and he stayed on with the Emperor in St Helena when even the most loyal of associates departed for France. Nor did Montholon object to Napoleon using his attractive wife Albine as a mistress.

Montholon was master of Napoleon's cellar, and Napoleon always drank from his own private barrel of Vin de Constance. It would have been a minute's work to poison the cask itself before the vintage was bottled.

It looks as though Montholon acted under orders as an assassin, and careful study of the Marchand diaries shows him adhering to the classical routine of the arsenic poisoner. First he dosed his victim repeatedly. Then in 1821 he stopped the arsenic, and induced the Emperor's physicians to prescribe a combination of otherwise innocuous drugs which would finish the patient without leaving arsenic residues for the autopsy. Thus, on 21 March 1821, Montholon ensured that Napoleon received a dose of tartar emetic, corroding the mucous lining of the stomach and destroying its capacity to vomit up further toxins. On 29 March, Montholon set up the daily tonic of 'orgeat', a drink of bitter almonds. Harmless of itself, the hydrocyanic acid in the orgeat combines with the inert mercury in calomel – another popular remedy – to produce lethal mercurous cyanide. On 3 May, Montholon persuaded the doctors to administer a huge dose of calomel. By the following evening the Emperor was dead and, in France, the cause of his death is still unknown.

Another murdered Napoleon, perhaps more familiar to True Crime enthusiasts, was Serge Rubinstein, the Napoleon of Fifth Avenue, discovered strangled in his five-storey home by his butler on the morning of 27 January 1955.

Rubinstein, a short individual, enjoyed dressing up as the Emperor for costume balls. He made his millions through stock market manipulation and insider-trading, driving companies into liquidation, defrauding stockholders, engineering currency fluctuations, and operating through aliases and nominees with such panache that on the eve of his 1941 marriage he was invited to dine at the Roosevelt White House.

Rubinstein liked women, and women liked him. He attended the 1955 New Year's Eve White Russian Ball with a bevy of seven lovelies in tow, juggled perhaps half a dozen lovers – actresses, singers and models – at a time, and handed out the keys of his Fifth Avenue Mansion to his current favourites.

Rubinstein was found trussed up on his bedroom floor in a silk dressing gown, and the police soon had a list of suspects. His loose-leaf notebooks provided the names of some 2,000 associates, lovers, pimps, politicians, business partners, creditors and informers, all of whom might have wanted him dead and any of whom could have secured access. After a sporting try, the police abandoned the case.

Another great admirer of Napoleon was Henry Fauntleroy (1785–1824), probably the first modern financial fraudster. Over the course of some nine years Fauntleroy embezzled £500,000 from the London bank, Marsh Sibbald and Company, in which he was a partner. Of diminutive stature, Fauntleroy had the drawing room of his mistress's Brighton villa decorated as a reproduction of the Emperor's travelling tent and, on his eventual arrest, inquired of the police officer, named Plank, 'Good God! Cannot this business be settled?'

But it could not, and Fauntleroy was sentenced to death for forgery, in part convicted on the evidence of Robert Browning's father, who worked for the Bank of England (see also **Wind in the Willows**). The tremendous public outcry on his behalf achieved nothing; even the entreaties of the language teacher Edmund Angelini to be executed in his stead fell on deaf ears. The financier met his end with dignity on 30 November 1824, but rose again – at least in legend – to start a new life abroad as a nineteenth-century Lord **Lucan**, saved not by a silver spoon in the mouth but by the silver pipe that popular myth adroitly inserted into his windpipe.

Apart from Napoleon himself, and Mussolini and Goebbels, the list of unusually short delinquents includes **Manson**, Issei **Sagawa** and **Bonnie** Parker.

Narcotics, smuggling

In January 1992, British Customs and Excise exhibited a captured false leg, former property of a smuggler hoping to walk 1.5 kilos of cocaine through Heathrow airport (see **Thiefrow**). Other containers include the stomach, spectacle frames, television cathode tubes, shoe heels, children's books, nuns' habits, fish cakes, artificial hair braids, factory-sealed liquor bottles, impregnated suitcases, antique chair-legs, hollowed-out jacket buttons, salsa records split down the centre (filled and re-bonded) and a St Bernard dog. A single dummy aerosol can hold several million dollars' worth of heroin at street prices.

In April 1992 the *Independent* newspaper referred to a deranged woman in Holloway, imprisoned for smuggling drugs in the body of a dead baby. Surgical implants are another innovation, with one Puerto Rican arrested with slabs of cocaine introduced into his thighs. He was stopped because of his waddling gait.

A recent stratagem of almost fiendish cunning has clean merchandise shipped in contaminated packaging. When the goods are extracted from their containers for scrutiny, the drugs are laid to one side; and, the examination over, they are replaced for onwards shipment. One version has the heroin stuffed into long, specially made straws inserted between the serrated walls of cardboard boxes; a large package can carry perhaps two kilos. The first Customs 'bust' was at Rotterdam when a crate accidentally dropped during handling. A variant secretes the contraband in the hollowed-out chocks of wooden pallets.

The latest high-technology ploy is infusion of fibre glass and plastic products with cocaine. The only recorded seizure was a batch of cocaine dog kennels imported from Colombia, surely the perfect mainspring for the plot of a 'mistaken identity' thriller. The three kennels were impounded on arrival in Los Angeles in October 1992 and, when ground to powder, yielded seventeen kilos of cocaine with a street value of $1.5 million.

More antiquated ruses include strips sewn into the bra, and vaginal caches; female crack vendors now employ an updated version with the 'rocks' first popped into a little plastic egg of the type found in Kinder chocolates.

With domestic vehicles, a favourite hiding place was a petrol tank rewelded to take drugs instead of fuel. This reduced range. In the era of the long overland haul from Spain to **Sweden**, cannabis smugglers made the journey with a one-gallon petrol capacity, allowing twenty-five-mile runs between fuel stops. Drug smugglers with camper vans prepared for their trip through Customs by a three-day in-vehicle stint of cooking onions.

Some 80 per cent of Europe's heroin now comes in through the Balkan route. For many years, the repressive regimes of Iran, Turkey and Eastern Europe, with their strict controls on through-traffic, kept the influx of drugs from Pakistan and Afghanistan in check. But the road to Istanbul is now clogged with tourists and lorries, and it can take a day to search a single vehicle; narcotics worth millions (or birds worth thousands) can be concealed in a compartment measured in cubic inches.

The illegal trade in rare birds, now attracting serious smugglers, has obvious financial parallels with the exponential mark-up on drugs: an African Grey plucked out of the jungle for almost nothing fetches £500 in the UK and £7,000 in Australia. The contraband is stuffed into tiny cardboard boxes or specially designed cavities in a dashboard; fatalities in transit are high. For the traffickers the penalties are trivial, a fine of £250 or maybe £400; for the birds, seventy-seven of the world's 300 species of parrots are facing extinction.

Lucky Luciano's horticultural contribution was the invention of wax oranges, injected with 100 grams of heroin, for shipment from Sicily to the United States.

See also **Condoms**, **Magic Eraser**, **Pizza Connection**, **Swallowers**

Negative blocking

A concept invented by the American penologist Dan McDougald. His views owed much to Jouvet's 1950s Harvard experiments on a cat wired for sound. When confronted by a jar of appetising white mice, both the cat and the oscilloscope (connected to its ear) ignored a sharp click. The machine itself no longer detected the sound. That is, the cat was so distracted by its prey that it somehow prevented the signal from reaching the eardrum.

As with cats, reasoned McDougald, so with criminals. He argued that 'negative blocking' ensured that a villain's fixation on Looking After Number One made him blind and deaf to the claims of love, honesty and fellow-feeling. Dyed-in-the-wool criminals would not know what these words meant. They were linguistically challenged, and the way to defeat their blocking mechanism was by inculcating the definitions of these key concepts, first persuading hard-core psychopaths to expose their defective preconceptions during conversation, and then subjecting them to a course of remedial tuition. When convicts grasped the basic vocabulary of ordinary life – that is, what the words really meant – they would be reformed. McDougald named his method 'Emotional Maturity Instruction'.

In 1967, McDougald decided to pit his theory against the toughest nuts in Georgia's maximum security prison near Reidesville. Shortly afterwards a startled Dr C. D. Warren, medical director to the penitentiary, reported: 'You would not believe the results. In two weeks with the twenty-two-man group, the constructive changes were impressive … In eight weeks, they had successfully rehabilitated 63 per cent of men under instruction.'

The important thing with prisoners is to make *some* attempt at re-education; anything is better than the standard policy of locking men up in cells and leaving them there. Today, Britain has only one jail – Grendon in Buckinghamshire – where sex-offenders are treated as opposed to being merely confined. The **prison** houses about 190 inmates from a national pool of 3,000 offenders.

Traditionally, sexual criminals are despised by everyone else, but at Grendon the men are marshalled into small groups where, during encounter sessions, their problems are brought nearer home. The men find that they despise each other, and, subsequently, themselves. Nationally, 42 per cent of prisoners reoffend. The figure for Grendon inmates after a year and a half of therapy is 18 per cent.

Neilson, Donald (1936–)

On 6 March 1975 the search for kidnap victim Lesley Whittle drew to its close as Detective Constable Phil Maskery clambered into the Glory Hole, a shoulder-high octagonal structure protecting the entrance to the Bath Pool drainage system in Britain's Midlands.

Maskery climbed down the rungs of the dark concrete shaft, and forty feet into his descent he reached the culvert, a five-feet-high sewer pipe. His torch picked out a Dymo lettering machine discarded among the debris and grime. The kidnapper had laid his trail of messages with trigger-gun strips, but there was no sign of his teenage captive, and Maskery returned to the surface, tramping over to the second entrance to the underground complex. This time he found nothing.

The third and deepest shaft started at the top of a nearby hill. But a gas gauge showed – incorrectly – that dangerous levels of methane were present, and the following morning Maskery made his descent with breathing apparatus. He reached the first metal inspection platform twenty-two feet down, and ducked through the grille to the next section of steel ladder. On the second platform twenty-three feet below, he peered into a narrow culvert at knee height and saw a tape recorder – presumably used to dictate the ransom demand. Then he lowered himself to the final level in the pitch dark.

It was soft underfoot. Maskery was standing on a foam mattress. His flashlight picked out a dressing gown dangling over the edge of the platform from an iron stanchion. A taut steel cable ran from the base of the ladder over the metal lip and, swinging below, with her toes seven inches above the tunnel's floor, was Lesley Whittle, naked, hanging by the neck. She had died not of strangulation but vagal inhibition, that is, fright.

Lesley spent the last days of her life in this concrete-and-iron dungeon, and had perished after falling off the platform. Divers later found a sticking-plaster blindfold, a gag, her blue slippers and her zipped-up sleeping bag, which had perhaps slithered from her body as she swung.

Lesley's death may have been an accident, as the kidnapper Donald Neilson claimed with disconcerting

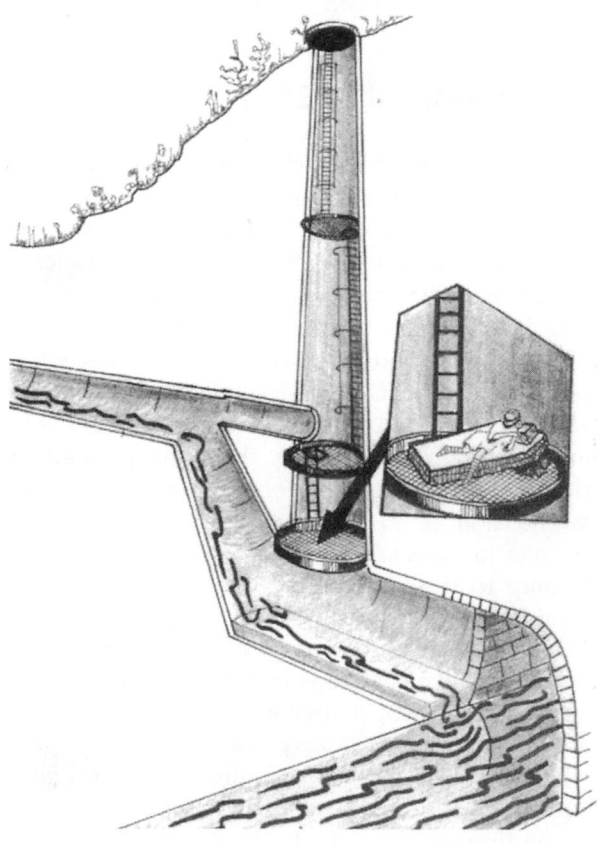

Lesley Whittle's last resting place

vagueness ('As I stood on the platform she went over the side and was suspended by the wire'), but it is unlikely the jury were in any mood to care, and he was jailed for life on 21 July 1976. To add to the family's torment, all attempts to ransom Lesley's life misfired. The first secret rendezvous, with £50,000 packed into a suitcase, was scheduled for the day of the kidnap, but the 'drop' aborted after an alert freelance journalist splashed the story over the news. The second demand miscarried when the kidnapper was interrupted while laying his trail. Gerald Smith, a British Rail overseer at the local freight depot, accosted a stranger skulking round his yard. The prowler shot him six times, and then pulled the trigger again with the pistol to Smith's head. But the magazine was empty.

The bullets extracted from Smith (who died a year later) proved a perfect ballistic match with ammunition used in a series of eighteen small-time robberies, in which three postmasters died. The raider, dubbed the 'Black Panther' for his habitual garb of a black hood with a slit for the eyes, was equated with the Whittle kidnapper a week later, on 23 April, after the discovery of his Morris saloon parked 250 yards from the scene of Smith's shooting. Inside was paraphernalia from the kidnapping – ropes, a mattress, plastic sheeting and four Dymo tape messages with ransom instructions.

By then, Ronald Whittle had tried to hand over the money for the last time. On 16 February a recorded message directed him to the Kidsgrove Post Office telephone box where it took an hour to find his next clue, a Dymo strip behind the back-board. This ordered him to Bathpool Park: 'Go to the wall and flash lights look for torch run to torch further instructions on torch then go home and await further instructions.' Ronald Whittle came so close, and yet so far. In the dark he drove through the grounds, with its football pitches, artificial ski slope and a dammed-up lake called the Bath Pool, from which the overflow was drained by an underground culvert accessed by three vertical concrete shafts. Unable to find the right wall or the torch, that night he stood alone in the park, above his entombed sister, shouting 'This is Ron Whittle. Is anybody there?'

Three weeks later, a schoolboy handed in a strip of Dymo tape found under some twigs two days after the kidnapping. It read, 'Drop suitcase into hole.' Next day some children produced the torch from which this message had worked loose. They had discovered it perched between the iron railings surrounding the first shaft of the Bath Pool drainage system. This was 'The Glory Hole' where Phil Maskery started his search on 6 March.

After his chance arrest five months later, Neilson began his interrogation in baby-talk. 'I no the shoot anybody,' he mouthed in a foreign accent. 'I would shoot dog but no policeman. I no Black Panther. When Black Panther work, he shoot to kill.' By then he was nearing forty. Born Donald Nappey, at school he was ragged and scruffy, known as 'Dirty Nappy', and in 1965 he changed his name to avoid the same fate for his daughter. After his mother's death when he was ten, Neilson became the household drudge, and grew into a shy, introverted youth. His happiest days came during Army National Service, serving in Kenya against the Mau Mau and in Cyprus against EOKA terrorists.

Neilson married his first girlfriend, and cajoled her into indulging his obsession with guerrilla warfare. Photographs recovered from his home showed the family at play, kitted out in combat fatigues, pitching dummy grenades at one another or lying 'wounded' in wrecked jeeps, and his home was stuffed with combat gear and equipment. In prison awaiting trial, Neilson continued his routine of 200 press-ups a day, and application of these specialist survival skills in the outside world had seemed to offer his only chance of decent money, which self-employment failed to deliver. As Neilson told Dr Hugo Milne, 'So there was only one thing left for me. There was no other way than crime', and by the late 1960s he started house-breaking. Then came armed robbery, then murder, then murder and **kidnapping**.

Four decades separated the Whittle case from a commensurate act of premature burial. On 25 April 1934, 6-year-old June Robles was walking back from kindergarten school in Tucson, Arizona, when a man beckoned her into his car. The stranger explained that her father had sent him. A ransom demand for $15,000, signed 'XYZ', arrived that afternoon, but nothing more was heard of the kidnap victim for nineteen days. 'Is little June dead?' asked New York's *Daily News*.

Then a letter to Governor B.B. Moeur of Arizona advised a search of the desert some ten miles east of Tuscon. There the rescue party pulled away at a pile of cactus and deadwood to reveal a crude box, six feet long and three feet high, dug into a sand pit. Its tin lid, burning hot and punched with ventilation holes, was ripped off to reveal a blistered and bleeding June, chained to a metal bar by a padlock round her ankles. She survived, and four days later President Roosevelt signed federal legislation making kidnapping punishable by death.

See also **Coffins**

Neo-Nazis

It is often commented that modern-day Germany is as far from its Nazi past as it is possible to imagine – the Germans have the highest proportion of declared pacifists in their population of any European country and the reunified Germany is considered a paragon of modern liberal democracy. Yet Germany's Nazi past still claims innocent victims.

In June 2000 three neo-Nazi youths in the eastern German town of Dessau deliberately kicked a man to death, simply because he was black. Enrico Hilprecht, aged 24, and Frank Miethbauer and Christian Richter, both 16, showed no remorse when arrested for the murder of Alberto Adriano, a Mozambican father of three who had emigrated legally to Germany twelve years before. Nor did the killers try to hide their Nazi affiliations – Hilprecht sported a Hitler moustache, albeit wispy blonde, and one of his co-defendants wore, tattooed on his forehead, the infamous SS lightning-bolt icon of the Nazi death squads.

Sentencing Hilprecht to life imprisonment and his juvenile co-defendants to nine years each, Judge Albrecht Hennig commented that the Adriano murder was 'the latest in a long chain of attacks to which we must put an end'. In this he was reflecting a growing public fear that the German neo-fascist movement was becoming a major problem.

Although few people believe that fascism could ever take over the reins of German government again – as the Nazis did in 1933 – the problem of bored, unemployed young men being inspired to racist violence by fascist doctrines remains a constant problem in Germany. After reunification the economy suffered a protracted downturn, and unemployment – especially in the former communist east of the country – rose year on year. Many of the youths left hanging around on street corners by the recession started to think of the Nazi regime as a golden age.

Germany has strict laws that forbid the spreading of

Nazi propaganda (and of even displaying Nazi symbols such as the swastika and the SS badge) but the universality of the internet and the difficulty of policing independent websites allowed many bored, jobless German youths access to any amount of neo-Nazi screeds. The result was a depressing increase in attacks on immigrants, who comprise 9 per cent of the German population.

An indication of just how bad Germany's underground fascist problem had become was inadvertently highlighted by the Adriano trial: Angelika Adriano, the victim's widow, received so many anonymous death threats during the trial that she and her three children were forced to go into hiding under police protection.

Newgate

A prison popularly known as 'hell on earth', built between 1130 and 1137 on the guardhouse site by the new gate of Roman London at a cost of £36 0s 11 d. Its administration hardly changed until well into the nineteenth century.

Gaolers had to pay their own turnkeys, so the prison was woefully understaffed, and inmates were kept in irons, fetters or the dreaded skull cap throughout their sentence. The warders' main source of income was the money wrested from their prisoners, and the staff sold or hired beds, blankets, sheets, mattresses, coal, firewood, candles, food and drink. In 1717 visits from friends were charged at six pence, furniture at a pound a fortnight, and whores for the night at a shilling a time.

Prisoners could 'choose' one of three standards of accommodation – the Master's Side, the Knight's Side or the Hole, roughly corresponding to First Class, Second Class and Steerage.

As money ran short, conditions deteriorated, and since everything had to be paid for repeatedly, funds never lasted long. On arrival, wealthy prisoners would subscribe to the Master's Side and, on payment of a bribe or 'garnish', were ushered through the appropriate doorway. This led to a passage at the end of which stood another locked door and another warden, exacting another bribe. This second payment only secured admittance to another Kafkaesque corridor. And so it went on.

As long as a Master's Side inmate could pay, there was meat and claret at every meal and plenty of

The main entrance

tobacco. Men of quality (see **Gordon**) dined alone or were waited on in the company of friends. For a few shillings more, the prisoner remained out of his cell after dinner, and his companions from outside might drop round for a game of cards. But every item, every service, entailed more garnish. Come the evil day, the prisoner was packed off to the Knight's Ward (again for a fee), and thence to the final indignity of the Condemned Hold, a large foetid dungeon underneath the prison gates with an open sewer oozing down the middle. Food was flung in through a hatch and, according to a Colonel John Turner, the prisoners 'lay like swine upon the ground, one upon another, howling and roaring'.

No public funds were set aside for poor convicts; if they lived, it was off citizens' bequests. Donations filtered through the warders' hands, to which they stuck and, at the end of Queen Elizabeth's reign, prisoners in the Hole submitted a petition complaining of their 'lying upon bare boards, still languishing in great need, cold and misery ... almost famished and half-starved to death; others very sore sick, and diseased for want of sustenance'. Fennor, author of *The Counter's Commonwealth*, writes of 'the child weeping over his dying father, the mother over her sick child; one friend over another … they lie together like so many graves'.

Constantly swept by epidemics of 'gaol fever', Newgate threatened those outside its walls with contagion. During the famous Black Assizes of May 1750 a hundred inmates were squeezed into Bail Dock and, in the ensuing outbreak of gaol fever, the Lord Mayor, two judges and over forty officials, barristers and jurymen lost their lives. Fee-paying was not abolished until 1823, when Newgate was found to house a man serving eleven years for a debt of 1s 5d and another incarcerated for **debts** of fourpence. The keepership became a valuable office, in 1696 reportedly sold for £3,500. In a 1708 pamphlet, it was said to give £8,000 security. Celebrated convicts provided windfall profits for the Warden, who charged admission for viewing. In 1724 the exhibition of highwayman Jack Sheppard netted £200.

Newgate had just been enlarged and rebuilt in 1780, after a fire in 1762, when it was put to the torch during the Gordon Riots. Some 300 prisoners were rescued from the flames and escorted by the jubilant mob to local blacksmiths, who struck off their irons. Puzzled by their new-found freedom, many drifted back to the smouldering debris, and were rounded up the following day.

Three years later the main London gallows were shifted from **Tyburn** to Newgate to eliminate the traditional procession of the condemned across the capital.

This was more convenient for the convicts, who could be executed on their own doorstep in the shadow of the Debtor's Gate, and the new gallows got off to a cracking start on 9 December 1783 when ten men were hanged in a single session. The impact on local property values was good; houses facing the gallows acquired new rental potential, charging three guineas a spectator for popular executions, and even the roofs could be filled at two guineas a place. But the new venue proved too cramped for proper crowd control. At the 1807 hanging of Haggerty and Holloway a mob of 40,000 gathered in the narrow streets; twenty-eight were killed in the crush when someone tripped over a pieman, and a further seventy were injured.

Newgate survived into the twentieth century as a relic of medieval barbarity at the heart of the Empire opposite the new Old Bailey. Demolished in 1902, the contents went to auction. The Tussaud brothers were enthusiastic bidders, acquiring the toll bell for £100 in addition to the complete cells of Lord George Gordon and Jack **Sheppard**. These were dismantled, carted down the Marylebone Road and reassembled in the Chamber of Horrors, where they remained until the 1970s. Newgate's plaster casts of hanged criminals fetched £5 each (many going to the Black Museum) and the execution shed, £5 15s 0d.

The gallows themselves went on to Pentonville, and were soon back in harness.

Ng, Charles Chiat (1961–)

One half of an American sex-killer duo. Ng met his partner, Leonard Lake, through a magazine personal advertisement. Ng was on the run from the Marines for stealing a brace of machine-guns in 1981, and ten years previously Lake had been released from the military with signs of an 'impending schizophrenic reaction'. Lake's in-laws gave him the freedom of a two-acre ranch north of San Francisco in the Sierra Nevada, and in 1984 and 1985 the pair made this Wisleyville property the base for their Nordic survivalist fantasies, of the variety where **slave** girls are tortured in dungeons. Together they snatched transient women, or men and women, or men and women and their babies, exercising the women as sexual drudges before they were discarded, dead. Meanwhile they stalked their male captives through grounds rigged with trip wires and booby traps in a crazed re-creation of the Vietnam War. Investigators were to remove forty-five pounds of bones from the compound.

The real 'fun' took place in the concrete bunker, built by local workmen as 'a food storage area, to keep apples and walnuts in a cool place'. The hut measured sixteen feet by fourteen, and behind a removable partition was a tiny bedroom with a viewing panel through a one-way mirror. In this torture chamber, which doubled as their home movie studio, the manacled women were terrorised, raped, mutilated with power tools and then murdered.

The case unravelled on 2 June 1985 when Ng ran off with a $75 vice from a San Francisco lumber yard. Lake, waiting in a car, was caught, and from this prosaic start flowed horror after horror. Lake requested a drink of water and then collapsed dead from a cyanide capsule. He had given his name as Robin Scott Stapely, and investigators identified Stapely as a San Diego Guardian Angel, reported missing some months before. Another Lake alias was Charles Gunnar (also missing), and Lake's 1980 Honda Prelude was registered to a car dealer, Paul Cosner (missing). Lake carried a bank card belonging to Randy Jacobson (missing), and when the San Francisco police contacted the Calaveras County Sheriff about the Wisleyville homestead, where Stapely had been Lake's immediate neighbour, they were dismayed to hear the fate of Stapely's three housemates: missing. The Sheriff drove to the ranch, where a pickup truck carried a sticker, 'If you love something, set it free. If it doesn't come back, hunt it down and kill it.' Ng and Lake were eventually linked to twenty-seven missing persons.

Lake was cremated with the exception of his brain, conserved for medical research. Ng escaped over the Canadian border to be captured a month later, down to his last ten dollars, shoplifting in a Calgary department store. He could not be extradited – Canada is opposed to capital punishment. But by September 1991 the Canadians were prepared to make an exception in Ng's case. In 1999, after a trial lasting eight months, he was found guilty of the murder of six men, three women and two male babies. The judge followed the jury's recommendation by imposing a sentence of death, although he had the option of handing down life imprisonment. An appeal is in progress against the 'harshness' of the sentence.

'Mike owes us and unfortunately he can't pay. We're going to give you a choice … You co-operate, and in approximately thirty days we'll take you back to the city and let you go … If you don't co-operate with us, we'll probably put a round through your head and take you out and bury you someplace … While you're here you'll wash for us, you'll clean for us, you'll fuck for us.' After this prologue Leonard Lake walked into shot and took off Kathy's handcuffs, put on her leg irons, and made her undress.

The tape cut to four days later. Kathy, strapped to the bed, listened as Lake castigated her for some bent hasps on a lock. In passing, he mentioned that they had killed Mike; it would soon be time for her to join him.

They did 'slay' Kathy, but not on screen. Instead the tape switched to a terrified Brenda O'Connor, with Ng slicing off her shirt with a knife and then shearing her bra in two. 'If you don't do what we tell you,' Ng threatened, 'we will tie you to the bed, rape you, shoot you in the head, and take you out and bury you.' Later footage showed Brenda imploring Ng for the life of her baby while he responded with taunts: 'I don't think you're a fit mother.'

A friend of Ng's, interviewed on the television show *Inside Edition*, said, 'The **torture**, the pure **terror** – Ng wanted to see terror … I don't think the sexual act was very gratifying … They had to beg for it to stop … And then, once they stopped, it was no longer fun. Then it's time to put a round in their head and move on to find another one.'

Lake, middle-aged and balding, wrote in his diary, 'There is no sexual problem with a submissive woman. There are no frustrations – only pleasure and contentment.' His idea that peace of mind was attainable through tying people up and killing them marked the intrusive triumph of long-nurtured fantasies over his nondescript everyday existence.

Although Lake maintained that his life started when he joined the Marines, he saw no active service in Vietnam. Instead, he bragged about his heroic exploits. After discharge, he degenerated into a gun freak, amassing scores of weapons, and thence into a paramilitary freak, stoking his dreams with war magazines. He wore combat fatigues round the neighbourhood, offered to instruct high school pupils in the use of explosives, liked to photograph his sex partners handcuffed, and progressed to pornographic home movies. His preoccupation with the John Fowles novel *The Collector* (in which the first kidnap victim is Miranda) cross-fertilised his survivalist obsessions. Hence Lake's 'Operation Miranda', where he would wait out the nuclear inferno in his bunker, consoled by weapons and sex slaves. In Lake's imagination, his insignificance was displaced by a sense of omnipotence, and he carried his philosophy through; the *San Jose Mercury News* quoted a neighbour who reported Lake saying, 'If somebody deserves to die they should be dead.'

Murder is no counterweight for personal inadequacy, and serial killers are typically left encumbered by gore with their troubles unresolved. Lake's later diary entries show that the growing number of bodies in the trench behind their bunker brought only misery. His problems can be traced to his childhood, when he was raised by his grandfather, a strict disciplinarian, and his sisters allowed Lake to have sex with them in return for protection from his brother.

Ng was a hard case from childhood. Of wealthy Hong Kong parents, he was expelled from two schools, the second time for stealing; he was caught shoplifting; became involved in a hit-and-run accident; intimidated his fellow-Marines; boasted about killings, and stole weapons before contacting Lake. In his Canadian prison, he compiled a **list** of seventy-seven witnesses and law officers scheduled for execution.

Sentenced to death in 1999, Ng is still on Death Row awaiting execution.

See also **Fantasising**, **Preview**, **Reading material**, **Souvenirs**, **Zodiac**

Nice, France

Scene of the 1976 bank raid on the Société Général, masterminded by Albert Spaggiari, an unsavoury right-wing criminal.

By his own account, Spaggiari's career started in 1948 with a bid to join a band of Sicilian bandits at the age of 16. He applied in writing. He served as a paratrooper in Indo-China, then robbed a nightclub, and later enlisted in the OAS where he tried to assassinate De Gaulle. It is said that Spaggiari had the President in his sights from an upper window above his mother's shop in Nice; but the order to fire never came.

After a four-year prison sentence for distributing inflammatory political pamphlets and the unlawful possession of firearms, Spaggiari hatched a plot for the perfect robbery. Despite its glamorous outcome, the project resembled a large-scale civil engineering exercise.

Spaggiari's first accomplice was a lady who tackled the undercover work with relish. She rented a safe deposit box in the underground vault of Nice's Société Général and arrived for her visits with a miniature spy-camera. She installed a concealed radio-transmitter to eavesdrop on the bank guards' daily routine, and her detailed questions about locks, alarm systems and patrols seemed perfectly natural for a nervous old woman nearing 80 who was worried about her savings.

Meanwhile Spaggiari boned up on commercial security from technical journals like *Science et Vie*. A frontal assault on the bank seemed bound to fail. The only remaining approach was through the walls or floor, but the vault was set into solid rock. Spaggiari experimented by leaving an alarm clock, then a radio with a timer, and finally a siren in the deposit box to prove that if ever the walls were breached he could work undisturbed.

Attempts to procure a thermal lance embroiled Spaggiari with a gang from Marseilles, to whom he divulged his plan. They 'wanted in' and undertook to supply seven men, leaving Spaggiari to rake up the rest from his military low-life acquaintances. Together they bought a van identical to the Public Works department's vehicles. Then they acquired official overalls, uniforms and a set of traffic signs, and mapped the sewers of Nice in broad daylight, setting up 'Roadworks' signs while they disappeared through manholes in the middle of the road. They needed an entrance large enough to admit heavy mechanical gear, giving good access to a point near the strongroom, preferably with electric power. They found it.

Spaggiari stockpiled equipment with the diligence of a quartermaster, making purchases in dispersed sorties to allay suspicion. In addition to hi-tech items like a small laser and walkie-talkie radios, and the basic requirements of electric drills and a heavy-duty hydraulic lever, he thought the plan through to the last details. After assembling their checklist of tool-bags, scissors, 300 metres of cable, chisels, hammers, jemmies, bolt cutters, oxyacetylene torches, gas cylinders, buckets, cement, boots, work gloves, surgical gloves, portable stove, smoke extractor and wheelbarrow, the gang took to the sewers, setting up first base in early May 1976 a hundred yards down a twisting route in the network of conduits, lugging eighty pounds of gear at a time during repeated trips.

Then they drilled towards the vault. The rockface was unyielding. Four inches an hour constituted good progress. Drill bits snapped and tempers flared, but after two weeks their shaft was twenty feet long, extending to the bank's concrete footings. Three pneumatic jacks and more than a hundred drill bits later, on 24 June, their seventh week in the sewers, the gang pierced the five-feet-thick foundations. The wall of the vault itself was the only remaining barrier.

They breached it easily. But the way was barred; they had come out behind a fifty-ton safe. First they tried budging it with jacks. Then they torched through its back. The steel casing yielded, but they were defeated by its concrete lining. Finally the entire unit was shifted and wedged out of the way, and on Friday 16 July the gang climbed into the strongroom with a whole weekend ahead.

The 1,500 deposit boxes were themselves inside safes, and Spaggiari assumed that the most strongly defended contained the most precious spoils. By four o'clock on Saturday afternoon only twenty-eight had been ruptured, sometimes disgorging cash, sometimes mouldy biscuits, or sugar, or jewels, gold, securities and pornographic pictures. The gang worked in relays, sleeping on the floor, slurping down hot soup prepared on their butane stove, and by Sunday evening they had opened a total of 317 boxes.

The value of their haul as they pulled out at midnight on Sunday, staggering under their sackloads in the rising sewers, is estimated at between a conservative $8 million and an extravagant $75 million. Behind them, the main door to the vault was welded shut from inside, and the walls bore their final message: 'No hate, no violence and no guns'.

The police were so impressed by the tunnelling, propped at the correct intervals, that they first suspected miners. Spaggiari, arrested three months later, was traced through one of the shops from which he bought his equipment, as well as by his predilection for Dom Miguel cigars; his butts littered the strongroom. But at a courtroom appearance on 10 March 1977 he broke free and leapt out of the window, breaking his fall with a paratrooper's roll on a parked car twenty feet below, and roared away on the back of an accomplice's motorcycle.

Spaggiari was never recaptured, and died on the run from natural causes. The money probably passed into the hands of sundry right-wing terrorist groups.

The best fictional account of the raid is Robert Pollock's novel *Loophole* published in 1972, four years before the event and a quarter of a century after the world's greatest robbery, when some £2,500 million of gold (at today's values) vanished from the Reichsbank following Germany's collapse in the spring of 1945.

Nicholl, Charles (1950–)

Author of one of the great passages of comedy-thriller crime reportage. In *The Fruit Palace* (1985), Nicholl recounts how an undercover story on the Colombian cocaine trade nearly came unstuck when his drug-dealing contacts discovered his true identity. The dealers considered 'checking his oil' with a knife in the guts, but veered in favour of giving him a little job: smuggling cocaine on to the *Nordic Star* in the Santa Marta docks. Nicholl had no choice but to comply.

He dressed in pristine whites as a *gringo* reporter for his big day out. A five-kilo sack of cocaine was thrown over the harbour's perimeter fence for him to collect once he had negotiated security, and Nicholl slunk unobserved through the harbour's outbuildings only to find that the bag had burst. Cocaine was blowing everywhere. He crammed the leaking sack into his briefcase. But it had been manufactured in Taiwan and the hinges broke. Nicholl tried to clean himself down with his hands, which were covered in oil, and in this state, smeared in grease and cocaine, he found himself button-holed at inordinate length by the harbour's Director of Operations.

In mid-conversation in his capacity of journalist, Nicholl looked down to find the white powder still trickling from the case's loose corner, making a little narcotic pyramid on the ground. He covered the cocaine pile with his foot. Still talking, he plugged the leak by clamping the briefcase close to his chest like a teddy bear, and the chit-chat droned on while the precious seconds of his hand-over time ticked away.

It was only by feigning convulsive diarrhoea that Nicholl tore himself away. He insisted on using the *Nordic Star*'s lavatories, where his hand-over was scheduled, and scampered up the gangplank with seconds to spare. But his contact, an irate Swede, refused to take delivery; the cocaine was spoiled, spilling loose inside the case. Wiping the briefcase down, Nicholl unthinkingly put his fingers to his nose, hoovering up pure 'Snow White'. As well as paralysing his speech centres, this laid waste to most of his motor co-ordination.

Nicholl's plight was now parlous. He could not deliver the consignment: it had been rejected. He could not dump it: he would be liquidated. He could hardly move; he was zinging at the eyeballs.

Luckily, what he lost in ability he gained in confidence, and he approached the task of running the drugs back out of the ship, down the gangplank and through the guarded harbour complex with unshakeable optimism. He attributes his survival to his innovation of smuggling cocaine *into* Colombia, for which the authorities were ill-prepared.

Nicholl is alive and well and still writing. The guards manning Colombian ports are open to financial persuasion; their weekly wage is £2.

Nilsen, Dennis (1945–)

One of Britain's most prolific serial killers, whose exploits are described elsewhere (see **Death**, **Life after** and **Mirror image**).

Why did Nilsen become a murderer? The best source is Brian Masters, author of *Killing for Company*, who makes the point that Nilsen's family were fishermen from eastern Scotland, a harsh coast savaged by wind and sea, where the inhabitants – fatalistic and suspicious – regarded good and evil not as thin religious concepts, but as reality. Inbreeding in the fishing villages was rife, stretching back for centuries, bringing in its wake mental and emotional disorders regarded locally as no more than quirks. Many of the menfolk were lost at sea. Life was poor and hard.

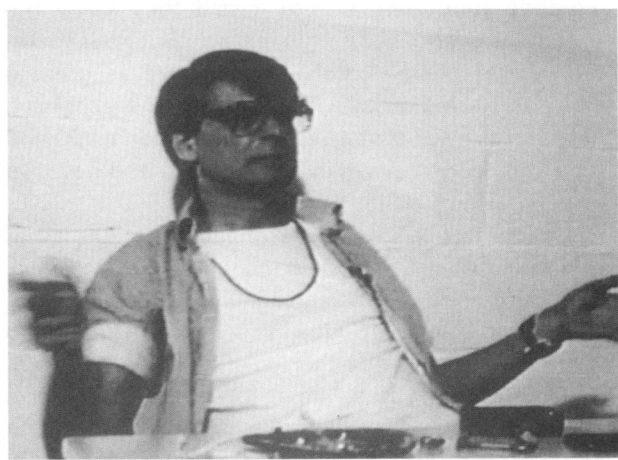

Dennis Nilsen, mass murderer

In 1942, Betty Whyte from Fraserburgh, a fisherman's daughter, rushed into marriage with an officer of the Free Norwegian Forces, Olav Magnus Nilsen. They lived in a single room in her mother's house, eventually with three children. In Nilsen's words, his

father 'in the heat and uncertainty of war, married my mother primarily on lustful grounds and ignoring irreconcilable cultural and personality differences which doomed the match to failure'.

During his early years Nilsen was quiet and withdrawn, liable to wander off on his own. He depicts himself as an 'unhappy, brooding child, secretive and stricken with inferiority'. He never saw his father, and remembers nothing of him save a photograph. His grandfather, Andrew Whyte, became his surrogate father and filled his head with tales of a seafarer's life, and this relationship became the core of the young Nilsen's life.

During 1951, Nilsen's grandfather weakened, and on the morning of 31 October his shipmates found him dead in his bunk. Whyte's body was despatched by train to the family home, where it lay in an open coffin amid the lamentations of his relatives and friends.

Nilsen knew something drastic had happened. Aged six, he was ushered into the parlour and lifted up to see the corpse in the coffin. His mother explained that grandfather – his 'father' – was asleep. Everyone cried, and Nilsen experienced a sense of dread and excitement. The next morning he watched a mysterious procession of besuited men troop past the window. He discovered that grandfather had disappeared without waking or saying goodbye, and from that day Andrew Whyte's name was never mentioned.

Nilsen waited patiently for his 'father' to return. He wrote later, 'It is the custom in Fraserburgh that when there is a death in a household they draw the blinds and curtains. When my grandfather died it seemed that these blinds were drawn across my life ... Relatives would pretend that he had gone to "a better place". "Why," I thought, "should he go to a better place and not take me with him?" "So death was a nice thing," I thought. "Then why does it make me miserable?" Father and grandfather had walked out on me, probably to a better place.'

Elsewhere Nilsen wrote of the 'emotional death' that stemmed from this incident. By the age of eight he would sit for hours on the rocks by the sea, watching its shifting patterns to the screech of gulls. He described his near-death by water in an incident that seems half-imagined: 'Many years ago I was a boy drowning in the sea ... The retreat of the wave carried me out further. I panicked, and waved my arms as I submerged. I could hear a loud buzzing in my head and kept gasping for air which wasn't there.

I thought that Grandad was bound to arrive and pull me out. I felt at ease, drugged and dreamlike under the silent green weight of water. I felt myself suspended in a void.'

Later, as a schoolboy, Nilsen helped in the search for an old man from the village who had wandered into the river to a watery grave. He found the corpse. 'He reminded me of my grandfather,' he noted, 'and the images were fixed firmly in my mind … I could never understand the reality of death.'

In a 1993 interview, Nilsen claimed twelve victims rather than the previously accepted figure of fifteen. He says that the misconception arose during an exchange in the police car immediately after his arrest. Asked how many men he had murdered, Nilsen reached for a number, and then stuck by his story to keep the police happy. During the interview, he pinpointed the high point of the killings. It came when he raised the dead bodies up, and their arms splayed back. 'The most exciting part of the little conundrum was when I lifted the corpses,' he recalled. 'It was an affirmation of my power to lift and carry and have control, and the dangling element of the limbs an expression of their passivity.'

Nonce

British prison slang for the lowest of the low, the sex offenders. Everyone needs someone to look down on, and 'nonce' means a nothing, a nonsense, a no one, or a non-thing. Nonces live in constant fear, always insulted and whenever possible pushed, tripped, beaten, burned and stabbed. They are generally segregated in Section 43, a prison within a prison, kept apart for their own protection.

There is a pecking order even for nonces; the sex offender spits on the child molester, in his turn a cut above the child killer. The bottom of the heap is Ian **Brady**, the child killer who tortured his victims. But even Brady found someone lower than himself. In 1967 this wretched individual, Raymond Morris, was convicted of the murder of seven-year-old Christine Darby on Cannock Chase in the West Midlands. Both Brady and Morris were confined to Durham Prison, and on 12 December 1969 Brady poured scalding tea over his inferior, earning himself twenty-eight days in solitary. Afterwards Brady went for Morris at every opportunity, on one occasion pushing him down the

stairs. 'Years later,' said Brady, 'I realised that, in a way, I was attacking myself.'

Norfolk Island

A stain on British history, Norfolk Island was 'the old hell' of the Australian penal colony. After its horrific opening stint under Major Foveaux, the settlement reopened in 1825 as the ultimate in convict degradation. A first-hand account of life under the regime of the new commandant, the sadistic Lieutenant-Colonel Morisset, survives in the memoir of transportee Laurence Frayne, an indomitable Irish thief who arrived on the island in late 1830.

Frayne had already taken fifty lashes for trying to jump ship and another 150 for cursing the overseer; he landed with his untended flesh ripped open, crawling with maggots. He was immediately set to work as a porter, his festering back piled high with heavy gear. 'I really longed for instant death,' he wrote. He soon came up before Morisset on another serious charge: he had broken a flagstone in the quarry. Frayne was awarded a further hundred lashes.

'After the sentence,' the undaunted Frayne recorded, 'I plainly told the Commandant in the Court that he was a Tyrant. He replied that no man had ever said that about him before. I said they knew the consequences too well to tell him so: "But I tell you in stark naked blunt English that you are as great a tyrant as Nero ever was." The moment I expressed these words I was sentenced to an additional 100 and to be kept ironed down in a cell for life and never to see daylight again.'

To allow Frayne's wounds to heal, these 200 lashes were administered over four sessions so that his back could be opened up time and again with special heavy-duty whips. Frayne's flogger was himself threatened with a flailing at any hint of leniency.

Frayne lived, to find himself up before Morisset a few weeks later on the pretext of assault. Again Frayne spoke out: 'It is useless for me to gainsay anything … If you actually knew my innocence yourself, I well know that you would punish me … If you acquit me for the assault you will flog me for what I have now said to you.' Morisset called Frayne a 'damned scoundrel', decreeing a further 300 lashes. Frayne took his life in his hands: 'I am no Scoundrel no more than yourself.'

After his second instalment of 100 lashes they banged Frayne untended into solitary, where he was reduced to pouring his miserly water ration on the floor and urinating into this puddle so that he could lie in a little lake of liquid to ease his agony. 'I was literally alive with Maggots and Vermin,' he noted. Next they cooped him up in a soundproof isolation chamber for two months' solitary and, on emerging, this remarkable man earned 100 supplementary lashes for consorting with women.

Frayne survived Norfolk Island. Others opted for suicide in semi-institutionalised rituals. William Ullathorn, Vicar-General of Australia, summarised the process in 1834: 'Lots were even cast; the man on whom it fell committed the deed, his comrades being witnesses, with the sole view of being taken to Sydney.'

For this temporary respite the men would kill. Convicts banded into co-operative units, about a dozen strong, choosing straws. The two finalists proceeded to a further draw to establish who was the murderer, and who the **murderee**. So one man died, meeting his end in a strange mixture of brutality and nobility: he gave his life that others might live. His attacker was arraigned on a capital charge, but at least he went to Sydney, accompanied by the witnesses, who provided muddling testimony at the trial and hoped for escape.

To end this practice, in September 1833 the authorities instituted kangaroo courts on Norfolk Island to hang the men there. On 15 January 1834 the convicts rose. The rebellion lasted seven hours and cost the lives of five prisoners, with about another fifty crippled. The guards resumed control, instigating months of what can only be described as systematic **torture**.

When fifty-five of the wretches came for trial they begged, in whispers, for death. One man, reprieved with his mates on a former occasion, told the court: 'We wish we had been executed then. It was no mercy to send us to this place. I do not ask for life. I do not want to be spared … Life is not worth living on such terms.'

Fourteen were condemned to be hanged. The men heard the news from Ullathorn, who recounted: 'Those who were to live wept bitterly, whilst those doomed to die, without exception, dropped on their knees, and with dry eyes, thanked God that they were to be delivered from such a place.' Ullathorn noted that the convicts' language had inverted: they transposed 'evil' with 'good', 'virtuous' with 'wicked' and so on. Prisoners habitually blinded themselves so

that they would be left alone as useless human trash, and it is worth remembering that the great majority were initially transported for subsistence thefts of clothes and food.

Norfolk Island improved dramatically under the influence of the penal reformer Alexander **Maconochie**. But in 1843 the settlement plunged back into the dark ages with the appointment of the abhorrent Major Joseph Childs, a flogger who distributed over 1,500 lashes a month.

Of this period the Reverend Thomas Rogers wrote that some mornings, 'The ground on which the men stood at the triangles was saturated with human gore as if a bucket of blood had been spilled on it, covering a space three feet in diameter and running out in various directions in little streams two or three feet long.' July 1846 saw another uprising, and after a hearing where the accused were allowed no representation and called no witnesses, twelve men swung. Then came the worst of all the Australian commandants, John Giles Price, who implemented a routine of savagery beyond anything previously imagined.

Price suffered a fitting retribution. After retiring in 1853 he secured an appointment as Inspector General of the Victoria hulks. Four years later in the quarry at Williamstown, on 26 March 1857, he was surrounded by a crowd of convicts, who closed in to trample, beat, kick and bludgeon him to a dead pulp.

In 2002, Norfolk Island hit the headlines after the murder there of Janelle Paton, the island's first killing for 150 years.

North Marshall Street

America's equivalent of **Rillington Place**. On 25 March 1987 the police, investigating the wild claims of a young hooker, Josefina Rivera, forced their way into 3520 North Marshall Street in a run-down residential district of Philadelphia.

Gary Michael Heidnik, the occupant, surrendered peaceably, mumbling about being late with his alimony payments, and at the station the police relieved their well-heeled captive of $2,000 in cash, numerous credit cards and the documents for four cars, including a Rolls-Royce, a Lincoln and a Cadillac Coupe de Ville.

Heidnik styled himself a Bishop, but only of his own sect, the United Church of the Ministers of God, and in his basement the officers found two semi-naked black women, brutally scarred and chained to a sewer pipe, huddling under a thin blanket. 'Hosanna – we're free,' they shouted, kissing the officer's hands. In a dark pit in the floor, covered by a board, crouched another woman, naked, manacled and handcuffed, too weak to move. A single bulb illuminated the mildewed, littered chamber. Upstairs, where Heidnik had conducted his bouts of sex and torture, was a stack of pornography. In the fridge, near the blackened stove surmounted by a sinister pan, an officer discovered a human forearm.

At his peak, Heidnik housed six women in the downstairs dungeon. He preferred mentally retarded black prostitutes, subjecting them to a routine of thrashings, rape, oral sex and three-in-a-bed sessions. Often he compelled the prisoners to beat each other. Two had perished: the troublesome Deborah Dudley, electrocuted on 18 March, and Sandra Lindsay, who expired on 7 February after swinging from the ceiling by her hands for a week. Heidnik roasted her dismembered body, ground up the remains, and mixed them with dog food in a processor to supplement the survivors' normal diet of gruel. He fed one of the arms intact to the Doberman in his yard.

Heidnik started his collection on 26 November 1986, picking up Josefina Rivera in his Lincoln. At North Marshall Street he clapped on handcuffs, threw her into the basement and outlined his plans for their future. Josefina represented the first of a projected harem of ten black women required to sire his children. 'We'll all be one big happy family,' he told her. 'Society owes me a wife and family.' But Heidnik resorted to extreme duress to keep his captives in order, and took pleasure in it, gouging out their eardrums with a screwdriver (so they could not hear any rescue attempt) and on occasions forcing the women into the pit and filling it with water. By degrees he came to rely on Josefina. She snitched on the others, reporting plans to escape and their disrespectful talk, and beat them to his command. Heidnik liked to watch, and he mistook this arrangement of convenience for a relationship, taking Josefina out for meals or rides in his Rolls. On 23 March they picked up his final captive, Agnes Adams, together. The following day he gave Josefina permission to visit her family on the strict understanding that she returned after setting their minds at rest but, unlike Colleen Stan, the sex-**slave** who endured years of such treatment, Josefina broke her word.

Opening the defence at Heidnik's trial on 20 June 1988, his attorney stated, 'My client is not innocent, he is very, very guilty', and asked for a verdict of insanity. Heidnik came from a broken home and a violent, loveless background. Born in 1943, his parents separated two years later. He last saw his father in 1967, his mother committed suicide in 1970, and in childhood he fell from a tree, injuring his head. It became slightly deformed, giving rise to a school nickname of 'football'. Discharged from the Army at the age of 18 as a schizophrenic with an IQ of 130, Heidnik committed himself to mental hospitals twenty-one times and survived thirteen suicide attempts. He registered his church, a delusion of grandeur, as a charity in 1971. Heidnik did hold services, but also ran it as a front for loan-sharking. Female members of his flock often finished up sharing his bed, two at a time.

An inadequate drawn to inadequates, in his midthirties Heidnik fathered one child by a semi-retarded black woman and helped her sister escape from a mental institution, installing her as a captive in his home where he subjected her to deviant sex. This led to a four-year prison sentence. Released in 1983, he continued to limp towards the goal of a family, impregnating Sandra Lindsay. But she had an abortion. A film, *The World of Susie Wong*, suggested that a compliant Oriental might provide the answer, and he obtained one from a matrimonial agency. A week after the wedding, his wife came back from a shopping expedition to find him bedding three women. She rejected his explanation that this was a standard American custom, and in 1986 brought charges of 'spouse rape'. Still impelled by matrimonial urgings, Heidnik blundered on towards the mirage of connubial harmony through the acquisition of multiple sex-slaves, capturing his first that November.

Heidnik could not hold down a relationship or a job, but one sector of his brain – the part that makes money – remained enviably intact. Within five years of opening a Merrill Lynch account with $1,500, he amassed half a million dollars. Josefina told the court that after making a killing, literally, Heidnik would stop off to check his stocks and shares. On 1 July 1988 he was sentenced to death.

Nuremberg, injustice at

The Americans made a botch of the Nazi executions in October 1946. A Master-Sergeant, John C. Woods, volunteered, putting on a brave face for an interview with the *Stars and Stripes:* 'I did a good job. Everything went Al … I wanted this job so terribly that I stayed here a bit longer.'

Woods had the requisite experience, with 347 hangings to his credit in America over a fifteen-year career. But the trap-door for each of the three specially-built gallows in the Nuremberg gymnasium proved too small, slicing off the noses of the descending Nazi leaders. Nor was the drop long enough. Keitel survived for twenty minutes dangling on the end of the rope, Jodi took eighteen minutes to die, and Ribbentrop ten. Goering attempted to 'cheat the hangman' by taking his own life, but in vain. They hanged his corpse.

The hanging impedimenta were burned. Woods had received an offer of $2,500 for one of the ropes from a souvenir hunter before the executions. Recently discovered documents from KGB files reveal that the corpses of the Nazi warlords were flown overnight to Munich, cremated, and then flown back to Nuremberg. During the return journey the ashes were vented over Germany.

Albert **Pierrepoint**, the famous hangman, was asked by the American United Press Association to contribute a critical review on the botched hangings. He declined, but he did agree to train the post-war Austrian executioners, who were addicted to a short drop, compensating by clinging to the condemned man's legs.

Nor did the Nuremberg trials provide a great advertisement for justice. At first Churchill wanted to shoot the Nazi leadership out of hand, and the political context of the hearings ensured that truth became the first casualty.

It remained so to the last. The authority of Air Chief Marshal Sholto Douglas, head of the Allied Control Commission, to review the sentences was taken out of his hands. The Russians blamed the Nazis for the massacres at Katyn, a fiction nodded through by the judges although Soviet responsibility must have been apparent, and, since the defendants were in the dock for waging a war of aggression, any allusion to Russia's attack on Poland or Finland was taboo, as was the British intervention in Norway.

The twenty-four defendants were selected with haste and negligence. Gustav Krupp, senile and bedridden, was indicted in place of his son Alfred. The duplicate charges against General Jodi served no purpose once General Keitel had been accused. Admiral Raeder and Doenitz landed in the dock, despite accurate evaluations by the British Foreign Office that the German Navy had 'behaved pretty well'. Even though Admiral Chester Nimitz let the side down, testifying that American naval practices were identical with the German, his opposite numbers were jailed.

During cross-examination, Goering was denounced for keeping the troop movements along the east bank of the Rhine secret, and the court could not restrain its mirth when he replied, 'I am not aware that the Americans ever informed us of their mobilisation plan.' Goering could only be tenuously linked to the shooting of escaping RAF officers. But he was a primary architect of the 1938 Munich conference, which temporarily averted war, and he endeavoured to dissuade Hitler from invading Poland the following year. Nevertheless he was found guilty.

Goering may have been repulsive, but it is bad law to condemn a man for crimes other than those with which he is charged; a tendency from which tribunals where the accusers sit as judges are not exempt.

O

Oakes, Sir Harry (1874–1943)

The rich may have more money, but this does not necessarily make them any nicer, and by the time Sir Harry Oakes's gold strike east of Swastika with his partners the Tough Boys made him the richest man in Canada, he lacked friends and social graces.

At smart dinner parties Sir Harry used foul language, whistled under his breath and spat grape-seeds across the table: the oblique legacy of two decades' hard graft, prospecting in Alaska, Canada, the Belgian Congo and Death Valley. But Oakes had to be invited everywhere as uncrowned king of his adopted home, where he maintained half a dozen residences, built a golf course, ran the British Colonial Hotel, and owned a third of New Providence Island, as well as an airline and an air-field. In 1937, the year Oakes settled in the Bahamas, the islands were a one-horse attraction, geared to the upper-crust few, playing host to a meagre 34,000 visitors during a three-month season. But the Bahamas had potential, particularly if gambling was legalised.

It is unlikely that Sir Harry saw it that way. He was happy with his bulldozer, and he went on buying land from the local real estate promoter, Harold Christie, so that he could knock down more trees. As the editor of the *Nassau Times* commented, 'As long as Christie could find something for Sir Harry to destroy, he knew he had a sale.' His other recreational outlet was golf, where he sparred with another unacknowledged king, the Duke of Windsor, posted to the Bahamas as Governor after the outbreak of World War II. The Duke found Bahamian society insufferably dull, and might well have considered a few casinos a welcome diversion.

As would *mafioso* Meyer Lansky, who acquired the gambling concession to Havana's Hotel Nacional in 1937 after a $250,000 bribe to Fulgencio Batista. But the war made life difficult for him. Passenger services to Cuba from the American mainland were in short supply, planes were scarce, and indigenous punters few and far between. From Lansky's perspective, the Bahamas lay nearer to America, were more stable politically, stocked with monied war-wives and Allied personnel, and made a nicer resort. A 1939 amendment to the Bahamas' Lotteries and Gaming Act of 1905 empowered the Duke to grant gaming licences as he saw fit – provided, of course, that its leading citizen, Sir Harry Oakes, assented.

Harold Christie, an astute operator, would have supported the move, like many other legitimate businessmen. For too long the Bahamas had been dependent on the whims of a few rich individuals, and the wartime boom was edging nearer to peacetime bust. Year-round mass tourism would ensure long-term prosperity, and Christie knew the man to put the package together: Meyer Lansky, to whom he ran bootleg liquor in Florida during Prohibition. Christie had access to the Duke and was a close associate of Sir Harry's.

On the night of 7 July 1943, Christie stayed at Westbourne, one of Sir Harry's homes. His host slept two bedrooms down the hall, and the following morning Christie discovered Sir Harry dead in bed, his body partially burned, and his skull fractured by four heavy blows. He had been set alight while alive and, intriguingly, the body was moved after the attack. Found face-up, it had blood from the back of the head running across the face. Mud tracks sullied the main staircase. But Christie declared that he had passed the entire evening and night at Westbourne without hearing a thing.

The killing created headlines round the world, ousting the Allied invasion of Sicily as the lead feature in American newspapers. It seemed that the Duke, who took personal charge of the investigation, delighted in another chance of snatching the lime-light. It is unfair to assume that the resulting bungle was deliberate, but he started on the wrong foot by dispensing with the services of the local police and Scotland Yard, instead summoning two Miami detectives (one of whom, it later transpired, was in the Mob's pay), reputedly asking them to 'confirm the details of a suicide'.

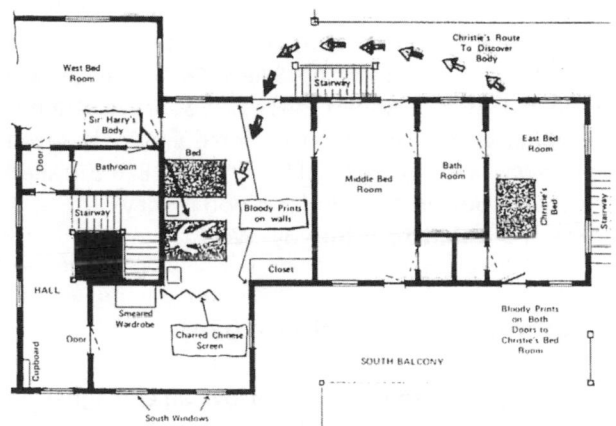

Plan of second storey at Westbourne

Soon an exotic playboy, Count Marie Alfred 'Freddie' Fouqereaux de Marigny, was under arrest, enhancing the case's newsworthiness. The Duke hated Freddie; he had not shown the deference due to an ex-monarch, and his caddish lifestyle represented an affront to the British community. Freddie bolstered his finances by marrying well, owned a speedboat called *Concubine*, was French, and had run off with Sir Harry's daughter when she was 17. In addition, he remarked to a detective, 'That guy, Sir Harry, the old bastard, should have been killed anyway.'

It is reasonably certain that Freddie was framed, perhaps with the Duke's collusion, and the Commissioner of Police, R. A. Erskine-Lindop, was transferred to Trinidad when he balked at pressing charges. This peremptory move prevented Erskine-Lindop from testifying. He would probably have expanded on his 1951 statement to the *Nassau Tribune* that an unnamed suspect, who 'continued to move about in high society … broke down under his cross-examination'. At the trial, the fingerprint evidence looked dubious in the extreme, and Police Captain Edward Sears gave evidence that he saw Christie on the murder night in downtown Nassau, on a route connecting Westbourne and Prince George's Wharf, three blocks from the sea. Sears had a good view of the Christie-lookalike; the two were both at the wheel, driving in opposite directions and passed only a couple of feet apart.

Freddie was discharged, and the murder remains unresolved. Solutions abound, but they are no more than scenarios, mostly orbiting round the casino issue, whereby Sir Harry refused to have his island paradise spoiled and was 'hit' by the Mafia. A Bahamian watchman at Lyford Cay reportedly watched as an unfamiliar, powerful speedboat docked on the night, disembarking two strangers who left before dawn; his story could not be verified because shortly afterwards he was 'found drowned'. Or perhaps Sir Harry and Christie kept a late-night rendezvous with Lansky's men on a boat. Discussions broke down, and Oakes was killed at sea, landed through the mud, and then driven back to Westbourne by a terrorised Christie.

In this version, Oakes's body was burned in ritual desecration to underline the lot of those who thwarted the Mafia, leaving Christie in no doubt that a dire fate awaited him and the Duke if they stepped out of line. The more drastic imputations against the Duke – for instance, that he had Freddie framed to avoid exposure of a proffered bribe for agreeing to legalise gambling – stem from his inexplicable conduct. But that is his hallmark.

Other theories range from robbery-gone-wrong to the exotic voodoo premise expounded by Charles Higham in his biography of the Duchess of Windsor. In this version, Christie imported a Brujeira dwarf from Florida to slaughter Sir Harry (to whom he was in debt) with a pronged fish spear, thus accounting both for the bloody hand-print four feet from the bedroom floor and the unusual wounds. A less exotic **weapon** would be a winch handle with a serrated spindle.

Casting Christie as the killer or witness to the killing has its attractions, and not just because newly declassified FBI documents name him as their front runner from the start. Christie is the most obvious suspect, a sound line to follow with murder. His bed was unrumpled on the morning of 8 July – not slept in, but merely lain on, and either he perjured himself by his insistence that he discovered Sir Harry on his back (and he had thus rearranged the body, or witnessed his rearrangement) or his slumbers, so light on the bedding, made him deaf to all comers.

The casinos finally arrived in 1963, four years after Castro's seizure of power in Cuba made a new locale a financial imperative. Patience is all: they were under Meyer Lansky's control.

Oaths

On 18 July 1816, the London *Times* – then known as 'The Thunderer' – called for an end to 'the horrible trade in blood demands'. This was during the last days of the old reward system. Thief-catchers and police received a capitation fee for the criminals they arrested, and the worse the crime, the greater the reward.

Thief-catchers were no fools and recognised that it made commercial sense to nurse a criminal along until he did something serious; the more avaricious would, through an intermediary, set up a dupe to commit a capital offence and then seize him, literally making a killing. Forty pounds was the price for death, 'weighing forty' the phrase as informers assessed a villain's worth.

The 1816 case which shocked the nation involved three Irish lads, Reardon, Quinn and Thomas Connell. Approached in London's Cheapside Market, they were offered work by Barry (the criminal intermediary). 'My master has plenty of employment for some smart fellows,' said Barry, 'but it is very *hard* work ... there is some *hazard* in it.' One of the boys replied: 'So has every kind of work; mounting a ladder five storeys high, with a heavy hod of mortar is attended with great hazard; but an Irish labourer does not care much for danger.'

Barry exacted a vow of secrecy: 'My master would not hire anyone, but such as will take a solemn oath that if he leaves the work, he will never speak about it.' Installed in a hired room, the boys were issued with base metal, files, scissors and tools and instructed to make things looking ominously like shillings. The penalty for forgery was death; they suddenly grasped their predicament and tried to leave, saying it was lunch-time. Barry countered that food was on its way. Meanwhile, police officer Brock obtained a search-warrant and together with Barry's contact, Constable Power, made the arrest. The boys went on trial for their lives.

The stark choice between a hanging and dishonouring their oaths was hardly an issue. As good Catholics the boys kept their word, offered no defence and were duly sentenced to death in Barry's presence. But Sir Matthew Wood, Chief Magistrate, overheard a chance remark during the trial and, discovering the obstacle, thought of the remedy. He summoned a priest, who assured the youths that in the circumstances their vows were not indissoluble. Thus the conspirators were exposed and, remarkably, the boys returned to Ireland with sufficient funds (from a subscription organised by Wood) to buy a smallholding.

The reputation of the London police had never been lower. There were not many of them, and most were corrupt. Little came of the Select Committee established in 1816, but Robert Peel's first abortive attempt to set up a centralised police force was only seven years away, and his Criminal Law Act of 1826 curtailed the courts' powers to disburse blood money.

See also **Ratcliffe Highway**, **Wild**

O'Bannion, Dion (1892–1924)

Chicago gang leader portrayed by James Cagney in *Public Enemy* and eventually eliminated, possibly by Capone, after an impressive sting. Born in Chicago's Little Hell, just by Death Corner, O'Bannion was noted for his fixed smile which remained in place even while he shot you. With one leg four inches shorter than the other, he was psychologically asymmetric: a bootlegger who deplored alcohol, a racketeer who eschewed prostitution, and an expert florist credited with twenty-five killings.

On his way up, O'Bannion served a stint as a singing waiter in McGovern's Cafe. At the top, he was Chicago's most dangerous mob-leader, carrying the North Side as well as three guns in his specially tailored pockets: one in his trousers, one in his overcoat and one under his armpit. Capone considered him cocky and impulsive, instancing O'Bannion's grudge shooting of Dave Miller in the La Salle Theater foyer on the first night of a musical comedy, but he received civic recognition at a 1924 banquet thrown in his honour by the Democrats. In addition to a shining galaxy of thugs, bodyguards, hitmen, plug-uglies, bludgeon men, bootleggers and pimps, the O'Bannion feast (the first blatant linking of politics and gangsterdom) was attended by upholders of Prohibition like the Chief of Detectives, police lieutenants, a County Clerk, a Commissioner of Public Works, a Union President and Secretary, an Assistant State Attorney and numerous

Chicago bootlegger Dion O'Bannion was said to look just as composed as he pumped bullets into you

other lesser police and politicians who, after downing quantities of illegal whisky, wooed O'Bannion to the Democrats' cause with a platinum watch encrusted with rubies and diamonds. It was money and effort wasted. Come the day, O'Bannion and his boys backed the Republicans.

In early 1924 he heard word that the Feds were moving to close the important Sieben Brewery, hitherto supervised by the precinct police. O'Bannion blithely told Capone and Torrio that he was contemplating retirement, and sold them his share in the brewery for $500,000. To allay suspicion, he arranged for a handover at Sieben's at the exact time of the raid. Any sooner, and the deal would abort; any later, and O'Bannion would go irritatingly scot-free.

The **Prohibition agents** hit the site on 19 May as soon as the money changed hands, grabbing Torrio and O'Bannion along with thirteen truckloads of beer. Despite a proffered $50,000 bribe, eleven defendants had to suffer the unusual inconvenience of a court hearing. But O'Bannion was not among them. Torrio smelt a rat, and exacted retribution.

At noon on 10 November 1934, O'Bannion was idling in his **flower** shop opposite the cathedral, clipping the stems from a bunch of chrysanthemums. Three customers entered. O'Bannion recognised them and turned to his young porter, saying, 'The floor's in a mess, Bill. Better brush all those leaves and petals up', and went forward, secateurs in one hand, the other arm outstretched in greeting. He shook hands with his killer, who did not let go.

Thus immobilised, O'Bannion was shot twice in the chest, twice in the throat, once through the cheek and then, sprawled among the lilies, in the head. A few days later one of his buddies, Two-gun (or sometimes Three-gun) Louis Alterie, issued a public challenge to the murderers to shoot it out fair and square on the corner of State and Madison Streets; Alterie was fresh in from the West and a life as a cowboy. Mayor Dever protested, 'Are we living by the code of the Dark Ages?'

O'Bannion's killers were almost certainly the Sicilian 'torpedoes' **Anselmi and Scalise**. As a minor refinement, they prepared for assignments by rubbing their bullets with garlic in the belief that this enhanced the likelihood of their victims' wounds turning gangrenous.

Oesterreich, Walburga (b. 1867)

A queer Californian case from 1922. The story started nineteen years before, when the redoubtable Walburga Oesterreich already felt disenchanted with her husband, Fred, a slave-driving drunk who owned a Milwaukee apron factory. In 1903 he hired a new repairman: an undersized, introverted 17-year-old, Otto Sanhuber.

Walburga, then 36, took a fancy to the newcomer. First the sewing-machines in the factory broke down continually; then the one in Walburga's bedroom malfunctioned. Otto started paying home calls, and soon Walburga's Singer needed his ministrations so regularly that her husband became jealous. He suggested that Walburga buy a new sewing-machine. 'No, I like this one,' she said firmly, and set off with Otto, by now her lover, for a protracted tour of Chicago and St Louis. Fred had them tailed, infuriating Walburga, and she cracked him over the head with a silver candlestick on her return.

Walburga realised that the only way to ensure that she was not followed when visiting her lover was for him to move in. So one day in 1905, while Fred went to work, Walburga installed Otto in the loft of their large mustard-coloured Milwaukee home, and there this shy, retiring man spent his next seventeen years. Walburga scratched three times on the ceiling when she wanted him, ascending through a trap-door in the master bedroom ceiling.

By day, Walburga lived with Otto. By night, she lived with Fred. So everything happened at different times, but in the same place, although there were occasional changes of scene when the Oesterreichs and Otto moved house. The three finished up in North St Andrews Place in Los Angeles.

Sometimes Fred heard scufflings overhead or noticed that this or that had been moved. His cigars kept disappearing and drink vanished at an alarming rate. Provisioning Otto was a major undertaking. Walburga ferried up armfuls of tinned meat, milk, bottled beer, canned fish, vegetables, bread, bolognas, whole liverwursts and entire cheeses. Otto's career provided another challenge, but convention has always allowed an outlet for solitary men of no particular aptitude confined to attics. They become writers, and after eleven years of rejection slips Otto's intensely visualised tales of sacred and profane love in the South Seas were eagerly sought by editors of pulp fiction.

When Fred heard things go bump in the night, Walburga responded with references to an infestation of rats, and his bewilderment at the way food seemed to eat itself made her heap scorn on his drunkard's memory. Finally, out in the garden, Fred swore that he discerned a face peering through the dusty attic window. This drove Walburga into a derisive frenzy.

The years passed, the First World War came and went, the Oesterreich Garment Company flourished. Then on 22 August 1922, Fred came back early from work and fell into an argument with Walburga while Otto, caught short, was downstairs. Intervening, he shot Fred dead with four bullets from his .25, a gift from Walburga.

Walburga called the police, explaining that her adored spouse, by now a millionaire, had been gunned down by a burglar. She was not believed. The .25-calibre weapon was a 'lady's gun' avoided by professional crooks, and everyone knew that Walburga detested her husband. She was arrested on suspicion after imprudently giving her lawyer, Herman Shapiro, a distinctive diamond-studded ring that she claimed had been stolen during the robbery.

In prison, Walburga sent for her attorney and asked him to call at her house, go to the bedroom, open the cupboard door, and scratch three times on a panel above a shelf. Then, Walburga explained, her ne'er-do-well half-brother in the attic would appear. Shapiro was to assure him that all was well.

But when pale Otto emerged, the truth came tumbling out; after nearly twenty years he was probably glad to talk to someone. Otto confessed to the shooting. What should he do? The attorney advised him to leave town. Otto did, settling in Portland, Oregon, where he married a compliant stenographer who accepted his selective **amnesia** covering the years from 1903 to 1922. Meanwhile, without Otto, the circumstantial case against Walburga folded.

Another seven years passed. By now Shapiro feared for his own life. Walburga had taken to paying threatening calls to his office, and he lodged an affidavit revealing the truth about Fred Oesterreich's murder.

In 1930 Otto and Walburga were indicted. Otto was tried first, and the jury convicted him of the lesser crime of manslaughter, an offence covered by a three-year Statute of Limitations. As the trial was out of time, Otto could not be guilty since he could not be prosecuted, and Walburga was absolved on account of the previous finding that Fred had been killed by Otto. In her declining years, she lost all her money and lived above a garage in the Wilshire district of Los Angeles.

Officer material

The **Kray** twins' unusual military career merits attention. Fierce and vicious fighters, they came from London's East End, an area largely beyond the law even in the 1950s. National Service provided the novel taste of an authority larger than their own: army discipline.

On 2 March 1952, their first day with the Royal Fusiliers, the brothers cut short a corporal's exposition on the virtues of highly polished boots. 'We don't care for it here,' they announced. 'We're off home to see our Mum.' The corporal grabbed one of the boys; they knocked him down and arrived home in time for tea. After recapture the next morning, each twin blamed the other, and the pair got off lightly with a week in the guardroom. On release, they went AWOL again, only to find that their diet of bar brawls at home palled after a couple of weeks. So when a policeman spotted them in a Mile End café, the twins meekly returned to the fray at the Fusiliers.

After their next sojourn in detention, the Krays beat up a sergeant. Separating the pair produced adverse results. Reggie honed his left hook on NCOs while Ronnie refused to shave or wear his uniform. Their next cells, in Colchester's Detention Barracks, supplied the twins' first encounter with hardened criminals, making a future of armed robbery a serious option.

The twins escaped again, were recaptured, and broke out once more, on Christmas Eve. A Constable Fisher spotted them in Mile End's 'Red Gaff' and, after offering to come quietly, they roughed him up and ran off. Collared a few weeks later, they served a month in the Scrubs before being locked in the Howe Barracks guardroom to await military trial. The worst they faced was a Dishonourable Discharge preceded by another spell in prison – exactly what they fancied.

So Ronnie and Reggie settled down to enjoy themselves. On their first day, after smashing the cell furniture, they ripped their bedding and uniforms into tiny shreds. When the colour sergeant arrived to restore discipline, the twins emptied the latrine bucket over his head. Caged up, they demanded water, and handcuffed the guard's outstretched wrists to the bars; it took an hour to cut him free. They burned their replacement bedding and uniforms, earning a drenching with fire hoses, and the following morning clambered on to the roof for a sing-song. But still they longed for home. Dressing up neat, they told the guards they were leaving, asked to visit the lavatory, put their escort in a necklock, stole the guardroom keys and broke out again.

Rather than lock the Krays away for five expensive years, the Army called a truce. A court martial on 11 June 1953 condemned the twins to spend their nine remaining months of military service in prison at Shepton Mallet, where they completed their criminal education.

The only soldier to overawe the Krays was a languid, upper-class cavalry captain, who interrupted the pair mid-rant: 'I know perfectly well what you're up to and it's all right by me. But for God's sake, *do* stop making such a bloody row. You'll frighten the horses.' In a seminal incident the year before their conscription, Ronnie was arrested for punching a constable on the jaw outside Pellici's café. The fight ended before

Reggie could come to his aid. Rather than let his twin down, Reggie spent the rest of the day hunting the policeman and, the moment he could, assaulted him. Thus did Reggie wangle his way *into* his brother's dungeon, a psychological pattern repeated in the years to come.

Oklahoma Bombing, The

On 19 April 1995 – on the second anniversary of the federal raid that led to the killing of most of David Koresh's Branch Davidian cult at the **Waco siege** – a bomb, hidden in a parked truck, demolished most of the Alfred P. Murrah Federal Building in Oklahoma City. One hundred and sixty-eight people were killed, including nineteen children in a crèche on the ground floor. Over five hundred people were injured in the blast.

(Some have suggested that the terrorist bomb was not the only cause of the disaster. Witnesses claimed to have heard a secondary explosion after the first and some claim that this was an armoury, maintained illegally in the public building by the federal authorities, that had been caused to explode by the bomb. This claim has been flatly denied by the FBI.)

The ruins of the Alfred P. Murrah Federal Building in Oklahoma City

One British tabloid newspaper echoed the suspicions of many in the immediate aftermath of the Oklahoma bombing, printing a full-page photograph of the shattered building under the headline 'IN THE NAME OF ALLAH', the suggestion being that Islamic terrorists had been responsible. It came as something of a shock to many, therefore, when investigators arrested American Gulf War veteran Timothy McVeigh.

McVeigh turned out to be a gun enthusiast and ultra-right-wing 'survivalist' (a highly mixed bag of libertarians, racists, fundamentalist Christians and some out-and-out paranoids who claim the US federal authorities and/or the United Nations are plotting to destroy the USA). He immediately confessed to the bombing, citing his opposition to federal gun-control laws as his motive. He also believed that the FBI had deliberately murdered the Branch Davidians in Waco; hence his choice of the anniversary of the end of the Waco siege to set off the Oklahoma bomb. McVeigh said that he regretted the deaths of the children, and would have chosen another target had he known there was a crèche in the building, but regarded the bombing as a legitimate act of war against a repressive regime.

Soldierly to the end, McVeigh requested the death sentence and flatly refused to string out his time on Death Row with appeals or insanity claims. He was executed on 11 June 2001.

Omerta

Strictly speaking, omerta means the ability to be a man, a key concept of the Sicilian Mafia. It involves double moral standards: those inside the group must be treated well whereas those outside are fair game, subject to false omerta (feigned courtesy, masking, for instance, the intent to deceive or kill).

Similarly, the ideal Sicilian male is virile, whereas the perfect woman is a virgin; there is an inherent contradiction here. In Sicily, either quality – virility and virginity – could be easily misplaced, the former by any momentary default in responding appropriately to a threat touching personal honour, and the latter in the usual way. But sexual honour might also be forfeit by a broken engagement, with its imputation that the intended bride was unworthy to be a wife.

Within the household, the two qualities were complementary: the men's virility shielded the women's virginity, and the women's virginity proclaimed their menfolk's virility. But beyond the family, all was marauding mayhem. Between 1940 and 1950, more than 60 per cent of Mafia murders in Calabria were sexually inspired.

A man could earn respect (uomo di rispetto) – no matter how humble his origins – by demonstrating omerta. The pursuit of honour was a democratic business; hence its appeal for the poor to whom no other avenues were open.

Today, omerta denotes **silence**. This is because, in Sicily, it was manly to stay quiet; in a society of oppressive injustice, little was gained by complaining. For almost thirty years in America, from Luciano's establishment of the 'Commission' in 1931 right through to the 1960s, if a gangster talked, he died. Some 5,000 mafiosi went through their lives, and even to their deaths, adhering to this doctrine in the face of law enforcement entreaties to co-operate.

Things are different now. In 1993 Sammy the Bull Gravano, former underboss of the Gambino family, occupied Court 318 on New York's Centre Street, testifying against his former associates, and the prospect that he will be hunted down by omniscient hoods seems remote.

See also **Decline**, **Inquisition**, **Murder Inc.**, **Vendetta**

One-way ride

Everything, no matter how mundane, has to be invented by someone and tested on someone else. In July 1921, Steve Wisiewski, picked up in Chicago's Maxwell Street ghetto, received an experimental 'one-way ride', the world's first, all the way to Libertyville twenty-five miles north of the city, where his body turned up the next day. The term was coined by the leading labour racketeer Big Tim Murphy, shot in 1928.

Wisiewski paid the price for hijacking a consignment of beer, becoming the first of Prohibition Chicago's 703 gangland killings.

Onoprienko, Anatoly

On the morning of Sunday 7 April 1996, police investigator Igor Khuney, in the Ukrainian town of Yavoriv, received a phone call from a man called Pyotr Onoprienko, complaining about his cousin Anatoly, who had until recently lived in his home. Pyotr had ejected him after finding a stock of firearms in his room, and Anatoly had threatened to 'take care' of Pyotr's family at Easter – which happened to be that day. Would the police go and see Anatoly? He was, said Pyotr, living with a woman in nearby Zhitomirskaya.

This caught Khuney's attention, for he had recently been informed of the theft of a shotgun in that area. And in recent months there had been an outbreak of appalling murders of whole families, most of them involving a rifle. On an intuition, Khuney's superior, Sergei Kryukov, decided to go and see Onoprienko. He took a squad of twenty policemen with him in squad cars.

They were taking no chances. When a small, balding man with piercing blue eyes opened the door, he was swiftly overpowered. Asked for identification, he led them to a closet, then, as a policeman opened the door, he dived for a pistol, but failed to reach it.

Anatoly Onoprienko, Ukrainian mass murderer

When Onoprienko's lady friend came home from church with her two small children, Kryukov told her that they thought her lover might be the suspected mass murderer, and she broke down and wept.

In police custody, Onoprienko refused to speak until he was questioned by a general. But when one was brought, he confessed that he had used the stolen shotgun in a recent murder. Then admissions to more than fifty murders came pouring out.

The mass murders began on Christmas Eve 1995, in the small village of Garmarnia, in central Ukraine, near the Polish border. A killer entered the home of a forester named Zaichenko, and killed the man, his wife

and two sons with a sawn-off double-barrelled hunting rifle. He stole a few items of jewellery and a bundle of clothes, then set the house on fire.

Five nights later he slaughtered another family of four – a young man, his wife and her twin sisters. It was again in a remote village, Bratkovychi, near the Polish border. He stole items of gold jewellery and an old jacket, and set fire to the house.

During the next three months there were eight similar attacks in two villages; twenty-eight people died and one woman was raped. In Enerhodar, seven were killed. The killer returned to Bratkovychi on 17 January 1996, to murder a family of five. In Fastov, near Kiev, he killed a family of four. In Olevsk, four women died. His usual method was to shoot the men, knife the women and bludgeon children to death. There was panic, and an army division began to patrol the villages. An enormous manhunt was mounted – even greater than for Andrei **Chikatilo**.

Anatoly Onoprienko, a 36-year-old former mental patient, went on to confess to a total of fifty-two murders. On one occasion, he admitted, he had raped a woman after shooting her in the face. On another, he had approached a young girl who had fallen on her knees to pray after seeing him kill her parents. He asked her to tell him where they kept the money, and she stared in his eyes and said defiantly, 'No.' Onoprienko killed her by smashing her skull; but he admitted that he was impressed by her courage.

Orphaned by the death of his mother when he was very young, Onoprienko felt a lifelong resentment against his father for agreeing to keep his brother while consigning him to an orphanage.

Onoprienko insisted that he felt nothing whatever during the murders. 'To me, killing people is like ripping up a duvet,' he told journalist Mark Franchetti, in his tiny prison cell in Zhitomir, where his trial had been held. He described how he had committed his first act of violence in his twenties, shooting a deer in the woods. But he felt sorry and upset to see the dead animal. 'I never had that feeling again,' he told Franchetti.

He also told how he had met a man called Sergei Rogozhin at a local gym in 1989, and the two began burgling homes to supplement their meagre incomes. One day they were interrupted by the householder and his wife. To escape, they killed both of them and their eight children.

As happens so often with mass murderers, it quickly became a powerful appetite.

In 1989, he said, 'driven by a rage at God and Satan', he had killed a couple standing by their Lada car on a motorway. He also killed five people in a car, then sat in the car for two hours, wondering what to do with the corpses, which quickly began to smell.

But the act of killing, he insisted, gave him no pleasure. On the contrary, he felt oddly detached from it. 'I watched all this as an animal would stare at a sheep,' he told police in a confession videotaped in 1997, 'I perceived it all as a kind of experiment. There can be no answer in this experiment to what you're trying to learn.' He said he felt like both perpetrator and spectator.

Onoprienko claimed that he was driven by some unknown force, and that voices ordered him to kill. 'I'm not a maniac,' he told Franchetti. 'I have been taken over by a higher force, something telepathic or cosmic, which drove me.' But he had to wait for this force to give him orders. 'For example, I wanted to kill my brother's first wife, because I hated her. I really wanted to kill her, but I couldn't, because I had to receive the order first. I waited for it, but it did not come.

'I am like a rabbit in a laboratory, a part of an experiment to prove that man is capable of murdering and learning to live with his crimes. It is to show that I can cope, that I can stand anything, forget anything.'

His trial began in Zhitomir in late November 1998. The delay was due to the fact that the authorities could not afford to try him, because his crimes had covered such a wide area. Eventually, after two years, his judges went on television to appeal for funds, and the Ukrainian government contributed the £30,000 for the trial.

Like Chikatilo, Onoprienko was kept in a metal cage in the courtroom. Sergei Rogozhin, accused of being an accomplice in nine of the killings, stood trial with him. It emerged that Onoprienko had spent three months in a Kiev mental hospital, where he had been diagnosed as schizophrenic. It was after his release that he had started his killing spree.

The trial ended four months later, on 31 March 1999, when Onoprienko was found guilty and sentenced to death. Rogozhin received thirteen years' imprisonment. Since there is a moratorium on capital punishment in his country, Onoprienko may never be executed. Leonid Kuchma, the Ukrainian president, spoke of temporarily lifting the moratorium in order to execute Onoprienko, who declared that, if ever released, he would immediately go back to killing.

Onorevole

More to do with strength than honour. Being *onorevole* was the other concept underpinning the Sicilian Mafia's code of conduct; it can be translated roughly as 'violently touchy'. Any successful act of aggression was *onorevole*, and the more aggressive the better. The traditional bandit Marlino Zappa attracted veneration because 'he wasn't violent as a rule, but when he had to be, then he amazed everyone, he stunned his enemies'.

Mafiosi always behave honourably; that is, they attain honour through violence. In Pitré's words from the turn of the century: 'The *mafioso* is simply a brave man, someone who will put up with no provocation … The Mafia is a certain consciousness of one's own being, an exaggerated notion of individual force and strength.'

In Sicily, those without honour were often physically segregated from the rest of the community. The writer Asprea describes a Calabrian village in the 1930s where the besmirched outcasts were cordoned off like lepers: 'To the south of *il Calvario* was *il Pilieri*. There, alongside the main sewer of the town was a string of huts, battered by the east wind.' These smoke-blackened hovels gave refuge to the most wretched dregs, feeble-hearted men whose defenceless womenfolk (and children) were at the mercy of anyone more powerful. Andrea described the killing of Pepinello, a prostitute's child from Oppido Mamertina, who was retained by local youths as a target for their shooting competition.

Failure to pursue a **vendetta** provided one sure means of forfeiting any claim to social standing. But it was not a bad plan. Before taking revenge on the violator of a daughter or on your wife's lover (for which you would die in turn), convention demanded you first dispose of your sullied offspring or unfaithful wife. For the squeamish, emigration provided the only way out.

See also **Contempt**

Opium

A drug with an extraordinary history. In nineteenth-century Britain, opium ('laudanum') was regarded as a relaxant, good for headaches or spicing up the after-dinner port. Devotees included Wordsworth, Coleridge, peasant women and babes-in-arms. In America, opium – known as the 'Mongolian curse' – reached San Francisco in 1853 along with the coolies working the railroads; by 1870, the town boasted a good 200 opium dens. Twenty-four were lavish joints with silk-lined bunks catering exclusively for whites, notably society matrons and their rich daughters.

Fortunately, as the grim facts of addiction emerged in the second half of the century, so did the cure, in the form of the opium derivative, morphine. When it transpired that this was no less habit-forming, doctors were relieved by the 1898 discovery of a heroic antidote to contain the morphine epidemic.

The new wonder-drug, heroin, not only weaned patients from their morphine dependence; it was, according to German chemists, a panacea for bronchitis and tuberculosis. By the turn of the century Bayer distributed heroin in a dozen countries, and in 1906 the American Medical Association approved it for general use. It acquired tens of thousands of followers through patent medicines like Dover's Powders or Sydenham's Syrup, and by the early 1920s, New York had 250,000 addicts, allegedly responsible for 95 per cent of the city's crime.

Opium has long been an instrument of national policy, political for the Americans and commercial for the British who, in the nineteenth century, became the largest organised drug traffickers in history, targeting China as their most profitable market. In 1800, 200 tons of Indian opium were shipped to China, a figure increased tenfold by 1840, and forty years later imports stood at 6,500 tons, supporting some 100 million users and 15 million addicts. Not until 1906 did the House of Commons pronounce the trade immoral, and opium was not banned in Hong Kong until 1946.

Decades before, Chinese smokers and licensed Chinese opium merchants had spread throughout South-east Asia, deriving additional stimulus from French colonial policies in Vietnam. This long-standing co-existence of the means of production and supply (an interlinked network of growers, Chinese traffickers and **Triad** distributors) ensured that opium became an ingrained part of South-east Asia's social fabric. Inevitably, any major player in the region was enmeshed in the heroin trade, and none more deeply than the CIA, who promoted the **Golden Triangle** into the world's foremost centre of opium production.

In 1945 the area yielded a hundred tons a year piecemeal. Within fifteen years, CIA policies had raised output by a factor of seven.

The post-war Truman administration wanted a bulwark against communist contagion, and in 1949 America backed the refugee troops fleeing from revolutionary China to northern Burma, arming and provisioning them through the CIA's Air America. But northern Burma was the Cradle of Opium and, once ensconced, the soldiers mutated into the world's largest private heroin armies.

Their leader, General Li, launched a couple of abortive strikes against China in 1951 and 1952. Meanwhile, he found himself commanding well-equipped forces in lawless territory. First Li extended his control throughout the Shan States. Then he taxed the hill tribes, then he taxed the smugglers, then he laid on protection for the smugglers, and finally he became a trafficker himself – buying direct, organising plantations, working hand-in-hand with the Triads. Still receiving CIA backing, he boosted production from its modest level of forty tons in 1949 to 350 tons within a decade. With 10,000 troops at his disposal, armed with the latest American weapons, General Li met the CIA's requirements for an anti-communist buffer state.

It was the same pattern elsewhere. In Laos, after Kennedy cut off the country's monthly drip-feed of $3 million aid in 1961, the CIA maintained their nominee (the right-wing Phoumi Nosavan) in power with funds raised through the opium trade. Taking the backward Laotian narcotics industry by the scruff of the neck, the American military encouraged farmers to cultivate opium and oversaw the crop. Output increased tenfold, to 200 tons a year. In Thailand, the CIA's principal government contact, Chief of Police General Phao Sriyanonda, went into partnership with the Triads to run the drugs business. Phao became a massive trafficker himself, inculcating widespread corruption, and when he took refuge in Switzerland in 1957 the Triads stepped into his shoes and into the regime, monopolising the trade.

Today, America reaps the harvest. As its forces poured into Vietnam, the dealers realised that here was a whole new mass market. In 1970 the Cholon Triad sponsored a test campaign, feeding the troops with free samples of injectable heroin; even when money changed hands, it was a pittance, with 99 per cent pure vials at five dollars. By mid-1971 some 40,000

GIs were hooked, and the Hong Kong Triads (the 14K and the Wo Shing Wo) were so impressed that they sent official observers to learn the business. The war's end saw 100,000 soldier-addicts; and the Triads, already billions of dollars to the good, viewed the American withdrawal with some chagrin.

Then the Triads regrouped under the far-sighted guidance of the Ma brothers from China's Chiu Chau region. Their customers might have left, but they had not ceased to exist. Why not establish a distribution network to trail the retreating troops home and supply the American market? And why stop there? Why not feed the world?

Hence today's international heroin traffic, dominated by billionaire Triads.

Optographs

In 1881, Professor Willi Kuhne of Heidelberg University peered into the eyes of a dead frog and discerned, etched on its retina, a faint impression of his laboratory bunsen burner. The frog had gazed fixedly at the flame before it died, and thus the professor could see an image of the last thing the frog saw.

Professor Kuhne realised that the criminological implications would be immense if the same held true for human beings: a deceased's eyes might 'photograph' his assailant. Kuhne could not conduct experiments on people, but he systematically repeated his work on frogs, confirming that images of bright, high-contrast objects remain imprinted on the retina for half an hour after death. The same applied to rabbits, and it was for this reason that in 1888 the British police took an 'optograph' of **Jack the Ripper**'s last victim, just in case.

To no avail. Nevertheless the legend of optographic images passed into criminal folklore. It inspired the grisly shooting of PC George William **Gutteridge** on 27 September 1927, and as late as 1947 an investigative photographer from California begged the coroner to release the Black Dahlia's eyeballs (see **False Confessions**) so that he could obtain a likeness of her murderer.

Research from the 1980s by Professors Sandheim and Alexandridis of Heidelberg suggests that people do 'photograph' the last thing they see. But the images, very poor at best, blur after the first half hour. Successful detection requires prompt development with specialised techniques, and a frontal assailant who remains immobile at length in bright sunlight.

Oral hygiene treatment

Invented by the Austrian nurse Waltraud Wagner at Vienna's Leinz hospital. Wagner devised her 'oral hygiene treatment' as a counter-measure to the interminable misery and suffering of her elderly charges.

In Britain, a concoction known as the 'Brompton Mixture', consisting of morphia, codeine, alcohol and syrup, provided a popular but informal method of euthanasia. During the final stages of terminal disease a large bottle was placed by the patient's bedside, with a warning that on no account should he or she drink it for fear of fatal consequences.

The medical profession at large, with its power to mete out life and death, has spawned its fair share of murderers. Pre-eminent among them is the industrious Dr Clarke Hyde of Kansas. Married to a niece of Thomas Swope, the millionaire founder of Kansas City, Hyde counted a total of seven relatives – surely a manageable total – interposed between him and inheritance, and in 1909 he set to work.

Swope perished in October, followed to the grave by his financial adviser James Hunton. Five brothers- and sisters-in-law fell ill from a familial epidemic of typhoid, and Chrisman Swope expired under Hyde's care. Suspicions against Hyde hardened when the condition of the survivors markedly improved during his absence on a trip to New York. He was followed, and observed discarding a capsule from his pocket which, on analysis, smelled of cyanide, as did the body of Thomas Swope after exhumation. Hyde was found guilty of murder, but a well-funded defence contrived his release in 1917.

Hyde's motive was clear, as is the ostensible element of perverted 'mercy-killings' for Waltraud Wagner. More obscure was the compulsion animating Britain's Nurse Beverley Allitt, who in February 1993 was charged with twenty-six counts of murder, attempted murder and causing grievous bodily harm. She worked on Ward 4 of the Grantham and Kesteven Hospital, where four children inexplicably died between February and April 1991. The body of the first victim, five-month-old Paul Crampton, contained a huge amount of **insulin**, and the duty roster showed that none of the twenty-five suspicious collapses occurred when Nurse Allitt was not on duty.

See also **In-laws**, **Münchausen**

Orfila, Joseph Bonaventure (b. 1787)

Father of modern toxicology. Orfila discovered his purpose in life halfway through a chemistry lecture to his students in April 1813. After summarising the standard tests for arsenious acid, he turned to his practical demonstration. It did not work.

At his bench after class, Orfila verified that most of the orthodox chemical tests for the better-known poisons were worthless. Toxic residues could not be detected in food, drink or bodies; the most reliable forensic indicator was to feed an animal with an extract of the suspect substance and see if it died. Orfila rapidly ascertained that no one knew anything. He wrote: 'The central fact that struck me had never been perceived by anyone else. My first words were these: *toxicology does not yet exist.*'

Orfila was a child prodigy. Born in a school-free Minorcan village, by the age of 14 he had mastered five languages and written a Latin thesis on philosophy. After a brief interlude as a sailor he won a chemistry scholarship to Barcelona and then took a medical degree in Paris. There he eked out his slender resources by teaching – hence his fateful lecture on poison.

Ambitious and energetic, Orfila signed up a bookseller to take on a two-volume textbook, *Treatise on Poison, or General Toxicology*, published that same year. Like today's unfathomable *Brief History of Time*, the title became a surprise best-seller and Orfila found himself catapulted into social prominence. He married well in 1815 and three years later was appointed professor in 'mental maladies' to the Paris Medical Faculty. As well as putting toxicology on a scientific footing, Orfila became a celebrated expert witness, perhaps most notably in the 1840 case of the romantic young Marie Lafarge.

The drawback with arsenic is that it does not readily dissolve, and when Marie Lafarge gave her husband a cup of poisoned milk after he became indisposed from poisoned cake, their maid noticed white flakes floating on the surface. The girl, Anna Brun, saw Marie surreptitiously taking pinches of white powder from a malachite box, and carried the milk dregs to the local doctor. Nine days after Charles Lafarge died on 16 January 1840 from an obscure gastric ailment, Marie was under arrest.

She cut an attractive and newsworthy figure, particularly when contrasted to her uncouth husband. Marie was well-born, of royal descent through an illegitimate line, and her cousin had married the Vicomte de Léautaud. Orphaned at the age of 18, Marie viewed with reserve the exertions of a wealthy aunt to offload her on to a suitable husband. The first contender, a local sub-prefect, did not correspond to her aristocratic expectations. But in 1839 a matrimonial agency proposed a candidate purportedly matching her 90,000-franc dowry. This was Charles Lafarge. He may have looked like a fat, crude rustic, but he was billed as a man of fortune, an ironmaster with 200,000 francs of property and an annual income of 30,000 francs.

The ill-matched pair were married in August that year, and a protesting Marie was dragged away to the social wastes of deepest Limousin. In her words, 'Upon arriving at Le Glandier, instead of the charming chateau I had been led to expect, I found a dilapidated ruin.' Her fashionable aspirations were utterly confounded. Her husband was a bankrupt, his family were peasants, and their farmhouse crawled with rats. A distraught Marie refused to consummate the marriage, and as the year progressed she discovered that her spouse, in his efforts to raise money, forged her signature, and that her mother-in-law had tampered with her will. At **Christmas** she sent Charles, on business in Paris, a large arsenic cake, and he died three weeks later.

The murder case was preceded by a preliminary trial for the theft of a diamond necklace which vanished from Léautaud's chateau while Marie was a guest. High-society allegations of Marie's kleptomania and compulsive lying monopolised the French headlines for months before she arrived to face capital charges in Tulle on 3 September 1840 as a convicted thief. The local chemist attested that he found arsenic traces in the fatal glass of milk and in the malachite box, as well as in her husband's stomach and vomit.

The defence consulted Orfila. He refuted the prosecution's case: the yellow precipitates discovered to be soluble in ammonia were not necessarily arsenic, and although boiling the dead man's stomach was said to have produced metallic deposits on the arsenic 'mirror' this could not be validated in court because the apparatus had exploded. Nor had the prosecution heard of the much more sensitive Marsh test, discovered ten years previously.

With their arguments in tatters, the prosecution volunteered to try the Marsh test themselves. Results were negative on the stomach contents – Marie was innocent – but positive on the malachite box and the suspect preparation of eggnog – Marie was guilty. Summoned to resolve the discrepancy, Orfila arrived by stagecoach on 13 September and worked well into the night in the presence of the local pharmacists.

The following afternoon he revealed that residues of arsenic (which did not originate from the soil) were present in Charles Lafarge's stomach, liver, heart, brain and intestines. Orfila left one tiny crack of hope; there was no trace of arsenic in the flesh, so perhaps Marie's husband had been contaminated *after* death. This was not sufficient to save her from a sentence of hard labour for life, later commuted to ten years, and she died a few months after her release in 1851.

See also **Poisoning**

Organised and disorganised

Interviews conducted by the FBI's Behavioral Science Unit in the early 1980s (see **Database**) resulted in the classification of sex killers into two major types: the 'organised nonsocial' and the 'disorganised asocial'. The first word of each designation means what it says. The murders are, to a greater or lesser extent, planned and controlled; and as so often happens, the 'organised' practitioner is a cut above his 'disorganised' counterpart – more intelligent, more employable, with his own car and perhaps a live-in lover.

Where the type of murderer can be gleaned from scene-of-the-crime evidence, investigators are provided with initial indicators on the suspect's characteristics: his type of job, whether he lives alone or with a partner, whether his home is near the scene of the crime, and so on. Sex killers leave few other clues, since the target is essentially random, making traditional detection (working back from the victim's identity) redundant.

The 'organised nonsocial' sex killer may dislike people in general. Superficially, however, he appears warm and even charming. Typically regarded as a troublemaker by acquaintances and colleagues, his prime concern is 'number one'. His latent social hostility materialises with the onset of adolescence, and the murder is generally triggered by some specific event, like losing a job.

As a rule, the organised killer does not take a local victim. He has the prudence to browse, cruising for the next hit, and the foresight to carry his weapon with him, both to and from the crime. He will not normally snatch his prey by immediate recourse to violence; his social skills beguile the prospect into going his way. The assault is a slow process as the victim is tortured and mutilated preparatory to the kill, making for a tidy crime scene. The infliction of **terror** and pain supplies the pay-off, and the organised killer lingers over his solitary pleasures, often elaborated into a ritual of **dismemberment**.

The organised killer obtains retrospective audience reaction, transporting the disfigured corpse to a place where someone is bound to stumble over it. As a follow-up he maintains an eye on the investigative progress, waiting to see if the body has been discovered, and ideally becomes peripherally involved in the investigation (see **Vocation**). He may taunt the police with messages. On his 'free' evenings he sometimes, like the Son-of-Sam, returns to the site of a previous killing and dreams of the parades gone by.

By contrast, the 'disorganised asocial' does not just dislike people deep down inside. A quiet loner unable to cope with personal relationships, he keeps himself to himself and is generally tied to a menial job. In adolescence, he steals women's clothes, particularly underwear; this is less risky than approaching them openly. In maturity, he is classified as 'sexually incompetent', and any sexual acts occur after the victim is safely dead. The disorganised killer finds his victims near home, overwhelming them in a frenzied 'blitz'. Up to the fatal moment, he may have had no intention to kill; the offence is unplanned, devoid of precipitating stress. Normally the body is abandoned where it lies with only a feeble attempt at concealment. There may be mess: bloody footprints and fingerprints. The murder weapon – often a weapon of opportunity – is frequently discarded nearby. Taking parts home to eat is a disorganised trait.

Thus the initial police investigation concentrates on the probable sequence of events during the killing (*in vivo*/posthumous mutilation), the location of the body (hidden/exposed) and the presence/absence of the weapon. Sometimes the signs are clear, sometimes they are mixed, but either way they form the basis of a psychological **'profile'**, quite possibly sufficiently revealing for the police to work a neighbourhood door-to-door asking questions beginning, 'Have you ever known someone who…', which lead to the culprit.

The system is by no means perfect. FBI Agent Robert Hazelwood keeps a profile on his office wall specifying that the suspect from a Georgia case was a divorced high-school drop-out from a broken home with a low-skill job who lived miles from the murder scene and hung around cheap bars. The culprit proved to be a non-drinking, married, high-flying executive from a reasonable family background with a neighbourhood home.

See also **Detection**, **Lines**, **Masturbation**, **Terminology**, **Torture**

Oxford Apartments, no. 213

Everybody likes good neighbours. Number 213 Oxford Apartments was home to Jeffrey **Dahmer**, the Milwaukee serial killer, and in the run-up to July 1991 the block's residents became acclimatised to the regular thumpings, crashings and screams from his flat.

Following Dahmer's arrest, it transpired that his neighbour Aaron Whitehead had listened to the sound of dismemberment, taking Dahmer for a hobbyist. 'I would hear a buzz saw running in the early evening,' he recalled. 'I thought he was building something.'

The noise was bad, but the stench was very nearly intolerable. Nanetta Lowery, who lived above Dahmer, commented, 'The smell got so bad, it got into my clothes and I couldn't get it out, even after washing.' According to neighbour John Batchelor, 'It was terrible. It almost made me throw up.'

The odour (see **Mothers**) was noticeable even from adjacent properties. Identifying its cause posed unfamiliar problems for civilians. After Dahmer's arrest, Ella Vickers, another neighbour, said, 'We've been smelling things for weeks, but we thought it was a dead animal, or something like that. We had no idea it was humans.' Larry Marion believed that combat experience would have helped. 'Had we been war veterans, we would have known the smell of death.'

Dahmer's neighbours constantly remonstrated with him; he attributed the stench of the dozen festering cadavers in his flat to a 'balky fish tank' or the 'spoiled meat' stored in his unreliable freezer. After the truth emerged, on the night of 22 July 1991, the building attracted such waves of antagonism that Milwaukee residents actually shot it, peppering it with random gunfire.

P

Packer, Alferd (d. 1907)

America's leading cannibal. In autumn 1873 Packer left Salt Lake City as one of twenty frontiersmen on an ill-fated expedition prospecting for gold. Close to starvation, ten men later turned back, and soon the expedition consisted of a rump of six survivors heading for the Rio Grande through the Colorado mountains under Packer's leadership.

Only Packer remained by the following spring. He dragged himself back from the wilds into the Los Pinos Indian Agency, exhausted but – all things considered – strangely plump.

The 2 April discovery of human flesh not far from the outpost prompted Packer's first confession. The famished prospectors had been reduced to eating roots over the winter; then one morning, after a fruit-less five-day scavenging foray, he staggered into their lakeside camp to find Israel Swan on the menu, his leg roasting on the camp-fire under the supervision of Shannon Wilson Bell. Everyone else was dead, either from hunger or from Bell's murderous hatchet.

Swan was the group's oldest, and after he ran out, fat Frank Miller was consumed. But it was clear that when James Humphrey and George Noon were exhausted, Packer and Bell would have no provisions left. Bell ran amok despite a non-aggression pact, and Packer shot him dead in self-defence, sitting out the winter on the remains. Come spring, he stripped Bell down for provisions and struggled away, discarding the last cuts of meat when he came in sight of the trading post. If Packer's story were believed, he was blameless. But it wasn't.

Packer's first bid to lead a party back to his encamp-ment in what is now known as Deadman's Gulch proved unsuccessful. By June, the team knew why. Near a cabin on the shores of Lake Christoval they found five corpses, four with their skulls shattered.

The brains of Frank Miller had been dashed out with a rifle butt.

Packer escaped from custody. Retaken in 1883, he was sentenced to death in ringing terms for the murder of Israel Swan. 'Stand up, y'voracious man-eating son of a bitch, stand up,' Judge Melville B. Gerry is said to have roared. 'There was seven democrats in Hinsdale County and you've ate five of them. God damn you. I sentence you to be hanged by the neck until you is dead, dead, dead, as a warning against reducing the Democrat population of the state.' More restrained versions of these sentiments appear in the published transcripts. On a retrial the charge was reduced to manslaughter, and a pardon trimmed Packer's forty-year term to eighteen years. He eventu-ally made good as a posthumous local hero, and his bust now stands in the Colorado State Capitol.

What really happened at Deadman's Gulch? Today, a replica of one of the prospectors' skulls squats on the desk of Professor James Starrs in Washington; massive photographic enlargements of the canni-balised bones grace the walls of his university office. In 1989 Starrs located the bodies with ground-pene-trating radar and subjected them to modern forensic techniques, putting it beyond doubt that the cadav-ers had been filleted; Starrs detected the carving nicks on the skeletons made by a skinning knife. No evidence of any gunshot wounds emerged, but exam-ination disclosed defence cuts on the upraised arms, indicating that the men had perished trying to ward off blows from a hatchet. Starrs confirmed the rifle butt injury to 'victim C'. Thus the prospectors were murdered and eaten, although there was nothing to show by whom, except that the manner of their deaths was inconsistent with Packer's story. Professor Starrs, clearly conversant with the intricacies of living off the land during a Colorado winter, commented, 'Packer was having his fillets morning, noon and night, even though he could have survived by killing rabbits.'

See also **Cannibalism**

Palmer, Dr William (1824–56)

A Victorian case of overpowering circumstantial evidence. Dr Palmer was a betting man accustomed to heavy losses, and on 12 November 1855 he accompanied a horse-owner called John Parsons Cook to the Shrewsbury races.

Cook's mare, Polestar, romped home and the two friends retired to the 'Talbot Arms' in Rugely to celebrate. Cook downed a glass of brandy and then leapt to his feet, exclaiming, 'Good God, there's something in that which burns my throat.' Palmer soothed him and appeared to sip the last drops without ill-effects. But Cook was taken ill, and the local physician, a venerable 80-year-old called Bamford, prescribed a diet of 'slops' together with a 'night pill'. Palmer fed the patient with capsules from his own hand, and his condition progressively deteriorated. On 20 November, Cook went into spasm and died as his heels arched back against his head.

The High Street, Rugby, showing the 'Talbot Arms' where Cook died (left)

Palmer fought a spirited rearguard action against growing suspicion. He attended Cook's autopsy in his medical capacity, and jostled the doctor's assistant against Charles Devonshire, the medical student who was, at that moment, slicing open Cook's stomach. Nearly all its contents spilled into the body cavity, but the organ was carefully placed in a sealed vessel, which Palmer attempted to steal. 'Where's the jar?' demanded Dr Harland. 'It's here,' called Palmer,

slinking towards the door at the other end of the room. 'I thought it more convenient to take it away.' Then Palmer offered the groom £10 to stage an accident destroying the specimen jars in transit.

Professor Alfred Swaine Taylor

When Cook's remains arrived unscathed at the London laboratory of Professor Taylor, the leading authority on poisons, they contained only a small quantity of antimony (rather than the expected **strychnine**, for which there was as yet no real test) and Palmer managed to intercept the post-mortem report in the post. Meanwhile he sweetened the local coroner with a bribe of a twenty-pound turkey, a brace of pheasants, a barrel of oysters and a fine cod.

But to no avail. By now the extensive conglomeration of Palmer's dead friends and relatives was a matter of public discussion, as was the imposing accretion of the fourteen illegitimate children he sired as a medical student. Palmer's first job with a Liverpool firm of druggists ended in embezzlement; his second apprenticeship was cancelled after difficulties over women and money. As a doctor, Palmer confined his interest to racing, which fuelled a downwards spiral into debt. But he was cheerful, a church-goer, and an inveterate liar whose bare-faced deceit inspired unwarranted credence.

First among the dead was a Mr Abley, who passed away after sharing a glass of brandy with Palmer in the Staffordshire Infirmary. Palmer was mid-affair with his wife. Then came the turn of Palmer's mother-in-law, reputedly worth £12,000. 'I know I shan't live long,' she had objected in January 1849 when invited for a visit which ended a week later, as she predicted, with her demise. This loss marked Palmer's first recourse to the obliging Dr Bamford, who ascribed the death to 'apoplexy'. Then a bookmaker, Leonard Bladen, came back from Chester Races, his pockets bulging with winnings of £1,000. Palmer asked him to stay. He too expired after a week, and both his money and his betting book (in which Palmer figured as a heavy loser) disappeared.

By now Palmer's wife, Annie, was fed up. 'When will it all end?' she asked. The answer was not with Palmer's four children, who perished in convulsions after licking honey from his fingers. Palmer next disposed of a creditor called Bly, to whom he owed £800, and an uncle, Joseph 'Beau' Bentley, who succumbed after a brandy-drinking competition. That left Annie herself. Palmer secured a policy of £13,000 on her life and paid the first premium. Then she died, goaded on her way by nine days of dosing with antimony. 'My poorest dear Annie expired at ten minutes past one,' Palmer noted in his diary before bedding their servant girl Eliza. 'She was called by God to the home of bliss she so well deserved.' Dr Bamford diagnosed 'English cholera'.

Now it was the turn of Palmer's younger brother Walter, an ailing alcoholic. Palmer insured him for £13,000, installed him in a local hotel and plied him with gin. But even on three bottles a day, it takes unremitting effort to drink a man to death, and on 15 August 1855 the landlord came upon Palmer at the bedside measuring out some accelerating medicine. He asked how the patient was. 'Very ill, very low,' conceded Palmer. 'I'm going to take him something stimulating.' Next day Walter was dead. This time the insurance company put an investigator on the case, and he learned from a boot boy, James Myatt, that Palmer was seen pouring something into Walter's glass. Palmer had a talk with this damaging witness over a drink; Myatt gradually made a full recovery.

Walter's widow unexpectedly claimed on the policy, so Palmer – harried by his creditors – cast around for another source of funds, and when Polestar came in at 7–1 at the Shrewsbury Races, Cook netted £2,050. He was ripe for the picking and, after his suspicious death, the authorities exhumed Annie's body. It too contained traces of antimony. At Palmer's trial the medical evidence was too weak to secure a conviction, but his general course of dealing proved overwhelming. The judge's summing-up was deadly, and, as Palmer told the prison governor, 'When the jury returned into Court, and I saw the cocked up nose of the perky little foreman, I knew it was a gooser with me.' His defence was assisted neither by

William Palmer

the forged cheque for £350 he drew on Cook's account as he lay dying, nor by his endeavour to forge a document showing that Cook owed him £4,000.

Palmer was hanged on 14 June 1856 after a hearing at the Old Bailey. It was felt that he would not receive a fair trial locally, and a special statute – the so-called Palmer Act – was passed for his benefit. Judge James Stephen observed that 'Palmer's career supplied one of the proofs of a fact of which many kind-hearted people seem to doubt, namely that such a thing as an atrocious wickedness is consistent with good education, perfect sanity, and everything in a word which deprives one of all excuse for crime.'

Palmer was not unique in turning children's sweet-tooths to fatal advantage. On Hallowe'en 1974, eight-year-old Timmy O'Bryan from Houston died in convulsions shortly after admission to hospital; his post-mortem suggested death by poisoning, confirmed by stomach analysis which detected traces of cyanide. This matched the cyanide discovered crammed into the candy straws – 'Pixy Sticks' – handed round as a Hallowe'en treat to Timmy and his friends. Police impounded the rest of the confectionary before it claimed more victims, finding six more Pixy Sticks laden with a fatal dose.

Timmy's father, who murdered his son for the insurance money, went to the electric chair.

Panopticon, The

In 1791, the British philosopher Jeremy Bentham published a pamphlet, 'The Panopticon or Inspection House', setting out his thinking on the perfect **prison**.

Bentham's edifice was to be constructed to the plan of a multi-storeyed wheel, with a circular rim housing the prisoners' individual dungeons and overlooked by a central hub, the inspection tower, a lay-out combining solitary confinement with a sense of continuous supervision from warders, who could peer in through the cell windows.

This represented the worst of both worlds.

Bentham submitted his proposal to successive governments to no avail, despite undertaking to run the concern himself at a modest profit derived from the prisoners' work.

In due course Bentham became such an enthusiastic proponent of his design that he advocated it as a substitute for Australia, arguing against the policy of transportation in his *Panopticon versus New South Wales*.

When this failed, Bentham tirelessly lobbied David Phillips, then setting off to colonise Port Phillip Bay, insisting that he build a Panopticon in Australia, a sort of a prison within a prison. Before Phillips sailed, Bentham demanded: 'Are you serious in your intention of building a prison, and moreover of building it on the central inspection principle?' Phillips was not, but he was too polite to say so. The thinking behind Bentham's scheme, intended to avoid 'contamination through association', gave rise to the catastrophes of the **Separate System**.

Panty Bandit *et al.*

In the summer of 1988, the Panty Bandit became California's Public Enemy Number One. He was a hybrid, a sex burglar.

First came the sex. The Panty Bandit would raid a Los Angeles beauty parlour and force a woman, at gunpoint, to remove her knickers. Then he draped the garment over his face and masturbated in front of the assembled customers. Phase two supplied the burglary. The Panty Bandit emptied the till and left. When arrested on 23 October 1988, the culprit Bruce Lyons was carrying a carton of trophy underwear in his Honda Civic.

People take their pleasures in different ways. An American, Edgar Jones, was detained in 1992 on suspicion of being the St Louis Serial Toe Sucker; he faced two charges of sexual abuse and five other related offences. His victims were all schoolgirls. Jones posed as a jogger, knocked the girls to the ground, ripped off their shoes and gave their toes a good sucking. In Britain, Jonathan Thomas of Oxford experienced a similar attack on the night of 10 April 1992 when he was bound, blindfolded, and remorselessly tickled on the soles of his feet.

Thomas informed the police, but the mute pavements, footpaths and underpass with which 20-year-old Karl Watkins from Worcestershire enjoyed sexual relations could take no such action.

Pedestrians and passers-by protested that Watkins would remove his trousers, lie down and make love to the flagstones, and on 19 February 1993 he was convicted on five charges of outraging public decency.

In Britain, Hampshire's Meon Valley became the favourite hunting ground of a sex attacker during 1991. Five of his twenty assaults included horrific mutilations to horses' genitals.

See also **Horse**, **Masturbation**, **Pets**

Parker, Marion (1925–27)

Los Angeles **kidnapping** victim. Marion was returned on 17 December 1927. The kidnapper pulled up at the handover location with the wide-eyed child in the front seat of his car. But after paying the $1,500 ransom, her father discovered that William Edward Hickman, the kidnapper, had already detached his child's hands, legs and intestines. Her eyes were wired open. Hickman was very definitely mad, but this proved insufficient to avert his execution on 4 February 1928.

His arrest followed a clear logical evolution. By the roadside near Marion's body, a woman noticed a suitcase stuffed with torn newspapers, some blood-drenched towels, a few scraps of wire and a paper pad identical to the one used in the ransom demand. The towels came from a nearby hotel, where traces of human flesh clogged the drains. A set of fingerprints enabled the police to broadcast Hickman's description and, a few days later, a Seattle haberdasher's suspicions were aroused by a young man trying to buy a change of clothing with a $20 bill. The note was traced to the ransom; and a local garage attendant reported that a man answering Hickman's description was driving a green Hudson. He was picked up heading back towards Los Angeles.

Parricides

In France, parricides were led in a black veil to the scaffold, where – until 1832 – their right hand was cut off prior to decapitation. Regicides suffered the same fate, since their crime was against the father of the nation.

This relatively humane treatment contrasts with the

staggering and extended brutality of the *amende honorable* with which the regicide Damiens was disjointed on 2 March 1757, a spectacle described with scrupulous particularity by a Monsieur Bouton, officer of the watch, in one of the most disgusting pas-sages ever printed. Interested readers are referred to *Discipline and Punish* (Allen Lane 1975).

Pax Capone

On 26 October 1926, Al Capone convened a mobster Summit at the Hotel Sherman to partition Chicago and Cook County into formal spheres of interest between the four main gangs. The delegates met without weapons or bodyguards, and agreed the framework of a treaty under Capone's Five Terms: 1. A general

Capone travelling in style to Atlanta Federal Penitentiary at the start of his eleven-year sentence

amnesty; 2. No future killings or beatings; 3. All past killings and beatings to be forgotten; 4. All malicious rumours to be ignored; 5. Gang leaders to be responsible for acts of their gang members.

'Let's give each other a break,' began Maxie Eisen in the chair to murmurs of assent. Then the hoodlums settled down to hard bargaining. This was fine-print business rather than thuggery, where (for instance) Drucci and Bugs Moran ceded their territorial gains south of Madison Street, limiting themselves to the Forty-second and Forty-third precincts; their rights for beer and spirits to be exclusive as to both retail and wholesale, with their North Side prostitution and gambling concessionaries operating henceforth as Capone licensees.

The convention concluded with warm hand-shakes, shoulder slapping and smiles all round. Then the colleagues fell to feasting, yarning about the old days. A newspaper man slipped in, later describing their celebratory supper as the ultimate in the macabre. 'Thugs who had taken a shot at each other with murderous intent admitted the effort to the proposed victim, laughing heartily. Thugs who had actually killed explained the details of the killing to friends of the deceased and gave their version why there was no way of getting out of it. The most frightful things in violence were discussed and chuckled over.'

Interviewed about the negotiations the next day, Capone said, 'I told them we were making a shooting gallery of a great business and that nobody profited by it. It's hard and dangerous work, aside from any hate at all, and when a fellow works hard at any line of business, he wants to go home and forget about it.'

For the next two months not a shot was fired. Capone's settlement worked tolerably well until Big Bill Thompson's re-election in April 1927 inaugurated Chicago's final free-for-all.

At the height of his powers, Capone ran his empire from a suite of six rooms on the fourth floor of the Hotel Lexington near the present-day McCormick Place. Staff patrolled the lobby, and their leader in Salon 430 was reached, via ranks of sentries and body-guards armed with .45s, through an oval vestibule where the initials AC were enclosed by a crest on the parquet floor. The bathroom – with purple tiles, gold fittings and an immense sunken tub – was off left. Capone liked to transact his morning business in a dressing gown and blue silk pyjamas with gold piping, sporting an eleven-carat blue-white diamond on his middle finger.

A New York dishwasher when Prohibition took effect, by 1925 Capone ruled a criminal empire with an annual income of $125 million. His house on Prairie Avenue was crammed with oriental rugs, antique furniture, jade and exquisite sculptures. Distended before his time by mountains of pasta, Capone was a music lover readily moved to tears and, unlike many of his colleagues, he held press conferences, attended opening nights at the opera and distributed $100 tips. People waved at the sight of him on city streets. One elderly widow knelt and kissed his hand and, on his appearances at the racetrack or Wrigley Field, hundreds rose to their feet in spontaneous applause. Today the Lexington is derelict; and on the warehouse site of the 1929 St Valentine's massacre they put up a parking lot.

The St Valentine's Day Massacre, 1929. Capone taught the Bugs Moran gang a lesson, but Bugs himself escaped, late for his appointment

Capone's machine-gunning of seven members of the North Side Gang proved a turning point, burying his affable reputation under the first real public outcry. Two prominent Chicago publishers, Knox of the *Daily News* and McCormick of the *Tribune*, travelled to Washington to complain to Hoover in person, and the upshot was a dual onslaught on Capone's kingdom. The Treasury Department, under Special Agent Frank J. Wilson, was instructed to build an income tax evasion case, and the Justice Department, not before time, enjoined to connect Capone with bootlegging. But their **Prohibition agents** were corrupt, and District Attorney George Q. Johnson determined to establish a special Capone squad. On 29 September 1929 he summoned a promising young agent, Eliot Ness by name, to his office. Thus were born the **Untouchables**.

In the event, Capone was indicted on 5 June 1931 and brought to justice by the Treasury's case (despite a $4 million bribe) with Ness's bootlegging charges kept in reserve. Sentenced to eleven years, Capone was paroled on 19 November 1939, 'nuttier than a fruit-cake' in the advanced stages of syphilis, and died eight years later.

In 1968 George Patty, a food company executive, bought the pock-marked St Valentine's Day garage wall at auction, intending to reassemble it for posterity. Capone's car became another curiosity. A real monster, his mobile fortress was based on a V8 40hp Cadillac, custom-built at a cost of £6,000, and its seven-ton mass owed much to the armour-plated bodywork, a steel-lined fuel tank and bullet-proof glass one and a half inches thick. The car featured a police siren, a secret gun-locker and a removable back window for the rear gunner.

Bought by a British speculator, in 1934 the vehicle, exhibited on a dais, toured England with Bertram Mills's Circus. A placard reading 'The Car of Scarface Al Capone, King of the Gangsters' stood alongside a photographic display of the great man together with his lieutenants, many pictured lying dead in the gutter amid pools of blood.

See also **Cicero**, **Eighteenth Amendment**, **Fallout**, **Hawthorne**, **Public relations**

Payne, A. D. (d. 1930)

A Texas lawyer. Payne was sentenced to death for exploding his wife and son on 27 June 1930; he wanted to be free to live with his secretary. Awaiting execution, he blew himself up in his prison cell by detonating a charge strapped to his chest.

Miami gangster Creighton Randall 'Randy' Bethell suffered a similar fate in February 1975. Acting on a tip-off, on 4 September 1975 police drove to the reported site of his corpse in a wood opposite utility pole 136 on Card Sound Road, only to find a four-foot crater. Bethell had been detonated with five sticks of dynamite.

But half-measures will not destroy a body. An intensive search of hundreds of square feet of woodland yielded myriads of bone shards. Enough of Bethell's shirt and wig survived to be recognised by his father. The skull was largely intact, showing the passage of a large calibre bullet, and a section of the lower jaw, containing teeth numbers 30, 31 and 32, displayed dental work that matched Bethell's army records.

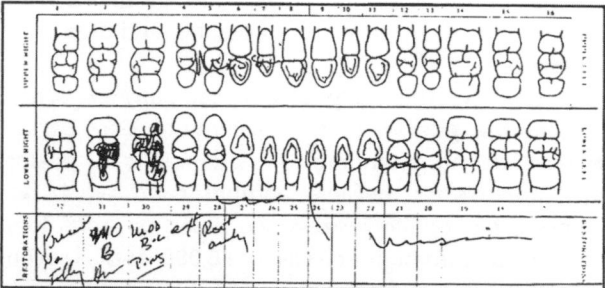

Bethell's dental chart, showing the pin work to teeth 30, 31 and 32 (lower left)

The medical examiner's report detailed the course of events. Bethell had been abducted from his home, driven to Card Sound Road and shot. Later the killers paid another visit to knock out his teeth and jaws, smashing his skull with a boulder. On ascertaining that both Bethell's knees were surgically pinned, they came back to blast his legs with a shotgun. Finally, they blew Bethell up, checked the site and gave it the all-clear.

Even so, his remains helped put Richard Douglas Cravero behind bars. Cravero headed a vicious team of drug-runners credited with thirty-five killings. Bethell, a former associate, had been executed for holding money back.

See also **Durability**

Pearce, Alexander (d. 1824)

Alexander Pearce's head was removed in 1824 by a Mr Crockett of the Hobart Colonial Hospital, Australia, who adapted it as a **souvenir**. Crockett stripped off the flesh, extracted its brains and eyes and then boiled it. In the 1850s the relic was presented to Dr Samuel Norton, the skull collector, who appended it to his one thousand other specimens in 'The American Golgotha'. Today, Pearce's head may be viewed in a display cabinet at the Academy of Natural Sciences in Philadelphia.

It is a head worth having. Pearce, its first owner, was born in Ireland in 1790. Sentenced at 29 to seven years' transportation for stealing six pairs of shoes, he wound up in the penal colony of Macquarie Harbour on Van Diemen's Land. There, on 20 September 1822, he commandeered an open boat and, together with seven companions and one axe, rowed across the bay and hightailed it into the forest.

The convicts found themselves entangled in rough terrain, battling up sharp mountainous escarpments through a morass of scrub, creepers and rotted trees. After a week their stores were exhausted. In Pearce's words, taken from his deposition: 'We then consulted who should fall. Greenhill said, "Dalton; as he volunteered to be a flogger, we will kill him."'

That night, while Dalton lay asleep, Greenhill's axe 'struck Dalton on the head, and he never spoke a word after ... Matthew Travers with a knife also came and cut his throat, and bled him; we then dragged him to a distance, and cut off his clothes, and tore out his inside, and cut off his head; then Matthew Travers and Greenhill put his heart and liver on the fire and ate it before it was right warm; they asked the rest would they have any, but they would not have any that night.'

Cannibalism exudes a terrible logic, immediately clear to the seven survivors. Dalton would soon run out and someone had to be next. The weakest were most in fear. Two slipped away in the forest mazes of the Engineer Ranges; the others hunted them, to kill, but the pair struggled back to Macquarie Harbour where they died from their privations. That left five convicts at large, and on 15 October, somewhere near the Loddon Plains, Greenhill rounded on Bodenham and split his skull. Then they devoured him.

Four remained. They reached the Western Tiers in a mania of sullen suspicion, vowing never to eat each other. But on the open plains, no man could hide, no man could hobble faster than his companions, no man could make a run for it, and still Greenhill had the axe. They were bound together in a stranglehold, destined to eat or be eaten, kill or be killed, and in late October, while Mather was sicking up some roots, 'Greenhill still showing his spontaneous habit of bloodshed seized the axe and crept up behind him and gave him a blow on the head'.

Mather beat off his attacker, and lived; that night the unhappy four gathered round the camp fire. Mather knew his time had come. 'They told him they would give him half an hour to pray for himself, which was agreed to; he then gave the prayer book to me, and laid down his head, and Greenhill took the axe and killed him.' And then there were three.

The next to go was Travers, Greenhill's bosom friend. So, at last, on the great Australian plains, just Pearce and Greenhill remained. Together this odd couple dragged through a pleasant landscape of undulating fields and copses, keeping a fixed distance apart, one stopping when the other did. Both knew that the first to sleep was a dead man. They eyed each other day and night, watching across the camp fire. One day passed, then another, and then another.

Finally Greenhill succumbed. He nodded off and Pearce killed him, continuing on his way alone but replenished, with his companion's arm and thigh for sustenance. A week later, after nearly two months of surviving on people, Pearce ran into a convict-shepherd, McGuire, on the edge of the River Ouse. McGuire gave him food and shelter, and Pearce avoided capture for two more months. Summoned before the acting magistrate, Reverend Robert Knopwood, he confessed everything.

But since his grotesque tale was not believed, the authorities sent Pearce back to Macquarie Harbour from which, on 16 November 1823, he escaped again. This time he headed north, making for Port Dalrymple with Thomas Cox, whom he ate on 19 November. On this occasion, Pearce's captors found a mangled body, cut through the middle and partially stripped.

Shipped down to Hobart, Pearce was tried, executed, and anatomised, with his head passing into the hands of Mr Crockett.

Pedigree Chum

Dogfood contaminated by Rodney Whitchelo, who blackmailed the manufacturers. He also spiked cans of Heinz babyfoods with caustic soda, razor blades and rat poison. At the height of the scare, Heinz and Cow & Gate – victims of a copycat threat – recalled 100 million units from the supermarket shelves after baby Victoria Coppock cut her lip on a razor implanted in a jar of yoghurt. Although Whitchelo only netted £32,000 from his £3.75 million demand before being caught in October 1989, he secured access of a peculiarly irritating kind to almost limitless funds.

As an Essex detective, Whitchelo formed a low opinion of police intelligence. He lived alone with his mother, founded the Sado Masochistic Pen Pal Club and rented hotel rooms for sex with women contacted through magazine advertisements. With the approach of his forties, he was loosely engaged on the early drafts of a book about the 'perfect crime', and the template for his blackmail scheme was a similar but secret plot by William Frary, an unemployed microbiologist who dosed Bernard Matthews's turkeyburgers with mercury. The Detective Training School attended by Whitchelo at Ripley put the clandestine details of Frary's scheme on their 1986 syllabus; Whitchelo, impressed, put them into action. He set up a mailing address in Hammersmith and whiled away two years before making his move, so that any recollection of his voice or appearance would have faded.

The crime was nearly perfect, and its ingenuity lay in the method of ransom collection. At first Whitchelo extorted £100,000 in a brisk letter explaining that he had poisoned the dog food with biocides because they were 'colourless, odourless and highly toxic'. The funds were paid into a building society account opened under a false name, and Whitchelo drove cross-country to make withdrawals from any one of 900 cash machines to a maximum of £300 per day. He reasoned that his colleagues could not mount a nationwide watch without his knowledge.

The police countered with Operation Roach, enlisting 3,000 officers for round-the-clock surveillance on building society branches on selected days. This massive undertaking required the collaboration of the Regional Crime Squads, and Whitchelo duly learned of the plan and its timing from his workmates in the pub. On Operation Roach days, he stayed home. He handled his cash-card with gloves, and when a machine 'ate' it acting under police orders it revealed no fingerprints. Caught on videotape at a branch in Ipswich, he was wearing a hood. And when a public reward was offered, Whitchelo applied for this too, requesting payment in his usual way.

The police guessed that the blackmailer had inside knowledge. So they set up an inner plan, Operation Agincourt, to disseminate the disinformation that Operation Roach was winding down. Whitchelo became careless. With no fears about his financial prospects, he took early retirement and confined his withdrawals to London. Meanwhile, Special Branch offered to maintain a discreet guard over the fifteen 'best-guess' **cash dispensers** on the night of 20 October 1989. Whitchelo went elsewhere, only to find the machine out of action. Workmen had severed an electric cable. So he drove to another cash point at Enfield, approached it wearing a mask, and was arrested.

Sentencing him to seventeen years, Judge Nina Lowry commented: 'You knew there were millions of dog owners in this country and a threat to poison dogs would be particularly compelling.' The case inspired copycat **blackmail** schemes by the sackload – 750 in all, triggering twenty-four charges for wasting police time.

Recent blackmail cases include threats of a poison gas blitz on Cyprus (1989), releasing animals injected with rabies (1989), poisoning a blind man's guide dog (1989), stuffing cyanide into cigarettes (1986) and threatening to destroy an original collection of photographs of Charlie **Chaplin** (1986). Robert Telford, a failed businessman, was jailed for ten years on 30 May 1991 for his million-pound plot to defile Cadbury's Creme Eggs with Paraquat weedkiller. The year 1980 furnished a relatively endearing scheme to spoil crumpets with cigarette-ends, and a recent attempt, from a duo calling themselves Laurel and Hardy, involved toothpaste contaminated with poison, an idea perhaps gleaned from the 1987 film *Black Widow*.

The British counselling experts in food contamination, public relations consultants Burson-Marseller, handle about a hundred incidents a year; about a quarter can be attributed to disaffected present and former employees. Insurance cover must be kept secret, and policies come complete with expert security services, including rehearsal of operational scenarios. Control Risks, leaders in the field, note that, 'Collecting the money is the most dangerous part for the criminal', and Whitchelo nearly had the problem licked.

Perera, Dr Samuel (1943–)

Sri Lankan dentist who killed his adopted daughter and used sections of her body as bedding soil for houseplants.

Perera settled in the West Yorkshire village of Sandal after winning a research post as a lecturer at the Dental Department of Leeds University. He had two children by his wife Dammika, but in December 1981 he decided (for reasons which remain obscure) to acquire another and flew to Colombo where he purchased a ten-year-old village girl, Nilanthe. Renamed Philomena, she was brought back to Sitwell Close, a series of redbrick 'executive style' dwellings.

In November 1983, Nilanthe disappeared. The neighbours asked what had happened. First Dr Perera's wife explained that she was banned from playing outside because 'she made eyes at all the men'. After Christmas the story changed: 'She grew homesick and my husband decided it was kindest to send her back to her father in Sri Lanka.'

Contrary to the general run of tales about compliant neighbours who listen unmoved to thuds and screams emanating from next door, the Sitwell Close residents called a community meeting and drafted a collective letter to the police. Detectives took Dr Perera to task, but he maintained that he had taken Nilanthe to Sicily for the weekend and handed her to his brother for repatriation.

Flight records showed no trace of Dr Perera's booking. And there the matter rested for nine months. The police had no body, but they pursued the case by talking to Dr Perera's colleagues at the Dental Department. Dr Perera shared a desk there, and on 4 February 1985 his fellow-lecturer happened on some human remains – a jawbone and segments of skull – in a manilla envelope in one of his drawers. A rapid scout through his office revealed a clutch of further fragments from the foot, pelvis, forearm, shoulder and neck – variously distributed in a five-litre glass beaker, a coffee jar and a stainless steel tray.

The next day the police searched 16 Sitwell Close. In the back garden they unearthed a shallow grave, recently vacated, containing a vestigial tooth, a hank of hair and one small bone.

Inside the house, three large plastic flowerpots stood on the hallway carpet and perspex sidetable. Two contained geraniums. In the words of forensic scientist Professor Usher, 'The plants were very small for such large pots, and did not seem to be doing very well; they were wilting somewhat.' Usher fetched a dustbin lid and placed it upside down on the carpet. On tipping out the contents of the largest pot, a complete human spine, coiled round the roots, slithered free. Decanting the geraniums disgorged semi-liquid clumps of decaying flesh. Then the police noticed a human rib in a butter dish.

In all, 105 bone fragments retrieved from Dr Perera's home were reunited with their associates from the University to form a total of 130 pieces, previously hidden in eight locations, and reassembled into a skeleton, in part to establish the age, sex and race of the deceased, but also to ensure that, say, two or more right arms were not present.

Perera was convicted on compelling evidence on 11 March 1986. As Professor Usher observed, 'I could conceive of no legitimate purpose for what was literally half a human torso being concealed in a domestic flowerpot.'

Perera's motive never emerged. Colleagues thought him a disagreeable, arrogant man, and perhaps the most revealing insight was afforded by a throwaway line to Detective Inspector Hodgson on his first visit to Sitwell Close: 'She's only a jungle girl, after all.'

'Planting a tree' is an arcane Trinidadian term meaning 'to kill'. The expression derives from Michael X, who issued orders for an execution in 1972 and then had the body buried in a trench, instructing his gardener to 'plant something in it'. In the case of Joseph Skerrit, decapitated for refusing to raid a country post office, the 'something' was lettuces. These grew tall and yellow, and his last bedding place came to light.

Pets

'Homicidal triangle' is the psychiatric term for the three character traits often found in serial killers: childhood bedwetting, acts of delinquency (especially arson), and a delight in torturing animals.

Cruelty to animals is usually as much as a child can manage, but when he becomes a man he progresses to people. Ian **Brady**, the Moors Murderer, flung cats out of tenement windows as a Glasgow child; Ed **Kemper**, from California, cut his family cat into pieces with a knife. **Kürten** mutilated dogs and, on one occasion, a swan. He sexually assaulted sheep. The underlying pattern is the pet today, the world tomorrow. The **torture** of animals is almost as satisfying as torturing people: pets can whimper, scream, struggle and bleed. But the essential difference remains. At the end of the day, they are only animals.

Jeffrey **Dahmer**, the Milwaukee serial killer, is not on the list of animal sadists, despite devoting much of his childhood to collecting insects in empty pickle jars and preserving them in formaldehyde. Dahmer started with butterflies and moths, and progressed via chipmunks, squirrels, raccoons, opossums and cats, often killed in road accidents. He carried a St

Bernard's body back to the woods, left it to rot, and then doused the remains in bleach to clean the bones.

Dahmer created an animal cemetery, spiking the skulls on crosses. Neighbours recollect that skinned and gutted dogs were nailed to nearby trees; one find had its gutted intestines draped round the tree. But on the best evidence, Dahmer's morbidity was restricted to creatures already dead, although on fishing expeditions he chopped up bluegills and bass, still alive and wriggling, into tiny pieces, before tossing them back. 'I want to see what it looks like inside, I like to see how things work,' he said. But fish hardly count, and Dahmer was not preoccupied with cruelty; he yearned for a relationship and, lacking the social skills to handle the living, lavished his attention on the dead, evolving a macabre preoccupation with his companions' innards – the mere *machinery* of life. He had a two-dimensional appreciation of the normal person's desire to see what makes his friends tick; in Dahmer's literal vision, it involved physical exposure of the heart.

His first human victim was Stephen Hicks, a hitchhiker. Dahmer smashed in his head on 18 June 1978 without preliminary torture, and then processed the body up at the shed in the usual way. Thus his lack of cruelty to animals presaged his lack of cruelty to people. But, like **Nilsen**, he still had to kill them.

Bedwetting only acquires significance if it persists beyond the age of twelve. **Arson** is considered separately.

Petty treason

A crime that embraced coining and other assaults on the body politic, murdering a husband among them. The sentence for women, whether for high or petty treason, was burning, a practice which continued until 1790.

But at least they were burned dead, not alive. The executioner tied the victim to a chair or to the stake and, after lighting the pyre, quickly strangled her with a noose round her neck. The timing could go awry, as with Catherine Hayes on 9 May 1726 (see **Head**). According to the *Newgate Calendar*, 'She rent the air with her cries and lamentations. Other firebrands were instantly thrown on her; but she survived among the flames for a considerable time.'

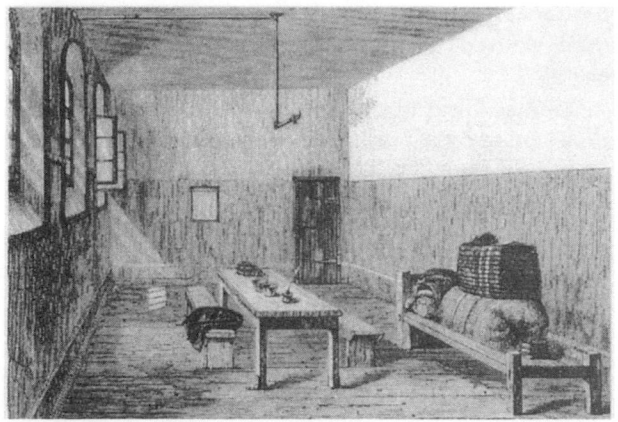

Condemned cell, Newgate

Using the term colloquially, the two notable transgressors of recent times were the writer P. G. Wodehouse and William Joyce, also known as Lord Haw Haw. Their treason was so petty it was not treason at all. In 1941

William Joyce, Lord Haw Haw

Wodehouse recorded a series of jocular (and even courageous) broadcasts to neutral America covering the Nazis' arrival in France, and was for ever after *persona non grata* with the British establishment. As for Joyce, his wartime broadcasts (which started 'This is Jairmany calling') may have annoyed the Allies, but his indiscretions were all abroad and, besides, he was not a British subject.

Joyce once owned a British passport, but he was not entitled to it and therefore was not British. His passport application gave his place of birth as Galway, Ireland instead of Brooklyn, New York.

In effect, the courts claimed jurisdiction over an alien for a crime committed abroad. If this were the law, the principle would be of limitless application and could, with similar justification, condemn anyone, anywhere, for anything unlawful in Britain. It was a political trial.

It is no matter for pride that Joyce was hanged, and on 3 January 1946 a crowd of 300 gathered round the prison gates. Some parents brought their children.

Philips, Judith

A 'cunning woman' who had it in for men. By and large, con-tricks from the Elizabethan era lose something in the telling; but not this one.

Judith Philips lived in Upper Sambourne, near Winchester, where her near neighbour was an unnamed but rich 'churl'. First Philips researched his background. Then, unobserved, she buried some money on his land and introduced herself as a white witch.

Philips intimated that she could tell by certain magical signs on his forehead that he was involved in a lawsuit with a local landowner, a fact she had already ascertained. Then she pointed out that the man's wife possessed a rather 'fortunate' face. This reminded Philips of the treasure she felt sure lay in his grounds, not least since she had just put it there. 'Have you not,' she enquired, 'a hollow tree standing near unto your house, with certain weeds growing about the root?'

It so happened that the neighbour had, and, after some testing excavations, a small gold coin and a silver sixpence were duly unearthed. Philips promised to find the rest of the buried hoard. But for her final act of divination she wanted £14 in cash together with a decent room, fit for an audience with the Fairy Queen.

Philips listed her requirements: 'You must set five

candlesticks in five several places in your chamber, and under every candlestick you must put a golden coin.' The apartment for the enchanted reception was to be sanctified with the finest linen and set about with the household's most precious objects. As a last detail, Philips insisted that her mark obtain a brand-new saddle and two girths.

Come evening, when all the valuables were neatly arrayed, Philips ordered her man into the yard. Then she saddled him up and rode him round and round the holly bush. Dismounting, she explained to the man and his wife: 'You must lie three hours one by another grovelling on your bellies under this tree, and stir not, I charge you, until I come back again. For I must go into the chamber to meet the Queen of the Fairies and welcome her to that holy spot.' Then she stripped the house bare and fled into the night with her spoils.

Sad to tell, Philips was caught and whipped through the City of London.

See also **Hopkins**

Pierrepoints

A Yorkshire 'family firm' of executioners who dominated the English **hanging** trade from 1900 to 1956. The first in the line was Old Harry Pierrepoint (1877–1922), a former butcher who resigned in 1916 with ninety-nine victims to his credit, including the last double female hanging. He passed on the torch to his elder brother Tom (1871–1955), a phlegmatic character given to sucking sweets during executions.

After the retirement of his rival John Ellis, Tom Pierrepoint rose to become Britain's chief hangman. By the time he hung up his rope in 1948, he had logged forty-five years in harness to become Britain's longest-serving executioner, often assisted by his nephew Albert (1905–92), selected at the age of 27 from a shortlist of ten applicants. During his interview Albert declared that the job was 'something to take pride in' and later referred favourably to the opportunities for travel.

Albert, an extremely fast worker, could clock in at somewhere between seventeen and twenty seconds. This included pinioning the victim, escorting him to the scaffold, and fitting the noose as well as pulling the lever. After the Second World War his professionalism was applied to despatching some 200 war criminals; he once hanged twenty-seven in twenty-four hours.

In 1946 Pierrepoint took over a pub, unremarkably named 'Help the Poor Struggler', known locally as 'Help the Poor Strangler'; one of his underlings, Harry Allen, ran the 'Rope and Anchor'. A publican's hours suited Pierrepoint well. As he wrote, 'I found that I could take a three o'clock plane from Dublin after conducting an execution there (Eire having no home-grown hangmen) and be opening my bar without comment at half-past five'.

Pierrepoint's pub sign

It was while emerging from another pub, the 'Fitzroy Tavern' in London's Charlotte Street, that Pierrepoint first laid eyes on the villains Jenkins and Geraghty who had just driven their stolen car through a jeweller's window in a smash and grab raid. They shot dead a passer-by who 'had a go', and five months later, on 19 September 1947, briefly met Pierrepoint again, when he hanged them. A fastidious man, he liked to be photographed in a bow-tie and, during the Royal Commission of 1953, confessed himself 'very much put out' by the impropriety of discussing his work in the proximity of a female typist. He retired in 1956.

In 1974, after profiting from the hanging of 530 men and twenty women during a career spanning three decades and nine countries, Albert Pierrepoint wrote: 'I do not believe that any of the hundreds of executions I have carried out has in any way acted as a deterrent against future murder. Capital punishment, in my view, achieves nothing except revenge.' This statement is often quoted by opponents of capital punishment, among whom Pierrepoint must rank as the most bizarre.

See also **Recruitment, Sansons**

Pillory *et al.*

A wooden clamp fixing a miscreant's arms and neck. The punishment, intended to expose its victims to ridicule rather than pain or injury, was in constant demand from the Anglo-Saxon era until its wholesale abolition in 1837. Its staple fodder was scolds, bakers adulterating their bread and suchlike, but it could rise to graver occasions. In May 1613 Messrs Waller and Bostock, seditious rumour-mongers, were fined 5,000 marks apiece and sentenced to 'stand on the pillory, to lose their ears and be whipped thence through the streets'.

By the end of the seventeenth century a spell in the pillory not infrequently ended in a public stoning. In 1756, when **highwaymen** M'Daniel and Barry were exhibited in London, 'it was with the utmost difficulty that one of the sheriffs and the keeper of Newgate, who stood on the balcony just by, prevented their being utterly destroyed'. Three days later their confederates, Eagan and Salmon, fared worse. They 'were instantly assaulted with showers of oystershells, stones, &c., and had not stood alive one half-hour before Eagan was struck dead and Salmon was so dangerously wounded in the head that it was thought impossible he could recover'. Clearly the bombardment could be vigorous in the extreme: in 1732 two men were convicted of murdering a prisoner in the pillory 'by pelting him with cauliflower stalks'.

Pillories were often combined with whipping posts and stocks to form a multiple facility, generally occupying the market square. The Manchester pillory remained in use until its removal in 1816. From then until 1837 the pillory was reserved for perjurers. Drunks and rowdies had their feet clamped in the stocks – a form of punishment that was never abolished but just faded away in the nineteenth century. The last recorded case was in Rugby in 1865, and the practice survived just long enough to be photographed, showing everyone (including the victim) smiling.

In the nineteenth century, some English local authorities would accept a public apology for a minor offence in lieu of prosecution. An otherwise obscure Mary Kelly made one such abject submission on a wall poster in Stockport on 27 July 1864 'for plucking flowers in Vernon Park'. The poster is signed with an 'X' placed in the space between the words 'Her Mark'.

Pizza Connection, The

On 24 October 1984, twenty-two members of the Sicilian and American Mafia were arraigned on conspiracy charges of smuggling heroin and cocaine into the United States by the ton. The gang's imports from 1979 to 1984 were estimated at $1.6 billion. Only $250 million in cash was recovered, but the Sicilian network – successor to the **French Connection** – was shattered by the eighteen convictions, which included a forty-five-year sentence for Gaetano Badalamenti, former head of the Sicilian Mafia's ruling commission.

The investigation started nearly five years before, in July 1979, after the murder of the Bonanno Family boss Carmine Galante, shot through the eye in a Brooklyn restaurant. The survival of his bodyguards suggested that they had sold his life, not theirs, dearly, in a pre-agreed hit probably engineered by the Gambino clan. Galante became a likely candidate for liquidation after his attempt to monopolise American heroin distribution, charging a 'licence fee' of $5,000 per kilo, but at the time these machinations were unknown, and surveillance agents found themselves stationed outside New York pizzerias, noting the delivery of mysterious cardboard cartons or paper shopping bags by hitherto unknown hoods.

Years passed before investigators realised that they had stumbled on the rear end of a vast heroin network. The bags contained kilos of money, and the bundles of cash were shipped out of America either as profits or as advance payment for the next consignment. Not until 7 March 1983 did the FBI accumulate sufficient evidence to run wiretaps; by the start of the court case two years later they had recorded approximately 100,000 conversations on hundreds of cassettes which, if played end to end, would last a year.

Transacting all the illegal business from pay-phones in code made it difficult to tell who was ringing whom about what. Officers had to put names to voices, and distinguish between genuine orders for pizzas and encoded exchanges about narcotics. The syndicate possessed no formal cypher; the glossary shifted from day to day, often depending on intonation. A typical snippet from 1983 had one conspirator saying to his wife: 'Tell them that I'm making a pizza and then I'm coming.'

What did this signify? 'And ask to bring the calzones,' someone chimed in from the background. These were real pizzas. But other innocuous commodities like lemons, shirts, tangerines, salted sardines, plants, tables, ovens, onions, suits, pants, pears, bread rolls, the 'thing that is being manufactured' or the state of the weather could allude to the shipment of merchandise. Again, 'My daughter wants a pizza with extra cheese, Sicilian not American' might mean just that. 'Is it still raining?' could refer to the level of police activity.

Perhaps the clearest sequence of dialogue was taped from 8 February 1984, recording Badalamenti masterminding the deal: 'I met the guy with the shirts of four years ago ... but there's a little problem ... There's another guy here that has, there's 10 per cent acrylic ... the good suits, you're talking 180 dollars ... 175 ... 185 ... it depends ... 190, it has also gone to. It depends on the situation.' The 'shirts' designated the cheaper heroin with 10 per cent impurity, the 'suits' the real McCoy, and the prices quoted were per kilo minus three noughts.

It was confusing for the agents and equally confusing for the slower conspirators, like Badalamenti's nephew Pietro Alfano from a pizzeria on South Fourth Street in Oregon. When he could not make up his mind if his instructions were in plain language or code, Alfano, the syndicate's Rosetta Stone, asked straight out over the wiretapped lines. Where were the 'salted sardines' kept? At Filippo's? Did 'town of the sun' mean Fort Lauderdale? What exactly was a '*little* shirt?' Were 'prickly pears' a place, a key of cocaine or ordinary fruit? Even references to a Howard Johnson threw Alfano; he thought it was a person. Understandably, he had problems calculating the syndicate's finances over the telephone by subtracting 'little things' from 'big shirts' to arrive at a dollar total.

Alfano's role was to assemble the syndicate's cash – no easy matter – for the next transaction. 'The thing is,' Alfano at last volunteered to Badalamenti on the telephone, 'I can do this thing tomorrow. Today is Tuesday.' 'Today is Thursday,' interjected Badalamenti while his nephew reckoned off the mid-week days still to come.

As the final deal started to fall apart, Alfano realised that without the cash the shippers were liable to turn nasty. He might be chopped into pizza: 'Ping, ping, ping, ping ... piece by piece.' In the event the Pizza Connection was busted in a series of co-ordinated raids on 9 April 1984. Alfano was arrested along with Badalamenti in Madrid, and in the second year of his trial he was shot in the back three times outside a delicatessen. He recovered, pleading guilty by telephone from hospital, paralysed from the waist down, and was jailed for ten to thirty years.

See also **World Wide Business Centre**

Planning Officers

The British Town and Country Planning Acts of 1947 empowered local authorities to control the right of ordinary citizens to build as they pleased. At a stroke, even the minor details of a small home extension could be indefinitely delayed or altogether banned. Planning Officers and council committees often imposed their personal taste on detailed questions of layout and appearance, deliberating for weeks, months or sometimes years on the precise type of glazing bars or railings on a residential extension, at the same time as authorising or encouraging the construction of large-scale developmental disasters.

It has long been the tradition for Planning Officers to claim that the real power is vested in their local councils. But in practice, councillors normally defer to the advice of their professionals, and thus Planning Officers can and do inflict almost limitless loss and distress on their applicants. So it is probable that most people with first-hand experience of the planning process have, at some stage, wanted to kill their Planning Officer, and thus even in law-abiding Britain it was only a matter of time before one got himself shot.

The man who did it was Albert Dryden. On 20 June 1991 he murdered Derwentside's Principal Planning Officer, Harry Collinson. As the confrontation and killing were filmed, Dryden became an instant television celebrity.

Albert Dryden was a well-liked local eccentric, a bachelor of 51 with a streak of self-taught mechanical ingenuity. In the 1970s he was known in the neighbourhood as the 'Rocket Man' for his hobby of building missiles which he launched from Stanhope Moors; the government took him to court because they flew too high. At the time of the killing, Dryden had the world's longest car under assembly.

After his redundancy from British Steel, Dryden invested his £15,000 pay-off in building a bungalow for his mother. He bought a plot of land and, in an off-the-record meeting as the planning wrangle developed, Collinson said he *could* put up a house – provided it was less than three feet high.

So Dryden built the bungalow in a hole. This meant that to all intents the structure could not be seen from the surrounding terrain. But, as many applicants for roof terraces can confirm, mere invisibility has never been an extenuating criterion for planners.

Dryden foolishly felt that he did not need permission for a building no one could see; quite properly, Collinson and the subsequent planning inquiry held otherwise. When Dryden's mother died, the *Northern Echo* ran the story that it was the row over the bungalow that killed her.

On the morning of 20 June 1991, the Council bulldozers arrived to flatten Dryden's bungalow. Harry Collinson was at their head, and Dryden shot him dead. According to eye-witness Michael Peckett: 'I saw Dryden straighten his arm and take very careful aim. When the gun went off, I jumped a foot in the air with surprise. To be honest, it was no noisier than a cap gun, not like you hear on TV.' Dryden shot Collinson four times.

In March 1992 Dryden was jailed for life despite pleading **amnesia** since, whether he could remember it or not, he had certainly committed murder. The public too felt strongly. That year Dryden received eighty-three Christmas cards.

Clearly Collinson had made many enemies. Terry Batson, an aggrieved town councillor for Tow Law outside Consett, commented: 'May you rot in hell, Harry Collinson, after what you did to my father.' Denise Bullivant, another local, was equally vehement: 'Harry Collinson was the officer who dealt with my planning application. He objected to the red tiles we wanted to use, even though they are traditional ... it changed the whole course of our lives. Mother had to sell the big house and ended up in Lanchester.'

Local hostility was intensified by Dryden's conviction. The chief executive of the Council, Neil Johnson, complained that 'some of the people around Mr Dryden have threatened and actually assaulted officers of the council. There've been threats of "We'll smash your car windows" and "We know where you all live."'

Other officials considered the episode and its outcome avoidable. For instance, Dryden and his mother could have been granted a purely personal right to occupy the bungalow, such right to cease on death. In retrospect, the Council escaped lightly with just the one fatality. Before the shooting, Dryden envisaged a kamikaze attack on the Town Hall. According to local newspaperman Garry Willey: 'Albert talked in the past about loading one of his American cars with explosives and ploughing it into the Civic Centre and taking eighty or ninety with him.'

Planning Officers in Turkey travel armed.

Poisoning

A source of macabre fascination but relatively few deaths, only accounting for about 5 per cent of murders. Generally the prosecution has little difficulty in proving malice aforethought. Extreme practitioners, like Graham **Young**, view their victims' protracted agonies as a spectator sport.

Although poisons are regarded as a 'coward's weapon' favoured by women, they are the special province of male doctors, with their unfettered access to lethal substances and their control over the legal formalities on death.

The wide latitude under which medical men can operate according to the dictates of their clinical opinion means that mere doubt about the propriety of any treatment is insufficient to establish guilt. Like everyone else, doctors disagree, and the main plank of the 1957 prosecution case against Dr Bodkin Adams (accused of giving lethal **injections** to his elderly patients) foundered when their expert witness was asked, 'Is there, in your opinion, any justification for injecting morphia and heroin immediately after a stroke?'

'No justification whatsoever,' replied Dr Douthwaite. But this was only Dr Douthwaite's opinion and it was, as it happened, incorrect.

From the other side of the fence, the allure of poison is that the resulting process often replicates the manifestations of an ordinary ailment, and few doctors query an apparently natural death. Death from arsenic evinces symptoms resembling those of severe gastroenteritis, and until quite recently a patient complaining of pain of obscure origin might have his condition diagnosed as 'neuralgia', which means no more than pain of obscure origin. In many cases a toxin degrades into the constituents conventionally found in a corpse; thus deadly succinylcholine chloride splits into the succinic acid and choline one would expect in body tissue. Other poisons have unknown active ingredients. They evidently work, because the recipient dies, but although modern laboratory techniques can discern quantities down to a single molecule, the pathologist does not know what to look for without advance knowledge of what the poison is. Despite progressive attempts at regulation, a murderer can generally get his hands on something lethal; Britain's Arsenic Act of 1851 represented an early attempt to prevent strangers or children from buying arsenic at will. Because of the relative scarcity both of black foodstuffs and beverages tasting of coal, the Act prescribed that soot, in the proportion of an ounce to a pound, be mixed with the poison prior to sale.

The diligent pathologist starts by evaluating the contents of a corpse's stomach and then samples the blood from at least six locations. Different organs favour different poisons. In the words of toxicologist Dr Alan Curry, 'The liver is a marvellous organ … That's where I'd look for inorganic material. There, and in the kidneys. The brain is where I'd look for volatile substances or solvents such as chloroform. Analysis of blood should reveal substances like strychnine.'

Perhaps the most famous delivery vehicle was the poisoned scone that the fastidious Major Herbert Armstrong handed Martin over tea in Hay-on-Wye in 1921, remarking 'Excuse fingers'. But, like the box of chocolates that Armstrong had sent to Martin's home earlier that week, the dosage proved too small to kill. The local chemist recognised Martin's symptoms, as did the Major when he passed his intended victim wobbling down the street. 'You must have eaten something which disagreed with you,' Armstrong pointed out, 'and I have a feeling you will have another illness very similar.'

It was easy to work out what the something was. On the day of Martin's stomach cramps he had eaten exactly the same as his wife, apart from the scone. A urine sample was despatched to the Home Office pathologist, together with the confectionery. Back came the reply: 'Two of the chocolates in this box had the appearance of being tampered with. A cylindrical hole nearly an inch long has apparently been bored and filled with a white powder … found on analysis to be white arsenic to the extent of 2.12 grains. Two grains of white arsenic has been known to cause death in an adult.'

The social imperative attaching to boxes of chocolates – they must be *shared* – invests the victim's precise identity with an element of uncertainty. It was not Oswald Martin who ate them, but his wife's sister. Similarly, the poisoned chocolates put in the mail by Professor John Buettner-Janusch in 1987 hit the wrong target. The professor, an American anthropologist of unusual brilliance, put the seal on his long record as a war protester and civil rights supporter with a 1980 conviction for making and possessing drugs. He was paroled, but the court case lay heavy on his mind, and

for St Valentine's Day in 1987, he sent the trial judge, Charles L. Brieant, a lethal box of 'Golden Godiva' chocolates. A former colleague at Duke University was another recipient, and two more boxes were intercepted in the post after the judge's wife nearly died.

Buettner-Janusch was caught by the imprint of his little finger on the packaging; five years into the sentence, a ruling that his release would not be before the year 2000 destroyed his will to live. He stopped eating and, despite force-feeding, died on 2 July 1992.

Poisons are either organic or inorganic (of mineral origin) and they work by latching on to enzymes, impeding their proper function. They can be classified into four main categories: those impairing the blood's ability to carry oxygen (carbon monoxide, cyanide); corrosive acids and alkalis which perforate the stomach (mustard gas, chloroform); systemic poisons causing widespread damage (**arsenic**, antimony, mercury, **strychnine**, morphine and hyoscine); and poisons which leave no trace on entry, like ricin, but wreak havoc only after their absorption.

Precociousness

Startling evidence was presented to the 1816 British Select Committee on the police. The Newgate chaplain, Reverend H. S. Cotton, a man with an advanced social conscience, was asked if the prisoner-boys in his charge kept mistresses. 'All of them,' he answered. 'Burnet, who is only nine years of age, has also a person he terms his girl.' Cotton affirmed that there was a constant procession of women at the prison gates 'calling themselves sisters and relations of the boys, who had been prevented afterwards from coming, from its being found out that they were common prostitutes and kept by the boys'.

'Prostitutes' was a term broadly used at the time, often designating an unmarried woman, other than of upper-class extraction, who had a boyfriend. 'Girl' or 'woman' would be a fair contemporary equivalent.

William Crawford, of the Society of Friends, provided the Committee corroborative testimony. He maintained that it was normal for boys on the loose to cohabit with girls of their own age. He cited the case of a youth lodging in a 'flash' house who 'had slept there upwards of thirty times with girls of his own age, and he particularly named five. This boy was fourteen.'

By this age, the reputation of the American Jesse Pomeroy (1860–1932) was already well-established. A double child killer, Pomeroy was a Bostonian child with a blind white eye and a hare-lip who murdered children. At 12 he was sent to the West Borough Reform School for his uncontrollable addiction to stripping youngsters naked, tying them up and beating them into unconsciousness. Paroled in February 1874, he turned to murder, stabbing four-year-old Horace Mullen thirty-one times before trying to cut off his head. He confessed to twenty-eight other killings, and the police unearthed twelve mutilated bodies buried round his mother's house.

Pomeroy's death sentence was commuted to solitary confinement because of his age; he served fifty-eight years, and perhaps the only uplifting feature of his life was an attempted jail-break of 1890. Chiselling away at his cell, Pomeroy's exertions exposed a gas pipe, and he hit on a four-stage escape plan. First, he took a deep breath. Second, he ruptured the pipe. Third, he held his breath. Fourth, he lit a match.

The explosion blew Pomeroy clear out of his cell but knocked him unconscious when he slammed into a wall. Meanwhile, the prison caught fire; three inmates perished in the blaze.

More recently, in April 1992 a girl of six was assaulted and allegedly raped in an Indianapolis junior school lavatory. The two males charged with the offence, aged seven, were confined to 'house arrest' with their parents.

At the other end of the scale, rapes of octogenarians are commonplace. A representative offender was Keith Walker, sentenced to life on 21 July 1992 for raping and then murdering an 82-year-old widow. He spent her savings of £70 in a Nottinghamshire nightclub.

Pregnancy

In the court of Henry VIII, a page's punishment was to go without beer for a month; the crime, making a chambermaid pregnant.

Until the twentieth century the social opprobrium directed at birth out of wedlock meant that the mother's fate might well be death. The centuries-long cycle consisted of poverty and pregnancy, followed by theft or prostitution to keep body and soul together. An expectant unmarried woman would be shown the door by any employer and probably turned on to the streets by her family.

Transportation or the gallows were thus frequent repercussions of sexual indiscretion, and the poor were often reduced to killing their illegitimate offspring. The better-off might foster them to the sinister 'baby farms' of the Victorian era; the most famous was run by a Mrs Amelia Dyer, whose main assets were a neat, bonneted appearance and a reassuring line in Salvation Army sentiments. With these she plied her trade for fifteen years, charging between £10 and £15 to relieve distressed mothers of their misbegotten children.

It was the dead baby she tossed into the Thames by Caversham Lock, trussed up in brown paper bearing her name and address, that brought Mrs Dyer to grief. The neat little parcel was fished out by a bargeman on 30 March 1896, and the wrapping tore to reveal a leg. In the five days it took the police to ascertain that '20 Wigott's Road, Caversham' should have read 20 Pigott's Road, and that the 'Mrs Harding' who had recently left was the same person as Amelia Dyer, now resident at 45 Kensington Road, she killed again.

Dyer drummed up custom by advertising in the *Bristol Times and Mirror*, posing as a childless woman yearning to care for a baby. She ran the operation in concert with her daughter and son-in-law, Polly and Ernest Palmer, who were forever picking up or dropping off Mrs Dyer from hand-overs at railway stations, watching a succession of babies arrive and heavily laden carpet-bags leave. The police dragged the Thames at Reading, dredging up another six bodies. 'You'll know mine by the tape around their necks,' Mrs Dyer observed, a point underlined in 1900 when four tiny skeletons were unearthed from the garden of a house she occupied in Bristol.

Polly gave evidence against her mother, and at the trial a Dr Lyttleton Stewart Forbes Winslow for the defence endeavoured to prove that his client was insane, a task to which Mrs Dyer had already applied herself with enthusiasm, inducing him to diagnose 'melancholia' and 'delusional insanity'. Forbes Winslow favoured the direct approach. 'Do you ever see any visions?' he demanded in a prison interview. 'Pray do not ask me,' Mrs Dyer replied, looking scared. 'What do you see?' Forbes Winslow continued. Mrs Dyer elaborated: 'I can't tell you; that is why I keep awake at night. The sounds I hear and the sights I see are dreadful.'

Dyer went to the gallows, as did many a mother who, in confusion or distress, slew her offspring within a year of birth. Only in 1938 did the Infanticide Act remove the onerous compulsion on judges to pass the death sentence in such cases; one beneficiary of this enlightened attitude was Australia's Barbara Wilkinson, who disposed of her six babies over a seven-year span, starting in 1961 at the age of 21. She killed the first because she was unmarried, the second because she conceived before marrying, and the next four because she could not face explaining their fate to a midwife or doctor (who would inevitably notice that the new child was not her firstborn).

Barbara Wilkinson produced all six infants without her husband, mother-in-law or friends noticing. She had two techniques. One was to understate the length of her term and, after the infanticide, conceal the corpse and claim a miscarriage. But when caught short staying at her mother-in-law's house at Mangrove Mountain, while her husband was away as a long-distance lorry driver, she explained that the swelling in her stomach came from an influx of 'fluid' which needed draining every year or so.

Wilkinson's past came to light when she haemorrhaged after having (and killing) her sixth. Her husband, Les, drove her to hospital where the doctors, like him, believed they were confronted by a still-pregnant woman. But foetal movement was completely lacking. They diagnosed and treated Barbara for an intra-uterine death, only to find no baby.

She was not a woman of great emotional depth. After telling the police about the 'binning' of her first child, she continued: 'After that, I went on to Les's place and that night I went to his twenty-first birthday party.'

See also **Münchausen**, **Weber**

Pressing

Not until 1827 were English courts empowered to enter a plea of 'Not Guilty' on behalf of an accused who stayed mute. His trial could not start without a plea, and thus an obdurate prisoner might defer his fate and, moreover, enrich his descendants by staying silent, since conviction as a felon entailed automatic forfeiture of all property to the Crown.

To prevent justice being cheated, taciturn suspects were sentenced to 'peine forte et dure'. They were 'pressed', that is, squashed. In about 1406 this supplanted the practice of starving them to death.

In **Newgate**'s dedicated Press Yard the prisoners, spreadeagled on their backs, had weights heaped on their chests until they spoke or died. Often the wretches' backs were snapped by positioning them over a central ridge. In Elizabethan times this served as a form of execution, but by the eighteenth century it was regarded as a **torture** to induce a plea. During the first twenty years of James I's reign, in Middlesex alone forty-four prisoners, including three women, were crushed to death.

In 1721 the highwayman William Spiggot withstood a load of 350 pounds for half an hour before a further fifty pounds compelled him to utter. He was hanged. In 1658 a Major Strangeways held out to the bitter end. To safeguard his estate from confiscation, a group of friends helped flatten him in a record eight minutes.

The practice was abolished in 1772.

See also **Insane**

Preview

Murder is such an obliterating event that it is hard to see where the sex comes in. What can be sexy about a sex killing?

A few weeks before the double murder at Lake Sammamish, Ted **Bundy** staged a dry run which stopped short of death. But the other constituents were in place, in diagrammatic form, and it is perhaps easier to discern the roots of Bundy's pleasure.

In June 1974, Bundy arranged a raft trip on the River Yakima with an acquaintance from the state legislature, Larry Voshall. The young men invited two women, Becky and Susan, buying life jackets because neither girl was a proficient swimmer. Three of the group took the raft, and the fourth was towed behind on a rubber inner-tube.

As they entered the white-water rapids, Bundy's mood suddenly changed. In Voshall's words, 'All at once, Ted who's behind Becky, unties the string of her halter top. It fell off, exposing her breasts. We were all just flabbergasted, embarrassed. You know, we didn't really know each other at all. Ted seemed to get some kick out of that. Later on we were in a pretty swift current, and Becky was behind the raft in the inner-tube. Ted reached for the rope and said,

"What'll you do if I untie this rope?" Well, Becky's screaming. Just scared to death. And I looked at Ted's face and I couldn't believe it. He had a look on his face as though he was enjoying subjecting her to that terror – hearing her scream. He had untied the rope. And I got really upset.'

Lust killers are normally highly '**organised**'. First comes the fantasy, replayed many times in the head, followed by the hunt, then the murder, an intensely personal act often preceded by mutilation and accompanied by extreme overkill; in a representative 1990 incident from Cardiff, shipping clerk Geraldine Palk was stabbed eighty-three times.

Bundy's dress rehearsal on the raft was aborted at a preliminary stage. He achieved sexual humiliation by ripping off Becky's clothes, and had settled into the phase of **terror** induced by domination: 'What'll you do if I untie this rope? What'll you do if I knife you just here?' There are clear parallels with an exaggerated version of sexual congress – the girl goes completely out of control, in a frenzy, she has eyes only for you, your slightest movement makes her squeal. Two thousand years ago, the amphitheatres of Rome were sexual arenas.

Normal intercourse is followed by psychic discharge, and sex killers like Bundy gradually devise the form of displaced sexual behaviour that meets their needs. In a hideously distorted form, many conventional motivational elements of the courtship ritual are embodied in a sex killing: the phase of establishing contact, the excitement, the 'intercourse' proper, and the afterglow. Although the killer adapts each stage to his own ends, the objectives remain the same.

Ordinary people may experience perfectly containable sadistic fantasies during sex. For a sex killer the two components (sex and sadism) diverge, with the killer's perverse sphere (sadism) progressively ousting the conventional side (sex) until it assumes an independent existence outside the sexual context, as a substitute for it.

Thus the Russian serial killer **Chikatilo** bit off his victims' nipples in mimicry of the love bite. **Masturbation** over the corpse is another common thread, as is the factor of the killer's sexual dysfunction, most often impotence, extending to an apparent lack of interest in sex and an awkwardness with women. The lethal combination is a desire to have sex coupled with the inability to have it, and the Russian investigator Kostoyev observed of Chikatilo that no one capable of having normal heterosexual relations would have needed to kill as he did. Sadism of this order may confer sexual ability, but not the partner, who is dead.

See **Cannibalism**, **Sex crimes**, **Torture**

Prison system, a brief history

Historically, Britain had little need of prisons. If guilty, the normal sentence was death, and if innocent, the accused was released. The idea of sentencing miscreants to a fixed term of confinement did not evolve until more civilised times.

Thomas More's *Utopia* (1516) contained an early proposal for imprisonment as a punishment. As an alternative to execution, More suggested that thieves should be locked up and reduced to slave status for a prescribed term of years. But there was hardly anywhere to send them. State prisons did not exist.

Until the nineteenth century, most prisoners were incarcerated not for crime but for **debt**. The remainder awaited their fate in a ragbag of local prisons, county prisons, debtors' prisons and private prisons. About half the jails were privately owned, rented out to subcontractors by their landlords, like the Duke of Portland or the Bishops of Ely or Leeds. Thus **Newgate** was a profit-making commercial enterprise run by and for the Warden, with any surplus after expenses accruing to his pocket. Unnecessary amelioration of the inmates' conditions was not a priority, and when the prison reformer John Howard began his visits in the 1770s, he preferred to travel by horse rather than carriage. His clothes became so heavily impregnated by their brief exposure to prison interiors that their stench in a post-chaise proved intolerable.

Transportation provided a long-standing alternative to the shortcomings of the prison system. From the seventeenth century onwards, the British shipped many of those who avoided execution to the plantations in Virginia or the last-ditch islands of Jamaica and Barbados. All went smoothly enough until 1775 and America's War of Independence. Thereafter, until the development of the Australian penal colony, convicts who were not hanged still had to be put somewhere.

Thus were born the **hulks**, clapped-out vessels where men and boys were kept ironed throughout their sentence. The ships' capacity was supplemented by the 1779 Act authorising the first state prison,

Millbank, which opened thirty-two years later on the site of today's Tate Gallery in London. Remarkably, it had individual lavatories in each cell, the outcome of the standing requirement for solitary confinement (the **Separate System**), but the contamination through substandard drainage claimed a dreadful death toll.

The policy of continuous solitary represented an abrupt volte-face on the previous regime of foul (but social) slumming, where inmates were bundled together in a heaving mass. Under the new order, convicts were obliged to contemplate their navels for years on end in supposed eradication of their criminality – a cruel distortion of the thinking of John Howard, who favoured classification into small groups of appropriately graded offenders.

Millbank may have been intended as a semi-religious reformatory, but its policies were conducive only to madness. This initial failure led to the implementation of steadily harsher measures, like flogging, until thirty years after its opening the government denounced Millbank as an 'entire failure'. By then the structure was little more than a reception centre before prisoners were farmed out to the hulks or transported.

But Australia increasingly resented the influx of unreformed convicts. So the government endorsed the construction of a new model prison, Pentonville, which espoused the Separate System with even greater ferocity. Opened in 1842, Pentonville ushered in an era of nationwide solitary confinement exacerbated by such soul-destroying devices as the **crank** and the **treadwheel**.

Discipline became stricter, and in 1877 prisons were unified into a monolithic state-run service under their first commissioner, Du Cane, architect of the great nineteenth-century prison construction programme of Wakefield, Reading, Wandsworth and the Scrubs (built entirely by convict labour). Du Cane enforced programmes of bread and water, solitary labour, religious instruction, and seclusion; more importantly, the cells were built without lavatories, and the ones in Pentonville were ripped out. Du Cane believed that the inmates had only to ring a little bell for attentive staff to come running.

Thereafter the prisons were closed to press and public alike, and the solitary rigours instigated at Pentonville extended throughout the system. Convicts had to maintain absolute silence, wear masks, and walk with their heads turned to face the wall when outside their cells to avoid eye contact. These practices continued into the present century; separate confinement was only abolished in 1922.

Today's regime represents a slightly mollified version of its nineteenth-century predecessor enacted within the same physical fabric. In 1991 an inmate commented, 'I've been on active service in Cyprus picking up dead bodies eaten by rabid dogs, but I found the conditions in Pentonville barbaric', and on 31 May 1992 the Human Rights Watch organisation characterised the British prison system as 'just coming out of the Dark Ages'. The next day the Chief Inspector of Prisons likened Dartmoor to a 'dustbin', lamenting the dual use of lavatory brushes for dish scrubbers. He pointed out that the inmates' only source of satisfaction was confrontation with the warders. Elsewhere, the twelve British mother-and-infant cells spawned a curious evolutionary mutation: babies who cannot crawl. Their mothers were afraid to let them loose on the cockroach-infested floors.

But things are worse in Thailand. In 1982 (and probably now) Bangkok's notorious Mahai Chai prison, with its design capacity of 600, housed 6,000 inmates, all without the benefit of plumbing. The only water was dumped into a large horse trough. The then commandant, Prasan Prasert Prasert, turned a blind eye to violence and torture by the guards; killings were particularly rife in the hospital unit. Overcrowding meant that prisoners were not alone even in 'solitary' confinement.

In America, more black men are in prison than in college. For the 15–25 age group, one quarter are in prison, or on bail, or on parole. But this is only the average. In Washington, the figure rises to 40 per cent.

Privilege

Some convicts are more equal than others. The murder-for-fun couple, Leopold and Loeb, were incarcerated in conditions of inexplicable luxury in the 1920s. The crowded Statesville penitentiary allocated them each a two-man cell, with space for a desk, a filing cabinet and a small library. The boys were allowed their own toiletries and their own meals, prepared to their personal specifications, and dined in private in the officers' mess. Special washing privileges gave them access to the officers' shower room, and the prison storeroom was available round the clock for telephone calls. Their doors were seldom locked, and the pair – lovers since the age of 14 – saw each other when they wanted, often taking a stroll outside the prison walls to visit Leopold's garden, or wandering off to buy dope or booze.

Photographs suggest that their standard of living was roughly comparable to a second-rate English public school, and indeed Leopold and Loeb were still teenagers at the start of their sentences in 1924. Had they been upper-crust English schoolboys, they would hardly have noticed the difference. As it was, they were upper-crust Americans, Leopold the son of a multi-millionaire shipping magnate, and Loeb the son of a vice-president of Sears, Roebuck. Both were law students.

The 1924 murder of Bobby Franks supposedly manifested their innate superiority over other mortals, who must have found the boys' immunity to the normal consequences of their actions very galling. Loeb was the leader of the two, and he accepted Leopold as his lover after insisting on a signed contract agreeing joint participation in teenage criminal ventures. The pair worked their way up through the petty thrill of stealing a typewriter from the fraternity house to their perfect version of the ultimate crime: murder 'for kicks'. According to Loeb, it was Leopold who 'suggested it as a means of having a great deal of excitement, together with getting quite a sum of money'. At the time, both ideas – kidnapping and recreational murder – were novelties.

On 21 May Leopold and Loeb hired a car and 'trolled' for a young victim, male or female, enhancing their excitement by watching through binoculars from the cover of an alley at some youths playing basketball, part of the selection process. Two hours passed before 14-year-old Bobby Franks hove into view. As a friend of Loeb's younger brother, Franks had no qualms about accepting a lift. He was killed with a chisel, stripped naked and disfigured with hydrochloric acid, and his parents received a pre-typed ransom demand for a meagre $10,000. But the next day their son's body was discovered wedged into a culvert on waste ground near Wold Lake outside Chicago.

Competent criminals might have concealed the body better. Its feet stuck out, and the boys were careless in three other respects. The Leopolds' chauffeur saw them scrubbing down blood from the back of the car; and they elected to dump Franks in a deserted marshy area which they were known to frequent as bird-watchers. Doubtless Leopold and Loeb were titillated by their inclusion in the initial investigative stages, but it was a more serious oversight to type the ransom note on their stolen portable, with its distinctive 'i', 't' and 'm'.

Bad luck took a hand in their conviction when Leopold mislaid his glasses near the culvert. They were picked up by one of the workmen summoned to shift the body, and the optical company Almer Coe recognised the spectacles as one of 54,000 pairs sold in Chicago, identical save for the refinement of the hinges machined by Bobrow Optical. Leopold's were one of only three sets made. He attempted to fob off his interrogators by describing how his glasses had slipped out of his top pocket when he tripped during a bird-watching expedition the previous week. Invited to replicate the incident, he fell forwards on his face. But the glasses stayed put.

Leopold and Loeb were saved from the death penalty by Clarence Darrow's sterling defence, and their lenient treatment meant the trial judge needed police protection for months afterwards. Family money ensured the boys a comfortable existence, but in 1935 a homosexual inmate razored Richard Loeb to death, inspiring the headline: 'Sentence ends with a proposition'. Leopold was released on parole in 1958, whereupon he sued the author of *Compulsion* (a novel and subsequently a film based on the case) for defamation. The $3 million action failed, and he died on parole in Puerto Rico in 1971.

More recently, white-collar criminal Ivan Boesky fared well in his jail of first choice, the minimum-security prison at Lompoc, Santa Barbara. Given the free run of the administrator's telephones, he habitually dined on steak and fresh fruit in the visitors' room and went into town whenever he wanted. Sometimes he was collected by a blonde in her early thirties.

Inside prison, men of importance do not lose caste. Lucky Luciano all but held court during his 1940s spell in the maximum-security State Penitentiary at Dannemora (known as 'Siberia'). According to a guard: 'He practically ran the place. He used to stand in the yard like he was the warden. Men waited in line to talk to him. Charlie Lucky would listen, say something and then wave his hand. The guy would actually *back* away.'

Procession

This is not the schematic disposition of a prison football team with the Chief Warder as goalkeeper:

Chief Warder
Warder   Warder
Warder   Chaplain   Warder
Convict
Executioner
Principal Warder   Principal Warder
Warder   Warder
Governor   Sheriff
Wand bearer   Wand bearer
Surgeon and Attendant

It was the rigid Victorian order of procession as the condemned man walked across the courtyard to the gallows. The strict protocol and the sheer number of state and institutional officials emphasised that his termination was very far from haphazard retaliation.

An unfortunate incident involving the murderer Andrew Carr at Dublin's Richmond Prison on 28 July 1870. His trunk continued to quiver for three minutes.

'Profiler'

Profiling is the buzz-word for the accurate psycho-logical portraits of serial killers constructed from seemingly trivial details; 'Profiler' is the FBI Behavioral Unit computer program. It operates according to rules culled from investigative experience. For instance, most violent crime is intra-racial: whites prefer slaughtering whites; and Hispanics, Hispanics. Most serial murderers are white; the majority take their first life between 25 and 30. Sexual assaults on the elderly are generally the province of blacks. Similarly, in British homicide cases with a female victim under 17, the assailant is 62 per cent likely to be single, rising to 83 per cent if the victim is male. In 70 per cent of child homicides unaccompanied by sexual molestation, the culprit is a parent or guardian, but in sexual cases parental involvement drops to near zero. And so on.

The FBI's Profiler prototype began with 150 rules; by 1990 this had topped 270, and the list is still growing. For each case, the input to Profiler is everything known about the crime and, in particular, about the victim and the state of the body. Profiler output is the *type* of culprit: his age, sex, race, marital status, IQ, school record, present type of job (if any), outline employment history, 'rearing environment', personality traits, hobbies, appearance and grooming; whether he is **organised** or disorganised, whether he is liable to return to the crime scene and whether he lives near to or far from it, his connection with the victim and, of course, the motive. More graphically, Profiler provides an itemised reconstruction of the murder, starting with Phase One (contact) and ending with Phase Four (disposal).

For fine tuning, results of the computer-generated profile are adjusted against the human operative's assessment. Even getting only five or six of the twenty-five personality 'indicators' right may pinpoint the culprit, and today the headquarters for the Analysis of Violent Crime at **Quantico** handles about 900 cases a year.

Profiling received an inauspicious start in the 1960s when the medical-psychiatric team deployed on the Boston Strangler case suggested that his killings were the handiwork of two people: one a schoolteacher and the other a man living alone. One was a homosexual. Both were consumed by a festering hatred for their domineering **mothers** who, it seemed, were probably dead. It seemed likely that during the killers' childhoods, their mothers walked about 'half-exposed in their apartment, but punished them severely for any curiosity'. These objectionable experiences encouraged the Stranglers to play out their resentments in adulthood, murdering and mutilating older women in a manner simultaneously 'loving and sadistic'. Both killers had a weak and distant father.

Arrested in one piece, DeSalvo proved a family man motivated by an **insatiable** sex-drive and a vitriolic hatred of his brutal, domineering *father*. DeSalvo actually liked his mother, who was still alive.

It was the alteration of DeSalvo's *modus operandi* during his criminal career that misled the profilers. In the initial stages he concentrated on elderly victims; later, he picked on his own age group. A dissenting member of the investigative team, Dr James Brussel (see **Mad Bomber**) correctly reconciled the apparent differences in the killers' style as a single individual's process of maturation. 'In this two-year period,' Brussel noted, 'he has suddenly grown from infancy to puberty to manhood.'

Profiling remains an inexact science, at least partly governed by psychiatrists' capacity to infer what they want to believe. Shrewder villains exploit this tendency. The Hillside Strangler, Kenneth Bianchi, nearly wriggled off the hook by feigning an exciting multiple personality disorder (**MPD**), fooling every expert apart from the police and a lone psychiatrist, Martin Orme, who happened to have read the books (*Three Faces of Eve*, *Sybil* etc.). Similarly, the **false** taped **confession** to the Yorkshire Ripper killings, which sidetracked the police investigation for months, may have invited belief by its conformity to the largely mythic stereotype of **Jack the Ripper**. Other critics maintain that psychiatrists are overly gratified by suggestions of a deranged mother–son relationship, regarding this as a touchstone indicative of authenticity.

In Britain, profiling was viewed with mistrust until very recently. But Professor David Canter of Surrey University has now collaborated with the police on fifty-two investigations, including the case of John **Duffy**, the first conviction secured by computer.

Jack the Ripper was profiled posthumously as a male in his late twenties living locally. Since the murders were associated with weekends, he was probably in employment – but free from family accountability, as the killings occurred between midnight and six in the morning. The profile pointed to someone from the lower classes, since the murders evinced 'marked unfastidiousness'. The Ripper was not surgically or anatomically skilled, and had probably been in some form of trouble with the police before. He would be regarded by his associates as a loner. And he was a likely victim of child abuse, especially from, or with the consent of, his mother.

Much of the scepticism about profiling centres round its clusters of jargon. Put more simply, many objections melt away. For instance, few people would dispute that it takes a particular type of cretin to be a serial killer; profiling tries to establish which. Professor Canter is admirably succinct: 'We can correlate the behaviour and the characteristics of the crime. From this we can draw indications of what sorts of criminals committed what sorts of murders. We will put a file of suspects into an order of priority.' Killings often throw up 'suspect lists' several thousand strong from their catchment area, and without a profiling system the police are left to plod endlessly through, say, reams of married businessmen when they should be concentrating on unemployed teenagers.

See also **Elveson**, **Mad Bomber**

Prohibition agents

A motley crew, despised by the Mob and public alike, and perhaps even more by the police as an unwarranted Federal intrusion.

Qualifications were minimal, the wages $200 dollars a month. But the prospects for extortion and kickbacks were without obvious limits, opening a vista of rich pickings which attracted the dregs of political appointees and near-criminals into the initial draft of 1,500 'Feds'. One agent was reportedly offered a bribe of $300,000 a week.

Prohibition agents became a byword for corruption, earning their first three indictments for selling confiscated liquor to bootleggers and accepting bribes within ten days of the **Eighteenth Amendment** coming into force; appropriately, the charges were issued in Chicago. Between 1920 and 1928, when the Department of Justice assumed control, the Treasury dismissed 706 agents for larceny. Too many of the remainder acquired justified reputations as hoodlums on the take, lolling in chauffeur-driven limousines with showgirl mistresses on their arms.

Captain Dan Chaplin, chief of the New York

Prohibition force, purged his squad in a few seconds. At a meeting of his agents round a large table, he rapped out, 'Put both hands on the table', then, 'Every one of you sons-of-bitches with a diamond ring is fired.' A good half left. In the Chicago of 1929, District Attorney George Emmerson Q. Johnson was perturbed by the young Eliot Ness's plan to form an elite caucus of a dozen **Untouchables**. 'Can we find enough honest agents?' he asked. Ness unearthed ten, most from outside Chicago.

New York agents Izzy Einstein and Moe Smith were men of integrity and substance, tipping the scales at 240 pounds each. Dubbed 'Tweedledum' and 'Tweedledee' by the press, the pair raided speakeasies in disguise, dressed up as rabbis, fishermen, bootleggers or football players.

The best evidence to make a charge stick in court was a sample of the liquor on sale. Einstein and Smith would order a drink at the bar and pour the tipple into a concealed funnel linked by a tube to a back-pocket flask. Between them, they were instrumental in making 4,392 arrests and impounding five million bottles of rotgut.

Prospects

According to the research of criminologist William West, professional criminals in America fare considerably better than their more opportunistic colleagues, who spend an average of two-thirds to three-quarters of their working lives in prison. A professional should get away with incarceration for about a quarter of his time.

The low clear-up rate presented by government statistics gives a different impression, but official figures relate only to the percentage of crimes solved on an annual basis. Habitual criminals commit more than one offence a year for more than one year. 'If you want to play, you have to pay' runs the adage.

According to Charles E. Silberman, author of *Criminal Violence, Criminal Justice*, 'None of the criminals I interviewed knew, or had ever heard of, anyone who had been a criminal for any length of time without having been imprisoned.'

An intractable problem is that after pulling off one paying job, the criminal must devise another. But any operation earning money through repetition is tantamount to business or, in other words, very like work,

requiring much the same qualities of reliability and applied intelligence. Thus a life of crime is not better than working for a living; it is working for a living. Mobster John Gotti put in fourteen-hour days under constant threat from law enforcement agents and his own colleagues.

In organised crime, the consequences of a hostile takeover or under-performance are often fatal. Although at first sight there is little to choose between Robert Maxwell and John Gotti as a boss, the blunt truth is that when Maxwell put his employees through the grinder it was only a figure of speech. Even the hoods assigned to mowing Gotti's garden lawn went in fear of their lives in case they tackled the task the wrong way and, under **Hoover**, the FBI achieved moblike status as a similarly terrorised organisation. John Dowd, the prosecuting attorney investigating misuse of Bureau funds in 1975, observed: 'There I was, interviewing employees just as scared as the people I'd had to deal with in pursuing Mafia chieftains. People in my office were absolutely trembling, relating twenty or thirty years of sordid conduct. They were still afraid, even though Hoover was dead.'

In America, a life of crime beckons early. It is as they enter Third Grade that pupils notice whether they form part of the cultural mainstream or its underclass. According to Dr James Comer, professor of psychiatry at Yale, the marginalised children appreciate what their background has failed to supply and what their future will fail to deliver, and slip off the edge academically as their attention fixes on two alternative scenarios: a life spent frying burgers for risible wages, or a bright-lights career for easy money dealing in drugs. The choice is theirs, to an extent, but the 1954 experiments of psychologist John B. Calhoun on the reaction of rat communities to gross overcrowding are not encouraging. Calhoun found that 5 per cent of the population turned into criminals, giving way to such anti-social ventures as rat rape and rat cannibalism. Contemporary statistics show parallel results with people, with the American urban homicide rate three times the norm for small towns, and the sex-crime rate up by a factor of four.

According to American criminologist Bruce Jackson, underworld figures spend an inordinate amount of time asleep. Lacking a proper job and, generally, the corrective framework of a wife and family, they have little reason to get up.

This has been true down the ages. In 1808 an English

seaman in Tunis recorded his impressions of the cele-brated pirate John Ward: 'Speaks little, and almost always swearing. Drunk from morn till night. Most prodigal and plucky. Sleeps a great deal and often on board when in port.'

Provenance

Technical term for corroborative evidence establishing the pedigree of a work of art. Until the Second World War, the authentification process tended to rely on the word of connoisseurs. But their opinions were erratic in the extreme. The art expert Abraham Bredius was over eighty and half blind when he accepted **Van Meegeren**'s pastiches as genuine Vermeers. Bernard Berenson too was famed for his partial, almost cantan-kerous attributions. Unsupported expert opinions can be just that: opinions. In 1984 a stone head dredged from a canal in Livorno, Italy, was proclaimed a price-less Modigliani by the curator of the local Museum of Modern Art before its exposure as a student prank, the fruit of four hours' work on a paving stone with two chisels, two hammers, a screwdriver and a power drill.

After the Second World War, academics like Anthony Blunt pioneered the careful inspection of the documentation related to a painting as an essential tool for the art historian. The legacy is a boom in forging not the paintings themselves but their authen-ticating papers. Even a genuine picture is more marketable with the appropriate paper-work. So the documents are faked. Since most galleries were extremely lax with their records until the 1960s, the door is wide open for imaginative interpolations.

Provenance can be established by almost anything: a letter, a diary entry, a line in an inventory or a receipt, and to mock up such scraps of paper is relatively straightforward. This means, paradoxically, that a fake provenance does not necessarily connote a bogus picture.

Intriguingly, there are a number of 'unclaimed' provenances. Thus a contemporary diary sometimes records that a famous artist painted a certain picture on such-and-such a day. But the picture itself may never have been discovered. A current example is the 1957 memoir of the French writer Jean Genet, 'The Studio of Giacometti', which details how Giacometti produced several versions of the writer's head, finally proffering one as a gift. Genet wrote: 'I decide to take a small head … it is only seven centimetres high and three-and-a-half or four wide.' Several versions of this painting exist, but none this size.

A competent forgery to these dimensions could beguile an unsuspecting art historian into the excited 'discovery' of the missing Genet head, easing its path to acceptance, and this project (suggested here for the first time) might well pay dividends. Similarly, an assiduous trawl through period diaries and letters would uncover other sitting targets, works of art known to have been created but which have never come to light.

Even today scientific tests are of limited application. Porcelain can be separated into 'ancient' and 'modern' by the thermo-luminescence test. But statues are beyond verification: all stone is old. Dendrochronology ascertains the age of wood in a Renaissance panel painting. Lead isotope ratios reveal whether paint includes American lead, which at least puts a work as before or after the sixteenth century, and patient scholarship has clarified various pockets of informa-tion, like the number of threads per inch in Rembrandt's canvases. But counts outside these norms are not of themselves conclusive.

Crystallography can distinguish without equivoca-tion between the regular machine-ground particles prevalent in nineteenth-century paint, and their rougher, earlier counterparts. But irrefutable evidence of counterfeit work most often comes from analysis of the pigments (and their binding medium) in the lower layers of a picture, indicating foul play if their ingre-dients post-date any overpainting, or the artist himself. But it is rare to expose a fake on scientific evidence alone. The great majority of artworks stand or fall on a rounded assessment of style, provenance and technical considerations conjointly, in other words, on opinion.

Save for his use of Bakelite, the physical constituents of the paintings by conscientious forgers like Hans Van Meegeren might pass muster today, but the paintings themselves are dreadful. Today's experts are astonished at how easily Van Meegeren duped yesterday's experts. Here the adage is that '**fakes** date'. The forger unwittingly absorbs stylistic nuances from his period, and a generation later it suddenly becomes clear that his compositions are distinctively of his own time. These days, with the perfect vision of hindsight, any fool can tell that Van Meegeren's *Christ* and the *Adulteress* was heavily influenced by Picasso's blue period.

Possibly the world's finest assemblage of forgeries was housed in Tito's Jesuistski's Museum outside Zagreb. The collection of 4,000 Old Masters, amassed by Ante Topic-Mimara and valued locally at $4 billion, contained hundreds of laughable Woolworth-style works in whose corners words like Turner, Michelangelo or Velazquez were written. Imelda Marcos is another mainline investor in expensive but obvious forgeries.

It is said that an expert cannot be fooled while drunk.

See also **Morals**

Public relations

One of the Mafia's more serious preoccupations In Sicily a 'man of respect' fulfilled a social function, wielding his power with a word here and there to straighten out day-to-day social conflicts. A mediator, even a public benefactor, he represented threatened individual or collective interests. According to the writer H. Hess: 'The *mafioso* recoils with shocked surprise from any suggestion that he is a criminal.'

The return of stolen goods is a Mafia speciality with an honourable lineage. In 1932, in Sicily, the bombastic Prefect Cesare Mori reported a 95 per cent success rate when the Mob was called in to mediate, and the semi-formalisation of this process of recovery (with a going rate of about one-third of the face value of the goods) epitomised the usurpation of the state's traditional monopoly of law and order.

When Mafia backs are against the wall, the gestures become grander. In his declining years, Capone spent time and money cultivating his role as a philanthropist. During the Depression, he set up Chicago's first soup-kitchens. 'Block restaurants for the unemployed, free food with compliments of the Organisation,' said a sociologist with first-hand knowledge, 'and you didn't have to listen to any sermons or get up and confess. You sat down and they gave you a real meal with tablecloths on the tables, and no one rescued you.'

The theft of national heirlooms provides real opportunities for gangland. After the Lindbergh kidnapping (see **Ladders**) of April 1932, Capone undertook to retrieve the child in return for temporary freedom. From Atlanta Penitentiary, he announced, 'I believe I can find the baby. I won't run away ... What a lot I could do outside! I don't know a thing about the Lindbergh kidnapping, but I'm known to all the racket crowd as an honest guy, an honest guy who would keep his word if it's money they're after.' Lindbergh accepted the offer; the authorities declined.

Joseph Profaci, reputed head of the Colombo family, reinforced the tradition in 1952 by arranging for the return of the jewel-encrusted golden crowns lifted from New York's Regina Pacis Votive Shrine; these plangent relics fashioned from the melted-down wedding rings of war widows. And when the icon from the Greek Orthodox church in Astoria, New York, was stolen at gunpoint on 23 December 1991, John Gotti put out word that he expected it to be returned. This was the famous 'weeping icon of peace' which shed tears at the start of the Gulf War.

At the time Gotti, in jail awaiting trial for racketeering, needed all the help he could get and, by the end of the week, amid much bell-ringing, the relic was safely back in the fold – minus its frame, a gold setting encrusted with rubies and diamonds, valued at $800,000.

It is not only *mafiosi* who crave respectability. Among the droves of Chinese drug traffickers infesting Bangkok, serious dealers who have made their fortune expend their millions on buying power and influential friends; for added social acceptability they distribute big money to worthy philanthropic causes. Accordingly, major traffickers make six-figure donations to anti-drug campaigns, helping to educate the public in the crusade against the addiction from which their riches sprang.

Puente, Dorothea (1928–)

Arsenic and Old Lace, the play by Joseph Kesselring, premièred at Broadway's Fulton Theater in 1938, with the comic theme of the two aged Brewster sisters who poisoned their way through a dozen lodgers, despatching them with arsenic-laced elderberry wine. Serial killers in America were then such rare aberrations that they made safe figures of fantasy; during the 1920s, a mere thirty-nine deaths were recognised as the handiwork of multiple murderers.

Today, serial killers are no longer a joke, and it is unlikely that a revival of *Arsenic and Old Lace* would attract wide audiences either in Milwaukee, the home town of Jeffrey **Dahmer**, or in Sacramento, California, where Dorothea Puente underwent a legal misunderstanding. Dorothea is the frail, diminutive grandmother who ran the boarding house on F Street. A keen gardener, she grew giant tomatoes, apricots and wonderful roses which sucked their nutrients from the lush soil near her back-door statuette of St Francis.

Dorothea provided work for prison parolees who sometimes laboured at digging her flower beds, and she turned her powder-blue Victorian home over to the welfare of the state's poor and muddled pensioners in their declining years, charging an affordable $350 for a month's board and lodging.

Dorothea prospered over the years. She took taxis everywhere, invested in a snappy wardrobe, favouring mauve and pink, and earned a reputation as a generous tipper at the local bar where she stood drinks all round. Always on the lookout for a new homeless senior citizen, she gave free financial advice on the welfare jungle, and many lodgers were picked up over a vodka-and-orange. When her guests fell ill, she dispensed special care upstairs in her sickroom. She replaced its carpet a number of times at her own expense; as she told friends, sometimes 'bad things' happened up there.

Two strict rules governed Dorothea's establishment.

First, guests had to be punctilious in the maintenance of their pension, welfare and disability allowances. Under the second, Dorothea alone could collect the post. Otherwise, her guests – and neighbours – only needed to acclimatise themselves to the F Street smell. For scrub as Dorothea might, spray what lemon deodorant she would, dump as much fish emulsion on the garden as she could, the place still stank.

In 1988 social worker Judy Moise enquired about the fate of one of the lodgers, a 52-year-old retarded immigrant from Costa Rica named Alvaro Montoya. Dorothea maintained that he had left to visit his relatives in Mexico.

But Moise knew that Montoya's only relatives lived in New Orleans. She called the police, who spent three days excavating Dorothea's garden, unearthing the decayed remains of seven tightly-wrapped bodies, all lodgers, buried under the rosebeds and the vegetable plot. Their former landlady was charged with a total of nine murders including another guest whose boxed corpse cropped up in the river, and yet another lodger previously regarded as a suicide. She was convicted for causing only three of these deaths but, as she was imprisoned for life, it might as well have been for all nine.

Q

Quantico

The US base forming the headquarters of the FBI's NCAVC: the National Centre for the Analysis of Violent Crime. Set up by Reagan in June 1984, its primary mission is the apprehension of serial killers, and its first investigative step to establish whether a new killing displays the hallmark of a villain already on file.

Operatives work sixty feet underground in an old nuclear bunker. The ten senior profilers are designated 'criminal investigative analysts' (the 'A team') and, since their job is analysis not arrest, the premises house neither cells nor offenders. The business end is the computer system, known formally as VICAP – the Violent Criminal Apprehension Program – and informally as 'Old Red-Eye' for the pulsing red light in the console's steel face.

Details of new cases come into Quantico clinically described on an exhaustive ten-part questionnaire completed by local police. Headings include everything known about the victim, the state of the body (including details of '**souvenirs**' removed, any **torture** and so on), the **modus operandi**, cause of death and forensic evidence. Thus Section VII ('Condition of Victim when Found') incorporates a sub-section, 'Restraints Used on Victim', beginning with Question 141 'Was the Victim bound?', followed by eight multiple-choice questions. Number 142 asks respondents to select between: restraint with an article of clothing; tape; cordage; chain; handcuffs; or other ('please specify').

These standardised data are sent down the line to the mainframe in Washington, which reciprocates with a print-out – the 'Template' – of the ten best matches: similar killings elsewhere, listed in order of resemblance. A junior analyst adds the human element, assessing which (if any) are the work of the same hand. A positive identification of two or more 'events' with a matching 'signature' means that the various law enforcement agencies involved are put in contact with each other and with Quantico which, on request (indicated by a tick in the relevant box), forwards a copy of the killer's 'profile'.

This system, the brainchild of Commander Pierce Brooks, represents the fruit of twenty-five years' work. The Commander's inspiration dates to 1958. Driven by a hunch that a murder victim had perished at the hands of an experienced killer, Brooks was reduced to combing through newspapers at public libraries to check for a previous mention of an unidentified killer. The search took a year of his free time, but it yielded a news clipping on an arrest for an analogous slaying in a different city. The fingerprints in that case matched those in his. As Brooks attested at the 1983 Senate Committee, 'Over the years that primitive system worked two or three times.'

Until the 1980s there was no alternative to similar feats of clerical drudgery. Local law officers remained in ignorance of the case-load of colleagues in other jurisdictions. Many forces in many states could want the same man, with no one the wiser, and police on the spot might be unaware that their murder was the work of a serial killer sought (or behind bars) elsewhere. In an era of advanced technology, American police lacked any means of pooling information, and the overwhelming consensus for reform voiced at the 1983 Senate Committee hearing prompted Reagan to implement the VICAP proposals without delay.

Today, VICAP constitutes a centralised, updated directory of homicides nationwide. Staff reckon on detecting the handiwork of about fifteen new serial killers a year. Perhaps half are caught.

One of Quantico's more unusual features is the mock town of 'Hogan's Alley' for anti-terrorist training, based on Hollywood's Universal Studios. Next to the Bank of Hogan, the most robbed financial institution in the world, stands the Biograph Theater, perpetually playing *Manhattan Melodrama* in tribute to the death of John **Dillinger**. Agents, brought up to regard themselves as 'doing God's work', incessantly rehearse tactical manoeuvres, scaling walls, firing at pop-up targets and simulating drug raids. Their FATS device (firearms training device) stages **virtual reality** gunfights where agents hone their skills on changing scenarios; one time, the electronic suspect reaches for a gun, the next for a cigarette, and the recorded fall of shot shows who dies when. In many ways, Quantico fosters a culture of action, and critics of the **Waco** débâcle, where more than eighty Davidians died in an inferno after the FBI rammed a tank into the compound, question whether the Agency is best equipped to handle situations of psychological stasis calling for protracted inaction.

See **Database, Organised, Profiler, Waco Siege**

Quartering

Unpopular with French executioners. The process was complicated and time-consuming since each of the condemned man's limbs had to be stoutly harnessed to a **horse**, and the four animals might strain for an hour before the victim was torn apart. Worse, each animal needed to be goaded by an assistant, whose fees came out of the executioner's pocket.

Queen Poison

Title awarded to Lydia Sherman, a manic American poisoner who escaped the death penalty. In 1864 Lydia grew tired of her whingeing husband, Edward Struck, a New York policeman who lost his job after flunking the arrest of a mad knife-man. First Lydia mocked her spouse into drink and despair; then she poisoned him with **arsenic**. Next she did away with her six children, including her nine-month-old baby, weaned on contaminated milk.

At last she was free, and in 1868 Lydia married the elderly Dennis Hurlbrut, whom she poisoned. Her third husband, Nelson Sherman, met the same fate on 12 May 1871, laid low by a mug of poisoned cocoa; by then she had already put his two daughters underground.

Altogether, Lydia is credited with forty-two killings. But she confessed to only eleven and another dozen or so 'possibles', and at her trial in April 1872 was convicted of second-degree murder. She died five years into her life sentence.

A strong British claimant for the epithet of Queen Poison is Mary Ann Cotton. Born in 1832 to a Durham miner, she was raised as a devout Methodist. At its maximum, Mary Ann's tally includes her own mother, two husbands, two lovers, her best friend, five of other people's children and ten of her own, but her fatal swathe is normally put at fourteen or fifteen, mostly identified by the tell-tale certification of death from 'gastric fever'. Mary Ann was atypical in her occasional poisonings to clear the way to a marriage rather than from one; other motives included insurance policies of a few pounds or even burial money. She often moved house, shedding spouses and children in her wake.

Mary Ann was arrested on 18 July 1872 after the unexpected demise of her stepson, Charles Edward, in the village of West Auckland. On 6 July she had implored the local public relief official, Thomas Riley, to make room for her boy in the workhouse. Riley enquired if she wanted to get married. 'It might be so,' responded Mary Ann, 'but the boy is in the way.' Six days later Charles Edward was dead. 'I was surprised,' Riley recounted. 'The boy had seemed a perfectly healthy little chap. I went straight to the police and the village doctor.' On exhumation, the child's viscera were found riddled with arsenic; £8 was due on a policy with the Prudential.

By the time Mary Ann came to court on 5 March 1873 her past was public knowledge, and the trial was a one-sided affair since the judge, Sir Thomas Archibald, admitted evidence of similarly suspicious deaths among her friends and relatives. Beyond arguing that Charles Edward had succumbed to some green floral wallpaper, heavily impregnated with arsenic, her counsel had nothing to say. Mary Ann was hanged on 24 March 1874, with the *Newcastle Journal* commenting: 'Perhaps the most astounding thought of all is that a woman could act thus without becoming horrible and repulsive. Mary Ann Cotton, on the contrary, seems to have possessed the faculty of getting a new husband whenever she wanted one. To her other children and her lodger, even when she was poisoning them, she is said to have maintained a rather kindly manner.'

R

Ramirez, Richard (1960–)

Julian and Mercedes Ramirez – poor Mexican immigrants – had seven children. Like all his family, Richard, the youngest, was brought up in the Catholic faith in El Paso, Texas. But by the age of nine he preferred glue-sniffing and video arcades to churchgoing.

Then Ramirez discovered dope, funding his habit by theft. Robbery led to burglary and school truancy. He dropped out at the age of 17, and on 7 December 1977 underwent his first arrest, for suspected possession of marijuana. He was carrying a ski mask and a toy gun at the time. After his fourth arrest he was sentenced to three years' parole. Thereafter Ramirez lived rough, subsisting on a diet of Coke and hamburgers. He stole cars. By 1983 he had moved to Los Angeles, where he slid into an existence in the abyss. A tall, lanky dope-head with hollow cheek-bones, obsessed with satanism and heavy metal rock'n'roll, Ramirez financed his injections of cocaine by stealing videos and microwaves.

He was caught, jailed for car theft, served his term and was released. Then in June 1984 Ramirez raped and killed Jennie Vincow. She was 79. Nine months later, on 17 March 1985, he broke into the apartment of Dayle Okazaki, a traffic-manager from Hawaii. In the kitchen he shot her dead, and when her flatmate returned, he shot her too. Then he pressed on to Monterey Park where he dragged Tsai Lian Yu from her car and killed her. On 27 March he forced his way into the home of Vincent and Maxine Zazzara; he owned a pizza restaurant, she was a lawyer. Ramirez shot him dead; she died after her eyes were cut out. On 14 May he broke into William Doi's home, shot him dead, beat his wife and raped his daughter. The next rape came on 30 May; the victim – Carol Kyle – survived, and on 27 June Ramirez slit the throat of Patty Elaine Higgins, and on 2 July Mary Louise Cannon suffered the same fate.

Five days later Ramirez bludgeoned to death Joyce Lucille Nelson, a grandmother. On 20 July Max Kneiding was shot dead in bed in his Glendale home. Ramirez stabbed Kneiding's wife, Lela, before attempting to cut off her head. That night he shot Chainarong Khovananth and raped his wife, and then on 5 August he left the Petersons for dead. Three days later he murdered Elyas Abowath in San Gabriel Valley before raping his wife. Then on 17 August he shot a man called Peter Pan and his wife Barbara through the head.

As early as June, Detective Sergeant Salerno of the LA County Sheriff's Department knew that a serial killer was on the loose. Salerno tracked Ramirez's progress through his persistent use of the same .22 calibre pistol and its matching bullets. Two hundred police were assigned to the case, but by August they had accumulated little more than an Avia shoeprint and various sightings indicating that the killer was tall, thin and dark-haired. When the detailed descriptions provided by the Petersons were converted into Identikit sketches and flooded on to the newspapers and television screens, Ramirez showed the results to a friend in San Francisco, Donna Myers, an older woman who did his laundry and was virtually his only stable relationship. 'Do you think that could be me?' he asked.

Donna said no. So after breaking into William Cairn's home on 24 August, shooting him dead and raping his fiancée Inez, Ramirez remained unconcerned. He went to Phoenix Arizona to buy cocaine and caught the Greyhound back on 31 August. At about 8.30 that evening he walked into Tito's liquor store on Towne Avenue to buy a can of Coke and some doughnuts. By the checkout he noticed a stack of newspapers with his clearly recognisable photograph on the front page. Ramirez panicked and ran, pursued by shoppers.

He was identified because, the week before, survivor Inez Erickson told the police that her assailant had driven an orange Toyota. That same day a sharp-eyed teenager, James Romero III, spotted a suspicious orange Toyota circling his home in Mission Viejo. He noted its number, which matched the registration of an orange Toyota abandoned in the Los Angeles suburb of Rampart. A fingerprint lifted from the vehicle by laser scanning was transmitted to the state computer in Sacramento, just updated with the prints of those born after 1 January 1960. Ramirez's birthday fell on 28 February 1960, and his photographs were on file.

Ramirez sprinted two miles down the broad Los Angeles avenues, twisting into the side streets to shake off a growing crowd of pursuers. Two teenagers, Jaime and Julio Burgoin, jumped him. Then the police arrived. 'Save me, please! Thank God you came,' blurted Ramirez. A mob gathered round Hollenbeck police station, eager for a lynching.

After legal manoeuvring his trial did not open until January 1989. A refurbished Ramirez appeared in the dock. No longer a shabby loner with T-shirt and decaying teeth, his hair was groomed, his dental work shone, and he wore a pinstripe suit. But he declined to testify and was sentenced to death on 20 September 1989.

What was the *point* of the murders? Ramirez bragged to a cellmate, 'I've killed twenty people, man. I love all that blood.' To Sheriff Jim Ellis he expanded, 'I love to kill people. I love watching them die. I would shoot them in the head ... or I would cut them with a bread knife and watch their faces turn real white. I love all that blood.'

After sentence Ramirez told the court, 'I have a lot to say, but now is not the time or place ... I am beyond your experience. I am beyond good and evil.' To the press he said, 'Death always went with the territory. See you in Disneyland.'

See also **de Sade**

Rape, Law of

In England, rape is punishable by a maximum of life imprisonment (Section 1, Offences Against the Person Act 1956) but the offence only received statutory definition in 1976 as 'unlawful sexual intercourse with a woman ... who does not consent'. Thus a woman cannot rape a man, although this exploit was attributed to Joyce **McKinney** in 1977 by the tabloid press. The word 'unlawful' appears – or did appear until 1991 – to mean extra-marital intercourse.

The basic constituents of rape have long been established. The 1841 case of *Hughes* laid down that the hymen need not be broken; in the words of the 1956 Act, 'it is not necessary to prove ... emission of seed, but intercourse shall be deemed to be complete upon proof of penetration'. Nor is it a defence that the victim was asleep (*R v. Mayers* 1872) or even unconscious (*R v. Camplin* 1845), since both states preclude the victim's consent. At the time of writing there remains an irrefutable legal presumption that a boy younger than 14 is incapable of sexual intercourse.

The fraud cases follow the firm stand taken by the American wit Dorothy Parker, who remarked to a diminutive colleague: 'Never make love to me again, and if I ever find out you have I shall be extremely annoyed.' In *R v. Case* (1850), a doctor duped his patient into having intercourse under the pretence that this constituted treatment. The victim regarded the insertion as a surgical operation.

In fact it was rape, and nearly seventy-five years later the principle was upheld in *R v. Williams*, where a singing master procured sex with a 16-year-old pupil by depicting intercourse as a method of voice training. It may be that with the greater emphasis on sexual education this particular approach is defunct; there are no recent cases. But Section 2 of the 1956 Act still prohibits the misguided venture of inducing a married woman to make love by impersonating her husband.

Dense thickets of problems surround the notion of 'consent', the absence of which turns sex into rape. This area was notoriously expounded by Lord Denning: 'If a lady says "no" she means maybe, if she says "maybe" she means yes and if she says "yes" she is no lady.'

It is clear from *Olugjuba* (1982) that rape need not entail violence or even the threat of violence. Nor is acquiescence during or after the act pertinent; it is the woman's state of mind immediately prior to penetration that matters. There is no requirement for the victim to put up resistance. But the accused has a good defence if he genuinely considers – however unreasonably – that the woman agreed to intercourse. In *DPP v. Morgan* (1975) three friends were invited back for sex with a man's wife. The husband cautioned that her protestations were not to be regarded as lack of enthusiasm; she enjoyed it better that way. Initially, the three were convicted on the grounds that their belief in the woman's willingness had to be reasonable, but this was overturned on appeal, a decision reinforced by *R v. Satnam and Kewel* (1983), when the victim's lack of consent should have been 'obvious to every ordinary observer' and the participants alone deluded. Provided the belief is genuine, it need not be reasonable; being stupid is one thing, reckless quite another.

American law has followed the alternative route, as the 1992 **Tyson** case exemplifies. Convictions are based not on whether the man thought he was raping the woman but on whether the woman thought she was being raped by the man.

In England, until 1991, a bizarre but absolute presumption remained that a woman consented to intercourse with her husband, irrespective of the facts. Over the years the exemption's broad sweep was progressively eroded. In 1949 legally separated couples were excluded (*Clarke*), nor has it applied during a decree nisi since 1974 (*O'Brien*), or where the husband was under an injunction not to cohabit with his victim.

The landmark case of *R v. R* abolished the defence, for which no authority later than 1736 could be found. Lord Lane commented that the exemption was socially outmoded, and in October 1991 Lord Keith averred that marriage was a partnership in which the wife no longer constituted a subservient chattel.

Judges' comments made after conviction but during sentencing often attract widespread press discussion, perhaps most notably when a young woman was deemed to have asked for it because she hitch-hiked home, after nightfall. A companion case from 1993 ended with the freeing of the 15-year-old assailant after Judge John Prosser ordered him pay £500 'compensation' to his schoolgirl victim so she could have a holiday 'to recover'.

But it is easy to make smoke without much fire. On 11 April 1991, Brian Huntley from Hull was convicted of raping a 19-year-old prostitute. When his intentions became clear, his victim begged him to use a contraceptive and, remarkably, he did. Judge Arthur Myerson took this act of vestigial concern into account when arriving at a sentence of three years' imprisonment. The following day, the *Daily Mirror* carried the headline 'Judge praises rapist who wore condom', printing calls from Women Against Rape for his dismissal. In America, a similar 1992 case caused even greater outcry when the request for a condom inspired a defence based on the victim's consent.

There were 4,110 reported rapes in Britain during 1992; the average sentence was six years four months. In America the total reached 160,000 – about ten times the British *per capita* rate. In Mississippi the offence carries the possibility of the death sentence, perhaps a historical legacy intended for blacks.

Probably the single greatest contributor to the global figures is Mustapha Tabet, the police commissioner of Casablanca. In three years 1990, he raped the astonishing total of 1,500 women in his *garçonnière* at 36 Boulevard Ben Yacine. Tabet was above the law. His bank account groaned under a credit balance of £l.8 million accumulated on an annual salary of £2,000, and he lived by rake-offs and bribes, the traditional perks of a local chief of police. But Tabet went further. He bought a blue Mercedes, hired a chauffeur and drove round Casablanca offering rides to young women. He video-taped his assaults, enabling identification of 516 of his victims. He was executed in 1993.

Ratcliffe Highway

The main thoroughfare running east out of London, through the worst districts of the capital. In 1811, Number 29 was occupied by a young linen-draper, Timothy Marr, his wife, their three-month-old baby, their maid and apprentice boy.

Late on 7 December 1811, the maid went out to buy oysters for the family supper. On her return, the Marrs could not be roused; it was as though they had all suddenly disappeared or died. She waited half an hour before waking her neighbour, who climbed over the backyard fence. In the shop he stumbled over the apprentice's body, his head smashed so badly that parts of his brains dripped from the ceiling. Nearby lay Mrs Marr, her skull likewise battered. Behind the counter was Timothy Marr's corpse, and downstairs the baby swung in its cradle, its head caved in and the throat cut to the bone. If the motive was burglary, the till was untouched, and a bedroom drawer still contained £152 in cash. Two sets of footprints led from the back of the house, and a long ripping chisel, perhaps used as a jemmy, reposed on the counter. Upstairs was a heavy iron mallet covered in blood.

A wave of horror and indignation swept the capital. *The Times* doubted the killings had any 'equal in atrocity', and sightseers clogged Ratcliffe Highway. Three separate authorities launched investigations: the parish churchwardens, the Shadwell magistrates and the River Thames Police. Their efforts were paltry, confused and disjointed. They failed to follow leads and fed on rumour, arresting dozens of suspects, most of them drunks, madmen or foreigners. The ripping chisel had last been seen in the possession of a carpenter, Cornelius Hart, who worked on Marr's shop, but his alibi went unchecked, and only on 19 December was it noticed that the iron mallet bore a set of dotted initials punched on its head: 'IP'.

Late that night, two minutes' walk from Marr's shop, a near-naked man lowered himself on a set of knotted sheets from the upper floors of the 'King's Arms', crying, 'They are murdering the people in the house.' Neighbours broke in and found three bodies, again with their throats slit and their heads pulped, this time with a three-foot crowbar. The intruder or intruders escaped out of the rear window, jumping on to a muddy bank.

John Turner, the lodger, had been saved by the housemaid's cry, 'Lord Jesus Christ! We shall all be murdered.' Tiptoeing down to the first floor he saw the killer, a tall man six feet high in a Flushing coat, with two brained bodies at his feet, his back turned as he rifled through the parlour cupboards. This tallied with a stranger in a brown jacket observed loitering outside the pub only minutes before. A tentative sighting of two suspects described one as lame.

According to crime writer Colin Wilson, public hysteria attained such heights because the murders were imputed to a single man rather than to run-of-the-mill gang violence. De Quincey put his literary seal on the concept of a demented individual in his fanciful 1854 essay, *Murder considered as one of the Fine Arts*, extolling the killings as 'the sublimest and most entire in their excellence that ever were committed'. Why, De Quincey demanded, cut a man's throat after beating out his brains? Why smash a baby's skull as it slept in its cot? Why razor its throat? De Quincey took hold of the cruelty and barbarity of the event, most probably an interrupted robbery, and added the thrilling element of pointless sadism. The scare had long tentacles. De Quincey mentions a friend in an isolated rural area in Grasmere, who 'never rested until she had placed eighteen doors … each secured and bolted, between her bedroom and any intruder of human build'. It only remained for **Jack the Ripper** to breathe life into the fantasies of recreational killing.

On 23 December, a young sailor of shabby elegance, John Williams, was summoned before the magistrates. A former shipmate of the dead linen-draper, he was a man of superior education and foppish disposition lodging at the 'Pear Tree Inn'. It was said that on the murder night Williams came home late and asked a roommate to extinguish the candle, as though anxious to conceal his appearance. He had been drinking at the 'King's Arms', starting the evening with sixpence and ending it with a pound. In addition, he was billed as short, lame and Irish (see **Xenophobia**)

On arrival in court, it was clear that at 5 feet 9 inches Williams was tall, even-limbed and Scottish. He admitted visiting the 'King's Arms', where he was friendly with the landlady, and accounted for his money with a tale of pawning his clothes. And, as a sailor with a dread of fire at sea, it was natural for him to be alarmed at finding his roommate lying in bed with a pipe in his mouth and a candle in his hand. Like many another suspect, Williams was consigned to Coldbath Fields Prison, but the next day the news broke that the 'Pear Tree''s landlord had recognised the iron mallet. It belonged to John Peterson, a German sailor, who stored his tool chest at the inn, and Williams was recalled for renewed questioning under mounting suspicion.

John Turner, the survivor from the 'King's Arms', failed to identify him, although a laundress testified that four or five days *before* the second murders she found lightly spattered blood round one of Williams's shirt collars. Clearly this had no bearing on the later killings, and Williams gave details of a scuffle after a drunken game of cards. But he was returned to custody. Then on Christmas Day, the 'Pear Tree' landlord stated that the crowbar also came from Peterson's tool chest, and Boxing Day brought the revelation that the morning after the murders Williams had washed a muddy pair of stockings. 'We are not yet certain he will prove the man,' the magistrates wrote to the Home Secretary. But charges were imminent.

On 27 December, the warders found Williams dead in his cell, suspended from an iron bar by his handkerchief. This dramatic development was interpreted as an admission of guilt, and the half-hearted examination of

John Williams, drawn in the prison cell soon after he was cut down

another suspect, William Ablass, the subject of much neighbourhood gossip for his unpleasant disposition, was not pursued. Following the route of least resistance, the magistrates concluded that Williams alone was guilty, and on 31 December his body was loaded on a cart, his head resting on a wooden stake, with the crowbar, mallet and ripping chisel arrayed around him. The corpse processed through Wapping, watched by a crowd of ten thousand in stony silence, and Williams was dumped in a hole at the crossroads of Back Lane and Cannon Street, with a stake hammered through his heart.

The case against him remains flimsy. Had the magistrates searched the 'Pear Tree' thoroughly, and cross-examined everyone with access to Peterson's tools, the truth might have been established. But, over-impressed by having a suspect in custody, they looked no further.

Was his death suicide? Williams left no note, and asked for no pen and paper. He was in confident mood when last seen, remarking that 'the saddle was on the wrong horse'. If innocent, he stood a fair chance of acquittal: his alibi might yet be confirmed, and he had not even been committed for trial. If guilty, he could save his skin by turning King's

Evidence. The individual most endangered by his existence was the true murderer, facing either betrayal or a renewed investigation.

The bar in Williams's cell stood 6 feet 2 inches from the floor, and he presumably jumped from his bed. But the *Morning Post* of 28 December states that 'the state of his body clearly demonstrated that he had struggled very hard'. If so, Williams could probably have saved himself in the minutes before asphyxiation, either with a toehold on his bed or by calling for help.

If Williams was not the culprit, then who? The Marrs' murderer did not act alone. Two, or possibly three, men loitered outside the shop earlier in the evening; two sets of footprints were found, and one man would hardly enter the premises encumbered by the long mallet and the long chisel as well as a razor. It would be interesting to put William Ablass back in the dock. He was tall, lame, and a dangerous man who had organised a mutiny on the *Roxburgh Castle*. He had access to Peterson's tools. The woman who vouchsafed his alibi was his wife, and he had money for which he could not account. Similarly, the armchair detective might recall Cornelius Hart and verify his alibi.

The Ratcliffe Highway murders made it very clear that London – still safeguarded by the antiquated system of decrepit **watchmen** – was unsafe for law-abiding citizens, and the idea of a 'police force' was hotly debated in the press. 'I had rather half-a-dozen people's throats be cut in the Ratcliffe Highway every three or four years,' affirmed one commentator just back from France, 'than be subject to the domiciliary

John Williams's burial

visits, spies and the rest of Fouché's contrivances.' A more vigorous Home Secretary than the incumbent, Richard Ryder, might have pushed through worthwhile legislation, but his proposals were costed at £74,000 and voted down for the 'alarming powers' they conferred. It was 1829 before Robert Peel set up the Metropolitan Police.

See also **Oaths**

Reading material

J. R. R. Tolkien's *The Lord of the Rings is* often dismissed by intellectual snobs as a literary ghetto for the emotionally retarded. One great fan was Jeffrey **Dahmer**.

For many serial killers, *The Collector* is a favourite choice. This 1963 novel by John Fowles tells the story of a shy young man who 'collects' a beautiful young girl and holds her captive until she perishes for want of medical attention. Then he looks for another specimen.

The would-be presidential **assassin**, John Hinckley, took his cue from J. D. Salinger's *The Catcher in the Rye*.

During Al Capone's brief 1929 spell in prison, his preferred authors were reputed to be Bernard Shaw and Shakespeare. At the time the public would swallow anything about Capone; 'genius' was a common epithet, and a Philadelphia newspaper characterised him as a 'stern highbrow'.

The reading list of actor Sean Penn, jailed for assaulting a photographer, was equally impressive. It included Montaigne and William Burroughs (see **Champagne**). But Penn says: 'I recommend Thurber for everyone in jail.' By a strange coincidence, British prisons are crammed with Walter Mitty characters professing to be Ulster secret agents or members of the Parachute Regiment and the SAS.

George Bernard Shaw was another perceptive man. According to his secretary, Bernard Blanche, in the early 1940s they were lunching together at London's Onslow Court Hotel when a sudden fracas broke out at a nearby table. A smart-looking gentleman shocked his fellow diners by savagely berating a troublesome child, snarling, 'If you do that again, I'll kill you.'

'That man will hang,' commented Shaw. Haigh did. Another writer imbued with prophetic powers was Mark Twain. In 1883, he published *Life on the Mississippi*. Chapter thirty-one described the identification of a murderer by a bloodstained **fingerprint**. This pre-dated the first such occurrence (Francisca Rojas,

Argentina) by nine years and was written before any police force anywhere was aware of the possibilities of fingerprints.

According to Shaw, the artist is judged by his highest moments, and the criminal by his lowest.

Recruitment

The Chinese street gangs infesting today's New York incorporate cultural elements derived in equal measure from the **Triads** and American gangster movies. Their members, who may live several to a room, can be as young as 13, and an unusually forthright – and cynical – description of their high school recruitment was given by David Chong, an undercover police officer and former *dai lo* (street boss) of the 'Flying Dragons'.

'I would have my kids go to a high school in Chinatown and look for the turkey right off the boat,' said Chong. 'You want him in ninth or tenth grade, he can't speak English, he's got a stupid hair-cut. And when you find this kid, you go beat the shit out of him. Tease him, beat him up, knock him around. We isolate this kid; he's our *target*. What will happen is one day I'll make sure I'm around when this kid is getting beaten up, and I'll stop it with the snap of my finger. He'll look at me – he'll see that I have a fancy car, girls, I'm wearing a beeper – and I'll turn around and say, "Hey, kid, how come these people are beating on you?" I'm gonna be this kid's hero, this kid's guru – I'm gonna be his *dai lo*.'

The softening-up complete, 'I'll take the kid for a drive, take him to a restaurant, order him the biggest lobster, the biggest steak. Eventually, I'll take him to the safe house where I keep kids and guns. Then I slowly break him in.'

Forty dollars a week and a bedroom shared with five others is a fair starting rate for a recruit. Training includes instruction on killing 'cleanly': shoot the victim repeatedly, make sure there are no witnesses, and – for economy – use a cheap gun. The murder weapon must always be discarded.

In Britain, finding a new recruit for the position of public hangman required no such coercion; the death of the executioner William Marwood on 2 September 1883 provoked a flood of unsolicited applications. Selected excerpts from assorted correspondents eager to prove their mettle read as follows [sic]: 'Dere Sir, I am waiting outside with a coil of rope, and should be glad to give you a personal proof of my method'; 'I would hang either brothers or sisters, or anyone else referred to me, without fear or favour'; 'I have witnessed Executions among all nations; consequently there is no fear of my getting sick at the right moment'; 'In my Line of Business as a Barber I have had some Great Experience of the Formation of necks and wind-pipes of all people'; 'Deer Sur, I am ankshus to be yure publick exechoner, and i hereby apply for the job. i am thurty yeres old, and am willing to hang one or two men for nothink'; and, 'I have at various times made some very successful experiments in the art of hanging (by means of life-size figures) with a view to making myself thoroughly proficient in the despatch of criminals.'

Thirty applicants were invited to an interview at the Old Bailey. Seventeen turned up, and after two hours the Sheriffs settled on Bartholomew Binns, a coalminer. He bungled his first four jobs, and was sacked after arriving drunk for the fifth. Thereafter, he briefly made a living in fairground booths demonstrating his prowess on wax effigies.

References

Like everyone else, hangmen must pitch for work. James **Berry**, the meticulous Victorian executioner, customarily issued new clients with a written estimate. His pre-printed form had various blanks to fill in, notably the Quote Number and the missing bits in the following sentence: 'I am prepared to undertake the execution you name of ... at ... on the ...'

As proof of his workmanship, Berry collected references. One testimonial, dated 2 September 1884 and signed by a Dr Bar, began: 'I have never seen an execution more satisfactorily performed ... This was very gratifying to me. Your rope was of excellent quality; fine, soft, pliable and strong.'

But few testimonials can have been as glowing as the one submitted by the serial killer Ted **Bundy** to bolster his 1973 application to law school. His reference, signed by Washington State Governor Dan Evans, read in part: 'It was the consensus among those of us who directed the operation that Ted's performance was outstanding. Given a key role in the issues, research, and strategy section, he demonstrated an ability to define and organise his own projects, to

effectively synthesise and clearly communicate factual information and to ... tolerate strain and sometimes critical situations. In the end it was probably his composure and discretion that allowed him to successfully carry out his assignments.'

Who could resist an applicant of this calibre? After Bundy's first conviction, Dr Carlisle of Utah State Penitentiary completed another assessment scarcely less flattering, although on careful reading the doctor's crucial final qualification is perceptive; anyone who needs to be 'clever' to appear 'close' to the 'edge' of normality must be way off beam.

'In general,' Dr Carlisle wrote, 'the scores for the objective tests portray the picture of a person who is happy, confident and very well adjusted ... In conclusion, I feel that Mr Bundy is either a man who has no problems or is smart and clever enough to appear close to the edge of "normal".'

It is probable that Bundy himself penned most of Governor Evans's panegyric. In prison awaiting trial, he sent the *Seattle Times* an open letter revealing a less confident touch: 'I address this letter to my many friends and acquaintances who have offered their prayers, concern and support in my behalf. When time permits, I shall do my best to reply personally to each of you. You are truly beautiful people.'

These are the flawed perceptions of a pop star, of a man with an admiring audience of depersonalised units.

'Reg Kray Book of Exercises for People in Confined Places, The'

Said in 1983 to be Reggie **Kray**'s joke title for a short manual compiled during his interminable prison sentence, setting out his physical fitness regime. The Kray twins' actual book *Our Story* is an affectionate piece of auto-hagiography, liberally sprinkled with photographs of the famous: Diana Dors ('a true friend'), Barbra Streisand ('To Ronnie, happiness!') and Lord Boothby ('a friend and business associate of Ron's').

Fifteen years in close confinement as a 'Category A' prisoner is generally reckoned sufficient to turn a jailbird into a human vegetable. Reggie was inside for more than twice that time: he was released in August 2000 and died in October that year. His brother, Ronnie, was in a bad way when he went into prison in 1969 and later became an inmate of

Broadmoor psychiatric hospital, where he died in 1995.

In August 1993 it finally emerged that the establishment politician Lord Boothby had indeed shared a joint enterprise with Ronald Kray: the pursuit of young men. Ronnie pandered for him. Scotland Yard's intelligence section, C11, kept them both under observation, and Boothby had to sue for libel after the *Sunday Mirror*, campaigning against organised crime in London, ran its July 1964 headline, 'Peer and a gangster: Yard inquiry'.

Ronnie's joint sexual escapades with a peer of the realm did more than titillate his appetite for celebrities. He hoped that the relationship would confer immunity from prosecution.

It did. Boothby's cronies rallied round to defend their colleague against the imputations of homosexuality, and Sir John Simpson, Scotland Yard's commissioner, denied ordering any investigation. The police inquiry was speedily wound down. Boothby won damages of £40,000, but, with incriminating letters and photographs in the Krays' possession, he remained wide open to **blackmail**. It seems that he bankrolled the twins' successful 1965 defence against extortion charges, and in February of that year spoke out on their behalf in the House of Lords.

It became increasingly clear that an attack on the Krays would involve tackling both Boothby and his influential friends, who had lied to maintain his innocence. The police backed off, as did the press, leaving evil alone. Thus began the Krays' four-year breathing-space, during which they constructed a criminal empire that was well-nigh impregnable.

See also **Attaché case, Bobettes**

Reis, Professor A. R.

Master detective and founder of the Lausanne Institute of Police Science, probably Europe's first forensic science laboratory. In October 1909, Reis performed a deductive feat worthy of Sherlock Holmes.

Reis received a summons from a baffled Préfet de Police in the south of France to assist in a murder investigation. After crawling round the crime scene with a magnifying glass and a pair of tweezers, Reis tendered the solution: 'The man you seek is a left-handed sailor who has recently been in Sicily. He has a cut on his left

hand and a red moustache.' This narrowed down the population of Marseilles to a field of one; and the arrest of the culprit Forfarazzo on board the *Donna Maria*, fresh in from Sicily, speedily followed.

The case involved the death of Marie Pallot, a receiver of stolen goods. Forfarazzo, the sailor, gashed his hand jemmying open her door, leaving a trail of blood down the left-hand side of the corridor and a trail of wax from a guttering candle down the right side. This suggested that he carried his weapon in his left hand, an observation confirmed by the damage to the left side of Mme Pallot's skull from a blow struck from behind.

Reis's magnifying glass located two **hairs** on the carpet which, under the microscope, proved red and of a length and width consistent with a moustache. Chemical analysis of the candle-wax – one of Reis's specialities – revealed that the candle was of a type made and sold only in Sicily. Since no one carries a candle around for ever, it seemed likely that the murderer had just been in Sicily, and since he was now in Marseilles, a port, he was probably a sailor.

Reis's deductions were correct. Tracked down by the police, Forfarazzo sealed his fate by taking a proffered slip of paper with his left hand. A search revealed the telltale candle stump in his pocket. Forfarazzo was tried, convicted, and later confessed.

See also **Locard**

Religion, abuse of

Down the ages, religious bigots have been accountable for untold suffering. But in Sicily, from the middle of the last century, Christianity degenerated into a straightforward criminal enterprise promoted for profit by the Mafia. The rot started in the outlying villages when the Mob seized control of the standing committees representing individual patron saints; maladministration of the funds earmarked for their annual feast days yielded easy money.

Thereafter the Mafia expropriated the religious function, monopolising the manufacture of devotional candles, hiring out church pews and, in the twentieth century, moving into mass production of religious relics. Many lines consisted of no more than statuettes and medallions churned out by the million, with the revenues creamed off by organised crime; others were hand-crafted speciality items. In 1962 the Italian newspaper *Le Ore* researched one distributor exporting to America and discovered that the year's sales included twenty suits of armour worn by St Joan, the same number of gowns (property of the late Francis of Assisi), fifty of St Bernadette's rosaries, and Moses' wand (one only).

The 'originals' of these and other artefacts were owned by the Mafia; to ensure a copy was infused with at least part of the original's rectitude, the two had only to be brought briefly into contact, a practice which lapsed into blessing dubious relics by the truckload, such as the ashes of Abraham (in presentation urns) or piscine bones from the Miracle of the Bread and Fishes.

When sales declined, a judiciously staged 'miracle' – like the stigmatisation of Padre Pio, the San Giovanni monk – drove pilgrims into a buying frenzy, transforming a locality's infrastructure. Mafia-run guest houses, hotels and hospitals burgeoned round the holy site, to which the pious flocked in their thousands, spending expensive weeks awaiting confession. The queue for absolution could be jumped, on payment of a fee. Or the unwary were confessed by false Padre Pios in back-street rooms, again for a fee. Meanwhile, sales of guidebooks and recordings of the priest at mass boosted the Mob's coffers, as did the merchandising of hundreds of yards of bloody bandages as authentic souvenirs of the monk's stigmata; even the 1960 newspaper revelation that they were steeped in the blood of chickens had no impact on income.

But the Franciscan fathers of Mazzarino take pride of place in the Sicilian annals of religious abuse. The monks were all gangsters, of itself nothing untoward in a country where as recently as 1923 a Benedictine mobster from Santo Stefano beheaded his Abbot on the refectory table. In Mazzarino the monks made their living from robbery and extortion, preying off the villagers. They dealt in property, traded as usurers, disposed of healthy bank accounts under their lay names, spent their nights whoring in the monastery and amassed a huge collection of pornography. One of the fathers, Guglielmo by name, blazed away at night with a heavy automatic, shooting at the stars; another, expelled by the brethren, was seen by a servant packing a sub-machine-gun as he left. Often the confessional box in the village church was used to transmit blackmail threats, and the nave became the 'drop' for payments.

In the late 1950s a prominent villager, Angelo Cannada, rejected the Franciscans' demand for ten million lire; he remained adamant even when the prior himself motored over to make him see sense. A few days later the intransigent Cannada was gunned down by four masked men in his vineyard, leaving his wife to inherit the bill. The aged prior, a malevolent octogenarian called Carmelo, conducted negotiations with the widow, dropping his fee to three million after threatening to kill her only son. The mere sighting of a monk in the village streets sent the locals scurrying for cover.

A new police chief, Di Stefano, started an inquiry. In 1961, one of his men was shot dead near the monastery. The three attackers fled, but one dropped his gun; this was recognised and the murderers arrested. In prison, they admitted to Cannada's murder, absolving themselves by blaming the monks' wicked gardener, who 'made' them do it. Within hours of his imprisonment in Caltanissetta, the gardener was found hanged in his cell.

A search of the monastery unearthed the typewriter used for the blackmail notes, and in March 1962 Padre Carmelo and three other monks were charged with extortion and complicity in murder. An ecstatic crowd greeted their arrival at the Messina courtroom; Padre Carmelo responded to the effusions of applause with the sign of the cross. While awaiting trial, the fathers continued to say mass and hear confessions and, when proceedings started, prominent ecclesiastics streamed over from the mainland to demonstrate solidarity. The prosecution agreed to stay its hand, withholding evidence about the orgies, the extortion and the secret bank accounts; and Cannada's widow refused to testify (see **Vendetta**).

The three **hitmen** accused the dead gardener; in the absence of religious orders they received thirty years apiece. The monks went free, successfully pleading duress, a defence which requires the physical impossibility of escape.

A 1963 appeal resulted in thirteen-year terms for the monks. With a parliamentary commission on the Mafia in the offing, the social climate had temporarily changed.

In medieval Britain, the Lord of the Manor was historically empowered to hang miscreants, as was every town and abbey. This gave rise to 'private' gallows, of which Edward I's Commissioners discovered ninety-four in Yorkshire alone, owned by such worthies as the Abbot, the Dean and the Archbishop of York.

See also **Inquisition**

Remorse

As they return from the sick moments of killing to more ordinary moral considerations, murderers often suffer extreme remorse. The nightmare of the event is succeeded by the nightmare of guilt from which there is no easy escape.

One-third of British killers commit suicide. Here are extracts from a letter from one who did not, written thirteen years after the spilling of blood. The exact wording posed its author with complex problems, since the recipient was the bereaved mother of the victim:

'My own mother, and my family have endured terrible sufferings through me, and are still serving, like yourself, an unbearable life sentence. This is yet another burden of guilt I carry, and the weight of it is almost more than I can bear. The same is true of the sufferings and heartaches I have caused you and the other families … I do understand your hatred, of course I do, but believe me Mrs West, you couldn't hate me more than I hate myself. I have asked God for his forgiveness, but I couldn't ask you for yours, for how can I expect you to forgive me when I cannot forgive myself? I have to live with the past for the rest of my life, with self-inflicted wounds to my mind and heart which I doubt will ever heal.

'Having finally and fully acknowledged and confessed these heinous crimes, and realised the dreadful enormity of them, the guilt and remorse I feel is agonising – the wounds have reopened and are raw-edged and festering. But I deserve it all … please don't add to your suffering by a hatred that I'm not worthy of.'

These words were sent by way of reply to Ann West, the mother of Lesley Anne Downey, murdered for kicks on 26 December 1964. The letter was published word for word in the *Daily Mirror* of 12 October 1987 and prompted renewed national vilification of its author, Myra **Hindley**.

Mrs West clearly remained locked in a psychological feud with her daughter's killer. 'I set a trap for Hindley,' she commented, 'and this letter proves she's fallen right into it. I've conned her … How can she lie like that? She obviously doesn't know I've heard the tapes and seen the photographs…'

Fury, bitterness and desolation are not easily reduced to words. Mrs West had written to Hindley in scrawled capitals: 'I could never forgive or forget my Lesley, I expect if you was in my position you would feel the same.' It may be that language, however used, is an inadequate vehicle to convey grief.

Murder is thus a crime for which it is difficult to apologise. There is no agreed protocol, nor is it clear what degree of personal abnegation can ever be acceptable to the bereaved. The serial killer Dennis **Nilsen** was not unreasonable in believing that mouthing the word 'Sorry' would add insult to injury. As author Anne Rule pointed out in her testimony to the 1983 Senate Committee (see **Repeat killers**): 'I have seen the agony of parents, children, spouses and friends of murder victims. For each of these violent deaths there is a ripple effect, and scores of lives are forever blighted. It is not just the victim who is lost; it becomes a kind of death for their families, and, indeed, the death of a small part of our entire society.'

To be included among a murder's detritus are the friends and family of the killer himself.

Removal, of fingerprints

After the FBI's establishment of a permanent Division of Identification and Information in 1930, harassed American gangsters toyed with the idea of having their **fingerprints** surgically removed, and in 1934 Freddy Barker and 'Creepy' Karpis – members of the Ma Barker gang – went under the knife only to find that as the fingerpads healed, so their fingerprints reappeared. But their doctor, Joe Moran, was never seen again.

In 1934, John **Dillinger** attempted a variant, scorching off his fingerprints with acid in a troublesome operation conducted at gunpoint, during the course of which he swallowed his tongue and nearly choked. But the telltale papillary patterns were already showing through when he was, they say, gunned down a few months later.

In 1941 Robert Pitts, a hold-up gangster, went one better with a bid to have 'neutral' skin grafted on to his surgically pruned fingertips, spending six weeks

FOR DETECTIVE WORK
£100 PRIZE
TO WHOM DO THESE FINGER-PRINTS BELONG?

A prize of ONE HUNDRED POUNDS is offered by the Editor of the
"DAILY EXPRESS"

for the best solution of the mystery WHO DID THE DEED? in connection with a novel and thrilling DETECTIVE STORY, which is to commence in the

"DAILY EXPRESS" on JULY 21st.

The interest of the story is centred upon the mysterious death of a solicitor, and the heroic efforts of his daughter to discover who did the deed. The clue is

A FINGER-PRINT

on a tumbler, and, in the course of the story, the finger-prints of all the characters are given, and by comparing them the problem can be solved.

On the day preceding the opening of the Story (JULY 20th) an interesting illustrated article by Dr. J. G Garson, the celebrated finger-print expert, will appear In the course of this article the writer explains the various patterns in the finger-print. Ridges (Fig. 1), Arches (Fig. 2), Whorls (Fig. 3), and Loops (Fig. 4).

In the competition for the hundred pounds Police Officers stand a splendid chance. Their experience in dealing with crime must materially assist them in solving the mystery. The story and the problem form a practical lesson in a branch of detective work that is coming more and more into prominence.

READ THE
Daily Express
On Thursday, July 20th.

Daily Express *fingerprint competition, 1905*

with his arms folded, fingerpads clamped to his chest while the graft took. But on his next arrest in Austin, Texas, it transpired that being the only man in the world with no fingerprints attracted almost equally unwelcome notice. Exhaustive research by the FBI produced a positive identification. This time the doctor, a Leopold Brandenburg of Union City, survived the operation but received a prison sentence, while his patient was sent down for a robbery where he left prints of the left ring-finger below the joint, the point where his skin graft stopped.

During the late 1950s and 1960s, Hong Kong deportees sought readmittance to the colony by having their fingerprints cut out and repositioned upside-down. But scar tissue round the join ensured that the inversion was easily spotted, and their true identity could thus be established by turning the records the other way up.

In 1933 a set of prints were accidentally detached by a natural process. The skin of the body's hands was 'sloughed off' by prolonged immersion in a river near Wagga Wagga, Australia. The fingerprints were later discovered intact, in the form of a detached skin 'glove' snagged on the river bank, enabling identification of the corpse, and hence of the murderer, Edward Morey.

Repeat killers

Ronald Reagan was prone to muddling up countries and calling Princess Diana 'David'. But when he announced the formation of the FBI's Behavioral Science Unit in 1984 to track 'repeat killers' this was the accepted terminology of the time. The phenomenon was so recently and dimly recognised that no one knew what to call it. The FBI had five categories of murder: felony murder (during a robbery), suspected felony murder (probably during a robbery), argument-motivated murder (domestic disputes), other motives (anything else, if known) and unknown (anything else, if unknown).

FBI special agent Robert Ressler, a **Quantico** instructor, gave birth to the media-friendly term 'serial killings'. According to a *New York Times* article of 26 October 1986: 'Mr Ressler started using the term because such an offender's behavior is so distinctly episodic, like the movie serials he enjoyed as a boy.'

Three years earlier, the phrase made its official debut during a 1983 Senate Judiciary Committee debating the unwieldy concept of 'patterns of murders committed by one person in large numbers with no apparent rhyme, reason or motivation'. One subheading was the more succinct 'Serial killers', and the American edge extends beyond the timely conferral of nomenclature. British serial killers can be counted on the fingers: Jack the Ripper, Christie, Brady and Hindley, Sutcliffe, Nilsen, Erskine, Duffy and Nurse Allitt. But America has everything, the biggest, the best, the most horrible. The names come tumbling out: Holmes, Manson, Bundy, Gacy, Gein, Panzram, Dahmer, DeSalvo, Fish, Ng, Kemper, the Night Stalker, the Skid Row Slasher, the Hillside Stranglers and so on.

The general American per capita murder rate is some eight times Britain's but, with 6,000 killings a year officially ascribed to 'unknown' motives, its pre-eminence in serial killings is probably by a factor of hundreds.

Puritanical zealotry gave birth to Prohibition, which

sired organised crime, and it is possible that the same repressive trait, directed at sexuality, has inspired the white American wave of middle-class sex killers. Early practitioners, like Gein and Heirens, raised to regard sex as a sin, fell into a greater heresy, and a common feature of the lust murder is the victim's denigration as a whore for indulging in sex, often under coercion.

Revelations, Book of

Charles **Manson** was inspired by the Book of Revelations which – with its emphasis on death, blood, judgment, and slaying the third part of men – provided a fertile stomping ground for his inflamed imagination. The ninth chapter provided his favourite reading.

The key biblical concept was the four angels 'standing at the four corners of the earth holding the four winds of the earth'. According to Manson, their names were John, Paul, George and Ringo. For the Bible says: 'Their faces were as the faces of men', although 'they had hair as the hair of women'. The Beatles were prophets, girded with 'breastplates of fire', updated as electric guitars, and their lyrics comprised the 'fire and brimstone' issuing from the angels' mouths.

Revelations 9:11 introduced the fifth angel: 'And they had a king over them, which is the angel of the bottomless pit.' Manson knew who this was: Charles Manson, a star descended from heaven to earth. In Latin, the fifth angel's name is Exterminans.

To Manson, the Armageddon of Revelations 9 was imminent and the 'bottomless pit' a real place. It had no zip code, but 'Crazie Sadie', a Family member, believed it was reached through the Hole in Death Valley to whose exact whereabouts only Manson was privy. There, beneath the ground, inside the earth, lay another civilisation with chocolate fountains and food trees. One of the entrance portals lay submerged in a lake off Route 127, just past the town of Death Valley Junction, and Manson obtained an estimate for pumping the water out. But the $33,000 price tag proved too steep for the privilege of direct access, so the Family devoted days to scouring the desert for another way in.

Similarly, Revelations 9 told the literal truth in verse 18: 'By these three plagues was the third part of men killed, by the fire and the smoke and the brimstone.' Manson could see the bloodshed coming to California

right then in 1969, for it was written, 'in those days men shall seek death'.

The carnage would be triggered by the black–white revolution. Blacks would surge into the exclusive Bel Air and Beverly Hills districts for an orgy of slaying – with stabbings, blood on the walls, and words like 'pigs' daubed in the victims' own blood. When the killing finally stopped, Manson divined that 'blackie' would be left in control of a devastated world, lumbered with his usual job of 'cleaning up the mess, like he always has'.

But the blacks needed leadership, and that was where Manson and his family came in. Out in the desert, their numbers swollen to 144,000, the Family would wait for the call, a world government under Jesus Charles Manson Christ.

To set this momentous train of events rolling, only the slightest of nudges was needed, and on the evening of 8 August 1969 Manson gave orders to one of his followers, Charles 'Tex' Watson, issuing him with a knife and a .22 revolver, and selecting two girls, Susan Atkins and Patricia Krenwinkel, to accompany him. 'Go with Tex,' he told them, 'and do whatever he tells you to do.' As they started up their '59 Ford, Manson leaned through the window and added: 'Leave a sign. You girls know what to write. Something witchy.' Then they headed off to 10050 Cielo Drive.

See also **White Album**

Rifkin, Joel

On 25 June 1993, soon after dawn, two New York State troopers were on patrol along Long Island's Southern State Parkway when they noticed that a Mazda pickup truck ahead of them lacked a licence plate. When flashing red lights failed to make it pull over they used the loudspeaker. But the driver accelerated and drove off the freeway at the next exit and through the streets of Wantagh. The chase often reached a speed of ninety miles an hour, and other patrol cars joined in. Finally, in Mineola, the driver lost control and hit a telephone pole. He proved to be a bespectacled man in his thirties, whose licence identified him as Joel Rifkin, 34, resident of Garden Street, East Meadow, Long Island.

A foul odour drew the police to the back of the truck, and there, wrapped in blue tarpaulin, police found the naked body of a young woman which was

Joel Rifkin

beginning to decompose. She was later identified as a 22-year-old prostitute named Tiffany Bresciani, who had vanished from her usual patch in Manhattan three days earlier. Rifkin confessed to strangling her as they had intercourse, then taking her back to the house where he lived with his mother and sister. When the body began to decompose in the hot weather, he decided to dump it among some bushes on rough ground near the local airport. He went on to admit that he had made a habit of picking up prostitutes and strangling them – seventeen in all. (The police decided the number was actually eighteen, and that Rifkin had simply lost count.)

Rifkin, an unemployed landscape gardener, freely admitted that he had been picking up prostitutes on average three times a week since he was 18. In his bedroom, police found victims' ID cards, driving licences, credit cards and piles of underwear: panties, bras and stockings. In the garage, which smelt of decaying flesh, they found the panties of his last victim, Tiffany Bresciani. In his bedroom there was a book about the **Green River Killer**, still at the time uncaught. It was a fair guess that Rifkin hoped to equal his score.

As information began to emerge, it became clear that Rifkin was basically an inadequate. Born on 20 January to an unwed college student, he had been adopted a few weeks after his birth by a Jewish couple, Ben and Jeanne Rifkin, who also adopted a girl, Jan, in 1962.

The children seemed to have been well treated, but Joel was backward at school; he mumbled, walked with rounded shoulders and was dyslexic. His schoolfellows called him 'the turtle' because of the hunched shoulders and slow walk, and made fun of him. When he left home he tried various jobs, on one occasion working in a record store; but he was usually late, and would turn up with rumpled clothes and dirty fingernails. Girls found him unattractive, and when his parents gave him a car at 18, he used it to pick up prostitutes, first in nearby Hempstead, then in Manhattan.

Rifkin's dream was to become a famous writer, and it could be argued that he had the right kind of preparation – a certain amount of childhood and adolescent frustration often seems to be good for writers. Rifkin spent hours writing poetry in his bedroom. But a few half-hearted attempts at further education fell through because he had no ability to concentrate. The exception was a two-year course in landscape gardening, where his exam results were excellent. But when he began to work as a landscape gardener it was with such inefficiency that he usually lost his customers within days.

He was already in his late twenties when his stepfather was diagnosed as suffering prostate cancer and committed suicide because he could not bear the pain. Jeanne Rifkin was shattered and went into depression.

Not long after, Rifkin met an attractive blonde in a coffee shop; he was scribbling, and they began a casual conversation; he was impressed when she told him she was writing a film script.

He told her – untruthfully – that he was also writing a film script, and that he was a university student. When she took a small apartment, she even invited him to move in, to help her with her script. Rifkin had hoped this was the beginning of a love affair; but she refused even to let him kiss him. A few weeks later she tired of his laziness and untidiness and threw him out.

After Rifkin's arrest it was reported that she had worked as a streetwalker and was suffering from AIDS, although it is not clear whether he was aware of this.

What is certain is that Rifkin began to kill prostitutes in 1989. The first victim was a girl called Susie, who was on crack. (Most of his victims would be drug addicts.) She made him stop several times to buy crack even before they reached his home, and when, after sex, she asked him to take her in search of more, he lost his temper and beat her with a souvenir howitzer shell, then strangled her. He disposed of the body by dismembering it with an X-acto knife, then put the parts in garbage bags, which he disposed of in the woods of New Jersey and the East River in Manhattan. After that, killing prostitutes became something of a habit; he picked them up on New York's Lower East Side and either had sex with them in his pickup or drove them home. On a few occasions he strangled women during oral sex

One drug addict, Mary DeLucca, was so addicted to crack that Rifkin spent $150 during a night driving her around, while she complained about her life. As she finally submitted to sex in a cheap motel, he asked her if she would like to die, and she said yes. Rifkin claimed that when he strangled her, she was passive, as if accepting it. He solved the problem of removing her body from the motel by going out and buying a cheap steamer trunk, which he dumped in a remote rural area.

Many prostitutes turned him down because he looked and smelled peculiar. But one with whom he had sex on two occasions said he seemed perfectly ordinary and normal, and made no unusual sexual demands. Another refused when he explained he wanted oral sex.

Rifkin continued to commit murder for almost five years, whenever the urge took him. He often took his victims home and kept them for days before he disposed of them. One body that he tossed on waste ground near JFK Airport was still there more than a year later, under a mattress, when he mentioned it after his arrest. Other bodies were placed in metal drums and thrown in the river. Rifkin found this method so labour-saving after dismembering them that he bought several metal drums for future use.

On the occasion of his final murder, when he had used his mother's car to pick up Tiffany Bresciani, his mother was waiting impatiently when he arrived home, and went straight off on a shopping trip with a corpse in the trunk. Fortunately, she did not open it. Yet although Rifkin was distraught with anxiety while she was gone, he moved the corpse only a few yards, into a wheelbarrow in the garage, when she returned, and then left it for three hot days, working on his truck while flies buzzed round the swiftly decomposing body. In a fit of oversight, he omitted to replace the licence plate on his car before he set out to dump the body. And although he had sprayed the corpse with the deodorant Noxema to lessen the stench – a notion he had picked up from the film *Silence of the Lambs* – he must have known that, in the event of his being stopped by police, the smell would give him away.

Rifkin's motivation has never been adequately explained. What is clear is that he was, like so many serial killers, an inadequate, a person who found life too much for him. As one of his schoolmates told a reporter, he was a lifelong loser. We can only assume that he killed because violence satisfied some long-held fantasy and because it gave him a bizarre sense of achievement, a feeling that, in spite of a lifetime of failure, he was a 'somebody', a multiple killer, a man to be reckoned with.

Yet soon after his arrest, one of the policemen involved in the chase commented that he had probably wanted to be caught, since driving with a corpse in a car without licence plates seems to be asking for trouble.

Tried first for the Bresciani killing, he was sentenced to twenty-five years to life. By the time several more trials were over, this had been increased to 203 years to life.

Rillington Place, Number 10

The London house in which a total of eight bodies were secreted, at least six by John Reginald Halliday Christie. The street was named Ruston Mews to escape its sinister reputation and, after demolition and redevelopment, the site was rechristened as Wesley Square, where Housing Association starter-homes for newly-weds now cluster round a pleasant garden.

The habitual watering holes of another resident at Number 10, Timothy Evans, are just down the way: the Kensington Park Hotel and the 'Elgin Arms'. They remain fairly startling places, comprising the backdrop to Martin Amis's murder novel *London Fields*.

Christie's 1953 arrest provided a double shock. Britons

were not accustomed to regard themselves as a nation in which a respectable citizen would occupy a home where he had buried two bodies in the garden, three in the outhouse and another under the living-room floorboards. The newly arrived Jamaican who moved into

The grimy exterior of 10 Rillington Place. Inset: John Reginald Halliday Christie

the empty flat in March 1953 and peered into the sealed-off kitchen recess may never have achieved the traditional, cosy image of the British as law-abiding sons of Empire, creators of an outstanding police force and a system of justice envied throughout the world. His surprising discovery of three stacked corpses in the cupboard brought in detectives, who unearthed another body and two skeletons, and the manhunt for the previous tenant of Rillington Place put the address back in the headlines. For it was in this same house that Timothy Evans, a mentally retarded illiterate from Wales, had strangled his wife and child in 1949.

Or so the court found. At his trial, Evans settled on the line – properly regarded by lawyers as the feeblest of inventions – that the principal witness against him, John Christie, was none other than the perpetrator of

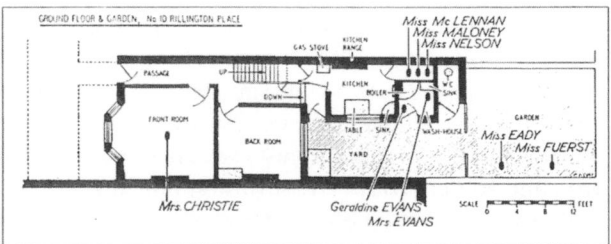

Ground-floor plan of 10 Rillington Place

his crimes. Evans was hanged on 5 March 1950, largely on the strength of a confession he subsequently withdrew, and three years later newspaper readers could not help wondering about the integrity of the original investigation and the fairness of the courts. The 1949 searches of the house had overlooked the two skeletons buried in shallow graves in the tiny back garden, where a bush grew through part of a human spine, and a femur stood upright, deployed as a fence post.

Was it likely that Evans, convicted as a strangler, lived in the same house as Christie, a strangler? And if not, how had the police obtained Evans's confession to the original murders? Why had Christie admitted to one of the same killings? Why were the case's shortcomings not exposed in court? And was execution an appropriate penalty when a man found guilty on capital charges might be innocent? The mood of public scepticism was heightened by the publication of John Scott Henderson's official report, which exonerated everyone except Timothy Evans.

The murder of Beryl and Geraldine Evans remains one of True Crime's most complex tangles. Sherlock Holmes's maxim may be of assistance: first eliminate the impossible, and whatever remains, however improbable, must contain the truth. Christie's confession to the murder of Beryl Evans included a description of how he 'turned the gas tap on and as near as I can make out, I held it clear to her face. When she became unconscious I turned the tap off.' Later he said, 'There is the possibility that as the gas tap was used for only a short time (1 to 1fi minutes) there may not have been signs in the body.'

But if Beryl was gassed into unconsciousness, however briefly, the cherry-pink signs of carbon-monoxide poisoning would have been evident on autopsy. No such traces were apparent in 1949, nor were they detected in her body tissues or **teeth** during the 1953 exhumation. So Beryl was not gassed, and thus the main component of Christie's confession is a fabrication. This reasonable starting point leads to the reasonable supposition that Christie's confession was false – he did not kill Beryl – and that Evans's confession was true.

Who killed baby Geraldine? With the mother dead, Evans's only hope of avoiding detection lay in disposing of the child. Provided the bodies were not found, he could brazen out their disappearance or flee. After his arrest, Evans talked with the murderer Donald Hume (see **Aeroplanes**) in Brixton prison.

Hume reported that Evans said: 'Christie came to an arrangement with his wife and that Christie had murdered her. Then Evans told me about the child. He said: "It was because the kid was crying." I said: "So you did it?" He said: "No, but I was there while it was done." He told me that he and Christie had gone into the bedroom together, that Christie had strangled the kid with a bit of rag while he stood and watched.' There are few compelling reasons for watching a man strangle your child, and being innocent of its mother's murder is not among them. Guilt might just suffice.

It is possible that the 'arrangement' mentioned by Evans has a bearing on the four clumps of pubic **hair** found in Christie's tobacco tin. One ringlet resembled Beryl's hair, but exhumation showed no sign that a tuft had been snipped from her pubis. Thus the trophy provided no support for Christie's confession to her murder unless he did have an 'arrangement', and it was of sufficient duration to allow Beryl's hair to regrow. An unsavoury dalliance would give *Evans* an additional reason for killing her. But this is to speculate.

Christie's motivation for his confirmed killings exemplifies the familiar paradox of sex murders by an impotent man. Desire plus inability creates frustration. After his first abortive attempt at sex as a youth, the shouted epithet of 'No-Dick Christie' in his home streets of Halifax can have done little to foster self-esteem. In maturer years Christie found that if he gassed the objects of his desire, he could manage intercourse just before, during, or after death.

Ripperology

Term coined by Colin Wilson in a review in *Books and Bookmen* in 1976.

Many – perhaps most – eminent Victorians have been fingered as the true **Jack the Ripper**; the suspects range from a future King of England downwards, with the added attraction of captivating conspiracy theories involving the Royals, the government, and the Freemasons. Many of the dozens of non-fiction books on the Ripper promote solutions devoid of evidential support which fly in the face of the evidence. The latest suspect is Virginia Woolf's cousin, James Kenneth Stephen, his culpability proved by a nonagenarian psychiatrist residing in New York.

Apparently Stephen acted in concert with his royal pupil as an early homosexual killer couple.

In more traditional versions, the story of the royal connection derives from Joseph Sickert, an artist and picture restorer, who alleged that Prince Albert Victor married Annie Crook, his grandmother; the Ripper murders were to cover up this shameful misalliance. But the marriage never happened and, as a suspect, the Prince is a non-starter. His movements are well documented from Court Circulars and diaries; thus for the double murder of 30 September 1888, which took place in London between one and two in the morning, the Prince was in Abergeldie, Scotland, as he had been for three days. On the 30th, he lunched with Queen Victoria.

The 'Freemason Connection' is based almost entirely on one word: 'Juwes'. This formed part of the graffiti found after one of the killings in Goulston Street: 'The Juwes are the men that will not be blamed for anything'. It is true that these words might have been scrawled by the killer, but not true that 'Juwes' is a collective noun for Jubela, Jubelo and Jubelum, the murderers of the master mason of Solomon's temple. Even if it were, 'Juwes' bears a more obvious interpretation. But Stephen Knight, champion of the Freemasons' involvement, expired shortly after publishing his views in *Jack the Ripper. The Final Solution*, thereby fuelling speculation that he was liquidated by the Brotherhood. In fact, Knight died of cancer.

Individual suspects include Dr Thomas Neill Cream (see **Strychnine**), incarcerated in Joliet Prison, Illinois, during the relevant period at the end of 1888 for the murder of a man called Stott; Sir William Gull, who suffered a severe stroke in 1887; the writer George Gissing, because he married a prostitute; the Prime Minister William Gladstone, because he took a charitable interest in prostitutes; and Randolph Churchill, because he went funny in the head. In 1888, the speculation was no less intense; a woman writing from the Isle of Wight affirmed that Jack was really a large ape on the loose from a wild beast show.

Beyond suggesting familiarity with the work of Edgar Allan Poe, her response constituted a denial that any member of the human species could be sufficiently depraved to perpetrate the revolting Ripper murders. Another popular theory promoted a disfigured murderer: 'He probably had his privy member destroyed and he is now revenging himself on the sex by these atrocities.' The concept of internal disfigurement was still to be accepted.

For murders dating back more than a century, new evidence comes to light with impressive regularity. Modern Ripperology started only in 1959 with the rediscovery of the 1894 Macnaghten Memorandum recording the views of the detectives on the spot. Six more years passed before a name was put to two of Macnaghten's prime suspects (Druitt and Kosminski); the third (Ostrog) was identified only after the 1987 discovery of the Swanson Marginalia and the unravelling of some thirty aliases. Similarly, the posthumous photographs of the victims unearthed by Francis Camps were not printed until 1972, and Dr Thomas Bond's autopsy report on Mary Jane Kelly was recovered by Scotland Yard only in 1987.

The proliferation of 'soft' theories, which evolve all by themselves, is scarcely affected by the continued emergence of 'hard' information, which may one day establish the true identity of the killer. And just such evidence may have now emerged. In 1992 a diary came to light in Liverpool. It was claimed that it had been written by cotton-broker James Maybrick, who in the diary confessed in detail to the Ripper murders and signed himself 'Jack the Ripper'. One excerpt read, 'Oh, what deeds I shall commit. For how could one suspect that I could be capable of such things? I will take the first whore I encounter and show what hell is really like.'

On the face of it, the diary seemed too good to be true, because its author was already famous in criminal annals – but as a victim of murder, not as a killer. Maybrick died in 1889, apparently poisoned by his wife, although it was never clear that she murdered him. As a gifted hypochondriac and a glutton for **arsenic**, which he regarded as a medicine, Maybrick may well have accidentally killed himself.

At the age of 42 he married Florence Elizabeth Chandler, twenty-three years his junior, and they led

James Maybrick, Jack the Ripper?

an extravagant life, which he could not afford, in a twenty-roomed Liverpool mansion named Battlecrease House. He also kept a mistress, and frequently travelled to London, where he visited his brother. The diary claimed that it was after Maybrick discovered that his wife was also having an affair that he decided to take revenge on the female sex as a whole by killing prostitutes. A few months after the last of the Ripper murders, Maybrick was dead too. Florence Maybrick was found guilty of his poisoning, but the jury were not told that Maybrick was an arsenic addict, so her commuted death sentence seems the least justice due to her.

Early critics of the diary seemed to be vindicated when Michael Barrett, the man who had brought the diary to public attention, claimed to have forged it on a blank Victorian ledger. However, since study of the ink in the diary has indicated that it is probably at least ninety years old, it would seem that Barrett's forgery claim is the fake. It later transpired that Barrett's estranged wife, Anne, had owned the diary, as a family

Early forensic detection from the Police News' *front page. Note the corpse undergoing assemblage (left)*

heirloom (it has been suggested, but not yet proved, that Anne is the descendant of Florence Maybrick). She says she gave the diary to her alcoholic, unemployed husband in the hopes it would give him something to occupy his mind. She says she knew little about Jack the Ripper (thinking him to be a fictional character) and was shocked and frightened by the media's reaction to the diary.

If the diary is indeed by Maybrick, he was clearly insane. Whether he was actually the Ripper or just a sick fantasist is moot, but it should be noted that arsenic, in non-fatal doses, has an effect much like cocaine – and, like cocaine, it can turn the user into a dangerously paranoid schizophrenic. It should also be noted that the diary mentions certain facts about the murders (the precise placing of neat piles of coins near one of the victims, for example) that did not come to public attention until decades after Maybrick's death.

See also **Solutions**

Ritual abuse, satanic

From the late 1980s, Britain was plagued by a series of 'satanic ritual abuse' (SRA) cases involving children. Caped adults were supposed to prance around, first molesting infants and then sacrificing them in late-night orgies of devil worship. These stories received wide press coverage; in February 1992 the respected television programme *Dispatches* produced conclusive evidence, broadcasting a grainy videotape with scenes of sexual mutilation and the buggery of young children.

A few days later it transpired that the tape was an old promo video made by an arts group. Such anticlimaxes have typified revelations; the caped molester of the Orkney Islands turned out to be the blameless local priest in his vestments, the Reverend Morris McKenzie.

Even a case reaching the Old Bailey proved without substance. In November 1991 five adults in a 'ring' were arraigned on twenty specimen counts of rape, buggery and assault, on the evidence of two sisters aged ten and 14. In the opening speeches the court heard how babies and little children – at least three of each – were slaughtered at a gypsy memorial stone in Epping Forest while the cloaked and masked adults sipped blood from a chalice and chanted 'Lucifer'. The two girls were obliged to dismember the corpses and eat their flesh; then they were raped, buggered and made to perform oral sex on each of the adults round the stone monument, which was surmounted by horns and a black cross.

On the fourth day of the trial, the basis of the case became clearer. The girls testified that they had made their stories up. The prosecution conceded that there were no bodies, no reports of missing children, and no reliable evidence of abuse. The stone memorial, which appeared in photographs to lurk deep in a creepy wood, lay a few yards from a main road; and one of the principal defendants, George Gibbard, was incapable of having sex due to horrific injuries suffered in the army. Meanwhile, the girls' parents – also among the accused – lost their homes and their jobs and were held in prison.

The credulity of the social workers, doctors, police, solicitors, barristers and the other myriads of professionals involved makes it easy to understand the former mania for burning witches (see **Witchcraze**). The parallels with the hysteria of Salem are distressingly clear. Today, a drawing of a love heart with 'Mum' in the middle has been interpreted as evidence of 'inappropriate sexual knowledge' and those sinister codewords used by children, like 'snow', 'rainbow' and 'brownie', regarded as Satanic indicators.

Transcripts of the Orkney Island interrogations by social workers anxious to procure convictions make pathetic reading. Here are fourteen consecutive answers of a child being browbeaten to admit that a party where a friend dressed up as a Teenage Ninja Turtle was in reality a Satanic Ritual. To save space, the questions have been omitted, but it is easy to get their general drift and assess the truth behind the allegations. Nothing happened.

First the child replies: 'I don't want to do that', then 'No', then 'No' again, then 'I don't want to do it. Can I play now?', then 'You are boring me', then 'That's all', then 'Morris', then 'I don't know', then 'Nobody else', then 'Who?', then 'I don't know', followed by 'I don't know' and 'I don't know', before concluding with the explanation 'Because I don't', at which stage the child bursts into tears.

These wayward stories pale into insignificance alongside American extravaganzas, which started in the early 1980s with imputations of sexual abuse in day-care centres, in part fuelled by the publication of *Michelle Remembers* cataloguing the ordeals endured by the Canadian Michelle Smith as a child. Smith recovered these buried **memories** while in therapy and, although there was no evidence to support her contentions, her story served as a blueprint for an escalating number of victims. In 1988 the first clinical study by the psychiatrist Bennett G. Braun unearthed common threads of being drugged during rituals; of witnessing the torture of others or the mutilation of animals; of attending the sacrifice of babies or adults, and the like, all features of *Michelle Remembers*.

By 1991, 30 per cent of the respondents to an American Psychological Association survey had treated patients suffering from SRA; 93 per cent of respondents believed that their patients' claims were true. In California, half the social workers interviewed accepted that SRA was a conspiracy of national proportions, extending through the generations, involving baby-killers who led otherwise exemplary lives and held respectable positions in the community.

In October 1988 the notion received a massive boost from two prime-time NBC television documentaries, 'Satanic Breeders: Babies for Sacrifice' and 'Devil Worship: Exposing Satan's Underground', which began with a voice-over intoning: 'No region in this country is beyond the reach of Devil worshippers … The children you're about to meet were born into it. They say their parents forced them to witness bloody rituals and even, they say, to participate in ritual murder.' The Satanist delusion is backed by fundamentalist Christians primed to drive the populace into the arms of God by scare stories about the Devil, their efforts aided by books like Lauren Stratford's autobiographical best-seller *Satan's Underground*, now said by her sister to be a work of fiction.

It is easy, but not necessarily facile, to draw comparisons between the communist threat and the onslaught of SRA. As international communism collapsed, so SRA replaced it. Bennett G. Braun drew an exact parallel, referring to the devil worshippers' 'national-international type of organisation' which exhibits a 'communist cell structure, where it goes from … small groups to local consuls, district consuls, national consuls, and they have meetings at different times'. The sophisticated use of brainwashing, drugs and hypnosis is supposed to keep members quiet for much of their lives.

The FBI's expert on SRA, a sceptical Kenneth V. Lanning, recently commented that the devil-stories are so unsubstantiated that it is 'up to mental health professionals, not law enforcement, to explain why victims are alleging things that don't seem to be true'.

By the mid-1980s, the number of SRA murders was said to be in the tens of thousands annually. A prison official from Utah revealed that sacrifices were running at 50,000 a year, a figure which became the accepted bench-mark. But the FBI have investigated 2,000 cases without uncovering any concrete evidence, the absence of which does little to curtail panics in rural areas, where distraught mothers drive to school to snatch their children back from class before marauding Satanists arrive.

America was the country briefly brought to its knees in 1938 by the Orson Welles-produced radio play *War of the Worlds*. Citizens fled the Men from Mars *en masse*, and the nearest to a solid SRA case is the trial of Paul **Ingram**, detailed elsewhere.

Rodine

A brand of rat poison containing phosphorus. In 1953 Rodine was still freely available over the counter at all good chemists. A one-shilling tin held enough to murder a large colony of humans; the phosphorus content was ten grains, and a lethal dose is one. Louisa Merrifield used it to poison Sarah Ricketts, an elderly widow who took her on as a live-in companion. Within a month of starting work Louisa was named as sole beneficiary under her employer's will and, a few days later, at 3.15 on the morning of 14 April 1953, the widow died in agony. Louisa waited until tea-time before summoning help, presumably animated by a justifiable sense of apprehension. 'It was not a nice time to go out on the streets and call a doctor,' she demurred. She was hanged on 18 September 1953, aged 46, and her husband, a quarter of a century her senior, was also charged with murder. But the jury could not agree and, notwithstanding his inheritance of a half-share in Ricketts's bungalow, he eked out his days as a sideshow on Blackpool promenade.

Four years later Mary Elizabeth Wilson, a serial husband-killer, used such quantities of phosphorus that her three exhumed spouses were found still glowing. The last two had survived only the first fortnight of their nuptials, and Wilson's total gross from these killings for profit exceeded £200. Aged 66, the 'Widow of Windy Nook' was regarded as past her prime for hanging and died soon after in prison. The sale of Rodine is now banned.

Rolling, Danny

The career of serial killer Danny Rolling, at present (2005) on Florida's death row, seems to raise the bizarre question of whether a criminal can be 'possessed' by demonic forces.

Rolling, an ex-convict, was arrested on 7 September 1990, after he had robbed a Winn-Dixie store in Ocala, Florida. It was not until January of the following year that the police decided to take a blood test. Rolling's DNA revealed that he was the man who had been involved in the sex murder of four young women, and also stabbed a man to death, on the campus of the University of Florida at Gainesville in the previous August. The crimes had caused such terror that half the students had gone home.

Rolling seemed an unlikely serial killer: 38 years old, tall, good-looking and articulate, a talented artist and guitar player, who looked more like a schoolteacher in his horn-rimmed glasses. But in due course he confessed to the Gainesville murders and eventually to three more, as well as a whole string of rapes.

He came to the attention of crime writer Sondra London when she was visiting the prison, and she became engaged to him. Through Sondra London, I (CW) came to write an introduction to Rolling's autobiography, *The Making of a Serial Killer* (1998), and even exchanged a few letters with him. He told me that he had no doubt that he had been possessed by some demonic force when he committed the murders, and after studying the case, I came close to agreeing with him.

Rolling was born in 1954 in Shreveport, Louisiana, the son of a police sergeant who had been a war hero. Unfortunately, the father was also what science-fiction writer A. E. Van Vogt has called a 'Right Man', someone who is obsessed by the need to be in the right. Such men are usually family tyrants. Rolling Snr seems to have had no love for his son, and lost no opportunity to tell him he was stupid and worthless.

Rolling also went into the military, but just before he was due to go to Vietnam he was caught with drugs and discharged. He was dismayed, for he had been enjoying the army. His father was furious and disgusted. But Rolling then experienced a religious conversion, and married a fellow-member of the Pentecostal Church. Unfortunately, he was unable to get rid of a habit he had acquired in childhood: peering through windows at women undressing.

When he was caught, the marriage began to disintegrate.

On the day he was served his divorce papers, he committed his first sex attack, breaking into a house and raping a young woman who was alone. He felt so remorseful that the next morning he made his way back to her house to apologise – then saw two grim, powerfully built men come out, and changed his mind. But soon after that he committed his first armed robbery. And it was not long before he was serving his first jail term.

The brutality and violence of prison life shocked him. Blacks and whites hated each other and often killed each other. He was nearly gang-raped in the shower by a crowd of blacks.

Free once more, he now experienced a compulsion to commit rape. He admits that what he enjoyed was the surrender of the terrified girl; it was balm to his badly bruised ego. Another term in jail only confirmed his self-image as a desperate criminal.

Back in his home town Shreveport in 1989, he began peeping through the window of a pretty model named Julie Grissom. One day, after missing work for three days in a row, he was fired from his job in a restaurant. He reacted just as he had reacted years before to his divorce papers. On 6 November 1989 he crept into the backyard of the Grissom household. Undeterred by the fact that there were three people in the house – Julie Grissom's father and her eight-year-old nephew – he burst in and tied up all three at gunpoint with duct tape. Then he stabbed to death the boy and the elder man, dragged Julie Grissom into the bathroom and raped her against the sink, forcing her to say, 'Fuck my pussy, daddy' (typical of the rapist's craving to feel 'in control'). After making her climb in the bath so he could wash out her vagina with a hosepipe, he stabbed her to death. Then he left after taking $200.

By now he was convinced that he had two 'demons', one a robber and rapist called Ennad and the other a killer called Gemini.

A violent quarrel with his father ended with James Rolling trying to shoot him, and with Danny shooting his father and leaving him for dead. In fact, Rolling survived, minus one eye. Danny Rolling committed more armed robberies and rapes, then went to Gainesville, where he bought a tent and pitched it in the woods.

There were more voyeur activities – on some occasions he stripped naked. On 24 August 1990 he broke into an apartment shared by two young women, Christina Powell and Sonja Larson, who were both asleep. He stabbed Sonja Larson to death in her bed. Then he went downstairs and woke up Christina Powell on the settee, and at gunpoint taped her hands. After raping her he stabbed her to death, making her lie on her face while he did it.

Two evenings later, on 26 August, he broke into the apartment of 18-year-old Christa Hoyt, on whom he had been spying, and waited for her to return home. When she did, he overpowered her, and raped and stabbed her to death, also disembowelling her.

On 28 August he broke into an apartment shared by two students, Tracy Paules and Manuel Taboada. The latter was stabbed as he lay asleep. Tracy Paules heard sounds of struggle and came to see what was happening. Rolling chased her to her bedroom, tied her up and raped her, afterwards stabbing her to death as she lay face down.

The murders caused widespread panic. By then Rolling had already moved south, living by burglary and armed robbery. He was caught in Ocala only ten days after his last murder.

Tried for the Gainesville murders in 1994, he was given five death sentences.

In *The Making of a Serial Killer* he tells how he tried to enter the apartment of Christina Powell and Sonja Larson and found the door locked. He claims that he then prayed to his demon Gemini, and that when he tried the door again, it was unlocked. And in a letter to me he described how, in his cell, a kind of grey gargoyle had leapt on to his chest, held him down with its claws and thrust its tongue down his throat. All this may, of course, be invention. Or it may be that Rolling really believes what he says. I am inclined to think that he does.

After thirty years studying the paranormal, I have slowly come to accept that 'possession' is a genuine possibility, and not a fantasy dreamed up by the feeble-minded and the sex-starved. But whether Rolling was possessed by some unpleasant paranormal entity is perhaps beside the point. As in the case of Ted Bundy, Rolling's life typifies the development of a sex killer: the childhood voyeurism culminating in his first rape (which was committed in a state of rage at the prospect of divorce), the murder of the Grissoms, again committed in a state of anger and defiance, then the orgy of rape and murder at Gainesville. It seems clear that, as in the case of Bundy, rape and murder proved

addictive. In a sense, Rolling *was* possessed – by his craving to violate and kill.

Rolling pin

The murder weapon in the 1992 June Scotland case. A century ago, bashing in a husband's head with a rolling pin and burying his body in the garden was the form expected from the worst murderesses of the melodramatic Victorian era. In those days, the perpetrator could count on general opprobrium and a well-received hanging. Today, June Scotland escaped a custodial sentence and left the court under a two-year probation order. Modern judges are more inclined to take into account the guilt of the accused, and June Scotland had withstood twenty-two years of domestic torture by her husband, driving her twice to attempted suicide.

There was no dispute as to the facts of the killing; to avoid the obligatory life sentence for murder, June Scotland's lawyers pleaded 'diminished responsibility'. But in successful cases the accused (although absolved of murder) is liable to confinement in Broadmoor for indefinite psychiatric detention, an outcome the judge avoided by conceding that June Scotland had been demented *at the time*. But now, five years later, with her husband dead, she felt much better.

The discovery of her husband's skeleton highlights the risks of shallow burial in a tiny back-garden near a neighbour's fence.

See also **Sexism**

Romances

There is a kind of security in loving a man behind bars. The prisoner is a sitting target for affection, liable to respond to any advances with enthusiasm. Men who kill have a certain glamour and Kenneth Bianchi killed a lot; as one of the Hillside Stranglers, his criminal career included schoolgirl victims, rapes committed with beer bottles and murders with plastic bags over the head, injections of cleaning fluid, gassing and electric shocks. Before strangling Lauren Rae Wagner, he plugged her into the mains.

Bianchi finally settled down to marry his pen-pal Shirlee J. Book in a prison ceremony during 1989. But Shirlee was not his first suitor. Veronica Lynn Compton stole his heart away in 1980.

Veronica was a fetching brunette aged 23 who loved True Crime murder and fancied her chances as a poet, playwright and actress. In June 1980 she mailed a fan letter to the imprisoned Bianchi, soliciting his expert advice on a play she was writing. Veronica's creation was a female serial killer who misled investigators by injecting semen into her victims' vaginas.

In fictional terms this is no mean ruse, and indeed Scott Turow's best-seller *Presumed Innocent* employs a similar plot-motif. Bianchi was intrigued by Veronica's request, and even more intrigued when he saw her in the flesh on a prison visit. Soon she visited twice a day, and together the couple concocted a dream future where they travelled the world on a voyage of murder, cutting off their victims' genitalia for permanent display in jars of embalming fluid.

Come to think of it, and they did, with Veronica at liberty this was perfectly feasible. Since Bianchi was locked up, she would kill for the two of them, and better still, provided she had the spunk, it could be just like her play. If she used Bianchi's, he would not just accompany her in spirit; he would be with her in spermatozoa, deposited in the corpse. Further, this might secure Bianchi's release by showing that an identical murderer remained at large.

And so it was. Before her next visit Bianchi masturbated into a rubber glove and later passed her the bulging finger concealed in the spine of a book. Veronica and her precious cargo flew to the small coastal town of Bellingham. There she checked into the Shangri-la motel, and in a local bar she identified a likely-looking cocktail waitress, Kim Breed. After a few drinks Veronica asked her new friend to drive her back to the hotel, where she lured her into the bedroom for a nightcap. Veronica slipped into the bathroom, took out her strangling rope, tiptoed behind her victim and drew the cord tight round her neck.

Kim Breed, a fitness fanatic, lofted Veronica over her head, and soon Bianchi's sweetheart was languishing unsubdued in jail for attempted murder, where she directed her love mail at a new beau, California's 'Sunset Strip Slayer' Douglas Clark. He reciprocated, sending her snaps of a body whose **head** he had cut off.

Bianchi was hardly more of a catch than his successor in Veronica's affections. Officially credited with a sequence of ten Californian murders starting in October 1977, he was finally caught in Washington after disposing of two co-ed students in January 1979.

Bianchi became a suspect when the police heard that he had offered the girls $200 to house-sit on the night they disappeared; in corroboration, police found the keys and address of the empty house in his car.

At first sight Bianchi made an improbable killer. Friendly, handsome and gentle, regarded by neighbours as a good family man, Bianchi lived amicably with his girlfriend, Kelli Boyd, and their young son. But the charm of serial murderers is an overrated commodity, and Bianchi may have been psychologically fissured almost at birth. From the age of only three months, after his adoption by Nicholas and Francis Bianchi, his upbringing was a model of stability and affection. But his true mother, a teenager with a drink problem and a reputation for promiscuity, handed Bianchi to a foster mother straight after delivery, and she, in turn, farmed him out to a series of neighbours. Bianchi matured as a liar, a thief and a two-timer. After visiting his cousin Angelo Buono in Los Angeles, he degenerated into a pimp, rapist and murderer.

Another prison liaison from the early 1970s involved Myra **Hindley**, the child killer, and Patricia Cairns, a former Carmelite nun turned warder. They met for sex in the prison chapel and, when apart, masturbated at pre-arranged times. Hindley was sentenced to an additional year inside, and Cairns to six years, for plotting an escape. Veronica succeeded; she is still at large.

Hindley's initiation into the world of romance was strikingly unfortunate. Just before Christmas 1961 she confided in her diary, 'Eureka! Today we have our first date. We are going to the cinema.' The film was *Trial at Nuremberg* and her escort Ian Brady.

See also **MPD**

Rummel, William James (1942–)

American drop-out whose plight was considered by the fearless Supreme Court. Born in 1942, Rummel was reared by his grandparents and left school to take up casual work in San Antonio, Texas. In 1964 he had his first brush with the law, pleading guilty to a minor credit fraud after running up an $80 debt on new tyres for his old Studebaker. Released in 1966, Rummel kept his nose clean until 1969 when he forged a cheque for $28.36 to cover his rent at the local Angeles Motel.

In August 1972, Rummel landed in trouble again when the owner of the local Captain Hook's Lounge, David Shaw, asked him to repair his air-conditioner.

Shaw produced an advance cheque of $120.75 for a new compressor; Rummel cashed it but never got round to doing the work.

At that date Texas had a 'Three Time Loser' law imposing a mandatory life sentence on anyone convicted of three felonies. It is far from clear that on the air-conditioning charge Rummel was guilty of theft, or of theft by pretext, or of anything, and in fact Shaw signed a non-prosecution agreement asking to withdraw the case. But Rummel's state-appointed lawyer, William B. Chenault III, on a fixed fee of $250, felt it would be irksome to call witnesses and advised his client not to testify. So Rummel, found guilty of wangling the $120 advance, was automatically sent to prison for life.

Several years later Rummel's cause was championed by a young lawyer, Scott Atlas, at a smart Houston firm. Against tooth-and-nail resistance from the state of Texas, by 1980 Atlas succeeded in referring the case to the Supreme Court.

There he argued that Rummel's sentence was so disproportionate that it constituted a 'cruel and unusual punishment' and hence was unconstitutional. But he was wrong. On 18 March 1980 both Rummel's sentence and the right of Texas to do what it wanted were upheld in a majority decision. Justice William Rehnquist explained that unlike mere traffic offences, for which life imprisonment would be excessive, Rummel's crimes were serious.

Later, after Rummel had served seven years, nine months and fifteen days, Atlas secured his release on the grounds of the inadequate defence by his first attorney, and in 1983 Texas deleted the mandatory life-sentence clause from the statute book.

See also **Attorneys**

Runyon, Damon (1884–1946)

Highly paid Hearst journalist and author of the *On Broadway* short stories. From his arrival in 1910 to his death from throat cancer in 1946, Runyon created the deadbeat folklore characters (immortalised in his *Guys and Dolls*) who encapsulated underworld New York, enriching our vocabulary with terms like 'monkey business', 'kisser' and 'croak'.

Some of his cast were based on real people. The last days of Arnold Rothstein (see **Great Gatsby**) are dramatised in the story *The Brain Goes Home*.

Nightclub hostess 'Texas' Guinan became 'Miss Missouri Martin', mobster Frank Costello (see **Head**) turned into 'Dave the Dude' and Al Capone made a starring appearance as 'Black Mike Mario'. 'Waldo Winchester' was the fictional alter ego of gossip columnist Walter Winchell, a late-night buddy on Runyon's forays with the police.

Winchell's unofficial office was his table at the New York's Stork Club, and from this vantage point two guests first spotted J. Edgar **Hoover** holding hands with his male lover, Clyde Tolson, on New Year's Eve 1936. It is unlikely that this particular cat stayed in the bag for long. Not only was Winchell a compulsive gossip anxious to impress the likes of mobster Costello; in addition, the front-man for the Stork Club, former bootlegger Sherman Billingsley, reportedly had the celebrity tables wired for sound and installed two-way mirrors in the lavatories. In any case, Billingsley was in Costello's pay.

Capone was a pal of Runyon's, and before his 1932 prison sentence presented him with his prize pair of whippets for safe-keeping.

R v. Collins

An English criminal case of 1973 dearly beloved by law students. The defendant, a youth called Collins, was tried on a technical charge of burglary contrary to Section 9 of the Theft Act 1968, in that he had entered a building as a trespasser with the intention of raping a girl.

The facts were that one night Collins, feeling randy, had determined to have sex – by force if necessary – with a distant female acquaintance. So he found a stepladder, went to her home, took off nearly all his clothes and ascended to her window. Case reports regard it as peculiarly comical that at this stage he was clad only in a pair of socks, left on to facilitate a rapid escape.

When Collins reached the top of the ladder he heaved himself on to the ledge of the bedroom's latticework window. Inside, the girl awoke and, observing a naked man with an erect penis crouching on the windowsill, mistakenly inferred that her boyfriend had arrived. She pulled Collins in. He had sex; she made love; they had sexual intercourse.

Afterwards the woman felt that 'somehow, something was different', perhaps the length of Collins's hair, or perhaps his voice as they exchanged pillow-talk, and he was exposed as an unwitting impostor. Captured despite his getaway socks, Collins presented the police with a legal dilemma. He could hardly be charged with rape; the girl had willingly submitted to his embraces.

So the police went for Section 9 burglary, citing his intention to rape at the moment of entry into the home. But on appeal Collins was exonerated. While outside the girl's window he had planned to rape her. But in the event she asked him in. The crux was that she extended her invitation to Collins while he remained *outside* the house. True, he was squatting on the windowsill, but he was not yet *in the house*. So he entered not as a trespasser but a guest.

Perhaps in a more solidly built home with a deeper window embrasure Collins would be adjudged as perching 'inside'. So burglars with charm should concentrate on houses of flimsy construction.

S

Sacco (1891–1927) and Vanzetti (1888–1927)

Electrocuted in 1927 and feted ever since as innocent victims of capitalist oppression. But there is little doubt of their guilt. The original 1921 trial took place in the infancy of forensic ballistics. The firearms evidence was unquestionably ambivalent, and although Sacco and Vanzetti were convicted, they were not executed. But when a 1927 committee re-examined the case, peering through the newly invented comparison microscope at slides of a test bullet fired from Nicola Sacco's Colt .32 into cotton wool, even defence firearms expert Augustus Gill conceded defeat, a conclusion confirmed in 1961 by another forensic team. The case against Bartolomeo Vanzetti is strong, but not conclusive.

The accused – a fish pedlar and a shoe-factory worker – were members of an anarchist cell advocating violence and, as labour agitators with communist sympathies who sidestepped the First World War by fleeing to Mexico, they presented an unsympathetic face to middle America, an impression enhanced by charges of a brutal double murder on 15 April 1920 when the paymaster and a guard at the Slater shoe factory in South Braintree were shot dead carrying two cashboxes containing $16,000. Frederick Parmenter was gunned down as he ran, even though he had already dropped his box, and the other victim, Alessandro Berardelli, was repeatedly shot as he lay wounded on the ground. By the time Sacco and Vanzetti came to trial, on 31 May 1921, Vanzetti was already serving ten years for an attempted hold-up at Bridgewater when he had again opened fire on payroll guards.

Their conviction on confusing evidence (including 158 identification witnesses) sparked an international outcry fostered by the defence attorney's insistence that this was a political trial dispensing capitalist justice. Judge Webster Thayer, presiding, did not allay these fears by calling the couple 'those anarchist bastards' in his club, and after the verdict his home was bombed. But the hearing was fairly conducted, the convictions proper and, despite the efforts of the Red Aid committee and numerous petitions (whose signatories included H. G. Wells, Albert Einstein and John Galsworthy), Sacco and Vanzetti died in the electric chair as propaganda heroes on 23 August 1927.

See also **Hamilton**

Sacco and Vanzetti, anarchists

Sacher-Masoch, Leopold von (1836–95)

Austrian inventor of masochism. A novelist by trade, Sacher-Masoch's literary endeavours were spurred on by his wife, who whipped him. A proponent of **torture** and subjugation, he particularly commended being lashed 'by a successful rival before the eyes of an adored woman', remarking that this sensation could not be described.

Sacher-Masoch devoted his life to refining the sources of pleasure, spiking himself on needles or adding flesh-retentive hooks to the tip of a whip. Like the celebrated serial murderer, A. H. **Fish**, he enjoyed slashing himself with razors, a tendency noted by his contemporary Richard von Krafft-Ebing, Professor of Psychiatry at the University of Vienna. Observing that some people derived gratification from inflicting pain and suffering on themselves, the professor (who pioneered the study of sexual deviation) coined the word 'masochism'.

Sadism differs only in that the discomfort is inflicted on someone else and hence is more popular. Krafft-Ebing's work led to the progressive recognition of 'lust murder', which we know today as sex killing; his *Psychopathia Sexualis* of 1886 incorporates a section on **sexual crimes** which encompasses the ritualised slaughter of women, anticipating **Jack the Ripper** by two years. 'Very likely,' Krafft-Ebing surmised, 'the murderous act and subsequent mutilation of the body were substitutes for the sexual act.'

Masochism may be fun, but is it legal? A related issue came before the British House of Lords in March 1993 after fifteen men in a homosexual ring were sentenced to prison for consensually assaulting each other. That is, they all agreed to it. The defence argued that it was not against the law to stick wires down a friend's penis, or sandpaper his testicles and nail his organ to a board through a hole in the foreskin, providing he made no objection, but their Lordships ruled that Sections 20 and 47 of the Offences Against the Person Act 1861 had been infringed. Lord Templeman commented, 'The victim was usually manacled so that the sadist could enjoy the thrill of power and the victim could enjoy the thrill of helplessness. But the victim had no control over the harm which the sadist, also stimulated by drugs and drink, might inflict. In one case a victim was branded twice on the thigh and there was some doubt as to whether he consented to or protested against the second branding.' It seems that these pleasures are best savoured in solitude.

Sade, Marquis de (1740–1814)

French inventor of sadism. The high point reached by the Marquis in real life was carving small slits in the skin of prostitute Rose Keller and pouring in hot wax.

This and similar misdemeanours, like administering sweetmeats containing aphrodisiacs to Marseille prostitutes, caused him to be locked up for thirteen years so that only his imagination could run riot. In prison Sade turned to literature, describing every sort of perversity by way of making a political rather than a sexual point.

Sade's premise was that there was no God. It followed that the dominant institutions of the state, like law and religion, were fraudulent in their efforts to bamboozle citizens into moral (or at least legal) conduct. Sade argued that to be selfish was to be honest, and the best an honest man could do was embark on a life of criminal debauchery. This is the 'plot' of *The 120 Days of Sodom*, where the four principal libertines include a bishop and a Lord Chief Justice, as well as a supporting cast of corrupt monks and nuns.

There was nothing too extreme about these views in the revolutionary France of 1789. So Sade was released. But theory is one thing, practice another. Once free, with both motive and opportunity, Sade passed up the chance to get even with his mother-in-law, responsible for his original incarceration. On his travels Sade professed to be outraged by the *castrati* and transvestites of Florence, and he was soon indicted by Robespierre's regime for excessive moderation. As from 1801 he spent the rest of his life in prison, dying in the madhouse at Charenton in 1814. His other books include *Justine* (1791) and *Juliette*.

Across the Channel, Sade's tracts became popular, inspiring English mutations which progressively eliminated the intellectual content and accentuated the sexual, until there emerged fully fledged Victorian pornography, precursor of the era of the **sex crime**.

The underlying aim of the sadist may not necessarily be the derivation of pleasure from another's agony. Ensuring compliance may be equally important. In words penned by one unusually articulate serial killer on the **Quantico** files, 'The wish to inflict pain is not the essence of sadism. One essential impulse: to have complete mastery over another person, to make him/her a helpless object of our will, to become the absolute ruler over her, to become her God. The most important radical aim is to make her suffer since there is no greater power over another person than that of inflicting pain.' For FBI Agent Robert Hazelwood, a sadist's hallmark is contempt for women as 'sluts and bitches', in part a defensive reaction to mask the perpetrator's own failure at normal interaction which simultaneously justifies brutality, forcing many a 'nice' girl to comply with deviant demands and thus justify her death as a whore.

See also **Slave**, **Torture**

Safes, how to crack

Of the two most comprehensive guides to safe-cracking, one was published by the American 'Commission of scientific or mechanical experts to report on the best methods of safe and vault construction'. It put the makes of safe on the market at the end of the last century through their paces and found all (with one exception) could be opened, whether with drills, wedges or explosives.

Through some oversight, the Commission released details of its deliberations, setting out exactly how each model should be tackled and producing comparative studies on the relative efficacy of different techniques. Thus it noted that 'the wedging off of sheet after sheet is found a better method of attack than drilling', thereby saving the inexperienced from hours of wasted exertion, quite apart from needless investment in costly drilling equipment.

On the delicate area of explosives the Commission promulgated clear guidelines on the appropriate type, quantity and technique. Best results were obtained when 'nitroglycerine was poured into the crack (between the door and frame) until three ounces had entered and it had begun to drip from the lower side of the door'. Did this work? Apparently, yes: the outcome was 'the complete destruction of the lower part of the door'. For the faint-hearted, the Commission offered reassurance that 'the sound of the explosion was not very startling'. To assist scheduling, it advised that a

The rotund Corliss, cast in a single piece of manganese steel

REWARD
$100,000

has been offered by BRINK'S, INCORPORATED, Chicago, Illinois, "for information leading to the Arrest and Conviction of the Persons involved in the Holdup of the Office of Brink's, Incorporated, 165 Prince Street, Boston, Massachusetts, on January 17, 1950." The person or persons to whom the reward shall be paid and the amount will be determined by a specially designated reward committee.

If you have any information concerning the identity or the whereabouts of any of the perpetrators of the robbery of Brink's, Incorporated, at Boston, Massachusetts, on January 17, 1950, please communicate with the undersigned or with the nearest office of the FEDERAL BUREAU OF INVESTIGATION, U. S. Department of Justice, the local address and telephone number of which are set forth on the reverse side of this notice. The telephone number can also be obtained from page one of your telephone directory.

If such information leads to the arrest and conviction and / or recovery of money, the FEDERAL BUREAU OF INVESTIGATION will, if specifically requested to do so by the person furnishing information advise the Reward Committee of the information so furnished.

JOHN EDGAR HOOVER, DIRECTOR
FEDERAL BUREAU OF INVESTIGATION
U. S. DEPARTMENT OF JUSTICE
WASHINGTON, D. C.
TELEPHONE NATIONAL 7117

well-conducted job took no longer than seven minutes. And so on, for page after page.

Corners were always a safe's most vulnerable point, and the only make to resist the Commission's attentions did without them. This was the Corliss, a strongbox shaped like a cannonball with a round door set in a round hole; circles are easier to engineer to fine tolerances than rectangles, making for a more exact fit, minimising the fatal gap between door and frame through which wedges or explosives could penetrate. A mere five-hundredth of an inch is sufficient for nitroglycerine to seep in.

One of few documented successes against the Corliss was achieved by Herbert Emmerson Wilson (with alleged career takings of $16 million), who adopted the alternative approach of an axe. First he torched a groove round the safe one inch deep, then he weakened it with his axe, tapping out the channel all the way round, and finally he split the 'egg' in two with a single mighty blow. He related: 'I took aim with the blacksmith's tool, prayed my hunch was right, hit the groove at the top of the safe only one sharp blow, just one … The haul came to $170,000.'

In the late nineteenth century, American cracksmen could learn their craft at Frederika Mandelbaum's educational establishment; she provided tuition in return for a percentage of her students' profits. In the 1920s, amateur cracksmen in Los Angeles took diplomas at the Wayne Strong School of Safework in 'safe opening, safe repairing and safe lockwork', and in the 1960s the Canadian police discovered a classroom in a Toronto garage, complete with sample oxyacetylene cutting gear, drills, nitroglycerine, detonators, and a course textbook footnoted, cross-referenced and divided into instructional modules.

In Britain, it was only in 1965 (when the era of safe-cracking had all but gone) that criminals received a properly printed thirteen-step guide to safeblowing, each stage illustrated with captioned photographs starting with removal of the keyhole cover. Pictures showed how to wire the detonator, drill the hole for the second charge (packed in a **condom**) and then fire the door itself. Only the amount of gelignite was omitted, but presumably the *Sunday Times*, with its several million readers, took legal advice on its liabilities.

See also **Gutshot**

Sagawa, Issei (1949–)

Japanese celebrity cannibal. On 11 June 1981, while studying at the Sorbonne in Paris, Sagawa invited a Dutch girl, Renee Hartevelt, to dinner. The pair had known each other for some time; Sagawa was a long-standing admirer, much taken by Renee's white arms, and had previously escorted her to the theatre and concerts. They had even danced together, their bodies touching. But this was the first time the diminutive Sagawa succeeded in enticing Renee back to his sixteenth *arrondissement* apartment. In Sagawa's words, she had 'nice breasts, a slender build, a long white neck, transparent white skin, and a beautiful and gorgeous face'.

After shooting her in the back of the neck, Sagawa chopped Renee up and consumed her. A student of comparative literature, he recorded his impressions meticulously. 'I touched her hip and wondered where I should eat first. After a little consideration, I ate right in the centre of the abundant, bouncing part of the right hip ... but I could not bite it out, so when I opened my mouth, I could see the teeth print in her

Issei Sagawa, cannibal killer

white hip ... so I took a meat knife, and when I stabbed, it went right in ... a little came out and I put it into my mouth ... it had no smell or taste, and melted in my mouth like raw tuna in a sushi restaurant. Finally I was eating a beautiful white woman, and I thought nothing was so delicious! Then I moved to the thighs ...'

Over the next few days Sagawa ate the rest, some fried in salt, pepper and mustard, and others sushi-style, raw. When the best parts were finished, Sagawa placed the leftovers into two cardboard suitcases and flung them into a pond in the Bois de Boulogne. But a severed arm and hand stuck out of one of the cases, so the incident attracted the attention of a watching couple. Arrested on 15 June, Sagawa confessed immediately.

Found insane by Judge Jean-Louis Brugière in 1983, Sagawa avoided a conviction for murder and was detained in Paris's Paul Guiraud asylum. But there were language difficulties. According to Dr Tsuguo Kaneko, the French mistook Sagawa's 'enteritis' (an inflammation of the intestines, like indigestion) for the more serious 'encephalitis', an inflammation of the brain (like incipient death). Regarding their patient as an incurable psychotic destined for an early grave, the French shipped him back to Tokyo after a year, on the understanding that he would be sequestered in a mental hospital. He was, but he did not enjoy it. 'My time in the mental ward was like hell,' Sagawa says. 'Everyone else in there was crazy.'

Problems arose because Sagawa had never been committed to Tokyo's Matsuzawa Hospital. His parents simply *consented* to his confinement. But their boy was not guilty of anything in Japan and, on reflection, he was not guilty of anything in France, where the charges were dropped because of his mental derangement. So after fifteen months his father, a company president, had him released. As Sagawa was not insane, he could not be detained.

By then he was moderately famous. In 1983 the Japanese playwright Kara wrote a 'factional' novel about him, *Letters from Sagawa*, which sold 320,000 copies in a month and won a literary prize. The same year Sagawa published his own memoirs, *In the Fog*, penned while in prison. His sales topped 200,000, and the book was acclaimed as 'beautifully done, outstanding amongst recent Japanese literature'. Forty pages were devoted to a detailed culinary description, starting with his first abortive attempts at eating Renee's corpse with his teeth (excerpted above).

Sagawa's *oeuvre* now comprises two more titles, *Health* and *Mirage*. In December 1991 he produced a magazine feature with the more graphic title of 'I ate her because of fetishism', and he is currently working on an anthology of **cannibalism**. In March 1992 Sagawa nearly precipitated an international diplomatic incident when he travelled to Germany for a television chat show with a regular audience of 9 million.

Like many famous trouble-makers, Sagawa is short, well under five feet. His hands and feet are undersized. Interviewed in January 1992, he said: 'I still adore the sight and shape of young Western women, particularly beautiful ones. I was a premature and unhealthy baby, I am ugly and small, but I indulge in fantasies about strong healthy bodies. I'm essentially a romantic.'

Sagawa's fetish took root at the age of five with a nightmare about being boiled inside a pot. By adolescence, this had transmuted from a fear of being eaten into a desire to eat, and that is what he still craves. But sometimes this finds expression as a desire to be devoured by a beautiful Western woman.

Conscientious reporters often point out that Renee's parents must find Sagawa's high profile extremely painful.

Saltillo Prison

Site of a famous Mexican jailbreak. In November 1975 the convicts started digging the tunnel through which, on 18 April 1976, some seventy-five escapists set off for the outside world. The tunnel came up in the nearby courtroom. All were recaptured.

In January 1913 an attempted escape from San Quentin by Herbert Repsold, a burglar, came to a more macabre end. Repsold had both nous and money, using the one to pull the fuses from the prison's power station and the other to pay for a boat waiting at the water's edge. In pitch darkness he scaled the prison wall and rowed out to sea. But his dinghy capsized and next morning he was taken back and dumped in the penitentiary's reception area where he remained on display for two days, dead, *pour décourager les autres*.

'Sam, Son of'

Pudgy David Richard Berkowitz turned violent at the age of 22. On Christmas Eve 1975 he drove to New York's Co-Op city looking for a woman to kill.

His intended target escaped. As Berkowitz ran off, his eye was caught by a 15-year-old in a doorway; he attacked her instead, stabbing the girl six times with his hunting knife. Elated by his success, that night he gorged himself on junk food. For the next venture he bought a pistol, a Charter Arms Special Bulldog, and in the year from 28 July 1976 he earned a name as 'The .44 Calibre Killer', attacking seventeen victims, killing six, blinding one and paralysing another. He concentrated on women, shooting courting couples through their car windows, sometimes gunning for the man too.

Like many 'dis**organised**' serial killers, Berkowitz was a no-hoper condemned to menial jobs, a shy recluse inhabiting a bare room with a blanket nailed over the window for a curtain and a dirty mattress on the floor. There he dreamed of women, of his enviable physique, of his superb stamina as a lover, and of the bouts of oral sex he later replicated by shooting Virginia Voskerichian through the mouth. This was the drab reality of his psychological state; but in court Berkowitz made much of the monsters, the demons, the voices in the head baying for blood and, most notably, the dog who urged him on.

Berkowitz claimed that he took his orders from a labrador belonging to his Yonkers neighbour, Sam Carr. The dog kept him awake with its barking, and at his trial Berkowitz declared that the animal had been possessed by the spirit of a 6,000-year-old demon who demanded sacrificial victims. Berkowitz assumed the name of 'Son of Sam' after the dog's owner, and only on his interview, post-conviction, for the FBI's Quantico **database** did a more sceptical picture surface.

In his cell, Berkowitz launched into his dog routine. FBI Special Agent Robert Ressler cut him off: 'Don't hand me that bullshit about the dog, David, I'm not buying.' Taken aback, Berkowitz replied, 'You're right', and conceded that the tales about demons were inventions concocted for the press. Under thorough questioning a more equivocal image emerged, of a timid loner given to sexual fantasies and addicted to TV horror movies.

Some shootings seemed almost reluctant. At his first killing, Berkowitz hoped the couple would drive away. Of the second, he said: 'I just wanted to get it over and head home', and of the seventh set of victims, Judy Placido and Salvatore Lupo, Berkowitz commented: 'I saw them and just finally decided that I must do it and get it over with.' But the afterglow was pleasant. 'You felt very good after you did it,' Berkowitz reported. 'It just happens to be satisfying, to get to the source of the blood.'

Berkowitz entered criminal record books as the only serial killer arrested on the strength of a parking ticket. Moments after his last attack on the night of 26 June 1977, a witness saw a man running to a car which had been ticketed only a few minutes previously. Police checked the parking records and found Berkowitz listed as the owner.

The cosmetics firm Max Factor made subliminal commercial capital from his 'reign of terror' by introducing a new female face moisturiser, 'Self-Defence', promoted by a poster reading, 'Warning! A Pretty Face Isn't Safe In This City. Fight Back With Self-Defence.' Berkowitz was well known for his pride in concentrating on shooting 'pretty girls', referring to them as 'tasty meat', and the linkage between sex, violence and fashion was underlined by the pop group, the Sex Pistols, who peaked at exactly the same time with a New York tour.

Sansons

Charles-Henri was probably the most famous of the great Sanson dynasty of French executioners, which included plain Charles (the first of the line, appointed in 1688), his successor Charles-Jean-Baptiste, and – in alphabetical order – Henri, Henri-Clèmont, Jean-Louis,

Louis-Charles-Martin, Louis-Cyr-Charlemagne, Louis Henri-Gabriel, and Nicholas-Charles-Gabriel.

The Sansons could not all trade as executioners in Paris, so they dispersed throughout the country, to Tours, Reims, Dijon and Provins. But it was Charles-Henri who cut off King Louis's head, and Robespierre's too; and his son who fell off the Paris scaffold and broke his neck.

In France, the selection process for executioners was analogous to the English procedure for choosing a monarch. There isn't one. French executioners, like kings, were born. Thus in 1706 Charles-Jean-Baptiste Sanson inherited his title at the age of seven, and a regent was appointed in the form of Francois Prud'homme until the lad came of age. So it was not just Charles-Henri's son who perished, but his apprentice and heir, and until 1775 it was a position worth inheriting. Executioners were entitled to the proceeds of *havage*, a tax levied on food which brought in revenues estimated at 60,000 livres a year. Charles-Jean-Baptiste maintained his large mansion in Paris in considerable style.

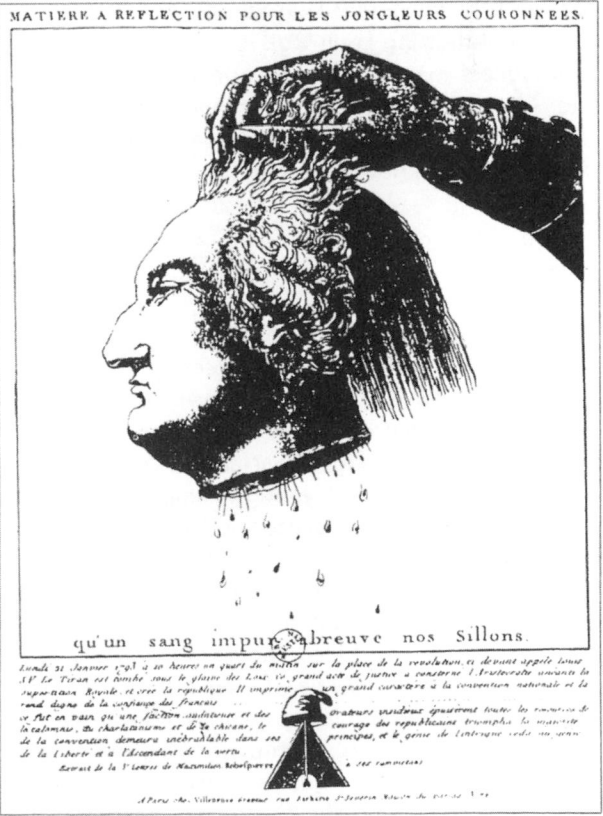

Their end-product

The black sheep of the family was Henri-Clement (1799–1889), a Regency buck of a fellow who dissipated his considerable inheritance on wine, women, gaming and the theatre. He took over the family business in 1840 and, as his fortune ran out, moved into harmless freelancing.

Henri stored his **guillotine** in a shed near home and, for a fee, would exhibit the machine in action, slicing straw-bales in half. But this additional income proved insufficient. So in 1847 Henri carted his guillotine round to the pawnbrokers. Inevitably, before it could be redeemed, he was instructed by the Procureur-général to cut off a head. In panic, Henri begged his creditor to release his equipment for just one day; then he would return it. But to no avail. Henri was obliged to make a full confession to his employers, who sacked him. By 1854 this guillotine was again in pawn when Henri, still struggling, had a windfall. A certain M. Tussaud bought the device outright for £220 (half due to the pawnbroker) for display in his waxworks; this particular model has a dubious but stimulating provenance as the specimen that Henri Sanson told Alexandre Dumas was used by his father to decapitate King Louis XVI.

Travellers may visit the Sanson family sepulchre in the Cimetière Montmartre, where the tombstone describes Charles-Henri as 'the benefactor of his whole family, who will never cease to pray for him'.

Sausages

The final format of Fritz Haarmann's victims. Haarmann (1879–1925), an epileptic homosexual butcher and police informer, frequented Hanover's railway station in Germany's depressed post-war years. The police issued him with a badge; Haarmann used it to pose as a policeman, picking up young unemployed workmen who slept rough on the platforms, part of the homeless flotsam tramping though the country in the 1920s.

Haarmann escorted the youths to his Neuestrasse lodgings in the thieves' quarter. There he violated them sexually, then killed them – supposedly with a bite through the windpipe – before selling their boned and dismembered bodies as meat. As the *News of the World* reported: 'All his victims were between twelve and eighteen years of age, and it was proved that the accused actually sold the flesh for human consumption. He once made sausages in his kitchen and,

Fritz Haarmann, mass murderer

together with his accomplice, cooked and ate them.' But more often Haarmann swept the boned chunks of youth into small buckets which he hawked round Hanover's open market, retailing the boys as horsemeat, selling their pathetic clothes and trinkets.

The butchery went on in the attic, its walls crusted with blood. Haarmann kept the neighbours awake chopping his way through the night. Bones were the problem. When Haarmann's neighbours started to query his persistent gifts of the suspiciously white bones for their stock-pots, he took to ejecting the mangled skeletons – including whole skulls – from his window into the river Leine which ran by the back of his house. In partnership with his lover Hans Grans, Haarmann ploughed through anywhere between twenty-seven and forty victims. Upper estimates of their toll extend into three figures; at this period, young men disappeared in Hanover at the rate of hundreds a year.

On 22 June 1924 Haarmann fell under suspicion for indecent behaviour, and when his rooms were searched the police discovered some of the missing boys' possessions. On the foreshore a heap of bones, 500 in all, from twenty-three bodies, came to light; skulls had been found by urchins on the river banks as early as 17 May. Haarmann confessed, and the evidence for the first few days of his trial was considered so revolting that proceedings were heard behind closed doors.

Like many of his ilk, Haarmann was a pleasant

enough man subject to periodic and irresistible urges. He claimed that he killed while in a trance-like state, unaware of the nature of his act. Court psychiatrists discerned a loathing of his father, who allegedly beat him. His three sisters became prostitutes while young; Haarmann himself was institutionalised at the age of 17 for sexual attacks on young children.

Haarmann kept his pride to the bitter end. Confronted with a picture of a missing boy, Herman Wolf, shown by his worried father, Haarmann exclaimed: 'Such an ugly creature as, according to his photographs, your son must have been, I would never have taken to ... You ought to be ashamed to have let him go about like that ... Such a youngster was far beneath my notice.'

He embraced the prospect of extinction with open arms, pleading: 'Condemn me to death. I only ask for justice. I am not mad. It is true that I often get into a state of which I know nothing, but that is not madness. Deliver me from this life which is a torment. I will not petition for mercy, nor will I appeal.' Before going to the guillotine, he insisted: 'On my tombstone must be inscribed, "Here rests the mass murderer, Haarmann."'

Schaefer, Gerard John (1947–)

Police deputy Gerard Schaefer of Martin County, California, brought about his own arrest in a rather unusual way. On 22 July 1972 he contacted his superior, Sheriff Robert Crowder. 'I've done something very foolish,' Schaefer said. 'You'll be mad at me.'

Crowder was. The previous day, cruising in his patrol car, Schaefer had given a lift to two girls on State Highway Al A, making a date to meet again and go to the beach. On 22 July the three set off as arranged but, with the girls safely in the vehicle, Schaefer settled into a long harangue about the dangers of hitch-hiking.

Then he handcuffed them, fitted gags, and dragged the women off the road into the swampland forests. There Schaefer slipped rope nooses round their necks and made them balance on the exposed tree roots to which their feet were bound. If they fell, they died.

At this stage Schaefer seemed to realise that he was late for an appointment, perhaps his call to Sheriff Crowder. Glancing at his watch, he exclaimed, 'Oh oh, I gotta go.' The girls wriggled free and, still gagged and handcuffed, struggled through the swamps to the road where they were collected by the sheriff. Schaefer was

charged with false imprisonment and aggravated assault. But as a law enforcement officer he remained at liberty until his trial some four months later and, on 27 September, local teenagers Susan Place and Georgia Jessup were last seen driving off with a new friend, 'Jerry Shepherd'. On 23 October, Mary Briscolina and Elsie Farmer, 14-year-olds from Fort Lauderdale, disappeared, and their sudden absence was linked to other neighbourhood 'missing persons', Leigh Hainline Bonadies, Carman Hallock and Belinda Hutchins.

When Schaefer's case came up in November he was sentenced to six months. Before his release date the skeletons and torsos of young girls were turning up around the county, the first on 17 January 1973 in the undergrowth near Plantation, the second 200 yards away a month later, and two more on 1 April in a pit hy Blind Creek on Hutchinson Island. The two known numerals – 42 – of 'Jerry Shepherd's' numberplate were traced to Gerard Schaefer's blue Datsun, and a search of his room yielded the usual clutch of **souvenirs**, weapons and aids to masturbation.

Gerard Schaefer, serial killer

Mementos taken from his victims included teeth, a driving licence, jewellery and a passport. Schaefer kept eleven guns, thirteen knives, pin-ups enhanced by the addition of pencilled ropes and bullet holes, 'live-action' blurred photographs of women being hanged and even a picture of Schaefer himself swinging from a tree in female underwear. A 300-page notebook meticulously detailed numerous murders including those of 'Belinda' and 'Carman'.

Schaefer had been divorced for 'extreme cruelty' five months into his 1970 marriage. Nor did he last long as a law officer. His previous job at Wilton Manors rapidly ended in dismissal for misuse of police computers to obtain the telephone numbers of girls he stopped while on traffic duty. In his student days at Broward Community College, he had avidly espoused clean-living, right-thinking values, joining a group called 'Sing Out 66' in reaction to the moral corrosion of his hippy contemporaries.

In September 1973 Schaefer was sentenced to two life terms, and in prison made money by publishing 'fictional' murder stories.

See also **Vocation**

Separate System, The

The nineteenth-century term for a supposedly elevating and actually extreme form of solitary confinement, enshrined by the Prison Act of 1839 as official government policy: 'Any prisoner may be separately confined during the whole or any part of the period of his or her imprisonment.'

The objective was the prisoners' permanent moral benefit, achieved by preventing contamination from association, and the idea followed the intense interest in the even more immoderate 'Silent System', an American regime which kept prisoners mute throughout their sentences while they contemplated their transgressions. But the British Prison Inspectors rejected the American model, recognising its overriding drawback. It was unenforceable. Instead, the Home Office plumped for the Separate (or 'Philadelphia') System, and as a showcase built the Model Penitentiary, Pentonville, really more of a convict academy. It boasted 500 separate cells of a relatively good size, each with its own lavatory.

The fact that Pentonville was accurately characterised as 'the culmination of three generations of thinking' provides a telling insight into the human condition. Inmates were rigorously isolated in continuous solitary, each convict identically regulated by an inflexible daily routine of twelve hours of repetitive task-work. Prisoners were known and addressed only by their numbers and, when they left their cells, were

obliged to don black hooded masks. They were thus incognito, incommunicado and deprived of all human contact.

In daily assembly at chapel, each man occupied his own box, a type of vertical coffin, preventing his gaze straying from the straight and narrow to his left or right, affording only a vision of the preacher. Prisoners left divine service one-by-one in a numerical sequence dictated by a silent, central numbering machine. The warders themselves knew neither the names nor the crimes of their charges; their shoes were soled in felt so that even the sound of footprints was erased, and no mail got through. The *Masked prisoner from* original allowance of one *Pentonville* fifteen-minute visit from the outside world every three months was pruned to a more ideologically pure twenty minutes twice a year.

Results were impressive. The insanity rate achieved at Pentonville was ten times higher than at any other British establishment. According to Ken Smith, author of *Inside Time*, 'After the experience most prisoners were found to be quite daft.' In 1861 the Reverend John Clay, Chaplain at Preston Gaol, said the same thing in different words: 'As a general rule, a few months in the separate cell can render a prisoner strangely impressible. The chaplain can then make the brawn navvy cry like a child; he can work his feelings in any way he pleases … and fill his mouth with his own phrases and language.'

This was considered so satisfactory that the system set the standard for forward-thinking penologists everywhere: an exact scaled-down replica was built on the far side of the globe in Australia's Port Arthur in 1848.

See also **Crank**, **Dickens**, **Treadwheel**

September 11 2001

Everyone remembers where they were when they first heard about the 'Twin Towers' atrocity. After a period of some confusion a final list of fatalities was published. But few, even years afterwards, can look at this terrible act of mass murder and say, with any degree of certainty, why it happened.

9/11

On the morning of 11 September 2001, two hijacked Boeing 757 passenger jets were deliberately crashed into the Twin Towers of the World Trade Center in New York; the first struck the North Tower at 8.45 a.m., the second hit the South Tower at 9.06 a.m. Both of the 110-storey, 1,350-feet-high skyscrapers collapsed within an hour and a half of the first impact.

The death toll caused by the destruction of the Twin Towers has been estimated as 2,752 people. This figure, however, remains debatable, as officials refused to include dozens of homeless people and illegal immigrants who were thought, but cannot be proved, to have been killed in the disaster area.

At 9.40 a.m. a third hijacked Boeing 757 struck the west side of the Pentagon building in Washington DC, the nerve centre of the US Military, killing 189 people.

At 10.37 a.m. the fourth and last hijacked plane crashed in open countryside near Shanksville, Pennsylvania, killing all forty-four people on board. A mobile phone message left by a passenger just before the crash said that he and others were going to try to recapture the plane from terrorists.

It has been speculated that, if the hijackers had not crashed the Shanksville plane prematurely, they would have tried to plunge the jet into Camp David – the presidential rural retreat in Maryland. American president George W. Bush was not in residence at the time, but Camp David was where the historic peace accord between Egypt's President Anwar Sadat and Israeli Prime Minister Menachem Begin was signed in 1978: a hated symbol of Arab–Israeli co-operation to many Muslim fundamentalists.

The death toll for what came to be known simply as '9/11' (11 September 2001) – including the nineteen suicide hijackers – is 2,985 people.

It is known that the hijackers were Islamic fundamentalists. The Al-Qaeda terrorist network, headed by the Saudi Arabian outlaw Osama bin Laden, was strongly suspected of being behind the hijacking of the four jets, but conclusive proof was never offered in open court.

What quickly became known as the 'Attack on America' shocked the world and emotionally traumatised the USA. No such large-scale attack on the North

Osama bin Laden

American mainland had taken place since the British invaded the East Coast during the War of 1812. Decades of American security – some might say complacency – came to an end in the instant the hijacked jet hit the North Tower.

Few people question that the Attack on America was a monstrous act of mass murder, but the question of *why* it happened remains a matter of debate. For many, 9/11 was simply an assault on Western democracy and secular freedom by rabid religious fanatics who irrationally hate both institutions. Others point out that American funding and training of Muslim fundamentalists (to attack the Soviet invasion army in Afghanistan in the 1980s) built up the very movement that now threatens the USA and its allies. Some Islamic extremists have even tried to condone the 9/11 atrocity by insisting that it was a legitimate act of revenge, a retaliation against the West – and the United States in particular – for supporting corrupt and repressive regimes around the world, all in the name of 'doing business'. The USA's dogged support for Israel – and the Israelis' illegal occupation of the West Bank – was another major cause of Islamic resentment.

As Noam Chomsky, the respected American academic and social commentator, observed only days after the 9/11 atrocity: '[It] is common knowledge among anyone who pays attention to the [Middle East] region, that the terrorists draw from a reservoir of desperation, anger, and frustration that extends from rich to poor, from secular to radical Islamist. That it is rooted in no small measure in US policies is evident and constantly articulated to those willing to listen.'

Sex crimes

Apart from the occasional wayward aristocrat, this staple of modern life hardly existed before the First World War. For centuries the term 'sex crime' had a different meaning imposed by the church, which can today be loosely translated by the word 'sex'. It included enterprises such as fellatio, masturbation, homosexuality and fornication.

The Ripper case of 1888 was probably the first modern sex murder, and the practice remained a rarity for several decades thereafter. The First World War, where horrors beyond imagination were played out in real life, brought a surge in the genre, as did the Second World War. It is argued that in previous centuries men had more important things to worry about, such as survival, and that the legacy of Victorian prudery was responsible not only for bizarre fetishistic fixations on anything remotely feminine (like footwear) but also for the pent-up frustration unleashed in frenzied killings. It seems likely that to earlier eras the idea of murdering for mere sex or sexual gratification would be incomprehensible.

Sex killings presented the police with a new problem. The absence of a clear connection between the killer and his particular victim left no line of enquiry to follow. But this has been counter-balanced both by tremendous strides in detection and by the tendency of many killers, once their violent spasm is over, almost to invite arrest (see **Jekyll and Hyde**) in sharp contrast to the self-protective instincts of the average criminal.

Criminologists regard the sex itself as a fairly unimportant component in a sex crime, a view shared by a multiple rapist who confided to FBI Agent Robert Hazelwood: 'Rape is the least enjoyable part of the entire crime.' Apparently, Charles **Ng** did not relish the sex; even in the absence of consent, it is a real experience between two parties, very fraught, most likely disappointing in the extreme, and one that makes reification of the victim a little bit harder. Other than **terror**, human interaction is not the sex criminal's purpose. Indeed, many victims are prostitutes, and if sex was what the attacker desired, he had only to ask. His craving for violative intimacy is typically reflected in a preference for a knife or an axe rather than an impersonal gun.

The 'sex' is furnished by the chosen method of assault and, even in the absence of ritual mutilation, the onslaught can be frenzied beyond any desire to extinguish life. The sex is often omitted. Instead, the sexual organs are attacked; tearing people to pieces is easier to do, easier to control, and more reliable. Moreover, it provides what the attacker wants: domination, so often sought by the weak.

A man capable of asserting himself in a socially acceptable fashion has no need to be vicious; it is the weak who are prone to stab in the back and, by extension, the impotent who gravitate towards sex crimes. Many serial killers are either pushed over the brink by imputations of impotence (**Sutcliffe**), are impotent (Christie), find they can only achieve erections during the frenzy of killing (**Chikatilo**) or have sex with corpses (**Dahmer**). Impotence, which does not negate sexual desire but merely prevents its release, is thus a potentially dangerous condition, and few experiences are as inimical to sexual fantasies as real life. Individuals reduced to inhabiting a world of sexual make-believe, having no other vent for their drive, often prefer their subjects dead, gaining transitory (and unsynchronised) potency in the process. In Chikatilo's words: 'I could not control my actions. What I did was not for sexual pleasure, rather it brought me peace of mind and soul for a long time.' But he obtained his satisfaction during the murders, and his killings represented a displaced sexual procedure, where his frenzy conferred release and, thereafter, calm.

Impotence has psychological roots, and one cause is repression stemming from childhood abuse or social conditioning. William Heirens's mother assured him at the age of 13, 'All sex is dirty, if you touch anyone you get a disease.' As a teenager locked in an embrace with a girlfriend, Heirens succumbed to an attack of revulsion at his fall from grace, first bursting into tears and then retching. Thereafter, his sexuality found other channels, coagulating into an obsessive fantasy involving female underwear, cross-dressing, photographs of Nazi leaders, masturbation, weapons and prowling through the unoccupied apartments of strange women. His sex life thus centred on almost anything apart from shared consensual heterosexual sex, which remained illicit, a depraved activity associated with degradation, thus putting Heirens's outlook on all fours with many victims of sexual abuse.

If sex is vile, then only vile people have sex, a proposition which (in the sadist's eyes) speaks volumes for the great hulk of the female population. They are whores. In the words of FBI Agent Robert Ressler, 'Most if not all the organised killers have tremendous anger towards women, often expressed in the belief that a certain female is not "woman enough" to "turn him on".' By this stage, the sexual criminal and his prey are trapped in a downward spiral. Women are filth. So they are treated like filth, coercing them into filthy behaviour, thus reinforcing the original premise. The FBI's working definition of a sex murder is a killing made 'in the context of power, sexuality and brutality', and its outer manifestations are 'the attire or lack of it found on the body; sexualised position of the body; sexual injury; evidence of sexual activity on, in or near the body and evidence of substitute sexual activity or sadistic fantasy'. The murders can normally be differentiated from run-of-the-mill sadistic homicides by the special emphasis placed on mutilation or removal of the breasts, rectum or genitals. The latest thinking on rapists (most of whom have been raped, making it an inherited condition) depicts them as depositing their self-hatred in another person, literally. On a practical level, rapists may feel obliged, against their better nature, to murder their victims to escape identification.

Triumphant armies have always raped their way through the womenfolk of their foes. In the recent Balkans conflict, the rape of Muslim village women by former neighbours evolved into an instrument of diplomatic policy. One 28-year-old mother from the town of Foca was raped perhaps 150 times in all, including thirty-three times in the course of her last night during a bout which presumably inflicted the last iota of defilement without producing the least tremor of recognisable sexual pleasure in her assailants. Humiliation of the enemy's women represents a triumph over, and attack on, their menfolk, and most assaults are conducted in groups, when the individual conscience is subservient to mob rule.

It might seem that murder for sexual gratification represents the end of the emotional road. But even at this stage, choices remain. At the outer reaches of the macabre, decapitators face a final option. Which part do they fancy? Edward **Kemper** made love to the torsos, but Douglas Clark preferred the severed **head**.

See also **Fantasising**, **Masturbation**, **Male rape**, **Preview**, **Terminology**, **Torture**, **Trolling**

Sexism

Women claim that they receive a rough deal from the courts. In 1991 the British discrepancy was encapsulated by the divergent fates of Sara Thornton (sentenced to life for murdering an alcoholic husband) and Joseph McGrail (given probation for disposing of his bullying wife). Similarly, on 29 January 1992 Bisla Rajinder Singh, aged 44, received a brief suspended sentence after killing his wife for nagging; she had shouted at him non-stop for (by some standards) a modest two hours.

According to the *New Law Journal*, 37.5 per cent of women who kill their spouses are found guilty of murder rather than manslaughter; the comparable level for men is 26.6 per cent. These figures conflict with official Home Office research, which shows almost the exact opposite. For the general record, of the thirty-three British women convicted of homicide in 1991, exactly one-third engaged in murder, as against a level of nearly half for the 408 male killers. Women tend to kill people they know.

Trial-by-media is no more reliable than trial by the courts. Press reports depicting Sara Thornton as a female scapegoat on the altar of male oppression do not always investigate her case thoroughly. It is true that her husband, Malcolm, was an alcoholic, but not a violent alcoholic. According to his previous wife, who tolerated him for fifteen years, after getting drunk he would go to sleep.

On all the evidence this was the pattern on the fatal night. His son last saw Malcolm dozing on the sofa. From his room upstairs, he heard no sound of the brutal altercation which Sara maintained triggered the killing. But her hunt for a knife in the kitchen was perfectly distinct, so the quarrel should have been audible. It seems as though Sara stabbed her husband while he slept; the couple had been married for ten months.

Apologists argue that the courts are perplexed by the differing gender-concepts of provocation. A man is taunted; he lashes out and kills, but he was provoked. A woman is taunted for twenty years. She does nothing, then suddenly, without apparent provocation, lashes out and kills. That looks like premeditation. Others believe a patriarchal court system treats the killing of a man by a woman as a violation of the natural order deserving of fearsome retribution.

One undeniable sign of sexism is that in the 1870s the women's cells in D Wing of Wormwood Scrubs were constructed to slightly smaller dimensions than their male counterparts. Another is that women are more likely to be jailed for non-violent minor offences. In September 1991 the British government's Inspectorate of Probation found that 2,650 women were sentenced to prison in 1989 but that, of these, over half were sent down for less than six months.

Had they been men, this group would be obvious candidates for community service or probation. But the women are regarded as unsuitable because they have young children, and thus end up in an even less suitable situation – prison, with an increased probability that their traumatised offspring will in due course follow suit.

Early female transportees fared worse. On arrival in Australia they were treated like cattle, and nowhere worse than on the hell-camp of **Norfolk Island**. As from 1800, under Major Foveaux's tenure, the new arrivals were sold off. A good specimen fetched as much as £10.

The role of auctioneer fell to the island's bell-man, Potter, who held the sales in an old store. The girls had to strip and race naked round the room while Potter kept up a running commentary on his nags. On Thursday nights the women were admitted to the barrack festivities where they performed (in the words of a witness, Robert Jones) 'the dance of the Mermaids, each one being naked with numbers painted on their backs so as to be recognised by their admirers who would clap their hands on seeing their favourite perform some grotesque action'.

Women, like the Aboriginals, were the blacks of the penal colony, the prisoners of prisoners, referred to as 'drunks and scum', often degenerating into terminally alcoholic sluts. Nor did Ronnie Kray speak highly of their contribution to gangland London. 'Always it's bloody women,' he would say. 'Women's our worstest enemy. Why can't they keep their places any more? They don't want men these days. They want bloody lap dogs.' It was a valid point. Stable relationships drained away promising criminals, luring them into home life and even steady jobs.

See also **Crime passionel**, **Female offender**, **Rolling pin**

Sheppard, Jack (1702–24)

Probably the single most famous highwayman, whose legendary cold genius and tragic fate continued to excite nursery tears into the nineteenth century.

In fact, Sheppard only traded as a highwayman for about a week, accumulating a total gross of thirty shillings and sixpence. He stopped a stagecoach once; a further half-crown was extracted from a lady's maid in Hampstead. The final six shillings belonged to a drunken grocer staggering out of a Hampstead pub, 'The Half Way House'.

But as an escapee Sheppard was without equal, notching up no fewer than four break-outs. First he broke out from St Giles's Roundhouse, clambering out through the roof. Then on 24 May 1724 at New Prison Clerkenwell, Sheppard extricated himself from his fourteen-pound leg-irons before hacking his way his cell, only to discover that the way was blocked by an iron rod across the flue. But he clawed out the masonry, knocked the bar free, eased his way up to the floor above and came out through a fireplace.

On the upper floor, Sheppard forced his way onwards through four successive locked and bolted doors, each of massive iron construction, picking them like a true locksmith or tearing them off their hinges, working in pitch darkness with nothing except odd metal scraps. An additional obstacle was provided by a 12-foot internal wall surmounted with spikes. At last he came to a window and flung it wide. But there was no safe way to climb down.

So Sheppard returned to his cell and fetched a blanket. Then he scrambled away to freedom, lowering himself on to the roof of a private house before disappearing through an open window. His feat remains one of history's greatest escapes.

But by the end of the week Sheppard was captured in a drunken stupor while celebrating his achievement with a girl called Moll Frisky. Their tavern party, just outside Newgate's walls, became so rowdy that the authorities went to investigate. In a way, the lad was a transitional criminal, bright enough to master the concept of escape but unfamiliar with the ins and outs of life as a hunted man. This is not so strange; British malefactors were hardly pursued until the introduction of the Bow Street Runners, and felt reasonably safe unless under lock and key.

This last time Sheppard was encumbered with 300 pounds of chains and manacles, fetters, leg-irons and padlocks. The warders watched him night and day. By now the most famous man in England, Sheppard filled pages of newsprint, inspired countless ballads, was depicted in thousands of prints (generally attached to a padlock about the size of a wheelbarrow), had his portrait painted by the fashionable Sir James Thornhill, inspired the Hogarth series 'Industry and Idleness', fathered nine stage plays in one year, enriched his Newgate jailer to the tune of £200 by his exhibition to crowds of the curious at three and sixpence a head, and went on to feature as the hero of the 1840s best-selling novel.

Sheppard's execution attracted a worshipping crowd estimated at 200,000; men fought for possession of his body, hoping to restore it to life. He did not die easy, struggling for several minutes as he choked. A riot raged outside the pub 'The Barley Mow' in Covent Garden where his battered corpse was finally

Sheppard's first escape, from the St Giles's Roundhouse in April

through a double grille of oak and iron bars. That left the obstacle of the prison walls. With a knotted rope of sheets, petticoats and a blanket, he shinned down a 25-foot drop before scaling the 22-foot wall on the other side, dragging his mistress, Edgeworth Bess, after him.

Sadly, Sheppard found it as easy to worm his way back into clink as to get out; on 3 July 1724 he was arrested and sentenced to death. But on 31 August, while awaiting execution in **Newgate**'s Condemned Hold, Bess smuggled in a file. Sheppard sawed through the barred window as she chatted to him across the grille in sight of the warders – and he was off.

Within a fortnight Sheppard was back in Newgate once more, this time thrown into the Stone Room festooned in chains: handcuffed, double irons on his legs, and shackled to the floor with a horse-lock. Now came his finest hour. On 15 September the warders tested his manacles at three in the afternoon; later that day, Sheppard freed his hands and, with a nail, opened the padlock fastening him to the floor and broke his chains. Then he wriggled up the chimney in secured by his admirers. After repeatedly reading the Riot Act without effect, the frightened magistrates restored order by summoning a company of foot guards, bayonets at the ready, from the Savoy.

Sheppard was buried in a graveyard of St Martin's-in-the-Fields; building works near the National Gallery unearthed his coffin in 1866. Today, one of his Newgate handcuffs survives in Scotland Yard's Black Museum and, if truth be told, it is easy to open, with a screwdriver, a nail or any metal lever.

Shipman, Dr Harold

The case of Harold Frederick Shipman, one of the most prolific serial killers of the twentieth century – at least 260 victims – is also one of the most baffling. Psychologically speaking, he remains an enigma.

It is clear from what we know about his life and background that Shipman was not one of those people who impress others with their vitality and charisma. On the contrary, he seemed a rather quiet and colourless little man. Born in Nottingham in 1946, he struggled out of his dull, working-class background because he wanted to live up to the expectations of his mother, Vera, for 'Fred' was her favourite, and she deeply believed in him. When she died of cancer when he was 17, he felt he had to justify her belief in him, and in spite of an initial failure, got into Leeds University Medical School, where he was a less than brilliant student.

His problem was always a certain lack of self-belief. At medical school he remained a loner, without close friends and without even that indispensable appendage of the randy medical student, a girlfriend.

Then came the event that transformed his life. On the bus that took him to medical school every morning, he noticed a plump, quiet girl among the teenagers. Primrose Oxtoby was a 'plain Jane', who was completely under the thumb of her parents. They were so straitlaced that they would not even allow her to attend a youth club – and Primrose would never have dreamed of trying to assert herself.

She was three years Shipman's junior, and when he realised that she regarded him with wide-eyed admiration, he was hooked. Because she adored him, this quiet, shy virgin became an addiction. Unfortunately, soon after she surrendered her virginity, she discovered she was pregnant. They married in 1966, but her

Harold Shipman

parents were so shocked that they broke with her.

Shipman later admitted her pregnancy was 'a mistake'. But it was a mistake he had to live with. The daydreams of a great career in medicine were over. Primrose was not even a very good housekeeper – police who later came to search their house were shocked by the dirt and general untidiness.

There were three years in which Shipman was a junior houseman in Pontefract General Infirmary, in Yorkshire. It was dull, grinding work, and by now there was a second baby. He must have felt that life was determined to drag him down.

There is a perfectly straightforward reason why a man like Shipman would have felt dissatisfied with himself. He was basically dominant and ambitious, and such people require, if possible, a partner like themselves. Primrose was quiet, plain and had a tendency to put on weight. No wonder Shipman became depressed and bad-tempered, and felt that life had turned into a disaster.

His first professional appointment, in March 1974, was in the small town of Todmorden, in the Pennines. And it was there he became a drug addict. He claimed later that he began taking pethidine, a morphine derivative, because of a back injury. Whether the excuse was true or not, Shipman certainly found that pethidine made life seem brighter and more bearable. He obtained the drug by forging prescriptions, and over-prescribing it for patients who needed it, and keeping the extra.

One year later, Dr John Dacre, a senior partner in the practice, checked the prescriptions and asked Shipman what was happening. Shipman confessed, and begged for a second chance. This was denied him, and at his trial for forging prescriptions in February 1976, he was temporarily suspended and fined £658. Primrose had to return to live with her family. He must have felt that fate was grinding him into the ground.

And it was probably after his drug habit had been exposed that he turned into a killer. At least one man in Todmorden, the husband of Eva Lyons – who was dying of cancer – believed that Shipman injected his elderly wife with an overdose of morphine as a mercy killing. Soon afterwards eight more elderly patients were found dead after Shipman had been to see them.

Had he discovered that watching someone die peacefully produced in him a sense of relief that was not unlike the effect of morphine?

It was a year later, in 1977, that Shipman became a member of the Donnybrook House practice in Hyde, in Greater Manchester, an area made notorious by former resident Ian **Brady**.

By this time he had developed the characteristics of a male whose attempts to express his dominance have always been frustrated: touchiness and swollen self-esteem. He enjoyed bullying, and taking it out on those over whom he had authority. He was brutal to a young female drugs representative, out on her first assignment, and browbeat her until she was in tears. When a receptionist forgot his coffee, he went white with rage. When his wife rang him to say that they were hungry and waiting to eat dinner he snapped, 'You'll wait until I get there.'

Oddly enough, his patients felt that he was the ideal doctor – caring, patient and endlessly helpful; but then a man of Shipman's immense self-centredness and ruthlessness would be a good doctor, for it was important to be liked and admired. However, to those who had nothing to contribute to his self-esteem, he could scarcely bring himself to be polite.

Shipman came under suspicion after the sudden death of an elderly patient named Kathleen Grundy on 24 June 1998. Mrs Grundy had apparently left a will in which her considerable fortune – over £300,000 – was left to her doctor, Harold Shipman. But the will was carelessly typed, and two witnesses who had also signed it would later explain that they had done so as a favour to Dr Shipman, who had folded the paper so they could not see what they were signing.

Mrs Grundy's daughter, Angela Woodruff, reported her suspicions to the police. Detective Inspector Stan Egerton noted that this looked like a case of attempted fraud. But could it be more than that? The death rate among Shipman's patients, especially elderly women, was remarkably high, but there seemed to be no other cases in which he had actually benefited from the death of one of them, at least not in their wills. (But when he was finally arrested, police found a large quantity of jewellery – worth around £10,000 – which clearly had been taken from dead patients.)

In fact, the above-average death rate had been noted by one of Shipman's colleagues, Dr Linda Reynolds. In 1997 she had realised that Shipman seemed to have been present at the deaths of an unusually high number of patients – three times as many as might have been expected – and reported her suspicions to the local coroner. This all came to nothing because there seemed to be no reason why a popular GP should kill his patients.

Mrs Grundy's body was now exhumed, and the post-mortem showed that she had died of an overdose of morphine. (This is easy to detect because it remains in the system.) After that, another fourteen exhumations of Shipman's patients revealed the same thing. Moreover, it was clear that these fifteen were only a small proportion of the victims.

When he was questioned on suspicion of fifteen murders, Shipman angrily denied any wrongdoing, sure that he had covered his trail so carefully that he was safe. But the investigators soon discovered that he had made extensive changes in his patients' records to make them seem more ill than they actually were. He was almost certainly unaware that the computer registered automatically the date and time of every one of these changes. On 7 October 1998 Shipman was full of self-confidence when he was interviewed by the police and confronted with evidence of his crimes. But when a woman detective constable began to question him about changes he had made in the patients' records, pointing out that many of them had been made within minutes of the death of the patient, he began to falter and flounder. That evening he broke down and sobbed.

Yet there was no confession. From that moment on, he simply refused to co-operate during interviews, often sitting with his back to the interviewer and refusing to speak.

In most cases of serial murder, there is a clear sexual element. Where Shipman was concerned, the only hint of a possible sexual hang-up can be found in the case of 17-year-old Lorraine Leighton, who went to see him about a lump in her breast. In her case, Shipman abandoned the kindly, sympathetic manner that endeared him to so many patients, and made such rude comments about the size of her breasts that she fled the surgery in tears.

One thing that seems clear is that Shipman felt no guilt about killing his patients. After his imprisonment, someone said something that implied a comparison with Myra **Hindley**, and Shipman snapped, 'She is a criminal. I am not a criminal.'

Shipman was given fifteen life sentences in January 2000 for murdering fifteen patients. On Tuesday 13 January 2004, he was discovered hanging in his cell. An official report later concluded he had killed between 215 and 260 people over a twenty-three-year period.

Shootists

The deranged Texas gunfighter Clay Allison (d. 1887) devised the word 'shootist' to describe himself. The term carries cool undertones of professional status redolent of, say, a chemist.

Allison peaked in 1870 when he went to the aid of a damsel in distress who claimed that her husband, a rancher named Kennedy, had murdered some strangers and her own infant to boot. Allison broke into the Elizabethtown jail where Kennedy was held, dragged the man out and lynched him in a slaughter-house. Then he cut off the head, impaled it on a pike, and rode twenty-nine miles to exhibit the trophy in his favourite drinking den in Cimarron.

It is often said that shootists could hardly hit a barn door. But this is to exaggerate. In 1879 at the Long Branch Saloon in Dodge City, buffalo hunter Levi Richardson attempted to gun down Cockeyed Frank Loving with six shots fired from a distance close enough to pick his target's pocket. Other commentators describe their pistols as 'nearly touching'. Returning fire in self-defence, the unscathed Loving shot his assailant dead.

Serious gunfights (as opposed to the practice of taking pot-shots) were generally fought at very close range: Frank Stilwell, killed by Doc Holliday and Wyatt Earp in March 1882, was found with powder burns on his clothes. His assailants' muzzles must have been almost in contact with his body and, according to Wyatt later, Stilwell was actually holding the barrel of the gun with which he was killed. The seminal gunfight at OK Corral began at a distance of six feet, with the range gradually opening out to something more like three yards for the closing shots between Billy Clanton and the brothers Earp. Many engagements were more like brawls, with added guns.

Silence

Like any other criminal cartel, Chicago gangsters operated on a sealed-lips basis. This frequently entailed denials of reality issued to the police from the death-bed. Examples include the dying words of Frank R. Thompson to Sheriff Harry Baldwin: 'Listen Harry, I've seen everything, done everything, and got everything, and you're smart enough to know I won't talk. Go to hell.' Or as Frank Gusenberg, the ephemeral survivor of the 1929 St Valentine's Day Massacre, explained to Sergeant Sweeney: 'Nobody shot me.' At the time, Gusenberg was bleeding from fourteen bullet wounds.

Interviewing gangsters *in vivo* was hardly more rewarding. At the inquest into his brother's death, witness Al Capone felt unable to contribute. Johnny Torrio, set up for a hit by Hymie Weiss on 24 January 1925, was lucky to escape with a bullet to his left arm and buckshot in his jaw and lungs after the *coup de grâce*, a shot to his brain, fell on an empty chamber. Torrio told the police, 'I know who they are and that's my business.' Likewise, on 10 August 1926 Vincent 'the Schemer' Drucci was involved in a prolonged gunfight at the junction of Michigan and Ninth Streets. After several minutes the exchange of shots was broken up by the police who, back at the station, produced one of Drucci's assailants for his inspection. Drucci took a good look at Capone gunman Louis Barko and said: 'Never seen him before. It wasn't no gang fight. It was a stick-up, that's all.'

The rule extended to wives of the deceased; Patsy Lolordo could never quite recall the names and faces of the three cronies who called round on 8 January

1929 to shoot her husband after pastries and cigars. Almost the only occasion the convention was contravened came after the St Valentine's Day Massacre when a shocked Bugs Moran let drop, 'Only the Capone gang kills like that', before clamming up.

Such 'Walls of Silence' have their roots in time immemorial and extend to the present day, binding individual interest groups in solidarity against outsiders. Doctors and solicitors are never negligent, judges never make mistakes, the police never assault suspects or fabricate evidence, drug companies never fix prices and criminals do not rat on their associates – unless they have to. A whistleblower from the professions must look to his future; an underworld grass needs eyes in the back of his head.

In Sicily, mortally wounded **vendetta** victims would respond to an invitation to identify their assailant with a muttered version of the formulaic 'If I die, may God forgive me, as I forgive the one who did this. If I manage to pull through, I know how to settle my own accounts.'

See also **Omerta**

Silicon Valley Murder

The town of Palo Alto, in Clara County, California, is a largely quiet, upmarket place thanks to its connections with the nearby Stanford University (to support which the town was originally developed) and because of the large amounts of money generated by the 1990s computer boom. Palo Alto is smack in the centre of Silicon Valley and so is at the heart of the US technology industry. Killings are comparatively rare in this affluent, civilised community (only eleven murders took place in the 1990s, for example) so police were reasonably unsuspicious when Kenneth Fitzhugh, a 57-year-old real-estate developer, reported that his wife had suffered a fatal accident.

On 5 May 2000, the school where Kristine Fitzhugh worked as a music teacher rang Kenneth to ask why she had not come into work that day. Despite his apparent anxiety, Kenneth took the time to collect two friends to help him investigate his wife's non-attendance. It was almost as if he thought he might need witnesses.

In the Fitzhugh home they found Kristine's body at the bottom of the cellar stairs with her head in a pool of blood. On Kenneth's insistence, one of his friends attempted CPU revival, but it was evident that Kristine had been dead some hours.

It was not long, however, before the police became suspicious of the apparent 'accident'. The autopsy showed that the 52-year-old woman had died of strangulation and repeated blows to the head. Forensic investigation of the Fitzhugh home showed that the killing had almost certainly taken place in the kitchen; police sprayed the chemical Luminol on seemingly clean surfaces to reveal numerous blood splashes that had recently been cleaned up there. It also became clear that the corpse had been arranged at the bottom of the cellar stairs to simulate an accident.

Kenneth Fitzhugh was the prime suspect; inspection of his bank account showed that his savings had dropped from $200,000 to $20,000 in just over a year, so he may have been trying to get his hands on his wife's money. Then another possible motive came to light when Kristine's ex-lover – disbarred lawyer and former drug addict Robert Brown – came forward to claim that Kristine's son, 23-year-old Justin, was actually *his* child, not Fitzhugh's. Kristine, he claimed, had been planning to tell her husband the truth and this might have pushed him over the edge into murder. Subsequent DNA testing backed Brown's paternity claim.

Kenneth Fitzhugh flatly denied the murder charge, suggesting that his wife had been killed by a burglar. However, few believed this explanation. Many asked, how many homicidal burglars take the time to make a killing look like an accident, then don't bother to steal anything? In an attempt to back his theory, Fitzhugh inventoried the contents of his house and showed that a few, largely worthless items, were missing. And it was this idiotic attempt to get himself off the hook that probably convicted him – among the missing items on the list he included a sponge, rubber gloves and cleaning supplies that could have been used to try to erase signs of the murder in the kitchen.

The jury found Kenneth Fitzhugh guilty of second-degree (unpremeditated) murder and he was sentenced to fifteen years to life in prison. A jury member later revealed that she and the other members believed that Fitzhugh *had* planned the killing – to get Kristine's money and avoid the social embarrassment of being revealed to be a cuckold – but they felt that the prosecution had not provided sufficient evidence to bring a sentence of first-degree murder.

Simpson, Orenthal James ('OJ')

Just after midnight on 13 June 1994, the attractive 35-year-old Nicole Brown Simpson, the estranged wife of American footballer and movie star OJ Simpson, was found dead in the garden of her Santa Monica home. Nearby lay the body of a young man called Ronald Goldman. Both had been hacked to death with a long-bladed weapon.

Los Angeles Police scene-of-crime officers quickly reconstructed the events of the two murders from the available evidence. The angle of the wound indicated that Nicole Brown Simpson had been standing near by and was probably conversing with the killer when he struck at her neck with the weapon, nearly severing Nicole's head from her body and killing her almost instantly. The 25-year-old Goldman then struggled with the murderer and was stabbed and slashed over thirty times. The murderer then escaped, leaving a trail of size-twelve footprints on the blood-muddied lawn.

Even from this initial evidence the police could make some preliminary guesses: the killer was quite possibly known to Nicole Brown Simpson, as he had been standing close to her when he attacked – people, especially women, tend to keep over an arm's length away when talking to total strangers. The killer was also almost certainly a man – to judge by the strength needed to make such damaging attacks on two unrestrained adults – and a very strong man at that. All the initial evidence seemed to point to Nicole's ex-husband.

Before he fell under suspicion as a double murderer, OJ Simpson's life had been a classic American success story. Starting his public career in American football in the 1970s, he was soon one of the most famous players in the game's history. He retired from professional football in 1979.

In 1985, Simpson married Nicole Brown. However, Nicole soon complained to friends and family members that OJ was violently jealous of her. She also showed them bruises that she claimed had come from beatings OJ had given her for playfully flirting with other men. Few of their friends were surprised, therefore, when Nicole filed for divorce from Simpson in 1992. She won a $433,000 cash settlement, plus $10,000 a month alimony and child support for their two children. It would seem that the affable ex-football star had at least a financial motive for murder.

Nicole Brown Simpson

Forensic examination placed the double killing at around ten that evening. OJ Simpson was in Santa Monica at the time of the murder, but caught a flight to Chicago at 11.45 p.m. – less than two hours after the killings. A limousine, booked to take him to the airport, had arrived at 10.25 p.m. but found that apparently nobody was at home. At 10.56 p.m. the driver saw a large but unidentifiable man enter Simpson's home, shortly after which Simpson emerged, claiming to have been deep asleep in the house for the past several hours and not to have heard the doorbell.

Later that night, when the police phoned Simpson in his Chicago hotel to tell him that his wife had been murdered, they noted that he did not ask how, when or where the crime had taken place – the usual questions asked by a relative of a murder victim. He didn't even ask if the police had caught the killer. Simpson later claimed to have been so grief-stricken on hearing the news that he had crushed a hotel water glass, badly cutting his hand. However, the prosecution at his trial claimed that this injury had actually been sustained by his own weapon while committing the murders.

Despite the fact he was clearly a prime suspect, the Los Angeles police (LAPD) treated Simpson with kid gloves – he was a popular celebrity, an African-American and, in fact, had several friends in the LAPD.

Investigators even allowed him to remain free until after Nicole's funeral, trustingly asking him to hand himself in for arrest the following day. This proved a mistake as Simpson failed to turn up. He was soon spotted, however, being driven by a friend in a white Ford Bronco.

There followed a farcical chase in which dozens of police cars and several news helicopters followed the slow-moving Bronco as it drove around the crowded Los Angeles road system. Simpson eventually had himself driven to his home, where he was finally arrested. The car was found to contain a gun, $8,750, a passport and a false beard.

Starting on 24 July 1995, a 133-day 'trial of the century' followed, with record media coverage. The prosecution sought to show that Simpson was a jealous and abusive husband who would have preferred to murder his estranged wife rather than see her with another man. Their chief evidence for their theory – aside from numerous witnesses who had seen or heard OJ threatening Nicole at one time or another – was the bad cut to his hand, apparently dating from the night of the murder.

A small herd of prosecution technical experts testified that hair, clothing fibres and footprints found at the murder scene indicated Simpson's presence. There was also the murderer's blood found there – from the cut on Simpson's hand, it was argued. DNA testing showed that only 0.5 per cent of the population could have deposited this blood; OJ Simpson was one of this very select group.

The police had also found a pair of bloodstained socks at the foot of OJ's bed and, even more damning, an extra-large Aris Light leather glove, of a type Simpson was known to wear, was found at the murder scene. Another such glove – apparently the partner of the murder scene glove – was found, soaked in blood, in a hallway of OJ's house. The likely inference was that OJ had attacked his victims with only his right hand gloved (there was no cut to the palm of the left glove), had sustained the wound to his left hand and had dropped the left glove at the crime scene. He then accidentally dropped the blood-soaked right glove in his hallway during his efforts to clean himself up before catching his flight to Chicago.

DNA testing pointed to a 6.8-billion-to-one likelihood that the blood on the gloves and socks belonged to Nicole Brown Simpson – she was probably the only person on earth with blood to match the samples.

The defence – dubbed the Dream Team by the press, because they comprised some of the most respected, and expensive, lawyers in the country – could only seek to sow a seed of doubt in the mind of the jury in the face of such apparently damning evidence. The police officer who had found the bloodied glove, Mark Fuhrman, was asked under oath if he ever used the 'n-word' ('nigger'). He replied that he never did. Tapes were then played to the court, featuring Fuhrman using the n-word with racist abandon – proving him to be a liar. Also on the tapes – made while he was acting as an adviser for a TV show about the LAPD – Fuhrman happily admitted to planting evidence to secure convictions.

The defence team suggested that Fuhrman had taken the bloodied right glove from the crime scene in order to 'find' it in Simpson's home. And the bloodied socks? Fuhrman had taken a pair of OJ's socks from his home, returned to the crime scene to dip them in blood, then hid them under OJ's bed to be found by another officer. Although the prosecution pointed out that there was not a shred of evidence to support such wild conjectures, Judge Ito allowed the jury to consider the theory.

OJ Simpson

Another key defence victory came when the prosecution asked Simpson to try on the gloves. They were self-evidently too small for him. Evidence came out later that the leather of the gloves had shrunk when the blood they had been soaked in dried. The damage to the prosecution had been done, however.

In a decisive move the head of the defence team, Johnny Cochrane, concluded his final statement by stressing that the jury should not convict if there was a shadow of a doubt in their minds. Echoing back to the dramatic moment when OJ put on the gloves and showed that they were too small (or shrunken) for his hands, Cochrane repeated several times: 'If it doesn't fit, you must acquit.'

The jury took just three hours to acquit OJ Simpson on all charges.

In his post-trial statement OJ Simpson insisted that he would dedicate the rest of his life to tracking down the actual killer of his ex-wife. He got little time to do this, however, as the bereaved families immediately filed a civil suit, demanding damages from OJ for killing their loved ones; civil cases can only award financial penalties.

Where Judge Ito in the criminal trial was often criticised for letting lawyers on both sides wander off on wild theories, Judge Hiroshi Fujisake, who sat in the civil proceedings, kept a tight ship. All attempts by OJ's defence team to suggest that their client was the victim of a huge, if unprovable, racist conspiracy were quashed by the bench. Only solid evidence was accepted on to the court record.

After a deliberation of seventeen hours, the civil jury concluded that OJ Simpson was guilty of the 'wrongfully caused deaths of Ronald Goldman and Nicole Brown Simpson'. He was ordered to pay compensatory damages of $8.5 million to the bereaved families plus a further $25 million in punitive damages. This did not reduce him to a pauper because, under California law, his $25,000-a-month pension fund from the National Football League could not be touched by any legal judgment against him.

In America, as under most democratic legal systems, OJ Simpson cannot be put before a criminal court twice for the same crime without dramatic new evidence coming to light that calls for a verdict of 'mistrial' on the first case. He is therefore likely to remain in legal limbo – found both guilty and not guilty of two particularly brutal murders.

Sinatra Connection, The

Was Frank Sinatra the decisive influence in the election of John **Kennedy**? We may never know, but we should be told that in the run-up to the 1960 presidential contest, Sinatra visited Sam Giancana at the Mob's Armory Lounge headquarters in the Chicago suburbs. 'Ole Blue Eyes' lobbied for the Mob to call in their political favours on JFK's behalf.

Sinatra's pitch was that after three approaches to Kennedy's father, he felt confident of halting the FBI's investigations into Giancana. We know this because FBI Agent Bill Roemer listened on the microphone, and it was a reasonable proposition. Harry Truman regarded Kennedy Snr, who made much of his fortune from complicity in bootlegging, as 'as big a crook as we've got anywhere in the country'.

In the event, the 1960 presidential election was too close to call until Illinois came in for Kennedy; the vital West Virginia primary may also have been swayed by Mob 'donations' elicited by JFK in direct contacts with Giancana. But Sinatra's plan backfired. Whatever his father's intentions, President Kennedy appointed his brother Attorney General, and Robert made the Mob – dismissed as a quaint superstition by **Hoover** – a top priority, quadrupling the staff and budget of the Department of Justice's Organised Crime Section. In Chicago, FBI agents assigned to the Mob rocketed from five to seventy, with Giancana heading the wanted list.

Robert Kennedy rapidly established supremacy over Hoover in the 1961 Buzzer Wars. Hoover had contrived a one-on-one right to confer personally with the President, thereby enshrining his bizarre whims as governmental policy, but Kennedy insisted that the line of communication went through him, and installed a buzzer to summon Hoover as required. Hoover had the buzzer removed. So Kennedy introduced a direct telephone link. So Hoover had it answered by a secretary. Kennedy lost his temper: 'When I pick up this telephone, there's only one man I want to talk to. Get this phone on the director's desk immediately.'

All Kennedy's good work was undone by his brother's indiscretions. Whether or not Hoover was blackmailed into quiescence by the Mob for his homosexuality, he made himself an irremovable government fixture by digging up dirt on the President's indiscriminate couplings and, after JFK's 1963 assassination, swiftly reasserted his deadening influence on the Justice Department's Organised Crime Section. By 1966 Hoover had forced the crime figures down: the number of man-days in the field dropped by 50 per cent, days before a grand jury against mobsters by 72 per cent, and the issue of court briefs by 82 per cent.

See also **Executive action**

Slave, sex

For a hitch-hiker, accepting a lift from a young couple *with a baby* might seem a safe bet. Under just such a misapprehension, on 19 May 1977 20-year-old Colleen Jean Stan climbed into a blue Dodge Colt driven by a bespectacled man with his wife and child.

Somewhere outside Red Bluff, Cameron Hooker pulled off the road and put a knife to Colleen's throat. Snapping on a pair of handcuffs, he encased her head in a purpose-built plywood box which had lain on the car seat. Hooker drove in silence to his home at 114 Oak Street, where he led the terrified Colleen to the basement and removed the head-clamp box. Next, she was blindfolded, stripped naked, hung from the ceiling by her wrists and whipped. Then she heard and – through her tiny field of vision – saw her captor and his wife enjoying inter-course while she swung overhead. By their side she glimpsed an open magazine depicting a tableau like the one of which she formed a part. After climaxing, Hooker lowered Colleen to the floor, replaced the box on her head, and shovelled her into a second, larger box about three feet high. Crammed inside, Colleen felt a hand between her thighs adjusting a small, spiny object. It was designed to give electric shocks, but the device malfunctioned. All this time, hardly a word was spoken, and after twenty-four hours Colleen, still in her hutch, received her first glass of water and a bowl of potatoes *au gratin*.

So began Colleen's seven-year routine of suspension, whipping, confinement, sexual abuse and half-drown-ing, for which Hooker espoused the immersion technique independently developed by George Joseph Smith, raising Colleen by the knees and forcing her head under whenever he gave her a **bath**. It made a nice picture for his photograph collection.

His unassuming wife, 20-year-old Janice, had long recognised something strange about her husband. Hooker, born into a traditional, warm family, was vari-ously regarded by neighbours as 'nice', 'courteous', 'quiet' and 'friendly', but he suspended Janice by the wrists from tree branches when courting, and she became accustomed to being trussed up and throttled

into unconsciousness as they made love. When she drew the line at wearing a gas mask for sex, Hooker, his imagination fired by underground literature, talked of a girl who could not say no. In part, Janice was relieved: a real slave would deflect his attentions.

After six months Hooker removed Colleen's blind-fold, and on 6 January 1978 he came across an engrossing feature in the magazine *Inside News*: 'They sell themselves body and soul when they sign THE SLAVERY CONTRACT.' On 25 January 1978 Colleen added her signature to an embellished 'Indenture'. At this stage, another player entered the scene, the ficti-tious 'Company' responsible for American slave management. It was they who countersigned the document. Two weeks later, Hooker showed Colleen a sealed plastic identification card, acknowledging receipt of the Company's $1,500 registration fee.

Under the deed, Colleen undertook to keep her body visually available, never wearing knickers and keeping her knees apart in Master's presence. This entitled her to menial chores upstairs or perhaps a little crochet work, which her owners sold in the San Jose market. If Hooker shouted 'Attention', Colleen stripped and stood on tip-toe with her hands above her head.

After the birth of her second child on 4 September 1978, Janice became jealous of the creature in the basement. Distressed, she took herself out of the house with a job in Silicon Valley, spending nights during the week with her sister. But this gave Hooker a free hand. In addition to scorching Colleen with a heat lamp and wiring her up to the mains, he made her fellate him, reassuring Janice that the absence of vaginal penetration betokened fidelity.

After a couple of years Colleen was rewarded with an evening off at a local dance. Divested of any will of her own, and with no understanding of her former life, she reported back at the end of the evening. Any threat to Hooker's domestic arrangements stemmed not from detection by the outside world, but from the enemy within, from disruption of the household's deli-cate triangular equilibrium. In one permutation, Janice took the initiative, suggesting that her husband would enjoy straight sex with Colleen. He did, first gagging the slave and then tying her spreadeagled to the bed. But watching made Janice physically sick. So it was back to the kennel for Colleen, and when Hooker bought a new mobile home off the Interstate 5 highway, he constructed a spacious new rabbit-hutch contraption under their waterbed. He stored Colleen there, letting her out for an hour every day to wash and clean, and every autumn he took her for runs in the mountains. But he still enforced the daily regimen of handcuffs, blindfolding, whipping, hanging, nipple burning and rape, stretched on a rack.

In early 1981, Hooker decided to take his slave for the weekend to her parents (who presumed her dead) in Riverside, California. Adopting a commonplace persona under which weirdos pass without comment, he posed as a computer buff, taking Colleen as his fiancée. The visit was preceded by intense security arrangements. For weeks, Hooker informed Colleen, Company operatives had mounted telephone surveillance on him, his associates and her parents, running up a bill of $30,000 before granting approval. On 20 March, the day of their trip, Hooker stopped off at the Company's headquarters in Sacramento. He disappeared into an office building, returning after a judicious interval looking relieved to report that security personnel had given clearance without the customary face-to-face briefing. They were free to go, and he handed her Company documentation authorising Colleen Stan, his slave, to bear money for the duration.

The stay passed off pleasantly, although Colleen's parents considered that their daughter looked pale. She spent one night with her father and another with her mother. When Hoooker collected her earlier than arranged, she left meekly but sulked on the drive home. So it was back to her box for another three years.

Janice and Hooker's marriage suffered from the attempt to compress three people into their relationship. They tried a new start, taking up Bible readings and asking Colleen to participate in their prayers for spiritual peace. Meanwhile Hooker started a new underground slave bunker, completing it in November 1983. But the winter rains poured in, and they gave Colleen house-room. In return, she had to earn her keep, and in May 1984 Hooker told her to be a domestic at a local motel. Each evening she returned home, but Janice disrupted their fragile tranquillity with muddled ideas about Christianity. Hooker reiterated the solid biblical precedent for his domestic arrangements. Abraham had sex with his wife's maid, so why shouldn't he? And why not make his wife engage in lesbian love, three-in-a-bed?

To Janice, slavery conflicted with the teachings of the church that the three now attended. So much so that she asked Hooker to kill her. When he declined, she decided to tell Colleen everything. On 9 August 1984 Janice met her at work and revealed that Colleen was not really a slave: she had been born free. Hooker was a filthy pervert. After a night of tears, the two women fled. Colleen reached her parents, but Janice reverted to Hooker for another fresh start. They all kept in touch.

Still the story did not break. Colleen had sworn never to involve the law, and took refuge behind a hazy account of her seven-year absence. But Janice snapped. On 7 November 1984 she poured out her tale to a doctor's receptionist, who referred her to the local pastor. He persuaded Janice to call the police, to whom she furnished a detailed description both of Colleen's abduction and a previous murder by Hooker in 1977. The body was never found.

But there was evidence enough to arrest Hooker. Nearly a year later, he came to trial on sixteen charges including kidnapping, rape, forced oral sex and penetration with a foreign body. His lawyers conceded that Colleen was abducted, but argued that thereafter she was free to leave; she stayed voluntarily because she loved Hooker. In this version, Janice betrayed Hooker out of jealousy because he reciprocated Colleen's affections. The trial was fiercely contested and the decision a close one, but Colleen's scars carried the day, and on 22 November 1985 Hooker, characterised by Judge Clarence B. Knight as 'the most dangerous psychopath I have ever dealt with', was sentenced to 104 years. The case echoes that other miracle of brainwashing, the Patty Hearst affair, and Colleen is the subject of a book aptly entitled *The Perfect Victim*.

Smokescreen

On 1 July 1930 Jack Zuta, Chicago racketeer, was hauled in by the police. After questioning, Lieutenant George Barker agreed to escort Zuta to Lake Street in his Pontiac.

In the bustling heart of Chicago, just past Quincy Street, a blue sedan drew alongside. A gunman standing on the running board drew a .45 automatic from his shoulder holster and poured seven shots into Barker's Pontiac, aiming for Zuta. Supporting fire came from the driver and a rear-window gunner.

Lieutenant Barker slammed on the brakes and leaped out, returning fire. Since he was in plain-clothes, Barker was nearly shot by a passing policeman, but the pair joined forces and traded bullets with their assailants for some thirty seconds while pedestrians scattered for cover. The assault car pulled away, Barker jumped into his Pontiac and roared off in pursuit up State Street. Suddenly the blue sedan ahead belched out clouds of black smoke and disappeared behind an impenetrable smokescreen, apparently activated by a special plunger positioned by the foot-pedals.

This fiendish device did not do much good, although the technique has an honourable record at sea. In Chicago, on the road, the intrepid Barker shot through the billowing fumes at fifty miles an hour. By the time his quarry reached Wabash Avenue, Barker was only fifty yards behind and gaining. There his engine died, the petrol tank punctured. The only fatality of the engagement was Elbert Lusader, a street-car driver hit in the neck by a stray round.

Jack Zuta survived for another month. On 1 August he was relaxing in his Lake View Hotel hide-out under the cover name of Goodman, slotting nickels into the electric piano. Couples were dancing, bathers swam from the beach. 'It may be Good for You, but it's So Bad for Me', played the piano. Behind Zuta's back, five of Capone's henchmen entered in single file, led by a man with tommy-gun; his four colleagues carried a rifle, two shotguns and a pistol. The silent intruders fanned out; Zuta turned and they cut him to pieces.

Soap

The final incarnation of Louise Luetgart. In 1897 her husband, Adolph Louis Luetgart, a compulsive womaniser known to chase his spouse down the street with a revolver, turned her into soap at his Chicago factory on Hermitage and Diversey. He was a prominent manufacturer of **sausages**.

Louise's disappearance was noted by her brother, Dietrich, on 4 May. Luetgart equivocated about his wife's whereabouts, saying that she had walked out with $18 in her handbag and had not been heard of since. After a few days of fruitless enquiries with her relatives, Dietrich called in the police, and Captain Schuettler interviewed a factory employee, 'Smokehouse Frank', who described an unusual industrial process undertaken with Luetgart on 24 April. Together they had boiled up 325 pounds of caustic potash (ordered a fortnight previously) in the sausage vat to produce an excoriating brew strong enough to dissolve human flesh on contact.

A week later, on 1 May, Louise was last seen late at night in an alley near the factory with her husband. The following morning, a Saturday, the nightwatchman was instructed by Luetgart, up early and fully dressed for work, to stoke the fires under the sausage vat. The watchman remarked that the meat factory floor was slimed by a gluey substance clogged with occasional pieces of bone and, after the weekend, Smokehouse Frank was told to tip the spillage down the drain and sling any residue on the nearby railway.

At the works, Captain Schuettler peered suspiciously into the middle vat, still two-thirds full of something very like brown soft soap. He had the sludge poured through a makeshift sacking filter and, sure enough, found two gold rings, one engraved 'L.L.', in the sediment. To make sure, on 7 August the investigators heaved another corpse into the same vat and stewed it in caustic potash for two hours. The results were suggestively similar; the new body changed into soap.

Luetgart insisted that his wife had simply left him, and claimed that he needed detergent in bulk to clean the factory. The prosecution countered that Luetgart kept a hundred boxes of soap in stock, and that more was superfluous. But the absence of Louise's body was exploited by defence allegations that she had been seen alive and well in New York, Wisconsin, here, there, and everywhere.

Today, the case would present few difficulties. But the turn-of-the-century jury distrusted experts, and felt unable to bring in a verdict despite scientific testimony that the soap's principal constituent was boiled human flesh, a finding corroborated by archaeologist Professor George Dorsey's demonstration that the bone fragments were human. At the second trial six weeks later, Luetgart received a life sentence, and he died in prison of a heart attack on 27 July 1899.

The widespread but misconceived view that Louise had been processed into sausages was reflected in poor seasonal sales by local butchers. But the case popularised the word 'sesamoid', hitherto a largely unknown bone.

Sodomy

In Georgia, USA, this happens whenever a person 'performs or submits to any sexual act involving the sex organs of one person and the mouth or anus of another'. The penalty is stiff (one to twenty years) and the drafting broad. Clearly heterosexual encounters are included, and – if nipples are sexual organs and kissing a sexual act – a man kissing his wife's breasts should think twice first.

On Valentine's Day 1983, GOAL (Georgian Citizens Opposed to Archaic Laws) brought a test case on behalf of a practising homosexual (Hardwick by name), alleging that the law infringed the rights of citizens wishing to engage in sodomy at home. Hardwick lost in the District Court but won on appeal. Georgia's Attorney General decided to contest the issue, and on 31 March 1986 the Supreme Court, ignoring the statute's heterosexual implications, upheld the law by a majority opinion. Justice Byron White pointed out – correctly – that Mr Hardwick 'would have us announce, as the Court of Appeals did, a fundamental right to engage in homosexual sodomy. This we are quite unwilling to do.' Today 'the abominable crime of sodomy' remains against the law in nineteen states.

Sodomy abounded in the early Australian penal colony, where it was punishable by death. The first governor, Arthur Phillip, took a resolute line: 'I would wish to confine the criminal until the opportunity offered of delivering him to New Zealand, and let them eat him.' Convictions were rare; one Australian sodomite was hanged in 1836, but anecdotal evidence puts the number of homosexual encounters on **Norfolk Island** alone at 'fifty or sixty cases a day'. For a convict population of only 600, this may seem high, but buggery has always formed an ineradicable part of jail culture, and the Australian continent was little more than a vast prison, with sex an instrument of dominance used by the strong against the weak.

Unlike under-age homosexuality, lesbianism is not illegal. The distinction arose because Queen Victoria struck the offence from the 1861 Offences Against the Person Act, esteeming the practice so vile that it could only reflect the fevered imaginations of Parliamentary draftsmen.

Soham Murders, The

The disappearance of two ten-year-old girls – Holly Wells and Jessica Chapman – was one of those heart-breaking cases that riveted the attention of a whole country. The pair had gone for a walk on the evening of 4 August 2002, dressed in bright red Manchester United football fan shirts, and had simply vanished. The chances that two happy girls might choose to run away with no coats and no money seemed slim, but few liked to contemplate the obvious alternative – that they had been kidnapped.

The infamous photo of Holly Wells and Jessica Chapman, taken just before they were murdered

The population of the girls' village, Soham, in Cambridgeshire, England, rallied around the frightened families, and many locals helped the police search the surrounding countryside. It was a particularly hot summer; perhaps the girls had decided to have a camping adventure?

However, over the following days hopes of finding the pair alive fell. All previous experience had showed the British public that child-kidnappers rarely risk keeping their victims alive, and the fact that two girls were missing only made their murder seem all the more likely. Agonised television pleas by the girls' parents only increased the general gloom over the case. A photograph of the pair, taken just moments before they went on their fateful walk, stared out from every news programme and newspaper.

Then, on 17 August, just under two weeks after

Holly and Jessica disappeared, police arrested two suspects, a man and a woman. The man led detectives to the bodies in the ditch where he had dumped them, just a few miles from Soham. The corpses had badly decomposed in the summer heat, indicating that they had probably been killed soon after they vanished. Their killer had also returned to the site at least once, as an attempt had been made to burn the bodies.

To the shock of the village, the arrested pair were revealed to be Ian Huntley, aged 29, the caretaker at Jessica and Holly's school, and his girlfriend, Maxine Carr, aged 26, who also worked at the school as a classroom assistant (a sort of deputy teacher). Maxine worked with the girls in some classes and Huntley had been prominent among the good neighbours who had helped in the search for the girls. He had even given a short interview to a TV journalist, speaking of his hopes that the pair would be found alive.

Carr and Huntley went on trial in December 2003. To everyone's surprise, Huntley admitted killing the children, but denied murdering them. He claimed that they had passed by his house on the evening of 4 August and had come in because Holly had a nosebleed. She had gone into his bathroom to wash her face and had somehow drowned in the bath (Huntley was vague on the details of just how a healthy ten-year-old girl can kill herself in an ordinary bath). Jessica, he continued, had panicked when she saw Holly was dead and he had covered her mouth to stifle her screams and accidentally smothered her to death. The fact that he would have had to cover her mouth and nose for at least three minutes to kill her (during much of which time she would have had to have stopped screaming) was also left unexplained by Huntley.

Maxine Carr was not charged with being involved with the murders, largely because she had been over 100 miles away in Grimsby on the evening of the killings. But she admitted lying to police to provide Huntley with an alibi, insisting she had not believed him guilty until he confessed. However, her insistence that she had covered up for Huntley because she wanted to start a family with him was somewhat shaken when it was revealed that she had been visiting her other lover, a 17-year-old rugby player, on the evening in question.

Huntley, unsurprisingly, was found guilty of double murder and sent down for two life sentences. It later emerged that he had to his name several accusations of sexual misconduct with under-aged girls, but the police had not passed on this information to the school authorities when he applied for the job of school caretaker. Maxine Carr was found guilty of perverting the course of justice and was sentenced to three and a half years.

Of course, the question remains as to what actually happened that August evening in Huntley's home. The autopsies made it clear that the girls had not been raped. That Huntley meant to sexually proposition or abuse them seems beyond doubt. That he killed them to stop them from telling anyone what he had attempted to do is certain.

Solution, The police's

Armchair detectives hoping to identify **Jack the Ripper** face a clear choice. One route is to follow hunches, attributing the means, motive and opportunity to a likely Victorian. A hundred years after the event, very few suspects can be excluded with complete confidence: hence the steady proliferation of 'final solutions'.

The alternative is to be guided by the police officers charged with the original investigation. We now know whom they suspected although, tantalisingly, we do not know why. There are two pieces of evidence, the Macnaghten Memorandum and the Swanson Marginalia.

Sir Melville Macnaghten was the Assistant Chief Constable from 1889 to 1890, and in 1894 he recorded his views on the Ripper case, first setting out his reasons for believing that a man called Cutbush was not the culprit, and then discussing his three preferred suspects, now identified as Druitt, Kosminski and Ostrog. In the early 1930s Macnaghten's memorandum was copied by his youngest daughter, Lady Christabel Aberconway, who typed out seven quarto sheets, the existence of which only came to public attention in 1959.

In his memorandum, Macnaghten concludes: 'I am inclined to exonerate the last two' – Kosminski and Ostrog – 'but I have always held strong opinions about No 1' – Druitt – 'and the more I think the matter over, the stronger these opinions become. The truth, however, will never be known.' Serious historical work on Jack the Ripper's identity started with the Macnaghten Memorandum.

Of the three suspects, Druitt was a barrister who committed suicide in December 1888 shortly after the last of the murders, leaving a note to the effect that 'since Friday I felt that I was going to be like Mother, and it would be best for all concerned if I were to die'. Druitt had recently been dismissed from Valentine's school at Blackheath for an unspecified but serious offence; according to Macnaghten he was 'sexually insane and from private information I have little doubt but that his family believed him to have been the murderer'. Macnaghten continued: 'The Whitechapel murderer in all probability put an end to himself soon after the Dorset Street affair in November 1888 … Certain facts, pointing to this conclusion, were not in possession of the police till some years after I became a police officer.'

No one knows what these 'certain facts' were; the only certainty is that Macnaghten, a sensible, reliable man who knew everything about the case, believed that Druitt was his man and put his suspicions on file.

Michael Ostrog proved the most difficult suspect to track down since he operated under at least thirty aliases. Macnaghten characterised him as 'a mad Russian doctor and convict and unquestionably a homicidal maniac. This man was said to have been habitually cruel to women and carried about with him surgical knives and other instruments.' A Russian or Polish Jew born in 1833, Ostrog traded as a confidence trickster. The year before the murders, in September 1887, he appeared at the Old Bailey accused of stealing a metal tankard. Ostrog pleaded insanity, but was sentenced to six months; he was discharged from Surrey Pauper Lunatic Asylum on 10 March 1888. Thereafter he failed to report to the police and his later movements, including his whereabouts during and after the vital period six months later, are vague, although Macnaghten notes he 'was subsequently detained in a lunatic asylum'.

Finally there is suspect number three: Aaron Kosminski, the Man Who Died of **Masturbation**. Kosminski was a Polish Jew, a bootmaker who arrived in Britain in 1882 at the age of 17. He lived at 15 Black Lion Yard in Whitechapel, and was diagnosed as syphilitic on 24 March 1888. According to the Macnaghten Memorandum, he inhabited the heart of the district where the murders were committed. He became 'insane owing to many years of indulgence in solitary vices. He had a great hatred of women with strong homicidal tendencies. He was and I believe is detained in a lunatic asylum about March 1889… There were many circumstances connected with this man which made him a strong "suspect".'

At this stage the Swanson Marginalia come into play. These are the recently discovered pencil notes made by Chief Inspector Donald Swanson in his personal copy of Sir Robert Anderson's memoirs, *The Lighter Side of My Official Life*. Anderson had early charge of the Ripper investigation; his book says: 'The conclusion we came to was that he and his people were certain low class Polish Jews; for it is remarkable that the people of that class in the East End will not give up one of their number to Gentile justice. And the result proved that our diagnosis was right on every point. I will merely add that the only person who ever had a good view of the murderer unhesitatingly identified the suspect the instant he was confronted with him, but he refused to give evidence against him. In saying that he was a Polish Jew I am merely stating a definitely ascertained fact. And my words are meant to specify race, not religion.'

For many decades these sentences were believed to refer to a suspect known as 'Leather Apron', or John Pizer. But Anderson's predecessor at the Yard, Chief Inspector Donald Swanson, owned a copy of Anderson's book, which he read and annotated. On Swanson's death, it passed to his daughter, and on her death it was inherited by his nephew who, in 1987, ninety-nine years after the murders, stumbled upon his grandfather's marginal notes.

The jottings identify Anderson's man as Kosminski, and explain the refusal of the eye-witness to confirm his identification thus: 'because the suspect was also a Jew and also because his evidence would convict the suspect'. Swanson commented that after Kosminski's identification the killings came to an end, 'and very shortly afterwards the suspect with his hands tied behind his hack was sent to Stepney Workhouse and thence to Colney Hatch; poor Polish Jews from Whitechapel, had a home to go to wash and people to shield him. Redischarged after three days, readmitted 4 Feb 1891. He took up a knife and threatened his sister.'

Kosminski died in confinement in 1919. Unlikely though it may be that the police allowed their prime suspect to go free from 1888 to 1891, the fact remains that the only candidates on a shortlist compiled by the handful of men versed in the full details of the police inquiry were Druitt, Osgood and Kosminski.

This trail is lukewarm at best. Macnaghten clearly knew little about Druitt, putting his age at 41 instead of 31 and describing him as a doctor not a barrister; and cricket enthusiasts point out that Druitt's fixtures show him taking wickets only a few hours after the killings, turning out on Blackheath's Rectory Field on the morning of 8

J. M. Druitt, Ripper suspect

September 1888. But if the Ripper's identity is to be revealed, it is by reliance on the written record through documentary research. A cold trail is better than no trail at all, and there is no reason why the murderer should have come to public attention in any other context. Who would have heard of Ramirez, or DeSalvo, or Bianchi, but for their killings?

The 1993 'Ripper diary' designates James Maybrick as the culprit, but pre-publication doubts have focused on the handwriting, which bears no overt resemblance to Maybrick's known script.

Souvenirs

Serial killers like their trophies. A few collect whole bodies (Christie), others keep trinkets and paste jewellery (**Hansen**) or keys (**Duffy**), while some enjoy reliving their golden moments with photographs (**Glatman**), videos (**Ng**) or tape recordings (**Brady** and **Hindley**). Sometimes the killer takes parts home (for instance, the **kidneys**) as a keepsake or, occasionally, to eat.

For these wretched individuals the murders represent moments of significant human contact, from which stems the ordinary desire to salvage a memento of their conquest, just as a hunter lines the walls of his home with trophy heads of the creatures he has killed. Retention of these keepsakes fulfils two functions, part visual reminder and part an expression of pride.

For **Dahmer**, the people he killed represented little more than potential skulls; once they were dead, he could have their heads to remember them by. This tendency ripened into a desire to take Polaroids of his 'conquests', so that what started as a human being ended as a little piece of card a few inches square bearing a printed image. This completed the reification of the victim. Whereas a dead body belongs to the deceased, a photograph of it belongs to the photographer, as his property and his creation, and, reciprocally, to derive emotional satisfaction from arranging dismembered limbs into pleasing photogenic compositions is an activity that emanates a near-terminal quality. The body parts of Dahmer's victims fulfilled a similar function; they were to be subsumed into the grand design towards which Dahmer was groping at the time of his arrest – the 'shrine' where his skulls could be laid out in a neat row, symmetrically displayed on a magic black table flanked by a pair of plastic gryphons. Thus people would become ornaments.

The excitement over **Jack the Ripper**'s gynaecological doodlings misled Victorians into thinking they might be dealing with something familiar, namely a doctor. In fact, they were confronted by the more or less standard mutilations of something new, a serial sex killer on the prowl, hunting for souvenirs.

Spanish Fly

An alleged aphrodisiac made from the dried beetle *Cantharis vesicatora*. It is poisonous.

A gram or so of the powder at the standard concentration of 0.6 per cent prepared insect is usually fatal; when used in Mediterranean countries as an abortifacient, it often kills both the foetus and the mother.

Very possibly, smaller doses may stimulate sexual activity by irritating the mucous membranes of the mouth, intestines and vagina.

In 1954 Spanish Fly's erotic properties were put to the test in Britain by the manager of a wholesale chemists, Arthur Kendrick Ford, who was powerfully attracted to a 27-year-old typist, Betty Grant. 'We were,' he said, 'very fond of each other, but she kept putting me off.' He claimed they had intercourse together, but she went to post-mortem a virgin. Betty was no great beauty, and Ford seemed to be happily married, the father of two children for whom she often acted as a babysitter.

Ten years before, in the army, Ford overheard barrack-room gossip about an aphrodisiac which drove women wild, and in early 1954 he made the dual discovery that canthardarin was the medical term for Spanish Fly and that his firm kept some in stock. He emptied forty grains into an envelope.

The idea took hold. On 26 April, Ford talked to the firm's senior chemist, Richard Lushington. 'This is a number one poison,' he was warned. Nevertheless, Ford purchased a bag of pink and white coconut confectionery into which he inserted quantities of the stolen drug with a pair of scissors. On Ford's reckoning, there was one piece for Betty and one for him. He offered the bag round the office. Betty ate one sweet, he downed another and – somehow – a seaside beauty queen, June Malins, also working as a typist, took a third. Other staff members guzzled up the remainder, with no ill-effects.

The two women died. Ford recovered and, lacking the intent to kill, got off with five years at the Old Bailey in a trial which he spent mostly in tears. In public his wife stood by him, writing in the press: 'Arthur Ford and I are still desperately in love with each other, and some day, somehow, we hope to regain the happiness we have known and restart our lives together.'

Spencer, Lady Diana

In the early hours of 31 August 1997, Lady Diana Spencer – the former Princess of Wales – and her lover Dodi Al Fayed, were killed in a high-speed car crash in a Paris underpass. The driver was also killed, but their bodyguard survived. The French inquest found that the driver had been drunk and ruled the deaths to be accidental. Nevertheless, rumours that the accident

had been deliberately orchestrated had already begun to circulate.

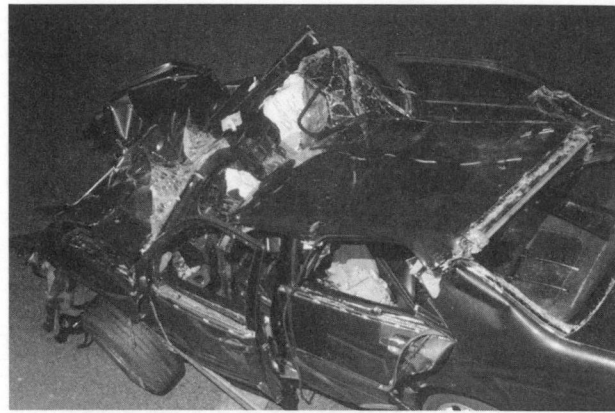

The Lady Diana car crash aftermath

These were given new life late in 2003, when Diana's former butler, Paul Burrell, revealed that she had sent him a letter, ten months before she died, mentioning that she feared that her former husband and the heir apparent to the British throne, Charles Windsor, Prince of Wales, was planning to kill her in a staged car accident.

Burrell himself stressed that he thought Diana's fears were groundless, and that the deaths were accidental. However, this is not the opinion of Dodi's father, Mohammed Al Fayed – millionaire owner of Harrods department store. He believes that his son and Diana were murdered by the British authorities. One reason for such a killing was the suggestion that Diana was planning to convert to Islam in order to marry Dodi – a shocking embarrassment for the Royal Family, with the potential to cause a constitutional crisis.

It is still illegal for the British head of state – either king or queen – to be a Roman Catholic. Diana was destined to be the Queen Mother when her elder son, Prince William, eventually ascended the throne. A Muslim Queen Mother? And what if her son were influenced to follow her lead and convert to Islam?

On the same day that a newspaper reported that Diana feared Prince Charles was going to have her murdered, a pathologist working for the royal household reported that Diana was definitely *not* pregnant at the time of her death. This may be so, but it is a fact that, just a few days before her death, Diana told pressmen that she would soon make 'a world-shattering announcement'. When time of the advertised press conference arrived, Diana suddenly decided to postpone it 'to a later date'. Before she could do so, she was killed.

It is hard not to suspect that Diana was planning to announce her marriage plans and/or admit to being pregnant by Dodi. How such a 'world-shattering' possibility would have been taken in the higher echelons of British power is anybody's guess.

Sperm, frozen

In July 1978 a 13-year-old Birmingham schoolgirl, Candice Williams, was raped and then strangled. Following normal procedure, the swabs of semen from her vagina were consigned to the freezer at the West Midlands Forensic Science Laboratory.

With his record of indecent assaults, local youth Patrick Hassett was the prime suspect. But his girlfriend supplied an alibi and the blood-grouping technology of the day proved inconclusive. Hassett went free, but five years later he was jailed for ten years after kidnapping and assaulting a mental defective.

In 1986 came the discovery of **genetic fingerprinting**. Another two years passed before samples of the type taken from Candice Williams could be processed. So it was not until 1988 that the bags of Hassett's semen were chemically analysed, yielding the requisite DNA fingerprint. But Hassett, still in prison, refused to supply a comparative sample.

The police waited until his 1991 release. Then they rearrested him. He agreed to provide some hair cuttings, and these matched the 1978 spermatozoa, a one-in-12,000 chance. On 18 March 1992, Hassett was sent to prison for life.

In America, the rapist and murderer Joseph O'Dell ran a 1992 campaign from **Death Row** for the right to impregnate his girlfriend, Sheryl, with frozen sperm. As an only son, O'Dell was concerned about his family's bloodline.

See also **Romances**

Spilsbury, Sir Bernard (1877–1947)

Spilsbury, the greatest medico-legal expert of his time, won his spurs for the destruction of Crippen's defence in 1910. A charismatic figure, habitually clad in a Savile Row suit with a carnation in his button-hole and a top hat from Lock's of St James's, Sir Bernard had his shirts tailor-made with detachable arms to avoid creasing his cuffs when he rolled up his sleeves for work. He conducted 25,000 post-mortems; a young barrister once courted his ire by demanding, 'When did you last examine a *live* patient, Sir Bernard?'

Few dared make such frontal assaults. Spilsbury's sway over the popular imagination and the courts was such that his word was seldom challenged. He delivered his opinions with confidence and clarity, and his cases read like a roll-call of famous British murders: Crippen, Frederick and Margaret Seddon, George Joseph Smith, Louis Voisin, Bywaters and Thompson, Herbert Armstrong, Patrick Mahon, Donald Merrett, the Brighton Trunk Murders and the like

In his later years, Spilsbury's court appearances became increasingly erratic. He intervened on behalf of the defence in the 1943 John Barleycorn murder, contending that the four-and-a-half-fingered Loughans lacked the strength to throttle his victim. When asked how he knew, Spilsbury said that he had visited Brixton Prison and enjoined Loughans to grip his hand 'with all the strength he had'. The great pathologist had been amazed at his client's weakness. 'I do not believe,' Spilsbury said, 'that he could strangle anyone with that hand.'

Spilsbury's reputation was sufficient to secure an acquittal from a deferential jury. Twenty years later, wasted by cancer, Loughans still showed a test grip of fourteen pounds. Spilsbury was accustomed to carry the day as much by sheer force of character as by his knowledge and experience; in the 1930 Merrett case (see **ears**), one of the opposing barristers referred to him as 'Saint Bernard'.

Similar prescience prevailed at the trial of the matricide Sidney Fox. By the time the corpse was examined by defence doctors, the crucial bruising round the victim's larynx had disappeared. Not surprisingly, the defence disputed the bruises, suggesting that Spilsbury was misled by incipient putrefaction. He brushed the objection aside: 'It was a bruise and nothing else. There are no two opinions about it.' Fox was hanged in 1930.

Spilsbury was not a man to overlook an injury, and never forgave the parsimonious Southwark coroner Douglas Cowburn for paying him a single fee for examining both bodies of a pair of Siamese twins.

His declining years were marked by domestic and

personal misfortune, and he committed suicide on 17 December 1947, gassing himself in his University College laboratory after dinner at his club.

Stabs

When examining stab wounds, it is best to concentrate on the cleanest slit. This indicates most clearly the type of weapon, for instance double-edged or single-edged; and the sharper the wound's outline, the sharper the instrument. Roughening or bruising round the aperture suggests something blunt, like a pair of scissors. The penetration of the deepest thrust indicates not the length of the knife but its minimum length.

Where suicide is to be weighed against murder, the corpse is studied for signs of defensive cuts. For suicides, the angulation and site of the stabs must be consistent with self-inflicted wounds. Most suicides go for the heart or thereabouts, with none of the hesitation cuts that characterise, say, self-administered throat-cutting. The murderer lands his hits wherever he can, most often on the upper chest.

What does this feel like for the the assailant? The murderer Jack Abbott, briefly the darling of New York's cocktail circuit for the literary accomplishments revealed by his *In the Belly of the Beast*, mentioned feeling the victim's 'life quivering on the end of the blade'. But there is probably no better authority than Susan Atkins of the **Manson** Family. Most discussions of **sex crimes** proceed by metaphor or analogy, drawing tentative parallels between the mutilatory and sexual processes. Atkins was more forthright. While in custody she told another inmate, Veronica Howard, about killing the pregnant Sharon Tate: 'It felt so good the first time I stabbed her, and when she screamed at me it did something to me, sent a rush through me and I stabbed her again … it was just like going into nothing, going into air … It's like a sexual release. Especially when you see the blood spurting out. It's better than a climax.'

Stalking

Technical term for the pursuit of celebrities by nonentities. Stalking can spill over into violence and even the final accolade of murder by a fan. Stalkers often subscribe to the view that their affections are reciprocated, although they may find that it needs some decisive act of armed confrontation to wring out the truth from their love-object. To date, the practice is illegal in forty-nine American states, the United Kingdom and many other countries.

Stalking is no new phenomenon. Roderick Maclean, incensed by Queen Victoria's refusal to read his poems, became one of her would-be assassins. A more recent pairing was of Jodie Foster and John Hinckley. Michael J. Fox, star of *Back to the Future*, received some 6,000 letters from 26-year-old Tina Ledbetter; the correspondence turned sour – 'very violent, very threatening', according to Fox – when he found a marriage partner elsewhere. Ledbetter was eventually arrested and packed off for psychiatric treatment.

In July 1992, Britain's *Sunday Times* reported an unusual case of an unnamed Hollywood actress who enjoyed a brief dalliance with an admirer, Susan Dyer; when the liaison ended, Dyer bombarded her target with telephone calls, stole her address book and then rang round the actress's friends to beg them to engineer a reconciliation. When this failed, Dyer broke into her former lover's home during a dinner party and threatened to shoot herself. A few weeks later, after Dyer's arrest, the actress called in an electrician to investigate a wiring problem and it emerged that Dyer had shared her home for months, taking up residence in a tiny space beneath the actress's bedroom floor.

Stalkers may fall prey to the delusion that their target is beaming them messages. Actress and singer Olivia Newton-John talked to Michael Perry with her eyes, and when Perry saw visions of dead bodies rising through his floor, he inferred that it was her way (as a goddess) of maintaining contact from an underground base in his home town of Lake Arthur. Later, he killed both his parents, two cousins and a nephew, but a court found him insane and thus 'incompetent' (see **Lunette**) to be executed. To end this impasse, it was proposed to treat Perry with drugs, on the one hand making him better which would, on the other hand, qualify him for electrocution. But in October 1990 a court ruled that enforced drug therapy was 'cruel and unusual', so Perry will only be killed if he recovers by more natural means.

The full-blown stalker kills his hero. But before Mark Chapman focused his grievances on John Lennon, his resentment was directed – at lower levels of harassment – towards other targets. He telephoned a bomb threat to Hawaii's Ili Kai Hotel, and watched from the balcony opposite as the police cars arrived. He would ring a street pay-phone, visible from his window, and tell whoever picked up the receiver, 'I'm watching you. I'm going to get you. I'm going to follow you home and kill you.'

Chapman became the stalkers' prototype. He used a .38 Charter Arms Special (see **Dumdums**), and took *The Catcher in the Rye* as his Bible. John Hinckley adopted the identical combination for his attempt on Ronald Reagan, as did Robert John Bardo when he gunned down actress Rebecca Schaeffer in June 1989. Hinckley told Jodie Foster that the **assassination** of Reagan was in retaliation for Lennon's death. Underlying these similarities is an obsession with celebrity. To their fans, celebrities lead mythic lives, flickering in the limelight. But what is fame? It may not reflect any achievement apart from fame itself. The celebrity projects a fantasy of celebrity, and his admirers project fantasies on to the celebrity. Confusion and disillusion can result.

Stomach analysis

Useful in determining not only the cause (in poison cases) but also the rough time of death. As a general rule, most food stays in the stomach for a couple of hours following consumption. A really large meal may linger a further hour and a rich creamy meal tarries for even longer.

As adults know, the stomach is emotionally responsive. In pathological terms it seems that fear slows, but anger hastens, gastric movement. Severe injury will stop it completely, so both the perpetrator and the victim of an assault are likely to have erratic digestive timetables and, according to some authorities, the best tactic is simply to recognise a meal, find out when it was eaten, and then assume that death occurred subsequently. But even this broad approach would have been difficult in the case of *mafioso* Dominick 'Big Trin' Trinchera, gunned down in 1981 during an internecine Bonnano feud. 'You should have seen it when they shot Big Trin,' one of the killers told the under-cover agent Joseph D. Pistone, 'fifty pounds of his stomach went flying.'

Given enough to work on, a conviction can be based on stomach analysis. On 10 June 1957, the body of Ontario schoolgirl Lynne Harper, missing since the previous night, was found in the undergrowth in Lawson's Bush. She had been raped and strangled. The time of death was critical, since Lynne's movements were well documented for much of her last evening.

Lynne was seen setting off on the cross-bar of a 14-year-old classmate, Stephen Truscott, at around 7.05 p.m. as he pedalled northwards down County Road. Travelling in the opposite direction were two boys returning from a dip in a local swimming hole; they started together, one on foot and the other going ahead on a bicycle. The first child crossed with Stephen and Lynne on the highway by the wood known as Lawson's Bush, but the second, a few minutes behind, did not meet them; he arrived home at 7.25 p.m. The inference was clear: the pair had struck off towards the spot where the body was discovered. A relaxed-looking Stephen arrived back in the school area around 8 p.m., when a friend asked, 'What did you do with Harper, throw her to the fishes?' Stephen replied that he had dropped her at the highway, a little north of the swimming hole and, questioned by police the next morning, he maintained that she had hitched a ride in a grey 1959 Chevrolet.

Lynne's temperature provided no assistance in determining the time of **death**; her body had lost all its natural heat. But the police knew what she had for her last meal: turkey, cranberry sauce, peas, potatoes and 'upside-down' pineapple cake. This distinctive intake remained in her stomach, and she had sat down to the fifteen-minute meal with her parents at 5.30 on the afternoon of her death.

Without realising that Stephen was a suspect, the pathologist wrote: 'I find it difficult to believe that this food could have been in the stomach for as long as two hours, unless some complicating factor was present, of which I have no knowledge. If the last meal was finished at 5.45 p.m., I would therefore conclude that death occurred prior to 7.45 p.m.' Truscott was arrested on 13 June and later found guilty of murder, incriminated by a wealth of circumstantial and forensic evidence. Eight years later the case became *a cause célèbre* when a crusading journalist, Isabel Lebourdais, heaped ill-informed scorn on the verdict, and in 1966 the case was retried, producing a rare gathering of the world's leading authorities on stomach emptying. A pathologist arguing that Lynne 'could have died within one hour – or up to nine or ten' of her supper found no support among his peers, who believed that the stomach does have its norms. The conviction was upheld.

Straighten, to

Criminal slang meaning, roughly, to bend. Villains 'straighten out' obstacles by removing or neutralising them. Thus a burglar alarm can be straightened by being cut, or a policeman straightened by bribery, resulting in the proverbial 'bent copper'.

Strangulation

According to Professor Keith Simpson, strangulation is not particularly painful. He established this empirically in the summer of 1941 by nearly murdering himself with a ligature in London's Euston Hotel lavatories. After winding a stocking twice round his neck and knotting it before losing consciousness, Simpson came sufficiently near to death to show that self-strangulation with a ligature is both feasible and tolerable. This is no party trick; it can kill suddenly, since even momentary compression of the neck may incur a reflex vagal nerve stoppage of the heart (see **Drowning**).

As recently as 1960 defence counsel suggested that a ligature round the neck of Frances Knight (found mummified after twenty years in a Welsh cupboard) was attributable to the deceased's faith in the procedure as a folk remedy for the common cold.

It is perhaps no coincidence that strangulation is the favoured murder method of many hardened serial killers, Christie, **Nilsen** and **Dahmer** among them. The process of extinguishing life can be prolonged almost at will by the exercise of self-control, with a diminution in applied pressure producing a temporary remission. According to the prosecution in the Dahmer trial, 'It takes five minutes to strangle a man to death.' Serial killers enjoy domination, and there can be few contexts more fraught with possibilities.

Death results from oxygen deprivation of the brain and, according to anaesthetist Nigel Robson, children can survive for longer than adults and cold people for longer than those who are warm. Even with the best will in the world, it is impossible to strangle yourself manually, as the loss of consciousness relaxes the grip, although it seems that Jeanne **Weber**, the famous French babysitter, died in the attempt. Another plucky

attempt was made by Amelia Dyer, the baby killer, after her arrest on 4 April 1896 (see **Pregnancy**). She failed with a ligature. Taken to Reading police station, Dyer removed her bootlaces, tied them together and, heaving with all her might, set about ending her life. Her eyes bulged, her tongue lolled and her face turned purple, but she survived, to be executed two months later. Otherwise, female stranglers are extremely rare. Simpson encountered none in a sequence of fifty-eight cases.

The hallmark of strangulation is a fracture limited to the upper horn of the thyroid cartilage. This little bone, the hyoid, is never broken on its own in any other way. As Sir Bernard **Spilsbury** pointed out with style under cross-examination, the converse is not always true. Asked if a murder victim's hyoid had been fractured, Spilsbury riposted, 'No. If it had, that would have made the strangling even more evident.' Most stranglings are ordinary domestic crimes and, after stabbing, it has long been the most popular British method of murder.

Body changes from death by asphyxia include a blueness in the face, and tiny haemorrhages in the eye membranes and the internal organs. Strangulation also diminishes bowel control, and semi-asphyxiation during masturbation heightens sexual pleasure, producing a surprising number of accidental hanging fatalities.

String

Getting the timing just right is important with electrocution. The moment to throw the switch is immediately after the condemned man empties his chest by exhaling. This prevents air from getting trapped in his lungs by the contraction of the glottis induced by the electric charge. Should this happen, the subsequent collapse of the chest when the current is switched off releases a lungful of escaping breath, engendering a highly distasteful sound and a foaming mouth (see **Allorto and Sellier**).

At the Sing Sing death house, matters were complicated by the executioner's special booth. This partitioned him from the condemned man so that he did not have to look at the prisoner while killing him. But it made the right moment impossible to judge.

It was the chief physician's job to watch the man die. So a little hole was drilled in the partition, and through it he passed a length of string with a ring attached to both ends. The executioner slipped one ring on his finger. The doctor put on the other and, when the prisoner was strapped in, he gauged the rhythm of his heaving chest and gave a tug. But stress left ample scope for misunderstanding, and the executioner's line of sight was later rearranged so the doctor was visible, allowing for visual hand-signals.

American executioners are typically called 'the electrician'. In Sing Sing the job paid $150 a head; for many years of his working life, John Hilbert used the extra income to make ends meet. He committed suicide in his cellar shortly after retirement.

Strychnine

In small doses a tonic. It comes from the orange-like fruit of the Strychnos nux-vomica tree and, after its 1817 discovery, strychnine was rapidly exploited by proprietary brands like Easton's Syrup as an aid to convalescence. It sharpened up the senses and promoted general well-being, but an overdose caused rapid or almost immediate death, an outcome demonstrated by many who forgot to shake the bottle, adequately distributing the concentrated sediment.

The poison is wholly inappropriate for discreet killing. Its use is better restricted to the random murder of strangers like the series devised by Dr Thomas Neill Cream, often believed to have made a truncated bid for immortality with his last words on the scaffold, 'I am Jack...' But this outburst can be interpreted in other ways (see **Hanging**) and, besides, the man was mad. Not only did Cream make a practice of inducing London prostitutes to swallow his pink pills just for the pleasure of watching them writhe, killing four, he wrote letters to public figures accusing them of his crimes.

Cream arrived in London in 1891 after serving ten years of a murder sentence. This charm-free man traded as an abortionist in Canada, where he once obliged a client to marry him at gunpoint, leaving her the next day. Within a month of setting foot in Britain, Cream poisoned Matilda Clover and Ellen Donworth. He tried to blackmail Lord Russell and a Dr William Broadbent for the killings, meanwhile writing to the coroner with an offer to solve the cases for £300,000. In April 1892, Cream accused a Dr Walter Harper of his next pair of murders, finally reporting

Title page of a contemporary account of Dr Cream's murders

him formally for the killing of Donworth and another prostitute, Louise Harvey. The police investigated, but Harvey was still very much alive; she told detectives that Cream had handed her some pills (which she did not take) for her complexion. And although Donworth was dead, her demise had been attributed to alcoholism. Exhumation detected substantial quantities of strychnine in her body, and Cream was hanged on 15 November 1892.

Death from strychnine is attended by some of the most startling symptoms known to medicine. A fatal dose is as little as 100 milligrams, and the victim suffers horrific spasms, his back arching over so that only the heels and back of the head stay in contact with the ground, a process known as 'opisthotonos'. The face becomes fixed in a grin ('risus sardonicus'), the muscles twitch and breathing becomes first laboured and then impossible. The spasms hit in two-minute waves until extinction results from suffocation or heart failure.

It is hard to see how anyone could hope to have such manifestations ascribed to natural causes, and in 1855 Dr William **Palmer** failed in just such an enterprise. Late on 19 November, having weakened the gambler John Parsons Cook with antimony, Palmer secured three grains of strychnine from the local chemist and returned to the sickbed at the 'Talbot Arms'. The inn's waitress reported that by midnight, 'Cook was screaming "Murder!" and was in violent pain. He said he was suffocating ... His eyes looked very wild, and were standing a great way out from his head. He was beating the bed with his hands.' A chambermaid noted of Cook, 'Sometimes he would throw back his head upon the pillow, and then he would raise himself up again. This jumping and jerking was all over his body... It was difficult for him to speak, he was so short of breath ... He called aloud: "Murder!"'

Cook survived this preliminary skirmish, perhaps the effects of antimony, and the following day Palmer gave him two 'ammonia pills'. The results were spectacular. According to Gordon Honeycombe's meticulous account, the patient at once 'began to scream, throwing himself back on the bed. He cried to Jones: "Raise me up – or I shall be suffocated!" Then his whole body was seized with violent convulsions, so extreme that his head and heels bent hack as if they would meet. Jones, with Palmer's assistance, tried to lift or control the contorting body but failed, because of the spasms and rigidity of Cook's limbs. The convulsions lasted for about ten minutes, after which Cook's agony diminished and his heartbeat faded.' On seeing the body, Cook's stepfather 'was greatly struck by the tightness of the muscles across his face', and on 14 June 1856, Palmer was hanged for murder.

Stupidity

No one knows the dumbest thing ever said by a mobster, but here is a recent crop of contenders. Gene Gotti, on being arrested for violation of the Racketeer Influenced Corrupt Organisation Act, demanded: 'Say, who is this Mr Rico, anyway?'

An unnamed gangster, acting as a security guard during a performance of *The Nutcracker*, inquired: 'Hey, how come there's no talking in this thing?'

Perhaps the strongest candidate is the wonderful exchange between another unknown goon and a policeman, as they stood watching a robot bomb-disposal device steer itself towards a suspicious package planted outside the Gambino family New York headquarters at the Ravenite Social Club.

'I don't see no wires, so how can they make it move around like that?' the mobster asked. A deadpan policeman replied, 'There's a tiny little cop inside.'

Success

Understandably, it can make someone's day to be mistaken for a world-famous desperado, a trait manifest in so-called 'motiveless' crimes where a murderer may kill just to achieve celebrity.

Thus in 1966, 18-year-old Robert Smith explained why he had blown out the brains of five women and two children in an Arizona beauty parlour: 'I wanted to get known, to get myself a name.' Kenneth Bianchi, the Hillside Strangler, wrote to the author Thomas Thomson shortly after his conviction in 1984 saying that his life would make a 'terrific movie' (see **Romances**). And Paul Knowles, finally arrested in Georgia in November 1974 after a massive manhunt following a murder spree which claimed eighteen lives, had a field day on his court outing. Crowds lined the streets, the courtroom was packed, the papers carried him all over the front pages.

Knowles had made it at last. Like royalty, he smiled graciously at everyone, reminding an interviewer that he was 'the only successful member' of his family. Jeffrey **Dahmer** rose further, to the coveted front cover of *Time* magazine and, after the 1991 success of the film *Silence of the Lambs*, American police were plagued with exaggerated claims from would-be serial killers. Henry Lee **Lucas**, a Texas drifter, confessed to a body count of 600, but later insisted it was just his mother he killed, and Britain produced an even more pitiful example in Ian Warby. If growing into a serial killer is an expression of failure, Warby was a failed failure. At 26 he was a worshipper of Nazism, the Devil, the Marquis de **Sade** and the fictional Hannibal Lecter, nicknaming himself The Panther and The Outsider. But, as Warby's lawyer declared in court, 'He is as physically weedy, pathetic and uncommunicative an individual as one could meet.'

On 12 October 1992, Warby went on the rampage in Essex, attacking a college boy with a hammer, a middle-aged man with a knife, hacking at two youths in a car and then going for an invalid, becoming a serial runner in the process, beaten off on every occasion. 'It doesn't say much for a serial killer when he can't even kill a victim in a wheelchair who is at his mercy,' commented his barrister. Warby was not so much a man driven to kill as a man who hoped to be driven to kill, the impetus seemingly derived from extrinsic rather than intrinsic sources, and it is rightly said that those who achieve their ambitions sometimes find the victory hollow.

Careful study of local newspaper files enables aspiring serial killers to restrict their **false confessions** to unsolved cases. Their braggardly tendency poses a temptation to police forces with an eye on clear-up rates. Critics now claim that officials used Lucas as a dustbin into which they dumped unsolved killings, taking a total of 210 murders in twenty-six states off the books, and in August 1991 officers were warily grappling with the case of ex-Marine Donald Leroy Evans. Arrested on a kidnapping charge in Mississippi, Evans confessed to 'more than eighty' killings in seventeen states. He was sentenced to death for the murder of a ten-year-old girl, but fellow-Mississippi Death Row inmate Jimmy Mack stabbed him to death in the shower in early January 1999. At the time of his death Evans was the prime suspect in at least twelve unsolved murders, but the rest of his claimed killings have been left largely uninvestigated.

A White Supremacist of low intelligence, Evans was believed by the majority of investigators to have invented most of his 'murders'. He told investigating officers that he was a committed Nazi, but then revealed that he thought the Nazi salutation 'Heil Hitler!' was actually a light-hearted greeting: 'Hi, Hitler!'

In the first half of the twentieth century, America produced serial killers at a rate of 1.2 per annum. Between 1960 and 1980 this had risen to around a dozen a year, and it is now approaching about two a month. Nearly all are men, nearly all are white, and many are prodigious drivers, logging up to 200,000 miles a year as they scour the country for their next victim.

See also **Canonisation**, **Locard**, **Puente**

Sunday Gentleman, The

Nickname of Daniel Defoe (1660–1731) when in Bristol; Sunday was the only day he dared show his face out of doors without risking arrest for **debt**.

His real name was Daniel Foe. After issuing the immensely popular 1701 pamphlet *The True Born Englishman*, inveighing against social snobbery, he spent a brief period as D. Foe before spreading his wings as De Foe and finally Defoe. Then in 1703 he penned a satirical tract that landed him in the **pillory**. There he was feted as a popular hero; the crowds showered him with flowers crying 'Good Old Dan'. His subsequent incarceration in **Newgate** bore fruit twenty years later, when he described his low-life experiences through the eyes of one Moll Flanders. At about the same time he published one of the many accounts of the life and adventures of the highwayman Jack **Sheppard**, interviewing his subject in the Condemned Hold.

Defoe launched his first newspaper while in Newgate in 1703, and secured his release by offering to work for the Lord Treasurer Robert Harley as a spy, setting up a network of informers to keep tabs on subversives like himself. Thus he became the father of the police state and of the British Secret Service.

Superhumans

The Denise Labbé case is perhaps one of the most sinister crimes of passion on record. Twenty-year-old Denise, a secretary, enjoyed mixing – and sleeping – with students at Rennes, in France, and had a baby daughter, Catherine, by one of them. Then she met officer cadet Jacques Algarron, a brilliant mathematician who believed ardently in Nietzsche's theory of the superman. He decided that he and Denise were a 'super-couple' and that, to prove that she was above conventional morality, she should kill her daughter. She was so besotted with him that she agreed. Delays brought threats to break off the affair.

Eventually she tried to throw Catherine from a high window, but found she could not bring herself to do it. Then she pushed her into the canal but relented and

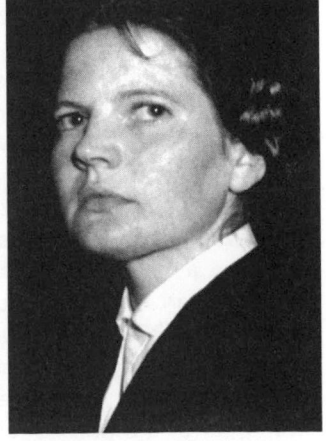

Denise Labbé

summoned help. A second attempt at drowning was frustrated when neighbours heard the child's cries and pulled her out of the river. On 8 November 1954 Denise Labbé eventually drowned Catherine in a stone wash basin. Friends were suspicious, and Denise was questioned by police. Finally, she confessed, implicating her lover: 'It was a ritual murder.' She was sentenced to life imprisonment, Algarron to twenty years' hard labour.

Sutcliffe, Peter (1946–)

The story of the Yorkshire Ripper well illustrates the point about the banality of evil. Almost the only interesting fact about Peter Sutcliffe is that between 1975 and 1980 he murdered thirteen women.

Sutcliffe was an unexceptional, inarticulate, taciturn and averagely coarse lorry driver, endowed with the normal complement of relatives, friends, workmates and drinking cronies, none of whom regarded him as anything special. Born on 2 June 1946 in Bingley, the turning point in Sutcliffe's life came in the summer of 1969 when he picked up a prostitute in Bradford's run-down Manningham Lane. She said it would cost £5. Sutcliffe became increasingly half-hearted at the prospect of back-street sex, but he handed over a £10 note; she went to a garage to change the note and then disappeared. This incident followed a row with his long-standing fiancée Sonia about a rival, an Italian with a sports car, and preceded a dressing-down the next morning for being late to work at the local Water Board, where his absence triggered an accident in which several men nearly drowned. All in all, it was a bad twenty-four hours.

Three weeks later, Sutcliffe found the woman who duped him out of his £5 drinking in another prostitutes' pub. He demanded his money back. In Sutcliffe's words: 'She thought this was a huge joke and, as luck would have it, she knew everybody else in the place and went round telling them. Before I knew what was happening, most of the people were having a good laugh.'

A week after this public humiliation, Sutcliffe assaulted a St Paul's Road whore chosen at random, cracking her on the head with a stone. Then in September 1969 he was arrested lurking behind a hedge in the red-light district armed with a heavy hammer and was – mistakenly – charged with 'going equipped for a theft'. As far as we know, that was the end of Sutcliffe's assaults for nearly six years.

Peter Sutcliffe, Yorkshire Ripper

In June 1975 a divorcée, Anna Rogulskyj, from the nearby town of Keighley, was repeatedly accosted and followed by a strange dark-haired man with a springy beard. On the night of 4 July 1975 Sutcliffe smashed her skull with a hammer. But he was interrupted, and Anna survived after a twelve-hour operation. On 29 October 1975, Sutcliffe gave a late-night lift to prostitute Wilma McCann. She upbraided him as a slow-starter and climbed out of the car saying: 'I'm going. It's going to take you all fucking day. You're fucking useless.' Incensed, Sutcliffe caved in McCann's head and then stabbed her fourteen times. After that he was away, killing his thirteenth and final victim five years later on 17 November 1980. In the meantime he continued his ordinary social rounds of friends and family.

Sutcliffe was finally picked up almost by chance on the evening of 2 January 1981 in a car with stolen numberplates. Unaware of his true identity, the police hung on to him overnight, and the next day a conscientious Sergeant Bob Ring searched the scene of the arrest. There he found a discarded knife and hammer, which Sutcliffe had concealed in a pile of leaves while urinating before going to the police station. Next day the giant 'Ripper' manhunt, during which 250,000 people were interviewed, 32,000 statements taken, 5.2

million car numbers checked and £4 million spent, drew to its close.

'I think you are in serious trouble,' said the interrogating officer, Inspector John Boyle. Sutcliffe replied, 'I think you have been leading up to it.'

'Leading up to what?'

'The Yorkshire Ripper.'

'What about the Yorkshire Ripper?' Boyle asked. 'Well,' said Sutcliffe, 'it's me.'

Sutcliffe came from a poor area of the West Riding with its rough and ready subculture. Women were habitually (and often affectionately) referred to as 'fucking cunts' and wives as 'cunts'; in the bars you could buy cocktails called 'Barbarella Legspreaders' and listen to pub DJs doing commercials between records, starting off 'Worried your willie's too short?' The prostitute areas were sleazy, run-down slums where junk shops and sex shops, betting offices and minicab rooms were interspersed between the patches of broken ground left by random demolition. Here the wretched prostitutes – often abandoned wives 'on the game' to feed their children – plied their trade in the open air. Piss-ups, brawls, violence against women, broken-down cars, cars on bricks, cars with Guinness labels for tax discs, unemployment, bailiffs, rat-catching, thieving, kerb crawling and trouble with the police were not unusual.

As a baby Sutcliffe was weak, and he developed into a shy, almost listless child who clung to his mother's skirts. At school he had a 'yonderly' glaze to his eyes; he was remembered by his teachers, if at all, as passive. At home it was not always possible to tell he was there. 'I've walked into the house many a time and he's been just sat quiet in the kitchen without me realising for ages,' recollected his sister. 'Not reading or anything; just sort of sat there staring at space.' One of Sutcliffe's few distinguishing traits was his passion for the bathroom, where he spent hours staring at himself in the mirror, occasionally snipping the odd millimetre off his hair. Most of his mid-teens were passed in his bedroom, with the door locked.

Three years after leaving school at fifteen Sutcliffe took a job as a gravedigger. To his workmates he seemed pleasant but shy, typically the one who tagged along. As girls started to feature in his mates' lives, Sutcliffe accompanied them drinking: looking, listening, and contributing nothing for hours, as though in a trance. Women found his dark and broody good looks an attraction until they tried to make conversation.

Somehow, in 1966, the young Sutcliffe hitched up with another loner, 16-year-old Sonia Szurma. She may have been an intelligent girl, even an intellectual snob by comparison with Sutcliffe; she was destined for teacher training college. But she was no more of a live wire. Uncommunicative in the extreme, she occasionally ventured into speech with remarks like 'Hello'. Sometimes she sat alone outside a pub while Sutcliffe drank inside it. She radiated disapproval, and after their 1974 wedding became obsessed with housework. Meanwhile she developed a considerable talent as a nag. For the married Sutcliffe, pubbing and cruising the red-light district provided a welcome diversion from his prim home life. In due course, one thing led to another.

Two months after his arrest, Sutcliffe pulled off a rather flashy coup. During his eighth interview with one of the Armley psychiatrists, he disclosed that his murders were at God's behest. The Almighty had ordered him to kill prostitutes. In corroboration, Sutcliffe furnished anecdotal material about voices, visions and hallucinations. The professionals trooped into line: Sutcliffe exhibited many 'first-rank signs' of mental disorder. So when he appeared in court on 29 April 1981, pleading guilty to thirteen charges not of murder, but of manslaughter, his future looked relatively rosy – the more so since the prosecution accepted his plea of diminished responsibility, guided by the evidence of three forensic psychiatrists.

The experts were unanimous in labelling Sutcliffe an 'encapsulated paranoid schizophrenic'. It was almost unheard of for three professionals to agree and, now they did, their views were dismissed. A week later the court reconvened, with the Old Bailey the improbable forum where twelve laymen spent thirteen working days deliberating the metaphysical issue of whether Sutcliffe was deranged; after all, anyone who thinks that killing people is right must be strange. The crux was whether Sutcliffe was mad or bad; his *acts* may have been 'insane', but insanity cannot be judged purely in terms of behaviour. Everyone behaves badly, but that does not prove that they suffer from a mental disorder and are entitled to disclaim responsibility for their actions. Common sense prevailed on 22 May when Sutcliffe was found guilty of murder and sentenced to life.

He took so long to catch because the police investigation, without computers, was swamped by the 151,000 reports laboriously cross-referenced by 150 officers on the case. Sutcliffe was interviewed nine times, with each report filed under a different heading. Enquiries were sidetracked for months by a 'hoaxer' who sent in an audio-cassette, beginning with the words 'I'm **Jack**', and the thousands of suspects whose voices were recognised by the public had to be individually checked.

Linguistic experts narrowed the accent on the tape to an area near Durham, but in 1980 an advisory team devised a simpler way of pinpointing the Ripper's home. There were seventeen known attack sites; clearly the murderer had to travel to each of them from home, and then return to home from each of them. So, 'What single point on the map was nearest to all the attack sites?' The answer was Heaton, between Manningham and Shipley, where Sutcliffe lived. Further corroboration came from the neat idea that the late-night attacks probably happened nearest home – he was nearly back – whereas those earlier in the evening would be further away, allowing more time to drive home. Coupled with two other 'hard' clues, the newly minted £5 note found in Jean Jordan's handbag after her murder on 1 October 1977 and issued two days previously in one of only 5,000 wage packets, and a set of tyre tracks common to 53,000 owners in the Midlands, Sutcliffe's detection was imminent at the time of his chance arrest.

Swallowers

Customs term for smugglers who take contraband through in their stomach, normally wrapped in **condoms** or surgical gloves. The technique first came to British attention at Heathrow in 1974 when three Americans were detained for the inexplicable profusions of condoms in their luggage; if the men had flown into the Republic of Ireland, they would have been accepted as no more than illicit condom smugglers. But British Customs had no easy explanation until it emerged *per rectum*, in the form of knotted rubbers filled with cannabis oil.

Heathrow's highest monthly tally of swallowers is a 1986 total of twenty-six. The record number of condoms secreted in a single stomach is in dispute. Gatwick has a confirmed 143; other reports claim 739 capsules of cannabis resin.

It is a good idea to take anti-diarrhoea tablets for added coagulation during transit, thereby minimising

the risk of premature evacuation. Working from the far end, the opposite of a 'swallower' is a 'stuffer'.

See also **White death**

Sweden

More Swedes are killed in collisions with elks than by unlawful assaults. It seems that Swedish criminals are a cosseted and endangered species, creating growing public resentment at the inferior treatment meted out to law-abiding citizens.

Featherbedding can disappoint. In early 1991, young offenders despatched on a six-month yacht cruise to 'find themselves' were recalled after rediscovering their identities as Viking marauders, running riot in the coastal ports, pillaging cars and shops.

Many commentators consider the Swedish machinery of justice a similar anachronism, harking back to the Dark Ages. The judiciary are not independent; judges are civil servants whose careers must progress, to some degree, according to the number of 'results'. The role of the jury is played by lay assessors; they too are political appointees. After arrest, suspects are kept in solitary, very often until they confess.

For all the faults of the adversarial system, the accused is tried before being sentenced. But in Sweden the real trial takes place before the court hearing, and consists of the pre-trial examination, for which almost anything is admissible in evidence. Specious allegations, hearsay and gossip can be accepted as fact, without the opportunity of rebuttal or cross-examination, and these pre-trial findings are presented to the court, which passes the appropriate sentence. There is no real presumption of innocence; on the contrary, the notorious 'Sanalika Skal' clause requires the prosecution not to prove that the defendant is guilty, but that he *could have* been guilty. This is hardly onerous, and only one or two per cent of defendants are discharged.

Thus the 1987 Captain Simon Hayward case is interesting not for whether Hayward 'did it' but for the light cast on Swedish justice. Hayward was arrested on 13 March 1987 in his brother's Jaguar; its door sills were crammed with cannabis. Captain Hayward did not know that the drugs were there, nor was he informed by the police. It was only after some days in prison that he learned the reason for his arrest.

Captain Hayward spent the next five months in

solitary while the prosecution went through the motions of proving that he *could* have acted knowingly as a courier. *Prima facie* it was unlikely that he *had*; couriers are typically individuals on their uppers with little to lose, whereas Hayward was a rising professional soldier in a good regiment on the eve of promotion. He did not need the money, and the alleged fee was way over the odds. Why give Hayward £8,000 when a professional would do the run for a fraction of the price?

Hayward's brother Christopher, on the other hand, was a drop-out living on uncertain income in Spain, and he went to ground shortly after Hayward's arrest. His role remains open to doubt. It was he who asked Hayward to drive his car to Sweden and deliver it to a cash buyer. Hayward decided to spend his few days' leave on the trip, squeezing in a couple of days' skiing at the far end. But, as the Judge later pointed out, Hayward's story was a lie because ... why would anyone go skiing in *Sweden*?

The physical evidence at the trial consisted of Captain Hayward's screwdriver. The Judge said that it was for levering open the panels and extricating the cannabis. In fact, the Swedish mechanics who dismantled the car knew that it was almost the only tool *not* needed to break into the door sills. Access required a small Phillips screwdriver, a flat-ended screwdriver, a chisel, and some wire hooks, none of which Hayward had. But there was no procedure whereby this point could be made in court.

Hayward's screwdriver was a special six-pointed Phillips, bought in Astorp to tighten the screws on the Jaguar's seat, which worked loose on the long, fast drive. Again, this explanation was ridiculed in court on the grounds that the seat was perfectly sound on arrival (after Hayward had fixed it) when driven round the state garage at three miles an hour. Why would Hayward buy a *screwdriver* to tighten up the screws on his seat?

Another talking point was the adverse testimony given by Inspector Larsen. His evidence consisted of information which had been submitted to (and rejected by) Scotland Yard, who thought it unreliable. Larsen would not say exactly whose testimony it was. Nor would he disclose his source's address; in fact Larsen had no idea of the man's whereabouts. As the informant was a criminal, Larsen had to protect his anonymity.

The court accepted these submissions at face value, and on 10 August 1987 a warder passing Hayward's cell let him know he had been sentenced to five years in his absence.

For the equally farcical appeal, London solicitors Kingsley Napley commissioned a report from Richard New, an experienced drugs officer. He wrote: 'In my considerable experience, I have never seen a verdict reached with such blatant disregard for the facts.'

Simon Hayward was released early, in September 1989, his life broken.

Sweeney Todd

The demon barber of Fleet Street. Careful tracking through the fictional accounts suggests that he may have existed in real life.

The story of a hairdresser who cut his customers' throats, pulled a lever to catapult them into the basement and then sold their remains as meat pies, was first serialised in *The People's Periodical and Family Library* of 1846 where it appeared under the demure title *The String of Pearls* and ran for eighteen episodes. The author was a little-known imitator of Edgar Allan Poe, Thomas Prest. In 1862 a journeyman writer, Frederick Hazelton, adapted Prest's serial for the stage, and it has rarely been out of production since. Before gracing the boards as a Stephen Sondheim musical, the story was filmed three times, once starring Tod Slaughter.

The cannibalistic elements of the plot are reminiscent of the Scottish legend of Sawney Beane, but an alternative inspiration is Prest's own version of the murders of the rue de la Harpe in Paris, in which he had the victims' bodies turned into savories by a pie-maker.

But the programme notes of a 1940 New York production refer to the *Newgate Calendar* of 29 January 1802, which described in detail the career of a twisted barber called Todd. Unfortunately, no copies of this issue have survived. But the anonymous *Romance of Newgate* (1884) contains an entry seemingly derived from this source, describing a 'Sweeney Todd' who traded for seventeen months as a hairdresser in Crutched-friars before moving into larger premises in Fleet Street.

It is likely that the house in question was 186 Fleet Street, and the *Annual Register* of 1880 recorded that when it was demolished a large pit of bones was found in its cellars. But these may have come from burials in nearby St Dunstan's Church.

The delicatessen in the story, Mrs Lovett's pie shop, was said to be in Bell Yard. Charles Fox, author of an 1878 retelling of the Sweeney Todd story, includes an account of an underground tunnel linking the barber's to the meat shop and it is possible that this passage existed prior to the rebuilding of the church 1831–3.

Another outside contender for derivation from a factual basis is Poo-Bah's ditty in Gilbert and Sullivan's 1885 *Mikado*. At the time, the fringes of the medical community were preoccupied with the debate on whether decapitated **heads** survived their removal from the main body trunk. Pooh-Bah himself had no doubts, and his words afford an uncannily accurate precognition of the fate of the convict Languille:

Now 'though you'd have said
That head was dead
For its owner dead was he
It stood on its neck
With a smile well bred
And bowed three times to me.

'Sweet Fanny Adams'

Expression indicating that there is nothing of value in a given situation; often reduced to 'sweet FA' or thence re-expanded into 'sweet fuck all'. It was coined by the Royal Navy, who felt their tins of chopped mutton bore a striking resemblance to the state of eight-year-old Fanny Adams on the evening of 24 August 1867.

Earlier that day Fanny's head was cut off, and at about 7 p.m. a labourer – part of a search party – discovered it balancing uneasily on two poles laid side by side several hours after her eyes were observed drifting down the River Wey through the Hampshire countryside. One ear had been removed, and a leg and an arm hacked from her trunk, itself disembowelled. The heart was displayed separately.

Fanny spent the last hours of her life, a warm summer's afternoon, playing in Flood Meadow about four hundred yards from her home in Alton with her sister Lizzie and their friend Minnie Warner.

Along came Frederick Baker, a personable 29-year-old solicitor's clerk. He helped the three children pick blackberries before presenting Minnie and Lizzie with a penny-ha'penny to buy some sweets while he stayed to look after Fanny. Then he lured her to a nearby hopfield. Then he ripped her to pieces.

Noticed in the meadow by local women, Baker was arrested with blood on his clothes and two knives in his pockets. His diary entry for the afternoon read, 'Killed a young girl today. It was fine and hot.' Baker contended that these words recorded no more than current gossip and should be construed as 'Killed today – a young girl. The weather was fine and hot.' But the jury believed the 'it' referred to his butchery-work.

Baker's family suffered from a history of mental illness, and contemporaries ascribed his crime to 'moral insanity'. With hindsight, the killing has all the hallmarks of an early sex murder.

Swordstick

The purported murder weapon in the curious case of Colin Chisam. This British trial turned on the arcane question of whether the deceased, a young man called Henderson, was killed by a bullet or a swordstick. Whatever it was had passed right through him, and thus the lawyers argued this important issue in the abstract. In 1962 the penalty for murder with a firearm was death but the legislature had, through some oversight, made no corresponding provision for death by swordstick, and the aftermath of the trial saw the first forensic application of the electron-beam probe.

Colin Chisam, a Berwick-on-Tweed garage owner and arms collector, opened fire with a .22 repeater from his front door at three passing youths on the night of 5 August 1962. They were playing their transistor radio too loudly. Infuriated, the young men ran back to Chisam's house, forced their way into the front hall and set about him and his adopted son. After a scuffle one of the intruders, Tait, died in hospital from a fatal wound which traversed his body, with an entry hole on one side and an exit hole at the other.

Except in the case of an alibi, lawyers are under no obligation to divulge their line of defence in advance. At the trial the prosecution was surprised to hear that Tait had died of a swordstick wound contracted by impaling himself on top of Chisam, and five days of expert medical evidence were insufficient to resolve the question. For the Crown, Dr H. J. Walls's half-hearted experiments with a swordstick on a laboratory corpse proved inconclusive; it was only after the trial that he realised an electron-beam probe would provide incontrovertible evidence. Too late, he discovered the tiny traces of lead from a bullet on the torn threads of the entry hole through Tait's clothing.

By then Chisam had been convicted of manslaughter, always the most likely outcome since psychiatric reports diagnosed him as subject to a condition considered exceptional by experts and near-universal by everyone else, namely 'a paranoid disorder that made him feel he was always right and everyone else was always wrong'.

T

Tapes

Few killings have shocked the British public as deeply as the Moors Murders of the 1960s, and at the heart of darkness is the sixteen-minute tape-recording, made by Ian **Brady** and Myra **Hindley**, of ten-year-old Lesley Ann Downey during the last minutes of her life.

Lesley was 'snatched' on 26 December 1964 while on her way home from a fair on the local recreation ground. Hindley made a show of dropping some parcels and asked Lesley to help, first, by taking the shopping to the car, and then by unloading the vehicle at her home. Brady was waiting in a prepared room with his lights and camera and a tape recorder. He hoped to make money by selling the pictures to child sex perverts, but this was probably the least important motivational component. His primary objective was a permanent memento (see **Souvenirs**) which would, at the same time, complete his victim's defilement, reducing her to the status of a 'performer' in his tape collection.

The tape was consigned to a left luggage suitcase, deposited at Manchester's Central Station, containing the pair's paraphernalia of coshes, wigs, masks and ammunition. The police came across the ticket, Number 74843, in Hindley's prayer book, *The Garden of the Soul*.

After stripping Lesley and photographing her naked apart from ankle-socks, Brady raped and killed her. The pictures do not show much, just a naked little girl in a sequence of semi-obscene poses, gagged with a man's scarf – one leg in the air, or arms outflung and the like, rather like childish ballet exercises. The tape was more explicit, starting with a scream and the words 'Don't… please God help me' and ending with the background recording of 'The Little Drummer Boy'.

More than twenty years later Hindley wrote to Lesley's mother from prison: 'I now want to say to you,

and I implore you to believe me, because it is the truth, that your child was not physically tortured, as is widely believed.' Taking the unpopular step of giving Hindley the benefit of the doubt, and limiting interpretation of the tape to the meaning of the recorded words, then it may represent nothing particularly unspeakable. But enlarging the frame by only a few minutes, Lesley was killed for pleasure, and the mere fact that the recording could be made, almost irrespective of its contents, under overhanging homicidal intent in a suburban living room, stained British conceptions about their society and the reach of evil just as surely as the Ripper murders did for the Victorians a hundred years ago.

Hindley was convicted as an accessory to two murders in 1966 and died in prison on 14 November 2002. She was not physically present at four of the five killings, withdrawing upstairs to the bathroom while Lesley was strangled, and otherwise busying herself parking their van as Brady guided the children across the moors to their doom. Nor did she strike their last victim, Edward Evans. Hindley served almost the longest sentence of any legally sane killer since the abolition of capital punishment. If standard parole rules had been applied to her case, she would have been eligible for release in the 1980s. But the Home Office's freedom of action was uniquely circumscribed by public opinion.

Tax havens

Tax havens attract drug dealers. The fundamentals for a narcotics syndicate laundering money are identical to the requirements of large conglomerates shifting funds offshore in a tax avoidance scheme. Both need corporate confidentiality, banking confidentiality and a stable government.

A good place to look is in the Caribbean. In 1986 the British Virgin Islands provided a home for a mere 5,000 companies. Six years later, 65,000 legal entities were registered through the competing services of forty-nine company formation agencies, advertised, in the manner of escort services, as 'Strictly Confidential' or 'Very Discreet'. Virtually no information is disclosed to the authorities: no list of shareholders, no list of directors, no annual returns, just the name and the company 'objects', typically as broad as the notorious CIA sweeper-up clause allowing the pursuit of 'any business whatsoever'. Local governments have no idea who owns the companies. Nor do the company formation agents.

Refuges like the Virgin Islands solve the drug dealers' long-standing problem of hanging on to their lucre. In a personal account, drug money is vulnerable to confiscation. Traffickers want resources on which they can draw freely which do not belong to them technically, and the ideal arrangement is as an authorised signatory for company funds. But standard national regulations for disclosure under local Companies Acts make this impracticable – except in tax havens.

Drug barons buy businesses off the shelf, thwarting investigation with a network whereby Company A is owned by Company B which in turn is owned by Company A. Thus true ownership can never be ascertained. Stratagems devised by lawyers, bankers and tax consultants representing legitimate concerns are adopted wholesale, and today the Caribbean islands are depositaries for the proceeds of the international drug business, conferring legitimate status on the cartels.

Some traffickers squander fortunes on flash consumer goods like helicopters and yachts, others on gambling; the major heroin dealer Frank Lucas dropped $15 million at blackjack in Las Vegas with apparent nonchalance. Other operators get serious, collecting skyscrapers, luxury apartments, shopping centres, hotels and even banks.

The Virgin Islands are by no means the worst offenders. Anguilla boasts a bank on the airport runway, enabling 'slush' funds to be dropped off without the depositor entering the territory, and St Martin has *no* Customs checks; you just walk your suitcases through the airport. One ton in four of the cocaine estimated to pass through the Caribbean each week enters by this route.

In 1989 the United Nations talked tough as part of its War on Drugs programme. But the Basle edict of 'Know Your Customer' encountered an insuperable obstacle: tax havens make money by not knowing their customers.

See also **World-Wide Business Centre**

Techies

FBI slang for their technical squads specialising in electronic eavesdropping. A full techie team calls on the services of locksmiths, burglars, undercover operatives, surveillance teams and electronic experts known as 'buggies' or 'Dr Bugs'. Their task is to penetrate sensitive locations – for instance a *mafioso*'s house – and plant a listening device consisting of three elements, a miniature microphone and a thin wire, leading to a battery as big as a fireplace log. Post-installation, the site is manicured so that not even a speck of dust is out of place.

The signal (scrambled to defeat scanners) is transmitted to electrical boosters maybe a quarter of a mile away and relayed to the monitoring station, where listeners are on constant alert for counter-surveillance 'sweepers'.

In the days of the **Pizza Connection**, conversations intercepted by wire-taps on public pay-phones were oblique in the extreme, with drug dealers rambling on about consignments of 'suits', 'shirts' or 'lemons'. By the 1992 Gotti case, the techies secured direct access to the homes of *mafiosi* like Paul Ruggiero and Paul Castellano. The under-boss of the Gambino family, Aniello Dellacroce, had a bug planted right beside his sickbed, effectively his office desk during his last years. John Gotti's sidekick Angelo Ruggiero, nicknamed 'Quack-quack' for his incessant chattering rather than his ducklike waddle, provided hours of easy listening, setting up a drugs link with the Bonanno family on the telephone, prattling away about his narcotics business for hours on end, threatening to lob creditors into a swimming pool with a man-eating shark or to chop rivals into pieces. By inextricably incriminating the entire upper echelons of the Gambino clan, he set it on a course of internal warfare.

Tapped at source, the Mafia verbals were unambiguous. Thus Alphonse Sciacia arrived at the Ruggerio home saying, 'I got thirty things of heroin. That's why I'm here.' John Gotti, overheard in Dellacroce's residence, was no less forthcoming: 'I'll kick his fucking brains in', or: ' I told him, you better come and check in every week. You miss one week, and I'll kill you, you cocksucker, fucking creep.' Evidence like this is hard to shrug off.

See also **Decline**, **Trial**

Teeth-marks

Identifying a corpse from its teeth is an obvious step when dental records are available. By the 1940s, forensic horizons extended to a study of bite-marks on the corpse. Perhaps the idea first came to Professor Keith Simpson on viewing Margery Gardner's body in Notting Hill's Pembridge Court Hotel in June 1946. Her corpse displayed seventeen lash-marks from a whip, its distinctive diamond-pattern hatched into her flesh. 'If you find that whip you've found your man,' Simpson told the police, and it was located a few days later in an attaché case belonging to Neville George Clevely Heath. He was executed on 16 October 1946 for two murders.

Neville Heath, sex murderer

Scrutinising Gardner's body, Simpson's interest was also engaged by the ferocious bite-marks on her nipples. But she had not died outright from the assault, and her bruising diffused into the surrounding tissues, blurring the outline of her assailant's dentistry. Two years later, Simpson was confronted by the corpse of a Mrs Margaret Gorringe, whose exposed right breast bore a usable impression of two upper front and four lower teeth. Their uncommon spacing, irregular shape and curious angles proved sufficient to convict her husband, already under suspicion. This was the first British case, but the body of 15-year-old Linda Peacock, discovered in a Glasgow cemetery on the morning of 7 August 1957, posed a tougher test of Simpson's ingenuity.

Linda died within minutes of being bitten, and her breast showed five distinct indentations. Two were no more than small dark rings with pale centres. The biggest measured 7mm by 13mm, the result either of two adjacent teeth or one badly compacted molar. The twenty-nine suspects were all borstal boys from a local detention centre, and plaster casts of their teeth suggested that number fourteen possessed the requisite dentistry in the form of a sharp-edged right canine. For confirmation, the cautious Simpson had the upper and lower teeth mounted on a hinged clamp and, when a suitable body arrived in the mortuary, bit it. The marks did not match.

Attention now focused on the two ring-shaped abrasions. The literature of bite-marks, mostly in Swedish and Japanese, cast no light on their origin, but Dr Warren Harvey, Scotland's leading odontologist, reasoned that they could derive from teeth with a pit in their tip, corresponding to craters in the upper and lower *right* canines of cast number eleven. But the marks on Linda's breast showed the ring marks to the *left*, indicating that the killer's head was upside-down at the time. In this orientation, number eleven's broken upper left incisor and its adjacent left lateral matched the large abrasion perfectly.

Medical evidence showed that the victim was strangled from behind, and the mud on suspect number eleven's trousers intimated that he pinioned his victim from behind while kneeling, and had leaned over her shoulder to exact his bite on her breast. One thousand canines from a test sample of 342 boys of similar age revealed that only two possessed the distinctive craters, the product of hypocalcination, and no single mouth contained two pits. Simpson wrote in his report, 'A jury should have no difficulty in understanding this evidence and appreciating its strength. It is akin to tool-marking evidence or fingerprints.' Gordon Hay, aged 17, was arrested and found guilty of murder.

Ted **Bundy** was another killer convicted by bite-marks. In 1979 Dr Richard Souviron was able to satisfy the court that his lower left incisors, sharply askew from the rest of his teeth, caused the distinctive indentations in Lisa Levy's buttock.

Teeth-snatching

A variant on **body-snatching**. During his medical career, English surgeon Astley Cooper (1768–1841) was supplied with cadavers by the proficient Tom Butler, a hard-drinking dissecting room porter. Cooper kept in touch after Butler left St Thomas's Hospital; and in 1811 Cooper sent him off to Spain with an introduction to his nephew Bransby Cooper, a surgeon serving with the Royal Artillery in the Peninsular War. 'My dear Bransby,' wrote Cooper, 'Butler will tell you the purpose of his visit.'

At that time, false teeth were made of boxwood or – preferably – someone else's molars. Those of relatively fresh origin commanded a high price. 'Oh sir,' enthused Butler to his contact in Portugal, 'only let there be a battle and there'll be no want of teeth. I'll draw them as fast as the men are knocked down.' He did, after each engagement following Bransby Cooper around the battlefield among the casualties. Pincers at the ready, Butler extracted teeth enough from the dead and dying to net £300 from their sale in England, where this practical man set up as a dentist (see **Perera**).

But drink dragged Butler into debt and serious trouble, and he was sentenced to death for passing a stolen £5 note. In prison awaiting appeal, Butler turned his hand to articulating the disassembled skeleton of the prison governor's favourite horse. His handiwork was much admired by an influential foreign visitor, an Austrian Archduke, who pulled rank to secure a pardon from the Prince Regent, and Butler is believed to have ended his days in Ireland, shipping bodies for the surgical trade into Scotland.

In 1801 Astley Cooper attracted a large crowd outside his London house in St Mary Axe by dissecting an elephant in the street.

Terminology

Mass killers must be distinguished from their counterparts, the serial killers and the spree killers. Mass murderers kill a lot of people in one place; serial murderers kill one person at a time in a lot of places.

The predominant mass killer profile is of a desolate white male in his thirties or forties overwhelmed by personal failure. For this, everyone is responsible except himself – women, workmates, teachers, bosses, entire towns and sometimes the Devil. The malevolent schemes of his tormentors infuse the killer with a festering desire for revenge, fuelled by get-even films and empowered by a fascination with guns. At this stage only a precipitating trigger is needed, like losing a job or being dumped by a girlfriend.

There are, to date, no female mass murderers, partly because they do not regard firearms as fitting objects of veneration. Further, women are more likely to admit to depression, telephone a friend, or go to therapy.

The spree killer – the next evolutionary step – takes lives without the essential 'cooling-off period' which marks out the serial killer. For an official 'spree' the killings take place in different locations; a simple walkabout during a twenty-minute 'event' will qualify.

Both the spree killer and the mass killer process undifferentiated consignments of victims; anyone crossing their path is at risk, as are the killers themselves. They often commit suicide or, in America, go on killing until they have to be shot.

The serial killer is unique in desiring both to kill and to live, achieving a delicate equilibrium that imbues his psyche with a certain fascination. More discriminating, he selects his targets, limiting them to a particular type of victim. The murder itself is more controlled, representing an endeavour to extract the maximum pleasure by proceeding deliberately from one stage to the next, for example from abduction through mutilation to termination and then ritual rearrangement of the corpse. Then comes the 'cooling-off period', varying anywhere between a day, several months or even years, which constitutes his inert emotional phase. The underlying pattern bears a correspondence to the process of sex or drugs, enhanced by near-infinite reverberations of self-disgust: first wanting to do it, then doing it, then regretting it, then coming to terms with having done it, and finally wanting it again. The serial killer may move on, change jobs, go to prison for something else or die, but he is unlikely to take his own life, even during the course of capture by the police.

Confusion can arise between the categories. In his final tailspin, a serial killer on the run may embark on a killing spree, like Florida's Christopher Wilder.

These seemingly academic distinctions hold great practical significance for detection, notably in the USA where the mosaic of unsolved 'incidents' are, state by state, reported back to FBI headquarters at **Quantico**, and then disentangled into distinct strands as the computer stitches together apparently unrelated homicides into the work of a single man.

The minimum FBI qualification for a serial killer is three clearly separated deaths.

See also **Sex crimes**, **Trolling**

Terror

Screaming can be a mistake, inciting the aggressor to shut his victim up. On his arrest in 1943, Harold Loughans, the John Barleycorn murderer, stated not untypically: 'I want to say I done a murder job in Hampshire about fourteen days ago … It's a relief to get it off my mind. I had to stop her screaming, but I didn't mean to kill the old girl, but you know what it is when a woman screams.'

Loughans led a chequered career in the courts, his tendency to confess only marginally exceeded by his verve at securing acquittals. At his first trial there was a hung jury and, at the second, the prestigious but misguided evidence of Sir Bernard **Spilsbury** got him off. Loughans was sent down for another attempted murder. On his emergence from jail in 1963 he sued the *People* for libel, but the civil courts adjudged him guilty of the murder for which he was discharged under the criminal jurisdiction. Then, learning he had cancer, Loughans confessed to everything and died.

With **sex crimes**, by the time the perpetrator has the victim safe within his lair, screaming may prolong life. The attacker's goal is not to cause death (a mere by-product) but fear and degradation. As long as the victim can yell he retains play value. As a friend of Charles **Ng**'s put it, 'The **torture**, the pure terror – Ng wanted to see terror. He wanted to see them beg, to plead. That's what he really got off on … They had to beg for it to stop … And then, once they stopped, it was no longer fun. Then it's time to put a round in their head and move on to find another one.'

In a less extreme context, running away may, like screaming, provoke a gunman to fire. Britain's Michael Peckett was given the option during the 1992 Dryden shooting (see **Planning Officer**). He reasoned: 'I'm not going to run and get it in the back. If a rabbit's running, you shoot it. If it's still, you don't.' Be that as it may, Peckett stood his ground and survived to tell the tale.

According to survivors, staring into a gun barrel is very, very frightening. In the words of Ann Bristow, a 1992 victim of a Yorkshire armed robbery, 'You don't take your eyes off the gun. It's not like you think it would be, not like on television. It's stark panic. I've never been so frightened. I can't even talk about it now without shaking.' Britain's Midland Bank retains a firm of industrial counsellors, who report that the initial post-raid reaction is uncontrollable crying coupled with endless mental replays of the incident and inability to sleep. In America, victims prefer to take in a violent film or two; apparently this consigns the trauma to the realms of fantasy. But the English Miss Bristow now leaves the room at any hint of television gunplay.

It may be worth reserving one's fear for the physical consequences of being shot rather than the pain. According to writer Auberon Waugh, who accidentally fired a machine-gun, inflicting six wounds on himself, four to the chest, the immediate experience is not unpleasant: 'To those who suffer from anxieties about being shot I can give the reassuring news that it is almost completely painless. Although the bullets caused considerable devastation on the way out, the only sensation at the time was of a mild tapping on the front of the chest. I also felt suddenly winded as they went through a lung. But there was virtually no pain for about three-quarters of an hour, and then only a dull ache.'

Thiefrow

Common parlance for Heathrow, the world's busiest international airport. Terminal One is the place to go. In a single year supercrook Geoffrey Senior stole £350,000 of property from the Heathrow baggage collection-points.

Senior hardly conforms to a master criminal's stereotype. An unemployed drifter with long greasy hair and no front teeth, he pitched up in London penniless at the age of 20 and was drawn to the airport because of its warmth. It provided somewhere to stand. After a while, he noticed that anyone could stroll up to the baggage carousels for domestic passengers and take a suitcase. So he did.

His first theft netted £7,000 in cash stuffed into a Jiffy bag. 'I couldn't believe it was such a doddle,' he said. 'Like any drug, I became addicted and just couldn't give it up. Sometimes I tried to keep away, but the easiness kept taking me back.' Day after day, Senior would pick up two or three bags at a time, pile them on to a trolley and wheel them to the Underground, where he rifled through the luggage in a lavatory cubicle. He found a mine of cameras, jewellery, word-processors, watches and money; after his arrest, police unearthed £15,000 in an overlooked envelope in one discarded bag.

Senior's one concession to technique was to watch from the balconies until the crowd thronging the carousels thinned out, although he varied the times of his thefts so that the security and airline staff changed with the shifts, and invested in two suits, six ties and fifteen shirts to rotate his appearance – the only tangible capital investments from a high-earning year. The rest he dissipated on premium drink, car-hire, travel and on five-star hotels, which made a change from his Hammersmith squat.

Senior estimated his profits at £80,000. Once, another passenger confronted him. 'I admitted the mistake. He smiled, and even seemed to feel sorry for me, because I had no bags,' Senior said. 'I thought I could go on for ever ... There was no security to penetrate.'

In September 1991 Senior was caught trundling away a set of golf clubs. Sentenced to three years, he reviewed his life contentedly: 'It were really amazing, it's hard to tell you exactly how wonderful it was.'

His story makes traditional forms of robbery, like bank raids, look old-fashioned, but the expenditure of greater ingenuity provides no guarantee of increased success – as witness the career of the miniaturised vacuum cleaner pioneered by the gem thief Julio Cesar de Monraes Barros.

A 28-year-old Brazilian in Bangkok, Barros installed a brachial implant of a long thin tube running subcutaneously from the tip of the little finger on his left hand to the wrist, where the conduit emerged to join thicker piping, in turn routed to a storage pouch in the armpit. Barros powered the system by flexing his muscles to activate a small pump.

Barros and his accomplice, Paulo dos Santos, called on a string of jewellers posing as customers. Out came the dealers' boxes of precious stones. While Santos distracted the staff's attention, Barros hoovered up loose diamonds, using his little finger as the nozzle.

But this clever ruse only solved half the thieves' problem. It is one thing for the dealer not to know *how* his baubles were stolen but quite another not to notice that they *have* been stolen. This remained a pitfall. On 12 December 1991 Barros was arrested with £7,000 of gems in his armpit. For the avoidance of incredulity, police introduced their human vacuum cleaner to journalists, still festooned with lengths of rubber hosing.

Another technological innovation brought Jenny Webb, the British eighteenth-century pickpocket, greater dividends. Supposedly the illegitimate daughter of an aristocrat and a serving girl, Jenny arrived in London in 1721, and by the age of 18 she ran a gang of forty pickpockets. Her particular contribution involved a special dress with slits cut in either side at waist level. She became adept at rifling her neighbours' purses through these apertures, generally in church, while seated with a pair of false, law-abiding arms reassuringly folded on her lap. Webb survived a sentence of transportation, bribing her way back to England, and was hanged at **Tyburn** in 1741.

Today, more money can be made by mundane pen-pushing occupations like mortgage fraud than armed robbery, as *mafioso* John Gotti noticed in the 1980s when he graduated to the New York concrete racket, which seemed easy meat compared to his previous daily grind of narcotics distribution, loan-sharking and gambling. In the eight years before the ring was smashed, the four participating families netted an estimated $8 million, extorting a levy of 1 per cent on all construction contracts over $2 million plus $2 for every cubic yard poured. But an infuriated Gotti discovered that an Israeli émigré, Michael Markowitz, had devised a way of creaming off federal and state revenues to the tune of $300 million in two years simply by shuffling paper.

Markowitz targeted the tax collected by wholesale gasoline distributors for remission to the authorities, setting up a string of dummy companies which collectively siphoned off somewhere in the region of a penny a gallon. Markowitz happily split his burgeoning proceeds with college-educated Michael Franzese of the Colombo family while Gotti slugged it out with the building trade and exacted rake-offs from flea-market operators. In the event, all the participants wound up dead or in prison, but, one step further towards legality, or at least sophistication, the criminal element fades away, leaving little more than a grey smudge of suspected fraud and exponentially increased takings.

See also **High finance**

Thompson, Edith (1894–1923)

Edith Thompson, an unhappily married book-keeper, lived with her husband Percy in the London suburb of Ilford. He beat her, but one day in June 1921 young Frederick Bywaters – a good-looking laundry steward on a P & O ocean liner – came to stay between voyages. He was a schoolmate of Edith's brother, and their families were longstanding friends.

The August Bank Holiday of 1921 turned out fine and sunny and, while sitting in the garden, the 19-year-old Bywaters overheard Percy quarrelling with his wife. The sound of Edith being thrown across the room, where she collided with a chair, prompted him to intervene. He brought the fight to a close; angry words were exchanged, the possibility of divorce mooted, and later a tearful Edith crept up the stairs to the young man's bedroom where, for the first time, they kissed. Shortly afterwards Bywaters left to live with his mother and, as extra-marital affairs go, their romance began on a relatively honourable footing. Over the next two months the pair enjoyed assignations in teashops, parks or at *thés dansants* where they shared covert embraces; 'their tune' was 'One Stolen Hour'. Percy refused to countenance a separation or a divorce and, on 9 September, the lovers finally had sexual intercourse after registering at a small hotel under false names. Bywaters sailed shortly afterwards and they consoled themselves with a passionate correspondence.

By September 1922 Bywaters was back in London. The liaison resumed, and on the afternoon of 3 October the lovers met in a London teashop. They parted to allow Edith to accompany her husband to the theatre, and that night the married couple caught the train back to Ilford and walked home down Belgrave Road.

Frederick Bywaters jumped out of the shadows. Seizing Percy by the arm, he cried, 'Why don't you get a divorce, you cad?'

'I've got her, I'll keep her and I'll shoot you,' said Percy. Bywaters pulled out his seafarer's knife. The two men struggled. 'Oh don't, don't,' Edith implored. Percy fell to the pavement, coughing blood, and Bywaters vanished into the dark while Edith rushed down the street towards a knot of distant onlookers crying, 'Oh my God, will you help me, my husband is ill; he is bleeding!' By the time a doctor arrived Percy was dead. 'Why did you not come sooner?' she sobbed.

Frederick Bywaters (left) at the October 1922 inquest into the death of his lover's husband, Percy Thompson (right). Edith, Percy's wife (centre), shows some of the sexuality she later exuded from the dock

On these unpromising facts Edith was hanged for her husband's murder. The prosecution contended that she plotted the killing with Bywaters over tea that afternoon, and in evidence – the only evidence – produced sixty-two love letters, some retrieved from Bywaters's ship's locker and others from his mother's home. In their totality Edith's letters were harmless: hundreds of pages of endearments interspersed with multitudinous schemes to break the *impasse* by elopement, divorce or even joint suicide. Among these vapourings were Edith's idiotic plans for murdering her husband. She would feed him lightbulbs 'big pieces too – not too powdered'.

According to the written record, she tried this method three times after wearying of her labours at **poisoning**. 'I'm going to try glass again occasionally – when it's safe,' she wrote. 'I've got an electric light globe this time.' Did this work? Apparently not. 'The third time he found a piece – so I've given it up – until you come home.'

The words 'until you come home' hold the key. Edith was frantic to bolster Bywaters's interest and ensure that he did come back, whatever the marital stalemate. The only avenue for progress lay in their imaginations, and Edith's medicinal constructions embraced exotic but unspecified toxins. She entreated Bywaters to send 'something to make him ill'. Then she complained, 'You said it was enough for an elephant. Perhaps it was. But you don't allow for the taste making it possible for only a small quantity to be taken.' Her husband was becoming suspicious: 'He puts great stress on the fact of the tea tasting bitter "as if something had been put in it".'

Nothing had. No trace of poison or glass was found in Percy's body. But when the extracts from her correspondence were joined end-to-end they sounded sinister in the extreme. Other incidental material made matters worse. 'I am still willing to dare all and risk all,' wrote Edith in reference to her intended abortion. It was already an uphill task to persuade the jury of the innocence of an adulteress, and her defence dared not attempt to exculpate her from husband-murder by depicting her as an adulterous abortionist, capable of child-murder.

Edith's ambiguous phrases such as 'drastic measures' were pulled into the web, and only occasionally could her barrister, Sir Henry Curtis-Bennett, demonstrate that sentences like 'He is still well' referred to the unsurprising well-being of a bronze monkey, a

gift from Bywaters. Edith tightened the noose round her neck by including news clippings of 'Poisoned chocolates' or 'Patient killed by an overdose' with her love letters. But 'Woman the Consoler' or 'Masterful Men' were the themes of more frequent inserts, and in the dock Bywaters was asked by the prosecution: 'Did you ever believe in your own mind that she herself had given any poison to her husband?'

'No,' he replied. 'It never entered my mind at all. She had been reading books. She had a vivid way of declaring herself. She would read a book and imagine herself as the character in the book.' Perhaps the defence could have dismissed Edith's letters as the gushings of a vain and silly romantic if she had kept silent in court. But, anxious to impress, this obstinate, highly strung woman insisted on testifying to prove her *truthfulness*, a grave tactical error compounded by the sexuality she oozed from the dock, and her cause suffered further damage from the judge, Mr Justice Shearman, who was opposed to adultery. He summed up against the defendants in a mood of strong moral indignation, ridiculing the notion (which had not been proposed) that 'the love of a husband for his wife is something improper because marriage is acknowledged by the law, and that the love of a woman for her lover – illicit and clandestine – is something great and noble'.

Both Bywaters and Thompson were sentenced to death. 'I say the verdict of the jury is wrong,' said Bywaters from the dock. 'Edith is not guilty.' The trial never addressed the issues. Had it been established that Edith did try to poison her husband (for which attempted murder would be the appropriate charge), it remained to prove a conspiracy for the stabbing. The **Court of Appeal** dismissed the affair as 'a squalid and rather indecent case of lust and adultery'. A petition for clemency many thousands strong was submitted to the Home Secretary, and on 6 January, as the fatal day approached, Bywaters said of Edith from his cell, 'I swear she is completely innocent. She never knew that I was going to meet them that night … She didn't commit the murder. I did. She never knew about it. She is innocent, absolutely innocent. I can't believe that they will hang her.'

Bywaters's 'confession' was driven 200 miles through the night to the Home Secretary at a country house weekend. But there was no reprieve. Edith broke down when they came to fetch her on 9 January 1923 after a night of semi-consciousness, the first woman to be executed in Britain for fifteen years. Two female warders carried her to the scaffold and there, in the words of Sir Henry Curtis-Brown, 'Mrs Thompson was hanged for immorality'.

Of necessity, Percy's role in the love triangle is as reported by Edith and Frederick.

Throne Room, The

Special lavatory. Smugglers suspected of 'body-packing' do their business in the Throne Room's dry lavatory under the watchful eye of Revenue men (or women) clad in white surgical outfits. A small quantity of water is admitted to wash the suspect's faeces into a stainless steel box fronted by a glass viewing panel and a rubber-glove insert; the compartment resembles a hi-tech nuclear enclosure. Inside this box, the precious excrement undergoes a full examination: it can be washed down with water jets, subjected to probes or gently palpated by the gloved hand. The detritus is flushed away, and any contraband collected in a shiny perspex container.

The preceding generation of equipment consisted of a colander.

Throwaways

Ted **Bundy**'s term for his victims, whom he *threw away* afterwards, dumping them from his car like garbage. But in the California of the 1970s, Patrick Kearney and David Hill, the 'Trashbag Killers', developed the idea a step further, as takeaways. They put their bagged-up victims out for collection.

Bundy was fastidious in his vocabulary, posing interrogators with delicate linguistic problems in their search for inoffensive euphemisms. To Bundy, 'people' or (even worse) 'victims' was not an acceptable wording, and one interviewer hit on the euphemism 'cargo', giving rise to the following exchange.

'Is the cargo dead or alive when you put it in the vehicle?'

'I don't like to use that terminology.'

'Is the cargo *damaged* when it's in the vehicle?'

'Yes, sometimes it's damaged and sometimes it's not.'

Thugs

The term derives from the Thuggee cult, prevalent in India from at least the middle of the sixteenth century until its suppression by the British in 1853. The devotional act consisted of strangling suitable travellers (ruling out Europeans, poets, women and defective specimens lacking a hand or nose) with a yellow and white silk strip called a *rhumal*. Since many Thugs held respectable positions in society, the act of worship entailed taking a month off to form a gang to ramble on the subcontinent's roads, killing as they went. Unsuspecting prospects were enjoined to look upwards at some fascinating sight in the sky, thus exposing their necks.

To avoid distension of the corpse, leading to discovery through disinterment, the body was slit up the stomach and, what with dead men telling no tales, the hereditary cult's existence remained largely unsuspected by Europeans. Rough estimates suggest that some 40,000 fell victim annually. A leading practitioner was one Behram, said at his trial to have 931 souls to his credit culled from the district of Oudh between 1790 and 1840. Another remarked in 1833: 'Sahib, I ceased counting when I was sure of my thousand victims.'

The sect was both discovered and ended in a few years by an English soldier-turned-magistrate, William Sleeman, who persuaded the first captured gang leader to turn Queen's evidence, betraying other gangs in return for his life. Sleeman repeated the technique, leapfrogging from gang to gang, and eventually attained the position of Superintendent for the Suppression of Thuggees.

Tichborne Claimant, The

Nineteenth-century British inheritance farce marking the outer reaches of either self-delusion or wilful cussedness.

In March 1854 the young Sir Roger Charles Tichborne set sail for South America in the hope of forgetting a blighted love affair with his cousin, Katherine Doughty. His ship, the *Bella*, foundered somewhere off Brazil; her log-book was recovered 400 miles from land.

Back in England his mother, Lady Henriette Tichborne, refused to accept that her son was dead. Said to be a woman 'of a singularly perverse, unamiable disposition', she kept a candle burning in her son's bedroom and eleven years later was still pursuing rumours of his survival with advertisements in the English and colonial press.

Over in Australia, the reading room of the Mechanics Institute in Wagga Wagga was frequented by an uncouth, semi-literate butcher, Tom Castro. There he saw the newspaper announcements, took a long hard look at the *Illustrated London News* of 1862 celebrating the enviable Tichborne estates complete with church and village in Hampshire's Itchen valley, and noted in his pocket-book: 'Some men has plenty money and no brains, and some men has plenty brains and no money. Surely men with plenty money and no brains were made for men with plenty brains and no money.'

Castro was verging on bankruptcy and so, one day in 1866, he scratched the missing baronet's initials 'RCT' on his pipe and called on his new solicitor, Mr Gibbes. At the meeting, Castro wondered aloud whether valuable property in England would be caught by any composition with his creditors. The astute Gibbes spotted the initials on the pipe-bowl and soon put two and two together, forcing Castro to admit that he was none other than the missing baronet. Then, in his new role as Sir Roger Charles Doughty Tichborne, Castro was coaxed into writing home to break the happy news of his survival.

Spelling – and grammar – were problems, but Castro requested funds by return 'has I can not get serfiance of money to come home with'. On receipt, the delighted Lady T. ascribed her long-lost son's poor showing to his expensive public school education, expressing concern that her 'poor dear Roger confuses everything in his head just as in a dream'. But neither her professional advisers nor her more conventional heirs, with whom she was already at loggerheads, were so sure.

Castro moved his family to Sydney, where he became a popular fixture, engaging a secretary, nursemaid and valet. Money flowed in, and out. Struggling to pay the bill of his hotel, he purchased it with a bouncing cheque signed 'Roger Tichborne'. By the time the draft was returned to drawer, Castro was en route to Paris, where mother and son finally met in a Paris hotel. The coarse-featured Castro, who weighed twenty-six stone and had at school been nicknamed

The effete Sir Roger (top left), Castro (second row, right), other principals and five prosperous lawyers

Bullocky on account of his near-limitless extent, was immediately recognised by Lady Tichborne as the slender, delicate nine-stone Sir Roger.

Despite her son's infirmity, which obliged him to lie facing the wall in a darkened room, Lady Tichborne (possibly out of malice) was able to pick out the unmistakable family ears. Her faith overcame Castro's childhood recollections of his grandfather (who died before he was born), the memories of his schooldays at Winchester (Sir Roger was educated at Stonyhurst) and tales of his early days as an Army trooper (Sir Roger was a commissioned officer). She arranged for Castro to receive a token allowance of £1,000 a year while the formalities were sorted out. These involved the ejection of a Colonel Lushington from Castro's ancestral seat at Tichborne House, but before matters reached this stage Lady Tichborne was dead.

Amid tremendous excitement the legal proceedings began on 10 May 1871 at the Westminster Session Court. The simple issue of whether Castro, an obvious impostor, was entitled to the Tichborne millions became obscured by so much detail that the trial ran for months. Favourable identification witnesses were called in droves; generals, colonels, JPs, clergymen, Deputy-Lieutenants, ladies and servants – over a hundred men and women of good standing swore that Castro was the long-lost baronet.

The only poor performance was put in by Castro, who displayed convincing ignorance of his former life first as a child, then as a student, and finally as an officer with the Sixth Dragoon Guards. There was

Castro doffs his hat as he arrives for his first day in court. Note his bulk

much ribaldry when he alleged that Caesar was a Greek; nor did he know what 'quadrangle' meant, although Stonyhurst boys talk of little else. Not that Castro was idle in the five years preceding the case; he studied the family's history, and hired two regimental servants to pad out gaps in his military career.

On the 102nd day of proceedings he withdrew his claim under a welter of inconsistencies. Then he was indicted for perjury in a hearing which ran for 188 days, notable for the weight of Lord Cockburn's summing-up, tipping the scales at eight and a half pounds in bound volume form. The court concluded, possibly erroneously, that Castro was a former immigrant from the East End, Arthur Orton, and sentenced him to fourteen years' hard labour. After remission for good conduct, he was released from Dartmoor in 1884 and died in destitution on April Fools' Day four years later.

Tobacco

Said, with minor inexactitude, to be prison currency. Until very recently tobacco was what was bought with prison currency, consisting of anything and everything.

In their impoverished environment, prisoners scavenge and swap what they can: pencil stubs, pins, hits of string, paper clips or scraps of cardboard. Give a man the striker from a gas lighter, add a scrap of wood, a twist of mop rope and a length of plug chain, and he will assemble a cigarette lighter. Matchsticks make matchstick models, rags turn into rag toys.

So bare and dead is life inside that released prisoners enthuse over mundane objects like door furniture. Paddy Hill, who spent sixteen years inside after his wrongful conviction for the Birmingham pub bombing, devoted his first morning of freedom in March 1991 to studying a doorknob as he allowed its implications to sink home. 'I stared at it for forty-five minutes,' he recalled a year later, 'I was almost paralysed.'

In the words of Ken Smith, author of *Inside Time*: 'In prison, which is all waste, nothing is wasted.' Discarded biros, for instance, can be turned into syringes, much in demand now that the traditional prison economy is under threat: tobacco has been replaced by narcotics. According to an inmate released in 1990, referred to in press reports as 'Cathy': 'I did my first stint in prison in the 1970s when cigarettes were the major currency.

Now money, jewellery and clothes are bartered for cannabis and heroin.'

The 1991 British report by Professor John Gunn estimated that one in ten male convicts, and one in four women, are hooked on hard drugs. No matter how resourceful the prisoners, injection equipment tends to be shared and, given the prevalence of anal sex, there can be few more fertile hotbeds for the spread of AIDS.

Tobacco smuggling remained big business with the Sicilian Mafia until the 1970s. They ran cigarettes into Italy, ultimately dealing in entire shiploads of 40,000 cases which provided gainful employment for thousands in the distribution chains. When the trade flagged towards the end of the decade, one of the old-time tobacco smugglers – the *mafioso* Nunzio La Mattina from Sicily – turned his expertise to narcotics. Thus was born the **Pizza Connection** – successor to the **French Connection** – which poured billions of dollars of heroin into America.

By 1980 La Mattina was in financial difficulties; he owed his supplier Yasar Musullu $11 million. But in the world of serious drug trafficking this is not an unimaginable sum. Musullu clocked up a career total of eight tons of **opium**, generating a profit of $57 million and, similarly, Colombia's **Escobar** cartel offered to wipe out the whole of their country's debt of $3 billion in return for legal immunity. But La Mattina was eventually murdered after reporting that one of his couriers had been taken for $1.3 million in a hold-up.

And lastly, during the Second World War, the issue of free tobacco was pressed into harness as an SS incentive scheme for shooting prisoners. Shortly after D-Day on 6 June 1944, the guards at Sylt, the most brutal of the Channel Islands' death camps, were told: 'Men, I remind you once again of the rules laid down in the sentries' orders, and I personally will give any SS man who shoots a prisoner attempting to escape three days' special leave and twenty-five cigarettes.'

As there was nowhere to escape to on the tiny island of Alderney the inmates had to be encouraged. According to survivor Otto Spehr (imprisoned as a socialist), the guards 'cut down the fence of the camp and pushed the men out – the moment they stepped over the camp boundary they were shot down'. The records of British Military Intelligence describe how the Sylt guards 'competed in getting leave by shooting prisoners for the smallest offences, for example, they threw away cigarette ends and as soon as an inmate bent down to pick them up they shot them'.

Tongs

Question: when is a **Triad** not a Triad? Answer: when it is a Tong. Or perhaps not. In America, the Chinese were long the subject of institutional racism, epitomised by the Chinese Exclusion Act of 1882 banning further immigration and denying citizenship to existing Chinese residents. So they remained (and remain) an exploited inward-looking ethnic group, crammed into the hermetic ghettos of Chinatown where they established their own town halls or 'Tongs'. It has never been clear whether these tongs are merely self-help associations or straightforward overseas branches for illegal Hong Kong syndicates. Nor did it seem to matter much, as long as the Chinese kept to themselves.

Mock Duck was an early Tong leader, head of New York's 'Hip Sings' (hence, to be 'hip'). From 1900 to 1906 Duck waged a bloody war with his rival Tom Lee for Chinatown's **opium** dens, and hundreds perished before the two gangs finally signed the 1906 peace treaty at the home of Judge Warren W. Foster. Duck was an idiosyncratic marksman. On scenting trouble, he would drop to a crouching position in the streets and close his eyes tight. Then he blazed away madly in all directions, accounting for dozens of 'enemies'.

Even the so-called 'hatchet wars' of the 1920s were regarded as a private affair, and it still takes a white corpse to flush out media attention, a trait manifested in San Francisco on 4 September 1977 after three Joe Boys raided the Golden Dragon restaurant gunning for the Wah Ching Sings in a struggle for dominion of the firework business. The attackers left four diners and one waiter dead, plus eleven wounded, all innocent bystanders, and suddenly the media were everywhere. In the words of a San Francisco cop, 'We had some fifty gang murders before the Golden Dragon, they were all Chinese-to-Chinese. The moment the violence spread beyond the Chinese, the politicians were jumping on camera.'

Certainly the Tongs are excellent in parts, fulfilling many charitable community functions. Membership is legal. But according to a Hong Kong police officer, the American Tongs are public fronts for the Triads: 'Rest assured some members are criminal and are using the Tong's apparatus to control everything from gambling to narcotics.'

Since the mid-1960s each Tong has attracted the

allegiance of a particular youth gang, such as the Green Dragons or the Ghost Shadows, who terrorise the neighbourhood, driving home the doctrine of government through intimidation. The gangs extort 'protection' from local tradesmen and make examples of those (like Mon Hsiung Ting of New York's Tien Chau chop house, shot on 16 July 1989) stubborn enough to refuse. Neighbourhood restaurant openings are welcome events, triggering an inaugural payment of 'lucky money', often a multiple of the number 108 in honour of the contingent of Buddhist monks who defended the Shaolin monastery in the seventeenth century. A thousand and eighty dollars is thus a common backhander, paid in the 'red envelope' traditional among the Chinese for gifts.

At the least, the Tongs provided a tempting takeover target in the Hong Kong criminal exodus of 1997, and the word is that the Tsung Tsin Association, one of New York's wealthiest, is now (if it was not before) a front for the Sun Yee On **triad**.

See also **Recruitment**

Torso Murders, The

In a three-year span between 1934 and 1938, someone in Cleveland, Ohio claimed the lives of a good dozen down-and-outs, some men, some women, in general mutilating or dismembering the bodies but invariably cutting off their heads, six of which were never found.

The 'Torso Murderer' is sometimes reckoned America's first serial killer and, as with **Jack the Ripper**, the phenomenon left the police floundering. The case shows detection in a transitional stage, with intensive and traditional efforts directed at establishing the victims' identities. With luck and application, this occasionally revealed who they were, but not who the killer was, and eventually a 'Torso Clinic', the forerunner of the DeSalvo seminar, was convened. The thirty-four professionals attending it included policemen, pathologists and medical consultants who agreed on seven 'points', groping their way towards a primitive profile. Otherwise, efforts concentrated on grilling those singled out by neighbours and acquaintances, including such exotic local deviants as the 'Voodoo Doctor', the 'Cave Dweller', the 'Chicken Freak', the 'Mad Russian' and the 'Crazy Greek'. Three hundred suspects were interviewed, thousands of telephone calls fielded, but for all his flair, Eliot Ness,

Cleveland's Director of Public Safety, was at a loss: 'The murderer doesn't seem to leave many clues. This man seems to specialise in the sort of person nobody is likely to miss.'

When Ness made his move, it was supremely ill-judged, sullying a fine career. On 17 August, backed by eleven squad cars, two vans and three firetrucks, he cordoned off the shantytown under the Eagle Street ramp at midnight and battered his way into the down-and-outs' hovels, dragging off sixty-three derelicts to the police cells and then searching shack-to-shack to discover nothing more incriminating than two dogs and three kittens. Ness defended his actions on the grounds that he was hunting for clues or, in the alternative, bent on saving potential victims, and then had the settlements razed to the ground.

The case started on 5 September 1934 when a carpenter out for a walk noticed a curious object protruding from the sands on the Lake Erie foreshore. It was the lower half of a woman, severed at the waist and knees, and this section proved a perfect match for the upper remains discovered in North Perry by a local handyman. A fortnight later two boys playing in the Kingsbury Run, a railway cutting site of a Great Depression shantytown, stumbled over a headless, emasculated body and, thirty feet away, in the thick brush, the police located another corpse. Both were cleanly presented and tidily arranged, legs and heels together. They had been killed elsewhere, washed, transported by car and then ferried down a steep incline to the burial site. Their genitalia lay discarded a few yards away, and ten feet beyond the detectives noticed hair growing out of the dirt. They exposed a severed head planted in the ground, and on post-mortem it emerged that decapitation was the cause of death. Although an inevitable consequence, the technique is rarely adopted by murderers.

The *Plain Dealer* reported it as 'the most bizarre double murder', and the smart money was on a perverted love triangle. The killings were not linked to the Lake Erie corpse, nor were the next three victims, all neatly dismembered. But the upper half of a headless trunk found in Kingsbury Run on 10 September 1936 ensured that twenty-five police were assigned to the case, with the perpetrator dubbed the 'Horrible Headhunter' by the press. In the absence of any promising leads, on 14 September Ness summoned a think-tank, the 'Torso Clinic', which agreed on the premise that the killer was demented but not insane and might well be leading an ostensibly normal life. It seemed that he possessed a definite knowledge of human anatomy on a par with, say, a hunter or a butcher; that he was large and strong, lived in or near Kingsbury Run and had access to a laboratory or workshop. His *modus operandi* was to befriend hobos and derelicts; the contents of their stomachs suggested that he snared them with offers of food and perhaps shelter; the lack of resistance cuts or signs of restraint implied that some were decapitated in their sleep. In today's parlance, the killings were highly **organised**, but at the time the sexual motivation was denied. Apparently, the bodies were dismembered simply to facilitate transportation, but it is hard to see how severing their genitalia helped.

Four more corpses were in the pipeline, and by the time the last two came to light on the waterfront on 16 August 1938 Cleveland was in a state of hysteria. The National Guard's 112th Observation Squadron overflew the city taking purposeless aerial photographs and, in the week starting 22 August, Ness organised a house-to-house search of the Roaring Third precinct. Six teams checked an area covering ten square miles, finding nothing. Perhaps they were expecting a blood-caked charnel house, but the dismembering room, its bodies flown, could have

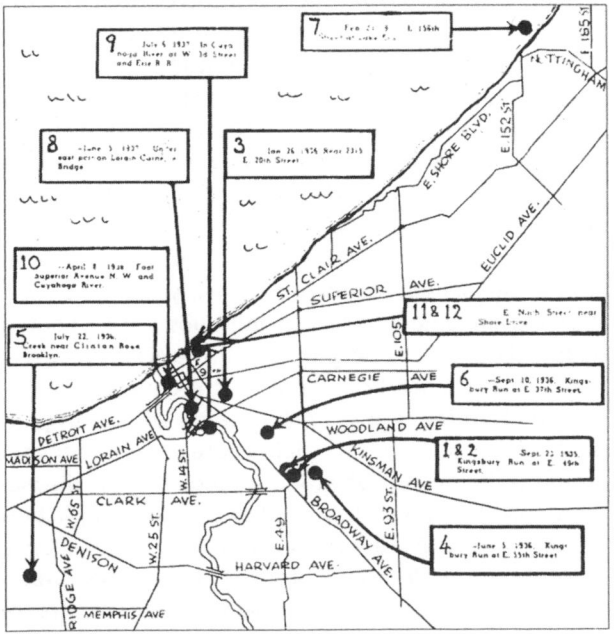

Locations of the 'torso' bodies in Cleveland

presented an innocuous aspect. Years later, Ness revealed that he had a homosexual suspect, pseudonymously known as Gaylord, under close watch. After repeated interviews, Gaylord put Ness to his proof, but before the case was fully established, he confined himself to a mental home and died the following year.

Ness made no mention of this lead at the time. Contemporary excitement centred on slaughter-house worker Frank Dolezal, arrested on 5 July 1939. He had actually lived with the victim of 26 January 1936, Florence Portillo, and was a habitué of a run-down corner tavern on 20th Street frequented by all three identified victims. Eventually he confessed: 'I hit her with my fist. She fell into the bathroom and hit her head ... Then I took a knife and cut off her head. Then I cut off her legs, then her arms ...' But none of Dolezal's dates or facts tallied and, the moment he gained access to a lawyer, he recanted, claiming that his admissions had been beaten out of him. After he committed suicide in police custody on 24 August, it emerged that his interrogation had left permanent scars and six broken ribs.

Then there was the letter, perhaps from the real killer, mailed to the Chief of Police on 21 December 1938: 'You can rest easy now as I have gone out to sunny California for the winter. I felt bad operating on those people but science must advance. I shall soon astound the medical profession ... What did their loss mean in comparison to all the hundreds of sick and disease-twisted bodies?' That same year a longshoreman, Emil Fronek, was almost kidnapped off his pitch by police and made to repeat a detailed story of his days as a drifter in 1935. Fronek related in convincing minutiae how a bogus doctor befriended him, inveigling him to a second-floor apartment on 55th Street with the promise of a meal and a pair of shoes. Fronek was convulsed by stomach pangs as he ate and, deducing that he had been drugged, staggered out before losing consciousness. He woke up three days later barely alive. His assailant was five feet six and weighed about 150 pounds, with a light complexion and sandy hair. Fronek spent several fruitless days with the police hunting the shifting tenements for the office.

Cleveland saw its last Torso corpse in 1938, but in 1942 three more corpses with comparable mutilations were discovered in freight cars outside New Castle, Pennsylvania. A final, similar body was discovered on 22 July 1950.

See also **Heads, living, Untouchables**

Torture

Like democracy, torture can be traced directly to the Greeks and is mentioned in Aristophanes' *The Frogs* as the appropriate method for interrogating 'human-footed stock' (slaves). It descended via the Romans without adulteration to the Middle Ages and beyond, playing a role in official criminal procedure until its abolition in the 1800s throughout most of Western Europe.

The ancient and irrational dogma of the exceptional crime, so dangerous to the state that anything (for instance, torture for treason) was permissible in its prosecution, has been largely superseded. In its stead stands the modern concept of subversive crimes against an all-powerful, but strangely vulnerable, state that are so dangerous that anything is permissible in their prosecution (for instance, torture for suspected treason). Following its primary eradication in the first quarter of the nineteenth century, torture proliferated like cancer, starting in the colonies and now practised officially or otherwise in one country out of three.

From the twelfth century the history of torture was entwined with the history of **justice**, except in England where the reforms of Henry II established a legal structure that all but dispensed with it. Elsewhere, torture became a means of obtaining justice. It extracted confessions, in many cases regarded as the only reliable form of first-hand evidence.

Since the systematic infliction of agony comprised part of the legal process, its Continental exercise was finely graded according to precedent and protocol, forming the subject of thousands of pages of learned discourse on a par with, say, ecclesiastical law; presumably, ambitious mothers boasted of their sons' preferment as attorneys in torture.

The public prosecutor's first duty was to establish the truth by other means; in theory, torture was his last resort for cases where other evidence proved insufficient. A strong *prima facie* case would automatically precipitate the procedure, but the accused could lodge an interlocutory appeal, contending either that the judge had failed to satisfy the prerequisite evidential criteria for torturing, or that he was an exempted person, for instance a knight, professor, pregnant woman or king.

Even if he went down on appeal, the defendant was entitled to a properly conducted torture session. First the instruments of his **dismemberment** were ritually displayed, and their anatomical application expounded in a last-ditch endeavour to concentrate his mind. During the session, a medical expert remained in attendance, together with a notary and, of course, the judge who put the questions. Prudent prosecutors restrained their zeal for fear of provoking a civil action for improper torturing, generally espousing methods hallowed by traditional usage. Nothing new, nothing showy, was the protocol; the infliction of finely calibrated torment was a Christian undertaking. Many tortures were only administered for a specific and limited time governed by however long it took the judge to recite the Creed – a ghastly process, but still infinitely preferable to the random barbarities inflicted outside the system by, for instance, the seventeenth-century French buccaneer Montbars of Languedoc, who would slit his victim's stomach, wrench out one end of the intestines, nail them to a post, and then use a firebrand to compel the man to dance to death as he unravelled his guts. He was particularly unpleasant to Spaniards.

Under the law, admissions counted for little until repeated in court. The defendant could recant, but his professional advisers would explain that this only courted another bout against an increased presumption of guilt, since he had already confessed. It is unlikely that hard-core enthusiasts ever observed the theoretical niceties, nor were the results entirely reliable. As the eighteenth century progressed, dispassionate observers discerned a definite tendency among tortured suspects to stake claims to murders which they could not conceivably have committed or even to admit responsibility for ones that had never happened (see **False confessions**).

In Britain, the best remembered torturer is Charles Richardson, sentenced to twenty-five years on 6 June 1967. His implements included golf clubs, knives, lighted cigars, pliers (for ripping out teeth), electric fires (for toasting) and a hand-operated electric generator.

Torture today is the stock-in-trade of the **organised** serial killer, who deliberately controls and prolongs the process of extinguishing life. Fine distinctions must be drawn. It is not the offender's infliction of pain that produces arousal but the victim's response to it. In the words of **Quantico**'s Gregg McCrary, 'These offenders make their victims scream and beg for mercy, beg for their lives and so on. This is why **Chikatilo** stabbed them in a way which would cause a slow and painful death. It was far more grati-fying for him to do so.'

Here, torture is equated with sex, but in another mutation the sadism is a prelude to sexual defilement, where the victim's degradation justifies her death. According to FBI Agent Robert Hazelwood, one killer explained to his victims, 'First I'm going to torture you in the most horrible and painful manner I can think of. Then I'm going to abuse you sexually in the most degrading way I can think of. Then I'll kill you in the slowest and most painful way I can conceive ... Do you have any questions?'

Another murderer tortured a prostitute for six weeks before the kill. Robert Andrew Berdella, from Kansas, tormented his bound captives for days, beating them with boards, spiking them with needles, using bleach, drain cleaner and electricity, and sticking his fingers into their eyeballs. Interviewed in 1992 he asserted that he 'never found bondage and non-consensual sex that stimulating'. Asked to reconcile this view with his track record, he replied: 'It was done to perhaps control these individ-uals, to modify them, to make them controllable so they would be consensual.'

After four days of torment, his sixth and last victim was too broken to run away and only required physi-cal restraint when Berdella went out. Otherwise, like one of Dahmer's **zombies**, the captive ambled round the house with his will broken. Asked what the process had accomplished, Berdella replied, 'A willing sex toy.' Individuals who were pre-consensual – that is, *willing* to be tied up – never became victims when they were at his mercy. They were happy to stay anyway.

See also **de Sade**, **Sex crimes**, **Terror**

Trading justice

Term for English parish magistrates from whom a convict could secure acquittal or release in return for drink, money or sex. The practice was widespread, perhaps the most famous exponent being Thomas De Veil (d. 1746), who needed supplementary income for his army of twenty-five legitimate children and droves of bastard offspring. An avid fornicator, De Veil had a special bedchamber leading off his Bow Street office.

De Veil's early life displayed a spectacular talent for dissipation, and as a trading justice he was unusual

not for his run-of-the-mill corruption but for his conscientious dedication. Not only did he think like a detective, he became one in response to approaches for outside advice, thereby anticipating the first fictional consulting sleuth – Sherlock Holmes – by more than a century.

De Veil's triumphs included having the rare acumen for the period to check a suspect's knife (with a broken-off tip) against the innards of a forced lock to a burgled house. In June 1741 he solved the mystery of the missing Mr Penny, Principal of Clement's Inn, by rational interrogation of the suspect and a thor-ough search for the body. These common-sense procedures were as rewarding as they were novel. Penny's body was found stuffed into an outside privy, head first, his throat slit by a disaffected servant with a fruit knife.

See also **Fielding**

Traffic lights

Until 1930, New York traffic lights were switched off at three in the morning. This gave late-night robbers a clear run in their getaway vehicles, and the decision to keep the signals on round the clock had an appreci-able impact on crime patterns. In Joe Valachi's words: 'It's getting tougher all the time ... After all, if I'm being chased by one cop's car and I go through these lights, I will draw attention and have a hundred cars chasing me. Jesus!'

So Valachi decided to get out of the uncertainties of robbery and into something more secure. He joined the Mafia. But perhaps he need not have worried. According to writer John Mortimer, the late and unlamented financial fraudster Robert Maxwell gave his chauffeur standing orders to shoot red lights at seventy miles an hour during his excursions through late-night London: presumably an indication of his disrespect for rules and regulations which, at the other end of the scale, impelled him to grand larceny.

In the paranoid regimes of modern Russia (see **Torture**), the Lubianka prison incorporated a compli-cated system of internal passageways with red and green signal lights at every corner. A warder escorting a prisoner who happened upon a red light knew that another inmate under guard was approaching in the opposite direction, and to prevent the minimal solace of the sight of another imprisoned wretch, the prisoner was pushed face first to the wall and stood in a recess until his fellow-sufferer had passed by.

See also **Separate System**

Train robbery, invention of

An American invention pioneered by the Reno Brothers, preying on the state of Indiana from their Rockford headquarters. In October 1866 they stopped an eastbound train on the Ohio and Mississippi Railroad and netted $13,000 from the first small safe. Their third train robbery on 22 May 1868 did better, yielding $97,000 in gold and government bonds.

The five brothers – one of whom, like Zeppo Marx, was out of his depth and bore the distinguishing soubriquet of 'Honest' Reno – excited such fear and loathing by their brutality that after three of them (two captured by Pinkerton's men) ended up in the New Albany jail it was stormed by a specially assembled party of fifty-six vigilantes. Capped in red flannel hoods, the lynch mob pulled in by train in the early hours of 12 December 1868. Outside the jail, lawman Thomas Fullenlove stood his ground.

'I am the sheriff,' he called to the threatening crowd, 'the highest peace officer in the county and if you respect the law you will not dare shoot me.' According to Dan Walsh's contemporary account, 'a dozen revolvers belched at him'.

The three Renos and an accomplice were hanged by the mob, swinging on the pendent bodies and nearly pulling off their heads. Previously, Frank and Simon

Reno had taken refuge across the border in Windsor – a sort of Canadian Dodge City – and narrowly escaped drowning during extradition when their tug was sliced in half by a steamer.

There are reports of train hold-ups in the American South dating to the 1850s. In a variant from this era, the outlaw John J. Moore was charged not with robbing a train but stealing it. In his endeavours to escape a frontier posse, Moore jumped a locomotive and then leaped to safety. The runaway engine ploughed up yards of track before grinding to a halt and, determined to get some satisfaction, the railroad prosecuted the outlaw with theft. With unwonted subtlety for a frontier court, Moore's attorney got his client off by arguing that a train could not be 'stolen' unless the thief first removed it from, rather than moved it along, the tracks.

Tranquilandia

The South American drugs industry was once a low-key affair, the cocaine brewed up in thousands of tiny 'kitchens', little more than ramshackle sheds producing five or ten kilos at a time. In 1982 the cartel put the business on a modern footing, appropriating an uninhabited 6.2-square-mile island in the province of Caqueta in southern Colombia, deep in the rain forests and surrounded by the Yari river. There they erected a streamlined industrial complex with a capacity of four tons a week, starting the operation by ferrying in tools and heavy materials by helicopter to build a landing strip.

Two gigantic cocaine laboratories, known as *Villa Coca* and *Coquilandia*, were constructed. Most of the site administration was handled from *Tranquilandia, a* third encampment that included executive offices, a clubhouse for the pilots, a canteen, a medical clinic and workshops. The buildings incorporated decent air-conditioning; the workers' sleeping quarters, furnished with bunk beds and mattresses, had pleasantly tiled washing and lavatory facilities. The overall workforce ran into the hundreds; there was no pension scheme, but the remuneration package included $100 a week (three times the local minimum wage), guaranteed flights home four times a year, and celebratory turkey dinners for exceeding production quotas. For leisure, staff amused themselves with videos, table games and porn magazines. Like any

Unidentified train robbers from 1878

other industrial facility, the factory was plastered with signs like 'Please keep this place tidy' or 'Do not enter without proper authorisation from the kitchen'.

For protection, the Cartel relied on the Communist Revolutionary Armed Forces of Colombia, a guerrilla group, and the dénouement, when it came, resembled the last reel of a James Bond film – the assault on Mr Big's lair.

Tranquilandia's existence came to light through its massive appetite for ethyl ether, the surgical anaesthetic constituting the single most efficient solvent for manufacturing cocaine. The Colombian government clamped down on imports, so it had to be sought abroad.

American manufacturers were briefed to tip off the Drugs Enforcement Agency when approached by a 'suspicious' character, and characters do not come any more suspicious than the Cartel's front man Francisco Torres. He ordered a huge consignment of ethyl ether from the J. T. Baker Company in unlabelled barrels, enough to process sixty-six tons of cocaine, and proffered the $300,000 purchase price in cash.

The DEA allowed the deal to go through, fitting the first batch of barrels with electronic transmitters the size of cigarette packs, and satellite surveillance garnered photographs of a busy jungle airstrip in a theoretically deserted part of Caqueta.

On 10 March 1984 the camp was hit by an armed raid backed by two helicopters and a light plane. The communist guerrillas fought a spirited rearguard action, allowing senior management to get clear by air. Another hundred employees melted into the jungle along specially prepared escape routes. Only forty-five of the most menial workers were captured.

But the haul in material was impressive. At Tranquilandia alone police recovered 2,500 kilos of cocaine, nineteen machine-guns and rifles, one mortar, four tractors, four electrical generators and seven portable radios; the other installations yielded fifteen laboratories, ten washing machines, four aeroplanes and a helicopter. The street value of the cocaine exceeded $1 billion; the river turned white when it was tipped.

The officer behind the raid, Colonel Jaime Ramirez, avoided retaliation for some time; he was not murdered until 17 November 1985. But the Justice Minister Rodrigo Lira Bonilla, who inspired the crackdown, paid for his temerity almost at once, on 30 April 1984, machine-gunned in his official Mercedes,

hit eight times with an Ingram .45. His head only just stayed on.

See also **Escobar**

Treadwheel

Invented by Samuel Cubitt, one of the dynasty who built Belgravia. He devised the treadwheel in 1817 after an approach from an Ipswich magistrate concerned to suppress widespread civil disorder in East Anglia, which was prompted largely by hunger. His prison machine would now rate as an instrument of **torture**.

The treadwheel, or treadmill, consisted of a revolving cylinder of iron and wood some six feet in diameter, like a paddle wheel with a stepped outside surface. As one more refinement of the **Separate System**, convicts were prevented from fraternising with their neighbours slaving alongside by the visual barrier of individual slatted stalls.

Generally the inmates faced two daily sessions of three hours. No one was exempt, neither old men nor pregnant women. The approved rate of climb was forty-eight to fifty steps a minute, and in the course of his day a man might ascend some 10,000 feet (about two vertical miles) while remaining exactly where he was.

The treadmill was enthusiastically embraced by the public who enjoyed the ponderous spectacle, rather as audiences used to flock to the films of Tarkovsky. Magistrates too were admirers, one accurately endorsing the device as 'the most tiresome, distressing, exemplary punishment that has ever been contrived by human ingenuity'. Sometimes careless prisoners were mangled in the machinery.

Unlike the **crank**, the treadmill was not invariably pointless. The occasional prison derived some small benefit by harnessing it to pump water or grind corn. At the turn of the twentieth century, thirteen remained in operation, and their use was not suspended (as an excessive form of hard labour) until April Fools' Day 1902. Five years later the installation at York Castle prison was dismantled and sold to Madame Tussaud's.

Triads

Chinese secret societies. Their **initiation** rite was recently described by a British recruit of the Sun Lee On Triad, inducted with twenty other participants:

'There was a small shrine in the room, with a statue of an ancient Chinese warlord. We were each given a stick or two of incense, which was lit. Then we recited the thirty-six oaths, extinguishing one incense after each oath. We all stood in a circle and they pricked our middle fingers with the needle. A drop of blood from each of us was mixed with water in a bowl. The bowl was passed around and we all had to take a drink.' Then an egg with a face drawn on it was put before the group. To symbolise the fate of informers, they each knifed it.

New recruits are known as Blue Lanterns in allusion to the lamps traditionally hung on the porches of bereaved families; the ceremony represents the end of the novice's former life and his rebirth as a hood.

Today's Triads are more interested in money than ritual, now regarded as mumbo jumbo for which an hour may suffice. In China, the rites originally lasted for up to three days, with recruits clad in silk robes, passing through the massed ranks of members, 'crossing the mountain of knives' before attaining the central altar. After the ceremonial decapitation of three dummies, demonstrating the penalty for betrayal, sharp swords were pressed into each initiate's chest. 'Which is stronger, the blade of the knife or your heart?' demanded the Master. The oath of loyalty was recited as the recruits rose to their feet; bamboo paraphernalia made it difficult to stand up without falling, and if the new member toppled forward, he could – theoretically at least – die on the sword.

In those days the Triads possessed a political purpose as Chinese nationalists. The first Triad was founded by the five surviving Foochow monks after their valiant 1674 resistance against the Manchu dynasty, and the gangs took popular root in Hong Kong following the failure of the 1851 Taiping Rebellion. It was during this period that they turned criminal and, after the 1911 revolution, General Chiang Kai-shek offered them unlimited underworld control in China and a leading role in his government.

The British kept the Triads in check in Hong Kong until the Japanese occupation of 1941, when the invaders delegated the gangs to control the colony's illegal businesses. As part of the deal, the invaders destroyed all Hong Kong police records and, after the war, in association with criminal elements from Triads in China monopolising the **opium** supply in South-east Asia, the Hong Kong syndicates were perfectly poised to play a leading role in the heroin bonanza.

Meanwhile, Triads infiltrated the Hong Kong Royal Police in strength. In the 1970s, the Independent Commission Against Corruption discovered that the five key Chinese staff sergeants inside the Triad Bureau were themselves Triads. Given advance warning, in 1974 the 'Five Dragons' fled to Vancouver where they spent staggeringly, acquiring an office building for $60 million. They paid cash.

Hong Kong today is riddled with Triads. Their traditional rackets in vice, protection, loan-sharking and gambling are themselves a billion-dollar business, permeating the minutiae of daily life, like buying a car, renting a flat or applying for a liquor licence. The dazzling **narcotics** profits of the past two decades enabled diversification into legitimate commercial operations – home decoration, wholesalers, hotels, car dealerships, casinos and banks. Meanwhile the income from narcotics continues unabated.

Comparatively, the Mafia are very small beer; their 'made' associates across the United States total perhaps 1,700 whereas Hong Kong is believed to contain some fifty gangs, with a membership between 150,000 and 300,000. Pitched gun-battles with the police are routine.

Triad control extends back to the **Golden Triangle** – where well-armed, private armies up to 15,000-strong protect the world's **opium** supply and its derivatives, morphine and heroin – and forwards to the international network of narcotics distribution.

With the expiration of the British lease on Hong Kong in 1997, Triads are searching for somewhere to settle. A vast criminal exodus looms; even the arrival of law-abiding Chinese in a host country establishes communities ripe for oppression. San Francisco is the likely first stop; advance teams have been in place since the mid-1980s, when the city was awash with independent Chinese banks and big buyers paying cash for prime property. New York may be next in line. The city contains about 50 per cent of America's half-million hard-core heroin addicts, each of whom (very roughly) has a $20,000-a-year habit, producing a gross revenue of $5 billion. This is a market worth going for, and the Triads have gone for it. In 1984, 5 per cent of the city's drugs came courtesy of the 'Chinese Connection' from South-east Asia; this is now closer to 80 per cent.

As ever, Britain lags behind. There are only four gangs, and police are currently investigating allegations about the stranglehold on the Chinese vegetable trade. But stories of protection, blackmail, loan sharking and credit card fraud are on the increase; in July 1992 the police raided a London brothel operated by the 14K gang. Working girls were flown in from Southeast Asia, and plied their trade in conditions little better than serfdom.

There is no call for complacency. According to a Hong Kong police superintendent: 'The Triads are a totally enclosed group of criminal societies. It has taken us years to try and understand the background of these criminal groups and to develop some methods of fighting them. In Canada and the United States and in Europe, law enforcement is at least thirty years behind.'

See also **Dutch**

Trials of life

John Gotti, the Mafia mobster, acquired a reputation as the 'Teflon Don' for his numerous non-sticking charges. But the first legal onslaught in 1986 never looked like achieving anything else.

During the early 1980s a woman prosecutor with New York's Eastern District, Diane Giacalone, decided to go it alone, mounting a case against Gotti without the help of either the FBI or the Organised Crime Task Force. Giacalone's principal information on Gotti's crimes centred on fragmentary suggestions of illegal 'tribute' skimmed from the 1980 neighbourhood robberies on IBI armoured cars.

It was Mafia custom to demand a percentage of the takings from unauthorised felonies on their patch; the payments made 'out of respect' constituted a tax on robbers. Repeated instances of such extortion could amount to 'a pattern of racketeering', and on this insubstantial basis Giacalone put in train the first Gotti case, *United States v. Aniello Dellacroce et al*.

Her legal colleagues were sceptical. But in 1985 she discovered that for sixteen years Willie Boy Johnson, a trusted Gotti aide, had played a double role as a deep-throat FBI informer. She charged him too, hoping to force Johnson to save his skin and talk in court.

Advice from her colleagues was unanimous: the case would merely blow Johnson's cover, jeopardising the FBI's operation against upper echelons of the Gambino clan. In any case they had Willie Boy figured as too loyal (rather than too scared) to betray Gotti.

This proved correct. Giacalone's other trump card, the informer Willie Batista, fled from his safe-house

Gambino family godfather John Gotti in transitional sartorial style, arriving for his 1986 trial in safari suit

as the pressure to testify mounted. With her two main witnesses *hors de combat*, there was hardly a case to answer. Nevertheless, Gotti spent much of the trial in prison, bail refused because of a 1984 fracas when he beat up a lorry driver for hooting; proceedings halted when the trucker saw his assailant's name in the papers and suffered an abrupt loss of memory, immortalised in the *New York Post* headline, 'I forgotti'.

The prosecution took refuge in the evidence of the hood James Cardinali, one of the original IBI robbers. But under cross-examination, Cardinali explained his prolific contradictions. 'Mr Slotnik,' he told defence counsel, 'I lie a lot.' Another prosecution witness, James Sanetore, failed to impress when asked whether his criminal career included scorching a woman's bosoms with cigarettes. 'Absolutely no,' he replied. 'All we did was tie her on the bed and throw burning matches on her breast.'

Gotti took violently against one of his more restrained attorneys, Jeffrey Hoffman. During cross-examination, Gotti sent a note saying, 'Sit down or you're dead'. Gotti preferred the ranting circus-style of Bruce Cutler, a former football player and wrestler who launched the defence by impugning the indictment as 'something to make anyone retch and vomit'. As the trial progressed, Cutler became assimilated into Mafia culture, affecting a *capo* outfit of blue socks, blue shirt and blue suit. His fellow-attorneys addressed him as *Don Brucino* and interrupted him, midflow, to hand advisory notes which read: 'Fuck you'. But Cutler proved unembarrassable, man enough to assert without shame that the Gambino headquarters at the Ravenite was a social club for doddery Italian gentlemen of leisure.

Detective Michael Falciano (see **Carrier pigeons**) also achieved fame with his characterisation of mobster Angelo Ruggerio. 'How should I describe him?' Falciano pondered. 'Animal or human? He looked like a fire pump.' Asked if he still had the notes he habitually scribbled on the back of his hands, Falciano replied: 'No, I bathe a lot.'

The trial dragged on for two sombre years, concluding with the performance of bank robber Matthew Traynor, originally earmarked as a prosecution witness. Appearing for the defence, Traynor came across as another obvious liar, affirming that Giacalone had offered the inducement of a pair of her panties to sniff in return for his allegiance. The outraged Giacalone attempted to strike his testimony from the record, in effect conceding that her potential witnesses were worthless.

On 13 March 1987 all the defendants were cleared of everything. Gotti emerged from the courtroom as an immortal, a gossip-column hero: 'Nobody can touch us now.' Willie Boy Johnson survived until 29 August 1988, cut down by nineteen bullets.

Gotti remained at liberty for two more trials and the best part of five years. But on 2 April 1992, with Cutler barred from the courtroom as the Mafia's 'house lawyer', he went down on charges of racketeering and murder, convicted on overwhelming evidence in a properly structured case (see **Techies**).

Gotti is scheduled to spend the rest of his life behind bars with little to look forward to, apart from film versions of his life, and the three shirts and trousers, 65 per cent polyester, that comprise standard prison issue.

He always seemed destined for some such fate. In his words, he 'wasn't born with four fucking cents', the youngest of a construction worker's five children, and his impressionable years in New York's Italian Harlem instilled a profound sense of awe for those mysterious men who spent all day lounging outside the local Palma Boys Club. Gotti's father sweated his life away for a pittance, but these men, topped by their standard grey fedoras with a three-inch brim and clad in immaculate pinstripe suits, never worked. Yet their pockets bulged with banknotes; diamond pinky rings flashed on their fingers, and they paid likely-looking kids $5 to fetch a coffee, or $10 for a shoe shine. Their black sedans gleamed in showroom condition, beautiful women hung on their arms, and the police treated them with deference. Much as his parents might decry these potent figures of respect as 'bad men' and insist on the alternative virtues of thrift, much as his school might promote the merits of self-help and citizenship, it proved hard to ignore the realities of ghetto life.

Gotti's role model, at the age of seven, was Albert 'the Executioner' Anastasia and, after his assassination on 25 October 1957, the neighbourhood hummed with speculation on the affairs of great men. At school Gotti developed a swagger, always fighting, always in trouble, using his explosive temper to secure loyalty. Teachers called it a 'discipline problem', but Gotti had followers enough at school and outside, dominating his local Fulton-Rockaway gang. He ended his education at sixteen and, hoping to emulate his hero Anastasia, modelled himself on Richard Widmark's Tommy Udo in *Kiss of Death* down to the death-rasp chuckle. Gotti found his first toehold running illegal bets for former schoolmates and, out in the world – its bars, pool halls, businesses and rackets regulated by Mafia-sanctioned operations – he inevitably came to the notice of organised crime in a trial of strength, taking them on in order to be taken on by them and, later, taking them over.

See also **Decline**

Trolling

An active search for victims. Serial killers operate on a highly individual emotional cycle; 'trolling' ('Whom shall I murder?') marks the compulsive stage following the so-called 'aura phase', the shadowy period when morality and taboos progressively fade away ('I might as well murder again') as the killer succumbs to obsessive **fantasising**.

For the hunt itself, each killer haunts a favoured locale, be it a department store, co-ed dormitory, playground or rural road: Gacy trolled in the demi-monde of male hustlers, **Bundy** on Seattle campus, and **Dahmer** in a shopping precinct.

Once a victim is identified, the killer 'stalks' from a distance before beginning the process of 'wooing' to secure the target's confidence as a preliminary to luring him or her into the trap. Gacy disarmed his targets by offering a job; Bundy would advance a self-effacing request for assistance; and Dahmer typically suggested that his mark share a couple of beers or pose as a photographic model for a few dollars.

The ensuing 'murder phase' is said by the psychologist Joel Norris to constitute a ritual re-enactment of the disastrous experiences of the killer's childhood. One murderer who chased a young playmate with a hatchet favoured a hatchet in his adult murders. Another, Gerald Stano (see **Body language**), acquired most of his estimated thirty-six victims by specialising in those wearing blue, a colour habitually worn by his brother and childhood rival. As a child the 'co-ed killer' Edmund **Kemper** stole his sister's Christmas present, a doll, and ripped off its head; as an adult, he did the same to his female victims. Gacy recited the 23rd psalm, from his purer days, while strangling his victims slowly in his basement, and in more general terms, the killers regurgitate the abuse, and particularly the sexual abuse, vented on them as children. Thus Philadelphia's Joseph Kallinger was adopted by Austrian immigrants who flogged him with a cat-o'-nine tails, held his hand over a naked flame as a punishment for stealing, and threatened to castrate him. After being abused at knife-point, he took to masturbating while clutching a knife and, his wiring irreparably crossed, experienced orgasm on killing his son in 1975.

After the death comes the totem phase (see **Souvenirs**), where the killer messes around with the body, dismembering it, taking pictures, and burying bits in special places. Then comes the aftermath, the pit of Phase Seven – black depression.

But one inexorable day, it is time to start all over again.

Tropmann, Jean Baptiste (1848–70)

An early French serial killer (concentrating on Kincks) who inspired a genuinely festive execution. A violent homosexual loner, the young Tropmann found his niche by disposing of an entire family. He picked one with six children.

First Tropmann befriended the prosperous Mr Kinck, and on 25 August 1869 he took his new acquaintance on a rural expedition to inspect an imaginary workshop making counterfeit gold coins. Out in the country, Tropmann murdered him with a glass of wine laced with prussic acid. He cut the body up, hiding it under a heap of stones in an old moat.

Thereafter Tropmann maintained contact with the family, assuring them of the father's well-being, and on 7 September he despatched his second Kinck, luring Master Gustave into the countryside and mangling rather than stabbing him to death. Next he persuaded Mrs Kinck to accompany him with her five surviving children to meet her husband, mysteriously insisting that she bring all their papers with her – birth certificates, title deeds and leases. Paying off their cab at Pantin, outside Paris, Tropmann dismounted announcing, 'Well, youngsters, we've decided to stay here.' Then he killed them in a field, disembowelling two-year-old Hortense, butchering little Achille with a spade, strangling Emile and Henry with their mufflers, impaling Alfred, the six-year-old, on a haft, and stabbing their mother thirty times.

The bodies were found on 23 September, half-buried, and a few days later Tropmann was arrested in Le Havre with 250 francs in his pocket. Paris became obsessed with the case.

The killings heralded a new type of crime. These were not primitive murders for food and drink, or (the next step up) for shelter and domestic security. Tropmann killed for obscure personal reasons; he liked sticking things into people, so there were strong sexual undertones. But the killings were not completely without purpose, however misconceived. In a break between the murders, Tropmann remarked to his brother-in-law (he still lodged at home): 'I have a business in hand which will surprise the whole world.' His plan, or megalomaniac delusion, was to *become* Mr Kinck, although it is hard to see how this would confer realisable riches.

Tropmann's last day dawned on 19 January 1870. In the prison courtyard, coffee was served to the assembled troops, and the official pharmacist entertained fifteen friends with truffled turkey. The prison Director threw a reception (one of his most successful) with pâté de foie gras, punch and wine. Outside, the mob gathered like the crowds at a Hollywood première, spotting celebrities. There was Maxime Du Camp! The man of letters, Victorien Sardou! And the Russian writer, Turgenev himself, was mistaken for the executioner, the famous and affable M. Heindrecht – who showed the guests round the guillotine and scaffold for some harmless horseplay, making his visitors lie in position millimetres from the blade's path as he triggered its descent.

Turgenev landed the plum job of walking Tropmann to the scaffold, marvelling at the killer's small stature and elongated thumbs. Tropmann too entered into the spirit of the thing. True, he failed in his last-minute bid to bribe the prison pharmacist to give him poison, but after his head had been cut off it was found attached to the assistant executioner's hand, the teeth deeply embedded by a last convulsive bite.

See also **Lunette**

Trousers, spare

Those who feel excluded from high office by mere lack of ability should take heart from the career of Rayner Goddard, appointed Lord Chief Justice in 1946 at the age of 69.

Goddard's supporters conceded that he 'rarely read the papers beforehand' (Lord Denning) and that he was 'contentious, cantankerous, prejudiced' (Lady Sachs, his daughter). His detractors are less complimentary. John Parris, one of the barristers in the **Craig and Bentley** case, decried Goddard as a judge who 'ignored precedents … His knowledge of law disgraced a first year law student … He lacked every judicial quality … He would not listen and made up his mind within minutes without hearing the evidence.' In sum, Parris depicts him as 'a dishonest political fascist'.

Worse, Goddard exhibited serious personality aberrations from an early age. At school, he was a notorious bully, his party piece to recite the death sentence in the dormitory. As a law student, he failed his bar exams five times. As a judge, his maiden speech in the House of Lords supported corporal punishment, and, as a pervert, he experienced emission every time he pronounced the death sentence. It was the task of the Lord Chief Justice's clerk, Arthur Harris, to take a spare pair of the standard striped trousers to court on sentencing days. When condemning a youth to be flogged or hanged, Goddard always ejaculated, and it is perhaps worth noting that, by contrast, a sex murderer is a man who kills for sexual gratification.

It is probably unfair to single Goddard out from the long tradition of Lord Chief Justices, who tend towards worthless political appointees. The first was Odo, younger brother to William the Conqueror, who attempted to buy the papacy on the death of Gregory VII. In 1350 the then incumbent, Sir William de Thorpe, was hanged for taking bribes. Robert Tresilian suffered the same fate after the Peasants' Revolt, during which he hanged the defendants without listening to the facts. He was done for a tax fiddle. The most execrated legal figure in British history held the post: Judge Jeffries, vividly described by King Charles II (who appointed him) as having 'no learning, no sense, no manners, and ten times more impudence than ten carted streetwalkers'. After sending 320 men to their deaths at the Bloody Assizes, Jeffries died in the Tower in April 1689 from a beating by the mob.

In the 1890s, the wife of John Duke Coleridge sat alongside her husband. Her duty was to nudge him awake. This century, Lord Reading whiled away the hours of courtroom drudgery by answering his correspondence; and Lord Widgery remained in office until 1980 despite his dementia.

See also **Birch**

Turpin, Dick (1705–39)

An English butcher who progressed via a career as a **highwayman** to his final status as a legend. Lack of social finesse precipitated Turpin's eventual downfall.

During life, Turpin was not so special; but after death his stature grew, fostered by ballads, prints, gossip, local history and burgeoning memorabilia – authentic 'Turpin' spurs, genuine 'Turpin' pistols and the extraordinary profusion of 'Turpin' inns where he spent the night. But what really launched his posthumous career was Harrison Ainsworth's 1824 romantic novel *Rookwood* where Turpin appeared as a secondary character. Ainsworth penned the hundred pages describing Turpin's epic but imaginary ride from Sussex to York in twenty-four hours, and the book was such a hit that seventy years later the novelist's biographer, S. M. Ellis, was shown the very hoof-marks made on five-bar gates by Turpin's mare along his way.

A famous but imaginary incident in Turpin's legend-encrusted life

The son of an Essex farmer, Turpin traded as a butcher and doubled as the neighbourhood sheep thief. After being discovered stealing oxen, Turpin moved into smuggling and joined a notorious group of burglars; soon he was leader of the Essex Gang. Their vicious exploits regularly made the columns of the *London Evening Post*, and by 1736 he and his accomplices had a price of £100 on their heads. Only by jumping out of a window did Turpin escape the hanging suffered by two other members of the gang.

Down on his luck, Turpin turned to highway robbery, operating out of a cave in Epping Forest, shooting dead a bounty hunter who cornered him in his lair. After that, killing came easily. The *Grub Street Journal* of 24 July 1736 reported that Turpin would have shot a robbery victim, Mr Omar, in cold blood had not his companion in crime 'pulled the pistol out of his hand'. Turpin became the scourge of Blackheath, and was a cool enough customer to take a short cut by riding through the middle of the City in broad daylight. Then in 1737 he shot his accomplice Tom King by accident, and by June of that year the price on his head had doubled.

The south was too hot, so Turpin headed north and set himself up as John Palmer, a country gentleman in Yorkshire where he earned his living as a horse thief. But one evening, returning home after a day's shooting, Turpin casually blasted a cockerel belonging to his landlord and threatened to kill a neighbour who remonstrated. He was arrested, imprisoned, investigated and finally identified by his old schoolmaster in Hempstead who, in his secondary capacity as postmaster, recognised his pupil's handwriting on a letter written from prison to his brother. Turpin was tried and condemned to death.

He died in style on 7 April 1739, buying a new suit for the occasion and hiring five men at ten shillings a head to act as mourners. Escorted to the gallows on what is now York racecourse, Turpin bowed to appreciative spectators with 'an air of the most astonishing indifference and intrepidity' and, it is said, chatted to his executioner for a good half-hour before a carefree jump from the ladder to his death started his post-mortem career as a celebrity. No sooner was Turpin buried than ruffians made off with his body. But the mob tracked it down to a garden, and Turpin's recaptured corpse was laid on a board, covered with straw, and borne nearly naked through the city in a triumphal parade.

Tyburn

A principal place of execution from 1177 to 1783. A plaque marks the spot at the junction of London's Oxford Street and Edgware Road where some 50,000 criminals met their deaths over the centuries. Nearby was a pleasant stream popular with anglers.

From 1571 to 1759 a permanent set of triangular gallows stood there, eighteen feet high, capable of hanging eight from each beam. With a maximum capacity of twenty-four they constituted a growing threat to traffic, and in 1759 the massive installation was removed, the timber sold to a carpenter who cut it into beer-butt stands for the nearby 'Carpenter's Arms'. A set of more modest removable gallows stood their turn until 1783, when the official place of execution was relocated at **Newgate**, which supplied the bulk of the condemned.

It was not before time. Tyburn hangings were an affront to public decency. Execution days – and there were many – incited mob violence. The long procession across London wound its way through the teeming crowds, with the death cart, crammed with prisoners seated on a coffin, preceded by the city marshal, sheriffs, peace officers and constables. The journey took three hours, and among the street vendors lining the roadside was the occasional carriage occupied by genteel spectators partaking of hampers and wine. The cortege repeatedly stopped at public houses for liquor to ease the men's fear.

Each prisoner travelled with a noose bound to his chest, and at the gallows' foot he donned a coarse white shroud. Even then he had a quarter of an hour to live. First the condemned were transferred to another cart, positioned under the beam and built unusually wide to permit multiple executions. The prisoners crowded at its rear while the hangman fussed with the noose and the Chaplain led them in prayers and the Psalms. All around jostled a scuffling throng of rich and poor, thieves, rogues, pickpockets and pedlars, thousands strong, shouting encouragement, hurling execration, cracking jokes or launching into bawdy songs as relatives climbed up to make their farewells. Among the audience would be calm family parties of tradesmen sipping tea, and the prisoners' last moments were overlooked by a grandstand for the well-to-do, called Mother Proctor's Pews after a commercially minded farmer's widow. When the cart finally lurched forwards the men still did not die, but were left to dangle, choking slowly to death. The crowd stood awestruck by their convulsions, greeting every new contortion of the limbs with a groan or a cheer.

Many contemporary observers regarded this spectacle as counter-productive, conferring fame and recognition on the condemned. Henry **Fielding** observed in 1751: 'The day appointed by law for the thief's shame is the day of glory in his own opinion. His procession to Tyburn, and his last moments there, are all triumphant, attended with the applause, admiration and envy of all the bold and hardened. His behaviour in his present condition, not the crimes, how atrocious soever, which brought him to it, is the subject of contemplation.'

Oxford Street was formerly known as Tyburn Road, and Park Lane used to be Tyburn Lane. 'Great Gibbet Field' was an expanse of land just off Tyburn in what is now Bayswater, and to 'dance the Tyburn jig' was to hang by the neck until dead.

Tyson, Mike (1966–)

On 26 March 1992 Mike Tyson, former world heavyweight boxing champion, was jailed for three years for the rape of Desiree Washington in Room 606 of the Canterbury Hotel, Indianapolis. The 18-year-old beauty queen accepted a telephone invitation to visit his bedroom shortly before two o'clock on a July morning the preceding year.

During the act of carnal knowledge, Tyson asked: 'Do you want to go on top?' Desiree replied 'Yeah', and did so. After ejaculating outside her Tyson said: 'Don't you love me now?'

The champion became convict 922335 at the Indiana Youth Correction Center, and this bizarre outcome highlights the law's complexities. The evidence supports Tyson's assumption that he was not engaged in **rape**; the fact that Miss Washington pressed charges suggests that she thought he was.

The issue is not only a matter of whom you believe, but whose belief is relevant. Criminal guilt can depend on whether the victim's or the perpetrator's point of view is paramount.

British convictions flow from the attacker's knowledge that he was committing a rape, and this produces seemingly outrageous acquittals when bone-headed dolts are convinced that the woman did not mind. American prosecutions are founded on the victim's reaction, and this means that, at its most extreme, seemingly outrageous convictions result when the accused had no idea, and received no indication, that anything was wrong.

Testimony barred by Judge Patricia Gifford from the first trial (because it was submitted too late) was presented to the Indiana Court of Appeal. The sworn statements of three friends – Carla Martin, Pamela Lawrence, Renee Deal – recorded their impressions on watching Tyson and Miss Washington emerge from the back seat of his gold limousine and walk through the hotel foyer at 1.30 a.m. The couple were all over each other. As Carla Martin put it, 'Desiree Washington had her tongue down Mike's throat and her hands on his crotch. She was really getting it on.'

Miss Washington filed a $10 million suit against Tyson and, within two days of the hotel episode, hired a lawyer to negotiate the book and movie rights to her story. A few hours after her horrific experience in Room 606, she was videoed in an apparently ebullient mood dancing and singing for the Miss Black America pageant.

According to some of the other twenty-two beauty contestants, Miss Washington flirted with Tyson before their assignation at his hotel room. Caroline Jones overheard her comment, 'That's twenty million dollars', as the boxer arrived at the rehearsal where they first made contact. Tanya St Claire-Gills listened to her speculate about the size of his penis. And when Madeline Whittingdon asked if she intended to keep her date, Miss Washington replied, 'Of course I'm going. This is

Mike Tyson. He's got a lot of money. He's dumb. You see what Robin Givens [his ex-wife] got out of him.'

Tyson's conviction was reaffirmed on appeal in August 1993, but the new testimony was not appraised, with the court ruling that it had been properly excluded from appraisal at the old hearing.

U

Ucciardone

Sicilian prison run by and for the Mafia where aged mobsters, as the saying went, 'retired into private life'. Until at least 1957 Ucciardone constituted a pleasant rest-home where the guards fell under direct Mafia control; the one governor who failed to toe the line had to pack his bags.

The cells were comfortably furnished, meals were sent in from the best Palermo restaurants, and *mafiosi* inside conducted their businesses outside with the help of warders acting as commission agents. If a prisoner's circumstances altered, as happened to Salvatore Malta (who needed a year off to run an armed band), he arranged for leave of absence while staying on the prison's books, nominally confined.

Institutional discipline for the less privileged was enforced with normal Mafia ferocity; the hospital register recorded injuries from these savage beatings as 'slipping on the stairs'. Five hundred inmates slipped on the stairs in twelve years.

Ucciardone's proudest accomplishment was a civil engineering project, tunnelling beneath the foundations to the underground pipeline running from the docks to the refinery. This the *mafiosi* tapped, syphoning off the petroleum for sale on the black market.

The vestiges of the Ucciardone tradition were not eradicated until June 1992, when the most recent anti-Mafia spasm exiled convicted mobsters from their power base to mainland 'hard' prisons.

See also **Cathedral**

Umbrellas

The existence of the most famous umbrella-gun in crime remains conjecture. Its victim, Georgi Markov, was a Bulgarian defector living in London, and on 7 September 1978 he queued for a bus on the south side of London's Waterloo Bridge. Jolted by a stab of pain in his upper thigh, he turned to notice a man picking up an umbrella as he hailed a cab. Markov continued to work, where he complained of a sore leg.

By the following morning Markov was sick. The doctor suspected 'flu, but three days later the patient was dead. In the circumstances, the bruise on the back of his right thigh was excised and forwarded to the chemical research establishment at Porton.

The tiny pellet, embedded in the inflamed tissues, consisted of a platinum and iridium sphere engineered to a diameter of 1.52mm, drilled with two 0.35mm holes. This exacting accomplishment represented the apex of a peculiarly Balkan arms race, backed by the KGB: the ammunition's manufacture entailed sophisticated micro-technology coupled with access to a defence industry high-temperature furnace. The Porton Down pathologists concluded that the cavities secreted something like 0.2 milligrams of a biotoxin, probably a first-use for ricin, an extremely potent derivative of castor-oil bean husks; hitherto, its effects were primarily known through the study of cattle. For humans, twenty-one millionths of a gram constitutes a fatal dose.

Despite the many published diagrams, the umbrella-gun hypothesis is supported only by Markov's equivocal impressions at the time of the shooting. Equally plausible variants are a straightforward gas or **airgun**, perhaps concealed in a furled umbrella. Some three months previously another Bulgarian, Kostov, survived a comparable incident on the Paris metro when he was apparently shot by a cardboard box, and the writer Alexander Solzhenitsyn weathered a similar attack.

The Bulgarian government has admitted culpability, placing the blame on their former security services, and in early 1992, the Bulgarian most closely linked to the murder, General Styoan Sanov, former deputy Interior Minister, was discovered dead in his apartment the day before his scheduled appearance in court to testify about Markov's files, which had vanished from state archives.

In America, umbrella-guns firing ordinary bullets continue in production, marketed to wealthy clients who fear violent attack, presumably in the rainy season. The weapons are indistinguishable from the genuine article except for their weight and the removable rubber tip protecting the barrel from abrasion on the pavement. On 2 June 1992 a specimen, confiscated from a John Portis by London magistrates, was destined for Scotland Yard's Black Museum.

One little-known criminal application is to poke an unopened umbrella through the ceiling from above. When unrolled, the brolly catches falling ceiling debris as the hole is enlarged, preventing any burglar-alarm wired to the floor below from detecting the incursion. This motif appeared in the film *Rififi*, and in real life was adopted by a German gang breaking into a strongroom during a 1907 hotel raid.

Unabomber, The

On 25 May 1978, a small parcel bomb mildly wounded a security guard at Northwestern University in Illinois. This was the first amateurish attack made by the serial killer who later became known as 'the Unabomber'. Over the next eighteen years the Unabomber sent home-made but increasingly sophisticated parcel bombs to educational establishments, technology companies and corporate businesses.

Between May 1978 and December 1985, the Unabomber is known to have sent out nine, fortunately non-fatal, parcel bombs. Two were intercepted and defused, but the others injured eighteen people, some seriously. One of these bombs, which wounded United Airlines' president, Percy A. Wood, earned the bomb-maker the media nickname 'the Un.A. bomber', later simplified to 'the Unabomber'.

Sacramento, California, saw the first fatal Unabomber attack, in December 1985. Hugh C. Scrutton tried to remove a package left lying in the car park behind his computer rental shop. It exploded, killing him.

The next three bombs – one in 1987, the other two in 1993 – did not kill their victims, but severely injured three people. The targets were unconnected except through their work with modern technology: a computer shop owner, a geneticist and a computer scientist.

In December 1994, a parcel bomb killed New York advertising executive Thomas Mosser. Some doubted that this was a genuine Unabomber attack until it was pointed out that one of Mosser's corporate clients was the Exxon oil company – responsible, in many people's eyes, for recklessly polluting the environment. Less than five months later, timber-industry lobbyist Gilbert B. Murray was killed by a parcel bomb. He was to be the Unabomber's last victim.

In 1995, in the wake of the **Oklahoma bombing**, the Unabomber sent a 'manifesto' to the *Washington Post* and the *New York Times* threatening to blow up a passenger jet if it were not promptly published. It proved to be a rambling and vitriolic screed that attacked big business, environmentally damaging government policies, academic and scientific research – and progress in general. It was plain that the Unabomber believed that all development since the Industrial Revolution was dangerous and damnable, and he was willing to kill to make his point.

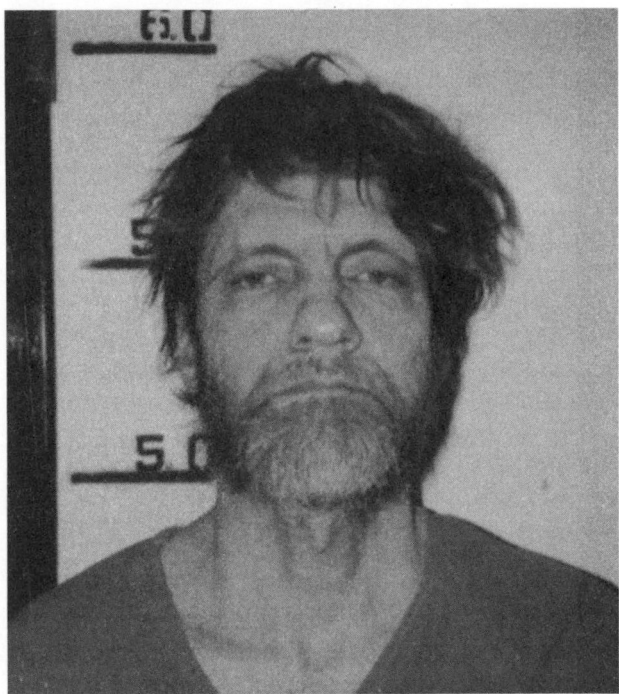

Theodore J. Kaczynski, the Unabomber

Fortunately, the manifesto was the last terrorist package the Unabomber was ever to send. David Kaczynski, in Montana, read the Unabomber's manifesto and realised with horror that it sounded just like the rantings of his hermit-like older brother, Theodore. With natural misgivings, David informed the FBI, who raided Theodore's isolated Montana cabin and found plenty of proof that he was the Unabomber.

Theodore J. Kaczynski had been a brilliant academic but in the late 1970s had suffered a total emotional breakdown and subsequently became a recluse. Living in an isolated log cabin, Kaczynski believed he followed a life in tune with nature – making bombs with some parts carefully hand carved from wood and roiling in hatred for the modern world.

In 1996, Ted Kaczynski was sentenced to four life sentences, with parole permanently denied.

Unfair arrest

Unlike today, in Elizabethan times you could be thrown into **prison** for practically anything: **debt**, petty theft, assault, slander, vagrancy, suspicion of witchcraft – the list is endless. It only needed someone to swear a warrant. Prison sergeants issued them at a shilling a time, sometimes releasing the intended victim in return for a bribe, sometimes threatening him with warrants unless they received a bribe, sometimes shopping the whereabouts of a debtor to a creditor for a bribe, and sometimes all three, after insisting on being primed with a bribe.

Getting in was easy. But there was no procedure for getting out. The better-off bribed their way to the outside world, or paid off their creditors and left. But the most widespread technique of modern times (serving the sentence) did not work. There was no sentence to serve.

Prisoners were not sent to prison for any particular length of time. They were simply sent to prison. Incarceration as punishment remained an uncrystallised concept; prison was a place to stay while awaiting release, trial or death, accelerated or otherwise.

Obviously things are better now, but once a prisoner is inside, protestations of innocence encounter almost insurmountable obstacles. One inmate had to set aside ten weeks of his prison wages to afford the photocopying of papers relevant to his case.

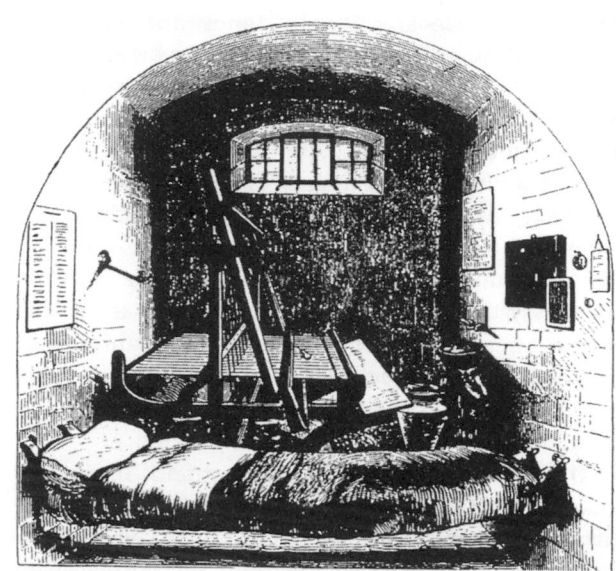

This Pentonville prisoner is lucky to have a loom rather than the dreaded crank for his task work. Note the basin with running water (right)

Other *prima facie* victims of injustice are pressurised to the limits of endurance. Bob Maynard and Reg Dudley, convicted of the 1974 Billy Moseley killing (see **Head**), learned that they had no prospect of release while they continued their protestations of innocence. This is standard practice: the Home Office informed Paul Cleeland (convicted of Terry Clarke's murder in November 1972) that he would be let out on licence if he admitted his guilt. After serving five years longer than the twenty years he had originally been given, he was released in 1998. Since going to prison in 1973 Cleeland had been trying to prove his innocence, and in 2002 he took new evidence to the Court of Appeal, where, however, three judges ruled that his grounds of appeal were without substance.

Jimmy O'Connor, a civilian convicted of murder in 1941, offers a different perspective. 'It was during the war,' he says of his trial. 'No one cared whether or not people were innocent. They had more important things to think about.' Prior to his execution, the principal prosecution witness, who had been pressurised by the police, withdrew his evidence, and with one day to run, after watching the digging of his grave through his Pentonville window, O'Connor was reprieved by the King. Released ten years later, he became a scriptwriter for the BBC, but thanks to a brilliant rearguard action by the Home Office, he could not be pardoned. The papers relating to his case were covered by the thirty-year secrecy rule, and time only started to run when his file was formally closed. Since O'Connor continued to ask to see his files, the Home Office had to open them to add his incoming letters. So his requests for disclosure became the reason for their non-disclosure.

The crime rate generally drops during wartime. Cynics say that this is because most criminals join the army.

See also **Virtual reality**

Unruth, Howard (1921–)

Howard Unruth was a 28-year-old former tank gunner from Camden, New Jersey, who went walk-about in his home town on 9 September 1949. He killed thirteen people in twelve minutes with his 9mm Luger, but then found himself penned into his house, surrounded by armed police. During the siege, an enterprising reporter dialled his home number for a telephone interview.

Unruth took the call. In a way, this was a golden opportunity to resolve the vexed issue of what makes mass murderers tick; one cannot always obtain the opinion of the man-on-the-spot, mid-massacre. The journalist came straight to the point: 'Why are you killing people, Howard?' he inquired. 'I don't know,' Howard replied.

Unruth survived his big day, telling the police, on capture: 'I'm no psycho.' To a psychiatrist he said later: 'I'd have killed a thousand if I'd had bullets enough.'

See also **Terminology**

Unterweger, Jack

Jack Unterweger, poet, dramatist and serial killer, qualifies as one of the strangest criminals of the twentieth century.

From the point of view of law enforcement, his case began on 14 September 1990, when the naked body of a shop assistant, Blanka Bockova, was found on the banks of the River Vltava, near Prague. She had been beaten and strangled with stockings. Although she was lying on her back with legs apart, a tampon was still in place and there were no traces of semen. She had been out drinking with friends in Wenceslas

Jack Unterweger

Square the previous evening, but had decided not to leave with them at 11.45 p.m. The police were baffled; there were simply no leads.

On New Year's Eve 1991, in a forest near Graz, Austria, nearly 300 miles south of Prague, another woman was found strangled with her pantyhose. She was Heidemarie Hammerer, a prostitute who had vanished from Graz on 26 October 1990. Although she was fully clothed, there were signs that she had been undressed and then re-dressed. Bruises on her wrist suggested rope or handcuffs. Again no semen was present. Some red fibres found on her clothes were preserved as forensic evidence, as were minute particles of leather, probably from a jacket.

Five days later a badly decomposed woman was found in a forest north of Graz. She had been stabbed, and probably strangled with her pantyhose. She was identified as Brunhilde Masser, another prostitute.

There was another disappearance from Graz on 7 March 1991, a prostitute named Elfriede Schrempf. Her decomposed body was found eight months later, on 5 October, in a forest near the city. And still the police had no clue to this multiple killer of prostitutes.

When four more prostitutes, Silvia Zagler, Sabine Moitzi, Regina Prem and Karin Eroglu, disappeared in Vienna during the next month, it looked as if the killer had changed his location.

Although the police claimed there was no established connection between the crimes, the press began to speak of a serial killer. They called him 'the Vienna Courier'.

And at this point they found their vital lead. Ex-policeman August Schenner, retired for five years from the Vienna force, was reminded of the MO of a murderer he had met seventeen years earlier, in 1974. His name was Jack Unterweger and he was now a famous writer and media personality. The case dated back to the time when Unterweger was 23. Two women had been strangled. The first, Margaret Schaefer, 18, was a friend of Barbara Scholz, a prostitute, who had turned him in. She told how they had robbed Schaefer's house, then taken her to the woods, where Unterweger had strangled her with her bra after she refused oral sex. He had left her naked and covered with leaves – as in most of the more recent killings.

The second victim, a prostitute named Marcia Horveth, had been strangled with her stockings and dumped in a lake. Unterweger was not charged with this murder, because he had already confessed to the first and been sentenced to life. He had pleaded guilty to the other murder, claiming that as he was making love he had seen the face of his mother before him. A psychologist had diagnosed him a sexually sadistic psychopath with narcissistic tendencies.

Unterweger, a good-looking youth who was the son of a prostitute and an American GI, had been illiterate when he went to jail. He had already been in prison fifteen times, for offences like rape and car theft. He had even been a pimp. But in prison for life, he set about learning to read and write. Then he edited the prison newspaper, started a literary review and wrote his autobiography, *Purgatory* (*Fegefeur*), which professed that he was totally rehabilitated and had killed the prostitute because he hated his mother.

The book made him an overnight literary celebrity,

and intellectuals began to lobby for his release. He was paroled on 23 May 1990, after sixteen years. And he was now a celebrity, who quickly became rich as his book was filmed. He had written plays, given readings of his poetry and became a guest on talk shows. He wore a white suit and drove expensive cars. Moreover, as a magazine writer, he had even interviewed the police about the Vienna Courier and been critical of their failure to catch him. Could this charming, brilliant new literary celebrity be a serial killer?

As they reviewed the evidence, the Vienna police – and especially the detective Ernst Geiger – decided the answer had to be yes.

To begin with, when they checked his credit card receipts, to establish his whereabouts at the times of crimes, they learned that he was in Graz in October, when Brunhilde Masser was killed, and again in March when Elfriede Schrempf vanished. He was in Bregenz, from where Heidemarie Hammerer was taken, in December, and resembled the last person with whom she was seen. This man had worn a red knitted scarf and a leather jacket.

Moreover, Unterweger had been in Prague the previous September, and when the police contacted their counterparts in Prague, they learned about the murder of Blanka Bockova. All this could hardly be coincidence. After months of secrecy it was time for the investigators to show their hand.

They interviewed Unterweger on 2 October 1991. Naturally, he denied everything. Moreover, he renewed criticism of the police for their failure to catch the Vienna Courier. And support for him among Viennese intellectuals and his society friends remained strong. (But how could they admit that their enthusiasm for his writing had unleashed a killer on Vienna? Was it not more likely, as Unterweger told them, that the authorities were persecuting this ex-criminal who had now become their scourge?)

Ernst Geiger went on with his search. Prostitutes who had been with Unterweger testified that he liked to handcuff them during sex – which was consistent with some of the marks on the wrists of victims. Police tracked down the BMW that Unterweger had bought on his release from prison, and found in it a dark hair with skin on the root. It was tiny, but using the PCR technique to make multiple copies of DNA, they were able to identify it as belonging to victim Blanka Bockova.

A search of his apartment revealed a red knitted

scarf whose fibres matched those found on her, as well as a leather jacket, and receipts from California, where Unterweger had gone to research a magazine article on prostitution in Hollywood. A check with the Los Angeles Police Department revealed that there had been three murders of prostitutes in the five weeks Unterweger was there, while the 'Courier's' activities in Vienna ceased. All three women – Irene Rodriguez, Shannon Exley and Sherri Long – had been strangled with their bras and left out in the open.

It seemed that Unterweger had gone to the LAPD and introduced himself as a European writer researching red-light areas. He went with police in patrol cars and was treated as a distinguished guest.

It was time to arrest the suspect. In February 1992 a judge signed a warrant. But when the police arrived at his apartment, Unterweger was gone. They learned from his friends that he had gone on holiday with his latest girlfriend, 18-year-old Bianca Mrak, whom he had picked up in a restaurant and with whom he had been living since the previous December.

It seemed they had gone to Switzerland, and then, when friends tipped him off by telephone that there was a warrant out for him, to New York.

Before leaving Europe, Unterweger had telephoned Vienna newspapers to insist that the police were trying to frame him. He also made an offer: if the officer in charge of the case would drop the warrant for his arrest, he would return voluntarily to 'clear his name'. He had alibis, he said, for all the murders – on one occasion had been giving a reading of his work.

Unterweger and Bianca moved to Miami, Florida, and rented a beach apartment. They were running short of money, so Bianca took a job as a topless dancer. Her mother kept them supplied with money by telegraph.

When the police learned about this, they called on the mother and prevailed on her to inform them next time her daughter made contact. And when Bianca asked her mother to telegraph more cash to the Western Union office in Miami, two agents were waiting for them. The alert Unterweger spotted them and fled, urging Bianca to go in another direction. But he was caught after running through a restaurant, causing havoc, and out at the back, where an agent with a gun arrested him. When told he was wanted for making a false customs declaration in New York – he had failed to admit his prison record – he looked relieved. But when they added that he was also wanted in Vienna for murder, he began to sob.

Learning that he was also wanted in California, where his semen had been found in one of the victims, he decided to resist extradition to Europe and opt for Los Angeles. But when told that California had a death penalty, he changed his mind.

Back in Vienna, the final outcome was inevitable. The strength of the evidence against him was overwhelming. As the trial – which began in April 1994 – dragged on for two and a half months – Unterweger's support among journalists and former admirers began to ebb away. He failed to produce any of the unshakeable alibis he had promised. On 28 June 1994 the jury found him guilty, and he was sentenced to life imprisonment.

American agent Gregg McCrary, who had been actively involved since 1992 as a psychological profiler, advised the Vienna police to keep a suicide watch on Unterweger, since he had frequently boasted that he would never spend another day in prison. They failed to heed his warning, and a few hours after being sentenced to life imprisonment he hanged himself in his cell with the cord from his jumpsuit.

Untouchables, The

As a child, Eliot Ness (1903–57) was exceptionally good. He worked a paper route, helped his father deliver pastries and loved books, particularly Sherlock Holmes. As an adult, he believed in the sanctity of the law, almost a unique attribute for a **Prohibition agent**. Perhaps surprisingly, departmental files commended his 'cool, aggressive and fearless manner' on raids, acknowledging that he made 'more than the average number of arrests' and that he never 'shirked assignments or complained'. Ness was well-dressed, well-educated, soft-spoken and clean-cut, and District Attorney George Q. Johnson, under orders to found a special Capone squad, looked no further. On 28 September 1929 he gave Ness, still residing with his parents, the assignment of crippling Capone financially.

Ness seconded nine men, four from outside Chicago, and by the end of the first year his elite cadre had captured nineteen distilleries and six breweries worth $1 million – a mere bagatelle to Capone, not one of whose men was arrested.

Ness's problem was that the bootleggers made good

By spring 1931 Ness had achieved ascendancy in his cat-and-mouse pursuit of the bootleggers. On 4 April, staking out a brewery, he was ringed by six armed hoods, who made another offer he could not refuse. But he did, drawling 'You haven't got enough money' before driving off. An outraged Capone assigned Michael Pitti to kill him. Ness, getting wind of the contract, drove everywhere with Pitti's mugshot at his side, eventually catching and disarming the hitman after a car chase. By mid-1931 Capone was in serious trouble, with busts at such a pitch that he could not maintain his customers in booze. Jake Guzik, a Capone henchman, was overheard on a wiretapped line telling a speakeasy that he was fresh out of liquor: the police would 'have to take a pass' on their monthly refreshers. Capone's alcohol production dropped by an estimated 80 per cent, compelling him to buy overpriced stock from out of town, and Ness staged a parade of forty-five impounded trucks past Capone's Lexington Hotel, reducing the great man to a frenzy. 'I'll kill 'im, I'll kill 'im with my own bare hands,' Capone fumed, but he delegated the job to someone else. In short order Ness survived three assassination attempts: a drive-by, a run-over and a car bomb wired to his ignition.

Although Ness secured indictments against Capone and sixty-eight confederates, citing 5,000 offences, his alcohol charges were kept in abeyance. Capone was convicted for income tax offences and, after forming his guard of honour at the station on his way to the penitentiary, the Untouchables were disbanded. Ness became Cleveland's Director of Public Safety, acquitting himself with his customary elan in the fight against civic corruption. 'Director Ness lifted fear from the hearts of honest men,' commented the press on his 1938 smashing of a union-racketeering case. But he met his match in the **Torso** serial killer, and a divorce, coupled with a drink-driving incident, tainted his squeaky-clean image. Ness resigned on 30 April 1942. After an abortive attempt at a political career he fell on hard times, once applying for a job at $60 a week, and by the 1950s eked out his life in obscurity on $150 a week as a salesman with a beaten-up car. In 1955 he ran into an old schoolfriend, Oscar Fraley, a journalist. Fraley sat up all night as Ness regaled him with half-remembered stories from his Prohibition days – about how he had gone eyeball to eyeball with 'Scarface' Capone and brought a criminal empire to its knees.

Handsome Eliot Ness, God's gift to public relations. But his reputation was deserved

their escape during the minutes it took to sledgehammer his way into their illicit premises. So he commandeered a ten-ton flatbed truck, welded a giant steel ram on to its cab and, on 13 June 1930, smashed his way into a brewery at 2108 South Wabash Avenue, taking five astonished hoods prisoner. Within days a youth, 'the Kid', presented himself at Ness's office bearing a bribe of $2,000, with $2,000 to follow for each week he behaved. 'Listen,' rasped Ness, 'and don't let me ever have to repeat it: I may be a poor baker's son, but I don't need this kind of money.' A few days later two of his agents on surveillance had a package hurled into their car. When it did not go off and, as expected, kill them, they unwrapped 'a wad of bills large enough to choke an ox'. They slung the bribe back into the mobsters' vehicle and told Ness of the incident. Fired with pride, he called in the press, and a *Tribune* writer christened his squad the 'Untouchables'. From then his fame grew, with Ness often accompanied by reporters as he set off riding shotgun on his sorties.

'You should write a book,' said Fraley, and Ness died on 16 December 1957, still poor, but a rightful legend in the making.

See also **Pax Capone**

Uranium

The Soviet Union's break-up led to a flurry of reports about nuclear material filtering on to the black market.

Russian inventory control of their nuclear arsenal has long been defective and their facilities woeful; newspapers commented unfavourably on warheads poking out through the windows of overloaded storage sites. Initially the nightmare spectre of unchecked nuclear proliferation went unrealised; the only corroborated reports involved conmen.

A typical incident from March 1992 culminated in the seizure of two Soviet-born Germans, one an unemployed fruit-and-veg merchant, during a car-boot sale of 1.2 kg of bomb-grade uranium (concealed in a sports bag) at an asking price of £650,000. On examination, the contents proved to be low-enriched uranium, worth about £50. Another gang arrested near Lake Como in October 1991 were hoping to shift the plutonium from a discarded heart pacemaker.

In the course of its nuclear career, Russia produced about 100 to 150 tons of weapons-grade plutonium and 1,000 tonnes of highly enriched uranium. Someone, somewhere, will want it. Worse, the break-up of the USSR left thousands of former Russian nuclear scientists scavenging for employment. Together they comprise a 'nuclear mafia', an illicit distribution network spreading outwards from Moscow to the former states of the Russian empire and probably further afield.

From 1992, the US Senate's 'Task Force on Terrorism and Unconventional Warfare' documented increasingly serious levels of nuclear trafficking in Europe, including an abortive endeavour in October of that year by Saddam Hussein of Iraq to procure 80 kilos of plutonium-239 (enough for twenty bombs). In the new millennium Iraq's putative nuclear capability has been used in part to justify invasion by a US-led coalition. After this campaign, Iran and North Korea became the most high-profile suspects in the eyes of the United States and its allies.

'Red mercury', that occasional feature of press reports, is a compound of unknown composition and unknown attributes. As David Kay, Secretary-General of the Uranium Institute, put it: 'A rumour started about fifteen years ago that the Soviets had found a new reactor base – something to do with mercury. Nobody knew quite what, but everybody got very excited. We thought it might be an ingredient in a hydrogen bomb, or facilitate a pressurised water reactor. It became known as "red mercury" purely because it was Russian. People try to sell off ordinary mercury tainted with colouring.'

The illicit trade in gaseous lithium (to 'enhance' nuclear detonations) poses a more serious threat.

Usual suspects, Round up the

One of the famous last lines from *Casablanca*, where Claude Rains, who witnessed the killing of a Nazi by Humphrey Bogart, orders the arrest of 'the usual suspects'.

After the death of the Fyffe banana couple James and Marjorie Etherington on 10 June 1971, this technique was employed with telling effect on the Caribbean island of St Lucia. Foul play was obvious when an insurance investigator noticed a garden hose, smelling strongly of petrol, running into the burned-out shell of the house where firemen had discovered the Etheringtons' charred remains. Within two days the suspects were under lock and key. The local Commissioner of Police explained: 'If I get any real trouble, I bring these three in: Florius the ringleader, Faucher, and Anthony Charles, who just does what he's told. If they haven't done it, they always know who has.'

The case had two notable features. First, the length of time taken to exhume the victims' bodies. Only one of St Lucia's gravediggers attended the excavation, arriving equipped with an old spade and two enamel bowls. These had holes in them. So every time the earth was ferried out of the grave, it dribbled in again. The gravedigger himself was ancient, and tired easily. But in front of a huge crowd of onlookers eating ice cream, the old-timer felt fiercely protective of his job and status, threatening to walk out if anyone helped. Sometimes he rested and sometimes he burst into tears, but after three hours the double coffin was finally exposed. Then, when the grave-pit sides collapsed, it was dug out again.

The Etheringtons had been burgled, beaten, tied up

and burned to cinders along with their house. In court, Faucher divulged that this last precaution was on the advice of Florius to prevent their victims, who were dead, from talking. Florius insisted that it was the only way to outwit Scotland Yard's posthumous electronic wizardry. 'If we burn them, ashes don't talk,' he explained. The three were hanged.

See also **Witchcrazes**

V

Vaginal devices, anti-rape

Very extreme. Theoretically, American women anticipating a **rape** can make a selection from a range of five patented intra-vaginal inserts.

All are tube-shaped. Patent number 4,167,183, registered at the US Patents Office in 1977, operates by harpooning the intruder's member with a miniature trident; number 4,508,114 encases the offending organ in a rigid sheath coated with a mixture of adhesives and acid; the 'Female Protective Device' spears it, and the creation of Joel D. Rumph administers it with a sedative injection.

All these contraptions suffer from the same drawbacks. First, they do not explain what happens next.

Another bizarre innovation. A baffled strangler from the 1860s registers chagrin as an unperturbed victim strolls by, thanks to his Antigarotte Collar

How should the woman deal with the encumbering rapist, who would still be attached? Second, the 'little and large' problem is unresolved: the devices are by definition big enough to accommodate the tumescent penis. Third, conventional difficulties in predicting the exact time of a rape would compel the user either to 'dress to kill' continuously or risk counter-allegations of penile entrapment by dressing up for, and then submitting to, a particular assault.

Valfierno, Marquis Eduardo de

Turn-of-the-century Argentinian conman operating in tandem with Yves Chaudron, an accomplished forger who churned out copies of the seventeenth-century Spanish painter Murillo. Together they crackled the newly finished canvases in front of an electric fan; sprayed on the dust of ages with a reversed vacuum cleaner; and simulated flyspecks by a scattering of coffee grains. For the period, the fakes were convincing.

The white-moustached Valfierno persuaded newly bereaved, wealthy widows to buy his Murillos for the family chapel in honour of their dear departed. But bilking widows one by one was time-consuming work, so the Marquis set himself up in a smart hotel in Mexico City. The capital had a genuine Murillo on public display; Valfierno's plan was to offer to steal it for gullible foreigners, mostly North Americans. Chaudron knocked up a copy, and the fake was smuggled *into* the gallery where it was slipped, a perfect fit, into the back of the original's frame, nestling unseen, face forwards behind Murillo's canvas.

Valfierno would escort his dupe into the gallery. 'That's the picture I told you about,' he would whisper, 'I can get my hands on it and arrange delivery to wherever you want.' The Marquis insisted that the buyer autograph the canvas on the back, 'so that you can be sure the painting you get is this very one.' The punter surreptitiously made his mark, sometimes snipping away a few centimetres of loose thread, while the Marquis briefly held the frame away from the wall, making a point of staring nervously out at the room.

What the punter actually signed was the concealed fake, which he later received together with a newspaper clipping reporting the theft of the original. The Marquis had these items specially printed. In a good week he could dispose of several Murillos; he hired local artists to boost production.

Word leaked out. Meanwhile the creative Chaudron grew frustrated at the limitations of his repertoire, always reworking the same masterpiece, and in 1907 the pair decamped to Paris to set up a gang, importing the talents of a monocled Englishman, a well-connected Frenchman and a socialite American, renting a villa near the Place de l'Etoile. Here they lavishly entertained selected visitors. The trap was baited by arranging some small favour for their client, perhaps a rendezvous with a Folies Bergères star, perhaps bypassing bureaucratic red tape or effecting an introduction. Then, confidence established, was there … anything else?

Valfierno's gang offered to steal to order from the Louvre. The purchaser obtained a facsimile of the designated object, along with impressive documentation on counterfeit museum stationery including a copy internal memo, marked 'confidential', stating that until the original was recovered a replica would be exhibited in its stead. All went well until, in June 1910, the gang nearly overreached themselves by 'stealing' the **Mona Lisa**. The client, bemused by the lack of international uproar, was only reassured after Valfierno persuaded amenable journalists to query the authenticity of the 'substitute' still on display.

Realising that if something was worth doing badly, it was worth doing well, the Marquis instructed Chaudron to embark on a production run of six Mona Lisas. Artists had always been permitted to set up their easels in the Louvre, provided their copy was to different dimensions. Chaudron slaved in the Salon Carré until he produced a perfect scale version, and carried it back to his studio for use as a master.

The Mona Lisa measures 30.32 by 20.86 inches, executed on close-grained Italian walnut one and a half inches thick weighing eighteen pounds. For added authenticity, the Marquis sacrificed an antique Italian bed, cannibalising its wooden panels for the walnut canvas. Meanwhile a circumspect marketing campaign secured six advance orders for the 'near' Mona Lisa, and these were shipped to America, passing through customs billed as copies. There they bided their time.

According to one account, Valfierno recruited a small-time crook, Vincenzo Perruggia, to purloin the original. When the news broke worldwide on 22 August 1911, Valfierno unloaded his fakes at $300,000 apiece. In this story, a disgruntled Perruggia stole the original back and, after storing it under his bed for two years, wrote to the Florentine dealer Alfredo Geri offering to sell. His exposure and arrest followed.

Valfierno's identity is unknown, and his involvement with Perruggia is no more than a persistent rumour defying verification; its source is a *Saturday Evening Post* article of 25 June 1932 by Carl Decker, who claimed friendship with the Marquis. By their nature, stories of successful con-artists tend to lack corroborative detail. The better the scam, the less it is reported or remembered, and on inspection the facts melt away to a series of hazy impressions.

Vampire of Sacramento (1950–79)

Regarded by his family as a peaceful child. But like the classic homicidal maniac he was, Richard Chase enjoyed playing with matches and wet his bed. Later, he amused himself with cruelty to animals and, conversely, was impotent with girls (see **Pets**, **Sex crimes**).

After high school, Chase – by then an unkempt loner, generally stoned – experienced difficulty in settling down, sometimes rambling round the house with his head wrapped in a cloth to make the blood run down properly inside his skull. Soon he became seriously worried that his head was changing shape and, in a hospital emergency room, complained that someone had misappropriated his pulmonary arteries. In 1973 a neurologist concluded that Chase suffered from a 'psychiatric disturbance of major proportions'.

At first his parents would not accept that he needed treatment. But after Chase took to disembowelling rabbits and eating their entrails raw, he fell ill and was put into Sacramento's American River Hospital. He escaped, but by 19 May he was back in an extended-care mental home where staff found dead, mauled birds cluttering the corridor outside his room. Chase was often seen smeared with blood; he explained that he cut himself shaving.

Diagnosed as a paranoid schizophrenic, Chase was

discharged from hospital; his mother, concerned at his zombie-like state, weaned him off medication. Left to his own devices, Chase realised that the reason that his heart had shrunk was through lack of blood.

By now he lived off a special cocktail of cola mixed in a blender with the innards of cats and dogs. In the spring of 1977 he banned his parents from his apartment, in any case too filthy for outsiders to stomach. He talked to them from his front porch, returning home just once to bring back their pet cat, which he had killed, eviscerating it and then smearing himself in its blood in his mother's presence. Neighbours saw animals aplenty entering his apartment. But none ever came out. Some were stolen, but others were bought, sometimes from the SPCA. Chase had an expensive dog habit to support and in June 1977 his mother handed over her savings from Social Security benefits, some $1,450. On 2 December 1977 Richard invested in a .22 semi-automatic pistol, firing it the day after Christmas through an open kitchen window selected at random. His bullet parted the hair on a stranger's head. Three days later he shot a passer-by dead in the street. The police investigation made no progress.

A reasonably accurate police sketch of the Wallin murder suspect, with a moustache and goatee added by Detective Roberts

On 23 January 1978, Chase broke into the house of Theresa Wallin, three months pregnant. After shooting her, he slit her stomach open and pulled out her intestines, loop after loop. He removed her kidneys, sliced her pancreas in two, stabbed her liver, severed her lung, knifed her in the heart, liver and, repeatedly, through the left nipple. Then he defecated, wedging his faeces into her mouth. Before leaving, he scooped her blood into an empty yogurt cup and drank it.

On 27 January, Chase forced his way into Evelyn Miroth's home. This time it was worse: there were children. The police hunted the neighbourhood house-to-house and, the following afternoon, met Chase on his doorstep carrying a large cardboard box.

Portions of the second child fell out.

His apartment – walls, floors, bed, clothing, bath, furniture, kitchen – was covered in blood. The freezer housed a half-gallon container filled with animal and human organs. On the bed lay a plate of fresh child's brain, but Chase denied everything. 'It wasn't me,' he said. 'No shit, I didn't do it.' Then he admitted cutting up dogs.

'Do you think it would be wrong if you ate people?' the police asked. After Chase replied, 'The Nazis ate a lot', a prolonged silence fell.

Under further questioning, Chase said that he was the victim of a conspiracy to poison him. His mother, father, Frank Sinatra, Hugh Hefner, the Mafia, Germans – they were all at it. In court, the district attorney argued that the killings were inspired by sexual sadism, and the anticipated defence of insanity did not succeed. Chase was sent to Death Row at San Quentin, where he repeatedly asked for fresh blood. Over time he stored up his medication and, on 24 December 1979, died of an overdose.

Van Meegeren, Hans (1889–1947)

Van Meegeren can be forgiven for the awful quality of his flat, soft-focus forgeries because they fooled so many experts. As a student he possessed a promising talent, taking the coveted Gold Medal at his Delft art school, and his first major one-man exhibition in The Hague in 1922 sold out. Van Meegeren prospered, but the more he painted low-brow pictures pandering to the public's taste, the better they sold. Critics, the influential Dr Abraham Bredius conspicuous among them, detested his work, and his output degenerated into commercial portraits of the nobility from London, Holland and the Riviera.

By the age of 43 Van Meegeren was based near Roquebrune in the South of France, sufficiently embittered with the Fine Art community to devote four years to perfecting the physical technicalities of forging Old Masters. He planned to debunk his critics. Taking an unwanted seventeenth-century canvas, the *Resurrection of Lazarus*, he prepared it by rubbing it down with pumice stone. He used badger-hair brushes, developed a special paint based on lilac oil hardened off with phenol-formaldehyde, baked the finished work at 105 degrees centigrade, rolled the canvas in a cylinder to reproduce 'crackling', rubbed Indian ink into the cracks to simulate antique dust, nailed the painting to a stretcher with period tacks and knocked the finished work about to justify slipshod repairs. For his blue pigments he hand-ground particles of lapis-lazuli, and, were phenol-formaldehyde (employed for its heat-resistant properties) not Bakelite, no scientific tests could have recognised the result as a fraud.

Whose work to forge? At first Van Meegeren considered Rembrandt and Leonardo. Then he chose a kindred spirit, the seventeenth-century Dutch artist, Jan Vermeer of Delft, whose reputation had languished for two centuries because his style failed to please a contemporary art historian.

For seven months in 1937 Van Meegeren worked up *Christ and the Disciples at Emmaus*, a hitherto unknown Vermeer measuring lm 20cm by 1m 17cm. He added a pinch of Caravaggio to the styling, in conformity with Dr Bredius's views – previously unconfirmed – on Vermeer's Italianate inheritance. Ten years later, Van Meegeren recalled this interlude with relish. 'It was the most thrilling, the most exciting period of my whole life! There were so many things to consider, so many traps to avoid … I was happy because I felt, yes, I was positive, that good old Vermeer would be satisfied with my job. He was keeping me company. He was always

Van Meegeren's signature on three of his forged Vermeers

with me. I sensed his presence; he encouraged me. He liked what I was doing. Yes, he really did.' Van Meegeren was proud to sign his work with the monogram for his master's I.V. Meer.

Posing as an agent for an anonymous Italian family fallen on hard times, who were smuggling out an Old Master in defiance of Fascist edicts, Van Meegeren took his picture to a discerning Amsterdam lawyer in Paris. The attorney recognised a work of quality, and appreciated that Van Meegeren's source had to be protected. So he concealed the painting's illicit **provenance**, devising a cover story of his own invention: the heirs of a Dutch businessman had found a canvas gathering dust in the deceased's Parisian apartment. They did not

rate it highly, but the attorney knew enough about art to catch the next train for Monte Carlo and consult the noted expert, Dr Abraham Bredius.

Over 80 and half-blind, Bredius spent two days closeted with *Christ at Emmaus* before making his triumphant attribution: 'this glorious work by Vermeer'. The *Burlington Magazine* published Bredius's rhapsodical discovery. 'It is a wonderful moment in the life of a lover of art when he finds himself suddenly confronted with a hitherto unknown painting by a great master, untouched, on the original canvas, and without any restoration, just as it left the artist's studio. Neither the beautiful signature nor the *pointillé* on the bread which Christ is blessing are necessary to convince us that we have here a – I am inclined to say *the* – masterpiece of Johannes Vermeer of Delft, and, moreover, one of his largest works, quite different from all his other works and yet *every inch a Vermeer.*'

The Netherlands seethed with excitement. Rotterdam's Boyman's Museum parted with 540,000 guilders for the canvas, popularly known as 'De Emmausgangers', and it formed the jewel in the crown of their 1938 exhibition, 'Masterpieces of Four Centuries'. Many eminent critics noted how badly underrated Vermeer had been as a religious artist, and soon millions of magazine reproductions of the Emmausgangers adorned walls throughout Europe.

So everyone was happy. Bredius had crowned his career, and Van Meegeren, something of a pragmatist, chose to omit his planned exposure of the art establishment as pompous, ignorant fools. He pocketed the money, and when friends inquired after the source of his monstrous wealth, he pointed to his regular purchases of lottery tickets. Van Meegeren returned to the Netherlands in 1939, acquiring a beautiful eighteenth-century mansion in the heart of Amsterdam, and the outbreak of World War II meant that his tranche of new Vermeers slipped on to the market without monopolising the headlines. There was a *Last Supper* (1,600,000 guilders), *The Blessing of Isaac* (1,275,000 guilders), *Christ's Ablution* and two spurious De Hoochs.

Meanwhile Van Meegeren's own reputation underwent a renaissance. But only with occupying Nazis. He specialised in black-and-white compositions of ferocious soldiers, ecstatic and libidinous nudes, Aryan pianists ringed by the Ghosts of the Great Composers, torture scenes and skeletons. These visual nightmares sold strongly to the SS, and his *oeuvre* was commemorated in book form; a personally signed and dedicated copy found its way into the Führer's library. Wearing his other hat, Van Meegeren's work caught the eye of the great collector Goering. A German banker, Herr Miedl, persuaded the Reichsmarschall to hand over 1,650,000 guilders for a Vermeer, *Christ and the Adulteress*.

But Germany lost the war, and in 1945 the Allied Military Government Art Commission discovered this heritage masterpiece among Goering's plundered hoard of art treasures stored in a salt mine near Salzburg. By then Miedl had fled to Franco's Spain, but the Dutch police tracked down his associate, the dismal hack Van Meegeren. He was arrested, thrown into prison and charged as a collaborator for selling off a priceless national asset. He faced the death penalty.

By then in his late fifties, Van Meegeren was a nervous chain smoker and heavy drinker dependent on sleeping pills. After six weeks pondering his fate, Van Meegeren revealed that he had not, after all, betrayed his country by selling a Vermeer. He had duped the state's enemies by painting it.

Van Meegeren went on repeating this preposterous assertion until, under strict police supervision and watched by professors, he was released to his studio to execute another Vermeer, *Young Jesus Teaching in the Temple*, which later fetched $600 and now hangs in a Johannesburg church. Doubters were convinced when they saw his studio littered with props – dishes, weapons, clothes, furniture – that figured in the background of previous Vermeers. In irrefutable confirmation, he sketched the underpainting of the *Resurrection of Lazarus* cloaked by his *Christ at Emmaus*. X-rays proved him correct.

Bredius was already dead. In short order Van Meegeren was bankrupted (being unable to repay what might be regarded as his well-deserved 8,000,000 guilders), and the collaboration charges reduced to 'deception'. The potential jamboree of his trial was rushed through in a few hours in 1947, and Van Meegeren died of a heart attack six weeks into his one-year sentence before Queen Juliana could effect a pardon.

See also **Morals**

Van Schoor, Louis (1953–)

South African security guard beached on the tide of history. Until he was 33, Van Schoor made very little of himself. He did badly at school, ran through four marriages, and served twelve years with the police, leaving with the same rank with which he joined – constable. But on starting work as a subcontractor for the security firms of Buffalo and Providence in 1986, Van Schoor discovered his forte. It was shooting blacks with **dumdum** bullets. His lawyer pleaded in mitigation that Van Schoor was not racially prejudiced; he would have shot whites just as happily.

In three years Van Schoor gunned his way through 101 people, killing thirty-nine. Cleared at inquest after inquest, he relied on Section 49(2) of the South African Penal Code permitting the shooting of anyone escaping from the scene of a serious crime. The word 'serious' was broadly construed to encompass petty theft while trespassing; the word 'escaping' included those hit in the chest while supposedly running away, or blown to pieces while trying to surrender, as well as those left to bleed to death.

By degrees, Van Schoor became trigger-happier. He shot Coleman Teto while he was walking to work, lured three victims to business premises to discuss job offers and then shot them, and shot another sixteen – on separate occasions – after they had surrendered. One magistrate listened patiently as Van Schoor explained a victim's frontal wound (contracted while running away) by a tale of running away backwards. 'Put it this way,' said a former client, 'I was a hell of a lot happier and I slept a lot easier when I knew Van Schoor was around.'

Detailed descriptions of the killings remove any element of ambiguity. On 11 July 1988 two youths, 13-year-old Liefe Peters and 14-year-old John Swarbooti, broke into an East London restaurant. Van Schoor found the boys hiding in the lavatories and ordered them to walk towards the shattered window. He shot Peters dead. Then he shot Swarbooti in the leg. Then he shot him in the buttock. Then he kicked him in the mouth. Then he picked him up, propped him against a table, and shot him again, in the shoulder.

Van Schoor's boss at Buffalo Security looked askance at the bodies piling up in the local morgue. So he took soundings from three senior policemen and a magistrate. Fine, they said. But the legal defence embodied in Section 49 has limitations; it only affords protection when shots are fired with intent to extinguish life.

This may sound tantamount to absolving a man of murder if he can prove that he meant to kill, but during the inquest into the January 1989 deaths of two blacks, Paliso and Bikitsha, an attentive magistrate noticed that Van Schoor had slipped up in his testimony. In attempted mitigation, Van Schoor misguidedly conceded that he only meant to wing his victims, thus laying himself open to charges of murder. But no matter. Van Schoor was acquitted because of his *constructive* intent to kill, charitably inferred by the court. 'In effect,' the magistrate concluded, 'by loosing a volley of shots he had from that moment decided to condemn them to death.'

But Section 49 has another requirement. People can only be shot if aware you are trying to arrest them – in other words, speak first, shoot later. An oversight in this department finally brought Van Schoor to book.

Apart from resigning his job, at first he did not suffer unduly. Public sentiment was reflected in the 'I love Louis' car-bumper stickers featuring a diagrammatic red heart stitched with three bullet holes. The local *Daily Dispatch* printed a letter beginning, 'I find it quite ludicrous that investigations are to be made into Mr Van Schoor, a security guard, for doing his job, and a very good job at that. In my opinion the man should be given a medal for bravery.'

But nemesis came in the wake of Nelson Mandela's release. The state needed a scapegoat as a token of its newfound good intentions, and on 10 April 1992 Van Schoor was convicted of five murders and two attempted murders. It is possible that he was not so much a luckless security guard as a blossoming serial killer suddenly presented with an endless supply of no-comeback victims. Reports depicted him as loner, of low intelligence, unable to cope with relationships and obsessed with the police and law enforcement – a perfect fit.

Vegetables

In Britain, where gun crime remains a relative rarity, it may be worth simulating a firearm with a vegetable during a robbery. The penalties on conviction are no less severe, but the chance of injury is substantially diminished, since (as a rule) the police do not carry weapons either. Shoot-outs under these conditions are risk-free. Nevertheless, most years bring a trickle of fatalities where the victim is found clasping an imitation gun.

The favoured assault vegetable is a cucumber, whether wrapped in a plastic bag or poking away menacingly in an anorak pocket. In October 1989,

Ernest Coverly was sent down for robbing fourteen building societies with a cucumber; Mark Fitzpatrick from Hampshire subjected five building societies to a reign of vegetable terror before being sentenced to five years in March 1991 for his haul of £4,750.

For his second robbery in two days at the same Shell petrol station in Old Street, London, young Carl Lancaster vacillated between cucumbers and bananas for his weapon of choice. He bought both at a local greengrocer's but, during the approach, one of the bananas was consumed by a cab-driver (Lancaster liked to rob in style) and he opted for the cucumber's superior fire-power. Lancaster relieved the cashier of £60, only to find his get-away (still by taxi) obstructed by irate customers on the forecourt. He was sentenced to three years in December 1990.

So it seems that Andrew Giles from West Yorkshire is a true innovator: in August 1991 he attempted to rob a shop assistant with a courgette.

In the 1992 British election campaign, Margaret Thatcher was attacked with a bunch of daffodils. Her aggressor, employing subterfuge, accosted the ex-Prime Minister with the pretext that the flowers were a gift. And in November 1991 Mohammed Jabber was jailed for three years for sexual assault with a vegetable after fitting a chili pepper into the rectum of a former Bangladeshi politician living in London.

Suitably concealed, French loaves constitute occasional stand-ins for vegetables (or sawn-off shotguns) and, in a forensic variation, pathologist Professor Keith Simpson detected signs of foul play when he unearthed what looked like a badly charred human forearm from the smouldering ruins of a Bedford pub. His find was gingerly boxed up and transported to the mortuary under police escort, where the blackened French loaf went under the knife in the expectant presence of Scotland Yard and CID chiefs, the local police surgeon and the Chief Fire Officer. Professor Simpson tells this undated story against himself in his autobiography, *40 Years of Murder*.

Vendetta

The most calamitous of the Sicilian vendettas raged between 1872 and 1878 in the towns of Bagheira and Monreale. For obvious reasons, detailed eye-witness descriptions from survivors are scarce; but the blood-bath's general course is clear.

Trouble started when a member of the Fratuzzi clan, Giuseppe Lipari, denounced a rival in the Stoppaglieri family to the police. The penalty for this breach of Mafia protocol was death, and the Stoppaglieri called for Lipari's execution.

The Fratuzzi's refusal to kill their own man started the feud. Soon all the close relatives of the original antagonists were dead in tit-for-tat killings, leaving families rummaging in terror through their ancestry in case some distant kinship put them in the firing line. Keeping count was complicated by the incidence of imprisonment or emigration, and strangers might be waylaid in the street by a grieving and unfamiliar crone – head of the female line – to learn that they were the surviving head of one clan or the other and hence in a state of ritual vendetta against a remote cousin. With progressive local depopulation, whether through death or prudence, youngsters were dragged into the dispute; one lad needed his blunderbuss loaded for him.

After six years the dispute hit the buffers when another Fratuzzi, Salvatore D'Amico, wearied of life; he too went to the police, in recognition of the consequences. This time the Fratuzzi took their cue and killed him, displaying his body in atonement.

In the 1960s a similar outbreak came close to cracking the Mafia's wall of **silence**. A feud between the Riccobonos, from the village of Tommaso Natale, and their neighbours left the Cracolici one down; denied an adult male for the next sacrificial offering, they resolved to make do with 13-year-old Paolino, who was machine-gunned to death on a mountain path.

His mother, Rosa Messina, courageously reported the killers to the police; Paolino was her second son to die, and her husband too had been murdered. On 19 September 1963 expectations ran high as she was called to the witness box at Palermo Assizes, where her disclosures had landed thirty *mafiosi* in the dock. But she lost her nerve, and the prosecution fell back on the testimony of Anna Galletti, who stated: 'I live alone at Tommaso Natale. I have four children. Therefore I know nothing about everything.'

Vendettas are a throwback almost to prehistory. For economies on the fringes of subsistence, unencumbered by central authority, infringements of grazing rights or access to a spring constituted an act of war punishable by death and, to this day, many Sicilians are forced to buy their water from Mafia-owned private wells. Even in Palermo, those wanting water daily negotiate their 'surplus' requirements from the Mob, and the trickle-down theory of wealth is rigidly enforced by systematically obstructing the construction of new aqueducts or dams. In Salvatore 'the beast' Riina's native Corleone, the plans for a barrage have been successfully kept at bay since the Second World War.

As justice goes, vendettas were very rough, but preferable to the feudal courts of the Sicilian aristocracy. In this harsh school a *mafioso*'s character was formed, and his outlook travelled well to gangland America where, until long after the First World War, Chicago featured a Dead Man's Tree, a sickly poplar in the heart of Little Italy. By old Sicilian custom it was here that the names of those condemned to die were posted in advance, a tradition honoured in the 1921 aldermanic campaign when thirty men lost their lives to bombings.

See also **Anselmi and Scalise, Inquisition**

Versace, Gianni

In 1994 the Hollywood director Oliver Stone released the movie *Natural Born Killers*, a deliberately shocking story of a young couple who travel around America brutally killing strangers for fun. A satire on the casual attitude towards violence and murder in the media, the movie was clearly meant to be controversial, but perhaps Stone got more than he bargained for. The very media he was satirising became almost hysterical over the film, with television and newspaper pundits wailing that it could inspire weak-minded people (not themselves, of course) to become serial killers. There is no evidence that *Natural Born Killers* ever did any such thing, but within three years the USA was traumatised by a series of killings that seemed as random and heartless as any of those depicted in Stone's movie.

The case started, some believe, when 28-year-old male prostitute Andrew Cunanan began to suspect had contracted AIDS. He went for a blood test in early 1997 but could not bring himself to collect the results. Soon his friends began to notice that the usually humorous and effervescent Cunanan seemed increasingly depressed – perhaps because he assumed that he indeed had the fatal disease.

Another cause of Cunanan's depression was his jealous fear that two of his ex-boyfriends, Jeffrey Trail (a former Navy officer) and David Madson (a

Minneapolis architect) were seeing each other behind his back. In an attempt to soothe his ex-lover's suspicions, Madson invited Cunanan to fly from his home in San Diego to Minneapolis to talk matters over with him and Trail. The meeting, on 27 April 1997 in Madson's apartment, proved stormy and ended with Cunanan grabbing a meat mallet from a kitchen drawer and smashing Trail's skull in.

It is a mystery just why David Madson – a respected and successful professional – helped Cunanan to roll the corpse in a rug and went on the run with the killer, but he did. The mystery will remain unsolved because Cunanan shot Madson dead and left him in a roadside ditch several days later. Ironically, the revolver Cunanan used had belonged to Trail.

At this point, Cunanan seems to have decided to live the life of a carefree outlaw, and never made any particular effort to cover his trail – even leaving photographs of himself in Madson's Cherokee Jeep when he abandoned it in Danville, Illinois, a week after the murder of Jeff Trail.

As he left no diaries, or similar indication of his mental workings, it is a matter of conjecture why Cunanan became a serial killer. However his next killing almost certainly stemmed from a sick urge to re-enact a scene from one of the sadomasochistic pornographic videos he loved to watch (and had at least once acted in). After abandoning Madson's Jeep, he walked a few blocks and approached 72-year-old Chicago-based property developer Lee Miglin. Drawing his revolver, Cunanan forced Miglin into the garage of Miglin's home and bound and gagged the old man with duct tape. Then, apparently re-creating a scene from a video called *Target for Torture*, he beat and kicked Miglin, stabbed him several times in the chest with a pair of pruning shears and slowly sawed the old man's throat open with a hacksaw. Cunanan then crushed the corpse to a pulp with Miglin's own car – driving over it backwards and forwards several times. Then, after stealing some ornamental gold coins from the house, he drove off.

As Miglin's murder took place in a different state from the site of the first two killings, the FBI became involved in the case. Realising that they had a very dangerous serial killer on the loose, they issued a nationwide police alert and placed Cunanan at the top of the Ten Most Wanted list. Yet he avoided all attempts to catch him, either through incredible luck or, more likely, grotesque police bungling. Cunanan

certainly wasn't making much effort to avoid detection, driving Miglin's stolen, blood-spattered Lexus all the way to New Jersey before dumping it to get a new vehicle.

To do this he murdered 45-year-old William Reece – a harmless groundsman at Finn's Point Cemetery, near Pennsville. It seems that Cunanan arrived at the cemetery, abandoned the Lexus and then approached Reece and asked for an aspirin and a glass of water (both were found spilled next to the body). Following him into the groundsman's lodge, Cunanan shot Reece dead and stole his Chevy pickup truck. Then he drove to Florida.

It seems certain that Cunanan pre-planned his next killing – that of the high-flying fashion designer Gianni Versace. At 50, Versace was at the top of his profession and counted among his closest friends international idols such as Princess Diana. When it was later discovered that, some years before, Versace had met

Gianni Versace

Cunanan at a San Francisco party, some wondered if the homosexual fashion designer and the gay toy boy had been lovers, but there is no evidence to back this conjecture. Whatever Cunanan's reason for deciding to kill Versace, the murder doesn't seem to have been a crime of passion.

For two months Cunanan wandered about Miami quite openly, keeping an eye on Versace's favourite clubs and restaurants. The fact that the Miami police failed to pick him up at this time is a matter of considerable embarrassment to the department – especially as it was quickly realised, as soon as Reece's abandoned Chevy was found, that Cunanan was at large in the city.

On the morning of 15 July 1997, Cunanan finally caught sight of Gianni Versace outside his Miami mansion. As the designer went to open the gate, Cunanan stepped up behind him and shot him twice in the head, killing him instantly. This was to be Cunanan's last murder. He went into hiding as hundreds of law officers and FBI agents flooded the city to hunt for him. Eight days after the Versace killing, he was discovered hiding in a luxury houseboat by the vessel's caretaker. Before the police could capture him, however, he shot himself in the temple with Jeff Trail's revolver.

Some psychiatrists believe that Cunanan went on his killing spree because he thought he was dying of AIDS and believed that he had nothing left to lose. However, although it has never been officially confirmed, it is rumoured that the AIDS test carried out during Cunanan's autopsy proved negative. If this is true, he might have never become a multiple murderer if he had had the courage to collect the results of his blood test earlier in the year.

Viaducts

Viaducts form an unusual focal point for sexual gratification, and the Hungarian Sylvestre Matuscka was probably unique in obtaining fulfilment from blowing up trains on them. At first he did so in his own time, but in later years he secured a paid position for his hobby.

On 12 September 1931, Matuscka detonated eighteen sticks of dynamite under the Budapest–Ostend express as it rumbled over the Biatorbagy viaduct. Transfixed in ecstasy, he watched as five coaches plunged eighty feet over the edge, resulting in billowing clouds of steam, the screech of tearing metal, twenty-five dead, 120 injured and dozens of exciting ambulances. It was a costly means of achieving orgasm, and the alert reader will note that Matuscka was a copycat fantasist. Peter **Kürten**, the Düsseldorf Vampire who derived the same satisfaction from dreams of blood that others procure from pornography, thrived on precisely this vision of railway catastrophes. Matuscka revelled in carnage, and his confession includes the words, 'I wrecked trains because I like to see people die. I like to hear them scream. I like to see them suffer', sentiments repeated almost verbatim, excepting the first four words, half a century later by the Los Angeles Night Stalker.

As an infantry officer decorated for bravery during the First World War, Matuscka was perhaps inured to slaughter, and by 1931, aged 40, he seemed a settled and prosperous businessman, married with a teenage daughter. But he was unable to experience emission without seeing trains crash, and the deaths at Biatorbagy represented the pinnacle of an escalating campaign. Nine months before, on 31 December 1930, the engine-cab crew of the Vienna–Passau express had brought their train to a halt ahead of a damaged section of track. A month later an engine was derailed by a steel bar across the lines, but there were no casualties.

On 8 August 1931, Matuscka drew his first blood with a home-made bomb at Juterborg, when seven coaches rolled down a thirty-foot embankment, and he took such delight in the Biatorbagy disaster that his arrest was inevitable. The day afterwards, Matuscka described the spectacle to an enthralled crowd, holding court in a local cafe. 'I saw one woman with her arm torn off!' he cried, and executed illustrative sketches before slipping away. Then he tried to wring blood-money from the atrocity, submitting a bogus compensation claim for facial injuries and loss of baggage as a passenger in the front coach.

But no one in the front coach had survived. Investigators found a map marked with the crash sites at Matuscka's home, and he was identified as the man who bought the explosives. During the trial, he pinned the blame on 'Leo', a spirit who never left him alone, and flirted from the dock with pretty female spectators. In his defence, Matuscka maintained that he had hoped to publicise a new patent safety device cold-shouldered by the railway companies, and he was lucky to be tried in Austria (which had no death penalty), where he was sentenced to serve life imprisonment in Hungary (which had).

In the aftermath of the Second World War it transpired that Matuscka had been released, probably at the Russians' behest. Crime writer Colin Wilson relates that he surfaced again in 1953, presumably happy as a sandboy, when a group of commandos about to blow a bridge surrendered to an American patrol in the Korean War. 'I am Matuscka, the train wrecker of Biatorbagy!' proclaimed their leader. After his capture, Matuscka again disappeared, possibly in a swap for communist secrets.

See also **Fantasising**, **Ramirez**, **Sade**, **Sex crimes**

Villa, Francisco 'Pancho' (d. 1923)

Revolutionary Mexican. Villa survived a firing squad in 1912 and, eleven years later, outlived most of his assassination.

Villa was an enthusiast of capital punishment for others, executing prisoners, traitors and suspected traitors out of hand. But when Villa himself went (on a trumped-up charge) to the firing squad on 4 June 1912, he spent so long pleading for his life – demanding a priest, then bringing out trinkets, coins and his gold watch in an attempt at bribery – that a reprieve arrived after the command 'Aim' but before the order 'Fire'.

Villa was finally killed on 20 July 1923 in his 1919 Dodge touring car, dying with four of his five bodyguards. By then the revolutionary general was in retirement, a pampered landowner possessed of thousands of acres. Eight gunmen lay in ambush in the town of Parra.

Villa took sixteen hits, four in the head and twelve in his body. With his chest ripped to pieces, the intestines slid on to the Dodge's floorboards. One of his arms swung free from a couple of shreds.

'The dirty pig, we taught him,' said Ramon Guerra, one of the assassins. With his other arm, Villa drew his Colt and blew off the approaching Guerra's face. After that, they shot the general dead.

Virginia Sword Parricide Case, The

On the evening of 8 December 2001, 19-year-old Kyle Hulbert entered the Virginia home of his girlfriend's father, the respected DNA expert Robert M. Schwartz. Hulbert found Schwartz on his own, about to eat his dinner. A heated argument took place, with Hulbert hurling accusations and Schwartz vehemently denying them. Then Hulbert pulled out a twenty-seven-inch-long sword and hacked the older man to death. Police later found forty-four wounds on the corpse, many on the hands and arms, indicating that he had been on his knees, trying to fend off the attack.

Gruesome as the use of a sword as a murder weapon was, this did not turn out to be the nastiest aspect of the case. Arrested, Kyle Hulbert told police that Robert Schwartz was a monster who had deserved to die. He had abused his daughter, Kyle's girlfriend Clara Schwarz, 20, and was in the process of slowly poisoning her to death. Only by killing Schwartz could Kyle save Clara.

Clara Schwartz and Kyle Hulbert were tried separately. Clara's defence lawyer admitted that Robert Schwartz was neither an abuser nor a poisoner; it was argued that Clara suffered emotional problems, including a persecution complex, and had fantasised it all. She had told Kyle that her father was a monster, but had never wanted her boyfriend to kill him.

However, this defence was undermined when the prosecution called one of Clara's previous boyfriends. He testified that while playing a fantasy role-playing game called Underworld, Clara – through her character in the game – had asked his character to kill her (character's) father. The implication was that she was testing the waters before really asking him to kill for her. This tortuous piece of circumstantial evidence was enough to convince the jury of Clara Schwartz's guilt and she was sentenced to life imprisonment.

Kyle Hulbert, tried some months later, showed remorse and apologised to the Schwartz family. He accepted he had been a fool and wished every day that he could undo the harm he had done. He too received a life sentence.

Virtual reality

In California, 'cyberspace' has reached the courtroom. Among the first cases was a pornographer who allegedly shot his brother eight times in one minute. This extended, complex incident made for descriptive problems, and in February 1992 the prosecution went to trial in San Rafael with a virtual reality animation of the shooting.

Over captions with digital time encoded, the court watched the victim get out of bed, walk to the door and get shot. With minimal reprogramming, the events could be viewed from eye-level or above the scene.

The defence appealed against the verdict, arguing that the prosecution relied on artistic merit and sound production values to sway the jury, and a similar debate preoccupied Britain after the May 1993 television screening of *Bad Company* had made it clear to millions of viewers that Michael Hickey, currently serving life for the murder of Carl Bridgewater in 1979, was innocent.

Bad Company was only a dramatisation of Hickey's story, and the British judiciary quite properly feel that prisoners should not be released simply because the audience enjoyed the show. A strictly factual documentary might carry greater weight – but the Bridgewater case received such treatment years ago. Thus the play, with its inescapable element of dramatic licence, was justified as a last recourse, adding visceral passion to what viewers already knew intellectually and, paradoxically, it is the weakness of the prosecution case that can make such convictions unassailable. There are almost no arguments to destroy, and whereas physical and forensic evidence can be reappraised with a degree of objectivity, a case founded solely on 'verbals' can only be challenged by more verbals, subject to judicial dismissal as mere verbals. Thus two truths run in companionable harness: Michael Hickey was acknowledged as innocent by a broad spectrum of the population, and their belief was vindicated in 1997 by the decision of three Court of Appeal judges to quash his conviction for murder, along with those of his three co-accused.

See also **Court of Appeal**

Vitiligo

An unusual clue in the case of John Hawkins, a Studio 54 hustler finally caught on 1 August 1991 in Sardinia, arrested in connection with Ellis Greene's murder in April 1988.

Greene's corpse served as a stand-in for the faked death of Gene Hanson, whose life was insured for a million dollars. Hawkins, the beneficiary, fled when the body-substitution came to light in June 1988, taking with him a further $240,000 of embezzled funds.

Hawkins was such a charmer that he could pull women off the street, the beach or the dance floor after a few minutes' chat. As a fugitive on the Caribbean island of St Thomas, he scored 'babes' at the rate of two a day, and many more were eager to claim intimate relations. This confusing trail of contacts brought little comfort to the officer on the case, Sergeant Jon Perkins. He wanted hard evidence, like fingerprints, to enable him to sift the deluge of sightings after successful television appeals on *Unsolved Mysteries* and *America's Most Wanted*.

In 1991 a Hollywood film mogul 'serviced' by Hawkins disclosed that he suffered from vitiligo, a skin-pigmentation disease which in Hawkins's case discoloured the penis. It had a big white blemish, known as 'Spot'. So for the next year of the man-hunt Sergeant Perkins weeded out attention-seekers from the women boasting of Hawkins as a conquest by insisting on a description of his genitalia.

It is true that Hawkins was eventually traced through his even more conspicuous red catamaran, moored in Sardinia's Cannigone dock, but the final identification came after the local *carabinieri* telephoned Interpol to ask if their suspect had any distinguishing features.

Vocations

Until the abolition of capital punishment in 1965, Britain carried a permanent complement of official executioners. This part-time occupation remained until the end a sought-after career. As the Royal Commission of 1953 observed: 'No doubt the ambition that prompts an average of five applicants a week for the post of hangman reveals psychological qualities of a sort no state would wish to foster in its citizens.' **Hanging** is now a bygone profession; but the vocation most missed by American serial killers remains available. Given the chance, most multiple murderers would plump for life as a cop.

In the words of FBI Agent John Douglas: 'Almost all serial killers are police buffs. When we ask them what they would do if they could start again and select another occupation, they choose law enforcement. Many of these guys in fact will have tried, but didn't make the grade. A lot end up as security guards.' A cursory glance at American periodicals like *True Police* reinforces this equation; the editorial content is mostly about sex killings ('Rape Slayer in Nunnery') and the advertisements mostly about sex ('Do You Want to Attract Women and Drive them Wild?').

Gerard **Schaefer**, sentenced to twenty years plus, actually was a policeman. He picked up female hitch-hikers, took them to a remote spot, hung them by their necks, force-fed them with beer, watched them urinate and defecate, and killed them – before having sex. Schaefer's other well-spring of moral authority was as a hyper-religious member of a Christian cult subscribing to literal adherence to the Bible, with its many strictures against wanton fornication.

Jeffrey **Dahmer** is probably alone among serial killers in wishing he had been a real estate agent.

Von Bülow, Claus (1926–)

The rich may have more money, but this does not necessarily make them happy. The $75 million heiress of the Crawford fortune, Martha 'Sunny' von Bülow, was frittering her life away in semi-isolation when she succumbed to an irreversible coma at the age of 50. Addicted to aspirin and laxatives, in a household devoid of friends and society, she teetered on the edge of divorce from an unsympathetic spouse (engaged in an affair) and had not indulged in sexual intercourse for at least five and perhaps thirteen years.

Her husband, Claus von Bülow, was born Claus Cecil Borberg, son of a Danish playwright. For the war years, his mother took refuge in Britain, sitting out hostilities in Claridges. Her son, an urbane sophisticate, evolved into a fearsome snob endowed with what writer Kirk Wilson's publishers call a 'plumy, upper-crest accent'. A capable, demanding man of great social refinement, von Bülow married into money. Sunny, unfamiliar with the world of work, reduced him to a house-husband; he complained of feeling like a gigolo. He stood to gain $14 million under her will of December 1979.

Von Bülow's lover, former soap opera actress Alexandra Isles, had issued him with an ultimatum some months before: get rid of your wife by the year's end or find another mistress. And on 27 December 1979 the obstacle to their future fell into a coma. Sunny's maid, the fiercely loyal Maria Shrallhammer, entered her employer's room to find von Bülow stretched out on one bed perusing a newspaper while her mistress lay unconscious on the other. Sunny could not be roused, but von Bülow assured Maria that there was no need for a doctor, an assertion reiterated throughout the day against Maria's deepening concern.

That evening, Sunny took an abrupt turn for the worse. Her breathing degenerated into a 'kind of rattle'. Alarmed, von Bülow telephoned for help, which arrived at the very moment his wife's heartbeats ceased and she stopped breathing. Sunny was revived by mouth-to-mouth resuscitation and rushed to hospital. Tests revealed a low blood-sugar level, 41 milligrams per 100 millilitres, outside the normal band of 70 to 110 mg. Glucose was injected, but still her blood-sugar level dropped, so five hours after admission Sunny was checked for **insulin**, which 'eats' sugar.

Her insulin reading was towards the upper end of the normal range. It gradually diminished, suggesting higher levels earlier in the day. Sunny regained consciousness twenty-four hours later with no ill effects. She suspected nothing untoward, but Maria remained on the alert, and in February 1980 Sunny succumbed to another unheralded attack, suddenly too weak to sit up in bed or speak distinctly. Von Bülow was inclined to suspect influenza. A few days later, Maria came across a black bag in one of his suitcases. Inside she saw pills, a white powder and a yellow paste. Analysed in secret by the family doctor, the first two were preparations of Valium, the last a sedative, neither available over the counter in paste or powder form.

In April, Sunny was hospitalised after another episode when her speech slurred and she lost motor-coordination. Over Thanksgiving, Maria checked von Bülow's bag and, as she testified later, found it contained a clear vial labelled 'Insulin', several needles and a syringe. On 19 December, Maria was given the weekend off. On her way out she peered into the bag: the insulin was still there. The following evening, Sunny collapsed without warning in the kitchen. Her son, Alexander, carried her to the bedroom and the following morning von Bülow discovered her unconscious in the bathroom in a pool of urine. On admission to Newport Hospital, her blood-sugar levels were extremely low (29 mg) and her insulin level extremely high (216 mg). A search of her apartment located the black bag inside a metal box in a locked cupboard. Among the bottles of pills and drugs was a used needle, which laboratory tests indicated to be encrusted with insulin, and on 16 March 1982 von Bülow was found guilty on two counts of attempted murder.

He never spent a night in prison. J. Paul Getty Jnr, an erstwhile employer, funded an appeal headed by Alan

Dershowitz, the Harvard Law professor. Dershowitz mobilised his students, assigning teams to different aspects of the case, and by the time the hearing opened in April 1985, Sunny's personal habits were acknowledged as less than pristine. An unreliable witness at the first trial had intimated that Sunny recommended self-inflicted insulin injections as an aid to slimming; now writer Truman Capote assured reporters that in the 1950s Sunny had offered to show him how to inject himself, and that during the late 1970s she was 'deep into drinking' and frequently experimented with amphetamines, Demerol and Quaaludes.

In court, medical experts for the defence pointed to inconsistencies in the damning needle. They maintained that the exterior aspect of a needle is wiped clean by its removal from the body tissues. In any case, the test result could be a false positive from two other drugs detected on its tip. Sunny's count of 216 mg insulin was dismissed as one of four conflicting readings, one higher, two lower. Both of Sunny's comas could have resulted from some unspecified combination of drugs and, under cross-examination, Maria admitted that she had made no mention of the insulin bottle when first questioned in January 1981. She maintained that she had not appreciated its significance at the time, but the defence only needed to insert an element of reasonable doubt into her testimony and the surrounding evidence. On 10 June 1985, after twelve hours' deliberation, von Bülow was discharged.

Perhaps the jury thought that Maria lied about the insulin. Perhaps they believed that the needle might have been dipped in insulin in order to incriminate von Bülow. Or perhaps insulin had never been present in Sunny's body.

But then why did she go into a coma? The most likely explanation for low blood-sugar which continues to drop under the impetus of a glucose injection is insulin, and the most likely reason for high test levels of insulin is … a high level of insulin. The only internal source, at anything approaching Sunny's readings, is a pancreatic tumour. But Sunny did not have a pancreatic tumour. The alternative is external administration, raising the macabre conjecture that Sunny *was* injected, and that an attempt followed to implicate von Bülow by tampering with, and embroidering, the evidence, thereby ensuring his eventual acquittal.

W

Waco Siege, The

Early in the afternoon of 19 April 1993, the TV news began to broadcast pictures of the final assault on the compound of the Branch Davidian religious cult in Waco, Texas, where David Koresh and his followers had been holding police and federal authorities at bay for fifty-one days. Koresh, who claimed to be the Son of God, had been wanted for questioning by the federal Bureau of Alcohol, Tobacco and Firearms (ATF) because he and his followers were known to be stockpiling weapons and explosives – the Branch Davidians believed that the war of Armageddon was imminent. Koresh had made several offers to allow the ATF to inspect his arsenal – all of it, he insisted, legal and licensed – but they had refused, preferring to make a surprise visit.

On 28 February, heavily armed agents from the ATF attempted to gain access to the Branch Davidians'

David Koresh

main building in the Waco compound. Someone started firing weapons, and in the ensuing battle four ATF officers and six Branch Davidians were killed.

The ATF later claimed that the cultists had fired first, and the Branch Davidians insisted that it was the ATF who had opened fire. (In fact, Koresh later claimed his people never shot anyone – he said that the ATF, firing wildly, had accidentally shot their own people.) Ironically, the Branch Davidians would have been within their rights to use their weapons, as the ATF agents did not have a valid search warrant and, under Texas law, a citizen is allowed to forcibly defend his property from attempts at illegal breaking and entry. But such petty legal points did not stop the federal authorities descending on the Koresh compound with military force after the gun battle.

Throughout March and early April, the surrounded cultists expressed defiance. On a number of occasions their leader agreed to surrender, then changed his mind at the last moment. To the worldwide audience that watched the siege daily on television, it seemed obvious that David Koresh was enjoying making fools of the authorities. Magazine articles about the 33-year-old rock guitarist talked about his harem of wives – which included under-age girls – and hordes of children, while ex-disciples described his self-glorifying sermons, which sometimes went on for sixteen hours. The result was that most people were impatient with the apparently 'softly softly' tactics of the authorities, and looked forward to the day when Koresh would be standing in court and sentenced to a long term of imprisonment.

So, on that April morning fifty-one days into the siege, when the federal agents decided to break in with tanks, there must have been few among the global audience who did not look forward to the prospect of Koresh getting his come-uppance.

It all began when an armoured vehicle rolled up to

the main building in the compound and a loudspeaker asked those inside to surrender. The answer was a barrage of bullets that bounced off the armour. The vehicle rolled forward and tore the corner off the building. Meanwhile, other tanks, with metal extension tubes attached to their barrels, knocked holes in the buildings, then pumped in clouds of CS tear gas. Then the vehicles withdrew and waited.

After six hours of standoff, the first wisps of smoke began to drift up from the buildings. It looked as if something had started a fire, perhaps igniting the CS gas. In a few minutes, flames were bursting out of upstairs windows. The TV cameras waited expectantly for fugitives to rush from the quickly burning building, but none was to be seen. No attempt was made by the FBI to stop the fire – none could, as no fire trucks had been called. In a few minutes, the wood and plasterboard buildings were a roaring inferno. At least eighty cult members, including twenty-seven children, died in the fire. Only nine people escaped from the inferno. Koresh was not among them.

The federal authorities, in the subsequent enquiry, claimed that Koresh had decided that he and his followers must die by fire and had stopped most of the cult members escaping to safety. Many of these were found lying face down, a position typical of death by smoke inhalation; others had died of gunshot wounds. Like the Reverend Jim Jones in Guyana in 1978, Koresh, the FBI said, had enforced a mass suicide.

Now, over a decade since the ashes of the siege have settled, pointed questions remain – and not about the cult's part in the tragedy. For example, the question of who fired first during the original, botched ATF raid might have been settled by the compound's metal front door. The ATF claimed the cultists initially opened fire through the door at them. Koresh, in telephone negotiations during the siege, said the ATF had first fired through it when he refused to come out. He pointed out that the bullet holes were all from the outside, coming inwards. This evidence could not be checked after the fire, however, as the door mysteriously disappeared from the crime scene.

More damningly, some now believe that the federal authorities deliberately murdered the Branch Davidians. They point out that the CS tear gas fired into the building by the FBI tanks was not only potentially lethal, it was also highly flammable. The makers of CS gas specifically insist that it should never be used in confined spaces. Unable to disperse in open air, it

The Waco fire

can cause fatal poisoning as it contains cyanide. Then, when it settles a short time after being released, CS gas forms a fine dust that burns very easily and rapidly. When the fire started, every surface and person within the compound would have had a dusting of this powder.

The nine surviving cult members have always maintained that there was no 'suicide pact' among the Branch Davidians, and some even claimed that FBI snipers shot at them as they escaped, preventing the others from leaving the building. Indeed, infrared aerial footage, taken by the FBI during the fire, reveals weapon flashes coming from outside the flaming compound, apparently confirming that the FBI fired at escapees. On the other hand, the survivors suggest, the only shooting done by the trapped cultists was to save each other and their children from being burned to death.

In August 1999, the FBI was forced to admit that 'pyrotechnic tear gas canisters' were fired into the Waco compound after the tanks had deployed the CS gas, but before the fire was seen to start. They flatly denied that these were responsible for starting the blaze, but the incendiaries certainly *could* have ignited the wooden, sun-dried, CS-powder-coated buildings. At the very least, the use of such weapons under such circumstances was highly questionable.

But why would the United States government ruthlessly murder over eighty adults and children? The cultists claimed, during the siege and after, that gunmen in federal helicopters had fired blindly through the roof of the building. If this is true, it was a blatant act of child endangerment – of the very children the FBI claimed to be so desperate to save. Perhaps it was thought that the only way to totally destroy the evidence of such a crime would be to burn the building – and its occupants.

The ATF bulldozed what little was left of the compound before it could be properly examined. The head of the subsequent Senate investigation of the Waco siege, while exonerating the FBI, noted that getting the authorities to hand over evidence 'was as difficult as pulling teeth'.

It has also been claimed that the US government wanted to frighten various groups, such as the Branch Davidians, who espoused anti-federalist doctrines (Koresh said the federal government was under the control of the Antichrist). These anti-federal religious sects, 'militias' and 'patriot groups' had been rapidly growing up across the country since the mid-1980s and were no longer composed of just a few extremists and crazies. Hundreds of thousands of ordinary, middle-class Americans, tired of big government and big business ruling their lives, had joined or indirectly supported groups who were calling for an end to federal income tax and the dismantling of the mono-lithic federal government machine.

Those who believe that the federal authorities were sending an intimidating message to these anti-federal groups by slaughtering the Branch Davidians point to the official title of the attack that ended the Waco siege: 'Operation Showtime'.

'Waldheim's disease'

A form of **amnesia** besetting war criminals. Kurt Waldheim, the Austrian President, used his affliction to avoid prison. Ernest Saunders, the former chief exec-utive convicted of the Guinness 'share-ramping' scandal, contracted Alzheimer's disease – supposedly an irreversible form of pre-senile dementia – to get out. But after his release ten months into a five-year sentence at Britain's Ford Open Prison, Saunders rapidly underwent a miraculous recovery. By early 1992 he was in fine fettle, hosting a business seminar at Cranfield, booked to lecture £350-a-head delegates on 'the lessons of turnaround'.

In Stuttgart, Josef Franz Leo Schwammberger spent early 1992 under impressive selective amnesia. Schwammberger remembered everything up to 1939 and everything after 1945, but the years in between were blank. He could recall nothing of his four years as a labour camp commandant in Poland. Day after day, Schwammberger sat in court listening, without a flicker of recollection, to survivors' accounts of how their genitals were branded, their babies smashed against walls to save bullets, and their lives valued at twelve pfennigs a thousand, the cost of a postcard to order up another batch of Jews.

Denial is a state known to therapists, but it is not a legal defence. On 18 May 1992 the 80-year-old Schwammberger was sentenced to life imprisonment on seven specimen counts of murder.

'Dementia Americana' is another affliction occa-sionally produced as a defence ploy. Diseases can also feature as an unreliable **weapon**. In 1912 Frenchman Henri Giraud tried to dispose of Louis Pernotte (whose life he insured for 300,000 francs) with typhoid. But the administration of his bacterial cultures was at first very non-specific; he confined the entire *famille* Pernotte to their sickbeds. In the end the resilient Louis required individual targeting with daily injections, said by Giraud to consist of restorative doses of chamomile. Six years later Giraud took his own life after falling under suspicion for the murder of a heavily insured widow.

In America, Dr Arthur Warren Waite from New York used diseases to despatch his wealthy in-laws, one by one. Waite was a bored and conscienceless society dentist who wanted to expedite his inheritance so that he could channel his energies more fully into tennis. In January 1916 he doctored his mother-in-law's rice pudding with tubes contaminated with a blunderbuss of typhoid, anthrax, diphtheria, tuberculosis and influenza. After she died, her grieving husband John E. Peck came to stay and it took Waite six weeks to polish him off. When poisoned desserts and an infected nasal spray failed to do the trick, he attempted to give his guest pneumonia; later he fell back on **arsenic** before suffocating Peck with a pillow on 12 March. In the witness box Waite related this *histoire* with such infec-tious good humour that the jury were reduced to sheepish giggles.

His trial was marked by that curious variant of the alibi defence, the Multiple Personality Disorder (see **MPD**). 'I believe,' Waite assured the court, 'that although my body lives in America, my soul lives in Egypt. It is the man from Egypt who has committed these foul crimes.' So Waite had really been some-where else at the critical moment, on the banks of the Nile during the time of the Pharaohs, and accordingly the dentist was cross-examined in detail about his Egyptian period. He too remembered nothing, was found sane and guilty, and went to the electric chair on 24 May 1917, still smiling.

Walpole, Horace (1717–97)

English man of letters and a good source on eighteenth-century robberies in the centre of fashionable London. In September 1750 Walpole was comfortably ensconced in his dining room when, as he wrote, 'I heard a loud cry of "Stop, thief."' A **highwayman** had attacked a post-chaise in Piccadilly. Walpole was later held up by a mounted robber in Hyde Park, and was lucky to escape with his life when the pistol went off (perhaps accidentally) in his face, scorching the skin with powder.

This incident was followed by a characteristic charade, played out with every appearance of courtesy. Walpole advertised, asking for the return of his property, and the reply showed 'less wit than the epistles of Voltaire, but had ten times more natural and easy politeness'. James M'Lean, the highwayman, agreed an exchange of goods through 'the same footman that was behind the Chariot when Rob'd … as We Intend Repaying him a trifle we took from him'.

M'Lean was the son of a Scottish Presbyterian minister. After wasting his inheritance, he applied himself to highway robbery with sufficient diligence to earn a smart mistress and a flat opposite White's, the London club for gentlemen. There he became a living embodiment of the highwayman myth. By day he promenaded up St James's, every inch a dandy, attired in white silk stockings, fine waistcoats and yellow Moroccan slippers; by night, he robbed.

Although some detractors averred that his lack of *true* breeding was easily discernible, at M'Lean's trial Lady Caroline Petersham testified on his behalf; while in **Newgate** he was visited (according to Walpole) by Lord Montford 'at the head of half White's', and the *Daily Journal* reported that hundreds of Ladies and Gentlemen attended his **Tyburn** execution.

Of all the acts of highwaymanly gallantry, the prize must go to Claude Duval (1643–70) for his *al fresco* dance with a lady of quality. She happened to have a flute in her pocket and, as the mounted robbers gained on her coach, she started playing to keep up her spirits. By a happy coincidence the accomplished Duval was also carrying a flute and reciprocated in kind. Drawing abreast of the carriage, he asked her to dance. 'Sir,' said she (according to Duval's 1670 biographer), 'I dare not deny anything to one of your quality and good mind. You seem a gentleman, and your request is very reasonable.'

So the couple tripped a light corranto on the heath. Duval demonstrated such consummate skill, despite his great French riding boots, that another passenger presented him with £100 in token of his esteem, and this touching scene became a favourite with Victorian narrative painters. In more robust vein, Duval is reported in the *Newgate Calendar* as snatching a silver feeding bottle from a baby, and at his arrest he would 'certainly have killed ten constables' had he not been drunk. Again, he was visited by scores of ladies in **Newgate**'s Condemned Hold; they later attended his hanging wearing masks. His tombstone can be seen in the Inigo Jones church in Covent Garden:

> *Here lies Du Vail: Reader, if male thou art*
> *Look to thy purse; if female, to thy Heart…*
> *Old **Tyburn's** Glory, England's illustrious thief,*
> *Du Vall, the ladies' joy, Du Vall the ladies' grief*

Washington Snipers, The

On 2 October 2002 James D. Spring, a program analyst at the National Oceanic and Atmospheric Administration, was crossing a car park in the **Weaton** district of Washington DC. There was the crack of a gunshot and Spring fell to the ground; he had been shot dead by a single, high-velocity rifle bullet.

It was immediately plain to investigators that this was no ordinary murder – even in crime-riddled Washington, police rarely see killings by sniper fire. Given the events of 9/11, just over a year before, some officers feared that the killing had been a terrorist incident.

Over the following twenty-four hours – between 3 and 4 October – five more of the city's residents were killed by long-range sniper shots. James Buchanan, aged 39, was killed while cutting the grass at a car dealership in the White Flint area. Prenkumar Walekar, 54 and a taxi driver, was killed as he filled up with petrol at a station in the Aspen Hill area. Sarah Ramos, a 34-year-old mother, was killed while reading a magazine on a bench outside a post office in the Silver Spring district. Lori Ann Lewis-Rivera, 25, was killed as she vacuumed her van at a petrol station in the Kensington district. The last fatality that grim day was a retired 72-year-old carpenter, Pascal Charlot, who was killed while standing at a bus stop in the inner city – however, he was not the last victim. A 43-year-old woman was shot while crossing a parking lot in Fredericksburg – a town forty miles south of Washington – but fortunately she survived. The assassin clearly like to move about and wasted no time. One harassed police officer grimly commented that his local county homicide rate 'just went up 25 per cent today'.

Panic spread as soon as the story hit the news: a sniper was stalking the capital and nobody was safe. Some people refused to leave their homes and many didn't dare use self-service petrol stations as these seemed one of the killer's favourite hunting areas. Suddenly Washington residents had a horrible taste of what life had been like in Sarajevo during the civil war in Yugoslavia in the 1990s.

After a few days' pause, the killing began again. A 13-year-old boy was shot in the stomach as he got off his school bus in the Maryland suburbs of Washington. Surgeons struggled to save his life, but he died of massive internal injuries. The following day the killer returned to the scene of the boy's murder and left a tarot card with the words 'Dear Mr Policeman. I am God' written on it.

On 9 October the sniper once again moved away from the suburbs of Washington, killing civil engineer Dean Harold Meyers, 53, at a petrol station in the Virginia town of Manassas. Two days later Kenneth H. Bridges, also 53, was shot dead at a petrol station near Fredericksburg. On 14 October the sniper killed Linda Franklin, 47, who was shot dead as she and her husband loaded their car outside a shop at the Seven Corners Shopping Center, on one of northern Virginia's busiest intersections. Ironically, Linda Franklin was an FBI analyst.

On 19 October the sniper attacked what was to be his last victim. A 37-year-old man was shot once in the stomach as he left a restaurant in the town of Ashland, seventy miles south of Washington. He suffered severe damage to his internal organs, but survived.

Suspicion that the sniper might be a Islamic terrorist seemed partly scotched by the bizarre tarot card note left at a crime scene: no true Muslim would claim to be 'God', not even in jest. More evidence to this effect came in the form of a letter found at the Ashland crime scene. The writer again referred to himself as God, and accused the police of incompetence, adding that it was their fault that five people had had to die. Presumably this indicated that he had expected to be caught after the first two days of his killing spree. The letter demanded a $10 million ransom to stop the killings and stated chillingly: 'Your children are not safe anywhere or at anytime.' Apparently the sniper was a murderous extortionist, not an Islamic terrorist.

By this stage the police were, understandably, becoming desperate. In an attempt to pacify the sniper they even complied with a bizarre demand he had made. A police spokesman read the statement 'We've caught the sniper like a duck in a noose' on national television. This was a reference to a folk tale in which an overconfident rabbit tried to catch a duck but ended up noosed itself. The sniper evidently wanted the authorities to feel that they were his playthings as much as his murder victims were.

Then, on 24 October, the police caught him – or rather, them. There turned out to be two killers working together: John Allen Muhammad, aged 41, and John Lee Malvo, aged 17, both Afro-American. On a tip-off from a member of the public, police caught the pair asleep in their car at a road stop on Virginia Interstate Route 70. Closer inspection of the car showed that it had been modified to allow a man to lie inside it and aim a rifle while remaining unseen.

John Allen Muhammad, the Washington Sniper

Muhammad turned out to be a former US soldier who had served in the 1992 Gulf War and had subsequently converted to Islam. Malvo was a Jamaican who lived with Muhammad and evidently regarded the older man as a father figure (nobody has ever suggested there was a sexual relationship between the pair). Both were convicted of murder, extortion and terrorism charges in 2003. Muhammad was sentenced to death and Malvo to life imprisonment without chance of parole.

Why the pair became spree killers remains something of a mystery. Malvo claims to have been brainwashed by Muhammad, but why the older man did so remains hard to pinpoint. Muhammad apparently had nothing against the USA and friends and former colleagues claim he was always a gentle, quiet man. It seems more likely he was simply a serial killer – a man addicted to murder. Investigating police believed that Muhammad was responsible for several, as yet unsolved murders.

Watchmen

Until the eighteenth century, London was policed by a combination of constables and geriatric watchmen, the latter too aged and infirm to earn their living by real work. Known as 'charleys', they were created under Charles II by a 1663 Act of the Common Court of Council, and were soon enshrined as a popular source of derision. Writer T. A. Critchley described them as 'contemptible, dissolute and drunken buffoons who shuffled along the darkened streets after sunset with their long staves and dim lanterns, calling out the time and the state of the weather.' When a charley wanted to summon help, he sounded a wooden rattle.

Often they took their job description literally, to 'watch men' being robbed. Francis Jackson, the eighteenth-century highwayman, reported in his *Recantation*: 'Every highwayman knows that these watchmen are silly old decrepit men who will run away rather than fight. I have seen a dozen of them stand with Halberds in their Hands, yet we have robbed before their very faces, and they stand still the while, not daring to oppose us in the least.' In more energetic mode, Jackson once had a batch trussed up and then took their place for the added ease with which he could accost passers-by. In 1737 a similarly effective system of day-policing was established in the capital.

Parish constables were both more vigorous and more corrupt. Of the eighty in Westminster, **Fielding** found that only six were trustworthy. But he used these **untouchables** to found the Bow Street Runners, the forebears of the modern police force.

See also **Ratcliffe Highway**

Weapons

Murder (and attempted murder) weapons have included: a golf tee (Queripetl), a lawnmower (Whybrow), paving slabs (the Stoneman), an umbrella (Markov), a television aerial (the Goodmans), a chainsaw (Gotti), a meat grinder (Gambino), a bucket (Kidd), a bath (Smith), a pillow (Waite), a poisoned raisin (Lamson), lightbulbs (Thompson), a rattlesnake (James), a life preserver (Kipnik), a putative poisoned suppository (Monroe), an exploding purse (Orchard), a particular object (Solzhenitsyn) and, in May 1982, a cookery-book gun. Sent through the mail to a Brooklyn housewife by an anonymous donor, the *Quick and Delicious Gourmet Cookbook* shot its recipient fatally through the chest with a couple of .22 bullets.

According to the *South Wales Echo*, on 5 June 1990 a Texas Pizza delivery man, Troy Brewer, was robbed in a Balch Springs phone booth. He handed over $50 when, threatened with a turtle, he was told, 'Don't move or you're gonna get bit.' In 1991, the Californian Kao Khae Saephan opened a one-inch gash over his wife's eye with a frozen squirrel.

In 1991, 40 per cent of Britain's 708 homicides were committed with a knife or sharp instrument; seventy-one victims were strangled and eight axed to death.

Weber, Jeanne (b. 1875)

A famous French bungle from the slums of Montmartre. So addicted was Jeanne Weber to **strangulation** that she died trying to throttle herself.

The daughter of a fisherman, Jeanne arrived in Paris in 1893 and married Marcel Weber, an impoverished drunk. Together they produced three children, but two died in infancy; this may have turned her mind and she took to drink. The lure of the cradle drew Jeanne to mind her friends' children, and almost at once two of her charges died. Then on 2 March 1905 she did away with her in-laws' daughter; the killing left telltale red marks round eighteen-month-old Georgette's throat, shrugged off by the parents. When they invited Jeanne to babysit again, she strangled their three-year-old Suzanne.

Brother-in-law Pierre now had no children left, so Jeanne turned to the family of Leon Weber. Throughout the day of 25 March his child Germaine experienced seizures when left alone with Jeanne, who was twice observed 'massaging the infant's heart'. On the third occasion the child died. On the morning of the little girl's funeral, Jeanne moved to quell mounting rumours by suffocating her last child, Marcel. Briefly the object of sympathy, on 5 April Jeanne was asked by another sister-in-law to look after ten-month-old Maurice while she went to the shops. The mother returned just in time to find him gasping for breath. He too had red marks round his throat.

Jeanne was dragged before Inspector Coiret, who established that three years previously two more children – young Alexandre and Marcel Poyatos – in her care had died from convulsive respiratory problems. He put Jeanne under arrest and she was lucky to escape a public lynching. But when the trial opened on 29 January 1906, the eminent medical expert Dr Leon Thoinot assured the court that Maurice, Georgette, Suzanne, Germaine and Marcel had all expired naturally from ailments like bronchitis. Jeanne, he said, was the victim of a witch-hunt, and his evidence secured her discharge. Thoinot's forensic deliberations were issued as an explanatory article for the medical press.

Jeanne left Paris to work as a housekeeper for a M. Bavouzet in a run-down smallholding in the remote countryside of Indre where, on 16 April 1907, she strangled his nine-year-old son Auguste. Noting the red marks round his neck, the local coroner diagnosed meningitis, but when the story reached Paris it exploded into scandal. Jeanne's former legal team, outraged by the new allegations, offered to defend her free of charge. At the inquest Thoinot ascribed Auguste's demise to 'intermittent fever', later denouncing the idiocy of provincial doctors to the Society of Forensic Medicine, and Jeanne found a new benefactor in Dr Georges Bonjeau, President of the Society for the Protection of Children. He gave her a job in one of the Society's homes at Orgeville.

Dismissed for attempted strangulation (which Bonjeau hushed up), Jeanne slid into the life of a prostitute and then joined forces with a lime-burner in a cheap hotel. There she throttled the inn-keeper's son and was discovered hunched over the corpse, covered in blood.

In Paris, Thoinot was asked for his comments. He conceded that this looked like murder. But it was her first. Jeanne, he said, had been 'animated by a frenzy at being accused and arraigned for crimes she did not commit'. Thoinot's influence prevented a further trial and Jeanne was sent to an island asylum off New Caledonia where she died two years later, foaming at the mouth, with her hands locked round her throat.

A recent rival was Marybeth Tinning from New York State. She killed all eight of her children between 1972 and 1985. Her special coup came in 1978 after the first six deaths, when she was taken on by an adoption agency familiar with her track record. They did not wish to increase Marybeth's problems by siding against her.

The adopted child, Michael, did well, lasting nearly three years. Despite a preliminary diagnosis of 'cot death', Marybeth's killing of four-month-old Tami Lynne in October 1985 aroused suspicions because of the blood on her pillow, and she was sentenced to life imprisonment two years later.

The practice of battering babies may be as old as time, but it first came to light in 1944, when it was mistaken for a disease. An American radiologist, Dr Gaffey, noted the first cases, ascribing the disorder to a congenital fragility of the bones causing spontaneous fractures in young infants.

This puzzling skeletal anomaly, the Gaffey Syndrome, was painstakingly explained to the parents, and nine years passed before another American, Dr Silverman, pointed out that victims were perfectly healthy apart from being knocked about. Only in 1955 did Doctors Wooley and Evans put the blame where it belonged, on parents and guardians.

Such was the professional and public ignorance that in Britain a grim line of cases unfolded before the condition was recognised and properly penalised. Thus in December 1963 Laurence Dean, father of four-month-old Susan Moon, left the coroner's court a free man after explaining that his child's fractured skull, the throttling marks round her neck, extensive bruising, several fractured ribs and a broken liver were attributable to bad luck rather than retrospective birth control. Only when his second child died of similar injuries was Dean brought to book for murder.

Perhaps more disquieting, in the mid-1960s many

British cases were heard in magistrates courts for a maximum penalty of six months or a £25 fine.

See also **Münchausen**, **Pregnancy**

Weiss, Dr Carl Austin (d. 1935)

Mild-mannered **assassin** of American demagogue Huey Long, the virtual dictator of the backward state of Louisiana. No one knows why Weiss wanted Huey Long dead more than anyone else, but by 1935 the embattled Senator was speaking out against his critics from behind ranks of armed men, bayonets at the ready, with machine-guns trained on his audience.

According to the generally accepted account, Weiss died immediately after mortally wounding Huey Long with a single shot to the abdomen on 9 September 1935; he hid behind a column in the state Capitol and stepped out as Long walked past. The Senator's body-guards returned fire, filling Weiss with sixty-one bullets at close range.

In November 1991 Weiss's embalmed body was exhumed by Professor James Starrs of Scientific Sleuthing Inc. to ascertain whether Huey Long was actually shot by his own bodyguards – who turned their guns on an innocent bystander to hide their guilt. This theory calls for a reconstruction of the shooting based on the angles of Weiss's numerous entry and exit holes.

But Weiss's perforated body is badly decayed, its preservation botched by the 1935 mortician. 'He lived all these years and died a month before the dig, expressly so as to avoid my wrath,' said Professor Starrs of the undertaker. 'He promised me a decent body.' In its present condition, the corpse is almost useless.

Westies

A particularly vicious New York **gang** of Irish-American criminals, responsible for at least thirty murders in the 1970s and 1980s. For light relief, the Westies played Russian roulette at a thousand dollars a throw. They operated as an Irish mini-Mafia, dealing in drugs, loan-sharking and labour racketeering, and their most baroque killing was the 1981 elimination of one of their own, Paddy Duggan, who defied the gang's leader James Coonan.

After cutting up Duggan's body with a machete, Coonan dropped the severed fingers into his variant of the handbag, the fingerbag, in which he habitually carried his victims' severed digits. Then he took Duggan's head out drinking to a local tavern, depositing it on the bar while he caroused with cronies, toasting his memory and stuffing a lighted cigarette – Duggan's favourite brand – into its lips.

Brutality of this order ensured that the Westies' patch along Manhattan's West Side stayed a no-go area for other gangs, and in 1977 even the Mafia negotiated terms. The Westies promised to stop roughing up *mafiosi* venturing on to their turf; instead, they would act as Gambino 'enforcers' in return for a percentage of their rake-offs.

A trouble-shooter was appointed to liaise between the two gangs and, after meeting his opposite number, Coonan remarked, 'I just met a greaseball tougher than we are.' It was John Gotti.

An earlier gang of contract killers operating out of Manhattan's Lower East Side in the 1870s was the Whyos, whose informal headquarters were a bar known as 'The Morgue'. In 1884 Piker Ryan was arrested with a printed price list in his pocket. Fees ranged from $2 ('punching') and $15 ('ear chawed of') to $25 ('shot in leg') and $100 up for 'doing the big job'; terms were cash in advance.

See also **Murder Inc**.

West Midlands Serious Crime Squad *et al.*

So called, according to the wags, for the serious crimes it committed in England's West Midlands. On 14 January 1992, Valentine Cooke of Birmingham became their ninth case to have his conviction quashed by the **Court of Appeal**. Cooke had been shopped by his 'partner-in-crime', supergrass Paul Jervis, who confessed to 1,510 offences.

As more than 200 of these supposed crimes occurred while Jervis was behind bars, his evidence was ruled unreliable. Two months later, Glen Lewis, serving ten years for burglary, explained why his confession proved so helpful to the prosecution. It had been made up by the police. They denied Lewis access to a solicitor, headbutted him, abused him, menaced him with a hypodermic syringe and then obtained his signature to blank sheets of statement paper. His case was sent for retrial. Delroy Hare, another West Midlands victim, said: 'My confession was totally made up by the police – they threatened to charge my mother if I didn't sign it.' His six-year sentence was quashed on 19 May 1992.

The discovery that the West Midlands Serious Crimes Squad systematically coerced suspects led to the unit's disbandment in August 1989 and the biggest-ever inquiry into police malpractice. Conducted by the police, it encountered strong internal opposition, stiffened by the fact that allegations against officers were entertained from convicted criminals. The investigation spent £1.8 million studying ninety-one complaint files against more than 226 officers, and culminated with sixteen recommendations for prosecution.

But in May 1992 the Director of Public Prosecutions found 'insufficient evidence' to bring charges – not unlikely, since it is one thing to quash a conviction because of a reasonable doubt, another to prove *beyond* doubt exactly who tampered with what and why. Similarly, the judge for the 1989 Guildford Four appeal had no doubt that their conviction was based on false evidence. 'The police officers must have lied,' he concluded. Twelve officers were named, three were charged and in May 1993 all were acquitted.

The case of Judith Minah Ward, convicted of the 1974 M62 bombing when twelve British servicemen lost their lives, contained more disturbing implications. As Miss Ward told the *Independent* seventeen years later: 'I was off my head at that stage. I was completely out of my tree. And after all the questioning, I would have said anything they wanted me to say.'

She did. Ward recalls: 'They would say: "I believe you are a member of the IRA," and I'd be saying "Oh yeah, sure, that's me."' But Ward's confessions went beyond the familiar domain of extorted admissions into the realms of incontrovertible mental derangement. She confessed that she was not Judith Ward, aged 24, but Teresa O'Connell, aged 14. Her claimed marriage to Michael McVerry, the Provisional IRA chief from South Armagh, was a fantasy; she had never met him. Her tales of multitudinous bombings with supposed accomplices never matched the facts. In all, thirty-four of her forty-four police interviews were withheld. Some contained retractions, others preposterous admissions, all were contradictory and highly suggestive of a suspect with a psychiatric disorder, a diagnosis confirmed by medical reports while she awaited trial. But defence lawyers were never informed, and Ward was presented to the court as a formidable terrorist.

Nor was the forensic evidence impartial. The Greiss test for explosives by Dr Frank Skuse proved positive.

But as it detects nitrates common in household cleaners, shoe polish, cigarettes, varnish, soap and so on, it is now regarded, at best, as preliminary screening; it recognises not nitroglycerine (used in explosives) but nitrocellulose (used in manufacturing). Crucially, two series of experiments before the original trial had exposed it as unreliable, but this was disclosed neither to the court, nor to the defence, nor to the prosecution. At Miss Ward's successful 1992 appeal, her original conviction was described by the judges as an 'ambush'.

This broad-brush approach to guilt raises the issue addressed head-on in 1927 by the courageous William O'Connor. As Chicago's Chief Detective, he determined to dispense with trials altogether, calling for a volunteer squad of 500 machine-gunners with war experience from the Flanders trenches.

Their assignment was to roam the Chicago streets in armoured cars and mow the prohibition gangsters down. In a ringing speech, O'Connor declared to his assembled force: 'Men, the war is on. We have got to show that society and the police department, and not a bunch of dirty rats, are running this town. It is the wish of the people of Chicago that you hunt these criminals down and kill them without mercy. Your cars are equipped with machine-guns and you will meet the enemies of society on equal terms. See to it that they do not have you pushing up daisies. Make them push up daisies. Shoot first and shoot to kill. If you kill a notorious feudist you will get a handsome reward and win promotion. If you meet a car containing bandits pursue them and fire. When I arrive on the scene my hopes will be fulfilled if you have shot off the top of their car and killed every criminal inside it.'

That very day, the detective machine-gunners raided the Candy Jobbers' Union and arrested forty-five gangsters for conscripting members by unlawful force. Then, acting on a tip-off, they proceeded to the Rex Hotel at 3142 North Ashland Avenue, where they captured the Milwaukee gunman La Mantio, thereby aborting his mission of killing Al Capone. Direct action, too, has its drawbacks.

See also **Sweden**

Whacks *et al.*

'Whack' is current Mafia jargon for 'to kill', and the New York Mafia made it a rule never to whack journalists. Until the Dios Unanue shooting of 1992 (see **Lingle**), the last murdered reporter died in 1943 for badmouthing Mussolini. According to a New York criminal pundit: 'Whacking a newspaperman, it's like the tide. You wash it out and it comes back in again. You kill a newsman, you get more coming in.'

Perhaps the first criminal laid low by the press was John Toms of Prescot, Lancashire. But this was a fluke, as was his conviction by forensic ballistics. In early 1794 Toms shot Edward Culshaw dead at close range in the head and, on examination, the deceased was found to have newspaper on the brain.

This proved to be the wadding originally rammed down Toms's pistol prior to discharge. The paper penetrated Culshaw's skull in the wake of the bullet and, when extracted, cleaned and unfolded, turned out to be a torn strip from a broadsheet which exactly matched the remainder of the page found in Toms's pocket. On 23 March 1794, he was sentenced to death.

The steady **decline** in the Mafia's fortunes has been matched by a deterioration in its whacking. According to former undercover agent Joe Pistone: 'There was a time when a guy was supposed to get whacked, he got whacked. Now they even have trouble getting that right.' A new low was set by the hit on the unmissable Mafia *capo* Peter Chiodo in May 1991. At 547 pounds (just under a quarter of a ton), Chiodo proved a surprisingly resilient target. Left for dead at Pellicano's gas station on Staten Island after absorbing twelve gunshot wounds, he survived to turn stool pigeon.

See also **Guldensuppe, Hamilton, Lingle**

White Album

Recording by the Beatles which inspired Charles **Manson**. A long-standing fan, he interpreted their double album in the light of The Book of **Revelations** which cast the Fab Four as God's mouthpieces. Manson was riveted by the *White Album* on its December 1968 release and swiftly intuited that its tracks were prophetic. The Beatles were sending him coded messages about the end of the world, and on New Year's Eve Manson arrived in Death Valley to tell the **Family**: 'Are you hep to what the Beatles are saying? Helter Skelter is coming down. The Beatles are telling it like it is.'

On careful listening, nearly all the *White Album*'s tracks bore out his views. The lyrics of 'I Will' formed a direct appeal to Manson to get into a recording studio: 'And when at last I find you, your song will fill the air, sing it loud so I can hear you.' The Beatles knew that their redeemer lived on the Pacific coast. Why else sing, 'Oh honey pie, you are driving me frantic, sail across the Atlantic, to be where you belong'?

It could only be Manson, and the time was now. In 'Blackbird', the Beatles reminded him, 'You were only waiting for this moment to arise.' The lyrics of 'Piggies' filled in the details, presaging a future where grotesque porcine couples dined out, stabbing at their food with knives and forks – which was what pigs deserved. They got it too, the following August, Rosemary LaBianca expiring from forty-one knife wounds and her husband Leno from twelve, with a fork in his stomach and 'Death to Pigs' scrawled in blood on the walls.

Then there was 'Helter Skelter', a song about a fairground ride. To Manson, it evoked the Family's dizzying descent into the 'bottomless pit' foretold in Revelations, when they would shelter from the coming bloodbath: 'Look out helter skelter, she's coming down fast.' Most of all, the extended sound-picture of 'Revolution 9' was a harbinger of the imminent carnage. In the background were machine-guns, oinking pigs and, very faintly, two minutes and thirty-four seconds into the track, the word 'Rise' repeated in a long drawn out scream, so like the same word daubed in blood on 10 August 1969 at the LaBiancas' residence, where the message 'Healther Skelter' was left on their fridge.

The killings came only a few days after Manson's humiliating musical rebuff of 5 August 1969 at the Esalen Institute, a 'personal growth' centre. He dropped by and (in the words of side-kick Paul Watkins) 'played his guitar for a bunch of people there … and they rejected his music. Some people pretended they were asleep, and others were saying, "This is too heavy for me" and "I'm not ready for that" … and some just got up and walked out.' It so happened that a record producer, Terry Melcher, who Manson had once hoped would land him a recording deal, owned an isolated house in Benedict Canyon, and three days later Manson sent Charles 'Tex' Watson, Susan Atkins, Patricia Krenwinkel and Linda Kasabian to start Helter Skelter there, at 10050 Cielo Drive.

On the night of 8 August, Watson cut the telephone wires before climbing over the fence. A car came through the grounds towards them; Watson flagged it down and shot the driver four times. Then they broke into the house through a window, marshalled the four occupants in the living room and forced them face-down on the floor. The two women, one with child, were roped to an overhead beam by their necks, but one of the men broke free and fought his way outside to collapse from two gunshots, thirteen blows to the head and fifty-one **stab** wounds. Meanwhile one of the women ran off, escaping through the french windows. She too was caught, slashed twenty-eight times. The other man was knifed seven times and shot once, and the pregnant woman knifed sixteen times. Atkins dipped a towel in her blood, and wrote 'Pigs' on the door.

The gang withdrew, tossing their bloodstained clothes down a hill from Benedict Canyon Road. Krenwinkel's hand ached, bruised from stabbing to the bone, and the other girls' scalps smarted from having their hair pulled.

Manson was waiting at Spahn Ranch. 'What are you doing home so early?' he asked. 'Boy,' said Watson, 'it sure was Helter Skelter.' The following night, Manson led another raiding party.

Today, an audio-cassette of Manson's music survives in specialist circulation. The lyrics disclose unusually high levels of hostility, with refrains like 'You'll get yours'.

White death

A serious risk for body-packing drug runners. The contraband is sealed into perhaps a hundred grape-sized pellets of four or five grams each, wrapped in **condoms**, surgical gloves or toy balloons. These are swallowed. Nine times out of ten a punctured capsule kills; only intensive hospital care with oxygen, short-acting barbiturates, psychiatric sedatives and constant maintenance of the air passages pulls the smuggler through the onslaught of undiluted cocaine in bulk hitting the lining of his gut. This state of acute toxic psychosis, of which the most prominent symptoms are euphoria, disorientation, behavioural change and fever, is known as White Death.

Problems most often arise when a capsule gets stuck in the caecum or blind gut at the entrance of the large intestine. When a smuggler counts all the capsules in but does not count them all out, his days are generally numbered; no enema or laxative will shift the tiny cargo of death. The gastric juices rumble on, slowly eating away the rubber protective cladding until one day it ruptures.

In 1992, four of the five cases diagnosed at British airports died.

White Mischief

At three o'clock on the morning of 24 January 1941 the body of Josslyn Hay, Lord Erroll, was found slumped underneath the steering wheel of his Buick, plunged halfway into a deep trench by the Ngong road eight miles from Nairobi. It looked like an accident, but the bullet hole by Erroll's ear was noticed later that day in the mortuary.

Lord Erroll, aged 39 and Scotland's premier earl, was an accomplished seducer of other men's wives; he pleasured one on the billiard table of Nairobi's Norfolk Hotel. Together with his first wife Idina, the twice-divorced daughter of Earl de La Warr, he helped found Kenya's 'Happy Valley'. At their ranch, 'Clouds', Joss and Idina entertained well-bred misfits who swilled cocktails and indulged in wife-swapping and high jinks; Idina held court, bathing and dressing in front of her guests and allocating bedroom keys at will. Cocaine and heroin were flown up from Nairobi and injected with silver syringes. Golf, bridge, horse-racing, backgammon, croquet and polo provided more serious occupations.

By 1941 any number of emotional casualties might have preferred Joss dead. But the main suspect was always Sir Jock Delves Broughton, the ageing husband of the desirable Diana who, in her turn, had become Erroll's very public mistress. Diana was 27. Sir Delves, thirty years her senior, suffered from an arthritic right hand and a dragging left foot. But he had money; in 1926 his spending topped £120,000. As he joylessly remarked: 'The first eighty was easy, but unless you gamble the rest is sheer extravagance.'

Sir Delves had known Diana for five years before proposing. An angelic blonde in appearance, Diana was a handsome divorcee who ran a London cocktail club, the Blue Goose. She pursued a hectic social life by private aeroplane, and if her lipstick was too red, her *penchant* for pearls too overt and her ancestry rather middlebrow, she had looks and style.

Diana's contemporaries were pairing off, and she accepted Broughton's offer. He closed the family seat, Doddington, and married her the week before they arrived in Kenya on 12 November 1940. She quickly clarified her position to her husband's old African friends: 'I'm not sharing a room with *that* dirty old man. I insist on a room to myself.' Less than three weeks later she met Lord Erroll and, the moment they were alone, he asked, 'Well, who's going to tell Jock? You or I?' Their affair ran wildfire, and on 6 January Broughton was tipped off about the romance.

Broughton had agreed to pay Diana £5,000 a year for at least five years after a divorce, making her doubly attractive to Erroll who, after the death of his second wife, an heiress, from heroin and champagne, was limping by on £300 a year. Broughton seemed to bow to the inevitable, accepting that he could not force his wife's affections. With great self-restraint he 'cut his losses', offering Diana the house at Karen while he left on a protracted trip to Ceylon.

'I am sorry it happened so soon,' she mouthed. That night Erroll, Diana, Broughton and June Carberry – an Erroll discard – sat down to a celebration supper. Broughton toasted the euphoric couple: 'I wish them every happiness and may their union be blessed with an heir.' The party broke up; Broughton and June returned to Karen where she helped him up the stairs. The maid fetched June a whisky and stayed chatting by her bedside. Erroll took Diana dancing, dropping her back at around 2.15 a.m. Still up, the maid let the young lovers in. June too remained awake. 'Please drive carefully,' said Diana as Joss left.

'Carefully but not slowly,' said the debonair Joss. Less than an hour later he was found dead two and a half miles away. The murder made the headlines in wartime London, where Broughton's acquaintances at White's and Brook's laid wagers on whether he would be hanged. His motive might be clear, but the evidence was circumstantial. The prosecution could never prove *how* Broughton killed Erroll while – apparently – lying sozzled and asleep in the bedroom of a crowded and wakeful house. Neither the maid nor June Carberry heard Broughton leave for, or return from, what would have been a five-mile round trip, and he was definitely at home at 3.30 a.m., when he called into June's bedroom 'to ask if she was all right'.

Ballistics provided the most incriminating evidence. The police recovered bullets which they claimed Broughton had fired during a practice shoot at another ranch (the 'Nanyuki' bullets). These matched the murder ammunition, and were linked to the obvious murder weapon: Broughton's registered pair of Colt .32s, reported stolen on 21 January. During a seven-hour cross-examination, the defence lawyer Harry Morris KC detailed endless tiny differences between the bullets. There always are. Then he played his trump card. 'In all these bullets was the direction uniform?' he demanded. 'Yes, it is right hand in all the bullets.'

'Is the direction in a Colt revolver right or left?'

'Left in the barrel,' admitted Harwich, the expert witness. The prosecution had not anticipated this simple point, which proved that the bullets had not come from a Colt. Their case foundered, and the explanation – that Broughton used some other make of .32 – hardly dared show its head for shame. Broughton was discharged on 1 July after withstanding twenty hours of cross-examination with *sang froid*. He set off for Ceylon with Diana, but their marriage soon crumbled, Diana effecting a smooth transition to the eccentric rancher Gilbert Colville, perhaps – in the words of a neighbour – 'the most boring man in the world', while Broughton left for England in September 1942 with the case still unsolved.

Kenyans discussed the crime for decades; alibis were complicated because many suspects were too drunk to remember where they were or with whom they were sleeping. Broughton remains the key. The Nanyuki bullets were charged with black powder, a propellant almost unobtainable since 1914, and black scorch marks were found on Joss's entry wound. Was Broughton's firearms certificate misleading? Were his guns really Colts? Did he have another gun? Was the gun robbery faked? Why had Broughton lit a bonfire the day after the murder in the Karen rubbish pit? A golfing stocking stained with blood smouldered in the embers, but Broughton disowned it; he never wore them.

Thirty years later Cyril Connolly and James Fox started a spirited investigation fuelled by lunches at the Savoy grill, the Connaught and the Ritz. Many 'survivors' were contacted. The Earl of Carnarvon, interviewed in Highclere Castle in May 1980, described Broughton as a weak man – vain, dishonest and a coward – who faked sunstroke to avoid war service. Behind the financial glamour, Broughton was a taciturn dullard, never known to make a joke, who allowed Lord Moyne to run off with his first wife without voicing any objection.

Despite an annual income of £80,000, Broughton dissipated his fortune in fifteen years. As money ran short he stole from the estate, appropriating £1.5 million from the sale of 32,500 acres of farmland. This too he squandered. The family found him out – hence the departure for Kenya ahead of disgrace. In June 1939 Broughton staged an insurance theft of pearls from Diana's car in the South of France, and blackmailed his accomplice, Hugh Dickinson, into stealing three over-insured pictures from Doddington, destroying two Romney portraits in the process. Broughton, in short, was bent.

In late 1942, the disconsolate Broughton was lodging alone in 'Badger's Bank', the butler's house on the estate. He ran into Alan Horn, a local horse breeder, and confessed in a Nantwich pub. Then on 30 November 1942 Broughton confided in his last remaining friend, Marie Woodhouse: 'You know I did it, I've never run so fast in my life.'

Two days later, while staying alone in Liverpool's Adelphi Hotel, he gave himself fourteen injections of Medinal and died on 5 December.

In 1980 June Carberry's stepdaughter told James Fox that Broughton had confessed to her too, at the Nyeri house the day after the murder. He arrived in a terrible state. No one else was there, and he related how everyone had mocked him and that he had shot Joss and thrown the gun into the Thika Falls.

Despite his impervious stance at the trial, Broughton was distraught at the loss of his wife, his resentment inflamed, Fox learned, by an accidental meeting with Joss and Diana glued together on the dance floor after the handover dinner. Paula Long, another old Kenya hand, said that Jock favoured golfing stockings and produced a photograph in proof.

In May 1993 the Broughton hypothesis was reinforced by the discovery of his letter to Diana of October 1942. It reveals her as more promiscuous than previously imagined, and Broughton as more deeply wounded and devious. The saga of the pearl theft reared its head anew, with Broughton blackmailing Diana. 'I have always been suspicious as to what you had inside the deed box you gave me to give to George Green [Broughton's solicitor],' he wrote. 'The penalty for this offence is fourteen years' hard labour.'

Broughton catalogued Diana's infidelities. 'On board the boat you became a stranger to me. You started a fuck with Tony Morrant under my eyes and I discovered the copy of a letter you wrote to your Italian, the most violent love letter … You made such a farce of our marriage that the registrar almost refused to marry you.' Then came her affair with a man named Orle. Of his fellow-dullard and successor Colville, Broughton noted, 'You knew he was the richest settler in Kenya… and laid yourself out to ensnare him.' An interlude with Hugh Strickland followed. 'You put him in a room with no lock on the door opening straight out into your rooms … I listened to him fuck you not more than three yards away. By the way the whole bed rocked, you evidently enjoyed it, like you used to with me.'

It is of such misalliances – unworkable, unleavable, tortured and, in this case, semi-voyeuristic – that domestic murders are born.

Wild, Jonathan (1683–1725)

An underworld receiver who ran with the hare and hunted with the hounds to become 'Thief-Taker General of Great Britain and Ireland'. Wild was the first mobster, a pioneering exponent of organised crime.

After imprisonment for **debt** as a young man, Wild set up as a pimp and accumulated enough money for his own London receiver-cum-brothel, in Cock Lane.

A successful receiver could eliminate the middleman. Instead of fencing his stolen property at a discount, Wild flogged it direct to a really appreciative end-buyer: the previous owner. Both the thief and the victim went straight to Wild, who split his take with the thief, paying an unusually generous rate. There was no law against letting owners know where their goods were or in sharing in the 'reward'. Wild was careful never to take possession of the loot, but compiled a list of hot merchandise and then approached the punter to put him in touch.

A talented businessman with a bureaucratic streak, Wild invested in his market by funding crime. He organised gangs throughout England, retaining jewellers to melt plate and cannibalise jewellery. He hired out burglars' tools and exported booty to Holland in his own sloop. Meanwhile, he collected incriminating files on his burgeoning armies of crooks.

Wild laid claim to the high rewards paid to informers which, starting under the reign of William and Mary, were set at £1 for betraying a deserter, £10 for a horse thief and £40 for a highwayman. Wild kept his underlings in line by threatening to turn them in and, with every man's neck on the line, he could fabricate charges or secure acquittals at will. In a submission to the Lord Mayor petitioning for elevation as a freeman of the City, Wild noted that he had, at some personal risk, sent

Invitation to an execution

a good sixty criminals to the gallows. Among them was Joseph 'Blueskin' Blake, Jack **Sheppard**'s whoring companion and accomplice, brought to trial in 1724 at the Old Bailey Sessions House on Wild's evidence.

Before the hearing, Wild approached Blake and offered a swig from his flask, hoping for information to turn to advantage. Blueskin misread the gesture and asked him to put in a good word. Wild laughed: 'I can't do that. You're a dead man and will be tucked up very speedily.' Hoping to decapitate Wild and throw his head to the rabble, Blake took out a penknife and soon had Wild's throat cut to the windpipe. But the blade was blunt and further progress of the assault was impeded by Wild's thick plaited muslin stock; two surgeons standing nearby saved the informer's life. This abortive onslaught assured Blake instant nationwide popularity fanned by numerous ballads. The best of these was by John Gay, to be sung to the tune of 'The Cut Purse':

Attend and draw near
Good news ye shall hear
How Jonathan's throat was cut from Ear to Ear.

Wild habitually dressed in lace finery, and carried a sword and a gold-topped cane. To the public, Wild and the law were synonymous, and his gang achieved a semi-legal, guildlike status. Parliament was not so pleased, and in 1718 the so-called 'Wild Act' created the new offence of accepting a reward without prosecuting the thief. So Wild changed tack, advising customers who wanted their goods back to abandon their money at a safe house, leaving nothing to prove that he had received payment or handled their property. Nevertheless, by a happy irony, in 1725 Wild was convicted under the Wild Act for pocketing a ten guinea finder's fee. He was hanged on 24 May of that year, pelted all the way to the **Tyburn** gallows, where the mob screamed at the hangman to hurry up. His dying act was to pick the executioner's pocket.

Wild was the eponymous hero of Henry Fielding's 1743 satirical novel *The Life of Jonathan Wild the Great* and, according to the American crime historian John Nash, inspired Conan Doyle's Moriarty, London's '**Napoleon** of Crime'. By a curious quirk of fate, for many years a publication called *Moriarty's Police Law* was the bible of the force.

Like Jonathan Wild, Scotland's Earl of Morton was hoist on his own petard. In 1565 Morton was so impressed by the **Halifax Gibbet** that he had a replica made, the Scottish Maiden, with which he himself was beheaded in 1581.

See also **Oaths**

Wind in the Willows

Kenneth Grahame was lucky to survive to write the children's classic *Wind in the Willows*.

Grahame worked at the Bank of England and, in December 1903, a young man called George Frederick Robinson was ushered into his office.

Robinson handed over some papers bound up with two ribbons, one black and one white, and since Grahame chose to untie the roll with the black ribbon, Robinson drew his revolver and banged off five shots at the future author. Grahame was only hit once (see **Shootist**); Robinson ran out, shouting, 'Come on, you cowards and curs', and took refuge in another room where he was subdued with a firehose.

At his trial, it transpired that the escapade was a mad political protest; political, because of Robinson's concern about the unequal distribution of wealth, and mad because a rabid dog had bitten him. Robinson would have spared Grahame had he chosen the white ribbon.

Witchcrazes

From about 1450 to 1750, Europe – with the exception of Britain (see **Hopkins**) – was gripped by a 'witch-craze'. Witches were exterminated in huge numbers, estimated at anywhere between 200,000 and 9 million. In the high period they were roped up and burned in groups of hundreds. According to Henry Charles Lea (*History of the Inquisition of the Middle Ages, 1906*): 'A bishop of Geneva is said to have burned five hundred within three months, a bishop of Bamberg six hundred, a bishop of Wurzburg, nine hundred. Eight hundred were condemned, apparently in one body, by the senate of Savoy.' It took the witch-finder Franz Buirman only five years from 1631 to incinerate half the population of a village of three hundred. Wurzburg lost 757 souls, including children as young as three.

Until the thirteenth century the church clung to the old-fashioned idea that night-riding groups of devil-worshipping women were a silly superstition. But the fledgling **Inquisition** had the concept of the female heretic on a firm scientific footing by about 1430, and the 1480s saw the publication of the standard text-book, *Malleus Maleficarum* (The Hammer of the Witches), and the papal bull *Sumnis desiderantes affectibus*, which declared open season on 'heretical pravities'. As the *Malleus* noted, 'All witchcraft comes from carnal lust, which is in women insatiable... wherefore for the sake of fulfilling their lusts they consort even with devils.'

Identifying a witch was best left to the professional 'witch-prickers', common throughout Europe. Armed with long needles, they roamed from town to town, exercising their right to strip, shave, rape and stab suspects in search of the telltale W-spot insensitive to pain. This was the Devil's Mark, the sure sign of a woman given over to debauchery. The guilty were burned or strangled to protect the religious and social order, including its highly vulnerable component of the male organ.

For it was well known to readers of the *Malleus* that witches caused impotence. 'They directly prevent the erection of the member which is accommodated to fructification ... they prevent the flow of the vital essences ... so that it cannot be ejaculated or is fruit-lessly spilled.' Countless unfortunates had their penises stolen, rounded up into early concentration camps: 'And what, then, is to be thought of those witches who in this way sometimes collect male organs in great numbers, as many as twenty or thirty members together, and put them in a bird's nest, or shut them up in a box where they move themselves like living members, and eat oats and corn, as has been seen by many and is a matter of common report?'

Indeed, as late as 1990 an outbreak of penis-snatch-ing surfaced in Lagos, Nigeria, when a scare ran through the city that evil magicians were spiriting away citizens' willies under the pretext of shaking hands. According to the *Nation* of 30 October 1990, the missing components reappeared for sale as luxury items in the thriving witchcraft market. People lost their lives to the craze. A typical incident in the town of Enugu started when a passenger boarding a bus noticed that his member had vanished. He shouted out; the man in front was dragged down and beaten; a policeman tried to restore calm by firing warning shots which wounded a woman and her child, and killed the bus driver. Other reports claim at least four suspects were killed by lynch mobs, the mania exacer-bated by hundreds of arrests for rumour-mongering after the Deputy Police Commissioner James Danbaba issued a plea for calm.

In Europe, popes, saints, theologians, scholars, and the well-known *penseur* Pascal, endorsed the only proper counter-measure of rounding up the usual suspects and burning them. Modern sociologists regard this impulse as a response to insecurity engen-dered by the breakdown of the medieval world in general and the emergence of a new and marginally less downtrodden role for women. Others find paral-lels between the witchcraze and the modern era's **sex crime**. In both, the intent is said to be gynocide; in both, the assaults are justified by manufactured cate-gories (witch-prickers/sexual psychopath) that obscure the basic gynocidal intent. Anyone looking for a pre-decessor to Peter **Sutcliffe** in his mission to 'clean the place up a bit' would find the fifteenth-century witch-prickers had relevant work experience; and impotence, or the fear of impotence, is a common thread uniting the two callings. Like the witches of yore, the serial killers of today are 'down on whores' for their carnal lust, 'which is in women insatiable', and are commonly unable to respond to normal sexual stimuli. In effect, their penises have been spirited away, and **Chikatilo**, the Russian Ripper, bared his in court for public denigration. He too regarded his underclass victims as sluts unworthy of life.

Perhaps the best-known witchcraze happened in Massachusetts at Salem Village, a settlement at the edge of the wilderness still at the mercy of scalping parties. Five witches were hanged on 19 July 1692, another five a month later, one on 19 September, and eight more three days later.

The trouble began in the kitchen of the Reverend Mr Parris, where his West Indian housewoman regaled his young class of a dozen adolescent girls with tales of palmistry, necromancy and wizards. Over the winter her impressionable charges began to see things that went bump in the night. The hysteria took root; rumours of covens proliferated, and when the girls went into fits, biting their lips until they bled, rolling on the floor and growling like animals, the local doctor diagnosed witchcraft. Their seizures, reproduced in court, may have been real, or feigned out of malice or peer-group pressure. Proof of enchantment was furnished by transference of the 'witch fluid' when a victim quietened after touching the witch – an easy courtroom stunt. Fifty-five suspects saved their lives by confessing, but the obdurate went to the gallows, among them Susanna Martin, convicted on overwhelming evidence on 29 June 1692.

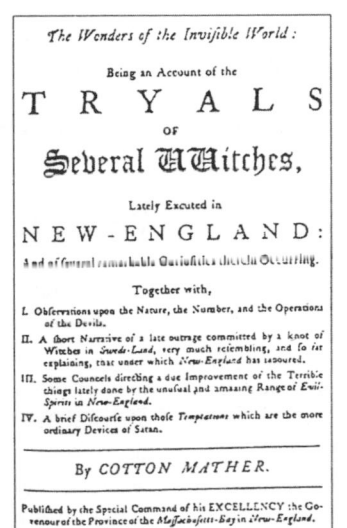

The Wonders of the Invisible World :

Being an Account of the

T R Y A L S

OF

Several Witches,

Lately Executed in

N E W - E N G L A N D :

And of several remarkable Curiosities therein Occurring.

Together with,

I. Observations upon the Nature, the Number, and the Operations of the Devils.

II. A short Narrative of a late outrage committed by a knot of Witches in Swords-Land, very much resembling, and so far explaining, that under which New-England has laboured.

III. Some Councels directing a due Improvement of the Terrible things lately done by the unusual and amazing Range of Evil-Spirits in New-England.

IV. A brief Discourse upon those Temptations which are the more ordinary Devices of Satan.

By COTTON MATHER.

Published by the Special Command of his EXCELLENCY the Governour of the Province of the Massachusetts-Bay in New-England.

Printed first, at Boston in New-England; and Reprinted at London, for John Dunton, at the Raven in the Poultry. 1693.

Her neighbour, Robert Downer, testified that Susanna had burst into his room looking just like a cat. And when he said, 'Avoid, thou she-devil', the creature ran away. While coming back from the woods, John Kembal got lost in a cloud which made him trip over tree stumps. Afterwards he was attacked by a brown puppy which fled when he cried 'Jesus Christ'. John Pressy had crossed words with Susanna twenty years before: she warned, 'That he should never have more than two cows; that tho' he was likely to have more, yet he should never have them.' And Pressy never did; something always cropped up.

Other witnesses told similar tales. When Susanna was asked what she had to say, 'Her chief plea was, "She had led a most virtuous and holy life."' In May 1693 the Salem episode ended with the Governor's issue of a pre-emptive group pardon, embracing both those found guilty and those awaiting trial.

There is, as yet, no sign of abatement in the American flood of satanic **ritual abuse** cases. 'In Salem,' according to psychiatrist Paul McHugh, 'the convictions depended on how judges thought the witches behaved. In our day, the conviction depends on how some therapists think a child's **memory** of trauma works.' That is, present allegations assume the reliability of 'recalled memories' stimulated under therapy.

The stories (where witches fly into bedrooms or meet in covens for human sacrifices) have not varied significantly over the centuries, unlike the status of those impeached and of their accusers. Formerly, witches were nearly all women, often misfits or outcasts; today, nearly all are men, generally of some standing and success. Research by Philadelphia's False Memory Syndrome Foundation shows that the majority of the accused had stable marriages, were college educated, on average commanding incomes in excess of $60,000, and that their families ate and vacationed together. Typically, they are denounced by their adult daughters, and those facing such charges may, with reason, evince the fashionable syndrome of white male paranoia.

Wobblies

Popular name for the anarchist wing of the revolutionary IWW group (Industrial Workers of the World) prevalent in the United States in the decade preceding the First World War. Their chief dynamiter was Harry Orchard, born Albert E. Horsley.

In 1903 Orchard blew up a mine shaft in Cripple Creek, Colorado, killing two. Next he detonated 100 pounds of explosive under a railway platform, despatching twenty-six miners – strikebreakers – and crippling fifty for life. Then Orchard singled out wealthy Fred Bradley, a member of the Mine Owners Association in San Francisco. But the taste of **strychnine** in Bradley's milk bottle made his cook throw away its contents. So Orchard blew up his target's house, completely destroying the three-storey façade as Bradley left for work, on this occasion flying across the street. He survived.

Next on Orchard's list was Luther M. Goddard, a Colorado Supreme Court judge. Planning to liquidate him with an exploding purse, Orchard deposited the device on a snow-swept path where it was picked up by another Denver citizen, Merrit W. Walley, parts of whom were found half a mile away.

Orchard was finally caught making a getaway from Caldwell, Idaho on 30 December 1905, shortly after vaporising the state's ex-Governor. He was condemned to death, but the unions exerted heavy influence to have the sentence commuted to life imprisonment.

Wolfsbane

Source of the deadly vegetable poison aconitine. Wolfsbane (*Aconitum napellus*) resembles parsley, but only in appearance; it attacks the central nervous system, causing nausea, vomiting, loss of muscle power, paralysis and death, on occasion producing death in eight minutes. A tiny dose of 1–2mg will kill, and the toxin was so fashionable among Romans that the Emperor Trajan had the plant banned. More recently, Dr George Henry Lamson was executed in April 1882 for murdering his brother-in-law Percy with an aconitine Madeira cake.

It was a tricky killing, since the crippled Percy was still at school in Wimbledon. The cake, which the prosecution argued contained a single poisoned raisin, was handed round slice by pre-cut slice in the presence of the lad's headmaster, Mr Bedbrook, while the grown-ups sipped sherry.

A misconceived diversionary ruse by Lamson accentuated suspicions. Anticipating that his nephew's abrupt demise would not pass without remark, he attempted to impress the gathering with irrefutable proof that he could not have poisoned Percy with sugar, and, calling for a bowl, spooned some into his sherry, drinking it without ill-effects. His cast-iron defence to contaminated sugar thus established, Lamson demonstrated the user-friendly qualities of a new American pill capsule to the party. Filling it from the same bowl, he said, 'Here, Percy, you are a champion pill-taker', and the lad swallowed it down.

Notwithstanding this harmless intake, Percy was dead within four hours, making it abundantly clear that he had eaten *something* that disagreed with him. That left the cake. Lamson stood to inherit through his wife; he fled to Paris, but returned to face trial. The toxicology of alkaloids was still very primitive, but Dr Thomas Stevenson, lecturer in medical jurisprudence at Guy's, processed Percy's innards for an extract of the poison. This he placed on his tongue and identified the aconitine by taste. Despite Lamson's efforts to gain a reprieve, he was executed on 28 April 1882, and during his last days hysterical women admirers sent him gifts of flowers and fruit.

See **Bobettes**

Wood, James

*'He who can smile when things go wrong
Has thought of someone he can blame it on.'*

This anonymous couplet encapsulates the psychology of most serial killers, who are basically driven by irrational resentment. But it applies to rapist and murderer James Wood more than most. He was a one-man crime wave, credited with sixty murders, eighty-five rapes and 185 robberies.

James Wood came to Pocatello, Idaho, at Halloween 1992, leaving behind a marriage that had been successful until he raped his 14-year-old stepdaughter.

James Wood

It was entirely her fault, he said, for dressing 'skimpily'. His wife ordered him out of the house.

On the way from Louisiana to Idaho, he kidnapped a teenage girl named Jeanne Faser at a petrol station near St Louis, raped her in the back of his truck, then shot her in the temple and left her for dead.

Six days later he called on his cousin, Dave Haggard, who had not seen him since childhood. Haggard made a living laying linoleum in Pocatello, and Wood became his house guest. Haggard was aware that his cousin had been in prison, although he was not sure why. But Wood seemed a nice enough character and was soon popular in the neighbourhood. He was tidy around the house, always ready to help and good with children.

He possessed artistic talent and would paint excellent nature scenes on old saws and metal milk jugs; he was also a skilled tattooist. Soon he was selling his artwork locally.

When an armed robbery took place at a nearby hot-dog counter, Wood was not even suspected. To begin with, he seemed to have a perfect alibi. He was with his cousin and some acquaintances when it took place, although he had been out of the room – presumably in the toilet – at the actual time of the hold-up. No one thought that he could have hurried down the street, held up the store and hurried back, all in ten minutes.

Neither did anyone suspect him when a pretty teenager named Beth Edwards was abducted and raped. She had been strapping her baby sister into the child seat in the back of the car when a man pushed a gun into her stomach and told her to get into the passenger seat. He drove her to a clearing near the main road and made her lie across the front seat. He played with her breasts, then removed her jeans and panties and performed oral sex on her, which brought him to a premature ejaculation.

Still not satisfied, he forced her to perform oral sex on him, then raped her. He then made her kneel and held the gun to her head; she expected to die, but it misfired. Instead he drove her some distance away and allowed her to go, carrying her sister. Twice during the assault he had told her: 'I'm in control.' Wood later returned the car to the place where he had kidnapped her.

An anonymous caller told the police that it would be worth checking out a man called James Woods as a suspect; but no James Woods in Pocatello corresponded to the rapist's description, with beard, moustache and two missing front teeth. If the caller had got the name right, it would have been the end of Wood's career of crime in Pocatello.

Wood was introduced to Brenda Davis, a single mother of three – two girls and a boy. He became a regular visitor at the house, and stayed the night. In the early hours of the morning Wood climbed into bed with the eleven-year-old girl, removed her pyjama bottoms and began kissing her buttocks. She screamed and ran down the corridor to join her brother. But she told no one what had happened. Not long afterwards Wood took the elder sister, Karen, who was 14, for a drive in a van. He dragged her by the hair into the back of the van, said, 'Now we're going to fuck', and raped her. Because he threatened he would kill her mother, she also told no one.

Soon after, Wood offered a lift to a blonde in a miniskirt, then forced her at gunpoint to fellate him, after which he raped her and pushed her out of the car.

On 29 June 1993 Wood picked up a ten-year-old girl, Jeralee Underwood, who was delivering newspapers. Jeralee vanished.

On a camping trip with his cousin and family members, Wood drew attention to himself by falling silent when everyone was discussing Jeralee's disappearance, then went into the camper van. Now someone recollected that the police drawing of the rapist of Beth Edwards had looked like Wood. They recalled that he had shaved off his goatee after the rape, and that he had stopped wearing a favourite fleece-lined jacket – which Beth reported the rapist as wearing. Dave Haggard recalled that Wood had been out all night when Jeralee disappeared, and the next day had carefully cleaned out his car and moved it behind a caravan so that it was not visible from the road.

Police Sergeant Scott Shaw had already received more tips that Wood might be the wanted man. A check into Wood's criminal record revealed that he had served time for the attempted murder of two girls by cutting their throats, and for raping one of them after he believed she was dead. Shaw lost no time in arresting him.

At the police station, Wood admitted immediately that he had pulled Jeralee Underwood into the car and driven off with her. But he claimed she had showed so much resistance when he tried to caress her buttocks that he had let her out alive.

Shaw treated Wood gently and sympathetically. He

may have been aware that most serial killers are dominant males who resent authority. When he said that he realised that Wood had had a bad childhood, and that everything in his life had turned out wrong, Wood looked at him in amazement and asked how he knew. In fact, Shaw knew that this is the story of most serial killers. Soon after, Wood admitted Jeralee was dead. He would also admit to returning to the corpse for sex, and finally dismembering it.

He confessed to other crimes, including the rape of Beth Edwards, and the attempt to shoot her in the back of the head when the gun jammed. Since he was 18, in 1965, his life had been a saga of robbery, rape and murder.

His father had gone to prison when Wood was a child, and his mother's new husband, Wood claimed, had abused him. After his mother died in a factory fire, he spent most of his teens in approved school. He committed his first rape at the age of 22 – in fact, two rapes on the same day. Soon after, he shot a horse he found tied to a tree (it was a Christmas present for a child), simply to see what it felt like to kill something.

Wood admitted to three murders: of Jeralee Underwood, of a teenage girl in Missouri and of a young mother of four children, Shirley Coleman, whom he kidnapped because she was driving an expensive car and 'had class' – he felt that he would never otherwise have sex with a woman who was his social superior.

He did not mention Jeanette Faser, the teenager he had kidnapped on his way to Pocatello and shot in the head. He had believed she was dead – until she later appeared at his trial. The shot had permanently disabled her, but she was alive.

Wood showed Shaw a self-portrait, with the background full of tiny figures of women. He told Shaw these were his victims. Shaw counted sixty of them.

In December 1993 James Wood was sentenced to die by lethal injection.

Woodward, Louise

It is a sad fact that, for all the talk of what Winston Churchill called 'the special relationship' between Britain and the USA, it doesn't take much to reveal the subsurface dislikes and irritations that lie between the two nations. The case of Louise Woodward is a good

example. Throughout the teenager's odyssey through the labyrinthine US legal system, UK opinion polls were of the overall view that she was innocent, while US poles on the same subject invariably leaned towards a verdict of guilt, and a lot of bad blood and bile was spouted by tabloids and the opinionated on both sides of the Atlantic.

Louise Woodward

In November 1996, Louise Woodward, from Elton in Cheshire, successfully interviewed for the job of live-in-nanny for the Eappens, a well-to-do family in Boston, Massachusetts. Unfortunately, there were problems from the start. The 18-year-old, new to the USA, wanted to stay up late and sample Boston's nightlife. The Eappens, on the other hand, told her that they wanted her back home no later than 11 p.m. Things got bad enough for Sunil and Deborah Eappen to draw up a set of their expectations from a nanny – the prime one being the 'safety and well-being' of their two children, baby Matthew and toddler Brendan.

On 4 February 1997, Louise Woodward called the emergency services and said that Matthew Eappen was having difficulty breathing. Rushed to hospital and put on a life-support machine, the eight-month-old baby died six days later. The autopsy showed that he had suffered a skull fracture and brain injuries. It was also noted that he had a month-old wrist fracture that had gone unnoticed by both Louise and his parents.

The police arrested Louise and later claimed that the teenager made a verbal confession, stating that, because he would not stop crying (presumably because of the pain in his wrist) she had shaken Matthew and thrown him on to a pile of towels shortly before his breathing had become erratic; a confession Louise later vehemently denied ever making.

Whoever was telling the truth over the confession, it came as a shock to many when the Massachusetts State Prosecutor pressed a charge of first-degree murder against Woodward (implying, of course, that she had deliberately murdered the baby). In another shock, Louise was denied bail and sent to a maximum-security prison for women to await her trial – harsh treatment that infuriated the British press.

The trial was held the following October. Two doctors who had examined Matthew – surgeon Joseph Medsen and pathologist Gerard Feigin – gave evidence that, in their professional opinion, Matthew's skull fracture might have been sustained days or even weeks before the claimed 'shaking incident'. Feigin also stated that he had found no conclusive evidence that the baby had been shaken at all.

The defence then called the respected forensics expert Barry Scheck, who suggested that Matthew might have suffered from a genetic disorder that caused his skull to be over-prone to fracturing. Alternatively, he added, two-year-old Brendan – the only other person in the Eappen house that night apart from Louise – might have caused the fracture.

At this stage it became clear to many just why the prosecution was pushing for the apparently overzealous charge of first-degree murder. Under Massachusetts state law, a charge of 'murder-one' cannot be reduced to manslaughter – the defendant is either deemed guilty or not guilty. Given the evidence, manslaughter was the natural choice for the jury if they believed the 'shaking incident' story, but now they would be forced to either find Woodward guilty of premeditated murder or let her go scot-free. The prosecution was clearly determined to win a murder charge, rather than just manslaughter, so was going for an all-or-nothing gamble.

They won. Louise Woodward was found guilty of deliberately murdering Matthew Eappen and was sentenced to life imprisonment – a minimum fifteen years in jail before getting even the possibility of winning a parole.

As it turned out, she served only 279 days in prison.

The day after the verdict, a jury member admitted to the press that none of the jury members 'thought she tried to murder him' but they couldn't countenance a verdict of 'not guilty' because they believed she had accidentally killed Matthew. An appeal was the obvious next step for Woodward and her supporters.

As it turned out, Judge Hiller Zobel, who had passed a life sentence on Louise, was one of those who had doubts about the murder-one verdict. At an appeal hearing a few weeks later, he reduced the charge to manslaughter and, since Woodward had already spent the minimum term in jail for manslaughter (ironically because the prosecution had blocked bail before the trial) Zobel ordered her immediate release. She was forced to remain in Massachusetts pending the prosecution's appeal against the appeal verdict, but when they lost she was allowed to return home to the UK. She is reported to have since taken a university degree in law in London.

Did Louise Woodward kill Matthew Eappen – deliberately or accidentally? She continues to deny the accusation and the Eappens continue to insist that she did. The gulf between the two positions seems as wide and cold as the Atlantic itself.

World-Wide Business Center

In August 1980 a tiny cubicle on the tenth floor of 575 Madison Avenue, New York, was briefly the world's biggest money laundry.

Salvatore Amendolito, a former financial analyst from Milan, set up as a New York fish exporter in 1977. Two years later, three Sicilians offered to load his fish, airfreight it to Italy and then unload it themselves, paying him when the cargo completed the journey. Amendolito declined, but when he went bankrupt the following year, his business agent in Milan telephoned with a similar proposal. He explained that many New York pizzerias needed to remit **cash** to Europe. The funds were destined for the construction of a hotel in Sicily; the owners wanted to bypass the taxman. 'How much money is it anyway?' asked Amendolito. 'Nine million dollars,' he was told.

Amendolito negotiated a 1 per cent handling charge. He began by dividing the stash, which arrived in cardboard boxes, into bundles of just under $10,000 – the level over which cash payments are reported to the Treasury – and spent days driving round New York making deposit after deposit at different banks. A sidekick checked the stacks as he sped along the New Jersey turnpike.

Amendolito met his punters on street corners, walking the city with $500,000 or even a million slung over his shoulder in a yellow leather bag. He picked up $3 million in three trips from the Roma Restaurant, and – after bribing a Bermudan official – flew over a metric *ton* of cash to the island.

By August, Amendolito's business was booming. He rented a proper office in the World-Wide Business Center where he installed a money-counting machine with a safe the size of two refrigerators. The floor needed reinforcement.

In late November 1980, acting on a tip-off, an undercover FBI team photographed a delivery of one of the mysterious cardboard cartons at the entrance of 575 Madison Avenue. To their dismay, the building housed a warren of hundreds of small firms, and it was not until the autumn of 1981 that Agent Robert Paquette tracked down the intended recipient. By then Amendolito had moved on, but this lead unravelled the Sicilian Mafia's American operation, the so-called **Pizza Connection**.

The cash mountains generated by today's international drugs business are too large for standard counting machines. Sophisticated traffickers value their takings by sorting them into different denomination bills and weighing the sackloads. A million dollars in $20 notes tips the balance at 107.4 pounds.

See also **Tax havens**

Wright, Whitaker (1845–1904)

A sixteen-stone financier of modest origins who committed suicide after his disgrace in 1904. At the height of his success and influence Wright was master of Witley Park, a 2,500-acre estate in Surrey girded by an eight-foot-high, fourteen-mile wall behind which lay farms, cottages, lodges, lakes and two old iron mines.

Wright spent his money with delectation and verve. He set an army of four or five hundred men to remodel his grounds and buildings, extending the old mansion until it boasted thirty-two bedrooms and a ballroom incorporating a theatre. He tacked a huge plant-house on to the east wing; the west wing culminated in an observatory with a dome and revolving roof.

After a hill had been removed, Wright's home commanded a fine view over his twenty-five-acre lake, stocked with a flotilla of the latest electric motor launches to tour the grottoes and underground galleries. A huge marble dolphin was transported from Italy to form a triumphal entrance to the lake; a railway bridge had to be demolished to allow the sculpture through. Under the lake's surface lay Wright's *pièce de résistance*, a glass-roofed underwater chamber built by first draining the waters. 'On summer nights,' wrote a contemporary, 'one looks through the green water at the stars and the moon, magnified quite ten times by the curved glass and the water.'

Born in northern England, Wright made and lost his first fortune in the Wild West and returned to Britain in the high noon of Empire. He turned his first-hand knowledge of mining to good advantage in the City, setting up groups of associated companies with dummy directors. At his trial, one co-director (General Gough-Calthorpe) explained that his role was 'to sign my name many thousands of times on share certificates', while another (Mr Worters) acknowledged that his duties were 'to confirm the transactions of the managing director'. When one of the companies, Lake View Consols, ran into trouble, Wright propped up the share price with funds from his London and Globe Company, driving it into insolvency. It transpired that Consols' balance sheet had been padded by over-valued shares.

Until the Companies Act of 1901 it was not illegal to issue a fraudulent balance sheet. Wright's offences predated its provisions, and he remained beyond the reach of law. But a consortium of out-of-pocket brokers brought a prosecution under the 1861 Larceny Act. Wright lacked the requisite criminal intent, but the hostile judge encouraged the jury to a finding of guilty, and he was sentenced to seven years' penal servitude. Led into the private room behind the court, the financier slipped a cyanide tablet into a glass of whisky and handed his watch to a friend, saying, 'I won't have any need of this where I'm going.' Then he fell down dead.

Wuornos, Aileen (1956–)

Dubbed 'The Damsel of Death' by the press, Aileen Wuornos (pronounced 'Warn-us') admitted to shooting seven men during 1989 and 1990 in self-defence, mostly middle-aged whites.

The Wuornos background is no fairy tale. Her father, a child molester, hanged himself in prison. Her mother abandoned her at three months. Sexually abused as a child, Wuornos attempted suicide by shooting herself in the stomach during adolescence, and was raped by her grandfather and (perhaps) her brother. After her illegitimate child was removed for adoption, she became a 14-year-old prostitute, maturing into an alcoholic lesbian with strong religious convictions, trawling the highways, motels and drive-ins as a hitch-hiking whore on Florida's Interstate 75.

Aileen Wuornos, the 'female serial killer'

She meant business with her .22 pistol: big business. As America's first female serial killer, Wuornos was worth serious money in movie deals, television docu-dramas, book rights and syndicated chat shows to anyone delivering her to the media – provided two conditions were met. First, the public had to be convinced that she was a serial killer, and second, she needed convicting. Properly handled, Wuornos could make a fortune; and she would have no *locus standi* to jeopardise her commercial exploitation when dead.

Wuornos played the husband to her lesbian lover, Tyrea Moore, principal prosecution witness. Coming from a solid family, Moore was an object of veneration to Wuornos, perhaps the only person she ever loved. Initially, both women were wanted as suspects, and Moore cajoled Wuornos into confessing after her

arrest at the 'Last Resort' bikers' bar. On 17 January 1991, Wuornos began a lengthy statement: 'Well, I came here to confess to murder, I just wish I'd never done this shit. I just wish I'd never bought that **gun**...'

Wuornos earned some sympathy at her trial for the murder of television repairman Richard Mallory, an ex-convict with a ten-year prison record for attempted rape. In her words, 'He put the cord around my neck and said, "You bitch, you're going to do everything I tell you to, and if you don't, I'll kill you right after-wards, just like the others."' Mallory threatened to have intercourse with Wuornos's still-warm corpse, and started to choke her. After various assaults, he poured medical alcohol into her bleeding orifices. He laughed at her screams, and she not unreasonably inferred that he would continue playing with her. 'I gotta fight or I'm gonna die', she thought, broke free, reached her gun, and shot Mallory dead.

Wuornos might have escaped with manslaughter had the judge barred evidence of six other killings. To shoot one assailant in self-defence may be bad luck, but seven looks like deliberation, and on 27 January 1992 Wuornos responded to the jury's 'guilty' verdict by shouting: 'I was raped, I hope you get raped, scumbags of America.' When Judge Thomas Sawaya sentenced her to death, Aileen yelled derisively at him: 'Thank you. I'll go to Heaven now, and you'll rot in Hell.'

She was on Death Row, but her fame as America's first female serial killer improved her lot. Arlene Pralles, a born-again Christian horse-farmer, was touched by Wuornos's plight, and adopted her. Pralles related, 'She is a beautiful woman, very kind, compas-sionate, with a heart of gold', and in fact, Wuornos cuts a surprisingly pleasant figure, an articulate woman with a talent for mimicry. At last someone cared for her, and she hired a new lawyer, Steven Glazer. Meanwhile, fifteen Hollywood companies competed for her story. A television film, *Overkill*, went into production, and Glazer acted as Pralles's agent; she collected 33 per cent royalties on every copy of 'On a Killing Day'.

But if Wuornos appealed against the 'similar facts' evidence of the first trial, she could overturn her convic-tion. Six more successes would save her life. As she said later, 'The principle is self-defence. They say it's the number. But it's still self-defence no matter how many people I shot. Two did rape me, five tried.' But Wuornos made no mention of this at the time. Instead, she deferred to the advice of her new lawyer and adoptive mother, and on 31 March 1992 pleaded 'no contest' to the next three charges. Arlene Pralles enthused, 'Our state has the death penalty, so why not go for it? I mean, Wow! She could be with Jesus in a few years.'

Importantly, this would make a better film. The police were rumoured to be turning their client investment to financial advantage. Tyrea Moore, no longer considered a suspect, was closeted with law enforcement officials, part of a witness-and-perpetrator package for the film industry. Wuornos objected to her own role, envisaged as a posthumous star. She told the court, 'I've been framed as a first-time female serial killer to make a better *title* and a bigger movie. The element of self-defence was hidden.'

The 1991 oil war precipitated Wuornos's downfall. As her 'regulars' were called up, so her earnings dwindled to $500 a month. Wuornos claimed that Tyrea Moore wanted $700 to $1,000 coming in a week and insisted that she take the risk of picking up strangers – hence the shootings. Wuornos may have been trigger-happy but, unlike her full-blown male counterparts, she never planned or stalked. Nor were her homicides recreational, and the tidy serial-killer deal was imperilled when police sergeant Brian Jervis expressed concern at departmental plans to work with Tyrea Moore in soliciting movie rights. After a month of harassment from colleagues, Jervis was transferred to patrol duties and resigned from the force. A break-in destroyed his home files on the Wuornos case and nothing else, but law enforcement agencies, up to and including the FBI, declined to investigate.

Meanwhile, a recalcitrant Wuornos had second thoughts about the wisdom of legal suicide, still promoted by her advisers, Glazer and Pralles. 'I do believe their main purpose is to see me die,' she complained from her cell. 'Arlene did not adopt me to be my mother, she adopted me to bury me and have easier visitation. Their motive was to make money ... They convinced me to plead "No contest". Arlene kept on saying, "If you don't attend the sentencing the cops won't have anything for the movie."' Wuornos said that both had suggested ways of killing herself, and her suicide would make a powerful last scene which could, alternatively, come up as a scrolled caption on a black screen for the end-titles.

From prison Wuornos urged assiduous investigators to obtain a copy of the Republican Pictures movie contract, believing it could secure a retrial, and on 10 November 1992, Sheriff Moorlands announced the transfer of two policemen from his Criminal Investigation Department together with the resignation of Major Dan Henry, Chief of Staff, after a bugged conversation about film rights.

The Wuornos story eventually spawned two movies, an opera and several books before she was executed by lethal injection on 9 October 2002. Shortly after her death, an anonymous joker posted a message on a website that was hosting an online discussion about the execution. Signed Satan, it simply read: 'Umm... Could you guys take her back?'

See also **Canonisation**

Xenophobia

The Portuguese were the supposed perpetrators of London's **Ratcliffe Highway** murders of 1811, considered far too horrible for an English killer. As the dramatist Sheridan later recounted in Parliament: 'People grew all of a sudden thoroughly persuaded that there was evidence that they were perpetrated by the Portuguese, and none but the Portuguese. "Oh, who would do it but the Portuguese?" was the general cry.' This was during the Peninsular War, when the Portuguese were Britain's *allies*.

Soon the prejudice switched to more traditional targets. As Sheridan recounted, 'The next tribe of foreigners were the Irish and it was none but an Irish murder and could only have been done by Irishmen.' Seven were arrested almost at random and flung into jail. Sheridan continued: 'Some noise being heard, the magistrates inquired into the cause of this uproar, and they were told, "Oh! It is nothing but those horrid Irish, who can never be quiet!" ... They had been confined to a hole of a room for twenty-two hours without a bed to lie upon, or a morsel of bread, or a drop of water to refresh them.' Whereupon they were released; nothing like this would happen today.

Currently occupying the racial limelight, after millennia of scant pickings in the desert, are Tuaregs. Press reports of attacks on intrepid package tourists first appeared in January 1992. A worker with an overland trekking company described the fate of two convoys ambushed in the remote Saharan border regions south of Tamanrasset. 'They lost everything except their passports, with the vehicles being driven away by the rebels into the Sahara, never to be seen again.' Tourists are held for maybe eight hours in the sands while their captors rummage through their possessions for money, cameras, personal cassette players and those puzzling coloured plastic cards. It is perhaps surprising that Toyota (see **Biggs**) have never based a publicity campaign round the desert marauders' preference for Land Cruisers, and equally surprising that Tuaregs are involved at all. For centuries they operated as peaceful traders in open markets with an innate respect for persons and property, and their popular image owes much to P. C. Wren's fiction and their stateless pedigree, making them easy scapegoats.

But at least these desert groups fared better than the British holiday-makers subjected to the spate of attacks on train journeys to the French Riviera in 1991. Overnight, their compartments were infiltrated with gas, leaving the tourists to come round with splitting headaches the following morning, still in their sleepwear, without money, luggage, ID, credit cards or clothes.

The French may have little good to say about the British. But they envied the high standards of our **highwaymen**. Abroad, the profession was all riff-raff; but visitors to England drew comfort from by the well-educated, polite bearing of the local villains, although they bridled at their sheer quantity. In the manner of a menu, roads round London were said to be '*garnis de voleurs à cheval*'. One well-informed foreigner noted in early Franglais that '*les highwaymen sont, en général, d'une classe supérieure ... They take a pride in carrying on their profession with distinction. One could say that they attach importance to honour, and that they think of their reputation as much as they do of their pockets.*'

Not so the Chinese who, in demonstration of their sovereignty as an occupying power, prefer to execute Tibetans in public. The condemned were apt to shout 'Long live the Dalai Lama' with their dying breath. So these days their vocal cords are prophylactically slit. Alternatively, Tibetans go to execution with their throats pre-garrotted with wire, and the more obstinate cases have their tongues hooked out.

The Chinese make the relatives of the deceased pay for the bullets with which they are shot. Since the 1950 invasion, the Tibetan population has fallen by 1.2 million and overall expenditure on ammunition must have been considerable.

According to American Drug Enforcement Agency officials, the Chinese make exemplary gangsters – patient, loyal, disciplined and low-profile. Under interrogation, they would rather die than talk, perhaps because, under the **Triad** oath of silence, they will die if they do.

Mexican criminals are reputedly the keenest to blab; the Italians also talk readily, but only about making a deal.

See also **Colombia**

X, Operation

'Operation X' was the French Secret Service's scheme for funding the unpopular Indo-Chinese War from 1951 to 1954. Starved of official funds from home, the French army earned their keep by collecting and distributing **opium** from the **Golden Triangle**. They paid a good price to the hill tribes, ensuring their loyalty, and flew the opium out to a military school for onward trucking to Saigon. There the opium was sold to river pirates, who refined it and marketed it locally, offloading any surplus to their **Triad** connections. Huge profits were shared with the French Secret Service, enabling the financing of a mercenary counter-insurgent army.

Before 1950, opium's physical bulk tended to restrict exports, but the French Secret Service showed the potential of international narcotics trafficking by deploying an efficient transportation system based round airforce planes – a lesson not lost on American intelligence, who flew opium from Laos to South Vietnam as late as 1973 on Air America, the CIA subsidiary.

The 1954 French surrender at Dien Bien Phu stemmed from the opium middlemen creaming off too much money. The disaffected Meo clan turned a blind eye while the area was infiltrated by hostiles.

Y

Yakuza

Japanese Mafia. In spring 1992 the Tokyo police inaugurated a telephone hotline for mobsters anxious to quit but unsure how.

Reformed gangsters remain conspicuous, thanks to their missing little fingers snipped off in an underworld **initiation** ritual. Police from the Kanagawa prefecture tempted converts with a packaged service offering referral to a surgeon specialising in grafting toes on to hands (see **Godmothers**).

These pathetic governmental inducements are symptomatic of a battle lost long ago. The police files on 3,200 Yakuza syndicates and 88,000 gangsters were easily amassed, the task simplified by legal membership: Yakuza members display their gang's name on calling cards and office doorplates.

The Yakuza's traditional remit was to regulate prostitution, gambling and – more recently – soft drugs. Someone had to do it, and the police left well alone. But in the 1970s the Yakuza diversified into loan-sharking and thence construction, acquiring substantial property holdings. By the economic boom of the 1980s they had infiltrated legitimate businesses, in 1989 raking in an estimated 1,300 billion yen from commercial blackmail, takeovers and extortion. But their links with blue-chip institutions remained invisible as long as asset prices inflated and rising wealth precluded financial investigation. The stock market collapse laid bare the dealings which destroyed mainstream companies like Itoman, a business of a hundred years' standing. Itoman fell into the clutches of a businessman, Suemsitsu Ito, with Yakuza connections through a Korean, Ho Yong Chung. Ito squandered company money on buying property and paintings from Ho at vastly inflated prices, creating a debt of 1,400 billion yen, and singlehandedly drove the business into the ground.

By the time this particular fraud was exposed in September 1990 it was evident that the Yakuza were rampant throughout Japanese society. A police survey of 2,106 Tokyo businesses found that 41 per cent had been approached with offers they could hardly refuse. One-third succumbed, and the bigger the company, the more enticing the target. The connections between the worlds of crime, business and politics were underlined by the discovery that the Prime Minister, Noboru Takeshita, secured his appointment by a deal with the Inagawi-kai, Tokyo's largest Yakuza gang, and when the first half-hearted anti-gang laws were passed in 1992 the Yakuza staged organised rallies and protest marches in the streets.

Yorkshire Ripper, alternative

Britain's second-ranking serial killer, arrested on 2 January 1981, was identified after a four-year manhunt as Peter **Sutcliffe**. But was he the right man? A persistent advertiser in the British satirical magazine *Private Eye* refuses to accept Sutcliffe as the real Yorkshire Ripper.

The theory is the brainchild of investigative writer Noel O'Gara, who has Sutcliffe down for a 'copy-cat' ripper, answerable only for the last four killings, as the police well knew. Supposedly, detectives were so keen for a conviction that they came to terms, offering Sutcliffe ten years in Broadmoor on diminished charges of manslaughter in exchange for his confessions, an arrangement scotched in court by an astute judge, Mr Justice Boreham. By then the true killer, William Tracey, had removed himself to Ireland.

With his beard and bushy eyebrows, Tracey is not dissimilar from Peter Sutcliffe. He fits survivors' descriptions. Like Sutcliffe, Tracey was of Irish extraction, in the 40-to-50 age range, stocky, tattooed, a

B-blood pimp with a gap tooth; and O'Gara presents evidence that Tracey had the means, motive and opportunity for the killings.

On 18 August 1983, the obsessive O'Gara extracted a written confession from his suspect: 'I William Tracey, aged 44, of 27 Kilcoursey, Clara, Co. Offaly, confess to the murders of the following women: McCann, Harrison, Jackson, Richardson, Atkinson, McDonald, Ryka, Millward, Whittaker, Leach. I have done the business on them. I have murdered them. I suppose I am unstable. I am perpetual, psychic, paranoid…'

But this admission was obtained by deception. O'Gara persuaded a friend to pose as a *News of the World* reporter and purchased two banker's drafts, one for £5 and one for £10. With a typewriter he inserted seven further noughts, and then invited Tracey to a videotaped presentation at the Prince of Wales Hotel in Athlone, offering £60,000 from the newspaper for his confession. Tracey obliged, but immediately after the formal ceremony smelt a rat and harried his tormentors round the car park with a Stanley knife. O'Gara made off with his precious confession, which he forwarded to the British police. Despite letters, telephone calls and a privately published book, he has heard no more. Doubtless he is regarded as a crank.

O'Gara's book has a frenetic 'round earth' feel that Galileo would recognise; he can prove his case time and again, but no one pays a blind bit of notice.

Young, Graham (1947–90)

A compulsive serial poisoner who assisted investigators by suggesting how his undiscovered murders were committed. When detectives checked his theory, they found it correct. So they arrested him. This happened not once, but twice.

Young's mother died of natural causes when he was a few months old, and in adolescence he developed into a loner whose heroes were Dr **Palmer** and Hitler. In 1961, aged 14, Young set about **poisoning** his family with antimony. Only his stepmother Molly died, the following April, but when his father was hospitalised the doctors outraged Young by a sloppy diagnosis of arsenic poisoning. 'How ridiculous not to be able to tell the difference between antimony and arsenic,' he scoffed.

Nine years later he was released from Broadmoor bearing the endorsement of a medical certificate from consultant psychiatrist E. L. Unwin. 'He has made an extremely full recovery,' it said of Young, 'and he is now entirely fit for discharge … He would fit in well and not draw any attention to himself in any community.'

Young's neat turn-out, meticulously backswept hair and grave, precise verbal mannerisms made him attractive to employers. Years of study in the Broadmoor library on chemistry and medicine had steeped him in the lore of lesser-known poisons, and the prospect of work at John Hadland's photographic works near Bovingdon held tantalising possibilities. In early 1971 Young accepted the post of assistant storeman. He laid his hands on a promising substance, thallium, a heavy metal (akin to mercury) both tasteless and easily soluble. All the auguries looked good: its curative properties on ringworm and unwanted facial hair were outweighed by serious side-effects, its medicinal use abandoned in the 1940s.

But would it kill? Young instigated a series of experiments. Each day he collected his workmates' tea from the storeroom hatch. Dosing their drinks was easy. First he tried the thallium salts on Bob Egle, the 60-year-old head warehouseman.

It made Egle throw up and, as the treatment progressed, so the symptoms increased in severity. Soon Egle evinced prolonged bouts of violent retching. Further doses engendered shooting pains in the chest and back. A touch more and he lost his balance. Finally Egle became delirious.

Young crowned these early successes on 13 July when, after weeks of agonising pain, Bob Egle died of 'peripheral neuritis' in St Alban's City Hospital. But could Young pull off the same trick on Egle's successor, 56-year-old Fred Biggs? Yes: by October, Biggs's hold on life was weakening and on 19 November he too perished. So presumably thallium would work on anyone? Yes: by then Jethro Batt and David Tilson were suffering severe stomach cramps, hair loss and attacks of numbness. And what about their four colleagues? They too fell ill.

Speculation about a 'Bovingdon Bug' encouraged the management to call in a team of toxicologists, headed by Dr Iain Anderson. He summoned a staff meeting and, hoping to quell the rumours, invited questions from the floor.

First to speak was Graham Young: didn't the doctors realise that the workers' symptoms were *obviously* consistent with thallium poisoning?

In court, the defence was handicapped by Young's diary. No special powers were required to interpret his entry for 31 October 1971: 'I have administered a fatal dose of the special compound to F... I gave him three separate doses.' Young enjoyed starring at his trial, and declared to the police, 'I could have killed them all if I wished ... But I allowed them to live.' He was no less munificent towards himself. After the discovery of an 'exit dose' sewn into the lining of his jacket, Young threatened to break his own neck on the courtroom dock rail if he was found guilty. But he stayed his hand.

Young was sent back to Broadmoor, where he died of a heart attack in August 1990. His sister Winifred, who nearly perished (and suffered protracted agonies) during his 1961 rehearsal, ascribes her brother's career to his 'craving for publicity'. It seems he did love his family, but not enough.

Young, John (d. 1750)

Until 1949, the death sentence in Scotland specified both the date and the time of a hanging. In 1750 John Young, a sergeant slated to swing in Edinburgh for forgery, assumed that time was of the essence. Condemned to hang between two and four in the afternoon, Young persuaded the officials presenting themselves at the appointed hour to give him a few moments' peace alone in his cell. Then he barricaded the door.

Outside, the clock ticked on while warders tried to force entry. The fateful hour of four o'clock came and went, and it was a quarter past before prison officers knocked a hole through the ceiling from the floor above.

But all Young's efforts came to nothing; the magistrates had stopped the city's clocks. So it still was between two and four in the afternoon when Young was dragged to the gallows.

Sixty-four years later Londoners were treated to the spectacle of a less grudging participant. The highwayman John Ashton went insane while awaiting his November 1814 execution at Newgate. When the moment came, Ashton dashed up the steps to the gallows as though unleashed and pranced up and down on top of the scaffold shouting to the crowds.

'Look at me!' he cried, 'I am the Lord Wellington.' They hanged him anyway and, after briefly vanishing from view beneath the trap-door, Ashton miraculously rebounded on to the platform with his delusions reinforced. He continued his dance, hopping up and down next to the chaplain. 'What do you think of me? Am I not Lord Wellington now?' he shouted, between cheering and clapping. The executioner remounted the scaffold to push him to his death.

Youngstown, Ohio

A statistical microcosm of American murder. With a population of 95,000, this depressed steel town (which lost 40,000 jobs in the 1970s and 1980s) recorded the country's biggest year-on-year increase in killings, up 310 per cent to a total of fifty-nine in 1991.

Part of the homicide toll was attributable to domestic and random violence, but its most striking feature was the surge in drug- and gang-related deaths among young adults. Three hundred dollars is the street price for a 9mm automatic; where once grandmothers looked after children, 30-year-old grandmother addicts now buy and sell **crack**. **Gangs** confer status on the young; there is little else that will. At least twenty-five killings involved drug disputes, whether for straightforward non-payment, territorial battles, disagreements over money or executions. Seven deaths came from rows between young lovers. Forty-six perished from gunfire. There were no killings for trainers, but Jermaine Williams, aged 17, died during a row over a gold chain.

Some murders had all the refinement of gang-land. Flip Williams, aged 34, masterminded the Labour Day killing of four drug-pushing rivals in their early twenties; his mob included a 16-year-old girl. Flip was captured himself in January 1992 breaking *into* jail to get at his captured lieutenants, who had turned state's evidence. When a Colombian dealer pulled into town with nine kilos of cocaine, he was kidnapped by local teenagers and tortured for four days until he met their ransom demand of $150,000; then they killed him.

According to 14-year-old Nathan Hayes, speaking from the refuge of the Boys and Girls Club: 'Pretty soon, if I stayed, I'd be shooting my friends, one way or another. Or they'd be shooting me.' Police noted that immediately after sentence the young killers could be calmed down, like babies with a bottle, by a bag of crisps or a can of Coke.

The risk of an American teenager being murdered doubled between 1985 and 1990; it is now the third highest cause of death among all young men and the highest for young black men. The sharp reduction of the homicide rate in the early 1980s was credited by Reagan to Reagan, but it reflects the temporary population dip in teenagers and young adult males.

In 1991, the American murder total was 24,020, putting the statistical likelihood at one in 10,400 (about eight times the British rate), a figure which varies widely from area to area. Washington DC (pop. 605,000) accounted for 489 killings at a rate of one in 1,200; the Washington body-count is well over half the figure for the whole of Britain.

Guns are used in 64 per cent of American cases. Blacks, a 12 per cent minority, constitute nearly half of all victims. The great majority of killings are confined to victims of the murderer's racial origin.

The 1990 clear-up rate was 67 per cent, proof again that even under the most extreme circumstances murder is a risky business for the perpetrator. But in the 1960s, 90 per cent or more of the annual harvest of 8,000 homicides were solved. In New York, the percentage of drug-related killings rose from about 20 per cent of the total in the early 1980s to some 40 per cent by the close of the decade.

Yuppies

Mafia boss John Gotti was often characterised as a hoodlums' hoodlum. He was also a hoodlums' yuppie.

His takeover of the Gambino family after the murder of Big Paul Castellano on 16 December 1985 marked a pronounced change in management style. Known as the 'Dapper Don', the flashy Gotti was seldom out of the pages of *Time*, *People* and *The New York Times Magazine*. For underlings jaded by years of low-profile leaders with zero *savoir faire*, it provided a welcome break from the endless niceties of outmoded Mafia protocol, derisively referred to as 'all this stupid *Cosa Nostra* crap'. Gotti was admired for his silk scarves and double-breasted $3,000 suits; the retail cost of his outfits was always quoted in the press, but reports did not mention that Gotti never bought a suit in his life. All were stolen.

At Gotti's trial the *Newsday* legal correspondent noted that the gangsters' courtroom benches were laden with men in 'calm stripes and turbulent ties'; younger members of the Gotti entourage were distinguished by more extreme peaked lapels and trousers with turn-ups. But Gotti's sartorial elegance

was of recent origin. As a teenage punk in the 1950s, taking bets from schoolchildren, he possessed a number of striking but simple outfits. There was the all-purple look, with purple shoes. And there was the all-green look, with green shoes. He also did a number in white shoes, black trousers and an orange shirt.

Come the late 1980s and the Wall Street boom, the Mafia blossomed. Gone was the fixation with dressing as peasants in baggy trousers belted round the midchest. Gone were the former obsessions with courtesy and rank, symbolised by old-style godfather Tony Corallo who entered restaurants flinging his camel hair coat to one side in the absolute certainty that some fawning henchman would catch it; gone were the days of mattress cash spent on mansions with downmarket pigeon-coops on the roof.

The boomtime mobster read the financial press, sported a power haircut, invested in handmade suits and, for preference, drove a BMW. Gotti, a youthful 47, appointed comparative youngsters like Salvatore Gravano to positions of influence, and their new broom swept away the Old World pretence of not dealing in drugs, a convention long more honoured in the breach than the observance.

Likewise, the mobsters of Prohibition Chicago were paragons of fashion. After the 'Diamond Jim' excesses of the previous era, correct menswear narrowed into a pearl-grey hat with black band, a dark, three-piece, double-breasted suit, handkerchief in breast pocket, white shirt, striped tie and – of course – spats; the famous photograph of 'Machine Gun' Jack McGurn's body shows that he died with his spats on (see **Names**). In his later days, Capone himself became a mite more relaxed, often photographed in a straw 'boater' with a fine watch-chain and a restrained tie.

In the late 1920s, smart mobster bodyguards were the elite of Chicago's youth: stereotypically good with *maître d's* and nightclub head waiters, at ease at the theatre or on the race track, snappy dressers with a keen eye for blondes, and good judges of diamonds. Capone's gunmen were the pick of the bunch. Said Harry Doremus, arrested in 1929: 'The Big Fellow hires nothing but gentlemen. They have to be well dressed at all times and must have cultured accents. They always say "Yes, Sir" and "No, Sir" to him.'

Physical fitness *was de rigueur*. Capone's Metropole headquarters boasted a two-room gymnasium with punch bags, horizontal bars, trapezes and rowing machines. According to Fred D. Pasley, an early Capone hagiographer, the bodyguards 'followed a schedule of training as methodical as that of college football athletes'. Their workouts included periodical trips to the Illinois outback, where the hoods practised on private machine-gun ranges. Being a mobster was a high-status, glamorous job, probably the best way the poor could make a dishonest living.

Yu, Wong

Inventor of hijacking. On 16 July 1947 Wong Yu and three Chinese accomplices staged a takeover of a Cathay Pacific flying boat on the Macao–Hong Kong route, planning to divert the flight and rob or ransom the passengers. But they panicked when the co-pilot set about them with an iron bar, and it was at this juncture that Wong Yu decided to shoot the pilot.

After the crash, Yu found himself the only survivor and might have escaped scot-free had he not, in hospital, related his misadventure to a fellow patient, a policeman. He was hanged.

The first American hijacking came in August 1971. Leon Bearden, an impecunious ex-convict, decided to emigrate. With his 16-year-old son, Cody, he commandeered a Continental Airlines Boeing 707 over New Mexico and demanded a passage to Cuba, but was overpowered while explaining to an FBI agent, during a pit stop in El Paso, that with 'less than twenty-five bucks to his name' he had no legitimate alternative. Bearden was sentenced to twenty years; Cody was paroled after two.

Some people nurture a sneaking admiration for the gallant D. B. Cooper, the one who got away, by parachute. On 24 November 1971, Cooper baled out of a North-West Airlines flight at 10,000 feet over the Cascade mountains south of Seattle, taking $200,000 in a rucksack, and he has never been seen since.

But a man called John List has. Or may have been. According to the police, on 9 November 1971 the 45-year-old List, a New Jersey insurance salesman, shot dead his mother, his wife and their three children with a 9mm automatic. Four were killed with a single bullet behind the ear; the fifth, their 15-year-old, was shot ten times. List disappeared, leaving a detailed account of his evening's work and a spate of press speculation about his financial double-dealing.

List was next heard of eighteen years later, featured on television as one of 'America's Most Wanted'. Visual aids for the broadcast included a computer-enhanced photograph and a sculptured bust of his head projected forwards by two decades to replicate ageing. A flood of 300 telephone calls led to the arrest of a Robert Clark, an elderly married man from Richmond, Virginia. 'Clark' was soon identified as John List.

At his trial, List admitted killing his family in a fit of depression. He had decided to send them to Heaven, he said, and would have killed himself if suicide had not meant he would be sent to Hell. He was given five consecutive life sentences.

On 8 June 1989 the FBI announced that they were reopening the case on D. B. Cooper, the hijacker who, it will be remembered, appeared fifteen days after List vanished. Unfortunately, the dull and depressive List was not the same man as the daring Cooper, so the mystery remains.

Z

Zapata, Emiliano (d. 1919)

Mexican folk-hero of the revolutionary war, elaborately liquidated by the half-breed Colonel Jesus Guajardo for $50,000 blood-money.

In 1919 the treacherous Guajardo defected to Zapata's cause, bringing 800 men as well as badly needed supplies of arms and ammunition, proving his loyalty by an attack on his own side at Jonacatepec where he executed the prisoners.

On 10 April, Zapata rode over to review Guajardo's incoming troops at the hacienda of San Juan Chinameca. As Zapata and ten aides jangled through the gates, a band began to play, and in the courtyard a guard of honour 200-strong paraded to attention. 'Present arms!' shouted Guajardo, standing slightly to one side, as Zapata halted to take the salute.

He was assassinated by volley, his blood-caked body put on display to show the Morelos peasantry that the government meant business.

Zebra Killings

A sequence of San Francisco murders claiming hundreds of lives during a 179-day period from October 1973. The zebra has alternating stripes of black and white, and the slayings were cross-racial, with blacks killing whites for religious reasons, inspired by the radical tract, 'Message to the Black Man', which embodied its precepts in question-and-answer form. Question four demanded: 'Does Allah have enemies and who are they?' The correct response was 'the white race'.

Answer ten explained the next step: 'All Muslims will murder the white devil because they know he is a snake. Each Muslim is required to kill four devils, and by bringing and presenting four at one time, his

reward is a button to wear on the lapel of his coat and free transportation to the Holy city of Mecca to see brother Mohammed.'

To beleaguered West Coast black fanatics this constituted an attractive offer, and a squad of Death Angels formed to snatch random whites off the street, as often as not raping and mutilating their victims before the kill.

The case was broken by Anthony Cornelius Harris, former prisoner B35599 of San Quentin and a judo expert. While inside, Harris was approached by Jesse Lee Cooks asking about the easiest way of killing people. In *The Zebra Killings* (1980) Cooks introduces himself with the words: 'I want to learn how to bust a heart with a punch to a chest. And how to come up behind somebody and snap their neck … See, man, in San Francisco they got what's called the Death Angels. It's a special part of the Muslims. The job of the Death Angels is to off white chumps, see? But you got to prove you can kill before they'll let you in.' Harris taught Cooks judo and kung fu.

The sect had a graded scoring system. Lukewarm devotees might have few qualms about murdering a white man, but women and children provided a tougher test of moral fibre, a distinction reflected in the 'points' for each kill. Nine adult males was the minimum qualification for admission through the pearly gates, but only five women or just four children. Elevation to the elect was signified by drawing a pair of celestial wings on the photographs of successful candidates kept at their San Francisco temple; these pictures were displayed on an easel at meetings held in the loft.

By October 1973, California had fifteen accredited Death Angels who between them killed 135 men, 75 women and 60 children, all white. Photographic evidence of the corpse *in situ* was helpful in substantiating a claim. Later, during the longest trial in

Californian history, Harris turned state's evidence and testified about his participation in ten murders, including the great binge of the Night of Five. The trial started on 3 March 1975 and ended a year and six days later; the jury reached a unanimous verdict of guilty and the four defendants received life sentences.

Zlotys, Polish

Poland's privatisation programme generated unprecedented opportunities for fraud as government officers jumped the gun on what belonged to whom. First came Cigarettesgate, then Schnappsgate and finally Roublesgate, where soft Soviet roubles were converted into fairly hard Polish zlotys, which could briefly be exchanged for completely hard American dollars, bequeathing a huge loss to the national treasury.

Next came the Finance Ministry's 'Fund for Foreign Debt', specialising in the sophisticated secondary-debt market. On these high-risk deals, you win some and you lose some. Those they lost the officials debited to the state's account. Those they won they credited to their own. The scam is under investigation with an expected deficit of four hundred million dollars.

For the Poles, one of the few heartening economic events of 1990 was the phenomenal rise of the company Art-B, living proof that under capitalism a hundred million zlotys could be made overnight by giving the public what they wanted. The brainchild of two musicians, Art-B started small in sacred Catholic songs, and finished big, sponsoring music festivals, film festivals, theatre festivals and art shows; they bailed out a hospital and nearly clinched a deal to rescue the Ursus tractor factory by buying an entire year's production.

It now seems that a provincial bank clerk founded Art-B's fortune in September 1990. He issued a letter confirming that they had $300,000 on deposit in return for a $5,000 bribe, and the document became collateral for a loan at a second bank, with these monies transferred to a third bank.

In Poland, cheques are cleared by post, which can take weeks, and interest accrued while the cheques were in transit at a dollar premium rate of 60 to 80 per cent. The Art-B con consisted of devising a way of transferring funds to outpace the postal system, making deposits before the notice of withdrawal was received. This entailed ferrying suitcases of cash around the country by helicopter, raking in interest from money simultaneously in two places, and investing the proceeds in a cascade of further accounts.

After washing $18 *billion* through the banking system in little more than a year, the Art-B boys decamped to Israel with $400 million from the last bank in the chain, and – excepting the initial bribe – it is not clear if the law was contravened. No free market meant no free market regulations, and today Poland remains open to the outdated, primitive financial swindles that had their heyday in the 1920s and 1930s – 'daisy chains', 'Ponzi schemes' and the like, no longer practicable in the West. In Poland, conmen pit their wits against the combined resources of the two officials in the State Prosecutor's office with a working grasp of financial corruption.

See also **Eastern bloc**, **High finance**

Zodiac Killer

An unidentified Californian murderer from the late 1960s. His continuing anonymity typifies the serial killer's insoluble dilemma in his drive for recognition: total success – evading capture – means oblivion.

Someone, somewhere may read these words knowing that the disclosure of his epic past will arouse not terror, but disgust, contempt and, perhaps, pity. There is little mileage in being a serial killer, but an unknown ex-serial killer is buried alive, a walking corpse – feckless before the murders started and a feckless murderer afterwards. It is the killings' continuance that establishes their necessity and imbues them and their author with interest and notoriety. Their cessation deprives the perpetrator of both his private justification and his public standing.

The Zodiac Killer shot courting couples: first David Faraday and Betty Lou Jensen on 20 December 1968, then Michael Mageau on 5 July 1969, then two student picnickers on 20 September, then two Pacific Union College students on 27 September 1969 and finally a San Francisco cab driver, Paul Stein, on 21 October. The murderer used the killings to elbow his way into newspapers, insisting that his letters (marked with the sign of the Zodiac) be published to prevent further bloodshed. There are other ways of getting into print, and similarly the airtime obtained by his telephone conversation with lawyer Melvin Belli during a television chat show on 21 October was available to callers with something to say. By 1974 'Zodiac' was threatening 'to do something nasty' if he did not receive more publicity. That meant more killing. But was it worth the effort or the risk?

The police came close to catching him. The hooded attacker of 20 September was overweight, and his telephone call to the Napa police left a clear palmprint on the receiver in the public call box. Bloodstained fingerprints were found in the back of Paul Stein's cab, but to date the podgy killer with horn-rimmed spectacles remains at large.

In June 1990 a copycat 'Zodiac Killer' set out his stall on the East Coast, sending the *New York Post* a *résumé* detailing his shooting of three men on the city streets. The note began, 'This is the Zodiac the twelve sign/will die when the belts in the heaven/are seen/the first sign is dead on march 8 1990 1:45 AM/white man with cane shoot on the back in street.' Checking their records, the police found that three men *had* been shot – although not fatally – at the designated times and places, and concluded that 'Zodiac' intended to kill once for each astrological sign. With three down, nine remained to go.

The case's enduring riddle was that each victim's astrological sign matched his attribution in the *New York Post* note. Chance odds were 1,584 to one against, but none of the wounded could recall volunteering their birthdays. Mario Orozoco, shot on 8 March, reported that his assailant 'was across the street from me and crossed to meet me. He just put a gun against my back and then, bang. He shot me in the spine.'

Behavioural scientists, astrologers and computer technologists pooled resources, producing the well-thumbed profile of a loner from a broken home with a menial job. Observing that the incidents occurred at twenty-one-day intervals, or multiples thereof, they deduced that the next attack was scheduled for 21 June, the first day of Cancer. That night a homeless man with a little black dog was shot at 3.52 a.m. sleeping on a Central Park bench. His star sign was Cancer, increasing the chance odds to 17,424 against, and the following day 'Zodiac' wrote to the *New York Post* correctly specifying the time of attack: 'Fourth sign dead shoot in Central Park white man sleeping on bench with little black dog shoot in chest.' That left eight to come.

At the same time 'Zodiac' asserted a pedigree as his illustrious Californian predecessor. But the New Yorker was tall (not shortish), slim (not podgy), the wrong age and the wrong colour (black not white). For the key dates of 12 July, 2 August and 23 August the streets were flooded with the officers of the Zodiac 'Operation Watchdog' Task Force, but by then, just like the original, his impetus was spent. He too languishes incognito.

See also **Jekyll and Hyde**

Zombie

A catatonic state achieved by Jeffrey **Dahmer**, the Milwaukee serial killer. During his stint as a professional soldier, Dahmer developed a serious drink problem.

On 29 December 1978, six months after his first murder, Dahmer joined the US Army at his father's insistence, hoping to become a military policeman. Reassigned as a medic, in July 1979 he was posted on exercises to Germany.

There Dahmer devised a singular way of passing the weekend. He converted his briefcase into a portable bar, and on Friday nights sat in an armchair, put his Black Sabbath tapes on the headphones and mixed up dry martinis from Beefeater gin. He neither moved nor spoke, and slugged shots back until he passed out. When he came round, still in the chair, he started drinking again, and continued in this manner until Monday.

Dahmer started on alcohol at the age of eleven as a counter to the objectionable ordeal of consciousness and, after his first murder in 1978, drank with ever-increasing fervour to blot out his guilt and cravings. In the process he blotted himself out, mutating into a dead zone incapable of human response. But Dahmer still needed company and, lacking the social skills to befriend the living, derived companionship from the dead.

Corpses do not make satisfactory partners for long. They decompose. In his final tailspin of 1991, Dahmer hit on the strategy of 'zombification'. As he said, 'I didn't want to keep killing people and have nothing left but the skull', and among the scant material resources in his apartment was an electric drill with two bits. Dahmer purchased a marinating syringe from 'Lecter's Kitchen Supply' and, in May 1991, after drugging Konerak Sinthasomphone, he bored a hole in the boy's cranium, angling the drill towards the frontal lobes. Then he slid the needle two inches into the skull and injected muriatic acid.

As related elsewhere (see **Edwards**), Sinthasomphone stumbled out of the apartment block while his tormentor went for a beer. Dahmer reclaimed the boy from a crowd in the streets and, safely back in his apartment, deduced that the first injection was too weak, since Sinthasomphone retained sufficient motive power and the will to leave. He administered another shot, resulting in death, and later explained the underlying rationale to Dr Wahlstrom: 'If they had their own thought processes, they might remember that they had to leave, or lived somewhere else.' This tallies with an exchange from the trial. 'What would it have taken to stop you killing?' Dahmer was asked. 'A permanent relationship.'

Zombification provided a good interim solution. As Dahmer observed of Jeremiah Weinberger, 'I wanted to find a way of keeping him with me without actually killing him.' Sinthasomphone had died from the acid, so Dahmer treated Weinberger with added circumspection, injecting him with boiling water. The patient later regained consciousness in a semi-functional state. 'He talked, it was like he was dazed,' Dahmer noted. 'I thought I would be able to keep him that way. He was walking around, going to the bathroom.'

The next evening Dahmer had to work, so he gave Weinberger 'another dose of pills and another shot of boiling water in the same hole'. Returning after the night shift, he found Weinberger dead. At the trial, this venture was discussed by prosecuting counsel and a psychiatrist, Dr Fosdal.

'Have you ever met a case of home-made lobotomy here?' Fosdal was asked.

'No, I think this is the first time internationally. Mr Dahmer is setting some precedents here.'

'It couldn't have worked, could it?'

'It's possible.'

'Did you ask him how long he was going to keep the zombie? Do you believe he would have created a zombie and never killed again?'

'Absolutely,' said Fosdal. 'That would have been the solution to his problem.' After arrest, Dahmer confided in Dr Dietz that he contemplated making a hole in the head of one of his subjects, inserting an electric cable, plugging it into the wall socket and then switching

him on. Other plans included freeze-drying the dead; Dahmer's initial attempt with domestic equipment on Eddie Smith in June 1990 failed when the body retained its moisture and acidified.

By 1991 Dahmer was little more than a zombie himself. At his trial the defence presented him as an automaton who killed and partially ate his fifteen victims because he suffered from necrophilia, defined as a compulsive desire to have sex with dead bodies. The prosecution agreed, but argued that this was not officially recognised as an allowable category of madness; in their book, he still knew it was wrong, and, were Dahmer adjudged insane, he could petition for release every six months after first undergoing a year's treatment in a mental institution.

In his entire life, Dahmer only once showed interest in something other than death: an aquarium. The fish he particularly favoured was the puffer fish, certain species of which are, by coincidence, the prime source for tetrodotoxin, used by Haitian witch-doctors in the creation of voodoo zombies.

Zoo, private

As built by Pablo **Escobar**, Colombia's cocaine billionaire, on his 7,000-acre estate on the Magdalena River. One of Escobar's diversions was a private zoo stocked with elephants, hippotami, rare birds and – apparently – a kangaroo footballer.

For many years, Escobar featured as a social benefactor. On the one hand, he put much of his profits into civic improvements for the city of **Medellin**, building swish shopping malls, gourmet restaurants, homes for the poor, sports pitches and street lighting, earning the title of 'Don Pablo'. On the other, the streets were paved with dead.

Escobar's hillside prison (see **Cathedral**) on the surrounding mountains lay above his old home town of Envigado, currently infested by banks. Escobar controlled its civic elections with huge influxes of drug money, endowing it as the only city in Colombia able to pay adequate welfare. Such largesse bought safety during his spells as a fugitive. In the words of a senior general, 'Escobar will not abandon Envigado. Two hundred thousand eyes and ears on his side ... maybe more than 100 taxis with radios, listening and informing.' Every night the city was patrolled by a vigilante force, the 'Department of Security and

Control', who took those they considered suspicious for a one-way walk, taped their mouths shut and hacked them to pieces.

Football was Escobar's great passion. He would play and referee at the same time, only blowing the final whistle when his team took the lead. In theory this should not have taken long; as an opponent from Magdalena Medio recalled, 'When Pablo kicked the ball, the other side moved away to let the ball through to the goal.' In practice, spectators recall four-hour marathons.

Zyklon B

Trade name for the Nazi concentration camps' extermination agent, hydrocyanic gas, employed today in American execution chambers.

Select Bibliography

Allsopp, Kenneth *The Bootleggers*: Arrow Books, London, 1970

Andrews, William *Bygone Punishments*: Andrews, 1899

Anspacher, Carolyn *The Acid Test*: Peter Dawnay, 1965

Arlacchi, Pino *Mafia Business*: Oxford University Press, 1988

Babington, Anthony *The English Bastille*: Macdonald, London, 1971

Bailey, Brian *Hangmen of England*: W H Allen, London, 1989

Ball, James Moores *The Body Snatchers*: Dorset Press, New York, 1989

Begg, Paul, Fido, Martin & Skinner, Keith *The Jack the Ripper A-Z*: Headline, London, 1991

Behn, Noel *Brink's!*: W H Allen, London, 1977

Berry-Dee, Christopher & Odell, Robin *The Long Drop*: Viking, London, 1993

Bland, James *Crime, Strange but True*: Futura, London, 1991

Blumenthal, Ralph *The Last Days of the Sicilian Mafia*: Bloomsbury, London, 1988

Blundell, Nigel *The World's Greatest Crooks and Conmen*: Hamlyn, London, 1991

Bolitho, William *Murder for Profit*: Cape, London, 1926

Bresler, Fenton *An Almanac of Murder*: Severn House, London, 1987

Brown, Peter *Marilyn, the Last Take*: Heinemann, London, 1992

Bugliosi, Vincent *Helter Skelter*: Penguin, London, 1977

Burn, Gordon *Somebody's Husband, Somebody's Son*: Heinemann, London, 1984

Byrne, Richard *Safecracking*: Grafton, London, 1992

Campbell, Duncan *That was Business, this is Personal*: Secker & Warburg, London, 1990

Carpozi, George *Bugsy*: SPI Books, New York, 1973

Chance, John Newton *Thieves' Kitchen*: Hale, London, 1989

Clark, Sir George *The Campden Wonder*: Oxford University Press, 1959

Conradi, Peter *The Red Ripper*: Virgin, London, 1993

Cordingly, David & Falconer, John *Pirates: Fact and Fiction*: Collins & Brown, London, 1992

Cornwell, John *A Thief in the Night*: Viking, London, 1989

Cowdery, Ray *Capone's Chicago*: Northstar Maschek Books, 1987

Craig, Mary *Tears of Blood*: HarperCollins, London, 1992

Crispin, Ken *The Dingo Baby Case*: Albatross Books, Australia, 1987

Critchley, T. A. & James, P. D. *The Maul and the Pear Tree*: Constable, London, 1971

Cummings, John & Volkman, Ernest *Mobster*: Futura, London, 1991

Davis, Don *The Milwaukee Murders*: St Martin's Press, USA, 1991

De Quincey, Thomas *On Murder Considered as One of the Fine Arts*: London, 1827

Duke, Thomas *Celebrated Criminal Cases of America*: James Barry, San Francisco, 1910

Dunstan, Keith *Saint Ned*: Methuen, Australia, 1980

Eddy, Paul *The Cocaine Wars*: Century, London, 1988

Emmons, Noel *Manson in His Own Words*: Grove Press, USA, 1986

Fletcher, Tony *Memories of Murder*: Weidenfeld & Nicolson, London, 1986

Foot, Paul *Who Killed Hanratty?*: Cape, London, 1971

Foucault, Michel *Discipline and Punish*: Allen Lane, London, 1977

Fox, Grace *British Admirals and Chinese Pirates*: Kegan Paul, London, 1940

Fox, James *White Mischief*: Cape, London, 1982

Gamini, Salgrado *The Elizabethan Underworld*: Dent, London, 1977

Garbutt, Paul *Assassins*: Ian Allen, London, 1992

Gaute, J. H. H. and Odell, Robin *Murder Whatdunit*: Harrap, London, 1982

Gilbert, Michael *Fraudsters*: Constable, London, 1986

Gollmar, Robert H. *Edward Gein*: Wisconsin, 1982

Goodman, Jonathan, ed. *Supernatural Murders*: Piatkus, London, 1992

Goodman, Jonathan, ed. *Trial of Ian Brady and Myra Hindley*: David & Charles, Devon, 1973

Goodman, Jonathan & Waddell, Bill *The Black Museum*: Harrap, London, 1987

Green, Jonathon *Directory of Infamy*: Mills & Boon, London, 1980

Haining, Peter *The English Highwayman*: Hale, London, 1991

Harris, Robert *Selling Hitler*: Faber & Faber, London, 1986

Harrison, Fred *Brady and Hindley*: Ashgrove Press, London, 1986

Hayward, Captain Simon *Under Fire*: W H Allen, London, 1989

Hobsbawm, E. J. *Bandits*: Nicolson, London, 1969

Holmes, Ronald *The Legend of Sawney Beane*: Muller, London, 1975

Honeycombe, Gordon *More Murders of the Black Museum*: Hutchinson, London, 1993

Houts, Marshall *Who Killed Sir Harry Oakes?*: Hale, London, 1976

Howard, Clark *The Zebra Killings*: New English Library, London, 1980

Hughes, Robert *The Fatal Shore*: Harvill, London, 1987

Jennings, Dean *We Only Kill Each Other*: Fawcett Crest, 1967

Jones, Jack *Let Me Take You Down*: Virgin, London, 1993

Kennedy, Ludovic *Ten Rillington Place*: Gollancz, London, 1982

Kray, Reginald & Ronald *Our Story*: Jackson, London, 1988

Laffin, John *Anatomy of Captivity*: Abelard-Schumann, 1968

Lambourne, Gerald *The Fingerprint Story*: Harrap, London, 1984

Lane, Brian & Gregg, Wilfred *The Encyclopedia of Serial Killers*: Headline, London, 1992

Lane, Brian *The Butchers*: Virgin, London, 1992

Larsen, Richard W. *Bundy: The Deliberate Stranger*: Prentice-Hall, USA, 1980

Lewis, Norman *The Honoured Society*: Eland Books, London, 1964

Lincoln, Victoria *Lizzie Borden. A Private Disgrace*: Souvenir, London, 1989

Linedecker, Clifford *Thrill Killers*: Futura, London, 1990

McGinniss, Joe *Fatal Vision*: André Deutsch, London, 1984

McGuire, Christine & Norton, Carla *The Perfect Victim*: Dell, New York, 1988

Maas, Peter *The Valachi Papers*: London, 1970

Markman, Ronald & Bosco, Dominic *Alone with the Devil*: Doubleday, New York, 1989

Marnham, Patrick *Trail of Havoc*: Viking, London, 1987

Marriner, Brian *A Century of Sex Killers*: Forum Press, London, 1992

Martin, Fido *Bodysnatchers*: Nicolson, London, 1988

Masters, Brian *Killing for Company*: Coronet, London, 1986

Masters, Brian *The Shrine of Jeffrey Dahmer*: Hodder & Stoughton, London, 1993

Mortimer, John *Famous Trials*: Penguin, London, 1984

Nash, J. Robert *Compendium of World Crimes*: McGraw-Hill, New York, 1983

Neustatter, W. Lindsay *The Mind of the Murderer*: Christopher Johnson, London, 1957

Nickel, Steven *Torso*: John Blair, North Carolina, 1989

Norris, Joel *Serial Killers.*: Doubleday, New York, 1988

Norman, Lucas *The Sex Killers*: W H Allen, London, 1974

Notable British Trials (series comprising 83 titles)

Parris, John *Scapegoat*: Duckworth, London, 1991

Paul, Philip *Murder under the Microscope*: Macdonald, London, 1990

Pearson, John *The Profession of Violence*: Granada, London, 1984

Peters, Edward *Torture*: Basil Blackwell, New York, 1985

Pope, Jeff & Shaps, Simon *True Crimes*: Boxtree, London, 1992

Posner, Gerald *Warlords of Crime*: Queen Anne Press, London, 1988

Rae, Simon, ed *Anthology of Drink* Faber & Faber, London, 1992

Ritchie, Jean *Inside the Mind of Murderers*: Angus & Robertson, 1988

Rose, Andrew *Scandal at the Savoy*: Bloomsbury, London, 1988

Rule, Ann *The Stranger Beside Me*: W W Norton, New York, 1980

Rumbelow, Donald *The Triple Tree: Newgate, Tyburn and Old Bailey*: Harrap, London, 1982

Rumbelow, Donald *Jack the Ripper: The Complete Casebook*: Penguin, London, 1988

Schechter, Harold *Deviant*: Pocket Books, New York, 1989

Scmalzbach, Oscar R. *Profiles in Murder*: Hodder, London, 1971

Scott, Sir Harold *Crime and Criminals*: André Deutsch, London 1961

Shears, Richard *Kingdom of Illusions*: Bandaid Publications, Australia, 1982

Simpson, Keith *Forty Years of Murder*: Harrap, London, 1978

Smart, Carol *Women, Crime and Criminology*: Routledge & Kegan Paul, London, 1976

Smith, Ken *Inside Time*: Harrap, London, 1989

Smyth, Frank *Cause of Death*: Orbis, London, 1980

Sondern, Frederick *The Mafia*: Panther, London, 1959

Sullivan, Robert *Goodbye Lizzie Borden*: Penguin, London, 1989

Summers, Anthony *The Secret Life of J. Edgar Hoover*: Gollancz, London, 1993

Templewood, Viscount *The Shadow of the Gallows*: Gollancz, London, 1951

Treherne, John *Bonnie and Clyde*: Cape, London, 1984

Turkus, Burton *Murder Inc*: Gollancz, London, 1952

Whittington-Egan, R. & M. *The Bedside Book of Murder*: David & Charles, Devon, 1988

Williams, Emlyn *Beyond Belief* Hamish Hamilton, London, 1967

Wilson, Colin *A Criminal History of Mankind*: Granada, London, 1984

Wilson, Colin *The Mammoth Book of True Crime*: Robinson, London, 1988

Wilson, Colin *Written in Blood*: Equation, Wellingborough, 1989

Wilson, Colin & Odell, Robert *Jack the Ripper: Summing Up and Verdict*: Transworld, London, 1987

Wilson, Kirk *Investigating Murder*: Robinson Publishing, London, 1990

Wilson, Robert *Return to Hell*: Javelin Books, 1988

Wyden, Peter *The Hired Killers*: W H Allen, London, 1964

Yallop, David *To Encourage the Others*: W H Allen, London, 1971

Yallop, David *In God's Name*: Cape, London, 1984

Sundry newspapers, crime periodicals and part works, supplemented by *Vanity Fair*, the *Fortean Times* and the *New Yorker*.

Picture Credits

Index